Current Law

Legislation Citator

STATUTE CITATOR 2014

STATUTORY INSTRUMENT CITATOR 2014

FOR REFERENCE

ONLY

Current Law

Legislation Citator

STATUTE CITATOR 2014
STATUTORY INSTRUMENT CITATOR 2014

SWEET & MAXWELL

 THOMSON REUTERS

Published in 2015 by Thomson Reuters (Professional) UK Limited, trading as Sweet & Maxwell,
Friars House, 160 Blackfriars Road, London, SE1 8EZ
(Registered in England & Wales, Company No.1679046. Registered Office and address
for service: 2nd floor, 1 Mark Square, Leonard Street, London EC2A 4EG).

Computerset by Sweet & Maxwell.

Printed and bound by CPI Group (UK) Ltd, Croydon, CR0 4YY.

For further information on our products and services, visit

http://www.sweetandmaxwell.co.uk.

No natural forests were destroyed to make this product:
only farmed timber was used and replanted.

A CIP catalogue record for this book is available from the
British Library.

Orders to: Sweet & Maxwell, PO Box 1000, Andover, SP10 9AF.
Tel: 0845 600 9355. Email: TRLUKI.orders@thomsonreuters.com.

ISBN: 978-0-414-03600-0

PREFACE

The Sweet & Maxwell Current Law Service

The Current Law Service began in 1947and provides a comprehensive guide to developments in case law, primary legislation and secondary legislation in the United Kingdom and mainland Europe. The Current Law service presently consists of the Monthly Digest and the Yearbook, Current Law Statutes Annotated and the Bound Volumes, European Current Law, Current Law Week, the Case Citator and the Legislation Citator.

The Legislation Citator

The Legislation Citator comprises the Statute Citator and the Statutory Instrument Citator and has been published annually in this format since 2005.The Citators list all amendments, modifications, repeals, etc. to primary and secondary legislation made in the years indicated.

Updates to these Citators are available in Current Law Statutes Annotated. This Volume of Legislation Citator contains the Statute Citator 2014 and the Statutory Instrument Citator 2014.

The Statute Citator

The material within the Statute Citator is arranged in chronological order and the following information is provided:

> (i) Statutes passed during the specified period;

> (ii) Statutes affected during the specified period by Statute or
> Statutory Instrument;

> (iii) Statutes judicially considered during the specified period;

> (iv)Statutes repealed and amended during the specified period; and

> (v) Statutes under which Statutory Instruments have been made
> during this period.

The Statutory Instrument Citator

The material within the Statutory Instrument Citator is arranged in chronological order and the following information is provided:

(i) Statutory Instruments amended, repealed, modified, etc. By Statute passed or Statutory Instrument issued during the specified period;

(ii) Statutory Instruments judicially considered during the specified period;

(iii) Statutory Instruments consolidated during the specified period; and

(iv) Statutory Instruments made under the powers of any Statutory Instrument issued during this period.

How To Use The Legislation Citator

The following example entries of the Statute and Statutory Instrument Citators indicate how to determine developments which have occurred to the piece of legislation in which you are interested. Entries to the Citators are arranged chronologically.

Statute Citator

7. Business Rates Supplement Act 2009	— Chapter number, name of Act and year
Commencement Orders: SI 2009/2892 Art.2	— Commencement orders bringing provisions into force
Royal Assent July 02, 2009	— Date of Royal Assent
s.12, enabling SI 2009/2542	— Statutory Instruments made under the powers of s.1 of the Act
s.2. see *R. v Brown* [2009] Crim. L.R. 43	— Case judicially considering s.2
s.3, amended: 2010 c.3 s.2	— s.3 amended by Act (s.2 of Ch.3 of 2010) and two SIs
s.3, enabling: SI 2009/82; SI 2010/70	
s.4, repealed: 2010 c.3 Sch.4	— s.4 repealed by Sch.4 of Ch.3 of 2010
s.4A added: SI 2009/42	— s.4A added by SI number 42 of 2009

SI Citator

3264 Agriculture (Cross compliance) Regulations 2009	— Number, name and year of SI
Reg.2, amended: SI 2010/65 Art.2	— reg.2 amended by art.2 of SI number 65 of 2010
Reg.3, revoked: 2010 c.23 Sch.15	— reg.3 revoked by Sch.15 of Ch.23 of 2010
Reg.4, see *R. v Smith* [2010] C.O.D. 54	— Case judicially considering reg.4

CONTENTS

CURRENT LAW

STATUTE CITATOR 2014

The Statute Citator covers the period 2014 and is up to date to February 13, 2015 (Orders and Acts received).

    (i)   Statutes passed between January 1, 2014 and February 13, 2015;
    (ii) Amendments, modifications and repeals made to existing Statutes during this period;
    (iii) Statutes judicially considered during this period;
    (iv) Statutes under which Statutory Instruments have been made during this period.

Definitions of legislative effects:

    ''added''   : new provisions are inserted by subsequent legislation

    ''amended''   : text of legislation is modified by subsequent legislation

    ''applied''   : brought to bear, or exercised by subsequent legislation

    ''consolidated'' : used where previous Acts in the same subject area are brought together in subsequent legislation, with or without amendments

    ''disapplied'' : an exception made to the application of an earlier enactment

    ''enabling''   : giving power for the relevant SI to be made

    ''referred to'' : direction from other legislation without specific effect or application

    ''repealed''   : rescinded by subsequent legislation

    ''restored''   : reinstated by subsequent legislation (where previously repealed/ revoked)

    ''substituted'' : text of provision is completely replaced by subsequent legislation

    ''varied''   : provisions modified in relation to their application to specified areas or circumstances, however the text itself remains unchanged

ACTS OF THE SCOTTISH PARLIAMENT

2000

asp 1. Public Finance and Accountability (Scotland) Act 2000
applied: SI 2014/2418 Sch.1
s.4, applied: 2014 asp 6 s.4, s.6
s.9, amended: 2014 asp 16 Sch.4 para.3
s.21, applied: SI 2014/2418 Sch.1
s.22, applied: SSI 2014/326 Reg.5
s.26D, amended: 2014 c.2 Sch.12 para.47

asp 4. Adults with Incapacity (Scotland) Act 2000
applied: SI 2014/3051 Reg.48, SSI 2014/360 Art.2
s.1, applied: SI 2014/2843 Reg.7
s.10, applied: SSI 2014/345 Sch.1 Part 1
s.10, referred to: 2014 asp 9 Sch.1 Part 1
s.10, enabling: SSI 2014/123, SSI 2014/157
s.12, applied: SSI 2014/345 Sch.1 Part 1
s.12, referred to: 2014 asp 9 Sch.1 Part 1
s.15, applied: SSI 2014/360 Art.2
s.16, applied: SSI 2014/360 Art.2
s.37, applied: SSI 2014/345 Sch.1 Part 1
s.37, referred to: 2014 asp 9 Sch.1 Part 1
s.39, applied: SSI 2014/345 Sch.1 Part 1
s.39, referred to: 2014 asp 9 Sch.1 Part 1
s.41, applied: SSI 2014/345 Sch.1 Part 1
s.86, enabling: SSI 2014/123, SSI 2014/157

asp 5. Abolition of Feudal Tenure etc (Scotland) Act 2000
Sch.12 Part 1 para.48, repealed (in part): 2014 asp 14 Sch.2 para.9

asp 6. Standards in Scotland's Schools etc Act 2000
s.34, amended: 2014 asp 8 Sch.5 para.7

asp 7. Ethical Standards in Public Life etc (Scotland) Act 2000
s.7, enabling: SSI 2014/50
s.19, applied: SSI 2014/281 Art.8, SSI 2014/285 Art.8
s.28, referred to: SI 2014/2418 Sch.1
Sch.3, amended: 2014 asp 16 Sch.4 para.4, 2014 asp 19 Sch.6 para.1

asp 10. National Parks (Scotland) Act 2000
s.6, applied: 2014 asp 12 Sch.1 para.39

asp 11. Regulation of Investigatory Powers (Scotland) Act 2000
s.7, applied: SSI 2014/339 Art.4, Art.5, Art.7, Art.9, Art.10, Art.11, Art.14

s.7, enabling: SSI 2014/339
s.8, enabling: SSI 2014/339
s.19, applied: SSI 2014/339 Art.4, Art.8
s.19, referred to: SSI 2014/339 Art.9
s.19, varied: SSI 2014/339 Art.6
s.19, enabling: SSI 2014/339
s.28, enabling: SSI 2014/339

2001

asp 7. Convention Rights (Compliance) (Scotland) Act 2001
s.12, applied: SSI 2014/98
s.12, enabling: SSI 2014/98
s.13, applied: SSI 2014/98

asp 8. Regulation of Care (Scotland) Act 2001
applied: SI 2014/2418 Sch.1
s.44, applied: SSI 2014/129
s.44, enabling: SSI 2014/129
s.70, repealed: SSI 2014/90 Sch.1 Part 1
s.73, amended: 2014 asp 8 Sch.5 para.8
s.77, referred to: 2014 asp 1 s.7

asp 10. Housing (Scotland) Act 2001
s.1, referred to: 2014 asp 9 Sch.1 Part 1
s.5, amended: 2014 asp 14 Sch.2 para.10
s.5, referred to: 2014 asp 9 Sch.1 Part 1
s.8, referred to: 2014 asp 9 Sch.1 Part 1
s.11, amended: 2014 asp 14 s.12
s.14, amended: 2014 asp 14 s.14
s.16, amended: 2014 asp 14 s.14
s.23, repealed (in part): 2014 asp 14 Sch.2 para.10
s.32, amended: 2014 asp 14 s.12
s.34, amended: 2014 asp 14 s.7, s.9
s.35, amended: 2014 asp 14 s.7, s.9
s.35A, added: 2014 asp 14 s.10
s.36, amended: 2014 asp 14 s.11
s.37, amended: 2014 asp 14 s.7, s.9, s.10
s.42, repealed: 2014 asp 14 Sch.2 para.10
s.52, repealed: 2014 asp 14 s.1
s.83, amended: 2014 c.14 Sch.4 para.79
s.92, applied: SSI 2014/345 Sch.1 Part 1
s.92, referred to: 2014 asp 9 Sch.1 Part 1
Sch.2 Part 1 para.11, amended: 2014 asp 14 s.15
Sch.2 Part 1 para.12, amended: 2014 asp 14 s.15
Sch.3 para.2, amended: 2014 asp 14 s.13

Sch.3 para.3, amended: 2014 asp 14 s.13
Sch.3 para.4, amended: 2014 asp 14 s.13
Sch.3 para.4A, added: 2014 asp 14 s.13
Sch.6 para.2A, added: 2014 asp 14 s.7
Sch.6 para.6, substituted: 2014 asp 14 s.7
Sch.6 para.7A, added: 2014 asp 14 s.8
Sch.10 para.2, repealed: 2014 c.14 Sch.7
Sch.10 para.13, repealed (in part): 2014 asp 14 Sch.2 para.10

asp 13. International Criminal Court (Scotland) Act 2001

Sch.6 para.8, amended: SSI 2014/293 Sch.1 para.2

asp 14. Protection from Abuse (Scotland) Act 2001

s.2, enabling: SSI 2014/371
s.3, enabling: SSI 2014/371

2002

asp 3. Water Industry (Scotland) Act 2002

applied: SI 2014/631 Art.3
Part 2, applied: SSI 2014/364 Reg.22
s.2A, amended: SI 2014/631 Sch.1 para.15
s.4, amended: SI 2014/631 Sch.1 para.15
s.5, amended: SI 2014/631 Sch.1 para.15
s.6, amended: SI 2014/631 Sch.1 para.15
s.20, applied: SSI 2014/164 Sch.2 Part 1
s.27, amended: SI 2014/631 Sch.1 para.15
s.28, amended: SI 2014/631 Sch.1 para.15
s.29B, amended: SI 2014/631 Sch.1 para.15
s.29D, amended: SI 2014/631 Sch.1 para.15
s.29D, applied: SSI 2014/3 Art.7
s.37, enabling: SSI 2014/3
s.42, applied: 2014 asp 6 Sch.3
s.56, applied: SSI 2014/364 Reg.7, Reg.33
s.56A, amended: SI 2014/631 Sch.1 para.15
s.57, amended: SI 2014/631 Sch.1 para.15
s.68, enabling: SSI 2014/3
s.70, amended: SI 2014/631 Sch.1 para.15
Sch.7 para.18, repealed (in part): 2014 asp 14 Sch.2 para.11
Sch.7 para.24, repealed (in part): 2014 asp 3 Sch.3 para.15

asp 5. Community Care and Health (Scotland) Act 2002

applied: SSI 2014/344 Sch.1, Sch.2
s.1, enabling: SSI 2014/91
s.2, enabling: SSI 2014/91
s.4, applied: SSI 2014/345 Sch.1 Part 2

s.4, referred to: 2014 asp 9 Sch.1 Part 2
s.5, amended: 2014 c.23 Sch.1 para.3, Sch.1 para.10
s.5, applied: SSI 2014/345 Sch.1 Part 1
s.5, referred to: 2014 asp 9 Sch.1 Part 1
s.5, substituted: 2014 c.23 Sch.1 para.10
s.7, repealed: SSI 2014/90 Sch.1 Part 1
s.13, enabling: SSI 2014/66
s.14, applied: SSI 2014/345 Sch.1 Part 1
s.14, referred to: 2014 asp 9 Sch.1 Part 1
s.15, applied: SSI 2014/164 Reg.4
s.15, repealed: 2014 asp 9 s.71
s.15, enabling: SSI 2014/66
s.23, applied: SSI 2014/91
s.23, enabling: SSI 2014/91
Sch.2 para.1, repealed (in part): SSI 2014/90 Sch.1 Part 1

asp 11. Scottish Public Services Ombudsman Act 2002

Sch.2 Part 2 para.21ZC, added: 2014 asp 8 s.81
Sch.2 Part 2 para.25ZA, added: 2014 asp 19 Sch.6 para.2
Sch.2 Part 2 para.34, repealed: 2014 asp 19 Sch.6 para.2
Sch.2 Part 2 para.44, repealed: 2014 asp 14 Sch.2 para.12
Sch.2 Part 2 para.70, repealed: SI 2014/1924 Sch.1
Sch.2 Part 2 para.79, repealed: SI 2014/631 Sch.1 para.16

asp 13. Freedom of Information (Scotland) Act 2002

applied: SI 2014/469 Sch.4 para.21
s.4, enabling: SSI 2014/354
Sch.1 Part 2 para.18AA, amended: 2014 asp 16 Sch.4 para.5
Sch.1 Part 2 para.18B, added: 2014 asp 14 Sch.2 para.13
Sch.1 Part 7 para.62ZC, added: 2014 asp 8 s.81
Sch.1 Part 7 para.62ZZA, substituted: SSI 2014/354 Art.2
Sch.1 Part 7 para.67B, added: SSI 2014/354 Sch.1
Sch.1 Part 7 para.67ZA, added: 2014 asp 19 Sch.6 para.3
Sch.1 Part 7 para.68ZA, added: SSI 2014/354 Sch.1
Sch.1 Part 7 para.71A, added: SSI 2014/354 Sch.1

Sch.1 Part 7 para.75A, repealed: SSI 2014/354 Art.2

Sch.1 Part 7 para.76, repealed: 2014 asp 19 Sch.6 para.3

Sch.1 Part 7 para.76A, added: 2014 asp 8 s.81

Sch.1 Part 7 para.79A, amended: SI 2014/631 Sch.1 para.17

Sch.1 Part 7 para.85B, repealed: 2014 asp 14 Sch.2 para.13

Sch.1 Part 7 para.94, repealed: SSI 2014/354 Art.2

asp 17. Debt Arrangement and Attachment (Scotland) Act 2002

Part 1, applied: SSI 2014/172 Art.3, SSI 2014/281 Art.8, SSI 2014/285 Art.8

s.1, amended: 2014 asp 11 s.53

s.2, applied: 2014 asp 19 Sch.1 para.4, SSI 2014/262 Reg.5, SSI 2014/263 Reg.5

s.2, enabling: SSI 2014/294

s.4, enabling: SSI 2014/294

s.5, enabling: SSI 2014/294

s.7, amended: 2014 asp 11 s.3, s.53

s.7, enabling: SSI 2014/290, SSI 2014/294

s.9, repealed (in part): 2014 asp 11 s.53

s.10, referred to: SSI 2014/296 Reg.5

s.39, applied: 2014 asp 16 s.225

s.62, amended: 2014 asp 11 Sch.3 para.38

s.62, applied: SSI 2014/290, SSI 2014/294

s.62, enabling: SSI 2014/294

2003

asp 1. Local Government in Scotland Act 2003

Part 1, applied: SSI 2014/326 Reg.5

asp 2. Land Reform (Scotland) Act 2003

s.40, repealed (in part): 2014 asp 14 Sch.2 para.14

s.65, repealed (in part): 2014 asp 14 Sch.2 para.14

s.84, repealed (in part): 2014 asp 14 Sch.2 para.14

asp 3. Water Environment and Water Services (Scotland) Act 2003

s.2, amended: 2014 asp 3 Sch.3 para.8

s.18, applied: SSI 2014/319 Sch.2 para.11

s.20, repealed: 2014 asp 3 Sch.3 para.8

s.21, repealed: 2014 asp 3 Sch.3 para.8

s.22, amended: 2014 asp 3 Sch.3 para.8

s.23, amended: 2014 asp 3 Sch.3 para.8

s.28, amended: 2014 asp 3 Sch.3 para.8

s.36, amended: 2014 asp 3 Sch.3 para.8

s.36, repealed (in part): 2014 asp 3 Sch.3 para.8

Sch.1 Part 1 para.10, amended: 2014 asp 3 Sch.3 para.8

Sch.2, repealed: 2014 asp 3 Sch.3 para.8

asp 4. Public Appointments and Public Bodies etc (Scotland) Act 2003

s.2, applied: SSI 2014/191 Art.2, SSI 2014/230 Art.2, SSI 2014/239 Art.2

s.3, enabling: SSI 2014/191, SSI 2014/230, SSI 2014/239

s.18, applied: SSI 2014/191, SSI 2014/230, SSI 2014/239

Sch.2, amended: 2014 asp 16 Sch.4 para.6, 2014 asp 19 Sch.6 para.4, 2014 asp 1 s.31, 2014 asp 8 s.81

asp 7. Criminal Justice (Scotland) Act 2003

s.14, amended: 2014 asp 1 s.23

s.14, repealed (in part): 2014 asp 1 s.23

s.16, amended: 2014 asp 1 s.23, s.27

s.16, repealed (in part): 2014 asp 1 s.23

s.17, amended: 2014 asp 1 s.28

s.17A, added: 2014 asp 1 s.29

s.22, applied: 2014 asp 1 s.8

s.88, amended: 2014 asp 1 s.23

asp 8. Building (Scotland) Act 2003

applied:

s.1, applied: SSI 2014/219

s.1, enabling: SSI 2014/219

s.24, amended: 2014 asp 14 s.89

s.27, applied: SSI 2014/369 Reg.2

s.27, referred to: SSI 2014/369 Reg.2

s.33, enabling: SSI 2014/369

s.36, enabling: SSI 2014/369

s.44, amended: 2014 asp 13 s.1

s.46A, added: 2014 asp 13 s.1

s.46A, applied: SSI 2014/369 Reg.2

s.46B, referred to: SSI 2014/369 Reg.2

s.47, amended: 2014 asp 13 s.1

s.47, applied: SSI 2014/369 Reg.2

s.54, enabling: SSI 2014/219

Sch.1 para.5, amended: SSI 2014/364 Reg.49

asp 9. Title Conditions (Scotland) Act 2003

s.10A, amended: 2014 asp 14 s.86

s.10A, applied: SSI 2014/313 Art.2

s.10A, enabling: SSI 2014/313

s.43, applied: SSI 2014/220 Art.2

s.43, referred to: SSI 2014/130, SSI
2014/220

s.43, enabling: SSI 2014/130, SSI 2014/220

**asp 11. Agricultural Holdings (Scotland) Act
2003**

applied: 2014 asp 18 s.94, SSI 2014/188
Art.3, Art.6

s.27, repealed (in part): 2014 asp 14 Sch.2
para.15

s.71, applied: SSI 2014/229 Sch.1

s.72, amended: SSI 2014/98 Art.2

s.72, applied: SSI 2014/98, SSI 2014/98
Art.3, Art.4, Art.5

s.72, referred to: SSI 2014/98 Art.4

s.72, repealed (in part): SSI 2014/98 Art.2

s.72A, added: SSI 2014/98 Art.2

s.72A, applied: SSI 2014/98 Art.4

s.73, applied: SSI 2014/98 Art.3, Art.5

**asp 13. Mental Health (Care and Treatment)
(Scotland) Act 2003**

s.1, applied: SSI 2014/344 Sch.1, Sch.2

s.4ZA, added: 2014 asp 1 s.30

s.4ZB, added: 2014 asp 1 s.30

s.17, applied: SSI 2014/345 Sch.1 Part 1

s.17, referred to: 2014 asp 9 Sch.1 Part 1

s.21, applied: 2014 asp 10 Sch.1 para.13

s.21, referred to: 2014 asp 18 Sch.4 para.3

s.22, disapplied: SSI 2014/344 Sch.1, Sch.2

s.23, applied: SSI 2014/344 Sch.1, Sch.2

s.25, applied: 2014 c.23 s.49, s.50, s.51,
Sch.1 para.3, SSI 2014/345 Sch.1 Part 1

s.25, disapplied: 2014 c.23 Sch.1 para.1,
Sch.1 para.2, Sch.1 para.4

s.25, referred to: 2014 asp 9 Sch.1 Part 1

s.33, applied: SSI 2014/345 Sch.1 Part 1

s.33, referred to: 2014 asp 9 Sch.1 Part 1

s.34, disapplied: SSI 2014/344 Sch.2

s.35, applied: SSI 2014/344 Sch.2

s.38, disapplied: SSI 2014/344 Sch.2

s.39, applied: SSI 2014/344 Sch.2

s.46, disapplied: SSI 2014/344 Sch.2

s.47, applied: SSI 2014/344 Sch.2

s.124, disapplied: SSI 2014/344 Sch.2

s.125, applied: SSI 2014/344 Sch.2

s.228, applied: SSI 2014/345 Sch.1 Part 1

s.228, disapplied: SSI 2014/344 Sch.2

s.228, referred to: 2014 asp 9 Sch.1 Part 1

s.229, applied: SSI 2014/344 Sch.2

s.230, disapplied: SSI 2014/344 Sch.2

s.231, applied: SSI 2014/344 Sch.2

s.259, applied: SSI 2014/345 Sch.1 Part 1

s.259, referred to: 2014 asp 9 Sch.1 Part 1

s.260, disapplied: SSI 2014/344 Sch.2

s.261, applied: SSI 2014/344 Sch.2

s.264, disapplied: SSI 2014/344 Sch.2

s.265, applied: SSI 2014/344 Sch.2

s.267, disapplied: SSI 2014/344 Sch.2

s.268, applied: SSI 2014/344 Sch.2

s.281, disapplied: SSI 2014/344 Sch.2

s.282, applied: SSI 2014/344 Sch.2

s.329, amended: 2014 asp 8 Sch.5 para.9

Sch.1, applied: SSI 2014/344 Sch.2

Sch.1 Part 1 para.2A, amended: 2014 asp 1
s.31

Sch.1 Part 1 para.2B, amended: 2014 asp 1
s.31

Sch.1A Part 1 para.1, added: 2014 asp 1 s.31

Sch.1A Part 1 para.3, added: 2014 asp 1 s.31

Sch.1A Part 1 para.5, added: 2014 asp 1 s.31

Sch.1A Part 2 para.6, added: 2014 asp 1 s.31

Sch.1A Part 3 para.7, amended: 2014 asp 1
s.31

Sch.1A Part 3 para.7, applied: SSI 2014/193

Sch.1A Part 3 para.7, enabling: SSI
2014/193

Sch.1A Part 4 para.8, added: 2014 asp 1 s.31

Sch.1A Part 7 para.14, added: 2014 asp 1
s.31

Sch.2 Part 1 para.3, applied: 2014 asp 18
Sch.4 para.3

Sch.2 Part 2 para.8, repealed (in part): 2014
asp 18 Sch.4 para.5

**asp 15. Salmon and Freshwater Fisheries
(Consolidation) (Scotland) Act 2003**

s.38, enabling: SSI 2014/327, SSI 2014/357

Sch.1 para.7, enabling: SSI 2014/327, SSI
2014/357

Sch.1 para.10, applied: SSI 2014/327, SSI
2014/357

Sch.1 para.14, applied: SSI 2014/357

Sch.1 para.14, enabling: SSI 2014/327, SSI
2014/357

**asp 17. Commissioner for Children and Young
People (Scotland) Act 2003**

s.7, amended: 2014 asp 8 s.5

s.7, repealed (in part): 2014 asp 8 s.5

s.8, amended: 2014 asp 8 s.5

s.11, amended: 2014 asp 8 s.5, s.6

s.14AA, added: 2014 asp 8 s.6

2004

asp 3. Vulnerable Witnesses (Scotland) Act 2004
s.11, amended: 2014 asp 1 s.22
asp 4. Education (Additional Support for Learning) (Scotland) Act 2004
s.1, amended: 2014 asp 8 Sch.5 para.10
s.1, applied: SSI 2014/116 Art.1
s.2, applied: SSI 2014/116 Art.1
s.5, amended: 2014 asp 8 Sch.5 para.10
s.17, applied: 2014 asp 10 Sch.1 para.13, 2014 asp 18 Sch.4 para.3
s.23, applied: SSI 2014/344 Sch.1, Sch.2
s.26, enabling: SSI 2014/103
s.29, amended: 2014 asp 8 Sch.5 para.10
Sch.1 para.9, repealed: 2014 asp 18 Sch.4 para.6
asp 7. National Health Service Reform (Scotland) Act 2004
s.2, repealed: 2014 asp 9 s.71
asp 8. Antisocial Behaviour etc (Scotland) Act 2004
applied: 2014 asp 14 s.94
Part 8, applied: 2014 asp 14 s.28
s.81, referred to: 2014 asp 14 s.28
s.84, amended: 2014 asp 14 s.60
s.85B, added: 2014 asp 14 s.21
s.86, amended: 2014 asp 14 s.21
s.88, amended: 2014 asp 14 s.60
s.89, amended: 2014 asp 14 s.60
s.90, amended: 2014 asp 14 s.60
s.91, amended: 2014 asp 14 s.60
s.92, amended: 2014 asp 14 s.19, s.60, Sch.1 para.57
s.92, repealed (in part): 2014 asp 14 Sch.1 para.57
s.92A, amended: 2014 asp 14 s.60
s.92A, applied: 2014 asp 14 s.34
s.92ZA, amended: 2014 asp 14 s.60, Sch.1 para.58
s.97, amended: 2014 asp 14 s.19, Sch.1 para.59
s.101, amended: 2014 asp 14 s.60, Sch.1 para.60
Sch.2 Part 1 para.2, repealed: 2014 asp 3 Sch.3 para.37
asp 11. Tenements (Scotland) Act 2004
s.4, amended: 2014 asp 14 s.85
s.4A, added: 2014 asp 14 s.85
s.13, amended: 2014 asp 14 s.85, s.86
s.13, applied: SSI 2014/313 Art.3

s.13, enabling: SSI 2014/313
s.29, amended: 2014 asp 14 s.86
Sch.1 Part RULEd, amended: 2014 asp 14 s.85
Sch.1 Part RULEg para.8_4, amended: 2014 asp 14 s.85

2005

asp 3. Water Services etc (Scotland) Act 2005
applied: SI 2014/631 Art.3
s.6, amended: 2014 c.21 s.7
s.14, applied: 2014 asp 6 Sch.3
s.19, amended: SI 2014/631 Sch.1 para.18
s.20B, amended: SI 2014/631 Sch.1 para.18
s.25, amended: 2014 asp 3 Sch.3 para.9
s.34, amended: 2014 c.21 s.7
Sch.2 para.1A, added: 2014 c.21 s.7
asp 5. Fire (Scotland) Act 2005
s.1A, applied: SSI 2014/164 Sch.2 Part 1
s.61, applied: SI 2014/469 Sch.4 para.12, Sch.4 para.13
Sch.1A para.5, amended: 2014 asp 11 Sch.3 para.39
Sch.3 para.13, repealed: 2014 asp 14 Sch.2 para.16
asp 6. Further and Higher Education (Scotland) Act 2005
applied: 2014 asp 8 s.31, s.56, Sch.2 para.13, Sch.3 para.14, Sch.4 para.24
s.7A, applied: SSI 2014/21 Art.4, Art.5, SSI 2014/22, SSI 2014/250
s.7A, enabling: SSI 2014/22, SSI 2014/250
s.7B, applied: SSI 2014/250
s.7B, enabling: SSI 2014/250
s.7C, applied: SSI 2014/21 Art.4, Art.5, SSI 2014/80, SSI 2014/146, SSI 2014/250
s.7C, enabling: SSI 2014/80, SSI 2014/146, SSI 2014/250
s.9, amended: SSI 2014/21 Art.3
s.9, repealed (in part): SSI 2014/21 Art.3
s.9B, amended: SSI 2014/21 Art.3
s.9B, repealed (in part): SSI 2014/21 Art.3
s.9D, amended: SSI 2014/21 Art.3
s.9D, repealed (in part): SSI 2014/21 Art.3
s.14A, amended: SSI 2014/21 Art.3
s.14A, repealed (in part): SSI 2014/21 Art.3
s.19A, amended: SSI 2014/21 Art.3
s.19A, repealed (in part): SSI 2014/21 Art.3
s.26A, disapplied: SSI 2014/21 Art.4

s.34, applied: SSI 2014/250
s.34, enabling: SSI 2014/22, SSI 2014/80,
SSI 2014/146, SSI 2014/250
s.35, amended: SSI 2014/21 Art.3
Sch.1 para.4, amended: SSI 2014/21 Art.3
Sch.2A Part 1, amended: SSI 2014/250 Art.3
Sch.2A Part 2, amended: SSI 2014/250 Art.3
Sch.2B para.3, amended: SSI 2014/79 Art.3
Sch.2B para.3, applied: SSI 2014/80 Art.3
Sch.2B para.4, applied: SSI 2014/80 Art.3
Sch.2B para.7, amended: SSI 2014/79 Art.3
Sch.2B para.7, disapplied: SSI 2014/80 Art.3
Sch.2B para.9, amended: SSI 2014/79 Art.3

asp 9. Protection of Children and Prevention of Sexual Offences (Scotland) Act 2005
s.7, amended: 2014 c.12 Sch.11 para.78
s.8, amended: 2014 c.12 Sch.11 para.79

asp 10. Charities and Trustee Investment (Scotland) Act 2005
applied: 2014 asp 16 Sch.1 para.2
s.3, applied: SI 2014/1960 Art.5
s.7, applied: 2014 asp 19 Sch.1 para.12
s.34, applied: SI 2014/1132 Sch.7 para.8, SI 2014/2709 Sch.2 para.8
s.44, applied: SSI 2014/200 Reg.12
s.44, enabling: SSI 2014/295, SSI 2014/335
s.56, amended: 2014 c.14 Sch.4 para.97
s.58, amended: 2014 c.14 Sch.4 para.98
s.70, amended: SSI 2014/293 Sch.1 para.3
s.75, applied: 2014 asp 10 Sch.1 para.13, 2014 asp 18 Sch.4 para.3
Sch.2 para.3, repealed: 2014 asp 18 Sch.4 para.7

asp 12. Transport (Scotland) Act 2005
s.1, applied: SSI 2014/164 Sch.2 Part 1
s.2, applied: SSI 2014/164 Sch.4 Part 2
s.10, applied: SSI 2014/164 Sch.4 Part 2

asp 14. Management of Offenders etc (Scotland) Act 2005
s.10, referred to: 2014 asp 9 Sch.1 Part 1

2006

asp 1. Housing (Scotland) Act 2006
applied: 2014 asp 14 s.94, SSI 2014/347 Reg.2
s.13, amended: 2014 asp 14 s.22, s.23
s.18, amended: 2014 asp 14 s.17
s.19A, added: 2014 asp 14 s.23
s.20A, added: 2014 asp 14 s.24

s.21, amended: 2014 asp 14 s.96
s.21, applied: 2014 asp 10 Sch.1 para.13
s.22, amended: 2014 asp 14 s.25
s.22, repealed (in part): 2014 asp 14 Sch.2 para.17
s.22A, amended: 2014 asp 14 s.25
s.23, amended: 2014 asp 14 s.25
s.24, amended: 2014 asp 14 s.25, Sch.1 para.50
s.30, amended: 2014 asp 14 s.87
s.42, amended: 2014 asp 14 s.88
s.47, amended: 2014 asp 14 s.89
s.57, amended: 2014 asp 14 s.17
s.61, repealed (in part): 2014 asp 14 s.89
s.64, amended: 2014 asp 14 s.27, Sch.1 para.53
s.64, repealed (in part): 2014 asp 14 Sch.1 para.53
s.65, amended: 2014 asp 14 s.27
s.65, repealed (in part): 2014 asp 14 Sch.1 para.54
s.66, amended: 2014 asp 14 s.27
s.66A, added: 2014 asp 14 s.18
s.67, repealed: 2014 asp 14 Sch.1 para.55
s.71, applied: SSI 2014/345 Sch.1 Part 1
s.71, referred to: 2014 asp 9 Sch.1 Part 1
s.75, applied: SSI 2014/347 Reg.3
s.117, amended: SI 2014/631 Sch.2 para.7
s.153, disapplied: 2014 asp 14 s.20
s.153, referred to: 2014 asp 14 s.20
s.158, applied: 2014 asp 14 s.20
s.159, disapplied: 2014 asp 14 s.20
s.172, amended: 2014 asp 14 s.85, s.90, s.91
s.172A, added: 2014 asp 14 s.91
s.173, amended: 2014 asp 14 s.90
s.174A, added: 2014 asp 14 s.85
s.181, amended: 2014 asp 14 s.25
s.182, amended: 2014 asp 14 s.25
s.184, amended: 2014 asp 14 s.25
s.187, amended: 2014 asp 14 s.25
s.191, amended: 2014 asp 14 s.24, s.85
s.194, amended: 2014 asp 14 s.25, Sch.1 para.51
Sch.2 para.1, amended: 2014 asp 14 s.26
Sch.2 para.2, amended: 2014 asp 14 s.26
Sch.2 para.3, amended: 2014 asp 14 s.26
Sch.2 para.5, amended: 2014 asp 14 s.26
Sch.2 para.6, amended: 2014 asp 14 s.26
Sch.2 para.7, amended: 2014 asp 14 s.26
Sch.2 para.8, amended: 2014 asp 14 s.26
Sch.4 para.9, applied: 2014 asp 14 s.20

Sch.4 para.9, disapplied: 2014 asp 14 s.20
Sch.5 para.2, applied: 2014 asp 14 s.20
Sch.5 para.3, disapplied: 2014 asp 14 s.20
asp 2. Family Law (Scotland) Act 2006
s.38, amended: SI 2014/560 Sch.1 para.31,
SI 2014/1110 Art.18
asp 10. Police, Public Order and Criminal Justice (Scotland) Act 2006
Sch.3 Part 1 para.2, applied: SSI 2014/164
Sch.4 Part 2
Sch.6 Part 1 para.5, repealed (in part): 2014
c.12 Sch.11 para.102
asp 11. Animal Health and Welfare (Scotland) Act 2006
s.40, applied: SI 2014/3266 Reg.10
asp 14. Local Electoral Administration and Registration Services (Scotland) Act 2006
s.55, enabling: SSI 2014/306
s.60, applied: SSI 2014/306
asp 15. Tourist Boards (Scotland) Act 2006
Sch.1 para.1, applied: SSI 2014/164 Sch.4
Part 2

2007

asp 3. Bankruptcy and Diligence etc (Scotland) Act 2007
Commencement Orders: SSI 2014/173 Art.2,
Art.3
Part 8, applied: 2014 asp 18 Sch.1 para.7
s.15, repealed (in part): 2014 asp 11 Sch.4
s.21, repealed: 2014 asp 11 Sch.4
s.49, amended: 2014 c.14 Sch.4 para.118,
Sch.4 para.119, Sch.4 para.120
s.62, repealed (in part): 2014 asp 11 Sch.4
s.182, applied: 2014 asp 18 Sch.1 para.8
s.217, applied: 2014 asp 18 Sch.1 para.9
s.224, enabling: SSI 2014/173
s.227, enabling: SSI 2014/173
Sch.6 Part 1, amended: 2014 asp 11 Sch.3
para.40
asp 4. Adoption and Children (Scotland) Act 2007
Part 1 c.1A, added: 2014 asp 8 s.75
s.1, referred to: 2014 asp 9 Sch.1 Part 1
s.4, referred to: 2014 asp 9 Sch.1 Part 1
s.4, repealed: 2014 asp 8 Sch.5 para.11
s.6, amended: 2014 asp 8 Sch.5 para.11
s.9, referred to: 2014 asp 9 Sch.1 Part 1
s.19, referred to: 2014 asp 9 Sch.1 Part 1

s.25, applied: SI 2014/3051 Sch.1 para.12
s.26, referred to: 2014 asp 9 Sch.1 Part 1
s.28, applied: 2014 asp 18 Sch.1 para.3
s.45, referred to: 2014 asp 9 Sch.1 Part 1
s.47, referred to: 2014 asp 9 Sch.1 Part 1
s.51, referred to: 2014 asp 9 Sch.1 Part 1
s.59, applied: 2014 asp 18 Sch.1 para.3
s.71, referred to: 2014 asp 9 Sch.1 Part 1
s.80, applied: 2014 asp 18 Sch.1 para.3
s.80, referred to: 2014 asp 9 Sch.1 Part 1
s.90, referred to: 2014 asp 9 Sch.1 Part 1
s.95, applied: SSI 2014/113 Reg.3
s.95, enabling: SSI 2014/113
s.99, referred to: 2014 asp 9 Sch.1 Part 1
s.101, referred to: 2014 asp 9 Sch.1 Part 1
s.105, referred to: 2014 asp 9 Sch.1 Part 1
s.114, enabling: SSI 2014/302
s.117, amended: 2014 asp 8 Sch.5 para.11
s.119, amended: 2014 asp 8 Sch.5 para.11
asp 5. Legal Profession and Legal Aid (Scotland) Act 2007
s.1, enabling: SSI 2014/272
s.2, amended: SSI 2014/232 Reg.2
s.4, amended: SSI 2014/232 Reg.2
s.5, repealed: SSI 2014/232 Reg.2
s.6, amended: SSI 2014/232 Reg.2
s.7, amended: SSI 2014/232 Reg.2
s.8, amended: SSI 2014/232 Reg.2
s.9, amended: SSI 2014/232 Reg.2
s.9A, added: SSI 2014/232 Reg.2
s.15, amended: SSI 2014/232 Reg.2
s.17, amended: SSI 2014/232 Reg.2
s.23, amended: SSI 2014/232 Reg.2
s.23, repealed (in part): SSI 2014/232 Reg.2
s.24, amended: SSI 2014/232 Reg.2
s.24, repealed (in part): SSI 2014/232 Reg.2
s.33, amended: SSI 2014/232 Reg.2
s.36, amended: SSI 2014/232 Reg.2
s.37, amended: SSI 2014/232 Reg.2
s.41, enabling: SSI 2014/232
s.46, amended: SSI 2014/232 Reg.2
s.47, amended: SSI 2014/232 Reg.2
s.79, applied: SSI 2014/232, SSI 2014/272
Sch.1 para.2, amended: SSI 2014/272 Art.2
Sch.1 para.2, enabling: SSI 2014/272
Sch.1 para.11A, added: SSI 2014/232 Reg.2
Sch.3 para.1, amended: SSI 2014/232 Reg.2
asp 6. Criminal Proceedings etc (Reform) (Scotland) Act 2007
s.56, amended: SI 2014/2947 Sch.4 para.6
s.56, enabling: SSI 2014/322

s.59, amended: 2014 asp 18 s.127
s.61, amended: 2014 asp 18 Sch.5 para.40
s.62, amended: 2014 asp 18 Sch.5 para.40
s.63, amended: 2014 asp 18 Sch.5 para.40
s.67, amended: SSI 2014/155 Art.4
s.70, repealed (in part): SSI 2014/155 Art.4
s.71, applied: 2014 asp 10 s.27
s.71A, added: SSI 2014/155 Art.4
s.74, amended: SSI 2014/155 Art.4
s.74, repealed: 2014 asp 18 Sch.5 para.40
s.74A, repealed: 2014 asp 18 Sch.5 para.40
s.75, amended: SSI 2014/155 Art.4
s.75, repealed: 2014 asp 18 Sch.5 para.40
s.76, amended: 2014 asp 18 Sch.5 para.40
s.77, amended: 2014 asp 18 Sch.5 para.40
s.77, repealed (in part): 2014 asp 18 Sch.5 para.40
s.81, amended: 2014 asp 18 s.127
s.81, applied: SSI 2014/322

asp 10. Adult Support and Protection (Scotland) Act 2007

s.4, applied: SSI 2014/345 Sch.1 Part 1
s.4, referred to: 2014 asp 9 Sch.1 Part 1
s.7, applied: SSI 2014/282 Sch.1
s.11, applied: SSI 2014/282 Sch.1, SSI 2014/345 Sch.1 Part 1
s.14, applied: SSI 2014/282 Sch.1, SSI 2014/345 Sch.1 Part 1
s.14, referred to: 2014 asp 9 Sch.1 Part 1
s.16, applied: SSI 2014/282 Sch.1
s.16, referred to: 2014 asp 9 Sch.1 Part 1
s.18, applied: SSI 2014/282 Sch.1, SSI 2014/345 Sch.1 Part 1
s.18, referred to: 2014 asp 9 Sch.1 Part 1
s.22, applied: SSI 2014/345 Sch.1 Part 1
s.22, referred to: 2014 asp 9 Sch.1 Part 1
s.40, applied: SSI 2014/345 Sch.1 Part 1
s.40, referred to: 2014 asp 9 Sch.1 Part 1
s.42, applied: SSI 2014/345 Sch.1 Part 1
s.42, referred to: 2014 asp 9 Sch.1 Part 1
s.63, repealed: SSI 2014/90 Sch.1 Part 1

asp 14. Protection of Vulnerable Groups (Scotland) Act 2007

s.94, amended: SSI 2014/90 Sch.1 Part 3
s.96, applied: SSI 2014/360 Art.2

2008

asp 4. Glasgow Commonwealth Games Act 2008
s.38, enabling: SSI 2014/197

s.39, applied: SSI 2014/92 Art.2
s.47, enabling: SSI 2014/92
s.50, enabling: SSI 2014/356

asp 5. Public Health etc (Scotland) Act 2008
s.2, applied: SSI 2014/344 Sch.1
s.7, applied: SSI 2014/344 Sch.1

asp 6. Judiciary and Courts (Scotland) Act 2008
Part 4, amended: 2014 asp 18 Sch.4 para.1
s.2, amended: 2014 asp 18 Sch.5 para.16
s.2, applied: 2014 asp 18 s.27, s.28, s.56, s.57
s.2, referred to: 2014 asp 10 s.27
s.10, amended: 2014 asp 10 Sch.9 para.12, 2014 asp 18 Sch.5 para.9
s.10, applied: 2014 asp 10 Sch.7 para.7
s.11, referred to: 2014 asp 18 s.3, s.4, s.5
s.21, substituted: 2014 asp 18 s.123
s.24, repealed: 2014 asp 18 Sch.5 para.9
s.30, amended: 2014 asp 10 Sch.9 para.12
s.35, applied: 2014 asp 10 s.27, SSI 2014/99 r.13, SSI 2014/102 r.13
s.37, enabling: SSI 2014/99, SSI 2014/102
s.38, applied: SSI 2014/99 r.14, r.15, SSI 2014/102 r.14, r.15
s.40, repealed: 2014 asp 18 Sch.5 para.9
s.43, amended: 2014 asp 18 Sch.5 para.9, Sch.5 para.16, Sch.5 para.38
s.43, repealed (in part): 2014 asp 18 Sch.5 para.41
s.47, repealed: 2014 asp 18 Sch.5 para.9
s.60, amended: 2014 asp 18 Sch.4 para.1
s.61, amended: 2014 asp 18 Sch.4 para.1
s.61A, added: 2014 asp 18 s.130
s.61A, applied: 2014 asp 18 Sch.4 para.3
s.61A, referred to: 2014 asp 18 Sch.4 para.3
s.62, amended: 2014 asp 18 Sch.4 para.1, Sch.5 para.9, Sch.5 para.16
s.63, amended: 2014 asp 18 Sch.4 para.1
s.63, referred to: SSI 2014/337 Sch.1 para.9
s.64, repealed (in part): 2014 asp 18 Sch.5 para.9, Sch.5 para.38
s.65, amended: 2014 asp 18 Sch.4 para.1
s.66, amended: 2014 asp 18 Sch.4 para.1
s.67, amended: 2014 asp 18 Sch.4 para.1
s.69, amended: 2014 asp 18 Sch.4 para.1
s.70, amended: 2014 asp 18 Sch.4 para.1
s.70, applied: 2014 asp 18 Sch.4 para.3
s.72, amended: 2014 asp 18 Sch.5 para.9, Sch.5 para.38
Sch.1 para.3, amended: 2014 asp 10 Sch.9 para.12

Sch.1 para.3, varied: 2014 asp 10 Sch.9 para.10

Sch.1 para.13A, added: 2014 asp 18 s.131

Sch.1 para.16A, added: 2014 asp 10 Sch.9 para.12

Sch.1 para.16A, amended: 2014 asp 18 s.131

Sch.1 para.16A, varied: 2014 asp 10 Sch.9 para.10

Sch.3, amended: 2014 asp 18 Sch.4 para.1

Sch.3 para.1, amended: 2014 asp 18 Sch.4 para.1

Sch.3 para.1, repealed: 2014 asp 18 Sch.4 para.1

Sch.3 para.2, amended: 2014 asp 18 Sch.4 para.1

Sch.3 para.2, applied: 2014 asp 18 Sch.4 para.3

Sch.3 para.3, amended: 2014 asp 18 Sch.4 para.1

Sch.3 para.4, amended: 2014 asp 18 Sch.4 para.1

Sch.3 para.5, amended: 2014 asp 18 Sch.4 para.1

Sch.3 para.6, amended: 2014 asp 18 Sch.4 para.1

Sch.3 para.7, amended: 2014 asp 18 Sch.4 para.1

Sch.3 para.9, amended: 2014 asp 18 Sch.4 para.1

Sch.3 para.10, amended: 2014 asp 18 Sch.4 para.1

Sch.3 para.11, amended: 2014 asp 18 Sch.4 para.1

Sch.3 para.12, amended: 2014 asp 18 Sch.4 para.1

Sch.3 para.13, amended: 2014 asp 18 Sch.4 para.1

Sch.3 para.13, referred to: 2014 asp 18 Sch.4 para.3

Sch.3 para.14, amended: 2014 asp 18 Sch.4 para.1

Sch.3 para.15, amended: 2014 asp 18 Sch.4 para.1

Sch.3 para.16, amended: 2014 asp 18 Sch.4 para.1

Sch.3 para.17, amended: 2014 asp 18 Sch.4 para.1

Sch.3 para.19, amended: 2014 asp 18 Sch.4 para.1

Sch.3 para.20, amended: 2014 asp 18 Sch.4 para.1

Sch.5 para.2, repealed: 2014 asp 18 Sch.5 para.9

2009

asp 6. Flood Risk Management (Scotland) Act 2009
s.47, applied: SSI 2014/319 Sch.2 para.17
s.78, repealed: 2014 asp 3 Sch.3 para.44

asp 12. Climate Change (Scotland) Act 2009
s.82A, added: 2014 asp 12 s.36
s.88, enabling: SSI 2014/161
s.88A, added: 2014 asp 3 s.43
s.89, enabling: SSI 2014/161
s.90, enabling: SSI 2014/161
s.96, applied: SSI 2014/161
s.96, enabling: SSI 2014/161
s.97, applied: SSI 2014/161
Sch.1A, added: 2014 asp 3 s.43

2010

asp 1. Arbitration (Scotland) Act 2010
applied: 2014 c.1 s.16
varied: 2014 c.1 s.16
s.16, referred to: 2014 c.1 s.16

asp 2. Schools (Consultation) (Scotland) Act 2010
applied: SSI 2014/262 Reg.2, Reg.6, SSI 2014/263 Reg.2, Reg.6
disapplied: SSI 2014/132 Art.2
s.1, amended: 2014 asp 8 s.80
s.2A, added: 2014 asp 8 s.77
s.4, amended: 2014 asp 8 s.78, s.81
s.5, amended: 2014 asp 8 s.79
s.10, amended: 2014 asp 8 s.79
s.11A, added: 2014 asp 8 s.80
s.12, amended: 2014 asp 8 s.80
s.12, repealed (in part): 2014 asp 8 s.80
s.12A, added: 2014 asp 8 s.80
s.13, substituted: 2014 asp 8 s.80
s.15, amended: 2014 asp 8 s.81
s.15, repealed (in part): 2014 asp 8 s.81
s.16, repealed: 2014 asp 8 s.81
s.17, amended: 2014 asp 8 s.81
s.17, repealed (in part): 2014 asp 8 s.81
s.17A, added: 2014 asp 8 s.81
s.17A, amended: 2014 asp 8 s.81
s.17B, amended: 2014 asp 8 s.81

s.19, substituted: 2014 asp 8 s.81
s.20, amended: 2014 asp 8 s.81
s.21, amended: 2014 asp 8 s.81
Sch.1 para.2, applied: SSI 2014/132 Sch.1
Sch.2A, added: 2014 asp 8 s.81
Sch.2A para.1, amended: 2014 asp 8 s.81
Sch.2A para.1, enabling: SSI 2014/262
Sch.2A para.2, amended: 2014 asp 8 s.81
Sch.2A para.2, applied: SSI 2014/263 Reg.7
Sch.2A para.2, enabling: SSI 2014/263

asp 5. Marine (Scotland) Act 2010
referred to: 2014 asp 19 s.17
Part 4, referred to: SSI 2014/324 Sch.1
para.13
s.38, amended: 2014 asp 3 s.54
s.63A, added: 2014 asp 3 s.54
s.80A, added: 2014 asp 19 Sch.4 para.2
s.82, amended: 2014 asp 19 Sch.4 para.3
s.83, amended: 2014 asp 19 Sch.4 para.4
s.84, amended: 2014 asp 19 Sch.4 para.5
s.85, applied: SSI 2014/260
s.85, enabling: SSI 2014/260, SSI 2014/297
s.86, enabling: SSI 2014/260, SSI 2014/297
s.87, applied: SSI 2014/297
s.88, enabling: SSI 2014/260
s.92, enabling: SSI 2014/260, SSI 2014/297
s.94, applied: SSI 2014/260 Art.6
s.95, applied: SSI 2014/260 Art.6
s.97, applied: SSI 2014/260 Art.6
s.117, applied: SSI 2014/185 Art.3
s.117, enabling: SSI 2014/185

asp 6. Home Owner and Debtor Protection (Scotland) Act 2010
s.13, repealed (in part): 2014 asp 11 Sch.4

asp 8. Public Services Reform (Scotland) Act 2010
applied: SI 2014/631 Art.3, SSI 2014/344
Sch.1
referred to: SI 2014/2418 Sch.1
s.1, applied: SSI 2014/344 Sch.1, Sch.2
s.3, amended: SI 2014/631 Sch.1 para.19
s.31, disapplied: SSI 2014/344 Sch.2
s.33, applied: SSI 2014/344 Sch.1, Sch.2
s.53, amended: 2014 asp 9 s.54
s.59, applied: 2014 c.23 s.73
s.78, enabling: SSI 2014/192
s.104, applied: SSI 2014/192
s.104, enabling: SSI 2014/192
s.115, amended: 2014 asp 9 s.56
s.116A, added: 2014 asp 9 s.56
s.117, amended: 2014 asp 9 s.56

Sch.2 Part 1 para.16, repealed: SI 2014/631
Sch.1 para.19
Sch.5, amended: 2014 asp 19 Sch.6 para.5
Sch.8, amended: 2014 asp 16 Sch.4 para.7,
2014 asp 19 Sch.6 para.5
Sch.12 para.20, applied: SSI 2014/360 Art.2

asp 10. Interpretation and Legislative Reform (Scotland) Act 2010
Sch.1, amended: 2014 asp 5 s.4, 2014 asp 18
Sch.5 para.45

asp 13. Criminal Justice and Licensing (Scotland) Act 2010
Part 6, applied: SSI 2014/159 Reg.4
s.6, amended: 2014 asp 18 Sch.5 para.17
s.8A, added: 2014 asp 18 Sch.5 para.17

asp 14. Crofting Reform (Scotland) Act 2010
s.4, applied: SSI 2014/188 Sch.1 Part 5
s.5, applied: SSI 2014/188 Sch.1 Part 5
s.24, applied: SSI 2014/188 Sch.1 Part 5
s.25, applied: SSI 2014/188 Sch.1 Part 5
s.32, applied: SSI 2014/188 Sch.1 Part 5

asp 17. Housing (Scotland) Act 2010
Commencement Orders: 2014 asp 14 s.1
Part 2, applied: 2014 c.14 s.118, SI
2014/2418 Sch.1
Part 10 c.3, added: 2014 asp 14 s.98
s.20, applied: 2014 c.14 s.84
s.23, applied: SI 2014/928 Sch.4 para.1
s.58, amended: 2014 asp 14 Sch.2 para.18
s.67, amended: 2014 asp 14 s.97
s.67, repealed (in part): 2014 asp 14 s.97
s.80, amended: SI 2014/3486 Art.31
s.104A, added: 2014 asp 14 s.98
s.108, repealed (in part): 2014 asp 14 Sch.2
para.18
s.110, amended: 2014 asp 14 Sch.2 para.18
s.124, amended: 2014 asp 14 Sch.2 para.18
s.140, repealed: 2014 asp 14 Sch.2 para.18
s.145, repealed: 2014 asp 14 s.1
s.147, repealed: 2014 asp 14 s.1
s.164, amended: 2014 asp 14 s.98
s.165, amended: 2014 asp 11 Sch.3 para.41,
2014 asp 14 s.98
Sch.2 para.3, repealed (in part): 2014 asp 14
Sch.2 para.18
Sch.2 para.9, repealed: 2014 asp 14 Sch.2
para.18

2011

asp 1. Children's Hearings (Scotland) Act 2011
 applied: 2014 asp 8 s.37, 2014 asp 18 s.41,
 s.88, Sch.1 para.4, SSI 2014/193 Art.3, SSI
 2014/337 Sch.2 para.16
 s.15, applied: SSI 2014/164 Sch.2 Part 1
 s.33, amended: 2014 asp 8 s.82
 s.35, referred to: 2014 asp 9 Sch.1 Part 1
 s.37, referred to: 2014 asp 9 Sch.1 Part 1
 s.42, referred to: 2014 asp 9 Sch.1 Part 1
 s.44, referred to: 2014 asp 9 Sch.1 Part 1
 s.48, referred to: 2014 asp 9 Sch.1 Part 1
 s.49, referred to: 2014 asp 9 Sch.1 Part 1
 s.54, amended: 2014 asp 8 s.83
 s.60, referred to: 2014 asp 9 Sch.1 Part 1
 s.79, amended: 2014 asp 8 s.84
 s.80, amended: 2014 asp 8 Sch.5 para.12
 s.81, amended: 2014 asp 8 Sch.5 para.12
 s.81A, added: 2014 asp 8 s.84
 s.90, amended: 2014 asp 8 s.85
 s.94, amended: 2014 asp 8 Sch.5 para.12
 s.95, amended: 2014 asp 8 s.86
 s.96, amended: 2014 asp 8 s.87
 s.105, amended: 2014 asp 8 Sch.5 para.12
 s.106, amended: 2014 asp 8 Sch.5 para.12
 s.131, referred to: 2014 asp 9 Sch.1 Part 1
 s.142, amended: 2014 asp 8 Sch.5 para.12
 s.144, referred to: 2014 asp 9 Sch.1 Part 1
 s.153, referred to: 2014 asp 9 Sch.1 Part 2
 s.160, amended: 2014 asp 8 Sch.5 para.12
 s.166, referred to: 2014 asp 9 Sch.1 Part 1
 s.180, referred to: 2014 asp 9 Sch.1 Part 1
 s.183, referred to: 2014 asp 9 Sch.1 Part 1
 s.202, amended: 2014 asp 8 Sch.5 para.12
 s.202, applied: 2014 asp 8 s.37
 s.204, enabling: SSI 2014/112, SSI 2014/137
 Sch.1 para.12, amended: 2014 asp 8 s.88
 Sch.1 para.13, amended: 2014 asp 8 s.88
 Sch.1 para.14, amended: 2014 asp 8 s.89
 Sch.6, amended: 2014 asp 8 Sch.5 para.12

asp 2. Forth Crossing Act 2011
 s.70, repealed (in part): 2014 asp 3 Sch.3
 para.38

asp 5. Patient Rights (Scotland) Act 2011
 applied: SSI 2014/344 Sch.1, Sch.2
 s.9, enabling: SSI 2014/93
 s.17, amended: 2014 asp 9 s.63
 s.17, repealed (in part): 2014 asp 9 s.71
 s.25, applied: SSI 2014/93
 s.25, enabling: SSI 2014/93

asp 8. Property Factors (Scotland) Act 2011
 s.16, amended: 2014 asp 14 s.96
 s.16, applied: 2014 asp 10 Sch.1 para.13

asp 9. Reservoirs (Scotland) Act 2011
 Commencement Orders: 2014 asp 3 Sch.3
 para.13; SSI 2014/348 Sch.1, Art.2
 s.5, applied: SSI 2014/319 Sch.2 para.22
 s.17, applied: SSI 2014/319 Sch.2 para.22
 s.42, applied: SSI 2014/319 Sch.1 para.12,
 Sch.2 para.22, Sch.3 para.12
 s.52, applied: SSI 2014/319 Sch.1 para.12,
 Sch.2 para.22, Sch.3 para.12
 s.58, applied: SSI 2014/319 Sch.2 para.22
 s.66, applied: SSI 2014/319 Sch.2 para.22
 s.70, applied: SSI 2014/319 Sch.1 para.12,
 Sch.2 para.22, Sch.3 para.12
 s.78, repealed: 2014 asp 3 Sch.3 para.13
 s.82, amended: 2014 asp 3 Sch.3 para.13
 s.82, repealed (in part): 2014 asp 3 Sch.3
 para.13
 s.83, repealed (in part): 2014 asp 3 Sch.3
 para.13
 s.84, repealed (in part): 2014 asp 3 Sch.3
 para.13
 s.86, amended: 2014 asp 3 Sch.3 para.13
 s.86, repealed (in part): 2014 asp 3 Sch.3
 para.13
 s.87, amended: 2014 asp 3 Sch.3 para.13
 s.87, repealed (in part): 2014 asp 3 Sch.3
 para.13
 s.89, amended: 2014 asp 3 Sch.3 para.13
 s.90, amended: 2014 asp 3 Sch.3 para.13
 s.90, repealed (in part): 2014 asp 3 Sch.3
 para.13
 s.99, applied: SSI 2014/319 Sch.2 para.22
 s.103, applied: SSI 2014/319 Sch.2 para.22
 s.114, amended: 2014 asp 3 Sch.3 para.13
 s.116, enabling: SSI 2014/348
 Sch.1, amended: 2014 asp 3 Sch.3 para.13

asp 12. Public Records (Scotland) Act 2011
 Sch.1, amended: 2014 asp 16 Sch.4 para.8,
 2014 asp 19 Sch.6 para.6

asp 14. Private Rented Housing (Scotland) Act 2011
 s.35, repealed (in part): 2014 asp 14 s.25

asp 15. Forced Marriage etc (Protection and Jurisdiction) (Scotland) Act 2011
 s.1, applied: 2014 asp 18 Sch.1 para.5
 s.5, applied: 2014 asp 18 Sch.1 para.5

2012

asp 5. Land Registration etc (Scotland) Act 2012
Commencement Orders: 2014 c.14 Sch.7;
SSI 2014/41 Art.2; SSI 2014/127 Art.2; SSI
2014/41 Sch.1 Part 1, 3, 2, Art.3
applied: SSI 2014/150 Sch.1 Part 4
referred to: SSI 2014/127 Art.2
s.4, applied: SSI 2014/150 Reg.10
s.6, applied: SSI 2014/150 Reg.12
s.7, applied: SSI 2014/150 Reg.12
s.13, applied: SSI 2014/150 Reg.14
s.17, applied: SSI 2014/188 Sch.1 para.1
s.21, applied: SSI 2014/150 Reg.7, SSI
2014/188 Sch.1 para.3, Sch.1 para.9, Sch.1
para.10, SSI 2014/347 Sch.2
s.22, applied: SSI 2014/347 Sch.2
s.27, applied: SSI 2014/150 Reg.7, SSI
2014/188 Sch.1 para.1
s.30, applied: SSI 2014/150 Reg.10
s.34, applied: SSI 2014/150 Reg.13, SSI
2014/188 Sch.1 para.3
s.43, applied: SSI 2014/150 Reg.18, Sch.2
s.43, referred to: SSI 2014/150 Reg.18
s.43, enabling: SSI 2014/150
s.56, applied: SSI 2014/150 Reg.4, Sch.1
Part 1, Sch.1 Part 2
s.56, enabling: SSI 2014/150
s.57, amended: SSI 2014/190 Art.4
s.57, applied: SSI 2014/150 Reg.2, Reg.5,
Sch.1 Part 1, Sch.1 Part 2, SSI 2014/188
Sch.1 para.3
s.62, enabling: SSI 2014/150
s.63, applied: SSI 2014/150 Reg.2, Sch.1
Part 3, SSI 2014/188 Sch.1 para.3
s.64, applied: SSI 2014/190
s.64, enabling: SSI 2014/190
s.65, applied: SSI 2014/150 Reg.17
s.67, applied: SSI 2014/150 Reg.15, SSI
2014/188 Sch.1 para.3
s.69, applied: SSI 2014/150 Reg.15, SSI
2014/188 Sch.1 para.3
s.70, applied: SSI 2014/150 Reg.15, SSI
2014/188 Sch.1 para.3
s.71, applied: SSI 2014/150 Reg.15, SSI
2014/188 Sch.1 para.3
s.72, applied: SSI 2014/150 Reg.15, SSI
2014/188 Sch.1 para.3
s.76, applied: SSI 2014/150 Reg.16, SSI
2014/188 Sch.1 para.3
s.79, applied: SSI 2014/194 Reg.2

s.79, enabling: SSI 2014/194
s.84, applied: SSI 2014/194 Reg.2
s.84, enabling: SSI 2014/194
s.95, applied: SSI 2014/194 Reg.2
s.95, enabling: SSI 2014/194
s.99, applied: SSI 2014/347
s.99, enabling: SSI 2014/347
s.100, applied: SSI 2014/347
s.100, enabling: SSI 2014/347
s.104, applied: SSI 2014/189 Art.3
s.107, enabling: SSI 2014/189
s.108, applied: 2014 asp 16 s.18
s.110, applied: SSI 2014/188, SSI 2014/346
s.110, referred to: SSI 2014/188
s.110, enabling: SSI 2014/188, SSI 2014/346
s.115, applied: SSI 2014/150
s.115, enabling: SSI 2014/150, SSI 2014/347
s.116, applied: SSI 2014/188, SSI 2014/189,
SSI 2014/190, SSI 2014/194, SSI 2014/346,
SSI 2014/347
s.116, enabling: SSI 2014/41, SSI 2014/150,
SSI 2014/188, SSI 2014/190, SSI 2014/346
s.117, enabling: SSI 2014/41, SSI 2014/188,
SSI 2014/190, SSI 2014/346
s.122, enabling: SSI 2014/127
s.123, enabling: SSI 2014/41
Sch.1 para.2, applied: SSI 2014/188 Sch.1
para.1
Sch.1 para.7, amended: SSI 2014/190 Art.5
Sch.3 para.27, amended: SSI 2014/346 Art.2
Sch.4, substituted: SSI 2014/346 Art.4
Sch.4 para.11A, added: SSI 2014/190 Art.6
Sch.4 para.11B, amended: SSI 2014/346
Art.4
Sch.5 para.14, amended: SSI 2014/346 Art.3
Sch.5 para.15, repealed: 2014 c.14 Sch.7
Sch.5 para.18, amended: SSI 2014/190 Art.2
Sch.5 para.18, repealed (in part): SSI
2014/190 Art.2

**asp 8. Police and Fire Reform (Scotland) Act
2012**
applied: SSI 2014/164 Sch.4 Part 2
s.1, applied: SSI 2014/164 Sch.2 Part 1
s.2, applied: SI 2014/1638 Reg.13
s.9, applied: SSI 2014/67 Reg.3, SSI
2014/68 Reg.3
s.15, applied: SSI 2014/67 Reg.3
s.16, applied: SSI 2014/67 Reg.3, SSI
2014/68 Reg.3
s.26, applied: SI 2014/1638 Reg.3

s.26, referred to: SI 2014/1638 Reg.2, Reg.3,
Sch.11 para.9
s.31, applied: 2014 asp 1 s.9
s.48, enabling: SSI 2014/1, SSI 2014/67, SSI
2014/68
s.54, applied: SSI 2014/1, SSI 2014/67, SSI
2014/68
s.54, referred to: SSI 2014/67, SSI 2014/68
s.56, applied: 2014 asp 10 Sch.1 para.13
s.125, enabling: SSI 2014/1, SSI 2014/67,
SSI 2014/68
Sch.5 para.8, applied: SSI 2014/67 Reg.3,
SSI 2014/68 Reg.3
Sch.7 Part 1 para.13, repealed (in part): 2014
c.12 Sch.11 para.102
Sch.7 Part 2 para.56, repealed: 2014 asp 14
Sch.2 para.19

asp 9. Long Leases (Scotland) Act 2012
s.8, referred to: SSI 2014/9 Reg.2
s.8, enabling: SSI 2014/9
s.14, referred to: SSI 2014/9 Reg.3
s.14, enabling: SSI 2014/9
s.17, referred to: SSI 2014/9 Reg.4
s.17, enabling: SSI 2014/9
s.23, referred to: SSI 2014/9 Reg.5
s.23, enabling: SSI 2014/9
s.24, referred to: SSI 2014/9 Reg.6
s.24, enabling: SSI 2014/9
s.25, referred to: SSI 2014/9 Reg.7
s.25, enabling: SSI 2014/9
s.26, referred to: SSI 2014/9 Reg.8
s.26, enabling: SSI 2014/9
s.27, referred to: SSI 2014/9 Reg.9
s.27, enabling: SSI 2014/9
s.28, referred to: SSI 2014/9 Reg.10
s.28, enabling: SSI 2014/9
s.45, referred to: SSI 2014/9 Reg.11
s.45, enabling: SSI 2014/9
s.50, referred to: SSI 2014/9 Reg.12
s.50, enabling: SSI 2014/9
s.54, referred to: SSI 2014/9 Reg.13
s.54, enabling: SSI 2014/9
s.56, referred to: SSI 2014/9 Reg.14
s.56, enabling: SSI 2014/9
s.57, referred to: SSI 2014/9 Reg.15
s.57, enabling: SSI 2014/9
s.63, referred to: SSI 2014/9 Reg.16
s.63, enabling: SSI 2014/9
s.64, referred to: SSI 2014/9 Reg.17
s.64, enabling: SSI 2014/9
s.67, referred to: SSI 2014/9 Reg.18

s.67, enabling: SSI 2014/9
s.68, referred to: SSI 2014/9 Reg.16, Reg.18
s.68, enabling: SSI 2014/9
s.71, referred to: SSI 2014/9 Reg.20
s.71, enabling: SSI 2014/9
s.74, referred to: SSI 2014/9 Reg.19
s.74, enabling: SSI 2014/9
s.75, referred to: SSI 2014/9 Reg.2, Reg.3,
Reg.4, Reg.5, Reg.6, Reg.7, Reg.8, Reg.9,
Reg.10
s.75, enabling: SSI 2014/9
s.78, applied: SSI 2014/8 Art.2
s.78, referred to: SSI 2014/8 Art.2
s.78, enabling: SSI 2014/8
s.81, applied: SSI 2014/190
s.81, enabling: SSI 2014/190
s.82, enabling: SSI 2014/9

2013

asp 1. Social Care (Self-directed Support)
(Scotland) Act 2013
Commencement Orders: SSI 2014/32 Art.2,
Art.3, Art.4
s.3, applied: 2014 c.23 s.73, SSI 2014/25
Reg.3A, SSI 2014/65 Reg.3, SSI 2014/345
Sch.1 Part 1
s.3, referred to: 2014 asp 9 Sch.1 Part 1
s.5, applied: 2014 c.23 s.49, s.50, s.51, Sch.1
para.9, SSI 2014/25 Reg.7, Reg.11, SSI
2014/345 Sch.1 Part 1
s.5, disapplied: SSI 2014/32 Art.4
s.5, referred to: 2014 asp 9 Sch.1 Part 1
s.7, applied: SSI 2014/25 Reg.11
s.8, applied: SSI 2014/25 Reg.7
s.8, disapplied: SSI 2014/32 Art.4
s.9, applied: SSI 2014/345 Sch.1 Part 1
s.11, applied: SSI 2014/345 Sch.1 Part 1
s.15, applied: SSI 2014/25 Reg.10
s.15, enabling: SSI 2014/25, SSI 2014/65
s.16, applied: SSI 2014/345 Sch.1 Part 1
s.16, referred to: 2014 asp 9 Sch.1 Part 1
s.19, applied: SSI 2014/345 Sch.1 Part 1
s.19, referred to: 2014 asp 9 Sch.1 Part 1
s.20, repealed: 2014 asp 9 s.71
s.22, enabling: SSI 2014/25, SSI 2014/65
s.26, applied: SSI 2014/90
s.26, enabling: SSI 2014/90
s.27, enabling: SSI 2014/90
s.28, enabling: SSI 2014/32

asp 3. Scottish Civil Justice Council and Criminal Legal Assistance Act 2013

    Part 1, applied: 2014 asp 10 s.68, 2014 asp 16 s.49

    s.2, amended: 2014 asp 10 Sch.9 para.13, 2014 asp 18 Sch.5 para.18, Sch.5 para.31

    s.4, amended: 2014 asp 10 Sch.9 para.13, 2014 asp 18 Sch.5 para.31

    s.4, applied: SSI 2014/119, SSI 2014/152, SSI 2014/201, SSI 2014/291, SSI 2014/302, SSI 2014/371

    s.6, amended: 2014 asp 10 Sch.9 para.13

    s.8, amended: 2014 asp 10 Sch.9 para.13

    s.13, amended: 2014 asp 10 Sch.9 para.13

    s.13A, added: 2014 asp 10 Sch.9 para.13

    s.16, substituted: 2014 asp 10 Sch.9 para.13

asp 4. Budget (Scotland) Act 2013

    Part 2, repealed: 2014 asp 6 s.8

    s.4, amended: SSI 2014/81 Art.2

    s.7, applied: SSI 2014/81

    s.7, enabling: SSI 2014/81

    Sch.1, amended: SSI 2014/81 Art.3

    Sch.2, amended: SSI 2014/81 Art.4

asp 5. Water Resources (Scotland) Act 2013

    s.5, amended: 2014 asp 3 Sch.3 para.10

    s.21, amended: 2014 asp 3 Sch.3 para.10

    s.50, amended: 2014 asp 3 Sch.3 para.10

asp 6. High Hedges (Scotland) Act 2013

    Commencement Orders: SSI 2014/54 Art.2

    s.26, applied: SSI 2014/55 Art.2

    s.29, applied: SSI 2014/55 Art.2

    s.36, enabling: SSI 2014/55

    s.38, enabling: SSI 2014/54

asp 7. Aquaculture and Fisheries (Scotland) Act 2013

    Part 1 c.3, applied: SSI 2014/176 Art.2

    s.11, enabling: SSI 2014/176

asp 11. Land and Buildings Transaction Tax (Scotland) Act 2013

    Commencement Orders: SSI 2014/279 Sch.1, Art.2

    applied: 2014 asp 16 s.81, s.108, SSI 2014/377 Art.6

    s.9, applied: SSI 2014/377 Art.3, Art.4

    s.10, amended: 2014 asp 16 Sch.4 para.9

    s.10, applied: SSI 2014/377 Art.3, Art.4

    s.11, amended: 2014 asp 16 Sch.4 para.9

    s.24, applied: 2014 asp 16 s.108

    s.25, applied: 2014 asp 16 s.182

    s.27, amended: 2014 asp 16 Sch.4 para.9

    s.29, applied: 2014 asp 16 s.159, s.182

    s.30, applied: SSI 2014/150 Sch.1 Part 4, SSI 2014/347 Sch.2, SSI 2014/376 Art.2

    s.31, applied: 2014 asp 16 s.159, s.182, SSI 2014/375 Reg.12

    s.32, amended: 2014 asp 16 Sch.4 para.9

    s.33, applied: 2014 asp 16 s.159, s.182

    s.34, applied: 2014 asp 16 s.182

    s.35, amended: 2014 asp 16 Sch.4 para.9

    s.37, repealed: 2014 asp 16 Sch.4 para.9

    s.37A, added: 2014 asp 16 Sch.4 para.9

    s.37A, applied: SSI 2014/375 Reg.9

    s.40, applied: 2014 asp 16 s.168

    s.41, applied: 2014 asp 16 s.182

    s.41, referred to: SSI 2014/375 Reg.9, Reg.12

    s.41, repealed (in part): 2014 asp 16 Sch.4 para.9

    s.42, enabling: SSI 2014/375

    s.43, applied: SSI 2014/376 Art.2

    s.48, amended: 2014 asp 16 Sch.4 para.9

    s.50, amended: 2014 asp 16 Sch.4 para.9

    s.54, amended: 2014 asp 16 Sch.4 para.9

    s.54, repealed (in part): 2014 asp 16 Sch.4 para.9

    s.55, repealed: 2014 asp 16 Sch.4 para.9

    s.56, repealed: 2014 asp 16 Sch.4 para.9

    s.63, amended: 2014 asp 16 Sch.4 para.9

    s.67, enabling: SSI 2014/376, SSI 2014/377

    s.68, amended: 2014 asp 16 Sch.4 para.9

    s.68, applied: 2014 asp 16 s.108

    s.68, repealed (in part): 2014 asp 16 Sch.4 para.9

    s.70, amended: 2014 asp 16 Sch.4 para.9

    s.70, enabling: SSI 2014/279

    Sch.1 para.2, amended: 2014 c.29 s.4

    Sch.2 para.16, amended: 2014 asp 16 Sch.4 para.9

    Sch.2 para.17, amended: SSI 2014/351 Art.2

    Sch.2 para.17, enabling: SSI 2014/351

    Sch.5 Part 4 para.11, applied: SSI 2014/350 Art.2

    Sch.5 Part 4 para.12, enabling: SSI 2014/350

    Sch.5 Part 5 para.18, amended: 2014 asp 16 Sch.4 para.9

    Sch.8 Part 3 para.11, applied: SSI 2014/375 Reg.16

    Sch.8 Part 3 para.11, enabling: SSI 2014/375

    Sch.8 Part 4 para.20, applied: SSI 2014/375 Reg.17

    Sch.8 Part 4 para.20, enabling: SSI 2014/375

Sch.8 Part 5 para.21, applied: SSI 2014/375
Reg.18, Reg.19
Sch.8 Part 5 para.21, enabling: SSI 2014/375
Sch.10 Part 1 para.1, amended: 2014 asp 16
Sch.4 para.9
Sch.10 Part 3A, added: 2014 asp 16 Sch.4
para.9
Sch.11 Part 1 para.1, amended: 2014 asp 16
Sch.4 para.9
Sch.11 Part 2 para.5, amended: 2014 asp 16
Sch.4 para.9
Sch.11 Part 3 para.6, applied: SSI 2014/350
Art.3
Sch.11 Part 3 para.6, enabling: SSI 2014/350
Sch.11 Part 3 para.9, amended: 2014 asp 16
Sch.4 para.9
Sch.11 Part 4A, added: 2014 asp 16 Sch.4
para.9
Sch.13 para.15, applied: SSI 2014/352 Reg.2
Sch.13 para.15, enabling: SSI 2014/352
Sch.17, applied: 2014 asp 16 s.247
Sch.17 Part 4 para.17, applied: SSI 2014/377
Art.7
Sch.17 Part 4 para.18, applied: SSI 2014/377
Art.8
Sch.17 Part 4 para.18, referred to: SSI
2014/377 Art.8
Sch.17 Part 5 para.25, applied: SSI 2014/377
Art.9
Sch.17 Part 5 para.26, applied: SSI 2014/377
Art.9
Sch.17 Part 7 para.35, amended: 2014 asp 16
Sch.4 para.9
Sch.17 Part 8 para.38, amended: 2014 asp 16
Sch.4 para.9
Sch.18, applied: 2014 asp 16 s.247, s.248
Sch.19 Part 2 para.3, applied: 2014 asp 16
s.108
Sch.19 Part 4 para.10, applied: 2014 asp 16
s.159, s.182
Sch.19 Part 4 para.11, applied: 2014 asp 16
s.182
Sch.19 Part 6 para.20, applied: 2014 asp 16
s.159, s.182
Sch.19 Part 6 para.22, applied: 2014 asp 16
s.159, s.182
Sch.19 Part 6 para.24, applied: SSI 2014/377
Art.10
Sch.19 Part 6 para.24, referred to: SSI
2014/377 Art.10

Sch.19 Part 6 para.25, amended: 2014 asp 16
Sch.4 para.9
Sch.19 Part 6 para.27, applied: SSI 2014/377
Art.11
Sch.19 Part 6 para.30, applied: 2014 asp 16
s.159, s.182

asp 12. Post-16 Education (Scotland) Act 2013
Commencement Orders: SSI 2014/21 Art.4,
Art.5, Sch.1, Art.2, Sch.2; SSI 2014/79
Sch.2; SSI 2014/144 Art.2; SSI 2014/79
Art.2, Sch.1
s.20, applied: SSI 2014/116
s.20, enabling: SSI 2014/116
s.23, enabling: SSI 2014/21, SSI 2014/79,
SSI 2014/144

asp 14. Scottish Independence Referendum Act 2013
s.9, enabling: SSI 2014/101
Sch.3 para.11, applied: SSI 2014/101 Art.8
Sch.4 Part 1 para.1, amended: 2014 c.29 s.4

2014

asp 1. Victims and Witnesses (Scotland) Act 2014
Commencement Orders: SSI 2014/117
Art.3; SSI 2014/210 Art.3, Sch.1, Art.2; SSI
2014/359 Art.1, Art.3, Sch.1, Art.2
Royal Assent, January 17, 2014
s.2, applied: SSI 2014/360 Art.2
s.2, enabling: SSI 2014/360
s.6, applied: SSI 2014/359 Art.1, SSI
2014/360 Art.2
s.6, enabling: SSI 2014/360
s.34, enabling: SSI 2014/117, SSI 2014/210,
SSI 2014/359

asp 2. Landfill Tax (Scotland) Act 2014
Commencement Orders: 2014 asp 16 Sch.4
para.10; SSI 2014/277 Sch.1, Art.2
Royal Assent, January 21, 2014
referred to: 2014 asp 16 s.108
s.5, applied: 2014 asp 16 s.108
s.6, applied: 2014 asp 16 s.108, SSI
2014/367 Art.3
s.6, enabling: SSI 2014/367
s.13, applied: 2014 asp 16 s.108
s.14, applied: 2014 asp 16 s.108
s.15, amended: 2014 asp 16 Sch.4 para.10
s.18, amended: 2014 asp 16 Sch.4 para.10

s.22, repealed (in part): 2014 asp 16 Sch.4
para.10
s.23, repealed (in part): 2014 asp 16 Sch.4
para.10
s.25, amended: 2014 asp 16 Sch.4 para.10
s.25, applied: 2014 asp 16 s.159, s.168
s.25A, added: 2014 asp 16 Sch.4 para.10
s.26, repealed: 2014 asp 16 Sch.4 para.10
s.28, repealed: 2014 asp 16 Sch.4 para.10
s.29, repealed: 2014 asp 16 Sch.4 para.10
s.30, amended: 2014 asp 16 Sch.4 para.10
s.30, applied: SSI 2014/367 Art.3
s.31, amended: 2014 asp 16 Sch.4 para.10
s.31, applied: SSI 2014/367 Art.3
s.32, repealed: 2014 asp 16 Sch.4 para.10
s.34, amended: 2014 asp 16 Sch.4 para.10
s.34, repealed (in part): 2014 asp 16 Sch.4
para.10
s.35, repealed: 2014 asp 16 Sch.4 para.10
s.36, repealed: 2014 asp 16 Sch.4 para.10
s.39, amended: 2014 asp 16 Sch.4 para.10
s.41, amended: 2014 asp 16 Sch.4 para.10
s.41, applied: 2014 asp 16 s.108
s.41, repealed (in part): 2014 asp 16 Sch.4
para.10
s.43, amended: 2014 asp 16 Sch.4 para.10
s.43, enabling: SSI 2014/277

asp 3. Regulatory Reform (Scotland) Act 2014
Commencement Orders: SSI 2014/160 Art.2,
Sch.1
Royal Assent, February 19, 2014
s.18, applied: SSI 2014/258 Sch.1 para.1
s.34, applied: SSI 2014/319 Art.2
s.35, applied: SSI 2014/319 Art.2
s.36, applied: SSI 2014/319 Art.2
s.38, applied: SSI 2014/319 Art.2
s.39, applied: SSI 2014/323 Art.2
s.39, enabling: SSI 2014/323
s.40, applied: SSI 2014/319 Sch.1 para.14,
Sch.2 para.26, Sch.3 para.14, Sch.4 para.9
s.40, enabling: SSI 2014/324
s.41, applied: SSI 2014/319 Sch.1 para.14,
Sch.2 para.26
s.53, enabling: SSI 2014/319
s.56, applied: SSI 2014/160 Art.3
s.58, enabling: SSI 2014/319
s.61, enabling: SSI 2014/160

**asp 4. Burrell Collection (Lending and
Borrowing) (Scotland) Act 2014**
Royal Assent, February 25, 2014

**asp 5. Marriage and Civil Partnership (Scotland)
Act 2014**
Commencement Orders: SSI 2014/121
Art.2; SSI 2014/212 Art.3, Sch.1, Art.2; SSI
2014/287 Art.3, Sch.1
Royal Assent, March 12, 2014
s.10, applied: SSI 2014/361
s.10, enabling: SSI 2014/361
s.12, referred to: SSI 2014/212 Art.3, SSI
2014/287 Art.4
s.13, referred to: SSI 2014/287 Art.4
s.14, referred to: SSI 2014/287 Art.4
s.28, disapplied: SSI 2014/212 Art.3
s.35, enabling: SSI 2014/287
s.36, enabling: SSI 2014/121, SSI 2014/212,
SSI 2014/218, SSI 2014/287

asp 6. Budget (Scotland) Act 2014
Royal Assent, March 12, 2014
s.4, amended: SSI 2014/363 Art.2
s.7, applied: SSI 2014/363
s.7, enabling: SSI 2014/363
Sch.1, amended: SSI 2014/363 Art.3
Sch.2, amended: SSI 2014/363 Art.4

**asp 7. City of Edinburgh Council (Leith Links
and Surplus Fire Fund) Act 2014**
Royal Assent, March 27, 2014

**asp 8. Children and Young People (Scotland)
Act 2014**
Commencement Orders: SSI 2014/131 Art.2,
Sch.1; SSI 2014/165 Sch.1, Art.2; SSI
2014/251 Art.2; SSI 2014/314 Art.2, Sch.1;
SSI 2014/353 Art.2, Sch.1; SSI 2014/365
Art.2
Royal Assent, March 27, 2014
s.7, amended: 2014 asp 9 s.58
s.47, applied: SSI 2014/132 Art.2, SSI
2014/196 Art.3
s.47, enabling: SSI 2014/196
s.49, varied: SSI 2014/131 Art.3
s.99, applied: SSI 2014/196
s.99, enabling: SSI 2014/196
s.101, enabling: SSI 2014/132, SSI 2014/315
s.102, enabling: SSI 2014/131, SSI
2014/165, SSI 2014/251, SSI 2014/314, SSI
2014/353, SSI 2014/365

**asp 9. Public Bodies (Joint Working) (Scotland)
Act 2014**
Commencement Orders: SSI 2014/202
Art.2; SSI 2014/231 Art.2, Art.3
Royal Assent, April 01, 2014
applied: SSI 2014/341 Sch.1

s.1, applied: SSI 2014/281 Art.2, SSI 2014/283 Reg.2, SSI 2014/285 Art.2, SSI 2014/341 Sch.1, SSI 2014/344 Reg.2, Reg.3, SSI 2014/345 Reg.2

s.1, referred to: SSI 2014/281 Art.3, Art.4

s.1, enabling: SSI 2014/341, SSI 2014/344, SSI 2014/345

s.2, applied: SSI 2014/281 Art.2, Art.4, SSI 2014/285 Art.2, SSI 2014/341 Sch.1

s.5, applied: SSI 2014/343, SSI 2014/343 Reg.2

s.5, enabling: SSI 2014/343

s.6, applied: SSI 2014/283 Reg.2, SSI 2014/341 Sch.1

s.6, enabling: SSI 2014/283

s.7, applied: SSI 2014/284 Reg.2

s.7, enabling: SSI 2014/284

s.9, applied: SSI 2014/284 Reg.3

s.9, enabling: SSI 2014/284

s.12, applied: SSI 2014/285

s.12, enabling: SSI 2014/285

s.15, applied: SSI 2014/284 Reg.3

s.15, enabling: SSI 2014/284

s.17, applied: SSI 2014/341 Sch.1

s.17, enabling: SSI 2014/281

s.20, enabling: SSI 2014/341

s.23, amended: SSI 2014/342 Art.2

s.23, applied: SSI 2014/282 Reg.2

s.23, enabling: SSI 2014/282

s.24, amended: SSI 2014/342 Art.2

s.26, amended: SSI 2014/342 Art.2

s.30, applied: SSI 2014/341 Sch.1

s.32, applied: SSI 2014/308 Reg.2

s.32, enabling: SSI 2014/308

s.33, applied: SSI 2014/283 Reg.3

s.33, enabling: SSI 2014/283

s.36, amended: SSI 2014/342 Art.2

s.36, applied: SSI 2014/326 Reg.3

s.39, applied: SSI 2014/341 Sch.1

s.41, applied: SSI 2014/283 Reg.4, SSI 2014/326 Reg.6

s.41, enabling: SSI 2014/283

s.42, applied: SSI 2014/326 Reg.2

s.42, enabling: SSI 2014/326

s.43, applied: SSI 2014/326 Reg.9

s.46, applied: SSI 2014/283 Reg.2

s.46, enabling: SSI 2014/283

s.51, applied: SSI 2014/284 Reg.3

s.51, enabling: SSI 2014/284

s.59, amended: SSI 2014/342 Art.2

s.62, amended: SSI 2014/342 Art.2

s.68, enabling: SSI 2014/307

s.69, applied: SSI 2014/341, SSI 2014/342, SSI 2014/343, SSI 2014/344, SSI 2014/345

s.69, enabling: SSI 2014/281, SSI 2014/283, SSI 2014/285, SSI 2014/326, SSI 2014/341, SSI 2014/344, SSI 2014/345

s.70, enabling: SSI 2014/342

s.72, enabling: SSI 2014/202, SSI 2014/231

Sch.1, referred to: SSI 2014/283 Reg.2

Sch.1 Part 1, amended: SSI 2014/345 Reg.3

asp 10. Tribunals (Scotland) Act 2014

Commencement Orders: SSI 2014/183 Art.2

Royal Assent, April 15, 2014

s.28, referred to: 2014 asp 18 Sch.4 para.3

s.57A, added: 2014 asp 18 Sch.5 para.24

s.77, repealed: 2014 asp 18 Sch.4 para.8

s.83, enabling: SSI 2014/183

Sch.1, referred to: 2014 asp 18 Sch.4 para.3

Sch.1 Part 1 para.10A, added: 2014 asp 16 Sch.4 para.11

Sch.1 Part 2 para.13, amended: 2014 asp 16 Sch.4 para.11

Sch.9 Part 1 para.10, amended: 2014 asp 18 s.131

asp 11. Bankruptcy and Debt Advice (Scotland) Act 2014

Commencement Orders: SSI 2014/172 Sch.1, Art.2; SSI 2014/261 Art.3

Royal Assent, April 29, 2014

s.8, disapplied: SSI 2014/261 Art.4

s.12, disapplied: SSI 2014/261 Art.4

s.20, disapplied: SSI 2014/261 Art.4

s.22, disapplied: SSI 2014/261 Art.4

s.24, disapplied: SSI 2014/261 Art.4, Art.8

s.25, disapplied: SSI 2014/261 Art.4, Art.9

s.26, disapplied: SSI 2014/261 Art.4

s.27, disapplied: SSI 2014/261 Art.4

s.34, disapplied: SSI 2014/261 Art.4

s.38, disapplied: SSI 2014/261 Art.4, Art.10

s.38, referred to: SSI 2014/261 Art.10

s.48, disapplied: SSI 2014/261 Art.4

s.49, disapplied: SSI 2014/261 Art.4, Art.11

s.50, disapplied: SSI 2014/261 Art.4

s.53, applied: SSI 2014/172 Art.3

s.55, enabling: SSI 2014/293

s.57, enabling: SSI 2014/172, SSI 2014/261

Sch.3 para.3, disapplied: SSI 2014/261 Art.4

Sch.3 para.12, disapplied: SSI 2014/261 Art.4

Sch.3 para.25, disapplied: SSI 2014/261 Art.4

Sch.3 para.31, disapplied: SSI 2014/261
Art.4
Sch.3 para.35, disapplied: SSI 2014/261
Art.4
Sch.3 para.38, applied: SSI 2014/172 Art.3

asp 12. Procurement Reform (Scotland) Act 2014
Royal Assent, June 17, 2014
Sch.1 Part 1 para.13A, added: 2014 asp 16
Sch.4 para.12

asp 13. Buildings (Recovery of Expenses) (Scotland) Act 2014
Royal Assent, July 24, 2014

asp 14. Housing (Scotland) Act 2014
Commencement Orders: SSI 2014/264 Art.3,
Art.4, Art.2, Art.6, Sch.1
Royal Assent, August 01, 2014
s.104, enabling: SSI 2014/264

asp 15. City of Edinburgh Council (Portobello Park) Act 2014
Royal Assent, August 01, 2014

asp 16. Revenue Scotland and Tax Powers Act 2014
Commencement Orders: SSI 2014/278
Sch.1, Art.2; SSI 2014/370 Sch.1, Art.2
Royal Assent, September 24, 2014
Part 7, applied: SSI 2014/375 Reg.6

s.15, applied: SI 2014/3294 Art.4
s.21, referred to: 2014 asp 18 Sch.4 para.3
s.22, applied: 2014 asp 18 Sch.4 para.3
s.58, repealed: 2014 asp 18 Sch.4 para.9
s.59, amended: 2014 asp 18 Sch.4 para.9
s.63, referred to: SSI 2014/375 Reg.10
s.64, referred to: SSI 2014/375 Reg.10
s.107, applied: 2014 asp 2 s.18
s.241, applied: SSI 2014/375 Reg.7
s.260, enabling: SSI 2014/278, SSI 2014/370
Sch.2 Part 1 para.1, referred to: SSI
2014/355 Reg.4
Sch.2 Part 1 para.2, enabling: SSI 2014/355
Sch.2 Part 1 para.4, referred to: SSI
2014/355 Reg.3
Sch.2 Part 1 para.6, referred to: SSI
2014/355 Reg.4
Sch.2 Part 1 para.9, enabling: SSI 2014/355

asp 17. Disabled Persons Parking Badges (Scotland) Act 2014
Royal Assent, September 24, 2014

asp 18. Courts Reform (Scotland) Act 2014
Royal Assent, November 10, 2014

asp 19. Historic Environment Scotland Act 2014
Commencement Orders: SSI 2014/368 Art.2
Royal Assent, December 09, 2014
s.31, enabling: SI 2014/3307

ACTS OF THE PARLIAMENT OF ENGLAND, WALES & THE UNITED KINGDOM

1351

2. Treason Act 1351
disapplied: SI 2014/3229 Sch.2 para.6

7 & 8 Will. 3 (1695)

69. Division of Commonties Act 1695
varied: 2014 asp 18 s.38

14 Geo. 3 (1774)

78. Fires Prevention (Metropolis) Act 1774
s.86, see *Gore v Stannard (t/a Wyvern Tyres)*
[2012] EWCA Civ 1248, [2014] Q.B. 1 (CA
(Civ Div)), Ward, L.J.

39 & 40 Geo. 3 (1800)

88. Crown Private Estate Act 1800
disapplied: SI 2014/3229 Sch.2 para.6

52 Geo. 3 (1812)

161. Duchy of Lancaster Act 1812
varied: SI 2014/2708 Art.5

3 Geo. 4 (1822)

33. Riotous Assemblies (Scotland) Act 1822
s.10, see *Board of Managers of St Mary's
Kenmure v East Dunbartonshire Council*
[2014] CSIH 46, 2014 S.C. 665 (IH (Ex
Div)), Lady Smith

6 Geo. 4 (1825)

50. Juries Act 1825
s.29, applied: SI 2014/1610 r.38_8

7 Geo. 4 (1826)

**16. Chelsea
and Kilmainham Hospitals Act 1826**
applied: SI 2014/2336 Reg.128
s.24, applied: SI 2014/2336 Reg.121

3 & 4 Will. 4 (1833)

85. Saint Helena Act 1833
s.112, enabling: SI 2014/269, SI 2014/497,
SI 2014/1098, SI 2014/1100, SI 2014/1368,
SI 2014/2703, SI 2014/2707, SI 2014/2710,
SI 2014/2711, SI 2014/2919

6 & 7 Will. 4 (1836)

71. Tithe Act 1836
applied: SI 2014/813 Sch.1

7 Will. 4 & 1 Vict. (1837)

26. Wills Act 1837
s.18, amended: SI 2014/3168 Sch.1 para.1
s.18D, added: SI 2014/3168 Sch.1 para.1

1 & 2 Vict. (1837-38)

110. Judgments Act 1838
see *Jones v Secretary of State for Energy
and Climate Change* [2014] EWCA Civ 363,
[2014] 3 All E.R. 956 (CA (Civ Div)),
Patten LJ; see *Societe pour la Recherche, la
Production, le Transport, la Transformation
et la Commercialisation des Hydrocarbures
SpA (Sonatrach) v Statoil Natural Gas LLC
(Statoil)* [2014] EWHC 875 (Comm), [2014]
2 All E.R. (Comm) 857 (QBD (Comm)),
Flaux J
s.17, see *Novoship (UK) Ltd v Mikhaylyuk*
[2014] EWCA Civ 908, [2014] W.T.L.R.
1521 (CA (Civ Div)), Longmore LJ
s.17, referred to: 2014 c.20 s.22, s.34, SI
2014/3238 Sch.2 para.2, Sch.4 para.2

4 & 5 Vict. (1841)

30. Ordnance Survey Act 1841
    applied: SI 2014/17 Art.7

8 & 9 Vict. (1845)

18. Lands Clauses Consolidation Act 1845
    applied: SI 2014/3038 Sch.4 para.8
    s.1, see *Stynes v Western Power (East Midlands) Plc* [2014] R.V.R. 15 (UT (Lands)), Sir Keith Lindblom P
    s.63, see *Stynes v Western Power (East Midlands) Plc* [2014] R.V.R. 15 (UT (Lands)), Sir Keith Lindblom P
    s.63, applied: SI 2014/2434 Art.17
    s.68, applied: SI 2014/2434 Art.17
20. Railways Clauses Consolidation Act 1845
    s.46, amended: SI 2014/909 Art.3
    s.46, applied: SI 2014/909 Art.3
    s.58, applied: SI 2014/909 Art.3, SI 2014/2027 Art.3
    s.61, applied: SI 2014/909 Art.3, SI 2014/2027 Art.3
    s.68, applied: SI 2014/909 Art.3, SI 2014/2027 Art.3
    s.71, applied: SI 2014/909 Art.3, SI 2014/2027 Art.3
    s.75, applied: SI 2014/2027 Art.3
    s.77, applied: SI 2014/909 Art.3, SI 2014/2027 Art.3
    s.85, applied: SI 2014/909 Art.3
    s.103, applied: SI 2014/2027 Art.3
    s.105, applied: SI 2014/909 Art.3, SI 2014/2027 Art.3
    s.145, applied: SI 2014/2027 Art.3
    Sch.1, applied: SI 2014/909 Art.3, SI 2014/2027 Art.3
118. Inclosure Act 1845
    s.2, referred to: SI 2014/3038 Sch.4 para.8
    s.147, applied: SI 2014/3038 Sch.4 para.8
    s.149, applied: SI 2014/3038 Sch.4 para.8

9 & 10 Vict. (1846)

70. Inclosure Act 1846
    s.11, applied: SI 2014/3038 Sch.4 para.8

10 & 11 Vict. (1847)

16. Commissioners Clauses Act 1847
    varied: SSI 2014/158 Art.3
    s.2, applied: SSI 2014/158 Art.3
    s.56, applied: SSI 2014/158 Art.3
    s.58, applied: SSI 2014/158 Art.3
    s.65, applied: SSI 2014/158 Art.3
27. Harbours, Docks, and Piers Clauses Act 1847
    disapplied: SI 2014/2935 Art.8
    varied: SSI 2014/158 Art.3
    s.1, applied: SSI 2014/158 Art.3, SSI 2014/224 Art.3
    s.1, varied: SI 2014/2935 Art.3
    s.3, applied: SI 2014/2935 Art.3
    s.3, varied: SSI 2014/224 Art.3
    s.26, varied: SI 2014/2935 Art.3
    s.28, varied: SI 2014/2935 Art.3
    s.29, varied: SI 2014/2935 Art.3
    s.32, applied: SSI 2014/158 Art.3
    s.32, varied: SI 2014/2935 Art.3
    s.33, applied: SSI 2014/224 Art.3
    s.33, disapplied: SI 2014/2935 Art.29
    s.33, varied: SI 2014/2935 Art.3
    s.37, applied: SSI 2014/158 Art.3, SSI 2014/224 Art.3
    s.37, varied: SI 2014/2935 Art.3
    s.40, varied: SI 2014/2935 Art.3
    s.42, applied: SSI 2014/158 Art.3, SSI 2014/224 Art.3
    s.44, varied: SI 2014/2935 Art.3
    s.46, varied: SI 2014/2935 Art.3
    s.51, applied: SSI 2014/158 Art.3, SSI 2014/224 Art.3
    s.51, varied: SI 2014/2935 Art.3
    s.52, applied: SI 2014/2935 Sch.9 para.19
    s.54, applied: SSI 2014/158 Art.3, SSI 2014/224 Art.3
    s.56, applied: SI 2014/2935 Sch.9 para.22
    s.56, varied: SI 2014/2935 Art.3
    s.57, applied: SI 2014/2935 Sch.9 para.19
    s.58, applied: SI 2014/2935 Art.29
    s.63, applied: SSI 2014/158 Art.3, SSI 2014/224 Art.3
    s.63, varied: SSI 2014/158 Art.3, SSI 2014/224 Art.3
    s.65, applied: SI 2014/2935 Sch.9 para.19

s.65, varied: SI 2014/2935 Art.3, SSI
2014/158 Art.3, SSI 2014/224 Art.3
s.69, applied: SSI 2014/224 Art.3
s.69, varied: SSI 2014/224 Art.3
s.70, varied: SI 2014/2935 Art.3
s.74, varied: SI 2014/2935 Art.3
s.77, varied: SI 2014/2935 Art.3
s.93, varied: SI 2014/2935 Art.3
s.99, varied: SI 2014/2935 Art.3
s.103, varied: SI 2014/2935 Art.3

14 & 15 Vict. (1851)

99. Evidence Act 1851
s.7, applied: SI 2014/1610 r.35_2

18 & 19 Vict. (1855)

81. Places of Worship Registration Act 1855
see *R. (on the application of Hodkin) v
Registrar General of Births, Deaths and
Marriages* [2014] A.C. 610 (SC), Lord
Neuberger JSC
s.2, see *R. (on the application of Hodkin) v
Registrar General of Births, Deaths and
Marriages* [2014] A.C. 610 (SC), Lord
Neuberger JSC
s.3, see *R. (on the application of Hodkin) v
Registrar General of Births, Deaths and
Marriages* [2014] A.C. 610 (SC), Lord
Neuberger JSC

20 & 21 Vict. (1857)

81. Burial Act 1857
s.25, applied: SI 2014/2077 Sch.1 para.1,
Sch.1 para.2, SI 2014/2950 Art.18
s.25, disapplied: SI 2014/2384 Art.23, SI
2014/2441 Art.32

24 & 25 Vict. (1861)

100. Offences against the Person Act 1861
s.18, see *Attorney General's Reference (No.9
of 2013)* [2013] EWCA Crim 597, [2014] 1
Cr. App. R. (S.) 3 (CA (Crim Div)),

Pitchford LJ; see *R. v Howe (Kevin James)*
[2014] EWCA Crim 114, [2014] 2 Cr. App.
R. (S.) 38 (CA (Crim Div)), Lord Thomas
LCJ
s.18, applied: SI 2014/1610 r.38_9
s.20, see *R. v Caceres (Jose)* [2013] EWCA
Crim 924, [2014] 1 Cr. App. R. (S.) 23 (CA
(Crim Div)), Sir John Thomas PQBD; see
R. v Edwards (Christopher James) [2013]
EWCA Crim 728, [2014] 1 Cr. App. R. (S.)
9 (CA (Crim Div)), Davis LJ; see *R. v Oye
(Seun)* [2013] EWCA Crim 1725, [2014] 1
W.L.R. 3354 (CA (Crim Div)), Davis LJ
s.20, applied: SI 2014/1610 r.38_9
s.47, see *R. v Caceres (Jose)* [2013] EWCA
Crim 924, [2014] 1 Cr. App. R. (S.) 23 (CA
(Crim Div)), Sir John Thomas PQBD
s.58, see *R. v Catt (Sarah Louise)* [2013]
EWCA Crim 1187, [2014] 1 Cr. App. R. (S.)
35 (CA (Crim Div)), Rafferty LJ

25 & 26 Vict. (1862)

37. Crown Private Estates Act 1862
s.1, applied: 2014 asp 19 s.30

26 & 27 Vict. (1863)

92. Railways Clauses Act 1863
s.5, applied: SI 2014/909 Art.3
s.7, applied: SI 2014/909 Art.3
s.12, applied: SI 2014/909 Art.3, SI
2014/2027 Art.3

28 & 29 Vict. (1865)

18. Criminal Procedure Act 1865
s.2, applied: SI 2014/1610 r.38_9, r.37_3
s.3, applied: SI 2014/1610 r.37_4
s.5, applied: SI 2014/1610 r.50_8, r.62_15

29 & 30 Vict. (1866)

122. Metropolitan Commons Act 1866
applied: SI 2014/3038 Reg.46
s.29, varied: SI 2014/2708 Art.5

30 & 31 Vict. (1867)

133. Consecration of Churchyards Act 1867
applied: SI 2014/895 Sch.2 para.1

31 & 32 Vict. (1868)

72. Promissory Oaths Act 1868
Sch.1 Part 1, varied: SI 2014/2708 Art.5
Sch.1 Part 2, amended: 2014 asp 18 Sch.5
para.1, Sch.5 para.34

32 & 33 Vict. (1869)

62. Debtors Act 1869
s.5, see *Constantinides v Constantinides*
[2013] EWHC 3688 (Fam), [2014] 1 W.L.R.
1934 (Fam Div), Holman J
107. Metropolitan Commons Amendment Act 1869
applied: SI 2014/3038 Reg.46
115. Metropolitan Public Carriage Act 1869
s.6, amended: SI 2014/560 Sch.1 para.1
s.6, repealed (in part): SI 2014/560 Sch.1
para.1

33 & 34 Vict. (1870)

23. Forfeiture Act 1870
s.2, disapplied: 2014 c.24 s.6
s.2, referred to: SI 2014/2336 Reg.121
35. Apportionment Act 1870
disapplied: SI 2014/512 Reg.166
s.2, see *Amey v Peter Symonds College*
[2013] EWHC 2788 (QB), [2014] I.R.L.R.
206 (QBD), Jay J
s.7, see *Amey v Peter Symonds College*
[2013] EWHC 2788 (QB), [2014] I.R.L.R.
206 (QBD), Jay J

34 & 35 Vict. (1871)

cciv. Wimbledon and Putney Commons Act 1871
s.34, see *Evans v Wimbledon and Putney
Commons Conservators* [2014] EWCA Civ

940, [2014] 2 P. & C.R. 17 (CA (Civ Div)),
Rimer LJ
s.35, see *Evans v Wimbledon and Putney
Commons Conservators* [2014] EWCA Civ
940, [2014] 2 P. & C.R. 17 (CA (Civ Div)),
Rimer LJ
s.36, see *Evans v Wimbledon and Putney
Commons Conservators* [2014] EWCA Civ
940, [2014] 2 P. & C.R. 17 (CA (Civ Div)),
Rimer LJ
s.39, see *Evans v Wimbledon and Putney
Commons Conservators* [2014] EWCA Civ
940, [2014] 2 P. & C.R. 17 (CA (Civ Div)),
Rimer LJ
21. Lloyd's Act 1871
applied: SI 2014/2418 Sch.1
24. Wimbledon and Putney Commons Act 1871
see *Evans v Wimbledon and Putney
Commons Conservators* [2014] EWCA Civ
940, [2014] 2 P. & C.R. 17 (CA (Civ Div)),
Rimer LJ
s.8, see *Evans v Wimbledon and Putney
Commons Conservators* [2014] EWCA Civ
940, [2014] 2 P. & C.R. 17 (CA (Civ Div)),
Rimer LJ
36. Pensions Commutation Act 1871
s.4, amended: SI 2014/560 Sch.1 para.2, SI
2014/3229 Sch.5 para.1
48. Promissory Oaths Act 1871
s.2, amended: 2014 asp 18 Sch.5 para.2

38 & 39 Vict. (1875)

17. Explosives Act 1875
s.23, repealed (in part): SI 2014/1638 Sch.13
para.1, Sch.14 Part 1
s.43, repealed: SI 2014/1639 Sch.3 Part 1
s.61, repealed (in part): SI 2014/1638 Sch.13
para.1, Sch.14 Part 1
s.74, amended: SI 2014/1638 Sch.13 para.1,
Sch.14 Part 1
s.74, applied: SI 2014/1638 Reg.3
s.74, referred to: SI 2014/1638 Reg.3
s.104, repealed: SI 2014/1639 Sch.3 Part 1
55. Public Health Act 1875
s.265, amended: 2014 c.2 Sch.12 para.1
s.265, applied: 2014 c.23 Sch.7 para.18
s.265, varied: 2014 c.23 Sch.5 para.24, Sch.7
para.18

39 & 40 Vict. (1876)

56. Commons Act 1876
applied: SI 2014/3038 Reg.46
s.27, see *Snelling v Burstow Parish Council*
[2013] EWCA Civ 1411, [2014] 1 W.L.R.
2388 (CA (Civ Div)), Patten LJ
70. Sheriff Courts (Scotland) Act 1876
s.54, repealed: 2014 asp 18 Sch.5 para.3
s.54, enabling: SSI 2014/265

41 & 42 Vict. (1878)

31. Bills of Sale Act 1878
applied: 2014 c.14 s.59
71. Metropolitan Commons Act 1878
applied: SI 2014/3038 Reg.46

42 & 43 Vict. (1879)

11. Bankers Books Evidence Act 1879
s.6, applied: SI 2014/1610 Part 28
s.7, applied: SI 2014/1610 r.28_1
s.8, applied: SI 2014/1610 r.76_1, r.76_7

43 & 44 Vict. (1880)

34. Debtors (Scotland) Act 1880
s.4, see *M, Petitioner* 2014 S.C. 165 (IH (2
Div)), The Lord Justice Clerk (Carloway)
41. Burial Laws Amendment Act 1880
applied: SI 2014/813 Sch.2 para.5

45 & 46 Vict. (1882)

31. Bills of Sale Act 1882
s.7, see *Evans v Finance-U-Ltd* [2013]
EWCA Civ 869, [2014] R.T.R. 8 (CA (Civ
Div)), Mummery, L.J.
**43. Bills of Sale Act (1878) Amendment Act
1882**
see *Bassano v Toft* [2014] EWHC 377 (QB),
[2014] E.C.C. 14 (QBD), Popplewell J
applied: 2014 c.14 s.59
75. Married Women's Property Act 1882
applied: SI 2014/840 Sch.1

46 & 47 Vict. (1883)

38. Trial of Lunatics Act 1883
s.2, applied: SI 2014/1610 r.38_14

49 & 50 Vict. (1886)

38. Riot (Damages) Act 1886
see *Mitsui Sumitomo Insurance Co (Europe)
Ltd v Mayor's Office for Policing and Crime*
[2013] EWHC 2734 (Comm), [2014] 1 All
E.R. 422 (QBD (Comm)), Flaux J
s.2, see *Mitsui Sumitomo Insurance Co
(Europe) Ltd v Mayor's Office for Policing
and Crime* [2013] EWHC 2734 (Comm),
[2014] 1 All E.R. 422 (QBD (Comm)),
Flaux J; see *Mitsui Sumitomo Insurance Co
(Europe) Ltd v Mayor's Office for Policing
and Crime* [2014] EWCA Civ 682, [2014] 3
W.L.R. 576 (CA (Civ Div)), Lord Dyson
MR
s.7, see *Mitsui Sumitomo Insurance Co
(Europe) Ltd v Mayor's Office for Policing
and Crime* [2013] EWHC 2734 (Comm),
[2014] 1 All E.R. 422 (QBD (Comm)),
Flaux J; see *Mitsui Sumitomo Insurance Co
(Europe) Ltd v Mayor's Office for Policing
and Crime* [2014] EWCA Civ 682, [2014] 3
W.L.R. 576 (CA (Civ Div)), Lord Dyson
MR

50 & 51 Vict. (1887)

54. British Settlements Act 1887
enabling: SI 2014/269, SI 2014/497, SI
2014/1098, SI 2014/1100, SI 2014/1368, SI
2014/2703, SI 2014/2707, SI 2014/2710, SI
2014/2711, SI 2014/2919

51 & 52 Vict. (1888)

21. Law of Distress Amendment Act 1888
s.7, applied: SI 2014/421 Reg.14, Reg.15
s.8, enabling: SI 2014/600

52 & 53 Vict. (1889)

39. Judicial Factors (Scotland) Act 1889
s.11A, applied: SI 2014/3051 Reg.45

53 & 54 Vict. (1890)

39. Partnership Act 1890
s.24, see *Trustees for S & A Kilcoyne v Sadiq's Judicial Factor* [2014] CSIH 34, 2014 G.W.D. 17-310 (IH (Ex Div)), Lord Brodie
s.35, see *Golstein v Bishop* [2013] EWHC 881 (Ch), [2014] Ch. 131 (Ch D), Christopher Nugee Q.C.; see *Golstein v Bishop* [2014] EWCA Civ 10, [2014] Ch. 455 (CA (Civ Div)), Maurice Kay LJ

54 & 55 Vict. (1891)

43. Forged Transfers Act 1891
s.3, amended: 2014 c.14 Sch.4 para.19

55 & 56 Vict. (1892)

23. Foreign Marriage Act 1892
applied: SI 2014/3061 Sch.4 para.2
s.9, applied: SI 2014/3061 Sch.4 para.3
s.10, applied: SI 2014/3061 Sch.4 para.1
43. Military Lands Act 1892
s.14, applied: SI 2014/862
s.14, enabling: SI 2014/855, SI 2014/862
s.17, applied: SI 2014/855

1893

39. Industrial and Provident Societies Act 1893
applied: 2014 c.14 Sch.3 para.2, Sch.3 para.3, Sch.3 para.7, Sch.3 para.15

71. Sale of Goods Act 1893
see *FG Wilson (Engineering) Ltd v John Holt & Co (Liverpool) Ltd* [2013] EWCA Civ 1232, [2014] 1 W.L.R. 2365 (CA (Civ Div)), Longmore LJ

57 & 58 Vict. (1894)

44. Heritable Securities (Scotland) Act 1894
see *Mortgages 1 Ltd v Chaudhary* 2014 S.L.T. (Sh Ct) 35 (Sh Ct (South Strathclyde) (Airdrie)), Sheriff Principal B A Lockhart
s.5, see *Mortgages 1 Ltd v Chaudhary* 2014 S.L.T. (Sh Ct) 35 (Sh Ct (South Strathclyde) (Airdrie)), Sheriff Principal B A Lockhart
s.5, amended: 2014 asp 18 Sch.5 para.20
73. Local Government Act 1894
s.6, see *Snelling v Burstow Parish Council* [2013] EWCA Civ 1411, [2014] 1 W.L.R. 2388 (CA (Civ Div)), Patten LJ

58 & 59 Vict. (1895)

14. Courts of Law Fees (Scotland) Act 1895
s.2, repealed: 2014 asp 18 Sch.5 para.26
16. Finance Act 1895
s.12, applied: 2014 c.26 Sch.24 para.7

61 & 62 Vict. (1898)

35. Vexatious Actions (Scotland) Act 1898
repealed: 2014 asp 18 Sch.5 para.27
36. Criminal Evidence Act 1898
s.1, applied: SI 2014/1610 r.38_11, r.37_4
s.2, applied: SI 2014/1610 r.38_9
s.3, applied: SI 2014/1610 r.38_9, r.37_3
43. Metropolitan Commons Act 1898
applied: SI 2014/3038 Reg.46
53. Libraries Offences Act 1898
s.3, amended: 2014 c.14 Sch.4 para.20

62 & 63 Vict. (1899)

30. Commons Act 1899
Part I, applied: SI 2014/3038 Reg.46
s.22, applied: SI 2014/3038 Sch.4 para.8

2 Edw. 7 (1902)

28. Licensing Act 1902
s.2, see *R. (on the application of A) v Lowestoft Magistrates' Court* [2013] EWHC

659 (Admin), [2014] 1 W.L.R. 1489 (QBD
(Admin)), Pitchford LJ

3 Edw. 7 (1903)

129. Pier and Harbour Orders Confirmation (No.3) Act 1903
s.2, amended: SSI 2014/158 Sch.3
s.5, amended: SSI 2014/158 Sch.3
s.6, repealed: SSI 2014/158 Sch.3
s.29, repealed: SSI 2014/158 Sch.3

6 Edw. 7 (1906)

25. Open Spaces Act 1906
s.20, see *Lake District National Park Authority v Grace (Valuation Officer)* [2014] R.A. 81 (VT), A Clark
32. Dogs Act 1906
s.1, see *Dickson v Brown* 2014 S.L.T. 126 (HCJ), Lady Smith
34. Prevention of Corruption Act 1906
s.1, see *R. v J* [2013] EWCA Crim 2287, [2014] 1 W.L.R. 1857 (CA (Crim Div)), Lord Thomas LCJ
s.2, see *R. v Hammond (Philip)* [2013] EWCA Crim 2636, [2014] 1 W.L.R. 4303 (CA (Crim Div)), Laws LJ
40. Marriage with Foreigners Act 1906
s.1, repealed: SI 2014/1110 Art.16
s.4, amended: SI 2014/1110 Art.16
Sch.1, repealed: SI 2014/1110 Art.16
41. Marine Insurance Act 1906
s.60, see *Venetico Marine SA v International General Insurance Co Ltd* [2013] EWHC 3644 (Comm), [2014] 1 Lloyd's Rep. 349 (QBD (Comm)), Andrew Smith J

S.C. 448 (IH (2 Div)), The Lord Justice Clerk (Carloway)
s.4, repealed: 2014 asp 18 Sch.5 para.4
s.10, repealed: 2014 asp 18 Sch.5 para.4
s.14, repealed: 2014 asp 18 Sch.5 para.4
s.17, repealed: 2014 asp 18 Sch.5 para.4
s.27, repealed: 2014 asp 18 Sch.5 para.4
s.34, see *Lormor Ltd v Glasgow City Council* [2014] CSIH 80, 2014 S.L.T. 1055 (IH (Ex Div)), Lady Paton
s.39, repealed: 2014 asp 18 Sch.5 para.4
s.40, enabling: SSI 2014/14
s.50, repealed: 2014 asp 18 Sch.5 para.4
Sch.1, repealed: 2014 asp 18 Sch.5 para.4
Sch.1 Part 6 paraA.4, substituted: SSI 2014/291 r.3
Sch.1 Part 28 para.3, substituted: SSI 2014/152 r.3
Sch.1 Part 28 para.8, amended: SSI 2014/152 r.3, SSI 2014/201 r.3
Sch.1 Part 33 para.1, amended: SSI 2014/302 r.5
Sch.1 Part 33 para.6ZA, added: SSI 2014/302 r.5
Sch.1 Part 33 para.28, amended: SSI 2014/302 r.5
Sch.1 Part 33 para.96, amended: SSI 2014/302 r.5
Sch.1 Part 36, amended: SSI 2014/152 r.3
Sch.1 Part 36, repealed (in part): SSI 2014/152 r.3
Sch.1 Part 36 paraH.1, amended: SSI 2014/152 r.3
Sch.1 Part 51, added: SSI 2014/291 r.3
Sch.1 Part 52, added: SSI 2014/371 r.3
53. Public Health Acts Amendment Act 1907
s.77, see *Redbridge LBC v Dhinsa* [2014] EWCA Civ 178, [2014] I.C.R. 834 (CA (Civ Div)), Longmore LJ

7 Edw. 7 (1907)

51. Sheriff Courts (Scotland) Act 1907
Appendix 1., amended: SSI 2014/152 Sch.1, SSI 2014/291 Sch.2, SSI 2014/302 r.6, SSI 2014/371 Sch.2
s.3, see *Chief Constable of the Police Service of Scotland v R* [2014] CSIH 8, 2014

8 Edw. 7 (1908)

36. Small Holdings and Allotments Act 1908
s.25, see *Snelling v Burstow Parish Council* [2013] EWCA Civ 1411, [2014] 1 W.L.R. 2388 (CA (Civ Div)), Patten LJ

s.32, see *Snelling v Burstow Parish Council*
[2013] EWCA Civ 1411, [2014] 1 W.L.R.
2388 (CA (Civ Div)), Patten LJ
s.33, see *Snelling v Burstow Parish Council*
[2013] EWCA Civ 1411, [2014] 1 W.L.R.
2388 (CA (Civ Div)), Patten LJ

1 & 2 Geo. 5 (1911)

6. **Perjury Act 1911**
    applied: SI 2014/3181 Reg.26
    s.3, amended: SI 2014/3168 Sch.1 para.2
    s.5, applied: 2014 c.4 s.10, SI 2014/1893
    Art.19
27. **Protection of Animals Act 1911**
    s.1, see *R. (on the application of Gray) v
    Aylesbury Crown Court* [2013] EWHC 500
    (Admin), [2014] 1 W.L.R. 818 (QBD
    (Admin)), Toulson, L.J.
28. **Official Secrets Act 1911**
    applied: SI 2014/512 Reg.181, SI 2014/1610
    r.16_1, SI 2014/2336 Reg.122, SSI 2014/164
    Reg.92, SSI 2014/217 Reg.175, SSI
    2014/292 Reg.175

4 & 5 Geo. 5 (1914)

47. **Deeds of Arrangement Act 1914**
    Royal Assent, August 10, 2014
    applied: SI 2014/2839 Reg.4

5 & 6 Geo. 5 (1914-15)

90. **Indictments Act 1915**
    s.3, see *R. v Stocker (Keith Anthony)* [2013]
    EWCA Crim 1993, [2014] 1 Cr. App. R. 18
    (CA (Crim Div)), Hallett LJ
    s.5, applied: SI 2014/1610 r.3_21, r.14_1

6 & 7 Geo. 5 (1916)

12. **Local Government (Emergency Provisions)
Act 1916**
    s.2, substituted: SI 2014/560 Sch.1 para.3, SI
    2014/3229 Sch.5 para.2

7 & 8 Geo. 5 (1917)

55. **Chequers Estate Act 1917**
    applied: SI 2014/2708 Art.2
    Sch.1, amended: SI 2014/2708 Art.6

7 & 8 Geo. 5 (1918)

40. **Income Tax Act 1918**
    s.37, see *Routier v Revenue and Customs
    Commissioners* [2014] EWHC 3010 (Ch),
    [2014] B.T.C. 42 (Ch D), Rose J

9 & 10 Geo. 5 (1919)

20. **Scottish Board of Health Act 1919**
    s.4, repealed (in part): 2014 asp 3 Sch.3
    para.17

10 & 11 Geo. 5 (1920)

33. **Maintenance Orders (Facilities for
Enforcement) Act 1920**
    applied: SI 2014/840 Sch.1
75. **Official Secrets Act 1920**
    applied: SI 2014/512 Reg.181, SI 2014/1610
    r.16_1, SSI 2014/164 Reg.92, SSI 2014/217
    Reg.175, SSI 2014/292 Reg.175
    s.8, applied: SI 2014/1610 r.16_1

13 & 14 Geo. 5 (1923)

34. **Agricultural Credits Act 1923**
    s.2, applied: 2014 c.14 s.24
    Sch.1 Part I para.2, applied: 2014 c.14 s.24

15 & 16 Geo. 5 (1925)

19. **Trustee Act 1925**
    s.15, see *MF Global UK Ltd (In Special
    Administration), Re* [2014] EWHC 2222
    (Ch), [2014] Bus. L.R. 1156 (Ch D
    (Companies Ct)), Richards J

s.31, amended: 2014 c.16 s.8
s.32, amended: 2014 c.16 s.9
s.57, see *English & American Insurance Co Ltd, Re* [2013] EWHC 3360 (Ch), [2014] W.T.L.R. 57 (Ch D), Clive Freedman, Q.C.
s.61, see *Ikbal v Sterling Law* [2013] EWHC 3291 (Ch), [2014] P.N.L.R. 9 (Ch D), Nicholas Davidson, Q.C.; see *Santander UK v RA Legal Solicitors* [2014] EWCA Civ 183, [2014] Lloyd's Rep. F.C. 282 (CA (Civ Div)), Sir Terence Etherton C; see *Sheffield v Sheffield* [2013] EWHC 3927 (Ch), [2014] W.T.L.R. 1039 (Ch D), Judge Pelling QC

20. Law of Property Act 1925
s.72, see *Lie v Mohile* [2014] EWCA Civ 728, [2014] 2 P. & C.R. 13 (CA (Civ Div)), Patten LJ
s.82, see *Lie v Mohile* [2014] EWCA Civ 728, [2014] 2 P. & C.R. 13 (CA (Civ Div)), Patten LJ
s.84, see *Morningside (Leicester) Ltd's Application, Re* [2014] UKUT 70 (LC), [2014] J.P.L. 674 (UT (Lands)), AJ Trott FRICS
s.91, see *Alpstream AG v PK Airfinance Sarl* [2013] EWHC 2370 (Comm), [2014] 1 All E.R. (Comm) 441 (QBD (Comm)), Burton J
s.115, applied: 2014 c.14 s.71
s.146, see *Telchadder v Wickland (Holdings) Ltd* [2014] UKSC 57, [2014] 1 W.L.R. 4004 (SC), Lady Hale DPSC
s.164, see *Trustees of the Travers Will Trust v Revenue and Customs Commissioners* [2014] S.F.T.D. 265 (FTT (Tax)), Judge Nicholas Paines QC
s.193, applied: SI 2014/3038 Reg.46

21. Land Registration Act 1925
see *Nugent v Nugent* [2013] EWHC 4095 (Ch), [2014] 3 W.L.R. 59 (Ch D (Bristol)), Morgan J

23. Administration of Estates Act 1925
s.35, see *Ross (Deceased), Re* [2013] EWHC 2724 (Ch), [2014] W.T.L.R. 321 (Ch D), Judge Behrens Q.C.
s.46, amended: 2014 c.16 s.1
s.46, repealed (in part): 2014 c.16 Sch.4 para.1
s.47A, repealed: 2014 c.16 Sch.4 para.1
s.48, amended: 2014 c.16 Sch.4 para.1
s.48, repealed (in part): 2014 c.16 Sch.4 para.1

s.49, repealed (in part): 2014 c.16 Sch.4 para.1
s.55, amended: 2014 c.16 s.3
s.55, referred to: 2014 c.16 s.3
Sch.1A, added: 2014 c.16 Sch.1

61. Allotments Act 1925
s.8, see *Snelling v Burstow Parish Council* [2013] EWCA Civ 1411, [2014] 1 W.L.R. 2388 (CA (Civ Div)), Patten LJ

86. Criminal Justice Act 1925
s.33, applied: 2014 c.23 s.94, SI 2014/195 Reg.15, SI 2014/517 Reg.19, SI 2014/1610 r.2_4, SI 2014/3085 Reg.23, SI 2014/3223 Reg.12, SI 2014/3263 Reg.17, Reg.26, SI 2014/3303 Reg.16
s.33, varied: SI 2014/3222 Reg.14
s.41, applied: SI 2014/1610 r.16_1
s.47, repealed: 2014 c.12 s.177

16 & 17 Geo. 5 (1926)

16. Execution of Diligence (Scotland) Act 1926
applied: 2014 asp 18 s.105, s.106
s.6, repealed: 2014 asp 18 Sch.5 para.28
61. Judicial Proceedings (Regulation of Reports) Act 1926
s.1, see *180 Irregular Divorces, Re* [2014] EWFC 1406, [2014] E.M.L.R. 26 (Fam Ct), Sir James Munby PFD
s.1, applied: SI 2014/1610 r.16_1

17 & 18 Geo. 5 (1927)

35. Sheriff Courts and Legal Officers (Scotland) Act 1927
s.1, amended: 2014 asp 18 Sch.5 para.10
s.8, amended: 2014 asp 18 Sch.5 para.5

18 & 19 Geo. 5 (1928)

32. Petroleum (Consolidation) Act 1928
repealed: SI 2014/1637 Sch.4 Part 1
s.1, applied: SI 2014/1637 Reg.22
s.2, applied: SI 2014/1637 Reg.22, Reg.23
s.9, applied: SI 2014/1637 Reg.24

43. Agricultural Credits Act 1928
s.9, applied: 2014 c.14 s.65
s.14, applied: 2014 c.14 s.59, s.65

19 & 20 Geo. 5 (1929)

13. Agricultural Credits (Scotland) Act 1929
Part II, applied: 2014 c.14 s.62
29. Government Annuities Act 1929
s.60, disapplied: SI 2014/3229 Sch.2 para.6

20 & 21 Geo. 5 (1930)

28. Finance Act 1930
s.40, applied: 2014 c.26 s.118

21 & 22 Geo. 5 (1931)

28. Finance Act 1931
s.2, referred to: 2014 c.26 s.118
s.28, amended: 2014 c.29 Sch.2 para.1

23 & 24 Geo. 5 (1932-33)

12. Children and Young Persons Act 1933
applied: 2014 c.12 Sch.2 para.4
Part I, amended: 2014 c.6 s.93
Part II, applied: SI 2014/3352 Sch.1 para.29
s.1, see *R. v J* [2014] EWCA Crim 1442,
[2014] 2 Cr. App. R. (S.) 77 (CA (Crim
Div)), Rafferty LJ
s.12A, amended: 2014 c.6 s.93
s.12B, amended: 2014 c.6 s.93
s.12C, amended: 2014 c.6 s.93
s.12D, amended: 2014 c.6 s.93
s.25, applied: SI 2014/3309 Reg.1, Reg.30,
Reg.31, SSI 2014/372 Reg.1, Reg.30,
Reg.31
s.25, enabling: SI 2014/3309, SSI 2014/372
s.34A, applied: SI 2014/1610 r.7_4, r.37_2,
r.38_1
s.36, applied: SI 2014/1610 r.16_1
s.39, see *R. (on the application of A) v
Lowestoft Magistrates' Court* [2013] EWHC
659 (Admin), [2014] 1 W.L.R. 1489 (QBD
(Admin)), Pitchford LJ; see *R. (on the
application of JC) v Central Criminal Court*

[2014] EWHC 1041 (Admin), [2014] 1
W.L.R. 3697 (DC), Sir Brian Leveson
PQBD; see *R. v Jolleys (Robert) Ex p. Press
Association* [2013] EWCA Crim 1135,
[2014] 1 Cr. App. R. 15 (CA (Crim Div)),
Leveson LJ; see *Surrey CC v ME* [2014]
EWHC 489 (Fam), [2014] 2 F.L.R. 1267
(Fam Div), Keehan J
s.39, applied: SI 2014/1610 r.16_1, r.29_19,
r.37_2
s.39, disapplied: 2014 c.12 s.23
s.45, applied: SI 2014/1610 r.37_1, r.63_10
s.46, applied: SI 2014/1610 r.37_2
s.47, applied: SI 2014/1610 r.16_1
s.48, applied: SI 2014/1610 r.37_1
s.49, applied: 2014 c.12 s.17, s.30, SI
2014/1610 r.16_1, r.37_2
s.49, disapplied: 2014 c.12 s.23
s.59, applied: SI 2014/1610 r.37_1
**36. Administration of Justice (Miscellaneous
Provisions) Act 1933**
s.2, applied: SI 2014/1610 r.14_1, r.3_1,
r.12_4, r.3_26, r.14_2

24 & 25 Geo. 5 (1933-34)

**41. Law Reform (Miscellaneous Provisions) Act
1934**
see *Haxton v Philips Electronics UK Ltd*
[2014] EWCA Civ 4, [2014] 1 W.L.R. 2721
(CA (Civ Div)), Elias LJ

26 Geo. 5 & Edw. 8 (1935-36)

27. Petroleum (Transfer of Licences) Act 1936
repealed: SI 2014/1637 Sch.4 Part 1
s.1, applied: SI 2014/1637 Reg.22
32. National Health Insurance Act 1936
s.36, amended: 2014 c.19 Sch.12 para.53
49. Public Health Act 1936
s.262, repealed: 2014 c.21 s.63
s.263, repealed: 2014 c.21 s.63

1 Edw. 8 & 1 Geo. 6 (1936-37)

37. Children and Young Persons (Scotland) Act 1937
s.12, see *B v Murphy* [2014] HCJAC 56, 2014 S.C.L. 563 (HCJ), Lady Paton

43. Public Records (Scotland) Act 1937
s.1A, added: 2014 asp 18 Sch.5 para.11
s.2, amended: 2014 asp 18 Sch.5 para.11
s.2A, amended: 2014 asp 18 Sch.5 para.11
s.14, amended: 2014 asp 18 Sch.5 para.11

67. Factories Act 1937
see *McDonald v Department for Communities and Local Government* [2013] EWCA Civ 1346, [2014] P.I.Q.R. P7 (CA (Civ Div)), Dyson LJ
s.47, see *McDonald v Department for Communities and Local Government* [2013] EWCA Civ 1346, [2014] P.I.Q.R. P7 (CA (Civ Div)), Dyson LJ; see *McDonald v Department for Communities and Local Government* [2014] UKSC 53, [2014] 3 W.L.R. 1197 (SC), Lord Neuberger PSC

1 & 2 Geo. 6 (1937-38)

12. Population (Statistics) Act 1938
Sch.1 para.1, amended: SI 2014/560 Sch.1 para.4

22. Trade Marks Act 1938
s.22, see *Iliffe News & Media Ltd v Revenue and Customs Commissioners* [2014] F.S.R. 6 (FTT (Tax)), Judge John Walters Q.C.

2 & 3 Geo. 6 (1938-39)

82. Personal Injuries (Emergency Provisions) Act 1939
s.1, enabling: SI 2014/444
s.2, enabling: SI 2014/444

121. Official Secrets Act 1939
applied: SI 2014/512 Reg.181, SSI 2014/164 Reg.92, SSI 2014/217 Reg.175, SSI 2014/292 Reg.175

3 & 4 Geo. 6 (1939-40)

19. Societies (Miscellaneous Provisions) Act 1940
s.8, applied: 2014 c.14 Sch.3 para.5

4 & 5 Geo. 6 (1940-41)

27. Justices (Supplemental List) Act 1941
s.2, varied: SI 2014/2708 Art.5

7 & 8 Geo. 6 (1943-44)

31. Education Act 1944
s.1, see *R. (on the application of Tigere) v Secretary of State for Business, Innovation and Skills* [2014] EWCA Civ 1216, [2014] H.R.L.R. 26 (CA (Civ Div)), Laws LJ

8 & 9 Geo. 6 (1944-45)

7. British Settlements Act 1945
enabling: SI 2014/269, SI 2014/497, SI 2014/1098, SI 2014/1100, SI 2014/1368, SI 2014/2703, SI 2014/2707, SI 2014/2710, SI 2014/2711, SI 2014/2919

28. Law Reform (Contributory Negligence) Act 1945
see *McLaughlin v Morrison* [2014] CSOH 123, 2014 S.L.T. 862 (OH), Lord Jones

9 & 10 Geo. 6 (1945-46)

36. Statutory Instruments Act 1946
s.1, applied: SI 2014/1887 Art.3
s.11A, amended: 2014 c.29 s.4

45. United Nations Act 1946
s.1, enabling: SI 2014/1368, SI 2014/2707, SI 2014/2711

55. Ministerial Salaries Act 1946
s.1, varied: SI 2014/2708 Art.5

59. Coal Industry Nationalisation Act 1946
s.37, enabling: SI 2014/1986

65. Appropriation Act 1946
Sch.4 Part 10, varied: SI 2014/2708 Art.5

73. Hill Farming Act 1946
s.23, referred to: SSI 2014/324 Sch.1 para.1

s.26A, referred to: SSI 2014/324 Sch.1
para.1

10 & 11 Geo. 6 (1946-47)

41. Fire Services Act 1947
    s.26, enabling: SI 2014/446, SI 2014/522,
    SSI 2014/59, SSI 2014/108
44. Crown Proceedings Act 1947
    s.17, applied: SI 2014/1610 r.17_28, r.65_12
    s.38, applied: SI 2014/507 Reg.17, SI
    2014/587 Reg.17, SI 2014/1826 Reg.17, SI
    2014/1827 Reg.17, SI 2014/2054 Reg.10, SI
    2014/3204 Sch.4 para.11
    s.38, varied: SI 2014/3349 Reg.17
48. Agriculture Act 1947
    s.109, applied: SI 2014/3318 Reg.4, Sch.2
51. Town and Country Planning Act 1947
    s.51, see *GPE (Hanover Square) Ltd v
    Transport for London* [2014] R.V.R. 77 (UT
    (Lands)), George Bartlett QC
52. Appropriation Act 1947. 1947
    Sch.4 Part 4, varied: SI 2014/2708 Art.5
    Sch.4 Part 8, varied: SI 2014/2708 Art.5

11 & 12 Geo. 6 (1947-48)

29. National Assistance Act 1948
    see *Aster Healthcare Ltd v Shafi* [2014]
    EWHC 77 (QB), [2014] 3 All E.R. 283
    (QBD), Andrews J; see *R. (on the
    application of Walford) v Worcestershire CC*
    [2014] EWHC 234 (Admin), [2014] 3 All
    E.R. 128 (QBD (Admin)), Supperstone J
    s.21, see *Aster Healthcare Ltd v Shafi* [2014]
    EWCA Civ 1350, [2014] P.T.S.R. 1507 (CA
    (Civ Div)), Lord Dyson MR; see *Aster
    Healthcare Ltd v Shafi* [2014] EWHC 77
    (QB), [2014] 3 All E.R. 283 (QBD),
    Andrews J; see *R. (on the application of
    Cornwall Council) v Secretary of State for
    Health* [2014] EWCA Civ 12, [2014] 1
    W.L.R. 3408 (CA (Civ Div)), Elias LJ; see
    *R. (on the application of Members of the
    Committee of Care North East
    Northumberland) v Northumberland CC*
    [2013] EWCA Civ 1740, [2014] P.T.S.R.
    758 (CA (Civ Div)), Aikens LJ
    s.21, applied: SI 2014/829 Sch.1 para.1

s.22, applied: SI 2014/666 Reg.2, SI
2014/829 Sch.1 para.2, SSI 2014/39 Reg.2
s.22, referred to: 2014 asp 9 Sch.1 Part 1
s.22, enabling: SI 2014/582, SI 2014/666,
SSI 2014/38, SSI 2014/39
s.24, see *R. (on the application of Cornwall
Council) v Secretary of State for Health*
[2014] EWCA Civ 12, [2014] 1 W.L.R.
3408 (CA (Civ Div)), Elias LJ
s.24, applied: SI 2014/829 Sch.1 para.3
s.26, see *Aster Healthcare Ltd v Shafi* [2014]
EWCA Civ 1350, [2014] P.T.S.R. 1507 (CA
(Civ Div)), Lord Dyson MR; see *Aster
Healthcare Ltd v Shafi* [2014] EWHC 77
(QB), [2014] 3 All E.R. 283 (QBD),
Andrews J; see *R. (on the application of
Members of the Committee of Care North
East Northumberland) v Northumberland
CC* [2013] EWCA Civ 1740, [2014]
P.T.S.R. 758 (CA (Civ Div)), Aikens LJ
s.26, applied: SI 2014/829 Sch.1 para.4
s.26, referred to: 2014 asp 9 Sch.1 Part 1
s.29, applied: SI 2014/829 Sch.1 para.5
s.45, referred to: 2014 asp 9 Sch.1 Part 1
s.47, repealed (in part): 2014 c.23 s.46
s.48, applied: SSI 2014/345 Sch.1 Part 1
s.48, referred to: 2014 asp 9 Sch.1 Part 1
50. Appropriation Act 1948. 1948
    Sch.4 Part II, varied: SI 2014/2708 Art.5
    Sch.4 Part 6, varied: SI 2014/2708 Art.5
56. British Nationality Act 1948
    s.3, applied: SI 2014/2926 Art.24
    s.5, see *Romein v Advocate General for
    Scotland* [2014] CSOH 174 (OH), Lord
    Brailsford
58. Criminal Justice Act 1948
    s.70, applied: SI 2014/2336 Reg.121
63. Agricultural Holdings Act 1948
    s.87, varied: SI 2014/2708 Art.5

12, 13 & 14 Geo. 6 (1948-49)

42. Lands Tribunal Act 1949
    applied: 2014 asp 10 Sch.1 para.13
    s.1, see *Ministry of Defence v Grampian
    Assessor* 2014 S.L.T. (Lands Tr) 44 (Lands
    Tr (Scot)), J N Wright, QC
    s.1, referred to: 2014 asp 18 Sch.4 para.3
    s.2, applied: 2014 asp 18 Sch.4 para.3

s.2, repealed (in part): 2014 asp 18 Sch.4
para.4
s.3, enabling: SSI 2014/24
48. Appropriation Act 1949
Sch.4 Part 5, varied: SI 2014/2708 Art.5
Sch.4 Part 10, varied: SI 2014/2708 Art.5
54. Wireless Telegraphy Act 1949
see *Recall Support Services Ltd v Secretary of State for Culture Media and Sport* [2013] EWHC 3091 (Ch), [2014] 2 C.M.L.R. 2 (Ch D), Rose J
67. Civil Aviation Act 1949
s.8, enabling: SI 2014/2925, SI 2014/2926, SI 2014/3281
74. Coast Protection Act 1949
s.16, disapplied: SI 2014/2384 Sch.19 para.10
s.18, disapplied: SI 2014/2384 Sch.19 para.10
76. Marriage Act 1949
applied: SI 2014/840 Sch.1, SI 2014/895 Sch.2 para.1
Part III, applied: SI 2014/1108 Art.8, SI 2014/1110 Art.5, SI 2014/3265 Art.5
s.1, applied: SI 2014/1110 Art.8, Art.14, SI 2014/3265 Art.8, Art.14, Art.16
s.2, see *A Local Authority v X* [2013] EWHC 3274 (Fam), [2014] 2 F.L.R. 123 (Fam Div (Birmingham)), Holman J
s.3, amended: 2014 c.6 Sch.2 para.42
s.5, amended: 2014 c.22 s.57
s.8, amended: 2014 c.22 s.57
s.9, applied: SI 2014/813 Sch.2 para.6
s.10, applied: SI 2014/3181 Reg.12
s.16, amended: 2014 c.22 s.57
s.26A, applied: SI 2014/106 Reg.4, SI 2014/544 Reg.4, Reg.10
s.26A, referred to: SI 2014/544 Reg.4
s.26B, applied: SI 2014/544 Reg.7
s.27, amended: 2014 c.22 Sch.4 para.2
s.27, applied: 2014 c.22 Sch.9 para.66, SI 2014/3265 Art.15
s.27A, repealed (in part): 2014 c.22 Sch.4 para.3
s.27E, added: 2014 c.22 Sch.4 para.4
s.27ZA, added: 2014 c.22 Sch.4 para.3
s.28, amended: 2014 c.22 Sch.4 para.5, SI 2014/560 Sch.1 para.5
s.28A, amended: 2014 c.22 Sch.4 para.6
s.28A, repealed (in part): 2014 c.22 Sch.4 para.6

s.28B, added: 2014 c.22 Sch.4 para.7
s.28H, added: 2014 c.22 Sch.4 para.8
s.28H, applied: 2014 c.22 s.48, s.61, Sch.6 para.1, Sch.6 para.2
s.31, amended: 2014 c.22 Sch.4 para.10, Sch.4 para.11
s.31, enabling: SI 2014/1790
s.31A, amended: 2014 c.22 Sch.4 para.11
s.31ZA, added: 2014 c.22 Sch.4 para.11
s.35, amended: 2014 c.22 Sch.4 para.12
s.37, amended: 2014 c.22 Sch.4 para.13
s.38, repealed: 2014 c.22 Sch.4 para.12
s.41, see *R. (on the application of Hodkin) v Registrar General of Births, Deaths and Marriages* [2014] A.C. 610 (SC), Lord Neuberger JSC
s.41, applied: SI 2014/106 Reg.4, Reg.5, Reg.9, Reg.10
s.41, varied: SI 2014/106 Reg.9
s.42, amended: SI 2014/560 Sch.1 para.5
s.43A, applied: SI 2014/106 Reg.4, Reg.7, Reg.9, Reg.10, SI 2014/544 Reg.4, Reg.5, Reg.8, Reg.9, Reg.10, Reg.11, SI 2014/3181 Reg.12
s.43A, referred to: SI 2014/106 Reg.4, SI 2014/544 Reg.4
s.43B, applied: SI 2014/106 Reg.6, SI 2014/815 Reg.4
s.43B, referred to: SI 2014/106 Reg.6
s.43C, applied: SI 2014/106 Reg.7, SI 2014/544 Reg.3, Reg.5
s.43D, enabling: SI 2014/106, SI 2014/1791
s.44A, applied: SI 2014/106 Reg.3, SI 2014/544 Reg.6, Reg.7
s.44B, referred to: SI 2014/544 Reg.3
s.44B, enabling: SI 2014/544
s.44C, enabling: SI 2014/544
s.44D, applied: SI 2014/106 Reg.3, SI 2014/544
s.44D, enabling: SI 2014/544
s.45, amended: SI 2014/3168 Sch.1 para.3
s.46, amended: SI 2014/3168 Sch.1 para.3
s.46, applied: SI 2014/3168 Sch.1 para.3, SI 2014/3181 Reg.12, Reg.13, Reg.40
s.46, referred to: SI 2014/3181 Reg.12
s.46A, applied: SI 2014/3181 Reg.6, Reg.11
s.48, amended: 2014 c.22 Sch.4 para.14
s.49A, amended: SI 2014/560 Sch.1 para.5
s.64, applied: SI 2014/3181 Reg.24
s.65, applied: SI 2014/3181 Reg.23
s.68, amended: 2014 c.20 s.44

s.68, applied: SI 2014/3181 Reg.12
s.70A, applied: SI 2014/815, SI 2014/815
Reg.4, Reg.5, SI 2014/3181 Reg.12
s.70A, enabling: SI 2014/815
s.74, amended: 2014 c.22 Sch.4 para.15
s.75, amended: 2014 c.22 Sch.4 para.16
s.78, amended: 2014 c.22 Sch.4 para.17
Sch.3A, added: 2014 c.22 Sch.4 para.9

88. Registered Designs Act 1949
s.2, amended: 2014 c.18 s.6
s.2, repealed (in part): 2014 c.18 s.6
s.3, amended: 2014 c.18 s.12
s.3, applied: 2014 c.18 s.12
s.3, repealed (in part): 2014 c.18 s.6
s.7B, added: 2014 c.18 s.7
s.11A, amended: SI 2014/892 Sch.1 para.20
s.11AB, amended: SI 2014/892 Sch.1
para.21
s.15ZA, added: 2014 c.18 s.8
s.19, repealed (in part): 2014 c.18 s.9
s.22, amended: 2014 c.18 s.9
s.24B, amended: 2014 c.18 s.10
s.27, amended: 2014 c.18 s.10
s.27A, added: 2014 c.18 s.10
s.28, repealed: 2014 c.18 s.10
s.28A, added: 2014 c.18 s.11
s.31A, added: 2014 c.18 s.12
s.35A, amended: 2014 c.18 s.14
s.35ZA, added: 2014 c.18 s.13
s.36, amended: 2014 c.18 s.12
s.36, applied: 2014 c.18 s.12
s.36, enabling: SI 2014/2405
s.37, amended: 2014 c.18 s.8, s.9, s.10, s.11
s.39, amended: 2014 c.18 s.12
s.39, applied: 2014 c.18 s.12
s.44, amended: 2014 c.18 s.10

97. National Parks and Access to the Countryside Act 1949
s.16, applied: SI 2014/3223 Sch.2 para.1, SI
2014/3263 Sch.3 para.1
s.51, disapplied: SI 2014/2384 Sch.19
para.12
s.55, disapplied: SI 2014/2384 Sch.19
para.12

14 Geo. 6 (1950)

16. Appropriation Act 1950
Sch.4 Part 3, varied: SI 2014/2708 Art.5
Sch.4 Part 8, varied: SI 2014/2708 Art.5

32. Army Reserve Act 1950
s.1, amended: 2014 c.20 s.44
s.2, amended: 2014 c.20 s.44
s.3, amended: 2014 c.20 s.44
s.4, amended: 2014 c.20 s.44
s.5, amended: 2014 c.20 s.44
s.6, amended: 2014 c.20 s.44
s.7, amended: 2014 c.20 s.44
s.8, amended: 2014 c.20 s.44
s.9, amended: 2014 c.20 s.44
s.10, amended: 2014 c.20 s.44
s.11, amended: 2014 c.20 s.44
s.12, amended: 2014 c.20 s.44
s.13, amended: 2014 c.20 s.44
s.14, amended: 2014 c.20 s.44
s.15, amended: 2014 c.20 s.44
s.16, amended: 2014 c.20 s.44
s.17, amended: 2014 c.20 s.44
s.18, amended: 2014 c.20 s.44
s.19, amended: 2014 c.20 s.44
s.20, amended: 2014 c.20 s.44
s.21, amended: 2014 c.20 s.44
s.22, amended: 2014 c.20 s.44
s.23, amended: 2014 c.20 s.44
s.24, amended: 2014 c.20 s.44
s.25, amended: 2014 c.20 s.44
s.26, amended: 2014 c.20 s.44
s.28, amended: 2014 c.20 s.44
s.29, amended: 2014 c.20 s.44
s.30, amended: 2014 c.20 s.44
Sch.1, amended: 2014 c.20 s.44
Sch.1 para.1, amended: 2014 c.20 s.44
Sch.1 para.2, amended: 2014 c.20 s.44
Sch.2, amended: 2014 c.20 s.44
Sch.3, amended: 2014 c.20 s.44

37. Maintenance Orders Act 1950
applied: SI 2014/840 Sch.1

14 & 15 Geo. 6 (1950-51)

35. Pet Animals Act 1951
s.5, applied: SI 2014/3266 Reg.10

44. Appropriation Act 1951
Sch.4 Part 9, varied: SI 2014/2708 Art.5

46. Courts-Martial (Appeals) Act 1951
s.30, applied: SI 2014/602 Art.2

58. Fireworks Act 1951
repealed: SI 2014/1638 Sch.13 para.3,
Sch.14 Part 1
s.1, amended: SI 2014/469 Sch.2 para.1

65. Reserve and Auxiliary Forces (Protection of Civil Interests) Act 1951
> Part V, applied: SI 2014/512 Reg.187, SI 2014/2848 Reg.114, SSI 2014/164 Reg.83, SSI 2014/217 Reg.181, SSI 2014/292 Reg.181
> s.46, amended: SI 2014/560 Sch.1 para.6, SI 2014/3229 Sch.5 para.3

15 & 16 Geo. 6 & 1 Eliz. 2 (1951-52)

12. Judicial Offices (Salaries, &c.) Act 1952
> repealed: 2014 asp 18 Sch.5 para.42

38. Appropriation Act 1952
> Sch.8 Part 5, varied: SI 2014/2708 Art.5
> Sch.13 Part 10, varied: SI 2014/2708 Art.5

44. Customs and Excise Act 1952
> s.275, see *R. (on the application of Eastenders Cash & Carry Plc) v Revenue and Customs Commissioners* [2014] UKSC 34, [2014] 2 W.L.R. 1580 (SC), Lord Neuberger PSC

52. Prison Act 1952
> applied: SI 2014/1788 Reg.2
> s.5A, amended: 2014 c.22 Sch.9 para.8
> s.37, enabling: SI 2014/3, SI 2014/2340
> s.47, enabling: SI 2014/2169
> s.49, amended: 2014 c.12 s.171
> Sch.A1 para.2, repealed (in part): 2014 c.2 Sch.12 para.2
> Sch.A1 para.3, repealed (in part): 2014 c.2 Sch.12 para.2
> Sch.A1 para.4, repealed (in part): 2014 c.2 Sch.12 para.2
> Sch.A1 para.6, amended: 2014 c.2 Sch.12 para.2

64. Intestates Estates Act 1952
> Sch.2 para.1, repealed (in part): 2014 c.16 Sch.4 para.2
> Sch.2 para.3, amended: 2014 c.16 Sch.4 para.2

66. Defamation Act 1952
> s.3, see *Niche Products Ltd v MacDermid Offshore Solutions LLC* [2013] EWHC 3540 (IPEC), [2014] E.M.L.R. 9 (IPEC), Birss J

1 & 2 Eliz. 2 (1952-53)

20. Births and Deaths Registration Act 1953
> s.10, amended: SI 2014/560 Sch.1 para.7

28. Dogs (Protection of Livestock) Act 1953
> s.1, see *Dickson v Brown* 2014 S.L.T. 126 (HCJ), Lady Smith

35. Appropriation Act, 1953
> Sch.16, varied: SI 2014/2708 Art.5

49. Historic Buildings and Ancient Monuments Act 1953
> s.4, amended: 2014 asp 19 s.20

2 & 3 Eliz. 2 (1953-54)

40. Protection of Animals (Amendment) Act 1954
> s.1, applied: SI 2014/3266 Reg.10

45. Appropriation Act 1954
> Sch.4 Part 4, varied: SI 2014/2708 Art.5
> Sch.4 Part 9, varied: SI 2014/2708 Art.5

56. Landlord and Tenant Act 1954
> see *Barclays Wealth Trustees (Jersey) Ltd v Erimus Housing Ltd* [2014] EWCA Civ 303, [2014] 2 P. & C.R. 4 (CA (Civ Div)), Longmore LJ
> Part II, disapplied: 2014 c.20 Sch.1 para.2
> Pt II., see *Martin Retail Group Ltd v Crawley BC* [2014] L. & T.R. 17 (CC (Central London)), Judge Dight; see *R. (on the application of Trafford) v Blackpool BC* [2014] EWHC 85 (Admin), [2014] 2 All E.R. 947 (QBD (Admin)), Judge Stephen Davies
> s.24, see *Lie v Mohile* [2014] EWCA Civ 728, [2014] 2 P. & C.R. 13 (CA (Civ Div)), Patten LJ; see *Siemens Hearing Instruments Ltd v Friends Life Ltd* [2014] EWCA Civ 382, [2014] 2 P. & C.R. 5 (CA (Civ Div)), Black LJ
> s.25, see *Lie v Mohile* [2014] EWCA Civ 728, [2014] 2 P. & C.R. 13 (CA (Civ Div)), Patten LJ
> s.26, see *Youssefi v Mussellwhite* [2014] EWCA Civ 885, [2014] 2 P. & C.R. 14 (CA (Civ Div)), Moore-Bick LJ
> s.30, see *Horne and Meredith Properties Ltd v Cox* [2014] EWCA Civ 423, [2014] 2 P. & C.R. 18 (CA (Civ Div)), Lewison LJ; see *Lie v Mohile* [2014] EWCA Civ 728, [2014]

2 P. & C.R. 13 (CA (Civ Div)), Patten LJ;
see *Youssefi v Mussellwhite* [2014] EWCA
Civ 885, [2014] 2 P. & C.R. 14 (CA (Civ
Div)), Moore-Bick LJ
s.34, see *Martineau Galleries No.1 Ltd v
Birmingham City Council* [2013] EWHC
3018 (Ch), [2014] 1 P. & C.R. 6 (Ch D
(Birmingham)), Judge Purle Q.C.
s.41A, see *Lie v Mohile* [2014] EWCA Civ
728, [2014] 2 P. & C.R. 13 (CA (Civ Div)),
Patten LJ
s.64, see *Youssefi v Mussellwhite* [2014]
EWCA Civ 885, [2014] 2 P. & C.R. 14 (CA
(Civ Div)), Moore-Bick LJ
Sch.8 para.4, varied: SI 2014/2708 Art.5
**64. Transport Charges &c (Miscellaneous
Provisions) Act 1954**
s.6, enabling: SI 2014/926
70. Mines and Quarries Act 1954
s.19, repealed: SI 2014/3248 Sch.3 Part 1
s.28, repealed: SI 2014/3248 Sch.3 Part 1
s.30, repealed: SI 2014/3248 Sch.3 Part 1
s.36, repealed: SI 2014/3248 Sch.3 Part 1
s.37, applied: SI 2014/3248 Reg.71
s.39, repealed: SI 2014/3248 Sch.3 Part 1
s.55, repealed: SI 2014/3248 Sch.3 Part 1
s.58, repealed: SI 2014/3248 Sch.3 Part 1
s.61, repealed: SI 2014/3248 Sch.3 Part 1
s.64, repealed: SI 2014/3248 Sch.3 Part 1
s.69, repealed: SI 2014/3248 Sch.3 Part 1
s.73, repealed: SI 2014/3248 Sch.3 Part 1
s.79, repealed: SI 2014/3248 Sch.3 Part 1
s.83, repealed: SI 2014/3248 Sch.3 Part 1
s.86, repealed: SI 2014/3248 Sch.3 Part 1
s.94, repealed: SI 2014/3248 Sch.3 Part 1
s.97, repealed: SI 2014/3248 Sch.3 Part 1
s.123, repealed: SI 2014/3248 Sch.3 Part 1
s.137, repealed: SI 2014/3248 Sch.3 Part 1
s.139, applied: SI 2014/3248 Reg.6
s.141, repealed (in part): SI 2014/3248 Sch.3
Part 1
s.143, repealed: SI 2014/3248 Sch.3 Part 1
s.150, repealed: SI 2014/3248 Sch.3 Part 1
s.170, repealed: SI 2014/3248 Sch.3 Part 1
s.171, repealed: SI 2014/3248 Sch.3 Part 1
s.174, repealed: SI 2014/3248 Sch.3 Part 1
s.180, substituted: SI 2014/3248 Sch.5
para.1
s.182, amended: SI 2014/3248 Sch.5 para.2
Sch.3, repealed: SI 2014/3248 Sch.3 Part 1

3 & 4 Eliz. 2 (1954-55)

16. Appropriation Act 1955
Sch.4 Part 2, varied: SI 2014/2708 Art.5
Sch.4 Part 7, varied: SI 2014/2708 Art.5

4 & 5 Eliz. 2 (1955-56)

34. Criminal Justice Administration Act 1956
varied: SI 2014/2708 Art.5
s.16, varied: SI 2014/2708 Art.5
Sch.2 para.6, varied: SI 2014/2708 Art.5
Sch.2 para.7, varied: SI 2014/2708 Art.5
**44. Magistrates Courts (Appeals from Binding
Over Orders) Act 1956**
s.1, applied: SI 2014/1610 r.63_1
46. Administration of Justice Act 1956
s.47, applied: 2014 asp 18 Sch.1 para.10
s.47E, applied: 2014 asp 18 Sch.1 para.10
52. Clean Air Act 1956
referred to: SI 2014/3318 Reg.2
55. Appropriation Act 1956
Sch.4 Part 3, varied: SI 2014/2708 Art.5
Sch.4 Part 8, varied: SI 2014/2708 Art.5
60. Valuation and Rating (Scotland) Act 1956
s.6, see *Happy Feet Nursery and Out of
School Club Ltd v Assessor for Lanarkshire*
[2014] CSIH 87, 2014 S.L.T. 1066 (LVAC),
The Lord President (Gill)
s.6, applied: SSI 2014/30 Reg.3
s.6A, applied: SSI 2014/64
s.6A, enabling: SSI 2014/64
s.7B, applied: SSI 2014/30 Reg.3
69. Sexual Offences Act 1956
see *R. v Stocker (Keith Anthony)* [2013]
EWCA Crim 1993, [2014] 1 Cr. App. R. 18
(CA (Crim Div)), Hallett LJ

5 & 6 Eliz. 2 (1957)

11. Homicide Act 1957
s.2, see *R. v Golds (Mark Richard)* [2014]
EWCA Crim 748, [2014] 4 All E.R. 64 (CA
(Crim Div)), Elias LJ; see *R. v Williams
(Dean)* [2013] EWCA Crim 2749, [2014] 1
Cr. App. R. 23 (CA (Crim Div)), Laws LJ

20. House of Commons Disqualification Act 1957
  Sch.1 Part I, varied: SI 2014/2708 Art.5
  Sch.2 Part I, varied: SI 2014/2708 Art.5
31. Occupiers Liability Act 1957
  see *Manolete Partners Plc v Hastings BC*
  [2014] EWCA Civ 562, [2014] 1 W.L.R.
  4030 (CA (Civ Div)), Jackson LJ
  s.2, see *West Sussex CC v Pierce* [2013]
  EWCA Civ 1230, [2014] E.L.R. 62 (CA
  (Civ Div)), Lord Dyson MR; see *Yates v
  National Trust* [2014] EWHC 222 (QB),
  [2014] P.I.Q.R. P16 (QBD), Nicol J
52. Geneva Conventions Act 1957
  referred to: SI 2014/2706 Art.2
**58. Registration of Births, Deaths and
Marriages (Special Provisions) Act 1957**
  s.1, amended: SI 2014/3168 Sch.1 para.4
  s.3, amended: SI 2014/3168 Sch.1 para.4
  s.5, amended: SI 2014/560 Sch.1 para.8
63. Appropriation Act 1957
  Sch.9 Part 6, varied: SI 2014/2708 Art.5
  Sch.14 Part 11, varied: SI 2014/2708 Art.5

6 & 7 Eliz. 2 (1957-58)

16. Commonwealth Institute Act 1958
  see *Commonwealth Institute (In Members'
  Voluntary Liquidation), Re* [2014] EWHC
  2218 (Ch), [2014] W.T.L.R. 1621 (Ch D
  (Companies Ct)), David Richards J
21. Life Peerages Act 1958
  s.1, applied: 2014 c.24 s.4
33. Disabled Persons (Employment) Act 1958
  s.3, applied: SSI 2014/345 Sch.1 Part 1
  s.3, referred to: 2014 asp 9 Sch.1 Part 1
39. Maintenance Orders Act 1958
  applied: SI 2014/840 Sch.1
  s.3, see *Constantinides v Constantinides*
  [2013] EWHC 3688 (Fam), [2014] 1 W.L.R.
  1934 (Fam Div), Holman J
**40. Matrimonial Proceedings (Children) Act
1958**
  s.11, referred to: 2014 asp 9 Sch.1 Part 1
47. Agricultural Marketing Act 1958
  s.19A, amended: SI 2014/892 Sch.1 para.23
  s.47, amended: SI 2014/892 Sch.1 para.24
51. Public Records Act 1958
  s.3, applied: SI 2014/3249 Art.2, Art.3
  s.5, applied: SI 2014/1610 r.5_4
  s.8, applied: SI 2014/1610 r.5_4

Sch.1 Part 2, amended: 2014 c.4 Sch.2
  para.11, 2014 c.23 Sch.5 para.29, Sch.7
  para.21, SI 2014/469 Sch.2 para.2, SI
  2014/631 Sch.1 para.1, SI 2014/892 Sch.1
  para.25, SI 2014/3184 Sch.1 para.8
57. Appropriation Act 1958
  Sch.4 Part 6, varied: SI 2014/2708 Art.5
  Sch.4 Part 11, varied: SI 2014/2708 Art.5

7 & 8 Eliz. 2 (1958-59)

22. County Courts Act, 1959
  s.5, varied: SI 2014/2708 Art.5
54. Weeds Act 1959
  applied: SSI 2014/325 Sch.1 para.1, Sch.1
  para.7
57. Street Offences Act 1959
  s.1, applied: SI 2014/1610 r.42_2
  s.1A, applied: SI 2014/1610 r.42_2, r.42_10
  Sch.1, applied: SI 2014/1610 r.44_1
59. Appropriation Act, 1959
  Sch.4 Part 5, varied: SI 2014/2708 Art.5
  Sch.4 Part 10, varied: SI 2014/2708 Art.5
72. Mental Health Act 1959
  s.8, applied: SI 2014/829 Sch.1 para.6

8 & 9 Eliz. 2 (1959-60)

30. Occupiers Liability (Scotland) Act 1960
  s.2, see *Leonard v Loch Lomond and the
  Trossachs National Park Authority* [2014]
  CSOH 38, 2014 Rep. L.R. 46 (OH), Lord
  Uist; see *Shepherd v Travelodge Hoteld Ltd*
  [2014] CSOH 162 (OH), Lord Boyd of
  Duncansby
45. Appropriation Act, 1960
  Sch.4 Part 5, varied: SI 2014/2708 Art.5
  Sch.4 Part 10, varied: SI 2014/2708 Art.5
46. Corporate Bodies Contracts Act 1960
  applied: 2014 c.14 s.54
**62. Caravan Sites and Control of Development
Act 1960**
  applied: SI 2014/442 Reg.3, SI 2014/1900
  Art.2
  Part IA, added: 2014 asp 14 s.63
  Part IA, disapplied: 2014 asp 14 s.83
  Part IA, referred to: 2014 asp 14 s.83
  s.3, amended: SI 2014/1900 Sch.1 para.2
  s.3, applied: SI 2014/816 Art.4, Art.5

s.3, enabling: SI 2014/442
s.5A, amended: SI 2014/1900 Sch.1 para.3
s.5A, applied: SI 2014/442 Reg.3
s.7, amended: SI 2014/1900 Sch.1 para.4
s.7, applied: SI 2014/816 Art.5
s.8, amended: SI 2014/1900 Sch.1 para.5
s.8, applied: SI 2014/816 Art.5
s.9A, amended: SI 2014/1900 Sch.1 para.6
s.9A, applied: SI 2014/442 Reg.3
s.9B, applied: SI 2014/442 Reg.3
s.9D, applied: SI 2014/442 Reg.3
s.9E, amended: SI 2014/1900 Sch.1 para.7
s.9F, amended: SI 2014/1900 Sch.1 para.8
s.9G, amended: SI 2014/1900 Sch.1 para.9
s.10, amended: SI 2014/1900 Sch.1 para.10
s.10, applied: SI 2014/816 Art.4
s.10, enabling: SI 2014/442
s.24, see *Slattery v Basildon BC* [2014]
EWCA Civ 30, [2014] H.L.R. 16 (CA (Civ
Div)), Sullivan LJ
s.29, amended: SI 2014/1900 Sch.1 para.11
s.32, amended: 2014 asp 14 s.63
s.32B, added: 2014 asp 14 s.64
s.32C, added: 2014 asp 14 s.64
s.32D, added: 2014 asp 14 s.65
s.32J, added: 2014 asp 14 s.66
s.32K, added: 2014 asp 14 s.67
s.32L, added: 2014 asp 14 s.68
s.32M, added: 2014 asp 14 s.69
s.32N, added: 2014 asp 14 s.70
s.32O, added: 2014 asp 14 s.71
s.32P, added: 2014 asp 14 s.72
s.32Q, added: 2014 asp 14 s.73
s.32R, added: 2014 asp 14 s.74
s.32W, added: 2014 asp 14 s.75
s.32X, added: 2014 asp 14 s.76
s.32Y, added: 2014 asp 14 s.77
s.32Z, added: 2014 asp 14 s.78
s.32Z1, added: 2014 asp 14 s.79
s.32Z2, added: 2014 asp 14 s.80
s.32Z5, added: 2014 asp 14 s.81
s.32Z6, added: 2014 asp 14 s.82

65. Administration of Justice Act 1960
s.12, see *E (A Child) (Care Proceedings:*
European Dimension), Re [2014] EWHC 6
(Fam), [2014] 1 W.L.R. 2670 (Fam Div), Sir
James Munby PFD; see *K (A Child)*
(Wardship: Publicity), Re [2013] EWHC
3748 (Fam), [2014] 2 F.L.R. 310 (Fam Div
(Coventry)), Judge Clifford Bellamy

s.13, applied: SI 2014/602 Art.2, SI
2014/1610 r.74_1, r.68_1
67. Public Bodies (Admission to Meetings) Act
1960
applied: 2014 c.2 s.40, Sch.7 para.5, Sch.7
para.8, Sch.7 para.9, Sch.7 para.10
s.1, amended: SI 2014/2095 Reg.3
s.1, applied: 2014 c.2 Sch.7 para.9, Sch.7
para.10
s.1A, added: SI 2014/2095 Reg.3
s.2, amended: SI 2014/2095 Reg.3
Sch.1 para.1, amended: 2014 c.21 Sch.10
para.1, 2014 c.23 Sch.5 para.30, Sch.7
para.22

9 & 10 Eliz. 2 (1960-61)

33. Land Compensation Act 1961
applied: SI 2014/310 Art.15, SI 2014/909
Art.11, SI 2014/1821 Art.11, SI 2014/2027
Art.24, SI 2014/2384 Art.24, Art.38
Part I, applied: SI 2014/310 Art.7, Art.13, SI
2014/909 Art.13, Art.17, Art.19, Art.23,
Art.27, Art.28, Art.29, Art.30, Art.35, SI
2014/1052 Art.18, Art.20, Art.26, Art.30,
Art.31, Art.32, SI 2014/1599 Art.14, Art.18,
Art.22, Art.23, Art.24, Art.32, SI 2014/1796
Art.12, Art.14, Art.18, Art.22, Art.26, SI
2014/1821 Art.7, Art.8, Art.9, Art.13, SI
2014/1873 Art.16, Art.21, Art.30, Art.31,
Art.32, Art.37, Art.38, SI 2014/2027 Art.8,
Art.9, Art.14, Art.15, Art.21, Art.22, Art.26,
Art.30, SI 2014/2269 Art.11, Art.12, Art.16,
Art.17, Art.21, Art.25, Art.26, Art.30, SI
2014/2384 Art.13, Art.15, Art.20, Art.21,
Art.22, Art.25, Art.26, Art.27, Art.28,
Art.29, Art.35, Art.36, Art.46, Art.48, SI
2014/2434 Art.10, Art.15, Art.16, Art.18,
Art.20, Art.24, Art.25, Art.26, Art.31,
Art.32, SI 2014/2441 Art.11, Art.14, Art.19,
Art.24, Art.28, SI 2014/2637 Art.12, Art.13,
Art.17, Art.18, Art.26, Art.27, Art.28,
Art.33, SI 2014/2846 Art.11, SI 2014/2935
Art.16, Art.21, Art.22, Art.30, Art.34,
Art.35, Art.39, Art.40, Art.41, Art.45,
Art.46, SI 2014/2950 Art.11, Art.16, Art.17,
Art.21, Art.22, Art.26, Art.27, Art.28,
Art.33, Art.34, SI 2014/3102 Art.10, Art.13,
Art.18, Art.20, Art.21, Art.29, Art.30,
Art.31, Art.35, SI 2014/3328 Art.15, Art.16,

Art.18, Art.20, Art.23, Art.24, Art.32, SI
2014/3331 Art.13, Art.16, Art.17, Art.18,
Art.22, Art.23, Art.24, Art.27, Art.28
Part I, referred to: SI 2014/3328 Art.25
Part III, applied: SI 2014/1052 Art.35,
Art.36
s.5, see *GPE (Hanover Square) Ltd v
Transport for London* [2014] R.V.R. 77 (UT
(Lands)), George Bartlett QC; see *Halpern v
Greater London Authority* [2014] UKUT
116 (LC), [2014] R.V.R. 166 (UT (Lands)),
Judge Mole QC; see *Ramac Holdings Ltd v
Kent CC* [2014] UKUT 109 (LC), [2014]
R.V.R. 207 (UT (Lands)), Judge Alice
Robinson
s.9, see *GPE (Hanover Square) Ltd v
Transport for London* [2014] R.V.R. 77 (UT
(Lands)), George Bartlett QC
s.14, see *Halpern v Greater London
Authority* [2014] UKUT 116 (LC), [2014]
R.V.R. 166 (UT (Lands)), Judge Mole QC
s.16, see *Halpern v Greater London
Authority* [2014] UKUT 116 (LC), [2014]
R.V.R. 166 (UT (Lands)), Judge Mole QC
s.17, see *Edwards v Rhondda Cynon Taff
CBC* [2014] UKUT 435 (LC) (UT (Lands)),
PR Francis

34. Factories Act 1961
s.39, repealed: SI 2014/486 Sch.1
s.56, repealed: SI 2014/486 Sch.1
s.117, repealed: SI 2014/486 Sch.1
s.119, repealed: SI 2014/486 Sch.1
s.121, repealed: SI 2014/486 Sch.1
s.153, repealed: SI 2014/486 Sch.1
s.163, repealed: SI 2014/486 Sch.1
s.169, repealed: SI 2014/486 Sch.1
s.176, applied: SI 2014/3318 Reg.4, Sch.2
s.181, repealed: SI 2014/486 Sch.1

60. Suicide Act 1961
s.2, see *R. (on the application of Nicklinson)
v Ministry of Justice* [2013] EWCA Civ 961,
[2014] 2 All E.R. 32 (CA (Civ Div)), Lord
Judge LCJ; see *R. (on the application of
Nicklinson) v Ministry of Justice* [2014]
UKSC 38, [2014] 3 W.L.R. 200 (SC), Lord
Neuberger PSC; see *R. v Howe (Kevin
James)* [2014] EWCA Crim 114, [2014] 2
Cr. App. R. (S.) 38 (CA (Crim Div)), Lord
Thomas LCJ

62. Trustee Investments Act 1961
s.1, varied: 2014 c.14 s.27

64. Public Health Act 1961
s.73, amended: SI 2014/1637 Sch.4 para.3
Sch.4, amended: SI 2014/3302 Sch.1 para.1

10 & 11 Eliz. 2 (1961-62)

**9. Local Government (Financial Provisions
etc.) (Scotland) Act 1962**
s.4, applied: SSI 2014/30 Reg.3, Reg.5
12. Education Act 1962
s.1, applied: SI 2014/3352 Sch.1 para.12,
Sch.1 para.13
s.2, applied: SI 2014/3352 Sch.1 para.13
45. Appropriation Act, 1962
Sch.4 Part 4, varied: SI 2014/2708 Art.5
Sch.4 Part 9, varied: SI 2014/2708 Art.5
46. Transport Act 1962
s.65, amended: SI 2014/560 Sch.1 para.9, SI
2014/3229 Sch.5 para.4

1963

18. Stock Transfer Act 1963
s.1, amended: 2014 c.14 Sch.4 para.21
**22. Sheriff Courts (Civil Jurisdiction and
Procedure) (Scotland) Act 1963**
repealed: 2014 asp 18 Sch.5 para.21
26. Appropriation Act 1963
Sch.4 Part 6, varied: SI 2014/2708 Art.5
Sch.4 Part 11, varied: SI 2014/2708 Art.5
37. Children and Young Persons Act 1963
s.18, applied: SI 2014/1610 r.37_1
s.28, applied: SI 2014/1610 r.38_11, r.37_4
s.37, applied: SI 2014/3309 Reg.1, Reg.19,
Reg.23, Sch.2 para.5, SSI 2014/372 Reg.1,
Reg.18, Sch.1
s.37, enabling: SI 2014/3309, SSI 2014/372
s.38, repealed (in part): 2014 asp 8 s.94,
2014 c.6 s.90
s.39, applied: SI 2014/3309 Reg.10
s.39, enabling: SI 2014/3309, SSI 2014/372
s.40, applied: SSI 2014/372 Sch.1
**41. Offices, Shops and Railway Premises Act
1963**
s.42, repealed: SI 2014/486 Sch.1
s.46, repealed: SI 2014/486 Sch.1
s.59, repealed: SI 2014/486 Sch.1
s.63, repealed: SI 2014/486 Sch.1
s.67, repealed: SI 2014/486 Sch.1

s.69, repealed: SI 2014/486 Sch.1
s.72, repealed: SI 2014/486 Sch.1
s.78, repealed: SI 2014/486 Sch.1
s.80, repealed: SI 2014/486 Sch.1
s.82, repealed: SI 2014/486 Sch.1
s.86, repealed: SI 2014/486 Sch.1
s.88, repealed: SI 2014/486 Sch.1
43. Animal Boarding Establishments Act 1963
s.3, applied: SI 2014/3266 Reg.10
51. Land Compensation (Scotland) Act 1963
s.25, see *Network Rail Infrastructure Ltd v Scottish Ministers* 2014 S.C. 15 (IH (2 Div)), The Lord Justice Clerk (Carloway)

1964

5. International Headquarters and Defence Organisations Act 1964
applied: SI 2014/1638 Reg.3
14. Plant Varieties and Seeds Act 1964
s.16, applied: SSI 2014/167
s.16, enabling: SI 2014/487, SI 2014/519, SSI 2014/167
s.36, enabling: SI 2014/519, SSI 2014/167
34. Criminal Procedure (Right of Reply) Act 1964
s.1, applied: SI 2014/1610 r.38_9
40. Harbours Act 1964
s.14, applied: SI 2014/17, SI 2014/1076, SI 2014/1277, SI 2014/2720, SI 2014/2933, SSI 2014/158, SSI 2014/224
s.14, referred to: SI 2014/17, SI 2014/2933
s.14, enabling: SI 2014/17, SI 2014/1076, SI 2014/1277, SI 2014/2720, SI 2014/2933, SSI 2014/158, SSI 2014/224
s.18, amended: SI 2014/560 Sch.1 para.10
s.26, applied: SI 2014/1076 Art.18
s.40A, referred to: SSI 2014/166 Art.2
s.40A, enabling: SSI 2014/166
s.42A, applied: SI 2014/17, SI 2014/1076, SI 2014/1277, SI 2014/2720, SI 2014/2933
s.48A, applied: SI 2014/2935 Sch.9 para.12
Sch.2, referred to: SSI 2014/158, SSI 2014/224
Sch.2 para.9B, applied: SI 2014/2720 Art.8
Sch.3 Part I para.4, applied: SSI 2014/224
Sch.3 Part I para.6, applied: SSI 2014/224
Sch.3 Part I para.8, applied: SSI 2014/224
Sch.3 Part I para.10, applied: SSI 2014/158, SSI 2014/224

Sch.3 Part I para.14, applied: SSI 2014/158
Sch.3 Part I para.15, applied: SSI 2014/224
Sch.3 Part I para.17, applied: SSI 2014/224
Sch.3 Part I para.19, applied: SSI 2014/224
62. Appropriation Act 1964
Sch.4 Part 5, varied: SI 2014/2708 Art.5
Sch.4 Part 10, varied: SI 2014/2708 Art.5
70. Riding Establishments Act 1964
s.4, applied: SI 2014/3266 Reg.10
75. Public Libraries and Museums Act 1964
s.7, see *Draper v Lincolnshire CC* [2014] EWHC 2388 (Admin), [2014] B.L.G.R. 673 (QBD (Admin)), Collins J
Sch.1 para.4, amended: SI 2014/3168 Sch.1 para.5
81. Diplomatic Privileges Act 1964
see *Al-Malki v Reyes* [2014] I.C.R. 135 (EAT), Langstaff J
s.4, see *Apex Global Management Ltd v Fi Call Ltd* [2013] EWCA Civ 642, [2014] 1 W.L.R. 492 (CA (Civ Div)), Maurice Kay LJ
84. Criminal Procedure (Insanity) Act 1964
applied: SI 2014/1610 r.76_4
s.4, applied: SI 2014/1610 r.38_10, r.33_1, r.42_8
s.4A, see *R. v A* [2014] EWCA Crim 299, [2014] 1 W.L.R. 2469 (CA (Crim Div)), Macur LJ
s.5, applied: SI 2014/1610 r.68_1, r.68_13
98. Ministers of the Crown Act 1964
Sch.2 Part II, varied: SI 2014/2708 Art.5

1965

11. Ministerial Salaries and Members Pensions Act 1965
s.1, varied: SI 2014/2708 Art.5
Sch.1, varied: SI 2014/2708 Art.5
12. Industrial and Provident Societies Act 1965
applied: 2014 c.14, s.150, Sch.3 para.9, SI 2014/229 Sch.1 para.1, SI 2014/574 Reg.2, SSI 2014/188 Sch.1 para.8, SSI 2014/296 Reg.4
repealed: 2014 c.14 Sch.7
s.2, amended: SI 2014/184 Art.2
s.6, amended: SI 2014/210 Art.2
s.6, applied: 2014 c.14 Sch.3 para.6
s.10, applied: SI 2014/210 Art.3
s.11, applied: 2014 c.14 Sch.3 para.5

s.43A, added: SI 2014/229 Art.17
s.44, applied: SI 2014/229 Sch.1 para.1
s.48, repealed: SI 2014/574 Reg.4
s.49, amended: SI 2014/229 Art.17
s.50, varied: SI 2014/229 Art.13
s.51, varied: SI 2014/229 Art.14
s.52, varied: SI 2014/229 Art.15
s.55, amended: SI 2014/229 Art.17
s.59, varied: SI 2014/229 Art.16
s.74, amended: SI 2014/229 Art.17
s.74, applied: SI 2014/574 Reg.2
Sch.1 para.7, applied: SI 2014/210 Art.3

22. Law Commissions Act 1965
s.3, amended: 2014 c.29 s.25
s.3A, amended: 2014 c.29 s.25
s.3C, added: 2014 c.29 s.25
s.5, amended: 2014 c.29 s.25

23. Appropriation Act 1965
Sch.4 Part 4, varied: SI 2014/2708 Art.5
Sch.4 Part 9, varied: SI 2014/2708 Art.5

32. Administration of Estates (Small Payments) Act 1965
s.1, referred to: 2014 c.14 s.40
s.2, referred to: 2014 c.14 s.36
s.6, applied: 2014 c.14 s.36, s.40, SI 2014/2848 Reg.169, SSI 2014/164 Reg.80, SSI 2014/217 Reg.173, SSI 2014/292 Reg.173
Sch.3, amended: 2014 c.14 Sch.7

45. Backing of Warrants (Republic of Ireland) Act 1965
applied: SI 2014/1610 r.2_1

49. Registration of Births, Deaths and Marriages (Scotland) Act 1965
s.24, enabling: SSI 2014/141
s.32, enabling: SSI 2014/306
s.39C, amended: 2014 asp 5 s.32
s.54, amended: 2014 asp 5 s.33
s.54, applied: SSI 2014/141, SSI 2014/306
s.54, enabling: SSI 2014/141, SSI 2014/306

51. National Insurance Act 1965
applied: 2014 c.19 s.21, SI 2014/3134 Sch.1 para.10
s.36, amended: SI 2014/516 Art.8
s.36, applied: 2014 c.19 Sch.1 para.3
s.37, amended: SI 2014/76 Reg.2, SI 2014/3229 Sch.5 para.5
s.37, disapplied: 2014 c.19 Sch.1 para.3
s.37, varied: SI 2014/516 Art.8

56. Compulsory Purchase Act 1965
applied: SI 2014/310 Art.9, Art.11, Art.16, Sch.3 para.3, SI 2014/909 Art.22, Art.26, SI 2014/1052 Art.29, SI 2014/1599 Art.17, Sch.7 para.3, SI 2014/1821 Art.6, Art.8, Art.12, SI 2014/1873 Art.25, Art.27, Art.29, SI 2014/2027 Art.19, Art.25, Sch.5 para.3, SI 2014/2269 Art.20, Art.24, SI 2014/2384 Art.32, Art.41, SI 2014/2434 Art.23, SI 2014/2441 Art.23, SI 2014/2637 Art.25, SI 2014/2935 Art.36, Art.38, SI 2014/2950 Art.21, Art.25, SI 2014/3038 Sch.4 para.8, SI 2014/3102 Art.34, SI 2014/3328 Sch.7 para.3, SI 2014/3331 Art.16, Art.21
referred to: SI 2014/310 Art.10, SI 2014/909 Art.24, SI 2014/1599 Art.19, SI 2014/1796 Art.21, SI 2014/1821 Art.5, SI 2014/2027 Art.18, SI 2014/2269 Art.22, SI 2014/2384 Art.34, SI 2014/2434 Art.21, SI 2014/2441 Art.25, SI 2014/2637 Art.21, Art.23, SI 2014/3102 Art.25, SI 2014/3331 Art.19
varied: SI 2014/1052 Sch.10 para.3, SI 2014/1599 Sch.7 para.3, SI 2014/2269 Sch.6 para.3, SI 2014/2441 Sch.7 para.3
applied: SI 2014/2441 Sch.7 para.3
Part I, applied: SI 2014/310 Art.9, Art.13, Art.16, Art.17, Sch.3 para.3, SI 2014/909 Art.21, Sch.8 para.3, SI 2014/1052 Art.24, SI 2014/1599 Sch.7 para.3, SI 2014/1796 Art.20, SI 2014/1821 Art.4, Art.14, SI 2014/1873 Art.24, Art.26, Sch.8 para.3, SI 2014/2027 Art.17, Art.26, Art.27, Sch.5 para.3, SI 2014/2269 Art.19, Sch.6 para.3, SI 2014/2384 Art.45, SI 2014/2434 Art.19, SI 2014/2441 Art.21, SI 2014/2935 Art.33, SI 2014/2950 Art.20, Sch.7 para.3, SI 2014/3102 Art.24, Art.36, Sch.3 para.3, SI 2014/3328 Art.17, Sch.7 para.3
Part I, varied: SI 2014/3102 Art.24
s.1, referred to: SI 2014/3038 Sch.4 para.8
s.4, varied: SI 2014/1821 Art.4
s.7, applied: SI 2014/909 Sch.8 para.2, SI 2014/2027 Sch.5 para.2, SI 2014/2384 Art.32, SI 2014/2434 Art.17, SI 2014/2935 Art.31, SI 2014/3102 Sch.3 para.2
s.7, varied: SI 2014/310 Sch.3 para.4, SI 2014/909 Sch.8 para.4, SI 2014/1052 Sch.10 para.4, SI 2014/1599 Sch.7 para.4, SI 2014/1873 Sch.8 para.4, SI 2014/2027 Sch.5 para.4, SI 2014/2269 Sch.6 para.4, SI 2014/2441 Sch.7 para.4, SI 2014/2637 Sch.8

41

para.4, SI 2014/2950 Sch.7 para.4, SI
2014/3102 Sch.3 para.4, SI 2014/3331 Sch.6
para.2
s.8, applied: SI 2014/310 Art.11, Art.16, SI
2014/909 Art.22, Art.26, Sch.8 para.2, SI
2014/1599 Art.17, Art.21, SI 2014/1821
Art.6, Art.12, SI 2014/1873 Art.29, SI
2014/2027 Art.19, Art.25, Sch.5 para.2, SI
2014/2269 Art.20, Art.24, SI 2014/2384
Art.29, Art.41, SI 2014/2434 Art.20, Art.23,
SI 2014/2441 Art.23, SI 2014/2935 Art.34,
SI 2014/2950 Art.21, Art.25, SI 2014/3102
Art.26, Art.34, Sch.3 para.2
s.8, disapplied: SI 2014/1052 Art.29, SI
2014/2637 Art.25, SI 2014/2935 Art.38, SI
2014/3331 Art.21
s.8, referred to: SI 2014/1052 Art.25, SI
2014/1873 Art.25, SI 2014/2637 Art.21, SI
2014/3331 Art.16
s.8, varied: SI 2014/310 Sch.3 para.5, SI
2014/909 Sch.8 para.5, SI 2014/1052 Sch.10
para.5, SI 2014/1599 Sch.7 para.5, SI
2014/1873 Sch.8 para.5, SI 2014/2027 Sch.5
para.5, SI 2014/2269 Sch.6 para.5, SI
2014/2441 Sch.7 para.5, SI 2014/2637 Sch.8
para.5, SI 2014/2950 Sch.7 para.5, SI
2014/3102 Sch.3 para.5, SI 2014/3331 Sch.6
para.3
s.9, varied: SI 2014/310 Sch.3 para.6, SI
2014/909 Sch.8 para.6, SI 2014/1052 Sch.10
para.6, SI 2014/1599 Sch.7 para.6, SI
2014/1873 Sch.8 para.6, SI 2014/2027 Sch.5
para.6, SI 2014/2269 Sch.6 para.6, SI
2014/2441 Sch.7 para.6, SI 2014/2637 Sch.8
para.6, SI 2014/2950 Sch.7 para.6, SI
2014/3102 Sch.3 para.6, SI 2014/3331 Sch.6
para.4
s.10, applied: SI 2014/310 Art.7, Art.13, SI
2014/1052 Art.18, SI 2014/1821 Art.9, SI
2014/2027 Art.14, Art.21, Art.22, SI
2014/2384 Art.20, Art.21, Art.32, Art.33,
Art.35, Art.36, SI 2014/2434 Art.17, Art.25,
Art.26, Art.32, SI 2014/2935 Art.31, SI
2014/3102 Art.18, Art.30, Art.31, SI
2014/3328 Art.19, SI 2014/3331 Art.24
s.10, varied: SI 2014/1873 Sch.8 para.6
s.11, applied: SI 2014/310 Art.13, SI
2014/909 Art.23, Art.28, SI 2014/1052
Art.26, Art.31, SI 2014/1599 Art.18, Art.23,
Sch.9 para.4, SI 2014/1796 Art.19, SI
2014/1821 Art.13, SI 2014/1873 Art.26,

Art.31, Sch.12 para.4, SI 2014/2027 Art.21,
Art.26, SI 2014/2269 Art.21, Art.26, SI
2014/2384 Art.35, Art.46, Sch.16 para.3,
Sch.16 para.4, SI 2014/2434 Art.18, Sch.8
para.4, SI 2014/2637 Art.22, Art.27, SI
2014/2935 Art.35, Art.40, Sch.9 para.35, SI
2014/2950 Art.22, Art.27, SI 2014/3102
Art.30, Art.35, Sch.8 para.4, Sch.8 para.53,
SI 2014/3328 Art.20, Art.24, Sch.7 para.4,
Sch.9 para.4, SI 2014/3331 Art.18, Art.23,
Sch.12 para.14
s.11, varied: SI 2014/310 Sch.3 para.7, SI
2014/909 Sch.8 para.7, SI 2014/1052 Sch.10
para.7, SI 2014/1599 Sch.7 para.7, SI
2014/1873 Sch.8 para.7, SI 2014/2027 Sch.5
para.7, SI 2014/2269 Sch.6 para.7, SI
2014/2441 Sch.7 para.7, SI 2014/2637 Sch.8
para.7, SI 2014/2950 Sch.7 para.7, SI
2014/3102 Sch.3 para.7, SI 2014/3331 Sch.6
para.5
s.13, applied: SI 2014/310 Art.13, SI
2014/909 Art.28, Art.29, Art.30, SI
2014/1052 Art.31, Art.32, SI 2014/1599
Art.23, Art.24, SI 2014/1821 Art.8, Art.9, SI
2014/1873 Art.31, Art.32, SI 2014/2027
Art.21, Art.22, SI 2014/2269 Art.26, SI
2014/2384 Art.35, Art.36, SI 2014/2434
Art.25, Art.26, SI 2014/2637 Art.27, Art.28,
SI 2014/2935 Art.40, Art.41, SI 2014/2950
Art.27, Art.28, SI 2014/3102 Art.30, Art.31,
SI 2014/3328 Art.24, Art.25, SI 2014/3331
Art.23, Art.24
s.20, varied: SI 2014/310 Sch.3 para.8, SI
2014/909 Sch.8 para.8, SI 2014/1052 Sch.10
para.8, SI 2014/1599 Sch.7 para.8, SI
2014/1873 Sch.8 para.8, SI 2014/2027 Sch.5
para.8, SI 2014/2269 Sch.6 para.8, SI
2014/2441 Sch.7 para.8, SI 2014/2637 Sch.8
para.8, SI 2014/2950 Sch.7 para.8, SI
2014/3102 Sch.3 para.8, SI 2014/3331 Sch.6
para.6
s.21, disapplied: SI 2014/1873 Sch.12 para.4
s.22, varied: SI 2014/310 Sch.3 para.9, SI
2014/909 Sch.8 para.9, SI 2014/1052 Sch.10
para.9, SI 2014/1599 Sch.7 para.9, SI
2014/1873 Sch.8 para.9, SI 2014/2027 Sch.5
para.9, SI 2014/2269 Sch.6 para.9, SI
2014/2441 Sch.7 para.9, SI 2014/2637 Sch.8
para.9, SI 2014/2950 Sch.7 para.9, SI
2014/3102 Sch.3 para.9, SI 2014/3331 Sch.6
para.7

s.23, disapplied: SI 2014/1873 Sch.12 para.4
s.25, disapplied: SI 2014/1873 Sch.12 para.4
s.28, disapplied: SI 2014/1873 Sch.12 para.4
s.31, disapplied: SI 2014/1873 Sch.12 para.4
Sch.1 para.10, varied: SI 2014/310 Sch.3
para.6, SI 2014/909 Sch.8 para.6, SI
2014/1052 Sch.10 para.6, SI 2014/1599
Sch.7 para.6, SI 2014/2027 Sch.5 para.6, SI
2014/2269 Sch.6 para.6, SI 2014/2441 Sch.7
para.6, SI 2014/2637 Sch.8 para.6, SI
2014/2950 Sch.7 para.6, SI 2014/3102 Sch.3
para.6, SI 2014/3331 Sch.6 para.4
Sch.2 para.2, varied: SI 2014/310 Sch.3
para.6, SI 2014/909 Sch.8 para.6, SI
2014/1052 Sch.10 para.6, SI 2014/1599
Sch.7 para.6, SI 2014/1873 Sch.8 para.6, SI
2014/2027 Sch.5 para.6, SI 2014/2269 Sch.6
para.6, SI 2014/2441 Sch.7 para.6, SI
2014/2637 Sch.8 para.6, SI 2014/2950 Sch.7
para.6, SI 2014/3102 Sch.3 para.6, SI
2014/3331 Sch.6 para.4
Sch.3 para.3, varied: SI 2014/1821 Art.4
Sch.4 para.2, varied: SI 2014/310 Sch.3
para.6, SI 2014/909 Sch.8 para.6, SI
2014/1052 Sch.10 para.6, SI 2014/1599
Sch.7 para.6, SI 2014/1873 Sch.8 para.6, SI
2014/2027 Sch.5 para.6, SI 2014/2269 Sch.6
para.6, SI 2014/2441 Sch.7 para.6, SI
2014/2637 Sch.8 para.6, SI 2014/2950 Sch.7
para.6, SI 2014/3102 Sch.3 para.6, SI
2014/3331 Sch.6 para.4
Sch.4 para.7, varied: SI 2014/310 Sch.3
para.6, SI 2014/909 Sch.8 para.6, SI
2014/1052 Sch.10 para.6, SI 2014/1599
Sch.7 para.6, SI 2014/1873 Sch.8 para.6, SI
2014/2027 Sch.5 para.6, SI 2014/2269 Sch.6
para.6, SI 2014/2441 Sch.7 para.6, SI
2014/2637 Sch.8 para.6, SI 2014/2950 Sch.7
para.6, SI 2014/3102 Sch.3 para.6, SI
2014/3331 Sch.6 para.4
57. Nuclear Installations Act 1965
referred to: SSI 2014/324 Sch.1 para.3
s.1, applied: 2014 c.20 Sch.1 para.3, SI
2014/469 Sch.4 para.22
s.1, referred to: 2014 c.20 Sch.1 para.3
s.1, varied: SI 2014/469 Art.7
s.4, applied: SI 2014/469 Sch.4 para.22
s.4, varied: SI 2014/469 Art.7
s.5, varied: SI 2014/469 Art.7
s.6A, varied: 2014 c.20 Sch.1 para.3
s.22, varied: SI 2014/469 Art.7

s.23, varied: 2014 c.20 Sch.1 para.3
s.24A, applied: SI 2014/469 Sch.4 para.23
Sch.1, varied: 2014 c.20 Sch.1 para.3
58. Ministerial Salaries Consolidation Act 1965
s.1, varied: SI 2014/2708 Art.5
s.7, varied: SI 2014/2708 Art.5
Sch.1, varied: SI 2014/2708 Art.5
64. Commons Registration Act 1965
see *Paddico (267) Ltd v Kirklees*
Metropolitan Council [2014] UKSC 7,
[2014] A.C. 1072 (SC), Lord Neuberger
PSC
applied: SI 2014/3038 Reg.1, Reg.6, Reg.14,
Reg.39, Sch.4 para.14, Sch.7 para.2, Sch.8
para.1, Sch.8 para.3
s.1, disapplied: SI 2014/3038 Reg.10
s.2, applied: SI 2014/3038 Reg.5
s.11, applied: SI 2014/3038 Reg.10
s.14, see *Paddico (267) Ltd v Kirklees*
Metropolitan Council [2014] UKSC 7,
[2014] A.C. 1072 (SC), Lord Neuberger
PSC
s.22, see *R. (on the application of Newhaven*
Port and Properties Ltd) v East Sussex CC
[2013] EWCA Civ 276, [2014] Q.B. 186
(CA (Civ Div)), Richards LJ
69. Criminal Procedure (Attendance of
Witnesses) Act 1965
s.2, see *DLA Piper UK LLP v BDO LLP*
[2013] EWHC 3970 (Admin), [2014] 1
W.L.R. 4425 (QBD (Admin)), Moses LJ
s.2, applied: SI 2014/1610 Part 28, r.61_7,
r.28_1
s.2A, applied: SI 2014/1610 r.28_5
s.2B, applied: SI 2014/1610 r.28_7
s.2C, applied: SI 2014/1610 r.76_1, r.76_7
s.2D, applied: SI 2014/1610 Part 28, r.28_1
s.2E, applied: SI 2014/1610 r.28_7
s.3, applied: SI 2014/1610 Part 28, r.62_5
s.4, applied: SI 2014/1610 r.18_2, r.28_3

1966

3. Appropriation Act 1966
Sch.4 Part 4, varied: SI 2014/2708 Art.5
Sch.4 Part 9, varied: SI 2014/2708 Art.5
26. Appropriation (No.2) Act 1966
Sch.4 Part 5, varied: SI 2014/2708 Art.5
35. Family Provision Act 1966
repealed: 2014 c.16 s.2

36. Veterinary Surgeons Act 1966
s.11, applied: SI 2014/3493 Sch.1
s.11, enabling: SI 2014/3493
s.16, applied: SI 2014/3493 Sch.1
s.25, applied: SI 2014/3493

51. Local Government (Scotland) Act 1966
s.24, applied: SSI 2014/30 Reg.3
s.24A, applied: SSI 2014/30 Reg.3
s.24B, enabling: SSI 2014/31
s.25A, applied: SSI 2014/30 Reg.5

1967

**v. Edinburgh Corporation Order
Confirmation Act 1967**
Sch.1, repealed: 2014 asp 7 s.5
7. Misrepresentation Act 1967
s.2, see *Burntcopper Ltd (t/a Contemporary
Design Unit) v International Travel Catering
Association Ltd* [2014] EWHC 148 (Comm),
[2014] 2 All E.R. (Comm) 1055 (QBD
(Comm)), Judge Mackie QC
s.2, amended: SI 2014/870 Reg.5
8. Plant Health Act 1967
s.2, enabling: SI 2014/521, SI 2014/979, SI
2014/981, SI 2014/1186, SI 2014/2368, SI
2014/2385, SI 2014/2420, SSI 2014/140
s.3, enabling: SI 2014/521, SI 2014/609, SI
2014/979, SI 2014/981, SI 2014/1186, SI
2014/1759, SI 2014/2368, SI 2014/2385, SI
2014/2420, SI 2014/2875, SSI 2014/122,
SSI 2014/140
s.4, enabling: SI 2014/2875, SSI 2014/140
s.4A, enabling: SI 2014/609, SI 2014/1759
9. General Rate Act 1967
s.19, see *Furlonger v Lalatta* [2014] EWHC
37 (Ch), [2014] L. & T.R. 14 (Ch D),
Jonathan Klein
10. Forestry Act 1967
s.9, applied: SI 2014/3223 Sch.1 para.15
s.9, disapplied: SI 2014/3263 Sch.2 para.2
s.24, applied: SI 2014/3223 Sch.1 para.15
s.24, disapplied: SI 2014/3263 Sch.2 para.2
13. Parliamentary Commissioner Act 1967
Sch.2, amended: 2014 c.4 Sch.2 para.12,
2014 c.20 Sch.4 para.18, 2014 c.23 Sch.5
para.31, Sch.7 para.23, SI 2014/631 Sch.1
para.2, SI 2014/892 Sch.1 para.26, SI
2014/1924 Sch.1, SI 2014/3184 Sch.1 para.9

22. Agriculture Act 1967
Part IV, repealed: SI 2014/1924 Sch.1
24. Slaughter of Poultry Act 1967
applied: SI 2014/951 Reg.8, Reg.10, Reg.16,
SI 2014/1240 Reg.8, Reg.10, Reg.16
48. Industrial and Provident Societies Act 1967
repealed: 2014 c.14 Sch.7
58. Criminal Law Act 1967
s.3, see *R. v Morris (Daryl Howard)* [2013]
EWCA Crim 436, [2014] 1 W.L.R. 16 (CA
(Crim Div)), Leveson LJ
s.6, applied: SI 2014/1610 r.38_14, r.3_24
59. Appropriation Act 1967
Sch.4 Part 5, varied: SI 2014/2708 Art.5
Sch.4 Part 10, varied: SI 2014/2708 Art.5
77. Police (Scotland) Act 1967
s.41, see *Middlemiss v Fraser* 2014 J.C. 111
(HCJ), Lady Smith
80. Criminal Justice Act 1967
s.9, see *P v Ealing LBC* [2013] EWCA Civ
1579, [2014] H.L.R. 5 (CA (Civ Div)),
Arden LJ
s.9, applied: SI 2014/1610 r.27_1, r.28_4,
r.33_4, r.3_26, r.17_15
s.10, applied: SI 2014/1610 r.33_3, r.35_2,
r.37_6, r.12_4, r.38_13
s.17, applied: SI 2014/1610 r.38_9
s.22, applied: SI 2014/1610 r.19_8
s.89, applied: SI 2014/1610 r.28_4
81. Companies Act 1967
referred to: 2014 c.2 Sch.5 para.3
84. Sea Fish (Conservation) Act 1967
s.5, applied: SSI 2014/2 Art.4
s.5, enabling: SSI 2014/2
s.15, enabling: SSI 2014/2
87. Abortion Act 1967
see *R. (on the application of A) v Secretary
of State for Health* [2014] EWHC 1364
(Admin), [2014] Med. L.R. 246 (QBD
(Admin)), King J
s.1, see *Doogan v Greater Glasgow and
Clyde Health Board* [2014] UKSC 68 (SC),
Lady Hale DPSC; see *X (A Child) (Capacity
to Consent to Termination), Re* [2014]
EWHC 1871 (Fam), (2014) 139 B.M.L.R.
143 (Fam Div), Sir James Munby PFD
s.4, see *Doogan v Greater Glasgow and
Clyde Health Board* [2014] UKSC 68 (SC),
Lady Hale DPSC

88. Leasehold Reform Act 1967
    see *Shebelle Enterprises Ltd v Hampstead
    Garden Suburb Trust Ltd* [2014] EWCA Civ
    305, [2014] 2 P. & C.R. 6 (CA (Civ Div)),
    Arden LJ
    Pt I., see *Helman v John Lyon Free
    Grammar School* [2014] EWCA Civ 17,
    [2014] 1 W.L.R. 2451 (CA (Civ Div)),
    Arden LJ
    s.1, see *Helman v John Lyon Free Grammar
    School* [2014] EWCA Civ 17, [2014] 1
    W.L.R. 2451 (CA (Civ Div)), Arden LJ
    s.9, see *Voyazides v Eyre* [2014] R.V.R. 38
    (UT (Lands)), Judge Alice Robinson
    s.19, see *Shebelle Enterprises Ltd v
    Hampstead Garden Suburb Trust Ltd* [2014]
    EWCA Civ 305, [2014] 2 P. & C.R. 6 (CA
    (Civ Div)), Arden LJ

1968

2. Provisional Collection of Taxes Act 1968
    s.1, repealed (in part): 2014 c.26 Sch.38
    para.13
    s.1, enabling: SI 2014/474
13. National Loans Act 1968
    s.4, amended: 2014 c.26 s.300
    Sch.5A para.1, applied: SI 2014/1327 Reg.9
    Sch.5A para.15, applied: SI 2014/1327
    Reg.9
14. Public Expenditure and Receipts Act 1968
    s.5, enabling: SI 2014/1790
    Sch.3, enabling: SI 2014/1790
19. Criminal Appeal Act 1968
    see *R. v Dobson (Anthony)* [2013] EWCA
    Crim 1416, [2014] 1 Cr. App. R. (S.) 54 (CA
    (Crim Div)), Leveson LJ; see *R. v Padda
    (Gurpreet Singh)* [2013] EWCA Crim 2330,
    [2014] 1 W.L.R. 1920 (CA (Crim Div)),
    Rafferty LJ; see *R. v Price (Jamie)* [2013]
    EWCA Crim 1283, [2014] 1 Cr. App. R. (S.)
    36 (CA (Crim Div)), Elias LJ
    applied: SI 2014/1610 r.68_3
    Part I, applied: SI 2014/1610 r.71_2, r.71_3,
    r.68_1, r.68_2, r.74_1, r.71_4, r.71_9
    s.1, applied: SI 2014/1610 r.68_1, r.68_3,
    r.68_4
    s.3A, see *R. v Lawrence (Nyira)* [2013]
    EWCA Crim 1054, [2014] 1 W.L.R. 106
    (CA (Crim Div)), Hallett LJ; see *R. v White

(Anthony Alan) [2014] EWCA Crim 714,
    [2014] 2 Cr. App. R. 14 (CA (Crim Div)),
    Sir Brian Leveson PQBD
    s.6, see *R. v Oye (Seun)* [2013] EWCA Crim
    1725, [2014] 1 W.L.R. 3354 (CA (Crim
    Div)), Davis LJ
    s.7, see *R. v Lawrence (Nyira)* [2013]
    EWCA Crim 1054, [2014] 1 W.L.R. 106
    (CA (Crim Div)), Hallett LJ
    s.7, applied: SI 2014/1610 r.68_14
    s.8, applied: SI 2014/1610 r.3_1, r.14_1
    s.8, referred to: SI 2014/1610 r.68_14
    s.9, applied: SI 2014/1610 r.68_1
    s.11, see *R. v Bailey (Wayne)* [2013] EWCA
    Crim 1551, [2014] 1 Cr. App. R. (S.) 59 (CA
    (Crim Div)), Leveson LJ; see *R. v Henry
    (Derek Nicholas)* [2013] EWCA Crim 1415,
    [2014] 1 Cr. App. R. (S.) 55 (CA (Crim
    Div)), Leveson LJ
    s.11, applied: SI 2014/1610 r.68_3, r.68_4
    s.12, applied: SI 2014/1610 r.68_1, r.68_3,
    r.68_4
    s.15, applied: SI 2014/1610 r.68_1, r.68_3,
    r.68_4
    s.16A, applied: SI 2014/1610 r.76_4, r.68_1,
    r.68_3, r.68_4
    s.18, applied: SI 2014/1610 r.65_3, r.68_2
    s.18A, applied: SI 2014/1610 r.68_1
    s.19, applied: SI 2014/1610 r.68_8
    s.20, see *R. v A* [2014] EWCA Crim 567,
    [2014] 2 Cr. App. R. 7 (CA (Crim Div)),
    Lord Thomas LCJ
    s.21, applied: SI 2014/1610 r.65_11
    s.22, applied: SI 2014/1610 r.65_5, r.68_11,
    r.68_12
    s.23, see *R. v Smith (Paul James)* [2013]
    EWCA Crim 2388, [2014] 2 Cr. App. R. 1
    (CA (Crim Div)), Jackson LJ
    s.23, applied: SI 2014/1610 r.68_7
    s.31, applied: SI 2014/1610 r.65_1, r.68_3,
    r.66_6, r.69_3, r.65_5
    s.31, referred to: SI 2014/1610 r.71_6,
    r.71_7, r.71_10
    s.31C, applied: SI 2014/1610 r.65_5
    s.32, applied: SI 2014/1610 r.65_9, r.5_5
    s.33, applied: SI 2014/1610 r.74_1, r.74_2
    s.36, applied: SI 2014/1610 r.74_2
    s.37, applied: SI 2014/1610 r.74_3
    s.38, applied: SI 2014/1610 r.74_2
    s.49, applied: SI 2014/1610 r.66_6
    s.50, applied: SI 2014/1610 r.68_1

23. Rent Act 1968
 see *Lie v Mohile* [2014] EWCA Civ 728,
 [2014] 2 P. & C.R. 13 (CA (Civ Div)),
 Patten LJ
27. Firearms Act 1968
 applied: SI 2014/1638 Reg.5
 s.5, see *R. v Bate (Jonathan)* [2013] EWCA
 Crim 1327, [2014] 1 Cr. App. R. (S.) 48 (CA
 (Crim Div)), Moore-Bick LJ; see *R. v Stoker
 (Graham)* [2013] EWCA Crim 1431, [2014]
 1 Cr. App. R. (S.) 47 (CA (Crim Div)),
 Aikens LJ
 s.5, amended: 2014 c.12 s.108, s.109
 s.5A, amended: 2014 c.12 s.108, s.109
 s.7, applied: SI 2014/1638 Sch.2 para.15
 s.10, amended: SI 2014/1240 Sch.6 para.1,
 SI 2014/2124 Reg.2
 s.21, amended: 2014 c.12 s.110, SI
 2014/2522 Art.2
 s.21, applied: 2014 c.12 s.110
 s.26A, enabling: SI 2014/1239
 s.26B, enabling: SI 2014/1239
 s.27, applied: SI 2014/1638 Sch.2 para.15
 s.27, enabling: SI 2014/1239
 s.28, applied: SI 2014/1638 Sch.2 para.15
 s.33, applied: SI 2014/1638 Sch.2 para.15
 s.51A, see *Attorney General's Reference
 (No.37 of 2013)* [2013] EWCA Crim 1466,
 [2014] 1 Cr. App. R. (S.) 62 (CA (Crim
 Div)), Rafferty LJ; see *Attorney General's
 Reference (No.51 of 2013)* [2013] EWCA
 Crim 1927, [2014] 1 Cr. App. R. (S.) 83 (CA
 (Crim Div)), Hallett LJ; see *Attorney
 General's Reference (Nos 4, 5, 6, 7 and 8 of
 2014)* [2014] EWCA Crim 651, [2014] 2 Cr.
 App. R. (S.) 51 (CA (Crim Div)), Davis LJ;
 see *R. v Bate (Jonathan)* [2013] EWCA
 Crim 1327, [2014] 1 Cr. App. R. (S.) 48 (CA
 (Crim Div)), Moore-Bick LJ; see *R. v
 Moffat (Kevin)* [2014] EWCA Crim 332,
 [2014] 2 Cr. App. R. (S.) 37 (CMAC),
 Pitchford LJ; see *R. v Stoker (Graham)*
 [2013] EWCA Crim 1431, [2014] 1 Cr. App.
 R. (S.) 47 (CA (Crim Div)), Aikens LJ
 s.51A, amended: 2014 c.12 s.108
 s.53, enabling: SI 2014/1239
 s.54, amended: 2014 c.12 s.112
 s.54, repealed (in part): 2014 c.12 s.112
 s.57, referred to: 2014 c.12 s.110
 s.58, amended: 2014 c.12 s.110
 Sch.6 Part I, amended: 2014 c.12 s.108

41. Countryside Act 1968
 s.6, see *Lake District National Park
 Authority v Grace (Valuation Officer)* [2014]
 R.A. 81 (VT), A Clark
 s.6, applied: SI 2014/3038 Sch.4 para.8
 s.6, referred to: SI 2014/3038 Sch.4 para.8
 s.9, applied: SI 2014/3038 Sch.4 para.8
 s.15, applied: SI 2014/3223 Sch.2 para.1, SI
 2014/3263 Sch.3 para.1
 Sch.2, applied: SI 2014/3038 Sch.4 para.8
43. Appropriation Act 1968
 Sch.4 Part 7, varied: SI 2014/2708 Art.5
 Sch.4 Part 10, varied: SI 2014/2708 Art.5
46. Health Services and Public Health Act 1968
 s.45, applied: SI 2014/829 Sch.1 para.7
 s.63, amended: 2014 c.23 s.97
 s.63, applied: 2014 c.23 s.97, SI 2014/2672
 Sch.1 para.42, Sch.2 para.33
 s.63, referred to: 2014 c.23 s.99
47. Sewerage (Scotland) Act 1968
 s.29A, amended: 2014 asp 3 Sch.3 para.1
 s.38H, amended: 2014 asp 3 Sch.3 para.1
48. International Organisations Act 1968
 s.1, enabling: SI 2014/1891
 s.10, applied: SI 2014/1891
49. Social Work (Scotland) Act 1968
 applied: SSI 2014/193 Art.3
 Part II, applied: 2014 c.23 Sch.1 para.1,
 Sch.1 para.2, Sch.1 para.4
 Part II, disapplied: 2014 c.23 Sch.1 para.1,
 Sch.1 para.2, Sch.1 para.4
 s.1, applied: SSI 2014/345 Sch.1 Part 1
 s.1, referred to: 2014 asp 9 Sch.1 Part 1
 s.4, applied: SSI 2014/345 Sch.1 Part 1
 s.4, referred to: 2014 asp 9 Sch.1 Part 1
 s.5, amended: 2014 asp 8 Sch.5 para.1
 s.5, varied: SSI 2014/131 Art.4
 s.5, enabling: SSI 2014/310
 s.5A, repealed: 2014 asp 9 s.71
 s.6B, referred to: 2014 asp 9 Sch.1 Part 1
 s.8, applied: SSI 2014/345 Sch.1 Part 1
 s.8, referred to: 2014 asp 9 Sch.1 Part 1
 s.10, applied: SSI 2014/345 Sch.1 Part 1
 s.10, referred to: 2014 asp 9 Sch.1 Part 1
 s.12, applied: 2014 c.23 s.49, s.50, s.51, s.73,
 Sch.1 para.3, SI 2014/2839 Reg.5, SSI
 2014/345 Sch.1 Part 1
 s.12, referred to: 2014 asp 9 Sch.1 Part 1
 s.12A, see *McCue v Glasgow City Council*
 [2014] CSOH 124, 2014 S.L.T. 891 (OH),
 Lord Jones

s.12A, applied: SSI 2014/32 Art.4

s.12B, applied: SI 2014/513 Art.3, SSI 2014/32 Art.5

s.13, applied: SSI 2014/345 Sch.1 Part 1

s.13, referred to: 2014 asp 9 Sch.1 Part 1

s.13A, applied: 2014 c.23 s.49, s.50, s.51, s.73, Sch.1 para.3, SI 2014/2839 Reg.5, SSI 2014/25 Reg.10

s.14, applied: SSI 2014/345 Sch.1 Part 1

s.27, referred to: 2014 asp 9 Sch.1 Part 1

s.28, applied: SSI 2014/345 Sch.1 Part 1

s.28, referred to: 2014 asp 9 Sch.1 Part 1

s.59, applied: SSI 2014/345 Sch.1 Part 1

s.59, referred to: 2014 asp 9 Sch.1 Part 1

s.78A, referred to: 2014 asp 9 Sch.1 Part 1

s.80, referred to: 2014 asp 9 Sch.1 Part 1

s.83, referred to: 2014 asp 9 Sch.1 Part 1

s.86, amended: 2014 c.23 Sch.1 para.7, SSI 2014/90 Sch.1 Part 3

s.86, referred to: 2014 asp 9 Sch.1 Part 1

s.87, applied: SSI 2014/38, SSI 2014/39, SSI 2014/39 Reg.2, SSI 2014/65 Reg.2

s.87, enabling: SSI 2014/65

s.97, amended: 2014 c.23 Sch.1 para.7

55. Friendly and Industrial and Provident Societies Act 1968

repealed: 2014 c.14 Sch.7

s.15, applied: SI 2014/574 Reg.2

60. Theft Act 1968

s.15A, see *R. v White (Anthony Alan)* [2014] EWCA Crim 714, [2014] 2 Cr. App. R. 14 (CA (Crim Div)), Sir Brian Leveson PQBD

s.16, see *R. v White (Anthony Alan)* [2014] EWCA Crim 714, [2014] 2 Cr. App. R. 14 (CA (Crim Div)), Sir Brian Leveson PQBD; see *R. v Wright (Robert)* [2014] EWCA Crim 382, [2014] 1 W.L.R. 2913 (CA (Crim Div)), Treacy LJ

s.25, see *R. v Sakalauskas (Gytis)* [2013] EWCA Crim 2278, [2014] 1 W.L.R. 1204 (CA (Crim Div)), Goldring LJ

64. Civil Evidence Act 1968

see *Rogers v Hoyle* [2014] EWCA Civ 257, [2014] 3 W.L.R. 148 (CA (Civ Div)), Arden LJ

s.3, see *Rogers v Hoyle* [2014] EWCA Civ 257, [2014] 3 W.L.R. 148 (CA (Civ Div)), Arden LJ

s.11, applied: SI 2014/2833 Reg.19

65. Gaming Act 1968

see *Revenue and Customs Commissioners v IFX Investment Co Ltd* [2014] UKUT 398 (TCC), [2014] B.V.C. 535 (UT (Tax)), Norris J

Pt III., see *Revenue and Customs Commissioners v Rank Group Plc* [2013] EWCA Civ 1289, [2014] S.T.C. 470 (CA (Civ Div)), Rimer LJ

s.26, see *Revenue and Customs Commissioners v Rank Group Plc* [2013] EWCA Civ 1289, [2014] S.T.C. 470 (CA (Civ Div)), Rimer LJ

67. Medicines Act 1968

applied: 2014 c.23 s.111

s.74, applied: SI 2014/2936 Sch.2 para.8

s.105, applied: SI 2014/1638 Sch.2 para.7

70. Law Reform (Miscellaneous Provisions) (Scotland) Act 1968

s.10, applied: SI 2014/2833 Reg.19

73. Transport Act 1968

Part II, disapplied: SI 2014/864 Art.7

s.9, amended: SI 2014/864 Sch.2 para.2, SI 2014/866 Sch.1 para.2

s.9, applied: SSI 2014/164 Sch.2 Part 1

s.9, repealed (in part): SI 2014/866 Sch.1 para.2

s.9A, amended: SI 2014/864 Sch.2 para.3, SI 2014/866 Sch.1 para.3

s.10, amended: SI 2014/864 Sch.2 para.4, SI 2014/866 Sch.1 para.4

s.10A, amended: SI 2014/866 Sch.1 para.5

s.10B, amended: 2014 c.14 Sch.4 para.22

s.11, amended: SI 2014/864 Sch.2 para.5

s.12, amended: SI 2014/864 Sch.2 para.6, SI 2014/866 Sch.1 para.6

s.13, substituted: SI 2014/864 Sch.2 para.7

s.14, amended: 2014 c.2 Sch.12 para.3, SI 2014/864 Sch.2 para.8, SI 2014/866 Sch.1 para.7

s.14, applied: 2014 c.2 s.32

s.15, amended: SI 2014/864 Sch.2 para.9, SI 2014/866 Sch.1 para.8

s.15A, amended: SI 2014/864 Sch.2 para.10

s.16, amended: SI 2014/864 Sch.2 para.11, SI 2014/866 Sch.1 para.9

s.20, amended: SI 2014/866 Sch.1 para.10

s.23, amended: SI 2014/866 Sch.1 para.11

s.116, applied: SI 2014/1604 Art.3

1969

10. Mines and Quarries (Tips) Act 1969
s.1, repealed: SI 2014/3248 Sch.3 Part 1
s.10, repealed: SI 2014/3248 Sch.3 Part 1
s.11, amended: SI 2014/3248 Sch.5 para.3
Sch.1, repealed: SI 2014/3248 Sch.3 Part 1

12. Genocide Act 1969
referred to: SI 2014/2706 Art.2

31. Appropriation Act 1969
Sch.4 Part 5, varied: SI 2014/2708 Art.5
Sch.5 Part 10, varied: SI 2014/2708 Art.5

38. Sharing of Church Buildings Act 1969
s.6, referred to: SI 2014/544 Reg.3
Sch.1 para.3, amended: SI 2014/560 Sch.1
para.11
Sch.1 para.3A, added: SI 2014/560 Sch.1
para.11
Sch.1 para.4, amended: SI 2014/560 Sch.1
para.11
Sch.1 para.5, amended: SI 2014/560 Sch.1
para.11

39. Age of Majority (Scotland) Act 1969
Sch.1 Part I, amended: 2014 c.14 Sch.7

46. Family Law Reform Act 1969
s.15, see *Holden-Hindley v Holden-Hindley*
[2013] EWHC 3053 (Ch), [2014] W.T.L.R.
275 (Ch D), Roth J
s.19, amended: 2014 c.14 Sch.7
s.19, repealed (in part): 2014 c.14 Sch.7
Sch.1 Part II, amended: 2014 c.14 Sch.7

51. Development of Tourism Act 1969
s.1, applied: SSI 2014/164 Sch.2 Part 1

54. Children and Young Persons Act 1969
s.70, amended: 2014 c.6 Sch.2 para.43

**57. Employers Liability (Compulsory
Insurance) Act 1969**
see *Campbell v Peter Gordon Joiners Ltd*
2014 S.L.T. 178 (OH), Lord Glennie
s.1, see *Campbell v Peter Gordon Joiners
Ltd* 2014 S.L.T. 178 (OH), Lord Glennie
s.3, applied: 2014 c.1 s.18
s.4, applied: SI 2014/469 Sch.4 para.13
s.5, see *Campbell v Peter Gordon Joiners
Ltd* 2014 S.L.T. 178 (OH), Lord Glennie

1970

9. Taxes Management Act 1970
see *MCashback Software 6 LLP v Revenue
and Customs Commissioners* [2014]
S.F.T.D. 510 (FTT (Tax)), Judge Jonathan
Cannan
Part V, applied: 2014 c.26 s.247, s.266, SI
2014/520 Reg.15, SI 2014/1506 Reg.23
Part VI, applied: SI 2014/2929 Reg.8
Part VI, varied: SI 2014/2929 Reg.8
s.7, amended: 2014 c.26 Sch.38 para.14,
2014 c.29 s.9
s.8, see *R. (on the application of de Silva) v
Revenue and Customs Commissioners*
[2014] UKUT 170 (TCC), [2014] S.T.C.
2088 (UT (Tax)), Sales J
s.9A, see *R. (on the application of Rouse) v
Revenue and Customs Commissioners*
[2014] S.T.C. 230 (UT (Tax)), Warren J
s.9B, amended: 2014 c.26 Sch.33 para.1
s.9C, see *Blum v Revenue and Customs*
[2014] R.V.R. 137 (UT (Lands)), PR Francis
FRICS
s.9ZB, see *R. (on the application of Rouse) v
Revenue and Customs Commissioners*
[2014] S.T.C. 230 (UT (Tax)), Warren J
s.12AA, applied: 2014 c.26 Sch.31 para.3
s.12AB, applied: 2014 c.26 Sch.31 para.3
s.12ADA, added: 2014 c.26 Sch.17 para.16
s.29, see *Fisher v Revenue and Customs
Commissioners* [2014] UKFTT 804 (TC),
[2014] S.F.T.D. 1341 (FTT (Tax)), Judge
Swami Raghavan; see *Hargreaves v
Revenue and Customs Commissioners*
[2014] UKUT 395 (TCC), [2014] B.T.C.
526 (UT (Tax)), Nugee J; see *Macklin v
Revenue and Customs Commissioners*
[2014] S.F.T.D. 290 (FTT (Tax)), Judge
John Walters Q.C.; see *Sanderson v
Revenue and Customs Commissioners*
[2014] S.T.C. 915 (UT (Tax)), Newey J
s.30, amended: SI 2014/992 Art.4
s.31, see *MCashback Software 6 LLP v
Revenue and Customs Commissioners*
[2014] S.F.T.D. 510 (FTT (Tax)), Judge
Jonathan Cannan
s.31, applied: 2014 c.26 s.208
s.33, see *Macklin v Revenue and Customs
Commissioners* [2014] S.F.T.D. 290 (FTT
(Tax)), Judge John Walters Q.C.; see

Tindale v Revenue and Customs Commissioners [2014] UKUT 324 (TCC) (UT (Tax)), Judge Timothy Herrington
s.36, amended: 2014 c.26 s.277
s.42, amended: 2014 c.26 s.11
s.43, see *Trustees of the BT Pension Scheme v Revenue and Customs Commissioners* [2014] EWCA Civ 23, [2014] S.T.C. 1156 (CA (Civ Div)), Longmore LJ
s.43A, amended: 2014 c.26 s.11
s.54, applied: 2014 c.28 s.59
s.54, varied: SI 2014/1933 Reg.3
s.55, amended: 2014 c.26 s.224
s.55, applied: 2014 c.26 s.227
s.56, amended: 2014 c.26 s.225
s.59D, applied: 2014 c.26 s.119
s.59E, enabling: SI 2014/2409
s.65, applied: SI 2014/2929 Reg.8
s.70A, amended: SI 2014/992 Art.4
s.73, see *Currie v Revenue and Customs Commissioners* [2014] UKFTT 882 (TC) (FTT (Tax)), Judge Anne Redston
s.97A, applied: 2014 c.26 s.212
s.98, amended: 2014 c.26 s.18, Sch.6 para.11, Sch.8 para.221, Sch.8 para.231, Sch.11 para.2, Sch.17 para.16
s.98A, see *Revenue and Customs Commissioners v Bosher* [2014] S.T.C. 617 (UT (Tax)), Warren J
s.98C, amended: 2014 c.26 s.275, s.284
s.100, see *Revenue and Customs Commissioners v Bosher* [2014] S.T.C. 617 (UT (Tax)), Warren J
s.100, varied: 2014 c.26 Sch.35 para.10
s.100B, see *Khawaja v Revenue and Customs Commissioners* [2014] S.T.C. 150 (UT (Tax)), Judge Roger Berner; see *Revenue and Customs Commissioners v Bosher* [2014] S.T.C. 617 (UT (Tax)), Warren J
s.102, see *Revenue and Customs Commissioners v Bosher* [2014] S.T.C. 617 (UT (Tax)), Warren J
s.103ZA, amended: 2014 c.26 Sch.33 para.2
s.113, enabling: SI 2014/472
s.118, applied: 2014 c.26 Sch.34 para.5
Sch.1A, see *R. (on the application of Rouse) v Revenue and Customs Commissioners* [2014] S.T.C. 230 (UT (Tax)), Warren J; see *Spring Salmon & Seafood Ltd v Revenue and Customs Commissioners* [2014] UKUT 488

(TCC), [2014] B.T.C. 529 (UT (Tax)), Warren J
Sch.1A, applied: 2014 c.7 s.10
Sch.1B, see *R. (on the application of de Silva) v Revenue and Customs Commissioners* [2014] UKUT 170 (TCC), [2014] S.T.C. 2088 (UT (Tax)), Sales J
Sch.1AB para.3A, see *Currie v Revenue and Customs Commissioners* [2014] UKFTT 882 (TC) (FTT (Tax)), Judge Anne Redston
Sch.1A para.3, see *R. (on the application of de Silva) v Revenue and Customs Commissioners* [2014] UKUT 170 (TCC), [2014] S.T.C. 2088 (UT (Tax)), Sales J
Sch.1A para.5, see *R. (on the application of de Silva) v Revenue and Customs Commissioners* [2014] UKUT 170 (TCC), [2014] S.T.C. 2088 (UT (Tax)), Sales J
Sch.1A para.9, see *Currie v Revenue and Customs Commissioners* [2014] UKFTT 882 (TC) (FTT (Tax)), Judge Anne Redston
Sch.1A para.9, applied: 2014 c.26 s.208
Sch.1B para.2, see *R. (on the application of de Silva) v Revenue and Customs Commissioners* [2014] UKUT 170 (TCC), [2014] S.T.C. 2088 (UT (Tax)), Sales J

25. Appropriation Act 1970
Sch.4 Part 6, varied: SI 2014/2708 Art.5
Sch.4 Part 8, varied: SI 2014/2708 Art.5

31. Administration of Justice Act 1970
s.11, see *Constantinides v Constantinides* [2013] EWHC 3688 (Fam), [2014] 1 W.L.R. 1934 (Fam Div), Holman J
s.36, see *Serious Organised Crime Agency v Szepietowski* [2014] A.C. 338 (SC), Lord Neuberger PSC
s.41, applied: SI 2014/1610 r.76_1
s.44A, see *Novoship (UK) Ltd v Mikhaylyuk* [2014] EWCA Civ 908, [2014] W.T.L.R. 1521 (CA (Civ Div)), Longmore LJ
Sch.8 para.11, amended: SI 2014/605 Art.3
Sch.8 para.13, amended: SI 2014/605 Art.3
Sch.8 para.13A, amended: SI 2014/605 Art.4
Sch.8 para.13B, amended: SI 2014/605 Art.3
Sch.8 para.13C, amended: SI 2014/605 Art.3

35. Conveyancing and Feudal Reform (Scotland) Act 1970
s.24, see *Mortgages 1 Ltd v Chaudhary* 2014 S.L.T. (Sh Ct) 35 (Sh Ct (South Strathclyde) (Airdrie)), Sheriff Principal B A Lockhart
s.24, amended: 2014 asp 18 Sch.5 para.22

36. Merchant Shipping Act 1970
s.43, applied: SI 2014/1613 Reg.39
39. Local Authorities (Goods and Services) Act 1970
s.1, see *Tayside Contracts v D Geddes (Contractors) Ltd* [2014] CSOH 105, 2014 S.L.T. 764 (OH), Lord Malcolm
s.1, applied: SI 2014/1197 Art.2
s.1, enabling: SI 2014/1197
41. Equal Pay Act 1970
s.1, see *Glasgow City Council v Fox Cross Claimants* [2014] CSIH 27, 2014 S.C. 610 (IH (Ex Div)), Lord Brodie
42. Local Authority Social Services Act 1970
s.1A, applied: 2014 c.12 Sch.2 para.4
s.7, see *R. (on the application of Members of the Committee of Care North East Northumberland) v Northumberland CC* [2013] EWCA Civ 1740, [2014] P.T.S.R. 758 (CA (Civ Div)), Aikens LJ
s.7A, applied: SI 2014/2821 Reg.5
Sch.1, amended: 2014 c.6 Sch.2 para.44
Sch.1, varied: SI 2014/829 Art.4
44. Chronically Sick and Disabled Persons Act 1970
s.1, applied: SI 2014/829 Sch.1 para.8
s.2, see *Robson v Salford City Council* [2014] EWHC 3481 (Admin), (2014) 17 C.C.L. Rep. 474 (QBD (Admin)), Judge Stephen Davies
s.2, applied: 2014 c.6 s.37, SI 2014/829 Sch.1 para.9, SI 2014/1530 Reg.12
s.2A, added: 2014 c.23 s.66
s.21, amended: 2014 asp 17 s.1, s.2, s.3, s.4, s.5
s.21, applied: 2014 asp 17 s.6
s.21, enabling: SI 2014/3082, SSI 2014/145
s.28A, applied: 2014 c.6 s.37

1971

19. Carriage of Goods by Sea Act 1971
s.1, see *Yemgas FZCO v Superior Pescadores SA Panama (The Superior Pescadores)* [2014] EWHC 971 (comm), [2014] 1 Lloyd's Rep. 660 (QBD (Comm)), Males J
29. National Savings Bank Act 1971
s.4, enabling: SI 2014/484
s.16, amended: 2014 c.14 Sch.4 para.23

32. Attachment of Earnings Act 1971
s.14, see *R. (on the application of Lawson) v Westminster Magistrates' Court* [2013] EWHC 2434 (Admin), [2014] 1 W.L.R. 2085 (DC), Treacy LJ
Sch.1 para.11, amended: SI 2014/605 Art.5
Sch.1 para.13, amended: SI 2014/605 Art.5
Sch.1 para.14, amended: SI 2014/605 Art.5
Sch.1 para.14A, amended: SI 2014/605 Art.5
Sch.1 para.14B, amended: SI 2014/605 Art.5
Sch.1 para.15, amended: SI 2014/605 Art.5
Sch.1 para.16, amended: SI 2014/605 Art.5
38. Misuse of Drugs Act 1971
s.2, applied: SI 2014/1106, SI 2014/1352, SI 2014/3271
s.2, enabling: SI 2014/1106, SI 2014/1352, SI 2014/3271
s.4, see *Gorrie v MacLeod* [2014] HCJAC 10, 2014 S.C.L. 293 (HCJ), The Lord Justice Clerk (Carloway); see *Griffiths v R* 2014 S.C.L. 61 (Sh Ct (Tayside) (Dundee)), Sheriff A N Brown; see *HM Advocate v McAllister (Jason)* [2014] HCJ 111, 2014 S.L.T. 1023 (HCJ), Lord Boyd of Duncansby; see *HM Advocate v McAllister (Jason)* [2014] HCJ 112, 2014 S.C.L. 807 (HCJ), Lord Boyd of Duncansby; see *R. v Dang (Manh Toan)* [2014] EWCA Crim 348, [2014] 1 W.L.R. 3797 (CA (Crim Div)), Pitchford LJ; see *R. v Khan (Kazim Ali)* [2013] EWCA Crim 800, [2014] 1 Cr. App. R. (S.) 10 (CA (Crim Div)), Treacy LJ
s.7, applied: SI 2014/1274, SI 2014/1376, SI 2014/3276
s.7, enabling: SI 2014/1274, SI 2014/1275, SI 2014/1376, SI 2014/1377, SI 2014/3276, SI 2014/3277
s.10, enabling: SI 2014/1275, SI 2014/1377, SI 2014/3277
s.22, enabling: SI 2014/1275, SI 2014/1377, SI 2014/2081, SI 2014/3277
s.23, see *Haashi (Shirwa) v HM Advocate* [2014] HCJAC 48, 2014 G.W.D. 17-313 (HCJ), The Lord Justice Clerk (Carloway); see *McAughey (Charles Gray) v HM Advocate* 2014 S.C.L. 165 (HCJ), Lord Menzies
s.31, applied: SI 2014/1275, SI 2014/2081, SI 2014/3277
s.31, enabling: SI 2014/1275, SI 2014/1377, SI 2014/2081, SI 2014/3277

Sch.2 Pt II para.1, see *R. v Brown (Michael)*
[2013] EWCA Crim 1726, [2014] 1 Cr. App.
R. (S.) 84 (CA (Crim Div)), Pitchford LJ
Sch.2 Part I para.1, amended: SI 2014/1106
Art.3, SI 2014/3271 Art.3, Art.4
Sch.2 Part II para.1, amended: SI 2014/1106
Art.4
Sch.2 Part III para.1, amended: SI
2014/1106 Art.5, SI 2014/1352 Art.3
Sch.2 Part IV, amended: SI 2014/1352 Art.4

56. Pensions (Increase) Act 1971
applied: SI 2014/512 Reg.41, Sch.2 para.3,
SI 2014/525 Reg.25, SI 2014/1964 Reg.85,
Reg.98, Reg.127, Reg.128, Reg.131, Sch.1
para.3, Sch.2 para.30, SI 2014/2328 Reg.6,
Reg.12, SI 2014/2336 Reg.77, Reg.81,
Reg.82, SI 2014/2848 Reg.25, Reg.61, SSI
2014/164 Reg.9, Reg.24, Reg.25, Reg.26,
Reg.27, Reg.28, Reg.30, Reg.39, Reg.40,
Reg.42, Reg.43, Reg.45, Reg.46, SSI
2014/217 Reg.43, Reg.146, Sch.2 para.3,
SSI 2014/233 Reg.13, Reg.25, SSI 2014/292
Reg.114, Reg.146
s.1, applied: SI 2014/668 Art.3
s.1, disapplied: SI 2014/3229 Sch.2 para.6
s.3, amended: SI 2014/560 Sch.3 para.1, SI
2014/3229 Sch.3 para.1
s.3, disapplied: SI 2014/3229 Sch.2 para.6
s.5, applied: SI 2014/512 Reg.117, Reg.149,
SSI 2014/217 Reg.114, Reg.146, SSI
2014/292 Reg.114, Reg.146
s.5, enabling: SI 2014/563
s.6, disapplied: SI 2014/3229 Sch.2 para.6
s.7, applied: SI 2014/1964 Reg.108
s.8, applied: SI 2014/563 Reg.3, SI 2014/668
Art.2, SI 2014/1964 Reg.131
s.17, amended: SI 2014/560 Sch.3 para.1, SI
2014/3229 Sch.3 para.1
s.17, disapplied: SI 2014/3229 Sch.2 para.6
Sch.3, applied: SI 2014/525 Reg.25, SSI
2014/233 Reg.25

58. Sheriff Courts (Scotland) Act 1971
Part I, repealed: 2014 asp 18 Sch.5 para.6
s.2, amended: 2014 asp 18 Sch.5 para.6
s.2, repealed (in part): 2014 asp 18 Sch.5
para.6
s.3, amended: 2014 asp 18 Sch.5 para.6
s.3, repealed (in part): 2014 asp 18 Sch.5
para.6
s.4, repealed: 2014 asp 18 Sch.5 para.6
s.11B, amended: SSI 2014/155 Art.3

s.11B, repealed (in part): SSI 2014/155 Art.3
s.12A, applied: 2014 asp 10 s.27, SSI
2014/99 r.13, SSI 2014/102 r.13
s.12C, enabling: SSI 2014/99, SSI 2014/102
s.12D, applied: SSI 2014/99 r.14, r.15, SSI
2014/102 r.14, r.15
s.14A, amended: SSI 2014/155 Art.3
s.32, amended: 2014 asp 11 Sch.3 para.1
s.32, enabling: SSI 2014/119, SSI 2014/152,
SSI 2014/201, SSI 2014/291, SSI 2014/302,
SSI 2014/371

60. Prevention of Oil Pollution Act 1971
s.11A, amended: 2014 asp 3 Sch.3 para.2

**61. Mineral Workings (Offshore Installations)
Act 1971**
s.12, applied: SI 2014/1638 Reg.31

67. Appropriation Act 1971
Sch.4 Part 2, varied: SI 2014/2708 Art.5
Sch.4 Part 5, varied: SI 2014/2708 Art.5

68. Finance Act 1971
Sch.8 para.3, see *Revenue and Customs
Commissioners v Lloyds TSB Equipment
Leasing (No.1) Ltd* [2014] EWCA Civ 1062,
[2014] S.T.C. 2770 (CA (Civ Div)), Rimer
LJ

77. Immigration Act 1971
see *Greenwood (Automatic Deportation:
Order of Events), Re* [2014] UKUT 342
(IAC), [2014] Imm. A.R. 1288 (UT (IAC)),
CMG Ockelton (Vice President); see *R. (on
the application of Thapa) v Secretary of
State for the Home Department* [2014]
EWHC 659 (Admin), [2014] 1 W.L.R. 4138
(QBD (Admin)), Helen Mountfield QC
applied: 2014 c.22 s.49, SI 2014/2604 Sch.1
para.2, SI 2014/2702 Art.2
s.3, see *R. (on the application of George) v
Secretary of State for the Home Department*
[2014] UKSC 28, [2014] 1 W.L.R. 1831
(SC), Lord Neuberger PSC; see *R. (on the
application of Pryor) v Secretary of State for
the Home Department* [2013] EWHC 2853
(Admin), [2014] Imm. A.R. 341 (QBD
(Admin)), Jeremy Baker J; see *R. (on the
application of Rostami) v Secretary of State
for the Home Department* [2013] EWHC
1494 (Admin), [2014] Imm. A.R. 56 (QBD
(Admin)), Hickinbottom J
s.3, applied: SI 2014/2771 Art.10, SI
2014/2928 Art.2

s.3C, see *Ahmadi (S.47 Decision: Validity: Sapkota: Afghanistan), Re* [2013] EWCA Civ 512, [2014] 1 W.L.R. 401 (CA (Civ Div)), Sullivan LJ; see *R. (on the application of Bhgat) v Secretary of State for the Home Department* [2014] EWHC 772 (Admin), [2014] 1 W.L.R. 3710 (QBD (Admin)), Clare Moulder

s.3C, amended: 2014 c.22 Sch.9 para.21

s.3D, see *Ahmadi (S.47 Decision: Validity: Sapkota: Afghanistan), Re* [2013] EWCA Civ 512, [2014] 1 W.L.R. 401 (CA (Civ Div)), Sullivan LJ

s.3D, amended: 2014 c.22 Sch.9 para.22

s.4, see *Ahmadi (S.47 Decision: Validity: Sapkota: Afghanistan), Re* [2013] EWCA Civ 512, [2014] 1 W.L.R. 401 (CA (Civ Div)), Sullivan LJ

s.5, see *R. (on the application of George) v Secretary of State for the Home Department* [2014] UKSC 28, [2014] 1 W.L.R. 1831 (SC), Lord Neuberger PSC

s.8B, enabling: SI 2014/1849

s.9, enabling: SI 2014/2475

s.25, see *R. v Bina (Arya)* [2014] EWCA Crim 1444, [2014] 2 Cr. App. R. 30 (CA (Crim Div)), McCombe LJ

s.25A, see *R. v Bina (Arya)* [2014] EWCA Crim 1444, [2014] 2 Cr. App. R. 30 (CA (Crim Div)), McCombe LJ

s.26A, applied: SI 2014/3181 Sch.1 para.1

s.27, amended: 2014 c.22 Sch.8 para.7

s.28C, varied: SI 2014/1704 Sch.2 para.1

s.28CA, varied: SI 2014/1704 Sch.2 para.2

s.28D, referred to: SI 2014/1610 r.6_30

s.28F, varied: SI 2014/1704 Sch.2 para.3

s.28FA, varied: SI 2014/1704 Sch.2 para.4

s.28J, amended: 2014 c.22 Sch.1 para.4

s.28K, amended: 2014 c.22 Sch.1 para.4

s.28K, varied: SI 2014/1704 Sch.2 para.5

s.32, enabling: SI 2014/2475

s.33, see *R. (on the application of Tigere) v Secretary of State for Business, Innovation and Skills* [2014] EWCA Civ 1216, [2014] H.R.L.R. 26 (CA (Civ Div)), Laws LJ

s.33, applied: SI 2014/581 Sch.4 para.2

s.33, referred to: 2014 c.22 s.49

s.33, varied: SI 2014/1704 Sch.2 para.6

Sch.2 Part I para.1, varied: SI 2014/1704 Sch.2 para.7

Sch.2 Part I para.2A, amended: 2014 c.22 Sch.9 para.23

Sch.2 Part I para.3, amended: 2014 c.22 Sch.8 para.2

Sch.2 Part I para.4, amended: 2014 c.22 s.13, Sch.2 para.1, Sch.8 para.3

Sch.2 Part I para.5, amended: 2014 c.22 Sch.8 para.4

Sch.2 Part I para.5, applied: 2014 c.22 Sch.9 para.72

Sch.2 Part I para.5A, added: 2014 c.22 Sch.8 para.5

Sch.2 Part I para.5B, added: 2014 c.22 Sch.8 para.6

Sch.2 Part I para.11, amended: 2014 c.22 Sch.9 para.1

Sch.2 Part I para.16, amended: 2014 c.22 s.5

Sch.2 Part I para.18, amended: 2014 c.22 s.5, s.9, s.13, Sch.1 para.1, Sch.2 para.1

Sch.2 Part I para.18A, added: 2014 c.22 Sch.1 para.2

Sch.2 Part I para.18B, added: 2014 c.22 s.5

Sch.2 Part I para.22, amended: 2014 c.22 s.7

Sch.2 Part I para.22, varied: SI 2014/1704 Sch.2 para.7

Sch.2 Part I para.25, amended: 2014 c.22 s.7

Sch.2 Part I para.25, referred to: SI 2014/2604 r.39

Sch.2 Part I para.25, enabling: SI 2014/2604

Sch.2 Part I para.25A, amended: 2014 c.22 Sch.1 para.3

Sch.2 Part I para.25A, repealed (in part): 2014 c.22 Sch.1 para.3

Sch.2 Part I para.25A, varied: SI 2014/1704 Sch.2 para.7

Sch.2 Part I para.27C, varied: SI 2014/1704 Sch.2 para.7

Sch.2 Part II para.29, amended: 2014 c.22 s.7

Sch.2 Part II para.30, amended: 2014 c.22 s.7

Sch.2 Part II para.33A, added: 2014 c.22 s.7

Sch.2 para.18, see *R. (on the application of Muaza) v Secretary of State for the Home Department* [2013] EWCA Civ 1561, [2014] 1 W.L.R. 1870 (CA (Civ Div)), Lewison LJ

Sch.3, see *R. (on the application of Nouazli) v Secretary of State for the Home Department* [2013] EWCA Civ 1608, [2014] 1 W.L.R. 3313 (CA (Civ Div)), Moore-Bick LJ

Sch.3 para.2, see *R. (on the application of Francis) v Secretary of State for the Home Department* [2013] EWHC 2115 (Admin), [2014] 1 All E.R. 68 (QBD (Admin)), McKenna, J.

Sch.3 para.2, amended: 2014 c.22 Sch.1 para.2

Sch.3 para.3, amended: 2014 c.22 Sch.9 para.9, Sch.9 para.24

80. Banking and Financial Dealings Act 1971

applied: SI 2014/2874 Art.6, SI 2014/3117 Reg.2

1972

3. Ministerial and other Salaries Act 1972

Sch.1 Part I, varied: SI 2014/2708 Art.5

Sch.3 para.3, varied: SI 2014/2708 Art.5

11. Superannuation Act 1972

see *Ellis v Cabinet Office* [2014] EWHC 2049 (Ch), [2014] Pens. L.R. 681 (Ch D), Rose J

applied: 2014 c.20 Sch.4 para.9, SI 2014/555 Art.2

s.1, see *Heron v Sefton MBC* [2014] Eq. L.R. 130 (EAT), Mitting J

s.1, applied: SI 2014/1964 Reg.3

s.1, enabling: SI 2014/555

s.7, applied: SI 2014/44, SI 2014/525, SSI 2014/23, SSI 2014/164 Reg.4, SSI 2014/233

s.7, enabling: SI 2014/44, SI 2014/525, SSI 2014/23, SSI 2014/233

s.9, applied: SI 2014/424, SI 2014/2651, SSI 2014/44, SSI 2014/69

s.9, referred to: SI 2014/424, SI 2014/2651

s.9, enabling: SI 2014/424, SI 2014/2651, SSI 2014/44, SSI 2014/69

s.10, applied: SI 2014/78, SI 2014/1607, SSI 2014/43, SSI 2014/154

s.10, enabling: SI 2014/78, SI 2014/570, SI 2014/1607, SSI 2014/43, SSI 2014/154

s.12, enabling: SI 2014/44, SI 2014/78, SI 2014/424, SI 2014/525, SI 2014/570, SI 2014/1607, SI 2014/2651, SSI 2014/23, SSI 2014/69

s.24, enabling: SI 2014/78, SSI 2014/23

Sch.1, see *Heron v Sefton MBC* [2014] Eq. L.R. 130 (EAT), Mitting J

Sch.1, amended: 2014 c.20 Sch.4 para.9, SI 2014/555 Art.2, SI 2014/892 Sch.1 para.27, SI 2014/3184 Sch.1 para.10

Sch.1, applied: SI 2014/1964 Reg.3

Sch.1, referred to: SI 2014/1964 Reg.3

Sch.3, enabling: SI 2014/78, SI 2014/424, SI 2014/525, SI 2014/570, SI 2014/1607, SI 2014/2651, SSI 2014/23, SSI 2014/43, SSI 2014/44, SSI 2014/69, SSI 2014/154

18. Maintenance Orders (Reciprocal Enforcement) Act 1972

applied: SI 2014/840 Sch.1

s.8, amended: SI 2014/605 Art.7

s.8, disapplied: SI 2014/605 Art.11

s.17, amended: SI 2014/605 Art.8

s.31, applied: 2014 asp 18 s.38

s.33, amended: SI 2014/605 Art.9

s.33, disapplied: SI 2014/605 Art.11

s.35, repealed (in part): SI 2014/605 Art.10

41. Finance Act 1972

Sch.5, see *Revenue and Customs Commissioners v IFX Investment Co Ltd* [2014] UKUT 398 (TCC), [2014] B.V.C. 535 (UT (Tax)), Norris J

52. Town and Country Planning (Scotland) Act 1972

applied: SI 2014/1686 Sch.2 para.15, Sch.3 para.3

56. Appropriation Act 1972

Sch.4 Part 3, varied: SI 2014/2708 Art.5

Sch.4 Part 5, varied: SI 2014/2708 Art.5

59. Administration of Justice (Scotland) Act 1972

s.1, see *Clark v TripAdvisor LLC* [2014] CSOH 20, 2014 S.L.T. 418 (OH), Temporary Judge P A Arthurson, QC; see *Martin and Co (UK) Ltd, Petitioners* 2014 S.L.T. 71 (IH (Ex Div)), Lady Smith; see *Ted Jacob Engineering Group Inc v RMJM* [2014] CSIH 18, 2014 S.C. 579 (IH (Ex Div)), Lady Paton

s.1, amended: 2014 asp 18 Sch.5 para.12, Sch.5 para.29

s.5, see *Clark v TripAdvisor LLC* [2014] CSOH 20, 2014 S.L.T. 418 (OH), Temporary Judge P A Arthurson, QC

62. Agriculture (Miscellaneous Provisions) Act 1972

s.20, enabling: SSI 2014/140

65. National Debt Act 1972

s.3, enabling: SI 2014/3214

s.11, enabling: SI 2014/1182

68. European Communities Act 1972

applied: SI 2014/656, SI 2014/1184, SI
2014/3348

referred to: SI 2014/1557

s.1, referred to: SI 2014/266 Art.3, SI
2014/1883 Art.3, SI 2014/1884 Art.3, SI
2014/1885 Art.2, SI 2014/1886 Art.3, SI
2014/1889 Art.3

s.1, enabling: SI 2014/266, SI 2014/1883, SI
2014/1884, SI 2014/1885, SI 2014/1886, SI
2014/1888, SI 2014/1889

s.2, see *United States v Nolan* [2014] EWCA
Civ 71, [2014] I.C.R. 685 (CA (Civ Div)),
Moore-Bick LJ

s.2, applied: 2014 asp 3 Sch.2 para.22, 2014
c.22 s.21, s.27, s.49, SI 2014/870, SI
2014/951, SI 2014/1240, SI 2014/1258, SI
2014/1616, SI 2014/1638, SI 2014/1638
Sch.12 para.1, SI 2014/1826, SI 2014/1827,
SI 2014/1937, SI 2014/1975, SI 2014/2361,
SI 2014/2400, SI 2014/2445, SI 2014/3079,
SI 2014/3329, SI 2014/3330

s.2, referred to: SI 2014/331, SI 2014/521, SI
2014/951, SI 2014/1240, SI 2014/2368, SI
2014/2385, SI 2014/2420, SI 2014/3079, SSI
2014/4

s.2, enabling: SI 2014/4, SI 2014/8, SI
2014/16, SI 2014/82, SI 2014/92, SI
2014/105, SI 2014/112, SI 2014/123, SI
2014/162, SI 2014/195, SI 2014/208, SI
2014/308, SI 2014/371, SI 2014/383, SI
2014/434, SI 2014/480, SI 2014/487, SI
2014/490, SI 2014/506, SI 2014/507, SI
2014/517, SI 2014/519, SI 2014/529, SI
2014/537, SI 2014/557, SI 2014/577, SI
2014/587, SI 2014/589, SI 2014/599, SI
2014/604, SI 2014/606, SI 2014/656, SI
2014/693, SI 2014/861, SI 2014/870, SI
2014/880, SI 2014/894, SI 2014/905, SI
2014/952, SI 2014/1067, SI 2014/1184, SI
2014/1261, SI 2014/1290, SI 2014/1292, SI
2014/1309, SI 2014/1313, SI 2014/1333, SI
2014/1362, SI 2014/1372, SI 2014/1384, SI
2014/1385, SI 2014/1403, SI 2014/1451, SI
2014/1459, SI 2014/1463, SI 2014/1512, SI
2014/1557, SI 2014/1613, SI 2014/1614, SI
2014/1615, SI 2014/1616, SI 2014/1643, SI
2014/1648, SI 2014/1663, SI 2014/1771, SI
2014/1803, SI 2014/1811, SI 2014/1816, SI
2014/1826, SI 2014/1827, SI 2014/1833, SI

2014/1835, SI 2014/1855, SI 2014/1858, SI
2014/1878, SI 2014/1890, SI 2014/1894, SI
2014/1896, SI 2014/1902, SI 2014/1937, SI
2014/1942, SI 2014/1975, SI 2014/1976, SI
2014/2007, SI 2014/2054, SI 2014/2124, SI
2014/2264, SI 2014/2303, SI 2014/2329, SI
2014/2356, SI 2014/2357, SI 2014/2361, SI
2014/2363, SI 2014/2367, SI 2014/2382, SI
2014/2400, SI 2014/2411, SI 2014/2437, SI
2014/2445, SI 2014/2705, SI 2014/2714, SI
2014/2715, SI 2014/2748, SI 2014/2761, SI
2014/2793, SI 2014/2833, SI 2014/2861, SI
2014/2879, SI 2014/2882, SI 2014/2883, SI
2014/2884, SI 2014/2885, SI 2014/2894, SI
2014/2916, SI 2014/2920, SI 2014/2932, SI
2014/2947, SI 2014/2975, SI 2014/3075, SI
2014/3076, SI 2014/3080, SI 2014/3081, SI
2014/3104, SI 2014/3120, SI 2014/3125, SI
2014/3135, SI 2014/3141, SI 2014/3158, SI
2014/3190, SI 2014/3191, SI 2014/3209, SI
2014/3219, SI 2014/3222, SI 2014/3223, SI
2014/3225, SI 2014/3230, SI 2014/3258, SI
2014/3259, SI 2014/3260, SI 2014/3263, SI
2014/3293, SI 2014/3298, SI 2014/3300, SI
2014/3302, SI 2014/3306, SI 2014/3322, SI
2014/3329, SI 2014/3330, SI 2014/3332, SI
2014/3333, SI 2014/3344, SI 2014/3345, SI
2014/3348, SI 2014/3349, SI 2014/3486, SSI
2014/6, SSI 2014/7, SSI 2014/33, SSI
2014/63, SSI 2014/72, SSI 2014/95, SSI
2014/111, SSI 2014/118, SSI 2014/155, SSI
2014/159, SSI 2014/213, SSI 2014/258, SSI
2014/312, SSI 2014/325, SSI 2014/333, SSI
2014/336, SSI 2014/337, SSI 2014/338, SSI
2014/364, SSI 2014/373, SSI 2014/379

s.3, see *Dawson v Thomson Airways Ltd*
[2014] EWCA Civ 845, [2014] 4 All E.R.
832 (CA (Civ Div)), Moore-Bick LJ

Sch.2 para.1A, applied: SI 2014/195, SI
2014/1894, SI 2014/2411, SI 2014/2437, SI
2014/3125

Sch.2 para.1A, referred to: SI 2014/331

Sch.2 para.1A, enabling: SI 2014/383, SI
2014/507, SI 2014/517, SI 2014/519, SI
2014/521, SI 2014/587, SI 2014/693, SI
2014/951, SI 2014/952, SI 2014/1240, SI
2014/1258, SI 2014/1557, SI 2014/1826, SI
2014/1827, SI 2014/1833, SI 2014/1835, SI
2014/1855, SI 2014/1858, SI 2014/1896, SI
2014/1942, SI 2014/2054, SI 2014/2303, SI
2014/2367, SI 2014/2368, SI 2014/2385, SI

2014/2420, SI 2014/2714, SI 2014/2748, SI
2014/2894, SI 2014/3079, SI 2014/3104, SI
2014/3158, SI 2014/3222, SI 2014/3223, SI
2014/3263, SI 2014/3345, SI 2014/3349, SSI
2014/4, SSI 2014/111, SSI 2014/118, SSI
2014/213, SSI 2014/312, SSI 2014/325, SSI
2014/337, SSI 2014/338, SSI 2014/364, SSI
2014/379
Sch.2 para.2, applied: SI 2014/1372, SI
2014/1384, SI 2014/1385, SI 2014/1803, SI
2014/2356, SI 2014/2361, SI 2014/2861, SI
2014/3141, SI 2014/3209, SI 2014/3219, SI
2014/3329, SI 2014/3330, SI 2014/3486, SSI
2014/155, SSI 2014/364
Sch.2 para.2A, applied: SSI 2014/155, SSI
2014/364

70. Local Government Act 1972
applied: 2014 c.2 Sch.7 para.8, Sch.7 para.10
Part VA, applied: 2014 c.2 s.40, Sch.7
para.5, Sch.7 para.9
Part VA, varied: 2014 c.2 Sch.7 para.9
s.26, amended: SI 2014/3033 Art.2
s.26, applied: SI 2014/3033 Art.3
s.26, varied: SI 2014/3033 Art.3
s.35, amended: SI 2014/3033 Art.2
s.35, applied: SI 2014/3033 Art.3
s.35, varied: SI 2014/3033 Art.3
s.86, amended: 2014 c.2 Sch.12 para.5
s.87, amended: 2014 c.2 Sch.12 para.6
s.100A, amended: SI 2014/2095 Reg.4
s.100A, applied: 2014 c.2 Sch.7 para.10, SI
2014/3224 Reg.9
s.100A, referred to: SI 2014/3224 Reg.9
s.100B, applied: 2014 c.2 Sch.7 para.9, SI
2014/3224 Reg.9
s.100B, referred to: SI 2014/3224 Reg.9
s.100C, applied: 2014 c.2 Sch.7 para.10
s.100C, varied: 2014 c.2 Sch.7 para.9
s.100E, amended: SI 2014/2095 Reg.4
s.100E, referred to: SI 2014/3224 Reg.9
s.100I, referred to: SI 2014/3224 Reg.9
s.100J, amended: SI 2014/2095 Reg.4
s.101, applied: 2014 c.2 s.15, Sch.3 para.1,
Sch.7 para.7, SI 2014/1710 Reg.5, SI
2014/3224 Reg.2
s.101, disapplied: 2014 c.2 Sch.3 para.1,
Sch.7 para.7
s.101, varied: SI 2014/863 Art.8, SI
2014/865 Art.10, Art.11, SI 2014/1012
Art.10
s.104, applied: SI 2014/3224 Reg.8

s.122, see *R. (on the application of Maries) v
Merton LBC* [2014] EWHC 2689 (Admin),
[2014] B.L.G.R. 756 (QBD (Admin)), King
J
s.123, see *R. (on the application of Trafford)
v Blackpool BC* [2014] EWHC 85 (Admin),
[2014] 2 All E.R. 947 (QBD (Admin)),
Judge Stephen Davies
s.137, amended: 2014 c.2 Sch.12 para.7
s.142, applied: SI 2014/864 Art.11, SI
2014/1012 Art.13
s.142, varied: SI 2014/863 Art.11, SI
2014/865 Art.14
s.144, applied: SI 2014/863 Sch.2 para.2, SI
2014/865 Sch.2 para.2, SI 2014/1012 Sch.2
para.2
s.150, repealed (in part): SI 2014/580 Art.2
s.151, applied: SI 2014/3352 Sch.1 para.20
s.222, see *Oldham MBC v Worldwide
Marketing Solutions Ltd* [2014] EWHC 1910
(QB), [2014] P.T.S.R. 1072 (QBD), Phillips
J
s.222, applied: SI 2014/864 Art.11, SI
2014/1012 Art.13
s.222, varied: SI 2014/863 Art.11, SI
2014/865 Art.14
s.223, applied: SI 2014/1610 r.2_4
s.228, applied: 2014 c.2 s.40
s.233, applied: SI 2014/3204 Sch.4 para.1,
SI 2014/3318 Reg.7
s.233, referred to: SI 2014/3204 Sch.4
para.1, Sch.4 para.12
s.237A, applied: SI 2014/865 Art.11
s.243, amended: 2014 c.2 s.42
s.246, applied: 2014 c.2 Sch.12 para.8
s.246, repealed (in part): SI 2014/580 Art.3
s.254, enabling: SI 2014/683
Sch.12, applied: 2014 c.2 Sch.7 para.5
Sch.12 Part I para.4, amended: 2014 c.2 s.40
Sch.12 Part I para.4, applied: 2014 c.2 s.40
Sch.12 Part III para.18, amended: 2014 c.2
s.42
Sch.12 Part III para.18, repealed (in part):
2014 c.2 s.42
Sch.12A Part I, referred to: SI 2014/3224
Reg.9
Sch.12A Part II para.8, amended: 2014 c.14
Sch.4 para.24
Sch.12A Part III para.11, applied: SI
2014/3224 Reg.9

Sch.12A Part V para.19, amended: 2014 c.14
Sch.4 para.24

71. Criminal Justice Act 1972
s.36, applied: SI 2014/1610 r.70_1, r.74_1,
r.74_2, r.76_1, r.76_4
s.36, disapplied: SI 2014/1610 r.74_2

1973

15. Administration of Justice Act 1973
s.9, applied: 2014 asp 18 s.124
s.9, repealed (in part): 2014 asp 18 Sch.5
para.35

18. Matrimonial Causes Act 1973
see *Asaad v Kurter* [2013] EWHC 3852
(Fam), [2014] 2 F.L.R. 833 (Fam Div),
Moylan J; see *CR v MZ (Financial
Remedies: Beneficial Ownership)* [2013]
EWHC 295 (Fam), [2014] 1 F.L.R. 22 (Fam
Div), Jonathan Cohen, Q.C.; see *Rubin v
Rubin* [2014] EWHC 611 (Fam), [2014] 1
W.L.R. 3289 (Fam Div), Mostyn J
applied: SI 2014/840 Sch.1
s.1, referred to: SI 2014/603 Sch.1
s.6, referred to: SI 2014/603 Sch.1
s.9, amended: 2014 c.6 s.17
s.10A, referred to: SI 2014/603 Sch.1
s.11, see *A Local Authority v X* [2013]
EWHC 3274 (Fam), [2014] 2 F.L.R. 123
(Fam Div (Birmingham)), Holman J
s.11, amended: SI 2014/3168 Sch.1 para.6
s.12, see *A Local Authority v X* [2013]
EWHC 3274 (Fam), [2014] 2 F.L.R. 123
(Fam Div (Birmingham)), Holman J
s.12, amended: SI 2014/3168 Sch.1 para.6
s.12A, added: SI 2014/3168 Sch.1 para.6
s.17, amended: 2014 c.6 s.17
s.17, referred to: SI 2014/603 Sch.1
s.19, applied: SI 2014/3296 r.15
s.22ZA, see *Rubin v Rubin* [2014] EWHC
611 (Fam), [2014] 1 W.L.R. 3289 (Fam
Div), Mostyn J
s.22ZB, see *Rubin v Rubin* [2014] EWHC
611 (Fam), [2014] 1 W.L.R. 3289 (Fam
Div), Mostyn J
s.23, see *P v P (Divorce: Financial Remedy
Order)* [2014] EWHC 1101 (Fam), [2014] 1
W.L.R. 4607 (Fam Div), Eleanor King J; see
Young v Young [2013] EWHC 3637 (Fam),
[2014] 2 Costs L.O. 136 (Fam Div), Moor J

s.23, applied: SI 2014/3037 Sch.2 para.1
s.24, see *Tchenguiz-Imerman v Imerman*
[2013] EWHC 3627 (Fam), [2014] 2 F.L.R.
939 (Fam Div), Moylan J
s.25, see *G v B (Financial Remedies: Asset
Beneficiaries)* [2013] EWHC 3414 (Fam),
[2014] 2 F.L.R. 292 (Fam Div), Blair J; see
Luckwell v Limata [2014] EWHC 502
(Fam), [2014] 2 F.L.R. 168 (Fam Div),
Holman J; see *M v M* [2013] EWHC 2534
(Fam), [2014] 1 F.L.R. 439 (Fam Div),
Eleanor King J; see *Tattersall v Tattersall*
[2013] EWCA Civ 774, [2014] 1 F.L.R. 997
(CA (Civ Div)), Hallett LJ; see *Tchenguiz-
Imerman v Imerman* [2013] EWHC 3627
(Fam), [2014] 2 F.L.R. 939 (Fam Div),
Moylan J
s.25B, applied: SI 2014/3037 Sch.2 para.1
s.25E, applied: SI 2014/3037 Sch.2 para.1
s.31, amended: 2014 c.6 s.18, 2014 c.16
Sch.3 para.1
s.33A, see *P v P (Divorce: Financial
Remedy Order)* [2014] EWHC 1101 (Fam),
[2014] 1 W.L.R. 4607 (Fam Div), Eleanor
King J
s.37, see *B v IB (Order to set aside
disposition under Insolvency Act)* [2013]
EWHC 3755 (Fam), [2014] 2 F.L.R. 273
(Fam Div), Parker J; see *R v R* [2013]
EWHC 4244 (Fam), [2014] 2 F.L.R. 699
(Fam Div), Sir James Munby PFD; see *UL v
BK (Freezing Orders: Safeguards: Standard
Examples)* [2013] EWHC 1735 (Fam),
[2014] Fam. 35 (Fam Div), Mostyn J
s.41, repealed: 2014 c.6 s.17

26. Land Compensation Act 1973
applied: SI 2014/909 Sch.8 para.2
Pt I., see *Dickinson v Network Rail
Infrastructure Ltd* [2014] UKUT 372 (LC)
(UT (Lands)), Sir Keith Lindblom P
s.20, applied: SI 2014/909 Art.40
s.28, applied: SI 2014/909 Art.40
s.30, amended: SI 2014/1966 Reg.2
s.30, applied: SI 2014/1966 Reg.2
s.30, enabling: SI 2014/1966
s.44, see *Stynes v Western Power (East
Midlands) Plc* [2014] R.V.R. 15 (UT
(Lands)), Sir Keith Lindblom P
s.44, varied: SI 2014/310 Sch.3 para.2, SI
2014/909 Sch.8 para.2, SI 2014/1052 Sch.10
para.2, SI 2014/1599 Sch.7 para.2, SI

2014/1873 Sch.8 para.2, SI 2014/2027 Sch.5
para.2, SI 2014/2269 Sch.6 para.2, SI
2014/2441 Sch.7 para.2, SI 2014/2637 Sch.8
para.2, SI 2014/2950 Sch.7 para.2, SI
2014/3102 Sch.3 para.2, SI 2014/3328 Sch.7
para.2, SI 2014/3331 Sch.6 para.2
s.58, varied: SI 2014/310 Sch.3 para.2, SI
2014/909 Sch.8 para.2, SI 2014/1052 Sch.10
para.2, SI 2014/1599 Sch.7 para.2, SI
2014/1873 Sch.8 para.2, SI 2014/2027 Sch.5
para.2, SI 2014/2269 Sch.6 para.2, SI
2014/2441 Sch.7 para.2, SI 2014/2637 Sch.8
para.2, SI 2014/2950 Sch.7 para.2, SI
2014/3102 Sch.3 para.2, SI 2014/3331 Sch.6
para.2

33. Protection of Wrecks Act 1973
s.1, enabling: SI 2014/753

35. Employment Agencies Act 1973
s.5, enabling: SI 2014/3351
s.9, applied: SI 2014/1615 Reg.12
s.12, applied: SI 2014/3351
s.12, enabling: SI 2014/3351
s.13, amended: 2014 c.6 Sch.4 para.64
s.13, referred to: SI 2014/1615 Reg.2

40. Appropriation Act 1973
Sch.4 Part 3, varied: SI 2014/2708 Art.5
Sch.4 Part 5, varied: SI 2014/2708 Art.5

41. Fair Trading Act 1973
s.137, amended: SI 2014/892 Sch.1 para.28

45. Domicile and Matrimonial Proceedings Act 1973
see *AB v CB (Divorce and Maintenance: Discretion to Stay)* [2013] EWCA Civ 1255, [2014] Fam. 102 (CA (Civ Div)), Rimer LJ
s.5, see *AB v CB (Divorce and Maintenance: Discretion to Stay)* [2013] EWCA Civ 1255, [2014] Fam. 102 (CA (Civ Div)), Rimer LJ; see *Jefferson v O'Connor* [2014] EWCA Civ 38, [2014] 2 F.L.R. 759 (CA (Civ Div)), Rimer LJ
s.8, amended: 2014 asp 5 s.23
s.8, applied: 2014 asp 18 s.43
s.8A, added: 2014 asp 5 Sch.1 para.1
s.10, amended: 2014 asp 5 Sch.1 para.1
Sch.A1 para.5, applied: SI 2014/543, SI 2014/543 Reg.3
Sch.A1 para.5, enabling: SI 2014/543
Sch.1B, added: 2014 asp 5 Sch.1 para.1
Sch.1B, applied: 2014 asp 18 s.43
Sch.1 para.8, amended: SI 2014/3168 Sch.1 para.7

Sch.1 para.9, see *AB v CB (Divorce and Maintenance: Discretion to Stay)* [2013] EWCA Civ 1255, [2014] Fam. 102 (CA (Civ Div)), Rimer LJ; see *Jefferson v O'Connor* [2014] EWCA Civ 38, [2014] 2 F.L.R. 759 (CA (Civ Div)), Rimer LJ
Sch.1 para.11, amended: 2014 c.6 Sch.2 para.45
Sch.1B para.2, referred to: SSI 2014/212 Sch.1
Sch.1B para.2, enabling: SSI 2014/362

50. Employment and Training Act 1973
s.2, applied: SI 2014/1892 Art.2

51. Finance Act 1973
applied: SI 2014/2117
s.50, amended: 2014 c.26 s.116
s.56, applied: SI 2014/599, SI 2014/951, SI 2014/1240, SI 2014/1258, SI 2014/1816, SI 2014/3263
s.56, enabling: SI 2014/568, SI 2014/599, SI 2014/601, SI 2014/1684, SI 2014/1792, SI 2014/1816, SI 2014/2117, SI 2014/2339, SI 2014/2557, SI 2014/3075, SI 2014/3243, SSI 2014/338, SSI 2014/364

52. Prescription and Limitation (Scotland) Act 1973
s.6, see *David T Morrison & Co Ltd (t/a Gael Home Interiors) v ICL Plastics Ltd* [2014] UKSC 48, 2014 S.C. (U.K.S.C.) 222 (SC), Lord Neuberger PSC; see *Dryburgh v Scotts Media Tax Ltd* [2014] CSIH 45, 2014 S.C. 651 (IH (Ex Div)), Lady Smith; see *Highlands and Islands Airports Ltd v Shetland Islands Council* [2014] CSOH 17, 2014 S.L.T. 424 (OH), Lady Scott
s.9, see *Highlands and Islands Airports Ltd v Shetland Islands Council* [2014] CSOH 17, 2014 S.L.T. 424 (OH), Lady Scott
s.11, see *David T Morrison & Co Ltd (t/a Gael Home Interiors) v ICL Plastics Ltd* [2014] UKSC 48, 2014 S.C. (U.K.S.C.) 222 (SC), Lord Neuberger PSC
s.17, see *A v N* 2014 S.C.L.R. 225 (OH), Lord Kinclaven; see *Jamieson v O'Neill* [2014] CSOH 117, 2014 Rep. L.R. 98 (OH), Lord Tyre
s.18, see *David T Morrison & Co Ltd (t/a Gael Home Interiors) v ICL Plastics Ltd* [2014] UKSC 48, 2014 S.C. (U.K.S.C.) 222 (SC), Lord Neuberger PSC

s.19A, see *A v N* 2014 S.C.L.R. 225 (OH),
Lord Kinclaven; see *Jamieson v O'Neill*
[2014] CSOH 117, 2014 Rep. L.R. 98 (OH),
Lord Tyre; see *Peat's Executors v Assembly
Theatre Ltd* [2014] CSOH 144, 2014 S.L.T.
1017 (OH), Lord Doherty
Sch.1 para.1, amended: SI 2014/870 Reg.7
Sch.1 para.2, amended: SSI 2014/190 Art.2

56. Land Compensation (Scotland) Act 1973
s.49, see *Emslie v Scottish Ministers* 2014
S.L.T. (Lands Tr) 39 (Lands Tr (Scot)), Lord
McGhie

60. Breeding of Dogs Act 1973
applied: SI 2014/3266 Reg.25
s.1, amended: SI 2014/3266 Reg.2
s.3, applied: SI 2014/3266 Reg.10
s.5, amended: SI 2014/3266 Sch.2 para.1

62. Powers of Criminal Courts Act 1973
s.31, see *R. (on the application of Gibson) v
Secretary of State for Justice* [2013] EWHC
2481 (Admin), [2014] 1 W.L.R. 2658 (QBD
(Admin)), Judge Gosnell
s.32, see *R. (on the application of Gibson) v
Secretary of State for Justice* [2013] EWHC
2481 (Admin), [2014] 1 W.L.R. 2658 (QBD
(Admin)), Judge Gosnell

63. Government Trading Funds Act 1973
applied: SI 2014/432
s.1, enabling: SI 2014/432, SI 2014/561
s.2, applied: SI 2014/432 Art.3
s.2, enabling: SI 2014/432
s.6, enabling: SI 2014/432, SI 2014/561

65. Local Government (Scotland) Act 1973
applied: SSI 2014/200 Reg.6
Part VI, applied: 2014 asp 15 s.1, s.2
s.31, repealed (in part): 2014 asp 11 Sch.4
s.56, see *Tayside Contracts v D Geddes
(Contractors) Ltd* [2014] CSOH 105, 2014
S.L.T. 764 (OH), Lord Malcolm
s.56, amended: 2014 asp 9 s.57
s.57, see *Tayside Contracts v D Geddes
(Contractors) Ltd* [2014] CSOH 105, 2014
S.L.T. 764 (OH), Lord Malcolm
s.62A, applied: 2014 asp 12 Sch.1 para.15
s.62B, applied: 2014 asp 12 Sch.1 para.15
s.95, applied: SSI 2014/281 Art.3, Art.4, SSI
2014/285 Art.3, Art.5
s.96, referred to: SSI 2014/3 Art.11
s.101, applied: SSI 2014/200 Reg.9
s.101, referred to: SSI 2014/200 Reg.9,
Reg.11

s.102, referred to: SSI 2014/200 Reg.11
s.103F, referred to: SSI 2014/200 Reg.11
s.105, applied: SSI 2014/200
s.105, enabling: SSI 2014/200
s.106, amended: 2014 asp 9 s.13
s.195, applied: SSI 2014/200 Reg.9
s.235, see *Tayside Contracts v D Geddes
(Contractors) Ltd* [2014] CSOH 105, 2014
S.L.T. 764 (OH), Lord Malcolm
Sch.27 Part II para.146, repealed: 2014 asp 3
Sch.3 para.18

1974

2. Appropriation Act 1974
Sch.4 Part 14, varied: SI 2014/2708 Art.5

3. Slaughterhouses Act 1974
applied: SI 2014/951 Reg.8, Reg.10, Reg.16,
SI 2014/1240 Reg.8, Reg.10, Reg.16
s.16, amended: SI 2014/1240 Sch.6 para.2,
SI 2014/2124 Reg.2

6. Biological Weapons Act 1974
s.1B, amended: SI 2014/834 Sch.2 para.1

7. Local Government Act 1974
Part III, applied: SI 2014/1492 Reg.6, SI
2014/1530 Reg.17, SI 2014/2359 Art.6
s.25, amended: 2014 c.21 Sch.10 para.2
s.29, applied: SI 2014/1492 Reg.6
s.32, applied: SI 2014/1492 Reg.6
Sch.5 para.5, amended: 2014 c.6 Sch.3
para.63

9. Pensions (Increase) Act 1974
applied: SI 2014/525 Reg.25, SSI 2014/233
Reg.25

21. Ministers of the Crown Act 1974
s.1, varied: SI 2014/2708 Art.5

23. Juries Act 1974
s.2, applied: SI 2014/1610 r.38_6
s.5, applied: SI 2014/1610 r.38_6
s.9, applied: SI 2014/1610 r.39_1
s.10, applied: SI 2014/1610 r.39_2
s.11, applied: SI 2014/1610 r.38_6
s.12, applied: SI 2014/1610 r.38_8
s.14, applied: SI 2014/1610 r.3_25
s.16, applied: SI 2014/1610 r.38_7
s.17, applied: SI 2014/1610 r.38_14
s.18, applied: SI 2014/1610 r.38_7
s.20, applied: SI 2014/1610 r.62_5, r.39_1

31. Appropriation (No.2) Act 1974
Sch.4 Part 3, varied: SI 2014/2708 Art.5

Sch.4 Part 16, varied: SI 2014/2708 Art.5

37. Health and Safety at Work etc Act 1974
applied: 2014 asp 12 s.15, SI 2014/469 Sch.4
para.14, Sch.4 para.15, Sch.4 para.21, SI
2014/1638 Reg.29, SI 2014/1663 Reg.30, SI
2014/3248 Reg.71, SI 2014/3352 Sch.1
para.20, Sch.5 para.21
see *Manolete Partners Plc v Hastings BC*
[2014] EWCA Civ 562, [2014] 1 W.L.R.
4030 (CA (Civ Div)), Jackson LJ
Part I, applied: 2014 c.20 Sch.1 para.4
Part I, referred to: 2014 c.20 Sch.1 para.4
s.1, applied: SI 2014/1638 Reg.3, SI
2014/1639 Reg.1, SI 2014/3248 Reg.1
s.2, applied: SI 2014/1637 Reg.18
s.2, varied: SI 2014/1663 Reg.4
s.2, see *Health and Safety Executive v
Polyflor Ltd* [2014] EWCA Crim 1522,
[2014] I.C.R. 1142 (CA (Crim Div)), Fulford
LJ; see *R. v Pyranha Mouldings Ltd* [2014]
EWCA Crim 533, [2014] 2 Cr. App. R. (S.)
43 (CA (Crim Div)), Elias LJ
s.3, varied: SI 2014/1663 Reg.4
s.3, see *R. v Sellafield Ltd* [2014] EWCA
Crim 49, [2014] Env. L.R. 19 (CA (Crim
Div)), Lord Thomas LCJ
s.7, applied: SI 2014/1637 Reg.18
s.7, varied: SI 2014/1663 Reg.4
s.11, applied: SI 2014/162, SI 2014/486, SI
2014/1637, SI 2014/1638, SI 2014/1639, SI
2014/1663, SI 2014/3248
s.13, applied: SI 2014/469 Art.5
s.14, applied: SI 2014/469 Sch.1 para.7,
Sch.4 para.9, Sch.4 para.10
s.15, applied: SI 2014/1663 Reg.30
s.15, enabling: SI 2014/162, SI 2014/486, SI
2014/1637, SI 2014/1638, SI 2014/1639, SI
2014/1663, SI 2014/3248
s.16, varied: SI 2014/1663 Reg.30
s.18, enabling: SI 2014/1637, SI 2014/1638,
SI 2014/3248
s.19, applied: SI 2014/469 Sch.4 para.13, SI
2014/1638 Reg.3, Sch.12 para.2
s.20, applied: SI 2014/469 Sch.4 para.21, SI
2014/1638 Reg.3, SI 2014/3248 Reg.71
s.20, varied: SI 2014/1638 Sch.12 para.3
s.21, applied: SI 2014/3109 Sch.1
s.22, applied: SI 2014/469 Sch.4 para.15
s.22, varied: SI 2014/1638 Sch.12 para.3
s.23, varied: SI 2014/1638 Sch.12 para.3

s.24, see *MWH UK Ltd v Wise (Inspector of
Health and Safety)* [2014] EWHC 427
(Admin), [2014] A.C.D. 96 (QBD (Admin)),
Popplewell J
s.25, applied: SI 2014/3248 Reg.71
s.27, applied: SI 2014/469 Sch.4 para.20
s.33, applied: SI 2014/1638 Sch.12 para.2
s.33, disapplied: SI 2014/1663 Reg.30
s.33, varied: SI 2014/1638 Sch.12 para.3, SI
2014/1663 Reg.30
s.33, see *Health and Safety Executive v
Polyflor Ltd* [2014] EWCA Crim 1522,
[2014] I.C.R. 1142 (CA (Crim Div)), Fulford
LJ; see *Pall Mall Investments (London) Ltd
v Gloucester City Council* [2014] EWHC
2247 (Admin), [2014] P.T.S.R. 1184 (DC),
Pitchford LJ
s.34, varied: SI 2014/1638 Sch.12 para.3
s.36, applied: SI 2014/1638 Sch.12 para.2
s.37, applied: SI 2014/1638 Sch.12 para.2
s.38, applied: SI 2014/1638 Sch.12 para.2
s.41, applied: SI 2014/1638 Sch.12 para.2
s.43, enabling: SI 2014/1637, SI 2014/1638,
SI 2014/1639
s.44, applied: SI 2014/1637 Reg.11, Reg.15
s.46, applied: SI 2014/1638 Reg.11
s.47, applied: SI 2014/469 Sch.4 para.24
s.50, applied: SI 2014/162, SI 2014/486, SI
2014/1637, SI 2014/1638, SI 2014/1639, SI
2014/1663, SI 2014/3248
s.52, varied: SI 2014/1663 Reg.4
s.52, enabling: SI 2014/1663
s.53, referred to: SI 2014/3352 Sch.1 para.20
s.80, applied: SI 2014/1637, SI 2014/1638,
SI 2014/1638 Reg.3, SI 2014/1639, SI
2014/1639 Reg.1, SI 2014/3248, SI
2014/3248 Reg.1
s.80, referred to: SI 2014/1637, SI
2014/1639
s.80, enabling: SI 2014/1637, SI 2014/1638,
SI 2014/1639, SI 2014/3248
s.82, enabling: SI 2014/486, SI 2014/1637,
SI 2014/1638, SI 2014/1639, SI 2014/1663,
SI 2014/3248
s.82, see *MWH UK Ltd v Wise (Inspector of
Health and Safety)* [2014] EWHC 427
(Admin), [2014] A.C.D. 96 (QBD (Admin)),
Popplewell J
Sch.1, amended: SI 2014/3248 Sch.3 Part 1
Sch.3A, applied: SI 2014/1638 Sch.12 para.2

Sch.3 para.1, enabling: SI 2014/162, SI 2014/1637, SI 2014/1638, SI 2014/1639, SI 2014/1663, SI 2014/3248

Sch.3 para.2, enabling: SI 2014/1638, SI 2014/1639

Sch.3 para.3, enabling: SI 2014/1637, SI 2014/1638, SI 2014/1639, SI 2014/1663, SI 2014/3248

Sch.3 para.4, enabling: SI 2014/1637, SI 2014/1638, SI 2014/1639, SI 2014/1663

Sch.3 para.5, enabling: SI 2014/1638, SI 2014/1663

Sch.3 para.6, enabling: SI 2014/1638, SI 2014/1663, SI 2014/3248

Sch.3 para.7, enabling: SI 2014/1638

Sch.3 para.8, enabling: SI 2014/1663, SI 2014/3248

Sch.3 para.9, enabling: SI 2014/1637, SI 2014/1639, SI 2014/1663, SI 2014/3248

Sch.3 para.10, enabling: SI 2014/3248

Sch.3 para.11, enabling: SI 2014/1663, SI 2014/3248

Sch.3 para.12, enabling: SI 2014/1637, SI 2014/1638, SI 2014/1639

Sch.3 para.13, enabling: SI 2014/1663, SI 2014/3248

Sch.3 para.14, enabling: SI 2014/1663, SI 2014/3248

Sch.3 para.15, enabling: SI 2014/1637, SI 2014/1638, SI 2014/1663

Sch.3 para.16, enabling: SI 2014/1638, SI 2014/1663, SI 2014/3248

Sch.3 para.17, enabling: SI 2014/1663

Sch.3 para.18, enabling: SI 2014/1638, SI 2014/3248

Sch.3 para.20, enabling: SI 2014/1638, SI 2014/1663, SI 2014/3248

Sch.3 para.21, enabling: SI 2014/3248

38. Land Tenure Reform (Scotland) Act 1974
s.11, amended: 2014 asp 14 s.93
s.21, amended: 2014 asp 14 s.93

39. Consumer Credit Act 1974
see *Bassano v Toft* [2014] EWHC 377 (QB), [2014] E.C.C. 14 (QBD), Popplewell J; see *Evans v Finance-U-Ltd* [2013] EWCA Civ 869, [2014] R.T.R. 8 (CA (Civ Div)), Mummery, L.J.; see *Jones v Secretary of State for Energy and Climate Change* [2014] EWCA Civ 363, [2014] 3 All E.R. 956 (CA (Civ Div)), Patten LJ; see *Salat v Barutis* [2013] EWCA Civ 1499, [2014] E.C.C. 2

(CA (Civ Div)), Moore-Bick LJ; see *Sutherland Professional Funding Ltd v Bakewells* [2013] EWHC 2685 (QB), [2014] C.T.L.C. 1 (QBD (Merc)), Judge Pelling QC
applied: SI 2014/366 Art.1, Art.20, SI 2014/506 Art.7, SI 2014/1850 Art.12
s.4, applied: SI 2014/506 Art.7
s.8, see *Durkin v DSG Retail Ltd* [2014] UKSC 21, [2014] 1 W.L.R. 1148 (SC), Lady Hale DPSC
s.8, amended: SI 2014/436 Art.3
s.12, see *Durkin v DSG Retail Ltd* [2014] UKSC 21, [2014] 1 W.L.R. 1148 (SC), Lady Hale DPSC; see *Scotland v British Credit Trust Ltd* [2014] EWCA Civ 790, [2014] Bus. L.R. 1079 (CA (Civ Div)), Moore-Bick LJ
s.16B, amended: SI 2014/436 Art.4
s.16C, amended: SI 2014/560 Sch.1 para.12
s.21, amended: SI 2014/436 Art.8
s.21, applied: SI 2014/208 Art.8
s.21, referred to: SI 2014/208 Art.8
s.25A, applied: SI 2014/506 Art.7
s.33E, applied: SI 2014/506 Art.7
s.39, see *R. v Firth (Peter)* [2013] EWCA Crim 1201, [2014] 1 Cr. App. R. (S.) 24 (CA (Crim Div)), Rafferty LJ
s.39C, applied: SI 2014/506 Art.7
s.51, applied: SI 2014/366 Art.13
s.55, disapplied: SI 2014/1850 Art.12
s.55C, disapplied: SI 2014/1850 Art.12
s.56, see *Scotland v British Credit Trust Ltd* [2014] EWCA Civ 790, [2014] Bus. L.R. 1079 (CA (Civ Div)), Moore-Bick LJ
s.60, disapplied: SI 2014/1850 Art.12
s.61, see *Bassano v Toft* [2014] EWHC 377 (QB), [2014] E.C.C. 14 (QBD), Popplewell J
s.61, disapplied: SI 2014/1850 Art.12
s.62, disapplied: SI 2014/1850 Art.12
s.65, see *London Scottish Finance Ltd (In Administration), Re* [2013] EWHC 4047 (Ch), [2014] Bus. L.R. 424 (Ch D (Companies Ct)), Sir Terence Etherton C;
see *Salat v Barutis* [2013] EWCA Civ 1499, [2014] E.C.C. 2 (CA (Civ Div)), Moore-Bick LJ
s.66A, disapplied: SI 2014/1850 Art.12
s.67, disapplied: SI 2014/1850 Art.12
s.75, see *Durkin v DSG Retail Ltd* [2014] UKSC 21, [2014] 1 W.L.R. 1148 (SC), Lady Hale DPSC; see *Scotland v British Credit*

Trust Ltd [2014] EWCA Civ 790, [2014]
Bus. L.R. 1079 (CA (Civ Div)), Moore-Bick
LJ
s.75A, disapplied: SI 2014/1850 Art.12
s.76, see *Evans v Finance-U-Ltd* [2013]
EWCA Civ 869, [2014] R.T.R. 8 (CA (Civ
Div)), Mummery, L.J.
s.76, disapplied: SI 2014/1850 Art.12
s.77, amended: SI 2014/436 Art.8
s.77, disapplied: SI 2014/1850 Art.12
s.77A, see *JP Morgan Chase Bank NA v
Northern Rock (Asset Management) Plc*
[2014] EWHC 291 (Ch), [2014] 1 W.L.R.
2197 (Ch D), Simon Monty Q.C.; see
*Sutherland Professional Funding Ltd v
Bakewells* [2013] EWHC 2685 (QB), [2014]
C.T.L.C. 1 (QBD (Merc)), Judge Pelling QC
s.77A, amended: SI 2014/436 Art.8
s.77A, enabling: SI 2014/2369
s.77B, amended: SI 2014/436 Art.8
s.77B, disapplied: SI 2014/1850 Art.12
s.78A, disapplied: SI 2014/1850 Art.12
s.80, disapplied: SI 2014/1850 Art.12
s.82, disapplied: SI 2014/1850 Art.12
s.82, enabling: SI 2014/2369
s.86, disapplied: SI 2014/1850 Art.12
s.86A, amended: SI 2014/366 Art.3
s.86A, applied: SI 2014/506 Art.7
s.86B, amended: SI 2014/436 Art.8
s.86E, disapplied: SI 2014/1850 Art.12
s.87, see *Evans v Finance-U-Ltd* [2013]
EWCA Civ 869, [2014] R.T.R. 8 (CA (Civ
Div)), Mummery, L.J.
s.87, disapplied: SI 2014/1850 Art.12
s.93, disapplied: SI 2014/1850 Art.12
s.94, disapplied: SI 2014/1850 Art.12
s.95B, amended: SI 2014/436 Art.8
s.98, see *Evans v Finance-U-Ltd* [2013]
EWCA Civ 869, [2014] R.T.R. 8 (CA (Civ
Div)), Mummery, L.J.
s.98, disapplied: SI 2014/1850 Art.12
s.102, disapplied: SI 2014/1850 Art.12
s.105, disapplied: SI 2014/1850 Art.12
s.106, see *London Scottish Finance Ltd (In
Administration), Re* [2013] EWHC 4047
(Ch), [2014] Bus. L.R. 424 (Ch D
(Companies Ct)), Sir Terence Etherton C
s.110, disapplied: SI 2014/1850 Art.12
s.113, see *London Scottish Finance Ltd (In
Administration), Re* [2013] EWHC 4047

(Ch), [2014] Bus. L.R. 424 (Ch D
(Companies Ct)), Sir Terence Etherton C
s.126, substituted: SI 2014/366 Art.3
s.127, see *London Scottish Finance Ltd (In
Administration), Re* [2013] EWHC 4047
(Ch), [2014] Bus. L.R. 424 (Ch D
(Companies Ct)), Sir Terence Etherton C;
see *Salat v Barutis* [2013] EWCA Civ 1499,
[2014] E.C.C. 2 (CA (Civ Div)), Moore-
Bick LJ
s.129, disapplied: SI 2014/1850 Art.12
s.130A, disapplied: SI 2014/1850 Art.12
s.136, disapplied: SI 2014/1850 Art.12
s.140, see *London Scottish Finance Ltd (In
Administration), Re* [2013] EWHC 4047
(Ch), [2014] Bus. L.R. 424 (Ch D
(Companies Ct)), Sir Terence Etherton C
s.140A, see *Binns v Firstplus Financial
Group Plc* [2013] EWHC 2436 (QB), [2014]
Bus. L.R. 110 (QBD), Judge Jeremy
Richardson QC; see *Link Financial Ltd v
Wilson* [2014] EWHC 252 (Ch), [2014]
C.T.L.C. 145 (Ch D), David Railton QC; see
*London Scottish Finance Ltd (In
Administration), Re* [2013] EWHC 4047
(Ch), [2014] Bus. L.R. 424 (Ch D
(Companies Ct)), Sir Terence Etherton C;
see *Plevin v Paragon Personal Finance Ltd*
[2013] EWCA Civ 1658, [2014] Bus. L.R.
553 (CA (Civ Div)), Moses LJ; see *Plevin v
Paragon Personal Finance Ltd* [2014]
UKSC 61, [2014] 1 W.L.R. 4222 (SC), Lady
Hale DPSC; see *Scotland v British Credit
Trust Ltd* [2014] EWCA Civ 790, [2014]
Bus. L.R. 1079 (CA (Civ Div)), Moore-Bick
LJ
s.140B, see *London Scottish Finance Ltd (In
Administration), Re* [2013] EWHC 4047
(Ch), [2014] Bus. L.R. 424 (Ch D
(Companies Ct)), Sir Terence Etherton C;
see *Scotland v British Credit Trust Ltd*
[2014] EWCA Civ 790, [2014] Bus. L.R.
1079 (CA (Civ Div)), Moore-Bick LJ
s.142, see *London Scottish Finance Ltd (In
Administration), Re* [2013] EWHC 4047
(Ch), [2014] Bus. L.R. 424 (Ch D
(Companies Ct)), Sir Terence Etherton C
s.173, disapplied: SI 2014/1850 Art.12
s.182, enabling: SI 2014/2369
s.189, amended: SI 2014/436 Art.5
s.189, enabling: SI 2014/2369

s.189B, added: SI 2014/436 Art.6
Sch.1, applied: SI 2014/366 Art.13
Sch.2A, added: SI 2014/436 Art.7

40. Control of Pollution Act 1974
applied: SI 2014/2935 Art.54
s.3, see *Walker and Son (Hauliers) Ltd v
Environment Agency* [2014] EWCA Crim
100, [2014] 4 All E.R. 825 (CA (Crim Div)),
Lord Thomas LCJ
s.5, applied: SSI 2014/4 Reg.3
s.30B, repealed (in part): 2014 asp 3 Sch.3
para.16
s.30C, repealed (in part): 2014 asp 3 Sch.3
para.16
s.30D, repealed (in part): 2014 asp 3 Sch.3
para.16
s.30E, repealed (in part): 2014 asp 3 Sch.3
para.16
s.30Y, amended: 2014 asp 3 Sch.3 para.16
s.31B, repealed (in part): 2014 asp 3 Sch.3
para.16
s.31C, repealed (in part): 2014 asp 3 Sch.3
para.16
s.41, repealed (in part): 2014 asp 3 Sch.3
para.16
s.42A, repealed (in part): 2014 asp 3 Sch.3
para.16
s.42B, repealed (in part): 2014 asp 3 Sch.3
para.16
s.43, repealed (in part): 2014 asp 3 Sch.3
para.16
s.44, repealed (in part): 2014 asp 3 Sch.3
para.16
s.45, repealed (in part): 2014 asp 3 Sch.3
para.16
s.51, amended: 2014 asp 3 Sch.3 para.16
s.52, repealed (in part): 2014 asp 3 Sch.3
para.16
s.55A, amended: 2014 asp 3 Sch.3 para.16
s.56, amended: 2014 asp 3 Sch.3 para.16
s.56, repealed (in part): 2014 asp 3 Sch.3
para.16
s.57, repealed (in part): 2014 asp 3 Sch.3
para.16
s.60, applied: SI 2014/310 Art.25, Sch.6
para.4, SI 2014/909 Art.37, SI 2014/1052
Art.40, SI 2014/1599 Art.7, SI 2014/1873
Art.14, SI 2014/2027 Art.28, SI 2014/2384
Art.7, Art.54, Sch.17 para.4, Sch.19 para.13,
SI 2014/2434 Art.8, SI 2014/2441 Art.9, SI
2014/2637 Art.36, SI 2014/2846 Art.8, SI

2014/2935 Art.51, SI 2014/2950 Art.8, SI
2014/3102 Art.43, SI 2014/3328 Art.30, SI
2014/3331 Art.31
s.60, disapplied: SI 2014/2384 Sch.19
para.13
s.61, applied: SI 2014/310 Sch.6 para.4, SI
2014/2950 Art.8, SI 2014/3328 Art.30
s.61, disapplied: SI 2014/310 Art.25, SI
2014/909 Art.37, SI 2014/1052 Art.40, SI
2014/1599 Art.7, SI 2014/1873 Art.14, SI
2014/2027 Art.28, SI 2014/2269 Art.32, SI
2014/2384 Art.7, Sch.19 para.13, SI
2014/2441 Art.9, SI 2014/2637 Art.36, SI
2014/2846 Art.8, SI 2014/2935 Art.51, SI
2014/3102 Art.43, SI 2014/3331 Art.31
s.63, repealed (in part): 2014 asp 3 Sch.3
para.16
s.65, applied: SI 2014/310 Art.25, SI
2014/909 Art.37, SI 2014/1052 Art.40, SI
2014/1599 Art.7, SI 2014/1873 Art.14, SI
2014/2027 Art.28, SI 2014/2384 Art.7, SI
2014/2434 Art.8, SI 2014/2441 Art.9, SI
2014/2637 Art.36, SI 2014/2846 Art.8, SI
2014/2935 Art.51, SI 2014/2950 Art.8, SI
2014/3102 Art.43, SI 2014/3328 Art.30, SI
2014/3331 Art.31
s.65, disapplied: SI 2014/310 Art.25, SI
2014/909 Art.37, SI 2014/1052 Art.40, SI
2014/1599 Art.7, SI 2014/1873 Art.14, SI
2014/2027 Art.28, SI 2014/2269 Art.32, SI
2014/2384 Art.7, SI 2014/2434 Art.8, SI
2014/2441 Art.9, SI 2014/2637 Art.36, SI
2014/2846 Art.8, SI 2014/2935 Art.51, SI
2014/3102 Art.43, SI 2014/3331 Art.31
s.69, repealed (in part): 2014 asp 3 Sch.3
para.16
s.71, enabling: SI 2014/2123
s.73, amended: 2014 asp 3 Sch.3 para.16,
Sch.3 para.39
s.74, amended: 2014 asp 3 Sch.3 para.16
s.82, disapplied: SI 2014/2434 Art.8
s.85, amended: 2014 asp 3 Sch.3 para.39
s.87, repealed (in part): 2014 asp 3 Sch.3
para.16
s.88, repealed (in part): 2014 asp 3 Sch.3
para.16
s.90, repealed (in part): 2014 asp 3 Sch.3
para.16
s.101, repealed (in part): 2014 asp 3 Sch.3
para.16
s.104, amended: 2014 asp 3 Sch.3 para.16

s.105, amended: 2014 asp 3 Sch.3 para.16,
Sch.3 para.39
Sch.1, repealed (in part): 2014 asp 3 Sch.3
para.16
Sch.1A, repealed (in part): 2014 asp 3 Sch.3
para.16

46. Friendly Societies Act 1974
applied: SI 2014/2418 Sch.1
s.40, amended: 2014 c.14 Sch.4 para.26
s.47, applied: 2014 c.14 s.21
s.82, amended: 2014 c.14 Sch.4 para.27
s.84A, amended: 2014 c.14 Sch.4 para.28
s.109, amended: 2014 c.14 Sch.4 para.29
Sch.6A para.1, amended: 2014 c.14 Sch.4
para.30
Sch.6A para.2, amended: 2014 c.14 Sch.4
para.30
Sch.6A para.3, amended: 2014 c.14 Sch.4
para.30
Sch.9 para.18, repealed: 2014 c.14 Sch.7
Sch.9 para.22, repealed: 2014 c.14 Sch.7

47. Solicitors Act 1974
see *Assaubayev v Michael Wilson and
Partners Ltd* [2014] EWCA Civ 1491,
[2014] 6 Costs L.R. 1058 (CA (Civ Div)),
Aikens LJ; see *Assaubayev v Michael
Wilson and Partners Ltd* [2014] EWHC 821
(QB), [2014] 3 Costs L.O. 446 (QBD),
Walker J; see *Bentine v Bentine* [2013]
EWHC 3098 (Ch), [2014] 1 All E.R. 983
(Ch D), Proudman J
Pt III., see *Assaubayev v Michael Wilson and
Partners Ltd* [2014] EWHC 821 (QB),
[2014] 3 Costs L.O. 446 (QBD), Walker J
s.9, see *Assaubayev v Michael Wilson and
Partners Ltd* [2014] EWHC 821 (QB),
[2014] 3 Costs L.O. 446 (QBD), Walker J
s.20, see *Assaubayev v Michael Wilson and
Partners Ltd* [2014] EWCA Civ 1491,
[2014] 6 Costs L.R. 1058 (CA (Civ Div)),
Aikens LJ
s.24, see *Assaubayev v Michael Wilson and
Partners Ltd* [2014] EWCA Civ 1491,
[2014] 6 Costs L.R. 1058 (CA (Civ Div)),
Aikens LJ
s.68, amended: SI 2014/605 Art.12
s.69, see *Alpha Rocks Solicitors v Alade*
[2014] EWHC 3606 (Ch), [2014] 6 Costs
L.R. 1039 (Ch D), Kevin Prosser QC; see
Kingstons Solicitors v Reiss Solicitors

[2014] EWCA Civ 172, [2014] 6 Costs L.R.
998 (CA (Civ Div)), Maurice Kay LJ
s.70, see *Bentine v Bentine* [2013] EWHC
3098 (Ch), [2014] 1 All E.R. 983 (Ch D),
Proudman J; see *Stone Rowe Brewer LLP v
Just Costs Ltd* [2014] EWHC 219 (QB),
[2014] 3 All E.R. 723 (QBD), Andrews J

53. Rehabilitation of Offenders Act 1974
see *R. (on the application of T) v Chief
Constable of Greater Manchester* [2014]
UKSC 35 (SC), Lord Neuberger JSC
applied: 2014 asp 14 s.34, SI 2014/1610
r.5_8, SI 2014/1977 Reg.2, Reg.5
s.4, applied: SI 2014/1977 Reg.2
s.4, enabling: SI 2014/1707
s.5, see *HHG (Iraq) v Secretary of State for
the Home Department* [2014] CSOH 48,
2014 S.L.T. 693 (OH), Lord Boyd of
Duncansby
s.5, referred to: SI 2014/1610 r.5_8
s.7, enabling: SI 2014/1707
s.10, applied: SI 2014/1707
s.10, enabling: SI 2014/1707
Sch.2, applied: SI 2014/1977 Reg.2
Sch.2 para.4, enabling: SI 2014/1707
Sch.2 para.6, enabling: SI 2014/1707

1975

14. Social Security Act 1975
applied: SI 2014/3134 Sch.1 para.10
s.126A, applied: SI 2014/516 Art.4

22. Oil Taxation Act 1975
applied: SI 2014/1686 Sch.2 para.13
Sch.2 para.12B, amended: 2014 c.26 s.277

**24. House of Commons Disqualification Act
1975**
Sch.1 Part II, amended: 2014 c.12 Sch.11
para.83, 2014 c.20 Sch.4 para.19, 2014 c.23
Sch.5 para.32, Sch.7 para.24, SI 2014/631
Sch.1 para.3, SI 2014/892 Sch.1 para.29, SI
2014/3294 Art.5
Sch.1 Part III, amended: 2014 c.18 s.10,
2014 c.21 Sch.10 para.3, 2014 c.2 Sch.12
para.9, SI 2014/631 Sch.1 para.3, SI
2014/1924 Sch.1, SI 2014/3184 Sch.1
para.11
Sch.2, varied: SI 2014/2708 Art.5

25. Northern Ireland Assembly Disqualification Act 1975
 s.1, amended: 2014 c.13 s.3, s.4
 s.1A, added: 2014 c.13 s.3
 s.1B, added: 2014 c.13 s.4
 Sch.1 Part II, amended: 2014 c.20 Sch.4 para.20, SI 2014/892 Sch.1 para.30, SI 2014/1924 Sch.1
 Sch.1 Part III, amended: 2014 c.13 s.25, SI 2014/631 Sch.1 para.20, SI 2014/3184 Sch.1 para.12

26. Ministers of the Crown Act 1975
 applied: 2014 c.20 Sch.5 para.5
 referred to: 2014 c.22 s.41
 s.1, enabling: SI 2014/268, SI 2014/500, SI 2014/2708

27. Ministerial and other Salaries Act 1975
 s.3, varied: SI 2014/2708 Art.5
 Sch.1 Part I, varied: SI 2014/2708 Art.5

30. Local Government (Scotland) Act 1975
 s.2, see *Assessor for Lothian Valuation Joint Board v Over The Counter Ltd* [2014] CSIH 28, [2014] R.V.R. 231 (LVAC), The Lord President (Gill)
 s.3, see *Happy Feet Nursery and Out of School Club Ltd v Assessor for Lanarkshire* [2014] CSIH 87, 2014 S.L.T. 1066 (LVAC), The Lord President (Gill); see *Schuh Ltd v Assessor for Glasgow* 2014 S.L.T. 184 (LVAC), The Lord President (Gill)
 s.7B, applied: SSI 2014/28 Art.2
 s.7B, enabling: SSI 2014/28
 s.37, see *Happy Feet Nursery and Out of School Club Ltd v Assessor for Lanarkshire* [2014] CSIH 87, 2014 S.L.T. 1066 (LVAC), The Lord President (Gill)
 s.37, enabling: SSI 2014/28

41. Industrial and Provident Societies Act 1975
 repealed: 2014 c.14 Sch.7
 s.1, applied: 2014 c.14 s.25, Sch.3 para.6
 s.2, enabling: SI 2014/210

44. Appropriation Act 1975
 Sch.4 Part 4, varied: SI 2014/2708 Art.5
 Sch.4 Part 16, varied: SI 2014/2708 Art.5

50. Guard Dogs Act 1975
 s.3, amended: SI 2014/3266 Sch.2 para.3

51. Salmon and Freshwater Fisheries Act 1975
 s.9, applied: 2014 c.21 Sch.8 para.30
 s.18, applied: 2014 c.21 Sch.8 para.30
 s.30, repealed (in part): SI 2014/3303 Reg.18
 s.31, referred to: 2014 c.21 Sch.8 para.20

52. Safety of Sports Grounds Act 1975
 applied: SI 2014/2523 Art.2
 s.1, enabling: SI 2014/2523
 s.18, applied: SI 2014/2523

60. Social Security Pensions Act 1975
 s.59, amended: SI 2014/560 Sch.1 para.13, Sch.3 para.2, SI 2014/3168 Sch.1 para.8, SI 2014/3229 Sch.4 para.1
 s.59, applied: SI 2014/668 Art.6
 s.59, disapplied: SI 2014/3229 Sch.2 para.6
 s.59, enabling: SI 2014/668
 s.59A, applied: SI 2014/668 Art.5

63. Inheritance (Provision for Family and Dependants) Act 1975
 see *Freud (Deceased), Re* [2014] EWHC 2577 (Ch), [2014] W.T.L.R. 1453 (Ch D), Richard Spearman QC; see *Kaur v Dhaliwal* [2014] EWHC 1991 (Ch), [2014] W.T.L.R. 1381 (Ch D), Barling J; see *King v Dubrey* [2014] EWHC 2083 (Ch), [2014] W.T.L.R. 1411 (Ch D), Charles Hollander Q.C.; see *Lim v Walia* [2014] EWCA Civ 1076, [2014] 3 F.C.R. 284 (CA (Civ Div)), Arden LJ
 s.1, see *King v Dubrey* [2014] EWHC 2083 (Ch), [2014] W.T.L.R. 1411 (Ch D), Charles Hollander Q.C.; see *Swetenham v Walkley* [2014] W.T.L.R. 845 (CC (Central London)), Judge Walden-Smith; see *Wright-Gordon v Legister* [2014] EWHC 2041 (Ch), [2014] W.T.L.R. 1675 (Ch D), Master Bowles
 s.1, amended: 2014 c.16 Sch.2 para.2, Sch.2 para.3
 s.2, see *Berger v Berger* [2013] EWCA Civ 1305, [2014] W.T.L.R. 35 (CA (Civ Div)), Moses LJ
 s.2, amended: 2014 c.16 Sch.2 para.4
 s.3, see *Berger v Berger* [2013] EWCA Civ 1305, [2014] W.T.L.R. 35 (CA (Civ Div)), Moses LJ
 s.3, amended: 2014 c.16 Sch.2 para.5
 s.4, see *Berger v Berger* [2013] EWCA Civ 1305, [2014] W.T.L.R. 35 (CA (Civ Div)), Moses LJ
 s.4, amended: 2014 c.16 Sch.2 para.6
 s.9, see *Lim v Walia* [2014] EWCA Civ 1076, [2014] 3 F.C.R. 284 (CA (Civ Div)), Arden LJ
 s.9, amended: 2014 c.16 Sch.2 para.7
 s.10, see *B v IB (Order to set aside disposition under Insolvency Act)* [2013]

EWHC 3755 (Fam), [2014] 2 F.L.R. 273
(Fam Div), Parker J
s.23, substituted: 2014 c.16 Sch.3 para.2

65. Sex Discrimination Act 1975
s.1, see *D v Royal Bank of Scotland* [2014]
I.R.L.R. 25 (IH (Ex Div)), Lady Paton; see
Little v Richmond Pharmacology Ltd [2014]
I.C.R. 85 (EAT), Judge Peter Clark
s.6, see *D v Royal Bank of Scotland* [2014]
I.R.L.R. 25 (IH (Ex Div)), Lady Paton; see
Little v Richmond Pharmacology Ltd [2014]
I.C.R. 85 (EAT), Judge Peter Clark

70. Welsh Development Agency Act 1975
Sch.3 para.3, repealed: 2014 c.29 s.21
Sch.3 para.6, repealed: 2014 c.29 s.21

71. Employment Protection Act 1975
see *United States v Nolan* [2014] EWCA Civ
71, [2014] I.C.R. 685 (CA (Civ Div)),
Moore-Bick LJ

72. Children Act 1975
s.34, referred to: 2014 asp 9 Sch.1 Part 1
s.39, referred to: 2014 asp 9 Sch.1 Part 1
s.40, referred to: 2014 asp 9 Sch.1 Part 1
s.50, referred to: 2014 asp 9 Sch.1 Part 1

1976

30. Fatal Accidents Act 1976
see *Cox v Ergo Versicherung AG (formerly
Victoria)* [2014] UKSC 22, [2014] A.C.
1379 (SC), Lord Neuberger PSC; see
Haxton v Philips Electronics UK Ltd [2014]
EWCA Civ 4, [2014] 1 W.L.R. 2721 (CA
(Civ Div)), Elias LJ; see *Yates v Revenue
and Customs Commissioners* [2014] EWHC
2311 (QB), [2014] P.I.Q.R. P24 (QBD),
Master McCloud
s.1, see *Brewster v Northern Ireland Local
Government Officers' Superannuation
Committee* [2014] Pens. L.R. 103 (CA (NI)),
Higgins LJ; see *Swift v Secretary of State
for Justice* [2013] EWCA Civ 193, [2014]
Q.B. 373 (CA (Civ Div)), Lord Dyson MR
s.1, amended: SI 2014/560 Sch.1 para.14
s.3, see *Cox v Ergo Versicherung AG
(formerly Victoria)* [2014] UKSC 22, [2014]
A.C. 1379 (SC), Lord Neuberger PSC

31. Legitimacy Act 1976
s.1, amended: SI 2014/560 Sch.1 para.15, SI
2014/3168 Sch.1 para.9

s.2, amended: SI 2014/560 Sch.1 para.15
s.2A, amended: SI 2014/560 Sch.1 para.15
s.3, amended: SI 2014/560 Sch.1 para.15

35. Police Pensions Act 1976
s.1, amended: 2014 c.12 s.133
s.1, applied: SI 2014/79, SI 2014/381
s.1, enabling: SI 2014/79, SI 2014/381, SSI
2014/62
s.2, enabling: SI 2014/79
s.3, enabling: SI 2014/79
s.4, enabling: SI 2014/79
s.5, enabling: SI 2014/79
s.6, enabling: SI 2014/79
s.7, amended: 2014 c.12 Sch.11 para.84
s.7, enabling: SI 2014/79
s.11, amended: 2014 c.12 Sch.11 para.85

36. Adoption Act 1976
see *A County Council v M* [2013] EWHC
1501 (Fam), [2014] 1 F.L.R. 881 (Fam Div),
Peter Jackson J

38. Dangerous Wild Animals Act 1976
s.6, amended: SI 2014/3266 Sch.2 para.4
s.6, applied: SI 2014/3266 Reg.10

39. Divorce (Scotland) Act 1976
s.1, amended: 2014 asp 5 s.5, s.31

43. Appropriation Act 1976
Sch.4 Part 4, varied: SI 2014/2708 Art.5

**57. Local Government (Miscellaneous
Provisions) Act 1976**
s.42, disapplied: SI 2014/2384 Sch.19 para.8
s.45, see *Aylesbury Vale DC v Call A Cab
Ltd* [2013] EWHC 3765 (Admin), [2014]
P.T.S.R. 523 (DC), Treacy LJ
s.46, see *Aylesbury Vale DC v Call A Cab
Ltd* [2013] EWHC 3765 (Admin), [2014]
P.T.S.R. 523 (DC), Treacy LJ

63. Bail Act 1976
applied: SI 2014/1610 r.19_1, SI 2014/3141
Reg.79
s.3, applied: SI 2014/1610 r.19_7, r.19_12,
r.68_8, r.19_17, SI 2014/3141 Reg.78
s.3AA, applied: SI 2014/3141 Reg.88
s.3AA, referred to: SI 2014/1610 r.19_12
s.3AA, varied: SI 2014/3141 Reg.78
s.3AB, applied: SI 2014/3141 Reg.88
s.3AB, referred to: SI 2014/1610 r.19_12
s.3AB, varied: SI 2014/3141 Reg.78
s.3AC, applied: SI 2014/1610 r.19_12, SI
2014/3141 Reg.88
s.3AC, varied: SI 2014/3141 Reg.78
s.3AC, enabling: SI 2014/163, SI 2014/669

s.4, applied: SI 2014/1610 r.19_17
s.5, applied: SI 2014/1610 r.5_4, r.68_9,
r.42_10, r.19_2, r.19_4, r.41_5
s.5B, applied: SI 2014/1610 r.19_6, r.19_7
s.5B, enabling: SI 2014/1610
s.6, applied: SI 2014/1610 r.19_17, r.62_5
s.7, applied: SI 2014/1610 r.18_2, r.37_11
Sch.1, referred to: SI 2014/1610 r.19_17
Sch.1 Part I, applied: SI 2014/1610 r.19_17
Sch.1 Part IA, applied: SI 2014/1610
r.19_17
Sch.1 Part II, applied: SI 2014/1610 r.19_17
Sch.1 Part IIA, applied: SI 2014/1610
r.19_7, r.19_17

64. Valuation and Rating (Exempted Classes) (Scotland) Act 1976
s.1, applied: SSI 2014/153
s.1, enabling: SSI 2014/153

67. Sexual Offences (Scotland) Act 1976
s.5, see *Branney (Leslie McPherson) v HM Advocate* [2014] HCJAC 78, 2014 S.C.L. 728 (HCJ), Lady Smith

74. Race Relations Act 1976
applied: SI 2014/820 Art.3
s.1, see *Taiwo v Olaigbe* [2014] EWCA Civ 279, [2014] 1 W.L.R. 3636 (CA (Civ Div)), Maurice Kay LJ
s.2, see *Burrell v Micheldever Tyre Services Ltd* [2014] EWCA Civ 716, [2014] I.C.R. 935 (CA (Civ Div)), Maurice Kay LJ
s.32, see *Ministry of Defence v Kemeh* [2014] EWCA Civ 91, [2014] I.C.R. 625 (CA (Civ Div)), Elias LJ
s.57, applied: SI 2014/820 Art.3
s.67A, applied: SI 2014/820 Art.3
s.72, applied: SI 2014/820 Art.3
Sch.1A Part I, amended: 2014 c.29 s.4

76. Energy Act 1976
s.1, applied: SI 2014/1509
s.1, referred to: SI 2014/1509
s.1, enabling: SI 2014/1509
s.17, enabling: SI 2014/1509

78. Industrial Common Ownership Act 1976
s.2, amended: 2014 c.14 Sch.4 para.31

1977

5. Social Security (Miscellaneous Provisions) Act 1977
s.12, enabling: SI 2014/505

s.24, enabling: SI 2014/505

15. Marriage (Scotland) Act 1977
applied: 2014 asp 5 s.11, s.30, SI 2014/3229 Art.12, Art.14
amended: 2014 asp 5 s.13
s.2, amended: 2014 asp 5 s.1
s.2, applied: SI 2014/1110 Art.8, Art.14, SI 2014/3265 Art.8, Art.16
s.3, amended: 2014 asp 5 s.3, s.8, s.17
s.3, applied: SSI 2014/287 Art.4
s.3, enabling: SSI 2014/306
s.5, amended: 2014 asp 5 s.2, s.8
s.5, applied: 2014 asp 5 s.9, s.11
s.5, repealed (in part): 2014 asp 5 s.2
s.5, varied: SSI 2014/361 Reg.7
s.6, amended: 2014 asp 5 s.15, s.18
s.6, enabling: SSI 2014/306
s.7, amended: 2014 asp 5 s.3, s.17, s.18, s.19
s.7, enabling: SSI 2014/306
s.8, amended: 2014 asp 5 s.12, s.20
s.8, applied: SSI 2014/287 Art.4, SSI 2014/304, SSI 2014/304 Reg.2, SSI 2014/305, SSI 2014/305 Reg.2
s.8, referred to: SSI 2014/212 Sch.1
s.8, enabling: SSI 2014/304, SSI 2014/305
s.9, amended: 2014 asp 5 s.13
s.9, applied: SSI 2014/287 Art.4
s.9, referred to: SSI 2014/212 Sch.1
s.10, amended: 2014 asp 5 s.13
s.11, amended: 2014 asp 5 s.15
s.12, amended: 2014 asp 5 s.14
s.12, applied: SSI 2014/287 Art.4
s.12, referred to: SSI 2014/212 Sch.1
s.13, amended: 2014 asp 5 s.15
s.14, amended: 2014 asp 5 s.12, s.13, s.15
s.15, amended: 2014 asp 5 s.15
s.18, amended: 2014 asp 5 s.21
s.18, repealed (in part): 2014 asp 5 s.21
s.18A, repealed: 2014 asp 5 s.21
s.19, amended: 2014 asp 5 s.18, s.21
s.19, repealed (in part): 2014 asp 5 s.21
s.20, amended: 2014 asp 5 s.22
s.20A, varied: SSI 2014/361 Reg.7
s.22, varied: SSI 2014/361 Reg.7
s.23A, varied: SSI 2014/361 Reg.7
s.24, amended: 2014 asp 5 s.13, s.14, s.28
s.24, varied: SSI 2014/361 Reg.7
s.25, applied: SSI 2014/306
s.26, amended: 2014 asp 5 s.4, s.12, s.21
s.26, varied: SSI 2014/361 Reg.7
Sch.1, substituted: 2014 asp 5 s.1

27. Presumption of Death (Scotland) Act 1977
s.1, amended: 2014 asp 5 Sch.1 para.2
s.13, amended: 2014 asp 5 s.28

37. Patents Act 1977
see *IPCom GmbH & Co KG v HTC Europe Co Ltd* [2013] EWCA Civ 1496, [2014] Bus. L.R. 187 (CA (Civ Div)), Patten LJ
s.1, see *HTC Corp v Gemalto SA* [2013] EWHC 1876 (Pat), [2014] R.P.C. 9 (Ch D (Patents Ct)), Birss J
s.5, see *HTC Corp v Gemalto SA* [2013] EWHC 1876 (Pat), [2014] R.P.C. 9 (Ch D (Patents Ct)), Birss J
s.5, amended: 2014 c.18 Sch.1 para.1
s.5, repealed (in part): 2014 c.18 Sch.1 para.1
s.20B, amended: 2014 c.18 Sch.1 para.2
s.25, enabling: SI 2014/2401
s.32, enabling: SI 2014/2401
s.37, amended: 2014 c.18 Sch.1 para.3
s.39, see *Shanks v Unilever Plc* [2014] EWHC 1647 (Pat), [2014] R.P.C. 29 (Ch D (Patents Ct)), Arnold J
s.40, see *Shanks v Unilever Plc* [2014] EWHC 1647 (Pat), [2014] R.P.C. 29 (Ch D (Patents Ct)), Arnold J
s.41, see *Shanks v Unilever Plc* [2014] EWHC 1647 (Pat), [2014] R.P.C. 29 (Ch D (Patents Ct)), Arnold J
s.43, see *Shanks v Unilever Plc* [2014] EWHC 1647 (Pat), [2014] R.P.C. 29 (Ch D (Patents Ct)), Arnold J
s.50A, amended: SI 2014/892 Sch.1 para.32
s.51, amended: SI 2014/892 Sch.1 para.33
s.52, amended: 2014 c.18 Sch.1 para.4
s.53, amended: SI 2014/892 Sch.1 para.34
s.58, amended: 2014 c.18 Sch.1 para.4
s.60, see *Actavis UK Ltd v Eli Lilly & Co* [2014] EWHC 1511 (Pat), [2014] 4 All E.R. 331 (Ch D (Patents Ct)), Arnold J; see *HTC Corp v Nokia Corp* [2013] EWHC 3247 (Pat), [2014] R.P.C. 19 (Ch D (Patents Ct)), Arnold J
s.60, amended: 2014 c.18 Sch.1 para.5, SI 2014/1997 Art.2
s.62, amended: 2014 c.18 s.15
s.72, amended: 2014 c.18 Sch.1 para.3
s.73, amended: 2014 c.18 s.16
s.74, amended: 2014 c.18 Sch.1 para.3
s.74A, amended: 2014 c.18 s.16
s.74A, enabling: SI 2014/2401

s.74B, repealed (in part): 2014 c.18 s.16
s.77, see *Virgin Atlantic Airways Ltd v Jet Airways (India) Ltd* [2013] EWCA Civ 1713, [2014] Bus. L.R. 491 (CA (Civ Div)), Patten LJ
s.77, amended: 2014 c.18 Sch.1 para.6
s.77, enabling: SI 2014/2401
s.82, see *Conductive Inkjet Technology Ltd v Uni-Pixel Displays Inc* [2013] EWHC 2968 (Ch), [2014] 1 All E.R. (Comm) 654 (Ch D (Patents Ct)), Roth J
s.88A, added: 2014 c.18 s.17
s.118, amended: 2014 c.18 s.18
s.118A, repealed: SI 2014/1385 Reg.3
s.123, enabling: SI 2014/578, SI 2014/2401
s.128B, amended: SI 2014/2411 Reg.2
Sch.4A, added: SI 2014/2411 Reg.2
Sch.4A para.1, amended: 2014 c.18 s.16
Sch.4A para.7, amended: SI 2014/2411 Reg.2

38. Administration of Justice Act 1977
s.28, repealed (in part): 2014 c.16 Sch.4 para.3

42. Rent Act 1977
see *Furlonger v Lalatta* [2014] EWHC 37 (Ch), [2014] L. & T.R. 14 (Ch D), Jonathan Klein
s.127, see *Furlonger v Lalatta* [2014] EWHC 37 (Ch), [2014] L. & T.R. 14 (Ch D), Jonathan Klein
Sch.1 Part I para.2, amended: SI 2014/560 Sch.1 para.16
Sch.1 Pt I para.2, see *Northumberland and Durham Property Trust Ltd v Ouaha* [2014] EWCA Civ 571, [2014] H.L.R. 31 (CA (Civ Div)), Vos LJ

43. Protection from Eviction Act 1977
see *Sims v Dacorum BC* [2014] UKSC 63, [2014] 3 W.L.R. 1600 (SC), Lord Neuberger PSC
s.3, see *R. (on the application of N) v Lewisham LBC* [2013] EWCA Civ 804, [2014] 2 W.L.R. 719 (CA (Civ Div)), Moses LJ; see *R. (on the application of N) v Lewisham LBC* [2014] UKSC 62, [2014] 3 W.L.R. 1548 (SC), Lord Neuberger PSC
s.3A, see *R. (on the application of N) v Lewisham LBC* [2014] UKSC 62, [2014] 3 W.L.R. 1548 (SC), Lord Neuberger PSC
s.5, see *R. (on the application of N) v Lewisham LBC* [2013] EWCA Civ 804,

[2014] 2 W.L.R. 719 (CA (Civ Div)), Moses
LJ

45. Criminal Law Act 1977

see *R. v Coulson (Andrew)* [2013] EWCA
Crim 1026, [2014] 1 W.L.R. 1119 (CA
(Crim Div)), Lord Judge LCJ

s.1, see *R. v Bina (Arya)* [2014] EWCA
Crim 1444, [2014] 2 Cr. App. R. 30 (CA
(Crim Div)), McCombe LJ; see *R. v Dang
(Manh Toan)* [2014] EWCA Crim 348,
[2014] 1 W.L.R. 3797 (CA (Crim Div)),
Pitchford LJ; see *R. v Pace (Martin
Edward)* [2014] EWCA Crim 186, [2014] 1
W.L.R. 2867 (CA (Crim Div)), Davis LJ

s.4, see *R. v Hammond (Philip)* [2013]
EWCA Crim 2636, [2014] 1 W.L.R. 4303
(CA (Crim Div)), Laws LJ

s.39, applied: SI 2014/1610 r.4_4

s.48, enabling: SI 2014/1610

49. National Health Service Act 1977

applied: SI 2014/3249 Sch.1

50. Unfair Contract Terms Act 1977

see *FG Wilson (Engineering) Ltd v John
Holt & Co (Liverpool) Ltd* [2013] EWCA
Civ 1232, [2014] 1 W.L.R. 2365 (CA (Civ
Div)), Longmore LJ; see *West v Ian Finlay
and Associates* [2014] EWCA Civ 316,
[2014] B.L.R. 324 (CA (Civ Div)), Moore-
Bick LJ

s.2, see *West v Ian Finlay and Associates*
[2014] EWCA Civ 316, [2014] B.L.R. 324
(CA (Civ Div)), Moore-Bick LJ

s.2, applied: 2014 c.2 s.14

s.3, see *West v Ian Finlay and Associates*
[2014] EWCA Civ 316, [2014] B.L.R. 324
(CA (Civ Div)), Moore-Bick LJ

s.3, applied: 2014 c.2 s.14

s.11, see *Lloyd v Browning* [2013] EWCA
Civ 1637, [2014] 1 P. & C.R. 11 (CA (Civ
Div)), Arden LJ; see *West v Ian Finlay and
Associates* [2014] EWCA Civ 316, [2014]
B.L.R. 324 (CA (Civ Div)), Moore-Bick LJ

Sch.2, see *West v Ian Finlay and Associates*
[2014] EWCA Civ 316, [2014] B.L.R. 324
(CA (Civ Div)), Moore-Bick LJ

1978

19. Oaths Act 1978

s.1, applied: SI 2014/1610 r.38_6, r.37_4,
r.38_11

s.3, applied: SI 2014/1610 r.38_6, r.37_4,
r.38_11

s.5, applied: SI 2014/1610 r.38_11, r.37_4,
r.32_5

**22. Domestic Proceedings and Magistrates
Courts Act 1978**

applied: SI 2014/840 Sch.1

s.28, amended: SI 2014/605 Art.13

23. Judicature (Northern Ireland) Act 1978

s.44, applied: SI 2014/3298 Reg.3

s.53, amended: 2014 c.13 Sch.1 para.2

s.56, amended: 2014 c.13 Sch.1 para.1

29. National Health Service (Scotland) Act 1978

see *Holdich v Lothian Health Board* 2014
S.L.T. 495 (OH), Lord Stewart; see *M v
State Hospitals Board for Scotland* [2014]
CSIH 71, 2014 S.L.T. 905 (IH (2 Div)), The
Lord Justice Clerk (Carloway)

applied: SI 2014/3282 Sch.1 para.25

referred to: 2014 c.23 Sch.1 para.1

s.1, applied: SSI 2014/344 Sch.1, Sch.2

s.2, applied: 2014 asp 8 Sch.1 para.5, Sch.4
para.8, 2014 asp 12 Sch.1 para.31, Sch.1
para.65, SI 2014/3282 Sch.1 para.18, SSI
2014/344 Sch.1, Sch.2

s.2, disapplied: SSI 2014/344 Sch.1, Sch.2

s.2, enabling: SSI 2014/148

s.2A, applied: SSI 2014/344 Sch.1, Sch.2

s.2C, applied: SSI 2014/344 Sch.3 para.3

s.2CB, disapplied: SSI 2014/344 Sch.2

s.2D, applied: SSI 2014/344 Sch.2

s.4A, repealed: 2014 asp 9 s.71

s.7, applied: SI 2014/3282 Sch.1 para.20

s.9, disapplied: SSI 2014/344 Sch.2

s.10, amended: 2014 asp 9 s.63

s.10, applied: SSI 2014/344 Sch.1, Sch.2

s.10, enabling: SSI 2014/100

s.10A, applied: SI 2014/2418 Sch.1

s.10I, amended: 2014 asp 9 s.55

s.10J, amended: 2014 asp 9 s.55

s.12K, added: 2014 asp 9 s.67

s.15, amended: 2014 asp 9 s.63

s.15, repealed (in part): 2014 asp 9 s.63

s.17A, disapplied: SSI 2014/344 Sch.1,
Sch.2

s.17AA, applied: SSI 2014/344 Sch.3 para.3

s.17B, applied: SSI 2014/344 Sch.1
s.17C, applied: SSI 2014/344 Sch.3 para.3
s.17C, disapplied: SSI 2014/344 Sch.1,
Sch.2
s.17CA, applied: SSI 2014/344 Sch.1, Sch.2
s.17E, enabling: SSI 2014/73, SSI 2014/148
s.17I, disapplied: SSI 2014/344 Sch.2
s.17J, disapplied: SSI 2014/344 Sch.1, Sch.2
s.17K, applied: SSI 2014/344 Sch.1, Sch.2
s.17N, enabling: SSI 2014/73, SSI 2014/148
s.17P, applied: SSI 2014/281 Art.3, Art.4,
SSI 2014/285 Art.3, Art.5
s.25, applied: SSI 2014/344 Sch.3 para.3
s.26, applied: SSI 2014/344 Sch.3 para.3
s.27, applied: SSI 2014/344 Sch.3 para.3
s.27, enabling: SSI 2014/73, SSI 2014/148
s.28, enabling: SSI 2014/148
s.28A, disapplied: SSI 2014/344 Sch.1,
Sch.2
s.28B, applied: SSI 2014/344 Sch.1, Sch.2
s.29, applied: 2014 asp 10 Sch.1 para.13
s.38, disapplied: SSI 2014/344 Sch.2
s.38B, applied: SSI 2014/344 Sch.2
s.39, disapplied: SSI 2014/344 Sch.2
s.40, applied: SSI 2014/344 Sch.2
s.48, disapplied: SSI 2014/344 Sch.1, Sch.2
s.49, applied: SSI 2014/344 Sch.1, Sch.2
s.55, disapplied: SSI 2014/344 Sch.2
s.56, applied: SSI 2014/344 Sch.2
s.57, disapplied: SSI 2014/344 Sch.1, Sch.2
s.58, applied: SSI 2014/344 Sch.1, Sch.2
s.64, disapplied: SSI 2014/344 Sch.1, Sch.2
s.65, applied: SSI 2014/344 Sch.1, Sch.2
s.69, enabling: SSI 2014/115
s.70, enabling: SSI 2014/61
s.73, enabling: SSI 2014/61
s.74, enabling: SSI 2014/61
s.75A, disapplied: SSI 2014/344 Sch.2
s.75BB, applied: SSI 2014/344 Sch.2
s.79, disapplied: SSI 2014/344 Sch.1, Sch.2
s.80, applied: SSI 2014/344 Sch.1, Sch.2
s.82, disapplied: SSI 2014/344 Sch.2
s.84, applied: SSI 2014/344 Sch.2
s.84A, disapplied: SSI 2014/344 Sch.2
s.84B, amended: 2014 asp 9 s.66
s.85B, amended: 2014 asp 9 s.65
s.86, applied: SSI 2014/344 Sch.2
s.86, disapplied: SSI 2014/344 Sch.1, Sch.2
s.87, applied: SSI 2014/344 Sch.1
s.88, disapplied: SSI 2014/344 Sch.1, Sch.2
s.89, applied: SSI 2014/344 Sch.1, Sch.2

s.98, disapplied: SSI 2014/344 Sch.2
s.98, enabling: SSI 2014/70
s.99, applied: SSI 2014/344 Sch.2
s.105, enabling: SSI 2014/61, SSI 2014/70,
SSI 2014/100, SSI 2014/115, SSI 2014/148
s.106, enabling: SSI 2014/148
s.108, enabling: SSI 2014/61
Sch.1A, applied: SSI 2014/344 Sch.1, Sch.2
Sch.1 Part I para.1, applied: SSI 2014/344
Sch.1, Sch.2
Sch.1 Part I para.4, disapplied: SSI 2014/344
Sch.1, Sch.2
Sch.1 Part I para.5A, applied: SSI 2014/344
Sch.1, Sch.2
Sch.1 Part II para.11A, disapplied: SSI
2014/344 Sch.1, Sch.2
Sch.1 Part II para.12, applied: SSI 2014/344
Sch.1, Sch.2
Sch.1 Part II para.13, disapplied: SSI
2014/344 Sch.1, Sch.2
Sch.1 Part II para.14, applied: SSI 2014/344
Sch.1, Sch.2
Sch.11 para.2, enabling: SSI 2014/61
Sch.11 para.2A, enabling: SSI 2014/61

30. Interpretation Act 1978
applied: 2014 c.14 Sch.5 para.6
s.7, applied: 2014 c.12 s.55, SI 2014/195
Reg.3, SI 2014/310 Art.29, SI 2014/951
Reg.42, SI 2014/1052 Art.44, SI 2014/1076
Art.24, SI 2014/1240 Reg.42, SI 2014/1796
Art.29, SI 2014/1894 Reg.32, SI 2014/2027
Art.37, SI 2014/2269 Art.35, SI 2014/2441
Art.34, SI 2014/2935 Art.56, SI 2014/3102
Art.46, SI 2014/3328 Art.36, SSI 2014/86
Reg.16, SSI 2014/171 Reg.16
s.16, applied: 2014 c.26 Sch.29 para.9
s.17, applied: 2014 c.14 Sch.5 para.6
Sch.1, applied: SI 2014/1610 r.10_1

33. State Immunity Act 1978
see *Harb v Aziz* [2014] EWHC 1807 (Ch),
[2014] 1 W.L.R. 4437 (Ch D), Rose J
s.1, see *Jones v United Kingdom (34356/06)*
(2014) 59 E.H.R.R. 1 (ECHR), Judge
Ziemele (President); see *London Steam Ship
Owners Mutual Insurance Association Ltd v
Spain (The Prestige)* [2013] EWHC 3188
(Comm), [2014] 1 Lloyd's Rep. 309 (QBD
(Comm)), Hamblen J
s.2, see *Embassy of Brazil v de Castro
Cerqueira* [2014] 1 W.L.R. 3718 (EAT),
Lewis J

s.4, see *Benkharbouche v Embassy of Sudan*
[2014] 1 C.M.L.R. 40 (EAT), Langstaff J
s.9, see *London Steam Ship Owners Mutual
Insurance Association Ltd v Spain (The
Prestige)* [2013] EWHC 3188 (Comm),
[2014] 1 Lloyd's Rep. 309 (QBD (Comm)),
Hamblen J
s.12, see *Embassy of Brazil v de Castro
Cerqueira* [2014] 1 W.L.R. 3718 (EAT),
Lewis J
s.13, see *Taurus Petroleum Ltd v State Oil
Marketing Co of the Ministry of Oil, Iraq*
[2013] EWHC 3494 (Comm), [2014] 1 All
E.R. (Comm) 942 (QBD (Comm)), Field J
s.14, see *Taurus Petroleum Ltd v State Oil
Marketing Co of the Ministry of Oil, Iraq*
[2013] EWHC 3494 (Comm), [2014] 1 All
E.R. (Comm) 942 (QBD (Comm)), Field J
s.16, see *Benkharbouche v Embassy of
Sudan* [2014] 1 C.M.L.R. 40 (EAT),
Langstaff J
s.20, see *Apex Global Management Ltd v Fi
Call Ltd* [2013] EWCA Civ 642, [2014] 1
W.L.R. 492 (CA (Civ Div)), Maurice Kay
LJ

34. Industrial and Provident Societies Act 1978
repealed: 2014 c.14 Sch.7
s.1, applied: 2014 c.14 s.68, Sch.3 para.8

**36. House of Commons (Administration) Act
1978**
see *Thorne v House of Commons
Commission* [2014] EWHC 93 (QB), [2014]
I.R.L.R. 260 (QBD), Supperstone J

37. Protection of Children Act 1978
s.1, applied: 2014 c.12 s.116

40. Rating (Disabled Persons) Act 1978
applied: SSI 2014/30 Reg.3

42. Finance Act 1978
s.12, see *Revenue and Customs
Commissioners v British
Telecommunications Plc* [2014] EWCA Civ
433, [2014] S.T.C. 1926 (CA (Civ Div)),
Rimer LJ

47. Civil Liability (Contribution) Act 1978
s.1, see *Bank of Ireland v Faithful & Gould
Ltd* [2014] EWHC 2217 (TCC), [2014]
T.C.L.R. 7 (QBD (TCC)), Edwards-Stuart J;
see *Feest v South West SHA* [2014] EWHC
177 (QB), [2014] 1 Lloyd's Rep. 419 (QBD
(Merc) (Bristol)), Judge Havelock-Allan
QC; see *Harrison v Technical Sign Co Ltd*

[2013] EWCA Civ 1569, [2014] P.N.L.R. 15
(CA (Civ Div)), Moore-Bick LJ

55. Transport Act 1978
s.21, amended: SI 2014/560 Sch.1 para.17,
SI 2014/3229 Sch.5 para.6

1979

2. Customs and Excise Management Act 1979
see *Lord Chancellor v Ahmed* [2013] EWHC
3642 (QB), [2014] 1 Costs L.R. 21 (QBD),
Andrews J
applied: SI 2014/2357 Art.11
s.1, amended: 2014 c.26 Sch.21 para.1,
Sch.28 para.11, 2014 c.29 s.7
s.1, repealed (in part): 2014 c.26 Sch.21
para.1
s.33, amended: SI 2014/3302 Sch.1 para.2
s.39, amended: 2014 c.26 Sch.21 para.2
s.50, amended: 2014 c.12 s.111
s.50, repealed (in part): 2014 c.12 s.111
s.50, varied: SI 2014/2357 Art.11
s.60A, added: 2014 c.26 Sch.21 para.3
s.60B, added: 2014 c.26 Sch.21 para.6
s.61, amended: 2014 c.26 Sch.21 para.4
s.61, repealed (in part): 2014 c.26 Sch.21
para.4
s.68, amended: 2014 c.12 s.111
s.68, repealed (in part): 2014 c.12 s.111
s.68, varied: SI 2014/2357 Art.11
s.75, amended: SI 2014/1638 Sch.13 para.4
s.77A, applied: SI 2014/2357 Art.12
s.77A, referred to: SI 2014/2357 Art.12
s.77A, varied: SI 2014/2357 Art.12
s.93, enabling: SI 2014/471
s.118A, enabling: SI 2014/471
s.118BCA, added: 2014 c.26 Sch.28 para.12
s.118BD, amended: 2014 c.26 Sch.28
para.13
s.118G, amended: 2014 c.26 Sch.28 para.14
s.138, applied: SI 2014/2357 Art.12, SI
2014/3258 Reg.10
s.139, see *R. (on the application of
Eastenders Cash & Carry Plc) v Revenue
and Customs Commissioners* [2014] UKSC
34, [2014] 2 W.L.R. 1580 (SC), Lord
Neuberger PSC
s.144, see *R. (on the application of
Eastenders Cash & Carry Plc) v Revenue
and Customs Commissioners* [2014] UKSC

34, [2014] 2 W.L.R. 1580 (SC), Lord
Neuberger PSC
s.145, amended: SI 2014/834 Sch.2 para.2
s.145, applied: SI 2014/2357 Art.12, SI
2014/3258 Reg.10
s.146A, amended: SI 2014/834 Sch.2 para.2
s.147, applied: SI 2014/1610 r.63_1
s.150, amended: SI 2014/834 Sch.2 para.2
s.150, applied: SI 2014/2357 Art.12, SI
2014/3258 Reg.10
s.154, applied: SI 2014/2357 Art.12, SI
2014/3258 Reg.10
s.170, see *Lord Chancellor v Ahmed* [2013]
EWHC 3642 (QB), [2014] 1 Costs L.R. 21
(QBD), Andrews J
s.170, amended: 2014 c.12 s.111
s.170, repealed (in part): 2014 c.12 s.111
s.170, varied: SI 2014/2357 Art.11
Sch.3 para.4, see *Wnek v Director of Border
Revenue* [2014] 1 C.M.L.R. 48 (FTT (Tax)),
Judge Charles Hellier
Sch.3 para.5, see *Wnek v Director of Border
Revenue* [2014] 1 C.M.L.R. 48 (FTT (Tax)),
Judge Charles Hellier

4. Alcoholic Liquor Duties Act 1979
s.36, amended: 2014 c.26 s.76
s.37, amended: 2014 c.26 s.76
s.62, amended: 2014 c.26 s.76
Sch.1, amended: 2014 c.26 s.76

5. Hydrocarbon Oil Duties Act 1979
s.6A, enabling: SI 2014/470
s.20AA, enabling: SI 2014/713
s.21, enabling: SI 2014/471
Sch.3 Part I para.3, enabling: SI 2014/471

7. Tobacco Products Duty Act 1979
s.1, see *Wnek v Director of Border Revenue*
[2014] 1 C.M.L.R. 48 (FTT (Tax)), Judge
Charles Hellier
Sch.1, amended: 2014 c.26 s.77

10. Public Lending Right Act 1979
s.3, enabling: SI 2014/1457, SI 2014/1945
s.5, varied: SI 2014/2708 Art.5

33. Land Registration (Scotland) Act 1979
see *Gray v Keeper of the Registers of
Scotland* 2014 S.L.T. (Lands Tr) 117 (Lands
Tr (Scot)), Lord McGhie
s.9, see *Burton v Keeper of the Registers of
Scotland* 2014 S.L.T. (Lands Tr) 69 (Lands
Tr (Scot)), J N Wright, QC; see *Gray v
Keeper of the Registers of Scotland* 2014
S.L.T. (Lands Tr) 117 (Lands Tr (Scot)),

Lord McGhie; see *Mirza v Salim* [2014]
CSIH 51, 2014 S.L.T. 875 (IH (Ex Div)),
Lady Paton; see *Van Eck v Keeper of the
Registers of Scotland* 2014 S.L.T. (Lands Tr)
92 (Lands Tr (Scot)), R Smith QC
s.12, disapplied: SSI 2014/55 Art.2
s.25, see *Burton v Keeper of the Registers of
Scotland* 2014 S.L.T. (Lands Tr) 69 (Lands
Tr (Scot)), J N Wright, QC; see *Miller
Homes Ltd v Keeper of the Registers of
Scotland* 2014 S.L.T. (Lands Tr) 79 (Lands
Tr (Scot)), J N Wright, QC

34. Credit Unions Act 1979
applied: SI 2014/2418 Sch.1
referred to: 2014 c.14 s.2
s.1, amended: 2014 c.14 Sch.4 para.2
s.1, applied: SSI 2014/296 Reg.4
s.1, substituted: 2014 c.14 Sch.4 para.2
s.2, amended: 2014 c.14 Sch.4 para.3
s.2, referred to: 2014 c.14 s.4
s.3, amended: 2014 c.14 Sch.4 para.4
s.4, amended: 2014 c.14 Sch.4 para.5
s.6, amended: 2014 c.14 Sch.4 para.6
s.7, amended: 2014 c.14 Sch.4 para.7
s.7A, amended: 2014 c.14 Sch.4 para.8
s.17, applied: SI 2014/574 Reg.8
s.17, substituted: SI 2014/574 Reg.5
s.18, amended: 2014 c.14 Sch.4 para.9
s.20, amended: 2014 c.14 Sch.4 para.10
s.21, amended: 2014 c.14 Sch.4 para.11
s.22, amended: 2014 c.14 Sch.4 para.12
s.23, amended: 2014 c.14 Sch.4 para.13
s.23, repealed (in part): 2014 c.14 Sch.4
para.13
s.26, amended: 2014 c.14 Sch.4 para.14
s.28, amended: 2014 c.14 Sch.4 para.15
s.31, amended: 2014 c.14 Sch.4 para.16
s.32, amended: 2014 c.14 Sch.4 para.17
Sch.1 para.1, amended: 2014 c.14 Sch.4
para.18
Sch.1 para.11, substituted: 2014 c.14 Sch.4
para.18

38. Estate Agents Act 1979
applied: SI 2014/631 Art.5, Sch.2 para.15
amended: SI 2014/631 Sch.2 para.1
s.3, amended: SI 2014/631 Sch.2 para.1
s.4, amended: SI 2014/631 Sch.2 para.1
s.5, amended: SI 2014/631 Sch.2 para.1
s.6, amended: SI 2014/631 Sch.2 para.1
s.7, amended: SI 2014/631 Sch.2 para.1
s.8, amended: SI 2014/631 Sch.2 para.1

s.9, amended: SI 2014/631 Sch.2 para.1
s.9A, added: SI 2014/631 Sch.2 para.1
s.11, repealed (in part): SI 2014/631 Sch.2
para.1
s.13, amended: SI 2014/631 Sch.2 para.1
s.15, amended: SI 2014/631 Sch.2 para.1
s.17, amended: SI 2014/631 Sch.2 para.1
s.19, amended: SI 2014/631 Sch.2 para.1
s.20, amended: SI 2014/631 Sch.2 para.1
s.21, amended: SI 2014/631 Sch.2 para.1
s.23A, amended: SI 2014/631 Sch.2 para.1
s.23B, amended: SI 2014/631 Sch.2 para.1
s.25, amended: SI 2014/631 Sch.2 para.1
s.26, amended: SI 2014/631 Sch.2 para.1
s.29, amended: SI 2014/631 Sch.2 para.1
s.30, amended: SI 2014/631 Sch.2 para.1
s.33, amended: SI 2014/631 Sch.2 para.1
s.34, amended: SI 2014/631 Sch.2 para.1
Sch.2 Part I para.1, amended: SI 2014/631
Sch.2 para.1
Sch.2 Part I para.2, amended: SI 2014/631
Sch.2 para.1
Sch.2 Part I para.3, amended: SI 2014/631
Sch.2 para.1
Sch.2 Part I para.4, amended: SI 2014/631
Sch.2 para.1
Sch.2 Part I para.5, amended: SI 2014/631
Sch.2 para.1
Sch.2 Part I para.6, amended: SI 2014/631
Sch.2 para.1
Sch.2 Part I para.7, amended: SI 2014/631
Sch.2 para.1
Sch.2 Part I para.8, amended: SI 2014/631
Sch.2 para.1
Sch.2 Part I para.9, amended: SI 2014/631
Sch.2 para.1
Sch.2 Part I para.10, amended: SI 2014/631
Sch.2 para.1
Sch.2 Part II para.11, amended: SI 2014/631
Sch.2 para.1
Sch.2 Part II para.12, amended: SI 2014/631
Sch.2 para.1
Sch.2 Part II para.13, amended: SI 2014/631
Sch.2 para.1
Sch.2 Part II para.14, amended: SI 2014/631
Sch.2 para.1
Sch.3, amended: SI 2014/631 Sch.2 para.1
Sch.3 para.1, amended: SI 2014/631 Sch.2
para.1
Sch.3 para.2, amended: SI 2014/631 Sch.2
para.1

Sch.3 para.3, amended: SI 2014/631 Sch.2
para.1
Sch.3 para.4, amended: SI 2014/631 Sch.2
para.1
Sch.3 para.5, amended: SI 2014/631 Sch.2
para.1
Sch.3 para.6, amended: SI 2014/631 Sch.2
para.1
Sch.3 para.7, amended: SI 2014/631 Sch.2
para.1
Sch.3 para.8, amended: SI 2014/631 Sch.2
para.1
Sch.3 para.9, amended: SI 2014/631 Sch.2
para.1
Sch.3 para.10, amended: SI 2014/631 Sch.2
para.1
Sch.3 para.11, amended: SI 2014/631 Sch.2
para.1
Sch.3 para.12, amended: SI 2014/631 Sch.2
para.1
Sch.3 para.13, amended: SI 2014/631 Sch.2
para.1
Sch.4 para.1, amended: SI 2014/631 Sch.2
para.1
Sch.4 para.10, amended: SI 2014/631 Sch.2
para.1

41. Pneumoconiosis etc (Workers Compensation) Act 1979
s.1, enabling: SI 2014/869
s.2, amended: 2014 c.1 Sch.2 para.1
s.3, amended: SI 2014/560 Sch.1 para.18, SI
2014/3229 Sch.5 para.7
s.3, applied: SI 2014/916 Sch.3 para.4
s.3, repealed (in part): SI 2014/560 Sch.1
para.18, SI 2014/3229 Sch.5 para.7
s.7, applied: SI 2014/869
s.7, enabling: SI 2014/869

43. Crown Agents Act 1979
Sch.5 para.24, applied: SI 2014/1366
Sch.5 para.24, enabling: SI 2014/1366

46. Ancient Monuments and Archaeological Areas Act 1979
applied: SI 2014/1873 Sch.1 para.25, SI
2014/2027 Art.15, SSI 2014/325 Sch.1
para.7
referred to: 2014 asp 19 s.15
s.1, amended: 2014 asp 19 Sch.2 para.2
s.1, applied: SSI 2014/325 Sch.1 para.7
s.1, repealed (in part): 2014 asp 19 Sch.2
para.2
s.1B, added: 2014 asp 19 Sch.2 para.3

s.1C, added: 2014 asp 19 Sch.2 para.32
s.2, amended: 2014 asp 19 Sch.2 para.5
s.2, applied: SI 2014/3223 Sch.1 para.12
s.2, disapplied: SI 2014/3263 Sch.2 para.2
s.3A, added: 2014 asp 19 Sch.2 para.6
s.3B, added: 2014 asp 19 Sch.2 para.35
s.4, amended: 2014 asp 19 Sch.2 para.7
s.4A, added: 2014 asp 19 Sch.2 para.8
s.4B, added: 2014 asp 19 Sch.2 para.33
s.5, amended: 2014 asp 19 Sch.2 para.9
s.6, amended: 2014 asp 19 Sch.2 para.10
s.7, amended: 2014 asp 19 Sch.2 para.11
s.8, amended: 2014 asp 19 Sch.2 para.12
s.9, amended: 2014 asp 19 Sch.2 para.13
s.9A, amended: 2014 asp 19 Sch.2 para.17
s.9B, amended: 2014 asp 19 Sch.2 para.18
s.9C, amended: 2014 asp 19 Sch.2 para.19
s.9C, repealed (in part): 2014 asp 19 Sch.2 para.19
s.9CA, added: 2014 asp 19 Sch.2 para.20
s.9D, amended: 2014 asp 19 Sch.2 para.21
s.9FA, added: 2014 asp 19 Sch.2 para.22
s.9G, amended: 2014 asp 19 Sch.2 para.24
s.9H, amended: 2014 asp 19 Sch.2 para.25
s.9HA, added: 2014 asp 19 Sch.2 para.26
s.9I, amended: 2014 asp 19 Sch.2 para.27
s.9K, amended: 2014 asp 19 Sch.2 para.28
s.9L, amended: 2014 asp 19 Sch.2 para.29
s.9N, amended: 2014 asp 19 Sch.2 para.30
s.9O, amended: 2014 asp 19 Sch.2 para.40
s.17, amended: 2014 asp 19 Sch.2 para.41
s.23A, added: 2014 asp 19 s.21
s.25, amended: 2014 asp 19 Sch.2 para.42
s.26, amended: 2014 asp 19 Sch.2 para.43
s.31, amended: 2014 asp 19 Sch.2 para.44
s.32A, amended: 2014 asp 19 Sch.2 para.37
s.32B, amended: 2014 asp 19 Sch.2 para.38
s.42, amended: 2014 asp 19 Sch.2 para.45
s.43, amended: 2014 asp 19 Sch.2 para.46
s.45A, repealed (in part): 2014 asp 19 s.20
s.46, amended: 2014 asp 19 Sch.2 para.47
s.50, amended: 2014 asp 19 Sch.2 para.48
s.54, amended: 2014 asp 19 Sch.2 para.49
s.55, amended: 2014 asp 19 Sch.2 para.50
s.57, amended: 2014 asp 19 Sch.2 para.51
s.61, amended: 2014 asp 19 Sch.2 para.52
Sch.1A, added: 2014 asp 19 Sch.2 para.34
Sch.1 Part I para.1, amended: 2014 asp 19 Sch.2 para.14
Sch.1 Part I para.2, amended: 2014 asp 19 Sch.2 para.14

Sch.1 Part I para.2B, amended: 2014 asp 19 Sch.2 para.14
Sch.1 Part I para.2C, added: 2014 asp 19 Sch.2 para.14
Sch.1 Part I para.3, amended: 2014 asp 19 Sch.2 para.14
Sch.1 Part I para.4, repealed (in part): 2014 asp 19 Sch.2 para.14
Sch.1 Part II para.5, repealed (in part): 2014 asp 19 Sch.2 para.15
Sch.1 Part II para.10, added: 2014 asp 19 Sch.2 para.15

53. Charging Orders Act 1979
s.1, amended: SI 2014/605 Art.15, Art.16

54. Sale of Goods Act 1979
s.14, see *R. v King (Scott)* [2014] EWCA Crim 621, [2014] 2 Cr. App. R. (S.) 54 (CA (Crim Div)), Fulford LJ
s.49, see *FG Wilson (Engineering) Ltd v John Holt & Co (Liverpool) Ltd* [2013] EWCA Civ 1232, [2014] 1 W.L.R. 2365 (CA (Civ Div)), Longmore LJ
s.50, see *Glencore Energy UK Ltd v Cirrus Oil Services Ltd* [2014] EWHC 87 (Comm), [2014] 1 All E.R. (Comm) 513 (QBD (Comm)), Cooke J

58. Isle of Man Act 1979
s.8, amended: SI 2014/1638 Sch.13 para.5

1980

9. Reserve Forces Act 1980
Part IV, amended: 2014 c.20 s.44
Part V, amended: 2014 c.20 s.44
s.10, amended: 2014 c.20 s.44
s.11, amended: 2014 c.20 s.44
s.13, amended: 2014 c.20 s.44
s.18, amended: 2014 c.20 s.44
s.19, amended: 2014 c.20 s.44
s.19A, amended: 2014 c.20 s.44
s.22, amended: 2014 c.20 s.44
s.32, amended: 2014 c.20 s.44
s.34, amended: 2014 c.20 s.44
s.36, amended: 2014 c.20 s.44
s.38, amended: 2014 c.20 s.44
s.39, amended: 2014 c.20 s.44
s.44, referred to: 2014 c.20 s.49
s.63, amended: 2014 c.20 s.44
s.93, amended: 2014 c.20 s.44
s.100, amended: 2014 c.20 s.44

s.101, amended: 2014 c.20 s.44
s.120, amended: 2014 c.20 s.44
s.158, applied: 2014 c.20 s.49
Sch.8, amended: 2014 c.20 s.44
Sch.8 para.8, amended: 2014 c.20 s.44
Sch.8 para.11, amended: 2014 c.20 s.44
Sch.8 para.16, amended: 2014 c.20 s.44
Sch.8 para.17, amended: 2014 c.20 s.44

11. Protection of Trading Interests Act 1980
s.5, see *Service Temps Inc v MacLeod* 2014
S.L.T. 375 (OH), Lord Hodge

21. Competition Act 1980
s.11B, amended: SI 2014/892 Sch.1 para.36
s.11B, applied: SI 2014/559
s.11B, referred to: SI 2014/892 Sch.2 para.2
s.11B, repealed (in part): SI 2014/892 Sch.1
para.36
s.11D, amended: SI 2014/892 Sch.1 para.37

23. Consular Fees Act 1980
applied: SI 2014/511 Reg.3
s.1, applied: 2014 c.22 s.70
s.1, referred to: 2014 c.22 s.69
s.1, enabling: SI 2014/509

**27. Import of Live Fish (England and Wales)
Act 1980**
s.1, applied: SI 2014/143, SI 2014/3303
Reg.17, SI 2014/3342
s.1, enabling: SI 2014/143, SI 2014/3342

43. Magistrates Courts Act 1980
applied: SI 2014/1610 r.52_1, r.7_2, SI
2014/3266 Reg.19
Part II, applied: SI 2014/1610 r.76_1
Part III, applied: SI 2014/1610 r.52_1
s.1, applied: SI 2014/1610 r.2_4, r.7_1,
r.18_2, r.37_8
s.2, amended: 2014 c.12 s.176
s.2, applied: SI 2014/1610 r.37_1
s.3, see *Constantinides v Constantinides*
[2013] EWHC 3688 (Fam), [2014] 1 W.L.R.
1934 (Fam Div), Holman J
s.6, applied: SI 2014/1610 r.14_1
s.8A, applied: SI 2014/1610 r.36_2, r.33_6,
r.3_26, r.9_12
s.8B, applied: SI 2014/1610 r.35_3, r.35_4,
r.34_3
s.8C, applied: SI 2014/1610 r.16_1
s.9, applied: SI 2014/1610 r.37_3, r.37_7,
r.37_10
s.10, applied: SI 2014/1610 r.37_1, r.37_2,
r.37_15, r.42_10, r.3_26
s.11, applied: SI 2014/1610 r.37_10, r.37_11

s.12, applied: SI 2014/1610 r.37_8, r.37_14
s.13, applied: SI 2014/1610 r.37_11
s.14, applied: SI 2014/1610 r.37_1, r.37_16
s.15, see *DPP v Jarman* [2013] EWHC 4391
(Admin), (2014) 178 J.P. 89 (QBD
(Admin)), Beatson LJ
s.15, applied: SI 2014/1610 r.37_11
s.17, applied: SI 2014/1610 r.38_1
s.17A, see *R. (on the application of
Rahmdezfouli) v Wood Green Crown Court*
[2013] EWHC 2998 (Admin), [2014] 1
W.L.R. 1793 (DC), Moses LJ
s.17A, applied: SI 2014/1610 r.9_1, r.9_2,
r.9_8, r.9_9, r.9_10
s.17E, applied: SI 2014/1610 r.9_1
s.18, applied: SI 2014/1610 r.9_1, r.9_2,
r.3_26, r.9_10
s.19, applied: SI 2014/1610 r.9_1, r.3_26
s.19, referred to: SI 2014/1610 r.9_10
s.20, applied: SI 2014/1610 r.5_4, r.9_5,
r.9_11
s.21, applied: SI 2014/1610 r.9_14
s.22, see *R. v de Brito (Paulo Aguiar)* [2013]
EWCA Crim 1134, [2014] 1 Cr. App. R. (S.)
38 (CA (Crim Div)), Keith J
s.22, applied: SI 2014/1610 r.9_8, r.9_10
s.22A, added: 2014 c.12 s.176
s.22A, applied: SI 2014/1610 r.9_7
s.23, applied: SI 2014/1610 r.5_4, r.9_2
s.24, applied: SI 2014/1610 r.9_1, r.38_1
s.24A, applied: SI 2014/1610 r.9_2, r.9_7,
r.9_10, r.9_13, r.9_14, r.3_26
s.24D, applied: SI 2014/1610 r.9_1
s.25, see *R. (on the application of Morales) v
Kettering Magistrates' Court* [2013] EWHC
1922 (Admin), (2014) 178 J.P. 22 (DC),
Laws LJ
s.25, applied: SI 2014/1610 r.9_12
s.26, applied: SI 2014/1610 r.9_2
s.27, see *R. v J* [2013] EWCA Crim 569,
[2014] Q.B. 561 (CA (Crim Div)), Sir John
Thomas PQBD
s.27, applied: SI 2014/1610 r.37_11
s.27A, applied: SI 2014/1610 r.18_2, r.37_1,
r.37_2
s.29, applied: SI 2014/1610 r.37_2
s.32, see *R. (on the application of Gibson) v
Secretary of State for Justice* [2013] EWHC
2481 (Admin), [2014] 1 W.L.R. 2658 (QBD
(Admin)), Judge Gosnell

s.43, applied: SI 2014/1610 r.19_4, SI 2014/3106 Sch.1

s.43B, applied: SI 2014/1610 r.19_6

s.46, applied: SI 2014/1610 r.2_4, SI 2014/3085 Reg.23

s.47, applied: SI 2014/1610 r.7_4

s.51, varied: SI 2014/1610 r.62_16

s.54, varied: SI 2014/1610 r.62_16

s.55, varied: SI 2014/1610 r.62_16

s.58, applied: SI 2014/1610 r.76_1

s.59B, applied: SI 2014/956 Art.6

s.65, see *Constantinides v Constantinides* [2013] EWHC 3688 (Fam), [2014] 1 W.L.R. 1934 (Fam Div), Holman J

s.75, applied: SI 2014/1610 r.76_2, r.52_5

s.76, applied: SI 2014/600 Art.4, SI 2014/1610 r.18_4, r.52_2, r.18_6

s.78, applied: SI 2014/1610 r.52_7

s.79, see *R. (on the application of Gibson) v Secretary of State for Justice* [2013] EWHC 2481 (Admin), [2014] 1 W.L.R. 2658 (QBD (Admin)), Judge Gosnell

s.79, applied: SI 2014/1610 r.18_6

s.80, applied: SI 2014/1610 r.18_4

s.82, see *R. (on the application of Lawson) v Westminster Magistrates' Court* [2013] EWHC 2434 (Admin), [2014] 1 W.L.R. 2085 (DC), Treacy LJ

s.82, amended: 2014 c.12 s.179

s.82, applied: SI 2014/1610 r.18_4

s.83, see *R. (on the application of Lawson) v Westminster Magistrates' Court* [2013] EWHC 2434 (Admin), [2014] 1 W.L.R. 2085 (DC), Treacy LJ

s.83, applied: SI 2014/1610 r.18_6

s.84, see *R. (on the application of Lawson) v Westminster Magistrates' Court* [2013] EWHC 2434 (Admin), [2014] 1 W.L.R. 2085 (DC), Treacy LJ

s.85, amended: 2014 c.12 s.179

s.86, applied: SI 2014/1610 r.18_6

s.89, applied: SI 2014/1610 r.42_10

s.93, see *Constantinides v Constantinides* [2013] EWHC 3688 (Fam), [2014] 1 W.L.R. 1934 (Fam Div), Holman J

s.97, applied: SI 2014/1610 Part 28, r.18_2, r.28_1, r.28_3, r.62_4, r.62_5

s.97, varied: SI 2014/1610 r.62_16

s.108, applied: SI 2014/1610 r.63_1, r.76_6

s.109, applied: SI 2014/1610 r.76_1, r.63_8

s.111, applied: SI 2014/1610 r.64_1, r.64_2

s.111A, applied: SI 2014/840 r.6

s.114, applied: SI 2014/1610 r.64_3

s.119, applied: SI 2014/1610 r.19_14, r.41_5

s.120, applied: SI 2014/1610 r.19_15

s.121, applied: SI 2014/1610 r.37_1, r.37_2, r.16_2, r.64_3

s.121, varied: SI 2014/1610 r.62_16

s.122, applied: SI 2014/1610 r.2_4

s.123, see *Foster v DPP* [2013] EWHC 2039 (Admin), (2014) 178 J.P. 15 (DC), Laws LJ

s.123, applied: SI 2014/1610 r.18_4

s.123, varied: SI 2014/1610 r.62_16

s.125, applied: SI 2014/1610 r.52_8, r.18_5, r.18_6

s.125A, applied: SI 2014/832 Art.2, SI 2014/1610 r.18_5, r.52_8

s.125A, enabling: SI 2014/832

s.125D, applied: SI 2014/1610 r.18_5, r.52_8

s.125ZA, applied: SI 2014/1610 r.52_7

s.127, applied: SI 2014/1610 r.62_16, r.7_2, SI 2014/3107 Sch.1, SI 2014/3108 Sch.1, SI 2014/3109 Sch.1

s.127, disapplied: SI 2014/951 Reg.41, SI 2014/1240 Reg.41, SI 2014/1615 Reg.9

s.128, applied: SI 2014/1610 r.5_4, r.3_26, r.19_1, r.18_3

s.128, varied: SI 2014/3141 Reg.91

s.129, applied: SI 2014/1610 r.3_26

s.133, see *R. v Jepson (Matthew Joseph)* [2013] EWCA Crim 1362, [2014] 1 Cr. App. R. (S.) 43 (CA (Crim Div)), Moore-Bick LJ

s.136, applied: SI 2014/1610 r.18_3, r.18_6

s.142, applied: SI 2014/1610 r.37_1, r.37_17, r.63_3, r.42_4

s.143, amended: 2014 c.12 s.176

s.143, repealed (in part): 2014 c.12 Sch.11 para.1

s.148, applied: SI 2014/1610 r.37_1

s.150, applied: SI 2014/1610 r.37_1, r.32_9, r.76_1

Sch.2, see *R. v de Brito (Paulo Aguiar)* [2013] EWCA Crim 1134, [2014] 1 Cr. App. R. (S.) 38 (CA (Crim Div)), Keith J

Sch.3, applied: 2014 c.23 s.94, SI 2014/195 Reg.15, SI 2014/517 Reg.19, SI 2014/1610 r.2_4, SI 2014/3223 Reg.12, SI 2014/3263 Reg.17, Reg.26, SI 2014/3303 Reg.16

Sch.3, varied: SI 2014/3222 Reg.14

44. Education (Scotland) Act 1980
applied: 2014 asp 8 s.37, 2014 asp 12 Sch.1
para.10, SSI 2014/217 Sch.1 para.1
s.1, amended: 2014 asp 8 s.54, Sch.5 para.2
s.1, applied: 2014 asp 8 s.47
s.1, repealed (in part): 2014 asp 8 Sch.5
para.2
s.17, applied: 2014 asp 15 s.1
s.23, applied: SSI 2014/116 Art.1
s.28D, applied: 2014 asp 10 Sch.1 para.13
s.53, amended: 2014 asp 8 s.93
s.53, applied: SSI 2014/318 Reg.2
s.53, repealed (in part): 2014 asp 8 s.93
s.53A, amended: 2014 asp 8 Sch.5 para.2
s.53B, amended: 2014 asp 8 Sch.5 para.2
s.53B, applied: SSI 2014/318 Reg.2
s.53B, enabling: SSI 2014/318
s.73, enabling: SSI 2014/143
s.73B, amended: SSI 2014/293 Sch.1 para.1
s.73B, applied: SI 2014/2929 Reg.4
s.74, enabling: SSI 2014/143
s.133, amended: 2014 asp 8 Sch.5 para.2
s.135, amended: 2014 asp 8 Sch.5 para.2
s.135, applied: SSI 2014/116 Art.1

45. Water (Scotland) Act 1980
applied: SSI 2014/364 Reg.45
Part VIA, applied: SSI 2014/364 Reg.4,
Reg.5
s.10, applied: SSI 2014/364 Reg.45
s.11, applied: SSI 2014/364 Reg.46
s.76A, applied: SSI 2014/364 Reg.14,
Reg.32
s.76A, enabling: SSI 2014/364
s.76B, applied: SSI 2014/364 Reg.46
s.76B, enabling: SSI 2014/364
s.76E, amended: SSI 2014/364 Reg.48
s.76E, applied: SSI 2014/364 Reg.37,
Reg.46
s.76E, repealed (in part): SSI 2014/364
Reg.48
s.76F, applied: SSI 2014/364 Reg.47
s.76F, enabling: SSI 2014/364
s.76FA, repealed (in part): SSI 2014/364
Reg.48
s.76FA, substituted: SSI 2014/364 Reg.48
s.76FB, amended: SSI 2014/364 Reg.48
s.76FB, applied: SSI 2014/364 Reg.20,
Reg.21, Reg.23
s.76J, enabling: SSI 2014/364
s.76L, amended: SSI 2014/364 Reg.48
s.101, enabling: SSI 2014/364

s.109, enabling: SSI 2014/364
46. Solicitors (Scotland) Act 1980
s.3A, amended: SSI 2014/232 Reg.3
s.15, amended: SSI 2014/232 Reg.3
s.39A, amended: SSI 2014/232 Reg.3
s.40, amended: SSI 2014/232 Reg.3
s.42ZA, amended: SSI 2014/232 Reg.3
51. Housing Act 1980
see *Furlonger v Lalatta* [2014] EWHC 37
(Ch), [2014] L. & T.R. 14 (Ch D), Jonathan
Klein
Sch.9 para.5, added: 2014 c.12 Sch.11 para.2
Sch.9 para.5, amended: 2014 c.12 Sch.11
para.2
55. Law Reform (Miscellaneous Provisions)
(Scotland) Act 1980
s.1, amended: 2014 asp 18 s.99
s.1, repealed (in part): 2014 asp 18 s.99
s.1A, amended: 2014 asp 18 s.99
s.2, amended: 2014 asp 18 Sch.5 para.19
s.11, amended: 2014 asp 18 Sch.5 para.19
Sch.1 Part III, substituted: 2014 asp 18 s.99
58. Limitation Act 1980
see *Collins v Secretary of State for Business
Innovation and Skills* [2014] EWCA Civ
717, [2014] C.P. Rep. 39 (CA (Civ Div)),
Jackson LJ; see *Page v Hewetts Solicitors*
[2013] EWHC 2845 (Ch), [2014] W.T.L.R.
479 (Ch D), Hildyard J; see *San Vicente v
Secretary of State for Communities and
Local Government* [2013] EWCA Civ 817,
[2014] 1 W.L.R. 966 (CA (Civ Div)), Lloyd
LJ
s.2, see *Co-operative Group Ltd v Birse
Developments Ltd (In Liquidation)* [2014]
EWHC 530 (TCC), [2014] B.L.R. 359 (QBD
(TCC)), Stuart-Smith J
s.9, see *Dawson v Thomson Airways Ltd*
[2014] EWCA Civ 845, [2014] 4 All E.R.
832 (CA (Civ Div)), Moore-Bick LJ
s.11, see *Collins v Secretary of State for
Business Innovation and Skills* [2014]
EWCA Civ 717, [2014] C.P. Rep. 39 (CA
(Civ Div)), Jackson LJ
s.14, see *Collins v Secretary of State for
Business Innovation and Skills* [2014]
EWCA Civ 717, [2014] C.P. Rep. 39 (CA
(Civ Div)), Jackson LJ
s.14A, see *Bellinger v Mercer Ltd* [2014]
EWCA Civ 996, [2014] 1 W.L.R. 3597 (CA
(Civ Div)), Lord Dyson MR; see *Chandra v*

Brooke North (A Firm) [2013] EWCA Civ 1559, [2014] T.C.L.R. 1 (CA (Civ Div)), Laws LJ; see *Schumann v Veale Wasbrough* [2013] EWHC 3730 (QB), (2014) 136 B.M.L.R. 214 (QBD), Dingemans J

s.21, see *Page v Hewetts Solicitors* [2013] EWHC 2845 (Ch), [2014] W.T.L.R. 479 (Ch D), Hildyard J; see *Sheffield v Sheffield* [2013] EWHC 3927 (Ch), [2014] W.T.L.R. 1039 (Ch D), Judge Pelling QC; see *Williams v Central Bank of Nigeria* [2014] UKSC 10, [2014] A.C. 1189 (SC), Lord Neuberger PSC

s.27A, repealed (in part): SI 2014/834 Sch.2 para.4

s.27AB, repealed (in part): SI 2014/834 Sch.2 para.5

s.27B, repealed (in part): SI 2014/834 Sch.2 para.6

s.32, see *Prudential Assurance Co Ltd v Revenue and Customs Commissioners* [2013] EWHC 3249 (Ch), [2014] S.T.C. 1236 (Ch D), Henderson J; see *Test Claimants in the FII Group Litigation v Inland Revenue Commissioners (C-362/12)* [2014] A.C. 1161 (ECJ (3rd Chamber)), Judge Ilesic (President)

s.33, see *Collins v Secretary of State for Business Innovation and Skills* [2014] EWCA Civ 717, [2014] C.P. Rep. 39 (CA (Civ Div)), Jackson LJ; see *Davidson v Aegis Defence Services (BVI) Ltd* [2013] EWCA Civ 1586, [2014] 2 All E.R. 216 (CA (Civ Div)), Longmore LJ

s.35, see *Co-operative Group Ltd v Birse Developments Ltd* [2014] EWCA Civ 707, [2014] B.L.R. 477 (CA (Civ Div)), Tomlinson LJ; see *Insight Group Ltd v Kingston Smith (A Firm)* [2012] EWHC 3644 (QB), [2014] 1 W.L.R. 1448 (QBD), Leggatt J; see *Nemeti v Sabre Insurance Co Ltd* [2013] EWCA Civ 1555, [2014] C.P. Rep. 16 (CA (Civ Div)), Sir Terence Etherton C; see *Wm Morrison Supermarkets Plc v MasterCard Inc* [2013] EWHC 3271 (Comm), [2014] U.K.C.L.R. 56 (QBD (Comm)), Field J

65. Local Government, Planning and Land Act 1980

s.2, amended: 2014 c.2 s.38, Sch.12 para.10
s.2, applied: SI 2014/2060, SI 2014/2680

s.3, applied: SI 2014/2060 Art.2, SI 2014/2680
s.3, enabling: SI 2014/2060, SI 2014/2680
s.134, enabling: SI 2014/683, SI 2014/1181
s.135, enabling: SI 2014/1181
s.148, enabling: SI 2014/683
s.149, enabling: SI 2014/683
s.156, repealed (in part): 2014 asp 14 Sch.2 para.1
s.165A, applied: SI 2014/217
s.165A, enabling: SI 2014/217
s.165B, applied: SI 2014/217
s.165B, enabling: SI 2014/217
s.166, applied: SI 2014/857
s.166, enabling: SI 2014/857
s.170, enabling: SI 2014/683
Sch.2 para.10, repealed (in part): 2014 asp 3 Sch.3 para.19
Sch.2 para.14, repealed (in part): 2014 asp 3 Sch.3 para.19
Sch.2 para.18, repealed (in part): 2014 asp 3 Sch.3 para.19
Sch.26 para.1, enabling: SI 2014/1181

66. Highways Act 1980

applied: SI 2014/466 Sch.1, SI 2014/941 Sch.1, SI 2014/2434 Art.28, SI 2014/2935 Art.47, SI 2014/3109 Sch.1, SI 2014/3310 Sch.1, SI 2014/3311 Sch.1
Part I, applied: SI 2014/1599 Art.16
Part VIIIA, applied: 2014 c.12 s.75
s.4, applied: SI 2014/2269 Art.19
s.8, applied: SI 2014/865 Art.11
s.10, applied: SI 2014/2269 Art.10
s.10, enabling: SI 2014/1043, SI 2014/1044, SI 2014/1045, SI 2014/1328, SI 2014/1330, SI 2014/1331, SI 2014/1337, SI 2014/1431, SI 2014/1708, SI 2014/1837, SI 2014/1918, SI 2014/2130, SI 2014/2141, SI 2014/2657, SI 2014/2716, SI 2014/3027, SI 2014/3343
s.12, applied: SI 2014/2269 Art.10, SI 2014/2637 Art.10
s.12, enabling: SI 2014/1329, SI 2014/1337, SI 2014/1431, SI 2014/2141
s.14, enabling: SI 2014/1329
s.16, enabling: SI 2014/1857, SI 2014/2127, SI 2014/2899, SI 2014/3007, SI 2014/3295
s.17, enabling: SI 2014/1857, SI 2014/2127, SI 2014/2899, SI 2014/3007, SI 2014/3295
s.19, enabling: SI 2014/1857, SI 2014/2127, SI 2014/2899, SI 2014/3007, SI 2014/3295

s.41, see *AC v Devon CC* [2013] EWCA Civ
418, [2014] R.T.R. 1 (CA (Civ Div)), Lloyd
LJ
s.41, enabling: SI 2014/1328, SI 2014/1329,
SI 2014/1330, SI 2014/1331, SI 2014/1337,
SI 2014/1708, SI 2014/1837, SI 2014/2130,
SI 2014/2657, SI 2014/3027, SI 2014/3343
s.58, see *AC v Devon CC* [2013] EWCA Civ
418, [2014] R.T.R. 1 (CA (Civ Div)), Lloyd
LJ
s.58, varied: SI 2014/2637 Art.9
s.64, applied: SI 2014/909 Art.12, SI
2014/1052 Art.13, SI 2014/2027 Art.4, SI
2014/2269 Art.8, SI 2014/2441 Art.13, SI
2014/2637 Art.8, SI 2014/3102 Art.3
s.106, applied: SI 2014/1666 Sch.1, SI
2014/1871 Sch.1
s.106, enabling: SI 2014/1666, SI
2014/1799, SI 2014/1871, SI 2014/2657
s.115E, applied: 2014 c.12 s.62
s.125, enabling: SI 2014/1329
s.129A, repealed: 2014 c.12 Sch.11 para.3
s.131A, disapplied: SI 2014/3263 Sch.2
para.2
s.134, disapplied: SI 2014/3263 Sch.2 para.2
s.137, disapplied: SI 2014/3263 Sch.2 para.2
s.141, disapplied: SI 2014/2384 Sch.19
para.2
s.146, disapplied: SI 2014/3263 Sch.2 para.2
s.167, disapplied: SI 2014/2384 Sch.19
para.2
s.169, disapplied: SI 2014/2384 Sch.19
para.2
s.171, applied: SI 2014/941 Sch.1, SI
2014/3109 Sch.1
s.172, disapplied: SI 2014/2384 Sch.19
para.2
s.184, applied: SI 2014/2269 Art.8, SI
2014/3102 Art.3
s.265, applied: SI 2014/2269 Art.9
s.278, applied: SI 2014/1796 Art.11, SI
2014/2434 Art.17
s.326, enabling: SI 2014/1329
s.339, applied: 2014 c.21 Sch.8 para.30
Sch.2 para.1, applied: SI 2014/1799 Art.1, SI
2014/1871 Art.1
Sch.4, referred to: SI 2014/1857 Art.3, SI
2014/2127 Art.3, SI 2014/2269 Art.10, SI
2014/2899 Art.3, SI 2014/3295 Art.3

1981

14. Public Passenger Vehicles Act 1981
s.5, enabling: SI 2014/3142
s.10, enabling: SI 2014/480
s.52, enabling: SI 2014/2118
s.60, enabling: SI 2014/480, SI 2014/2118,
SI 2014/3142
s.61, applied: SI 2014/480, SI 2014/2118, SI
2014/3142
20. Judicial Pensions Act 1981
s.23, enabling: SI 2014/288
s.33ZA, enabling: SI 2014/483
22. Animal Health Act 1981
s.1, enabling: SI 2014/331, SI 2014/632, SI
2014/714, SI 2014/2337, SI 2014/2383, SSI
2014/71
s.7, enabling: SI 2014/2337, SI 2014/2383
s.8, enabling: SI 2014/331, SI 2014/632, SI
2014/714, SI 2014/2337, SI 2014/2383, SSI
2014/71
s.15, enabling: SI 2014/632, SI 2014/714, SI
2014/2337, SI 2014/2383, SSI 2014/71
s.25, enabling: SI 2014/632, SI 2014/714, SI
2014/2337, SI 2014/2383, SSI 2014/71
s.31, disapplied: SI 2014/1894 Reg.43
s.32, applied: SI 2014/2338 Art.3, Art.4,
Art.5, SSI 2014/151 Art.3
s.32, referred to: SI 2014/2337 Art.7, Art.15
s.32, enabling: SI 2014/2338, SSI 2014/151
s.34, enabling: SI 2014/2337
s.73, applied: SI 2014/2337 Art.16, SI
2014/2383 Art.23
s.83, enabling: SI 2014/632, SI 2014/714, SI
2014/2337, SSI 2014/71
s.87, enabling: SI 2014/2383, SSI 2014/151
s.88, enabling: SI 2014/2383, SSI 2014/63
Sch.3 para.4, disapplied: SI 2014/1894
Reg.43
29. Fisheries Act 1981
s.15, enabling: SI 2014/3363
37. Zoo Licensing Act 1981
s.4, amended: SI 2014/3266 Sch.2 para.5
45. Forgery and Counterfeiting Act 1981
applied: SI 2014/3181 Reg.26
s.5, amended: SI 2014/3168 Sch.1 para.10
47. Criminal Attempts Act 1981
s.1, see *R. v Pace (Martin Edward)* [2014]
EWCA Crim 186, [2014] 1 W.L.R. 2867
(CA (Crim Div)), Davis LJ
s.1, amended: 2014 c.12 s.176

s.4, amended: 2014 c.12 s.176

49. Contempt of Court Act 1981

s.2, applied: SI 2014/1610 r.16_1

s.4, see *Guardian News and Media Ltd v AB*
Times, June 18, 2014 (CA (Crim Div)),
Gross LJ; see *PNM v Times Newspapers Ltd*
[2014] EWCA Civ 1132, [2014] C.P. Rep.
48 (CA (Civ Div)), Lord Dyson MR; see *R.
v ITN News* [2013] EWCA Crim 773, [2014]
1 W.L.R. 199 (CA (Crim Div)), Lord Judge
LCJ

s.4, applied: SI 2014/1610 r.69_1, r.16_1,
r.37_2

s.8, applied: SI 2014/1610 r.62_5

s.9, applied: SI 2014/1610 r.16_1, r.62_5,
r.16_10

s.11, see *BBC, Re* [2014] UKSC 25, [2014] 2
W.L.R. 1243 (SC), Lady Hale DPSC; see
Guardian News and Media Ltd v AB Times,
June 18, 2014 (CA (Crim Div)), Gross LJ;
see *HM Advocate v McAllister (Jason)*
[2014] HCJ 111, 2014 S.L.T. 1023 (HCJ),
Lord Boyd of Duncansby

s.11, applied: SI 2014/1610 r.16_1, r.69_1,
r.37_2

s.12, applied: SI 2014/1610 r.62_4, r.62_5,
r.63_1

s.14, see *Button v Salama* [2013] EWHC
4152 (Fam), [2014] 2 F.L.R. 488 (Fam Div),
Holman J

s.14, applied: SI 2014/956 Art.7, SI
2014/1610 r.62_5, r.62_9, r.62_12

Sch.3, applied: SI 2014/1610 r.62_16

53. Deep Sea Mining Act 1981

s.1, amended: 2014 c.15 Sch.1 para.2

s.2, amended: 2014 c.15 Sch.1 para.3

s.2, repealed (in part): 2014 c.15 Sch.1
para.3

s.3, substituted: 2014 c.15 Sch.1 para.4

s.4, amended: 2014 c.15 Sch.1 para.5

s.5, amended: 2014 c.15 Sch.1 para.6

s.6, amended: 2014 c.15 Sch.1 para.7

s.8, amended: 2014 c.15 Sch.1 para.8

s.8A, added: 2014 c.15 Sch.1 para.9

s.9, repealed: 2014 c.15 Sch.1 para.10

s.11, amended: 2014 c.15 Sch.1 para.11

s.12, substituted: 2014 c.15 Sch.1 para.12

s.13, amended: 2014 c.15 Sch.1 para.13

s.16, substituted: 2014 c.15 Sch.1 para.14

s.17A, added: 2014 c.15 Sch.1 para.15

s.18, amended: 2014 c.15 Sch.1 para.16

s.18, applied: 2014 c.15 s.2

s.18, repealed (in part): 2014 c.15 Sch.1
para.16

Sch.1 para.5, amended: 2014 c.15 Sch.1
para.17

54. Senior Courts Act 1981

s.8, applied: SI 2014/1610 r.6_1, r.63_10

s.15, see *A (A Patient) (Court of Protection:
Appeal), Re* [2013] EWCA Civ 1661, [2014]
1 W.L.R. 3773 (CA (Civ Div)), Moses LJ

s.15, applied: SI 2014/1610 r.16_1, r.62_3,
r.62_4, r.62_5, r.62_12

s.19, applied: SI 2014/1610 r.17_30

s.19, enabling: SI 2014/1610

s.28, see *DLA Piper UK LLP v BDO LLP*
[2013] EWHC 3970 (Admin), [2014] 1
W.L.R. 4425 (QBD (Admin)), Moses LJ; see
Hunter v Newcastle Crown Court [2013]
EWHC 191 (Admin), [2014] Q.B. 94 (DC),
Leveson LJ; see *R. (on the application of
DPP) v Sheffield Crown Court* [2014]
EWHC 2014 (Admin), [2014] 1 W.L.R.
4639 (QBD (Admin)), Lord Thomas LCJ

s.28, applied: SI 2014/1610 r.64_1

s.29, see *DLA Piper UK LLP v BDO LLP*
[2013] EWHC 3970 (Admin), [2014] 1
W.L.R. 4425 (QBD (Admin)), Moses LJ; see
Hunter v Newcastle Crown Court [2013]
EWHC 191 (Admin), [2014] Q.B. 94 (DC),
Leveson LJ; see *R. (on the application of
DPP) v Sheffield Crown Court* [2014]
EWHC 2014 (Admin), [2014] 1 W.L.R.
4639 (QBD (Admin)), Lord Thomas LCJ;
see *R. (on the application of Uddin) v Leeds
Crown Court* [2013] EWHC 2752 (Admin),
[2014] 1 W.L.R. 1742 (QBD (Admin)),
Judge Jeremy Richardson QC

s.31, see *R. (on the application of Ellaway) v
Cardiff CC* [2013] EWHC 2907 (Admin),
[2014] Env. L.R. 12 (QBD (Admin)), Judge
Curran QC

s.31, applied: 2014 c.2 s.31

s.34, applied: SI 2014/840 Sch.2

s.35A, see *National Museums and Galleries
on Merseyside Board of Trustees v AEW
Architects and Designers Ltd* [2013] EWHC
3025 (TCC), [2014] 1 Costs L.O. 39 (QBD
(TCC)), Akenhead J; see *Yukos Capital Sarl
v OJSC Oil Co Rosneft* [2014] EWHC 2188
(Comm), [2014] 2 Lloyd's Rep. 435 (QBD
(Comm)), Simon J

s.37, see *Barnwell Enterprises Ltd v ECP Africa FII Investments LLC* [2013] EWHC 2517 (Comm), [2014] 1 Lloyd's Rep. 171 (QBD (Comm)), Hamblen J; see *R v R* [2013] EWHC 4244 (Fam), [2014] 2 F.L.R. 699 (Fam Div), Sir James Munby PFD; see *UL v BK (Freezing Orders: Safeguards: Standard Examples)* [2013] EWHC 1735 (Fam), [2014] Fam. 35 (Fam Div), Mostyn J
s.45, applied: SI 2014/1610 r.16_1, r.6_13, r.62_3, r.62_4, r.62_5, r.62_9, r.38_1, r.6_22, r.59_6, r.62_12
s.48, applied: SI 2014/1610 r.63_1
s.49, see *AB v CB (Divorce and Maintenance: Discretion to Stay)* [2013] EWCA Civ 1255, [2014] Fam. 102 (CA (Civ Div)), Rimer LJ; see *Fondazione Enasarco v Lehman Brothers Finance SA* [2014] EWHC 34 (Ch), [2014] 2 B.C.L.C. 662 (Ch D (Companies Ct)), David Richards J; see *IPCom GmbH & Co KG v HTC Europe Co Ltd* [2013] EWCA Civ 1496, [2014] Bus. L.R. 187 (CA (Civ Div)), Patten LJ; see *Plantation Holdings (FZ) LLC v Dubai Islamic Bank PJSC* [2013] EWCA Civ 1229, [2014] C.P. Rep. 7 (CA (Civ Div)), Moore-Bick LJ
s.51, see *Deutsche Bank AG v Sebastian Holdings Inc* [2014] EWHC 2073 (Comm), [2014] 4 Costs L.R. 711 (QBD (Comm)), Cooke J; see *Heron v TNT (UK) Ltd* [2013] EWCA Civ 469, [2014] 1 W.L.R. 1277 (CA (Civ Div)), Leveson LJ; see *Herridge v Parker* [2014] Lloyd's Rep. I.R. 177 (CC (Cardiff)), Recorder James Thom QC; see *Murphy v Rayner* [2013] EWHC 3878 (Ch), [2014] 1 W.L.R. 677 (Ch D), Nicholas Strauss QC; see *Portsmouth City Football Club Ltd (In Liquidation), Re* [2013] EWCA Civ 916, [2014] 1 All E.R. 12 (CA (Civ Div)), Mummery, L.J.; see *Salekipour v Parmar* [2013] EWCA Civ 1376, [2014] 1 Costs L.O. 81 (CA (Civ Div)), Arden LJ; see *Tasleem v Beverley* [2013] EWCA Civ 1805, [2014] 1 W.L.R. 3567 (CA (Civ Div)), Sir Terence Etherton C; see *Threlfall v ECD Insight Ltd (Costs)* [2013] EWCA Civ 1444, [2014] 2 Costs L.O. 129 (CA (Civ Div)), Richards LJ; see *Wagenaar v Weekend Travel Ltd (t/a Ski Weekend)* [2014] EWCA Civ 1105, [2014] C.P. Rep. 46 (CA (Civ Div)), Laws LJ; see *X Local Authority v Trimega Laboratories Ltd* [2014] 2 F.L.R. 232 (Fam Div), Judge Williams
s.52, applied: SI 2014/1610 r.76_1, r.63_8, r.76_6, r.61_19, r.76_7
s.52, enabling: SI 2014/1610
s.53, applied: SI 2014/1610 r.65_1
s.55, applied: SI 2014/1610 r.65_1
s.61, applied: SI 2014/3257
s.61, enabling: SI 2014/3257
s.66, applied: SI 2014/1610 r.17_30
s.66, enabling: SI 2014/1610
s.67, enabling: SI 2014/1610
s.70, applied: SI 2014/1610 r.76_13
s.73, applied: SI 2014/1610 r.63_10
s.73, enabling: SI 2014/1610
s.74, applied: SI 2014/1610 r.6_26
s.74, enabling: SI 2014/1610
s.78, applied: SI 2014/1610 r.18_2
s.79, applied: SI 2014/1610 r.18_2, r.63_1
s.81, applied: SI 2014/1610 r.19_1, r.19_8, r.68_3, r.68_4, r.68_8, r.18_2
s.82, applied: SI 2014/1610 r.38_18
s.87, applied: SI 2014/1610 r.65_8
s.87, enabling: SI 2014/1610
s.99, enabling: SI 2014/819
s.102, applied: SI 2014/602 Art.2
s.116, see *Goodman v Goodman* [2013] EWHC 758 (Ch), [2014] Ch. 186 (Ch D), Newey J
Sch.1 para.2, amended: SI 2014/3257 Art.4
Sch.1 para.3, amended: SI 2014/3257 Art.4, SI 2014/3298 Reg.3

59. Matrimonial Homes (Family Protection) (Scotland) Act 1981
s.3, applied: SSI 2014/287 Art.5
s.3, varied: 2014 asp 5 s.11
s.4, applied: 2014 asp 18 Sch.1 para.2, SSI 2014/287 Art.5
s.13, repealed (in part): 2014 asp 14 Sch.2 para.2
s.14, applied: 2014 asp 18 Sch.1 para.2
s.18A, applied: 2014 asp 18 Sch.1 para.2

61. British Nationality Act 1981
see *AHK v Secretary of State for the Home Department* [2013] EWHC 1426 (Admin), [2014] Imm. A.R. 32 (QBD (Admin)), Ouseley J; see *R. (on the application of Kaziu) v Secretary of State for the Home Department* [2014] EWHC 832 (Admin),

[2014] 4 All E.R. 133 (QBD (Admin)),
Ouseley J
applied: SI 2014/511 Reg.5, SI 2014/922
Sch.4 para.2
s.2, applied: SI 2014/511 Reg.5
s.4C, see *Romein v Advocate General for
Scotland* [2014] CSOH 174 (OH), Lord
Brailsford
s.4E, added: 2014 c.22 s.65
s.12, applied: SI 2014/581 Sch.4 para.2
s.14, amended: 2014 c.22 Sch.9 para.70
s.24, applied: SI 2014/581 Sch.4 para.2
s.29, applied: SI 2014/581 Sch.4 para.2
s.34, applied: SI 2014/581 Sch.4 para.2
s.40, see *Al-Jedda v Secretary of State for
the Home Department* [2014] A.C. 253 (SC),
Lord Neuberger PSC
s.40, amended: 2014 c.22 s.66
s.40, applied: 2014 c.22 s.66
s.40A, amended: 2014 c.22 Sch.9 para.25
s.40A, repealed (in part): 2014 c.22 Sch.9
para.25
s.40A, enabling: SI 2014/2604
s.40B, added: 2014 c.22 s.66
s.41, amended: 2014 c.22 s.10, SI 2014/542
Art.2
s.41, applied: 2014 c.22 Sch.9 para.71
s.41, repealed (in part): SI 2014/542 Art.2
s.41, enabling: SI 2014/511, SI 2014/1465
s.41A, amended: 2014 c.22 Sch.9 para.70
s.42, applied: SI 2014/581 Sch.4 para.4
s.50, applied: SI 2014/511 Reg.6, SI
2014/581 Sch.4 para.2, Sch.5 para.2
Sch.1 para.2, substituted: 2014 c.8 s.1
Sch.3, applied: SI 2014/3265 Art.14
Sch.3, referred to: SI 2014/511 Reg.5, Reg.8,
SI 2014/581 Sch.5 para.2

63. Betting and Gaming Duties Act 1981
see *Aspinalls Club Ltd v Revenue and
Customs Commissioners* [2013] EWCA Civ
1464, [2014] 2 W.L.R. 1574 (CA (Civ Div)),
Moses LJ
applied: 2014 c.26 Sch.29 para.5, Sch.29
para.9
s.1, repealed: 2014 c.26 Sch.28 para.2
s.2, applied: 2014 c.26 Sch.29 para.3, Sch.29
para.4, Sch.29 para.7, Sch.29 para.9
s.3, applied: 2014 c.26 Sch.29 para.3, Sch.29
para.4, Sch.29 para.6, Sch.29 para.7, Sch.29
para.9

s.4, applied: 2014 c.26 Sch.29 para.3, Sch.29
para.4, Sch.29 para.6, Sch.29 para.7, Sch.29
para.9
s.5, applied: 2014 c.26 Sch.29 para.3, Sch.29
para.4, Sch.29 para.6
s.5AA, applied: 2014 c.26 Sch.29 para.6
s.5AB, applied: 2014 c.26 Sch.29 para.9
s.5E, applied: 2014 c.26 Sch.29 para.2
s.7, applied: 2014 c.26 Sch.29 para.9
s.7A, applied: 2014 c.26 Sch.29 para.6
s.7B, applied: 2014 c.26 Sch.29 para.3,
Sch.29 para.4, Sch.29 para.7
s.7D, applied: 2014 c.26 Sch.29 para.3
s.7F, applied: 2014 c.26 Sch.29 para.4
s.7ZA, applied: 2014 c.26 Sch.29 para.6
s.8ZA, applied: 2014 c.26 Sch.29 para.2
s.17, amended: 2014 c.26 s.122, Sch.28
para.3
s.17, applied: 2014 c.26 Sch.29 para.9
s.17, referred to: 2014 c.26 s.154
s.19, see *Thomas Estates Ltd (t/a Beacon
Bingo) v Revenue and Customs
Commissioners* [2014] S.F.T.D. 651 (FTT
(Tax)), Judge Roger Berner
s.20C, referred to: 2014 c.26 s.161
s.26A, repealed: 2014 c.26 Sch.28 para.4
s.26B, applied: 2014 c.26 Sch.29 para.8,
Sch.29 para.9
s.26B, repealed (in part): 2014 c.17 s.1
s.26C, applied: 2014 c.26 Sch.29 para.6
s.26E, applied: 2014 c.26 Sch.29 para.5
s.26F, see *Aspinalls Club Ltd v Revenue and
Customs Commissioners* [2013] EWCA Civ
1464, [2014] 2 W.L.R. 1574 (CA (Civ Div)),
Moses LJ
s.26F, applied: 2014 c.26 Sch.29 para.5
s.26G, applied: 2014 c.26 Sch.29 para.6
s.26H, applied: 2014 c.26 Sch.29 para.5,
Sch.29 para.8
s.26IA, applied: 2014 c.26 Sch.29 para.2
s.26J, applied: SI 2014/2257 Reg.5
s.27, amended: 2014 c.26 Sch.28 para.5
s.27, applied: 2014 c.17 s.2
s.31, amended: 2014 c.26 Sch.28 para.6
Sch.A1, repealed: 2014 c.26 Sch.28 para.7
Sch.1, repealed: 2014 c.26 Sch.28 para.8
Sch.3 Part I para.5, amended: 2014 c.26
s.123
Sch.4B, repealed: 2014 c.26 Sch.28 para.9
64. New Towns Act 1981
applied: SI 2014/3038 Sch.4 para.8

s.80, referred to: SI 2014/3038 Sch.4 para.8

66. Compulsory Purchase (Vesting Declarations) Act 1981

applied: SI 2014/310 Art.10, Art.17, SI 2014/909 Art.24, SI 2014/1599 Art.19, SI 2014/2027 Art.18, SI 2014/2637 Art.23, SI 2014/2935 Art.36, SI 2014/3102 Sch.8 para.4, SI 2014/3328 Art.21

referred to: SI 2014/909 Art.24

s.1, applied: SI 2014/2384 Art.34

s.1, varied: SI 2014/2269 Art.22

s.3, varied: SI 2014/310 Art.10, SI 2014/909 Art.24, SI 2014/1052 Art.27, SI 2014/1599 Art.19, SI 2014/1796 Art.21, SI 2014/1821 Art.5, SI 2014/1873 Art.27, SI 2014/2027 Art.18, SI 2014/2269 Art.22, SI 2014/2384 Art.34, SI 2014/2434 Art.21, SI 2014/2441 Art.25, SI 2014/2637 Art.23, SI 2014/2935 Art.36, SI 2014/2950 Art.23, SI 2014/3102 Art.25, SI 2014/3331 Art.19

s.4, applied: SI 2014/310 Art.13, Art.17, SI 2014/909 Art.21, Art.28, SI 2014/1052 Art.24, Art.31, SI 2014/1599 Art.16, Art.23, SI 2014/1796 Art.20, SI 2014/1821 Art.14, SI 2014/1873 Art.24, Art.31, SI 2014/2027 Art.21, Art.27, SI 2014/2269 Art.26, SI 2014/2384 Art.35, Art.45, SI 2014/2434 Art.19, SI 2014/2441 Art.21, SI 2014/2637 Art.20, Art.27, SI 2014/2935 Art.33, Art.40, SI 2014/2950 Art.20, Art.27, SI 2014/3102 Art.30, Art.36, SI 2014/3328 Art.17, SI 2014/3331 Art.17, Art.23

s.5, varied: SI 2014/310 Art.10, SI 2014/909 Art.24, SI 2014/1052 Art.27, SI 2014/1599 Art.19, SI 2014/1796 Art.21, SI 2014/1821 Art.5, SI 2014/1873 Art.27, SI 2014/2027 Art.18, SI 2014/2269 Art.22, SI 2014/2384 Art.34, SI 2014/2434 Art.21, SI 2014/2441 Art.25, SI 2014/2637 Art.23, SI 2014/2935 Art.36, SI 2014/2950 Art.23, SI 2014/3102 Art.25, SI 2014/3331 Art.19

s.7, varied: SI 2014/310 Art.10, SI 2014/909 Art.24, SI 2014/1052 Art.27, SI 2014/1599 Art.19, SI 2014/1796 Art.21, SI 2014/1821 Art.5, SI 2014/1873 Art.27, SI 2014/2027 Art.18, SI 2014/2269 Art.22, SI 2014/2384 Art.34, SI 2014/2434 Art.21, SI 2014/2441 Art.25, SI 2014/2637 Art.23, SI 2014/2935 Art.36, SI 2014/2950 Art.23, SI 2014/3102 Art.25, SI 2014/3331 Art.19

67. Acquisition of Land Act 1981

applied: SI 2014/310 Art.9, SI 2014/1821 Art.4, SI 2014/3102 Art.24

s.7, referred to: SI 2014/3038 Sch.4 para.8

s.19, applied: SI 2014/3038 Sch.4 para.8

Sch.2, applied: SI 2014/2441 Art.22

Sch.2 Part II, applied: SI 2014/1052 Art.23

Sch.2 Part II, varied: SI 2014/1052 Art.23, SI 2014/2384 Art.40, SI 2014/2935 Art.32

Sch.2 Part III para.8, varied: SI 2014/1052 Art.23

Sch.3 Part II para.6, applied: SI 2014/3038 Sch.4 para.8

69. Wildlife and Countryside Act 1981

applied: SI 2014/219 Art.4, SI 2014/2935 Art.22, SI 2014/3223 Sch.1 para.1

s.9, applied: SI 2014/2935 Sch.11 para.28

s.14, applied: SI 2014/538 Art.2

s.14K, applied: SSI 2014/319 Sch.2 para.1

s.14ZA, applied: SI 2014/538 Art.2

s.14ZA, enabling: SI 2014/538

s.16, referred to: SSI 2014/324 Sch.1 para.2

s.26, applied: SI 2014/538

s.26, enabling: SI 2014/538

s.28E, see *Royal Society for the Protection of Birds v Secretary of State for Environment Food & Rural Affairs* [2014] EWHC 1645 (Admin), [2014] Env. L.R. 29 (QBD (Admin)), Mitting J

s.28E, disapplied: SI 2014/3263 Sch.2 para.2

s.28P, disapplied: SI 2014/3263 Sch.2 para.2

s.31, disapplied: SI 2014/3263 Sch.2 para.2

s.37A, referred to: SI 2014/3303 Reg.5

s.39, applied: SI 2014/3223 Sch.2 para.1, SI 2014/3263 Sch.3 para.1

s.52, referred to: SI 2014/3303 Reg.5

s.53, see *R. (on the application of Trail Riders' Fellowship) v Dorset CC* [2013] EWCA Civ 553, [2014] 3 All E.R. 429 (CA (Civ Div)), Maurice Kay LJ

Sch.5, applied: SI 2014/2935 Sch.11 para.28

Sch.9 Part II, referred to: SI 2014/538 Art.2

Sch.14 para.1, see *R. (on the application of Trail Riders' Fellowship) v Dorset CC* [2013] EWCA Civ 553, [2014] 3 All E.R. 429 (CA (Civ Div)), Maurice Kay LJ

1982

10. Industrial Training Act 1982
s.11, applied: SI 2014/791
s.11, referred to: SI 2014/791
s.11, enabling: SI 2014/791
s.12, applied: SI 2014/791, SI 2014/791
Art.14
s.12, enabling: SI 2014/791

16. Civil Aviation Act 1982
s.4, amended: SI 2014/892 Sch.1 para.38
s.5, amended: SI 2014/3302 Sch.1 para.3
s.38, amended: SI 2014/3302 Sch.1 para.3
s.39, amended: SI 2014/3302 Sch.1 para.3
s.46, amended: SI 2014/3302 Sch.1 para.3
s.47, amended: SI 2014/3302 Sch.1 para.3
s.50, amended: SI 2014/3302 Sch.1 para.3
s.60, enabling: SI 2014/508, SI 2014/1888,
SI 2014/2713, SI 2014/2920, SI 2014/3302
s.61, enabling: SI 2014/508, SI 2014/2713,
SI 2014/3302
s.77, enabling: SI 2014/2713
s.79, applied: SI 2014/3233
s.79, enabling: SI 2014/3233
s.84, amended: SI 2014/3302 Sch.1 para.3
s.101, enabling: SI 2014/2713
s.102, enabling: SI 2014/2713, SI
2014/2920, SI 2014/3302
s.105, amended: SI 2014/3302 Sch.1 para.3
s.108, applied: SI 2014/2926
Sch.1 para.15, applied: SI 2014/469 Art.5
Sch.13, enabling: SI 2014/2713

27. Civil Jurisdiction and Judgments Act 1982
applied: 2014 asp 18 s.43, SI 2014/840 Sch.1
s.1, see *Seakom Ltd v Knowledgepool Group
Ltd* [2014] EWCA Civ 1164, [2014] 5 Costs
L.R. 820 (CA (Civ Div)), Gloster LJ
s.1, amended: SI 2014/2947 Sch.1 para.2
s.16, amended: SI 2014/2947 Sch.1 para.3
s.20, amended: 2014 asp 18 Sch.5 para.7
s.25, see *United States v Abacha* [2014]
EWHC 993 (Comm), [2014] Lloyd's Rep.
F.C. 392 (QBD (Comm)), Field J
s.28, see *Clark v TripAdvisor LLC* [2014]
CSOH 20, 2014 S.L.T. 418 (OH),
Temporary Judge P A Arthurson, QC
s.48, amended: SI 2014/2947 Sch.1 para.4
s.50, amended: 2014 asp 18 Sch.5 para.13
29. Supply of Goods and Services Act 1982

s.4, see *XYZ v Various Companies* [2013]
EWHC 3643 (QB), [2014] 2 Costs L.O. 197
(QBD), Thirlwall J
s.13, see *Equitas Ltd v Walsham Bros & Co
Ltd* [2013] EWHC 3264 (Comm), [2014]
Lloyd's Rep. I.R. 398 (QBD (Comm)),
Males J
**30. Local Government (Miscellaneous
Provisions) Act 1982**
see *R. (on the application of Bridgerow Ltd)
v Cheshire West and Chester BC* [2014]
EWHC 1187 (Admin), [2014] B.L.G.R. 485
(QBD (Admin)), Stuart-Smith J
s.3, applied: SI 2014/2469 Art.5, SI
2014/3384 Art.5
Sch.3, see *R. (on the application of
Thompson) v Oxford City Council* [2014]
EWCA Civ 94, [2014] 1 W.L.R. 1811 (CA
(Civ Div)), Lord Dyson MR
Sch.4, applied: SI 2014/2469 Art.5, SI
2014/3384 Art.5
31. Firearms Act 1982
applied: SI 2014/1638 Reg.5
34. Forfeiture Act 1982
s.4, amended: 2014 c.19 Sch.12 para.1,
Sch.16 para.1
**37. Merchant Shipping (Liner Conferences) Act
1982**
s.5, amended: SI 2014/2947 Sch.4 para.1
42. Derelict Land Act 1982
s.1, applied: SI 2014/1508 Art.3
**43. Local Government and Planning (Scotland)
Act 1982**
s.14, applied: 2014 asp 15 s.2
s.24, applied: SSI 2014/345 Sch.1 Part 1
s.24, referred to: 2014 asp 9 Sch.1 Part 1
45. Civic Government (Scotland) Act 1982
s.10, see *Spring Radio Cars Ltd v Glasgow
City Council* [2014] CSIH 21, 2014 S.C. 529
(IH (Ex Div)), Lord Menzies
s.39, amended: 2014 asp 3 s.56
s.39, applied: SSI 2014/160 Art.3
s.52, see *Archer (Paul Graham) v HM
Advocate* 2014 S.L.T. 133 (HCJ), Lady
Paton; see *Connal v Dunn* [2014] HCJAC
57, 2014 S.L.T. 786 (HCJ), The Lord Justice
Clerk (Carloway); see *Murphy v B* [2014]
HCJAC 82, 2014 S.C.L. 648 (HCJ), Lord
Brodie
s.94, amended: SI 2014/1637 Sch.4 para.4
s.108, amended: 2014 asp 14 s.92

52. Industrial Development Act 1982
    applied: SI 2014/1508 Art.3
    s.1, enabling: SI 2014/1508
53. Administration of Justice Act 1982
    see *Young v MacVean* [2014] CSOH 133,
    2014 S.L.T. 934 (OH), Lady Rae
    s.8, see *McPake v SRCL Ltd* 2014 S.C.L.R.
    199 (OH), Lord Stewart
    s.9, see *McPake v SRCL Ltd* 2014 S.C.L.R.
    199 (OH), Lord Stewart; see *Young v*
    MacVean [2014] CSOH 133, 2014 S.L.T.
    934 (OH), Lady Rae
    s.12, see *Talbot v Babcock International Ltd*
    [2014] CSOH 160, 2014 S.L.T. 1077 (OH),
    Lord Brailsford
    s.20, see *Huntley (Deceased), Re* [2014]
    EWHC 547 (Ch), [2014] W.T.L.R. 745 (Ch
    D), David Donaldson QC; see *Marley v*
    Rawlings [2014] UKSC 2, [2014] 2 W.L.R.
    213 (SC), Lord Neuberger JSC
    s.20, amended: 2014 c.16 Sch.3 para.3
    s.21, see *Freud (Deceased), Re* [2014]
    EWHC 2577 (Ch), [2014] W.T.L.R. 1453
    (Ch D), Richard Spearman QC; see *Huntley*
    (Deceased), Re [2014] EWHC 547 (Ch),
    [2014] W.T.L.R. 745 (Ch D), David
    Donaldson QC; see *Loring v Woodland*
    Trust [2013] EWHC 4400 (Ch), [2014] 2 All
    E.R. 836 (Ch D), Asplin J; see *Marley v*
    Rawlings [2014] UKSC 2, [2014] 2 W.L.R.
    213 (SC), Lord Neuberger JSC
    s.38, amended: SI 2014/605 Art.17

1983

2. Representation of the People Act 1983
    see *Moohan, Petitioner* [2014] UKSC 67
    (SC), Lord Neuberger PSC
    applied: 2014 c.25 Sch.1
    referred to: 2014 c.5 Sch.1 para.1
    s.2, see *Moohan, Petitioner* [2014] UKSC 67
    (SC), Lord Neuberger PSC
    s.2, applied: 2014 c.29 Sch.1 para.1
    s.3, see *Moohan, Petitioner* [2014] CSIH 56,
    2014 S.L.T. 755 (IH (1 Div)), The Lord
    President (Gill); see *Moohan, Petitioner*
    [2014] UKSC 67 (SC), Lord Neuberger
    PSC; see *Moohan, Petitioner* 2014 S.L.T.
    213 (OH), Lord Glennie; see *R. (on the*
    application of Chester) v Secretary of State

for Justice [2014] A.C. 271 (SC), Lady Hale
JSC; see *Teshome v Lord President of the*
Council [2014] EWHC 1468 (Admin),
[2014] 3 C.M.L.R. 28 (QBD (Admin)),
Moses LJ
s.4, repealed (in part): 2014 c.13 s.14
s.7, applied: SI 2014/2764 Reg.2
s.7A, applied: SI 2014/2764 Reg.2
s.7B, repealed (in part): 2014 c.13 s.14
s.7C, repealed (in part): 2014 c.13 s.14
s.9, repealed (in part): 2014 c.13 s.18
s.9A, amended: 2014 c.13 s.18
s.9B, amended: SI 2014/1116 Art.3
s.9B, enabling: SI 2014/1808
s.9C, amended: SI 2014/1116 Art.3
s.9C, enabling: SI 2014/1808
s.9E, enabling: SI 2014/1234, SI 2014/1250
s.10, amended: 2014 c.13 s.13
s.10, repealed (in part): 2014 c.13 s.14
s.10A, repealed (in part): 2014 c.13 s.14
s.10A, enabling: SI 2014/1808
s.10ZC, applied: SI 2014/2764 Reg.2
s.10ZC, enabling: SI 2014/1250
s.10ZD, enabling: SI 2014/1250
s.10ZE, enabling: SI 2014/1250
s.13, applied: SI 2014/2764 Reg.2
s.13A, repealed (in part): 2014 c.13 s.14
s.13A, enabling: SI 2014/1808
s.13BA, repealed (in part): 2014 c.13 s.16
s.13CZA, added: 2014 c.13 s.17
s.14, repealed (in part): 2014 c.13 s.14
s.16, enabling: SI 2014/3124, SI 2014/3161
s.17, repealed (in part): 2014 c.13 s.14
s.35, applied: SI 2014/3204 Reg.7
s.36, enabling: SI 2014/492, SI 2014/494
s.37, applied: SI 2014/2172 Reg.3
s.53, amended: 2014 c.13 s.20
s.53, applied: SI 2014/450, SI 2014/1234, SI
2014/1250, SI 2014/3124
s.53, referred to: SI 2014/3161
s.53, enabling: SI 2014/450, SI 2014/1234,
SI 2014/1250, SI 2014/1808, SI 2014/2764,
SI 2014/3124, SI 2014/3161
s.58, amended: SI 2014/1116 Art.3
s.75, amended: 2014 c.4 s.36
s.75ZA, added: 2014 c.4 s.36
s.75ZB, applied: 2014 c.4 s.36
s.76, amended: 2014 c.4 s.37, SI 2014/1870
Art.4, Art.5
s.76, applied: 2014 c.4 s.37
s.76A, enabling: SI 2014/1870

s.76ZA, amended: SI 2014/1870 Art.6
s.201, amended: 2014 c.13 s.13
s.201, applied: SI 2014/450, SI 2014/920, SI 2014/1234, SI 2014/1250, SI 2014/1805, SI 2014/1808, SI 2014/2764, SI 2014/3124, SI 2014/3161
s.201, enabling: SI 2014/1234, SI 2014/1250, SI 2014/1808
s.202, applied: 2014 c.29 Sch.1 para.1
s.202, referred to: SI 2014/3161
s.202, enabling: SI 2014/1808
Sch.ZA1, enabling: SI 2014/1250
Sch.1 Part III para.24, enabling: SI 2014/1808
Sch.1 Part III para.28, amended: SI 2014/1880 Art.2
Sch.1 Part III para.28, enabling: SI 2014/1808
Sch.1 Part III para.31A, amended: SI 2014/1116 Art.3
Sch.1 Part III para.40, amended: SI 2014/1116 Art.3
Sch.1 Part III para.40ZA, added: SI 2014/1116 Art.3
Sch.1 Part III para.45, amended: SI 2014/336 Art.3, SI 2014/1116 Art.3
Sch.1 Part V para.54, amended: SI 2014/1116 Art.3
Sch.1 Part V para.55, amended: SI 2014/1116 Art.3
Sch.1 Part V para.55, enabling: SI 2014/1808
Sch.1 Part V para.57, enabling: SI 2014/1808
Sch.2 para.1, amended: 2014 c.13 s.20
Sch.2 para.1, repealed (in part): 2014 c.13 s.20
Sch.2 para.1, enabling: SI 2014/1234, SI 2014/1250
Sch.2 para.1A, amended: 2014 c.13 s.20
Sch.2 para.1A, enabling: SI 2014/450, SI 2014/1234, SI 2014/1250, SI 2014/3124
Sch.2 para.2A, enabling: SI 2014/3124, SI 2014/3161
Sch.2 para.2B, enabling: SI 2014/1808
Sch.2 para.3A, enabling: SI 2014/1808
Sch.2 para.3B, enabling: SI 2014/1808
Sch.2 para.3ZA, enabling: SI 2014/1250
Sch.2 para.4, enabling: SI 2014/3124, SI 2014/3161
Sch.2 para.5, enabling: SI 2014/1808

Sch.2 para.5A, enabling: SI 2014/1808
Sch.2 para.7, enabling: SI 2014/1808
Sch.2 para.8, enabling: SI 2014/1808
Sch.2 para.8A, enabling: SI 2014/1808
Sch.2 para.8C, amended: 2014 c.13 s.20
Sch.2 para.8C, enabling: SI 2014/1250
Sch.2 para.9C, enabling: SI 2014/1808
Sch.2 para.10, enabling: SI 2014/1808
Sch.2 para.10B, enabling: SI 2014/1808, SI 2014/2764
Sch.2 para.11, enabling: SI 2014/1250
Sch.2 para.11A, repealed (in part): 2014 c.13 s.20
Sch.2 para.11A, enabling: SI 2014/2764
Sch.2 para.12, enabling: SI 2014/1808
Sch.2 para.13, repealed (in part): 2014 c.13 s.20
Sch.2 para.13, enabling: SI 2014/1250
Sch.2A Part III para.10, applied: SI 2014/1805 Reg.2
Sch.2A Part III para.10, enabling: SI 2014/1805

3. Agricultural Marketing Act 1983
repealed: SI 2014/1924 Sch.1
s.1, applied: SI 2014/1924 Art.2

20. Mental Health Act 1983
see *Coombs v Dorset NHS Primary Care Trust* [2013] EWCA Civ 471, [2014] 1 W.L.R. 111 (CA (Civ Div)), Rix LJ; see *NHS Trust v FG* [2014] EWCOP 30, [2014] C.O.P.L.R. 598 (CP), Keehan J; see *R. (on the application of Das) v Secretary of State for the Home Department* [2014] EWCA Civ 45, [2014] 1 W.L.R. 3538 (CA (Civ Div)), Moses LJ; see *R. v Catchpole (Scott Jamie)* [2014] EWCA Crim 1037, [2014] 2 Cr. App. R. (S.) 66 (CA (Crim Div)), Treacy LJ; see *R. v Edgington (Nicola Caroline)* [2013] EWCA Crim 2185, [2014] 1 Cr. App. R. 24 (CA (Crim Div)), Treacy LJ; see *R. v Fort (Jamie Daniel)* [2013] EWCA Crim 2332, [2014] 2 Cr. App. R. (S.) 24 (CA (Crim Div)), Aikens LJ; see *Westminster City Council v Sykes* (2014) 17 C.C.L. Rep. 139 (CP), District Judge Eldergill
applied: SI 2014/1132 Sch.7 para.4, SI 2014/2709 Sch.2 para.4, SI 2014/2936 Sch.1 para.4, Sch.1 para.5
Part II, applied: SI 2014/2936 Sch.1 para.1
Part III, applied: SI 2014/1610 r.33_1

Part IV, applied: SI 2014/2936 Reg.9,
Reg.11, Sch.1 para.5
s.2, see *A (A Patient) (Court of Protection:
Appeal), Re* [2013] EWCA Civ 1661, [2014]
1 W.L.R. 3773 (CA (Civ Div)), Moses LJ;
see *Aster Healthcare Ltd v Shafi* [2014]
EWHC 77 (QB), [2014] 3 All E.R. 283
(QBD), Andrews J; see *Great Western
Hospitals NHS Foundation Trust v AA*
[2014] EWHC 1666 (Fam), [2014] 2 F.L.R.
1206 (Fam Div), Moor J; see *UF, Re* [2013]
EWHC 4289 (COP), [2014] C.O.P.L.R. 93
(CP), Charles J; see *Webley v St George's
Hospital NHS Trust* [2014] EWHC 299
(QB), (2014) 138 B.M.L.R. 190 (QBD),
Bean J
s.3, see *A (A Patient) (Court of Protection:
Appeal), Re* [2013] EWCA Civ 1661, [2014]
1 W.L.R. 3773 (CA (Civ Div)), Moses LJ;
see *AA (Compulsorily Detained Patient:
Elective Caesarean), Re* [2012] EWHC 4378
(COP), [2014] 2 F.L.R. 237 (CP), Mostyn J;
see *Coombs v Dorset NHS Primary Care
Trust* [2013] EWCA Civ 471, [2014] 1
W.L.R. 111 (CA (Civ Div)), Rix LJ; see
Islington LBC v QR [2014] EWCOP 26,
(2014) 17 C.C.L. Rep. 344 (CP), District
Judge Batten; see *K v Kingswood Centre
Hospital Managers* [2014] EWCA Civ 1332,
[2014] Med. L.R. 497 (CA (Civ Div)),
Moore-Bick LJ; see *Obrey v Secretary of
State for Work and Pensions* [2013] EWCA
Civ 1584, [2014] H.L.R. 12 (CA (Civ Div)),
Laws LJ; see *P (A Child) (Enforced
Caesarean: Reporting Restrictions), Re*
[2013] EWHC 4048 (Fam), [2014] 2 F.L.R.
410 (Fam Div), Sir James Munby PFD; see
*R. (on the application of Das) v Secretary of
State for the Home Department* [2014]
EWCA Civ 45, [2014] 1 W.L.R. 3538 (CA
(Civ Div)), Moses LJ; see *R. (on the
application of Wiltshire Council) v
Hertfordshire CC* [2014] EWCA Civ 712,
[2014] P.T.S.R. 1066 (CA (Civ Div)), Moses
LJ
s.5, see *Great Western Hospitals NHS
Foundation Trust v AA* [2014] EWHC 132
(Fam), [2014] 2 F.L.R. 1209 (Fam Div),
Hayden J; see *Great Western Hospitals
NHS Foundation Trust v AA* [2014] EWHC

1666 (Fam), [2014] 2 F.L.R. 1206 (Fam
Div), Moor J
s.11, see *TW v Enfield LBC* [2014] EWCA
Civ 362, [2014] 1 W.L.R. 3665 (CA (Civ
Div)), Arden LJ
s.17E, applied: SI 2014/2936 Sch.1 para.5
s.25, see *K v Kingswood Centre Hospital
Managers* [2014] EWCA Civ 1332, [2014]
Med. L.R. 497 (CA (Civ Div)), Moore-Bick
LJ
s.26, see *Nottinghamshire Healthcare NHS
Trust v RC* [2014] EWCOP 1317, [2014]
C.O.P.L.R. 468 (CP), Mostyn J
s.28, amended: 2014 c.6 Sch.2 para.46
s.31, applied: 2014 c.23 Sch.4 para.1
s.31, varied: 2014 c.23 Sch.4 para.1
s.32, see *K v Kingswood Centre Hospital
Managers* [2014] EWCA Civ 1332, [2014]
Med. L.R. 497 (CA (Civ Div)), Moore-Bick
LJ
s.35, see *R. v Catchpole (Scott Jamie)* [2014]
EWCA Crim 1037, [2014] 2 Cr. App. R. (S.)
66 (CA (Crim Div)), Treacy LJ
s.35, applied: SI 2014/1610 r.42_8, r.42_9
s.35, varied: 2014 c.12 Sch.1 para.6
s.36, applied: SI 2014/1610 r.42_8
s.37, see *R. (on the application of Wiltshire
Council) v Hertfordshire CC* [2014] EWCA
Civ 712, [2014] P.T.S.R. 1066 (CA (Civ
Div)), Moses LJ; see *R. v Catchpole (Scott
Jamie)* [2014] EWCA Crim 1037, [2014] 2
Cr. App. R. (S.) 66 (CA (Crim Div)), Treacy
LJ; see *R. v Fort (Jamie Daniel)* [2013]
EWCA Crim 2332, [2014] 2 Cr. App. R. (S.)
24 (CA (Crim Div)), Aikens LJ
s.37, applied: SI 2014/1610 r.42_8, r.42_9,
r.68_13, r.37_3
s.39, applied: SI 2014/1610 r.42_8
s.41, see *R. (on the application of Wiltshire
Council) v Hertfordshire CC* [2014] EWCA
Civ 712, [2014] P.T.S.R. 1066 (CA (Civ
Div)), Moses LJ; see *R. v Fort (Jamie
Daniel)* [2013] EWCA Crim 2332, [2014] 2
Cr. App. R. (S.) 24 (CA (Crim Div)), Aikens
LJ
s.42, see *R. (on the application of Wiltshire
Council) v Hertfordshire CC* [2014] EWCA
Civ 712, [2014] P.T.S.R. 1066 (CA (Civ
Div)), Moses LJ
s.43, applied: SI 2014/1610 r.42_10
s.44, applied: SI 2014/1610 r.42_9

s.45, see *R. v Fort (Jamie Daniel)* [2013] EWCA Crim 2332, [2014] 2 Cr. App. R. (S.) 24 (CA (Crim Div)), Aikens LJ

s.45, applied: SI 2014/1610 r.76_6, r.63_1

s.47, see *R. (on the application of Muaza) v Secretary of State for the Home Department* [2013] EWCA Civ 1561, [2014] 1 W.L.R. 1870 (CA (Civ Div)), Lewison LJ

s.48, see *R. (on the application of Muaza) v Secretary of State for the Home Department* [2013] EWCA Civ 1561, [2014] 1 W.L.R. 1870 (CA (Civ Div)), Lewison LJ

s.52, applied: SI 2014/1610 r.19_4

s.57, applied: SI 2014/2936 Sch.1 para.5

s.58, applied: SI 2014/2936 Sch.1 para.5

s.63, see *Nottinghamshire Healthcare NHS Trust v RC* [2014] EWCOP 1317, [2014] C.O.P.L.R. 468 (CP), Mostyn J

s.83, see *An NHS Trust v A* [2013] EWHC 2442 (COP), [2014] Fam. 161 (CP), Baker J

s.117, see *R. (on the application of Wiltshire Council) v Hertfordshire CC* [2014] EWCA Civ 712, [2014] P.T.S.R. 1066 (CA (Civ Div)), Moses LJ

s.117, amended: 2014 c.23 s.75

s.117, applied: 2014 c.23 s.39, s.75, s.79, SI 2014/829 Sch.1 para.10, SI 2014/2670 Reg.4, SI 2014/2821 Reg.3, SI 2014/2871 Reg.11

s.117, referred to: 2014 c.23 Sch.4 para.1

s.117A, added: 2014 c.23 s.75

s.117A, applied: SI 2014/2670 Reg.4

s.117A, enabling: SI 2014/2670

s.134, amended: 2014 c.29 s.4

s.135, disapplied: SI 2014/2936 Sch.1 para.5

s.145, see *An NHS Trust v A* [2013] EWHC 2442 (COP), [2014] Fam. 161 (CP), Baker J; see *Nottinghamshire Healthcare NHS Trust v RC* [2014] EWCOP 1317, [2014] C.O.P.L.R. 468 (CP), Mostyn J; see *R. (on the application of Muaza) v Secretary of State for the Home Department* [2013] EWCA Civ 1561, [2014] 1 W.L.R. 1870 (CA (Civ Div)), Lewison LJ

s.145, amended: 2014 c.23 s.75

34. Mobile Homes Act 1983

applied: SI 2014/5 Sch.5 para.2

referred to: 2014 c.22 Sch.3 para.9

s.1, referred to: SI 2014/5 Sch.5 para.2

s.1, enabling: SI 2014/5

s.2C, applied: SI 2014/5 Reg.4, Reg.6, Reg.14, Sch.5

s.2C, referred to: SI 2014/5 Sch.5

s.2C, enabling: SI 2014/5, SI 2014/3073

s.2D, enabling: SI 2014/5, SI 2014/3073

s.4, applied: SI 2014/11 Art.4

Sch.1 Part I para.1A, added: 2014 asp 14 s.84

Sch.1 Part I para.7B, enabling: SI 2014/5, SI 2014/442

Sch.1 Part I para.7C, enabling: SI 2014/5, SI 2014/442

Sch.1 Part I para.8, applied: SI 2014/11 Art.4

Sch.1 Part I para.8, referred to: SI 2014/11 Art.4

Sch.1 Part I para.8B, enabling: SI 2014/5, SI 2014/442

Sch.1 Part I para.8C, enabling: SI 2014/5, SI 2014/442

Sch.1 Part I para.9, applied: SI 2014/11 Art.4

Sch.1 Part I para.23, amended: 2014 asp 14 s.84

Sch.1 Pt I para.4, see *Telchadder v Wickland (Holdings) Ltd* [2014] UKSC 57, [2014] 1 W.L.R. 4004 (SC), Lady Hale DPSC

35. Litter Act 1983

s.4, repealed (in part): 2014 asp 3 Sch.3 para.20

s.9, repealed (in part): 2014 asp 3 Sch.3 para.20

s.13, repealed (in part): 2014 asp 3 Sch.3 para.20

41. Health and Social Services and Social Security Adjudications Act 1983

s.21, referred to: 2014 asp 9 Sch.1 Part 1

44. National Audit Act 1983

s.7ZA, added: 2014 c.2 s.35

s.8, amended: 2014 c.2 s.35

54. Medical Act 1983

applied: SI 2014/3215 Reg.2, Reg.3

Part IIIA, applied: SI 2014/1101 Art.12

s.1, see *Goodchild-Simpson v General Medical Council* [2014] EWHC 1343 (Admin), (2014) 139 B.M.L.R. 128 (QBD (Admin)), Green J

s.2, amended: SI 2014/1101 Art.2

s.3, see *Kapenova v Department of Health* [2014] I.C.R. 884 (EAT), Slade J

s.19, see *Alacakanat v General Medical Council* [2013] EWHC 1866 (Admin), [2014] 1 C.M.L.R. 5 (QBD (Admin)), Edwards-Stuart J

s.21B, see *Alacakanat v General Medical Council* [2013] EWHC 1866 (Admin), [2014] 1 C.M.L.R. 5 (QBD (Admin)), Edwards-Stuart J

s.29A, applied: SI 2014/1273 Sch.1

s.29A, enabling: SI 2014/1273

s.29B, amended: SI 2014/1101 Art.3

s.29B, applied: SI 2014/1273 Sch.1

s.29B, enabling: SI 2014/1273

s.29E, applied: SI 2014/1273 Sch.1

s.29E, enabling: SI 2014/1273

s.29F, amended: SI 2014/1887 Sch.1 para.1

s.29G, amended: SI 2014/1101 Art.4

s.29J, amended: SI 2014/1101 Art.5

s.29J, applied: SI 2014/1273, SI 2014/1273 Sch.1

s.29J, enabling: SI 2014/1273

s.31, applied: SI 2014/1276

s.31, enabling: SI 2014/1276

s.31A, applied: SI 2014/1272, SI 2014/1272 Sch.1

s.31A, enabling: SI 2014/1272

s.35C, amended: SI 2014/1101 Art.6

s.35CC, applied: SI 2014/1270 Sch.1

s.35CC, enabling: SI 2014/1270

s.35D, amended: SI 2014/1101 Art.7

s.35E, amended: SI 2014/1101 Art.8

s.44C, applied: SI 2014/1887 Sch.3 para.2

s.44C, disapplied: SI 2014/1887 Sch.3 para.2

s.44C, substituted: SI 2014/1887 Sch.1 para.1

s.55, amended: SI 2014/1101 Art.10

Sch.4 para.1, applied: SI 2014/1270, SI 2014/1270 Sch.1

Sch.4 para.1, enabling: SI 2014/1270

Sch.4 para.5A, amended: SI 2014/1101 Art.9

Sch.4 para.5A, applied: SI 2014/1270, SI 2014/1270 Sch.1

Sch.4 para.5A, enabling: SI 2014/1270

Sch.4 para.5C, added: SI 2014/1101 Art.9

Sch.4 para.5C, applied: SI 2014/1270, SI 2014/1270 Sch.1

Sch.4 para.5C, enabling: SI 2014/1270

Sch.4 para.8, amended: SI 2014/1101 Art.9

Sch.4 para.9, amended: SI 2014/1101 Art.9

Sch.4 para.10B, added: SI 2014/1101 Art.9

Sch.4 para.11, amended: SI 2014/1101 Art.9

Sch.4 para.12, amended: SI 2014/1101 Art.9

55. Value Added Tax Act 1983

s.22, see *Revenue and Customs Commissioners v British Telecommunications Plc* [2014] EWCA Civ 433, [2014] S.T.C. 1926 (CA (Civ Div)), Rimer LJ

Sch.6 Pt 7 para.4, see *Nuffield Health v Revenue and Customs Commissioners* [2014] S.F.T.D. 164 (FTT (Tax)), Judge John Brooks

1984

12. Telecommunications Act 1984

applied: SI 2014/2269 Art.14

referred to: SSI 2014/197 Art.4, SSI 2014/269 Art.7, SSI 2014/378 Art.4

s.60, see *BT Pension Scheme Trustees Ltd v British Telecommunications Plc* [2014] EWCA Civ 958, [2014] Pens. L.R. 647 (CA (Civ Div)), Rimer LJ

s.68, see *BT Pension Scheme Trustees Ltd v British Telecommunications Plc* [2014] EWCA Civ 958, [2014] Pens. L.R. 647 (CA (Civ Div)), Rimer LJ

s.101, amended: SI 2014/892 Sch.1 para.40

s.106, amended: SI 2014/892 Sch.1 para.41

Sch.2, referred to: SI 2014/790 Reg.5, SI 2014/2269 Art.14, SI 2014/2306 Art.4, SI 2014/2469 Art.4, SI 2014/2907 Art.4, SI 2014/3384 Art.4, SI 2014/3401 Art.4

Sch.2 para.23, applied: SI 2014/909 Sch.10 para.12, SI 2014/1052 Sch.13 para.3, SI 2014/1599 Sch.9 para.2, SI 2014/2269 Sch.8 para.16, SI 2014/2950 Sch.12 para.2, SI 2014/3328 Sch.9 para.3, SI 2014/3331 Sch.12 para.32

Sch.2 para.23, referred to: SI 2014/2384 Sch.16 para.3

16. Foreign Limitation Periods Act 1984

s.2, see *Bank St Petersburg v Arkhangelsky* [2014] EWCA Civ 593, [2014] 1 W.L.R. 4360 (CA (Civ Div)), Longmore LJ

22. Public Health (Control of Disease) Act 1984

s.2, applied: SI 2014/517 Reg.21

24. Dentists Act 1984

s.3, applied: SI 2014/936 Art.2, SI 2014/1981 Art.2

s.18, amended: SI 2014/1887 Sch.1 para.3

s.26A, substituted: SI 2014/1887 Sch.1
para.4
s.36L, substituted: SI 2014/1887 Sch.1
para.5
Sch.4A para.2, amended: SI 2014/1887
Sch.1 para.6
27. Road Traffic Regulation Act 1984
see *Hamnett v Essex CC* [2014] EWHC 246
(Admin), [2014] 1 W.L.R. 2562 (QBD
(Admin)), Singh J; see *R. (on the
application of Attfield) v Barnet LBC* [2013]
EWHC 2089 (Admin), [2014] 1 All E.R. 304
(QBD (Admin)), Lang J
applied: SI 2014/310 Art.22, Art.23, SI
2014/466 Sch.1, SI 2014/865 Art.11, SI
2014/909 Art.38, SI 2014/941 Sch.1, SI
2014/1033 Art.3, SI 2014/1052 Art.41, SI
2014/1059 Art.5, SI 2014/2027 Art.8, SI
2014/2269 Art.37, SI 2014/2384 Art.18, SI
2014/2441 Art.14, SI 2014/2637 Art.15, SI
2014/3102 Art.40, SI 2014/3105 Sch.1, SI
2014/3106 Sch.1, SI 2014/3107 Sch.1, SI
2014/3109 Sch.1, SI 2014/3110 Sch.1, SI
2014/3112 Sch.1, SI 2014/3310 Sch.1, SI
2014/3311 Sch.1
s.1, applied: SSI 2014/378
s.1, enabling: SI 2014/137, SI 2014/741, SI
2014/1029, SI 2014/1059, SI 2014/1064, SI
2014/1397, SI 2014/2151, SI 2014/2304, SI
2014/2306, SI 2014/2469, SI 2014/2518, SI
2014/2610, SI 2014/2612, SI 2014/2658, SI
2014/2678, SI 2014/2694, SI 2014/2907, SI
2014/2927, SI 2014/2938, SI 2014/2946, SI
2014/3384, SI 2014/3401, SI 2014/3472, SSI
2014/174, SSI 2014/269, SSI 2014/271, SSI
2014/378
s.2, enabling: SI 2014/137, SI 2014/741, SI
2014/1029, SI 2014/1059, SI 2014/1064, SI
2014/1397, SI 2014/2151, SI 2014/2304, SI
2014/2306, SI 2014/2469, SI 2014/2518, SI
2014/2610, SI 2014/2612, SI 2014/2658, SI
2014/2678, SI 2014/2694, SI 2014/2907, SI
2014/2927, SI 2014/2938, SI 2014/2946, SI
2014/3384, SI 2014/3401, SI 2014/3472, SSI
2014/10, SSI 2014/11, SSI 2014/16, SSI
2014/17, SSI 2014/18, SSI 2014/19, SSI
2014/20, SSI 2014/45, SSI 2014/46, SSI
2014/47, SSI 2014/48, SSI 2014/75, SSI
2014/76, SSI 2014/77, SSI 2014/78, SSI
2014/82, SSI 2014/104, SSI 2014/105, SSI
2014/106, SSI 2014/107, SSI 2014/120, SSI

2014/124, SSI 2014/128, SSI 2014/133, SSI
2014/134, SSI 2014/135, SSI 2014/136, SSI
2014/138, SSI 2014/156, SSI 2014/168, SSI
2014/174, SSI 2014/175, SSI 2014/177, SSI
2014/178, SSI 2014/179, SSI 2014/180, SSI
2014/181, SSI 2014/182, SSI 2014/195, SSI
2014/197, SSI 2014/198, SSI 2014/199, SSI
2014/203, SSI 2014/204, SSI 2014/205, SSI
2014/206, SSI 2014/207, SSI 2014/208, SSI
2014/209, SSI 2014/211, SSI 2014/216, SSI
2014/223, SSI 2014/228, SSI 2014/234, SSI
2014/235, SSI 2014/236, SSI 2014/237, SSI
2014/240, SSI 2014/241, SSI 2014/244, SSI
2014/245, SSI 2014/248, SSI 2014/253, SSI
2014/254, SSI 2014/255, SSI 2014/256, SSI
2014/259, SSI 2014/266, SSI 2014/269, SSI
2014/270, SSI 2014/271, SSI 2014/273, SSI
2014/275, SSI 2014/276, SSI 2014/280, SSI
2014/286, SSI 2014/288, SSI 2014/299, SSI
2014/329, SSI 2014/330, SSI 2014/331, SSI
2014/332, SSI 2014/340, SSI 2014/378, SSI
2014/380, SSI 2014/381, SSI 2014/382, SSI
2014/383, SSI 2014/384, SSI 2014/385
s.4, enabling: SI 2014/1059, SI 2014/2304,
SI 2014/2306, SI 2014/2469, SI 2014/2694,
SI 2014/2907, SI 2014/2938, SI 2014/3384,
SI 2014/3401, SSI 2014/10, SSI 2014/11,
SSI 2014/16, SSI 2014/17, SSI 2014/18, SSI
2014/19, SSI 2014/20, SSI 2014/45, SSI
2014/46, SSI 2014/47, SSI 2014/48, SSI
2014/75, SSI 2014/76, SSI 2014/77, SSI
2014/78, SSI 2014/82, SSI 2014/104, SSI
2014/105, SSI 2014/106, SSI 2014/107, SSI
2014/120, SSI 2014/124, SSI 2014/128, SSI
2014/133, SSI 2014/134, SSI 2014/135, SSI
2014/136, SSI 2014/138, SSI 2014/156, SSI
2014/168, SSI 2014/177, SSI 2014/178, SSI
2014/179, SSI 2014/180, SSI 2014/181, SSI
2014/182, SSI 2014/195, SSI 2014/197, SSI
2014/198, SSI 2014/199, SSI 2014/203, SSI
2014/204, SSI 2014/205, SSI 2014/206, SSI
2014/207, SSI 2014/208, SSI 2014/209, SSI
2014/211, SSI 2014/216, SSI 2014/223, SSI
2014/228, SSI 2014/234, SSI 2014/235, SSI
2014/236, SSI 2014/237, SSI 2014/240, SSI
2014/241, SSI 2014/244, SSI 2014/245, SSI
2014/248, SSI 2014/253, SSI 2014/254, SSI
2014/255, SSI 2014/256, SSI 2014/259, SSI
2014/266, SSI 2014/270, SSI 2014/271, SSI
2014/273, SSI 2014/275, SSI 2014/276, SSI
2014/280, SSI 2014/286, SSI 2014/288, SSI

2014/299, SSI 2014/329, SSI 2014/330, SSI
2014/331, SSI 2014/332, SSI 2014/340, SSI
2014/380, SSI 2014/381, SSI 2014/382, SSI
2014/383, SSI 2014/384, SSI 2014/385
s.9, enabling: SI 2014/1995
s.14, see *Castle v Crown Prosecution
Service* [2014] EWHC 587 (Admin), [2014]
1 W.L.R. 4279 (DC), Pitchford LJ
s.14, applied: SI 2014/399, SI 2014/466
Sch.1, SI 2014/687, SI 2014/688, SI
2014/941 Sch.1, SI 2014/1010, SI
2014/1393, SI 2014/1394, SI 2014/1395, SI
2014/2360, SI 2014/2513, SI 2014/2514, SI
2014/2602, SI 2014/3105 Sch.1, SI
2014/3109 Sch.1, SI 2014/3110 Sch.1, SI
2014/3112 Sch.1, SI 2014/3310 Sch.1, SI
2014/3311 Sch.1, SSI 2014/10, SSI 2014/11,
SSI 2014/16, SSI 2014/17, SSI 2014/18, SSI
2014/19, SSI 2014/20, SSI 2014/45, SSI
2014/46, SSI 2014/47, SSI 2014/48, SSI
2014/75, SSI 2014/76, SSI 2014/77, SSI
2014/78, SSI 2014/82, SSI 2014/104, SSI
2014/105, SSI 2014/106, SSI 2014/107, SSI
2014/120, SSI 2014/124, SSI 2014/133, SSI
2014/134, SSI 2014/135, SSI 2014/136, SSI
2014/138, SSI 2014/156, SSI 2014/168, SSI
2014/177, SSI 2014/178, SSI 2014/179, SSI
2014/180, SSI 2014/181, SSI 2014/182, SSI
2014/195, SSI 2014/197, SSI 2014/206, SSI
2014/207, SSI 2014/208, SSI 2014/209, SSI
2014/216, SSI 2014/223, SSI 2014/228, SSI
2014/234, SSI 2014/235, SSI 2014/236, SSI
2014/237, SSI 2014/240, SSI 2014/241, SSI
2014/244, SSI 2014/245, SSI 2014/248, SSI
2014/253, SSI 2014/254, SSI 2014/255, SSI
2014/256, SSI 2014/259, SSI 2014/266, SSI
2014/270, SSI 2014/271, SSI 2014/273, SSI
2014/275, SSI 2014/276, SSI 2014/286, SSI
2014/299, SSI 2014/329, SSI 2014/330, SSI
2014/331, SSI 2014/332, SSI 2014/340, SSI
2014/381, SSI 2014/382, SSI 2014/383, SSI
2014/384, SSI 2014/385
s.14, enabling: SI 2014/12, SI 2014/15, SI
2014/29, SI 2014/30, SI 2014/31, SI
2014/32, SI 2014/33, SI 2014/34, SI
2014/37, SI 2014/38, SI 2014/49, SI
2014/50, SI 2014/51, SI 2014/52, SI
2014/53, SI 2014/54, SI 2014/56, SI
2014/57, SI 2014/59, SI 2014/60, SI
2014/61, SI 2014/62, SI 2014/63, SI
2014/64, SI 2014/65, SI 2014/67, SI

2014/68, SI 2014/69, SI 2014/70, SI
2014/71, SI 2014/72, SI 2014/73, SI
2014/74, SI 2014/83, SI 2014/84, SI
2014/85, SI 2014/86, SI 2014/87, SI
2014/95, SI 2014/97, SI 2014/99, SI
2014/100, SI 2014/101, SI 2014/102, SI
2014/103, SI 2014/108, SI 2014/111, SI
2014/113, SI 2014/114, SI 2014/115, SI
2014/116, SI 2014/117, SI 2014/118, SI
2014/119, SI 2014/121, SI 2014/125, SI
2014/126, SI 2014/127, SI 2014/128, SI
2014/132, SI 2014/145, SI 2014/146, SI
2014/148, SI 2014/150, SI 2014/151, SI
2014/152, SI 2014/153, SI 2014/154, SI
2014/155, SI 2014/157, SI 2014/158, SI
2014/159, SI 2014/160, SI 2014/161, SI
2014/164, SI 2014/167, SI 2014/169, SI
2014/170, SI 2014/171, SI 2014/172, SI
2014/173, SI 2014/174, SI 2014/176, SI
2014/177, SI 2014/185, SI 2014/186, SI
2014/187, SI 2014/188, SI 2014/189, SI
2014/190, SI 2014/191, SI 2014/192, SI
2014/193, SI 2014/197, SI 2014/199, SI
2014/200, SI 2014/201, SI 2014/202, SI
2014/203, SI 2014/207, SI 2014/221, SI
2014/222, SI 2014/224, SI 2014/225, SI
2014/226, SI 2014/227, SI 2014/232, SI
2014/233, SI 2014/234, SI 2014/235, SI
2014/236, SI 2014/241, SI 2014/246, SI
2014/247, SI 2014/249, SI 2014/250, SI
2014/252, SI 2014/277, SI 2014/278, SI
2014/279, SI 2014/280, SI 2014/281, SI
2014/282, SI 2014/283, SI 2014/284, SI
2014/285, SI 2014/289, SI 2014/291, SI
2014/292, SI 2014/293, SI 2014/294, SI
2014/295, SI 2014/296, SI 2014/297, SI
2014/298, SI 2014/300, SI 2014/301, SI
2014/302, SI 2014/303, SI 2014/304, SI
2014/305, SI 2014/306, SI 2014/307, SI
2014/309, SI 2014/311, SI 2014/312, SI
2014/313, SI 2014/314, SI 2014/315, SI
2014/316, SI 2014/317, SI 2014/319, SI
2014/320, SI 2014/321, SI 2014/323, SI
2014/324, SI 2014/327, SI 2014/328, SI
2014/337, SI 2014/338, SI 2014/339, SI
2014/341, SI 2014/342, SI 2014/343, SI
2014/344, SI 2014/345, SI 2014/346, SI
2014/347, SI 2014/349, SI 2014/350, SI
2014/351, SI 2014/352, SI 2014/353, SI
2014/354, SI 2014/355, SI 2014/356, SI
2014/359, SI 2014/361, SI 2014/362, SI

2014/363, SI 2014/364, SI 2014/365, SI
2014/387, SI 2014/388, SI 2014/390, SI
2014/391, SI 2014/392, SI 2014/393, SI
2014/394, SI 2014/396, SI 2014/397, SI
2014/398, SI 2014/399, SI 2014/400, SI
2014/401, SI 2014/403, SI 2014/405, SI
2014/408, SI 2014/419, SI 2014/420, SI
2014/425, SI 2014/426, SI 2014/427, SI
2014/428, SI 2014/429, SI 2014/441, SI
2014/454, SI 2014/457, SI 2014/464, SI
2014/477, SI 2014/541, SI 2014/616, SI
2014/617, SI 2014/619, SI 2014/620, SI
2014/621, SI 2014/622, SI 2014/624, SI
2014/625, SI 2014/626, SI 2014/627, SI
2014/628, SI 2014/629, SI 2014/636, SI
2014/637, SI 2014/638, SI 2014/639, SI
2014/640, SI 2014/641, SI 2014/642, SI
2014/643, SI 2014/644, SI 2014/645, SI
2014/646, SI 2014/647, SI 2014/648, SI
2014/650, SI 2014/652, SI 2014/653, SI
2014/655, SI 2014/657, SI 2014/659, SI
2014/660, SI 2014/661, SI 2014/662, SI
2014/663, SI 2014/664, SI 2014/665, SI
2014/671, SI 2014/672, SI 2014/673, SI
2014/674, SI 2014/676, SI 2014/677, SI
2014/678, SI 2014/679, SI 2014/680, SI
2014/681, SI 2014/682, SI 2014/686, SI
2014/687, SI 2014/688, SI 2014/689, SI
2014/690, SI 2014/691, SI 2014/696, SI
2014/697, SI 2014/698, SI 2014/701, SI
2014/705, SI 2014/706, SI 2014/708, SI
2014/709, SI 2014/710, SI 2014/711, SI
2014/712, SI 2014/716, SI 2014/717, SI
2014/718, SI 2014/719, SI 2014/720, SI
2014/721, SI 2014/722, SI 2014/723, SI
2014/724, SI 2014/725, SI 2014/727, SI
2014/728, SI 2014/729, SI 2014/730, SI
2014/731, SI 2014/732, SI 2014/733, SI
2014/734, SI 2014/735, SI 2014/736, SI
2014/737, SI 2014/738, SI 2014/739, SI
2014/740, SI 2014/742, SI 2014/743, SI
2014/744, SI 2014/745, SI 2014/747, SI
2014/748, SI 2014/749, SI 2014/750, SI
2014/751, SI 2014/752, SI 2014/754, SI
2014/755, SI 2014/756, SI 2014/757, SI
2014/758, SI 2014/759, SI 2014/760, SI
2014/761, SI 2014/762, SI 2014/763, SI
2014/764, SI 2014/765, SI 2014/766, SI
2014/767, SI 2014/769, SI 2014/770, SI
2014/773, SI 2014/775, SI 2014/776, SI
2014/777, SI 2014/778, SI 2014/779, SI

2014/780, SI 2014/781, SI 2014/782, SI
2014/789, SI 2014/795, SI 2014/796, SI
2014/799, SI 2014/801, SI 2014/803, SI
2014/804, SI 2014/805, SI 2014/806, SI
2014/807, SI 2014/808, SI 2014/810, SI
2014/811, SI 2014/827, SI 2014/858, SI
2014/873, SI 2014/903, SI 2014/914, SI
2014/915, SI 2014/930, SI 2014/935, SI
2014/937, SI 2014/938, SI 2014/946, SI
2014/947, SI 2014/948, SI 2014/957, SI
2014/958, SI 2014/959, SI 2014/960, SI
2014/961, SI 2014/962, SI 2014/963, SI
2014/964, SI 2014/965, SI 2014/966, SI
2014/967, SI 2014/968, SI 2014/969, SI
2014/970, SI 2014/971, SI 2014/972, SI
2014/973, SI 2014/974, SI 2014/975, SI
2014/976, SI 2014/977, SI 2014/978, SI
2014/980, SI 2014/983, SI 2014/984, SI
2014/985, SI 2014/986, SI 2014/987, SI
2014/988, SI 2014/989, SI 2014/990, SI
2014/991, SI 2014/993, SI 2014/994, SI
2014/995, SI 2014/996, SI 2014/997, SI
2014/998, SI 2014/999, SI 2014/1000, SI
2014/1001, SI 2014/1009, SI 2014/1010, SI
2014/1014, SI 2014/1015, SI 2014/1018, SI
2014/1019, SI 2014/1020, SI 2014/1021, SI
2014/1022, SI 2014/1023, SI 2014/1025, SI
2014/1026, SI 2014/1031, SI 2014/1032, SI
2014/1035, SI 2014/1037, SI 2014/1038, SI
2014/1039, SI 2014/1040, SI 2014/1048, SI
2014/1049, SI 2014/1050, SI 2014/1051, SI
2014/1053, SI 2014/1054, SI 2014/1055, SI
2014/1056, SI 2014/1057, SI 2014/1058, SI
2014/1060, SI 2014/1061, SI 2014/1062, SI
2014/1071, SI 2014/1072, SI 2014/1073, SI
2014/1074, SI 2014/1075, SI 2014/1077, SI
2014/1078, SI 2014/1079, SI 2014/1080, SI
2014/1081, SI 2014/1082, SI 2014/1083, SI
2014/1084, SI 2014/1085, SI 2014/1086, SI
2014/1087, SI 2014/1088, SI 2014/1089, SI
2014/1090, SI 2014/1091, SI 2014/1092, SI
2014/1093, SI 2014/1094, SI 2014/1095, SI
2014/1096, SI 2014/1104, SI 2014/1109, SI
2014/1113, SI 2014/1114, SI 2014/1115, SI
2014/1117, SI 2014/1118, SI 2014/1119, SI
2014/1122, SI 2014/1123, SI 2014/1124, SI
2014/1125, SI 2014/1126, SI 2014/1127, SI
2014/1128, SI 2014/1135, SI 2014/1136, SI
2014/1137, SI 2014/1138, SI 2014/1145, SI
2014/1147, SI 2014/1148, SI 2014/1149, SI
2014/1150, SI 2014/1151, SI 2014/1152, SI

2014/1153, SI 2014/1154, SI 2014/1155, SI
2014/1156, SI 2014/1157, SI 2014/1158, SI
2014/1159, SI 2014/1160, SI 2014/1161, SI
2014/1162, SI 2014/1163, SI 2014/1164, SI
2014/1165, SI 2014/1166, SI 2014/1167, SI
2014/1168, SI 2014/1169, SI 2014/1170, SI
2014/1171, SI 2014/1172, SI 2014/1173, SI
2014/1174, SI 2014/1175, SI 2014/1176, SI
2014/1177, SI 2014/1178, SI 2014/1179, SI
2014/1200, SI 2014/1201, SI 2014/1202, SI
2014/1203, SI 2014/1204, SI 2014/1205, SI
2014/1206, SI 2014/1207, SI 2014/1208, SI
2014/1209, SI 2014/1210, SI 2014/1211, SI
2014/1213, SI 2014/1214, SI 2014/1215, SI
2014/1216, SI 2014/1217, SI 2014/1218, SI
2014/1219, SI 2014/1220, SI 2014/1221, SI
2014/1222, SI 2014/1223, SI 2014/1224, SI
2014/1225, SI 2014/1227, SI 2014/1228, SI
2014/1242, SI 2014/1243, SI 2014/1244, SI
2014/1245, SI 2014/1246, SI 2014/1247, SI
2014/1248, SI 2014/1251, SI 2014/1254, SI
2014/1255, SI 2014/1256, SI 2014/1259, SI
2014/1260, SI 2014/1265, SI 2014/1266, SI
2014/1267, SI 2014/1268, SI 2014/1269, SI
2014/1271, SI 2014/1279, SI 2014/1280, SI
2014/1282, SI 2014/1284, SI 2014/1285, SI
2014/1286, SI 2014/1288, SI 2014/1289, SI
2014/1296, SI 2014/1297, SI 2014/1298, SI
2014/1299, SI 2014/1300, SI 2014/1301, SI
2014/1302, SI 2014/1303, SI 2014/1305, SI
2014/1306, SI 2014/1307, SI 2014/1310, SI
2014/1311, SI 2014/1312, SI 2014/1315, SI
2014/1316, SI 2014/1317, SI 2014/1319, SI
2014/1320, SI 2014/1321, SI 2014/1322, SI
2014/1323, SI 2014/1324, SI 2014/1325, SI
2014/1326, SI 2014/1336, SI 2014/1338, SI
2014/1339, SI 2014/1340, SI 2014/1341, SI
2014/1342, SI 2014/1343, SI 2014/1344, SI
2014/1345, SI 2014/1346, SI 2014/1347, SI
2014/1348, SI 2014/1349, SI 2014/1350, SI
2014/1351, SI 2014/1373, SI 2014/1379, SI
2014/1381, SI 2014/1392, SI 2014/1393, SI
2014/1394, SI 2014/1395, SI 2014/1396, SI
2014/1399, SI 2014/1400, SI 2014/1401, SI
2014/1402, SI 2014/1404, SI 2014/1405, SI
2014/1406, SI 2014/1407, SI 2014/1408, SI
2014/1409, SI 2014/1410, SI 2014/1411, SI
2014/1412, SI 2014/1425, SI 2014/1426, SI
2014/1427, SI 2014/1428, SI 2014/1429, SI
2014/1430, SI 2014/1432, SI 2014/1433, SI
2014/1434, SI 2014/1435, SI 2014/1436, SI

2014/1437, SI 2014/1439, SI 2014/1440, SI
2014/1441, SI 2014/1442, SI 2014/1443, SI
2014/1466, SI 2014/1467, SI 2014/1468, SI
2014/1469, SI 2014/1470, SI 2014/1471, SI
2014/1472, SI 2014/1473, SI 2014/1474, SI
2014/1475, SI 2014/1476, SI 2014/1477, SI
2014/1478, SI 2014/1479, SI 2014/1480, SI
2014/1481, SI 2014/1482, SI 2014/1483, SI
2014/1485, SI 2014/1486, SI 2014/1487, SI
2014/1488, SI 2014/1489, SI 2014/1490, SI
2014/1491, SI 2014/1493, SI 2014/1494, SI
2014/1496, SI 2014/1498, SI 2014/1499, SI
2014/1500, SI 2014/1501, SI 2014/1502, SI
2014/1504, SI 2014/1515, SI 2014/1516, SI
2014/1517, SI 2014/1518, SI 2014/1519, SI
2014/1520, SI 2014/1521, SI 2014/1522, SI
2014/1523, SI 2014/1524, SI 2014/1525, SI
2014/1526, SI 2014/1527, SI 2014/1529, SI
2014/1535, SI 2014/1536, SI 2014/1537, SI
2014/1538, SI 2014/1539, SI 2014/1540, SI
2014/1541, SI 2014/1542, SI 2014/1543, SI
2014/1544, SI 2014/1545, SI 2014/1546, SI
2014/1547, SI 2014/1548, SI 2014/1549, SI
2014/1550, SI 2014/1552, SI 2014/1553, SI
2014/1554, SI 2014/1564, SI 2014/1565, SI
2014/1566, SI 2014/1568, SI 2014/1569, SI
2014/1570, SI 2014/1571, SI 2014/1572, SI
2014/1573, SI 2014/1574, SI 2014/1575, SI
2014/1581, SI 2014/1582, SI 2014/1584, SI
2014/1585, SI 2014/1586, SI 2014/1587, SI
2014/1588, SI 2014/1589, SI 2014/1590, SI
2014/1591, SI 2014/1592, SI 2014/1595, SI
2014/1598, SI 2014/1600, SI 2014/1617, SI
2014/1618, SI 2014/1619, SI 2014/1630, SI
2014/1631, SI 2014/1632, SI 2014/1633, SI
2014/1634, SI 2014/1642, SI 2014/1644, SI
2014/1645, SI 2014/1646, SI 2014/1647, SI
2014/1649, SI 2014/1653, SI 2014/1654, SI
2014/1655, SI 2014/1658, SI 2014/1668, SI
2014/1669, SI 2014/1670, SI 2014/1671, SI
2014/1672, SI 2014/1673, SI 2014/1674, SI
2014/1676, SI 2014/1677, SI 2014/1678, SI
2014/1679, SI 2014/1680, SI 2014/1681, SI
2014/1682, SI 2014/1688, SI 2014/1689, SI
2014/1690, SI 2014/1691, SI 2014/1692, SI
2014/1693, SI 2014/1694, SI 2014/1695, SI
2014/1696, SI 2014/1697, SI 2014/1698, SI
2014/1699, SI 2014/1700, SI 2014/1701, SI
2014/1702, SI 2014/1703, SI 2014/1716, SI
2014/1717, SI 2014/1718, SI 2014/1719, SI
2014/1720, SI 2014/1721, SI 2014/1723, SI

2014/1724, SI 2014/1725, SI 2014/1726, SI
2014/1727, SI 2014/1728, SI 2014/1729, SI
2014/1730, SI 2014/1731, SI 2014/1732, SI
2014/1733, SI 2014/1734, SI 2014/1735, SI
2014/1736, SI 2014/1737, SI 2014/1738, SI
2014/1739, SI 2014/1741, SI 2014/1742, SI
2014/1744, SI 2014/1745, SI 2014/1746, SI
2014/1747, SI 2014/1748, SI 2014/1749, SI
2014/1750, SI 2014/1752, SI 2014/1753, SI
2014/1754, SI 2014/1755, SI 2014/1756, SI
2014/1757, SI 2014/1758, SI 2014/1765, SI
2014/1767, SI 2014/1774, SI 2014/1775, SI
2014/1776, SI 2014/1778, SI 2014/1779, SI
2014/1780, SI 2014/1781, SI 2014/1782, SI
2014/1785, SI 2014/1786, SI 2014/1839, SI
2014/1841, SI 2014/1844, SI 2014/1845, SI
2014/1853, SI 2014/1854, SI 2014/1856, SI
2014/1859, SI 2014/1861, SI 2014/1863, SI
2014/1864, SI 2014/1914, SI 2014/1927, SI
2014/1934, SI 2014/1935, SI 2014/1936, SI
2014/1944, SI 2014/1946, SI 2014/1947, SI
2014/1948, SI 2014/1949, SI 2014/1950, SI
2014/1951, SI 2014/1952, SI 2014/1953, SI
2014/1955, SI 2014/1956, SI 2014/1968, SI
2014/1969, SI 2014/1970, SI 2014/1972, SI
2014/1974, SI 2014/1978, SI 2014/1979, SI
2014/1980, SI 2014/1982, SI 2014/1983, SI
2014/1984, SI 2014/1985, SI 2014/1987, SI
2014/1988, SI 2014/1989, SI 2014/1990, SI
2014/1991, SI 2014/1992, SI 2014/1993, SI
2014/1994, SI 2014/2000, SI 2014/2002, SI
2014/2003, SI 2014/2004, SI 2014/2005, SI
2014/2008, SI 2014/2016, SI 2014/2017, SI
2014/2018, SI 2014/2019, SI 2014/2021, SI
2014/2022, SI 2014/2023, SI 2014/2024, SI
2014/2025, SI 2014/2028, SI 2014/2029, SI
2014/2030, SI 2014/2031, SI 2014/2032, SI
2014/2034, SI 2014/2035, SI 2014/2036, SI
2014/2037, SI 2014/2041, SI 2014/2046, SI
2014/2047, SI 2014/2048, SI 2014/2049, SI
2014/2050, SI 2014/2051, SI 2014/2052, SI
2014/2053, SI 2014/2055, SI 2014/2058, SI
2014/2061, SI 2014/2062, SI 2014/2063, SI
2014/2064, SI 2014/2065, SI 2014/2066, SI
2014/2073, SI 2014/2074, SI 2014/2075, SI
2014/2076, SI 2014/2078, SI 2014/2079, SI
2014/2082, SI 2014/2084, SI 2014/2085, SI
2014/2086, SI 2014/2088, SI 2014/2089, SI
2014/2090, SI 2014/2091, SI 2014/2092, SI
2014/2093, SI 2014/2094, SI 2014/2098, SI
2014/2099, SI 2014/2100, SI 2014/2101, SI

2014/2102, SI 2014/2104, SI 2014/2105, SI
2014/2106, SI 2014/2107, SI 2014/2108, SI
2014/2109, SI 2014/2110, SI 2014/2111, SI
2014/2129, SI 2014/2131, SI 2014/2132, SI
2014/2133, SI 2014/2134, SI 2014/2135, SI
2014/2136, SI 2014/2137, SI 2014/2138, SI
2014/2139, SI 2014/2140, SI 2014/2142, SI
2014/2143, SI 2014/2144, SI 2014/2145, SI
2014/2146, SI 2014/2149, SI 2014/2150, SI
2014/2152, SI 2014/2153, SI 2014/2154, SI
2014/2155, SI 2014/2156, SI 2014/2157, SI
2014/2159, SI 2014/2160, SI 2014/2161, SI
2014/2163, SI 2014/2164, SI 2014/2165, SI
2014/2166, SI 2014/2167, SI 2014/2168, SI
2014/2170, SI 2014/2171, SI 2014/2173, SI
2014/2174, SI 2014/2175, SI 2014/2176, SI
2014/2177, SI 2014/2180, SI 2014/2181, SI
2014/2182, SI 2014/2183, SI 2014/2184, SI
2014/2185, SI 2014/2186, SI 2014/2187, SI
2014/2188, SI 2014/2189, SI 2014/2190, SI
2014/2191, SI 2014/2192, SI 2014/2193, SI
2014/2194, SI 2014/2195, SI 2014/2196, SI
2014/2197, SI 2014/2199, SI 2014/2200, SI
2014/2201, SI 2014/2202, SI 2014/2203, SI
2014/2204, SI 2014/2205, SI 2014/2207, SI
2014/2208, SI 2014/2209, SI 2014/2211, SI
2014/2212, SI 2014/2213, SI 2014/2214, SI
2014/2215, SI 2014/2217, SI 2014/2218, SI
2014/2219, SI 2014/2220, SI 2014/2221, SI
2014/2222, SI 2014/2223, SI 2014/2224, SI
2014/2226, SI 2014/2227, SI 2014/2229, SI
2014/2230, SI 2014/2231, SI 2014/2232, SI
2014/2233, SI 2014/2239, SI 2014/2240, SI
2014/2241, SI 2014/2242, SI 2014/2243, SI
2014/2244, SI 2014/2245, SI 2014/2246, SI
2014/2247, SI 2014/2248, SI 2014/2249, SI
2014/2250, SI 2014/2253, SI 2014/2255, SI
2014/2256, SI 2014/2258, SI 2014/2259, SI
2014/2261, SI 2014/2262, SI 2014/2265, SI
2014/2266, SI 2014/2267, SI 2014/2268, SI
2014/2271, SI 2014/2272, SI 2014/2273, SI
2014/2274, SI 2014/2275, SI 2014/2276, SI
2014/2277, SI 2014/2278, SI 2014/2279, SI
2014/2280, SI 2014/2282, SI 2014/2283, SI
2014/2284, SI 2014/2285, SI 2014/2286, SI
2014/2287, SI 2014/2288, SI 2014/2289, SI
2014/2290, SI 2014/2292, SI 2014/2293, SI
2014/2294, SI 2014/2296, SI 2014/2297, SI
2014/2298, SI 2014/2299, SI 2014/2300, SI
2014/2301, SI 2014/2302, SI 2014/2307, SI
2014/2308, SI 2014/2310, SI 2014/2311, SI

2014/2312, SI 2014/2313, SI 2014/2314, SI
2014/2315, SI 2014/2316, SI 2014/2317, SI
2014/2318, SI 2014/2322, SI 2014/2323, SI
2014/2324, SI 2014/2325, SI 2014/2327, SI
2014/2331, SI 2014/2332, SI 2014/2333, SI
2014/2334, SI 2014/2335, SI 2014/2343, SI
2014/2344, SI 2014/2345, SI 2014/2346, SI
2014/2347, SI 2014/2348, SI 2014/2349, SI
2014/2350, SI 2014/2351, SI 2014/2352, SI
2014/2353, SI 2014/2354, SI 2014/2360, SI
2014/2390, SI 2014/2408, SI 2014/2412, SI
2014/2413, SI 2014/2414, SI 2014/2415, SI
2014/2419, SI 2014/2421, SI 2014/2424, SI
2014/2425, SI 2014/2426, SI 2014/2427, SI
2014/2428, SI 2014/2429, SI 2014/2431, SI
2014/2432, SI 2014/2433, SI 2014/2435, SI
2014/2442, SI 2014/2443, SI 2014/2446, SI
2014/2447, SI 2014/2449, SI 2014/2451, SI
2014/2452, SI 2014/2453, SI 2014/2455, SI
2014/2463, SI 2014/2464, SI 2014/2465, SI
2014/2466, SI 2014/2467, SI 2014/2468, SI
2014/2470, SI 2014/2471, SI 2014/2472, SI
2014/2474, SI 2014/2476, SI 2014/2477, SI
2014/2478, SI 2014/2479, SI 2014/2480, SI
2014/2482, SI 2014/2484, SI 2014/2487, SI
2014/2488, SI 2014/2489, SI 2014/2490, SI
2014/2491, SI 2014/2492, SI 2014/2493, SI
2014/2494, SI 2014/2495, SI 2014/2496, SI
2014/2497, SI 2014/2498, SI 2014/2499, SI
2014/2500, SI 2014/2501, SI 2014/2502, SI
2014/2503, SI 2014/2504, SI 2014/2505, SI
2014/2506, SI 2014/2507, SI 2014/2508, SI
2014/2509, SI 2014/2510, SI 2014/2512, SI
2014/2513, SI 2014/2514, SI 2014/2515, SI
2014/2516, SI 2014/2517, SI 2014/2521, SI
2014/2525, SI 2014/2526, SI 2014/2527, SI
2014/2528, SI 2014/2529, SI 2014/2530, SI
2014/2531, SI 2014/2532, SI 2014/2533, SI
2014/2534, SI 2014/2535, SI 2014/2536, SI
2014/2537, SI 2014/2538, SI 2014/2539, SI
2014/2540, SI 2014/2541, SI 2014/2542, SI
2014/2543, SI 2014/2544, SI 2014/2545, SI
2014/2546, SI 2014/2547, SI 2014/2548, SI
2014/2549, SI 2014/2550, SI 2014/2551, SI
2014/2552, SI 2014/2556, SI 2014/2560, SI
2014/2561, SI 2014/2563, SI 2014/2564, SI
2014/2565, SI 2014/2566, SI 2014/2567, SI
2014/2568, SI 2014/2569, SI 2014/2570, SI
2014/2571, SI 2014/2572, SI 2014/2573, SI
2014/2574, SI 2014/2575, SI 2014/2576, SI
2014/2577, SI 2014/2578, SI 2014/2579, SI

2014/2581, SI 2014/2582, SI 2014/2583, SI
2014/2584, SI 2014/2585, SI 2014/2586, SI
2014/2592, SI 2014/2593, SI 2014/2595, SI
2014/2596, SI 2014/2597, SI 2014/2598, SI
2014/2599, SI 2014/2600, SI 2014/2601, SI
2014/2602, SI 2014/2605, SI 2014/2606, SI
2014/2607, SI 2014/2608, SI 2014/2611, SI
2014/2614, SI 2014/2615, SI 2014/2616, SI
2014/2617, SI 2014/2618, SI 2014/2619, SI
2014/2620, SI 2014/2621, SI 2014/2622, SI
2014/2623, SI 2014/2624, SI 2014/2625, SI
2014/2626, SI 2014/2627, SI 2014/2628, SI
2014/2629, SI 2014/2630, SI 2014/2633, SI
2014/2636, SI 2014/2638, SI 2014/2639, SI
2014/2640, SI 2014/2641, SI 2014/2642, SI
2014/2643, SI 2014/2644, SI 2014/2645, SI
2014/2647, SI 2014/2648, SI 2014/2649, SI
2014/2654, SI 2014/2655, SI 2014/2656, SI
2014/2659, SI 2014/2661, SI 2014/2662, SI
2014/2663, SI 2014/2664, SI 2014/2666, SI
2014/2668, SI 2014/2674, SI 2014/2675, SI
2014/2681, SI 2014/2682, SI 2014/2683, SI
2014/2684, SI 2014/2685, SI 2014/2686, SI
2014/2688, SI 2014/2690, SI 2014/2695, SI
2014/2698, SI 2014/2699, SI 2014/2700, SI
2014/2723, SI 2014/2724, SI 2014/2728, SI
2014/2729, SI 2014/2730, SI 2014/2731, SI
2014/2732, SI 2014/2733, SI 2014/2734, SI
2014/2736, SI 2014/2737, SI 2014/2738, SI
2014/2739, SI 2014/2740, SI 2014/2741, SI
2014/2742, SI 2014/2743, SI 2014/2744, SI
2014/2745, SI 2014/2750, SI 2014/2751, SI
2014/2752, SI 2014/2755, SI 2014/2756, SI
2014/2757, SI 2014/2758, SI 2014/2759, SI
2014/2760, SI 2014/2762, SI 2014/2763, SI
2014/2767, SI 2014/2769, SI 2014/2770, SI
2014/2772, SI 2014/2774, SI 2014/2778, SI
2014/2779, SI 2014/2781, SI 2014/2782, SI
2014/2783, SI 2014/2784, SI 2014/2785, SI
2014/2786, SI 2014/2787, SI 2014/2788, SI
2014/2789, SI 2014/2790, SI 2014/2791, SI
2014/2792, SI 2014/2794, SI 2014/2795, SI
2014/2797, SI 2014/2798, SI 2014/2799, SI
2014/2800, SI 2014/2801, SI 2014/2802, SI
2014/2803, SI 2014/2804, SI 2014/2805, SI
2014/2806, SI 2014/2808, SI 2014/2809, SI
2014/2810, SI 2014/2811, SI 2014/2812, SI
2014/2813, SI 2014/2814, SI 2014/2815, SI
2014/2817, SI 2014/2818, SI 2014/2820, SI
2014/2826, SI 2014/2831, SI 2014/2834, SI
2014/2835, SI 2014/2836, SI 2014/2837, SI

2014/2838, SI 2014/2851, SI 2014/2853, SI
2014/2859, SI 2014/2860, SI 2014/2869, SI
2014/2870, SI 2014/2876, SI 2014/2877, SI
2014/2878, SI 2014/2891, SI 2014/2892, SI
2014/2895, SI 2014/2900, SI 2014/2901, SI
2014/2902, SI 2014/2903, SI 2014/2905, SI
2014/2906, SI 2014/2909, SI 2014/2910, SI
2014/2911, SI 2014/2913, SI 2014/2914, SI
2014/2915, SI 2014/2930, SI 2014/2940, SI
2014/2941, SI 2014/2943, SI 2014/2944, SI
2014/2945, SI 2014/2951, SI 2014/2952, SI
2014/2953, SI 2014/2954, SI 2014/2955, SI
2014/2956, SI 2014/2957, SI 2014/2959, SI
2014/2960, SI 2014/2961, SI 2014/2962, SI
2014/2963, SI 2014/2964, SI 2014/2965, SI
2014/2966, SI 2014/2967, SI 2014/2968, SI
2014/2969, SI 2014/2970, SI 2014/2971, SI
2014/2972, SI 2014/2973, SI 2014/2974, SI
2014/2976, SI 2014/2977, SI 2014/2978, SI
2014/2979, SI 2014/2980, SI 2014/2981, SI
2014/2982, SI 2014/2983, SI 2014/2984, SI
2014/2985, SI 2014/2986, SI 2014/2987, SI
2014/2988, SI 2014/2990, SI 2014/2991, SI
2014/2992, SI 2014/2995, SI 2014/2996, SI
2014/2997, SI 2014/2998, SI 2014/2999, SI
2014/3000, SI 2014/3002, SI 2014/3003, SI
2014/3004, SI 2014/3005, SI 2014/3006, SI
2014/3008, SI 2014/3009, SI 2014/3010, SI
2014/3011, SI 2014/3012, SI 2014/3013, SI
2014/3014, SI 2014/3015, SI 2014/3016, SI
2014/3017, SI 2014/3019, SI 2014/3020, SI
2014/3021, SI 2014/3022, SI 2014/3023, SI
2014/3024, SI 2014/3025, SI 2014/3028, SI
2014/3029, SI 2014/3030, SI 2014/3031, SI
2014/3032, SI 2014/3034, SI 2014/3035, SI
2014/3036, SI 2014/3039, SI 2014/3040, SI
2014/3041, SI 2014/3042, SI 2014/3043, SI
2014/3044, SI 2014/3045, SI 2014/3046, SI
2014/3047, SI 2014/3048, SI 2014/3049, SI
2014/3063, SI 2014/3064, SI 2014/3065, SI
2014/3069, SI 2014/3071, SI 2014/3072, SI
2014/3113, SI 2014/3114, SI 2014/3115, SI
2014/3121, SI 2014/3122, SI 2014/3123, SI
2014/3129, SI 2014/3130, SI 2014/3131, SI
2014/3132, SI 2014/3136, SI 2014/3143, SI
2014/3144, SI 2014/3145, SI 2014/3146, SI
2014/3147, SI 2014/3148, SI 2014/3149, SI
2014/3150, SI 2014/3151, SI 2014/3152, SI
2014/3153, SI 2014/3154, SI 2014/3164, SI
2014/3165, SI 2014/3166, SI 2014/3167, SI
2014/3170, SI 2014/3171, SI 2014/3172, SI

2014/3173, SI 2014/3174, SI 2014/3175, SI
2014/3176, SI 2014/3177, SI 2014/3179, SI
2014/3180, SI 2014/3182, SI 2014/3198, SI
2014/3201, SI 2014/3202, SI 2014/3203, SSI
2014/3208, SI 2014/3353, SI 2014/3355, SI
2014/3356, SI 2014/3357, SI 2014/3358, SI
2014/3359, SI 2014/3360, SI 2014/3365, SI
2014/3366, SI 2014/3367, SI 2014/3368, SI
2014/3369, SI 2014/3370, SI 2014/3371, SI
2014/3372, SI 2014/3373, SI 2014/3374, SI
2014/3375, SI 2014/3376, SI 2014/3377, SI
2014/3378, SI 2014/3379, SI 2014/3380, SI
2014/3381, SI 2014/3382, SI 2014/3383, SI
2014/3386, SI 2014/3387, SI 2014/3388, SI
2014/3389, SI 2014/3390, SI 2014/3391, SI
2014/3392, SI 2014/3393, SI 2014/3394, SI
2014/3395, SI 2014/3396, SI 2014/3397, SI
2014/3398, SI 2014/3399, SI 2014/3400, SI
2014/3403, SI 2014/3404, SI 2014/3405, SI
2014/3406, SI 2014/3407, SI 2014/3408, SI
2014/3409, SI 2014/3410, SI 2014/3411, SI
2014/3412, SI 2014/3413, SI 2014/3414, SI
2014/3415, SI 2014/3416, SI 2014/3417, SI
2014/3418, SI 2014/3419, SI 2014/3420, SI
2014/3421, SI 2014/3422, SI 2014/3423, SI
2014/3424, SI 2014/3425, SI 2014/3426, SI
2014/3427, SI 2014/3428, SI 2014/3429, SI
2014/3430, SI 2014/3431, SI 2014/3432, SI
2014/3433, SI 2014/3434, SI 2014/3435, SI
2014/3436, SI 2014/3437, SI 2014/3438, SI
2014/3440, SI 2014/3441, SI 2014/3442, SI
2014/3443, SI 2014/3444, SI 2014/3445, SI
2014/3446, SI 2014/3447, SI 2014/3448, SI
2014/3449, SI 2014/3450, SI 2014/3451, SI
2014/3452, SI 2014/3453, SI 2014/3454, SI
2014/3455, SI 2014/3456, SI 2014/3457, SI
2014/3458, SI 2014/3459, SI 2014/3460, SI
2014/3461, SI 2014/3462, SI 2014/3463, SI
2014/3464, SI 2014/3465, SI 2014/3467, SI
2014/3468, SI 2014/3469, SI 2014/3470, SI
2014/3471, SI 2014/3473, SI 2014/3474, SI
2014/3475, SI 2014/3476, SI 2014/3477, SI
2014/3478, SI 2014/3479, SI 2014/3480, SI
2014/3481, SI 2014/3482, SI 2014/3483, SI
2014/3484, SI 2014/3485, SI 2014/3488, SI
2014/3489, SI 2014/3490, SI 2014/3491, SI
2014/3494, SI 2014/3496, SI 2014/3497, SI
2014/3498, SI 2014/3499, SI 2014/3500, SI
2014/3502, SI 2014/3504, SI 2014/3505, SI
2014/3506, SI 2014/3507, SI 2014/3509, SSI
2014/10, SSI 2014/11, SSI 2014/16, SSI

2014/17, SSI 2014/18, SSI 2014/19, SSI
2014/20, SSI 2014/45, SSI 2014/46, SSI
2014/47, SSI 2014/48, SSI 2014/75, SSI
2014/76, SSI 2014/77, SSI 2014/78, SSI
2014/82, SSI 2014/104, SSI 2014/105, SSI
2014/106, SSI 2014/107, SSI 2014/120, SSI
2014/124, SSI 2014/128, SSI 2014/133, SSI
2014/134, SSI 2014/135, SSI 2014/136, SSI
2014/138, SSI 2014/156, SSI 2014/168, SSI
2014/177, SSI 2014/178, SSI 2014/179, SSI
2014/180, SSI 2014/181, SSI 2014/182, SSI
2014/195, SSI 2014/197, SSI 2014/198, SSI
2014/204, SSI 2014/206, SSI 2014/207, SSI
2014/208, SSI 2014/209, SSI 2014/216, SSI
2014/223, SSI 2014/228, SSI 2014/234, SSI
2014/235, SSI 2014/236, SSI 2014/237, SSI
2014/240, SSI 2014/241, SSI 2014/244, SSI
2014/245, SSI 2014/248, SSI 2014/253, SSI
2014/254, SSI 2014/255, SSI 2014/256, SSI
2014/259, SSI 2014/266, SSI 2014/270, SSI
2014/271, SSI 2014/273, SSI 2014/275, SSI
2014/276, SSI 2014/286, SSI 2014/299, SSI
2014/329, SSI 2014/330, SSI 2014/331, SSI
2014/332, SSI 2014/340, SSI 2014/381, SSI
2014/382, SSI 2014/383, SSI 2014/384, SSI
2014/385
s.15, applied: SI 2014/3420 Art.9
s.15, varied: SSI 2014/92 Art.2
s.15, enabling: SI 2014/338, SI 2014/398, SI
2014/993, SI 2014/1164, SI 2014/1680, SI
2014/1689, SI 2014/2221, SI 2014/2636, SI
2014/2984, SI 2014/2985, SI 2014/3064, SSI
2014/228, SSI 2014/241, SSI 2014/245
s.16A, applied: SSI 2014/175, SSI 2014/199,
SSI 2014/203, SSI 2014/205, SSI 2014/211,
SSI 2014/280, SSI 2014/288, SSI 2014/380
s.16A, enabling: SI 2014/1036, SI
2014/1380, SI 2014/1567, SI 2014/1656, SI
2014/1743, SI 2014/1783, SI 2014/1784, SI
2014/1846, SI 2014/1851, SI 2014/1852, SI
2014/1967, SI 2014/2001, SI 2014/2056, SI
2014/2251, SI 2014/2281, SI 2014/2326, SI
2014/2416, SI 2014/2423, SI 2014/2989, SI
2014/2993, SI 2014/2994, SSI 2014/175,
SSI 2014/199, SSI 2014/203, SSI 2014/205,
SSI 2014/211, SSI 2014/280, SSI 2014/288,
SSI 2014/380
s.17, enabling: SI 2014/790
s.26, applied: SI 2014/3352 Reg.7

s.32, applied: SI 2014/909 Art.38, SI
2014/2269 Art.37, SI 2014/2384 Art.18, SI
2014/2637 Art.15
s.45, see *R. (on the application of Attfield) v
Barnet LBC* [2013] EWHC 2089 (Admin),
[2014] 1 All E.R. 304 (QBD (Admin)), Lang
J
s.46, varied: SSI 2014/84 Sch.3 para.1, SSI
2014/169 Sch.3 para.1
s.55, varied: SSI 2014/84 Sch.3 para.2, SSI
2014/169 Sch.3 para.2
s.63A, applied: SSI 2014/85 Reg.2, SSI
2014/170 Reg.2
s.63A, varied: SSI 2014/84 Sch.3 para.3, SSI
2014/169 Sch.3 para.3
s.63A, enabling: SSI 2014/85, SSI 2014/170
s.64, applied: SI 2014/56 Art.3, SI 2014/60
Art.4, SI 2014/75 Art.3, SI 2014/103 Art.4,
SI 2014/156 Art.4, SI 2014/157 Art.4, SI
2014/172 Art.4, SI 2014/224 Art.3, SI
2014/228 Art.4, SI 2014/283 Art.3, SI
2014/295 Art.4, SI 2014/310 Art.22, SI
2014/311 Art.4, SI 2014/365 Art.4, SI
2014/392 Art.4, SI 2014/393 Art.4, SI
2014/425 Art.3, SI 2014/429 Art.4, SI
2014/674 Art.4, SI 2014/679 Art.3, SI
2014/734 Art.3, SI 2014/960 Art.3, SI
2014/984 Art.3, SI 2014/989 Art.4, SI
2014/999 Art.5, SI 2014/1018 Art.3, SI
2014/1072 Art.3, SI 2014/1079 Art.3, SI
2014/1081 Art.3, SI 2014/1122 Art.3, SI
2014/1150 Art.4, SI 2014/1166 Art.5, SI
2014/1175 Art.3, SI 2014/1214 Art.4, SI
2014/1216 Art.4, SI 2014/1298 Art.3, SI
2014/1299 Art.3, SI 2014/1320 Art.3, SI
2014/1336 Art.2, SI 2014/1339 Art.3, SI
2014/1342 Art.4, SI 2014/1343 Art.4, SI
2014/1346 Art.6, SI 2014/1392 Art.4, SI
2014/1496 Art.3, SI 2014/1547 Art.3, SI
2014/1647 Art.3, SI 2014/1658 Art.3, SI
2014/1690 Art.6, SI 2014/1735 Art.4, SI
2014/1745 Art.4, SI 2014/1927 Art.3, SI
2014/1950 Art.4, SI 2014/1968 Art.3, SI
2014/1979 Art.4, SI 2014/2041 Art.4, SI
2014/2048 Art.3, SI 2014/2078 Art.5, SI
2014/2145 Art.3, SI 2014/2188 Art.4, SI
2014/2253 Art.3, SI 2014/2256 Art.3, SI
2014/2292 Art.4, SI 2014/2293 Art.4, SI
2014/2312 Art.3, SI 2014/2314 Art.3, SI
2014/2324 Art.3, SI 2014/2345 Art.3, SI
2014/2351 Art.3, SI 2014/2352 Art.4, SI

2014/2414 Art.4, SI 2014/2428 Art.3, SI
2014/2432 Art.4, SI 2014/2471 Art.4, SI
2014/2480 Art.4, SI 2014/2489 Art.5, SI
2014/2499 Art.3, SI 2014/2512 Art.3, SI
2014/2517 Art.4, SI 2014/2521 Art.5, SI
2014/2538 Art.4, SI 2014/2547 Art.5, SI
2014/2571 Art.3, SI 2014/2600 Art.4, SI
2014/2626 Art.4, SI 2014/2633 Art.4, SI
2014/2645 Art.4, SI 2014/2663 Art.3, SI
2014/2743 Art.4, SI 2014/2752 Art.4, SI
2014/2779 Art.3, SI 2014/2782 Art.4, SI
2014/2785 Art.3, SI 2014/2820 Art.4, SI
2014/2876 Art.3, SI 2014/2967 Art.3, SI
2014/2969 Art.3, SI 2014/3003 Art.4, SI
2014/3030 Art.3, SI 2014/3031 Art.4, SI
2014/3034 Art.3, SI 2014/3044 Art.4, SI
2014/3045 Art.3, SI 2014/3047 Art.4, SI
2014/3048 Art.4, SI 2014/3123 Art.5, SI
2014/3132 Art.3, SI 2014/3151 Art.3, SI
2014/3154 Art.3, SI 2014/3375 Art.4, SI
2014/3386 Art.3, SI 2014/3476 Art.4, SI
2014/3497 Art.4, SSI 2014/197 Art.3
s.65, applied: SI 2014/310 Art.22
s.81, see *Cusick (Gary) v McPherson* [2014]
HCJAC 39, 2014 G.W.D. 17-314 (HCJ),
The Lord Justice Clerk (Carloway)
s.81, applied: SI 2014/136 Art.6, SI
2014/1011 Art.2, SI 2014/1013 Art.2, SI
2014/1027 Art.2, SI 2014/1028, SI
2014/1034 Art.5, SI 2014/1046 Art.2, SI
2014/1047 Art.2, SI 2014/2305 Art.2, SI
2014/2855 Art.2, SSI 2014/247 Art.2
s.82, enabling: SI 2014/136, SI 2014/1011,
SI 2014/1013, SI 2014/1027, SI 2014/1028,
SI 2014/1034, SI 2014/1046, SI 2014/1047,
SI 2014/1455, SI 2014/1650, SI 2014/2305,
SI 2014/2855, SSI 2014/247
s.83, enabling: SI 2014/136, SI 2014/1011,
SI 2014/1013, SI 2014/1027, SI 2014/1028,
SI 2014/1034, SI 2014/1046, SI 2014/1047,
SI 2014/1455, SI 2014/1650, SI 2014/2305,
SI 2014/2855, SSI 2014/247
s.84, applied: SI 2014/2519, SI 2014/2637
Art.11, SSI 2014/96, SSI 2014/97, SSI
2014/125, SSI 2014/126, SSI 2014/198, SSI
2014/204, Sch.3 para.2
s.84, enabling: SI 2014/136, SI 2014/348, SI
2014/726, SI 2014/1033, SI 2014/1034, SI
2014/1041, SI 2014/1455, SI 2014/1503, SI
2014/1650, SI 2014/1722, SI 2014/2033, SI
2014/2148, SI 2014/2198, SI 2014/2519, SI

2014/2819, SI 2014/2855, SI 2014/2893, SI
2014/3018, SI 2014/3116, SI 2014/3385, SI
2014/3402, SI 2014/3439, SSI 2014/96, SSI
2014/97, SSI 2014/125, SSI 2014/126, SSI
2014/198, SSI 2014/204, SSI 2014/222
s.86, applied: SSI 2014/274
s.86, enabling: SSI 2014/274
s.89, see *Cusick (Gary) v McPherson* [2014]
HCJAC 39, 2014 G.W.D. 17-314 (HCJ),
The Lord Justice Clerk (Carloway)
s.99, applied: SSI 2014/85 Reg.2
s.99, referred to: SSI 2014/170 Reg.2
s.99, enabling: SI 2014/1388
s.101, varied: SSI 2014/84 Sch.3 para.4, SSI
2014/169 Sch.3 para.4
s.102, varied: SSI 2014/84 Sch.3 para.5, SSI
2014/169 Sch.3 para.5
s.112, applied: SI 2014/1610 r.4_1, r.4_7
s.117, amended: 2014 asp 17 s.4
s.122, see *AA and Sons Ltd v Slough BC*
[2014] EWHC 1127 (Admin), [2014] R.T.R.
29 (QBD (Admin)), Green J; see *Isle of
Wight Council v Revenue and Customs
Commissioners* [2014] UKUT 446 (TCC),
[2014] B.V.C. 538 (UT (Tax)), Proudman J;
see *R. (on the application of Attfield) v
Barnet LBC* [2013] EWHC 2089 (Admin),
[2014] 1 All E.R. 304 (QBD (Admin)), Lang
J
s.122, enabling: SI 2014/2655
s.122A, enabling: SI 2014/1018, SI
2014/1164, SI 2014/1172, SI 2014/2243, SI
2014/2304, SI 2014/2306, SI 2014/2346, SI
2014/3384, SI 2014/3385, SI 2014/3401, SI
2014/3402
s.124, enabling: SI 2014/348, SI 2014/1059,
SI 2014/1065, SI 2014/1455, SI 2014/1650,
SI 2014/2308, SI 2014/2892, SI 2014/2893,
SI 2014/2927, SI 2014/3116, SI 2014/3377,
SSI 2014/97, SSI 2014/198, SSI 2014/204,
SSI 2014/222, SSI 2014/228, SSI 2014/269
s.126, enabling: SI 2014/2519
s.134, applied: SI 2014/790, SI 2014/1388,
SSI 2014/85, SSI 2014/170
s.134, varied: SSI 2014/84 Sch.3 para.6, SSI
2014/169 Sch.3 para.6
s.138, referred to: SSI 2014/378 Art.2
s.140, applied: SSI 2014/104 Art.4, SSI
2014/105 Art.4, SSI 2014/106 Art.4, SSI
2014/107 Art.4, SSI 2014/124 Art.3, SSI
2014/179 Art.4, SSI 2014/206 Art.4, SSI

2014/207 Art.4, SSI 2014/208 Art.4, SSI
2014/209 Art.4, SSI 2014/271 Art.4, SSI
2014/286 Art.3, SSI 2014/381 Art.4, SSI
2014/382 Art.4, SSI 2014/383 Art.4, SSI
2014/384 Art.4
s.142, varied: SSI 2014/84 Sch.3 para.7, SSI
2014/169 Sch.3 para.7
Sch.5, amended: SI 2014/3302 Sch.1 para.4
Sch.6 Part I, amended: SSI 2014/274 Reg.2
Sch.6 Part I, referred to: SSI 2014/274
Reg.2, Reg.3
Sch.9 Part IV para.27, enabling: SI
2014/136, SI 2014/137, SI 2014/348, SI
2014/405, SI 2014/420, SI 2014/741, SI
2014/1027, SI 2014/1033, SI 2014/1034, SI
2014/1046, SI 2014/1059, SI 2014/1065, SI
2014/1164, SI 2014/1455, SI 2014/1650, SI
2014/1654, SI 2014/1785, SI 2014/2008, SI
2014/2037, SI 2014/2102, SI 2014/2148, SI
2014/2173, SI 2014/2198, SI 2014/2272, SI
2014/2304, SI 2014/2306, SI 2014/2308, SI
2014/2353, SI 2014/2412, SI 2014/2469, SI
2014/2488, SI 2014/2518, SI 2014/2519, SI
2014/2541, SI 2014/2549, SI 2014/2675, SI
2014/2699, SI 2014/2892, SI 2014/2893, SI
2014/2927, SI 2014/2946, SI 2014/2999, SI
2014/3116, SI 2014/3377, SI 2014/3384, SI
2014/3402, SI 2014/3473, SSI 2014/97, SSI
2014/198, SSI 2014/204, SSI 2014/222, SSI
2014/228, SSI 2014/247, SSI 2014/269

28. County Courts Act 1984
s.8, applied: SI 2014/602 Art.2
s.14, see *Chelmsford County Court v Ramet*
[2014] EWHC 56 (Fam), [2014] 2 F.L.R.
1081 (Fam Div), Sir James Munby PFD
s.15, see *Cussens v Realreed Ltd* [2013]
EWHC 1229 (QB), [2014] 1 W.L.R. 275
(QBD), Andrew Smith J
s.38, applied: SI 2014/982, SI 2014/982
Reg.3
s.38, enabling: SI 2014/982
s.53, applied: SI 2014/840 Sch.2
s.74, amended: SI 2014/1773 Art.2
s.74, applied: SI 2014/2604 r.9
s.77, applied: 2014 c.14 s.42
s.118, see *Chelmsford County Court v Ramet*
[2014] EWHC 56 (Fam), [2014] 2 F.L.R.
1081 (Fam Div), Sir James Munby PFD
s.145, enabling: SI 2014/503
Sch.2 Part V para.29, repealed: 2014 c.14
Sch.7

37. Child Abduction Act 1984
see *Button v Salama* [2013] EWHC 4152
(Fam), [2014] 2 F.L.R. 488 (Fam Div),
Holman J
s.1, amended: 2014 c.6 Sch.2 para.47
39. Video Recordings Act 1984
s.2, amended: SI 2014/2097 Reg.2
s.2, enabling: SI 2014/2097
s.3, amended: SI 2014/2097 Reg.3
s.3, enabling: SI 2014/2097
s.22A, applied: SI 2014/2097
s.22A, enabling: SI 2014/2097
42. Matrimonial and Family Proceedings Act 1984
see *MT v T (Marriage: Strike-Out)* [2013]
EWHC 2061 (Fam), [2014] 1 F.L.R. 1352
(Fam Div), Charles J
Pt III., see *M v M (Costs)* [2013] EWHC
3372 (Fam), [2014] 1 F.L.R. 499 (Fam Div),
Eleanor King J; see *M v M* [2013] EWHC
2534 (Fam), [2014] 1 F.L.R. 439 (Fam Div),
Eleanor King J; see *Sharbatly v Shagroon*
[2013] EWHC 3756 (Fam), [2014] 2 F.L.R.
209 (Fam Div), Parker J
s.12, applied: SI 2014/840 Sch.1
s.18, see *M v M* [2013] EWHC 2534 (Fam),
[2014] 1 F.L.R. 439 (Fam Div), Eleanor
King J
s.22, amended: 2014 c.6 s.18
s.31D, applied: SI 2014/840, SI 2014/3297
s.31D, enabling: SI 2014/840, SI 2014/3297
s.31E, applied: SI 2014/840 Sch.2
s.31G, referred to: SI 2014/603 Sch.1
s.31H, applied: SI 2014/833
s.31H, enabling: SI 2014/833
s.31K, applied: SI 2014/602 Art.2
s.31O, applied: SI 2014/603, SI 2014/841
s.31O, referred to: SI 2014/603 r.3
s.31O, enabling: SI 2014/603, SI 2014/841
s.31P, applied: SI 2014/603
s.31P, enabling: SI 2014/603, SI 2014/841
47. Repatriation of Prisoners Act 1984
s.3A, amended: SI 2014/3141 Reg.114
s.6A, amended: SI 2014/3141 Reg.114
s.6B, amended: SI 2014/3141 Reg.114
s.6C, substituted: SI 2014/3141 Reg.114
s.6D, amended: SI 2014/3141 Reg.114
s.8, amended: SI 2014/3141 Reg.114
s.9, amended: SI 2014/3141 Reg.114
s.9, repealed (in part): SI 2014/3141 Reg.114

51. Inheritance Tax Act 1984
  s.8, disapplied: 2014 c.26 Sch.25 para.2
  s.8A, see *Loring v Woodland Trust* [2013]
  EWHC 4400 (Ch), [2014] 2 All E.R. 836
  (Ch D), Asplin J
  s.13A, added: 2014 c.26 Sch.37 para.10
  s.17, repealed (in part): 2014 c.16 Sch.4
  para.4
  s.21, see *AK (Gift Application), Re* [2014]
  C.O.P.L.R. 180 (CP), Senior Judge Denzil
  Lush
  s.23, see *Giles v Royal National Institute for
  the Blind* [2014] EWHC 1373 (Ch), [2014]
  S.T.C. 1631 (Ch D), Barling J; see *Routier v
  Revenue and Customs Commissioners*
  [2014] EWHC 3010 (Ch), [2014] B.T.C. 42
  (Ch D), Rose J
  s.28A, added: 2014 c.26 Sch.37 para.11
  s.29A, amended: 2014 c.26 Sch.37 para.12
  s.64, amended: 2014 c.26 Sch.25 para.4
  s.66, amended: 2014 c.26 Sch.25 para.4
  s.72, amended: 2014 c.26 Sch.37 para.13
  s.75A, added: 2014 c.26 Sch.37 para.14
  s.86, amended: 2014 c.26 Sch.37 para.15
  s.89, applied: 2014 c.26 s.291
  s.104, see *Best v Revenue and Customs
  Commissioners* [2014] UKFTT 77 (TC),
  [2014] W.T.L.R. 409 (FTT (Tax)), Judge
  Jonathan Cannan
  s.142, see *Giles v Royal National Institute
  for the Blind* [2014] EWHC 1373 (Ch),
  [2014] S.T.C. 1631 (Ch D), Barling J; see
  Kevern v Ayres [2014] EWHC 165 (Ch),
  [2014] W.T.L.R. 441 (Ch D), David
  Donaldson QC
  s.144, amended: 2014 c.26 Sch.37 para.16
  s.145, repealed: 2014 c.16 Sch.4 para.4
  s.162AA, added: 2014 c.26 Sch.25 para.3
  s.162C, amended: 2014 c.26 Sch.25 para.3
  s.175A, amended: 2014 c.26 Sch.25 para.3
  s.216, amended: 2014 c.26 Sch.25 para.5
  s.226, amended: 2014 c.26 Sch.25 para.5
  s.227, applied: 2014 c.26 s.223
  s.233, amended: 2014 c.26 Sch.25 para.5
  s.240, amended: 2014 c.26 s.277
  s.242, amended: 2014 c.26 s.224
  s.256, applied: SI 2014/488
  s.256, enabling: SI 2014/488
54. Roads (Scotland) Act 1984
  s.5, enabling: SSI 2014/27, SSI 2014/215,
  SSI 2014/309

  s.9, applied: SSI 2014/238
  s.9, enabling: SSI 2014/238
  s.12, applied: SSI 2014/311
  s.12, enabling: SSI 2014/246, SSI 2014/311
  s.20A, applied: SSI 2014/309, SSI 2014/311
  s.55A, applied: SSI 2014/309, SSI 2014/311
  s.70, enabling: SSI 2014/246, SSI 2014/311
  s.71, applied: SSI 2014/246
  s.143, enabling: SSI 2014/238
  s.145, enabling: SSI 2014/246
  Sch.1 Part I, applied: SSI 2014/27, SSI
  2014/215, SSI 2014/238, SSI 2014/246
  Sch.1 Part III, applied: SSI 2014/27, SSI
  2014/215, SSI 2014/246
55. Building Act 1984
  Part I, disapplied: SI 2014/2384 Sch.19
  para.3
  s.1, enabling: SI 2014/58, SI 2014/110, SI
  2014/579, SI 2014/2362
  s.3, enabling: SI 2014/579, SI 2014/2362
  s.14, applied: SI 2014/110, SI 2014/579
  s.16, enabling: SI 2014/58
  s.17, enabling: SI 2014/58
  s.34, enabling: SI 2014/110, SI 2014/579, SI
  2014/2362
  s.47, enabling: SI 2014/58
  s.49, enabling: SI 2014/58
  s.50, enabling: SI 2014/58
  s.51, enabling: SI 2014/58
  s.51A, enabling: SI 2014/58
  s.77, see *Manolete Partners Plc v Hastings
  BC* [2014] EWCA Civ 562, [2014] 1 W.L.R.
  4030 (CA (Civ Div)), Jackson LJ
  s.78, see *Manolete Partners Plc v Hastings
  BC* [2014] EWCA Civ 562, [2014] 1 W.L.R.
  4030 (CA (Civ Div)), Jackson LJ
  s.81, amended: SI 2014/469 Sch.2 para.3
  s.106, see *Manolete Partners Plc v Hastings
  BC* [2014] EWCA Civ 562, [2014] 1 W.L.R.
  4030 (CA (Civ Div)), Jackson LJ
  s.115, repealed (in part): 2014 c.2 Sch.12
  para.11
  Sch.1 para.1, enabling: SI 2014/110, SI
  2014/579, SI 2014/2362
  Sch.1 para.2, enabling: SI 2014/58, SI
  2014/579, SI 2014/2362
  Sch.1 para.4, enabling: SI 2014/58, SI
  2014/110, SI 2014/579, SI 2014/2362
  Sch.1 para.4A, enabling: SI 2014/58, SI
  2014/579, SI 2014/2362

Sch.1 para.7, enabling: SI 2014/110, SI 2014/579, SI 2014/2362

Sch.1 para.8, enabling: SI 2014/579, SI 2014/2362

Sch.1 para.10, enabling: SI 2014/58, SI 2014/110, SI 2014/579, SI 2014/2362

56. Foster Children (Scotland) Act 1984

s.3, referred to: 2014 asp 9 Sch.1 Part 1

s.5, referred to: 2014 asp 9 Sch.1 Part 1

s.8, referred to: 2014 asp 9 Sch.1 Part 1

58. Rent (Scotland) Act 1984

s.7, amended: 2014 asp 14 Sch.1 para.2

s.8, applied: 2014 asp 14 s.16

s.11, amended: 2014 asp 14 Sch.1 para.3

s.12, amended: 2014 asp 14 Sch.1 para.4

s.19, amended: 2014 asp 14 Sch.1 para.5

s.21, amended: 2014 asp 14 Sch.1 para.6

s.23, amended: 2014 asp 14 Sch.1 para.7

s.24, amended: 2014 asp 14 Sch.1 para.8

s.25, amended: 2014 asp 14 Sch.1 para.9

s.26, amended: 2014 asp 14 Sch.1 para.10

s.27, repealed: 2014 asp 14 Sch.1 para.11

s.31, amended: 2014 asp 14 Sch.1 para.12

s.32, amended: 2014 asp 14 Sch.1 para.13

s.35, amended: 2014 asp 14 Sch.1 para.14

s.39, amended: 2014 asp 14 Sch.1 para.15

s.43B, amended: 2014 asp 14 Sch.1 para.16

s.45, amended: 2014 asp 14 Sch.1 para.17

s.60, amended: 2014 asp 14 Sch.1 para.18

s.63, applied: 2014 asp 14 s.16

s.64, amended: 2014 asp 14 Sch.1 para.19

s.75, amended: 2014 asp 14 Sch.1 para.20

s.76, amended: 2014 asp 14 Sch.1 para.21

s.77, amended: 2014 asp 14 Sch.1 para.22

s.82, see *Cross v Aberdeen Property Leasing* 2014 S.L.T. (Sh Ct) 46 (Sh Ct (Grampian) (Aberdeen)), Sheriff M Lewis

s.90, see *Cross v Aberdeen Property Leasing* 2014 S.L.T. (Sh Ct) 46 (Sh Ct (Grampian) (Aberdeen)), Sheriff M Lewis

s.97, amended: 2014 asp 14 Sch.1 para.23

s.102, amended: 2014 asp 14 Sch.1 para.24

s.102, repealed (in part): 2014 asp 14 Sch.1 para.24

s.103, amended: 2014 asp 14 Sch.1 para.25

s.104, amended: 2014 asp 14 Sch.1 para.26

s.115, amended: 2014 asp 14 Sch.1 para.27

s.116, varied: SI 2014/2708 Art.5

Sch.1 para.3, amended: 2014 asp 14 Sch.1 para.28

Sch.1 para.7, amended: 2014 asp 14 Sch.1 para.28

Sch.1A para.3, amended: 2014 asp 14 Sch.1 para.29

Sch.1A para.6, amended: 2014 asp 14 Sch.1 para.29

Sch.1B para.3, amended: 2014 asp 14 Sch.1 para.30

Sch.2 Part I, amended: 2014 asp 14 Sch.1 para.31, Sch.2 para.3

Sch.2 Part II, amended: 2014 asp 14 Sch.1 para.31

Sch.2 Part III para.1, amended: 2014 asp 14 Sch.1 para.31

Sch.2 Part IV para.2, amended: 2014 asp 14 Sch.1 para.31

Sch.2 Part IV para.3, amended: 2014 asp 14 Sch.1 para.31

Sch.4, referred to: 2014 asp 18 Sch.4 para.3

Sch.4 para.1A, added: 2014 asp 14 s.95

Sch.4 para.4, applied: 2014 asp 18 Sch.4 para.3

60. Police and Criminal Evidence Act 1984

see *Beghal v DPP* [2013] EWHC 2573 (Admin), [2014] Q.B. 607 (DC), Gross LJ; see *R. (on the application of HC) v Secretary of State for the Home Department* [2013] EWHC 982 (Admin), [2014] 1 W.L.R. 1234 (DC), Moses LJ; see *R. (on the application of Roberts) v Commissioner of Police of the Metropolis* [2014] EWCA Civ 69, [2014] 1 W.L.R. 3299 (CA (Civ Div)), Maurice Kay LJ; see *R. v Hammond (Philip)* [2013] EWCA Crim 2636, [2014] 1 W.L.R. 4303 (CA (Crim Div)), Laws LJ

applied: SI 2014/1610 r.6_1

Part V, applied: SI 2014/1610 r.6_35

s.2, varied: SI 2014/1704 Sch.1 para.2

s.4, varied: 2014 c.12 s.176, SI 2014/1704 Sch.1 para.3

s.8, see *Lees v Solihull Magistrates' Court* [2013] EWHC 3779 (Admin), [2014] Lloyd's Rep. F.C. 233 (DC), Treacy LJ; see *R. (on the application of AB) v Huddersfield Magistrates' Court* [2014] EWHC 1089 (Admin), [2014] 4 All E.R. 500 (QBD (Admin)), Rafferty LJ; see *Sweeney v Westminster Magistrates' Court* [2014] EWHC 2068 (Admin), (2014) 178 J.P. 336 (DC), Pitchford LJ

s.8, applied: SI 2014/1610 r.6_1, r.6_30, SI 2014/1942 Reg.14

s.8, varied: 2014 c.12 s.176

s.9, see *R. (on the application of British Sky Broadcasting Ltd) v Central Criminal Court* [2014] UKSC 17, [2014] A.C. 885 (SC), Lady Hale DPSC; see *R. (on the application of S) v Chief Constable of the British Transport Police* [2013] EWHC 2189 (Admin), [2014] 1 W.L.R. 1647 (QBD (Admin)), Aikens LJ

s.10, applied: SI 2014/1610 r.6_3

s.11, applied: SI 2014/1610 r.6_3

s.12, applied: 2014 c.26 s.269

s.13, applied: 2014 c.26 s.269

s.14, see *R. (on the application of S) v Chief Constable of the British Transport Police* [2013] EWHC 2189 (Admin), [2014] 1 W.L.R. 1647 (QBD (Admin)), Aikens LJ; see *R. (on the application of Secretary of State for the Home Department) v Southwark Crown Court* [2013] EWHC 4366 (Admin), [2014] 1 W.L.R. 2529 (QBD (Admin)), Moses LJ

s.15, see *Lees v Solihull Magistrates' Court* [2013] EWHC 3779 (Admin), [2014] Lloyd's Rep. F.C. 233 (DC), Treacy LJ; see *R. (on the application of AB) v Huddersfield Magistrates' Court* [2014] EWHC 1089 (Admin), [2014] 4 All E.R. 500 (QBD (Admin)), Rafferty LJ; see *R. (on the application of S) v Chief Constable of the British Transport Police* [2013] EWHC 2189 (Admin), [2014] 1 W.L.R. 1647 (QBD (Admin)), Aikens LJ; see *Sweeney v Westminster Magistrates' Court* [2014] EWHC 2068 (Admin), (2014) 178 J.P. 336 (DC), Pitchford LJ

s.15, applied: SI 2014/1610 r.6_1, r.6_29, r.6_32

s.16, see *Lees v Solihull Magistrates' Court* [2013] EWHC 3779 (Admin), [2014] Lloyd's Rep. F.C. 233 (DC), Treacy LJ

s.16, applied: SI 2014/1610 r.6_5, r.6_30, r.6_31, r.6_32, r.6_33, SI 2014/2402 Sch.1

s.16, varied: SI 2014/1704 Sch.1 para.4

s.17, applied: SI 2014/1942 Reg.14

s.17, varied: SI 2014/1704 Sch.1 para.5

s.18, applied: SI 2014/2402 Sch.1

s.18, varied: SI 2014/1704 Sch.1 para.6

s.21, varied: SI 2014/1704 Sch.1 para.7

s.22, varied: SI 2014/1704 Sch.1 para.8

s.23, applied: SI 2014/1610 r.6_30

s.24A, varied: 2014 c.12 s.176

s.28, see *Walker v Commissioner of Police of the Metropolis* [2014] EWCA Civ 897, Times, July 16, 2014 (CA (Civ Div)), Rimer LJ

s.29, varied: SI 2014/1704 Sch.1 para.9

s.32, varied: 2014 c.12 s.176

s.37, applied: SI 2014/1610 r.19_6, r.7_1

s.37C, applied: SI 2014/1610 r.19_6

s.37CA, applied: SI 2014/1610 r.19_6

s.38, applied: SI 2014/1610 r.7_1

s.41, varied: SI 2014/1704 Sch.1 para.10

s.43, varied: 2014 c.12 s.176, SI 2014/1704 Sch.1 para.11

s.45A, enabling: SI 2014/3279

s.46A, applied: SI 2014/1610 r.19_6

s.47, applied: SI 2014/1610 r.19_6

s.56, varied: 2014 c.12 s.176

s.58, see *Beeres v Crown Prosecution Service (West Midlands)* [2014] EWHC 283 (Admin), [2014] 2 Cr. App. R. 8 (QBD (Admin)), Green J; see *R. (on the application of Elosta) v Commissioner of Police of the Metropolis* [2013] EWHC 3397 (Admin), [2014] 1 W.L.R. 239 (QBD (Admin)), Bean J

s.58, applied: SI 2014/2402 Sch.1

s.58, varied: 2014 c.12 s.176

s.61, amended: 2014 c.12 s.144

s.61, varied: SI 2014/1704 Sch.1 para.12

s.61A, varied: SI 2014/1704 Sch.1 para.13

s.62, varied: SI 2014/1704 Sch.1 para.14

s.63, see *R. (on the application of R) v A Chief Constable* [2013] EWHC 2864 (Admin), [2014] 1 Cr. App. R. 16 (DC), Pitchford LJ

s.63, amended: 2014 c.12 s.144

s.63, varied: SI 2014/1704 Sch.1 para.15

s.63AB, varied: SI 2014/1704 Sch.1 para.16

s.63B, varied: SI 2014/1704 Sch.1 para.17

s.63D, applied: SI 2014/1610 r.6_35

s.63D, varied: SI 2014/1704 Sch.1 para.18

s.63F, applied: SI 2014/1610 r.6_1, r.6_35, r.6_36

s.63F, varied: SI 2014/1704 Sch.1 para.19

s.63G, varied: SI 2014/1704 Sch.1 para.20

s.63M, varied: SI 2014/1704 Sch.1 para.21

s.63P, substituted: 2014 c.12 s.145

s.63Q, varied: SI 2014/1704 Sch.1 para.22

s.63R, applied: SI 2014/1610 r.6_1, r.6_35
s.63R, varied: SI 2014/1704 Sch.1 para.23
s.63S, varied: SI 2014/1704 Sch.1 para.24
s.63U, amended: 2014 c.12 s.146
s.64A, amended: 2014 c.12 Sch.11 para.4
s.66, applied: SI 2014/1610 r.6_30
s.66, referred to: SI 2014/1237 Art.2
s.67, applied: SI 2014/1237
s.67, enabling: SI 2014/1146, SI 2014/1237
s.73, see *R. v M* [2014] EWCA Crim 1523,
[2014] 2 Cr. App. R. 29 (CA (Crim Div)),
Pitchford LJ
s.73, applied: SI 2014/1610 r.5_9, r.35_2
s.74, see *R. v M* [2014] EWCA Crim 1523,
[2014] 2 Cr. App. R. 29 (CA (Crim Div)),
Pitchford LJ
s.76, see *Beeres v Crown Prosecution
Service (West Midlands)* [2014] EWHC 283
(Admin), [2014] 2 Cr. App. R. 8 (QBD
(Admin)), Green J
s.77, varied: SI 2014/1704 Sch.1 para.25
s.78, see *Beeres v Crown Prosecution
Service (West Midlands)* [2014] EWHC 283
(Admin), [2014] 2 Cr. App. R. 8 (QBD
(Admin)), Green J; see *Beghal v DPP*
[2013] EWHC 2573 (Admin), [2014] Q.B.
607 (DC), Gross LJ; see *Bodhaniya v CPS*
[2013] EWHC 1743 (Admin), (2014) 178
J.P. 1 (QBD (Admin)), Moses LJ; see *Lees v
Solihull Magistrates' Court* [2013] EWHC
3779 (Admin), [2014] Lloyd's Rep. F.C. 233
(DC), Treacy LJ; see *R. v Ferdinand (Sean)*
[2014] EWCA Crim 1243, [2014] 2 Cr. App.
R. 23 (CA (Crim Div)), Pitchford LJ; see *R.
v Haq (Shakeel Ahmed)* [2014] EWCA Crim
2216, (2014) 178 J.P. 528 (CA (Crim Div)),
Macur LJ; see *R. v M* [2014] EWCA Crim
1523, [2014] 2 Cr. App. R. 29 (CA (Crim
Div)), Pitchford LJ
s.79, applied: SI 2014/1610 r.38_9
s.81, applied: SI 2014/1610 r.33_3, r.3_5
s.81, enabling: SI 2014/1610
s.114, enabling: SI 2014/788
s.114A, varied: 2014 c.12 s.176
s.118, varied: SI 2014/1704 Sch.1 para.26
Sch.1, see *R. (on the application of British
Sky Broadcasting Ltd) v Central Criminal
Court* [2014] UKSC 17, [2014] A.C. 885
(SC), Lady Hale DPSC; see *R. (on the
application of S) v Chief Constable of the
British Transport Police* [2013] EWHC

2189 (Admin), [2014] 1 W.L.R. 1647 (QBD
(Admin)), Aikens LJ; see *R. (on the
application of Secretary of State for the
Home Department) v Southwark Crown
Court* [2013] EWHC 4366 (Admin), [2014]
1 W.L.R. 2529 (QBD (Admin)), Moses LJ
Sch.1 para.2, see *R. (on the application of S)
v Chief Constable of the British Transport
Police* [2013] EWHC 2189 (Admin), [2014]
1 W.L.R. 1647 (QBD (Admin)), Aikens LJ
Sch.1 para.2, varied: 2014 c.12 s.176
Sch.1 para.3, see *R. (on the application of S)
v Chief Constable of the British Transport
Police* [2013] EWHC 2189 (Admin), [2014]
1 W.L.R. 1647 (QBD (Admin)), Aikens LJ
Sch.1 para.4, see *R. (on the application of S)
v Chief Constable of the British Transport
Police* [2013] EWHC 2189 (Admin), [2014]
1 W.L.R. 1647 (QBD (Admin)), Aikens LJ
Sch.1 para.7, see *R. (on the application of
British Sky Broadcasting Ltd) v Central
Criminal Court* [2014] UKSC 17, [2014]
A.C. 885 (SC), Lady Hale DPSC
Sch.1 para.14, see *R. (on the application of
S) v Chief Constable of the British Transport
Police* [2013] EWHC 2189 (Admin), [2014]
1 W.L.R. 1647 (QBD (Admin)), Aikens LJ
Sch.2A, varied: SI 2014/1704 Sch.1 para.27
Sch.2A Part I para.1, amended: 2014 c.12
Sch.11 para.86
Sch.2A Part I para.2, amended: 2014 c.12
Sch.11 para.86
Sch.2A Part I para.3, varied: SI 2014/1704
Sch.1 para.27
Sch.2A Part I para.6, varied: SI 2014/1704
Sch.1 para.27
Sch.2A Part III para.9, amended: 2014 c.12
Sch.11 para.86
Sch.2A Part III para.10, amended: 2014 c.12
Sch.11 para.86
Sch.2A Part III para.11, varied: SI
2014/1704 Sch.1 para.27
Sch.2A Part III para.14, varied: SI
2014/1704 Sch.1 para.27
Sch.2A Part IV para.16, varied: SI
2014/1704 Sch.1 para.27
Sch.2A Pt III para.11, see *R. (on the
application of R) v A Chief Constable* [2013]
EWHC 2864 (Admin), [2014] 1 Cr. App. R.
16 (DC), Pitchford LJ

Sch.2A Pt IV para.15, see *R. (on the application of R) v A Chief Constable* [2013] EWHC 2864 (Admin), [2014] 1 Cr. App. R. 16 (DC), Pitchford LJ
Sch.7 Part VI, varied: 2014 c.12 s.176

1985

6. Companies Act 1985
applied: 2014 c.14 s.115, s.135
Part XIV, referred to: 2014 c.14 s.135, SI 2014/574 Reg.2
Part XVIII c.I, applied: 2014 c.14 s.62
Part XVIII c.I, varied: 2014 c.14 s.62
s.130, see *Vocalspruce Ltd v Revenue and Customs Commissioners* [2014] EWCA Civ 1302, [2014] B.T.C. 50 (CA (Civ Div)), Gross LJ
s.194, see *DMWSHNZ Ltd v Revenue and Customs Commissioners* [2014] UKUT 98 (TCC), [2014] S.T.C. 1440 (UT (Tax)), Rose J
s.322, see *Dryburgh v Scotts Media Tax Ltd* [2014] CSIH 45, 2014 S.C. 651 (IH (Ex Div)), Lady Smith
s.353, see *Burry & Knight Ltd, Re* [2014] EWCA Civ 604, [2014] 1 W.L.R. 4046 (CA (Civ Div)), Arden LJ
s.432, varied: SI 2014/574 Reg.2
s.433, varied: SI 2014/574 Reg.2
s.434, varied: SI 2014/574 Reg.2
s.436, varied: SI 2014/574 Reg.2
s.437, applied: SI 2014/574 Reg.2
s.437, varied: SI 2014/574 Reg.2
s.439, varied: SI 2014/574 Reg.2
s.441, varied: SI 2014/574 Reg.2
s.446A, varied: SI 2014/574 Reg.2
s.446B, varied: SI 2014/574 Reg.2
s.446C, varied: SI 2014/574 Reg.2
s.446D, varied: SI 2014/574 Reg.2
s.446E, varied: SI 2014/574 Reg.2
s.447, varied: SI 2014/574 Reg.2
s.447A, varied: SI 2014/574 Reg.2
s.448, varied: SI 2014/574 Reg.2
s.448A, varied: SI 2014/574 Reg.2
s.449, varied: SI 2014/574 Reg.2
s.450, varied: SI 2014/574 Reg.2
s.451, varied: SI 2014/574 Reg.2
s.451A, varied: SI 2014/574 Reg.2
s.452, varied: SI 2014/574 Reg.2

s.453A, varied: SI 2014/574 Reg.2
s.453B, varied: SI 2014/574 Reg.2
s.453C, varied: SI 2014/574 Reg.2
s.453D, varied: SI 2014/574 Reg.2
s.462, varied: 2014 c.14 s.62
s.463, applied: 2014 c.14 s.62
s.464, applied: 2014 c.14 s.62
s.466, varied: 2014 c.14 s.62
s.727, see *Santander UK v RA Legal Solicitors* [2014] EWCA Civ 183, [2014] Lloyd's Rep. F.C. 282 (CA (Civ Div)), Sir Terence Etherton C
Sch.15C para.1, varied: SI 2014/574 Reg.2
Sch.15C para.11, varied: SI 2014/574 Reg.2
Sch.15D para.2, varied: SI 2014/574 Reg.2
Sch.15D para.3, varied: SI 2014/574 Reg.2
Sch.15D para.17, amended: SI 2014/892
Sch.1 para.42
Sch.15D para.17, repealed (in part): SI 2014/631 Sch.2 para.2
Sch.15D para.18, repealed: SI 2014/892
Sch.1 para.42
Sch.15D para.27A, added: SI 2014/631
Sch.2 para.2

9. Companies Consolidation (Consequential Provisions) Act 1985
applied: 2014 c.14 s.115, s.135

17. Reserve Forces (Safeguard of Employment) Act 1985
applied: SI 2014/3051 Reg.38, SSI 2014/225 Reg.21
s.1, applied: SI 2014/3051 Reg.38

21. Films Act 1985
Sch.1 para.4, enabling: SI 2014/1561

23. Prosecution of Offences Act 1985
applied: SI 2014/1610 r.19_1
Part II, applied: SI 2014/1610 r.76_1
s.3, amended: 2014 c.12 Sch.11 para.5, SI 2014/834 Sch.1 para.2
s.3, applied: SI 2014/834 Art.8, SI 2014/1610 r.17_19, r.2_4
s.3, repealed (in part): 2014 c.12 Sch.11 para.5
s.3, enabling: SI 2014/1229
s.5, amended: SI 2014/834 Sch.1 para.3
s.5, applied: SI 2014/834 Art.5, Art.6, Art.7
s.6, see *R. v Zinga (Munaf Ahmed)* [2014] EWCA Crim 52, [2014] 1 W.L.R. 2228 (CA (Crim Div)), Lord Thomas LCJ
s.6, applied: SI 2014/1610 r.2_4

s.7A, see *DPP v Radziwilowicz* [2014]
EWHC 2283 (Admin), (2014) 178 J.P. 432
(DC), Sir Brian Leveson PQBD
s.7A, amended: SI 2014/834 Sch.1 para.4
s.16, see *Hunter v Newcastle Crown Court*
[2013] EWHC 191 (Admin), [2014] Q.B. 94
(DC), Leveson LJ; see *R. (on the*
application of Virgin Media Ltd) v Zinga
[2014] EWCA Crim 1823, [2014] 5 Costs
L.R. 879 (CA (Crim Div)), Lord Thomas
LCJ; see *R. v Banfield (Shirley)* [2014]
EWCA Crim 1824, [2014] 5 Costs L.R. 896
(CA (Crim Div)), Lord Thomas LCJ
s.16, applied: SI 2014/1610 r.76_1, r.76_4
s.16A, amended: SI 2014/130 Reg.2
s.16A, applied: SI 2014/1610 r.76_2
s.16A, enabling: SI 2014/130
s.17, see *R. (on the application of Virgin*
Media Ltd) v Zinga [2014] EWCA Crim
1823, [2014] 5 Costs L.R. 879 (CA (Crim
Div)), Lord Thomas LCJ
s.17, applied: SI 2014/1610 r.76_1
s.18, applied: SI 2014/1610 r.76_5, r.76_6
s.19, see *R. (on the application of DPP) v*
Sheffield Crown Court [2014] EWHC 2014
(Admin), [2014] 1 W.L.R. 4639 (QBD
(Admin)), Lord Thomas LCJ; see *R. (on the*
application of Singh) v Ealing Magistrates'
Court [2014] EWHC 1443 (Admin), (2014)
178 J.P. 253 (QBD (Admin)), Beatson LJ
s.19, applied: SI 2014/1610 r.3_5, r.76_1,
r.76_8
s.19A, see *DLA Piper UK LLP v BDO LLP*
[2013] EWHC 3970 (Admin), [2014] 1
W.L.R. 4425 (QBD (Admin)), Moses LJ
s.19A, applied: SI 2014/1610 r.76_1, r.63_1,
r.76_9, r.68_1
s.19B, applied: SI 2014/1610 r.76_10
s.22, applied: SI 2014/1610 r.19_16, r.19_17
s.23, applied: SI 2014/1610 r.8_1, r.8_2
s.23A, applied: SI 2014/1610 r.8_1
s.29, applied: SI 2014/130
s.29, enabling: SI 2014/130

29. Enduring Powers of Attorney Act 1985
s.3, see *Day v Royal College of Music* [2013]
EWCA Civ 191, [2014] Ch. 211 (CA (Civ
Div)), Rix LJ
s.7, see *Day v Royal College of Music* [2013]
EWCA Civ 191, [2014] Ch. 211 (CA (Civ
Div)), Rix LJ

37. Family Law (Scotland) Act 1985
applied: SSI 2014/287 Art.5, SSI 2014/290
Reg.3
s.2, applied: 2014 asp 18 s.74
s.3, applied: 2014 asp 5 s.11, SSI 2014/287
Art.5
s.8, see *M v M* [2014] CSOH 136, 2014
Fam. L.R. 116 (OH), Lord Armstrong; see
W v W 2014 S.C.L.R. 63 (OH), Lord Tyre
s.9, see *M v M* [2014] CSOH 136, 2014
Fam. L.R. 116 (OH), Lord Armstrong
s.10, see *M v M* [2014] CSOH 136, 2014
Fam. L.R. 116 (OH), Lord Armstrong; see
TCM v AFMM 2014 Fam. L.R. 11 (Sh Ct
(Lothian) (Edinburgh)), Sheriff W Holligan
s.11, see *M v M* [2014] CSOH 136, 2014
Fam. L.R. 116 (OH), Lord Armstrong
s.27, amended: 2014 c.19 Sch.11 para.1

47. Further Education Act 1985
s.1, applied: SI 2014/1638 Sch.2 para.12
s.3, amended: 2014 c.2 Sch.12 para.12

48. Food and Environment Protection Act 1985
Part II, referred to: SSI 2014/324 Sch.1
para.4

50. Representation of the People Act 1985
s.1, see *Shindler v United Kingdom*
(19840/09) (2014) 58 E.H.R.R. 5 (ECHR),
Judge Ziemele (President)
s.1, varied: 2014 c.24 s.4
s.2, amended: 2014 c.13 s.15
s.5, amended: SI 2014/1116 Art.5
s.6, amended: SI 2014/1116 Art.5
s.6, enabling: SI 2014/1808
s.7, amended: SI 2014/1116 Art.5
s.7, enabling: SI 2014/1808
s.8, enabling: SI 2014/1808
s.9, amended: SI 2014/1116 Art.5
s.9, enabling: SI 2014/1808
s.15, enabling: SI 2014/920
s.22, applied: SI 2014/918, SI 2014/919
s.27, applied: SI 2014/920

51. Local Government Act 1985
Part IV, applied: 2014 c.2 s.40, Sch.2 para.5,
SI 2014/3224 Reg.8
s.29, applied: SI 2014/1180
s.29, enabling: SI 2014/1180
s.88, applied: SI 2014/863 Art.12, SI
2014/865 Art.15
s.88, referred to: SI 2014/864 Art.12, SI
2014/865 Art.15, SI 2014/1012 Art.14

s.88, varied: SI 2014/863 Art.12, SI
2014/864 Art.12, SI 2014/865 Art.15, SI
2014/1012 Art.14
Sch.10 Part VI, amended: SI 2014/1180
Art.2

55. Appropriation Act 1985
Sch.4 Part 2, varied: SI 2014/2708 Art.5
Sch.4 Part 15, varied: SI 2014/2708 Art.5

60. Child Abduction and Custody Act 1985
see *F (A Child) (Abduction: Art.13(b):
Psychiatric Assessment), Re* [2014] EWCA
Civ 275, [2014] 2 F.L.R. 1115 (CA (Civ
Div)), Sullivan LJ; see *R, Petitioner* [2014]
CSIH 95, 2014 S.L.T. 1080 (IH (Ex Div)),
Lady Paton
Sch.3 Part I para.1, amended: 2014 c.6 Sch.2
para.48

61. Administration of Justice Act 1985
s.9, see *Assaubayev v Michael Wilson and
Partners Ltd* [2014] EWHC 821 (QB),
[2014] 3 Costs L.O. 446 (QBD), Walker J
s.50, see *Goodman v Goodman* [2013]
EWHC 758 (Ch), [2014] Ch. 186 (Ch D),
Newey J
Sch.2 para.27, amended: SI 2014/605 Art.18

66. Bankruptcy (Scotland) Act 1985
applied: SI 2014/882 Reg.5, SSI 2014/225
Reg.8, SSI 2014/226 Reg.5, Reg.6, Reg.20,
SSI 2014/261 Art.4, Art.7, Art.12, SSI
2014/296 Reg.3
referred to: SSI 2014/225 Reg.8, SSI
2014/226 Reg.5, Reg.6, Reg.7, Reg.20
varied: SSI 2014/225 Reg.8
s.1, applied: SSI 2014/226 Reg.21
s.1A, amended: 2014 asp 11 s.22, Sch.3
para.3
s.1A, applied: SSI 2014/225 Reg.4
s.1A, enabling: SSI 2014/225
s.1D, added: 2014 asp 11 s.44
s.2, amended: 2014 asp 11 s.6, s.9
s.2, repealed (in part): 2014 asp 11 Sch.4
s.2, enabling: SSI 2014/225
s.3, amended: 2014 asp 11 s.25
s.3A, added: 2014 asp 11 s.25
s.3A, applied: SSI 2014/226 Reg.8, Reg.20
s.4A, added: 2014 asp 11 s.8
s.4A, applied: SSI 2014/225 Reg.22, SSI
2014/261 Art.7
s.4B, applied: SSI 2014/225 Reg.22, SSI
2014/261 Art.7

s.5, amended: 2014 asp 11 s.1, s.5, s.9, s.11,
s.45, Sch.3 para.4
s.5, applied: SSI 2014/225 Reg.6, Reg.7
s.5, disapplied: SSI 2014/225 Reg.7
s.5, repealed (in part): 2014 asp 11 s.45,
Sch.4
s.5, enabling: SSI 2014/225
s.5A, applied: SSI 2014/261 Art.6
s.5A, repealed: 2014 asp 11 Sch.4
s.5A, enabling: SSI 2014/296
s.5B, amended: 2014 asp 11 Sch.3 para.5
s.5B, repealed (in part): 2014 asp 11 Sch.4
s.5B, enabling: SSI 2014/296
s.5C, added: 2014 asp 11 s.1
s.5C, applied: SSI 2014/261 Art.5, SSI
2014/296 Reg.3, Reg.5, Reg.6
s.5C, enabling: SSI 2014/296
s.5D, added: 2014 asp 11 s.3
s.5D, applied: SSI 2014/261 Art.6
s.5D, enabling: SSI 2014/290
s.6, amended: 2014 asp 11 Sch.3 para.6
s.6, referred to: SSI 2014/225 Reg.5
s.6, enabling: SSI 2014/225
s.6B, amended: 2014 asp 11 s.11
s.7, amended: 2014 asp 11 Sch.3 para.7
s.7, applied: SSI 2014/225 Reg.9
s.7, enabling: SSI 2014/225
s.8, amended: 2014 asp 11 s.46
s.8, repealed (in part): 2014 asp 11 Sch.4
s.8A, amended: 2014 asp 11 s.11, s.46
s.9, amended: 2014 asp 11 Sch.3 para.8
s.9, applied: SSI 2014/225 Reg.8
s.10, amended: 2014 asp 11 Sch.4
s.10A, amended: 2014 asp 11 s.12
s.11, enabling: SSI 2014/225
s.11A, added: 2014 asp 11 s.10
s.11A, applied: SSI 2014/261 Art.5
s.12, amended: 2014 asp 11 s.11, s.47, Sch.3
para.9, Sch.4
s.12, applied: SI 2014/2839 Reg.4
s.13A, amended: 2014 asp 11 s.38, Sch.4
s.13A, applied: SSI 2014/226 Reg.20, SSI
2014/261 Art.10
s.13A, repealed (in part): 2014 asp 11 Sch.4
s.13B, amended: 2014 asp 11 s.38, Sch.3
para.10
s.13B, applied: SSI 2014/226 Reg.20, SSI
2014/261 Art.10
s.13B, repealed (in part): 2014 asp 11 Sch.4
s.14, amended: 2014 asp 11 s.48, Sch.3
para.11, Sch.3 para.12, Sch.4

s.14, applied: SSI 2014/225 Reg.8
s.14, referred to: SSI 2014/225 Reg.5
s.14, repealed (in part): 2014 asp 11 Sch.4
s.15, amended: 2014 asp 11 s.39, Sch.3
para.13
s.15, applied: SSI 2014/225 Reg.8, SSI
2014/226 Reg.20, SSI 2014/261 Art.10
s.16, amended: 2014 asp 11 s.24, s.26
s.16, repealed (in part): 2014 asp 11 s.26
s.17, amended: 2014 asp 11 s.26, Sch.3
para.14, Sch.4
s.17, applied: SSI 2014/225 Reg.8
s.17A, added: 2014 asp 11 s.27
s.17A, applied: SSI 2014/226 Reg.4
s.17A, referred to: SSI 2014/226 Reg.9
s.17B, applied: SSI 2014/226 Reg.9
s.17D, applied: SSI 2014/226 Reg.9
s.17E, applied: SSI 2014/226 Reg.9
s.17G, added: 2014 asp 11 s.27
s.17G, applied: SSI 2014/226 Reg.20
s.17G, referred to: SSI 2014/261 Art.3
s.18, amended: 2014 asp 11 s.38
s.18, applied: SSI 2014/226 Reg.20, SSI
2014/261 Art.10
s.19, amended: 2014 asp 11 s.45
s.19, repealed (in part): 2014 asp 11 s.45
s.19, enabling: SSI 2014/225
s.20, amended: 2014 asp 11 Sch.3 para.15
s.22, applied: SSI 2014/225 Reg.10
s.22, enabling: SSI 2014/225
s.23, amended: 2014 asp 11 Sch.3 para.16
s.23, applied: SSI 2014/225 Reg.11
s.23, enabling: SSI 2014/225
s.25, applied: SSI 2014/226 Reg.4, Reg.10
s.25, substituted: 2014 asp 11 s.28
s.25A, applied: SSI 2014/226 Reg.10,
Reg.20
s.26, amended: 2014 asp 11 Sch.3 para.17,
Sch.4
s.26, repealed (in part): 2014 asp 11 Sch.4
s.26A, amended: 2014 asp 11 s.40
s.26A, applied: SSI 2014/226 Reg.20, SSI
2014/227 Reg.5, SSI 2014/261 Art.10
s.26A, repealed (in part): 2014 asp 11 Sch.4
s.27, amended: 2014 asp 11 s.40, Sch.3
para.18, Sch.4
s.27, applied: SSI 2014/226 Reg.20, SSI
2014/261 Art.10
s.27, repealed (in part): 2014 asp 11 Sch.4
s.28, amended: 2014 asp 11 s.28
s.28, applied: SSI 2014/225 Reg.12

s.28A, applied: SSI 2014/226 Reg.4, Reg.11
s.28A, substituted: 2014 asp 11 s.29
s.28B, applied: SSI 2014/226 Reg.20
s.29, amended: 2014 asp 11 s.30, Sch.3
para.19
s.29, applied: SSI 2014/226 Reg.4, Reg.12,
Reg.20
s.29, referred to: SSI 2014/226 Reg.12
s.30, amended: 2014 asp 11 s.31
s.31, amended: 2014 asp 11 s.16
s.31B, applied: SI 2014/1610 r.60_4
s.32, amended: 2014 asp 11 s.13, s.16, Sch.3
para.20, Sch.4
s.32, applied: SSI 2014/164 Reg.82, SSI
2014/217 Reg.174, SSI 2014/225 Reg.13,
SSI 2014/261 Art.6, SSI 2014/292 Reg.174
s.32, repealed (in part): 2014 asp 11 Sch.4
s.32, enabling: SSI 2014/225
s.32A, added: 2014 asp 11 s.4
s.32A, applied: SSI 2014/225 Reg.14, SSI
2014/290 Reg.4
s.32B, applied: SSI 2014/296 Reg.8
s.32C, applied: SSI 2014/226 Reg.20, SSI
2014/290 Reg.4
s.32E, applied: SSI 2014/296 Reg.8
s.32E, enabling: SSI 2014/296
s.32F, applied: SSI 2014/261 Art.6, SSI
2014/290 Reg.3
s.32H, applied: SSI 2014/226 Reg.20, SSI
2014/290 Reg.4
s.34, amended: 2014 asp 11 Sch.4
s.34, repealed (in part): 2014 asp 11 Sch.4
s.35, repealed (in part): 2014 asp 11 Sch.4
s.36, amended: 2014 asp 11 Sch.4
s.36, repealed (in part): 2014 asp 11 Sch.4
s.38, amended: 2014 asp 11 Sch.4
s.39A, amended: 2014 asp 11 Sch.3 para.21,
Sch.4, SSI 2014/296 Reg.9
s.39A, enabling: SSI 2014/296
s.40, amended: 2014 asp 11 s.49
s.40, applied: SSI 2014/225 Reg.15
s.40, enabling: SSI 2014/225
s.42, amended: 2014 asp 11 s.32
s.42, applied: SSI 2014/226 Reg.4, Reg.13,
Reg.20
s.43A, amended: 2014 asp 11 Sch.3 para.22
s.43A, applied: SSI 2014/225 Reg.16
s.43A, enabling: SSI 2014/225
s.43B, added: 2014 asp 11 s.2
s.43B, applied: SSI 2014/225 Reg.17
s.43B, enabling: SSI 2014/225

s.45, amended: 2014 asp 11 s.24
s.45, enabling: SSI 2014/225
s.47, amended: 2014 asp 11 Sch.3 para.23, Sch.4
s.48, amended: 2014 asp 11 s.14, Sch.3 para.24
s.48, applied: SSI 2014/225 Reg.10
s.49, amended: 2014 asp 11 s.41, Sch.4
s.49, applied: SSI 2014/225 Reg.11, SSI 2014/226 Reg.20, SSI 2014/261 Art.10
s.49, enabling: SSI 2014/225
s.50, amended: 2014 asp 11 Sch.3 para.25
s.51, amended: SI 2014/3486 Art.28
s.51, applied: SSI 2014/225 Reg.18
s.51, enabling: SSI 2014/225
s.52, amended: 2014 asp 11 s.15, Sch.3 para.26, Sch.4
s.53, amended: 2014 asp 11 Sch.3 para.27
s.53, applied: SSI 2014/227 Reg.5
s.53, repealed (in part): 2014 asp 11 Sch.4
s.53A, applied: SSI 2014/227 Reg.5
s.54, substituted: 2014 asp 11 s.17
s.54, enabling: SSI 2014/225
s.54A, enabling: SSI 2014/225
s.54B, applied: SSI 2014/226 Reg.20
s.54C, added: 2014 asp 11 s.7
s.54C, enabling: SSI 2014/225
s.54D, added: 2014 asp 11 s.19
s.54D, applied: SSI 2014/225 Reg.19
s.54D, enabling: SSI 2014/225
s.54E, enabling: SSI 2014/225
s.54G, applied: SSI 2014/226 Reg.20
s.55, amended: 2014 asp 11 s.50, Sch.3 para.28, Sch.3 para.29
s.55, repealed (in part): 2014 asp 11 Sch.4
s.55A, added: 2014 asp 11 s.7
s.56, repealed: 2014 asp 11 s.18
s.56A, applied: SSI 2014/226 Reg.14, SSI 2014/227 Reg.12, SSI 2014/281 Art.8, SSI 2014/285 Art.8, SSI 2014/296 Reg.4
s.56A, substituted: 2014 asp 11 s.33
s.56B, amended: 2014 asp 11 s.33
s.56C, amended: 2014 asp 11 s.33
s.56D, amended: 2014 asp 11 s.33
s.56E, amended: 2014 asp 11 s.33
s.56E, applied: SSI 2014/226 Reg.4, Reg.15
s.56F, amended: 2014 asp 11 s.33
s.56F, applied: SSI 2014/296 Reg.4
s.56F, repealed (in part): 2014 asp 11 s.33
s.56G, applied: SSI 2014/281 Art.8, SSI 2014/285 Art.8

s.56G, repealed: 2014 asp 11 s.52
s.56H, repealed: 2014 asp 11 Sch.4
s.56J, amended: 2014 asp 11 s.33, Sch.3 para.30
s.56J, applied: SSI 2014/226 Reg.9, Reg.15, Reg.20
s.56J, repealed (in part): 2014 asp 11 Sch.4
s.56K, repealed: 2014 asp 11 s.18
s.57, amended: 2014 asp 11 s.20, s.23, s.42
s.57, applied: SSI 2014/226 Reg.20, SSI 2014/227 Reg.8, SSI 2014/261 Art.10
s.58, amended: 2014 asp 11 Sch.3 para.31
s.58A, amended: 2014 asp 11 s.23, s.42, Sch.3 para.32
s.58A, applied: SSI 2014/226 Reg.20, SSI 2014/227 Reg.5, SSI 2014/261 Art.10
s.58A, repealed (in part): 2014 asp 11 Sch.4
s.58B, added: 2014 asp 11 s.21
s.59A, amended: 2014 asp 11 s.34
s.59A, applied: SSI 2014/226 Reg.16
s.59B, amended: 2014 asp 11 s.34
s.59C, amended: 2014 asp 11 s.34
s.59C, applied: SSI 2014/226 Reg.16
s.60, repealed (in part): 2014 asp 11 Sch.4
s.60B, amended: 2014 asp 11 Sch.3 para.33
s.62, amended: 2014 asp 11 s.23
s.63, amended: 2014 asp 11 s.35
s.63, repealed (in part): 2014 asp 11 Sch.4
s.63A, added: 2014 asp 11 s.35
s.63A, applied: SSI 2014/226 Reg.4, Reg.17
s.63B, applied: SSI 2014/226 Reg.20
s.63C, added: 2014 asp 11 s.43
s.65, repealed (in part): 2014 asp 11 Sch.4
s.67, amended: 2014 asp 11 s.51
s.69, enabling: SSI 2014/225
s.69A, enabling: SSI 2014/227
s.71, repealed: 2014 asp 11 s.24
s.71B, repealed (in part): 2014 asp 11 Sch.4
s.71C, added: 2014 asp 11 s.36
s.71C, enabling: SSI 2014/225, SSI 2014/226, SSI 2014/290, SSI 2014/296
s.72, amended: 2014 asp 11 Sch.3 para.34, Sch.4
s.72, applied: SSI 2014/290, SSI 2014/296
s.72, repealed (in part): 2014 asp 11 Sch.4
s.72, enabling: SSI 2014/225, SSI 2014/226, SSI 2014/227, SSI 2014/290, SSI 2014/296
s.72A, enabling: SSI 2014/226
s.73, amended: 2014 asp 11 Sch.3 para.35, Sch.4
s.73, applied: SSI 2014/293 Art.2

s.73, enabling: SSI 2014/225
s.74, repealed (in part): 2014 asp 11 Sch.4
s.74, varied: SI 2014/229 Sch.3 para.3
Sch.A1, added: 2014 asp 11 Sch.1
Sch.A1 para.1, applied: SSI 2014/227 Reg.8
Sch.1 para.2, amended: 2014 asp 11 Sch.3
para.36
Sch.1 para.3, amended: 2014 asp 11 s.37
Sch.1 para.3, applied: SSI 2014/226 Reg.4,
Reg.18, Reg.20
Sch.1 para.4, repealed: 2014 asp 11 Sch.4
Sch.3A, added: 2014 asp 11 Sch.2
Sch.3 Part I para.5, applied: SSI 2014/225
Reg.21
Sch.3 Part I para.5, enabling: SSI 2014/225
Sch.3 Part I para.6, applied: SSI 2014/225
Reg.21
Sch.3 Part I para.6, enabling: SSI 2014/225
Sch.3 Part I para.6C, added: SI 2014/3486
Art.28
Sch.3 Part II para.9A, amended: SI
2014/3486 Art.28
Sch.4, repealed: 2014 asp 11 s.18
Sch.5 para.4, repealed (in part): 2014 asp 11
Sch.4
Sch.5 para.5, repealed (in part): 2014 asp 11
Sch.4
Sch.5 para.5, enabling: SSI 2014/290
Sch.6 Part I para.7, amended: 2014 asp 11
Sch.4
Sch.6 Part III para.20, amended: 2014 asp 11
Sch.4
Sch.6 Part III para.21, amended: 2014 asp 11
Sch.4
Sch.6 Part III para.23, amended: 2014 asp 11
Sch.4
Sch.7 Part II para.24, amended: 2014 asp 11
Sch.3 para.37

67. Transport Act 1985
Part IV, applied: SI 2014/865 Art.8, SI
2014/1012 Art.8
Part V, applied: SI 2014/865 Art.8
s.60, enabling: SI 2014/1364
s.76, amended: 2014 c.2 Sch.12 para.13
s.85, enabling: SI 2014/864
s.95, disapplied: SI 2014/864 Art.8
s.104, disapplied: SI 2014/864 Art.8
s.137, disapplied: SI 2014/864 Art.8

68. Housing Act 1985
see *Haile v Waltham Forest LBC* [2014]
EWCA Civ 792, [2014] P.T.S.R. 1376 (CA
(Civ Div)), Jackson LJ
referred to: SI 2014/1915 Art.1
Part V, applied: SI 2014/1378 Art.3, SI
2014/1915 Art.3, SI 2014/3219 Sch.4 para.1
s.5, amended: 2014 c.14 Sch.4 para.33
s.6A, amended: 2014 c.14 Sch.4 para.34
s.8, applied: SI 2014/863 Sch.2 para.3, SI
2014/865 Sch.2 para.5
s.12, see *R. (on the application of Barkas) v
North Yorkshire CC* [2014] UKSC 31,
[2014] 2 W.L.R. 1360 (SC), Lord Neuberger
PSC
s.27AB, amended: 2014 c.14 Sch.4 para.35
s.58, applied: 2014 c.14 s.24
s.59, applied: 2014 c.14 s.24
s.82A, amended: 2014 c.12 Sch.11 para.6
s.83, amended: 2014 c.12 Sch.11 para.7
s.83A, amended: 2014 c.12 Sch.11 para.8
s.83ZA, added: 2014 c.12 s.95
s.84, see *Holt v Reading BC* [2013] EWCA
Civ 641, [2014] P.T.S.R. 444 (CA (Civ
Div)), Arden LJ
s.84, amended: 2014 c.12 Sch.11 para.9
s.84A, added: 2014 c.12 s.94
s.84A, referred to: SI 2014/2830 Art.3
s.85A, amended: 2014 c.12 Sch.11 para.10
s.85ZA, added: 2014 c.12 s.96
s.85ZA, enabling: SI 2014/2554, SI
2014/3278
s.87, see *Birmingham City Council v Beech
(aka Howell)* [2014] EWCA Civ 830, [2014]
H.L.R. 38 (CA (Civ Div)), Sir Terence
Etherton C
s.88, see *Birmingham City Council v Beech
(aka Howell)* [2014] EWCA Civ 830, [2014]
H.L.R. 38 (CA (Civ Div)), Sir Terence
Etherton C
s.121A, amended: 2014 c.12 Sch.11 para.11
s.125, applied: SI 2014/1915 Art.3
s.129, applied: SI 2014/1915 Art.3
s.129, enabling: SI 2014/1915
s.131, enabling: SI 2014/1378, SI 2014/1865
s.136, applied: SI 2014/1915 Art.3
s.138, amended: 2014 c.12 s.100, SI
2014/949 Art.11, SI 2014/1241 Art.3
s.176, enabling: SI 2014/1797

Sch.1 para.4ZA, amended: 2014 c.12 Sch.11
para.12, SI 2014/949 Art.11, SI 2014/1241
Art.3
Sch.2 Pt IV, see *Holt v Reading BC* [2013]
EWCA Civ 641, [2014] P.T.S.R. 444 (CA
(Civ Div)), Arden LJ
Sch.2A, added: 2014 c.12 Sch.3
Sch.2 Part I, added: 2014 c.12 s.98, s.99
Sch.2 Part I, applied: SI 2014/949 Art.7
Sch.2 Part V para.5, amended: 2014 c.12
Sch.11 para.13
Sch.3 Part 2, amended: 2014 c.12 Sch.11
para.14
Sch.3 Part 2A, amended: 2014 c.12 Sch.11
para.15
Sch.3 Part 2B, added: 2014 c.12 Sch.11
para.16
Sch.3 Part 2ZA, added: 2014 c.12 s.100

69. Housing Associations Act 1985
s.1, amended: 2014 c.14 Sch.4 para.36
s.75, repealed (in part): 2014 c.2 Sch.12
para.14

70. Landlord and Tenant Act 1985
s.5, enabling: SI 2014/493
s.19, see *Blackpool BC v Cargill* [2014] L.
& T.R. 2 (UT (Lands)), Judge Huskinson
s.20, see *BDW Trading Ltd v South Anglia
Housing Ltd* [2013] EWHC 2169 (Ch),
[2014] 1 W.L.R. 920 (Ch D), Nicholas
Strauss QC
s.20ZA, see *BDW Trading Ltd v South
Anglia Housing Ltd* [2013] EWHC 2169
(Ch), [2014] 1 W.L.R. 920 (Ch D), Nicholas
Strauss QC
s.21, see *Di Marco v Morshead Mansions
Ltd* [2014] EWCA Civ 96, [2014] 1 W.L.R.
1799 (CA (Civ Div)), Patten LJ
s.22, see *Di Marco v Morshead Mansions
Ltd* [2014] EWCA Civ 96, [2014] 1 W.L.R.
1799 (CA (Civ Div)), Patten LJ
s.27A, see *Blackpool BC v Cargill* [2014] L.
& T.R. 2 (UT (Lands)), Judge Huskinson;
see *Christoforou v Standard Apartments Ltd*
[2014] L. & T.R. 12 (UT (Lands)), Martin
Rodger Q.C.
s.30, see *BDW Trading Ltd v South Anglia
Housing Ltd* [2013] EWHC 2169 (Ch),
[2014] 1 W.L.R. 920 (Ch D), Nicholas
Strauss QC
s.36, see *BDW Trading Ltd v South Anglia
Housing Ltd* [2013] EWHC 2169 (Ch),

[2014] 1 W.L.R. 920 (Ch D), Nicholas
Strauss QC
**71. Housing (Consequential Provisions) Act
1985**
Sch.2 para.8, repealed: 2014 c.14 Sch.7
72. Weights and Measures Act 1985
s.27, amended: SI 2014/2975 Reg.3
s.30, amended: SI 2014/2975 Reg.4
s.31A, added: SI 2014/2975 Reg.5
s.32, amended: SI 2014/2975 Reg.6
s.35, amended: SI 2014/2975 Reg.7
s.37, amended: SI 2014/2975 Reg.8
s.38, amended: SI 2014/2975 Reg.9
s.42, amended: SI 2014/2975 Reg.10
s.69, referred to: SI 2014/2418 Sch.1
s.94, amended: SI 2014/2975 Reg.11
Sch.7 para.2, amended: SI 2014/2975
Reg.12
Sch.7 para.3, amended: SI 2014/2975
Reg.12
Sch.7 para.4, amended: SI 2014/2975
Reg.12
**73. Law Reform (Miscellaneous Provisions)
(Scotland) Act 1985**
s.4, see *Shetland Leasing & Property
Developments Ltd v Younger* 2014 Hous.
L.R. 9 (Sh Ct (Grampian) (Lerwick)),
Sheriff P Mann
s.8, see *Archid Architecture and Interior
Design v Dundee City Council* 2014 S.L.T.
81 (OH), Lord Glennie; see *Mirza v Salim*
[2014] CSIH 51, 2014 S.L.T. 875 (IH (Ex
Div)), Lady Paton
s.9, see *Mirza v Salim* [2014] CSIH 51, 2014
S.L.T. 875 (IH (Ex Div)), Lady Paton
s.10, see *Cramaso LLP v Viscount
Reidhaven's Trustees* [2014] UKSC 9,
[2014] A.C. 1093 (SC), Lord Mance JSC
s.10, amended: SI 2014/870 Reg.8
s.14, repealed: 2014 asp 18 Sch.5 para.25
s.22, repealed: 2014 asp 18 Sch.5 para.36

1986

5. Agricultural Holdings Act 1986
s.92, applied: SI 2014/1068 Art.2
s.92, repealed: SI 2014/1068 Art.3
s.95, varied: SI 2014/2708 Art.5
Sch.6 Part I para.3, applied: SI 2014/41
Art.2, SI 2014/2712 Art.2

Sch.6 Part I para.4, enabling: SI 2014/41, SI 2014/2712

9. Law Reform (Parent and Child) (Scotland) Act 1986

s.5, see *S v S* 2014 S.L.T. (Sh Ct) 165 (Sh Ct (Lothian) (Livingston)), Sheriff D A Kinloch

10. Local Government Act 1986

s.4A, added: 2014 c.2 s.39

s.5, amended: 2014 c.2 Sch.12 para.15

s.12, amended: 2014 c.2 s.39

14. Animals (Scientific Procedures) Act 1986

applied: 2014 c.23 s.110, SI 2014/951 Sch.4 para.3

s.2B, applied: SI 2014/3266 Reg.6

s.2C, referred to: SI 2014/3266 Reg.6

s.30, referred to: SI 2014/3266 Reg.6

Sch.1, amended: SI 2014/1240 Sch.6 para.3, SI 2014/2124 Reg.2

31. Airports Act 1986

s.22, amended: 2014 c.2 Sch.12 para.17

s.24, amended: 2014 c.2 Sch.12 para.18

s.35, enabling: SI 2014/2713

s.74, amended: SI 2014/892 Sch.1 para.43

s.74, repealed (in part): SI 2014/892 Sch.1 para.43

33. Disabled Persons (Services, Consultation and Representation) Act 1986

s.2, applied: SSI 2014/345 Sch.1 Part 1

s.2, referred to: 2014 asp 9 Sch.1 Part 1

s.4, applied: SI 2014/829 Sch.1 para.11

s.5, amended: 2014 c.6 Sch.3 para.64

s.5, applied: SI 2014/1530 Reg.17

s.7, applied: SSI 2014/344 Sch.1, Sch.2, SSI 2014/345 Sch.1 Part 1

s.7, referred to: 2014 asp 9 Sch.1 Part 1

s.8, applied: SI 2014/829 Sch.1 para.12

s.16, applied: SSI 2014/345 Sch.1 Part 1

41. Finance Act 1986

s.24, amended: 2014 c.14 Sch.4 para.37

s.24, repealed (in part): 2014 c.14 Sch.4 para.37, Sch.7

s.66, applied: 2014 c.26 Sch.24 para.6

s.67, amended: 2014 c.26 Sch.24 para.9

s.80B, applied: SI 2014/2942 Reg.2

s.80B, enabling: SI 2014/2942

s.80C, applied: SI 2014/9 Reg.4

s.89AA, applied: SI 2014/9 Reg.4

s.90, amended: 2014 c.26 s.114

s.98, applied: 2014 c.26 s.114

s.98, enabling: SI 2014/1932

s.99, amended: 2014 c.26 Sch.24 para.2

s.99A, amended: 2014 c.26 Sch.24 para.3

s.99A, applied: 2014 c.26 Sch.24 para.8

s.102, see *Buzzoni v Revenue and Customs Commissioners* [2013] EWCA Civ 1684, [2014] 1 W.L.R. 3040 (CA (Civ Div)), Moses LJ

s.102, amended: 2014 c.26 Sch.37 para.17

42. Appropriation Act 1986

Sch.4 Part 9, varied: SI 2014/2708 Art.5

44. Gas Act 1986

see *Laverty v British Gas Trading Ltd* [2014] EWHC 2721 (Ch), [2014] B.C.C. 701 (Ch D (Companies Ct)), Sir Terence Etherton C

applied: 2014 c.5 Sch.1 para.1, 2014 c.25 Sch.1, SI 2014/631 Art.3

Part I, applied: SI 2014/3219 Art.34

s.4AB, amended: SI 2014/631 Sch.1 para.4

s.4B, amended: SI 2014/892 Sch.1 para.45

s.4D, amended: SI 2014/892 Sch.1 para.46

s.4D, repealed (in part): SI 2014/892 Sch.1 para.46

s.5, referred to: SI 2014/2418 Sch.1

s.6A, amended: SI 2014/631 Sch.1 para.4

s.6A, applied: SI 2014/528

s.6A, enabling: SI 2014/528

s.7, applied: SI 2014/826 Reg.4, SI 2014/899 Reg.4

s.7A, applied: SI 2014/826 Reg.4, SI 2014/899 Reg.4, SI 2014/1648 Reg.3

s.8, amended: SI 2014/631 Sch.1 para.4

s.8, applied: SI 2014/1648 Reg.3

s.8D, applied: SI 2014/3333 Reg.4

s.8H, amended: SI 2014/3333 Reg.2

s.8K, amended: SI 2014/3333 Reg.2

s.8K, applied: SI 2014/3333 Reg.4

s.8N, amended: SI 2014/3333 Reg.2

s.23, amended: SI 2014/631 Sch.1 para.4

s.23B, amended: SI 2014/631 Sch.1 para.4

s.27, amended: SI 2014/892 Sch.1 para.47

s.27A, amended: SI 2014/631 Sch.1 para.4

s.30A, amended: SI 2014/631 Sch.1 para.4

s.33AB, amended: SI 2014/631 Sch.1 para.4

s.33BAA, amended: SI 2014/631 Sch.1 para.4

s.33BC, amended: SI 2014/631 Sch.1 para.4

s.33BC, applied: SI 2014/1131, SI 2014/3219, SI 2014/3231

s.33BC, enabling: SI 2014/1131, SI 2014/2897, SI 2014/3219, SI 2014/3231

s.33BD, applied: SI 2014/1131, SI 2014/3219, SI 2014/3231

s.33BD, enabling: SI 2014/1131, SI
2014/2897, SI 2014/3219, SI 2014/3231
s.33DA, amended: SI 2014/631 Sch.1 para.4
s.34, amended: SI 2014/892 Sch.1 para.48
s.35, amended: SI 2014/892 Sch.1 para.49
s.36A, amended: SI 2014/892 Sch.1 para.50
s.41D, amended: SI 2014/631 Sch.1 para.4
s.41E, amended: SI 2014/631 Sch.1 para.4
s.41EB, amended: SI 2014/892 Sch.1
para.51
s.41EB, applied: SI 2014/559
s.41EB, referred to: SI 2014/892 Sch.2
para.2
s.41F, amended: SI 2014/631 Sch.1 para.4
s.41G, amended: SI 2014/631 Sch.1 para.4
s.41H, amended: SI 2014/631 Sch.1 para.4
s.41I, amended: SI 2014/631 Sch.1 para.4
s.48, amended: SI 2014/3332 Reg.2
s.66, amended: SI 2014/631 Sch.1 para.4
Sch.2A para.1, applied: SI 2014/1458 Art.5
Sch.2A para.4, applied: SI 2014/1458 Art.5
Sch.2B para.6A, amended: SI 2014/631
Sch.1 para.4
Sch.2B para.8, amended: SI 2014/631 Sch.1
para.4
Sch.2B para.8, applied: SI 2014/1458 Art.5
Sch.4B para.3, amended: SI 2014/3332
Reg.3
Sch.4B para.10, repealed: SI 2014/3332
Reg.3

45. Insolvency Act 1986
see *Hotel Company 42 The Calls Ltd, Re*
[2013] EWHC 3925 (Ch), [2014] B.C.C. 136
(Ch D), Judge Purle Q.C.; see *Icopal AS, Re*
[2013] EWHC 3469 (Ch), [2014] 2 All E.R.
(Comm) 1183 (Ch D), Proudman J; see
Kavanagh v Crystal Palace FC 2000 Ltd
[2013] EWCA Civ 1410, [2014] 1 All E.R.
1033 (CA (Civ Div)), Maurice Kay LJ; see
Kaye v South Oxfordshire DC [2013] EWHC
4165 (Ch), [2014] 2 All E.R. 1019 (Ch D
(Manchester)), Judge Hodge Q.C.; see
Kirkpatrick v Snoozebox Ltd [2014] B.C.C.
477 (QBD), Master Leslie; see *Magyar
Telecom BV, Re* [2013] EWHC 3800 (Ch),
[2014] B.C.C. 448 (Ch D), Richards J; see
Salliss v Hunt [2014] EWHC 229 (Ch),
[2014] 1 W.L.R. 2402 (Ch D), Sir Terence
Etherton C; see *Thomas v Edmondson*
[2014] EWHC 1494 (Ch), [2014] 3 All E.R.
976 (Ch D), Asplin J; see *Zodiac Pool

Solutions SAS, Re* [2014] EWHC 2365 (Ch),
[2014] B.C.C. 569 (Ch D (Companies Ct)),
Morgan J
applied: SI 2014/229 Sch.4 para.4, SI
2014/2068 Sch.1 para.6, SI 2014/2839
Reg.4, SI 2014/3348 Art.217
referred to: SI 2014/229 Art.10, Sch.1
para.1, Sch.4 para.4
Part I, applied: SI 2014/229 Art.6, Sch.4
para.5, SI 2014/512 Sch.1 para.2, Sch.1
para.3, Sch.1 para.8, SI 2014/817 r.2, SI
2014/882 Reg.5, SI 2014/2839 Reg.4, SI
2014/3051 Reg.45, SI 2014/3486 Art.3
Part I, referred to: SI 2014/229 Sch.4 para.4
Part II, applied: SI 2014/2839 Reg.4
Part III, applied: SI 2014/512 Sch.1 para.2,
Sch.1 para.3, Sch.1 para.8
Part IV, applied: SI 2014/512 Sch.1 para.2,
Sch.1 para.3, Sch.1 para.8, SI 2014/2839
Reg.4
Part IV, referred to: SI 2014/229 Sch.4
para.4
Part VI, referred to: SI 2014/229 Sch.4
para.4
Part VIIA, applied: SI 2014/817 r.3, SI
2014/2936 Sch.4 para.3
Part VIII, applied: SI 2014/2839 Reg.4, SI
2014/3486 Art.3, SSI 2014/281 Art.8, SSI
2014/285 Art.8
Part IX, applied: SI 2014/882 Reg.5
Part XVII, referred to: SI 2014/229 Sch.4
para.4
Pt IX s.279, see *Tucker v Atkins* [2013]
EWHC 4469 (Ch), [2014] B.P.I.R. 1359 (Ch
D), Barling J
Pt IX s.282, see *Yang v Official Receiver*
[2013] EWHC 3577 (Ch), [2014] B.P.I.R.
826 (Ch D (Manchester)), Judge Hodge Q.C.
Pt VIII s.257, see *Davis v Price* [2014]
EWCA Civ 26, [2014] 1 W.L.R. 2129 (CA
(Civ Div)), Arden LJ; see *Smith-Evans v
Smailes* [2013] EWHC 3199 (Ch), [2014] 1
W.L.R. 1548 (Ch D), Judge Purle Q.C.
s.1, applied: SI 2014/229 Art.11
s.1, varied: SI 2014/229 Sch.1 para.3
s.1A, applied: 2014 c.14 s.106
s.2, applied: SI 2014/2839 Reg.4
s.3, applied: SI 2014/2839 Reg.4
s.3, varied: SI 2014/229 Sch.1 para.4
s.4, amended: SI 2014/3486 Art.4

s.5, see *Westshield Ltd v Whitehouse* [2013]
EWHC 3576 (TCC), [2014] Bus. L.R. 268
(QBD (TCC)), Akenhead J
s.6, applied: SI 2014/229 Art.6
s.7, applied: SI 2014/229 Art.6, SI
2014/3204 Sch.4 para.14
s.7A, varied: SI 2014/229 Sch.1 para.5
s.51, applied: SSI 2014/114 r.29
s.51, repealed (in part): 2014 asp 11 Sch.4
s.74, see *Hamilton & Kinneil (Archerfield)
Ltd v Revenue and Customs Commissioners*
[2014] UKFTT 350 (TC), [2014] S.F.T.D.
1008 (FTT (Tax)), Judge Swami Raghavan
s.89, applied: SI 2014/2839 Reg.4
s.95, applied: SI 2014/2839 Reg.4
s.117, applied: SI 2014/817 r.2
s.122, applied: 2014 c.14 s.62
s.122, varied: 2014 c.14 s.62
s.123, see *Casa Estates (UK) Ltd (In
Liquidation), Re* [2014] EWCA Civ 383,
[2014] B.C.C. 269 (CA (Civ Div)), Sullivan
LJ; see *HLC Environmental Projects Ltd,
Re* [2013] EWHC 2876 (Ch), [2014] B.C.C.
337 (Ch D (Companies Ct)), John Randall
QC
s.127, see *Fuglers LLP v Solicitors
Regulation Authority* [2014] EWHC 179
(Admin), [2014] B.P.I.R. 610 (QBD
(Admin)), Popplewell J; see *Revenue and
Customs Commissioners v SED Essex Ltd*
[2013] EWHC 1583 (Ch), [2014] B.C.C. 628
(Ch D), John Randall QC
s.130, see *ARM Asset Backed Securities SA,
Re* [2014] EWHC 1097 (Ch), [2014] B.C.C.
260 (Ch D), Nugee J
s.135, applied: SSI 2014/114 r.29
s.175, amended: SI 2014/3486 Art.5
s.175, repealed (in part): SI 2014/3486 Art.5
s.176A, applied: SI 2014/229 Art.3
s.176A, referred to: SI 2014/229 Sch.5
para.1
s.178, see *Joint Liquidators of the Scottish
Coal Co Ltd, Noters* 2014 S.C. 372 (IH (2
Div)), The Lord Justice Clerk (Carloway);
see *Schroder Exempt Property Unit Trust v
Birmingham City Council* [2014] EWHC
2207 (Admin), [2014] B.C.C. 690 (QBD
(Admin)), Hickinbottom J
s.183, see *Science & Media LLP, Re* [2014]
B.P.I.R. 774 (Ch D (Companies Ct)),
Registrar Baister

s.212, see *HLC Environmental Projects Ltd,
Re* [2013] EWHC 2876 (Ch), [2014] B.C.C.
337 (Ch D (Companies Ct)), John Randall
QC
s.213, see *Bilta (UK) Ltd (In Liquidation) v
Nazir* [2013] EWCA Civ 968, [2014] Ch. 52
(CA (Civ Div)), Lord Dyson MR
s.220, see *Baker v West Reading Social Club*
[2014] EWHC 3033 (Ch), [2014] B.C.C. 575
(Ch D), Edward Murray
s.221, see *ARM Asset Backed Securities SA,
Re* [2013] EWHC 3351 (Ch), [2014] B.C.C.
252 (Ch D (Companies Ct)), David Richards
J
s.221, applied: SI 2014/3204 Sch.4 para.14
s.221, referred to: SI 2014/3204 Sch.4
para.14
s.233, see *Laverty v British Gas Trading Ltd*
[2014] EWHC 2721 (Ch), [2014] B.C.C. 701
(Ch D (Companies Ct)), Sir Terence
Etherton C
s.234, see *Kirkpatrick v Snoozebox Ltd*
[2014] B.C.C. 477 (QBD), Master Leslie
s.238, see *Bilta (UK) Ltd (In Liquidation) v
Nazir* [2013] EWCA Civ 968, [2014] Ch. 52
(CA (Civ Div)), Lord Dyson MR; see *Casa
Estates (UK) Ltd (In Liquidation), Re* [2014]
EWCA Civ 383, [2014] B.C.C. 269 (CA
(Civ Div)), Sullivan LJ; see *Ovenden
Colbert Printers Ltd (In Liquidation), Re*
[2013] EWCA Civ 1408, [2014] 1 B.C.L.C.
291 (CA (Civ Div)), Elias LJ; see *Sofra
Bakery Ltd (In Liquidation), Re* [2013]
EWHC 1499 (Ch), [2014] B.P.I.R. 435 (Ch
D (Leeds)), Andrew Sutcliffe, QC
s.240, see *Ovenden Colbert Printers Ltd (In
Liquidation), Re* [2013] EWCA Civ 1408,
[2014] 1 B.C.L.C. 291 (CA (Civ Div)), Elias
LJ
s.241, see *Ovenden Colbert Printers Ltd (In
Liquidation), Re* [2013] EWCA Civ 1408,
[2014] 1 B.C.L.C. 291 (CA (Civ Div)), Elias
LJ
s.242, varied: SI 2014/229 Sch.3 para.3
s.251, applied: SI 2014/2839 Reg.4
s.251, varied: SI 2014/229 Sch.3 para.4
s.251C, see *R. (on the application of
Howard) v Official Receiver* [2013] EWHC
1839 (Admin), [2014] Q.B. 930 (QBD
(Admin)), Stadlen J

s.251L, see *R. (on the application of Howard) v Official Receiver* [2013] EWHC 1839 (Admin), [2014] Q.B. 930 (QBD (Admin)), Stadlen J

s.252, see *Davis v Price* [2014] EWCA Civ 26, [2014] 1 W.L.R. 2129 (CA (Civ Div)), Arden LJ; see *Dewji v Banwaitt* [2013] EWHC 3746 (QB), [2014] B.P.I.R. 63 (QBD), Andrews J; see *Tucker v Atkins* [2013] EWHC 4469 (Ch), [2014] B.P.I.R. 1359 (Ch D), Barling J

s.256, applied: SI 2014/2839 Reg.4

s.256A, applied: SI 2014/2839 Reg.4

s.258, see *Narandas-Girdhar v Bradstock* [2014] EWHC 1321 (Ch), [2014] B.P.I.R. 1014 (Ch D), Jonathan Klein; see *Smith-Evans v Smailes* [2013] EWHC 3199 (Ch), [2014] 1 W.L.R. 1548 (Ch D), Judge Purle Q.C.

s.258, amended: SI 2014/3486 Art.6

s.260, see *Davis v Price* [2014] EWCA Civ 26, [2014] 1 W.L.R. 2129 (CA (Civ Div)), Arden LJ; see *Smith-Evans v Smailes* [2013] EWHC 3199 (Ch), [2014] 1 W.L.R. 1548 (Ch D), Judge Purle Q.C.; see *Thomas v Edmondson* [2014] EWHC 1494 (Ch), [2014] 3 All E.R. 976 (Ch D), Asplin J

s.262, see *Davis v Price* [2014] EWCA Civ 26, [2014] 1 W.L.R. 2129 (CA (Civ Div)), Arden LJ; see *Narandas-Girdhar v Bradstock* [2014] EWHC 1321 (Ch), [2014] B.P.I.R. 1014 (Ch D), Jonathan Klein; see *Smith-Evans v Smailes* [2013] EWHC 3199 (Ch), [2014] 1 W.L.R. 1548 (Ch D), Judge Purle Q.C.

s.264, see *JSC Bank of Moscow v Kekhman* [2014] B.P.I.R. 959 (Ch D (Bankruptcy Ct)), Registrar Baister

s.265, see *JSC Bank of Moscow v Kekhman* [2014] B.P.I.R. 959 (Ch D (Bankruptcy Ct)), Registrar Baister; see *Lombard North Central Plc v Blower* [2014] EWHC 2267 (Ch), [2014] I.L.Pr. 46 (Ch D), Amanda Tipples QC

s.267, see *Cahillane v National Asset Loan Management Ltd* [2014] EWHC 1992 (Ch), [2014] B.P.I.R. 1093 (Ch D), Judge Pelling QC; see *Lombard North Central Plc v Blower* [2014] EWHC 2267 (Ch), [2014] I.L.Pr. 46 (Ch D), Amanda Tipples QC; see *Rightmatch Ltd v Meisels* [2014] B.P.I.R.

733 (Ch D), Registrar Jones; see *Yang v Official Receiver* [2013] EWHC 3577 (Ch), [2014] B.P.I.R. 826 (Ch D (Manchester)), Judge Hodge Q.C.

s.268, see *Rightmatch Ltd v Meisels* [2014] B.P.I.R. 733 (Ch D), Registrar Jones

s.269, see *Cahillane v National Asset Loan Management Ltd* [2014] EWHC 1992 (Ch), [2014] B.P.I.R. 1093 (Ch D), Judge Pelling QC

s.271, see *Rightmatch Ltd v Meisels* [2014] B.P.I.R. 733 (Ch D), Registrar Jones

s.281A, applied: SSI 2014/281 Art.8, SSI 2014/285 Art.8

s.283A, see *Blemain Finance Ltd v Cugley* [2014] B.P.I.R. 20 (CC (Bristol)), Recorder Stead; see *Hunt v Conwy CBC* [2013] EWHC 1154 (Ch), [2014] 1 W.L.R. 254 (Ch D), Sir William Blackburne

s.284, see *Blemain Finance Ltd v Cugley* [2014] B.P.I.R. 20 (CC (Bristol)), Recorder Stead; see *Jones v Wealth Management (UK) Ltd* [2014] EWHC 842 (Ch), [2014] B.P.I.R. 948 (Ch D), Arnold J; see *National Westminster Bank Plc v Lucas* [2014] EWHC 653 (Ch), [2014] B.P.I.R. 551 (Ch D), Sales J

s.285, see *Evans v Finance-U-Ltd* [2013] EWCA Civ 869, [2014] R.T.R. 8 (CA (Civ Div)), Mummery, L.J.; see *Hellard v Chadwick* [2014] B.P.I.R. 163 (Ch D), Registrar Barber; see *Hellard v Chadwick* [2014] EWHC 2158 (Ch), [2014] B.P.I.R. 1234 (Ch D (Bankruptcy Ct)), Charles Hollander Q.C.

s.291, see *Blemain Finance Ltd v Cugley* [2014] B.P.I.R. 20 (CC (Bristol)), Recorder Stead

s.303, see *Aslam v Finn* [2013] EWHC 3405 (Ch), [2014] B.P.I.R. 1 (Ch D), Newey J

s.306, see *Blemain Finance Ltd v Cugley* [2014] B.P.I.R. 20 (CC (Bristol)), Recorder Stead; see *Helman v John Lyon Free Grammar School* [2014] EWCA Civ 17, [2014] 1 W.L.R. 2451 (CA (Civ Div)), Arden LJ

s.306B, applied: SI 2014/1610 r.60_4

s.307, see *Official Receiver v Baker* [2013] EWHC 4594 (Ch), [2014] B.P.I.R. 724 (Ch D), Warren J

s.310, see *Official Receiver v Baker* [2013] EWHC 4594 (Ch), [2014] B.P.I.R. 724 (Ch D), Warren J; see *Thomas v Edmondson* [2014] EWHC 1494 (Ch), [2014] 3 All E.R. 976 (Ch D), Asplin J; see *X (Application for Income Payments Order), Re* [2014] B.P.I.R. 1081 (Ch D), District Judge Smith
s.310, applied: SSI 2014/217 Reg.174, SSI 2014/292 Reg.174
s.310A, see *Thomas v Edmondson* [2014] EWHC 1494 (Ch), [2014] 3 All E.R. 976 (Ch D), Asplin J
s.313, see *Official Receiver v Parkins* [2014] B.P.I.R. 1054 (Ch D), Chief Registrar Baister
s.315, see *Hunt v Conwy CBC* [2013] EWHC 1154 (Ch), [2014] 1 W.L.R. 254 (Ch D), Sir William Blackburne
s.320, see *Hunt v Conwy CBC* [2013] EWHC 1154 (Ch), [2014] 1 W.L.R. 254 (Ch D), Sir William Blackburne
s.322, see *Hellard v Chadwick* [2014] B.P.I.R. 163 (Ch D), Registrar Barber
s.328, amended: SI 2014/3486 Art.7
s.328, repealed (in part): SI 2014/3486 Art.7
s.339, see *Bramston v Riaz* [2014] B.P.I.R. 42 (CC (Wakefield)), Deputy District Judge Josling; see *Hellard v Chadwick* [2014] EWHC 2158 (Ch), [2014] B.P.I.R. 1234 (Ch D (Bankruptcy Ct)), Charles Hollander Q.C.
s.340, see *Hellard v Chadwick* [2014] EWHC 2158 (Ch), [2014] B.P.I.R. 1234 (Ch D (Bankruptcy Ct)), Charles Hollander Q.C.
s.349A, see *Bannai v Erez* [2013] EWHC 3689 (Comm), [2014] B.P.I.R. 4 (QBD (Comm)), Burton J
s.365, see *Nicholson v Fayinka* [2014] B.P.I.R. 692 (Ch D (Bankruptcy Ct)), Registrar Baister
s.374, enabling: SI 2014/818
s.375, see *Yang v Official Receiver* [2013] EWHC 3577 (Ch), [2014] B.P.I.R. 826 (Ch D (Manchester)), Judge Hodge Q.C.
s.382, see *Hellard v Chadwick* [2014] B.P.I.R. 163 (Ch D), Registrar Barber; see *Hellard v Chadwick* [2014] EWHC 2158 (Ch), [2014] B.P.I.R. 1234 (Ch D (Bankruptcy Ct)), Charles Hollander Q.C.
s.385, see *Hunt v Conwy CBC* [2013] EWHC 1154 (Ch), [2014] 1 W.L.R. 254 (Ch D), Sir William Blackburne

s.386, amended: SI 2014/3486 Art.8
s.388, varied: SI 2014/229 Sch.3 para.5
s.390, applied: SSI 2014/296 Reg.3
s.411, applied: SI 2014/817
s.411, enabling: SI 2014/817, SSI 2014/114
s.412, applied: SI 2014/817
s.412, enabling: SI 2014/817
s.413, applied: SI 2014/817
s.414, applied: SI 2014/590
s.414, enabling: SI 2014/583, SI 2014/590, SI 2014/874, SI 2014/1834
s.415, applied: SI 2014/590
s.415, enabling: SI 2014/583, SI 2014/590, SI 2014/874, SI 2014/1834
s.420, applied: SI 2014/2839 Reg.4
s.421, applied: SI 2014/3051 Reg.45
s.423, see *B v IB (Order to set aside disposition under Insolvency Act)* [2013] EWHC 3755 (Fam), [2014] 2 F.L.R. 273 (Fam Div), Parker J; see *Erste Group Bank AG (London) v JSC (VMZ Red October)* [2013] EWHC 2926 (Comm), [2014] B.P.I.R. 81 (QBD (Comm)), Flaux J
s.426, see *Tambrook Jersey Ltd, Re* [2013] EWCA Civ 576, [2014] Ch. 252 (CA (Civ Div)), Longmore LJ
s.426A, disapplied: 2014 c.24 s.6
s.427, disapplied: 2014 c.24 s.6
s.429, applied: SI 2014/1132 Sch.7 para.7, SI 2014/2709 Sch.2 para.7
s.430, varied: SI 2014/229 Sch.3 para.6
s.436, see *GP Aviation Group International Ltd, Re* [2013] EWHC 1447 (Ch), [2014] 1 W.L.R. 166 (Ch D), Judge Pelling QC; see *Ovenden Colbert Printers Ltd (In Liquidation), Re* [2013] EWCA Civ 1408, [2014] 1 B.C.L.C. 291 (CA (Civ Div)), Elias LJ
Sch.A1, applied: SI 2014/229 Sch.4 para.4, Sch.4 para.37
Sch.A1 Part I para.1, varied: SI 2014/229 Sch.1 para.6
Sch.A1 Part I para.1A, varied: SI 2014/229 Sch.1 para.7
Sch.A1 Part I para.2, varied: SI 2014/229 Sch.1 para.8
Sch.A1 Part I para.3, varied: SI 2014/229 Sch.1 para.8
Sch.A1 Part I para.5, varied: SI 2014/229 Sch.1 para.8

Sch.A1 Part II para.7, applied: SI 2014/2839
Reg.4
Sch.A1 Part III para.12, applied: 2014 c.14
s.106
Sch.A1 Part V para.31, amended: SI
2014/3486 Art.9
Sch.B1, applied: SI 2014/229 Art.5, SI
2014/512 Sch.1 para.2, Sch.1 para.3, Sch.1
para.8
Sch.B1 Part 1 para.1, applied: SI 2014/2839
Reg.4
Sch.B1 Part 1 para.3, varied: SI 2014/229
Sch.1 para.11
Sch.B1 Pt 1 para.3, see *Kavanagh v Crystal
Palace FC 2000 Ltd* [2013] EWCA Civ
1410, [2014] 1 All E.R. 1033 (CA (Civ
Div)), Maurice Kay LJ
Sch.B1 Part 2 para.12, varied: SI 2014/229
Sch.1 para.12
Sch.B1 Part 3 para.14, varied: SI 2014/229
Sch.1 para.13
Sch.B1 Pt 3 para.14, see *Closegate Hotel
Development (Durham Ltd) v McLean*
[2013] EWHC 3237 (Ch), [2014] Bus. L.R.
405 (Ch D (Companies Ct)), Richard
Snowden QC
Sch.B1 Part 3 para.15, varied: SI 2014/229
Sch.1 para.14
Sch.B1 Part 3 para.18, applied: SI
2014/3486 Art.3
Sch.B1 Part 4 para.29, applied: SI
2014/3486 Art.3
Sch.B1 Part 6 para.41, varied: SI 2014/229
Sch.1 para.15
Sch.B1 Part 6 para.45, varied: SI 2014/229
Sch.1 para.16
Sch.B1 Part 7 para.46, varied: SI 2014/229
Sch.1 para.17
Sch.B1 Part 7 para.49, applied: SI 2014/229
Art.13, Art.14
Sch.B1 Part 7 para.49, varied: SI 2014/229
Sch.1 para.18
Sch.B1 Part 7 para.51, varied: SI 2014/229
Sch.1 para.19
Sch.B1 Part 7 para.52, varied: SI 2014/229
Sch.1 para.20
Sch.B1 Part 7 para.53, varied: SI 2014/229
Sch.1 para.21
Sch.B1 Part 7 para.54, applied: SI 2014/229
Art.13, Art.14

Sch.B1 Part 7 para.54, varied: SI 2014/229
Sch.1 para.22
Sch.B1 Part 7 para.55, varied: SI 2014/229
Sch.1 para.23
Sch.B1 Part 7 para.56, varied: SI 2014/229
Sch.1 para.24
Sch.B1 Part 7 para.57, applied: SI 2014/229
Sch.4 para.5
Sch.B1 Part 7 para.58, varied: SI 2014/229
Sch.1 para.25
Sch.B1 Part 8 para.59, varied: SI 2014/229
Sch.1 para.26
Sch.B1 Part 8 para.61, varied: SI 2014/229
Sch.1 para.27
Sch.B1 Part 8 para.64, varied: SI 2014/229
Sch.1 para.28
Sch.B1 Part 8 para.65, varied: SI 2014/229
Sch.1 para.29
Sch.B1 Part 8 para.73, amended: SI
2014/3486 Art.10
Sch.B1 Part 9 para.80, varied: SI 2014/229
Sch.1 para.30
Sch.B1 Part 9 para.83, applied: SI
2014/2839 Reg.4
Sch.B1 Part 9 para.84, applied: 2014 c.14
s.125
Sch.B1 Part 9 para.84, varied: SI 2014/229
Sch.1 para.31
Sch.B1 Part 10 para.91, varied: SI 2014/229
Sch.1 para.32
Sch.B1 Part 10 para.96, varied: SI 2014/229
Sch.1 para.33
Sch.B1 Part 11 para.111, varied: SI
2014/229 Sch.1 para.34
Sch.B1 para.49, see *Registrar of Companies
v Swarbrick* [2014] EWHC 1466 (Ch),
[2014] Bus. L.R. 625 (Ch D), Richard
Spearman QC; see *UK Coal Operations Ltd,
Re* [2013] EWHC 2581 (Ch), [2014] 1
B.C.L.C. 471 (Ch D), Judge Purle Q.C.
Sch.B1 para.51, see *UK Coal Operations
Ltd, Re* [2013] EWHC 2581 (Ch), [2014] 1
B.C.L.C. 471 (Ch D), Judge Purle Q.C.
Sch.B1 para.52, see *UK Coal Operations
Ltd, Re* [2013] EWHC 2581 (Ch), [2014] 1
B.C.L.C. 471 (Ch D), Judge Purle Q.C.
Sch.B1 para.55, see *Parmeko Holdings Ltd
(In Administration), Re* [2014] B.C.C. 159
(Ch D (Birmingham)), Judge Cooke

Sch.B1 para.59, see *Maxwell v Brookes* [2014] B.P.I.R. 1395 (Ch D (Companies Ct)), Registrar Jones

Sch.B1 para.60, see *MF Global UK Ltd (In Special Administration), Re* [2014] EWHC 2222 (Ch), [2014] Bus. L.R. 1156 (Ch D (Companies Ct)), Richards J

Sch.B1 para.63, see *Lehman Brothers International (Europe) (In Administration), Re* [2013] EWHC 1664 (Ch), [2014] B.C.C. 132 (Ch D), David Richards J

Sch.B1 para.64, see *Closegate Hotel Development (Durham Ltd) v McLean* [2013] EWHC 3237 (Ch), [2014] Bus. L.R. 405 (Ch D (Companies Ct)), Richard Snowden QC

Sch.B1 para.67, see *GSM Export (UK) Ltd (In Administration) v Revenue and Customs Commissioners* [2014] UKUT 457 (TCC), [2014] B.V.C. 539 (UT (Tax)), Judge Roger Berner

Sch.B1 para.69, see *Hellas Communications (Luxembourg) II SCA, Re* [2014] B.P.I.R. 179 (Ch D), Registrar Jones

Sch.B1 para.74, see *Hockin v Marsden* [2014] EWHC 763 (Ch), [2014] Bus. L.R. 441 (Ch D (Companies Ct)), Nicholas le Poidevin QC

Sch.B1 para.83, see *UK Coal Operations Ltd, Re* [2013] EWHC 2581 (Ch), [2014] 1 B.C.L.C. 471 (Ch D), Judge Purle Q.C.

Sch.B1 para.99, see *Hotel Company 42 The Calls Ltd, Re* [2013] EWHC 3925 (Ch), [2014] B.C.C. 136 (Ch D), Judge Purle Q.C.

Sch.B1 para.111, see *Mackellar v Griffin* [2014] EWHC 2644 (Ch), [2014] B.P.I.R. 1516 (Ch D), Mann J

Sch.1, see *Maxwell v Brookes* [2014] B.P.I.R. 1395 (Ch D (Companies Ct)), Registrar Jones

Sch.1 para.3, varied: SI 2014/229 Sch.1 para.38

Sch.1 para.15, varied: SI 2014/229 Sch.1 para.39

Sch.1 para.16, varied: SI 2014/229 Sch.1 para.40

Sch.1 para.18, see *MF Global UK Ltd (In Special Administration), Re* [2014] EWHC 2222 (Ch), [2014] Bus. L.R. 1156 (Ch D (Companies Ct)), Richards J

Sch.3 Part I, applied: SI 2014/3204 Sch.4 para.14

Sch.4A, applied: SI 2014/512 Sch.1 para.2, SSI 2014/281 Art.8, SSI 2014/285 Art.8, SSI 2014/296 Reg.4

Sch.4 Pt II para.4, see *Kirkpatrick v Snoozebox Ltd* [2014] B.C.C. 477 (QBD), Master Leslie

Sch.4 Pt III para.6, see *GP Aviation Group International Ltd, Re* [2013] EWHC 1447 (Ch), [2014] 1 W.L.R. 166 (Ch D), Judge Pelling QC

Sch.4ZA Pt I, see *R. (on the application of Howard) v Official Receiver* [2013] EWHC 1839 (Admin), [2014] Q.B. 930 (QBD (Admin)), Stadlen J

Sch.6, amended: SI 2014/3486 Art.11

Sch.6 para.15BA, added: SI 2014/3486 Art.11

Sch.6 para.15C, amended: SI 2014/3486 Art.11

Sch.10, varied: SI 2014/229 Sch.3 para.7

46. Company Directors Disqualification Act 1986

applied: 2014 asp 16 Sch.1 para.2, SI 2014/1132 Sch.7 para.7, SI 2014/1825 Art.3, SI 2014/2709 Sch.2 para.7, SI 2014/3348 Art.217

s.1A, see *Harris v Secretary of State for Business, Innovation and Skills* [2013] EWHC 2514 (Ch), [2014] 1 B.C.L.C. 447 (Ch D), Judge Simon Barker QC

s.1A, applied: SSI 2014/296 Reg.4

s.2, see *Secretary of State for Business, Innovation and Skills v Weston* [2014] EWHC 2933 (Ch), [2014] B.C.C. 581 (Ch D (Birmingham)), Judge David Cooke

s.4, see *Secretary of State for Business, Innovation and Skills v Weston* [2014] EWHC 2933 (Ch), [2014] B.C.C. 581 (Ch D (Birmingham)), Judge David Cooke

s.6, see *Secretary of State for Business, Innovation and Skills v Weston* [2014] EWHC 2933 (Ch), [2014] B.C.C. 581 (Ch D (Birmingham)), Judge David Cooke

s.7, applied: SI 2014/882 Reg.5

s.8A, amended: SI 2014/892 Sch.1 para.53

s.9A, amended: SI 2014/892 Sch.1 para.53

s.9B, amended: SI 2014/892 Sch.1 para.53

s.9C, amended: SI 2014/892 Sch.1 para.53

s.9D, amended: SI 2014/892 Sch.1 para.54

s.16, amended: SI 2014/892 Sch.1 para.53
s.17, amended: SI 2014/892 Sch.1 para.53
s.18, amended: SI 2014/892 Sch.1 para.53
s.22E, amended: 2014 c.14 Sch.4 para.38, SI
2014/574 Reg.6

47. Legal Aid (Scotland) Act 1986
s.6, see *Donaldson v Scottish Legal Aid
Board* [2014] CSIH 31, 2014 S.C. 689 (IH
(Ex Div)), Lady Paton
s.9, enabling: SSI 2014/366
s.20, amended: 2014 asp 8 Sch.5 para.4
s.21, amended: 2014 asp 18 Sch.5 para.14
s.25, amended: 2014 asp 18 Sch.5 para.14
s.28F, amended: 2014 asp 8 Sch.5 para.3
s.28L, amended: 2014 asp 8 s.92
s.28LA, added: 2014 asp 8 s.92
s.33, applied: 2014 asp 18 s.105, s.106
s.33, enabling: SSI 2014/257, SSI 2014/366
s.34, amended: SSI 2014/232 Reg.3
s.36, enabling: SSI 2014/366
s.37, amended: 2014 asp 8 Sch.5 para.3
s.37, applied: SSI 2014/366
Sch.2 Part I para.1, amended: 2014 asp 18
Sch.5 para.14
Sch.2 Part II para.3, repealed (in part): 2014
asp 18 Sch.5 para.23
Sch.2 Part II para.3A, added: 2014 asp 18
Sch.5 para.23

49. Agriculture Act 1986
s.8, repealed: SI 2014/1924 Sch.1
s.24, amended: SI 2014/1924 Sch.1
s.24, repealed (in part): SI 2014/1924 Sch.1
Sch.1 Part III para.17, varied: SI 2014/2708
Art.5

50. Social Security Act 1986
s.63, applied: SI 2014/516 Art.4

53. Building Societies Act 1986
applied: SI 2014/2418 Sch.1
s.74, enabling: SI 2014/48
s.90B, applied: SI 2014/3486
s.90B, enabling: SI 2014/3486
s.90D, amended: SI 2014/3344 Art.4
s.90D, repealed (in part): SI 2014/3344 Art.4
s.119, applied: SI 2014/3330 Reg.12
Sch.2 Part I para.3, amended: SI 2014/3486
Art.35
Sch.2 Part I para.5, applied: SI 2014/3330
Reg.12
Sch.15 Part I para.1A, added: SI 2014/3486
Art.32

Sch.15 Part I para.3, amended: SI 2014/3486
Art.32
Sch.15 Part II para.6A, added: SI 2014/3486
Art.33
Sch.15 Part II para.7, amended: SI
2014/3486 Art.33
Sch.15 Part II para.12, amended: SI
2014/3486 Art.33
Sch.15 Part II para.23A, added: SI
2014/3486 Art.33
Sch.15 Part III para.34A, added: SI
2014/3486 Art.34
Sch.15 Part III para.35, amended: SI
2014/3486 Art.34
Sch.15 Part III para.40, amended: SI
2014/3486 Art.34
Sch.15 Part III para.50A, added: SI
2014/3486 Art.34
Sch.18 Part I para.6, repealed: 2014 c.14
Sch.7

55. Family Law Act 1986
Part I c.III, applied: 2014 asp 18 s.43
s.1, see *A v A (Children) (Habitual
Residence)* [2014] A.C. 1 (SC), Lady Hale
JSC
s.1, amended: 2014 c.6 s.9
s.2, see *A v A (Children) (Habitual
Residence)* [2014] A.C. 1 (SC), Lady Hale
JSC
s.2, amended: 2014 c.6 s.9
s.5, amended: 2014 c.6 Sch.2 para.50
s.6, amended: 2014 c.6 Sch.2 para.51
s.6, repealed (in part): 2014 c.6 Sch.2
para.51
s.33, applied: SI 2014/840 r.16
s.34, applied: SI 2014/840 r.16
s.51, see *Ivleva (formerly Yates) v Yates*
[2014] EWHC 554 (Fam), [2014] 2 F.L.R.
1126 (Fam Div), Peter Jackson J
s.54, see *NP v KRP (Recognition of Foreign
Divorce)* [2013] EWHC 694 (Fam), [2014] 2
F.L.R. 1 (Fam Div), Parker J
s.55, see *NP v KRP (Recognition of Foreign
Divorce)* [2013] EWHC 694 (Fam), [2014] 2
F.L.R. 1 (Fam Div), Parker J
s.55, applied: SI 2014/840 Sch.1
s.55A, applied: SI 2014/840 Sch.1
s.56, applied: SI 2014/840 Sch.1
s.57, see *A County Council v M* [2013]
EWHC 1501 (Fam), [2014] 1 F.L.R. 881
(Fam Div), Peter Jackson J

s.58, see *A Local Authority v X* [2013]
EWHC 3274 (Fam), [2014] 2 F.L.R. 123
(Fam Div (Birmingham)), Holman J

63. Housing and Planning Act 1986
s.42, enabling: SI 2014/692

64. Public Order Act 1986
see *Walker v Commissioner of Police of the
Metropolis* [2014] EWCA Civ 897, Times,
July 16, 2014 (CA (Civ Div)), Rimer LJ
s.1, see *Mitsui Sumitomo Insurance Co
(Europe) Ltd v Mayor's Office for Policing
and Crime* [2013] EWHC 2734 (Comm),
[2014] 1 All E.R. 422 (QBD (Comm)),
Flaux J
s.8, see *Mitsui Sumitomo Insurance Co
(Europe) Ltd v Mayor's Office for Policing
and Crime* [2013] EWHC 2734 (Comm),
[2014] 1 All E.R. 422 (QBD (Comm)),
Flaux J
s.11, see *Powlesland v DPP* [2013] EWHC
3846 (Admin), [2014] 1 W.L.R. 2984 (DC),
Goldring LJ
s.11, applied: 2014 c.12 s.36
s.12, see *Powlesland v DPP* [2013] EWHC
3846 (Admin), [2014] 1 W.L.R. 2984 (DC),
Goldring LJ

1987

4. Ministry of Defence Police Act 1987
s.2, applied: 2014 c.20 s.5
s.2, varied: 2014 c.20 s.5

12. Petroleum Act 1987
s.21, applied: SI 2014/1253 Art.2, SI
2014/2260 Art.2, SI 2014/3212 Art.2
s.22, enabling: SI 2014/1253, SI 2014/2260,
SI 2014/3212
s.24, applied: SI 2014/3212(b), SI
2014/1253, SI 2014/2260

15. Reverter of Sites Act 1987
applied: SI 2014/2295, SI 2014/2631
s.1, applied: SI 2014/1836, SI 2014/1836
Art.3, SI 2014/2235, SI 2014/2235 Art.3,
Art.4, SI 2014/2236, SI 2014/2236 Art.3,
Art.4, SI 2014/2295, SI 2014/2295 Art.3, SI
2014/2631
s.5, applied: SI 2014/1836, SI 2014/2235, SI
2014/2236
s.5, enabling: SI 2014/1836, SI 2014/2235,
SI 2014/2236, SI 2014/2295

16. Finance Act 1987
s.55, amended: 2014 c.29 s.4

18. Debtors (Scotland) Act 1987
Part IA, applied: 2014 asp 18 Sch.1 para.7
Part III, applied: 2014 asp 18 Sch.1 para.7
Part IIIA, applied: 2014 asp 18 Sch.1 para.7
s.1, amended: 2014 asp 16 Sch.4 para.1
s.1, applied: 2014 asp 18 Sch.1 para.11
s.5, amended: 2014 asp 16 Sch.4 para.1
s.5, applied: 2014 asp 18 Sch.1 para.11
s.15K, enabling: SSI 2014/291
s.15N, applied: 2014 asp 18 Sch.1 para.7
s.71, applied: SSI 2014/296 Reg.8
s.75, enabling: SSI 2014/29
s.90, see *Little Cumbrae Estate Ltd v
Rolyat1 Ltd* [2014] CSOH 163, 2014 S.L.T.
1118 (OH), Lord Woolman
s.106, amended: 2014 asp 16 Sch.4 para.1

26. Housing (Scotland) Act 1987
applied: 2014 c.22 Sch.3 para.2
Part I, applied: 2014 c.22 Sch.3 para.2
Part XIV, repealed: 2014 asp 14 s.99
s.4, referred to: 2014 asp 9 Sch.1 Part 1
s.19, amended: 2014 asp 14 Sch.2 para.4
s.20, amended: 2014 asp 14 s.3, s.5, s.6,
Sch.2 para.4
s.20A, added: 2014 asp 14 s.4
s.20B, added: 2014 asp 14 s.6
s.21, amended: 2014 asp 14 s.4
s.21, repealed (in part): 2014 asp 14 Sch.2
para.4
s.24, amended: 2014 asp 14 Sch.2 para.4
s.24, applied: 2014 c.22 Sch.3 para.7
s.29, applied: SSI 2014/243 Art.3, Art.5
s.29, enabling: SSI 2014/243
s.31, amended: 2014 asp 14 s.7, Sch.2 para.4
s.61, see *Maclennan v Dunedin Canmore
Housing Association Ltd* 2014 S.L.T. (Lands
Tr) 25 (Lands Tr (Scot)), J N Wright, QC;
see *McIntosh v Castle Rock Edinvar
Housing Association Ltd* 2014 S.L.T. (Lands
Tr) 35 (Lands Tr (Scot)), J N Wright, QC
s.61, applied: SI 2014/3219 Sch.4 para.1
s.61, repealed: 2014 asp 14 s.1
s.61A, see *Maclennan v Dunedin Canmore
Housing Association Ltd* 2014 S.L.T. (Lands
Tr) 25 (Lands Tr (Scot)), J N Wright, QC
s.61F, amended: 2014 asp 14 s.2
s.61ZA, amended: 2014 asp 14 s.2

s.63, see *Maclennan v Dunedin Canmore Housing Association Ltd* 2014 S.L.T. (Lands Tr) 25 (Lands Tr (Scot)), J N Wright, QC
s.71, see *Maclennan v Dunedin Canmore Housing Association Ltd* 2014 S.L.T. (Lands Tr) 25 (Lands Tr (Scot)), J N Wright, QC
s.82, amended: 2014 asp 14 Sch.2 para.4
s.84, repealed: 2014 asp 14 s.1
s.84A, referred to: SI 2014/3219 Sch.4 para.1
s.300, amended: 2014 c.14 Sch.4 para.39
s.338, amended: 2014 asp 14 Sch.2 para.4
Sch.9 para.2, amended: 2014 asp 14 s.92
Sch.9 para.2A, added: 2014 asp 14 s.92
Sch.9 para.3A, added: 2014 asp 14 s.92
Sch.9 para.4, repealed (in part): 2014 asp 14 s.92
Sch.9 para.5A, added: 2014 asp 14 s.92
Sch.9 para.6, repealed: 2014 asp 14 s.92
Sch.20, repealed: 2014 asp 14 s.99
Sch.21, repealed: 2014 asp 14 s.99

38. Criminal Justice Act 1987
see *Tchenguiz v Director of the Serious Fraud Office* [2013] EWHC 2128 (QB), [2014] 1 W.L.R. 1476 (QBD), Eder J
applied: SI 2014/1610 r.6_1
s.1, applied: SI 2014/2418 Sch.1
s.2, see *Tchenguiz v Director of the Serious Fraud Office* [2013] EWHC 2128 (QB), [2014] 1 W.L.R. 1476 (QBD), Eder J
s.2, applied: SI 2014/1610 r.6_1, r.6_29, r.6_31
s.3, see *Tchenguiz v Director of the Serious Fraud Office* [2013] EWHC 2128 (QB), [2014] 1 W.L.R. 1476 (QBD), Eder J
s.3, amended: 2014 c.12 s.149, SI 2014/834 Sch.2 para.7
s.4, applied: SI 2014/1610 r.14_1
s.7, applied: SI 2014/1610 r.3_14, r.3_26
s.8, applied: SI 2014/1610 r.3_18
s.9, applied: SI 2014/1610 r.74_1, r.35_3, r.36_2, r.34_3, r.33_6, r.35_4, r.3_14, r.66_1, r.66_4
s.10, applied: SI 2014/1610 r.3_14
s.11, applied: SI 2014/1610 r.16_1

42. Family Law Reform Act 1987
s.1, amended: SI 2014/560 Sch.1 para.19
s.18, amended: 2014 c.16 s.5

43. Consumer Protection Act 1987
see *Hufford v Samsung Electronics (UK) Ltd* [2014] EWHC 2956 (TCC), [2014] B.L.R. 633 (QBD (TCC)), Judge David Grant
s.2, see *Hufford v Samsung Electronics (UK) Ltd* [2014] EWHC 2956 (TCC), [2014] B.L.R. 633 (QBD (TCC)), Judge David Grant
s.11, applied: SI 2014/1130
s.11, enabling: SI 2014/1130

49. Territorial Sea Act 1987
s.1, varied: SI 2014/1105 Sch.1
s.1, enabling: SI 2014/1353
s.4, enabling: SI 2014/1105

51. Finance (No.2) Act 1987
s.102, applied: 2014 c.22 s.70
s.102, referred to: 2014 c.22 s.69
s.103, repealed (in part): 2014 c.26 Sch.21 para.5

53. Channel Tunnel Act 1987
s.11, enabling: SI 2014/409, SI 2014/1814

1988

1. Income and Corporation Taxes Act 1988
see *Felixstowe Dock and Railway Co Ltd v Revenue and Customs Commissioners (C-80/12)* [2014] S.T.C. 1489 (ECJ (Grand Chamber)), Judge Skouris (President)
Part VII c.I, applied: SI 2014/3037 Sch.2 para.4
Pt X., see *R. (on the application of Bampton Property Group Ltd) v King* [2012] EWCA Civ 1744, [2014] S.T.C. 56 (CA (Civ Div)), Rix LJ
Pt XV s.686, see *Gilchrist v Revenue and Customs Commissioners* [2014] UKUT 169 (TCC) (UT (Tax)), David Richards J; see *Trustees of the Travers Will Trust v Revenue and Customs Commissioners* [2014] S.F.T.D. 265 (FTT (Tax)), Judge Nicholas Paines QC
s.13, see *Ghelanis Superstore and Cash & Carry Ltd v Revenue and Customs Commissioners* [2014] UKFTT 111 (TC), [2014] S.F.T.D. 835 (FTT (Tax)), Judge J Blewitt
s.18, see *Prudential Assurance Co Ltd v Revenue and Customs Commissioners* [2013] EWHC 3249 (Ch), [2014] S.T.C.

1236 (Ch D), Henderson J; see *Shop Direct Group v Revenue and Customs Commissioners* [2014] EWCA Civ 255, [2014] S.T.C. 1383 (CA (Civ Div)), Rimer LJ; see *Versteegh Ltd v Revenue and Customs Commissioners* [2014] S.F.T.D. 547 (FTT (Tax)), Judge Roger Berner

s.74, see *Interfish Ltd v Revenue and Customs Commissioners* [2014] S.T.C. 79 (UT (Tax)), Birss J; see *McLaren Racing Ltd v Revenue and Customs Commissioners* [2014] UKUT 269 (TCC), [2014] S.T.C. 2417 (UT (Tax)), Warren J; see *Samadian v Revenue and Customs Commissioners* [2014] UKUT 13 (TCC), [2014] S.T.C. 763 (UT (Tax)), Sales J

s.103, see *Shop Direct Group v Revenue and Customs Commissioners* [2014] EWCA Civ 255, [2014] S.T.C. 1383 (CA (Civ Div)), Rimer LJ

s.106, see *Shop Direct Group v Revenue and Customs Commissioners* [2014] EWCA Civ 255, [2014] S.T.C. 1383 (CA (Civ Div)), Rimer LJ

s.118ZC, see *Hamilton & Kinneil (Archerfield) Ltd v Revenue and Customs Commissioners* [2014] UKFTT 350 (TC), [2014] S.F.T.D. 1008 (FTT (Tax)), Judge Swami Raghavan

s.160, see *Leeds Design Innovation Centre Ltd v Revenue and Customs Commissioners* [2014] UKFTT 9 (TC), [2014] S.F.T.D. 681 (FTT (Tax)), Judge Rachel Short

s.187, amended: 2014 c.14 Sch.4 para.40

s.203, see *Aberdeen Asset Management Plc v Revenue and Customs Commissioners* [2014] S.T.C. 438 (IH (1 Div)), The Lord President (Gill)

s.203F, see *Aberdeen Asset Management Plc v Revenue and Customs Commissioners* [2014] S.T.C. 438 (IH (1 Div)), The Lord President (Gill)

s.231, see *Prudential Assurance Co Ltd v Revenue and Customs Commissioners* [2013] EWHC 3249 (Ch), [2014] S.T.C. 1236 (Ch D), Henderson J; see *Trustees of the BT Pension Scheme v Revenue and Customs Commissioners* [2014] EWCA Civ 23, [2014] S.T.C. 1156 (CA (Civ Div)), Longmore LJ

s.249, see *Gilchrist v Revenue and Customs Commissioners* [2014] UKUT 169 (TCC) (UT (Tax)), David Richards J

s.289, see *Harvey's Jersey Cream Ltd v Revenue and Customs Commissioners* [2014] S.F.T.D. 599 (FTT (Tax)), Judge Charles Hellier

s.362, see *Vaccine Research LP v Revenue and Customs Commissioners* [2014] UKUT 389 (TCC), [2014] B.T.C. 525 (UT (Tax)), Sales J

s.380, see *Acornwood LLP v Revenue and Customs Commissioners* [2014] UKFTT 416 (TC), [2014] S.F.T.D. 694 (FTT (Tax)), Judge Colin Bishopp

s.381, see *Acornwood LLP v Revenue and Customs Commissioners* [2014] UKFTT 416 (TC), [2014] S.F.T.D. 694 (FTT (Tax)), Judge Colin Bishopp; see *Vaccine Research LP v Revenue and Customs Commissioners* [2014] UKUT 389 (TCC), [2014] B.T.C. 525 (UT (Tax)), Sales J

s.393A, see *Glapwell Football Club Ltd v Revenue and Customs Commissioners* [2014] S.F.T.D. 485 (FTT (Tax)), Judge John Walters Q.C.

s.402, see *Felixstowe Dock and Railway Co Ltd v Revenue and Customs Commissioners* [2014] UKFTT 452 (TC), [2014] S.F.T.D. 955 (FTT (Tax)), Judge Roger Berner

s.403, see *BUPA Insurance Ltd v Revenue and Customs Commissioners* [2014] UKUT 262 (TCC), [2014] S.T.C. 2615 (UT (Tax)), Asplin J; see *Glapwell Football Club Ltd v Revenue and Customs Commissioners* [2014] S.F.T.D. 485 (FTT (Tax)), Judge John Walters Q.C.

s.403C, see *BUPA Insurance Ltd v Revenue and Customs Commissioners* [2014] UKUT 262 (TCC), [2014] S.T.C. 2615 (UT (Tax)), Asplin J

s.406, see *Felixstowe Dock and Railway Co Ltd v Revenue and Customs Commissioners* (C-80/12) [2014] S.T.C. 1489 (ECJ (Grand Chamber)), Judge Skouris (President); see *Felixstowe Dock and Railway Co Ltd v Revenue and Customs Commissioners* [2014] UKFTT 452 (TC), [2014] S.F.T.D. 955 (FTT (Tax)), Judge Roger Berner

s.416, see *Ghelanis Superstore and Cash & Carry Ltd v Revenue and Customs*

Commissioners [2014] UKFTT 111 (TC), [2014] S.F.T.D. 835 (FTT (Tax)), Judge J Blewitt; see *UBS AG v Revenue and Customs Commissioners* [2014] EWCA Civ 452, [2014] S.T.C. 2278 (CA (Civ Div)), Rimer LJ

s.416, applied: SI 2014/1686 Sch.2 para.41

s.416, varied: SI 2014/1686 Sch.2 para.40

s.419, see *Aspect Capital Ltd v Revenue and Customs Commissioners* [2014] UKUT 81 (TCC), [2014] S.T.C. 1360 (UT (Tax)), Warren J

s.591B, see *John Mander Pension Scheme Trustees Ltd v Revenue and Customs Commissioners* [2013] EWCA Civ 1683, [2014] 1 W.L.R. 2209 (CA (Civ Div)), Moses LJ

s.591C, see *John Mander Pension Scheme Trustees Ltd v Revenue and Customs Commissioners* [2013] EWCA Civ 1683, [2014] 1 W.L.R. 2209 (CA (Civ Div)), Moses LJ

s.591D, see *John Mander Pension Scheme Trustees Ltd v Revenue and Customs Commissioners* [2013] EWCA Civ 1683, [2014] 1 W.L.R. 2209 (CA (Civ Div)), Moses LJ

s.592, see *Trustees of the BT Pension Scheme v Revenue and Customs Commissioners* [2014] EWCA Civ 23, [2014] S.T.C. 1156 (CA (Civ Div)), Longmore LJ

s.710, see *Barnes v Revenue and Customs Commissioners* [2014] EWCA Civ 31, [2014] B.T.C. 5 (CA (Civ Div)), McFarlane LJ

s.713, see *Barnes v Revenue and Customs Commissioners* [2014] EWCA Civ 31, [2014] B.T.C. 5 (CA (Civ Div)), McFarlane LJ

s.714, see *Barnes v Revenue and Customs Commissioners* [2014] EWCA Civ 31, [2014] B.T.C. 5 (CA (Civ Div)), McFarlane LJ

s.727, see *Barnes v Revenue and Customs Commissioners* [2014] EWCA Civ 31, [2014] B.T.C. 5 (CA (Civ Div)), McFarlane LJ

s.739, see *Fisher v Revenue and Customs Commissioners* [2014] UKFTT 804 (TC),

[2014] S.F.T.D. 1341 (FTT (Tax)), Judge Swami Raghavan

s.741, see *Fisher v Revenue and Customs Commissioners* [2014] UKFTT 804 (TC), [2014] S.F.T.D. 1341 (FTT (Tax)), Judge Swami Raghavan

s.744, see *Fisher v Revenue and Customs Commissioners* [2014] UKFTT 804 (TC), [2014] S.F.T.D. 1341 (FTT (Tax)), Judge Swami Raghavan

s.786, see *Versteegh Ltd v Revenue and Customs Commissioners* [2014] S.F.T.D. 547 (FTT (Tax)), Judge Roger Berner

s.790, see *Prudential Assurance Co Ltd v Revenue and Customs Commissioners* [2013] EWHC 3249 (Ch), [2014] S.T.C. 1236 (Ch D), Henderson J

s.826, amended: 2014 c.26 Sch.4 para.2

s.839, see *University of Huddersfield Higher Education Corp v Revenue and Customs Commissioners* [2014] S.F.T.D. 78 (FTT (Tax)), Judge David Demack

Sch.9 Part I, applied: 2014 c.14 s.4

Sch.23A para.3, see *Barnes v Revenue and Customs Commissioners* [2014] EWCA Civ 31, [2014] B.T.C. 5 (CA (Civ Div)), McFarlane LJ

4. Norfolk and Suffolk Broads Act 1988
s.17, amended: 2014 c.2 Sch.12 para.19
s.25, applied: 2014 c.2 s.44

9. Local Government Act 1988
see *Church of Jesus Christ of Latter-Day Saints v United Kingdom (7552/09)* (2014) 59 E.H.R.R. 18 (ECHR), Judge Ziemele (President)
Sch.2, disapplied: SI 2014/864 Art.8

14. Immigration Act 1988
applied: SI 2014/2604 Sch.1 para.2

20. Dartford-Thurrock Crossing Act 1988
s.25, enabling: SI 2014/2949
s.44, enabling: SI 2014/2949

30. Environment and Safety Information Act 1988
s.1, applied: SI 2014/469 Sch.4 para.26
s.3, applied: SI 2014/469 Sch.4 para.26
s.3, referred to: SI 2014/469 Sch.4 para.26
s.4, applied: SI 2014/469 Sch.4 para.26
s.4, referred to: SI 2014/469 Sch.4 para.26
Sch.1, amended: SI 2014/469 Sch.2 para.4

33. Criminal Justice Act 1988
see *R. v Boughton-Fox (Christopher)* [2014]
EWCA Crim 227, [2014] Lloyd's Rep. F.C.
343 (CA (Crim Div)), Pitchford LJ
applied: 2014 c.5 Sch.1 para.1, 2014 c.25
Sch.1, SI 2014/1610 r.29_26
Part IV, applied: SI 2014/1610 r.70_1
Part VI, applied: SI 2014/1610 r.56_1
s.30, applied: SI 2014/1610 r.33_3
s.32, applied: SI 2014/1610 r.38_11, r.37_4,
r.29_1, r.29_24, r.29_25, r.29_26
s.33, applied: SI 2014/1610 r.65_3
s.35, applied: SI 2014/1610 r.70_1
s.35, enabling: SI 2014/1651
s.36, applied: SI 2014/1610 r.70_1, r.74_2
s.39, see *R. v J* [2013] EWCA Crim 569,
[2014] Q.B. 561 (CA (Crim Div)), Sir John
Thomas PQBD
s.40, see *R. v J* [2013] EWCA Crim 569,
[2014] Q.B. 561 (CA (Crim Div)), Sir John
Thomas PQBD; see *R. v Lewis (Leroy)*
[2013] EWCA Crim 2596, [2014] 1 W.L.R.
2027 (CA (Crim Div)), McCombe LJ
s.40, applied: SI 2014/1610 r.14_2
s.41, see *R. v J* [2014] EWCA Crim 1442,
[2014] 2 Cr. App. R. (S.) 77 (CA (Crim
Div)), Rafferty LJ
s.71, applied: SI 2014/3141 Reg.20
s.72A, applied: SI 2014/1610 r.56_2
s.73, applied: SI 2014/1610 r.56_1
s.74A, applied: SI 2014/1610 r.56_3
s.75A, applied: SI 2014/1610 r.56_5
s.77, applied: SI 2014/3141 Reg.19
s.93A, see *R. v Onuigbo (aka Okoronkwo)*
(Unoamaka) [2014] EWCA Crim 65, [2014]
Lloyd's Rep. F.C. 302 (CA (Crim Div)),
Pitchford LJ
s.93H, applied: SI 2014/1610 r.56_4
s.122, applied: SI 2014/1610 r.3_24
s.133, see *R. (on the application of Ali) v*
Secretary of State for Justice [2014] EWCA
Civ 194, [2014] 1 W.L.R. 3202 (CA (Civ
Div)), Maurice Kay LJ
s.133, amended: 2014 c.12 s.175
s.133, applied: 2014 c.12 s.175
s.152, applied: SI 2014/1610 r.18_3
s.159, applied: SI 2014/1610 r.69_1, r.74_1,
r.69_8, r.76_1, r.76_6
Sch.3 para.1, applied: SI 2014/1610 r.70_2
Sch.3 para.4, applied: SI 2014/1610 r.74_2
Sch.3 para.6, applied: SI 2014/1610 r.70_7

Sch.3 para.9, applied: SI 2014/1610 r.74_2
Sch.3 para.11, applied: SI 2014/1610 r.76_1,
r.76_4
Sch.4, referred to: SI 2014/1610 r.56_1
36. Court of Session Act 1988
see *SA (Nigeria) v Secretary of State for the*
Home Department 2014 S.C. 1 (IH (2 Div)),
The Lord Justice Clerk (Carloway)
s.2, amended: 2014 asp 18 Sch.5 para.30
s.5, repealed: 2014 asp 18 Sch.5 para.30
s.5, enabling: SSI 2014/15, SSI 2014/119,
SSI 2014/152, SSI 2014/201, SSI 2014/291,
SSI 2014/302, SSI 2014/371
s.9, applied: 2014 asp 18 s.63
s.24, repealed: 2014 asp 18 Sch.5 para.32
s.26, amended: 2014 asp 18 Sch.5 para.30
s.27A, added: 2014 asp 18 s.89
s.27A, applied: 2014 asp 16 s.41
s.27B, applied: 2014 asp 16 s.41
s.27C, applied: 2014 asp 16 s.41
s.27C, referred to: 2014 asp 16 s.41
s.28, see *Scottish Ministers v Mirza* [2014]
CSIH 103 (IH (Ex Div)), Lady Clark of
Calton
s.31A, added: 2014 asp 18 s.115
s.32, amended: 2014 asp 18 Sch.5 para.32
s.40, see *Forbes v Strathclyde Partnership*
for Transport [2014] CSIH 33, 2014 S.C.
717 (IH (Ex Div)), Lord Brodie
s.40, substituted: 2014 asp 18 s.117
s.45, applied: SI 2014/2042 Reg.15
s.47, amended: 2014 asp 18 s.90
s.47A, added: 2014 asp 18 s.91
s.51, amended: 2014 asp 18 Sch.5 para.43
s.52, repealed (in part): 2014 asp 18 Sch.5
para.32
40. Education Reform Act 1988
s.122A, applied: SI 2014/1507
s.122A, enabling: SI 2014/1507
s.124B, repealed (in part): 2014 c.2 Sch.12
para.21
s.198, applied: SI 2014/1132 Reg.13,
Reg.84, Reg.91
s.216, applied: SI 2014/1530 Reg.49
Sch.7 para.18, amended: 2014 c.2 Sch.12
para.22
Sch.7 para.18, repealed (in part): 2014 c.2
Sch.12 para.22
Sch.10, applied: SI 2014/1132 Reg.84,
Reg.91

41. Local Government Finance Act 1988
see *Furlonger v Lalatta* [2014] EWHC 37
(Ch), [2014] L. & T.R. 14 (Ch D), Jonathan
Klein
s.42, applied: SI 2014/3204 Sch.2 para.4
s.43, see *Kenya Aid Programme v Sheffield
City Council* [2013] EWHC 54 (Admin),
[2014] Q.B. 62 (DC), Treacy LJ
s.43, applied: SI 2014/98 Sch.2 para.2
s.43, enabling: SI 2014/43, SI 2014/372
s.44, enabling: SI 2014/43, SI 2014/372
s.45, see *Pall Mall Investments (London) Ltd
v Gloucester City Council* [2014] EWHC
2247 (Admin), [2014] P.T.S.R. 1184 (DC),
Pitchford LJ; see *Pall Mall Investments Ltd
v Castle Point BC* [2013] EWHC 4238
(Admin), [2014] R.V.R. 236 (QBD
(Admin)), Phillips J; see *Schroder Exempt
Property Unit Trust v Birmingham City
Council* [2014] EWHC 2207 (Admin),
[2014] B.C.C. 690 (QBD (Admin)),
Hickinbottom J
s.45, applied: SI 2014/98 Sch.2 para.2
s.46A, see *Tull Properties Ltd v South
Gloucestershire Council* [2014] R.A. 180
(VT), Graham Zellick Q.C. (President)
s.54A, applied: SI 2014/1370 Art.2
s.54A, enabling: SI 2014/1370
s.60, enabling: SI 2014/3193
s.62, enabling: SI 2014/379
s.64, applied: SI 2014/98 Sch.2 para.2
s.65, see *Pall Mall Investments Ltd v Castle
Point BC* [2013] EWHC 4238 (Admin),
[2014] R.V.R. 236 (QBD (Admin)), Phillips
J; see *Schroder Exempt Property Unit Trust
v Birmingham City Council* [2014] EWHC
2207 (Admin), [2014] B.C.C. 690 (QBD
(Admin)), Hickinbottom J
s.66, see *Seabrook v Alexander (Valuation
Officer)* [2014] R.A. 382 (VT), Graham
Zellick Q.C. (President)
s.74, applied: SI 2014/863 Art.9, SI
2014/864 Art.9, SI 2014/865 Art.5, Art.11,
SI 2014/1012 Art.5, Sch.1 para.3
s.99, enabling: SI 2014/96
s.114, applied: 2014 c.2 Sch.7 para.5, Sch.7
para.6, SI 2014/2418 Sch.1
s.140, enabling: SI 2014/554
s.143, applied: SI 2014/822, SI 2014/1370

s.143, enabling: SI 2014/43, SI 2014/372, SI
2014/379, SI 2014/404, SI 2014/479, SI
2014/554, SI 2014/822, SI 2014/2841
s.146, enabling: SI 2014/372
Sch.4A, see *Metis Apartments Ltd v Grace
(Valuation Officer)* [2014] R.A. 222 (VT),
Graham Zellick Q.C. (President)
Sch.4A para.1, see *Tull Properties Ltd v
South Gloucestershire Council* [2014] R.A.
180 (VT), Graham Zellick Q.C. (President);
see *UKI (Kingsway) Ltd v Westminster City
Council* [2014] R.A. 367 (VT), Graham
Zellick Q.C. (President)
Sch.4A para.2, see *UKI (Kingsway) Ltd v
Westminster City Council* [2014] R.A. 367
(VT), Graham Zellick Q.C. (President)
Sch.4A para.8, see *UKI (Kingsway) Ltd v
Westminster City Council* [2014] R.A. 367
(VT), Graham Zellick Q.C. (President)
Sch.5 para.1, see *A&N Frozen Foods v
Alexander (Valuation Officer)* [2014] R.V.R.
326 (VT), Graham Zellick Q.C. (President);
see *Tunnel Tech Ltd v Reeves (Valuation
Officer)* [2014] UKUT 159 (LC), [2014]
R.A. 293 (UT (Lands)), Judge Mole QC
Sch.5 para.2, see *Tunnel Tech Ltd v Reeves
(Valuation Officer)* [2014] UKUT 159 (LC),
[2014] R.A. 293 (UT (Lands)), Judge Mole
QC
Sch.5 para.3, see *Tunnel Tech Ltd v Reeves
(Valuation Officer)* [2014] UKUT 159 (LC),
[2014] R.A. 293 (UT (Lands)), Judge Mole
QC
Sch.5 para.8, see *A&N Frozen Foods v
Alexander (Valuation Officer)* [2014] R.V.R.
326 (VT), Graham Zellick Q.C. (President)
Sch.5 para.9, see *A&N Frozen Foods v
Alexander (Valuation Officer)* [2014] R.V.R.
326 (VT), Graham Zellick Q.C. (President)
Sch.5 para.15, see *Lake District National
Park Authority v Grace (Valuation Officer)*
[2014] R.A. 81 (VT), A Clark
Sch.6, see *Cerep III TW Sarl v Kendrick
(Valuation Officer)* [2014] R.V.R. 331 (VT),
A Ramsay
Sch.6 para.2, see *Pearce's Appeal, Re* [2014]
UKUT 291 (LC), [2014] R.A. 341 (UT
(Lands)), Martin Rodger Q.C.; see *R3
Products Ltd v Salt (Valuation Officer)*
[2014] UKUT 333 (LC) (UT (Lands)), PD
McCrea FRICS

Sch.6 para.2, referred to: SI 2014/2917 Art.2
Sch.6 para.2, enabling: SI 2014/2841, SI 2014/2917
Sch.7B, applied: SI 2014/98 Reg.5
Sch.7 Part I para.3B, applied: SI 2014/124 Art.2
Sch.7 Part I para.5, applied: SI 2014/124
Sch.7 Part I para.5, enabling: SI 2014/2, SI 2014/124
Sch.7B Part III para.6, applied: SI 2014/98 Reg.5
Sch.7B Part III para.7, applied: SI 2014/98 Reg.5
Sch.7B Part IV para.9, applied: SI 2014/98 Reg.5
Sch.7B Part IV para.10, applied: SI 2014/98 Reg.5
Sch.7B Part V para.13, applied: SI 2014/98 Reg.5
Sch.7B Part V para.16, applied: SI 2014/98 Reg.5
Sch.7B Part VII para.22, enabling: SI 2014/822
Sch.7B Part VII para.23, applied: SI 2014/98 Reg.5
Sch.7B Part VII para.25, enabling: SI 2014/822
Sch.7B Part VII para.26, applied: SI 2014/98 Reg.5
Sch.7B Part VII para.28, applied: SI 2014/98 Reg.5
Sch.7B Part VII para.30, applied: SI 2014/98 Reg.5
Sch.7B Part VIII para.33, applied: SI 2014/98 Sch.2 para.2
Sch.7B Part IX para.37, enabling: SI 2014/822
Sch.7B Part X para.39, applied: SI 2014/98
Sch.7B Part X para.39, enabling: SI 2014/98
Sch.8 Part I para.3, varied: SI 2014/939 Art.4
Sch.8 Part II para.4, applied: SI 2014/939 Art.3
Sch.8 Part II para.4, enabling: SI 2014/3193
Sch.8 Part II para.5, applied: SI 2014/939 Art.3
Sch.8 Part II para.6, applied: SI 2014/939 Art.3
Sch.8 Part II para.6, enabling: SI 2014/3193
Sch.8 Part III para.12, applied: SI 2014/939 Art.3

Sch.8 Part III para.15, applied: SI 2014/939 Art.3
Sch.9 para.1, enabling: SI 2014/379, SI 2014/479
Sch.9 para.2, enabling: SI 2014/379, SI 2014/404, SI 2014/479
Sch.11 Part 2 para.1, enabling: SI 2014/554
Sch.11 Part 3 para.8, enabling: SI 2014/554

43. Housing (Scotland) Act 1988
s.12, applied: 2014 asp 14 s.16
s.16, amended: 2014 asp 14 Sch.1 para.33
s.17, amended: 2014 asp 14 Sch.1 para.34
s.18, amended: 2014 asp 14 Sch.1 para.35
s.19, amended: 2014 asp 14 Sch.1 para.36
s.20, amended: 2014 asp 14 Sch.1 para.37
s.21, amended: 2014 asp 14 Sch.1 para.38
s.22, amended: 2014 asp 14 Sch.1 para.39
s.25, amended: 2014 asp 14 Sch.1 para.40
s.28, amended: 2014 asp 14 Sch.1 para.41
s.29, amended: 2014 asp 14 Sch.1 para.42
s.30, amended: 2014 asp 14 Sch.1 para.43
s.33, amended: 2014 asp 14 Sch.1 para.44
s.36, amended: 2014 asp 14 Sch.1 para.45
s.42, amended: 2014 asp 14 Sch.1 para.46, Sch.2 para.5
s.55, amended: 2014 asp 14 Sch.1 para.47
Sch.2 para.7, repealed: 2014 asp 14 Sch.2 para.5
Sch.5 Part I, amended: 2014 asp 14 Sch.1 para.48
Sch.5 Part II, amended: 2014 asp 14 Sch.1 para.48
Sch.5 Part III para.2, amended: 2014 asp 14 Sch.1 para.48
Sch.5 Part III para.3, amended: 2014 asp 14 Sch.1 para.48
Sch.7 para.19, repealed: 2014 asp 14 Sch.2 para.5

45. Firearms (Amendment) Act 1988
applied: SI 2014/1638 Reg.5
s.17, applied: SI 2014/1638 Sch.2 para.15

48. Copyright, Designs and Patents Act 1988
Part I c.III, amended: SI 2014/1384 Reg.2
Part I c.IIIA, added: SI 2014/2861 Reg.3
Part I c.IV, applied: SI 2014/2863 Art.6
Part II c.III, applied: SI 2014/2863 Art.6
s.4, see *Taylor v Maguire* [2013] EWHC 3804 (IPEC), [2014] E.C.D.R. 4 (IPEC), District Judge Clarke
s.20, see *Paramount Home Entertainment International Ltd v British Sky Broadcasting*

Ltd [2013] EWHC 3479 (Ch), [2014]
E.C.D.R. 7 (Ch D), Arnold J
s.27, amended: SI 2014/1372 Sch.1 para.2,
SI 2014/1384 Sch.1 para.1, SI 2014/2361
Reg.4
s.27, applied: SI 2014/2361 Reg.5
s.28B, added: SI 2014/2361 Reg.3
s.28B, applied: SI 2014/2361 Reg.5
s.29, amended: SI 2014/1372 Reg.3
s.29, repealed (in part): SI 2014/1372 Reg.3
s.29A, added: SI 2014/1372 Reg.3
s.30, amended: SI 2014/2356 Reg.3
s.30A, added: SI 2014/2356 Reg.5
s.31A, substituted: SI 2014/1384 Reg.2
s.31B, substituted: SI 2014/1384 Reg.2
s.31C, repealed: SI 2014/1384 Sch.1 para.8
s.31F, substituted: SI 2014/1384 Reg.2
s.32, substituted: SI 2014/1372 Reg.4
s.35, substituted: SI 2014/1372 Reg.4
s.36, substituted: SI 2014/1372 Reg.4
s.37, repealed: SI 2014/1372 Sch.1 para.14
s.40A, amended: SI 2014/1372 Sch.1 para.3
s.40B, added: SI 2014/1372 Reg.5
s.41, substituted: SI 2014/1372 Reg.5
s.44B, added: SI 2014/2861 Reg.3
s.47, amended: SI 2014/1385 Reg.2
s.48, amended: 2014 c.23 Sch.5 para.33,
Sch.7 para.25, SI 2014/1385 Reg.2
s.51, amended: 2014 c.18 s.1
s.53, amended: 2014 c.18 s.5
s.61, amended: SI 2014/1372 Reg.7
s.74, repealed: SI 2014/1384 Sch.1 para.8
s.75, substituted: SI 2014/1372 Reg.8
s.79, amended: SI 2014/1372 Sch.1 para.4
s.79, repealed (in part): SI 2014/1372 Sch.1
para.4
s.91, see *Performing Right Society Ltd v
B4U Network (Europe) Ltd* [2013] EWCA
Civ 1236, [2014] Bus. L.R. 207 (CA (Civ
Div)), Moses LJ
s.96, see *Twentieth Century Fox Film Corp v
Harris* [2013] EWHC 159 (Ch), [2014] Ch.
41 (Ch D), Newey J
s.97A, see *Paramount Home Entertainment
International Ltd v British Sky Broadcasting
Ltd* [2013] EWHC 3479 (Ch), [2014]
E.C.D.R. 7 (Ch D), Arnold J
s.98, amended: SI 2014/892 Sch.1 para.56
s.116, enabling: SI 2014/898
s.116A, enabling: SI 2014/2863
s.116B, enabling: SI 2014/2588

s.116C, enabling: SI 2014/2588, SI
2014/2863
s.116D, applied: SI 2014/2863
s.116D, enabling: SI 2014/2588, SI
2014/2863
s.143, amended: SI 2014/1372 Sch.1 para.5,
SI 2014/1384 Sch.1 para.2
s.143, repealed (in part): SI 2014/1372 Sch.1
para.5, SI 2014/1384 Sch.1 para.2
s.144, amended: SI 2014/892 Sch.1 para.57
s.144, substituted: SI 2014/892 Sch.1
para.57
s.149, amended: SI 2014/2861 Reg.3
s.154, amended: 2014 c.18 s.22
s.155, amended: 2014 c.18 s.22
s.156, amended: 2014 c.18 s.22
s.159, substituted: 2014 c.18 s.22
s.179, amended: SI 2014/1372 Sch.1 para.6,
SI 2014/1384 Sch.1 para.3
s.182, applied: SI 2014/2863 Art.4, Art.6,
Art.7
s.183, applied: SI 2014/2863 Art.4, Art.6,
Art.7
s.191HA, amended: SI 2014/434 Reg.2
s.197, amended: SI 2014/1372 Sch.1 para.7,
SI 2014/1384 Sch.1 para.4, SI 2014/2361
Reg.4
s.206, amended: 2014 c.18 s.22
s.208, amended: 2014 c.18 s.22
s.212, amended: SI 2014/1384 Sch.1 para.5
s.212A, added: 2014 c.18 s.22
s.213, see *Utopia Tableware Ltd v BBP
Marketing Ltd* [2013] EWHC 3483 (IPEC),
[2014] E.C.C. 34 (IPEC), Recorder Douglas
Campbell
s.213, amended: 2014 c.18 s.1, s.2
s.215, amended: 2014 c.18 s.2
s.215, repealed (in part): 2014 c.18 s.2
s.217, amended: 2014 c.18 s.3
s.217, repealed (in part): 2014 c.18 s.3
s.218, amended: 2014 c.18 s.2, s.3
s.219, amended: 2014 c.18 s.2
s.220, amended: 2014 c.18 s.2, s.3
s.220, repealed (in part): 2014 c.18 s.3
s.238, amended: SI 2014/892 Sch.1 para.58
s.244A, added: 2014 c.18 s.4
s.249, amended: 2014 c.18 s.10
s.249, repealed (in part): 2014 c.18 s.10
s.249A, added: 2014 c.18 s.11
s.251, amended: 2014 c.18 s.10
s.263, amended: 2014 c.18 s.2, 2014 c.29 s.4

s.264, amended: 2014 c.18 s.2, s.3
s.275, applied: SI 2014/3238 Sch.2 para.8
s.275A, applied: SI 2014/3238 Art.4, Art.5,
Sch.1 para.2, Sch.1 para.5, Sch.2 para.2
s.296ZEA, added: SI 2014/2361 Reg.3
s.296ZF, amended: SI 2014/2361 Reg.4
s.297, see *Federation Against Copyright
Theft Ltd v Ashton* [2013] EWHC 1923
(Admin), [2014] 1 W.L.R. 1322 (DC), Laws
LJ
Sch.A1 para.1, enabling: SI 2014/898
Sch.A1 para.2, enabling: SI 2014/898
Sch.A1 para.3, enabling: SI 2014/898
Sch.A1 para.4, enabling: SI 2014/898
Sch.A1 para.5, enabling: SI 2014/898
Sch.A1 para.6, enabling: SI 2014/898
Sch.A1 para.7, applied: SI 2014/898
Sch.A1 para.7, enabling: SI 2014/898
Sch.ZA1, added: SI 2014/2861 Sch.1 para.1
Sch.ZA1 Part II, applied: SI 2014/2863 Art.4
Sch.2, amended: SI 2014/2356 Reg.4
Sch.2 para.1B, added: SI 2014/2361 Reg.3
Sch.2 para.1B, applied: SI 2014/2361 Reg.5
Sch.2 para.1C, added: SI 2014/1372 Reg.3
Sch.2 para.2, amended: SI 2014/2356 Reg.4
Sch.2 para.2A, added: SI 2014/2356 Reg.5
Sch.2 para.3A, added: SI 2014/1384 Reg.3
Sch.2 para.4, substituted: SI 2014/1372
Reg.4
Sch.2 para.6, substituted: SI 2014/1372
Reg.4
Sch.2 para.6B, amended: SI 2014/1372
Sch.1 para.8
Sch.2 para.6B, repealed (in part): SI
2014/1372 Sch.1 para.8
Sch.2 para.6C, added: SI 2014/1372 Reg.6
Sch.2 para.6I, added: SI 2014/2861 Reg.3
Sch.2 para.14, amended: SI 2014/1372
Reg.7
Sch.2 para.20, repealed: SI 2014/1384 Sch.1
para.8
Sch.2 para.21, substituted: SI 2014/1372
Reg.8
Sch.2A para.1A, enabling: SI 2014/2863
Sch.2A para.1B, enabling: SI 2014/2588
Sch.2A para.1C, enabling: SI 2014/2588, SI
2014/2863
Sch.2A para.1D, applied: SI 2014/2863
Sch.2A para.1D, enabling: SI 2014/2588, SI
2014/2863

Sch.2A para.16, amended: SI 2014/1372
Sch.1 para.9, SI 2014/1384 Sch.1 para.6
Sch.2A para.17, amended: SI 2014/892
Sch.1 para.59
Sch.5A Part I, amended: SI 2014/1372 Sch.1
para.10, SI 2014/1384 Sch.1 para.7
Sch.5A Part II, amended: SI 2014/1372
Sch.1 para.10, SI 2014/1384 Sch.1 para.7
49. Health and Medicines Act 1988
s.23, enabling: SI 2014/256, SI 2014/451,
SSI 2014/42
50. Housing Act 1988
s.5, see *Taylor v Spencer* [2013] EWCA Civ
1600, [2014] H.L.R. 9 (CA (Civ Div)), Sir
Brian Leveson PQBD
s.6A, amended: 2014 c.12 Sch.11 para.17
s.7, see *Nelson v Circle Thirty Three
Housing Trust Ltd* [2014] EWCA Civ 106,
[2014] 3 Costs L.O. 355 (CA (Civ Div)),
Rimer LJ
s.7, amended: 2014 c.12 Sch.11 para.18
s.8, see *Masih v Yousaf* [2014] EWCA Civ
234, [2014] H.L.R. 27 (CA (Civ Div)),
Hallett LJ
s.8, amended: 2014 c.12 s.97
s.9A, amended: 2014 c.12 Sch.11 para.19
s.13, enabling: SI 2014/374, SI 2014/910
s.17, amended: SI 2014/560 Sch.1 para.20
s.21, see *McDonald v McDonald* [2014]
EWCA Civ 1049, [2014] B.P.I.R. 1270 (CA
(Civ Div)), Arden LJ; see *Taylor v Spencer*
[2013] EWCA Civ 1600, [2014] H.L.R. 9
(CA (Civ Div)), Sir Brian Leveson PQBD
s.27, see *Lambeth LBC v Loveridge* [2014]
UKSC 65, [2014] 1 W.L.R. 4516 (SC), Lord
Neuberger PSC
s.28, see *Lambeth LBC v Loveridge* [2014]
UKSC 65, [2014] 1 W.L.R. 4516 (SC), Lord
Neuberger PSC
s.44, varied: SI 2014/2708 Art.5
s.45, enabling: SI 2014/374, SI 2014/910
Sch.1 Part I para.12ZA, amended: 2014 c.12
Sch.11 para.20, SI 2014/949 Art.11, SI
2014/1241 Art.3
Sch.2, see *Masih v Yousaf* [2014] EWCA
Civ 234, [2014] H.L.R. 27 (CA (Civ Div)),
Hallett LJ
Sch.2 Part I, added: 2014 c.12 s.97
Sch.2 Part I, referred to: SI 2014/2830 Art.3
Sch.2 Part II, added: 2014 c.12 s.99
Sch.2 Part II, amended: 2014 c.12 s.98

Sch.2 Part II, applied: SI 2014/949 Art.7

52. Road Traffic Act 1988

s.2, see *Young (Adam Clark) v MacDonald* [2014] HCJAC 42, 2014 G.W.D. 17-316 (HCJ), Lord Eassie

s.2B, see *Morrison (Adam Edward) v HM Advocate* 2014 J.C. 74 (HCJ), Lord Eassie

s.5A, applied: SI 2014/2868 Reg.2

s.6, see *Arthur v Murphy* [2014] HCJAC 4, 2014 S.C.L. 218 (HCJ), Lord Drummond Young

s.7, see *Bodhaniya v CPS* [2013] EWHC 1743 (Admin), (2014) 178 J.P. 1 (QBD (Admin)), Moses LJ

s.8, amended: SSI 2014/328 Reg.3

s.8, enabling: SSI 2014/328

s.11, applied: SSI 2014/328 Reg.2

s.11, enabling: SSI 2014/328

s.22A, see *R. v Maxwell (Benjamin Joseph)* [2014] EWCA Crim 417, [2014] R.T.R. 27 (CA (Crim Div)), Davis LJ

s.31, enabling: SI 2014/887

s.38, see *Morrison (Adam Edward) v HM Advocate* 2014 J.C. 74 (HCJ), Lord Eassie

s.41, enabling: SI 2014/264, SI 2014/480, SI 2014/1862

s.42, see *DPP v Issler* [2014] EWHC 669 (Admin), [2014] 1 W.L.R. 3686 (DC), Rafferty LJ

s.45, enabling: SI 2014/480, SI 2014/2114

s.46, enabling: SI 2014/480, SI 2014/2114

s.49, enabling: SI 2014/480, SI 2014/2115

s.51, enabling: SI 2014/2115

s.63A, enabling: SI 2014/2115

s.89, amended: 2014 c.22 Sch.9 para.63

s.89, applied: SI 2014/1816

s.89, repealed (in part): 2014 c.22 Sch.9 para.63

s.89, enabling: SI 2014/480, SI 2014/613, SI 2014/1816, SI 2014/3190

s.91, enabling: SI 2014/480

s.92, enabling: SI 2014/613

s.97, amended: 2014 c.22 s.46

s.97, enabling: SI 2014/2580

s.97A, added: 2014 c.22 s.46

s.97A, amended: SI 2014/3190 Reg.10

s.99, amended: 2014 c.22 s.47, SI 2014/3190 Reg.10

s.99, enabling: SI 2014/2580

s.100, amended: 2014 c.22 s.47

s.101, enabling: SI 2014/613

s.105, applied: SI 2014/2580

s.105, enabling: SI 2014/480, SI 2014/613, SI 2014/1816, SI 2014/2580, SI 2014/3190

s.108, amended: SI 2014/3190 Reg.10

s.129, enabling: SI 2014/480

s.132, enabling: SI 2014/1816, SI 2014/2216

s.135, enabling: SI 2014/480

s.141, enabling: SI 2014/480, SI 2014/1816, SI 2014/2216

s.151, see *Nemeti v Sabre Insurance Co Ltd* [2013] EWCA Civ 1555, [2014] C.P. Rep. 16 (CA (Civ Div)), Sir Terence Etherton C

s.172, see *Foster v DPP* [2013] EWHC 2039 (Admin), (2014) 178 J.P. 15 (DC), Laws LJ; see *Krishevsky v DPP* [2014] EWHC 1755 (Admin), (2014) 178 J.P. 369 (DC), Moses LJ

s.172, applied: SI 2014/1610 r.4_1, r.4_7

s.195, applied: SI 2014/264, SI 2014/480, SI 2014/613, SI 2014/1816, SI 2014/1862, SI 2014/2114, SI 2014/2115, SI 2014/2868, SI 2014/3190, SSI 2014/328

53. Road Traffic Offenders Act 1988

applied: SI 2014/1610 r.55_2

s.1, see *Krishevsky v DPP* [2014] EWHC 1755 (Admin), (2014) 178 J.P. 369 (DC), Moses LJ

s.9, applied: SI 2014/1610 r.55_2

s.12, applied: SI 2014/1610 r.4_1, r.4_7

s.12, enabling: SI 2014/1610

s.20, see *Cusick (Gary) v McPherson* [2014] HCJAC 39, 2014 G.W.D. 17-314 (HCJ), The Lord Justice Clerk (Carloway)

s.20, amended: SI 2014/260 Art.2

s.20, enabling: SI 2014/260

s.25, applied: SI 2014/1610 r.38_18, r.37_15, r.55_2

s.26, applied: SI 2014/1610 r.55_2

s.27, applied: SI 2014/1610 r.55_2

s.30A, applied: SI 2014/1610 r.55_4

s.34, applied: SI 2014/1610 r.55_1, r.55_2, r.37_10, r.38_16

s.34A, applied: SI 2014/1610 r.55_4

s.34D, applied: SI 2014/1610 r.55_4

s.35, applied: SI 2014/1610 r.55_1, r.55_2, r.37_10, r.38_16

s.36, applied: SI 2014/1610 r.55_2

s.39, applied: SI 2014/1610 r.64_2, r.55_2, r.63_2

s.42, applied: SI 2014/1610 r.55_1, r.55_2

s.44, applied: SI 2014/1610 r.55_2, r.37_10, r.38_16

s.44A, applied: SI 2014/1610 r.55_2

s.47, applied: SI 2014/1610 r.55_2, r.5_4, r.42_1

s.53, enabling: SI 2014/259

s.54, applied: SI 2014/1610 r.55_3

s.57, applied: SI 2014/1610 r.5_4

s.62, applied: SI 2014/1610 r.55_3

s.70, applied: SI 2014/1610 r.55_3

s.71, applied: SI 2014/1610 r.5_4

s.72, applied: SI 2014/1610 r.55_3

s.73, applied: SI 2014/1610 r.55_3

s.74, applied: SI 2014/1610 r.55_3

s.88, applied: SI 2014/259

s.90A, enabling: SI 2014/267

s.90B, enabling: SI 2014/802, SI 2014/2766

s.90E, applied: SI 2014/267, SI 2014/802, SI 2014/2766

s.90E, enabling: SI 2014/802, SI 2014/2766

s.96, applied: SI 2014/1610 r.55_2

s.97A, applied: SI 2014/1610 r.55_2

s.97A, referred to: SI 2014/3178 Art.4

Sch.2, see *DPP v Issler* [2014] EWHC 669 (Admin), [2014] 1 W.L.R. 3686 (DC), Rafferty LJ

Sch.2, applied: SI 2014/1610 r.55_2

Sch.3, amended: 2014 c.26 Sch.19 para.21

1989

3. Elected Authorities (Northern Ireland) Act 1989

Sch.1 Part I, amended: 2014 c.13 s.14, s.18, s.20, SI 2014/1116 Art.8

Sch.1 Part II para.7, repealed (in part): 2014 c.13 s.14

Sch.1 Part II para.8A, repealed: 2014 c.13 s.16

6. Official Secrets Act 1989

applied: SI 2014/512 Reg.181, SI 2014/1964 Reg.120, Reg.164, SSI 2014/164 Reg.92, SSI 2014/217 Reg.175, SSI 2014/292 Reg.175

14. Control of Pollution (Amendment) Act 1989

s.1, applied: SSI 2014/319 Sch.2 para.3, Sch.4 para.2

s.2, applied: SSI 2014/4 Reg.3

s.3, amended: 2014 asp 3 s.47

s.5, applied: SSI 2014/319 Sch.2 para.3

s.5, enabling: SI 2014/656

s.7, applied: SSI 2014/319 Sch.2 para.3

s.8, enabling: SI 2014/656

15. Water Act 1989

see *Manchester Ship Canal Co Ltd v United Utilities Water Plc* [2014] UKSC 40, [2014] 1 W.L.R. 2576 (SC), Lord Neuberger PSC

s.4, applied: SI 2014/2679

s.4, enabling: SI 2014/2679

s.174, amended: 2014 c.21 Sch.7 para.1, SI 2014/892 Sch.1 para.60

s.174, repealed (in part): SI 2014/892 Sch.1 para.60

Sch.2, applied: SI 2014/2679

Sch.23 para.2, repealed: 2014 asp 3 Sch.3 para.21

18. Common Land (Rectification of Registers) Act 1989

applied: SI 2014/3038 Reg.14

24. Social Security Act 1989

Sch.5 Part I para.5A, amended: 2014 c.6 Sch.7 para.2

Sch.5 Part I para.5A, applied: SI 2014/3050 Reg.41

Sch.5 Part I para.5A, repealed (in part): 2014 c.6 Sch.7 para.2

Sch.5 Part I para.5A, varied: 2014 c.6 s.126

Sch.5 Part I para.5B, amended: 2014 c.6 Sch.7 para.3

Sch.5 Part I para.5C, added: 2014 c.6 Sch.7 para.4

Sch.5 Part I para.7, applied: SI 2014/3050 Reg.38, Reg.41

26. Finance Act 1989

s.178, amended: 2014 c.26 Sch.35 para.11

s.178, applied: 2014 c.26 Sch.35 para.11

s.178, enabling: SI 2014/496

s.182, amended: 2014 c.6 Sch.7 para.5

s.182, applied: SI 2014/1640 Art.17

s.182, varied: 2014 c.6 s.126, SI 2014/1640 Art.17

29. Electricity Act 1989

see *Laverty v British Gas Trading Ltd* [2014] EWHC 2721 (Ch), [2014] B.C.C. 701 (Ch D (Companies Ct)), Sir Terence Etherton C;

see *Trump International Golf Club Scotland Ltd v Scottish Ministers* [2014] CSOH 22, 2014 S.L.T. 406 (OH), Lord Doherty

applied: 2014 c.5 Sch.1 para.1, 2014 c.25 Sch.1, SI 2014/631 Art.3, SI 2014/826 Reg.4, SI 2014/899 Reg.4, SI 2014/1052

Art.9, SI 2014/1599 Art.5, SI 2014/1873
Art.7, SI 2014/2043 Reg.67, SI 2014/2950
Art.5
Part I, applied: SI 2014/3219 Art.34
s.3B, amended: SI 2014/631 Sch.1 para.5
s.3D, amended: SI 2014/892 Sch.1 para.62
s.3F, amended: SI 2014/892 Sch.1 para.63
s.3F, repealed (in part): SI 2014/892 Sch.1
para.63
s.4, see *Sustainable Shetland v Scottish
Ministers* [2014] CSIH 60, 2014 S.L.T. 806
(IH (1 Div)), The Lord President (Gill)
s.4, applied: SI 2014/94 Art.3
s.4, referred to: SI 2014/2418 Sch.1
s.5, see *Sustainable Shetland v Scottish
Ministers* [2014] CSIH 60, 2014 S.L.T. 806
(IH (1 Div)), The Lord President (Gill); see
*Trump International Golf Club Scotland Ltd
v Scottish Ministers* [2014] CSOH 22, 2014
S.L.T. 406 (OH), Lord Doherty
s.5, amended: SI 2014/631 Sch.1 para.5
s.5, applied: SI 2014/94, SI 2014/2587
s.5, enabling: SI 2014/94, SI 2014/2587
s.6, see *Sustainable Shetland v Scottish
Ministers* [2014] CSIH 60, 2014 S.L.T. 806
(IH (1 Div)), The Lord President (Gill); see
*Trump International Golf Club Scotland Ltd
v Scottish Ministers* [2014] CSOH 22, 2014
S.L.T. 406 (OH), Lord Doherty
s.6, applied: SI 2014/94 Art.3, SI 2014/1648
Reg.2, SI 2014/2043 Reg.2, Reg.79, SI
2014/2441 Art.4, SI 2014/2594 Art.6, SI
2014/2846 Art.4, Art.13, SI 2014/2950
Art.5, Art.9, SI 2014/3328 Art.3, SI
2014/3331 Sch.12 para.109
s.8, enabling: SI 2014/2587
s.8A, amended: SI 2014/631 Sch.1 para.5
s.8A, applied: SI 2014/1648 Reg.2
s.10, see *Stynes v Western Power (East
Midlands) Plc* [2014] R.V.R. 15 (UT
(Lands)), Sir Keith Lindblom P
s.10B, applied: SI 2014/3333 Reg.4
s.10F, amended: SI 2014/3333 Reg.3
s.10I, amended: SI 2014/3333 Reg.3
s.10I, applied: SI 2014/3333 Reg.4
s.10L, amended: SI 2014/3333 Reg.3
s.11A, amended: SI 2014/631 Sch.1 para.5
s.11C, amended: SI 2014/631 Sch.1 para.5
s.15, amended: SI 2014/892 Sch.1 para.64
s.23, amended: SI 2014/631 Sch.1 para.5

s.25, applied: SI 2014/2011 Reg.55, SI
2014/2013 Reg.5, Reg.6, Reg.7, Reg.8, SI
2014/2014 Reg.25, SI 2014/2043 Reg.67,
Reg.77, SI 2014/2511 Reg.29
s.27, applied: SI 2014/2013 Reg.15, SI
2014/2043 Reg.85
s.27A, amended: SI 2014/631 Sch.1 para.5
s.32, enabling: SI 2014/893, SSI 2014/94
s.32A, enabling: SI 2014/893, SSI 2014/94
s.32B, enabling: SSI 2014/94
s.32C, enabling: SI 2014/893, SSI 2014/94
s.32D, applied: SSI 2014/94
s.32D, enabling: SSI 2014/94
s.32J, enabling: SI 2014/893, SSI 2014/94
s.32K, enabling: SI 2014/893, SI 2014/2388,
SSI 2014/94
s.32L, amended: SI 2014/631 Sch.1 para.5
s.32L, applied: SI 2014/893, SSI 2014/94
s.32LA, enabling: SI 2014/2388
s.32LB, applied: SI 2014/2388
s.32M, enabling: SI 2014/893
s.36, see *Sustainable Shetland v Scottish
Ministers* [2014] CSIH 60, 2014 S.L.T. 806
(IH (1 Div)), The Lord President (Gill); see
*Trump International Golf Club Scotland Ltd
v Scottish Ministers* [2014] CSOH 22, 2014
S.L.T. 406 (OH), Lord Doherty
s.37, see *Trump International Golf Club
Scotland Ltd v Scottish Ministers* [2014]
CSOH 22, 2014 S.L.T. 406 (OH), Lord
Doherty
s.39B, amended: SI 2014/631 Sch.1 para.5
s.40B, amended: SI 2014/631 Sch.1 para.5
s.41A, amended: SI 2014/631 Sch.1 para.5
s.41A, applied: SI 2014/1131, SI 2014/3219,
SI 2014/3231
s.41A, enabling: SI 2014/1131, SI
2014/2897, SI 2014/3219, SI 2014/3231
s.41B, applied: SI 2014/1131, SI 2014/3219,
SI 2014/3231
s.41B, enabling: SI 2014/1131, SI
2014/2897, SI 2014/3219, SI 2014/3231
s.42AA, amended: SI 2014/631 Sch.1 para.5
s.43, amended: SI 2014/892 Sch.1 para.65
s.47, amended: SI 2014/892 Sch.1 para.66
s.47ZA, repealed: SI 2014/2043 Reg.88
s.48, amended: SI 2014/892 Sch.1 para.67
s.56B, amended: SI 2014/631 Sch.1 para.5
s.56C, amended: SI 2014/631 Sch.1 para.5
s.56CB, amended: SI 2014/892 Sch.1
para.68

s.56CB, applied: SI 2014/559
s.56CB, referred to: SI 2014/892 Sch.2
para.2
s.56D, amended: SI 2014/631 Sch.1 para.5
s.56E, amended: SI 2014/631 Sch.1 para.5
s.56F, amended: SI 2014/631 Sch.1 para.5
s.56G, amended: SI 2014/631 Sch.1 para.5
s.64, amended: SI 2014/3332 Reg.5
s.111, amended: SI 2014/631 Sch.1 para.5
Sch.3, see *Stynes v Western Power (East Midlands) Plc* [2014] R.V.R. 15 (UT (Lands)), Sir Keith Lindblom P
Sch.4, see *Stynes v Western Power (East Midlands) Plc* [2014] R.V.R. 15 (UT (Lands)), Sir Keith Lindblom P
Sch.4 para.6, see *Arnold White Estates Ltd v National Grid Electricity Transmission Plc* [2014] EWCA Civ 216, [2014] Ch. 385 (CA (Civ Div)), Lord Dyson MR; see *Stynes v Western Power (East Midlands) Plc* [2014] R.V.R. 15 (UT (Lands)), Sir Keith Lindblom P
Sch.4 para.7, see *Arnold White Estates Ltd v National Grid Electricity Transmission Plc* [2014] EWCA Civ 216, [2014] Ch. 385 (CA (Civ Div)), Lord Dyson MR; see *Stynes v Western Power (East Midlands) Plc* [2014] R.V.R. 15 (UT (Lands)), Sir Keith Lindblom P
Sch.6 para.3, amended: SI 2014/631 Sch.1 para.5
Sch.6 para.3, applied: SI 2014/1458 Art.5
Sch.6A para.11, repealed: SI 2014/3332 Reg.6
Sch.7 para.12, amended: SI 2014/631 Sch.1 para.5
Sch.9 para.3, see *Trump International Golf Club Scotland Ltd v Scottish Ministers* [2014] CSOH 22, 2014 S.L.T. 406 (OH), Lord Doherty

33. Extradition Act 1989
see *Director of the Serious Fraud Office v O'Brien* [2014] UKSC 23, [2014] A.C. 1246 (SC), Lord Mance JSC
applied: SI 2014/1610 r.2_1

34. Law of Property (Miscellaneous Provisions) Act 1989
s.1, see *Gleeds Retirement Benefits Scheme, Re* [2014] EWHC 1178 (Ch), [2014] 3 W.L.R. 1469 (Ch D), Newey J

37. Football Spectators Act 1989
Part II, applied: SI 2014/144, SI 2014/144 Art.3, SI 2014/220
s.14, varied: SI 2014/144 Art.2
s.14, enabling: SI 2014/144, SI 2014/220
s.14A, applied: SI 2014/1610 r.50_1, r.50_2, r.68_1, r.74_1, r.63_1, r.68_3, r.68_4
s.14H, applied: SI 2014/1610 r.76_1, r.76_7
s.22, applied: SI 2014/1610 r.63_1
s.22A, enabling: SI 2014/144

39. Self-Governing Schools etc (Scotland) Act 1989
s.19, applied: SSI 2014/164 Sch.2 Part 1
s.68, applied: SSI 2014/217 Sch.1 para.5, SSI 2014/292 Sch.1 para.5

40. Companies Act 1989
s.87, amended: SI 2014/892 Sch.1 para.69
s.183, amended: SI 2014/2947 Sch.4 para.2

41. Children Act 1989
see *DW (A Child) (Termination of Parental Responsibility), Re* [2014] EWCA Civ 315, [2014] 3 F.C.R. 314 (CA (Civ Div)), Arden LJ; see *JG (A Child) v Legal Services Commission* [2014] EWCA Civ 656, [2014] 5 Costs L.O. 708 (CA (Civ Div)), Richards LJ; see *R. (on the application of N) v Lewisham LBC* [2014] UKSC 62, [2014] 3 W.L.R. 1548 (SC), Lord Neuberger PSC; see *W (A Child) (Proportionality of Interim Care Order), Re* [2014] EWCA Civ 772, [2014] 3 F.C.R. 339 (CA (Civ Div)), Laws LJ
applied: SI 2014/1492 Reg.6, SI 2014/1795 Reg.3, SI 2014/3352 Sch.1 para.6
referred to: SI 2014/2418 Sch.1
Part IV, applied: SI 2014/1795 Reg.8
Part XA, applied: SI 2014/1132 Sch.7
para.9, SI 2014/2709 Sch.2 para.9
Pt II., see *X (Deprivation of Liberty), Re* [2014] EWCOP 37, (2014) 17 C.C.L. Rep. 464 (CP), Sir James Munby PFD
Pt IV., see *E (A Child) (Care Proceedings: European Dimension), Re* [2014] EWHC 6 (Fam), [2014] 1 W.L.R. 2670 (Fam Div), Sir James Munby PFD; see *S (A Child) v Nottingham City Council* [2013] EWCA Civ 771, [2014] 1 F.L.R. 739 (CA (Civ Div)), McCombe LJ
s.1, see *Al-Hilli (Summary of Final Judgment), Re* [2013] EWHC 2299 (Fam), [2014] 1 F.L.R. 428 (Fam Div), Baker J; see *C (A Child) (Placement for Adoption:*

Judicial Approach), Re [2013] EWCA Civ
1257, [2014] 1 W.L.R. 2247 (CA (Civ Div)),
Patten LJ; see *F v F (MMR Vaccine)* [2013]
EWHC 2683 (Fam), [2014] 1 F.L.R. 1328
(Fam Div), Theis J; see *G (A Child) (Care
Proceedings: Welfare Evaluation), Re*
[2013] EWCA Civ 965, [2014] 1 F.L.R. 670
(CA (Civ Div)), Longmore LJ; see *HA
(Capacity to Change), Re* [2013] EWHC
3634 (Fam), [2014] 2 F.L.R. 540 (Fam Div),
Baker J; see *M (A Child) (Parental
Responsibility Order), Re* [2013] EWCA Civ
969, [2014] 1 F.L.R. 339 (CA (Civ Div)),
Lloyd LJ; see *S (A Child) v Nottingham City
Council* [2013] EWCA Civ 771, [2014] 1
F.L.R. 739 (CA (Civ Div)), McCombe LJ;
see *Surrey CC v Al-Hilli* [2013] EWHC
3404 (Fam), [2014] 2 F.L.R. 217 (Fam Div),
Baker J; see *W (A Child) (Proportionality of
Interim Care Order), Re* [2014] EWCA Civ
772, [2014] 3 F.C.R. 339 (CA (Civ Div)),
Laws LJ
s.1, amended: 2014 c.6 s.11
s.3, see *G (Children) (Shared Residence
Order: Biological Non-Birth Mother), Re*
[2014] EWCA Civ 336, [2014] 2 F.L.R. 897
(CA (Civ Div)), Moses LJ
s.3, applied: 2014 c.12 Sch.2 para.4
s.5, amended: 2014 c.6 Sch.2 para.2
s.7, referred to: SI 2014/603 Sch.1
s.8, see *G (Children) (Shared Residence
Order: Biological Non-Birth Mother), Re*
[2014] EWCA Civ 336, [2014] 2 F.L.R. 897
(CA (Civ Div)), Moses LJ
s.8, amended: 2014 c.6 s.12, Sch.2 para.3
s.8, applied: SI 2014/3352 Reg.16
s.9, amended: 2014 c.6 s.9, Sch.2 para.4
s.10, amended: 2014 c.6 Sch.2 para.5
s.10, referred to: SI 2014/603 Sch.1
s.11, amended: 2014 c.6 s.14, Sch.2 para.6
s.11, repealed (in part): 2014 c.6 Sch.2
para.6
s.11A, amended: 2014 c.6 Sch.2 para.7
s.11B, amended: 2014 c.6 Sch.2 para.8
s.11C, amended: 2014 c.6 Sch.2 para.9
s.11D, amended: 2014 c.6 Sch.2 para.10
s.11E, amended: 2014 c.6 Sch.2 para.11
s.11F, amended: 2014 c.6 Sch.2 para.12
s.11G, amended: 2014 c.6 Sch.2 para.13
s.11H, amended: 2014 c.6 Sch.2 para.14
s.11I, amended: 2014 c.6 Sch.2 para.15

s.11J, amended: 2014 c.6 Sch.2 para.16
s.11J, applied: SI 2014/1042 Art.7
s.11K, amended: 2014 c.6 Sch.2 para.17
s.11L, amended: 2014 c.6 Sch.2 para.18
s.11L, applied: SI 2014/1042 Art.7
s.11O, amended: 2014 c.6 Sch.2 para.19
s.11O, applied: SI 2014/1042 Art.7
s.11P, amended: 2014 c.6 Sch.2 para.20
s.12, see *B (A Child) (Looked After Child),
Re* [2013] EWCA Civ 964, [2014] 1 F.L.R.
277 (CA (Civ Div)), Richards LJ
s.12, amended: 2014 c.6 Sch.2 para.21
s.13, amended: 2014 c.6 Sch.2 para.22
s.14, repealed: 2014 c.6 Sch.2 para.23
s.14A, amended: 2014 c.6 Sch.2 para.24
s.14A, applied: SI 2014/3352 Reg.16
s.14B, amended: 2014 c.6 Sch.2 para.25
s.14D, amended: 2014 c.6 Sch.2 para.26
s.14E, amended: 2014 c.6 s.14
s.14F, applied: SI 2014/2672 Sch.1 para.43,
Sch.2 para.34
s.15, applied: SI 2014/2672 Sch.1 para.25,
SI 2014/3037 Reg.25
s.16, amended: 2014 c.6 Sch.2 para.27
s.17, see *Mensah v Salford City Council*
[2014] EWHC 3537 (Admin), (2014) 17
C.C.L. Rep. 492 (QBD (Admin)), Lewis J;
see *R. (on the application of J) v
Worcestershire CC* [2013] EWHC 3845
(Admin), [2014] P.T.S.R. 537 (QBD
(Admin)), Holman J; see *R. (on the
application of N) v Newham LBC* [2013]
EWHC 2475 (Admin), [2014] 1 F.C.R. 1
(QBD (Admin)), Swift J; see *R. (on the
application of PO) v Newham LBC* [2014]
EWHC 2561 (Admin), (2014) 17 C.C.L.
Rep. 325 (QBD (Admin)), John Howell
Q.C.; see *R. (on the application of West) v
Rhondda Cynon Taff CBC* [2014] EWHC
2134 (Admin), [2014] E.L.R. 396 (QBD
(Admin)), Supperstone J
s.17, applied: 2014 c.23 s.62, SI 2014/1530
Sch.2 para.13
s.17ZA, added: 2014 c.6 s.96
s.17ZD, added: 2014 c.6 s.97
s.17ZG, added: 2014 c.6 s.50
s.17ZG, amended: 2014 c.23 s.66
s.17ZH, added: 2014 c.23 s.66
s.20, see *B (A Child) (Looked After Child),
Re* [2013] EWCA Civ 964, [2014] 1 F.L.R.
277 (CA (Civ Div)), Richards LJ; see

Bedford v Bedfordshire CC [2013] EWHC 1717 (QB), [2014] P.T.S.R. 351 (QBD), Jay J; see *C (A Child) (Care Proceedings: Deaf Parent), Re* [2014] EWCA Civ 128, [2014] 1 W.L.R. 2495 (CA (Civ Div)), Rimer LJ; see *KS v Bradford MDC* [2014] EWHC 11 (Admin), [2014] 3 F.C.R. 164 (QBD (Admin)), Judge Clive Heaton, Q.C.; see *R. (on the application of Cornwall Council) v Secretary of State for Health* [2014] EWCA Civ 12, [2014] 1 W.L.R. 3408 (CA (Civ Div)), Elias LJ; see *R. (on the application of GE (Eritrea)) v Secretary of State for the Home Department* [2013] EWHC 2186 (Admin), [2014] P.T.S.R. 124 (QBD), CMG Ockelton (Vice President); see *R. (on the application of Kebede) v Newcastle City Council* [2013] EWCA Civ 960, [2014] P.T.S.R. 82 (CA (Civ Div)), Laws LJ; see *Surrey CC v M* [2013] EWHC 2400 (Fam), [2014] 1 F.C.R. 429 (Fam Div), Theis J
s.20, amended: 2014 c.6 Sch.2 para.28
s.22, see *B (A Child) (Looked After Child), Re* [2013] EWCA Civ 964, [2014] 1 F.L.R. 277 (CA (Civ Div)), Richards LJ; see *KS v Bradford MDC* [2014] EWHC 11 (Admin), [2014] 3 F.C.R. 164 (QBD (Admin)), Judge Clive Heaton, Q.C.; see *R. (on the application of GE (Eritrea)) v Secretary of State for the Home Department* [2013] EWHC 2186 (Admin), [2014] P.T.S.R. 124 (QBD), CMG Ockelton (Vice President)
s.22, amended: 2014 c.6 s.99
s.22, applied: SI 2014/1530 Reg.17, SI 2014/2319 Reg.3
s.22C, amended: 2014 c.6 s.2, Sch.2 para.29
s.22C, applied: SI 2014/1492 Reg.4, SI 2014/3051 Sch.1 para.12
s.22C, enabling: SI 2014/1556, SI 2014/1917
s.23, see *KS v Bradford MDC* [2014] EWHC 11 (Admin), [2014] 3 F.C.R. 164 (QBD (Admin)), Judge Clive Heaton, Q.C.
s.23, amended: 2014 c.6 Sch.2 para.30
s.23, applied: SI 2014/3037 Reg.25
s.23A, see *R. (on the application of GE (Eritrea)) v Secretary of State for the Home Department* [2013] EWHC 2186 (Admin), [2014] P.T.S.R. 124 (QBD), CMG Ockelton (Vice President)
s.23C, see *R. (on the application of Cornwall Council) v Secretary of State for Health*

[2014] EWCA Civ 12, [2014] 1 W.L.R. 3408 (CA (Civ Div)), Elias LJ; see *R. (on the application of GE (Eritrea)) v Secretary of State for the Home Department* [2013] EWHC 2186 (Admin), [2014] P.T.S.R. 124 (QBD), CMG Ockelton (Vice President); see *R. (on the application of Kebede) v Newcastle City Council* [2013] EWCA Civ 960, [2014] P.T.S.R. 82 (CA (Civ Div)), Laws LJ
s.23C, applied: SI 2014/3037 Reg.25
s.23CZA, added: 2014 c.6 s.98
s.23E, amended: 2014 c.6 Sch.3 para.65
s.23E, enabling: SI 2014/1917
s.24, applied: SI 2014/3037 Reg.25
s.24B, see *R. (on the application of Kebede) v Newcastle City Council* [2013] EWCA Civ 960, [2014] P.T.S.R. 82 (CA (Civ Div)), Laws LJ
s.24D, enabling: SI 2014/1795
s.26, applied: SI 2014/1795 Reg.8, Reg.9, Reg.15
s.26, enabling: SI 2014/1795, SI 2014/1917
s.26A, enabling: SI 2014/1795
s.27, see *R. (on the application of J) v Worcestershire CC* [2013] EWHC 3845 (Admin), [2014] P.T.S.R. 537 (QBD (Admin)), Holman J
s.31, see *A (Placement Order: Imposition of Conditions on Adoption), Re* [2013] EWCA Civ 1611, [2014] 1 W.L.R. 2139 (CA (Civ Div)), Laws LJ; see *A Local Authority v DG (Concurrent Care and Criminal Proceedings)* [2014] EWHC 63 (Fam), [2014] 2 F.L.R. 713 (Fam Div), Keehan J; see *A v A (Abducted Children: Interim Care Order)* [2013] EWHC 3554 (Fam), [2014] 2 F.L.R. 365 (Fam Div), Parker J; see *C (A Child) (Care Proceedings: Deaf Parent), Re* [2014] EWCA Civ 128, [2014] 1 W.L.R. 2495 (CA (Civ Div)), Rimer LJ; see *C (A Child) (Placement for Adoption: Judicial Approach), Re* [2013] EWCA Civ 1257, [2014] 1 W.L.R. 2247 (CA (Civ Div)), Patten LJ; see *J (A Child) (Final Care Order: Threshold Criteria), Re* [2013] EWCA Civ 1685, [2014] 2 F.L.R. 1351 (CA (Civ Div)), Black LJ; see *N-D (Children) (Care and Placement Orders: Sufficiency of Welfare Determination), Re* [2014] EWCA Civ 1226, [2014] 3 F.C.R. 493 (CA (Civ

Div)), Longmore LJ; see *P (A Child) (Care and Placement: Evidential Basis of Local Authority Case), Re* [2013] EWCA Civ 963, [2014] 1 F.L.R. 824 (CA (Civ Div)), Lloyd LJ; see *S (A Child) (Split Hearing: Fact Finding), Re* [2014] EWCA Civ 25, [2014] 1 F.L.R. 1421 (CA (Civ Div)), Tomlinson LJ; see *S (A Child), Re* [2013] EWCA Civ 926, [2014] 2 F.C.R. 62 (CA (Civ Div)), Arden LJ; see *W (A Child) (Care Proceedings: Welfare Evaluation: Functions of Local Authority), Re* [2013] EWCA Civ 1227, [2014] 1 W.L.R. 1611 (CA (Civ Div)), Sir James Munby PFD

s.31, amended: 2014 c.6 s.15

s.31, applied: SI 2014/1042 Art.10, SI 2014/1794 Reg.12, SI 2014/1795 Reg.8, Reg.12

s.31A, amended: 2014 c.6 s.15

s.31A, enabling: SI 2014/1556, SI 2014/1917

s.32, see *S (Parenting Assessment), Re* [2014] 2 F.L.R. 575 (CC (Bournemouth)), Sir James Munby PFD

s.32, amended: 2014 c.6 s.14

s.32, applied: SI 2014/1042 Art.8

s.32, referred to: SI 2014/603 Sch.1

s.33, applied: SI 2014/1795 Reg.8

s.34, amended: 2014 c.6 s.8, Sch.2 para.31

s.34, applied: SI 2014/1795 Reg.8

s.34, enabling: SI 2014/1556

s.35, applied: SI 2014/1795 Reg.8

s.37, see *A v A (Abducted Children: Interim Care Order)* [2013] EWHC 3554 (Fam), [2014] 2 F.L.R. 365 (Fam Div), Parker J; see *W (A Child) (Proportionality of Interim Care Order), Re* [2014] EWCA Civ 772, [2014] 3 F.C.R. 339 (CA (Civ Div)), Laws LJ

s.38, see *AA (Compulsorily Detained Patient: Elective Caesarean), Re* [2012] EWHC 4378 (COP), [2014] 2 F.L.R. 237 (CP), Mostyn J; see *S (Parenting Assessment), Re* [2014] 2 F.L.R. 575 (CC (Bournemouth)), Sir James Munby PFD; see *W (A Child) (Proportionality of Interim Care Order), Re* [2014] EWCA Civ 772, [2014] 3 F.C.R. 339 (CA (Civ Div)), Laws LJ

s.38, amended: 2014 c.6 s.13, s.14, Sch.2 para.32

s.38, applied: SI 2014/1042 Art.9

s.38, referred to: SI 2014/603 Sch.1

s.38, repealed (in part): 2014 c.6 s.14

s.41, amended: 2014 c.6 Sch.2 para.33

s.41, referred to: SI 2014/603 Sch.1

s.43, amended: 2014 c.6 Sch.2 para.34

s.43, applied: SI 2014/1795 Reg.8

s.44, see *K v Crown Prosecution Service* [2014] EWHC 1606 (Admin), (2014) 178 J.P. 259 (DC), Beatson LJ

s.44, amended: 2014 c.6 Sch.2 para.35

s.44, applied: SI 2014/840 r.16, SI 2014/1795 Reg.8

s.45, applied: SI 2014/840 r.16

s.46, see *AA (Compulsorily Detained Patient: Elective Caesarean), Re* [2012] EWHC 4378 (COP), [2014] 2 F.L.R. 237 (CP), Mostyn J; see *K v Crown Prosecution Service* [2014] EWHC 1606 (Admin), (2014) 178 J.P. 259 (DC), Beatson LJ

s.46, amended: 2014 c.6 Sch.2 para.36

s.47, applied: SI 2014/1795 Reg.8

s.48, applied: SI 2014/840 r.16

s.50, applied: SI 2014/840 r.16

s.52, see *C (A Child) (Placement for Adoption: Judicial Approach), Re* [2013] EWCA Civ 1257, [2014] 1 W.L.R. 2247 (CA (Civ Div)), Patten LJ

s.53, applied: SI 2014/512 Sch.1 para.16

s.60, applied: SI 2014/512 Sch.1 para.16

s.65, amended: 2014 c.6 s.105

s.82, applied: SI 2014/512 Sch.1 para.16

s.85, applied: SI 2014/1530 Reg.17

s.86, applied: SI 2014/1530 Reg.17

s.87, applied: SI 2014/1530 Reg.17, SI 2014/2418 Sch.1, SI 2014/3283 Sch.1 para.8, Sch.1 para.32

s.87A, applied: SI 2014/2158 Reg.2

s.87A, enabling: SI 2014/2158

s.87D, enabling: SI 2014/410, SI 2014/670

s.91, see *B (A Child) (Looked After Child), Re* [2013] EWCA Civ 964, [2014] 1 F.L.R. 277 (CA (Civ Div)), Richards LJ; see *M (A Child) (Parental Responsibility Order), Re* [2013] EWCA Civ 969, [2014] 1 F.L.R. 339 (CA (Civ Div)), Lloyd LJ; see *N v B (Adoption by Grandmother)* [2013] EWHC 820 (Fam), [2014] 1 F.L.R. 369 (Fam Div), Theis J

s.91, amended: 2014 c.6 Sch.2 para.37

s.97, see *J (A Child) (Reporting Restriction: Internet: Video), Re* [2013] EWHC 2694

(Fam), [2014] E.M.L.R. 7 (Fam Div), Sir
James Munby PFD
s.97, amended: 2014 c.6 s.7
s.98, see *A Local Authority v DG
(Concurrent Care and Criminal
Proceedings)* [2014] EWHC 63 (Fam),
[2014] 2 F.L.R. 713 (Fam Div), Keehan J
s.102, applied: SI 2014/840 r.16
s.104, amended: 2014 c.6 s.16, s.96, s.97
s.104, enabling: SI 2014/410, SI 2014/670,
SI 2014/1556, SI 2014/1795, SI 2014/1917
s.104A, amended: 2014 c.6 s.16
s.104A, enabling: SI 2014/1795
s.105, amended: 2014 c.6 Sch.2 para.38
s.105, repealed (in part): 2014 c.6 Sch.2
para.38
Sch.A1 Part I para.3, amended: 2014 c.11
s.18
Sch.A1 Part I para.3, repealed (in part): 2014
c.11 Sch.4 para.9
Sch.A1 Part II para.4, amended: 2014 c.6
Sch.2 para.39
Sch.A1 Part II para.5, amended: 2014 c.6
Sch.2 para.39
Sch.A1 Part II para.6, amended: 2014 c.6
Sch.2 para.39
Sch.A1 Part II para.7, amended: 2014 c.6
Sch.2 para.39
Sch.A1 Part II para.8, amended: 2014 c.6
Sch.2 para.39
Sch.A1 Part II para.9, amended: 2014 c.6
Sch.2 para.39
Sch.1, see *EA v AP (Schedule I Proceedings:
Jurisdiction: Stay)* [2013] EWHC 2344
(Fam), [2014] I.L.Pr. 17 (Fam Div), Parker
J; see *M-M (A Child) (Financial Provision:
Father Resident Abroad), Re* [2014] EWCA
Civ 276, [2014] 2 F.L.R. 1391 (CA (Civ
Div)), Moore-Bick LJ; see *PG v TW (Child:
Financial Provision)* [2014] 1 F.L.R. 923
(Fam Div), Judge Horowitz QC
Sch.1, applied: SI 2014/840 Sch.1, SI
2014/3037 Reg.25
Sch.1 para.1, amended: 2014 c.6 Sch.2
para.40
Sch.1 para.7, amended: 2014 c.16 Sch.3
para.4
Sch.1 para.8, amended: 2014 c.6 Sch.2
para.40
Sch.1 para.11, amended: 2014 c.16 Sch.3
para.4

Sch.1 para.15, amended: 2014 c.6 Sch.2
para.40
Sch.1 para.15, applied: SI 2014/2672 Sch.1
para.25
Sch.2 Part I para.3, amended: 2014 c.6 Sch.3
para.65
Sch.2 Part II para.12E, enabling: SI
2014/1556
Sch.2 Part II para.12F, applied: SI
2014/3050 Reg.3
Sch.2 Part II para.19B, enabling: SI
2014/1917
Sch.2 Part II para.19BA, added: 2014 c.6
s.98
Sch.2 para.19B, see *R. (on the application of
GE (Eritrea)) v Secretary of State for the
Home Department* [2013] EWHC 2186
(Admin), [2014] P.T.S.R. 124 (QBD), CMG
Ockelton (Vice President)
Sch.7 para.6, applied: SI 2014/1795 Reg.9
Sch.7 para.6, enabling: SI 2014/1795
Sch.12 para.31, repealed: 2014 c.6 s.17
Sch.14 Part 3 para.10, repealed: 2014 c.6
Sch.2 para.41

42. Local Government and Housing Act 1989
s.4, applied: SI 2014/826 Reg.3, SI 2014/899
Reg.3, SI 2014/2418 Sch.1
s.5, applied: 2014 c.2 Sch.7 para.5, Sch.7
para.6, SI 2014/826 Reg.3, SI 2014/899
Reg.3, SI 2014/2359 Art.10
s.8, enabling: SI 2014/165, SI 2014/1514
s.11, amended: 2014 c.2 Sch.12 para.23
s.13, varied: SI 2014/863 Art.13, SI
2014/864 Art.13, SI 2014/865 Art.16, SI
2014/1012 Art.15
s.20, enabling: SI 2014/165, SI 2014/1514
s.67, amended: 2014 c.14 Sch.4 para.42
s.69, amended: 2014 c.14 Sch.4 para.43
s.70, amended: 2014 c.2 Sch.12 para.24
s.74, applied: SI 2014/3362 Reg.8
s.76A, added: 2014 c.29 s.24
s.87, amended: 2014 c.29 s.24
s.87, applied: SI 2014/2418 Sch.1
s.150, applied: SI 2014/3204
s.150, enabling: SI 2014/3204
s.166, repealed (in part): 2014 asp 14 Sch.2
para.6
s.190, enabling: SI 2014/165, SI 2014/1514
Sch.1 para.1, enabling: SI 2014/476
Sch.1 para.2, applied: SI 2014/3224 Reg.10
Sch.10 para.22, varied: SI 2014/2708 Art.5

44. Opticians Act 1989
s.9, amended: 2014 c.14 Sch.4 para.44
s.10A, applied: SI 2014/1887 Sch.3 para.6
s.10A, disapplied: SI 2014/1887 Sch.3
para.6
s.10A, substituted: SI 2014/1887 Sch.1
para.7
45. Prisons (Scotland) Act 1989
applied: 2014 asp 8 s.7, s.21
s.8, enabling: SSI 2014/26
s.22, applied: SI 2014/2871 Sch.1
s.26, applied: SI 2014/2871 Sch.1
s.37, enabling: SSI 2014/13
s.39, enabling: SSI 2014/26

1990

1. Capital Allowances Act 1990
s.18, see *Next Distribution Ltd v Revenue
and Customs Commissioners* [2014] UKUT
227 (TCC), [2014] S.T.C. 2682 (UT (Tax)),
David Richards J
**5. Criminal Justice (International Co-
operation) Act 1990**
see *R. (on the application of Secretary of
State for the Home Department) v Southwark
Crown Court* [2013] EWHC 4366 (Admin),
[2014] 1 W.L.R. 2529 (QBD (Admin)),
Moses LJ
s.21, amended: SI 2014/834 Sch.2 para.8
8. Town and Country Planning Act 1990
applied: SI 2014/1052 Sch.3 para.4, SI
2014/1599 Art.31, Art.35, SI 2014/1686
Sch.2 para.15, Sch.3 para.3, SI 2014/1796
Art.5, SI 2014/2027 Sch.7 para.2, SI
2014/2384 Art.42, Sch.19 para.9, SI
2014/2933 Sch.1 para.1, SI 2014/2935
Art.54, SI 2014/2950 Art.32
referred to: SI 2014/2027 Sch.7 para.5
Part III, applied: SI 2014/1052 Art.37, SI
2014/1761 Reg.5
Pt VII s.191, see *Hannan v Newham LBC*
[2014] EWHC 1424 (Admin), [2014] J.P.L.
1101 (QBD (Admin)), Ouseley J; see *R. (on
the application of Freedman) v Wiltshire
Council* [2014] EWHC 211 (Admin), [2014]
P.T.S.R. 696 (QBD (Admin)), Lewis J; see
*R. (on the application of Sellars) v
Basingstoke and Deane BC* [2013] EWHC

3673 (Admin), [2014] J.P.L. 643 (QBD
(Admin)), CMG Ockelton (Vice President)
s.2, repealed (in part): 2014 c.2 Sch.12
para.25
s.16, applied: SI 2014/333
s.19, applied: SI 2014/3038 Sch.4 para.8
s.55, applied: SI 2014/2384 Art.51
s.59, enabling: SI 2014/564, SI 2014/592, SI
2014/683, SI 2014/1532, SI 2014/2692
s.60, enabling: SI 2014/564, SI 2014/592, SI
2014/683, SI 2014/2692
s.61, enabling: SI 2014/564, SI 2014/592, SI
2014/1532, SI 2014/2692
s.61F, see *R. (on the application of Daws
Hill Neighbourhood Forum) v Wycombe DC*
[2014] EWCA Civ 228, [2014] 1 W.L.R.
1362 (CA (Civ Div)), Lord Dyson MR
s.61G, see *R. (on the application of Daws
Hill Neighbourhood Forum) v Wycombe DC*
[2014] EWCA Civ 228, [2014] 1 W.L.R.
1362 (CA (Civ Div)), Lord Dyson MR
s.69, enabling: SI 2014/1772
s.70, see *R. (on the application of HS2
Action Alliance Ltd) v Secretary of State for
Transport* [2014] EWHC 2759 (Admin),
[2014] P.T.S.R. 1334 (QBD (Admin)),
Lindblom J; see *R. (on the application of
Marton-cum-Grafton Parish Council) v
North Yorkshire CC* [2013] EWHC 2406
(Admin), [2014] Env. L.R. 10 (QBD
(Admin)), Judge Gosnell
s.70A, see *R. (on the application of
Skillcrown Homes Ltd) v Dartford BC*
[2014] EWHC 365 (Admin), [2014] J.P.L.
988 (QBD (Admin)), Singh J
s.72, applied: SI 2014/1599 Art.35
s.73A, see *Revenue and Customs
Commissioners v Patel* [2014] UKUT 361
(TCC) (UT (Tax)), Judge Colin Bishopp
s.74, see *R. (on the application of HS2
Action Alliance Ltd) v Secretary of State for
Transport* [2014] EWHC 2759 (Admin),
[2014] P.T.S.R. 1334 (QBD (Admin)),
Lindblom J
s.74, enabling: SI 2014/1532
s.76C, enabling: SI 2014/1532
s.77, amended: SI 2014/2773 Sch.1 para.2
s.78, see *Hunston Properties Ltd v Secretary
of State for Communities and Local
Government* [2013] EWCA Civ 1610,
[2014] J.P.L. 599 (CA (Civ Div)), Maurice

Kay LJ; see *Hunston Properties Ltd v Secretary of State for Communities and Local Government* [2013] EWHC 2678 (Admin), [2014] J.P.L. 240 (QBD (Admin)), Judge Pelling QC; see *R. (on the application of Gleeson Developments Ltd) v Secretary of State for Communities and Local Government* [2014] EWCA Civ 1118, [2014] P.T.S.R. 1226 (CA (Civ Div)), Laws LJ

s.78, amended: SI 2014/2773 Sch.1 para.3

s.78, applied: SI 2014/1599 Art.35, SI 2014/1796 Art.8, SI 2014/1873 Art.6, SI 2014/2441 Art.4, SI 2014/2637 Art.40, SI 2014/2846 Art.4, SI 2014/2935 Art.58, SI 2014/2950 Art.9, SI 2014/3328 Art.3, SI 2014/3331 Art.32

s.78, varied: SI 2014/1599 Art.35

s.79, amended: SI 2014/2773 Sch.1 para.4

s.79, applied: SI 2014/1599 Art.35, SI 2014/1873 Art.6, SI 2014/2441 Art.4, SI 2014/2637 Art.40, SI 2014/2846 Art.4, SI 2014/2935 Art.58, SI 2014/2950 Art.9, SI 2014/3328 Art.3, SI 2014/3331 Art.32

s.85, see *Lewis v Three Rivers DC* [2013] EWHC 3250 (Admin), [2014] J.P.L. 636 (DC), Richards LJ

s.90, applied: SI 2014/2027 Art.29, SI 2014/3102 Art.19

s.96A, amended: SI 2014/1770 Art.2

s.96A, applied: SI 2014/1761 Reg.1, Reg.3

s.96A, enabling: SI 2014/1772

s.97, see *R. (on the application of Gleeson Developments Ltd) v Secretary of State for Communities and Local Government* [2014] EWCA Civ 1118, [2014] P.T.S.R. 1226 (CA (Civ Div)), Laws LJ

s.100, see *R. (on the application of Gleeson Developments Ltd) v Secretary of State for Communities and Local Government* [2014] EWCA Civ 1118, [2014] P.T.S.R. 1226 (CA (Civ Div)), Laws LJ

s.106, see *Newham LBC v Ali* [2014] EWCA Civ 676, [2014] 1 W.L.R. 2743 (CA (Civ Div)), Lord Dyson MR; see *R. (on the application of Thakeham Village Action Ltd) v Horsham DC* [2014] EWHC 67 (Admin), [2014] Env. L.R. 21 (QBD (Admin)), Lindblom J

s.106, applied: SI 2014/2384 Sch.19 para.9, SI 2014/2434 Art.17

s.106A, see *Newham LBC v Ali* [2014] EWCA Civ 676, [2014] 1 W.L.R. 2743 (CA (Civ Div)), Lord Dyson MR

s.106B, see *Newham LBC v Ali* [2014] EWCA Civ 676, [2014] 1 W.L.R. 2743 (CA (Civ Div)), Lord Dyson MR

s.108, applied: SI 2014/593 Reg.2, Reg.3, Reg.4, Reg.5, SI 2014/2693 Reg.2, Reg.3, Reg.4, Reg.5

s.108, enabling: SI 2014/565, SI 2014/593, SI 2014/2693

s.150, applied: SI 2014/2384 Art.35

s.171, see *Sanger v Newham LBC* [2014] EWHC 1922 (Admin), [2014] 2 Cr. App. R. 27 (DC), Sir Brian Leveson PQBD

s.171B, see *R. (on the application of Evans) v Basingstoke and Deane BC* [2013] EWCA Civ 1635, [2014] 1 W.L.R. 2034 (CA (Civ Div)), Aikens LJ; see *R. (on the application of Lambrou) v Secretary of State for Communities and Local Government* [2013] EWHC 325 (Admin), [2014] J.P.L. 538 (QBD (Admin)), David Elvin QC; see *R. (on the application of Sellars) v Basingstoke and Deane BC* [2013] EWHC 3673 (Admin), [2014] J.P.L. 643 (QBD (Admin)), CMG Ockelton (Vice President)

s.173, see *Ioannou v Secretary of State for Communities and Local Government* [2013] EWHC 3945 (Admin), [2014] J.P.L. 608 (QBD (Admin)), Ouseley J

s.174, see *Ahmed v Secretary of State for Communities and Local Government* [2013] EWHC 2084 (Admin), [2014] 2 P. & C.R. 11 (QBD (Admin)), Ben Emmerson QC; see *Ioannou v Secretary of State for Communities and Local Government* [2013] EWHC 3945 (Admin), [2014] J.P.L. 608 (QBD (Admin)), Ouseley J; see *Makanjuola v Secretary of State for Communities and Local Government* [2013] EWHC 3528 (Admin), [2014] J.P.L. 439 (QBD (Admin)), Stewart J; see *R. (on the application of Flynn) v Secretary of State for Communities and Local Government* [2014] EWHC 390 (Admin), [2014] 1 W.L.R. 3270 (QBD (Admin)), Lewis J; see *Williams v Secretary of State for Communities and Local Government* [2013] EWCA Civ 958, [2014] J.P.L. 124 (CA (Civ Div)), Arden LJ

s.175, amended: SI 2014/2773 Sch.1 para.5

s.176, see *Ahmed v Secretary of State for Communities and Local Government* [2013] EWHC 2084 (Admin), [2014] 2 P. & C.R. 11 (QBD (Admin)), Ben Emmerson QC
s.177, see *Ahmed v Secretary of State for Communities and Local Government* [2013] EWHC 2084 (Admin), [2014] 2 P. & C.R. 11 (QBD (Admin)), Ben Emmerson QC; see *Ioannou v Secretary of State for Communities and Local Government* [2013] EWHC 3945 (Admin), [2014] J.P.L. 608 (QBD (Admin)), Ouseley J
s.179, see *Sanger v Newham LBC* [2014] EWHC 1922 (Admin), [2014] 2 Cr. App. R. 27 (DC), Sir Brian Leveson PQBD
s.187, see *Lewis v Three Rivers DC* [2013] EWHC 3250 (Admin), [2014] J.P.L. 636 (DC), Richards LJ
s.188, see *Sanger v Newham LBC* [2014] EWHC 1922 (Admin), [2014] 2 Cr. App. R. 27 (DC), Sir Brian Leveson PQBD
s.195, amended: SI 2014/2773 Sch.1 para.6
s.196, amended: SI 2014/2773 Sch.1 para.7
s.198, applied: SI 2014/3223 Sch.1 para.13
s.206, applied: SI 2014/1873 Art.38, SI 2014/2384 Art.26, SI 2014/2950 Art.34, SI 2014/3331 Art.28
s.206, disapplied: SI 2014/2935 Art.46
s.208, amended: SI 2014/2773 Sch.1 para.8
s.210, disapplied: SI 2014/3263 Sch.2 para.2
s.211, applied: SI 2014/2384 Art.27
s.211, disapplied: SI 2014/3263 Sch.2 para.2
s.212, applied: SI 2014/2384 Art.27
s.213, applied: SI 2014/2384 Art.27
s.229, applied: SI 2014/3038 Sch.4 para.8
s.238, applied: SI 2014/2384 Sch.19 para.9
s.247, applied: SI 2014/2441 Art.11, Art.12
s.257, applied: SI 2014/2441 Art.11, Art.12
s.262, applied: SI 2014/2441 Art.4, SI 2014/2846 Art.4, SI 2014/2950 Art.9
s.264, applied: SI 2014/909 Art.36, SI 2014/1052 Art.39, SI 2014/1599 Art.31, SI 2014/1873 Art.36, SI 2014/2027 Art.29, SI 2014/2269 Art.31, SI 2014/2384 Art.51, SI 2014/2434 Art.30, SI 2014/2441 Art.27, SI 2014/2637 Art.35, SI 2014/2846 Art.13, SI 2014/2935 Art.50, SI 2014/2950 Art.32, SI 2014/3328 Art.31, SI 2014/3331 Art.29
s.266, applied: SI 2014/3328 Art.3
s.271, applied: SI 2014/1599 Sch.9 para.4, SI 2014/1821 Art.13, SI 2014/1873 Sch.12

para.4, SI 2014/2027 Art.26, Sch.7 para.1, Sch.7 para.3, SI 2014/2384 Art.42, Sch.16 para.4, SI 2014/3102 Art.35, Sch.7 para.1, Sch.7 para.3, Sch.8 para.4, SI 2014/3328 Sch.9 para.4, SI 2014/3331 Sch.12 para.14
s.274, applied: SI 2014/2384 Sch.16 para.4
s.275, applied: SI 2014/2027 Sch.7 para.1
s.279, applied: SI 2014/2027 Sch.7 para.1
s.280, applied: SI 2014/2027 Sch.7 para.1
s.282, applied: SI 2014/2027 Sch.7 para.1
s.285, see *R. v Clayton (Jonathan James)* [2014] EWCA Crim 1030, [2014] 1 W.L.R. 3994 (CA (Crim Div)), Elias LJ; see *Sanger v Newham LBC* [2014] EWHC 1922 (Admin), [2014] 2 Cr. App. R. 27 (DC), Sir Brian Leveson PQBD
s.288, see *Hunston Properties Ltd v Secretary of State for Communities and Local Government* [2013] EWCA Civ 1610, [2014] J.P.L. 599 (CA (Civ Div)), Maurice Kay LJ; see *Hunston Properties Ltd v Secretary of State for Communities and Local Government* [2013] EWHC 2678 (Admin), [2014] J.P.L. 240 (QBD (Admin)), Judge Pelling QC; see *JB Trustees Ltd v Secretary of State for Communities and Local Government* [2013] EWHC 3555 (Admin), [2014] J.P.L. 656 (QBD (Admin)), Lindblom J; see *San Vicente v Secretary of State for Communities and Local Government* [2013] EWCA Civ 817, [2014] 1 W.L.R. 966 (CA (Civ Div)), Lloyd LJ; see *Skrytek v Secretary of State for Communities and Local Government* [2013] EWCA Civ 1231, [2014] Env. L.R. 15 (CA (Civ Div)), Maurice Kay LJ; see *Venn v Secretary of State for Communities and Local Government* [2013] EWHC 3546 (Admin), [2014] J.P.L. 447 (QBD (Admin)), Lang J
s.289, see *San Vicente v Secretary of State for Communities and Local Government* [2013] EWCA Civ 817, [2014] 1 W.L.R. 966 (CA (Civ Div)), Lloyd LJ
s.303, applied: SI 2014/357, SI 2014/1052 Sch.3 para.2, SI 2014/2026
s.303, enabling: SI 2014/357, SI 2014/1761, SI 2014/2026
s.303A, enabling: SI 2014/692
s.319B, added: SI 2014/2773 Art.2
s.319B, applied: SI 2014/2775 Reg.2
s.319B, enabling: SI 2014/2775

s.321B, amended: 2014 c.29 s.4
s.322, amended: SI 2014/2773 Sch.1 para.9
s.322A, amended: SI 2014/2773 Sch.1
para.10
s.323, amended: SI 2014/2773 Sch.1 para.11
s.333, amended: SI 2014/2773 Sch.1 para.12
s.333, applied: SI 2014/333, SI 2014/1052
Sch.3 para.2
s.333, enabling: SI 2014/333, SI 2014/357,
SI 2014/564, SI 2014/683, SI 2014/1772, SI
2014/2026, SI 2014/2692, SI 2014/2775
s.337, enabling: SI 2014/592
Sch.4B para.16, enabling: SI 2014/333
Sch.6 para.2, amended: SI 2014/2773 Sch.1
para.13
Sch.6 para.3, see *R. (on the application of
Gleeson Developments Ltd) v Secretary of
State for Communities and Local
Government* [2013] EWHC 3166 (Admin),
[2014] P.T.S.R. 135 (QBD (Admin)),
Cranston J; see *R. (on the application of
Gleeson Developments Ltd) v Secretary of
State for Communities and Local
Government* [2014] EWCA Civ 1118,
[2014] P.T.S.R. 1226 (CA (Civ Div)), Laws
LJ
Sch.6 para.3, amended: SI 2014/2773 Sch.1
para.13
Sch.6 para.6, amended: SI 2014/2773 Sch.1
para.13

**9. Planning (Listed Buildings and
Conservation Areas) Act 1990**

Part III, varied: SI 2014/550 Reg.7
s.12, amended: SI 2014/2773 Sch.1 para.15
s.12, varied: SI 2014/550 Reg.7
s.16, varied: SI 2014/550 Reg.7
s.17, varied: SI 2014/550 Reg.7
s.20, amended: SI 2014/2773 Sch.1 para.16
s.22, amended: SI 2014/2773 Sch.1 para.17
s.26, applied: SI 2014/550 Reg.7
s.26, varied: SI 2014/550 Reg.7
s.26B, enabling: SI 2014/550
s.26H, applied: SI 2014/552 Reg.2, Reg.3,
Reg.4
s.26I, applied: SI 2014/552 Reg.4
s.26I, enabling: SI 2014/552
s.26K, applied: SI 2014/552 Reg.2, Reg.4
s.26K, enabling: SI 2014/552
s.28, applied: SI 2014/550 Reg.7
s.28, referred to: SI 2014/550 Reg.7
s.28, varied: SI 2014/550 Reg.7

s.28A, applied: SI 2014/551 Reg.7
s.28A, enabling: SI 2014/551
s.30, varied: SI 2014/550 Reg.7
s.40, amended: SI 2014/2773 Sch.1 para.18
s.41, amended: SI 2014/2773 Sch.1 para.19
s.62, varied: SI 2014/550 Reg.7
s.69, applied: SI 2014/2384 Art.27
s.74, amended: SI 2014/2773 Sch.1 para.20
s.88D, amended: SI 2014/2773 Art.2
s.88E, added: SI 2014/2773 Art.2
s.88E, applied: SI 2014/2776 Reg.2
s.88E, enabling: SI 2014/2776
s.89, amended: SI 2014/2773 Sch.1 para.21
s.93, amended: SI 2014/2773 Sch.1 para.22
s.93, enabling: SI 2014/550, SI 2014/551, SI
2014/552, SI 2014/2776
Sch.2A, enabling: SI 2014/551
Sch.3, enabling: SI 2014/552
Sch.3 para.2, amended: SI 2014/2773 Sch.1
para.23
Sch.3 para.3, amended: SI 2014/2773 Sch.1
para.23
Sch.3 para.6, amended: SI 2014/2773 Sch.1
para.23
Sch.3 para.8, amended: 2014 c.29 s.4

10. Planning (Hazardous Substances) Act 1990

s.5, enabling: SI 2014/162, SI 2014/375
s.7, amended: SI 2014/469 Sch.2 para.6
s.9, amended: SI 2014/469 Sch.2 para.7
s.10, amended: SI 2014/469 Sch.2 para.8
s.18, amended: SI 2014/469 Sch.2 para.9
s.20, amended: SI 2014/2773 Sch.1 para.25
s.21, amended: SI 2014/2773 Sch.1 para.26
s.21, applied: SI 2014/162 Reg.3, SI
2014/375 Reg.3
s.21B, added: SI 2014/2773 Art.2
s.21B, applied: SI 2014/2777, SI 2014/2777
Reg.2
s.21B, enabling: SI 2014/2777
s.23, applied: SI 2014/162 Reg.3, SI
2014/375 Reg.3
s.25, amended: SI 2014/2773 Sch.1 para.27
s.29, amended: SI 2014/469 Sch.2 para.10
s.37, amended: SI 2014/2773 Sch.1 para.28
s.39, amended: SI 2014/469 Sch.2 para.10
s.40, enabling: SI 2014/162, SI 2014/375, SI
2014/2777
Sch.1 para.2, amended: SI 2014/2773 Sch.1
para.29
Sch.1 para.3, amended: SI 2014/2773 Sch.1
para.29

Sch.1 para.6, amended: SI 2014/2773 Sch.1 para.29

Sch.1 para.8, amended: 2014 c.29 s.4

11. Planning (Consequential Provisions) Act 1990

Sch.2 para.31, repealed (in part): 2014 asp 3 Sch.3 para.22

16. Food Safety Act 1990

applied: SI 2014/1855, SI 2014/2303, SI 2014/3001, SI 2014/3079, SI 2014/3080, SSI 2014/312

enabling: SI 2014/1855

s.2, varied: SI 2014/3001 Sch.2, SI 2014/3087 Sch.2, SSI 2014/289 Reg.7

s.3, applied: SSI 2014/312 Reg.12

s.3, varied: SI 2014/1855 Sch.4 Part 5, SI 2014/2303 Sch.4 Part 5, SI 2014/3001 Sch.2, SI 2014/3087 Sch.2, SSI 2014/289 Reg.7

s.5, applied: SI 2014/2418 Sch.1

s.6, enabling: SI 2014/1102, SI 2014/1855, SI 2014/2303, SI 2014/3001, SI 2014/3087, SI 2014/3104, SSI 2014/289, SSI 2014/312

s.8, applied: SSI 2014/289 Reg.7

s.10, applied: SI 2014/1855 Reg.12, SI 2014/2303 Reg.12

s.10, referred to: SI 2014/1855 Reg.12

s.10, varied: SI 2014/1855 Sch.4 para.1, SI 2014/2303 Sch.4 para.1, SI 2014/3001 Reg.7, SI 2014/3087 Reg.7

s.14, applied: SSI 2014/289 Reg.7

s.16, enabling: SI 2014/123, SI 2014/440, SI 2014/1102, SI 2014/1855, SI 2014/2303, SI 2014/3001, SI 2014/3079, SI 2014/3080, SI 2014/3087, SI 2014/3104, SSI 2014/12, SSI 2014/289, SSI 2014/312

s.17, enabling: SI 2014/123, SI 2014/440, SI 2014/1102, SI 2014/1855, SI 2014/2303, SI 2014/3079, SI 2014/3104, SSI 2014/12, SSI 2014/312

s.18, enabling: SI 2014/1855, SI 2014/2303, SSI 2014/312

s.20, applied: SSI 2014/312 Reg.12

s.20, varied: SI 2014/1855 Sch.4 Part 5, SI 2014/2303 Sch.4 Part 5, SI 2014/3001 Sch.2, SI 2014/3087 Sch.2, SSI 2014/289 Reg.7

s.21, applied: SSI 2014/312 Reg.12

s.21, varied: SI 2014/1855 Sch.4 Part 5, SI 2014/2303 Sch.4 Part 5, SI 2014/3001 Sch.2, SI 2014/3087 Sch.2, SSI 2014/289 Reg.7

s.22, applied: SSI 2014/312 Reg.12

s.22, varied: SI 2014/1855 Sch.4 Part 5, SI 2014/2303 Sch.4 Part 5, SSI 2014/312 Reg.12

s.26, enabling: SI 2014/440, SI 2014/1102, SI 2014/1855, SI 2014/2303, SI 2014/3001, SI 2014/3079, SI 2014/3087, SI 2014/3104, SSI 2014/289, SSI 2014/312

s.27, applied: SI 2014/1942 Reg.12

s.29, varied: SI 2014/1855 Sch.4 Part 5, SI 2014/2303 Sch.4 Part 5

s.30, applied: SSI 2014/312 Reg.12

s.30, varied: SI 2014/1855 Sch.4 Part 5, SI 2014/2303 Sch.4 Part 5, SI 2014/3001 Sch.2, SI 2014/3087 Sch.2, SSI 2014/289 Reg.7

s.32, applied: SI 2014/1855 Reg.12, SI 2014/2303 Reg.12, SSI 2014/312 Reg.12

s.32, disapplied: SSI 2014/312 Reg.12

s.32, referred to: SI 2014/1855 Reg.12

s.32, varied: SI 2014/1855 Sch.4 para.2, SI 2014/2303 Sch.4 para.2

s.33, applied: SSI 2014/289 Reg.7, SSI 2014/312 Reg.12

s.33, varied: SI 2014/1855 Sch.4 Part 5, SI 2014/2303 Sch.4 Part 5, SI 2014/3001 Sch.2, SI 2014/3087 Sch.2, SSI 2014/289 Reg.7

s.35, applied: SSI 2014/312 Reg.12

s.35, varied: SI 2014/1855 Sch.4 Part 5, SI 2014/2303 Sch.4 Part 5, SI 2014/3001 Sch.2, SI 2014/3087 Sch.2, SSI 2014/289 Reg.7

s.36, applied: SSI 2014/312 Reg.12

s.36, varied: SI 2014/1855 Sch.4 Part 5, SI 2014/2303 Sch.4 Part 5, SI 2014/3001 Sch.2, SI 2014/3087 Sch.2, SSI 2014/289 Reg.7

s.36A, applied: SSI 2014/312 Reg.12

s.36A, varied: SI 2014/1855 Sch.4 Part 5, SI 2014/2303 Sch.4 Part 5, SI 2014/3001 Sch.2, SI 2014/3087 Sch.2, SSI 2014/289 Reg.7

s.37, applied: SI 2014/1855 Reg.12, SI 2014/2303 Reg.12

s.37, referred to: SI 2014/1855 Reg.12

s.37, varied: SI 2014/1855 Sch.4 para.3, Sch.4 para.4, SI 2014/2303 Sch.4 para.3, Sch.4 para.4, SI 2014/3001 Reg.7, SI 2014/3087 Reg.7

s.39, applied: SI 2014/1855 Reg.12, SI 2014/2303 Reg.12

s.39, referred to: SI 2014/1855 Reg.12

s.39, varied: SI 2014/1855 Sch.4 para.5, Sch.4 para.6, SI 2014/2303 Sch.4 para.5, Sch.4 para.6, SI 2014/3001 Reg.7, SI 2014/3087 Reg.7

s.44, applied: SSI 2014/312 Reg.12
s.44, varied: SI 2014/1855 Sch.4 Part 5, SI
2014/2303 Sch.4 Part 5, SI 2014/3001 Sch.2,
SI 2014/3087 Sch.2, SSI 2014/289 Reg.7
s.45, enabling: SI 2014/1855, SI 2014/2303,
SSI 2014/312
s.48, applied: SI 2014/123, SI 2014/440, SI
2014/1855, SI 2014/2303, SI 2014/3001, SI
2014/3079, SI 2014/3080, SI 2014/3087, SI
2014/3104, SSI 2014/12, SSI 2014/289, SSI
2014/312
s.48, enabling: SI 2014/123, SI 2014/440, SI
2014/1102, SI 2014/1855, SI 2014/2303, SI
2014/3001, SI 2014/3079, SI 2014/3080, SI
2014/3087, SI 2014/3104, SSI 2014/12, SSI
2014/289, SSI 2014/312
Sch.1 para.1, enabling: SI 2014/1855, SI
2014/2303, SSI 2014/312
Sch.1 para.4, enabling: SI 2014/1855, SI
2014/2303, SSI 2014/312

18. Computer Misuse Act 1990
see *R. v Martin (Lewys Stephen)* [2013]
EWCA Crim 1420, [2014] 1 Cr. App. R. (S.)
63 (CA (Crim Div)), Leveson LJ

**19. National Health Service and Community
Care Act 1990**
Pt III., see *Aster Healthcare Ltd v Shafi*
[2014] EWHC 77 (QB), [2014] 3 All E.R.
283 (QBD), Andrews J
s.47, see *Aster Healthcare Ltd v Shafi* [2014]
EWHC 77 (QB), [2014] 3 All E.R. 283
(QBD), Andrews J
s.47, applied: SI 2014/829 Sch.1 para.13

27. Social Security Act 1990
s.15, enabling: SSI 2014/40

28. Appropriation Act 1990
Sch.4 Part 21, varied: SI 2014/2708 Art.5

31. Aviation and Maritime Security Act 1990
s.9, varied: SI 2014/265 Sch.1
s.27, varied: SI 2014/265 Sch.1
s.28, varied: SI 2014/265 Sch.1
s.34, varied: SI 2014/265 Sch.1
s.35, varied: SI 2014/265 Sch.1
s.37, varied: SI 2014/265 Sch.1
s.45, varied: SI 2014/265 Sch.1
s.50, varied: SI 2014/265 Sch.1
s.51, enabling: SI 2014/265
Sch.2 para.2, varied: SI 2014/265 Sch.1
Sch.2 para.5, varied: SI 2014/265 Sch.1

**35. Enterprise and New Towns (Scotland) Act
1990**
s.8, amended: 2014 c.14 Sch.4 para.45
s.25, applied: 2014 asp 6 Sch.3
s.26, applied: 2014 asp 6 Sch.3

**37. Human Fertilisation and Embryology Act
1990**
see *R. (on the application of Assisted
Reproduction and Gynaecology Centre) v
Human Fertilisation and Embryology
Authority* [2013] EWHC 3087 (Admin),
[2014] 1 W.L.R. 2540 (QBD (Admin)),
Patterson J
s.1A, amended: SI 2014/2884 Reg.2
s.5, see *R. (on the application of Assisted
Reproduction and Gynaecology Centre) v
Human Fertilisation and Embryology
Authority* [2013] EWHC 3087 (Admin),
[2014] 1 W.L.R. 2540 (QBD (Admin)),
Patterson J
s.16, applied: SI 2014/1788 Sch.1, SI
2014/2936 Sch.1 para.7
s.17, see *R. (on the application of Assisted
Reproduction and Gynaecology Centre) v
Human Fertilisation and Embryology
Authority* [2013] EWHC 3087 (Admin),
[2014] 1 W.L.R. 2540 (QBD (Admin)),
Patterson J
s.19, see *R. (on the application of Assisted
Reproduction and Gynaecology Centre) v
Human Fertilisation and Embryology
Authority* [2013] EWHC 3087 (Admin),
[2014] 1 W.L.R. 2540 (QBD (Admin)),
Patterson J
s.20, see *R. (on the application of Assisted
Reproduction and Gynaecology Centre) v
Human Fertilisation and Embryology
Authority* [2013] EWHC 3087 (Admin),
[2014] 1 W.L.R. 2540 (QBD (Admin)),
Patterson J
s.27, see *G (Children) (Shared Residence
Order: Biological Non-Birth Mother), Re*
[2014] EWCA Civ 336, [2014] 2 F.L.R. 897
(CA (Civ Div)), Moses LJ
Sch.2, referred to: SI 2014/1788 Sch.1, SI
2014/2936 Sch.1 para.7
Sch.2 para.1, applied: SI 2014/2936 Sch.1
para.4

**40. Law Reform (Miscellaneous Provisions)
(Scotland) Act 1990**
s.20, amended: SSI 2014/232 Reg.3

s.20ZB, amended: SSI 2014/232 Reg.3
s.25, amended: SSI 2014/232 Reg.3
s.27, applied: 2014 asp 18 s.103, s.104
s.35, amended: 2014 asp 18 Sch.5 para.37
s.35, repealed (in part): 2014 asp 18 Sch.5 para.37
Sch.4 para.1, repealed: 2014 asp 18 Sch.5 para.37
Sch.4 para.5, repealed: 2014 asp 18 Sch.5 para.37

41. Courts and Legal Services Act 1990
see *Coventry v Lawrence* [2014] UKSC 46 (SC), Lord Neuberger PSC
s.1, applied: SI 2014/821
s.1, enabling: SI 2014/821
s.15, amended: SI 2014/605 Art.19
s.58, see *Rees v Gateley Wareing (A Firm)* [2013] EWHC 3708 (Ch), [2014] 2 Costs L.O. 210 (Ch D), Morgan J; see *Rees v Gateley Wareing (A Firm)* [2014] EWCA Civ 1351, [2014] 6 Costs L.O. 953 (CA (Civ Div)), Elias LJ
s.119, see *Rees v Gateley Wareing (A Firm)* [2013] EWHC 3708 (Ch), [2014] 2 Costs L.O. 210 (Ch D), Morgan J; see *Rees v Gateley Wareing (A Firm)* [2014] EWCA Civ 1351, [2014] 6 Costs L.O. 953 (CA (Civ Div)), Elias LJ
s.120, enabling: SI 2014/821

42. Broadcasting Act 1990
Part I, applied: SI 2014/774 Sch.1 para.1
Part III, applied: SI 2014/774 Sch.1 para.1
s.185, repealed (in part): SI 2014/1372 Sch.1 para.11
s.193, amended: SI 2014/892 Sch.1 para.71
s.194A, amended: SI 2014/892 Sch.1 para.72

43. Environmental Protection Act 1990
Commencement Orders: 2014 asp 3 Sch.3 para.23
Part I, applied: SSI 2014/258 Sch.1 para.1
Part II, applied: 2014 asp 3 Sch.2 para.22
Part IIA, applied: SI 2014/2846 Sch.2 para.9
s.33, see *Doonin Plant Ltd v HM Advocate* [2014] HCJAC 26, 2014 J.C. 207 (HCJ), The Lord Justice Clerk (Carloway); see *R. v Morgan (Christopher Lynn)* [2013] EWCA Crim 1307, [2014] 1 W.L.R. 3450 (CA (Crim Div)), Aikens LJ; see *Walker and Son (Hauliers) Ltd v Environment Agency* [2014]

EWCA Crim 100, [2014] 4 All E.R. 825 (CA (Crim Div)), Lord Thomas LCJ
s.33, amended: 2014 asp 3 Sch.3 para.40
s.33, applied: SSI 2014/4 Reg.3, SSI 2014/319 Sch.1 para.2, Sch.2 para.4, Sch.3 para.2, Sch.4 para.3
s.33, disapplied: SSI 2014/4 Reg.3
s.33, referred to: SSI 2014/320 Art.2
s.33A, amended: 2014 asp 3 Sch.3 para.11
s.33A, applied: SSI 2014/320 Art.2
s.33A, repealed (in part): 2014 asp 3 Sch.3 para.11
s.33A, enabling: SSI 2014/320
s.34, applied: SSI 2014/4 Reg.3, SSI 2014/319 Sch.2 para.4, Sch.4 para.3
s.34, enabling: SSI 2014/4
s.35, amended: 2014 asp 3 Sch.3 para.3
s.35, applied: SSI 2014/4 Reg.3, SSI 2014/319 Sch.2 para.4
s.35, referred to: SSI 2014/324 Sch.1 para.6
s.36, amended: SI 2014/469 Sch.2 para.12
s.38, applied: SSI 2014/319 Sch.2 para.4
s.44, applied: SSI 2014/319 Sch.2 para.4
s.46, amended: 2014 asp 3 Sch.3 para.3
s.47, amended: 2014 asp 3 Sch.3 para.3
s.57, amended: 2014 asp 3 Sch.3 para.40
s.59, amended: 2014 asp 3 Sch.3 para.11
s.59, applied: SSI 2014/319 Sch.1 para.2, Sch.2 para.4, Sch.3 para.2
s.63, amended: 2014 asp 3 Sch.3 para.40
s.63, applied: SSI 2014/319 Sch.1 para.2, Sch.2 para.4, Sch.3 para.2, Sch.4 para.3
s.71, applied: SSI 2014/319 Sch.2 para.4
s.73, amended: 2014 asp 3 Sch.3 para.40
s.74, amended: 2014 asp 3 s.48
s.78F, amended: 2014 asp 3 s.45
s.78M, applied: SSI 2014/319 Sch.1 para.2, Sch.2 para.4, Sch.3 para.2
s.78QA, added: 2014 asp 3 s.45
s.78TA, added: 2014 asp 3 s.45
s.78X, amended: 2014 asp 3 s.45, Sch.3 para.40
s.78YA, amended: 2014 asp 3 s.45
s.79, see *North Lincolnshire CC v Act Fast North Lincolnshire (CIC)* [2013] EWHC 2890 (Admin), [2014] Env. L.R. 7 (QBD (Admin)), Judge Behrens
s.79, amended: 2014 asp 3 Sch.3 para.3, Sch.3 para.23, Sch.3 para.40
s.79, applied: SI 2014/310 Art.25, SI 2014/909 Art.37, SI 2014/1052 Art.40, SI

2014/1599 Art.7, SI 2014/1873 Art.14, SI
2014/2027 Art.28, SI 2014/2269 Art.32, SI
2014/2384 Art.7, SI 2014/2434 Art.8, SI
2014/2441 Art.9, SI 2014/2637 Art.36, SI
2014/2846 Art.8, SI 2014/2935 Art.51, SI
2014/2950 Art.8, SI 2014/3102 Art.43, SI
2014/3328 Art.30, SI 2014/3331 Art.31
s.80, see *North Lincolnshire CC v Act Fast
North Lincolnshire (CIC)* [2013] EWHC
2890 (Admin), [2014] Env. L.R. 7 (QBD
(Admin)), Judge Behrens
s.80, amended: 2014 asp 3 Sch.3 para.23
s.80, applied: SI 2014/2830 Art.3
s.80, repealed (in part): 2014 asp 3 Sch.3
para.23
s.82, applied: SI 2014/310 Art.25, SI
2014/909 Art.37, SI 2014/1052 Art.40, SI
2014/1599 Art.7, SI 2014/1873 Art.14, SI
2014/2027 Art.28, SI 2014/2269 Art.32, SI
2014/2384 Art.7, SI 2014/2434 Art.8, SI
2014/2441 Art.9, SI 2014/2637 Art.36, SI
2014/2830 Art.3, SI 2014/2846 Art.8, SI
2014/2935 Art.51, SI 2014/2950 Art.8, SI
2014/3102 Art.43, SI 2014/3328 Art.30, SI
2014/3331 Art.31
s.82, referred to: SI 2014/2935 Art.51
s.84, repealed (in part): 2014 asp 3 Sch.3
para.23
s.88, amended: 2014 asp 3 Sch.3 para.11
s.88, applied: SSI 2014/321 Art.2
s.88, enabling: SSI 2014/321
s.88A, added: 2014 c.12 s.154
s.92, applied: 2014 c.12 s.58
s.92, repealed: 2014 c.12 Sch.11 para.21
s.92A, applied: 2014 c.12 s.58
s.93, applied: 2014 c.12 s.58
s.98, amended: 2014 asp 3 Sch.3 para.40
s.111, applied: SI 2014/1663 Reg.3
s.122, applied: SI 2014/3102 Art.43
s.140, amended: 2014 asp 3 Sch.3 para.40
s.142, amended: SI 2014/1638 Sch.13 para.6
s.145, repealed (in part): 2014 asp 3 Sch.3
para.23
s.161, amended: 2014 c.12 s.154
Sch.3 para.5, amended: 2014 c.2 Sch.12
para.26
Sch.4 para.1, amended: 2014 asp 3 Sch.3
para.40
Sch.13 Part I para.2, repealed (in part): SI
2014/469 Sch.2 para.13

Sch.15 para.2, repealed (in part): 2014 asp 3
Sch.3 para.23
Sch.15 para.15, repealed (in part): 2014 asp
3 Sch.3 para.23
Sch.15 para.17, repealed: 2014 asp 3 Sch.3
para.23
Sch.16 Part I, amended: 2014 asp 3 Sch.3
para.23

1991

22. New Roads and Street Works Act 1991
applied: SI 2014/466 Sch.1, SI 2014/909
Sch.10 para.3, SI 2014/941 Sch.1, SI
2014/2269 Art.8, SI 2014/3105 Sch.1, SI
2014/3106 Sch.1, SI 2014/3107 Sch.1, SI
2014/3108 Sch.1, SI 2014/3109 Sch.1, SI
2014/3110 Sch.1, SI 2014/3112 Sch.1, SI
2014/3310 Sch.1, SI 2014/3311 Sch.1
referred to: SI 2014/941 Sch.1, SI 2014/1599
Sch.9 para.7, Sch.9 para.8, SI 2014/1796
Sch.6 para.6, SI 2014/1873 Sch.12 para.8,
Sch.12 para.9, SI 2014/2384 Sch.16 para.10,
Sch.16 para.11, SI 2014/2434 Sch.8 para.10,
SI 2014/2441 Art.13, SI 2014/2637 Sch.10
para.8, Sch.10 para.13, SI 2014/2935 Sch.9
para.82, SI 2014/3105 Sch.1, SI 2014/3106
Sch.1, SI 2014/3107 Sch.1, SI 2014/3109
Sch.1, SI 2014/3328 Sch.9 para.7, Sch.9
para.8
Part III, applied: SI 2014/909 Art.10, Art.12,
Art.32, Sch.10 para.14, SI 2014/1052 Art.10,
Art.13, Sch.13 para.5, SI 2014/1599 Art.27,
Sch.9 para.3, Sch.9 para.4, SI 2014/1796
Art.23, SI 2014/1873 Art.34, Sch.12 para.3,
SI 2014/2027 Art.4, Sch.7 para.5, Sch.8
para.3, SI 2014/2269 Art.8, Art.27, Art.28,
Art.29, Sch.8 para.3, Sch.8 para.18, SI
2014/2384 Art.10, Art.11, Art.12, Art.44,
Sch.16 para.3, SI 2014/2434 Art.28, Sch.8
para.3, SI 2014/2441 Art.13, Art.16, Art.30,
Art.31, SI 2014/2637 Art.8, Art.31, Art.32,
Sch.10 para.6, SI 2014/2935 Art.43, Art.47,
SI 2014/2950 Sch.12 para.3, Sch.12 para.4,
SI 2014/3102 Art.3, Sch.7 para.5, Sch.8
para.44, Sch.8 para.57, SI 2014/3106 Sch.1,
SI 2014/3107 Sch.1, SI 2014/3109 Sch.1, SI
2014/3328 Art.29, Sch.9 para.3, Sch.9
para.5, Sch.9 para.15, SI 2014/3331 Sch.12
para.34, Sch.12 para.37

Part III, disapplied: SI 2014/2441 Sch.8
para.3
Part III, referred to: SI 2014/2269 Art.8, SI
2014/2637 Art.8, SI 2014/3102 Art.3
s.48, applied: SI 2014/1052 Art.9, SI
2014/1599 Art.8, SI 2014/1873 Art.15, SI
2014/2384 Art.10, SI 2014/2434 Art.9, SI
2014/2935 Art.15, SI 2014/2950 Art.10, SI
2014/3328 Art.10
s.48, referred to: SI 2014/3105 Sch.1, SI
2014/3110 Sch.1, SI 2014/3112 Sch.1, SI
2014/3310 Sch.1, SI 2014/3311 Sch.1
s.49, applied: SI 2014/865 Art.11
s.50, applied: SI 2014/466 Sch.1, SI
2014/941 Sch.1, SI 2014/3105 Sch.1, SI
2014/3106 Sch.1, SI 2014/3107 Sch.1, SI
2014/3108 Sch.1, SI 2014/3109 Sch.1, SI
2014/3110 Sch.1, SI 2014/3112 Sch.1, SI
2014/3310 Sch.1, SI 2014/3311 Sch.1
s.51, applied: SI 2014/1052 Art.9, SI
2014/1599 Art.8, SI 2014/1873 Art.15, SI
2014/2384 Art.10, SI 2014/2434 Art.9, SI
2014/2935 Art.15, SI 2014/2950 Art.10, SI
2014/3328 Art.10
s.52, applied: SI 2014/3108 Sch.1, SI
2014/3112 Sch.1, SI 2014/3310 Sch.1, SI
2014/3311 Sch.1
s.52, referred to: SI 2014/466 Sch.1, SI
2014/941 Sch.1, SI 2014/3105 Sch.1, SI
2014/3106 Sch.1, SI 2014/3107 Sch.1, SI
2014/3109 Sch.1, SI 2014/3110 Sch.1
s.53, applied: SI 2014/466 Sch.1, SI
2014/3106 Sch.1, SI 2014/3107 Sch.1, SI
2014/3108 Sch.1, SI 2014/3109 Sch.1, SI
2014/3310 Sch.1
s.53, disapplied: SI 2014/466 Sch.1, SI
2014/941 Sch.1, SI 2014/3105 Sch.1, SI
2014/3106 Sch.1, SI 2014/3107 Sch.1, SI
2014/3108 Sch.1, SI 2014/3109 Sch.1, SI
2014/3110 Sch.1, SI 2014/3112 Sch.1, SI
2014/3310 Sch.1, SI 2014/3311 Sch.1
s.54, applied: SI 2014/466 Sch.1, SI
2014/909 Art.12, SI 2014/941 Sch.1, SI
2014/1052 Art.13, SI 2014/1599 Art.8, SI
2014/1873 Art.15, SI 2014/2027 Art.4, SI
2014/2269 Art.8, SI 2014/2384 Art.10,
Art.11, Sch.19 para.4, SI 2014/2434 Art.9,
SI 2014/2441 Art.13, SI 2014/2637 Art.8, SI
2014/2935 Art.15, SI 2014/2950 Art.10, SI
2014/3102 Art.3, SI 2014/3105 Sch.1, SI
2014/3110 Sch.1, SI 2014/3112 Sch.1, SI

2014/3310 Sch.1, SI 2014/3311 Sch.1, SI
2014/3328 Art.10, SI 2014/3331 Art.7
s.54, disapplied: SI 2014/466 Sch.1, SI
2014/941 Sch.1, SI 2014/3105 Sch.1, SI
2014/3106 Sch.1, SI 2014/3107 Sch.1, SI
2014/3108 Sch.1, SI 2014/3109 Sch.1, SI
2014/3110 Sch.1, SI 2014/3112 Sch.1, SI
2014/3310 Sch.1, SI 2014/3311 Sch.1
s.54, referred to: SI 2014/909 Art.12, SI
2014/2441 Art.13
s.54, varied: SI 2014/1052 Art.13, SI
2014/3102 Art.3, SI 2014/3331 Art.7
s.55, applied: SI 2014/2637 Art.8
s.55, referred to: SI 2014/2441 Art.13
s.56, applied: SI 2014/2384 Sch.19 para.4
s.56, disapplied: SI 2014/909 Art.12, SI
2014/2027 Art.4, SI 2014/2269 Art.8, SI
2014/2637 Art.8, SI 2014/3102 Art.3
s.56A, applied: SI 2014/941 Sch.1, SI
2014/3105 Sch.1, SI 2014/3110 Sch.1, SI
2014/3112 Sch.1
s.56A, disapplied: SI 2014/2384 Sch.19
para.4
s.57, applied: SI 2014/466 Sch.1, SI
2014/1052 Art.13, SI 2014/2027 Art.4, SI
2014/2269 Art.8, SI 2014/2637 Art.8, SI
2014/3102 Art.3, SI 2014/3105 Sch.1, SI
2014/3110 Sch.1, SI 2014/3112 Sch.1, SI
2014/3310 Sch.1, SI 2014/3311 Sch.1, SI
2014/3331 Art.7
s.57, disapplied: SI 2014/466 Sch.1, SI
2014/941 Sch.1, SI 2014/3105 Sch.1, SI
2014/3106 Sch.1, SI 2014/3107 Sch.1, SI
2014/3108 Sch.1, SI 2014/3109 Sch.1, SI
2014/3110 Sch.1, SI 2014/3112 Sch.1, SI
2014/3310 Sch.1, SI 2014/3311 Sch.1
s.57, referred to: SI 2014/909 Art.12, SI
2014/2441 Art.13, SI 2014/3102 Art.3
s.57, varied: SI 2014/2269 Art.8
s.58, applied: SI 2014/466 Sch.1, SI
2014/941 Sch.1, SI 2014/2384 Sch.19
para.4, SI 2014/3106 Sch.1, SI 2014/3107
Sch.1, SI 2014/3108 Sch.1, SI 2014/3109
Sch.1, SI 2014/3110 Sch.1, SI 2014/3112
Sch.1, SI 2014/3310 Sch.1, SI 2014/3311
Sch.1
s.58, disapplied: SI 2014/909 Art.12, SI
2014/2027 Art.4, SI 2014/2269 Art.8, SI
2014/2637 Art.8, SI 2014/3102 Art.3
s.58, varied: SI 2014/3105 Sch.1, SI
2014/3106 Sch.1, SI 2014/3107 Sch.1, SI

2014/3108 Sch.1, SI 2014/3109 Sch.1, SI
2014/3110 Sch.1, SI 2014/3112 Sch.1
s.58A, applied: SI 2014/3109 Sch.1
s.58A, varied: SI 2014/466 Sch.1, SI
2014/941 Sch.1
s.59, applied: SI 2014/466 Sch.1, SI
2014/941 Sch.1, SI 2014/1052 Art.13, SI
2014/2027 Art.4, SI 2014/2269 Art.8, SI
2014/2637 Art.8, SI 2014/3102 Art.3, Sch.8
para.23, SI 2014/3109 Sch.1, SI 2014/3310
Sch.1, SI 2014/3311 Sch.1, SI 2014/3331
Art.7
s.59, referred to: SI 2014/909 Art.12, SI
2014/2441 Art.13
s.60, applied: SI 2014/2637 Art.8, SI
2014/3311 Sch.1
s.60, referred to: SI 2014/2441 Art.13
s.61, applied: SI 2014/941 Sch.1, SI
2014/3109 Sch.1, SI 2014/3310 Sch.1, SI
2014/3311 Sch.1
s.61, disapplied: SI 2014/2384 Sch.19 para.4
s.61, referred to: SI 2014/466 Sch.1
s.62, applied: SI 2014/941 Sch.1, SI
2014/3109 Sch.1, SI 2014/3310 Sch.1, SI
2014/3311 Sch.1
s.62, disapplied: SI 2014/2384 Sch.19 para.4
s.62, referred to: SI 2014/466 Sch.1
s.63, disapplied: SI 2014/2384 Sch.19 para.4
s.64, varied: SI 2014/466 Sch.1, SI 2014/941
Sch.1, SI 2014/3106 Sch.1, SI 2014/3108
Sch.1
s.66, applied: SI 2014/3109 Sch.1, SI
2014/3110 Sch.1
s.66, disapplied: SI 2014/466 Sch.1, SI
2014/941 Sch.1, SI 2014/3105 Sch.1, SI
2014/3106 Sch.1, SI 2014/3107 Sch.1, SI
2014/3108 Sch.1, SI 2014/3109 Sch.1, SI
2014/3110 Sch.1, SI 2014/3112 Sch.1, SI
2014/3310 Sch.1, SI 2014/3311 Sch.1
s.68, applied: SI 2014/1052 Art.13, SI
2014/2027 Art.4, SI 2014/2269 Art.8, SI
2014/2637 Art.8, SI 2014/3102 Art.3, SI
2014/3331 Art.7
s.68, referred to: SI 2014/909 Art.12, SI
2014/2441 Art.13
s.69, applied: SI 2014/2637 Art.8, SI
2014/3109 Sch.1, SI 2014/3310 Sch.1, SI
2014/3311 Sch.1
s.69, referred to: SI 2014/2441 Art.13

s.69, varied: SI 2014/466 Sch.1, SI 2014/941
Sch.1, SI 2014/3106 Sch.1, SI 2014/3108
Sch.1
s.70, applied: SI 2014/466 Sch.1, SI
2014/941 Sch.1, SI 2014/3106 Sch.1, SI
2014/3107 Sch.1, SI 2014/3108 Sch.1, SI
2014/3109 Sch.1, SI 2014/3310 Sch.1, SI
2014/3311 Sch.1
s.70, disapplied: SI 2014/466 Sch.1
s.71, applied: SI 2014/1052 Sch.13 para.17
s.73A, applied: SI 2014/2384 Sch.19 para.4
s.73A, disapplied: SI 2014/909 Art.12, SI
2014/2027 Art.4, SI 2014/2269 Art.8, SI
2014/2637 Art.8, SI 2014/3102 Art.3
s.73A, varied: SI 2014/3105 Sch.1, SI
2014/3106 Sch.1, SI 2014/3107 Sch.1, SI
2014/3108 Sch.1, SI 2014/3109 Sch.1, SI
2014/3110 Sch.1, SI 2014/3112 Sch.1
s.74, applied: SI 2014/466 Sch.1, SI
2014/941 Sch.1, SI 2014/3105 Sch.1, SI
2014/3106 Sch.1, SI 2014/3107 Sch.1, SI
2014/3108 Sch.1, SI 2014/3109 Sch.1, SI
2014/3110 Sch.1, SI 2014/3112 Sch.1, SI
2014/3310 Sch.1, SI 2014/3311 Sch.1
s.74, disapplied: SI 2014/2384 Sch.19 para.4
s.74, referred to: SI 2014/466 Sch.1, SI
2014/3310 Sch.1
s.74, varied: SI 2014/3105 Sch.1, SI
2014/3106 Sch.1, SI 2014/3107 Sch.1, SI
2014/3108 Sch.1, SI 2014/3109 Sch.1, SI
2014/3110 Sch.1, SI 2014/3112 Sch.1
s.74A, applied: SI 2014/941 Sch.1, SI
2014/3109 Sch.1, SI 2014/3310 Sch.1, SI
2014/3311 Sch.1
s.74A, referred to: SI 2014/466 Sch.1
s.75, applied: SI 2014/2269 Art.8, SI
2014/2637 Art.8
s.76, applied: SI 2014/1052 Art.13, SI
2014/2027 Art.4, SI 2014/2637 Art.8, SI
2014/3102 Art.3, SI 2014/3310 Sch.1, SI
2014/3331 Art.7
s.76, referred to: SI 2014/909 Art.12, SI
2014/2441 Art.13
s.77, applied: SI 2014/2637 Art.8
s.77, referred to: SI 2014/2441 Art.13
s.78A, applied: SI 2014/2384 Sch.19 para.4
s.78A, disapplied: SI 2014/909 Art.12, SI
2014/2027 Art.4, SI 2014/2269 Art.8, SI
2014/2637 Art.8, SI 2014/3102 Art.3
s.80, applied: SI 2014/466 Sch.1, SI
2014/3106 Sch.1, SI 2014/3107 Sch.1, SI

2014/3108 Sch.1, SI 2014/3109 Sch.1, SI
2014/3310 Sch.1, SI 2014/3311 Sch.1
s.81, applied: SI 2014/941 Sch.1, SI
2014/3105 Sch.1, SI 2014/3109 Sch.1, SI
2014/3110 Sch.1, SI 2014/3112 Sch.1, SI
2014/3310 Sch.1, SI 2014/3311 Sch.1
s.82, referred to: SI 2014/2441 Art.13
s.84, applied: SI 2014/941 Sch.1, SI
2014/3109 Sch.1, SI 2014/3310 Sch.1, SI
2014/3311 Sch.1
s.84, referred to: SI 2014/466 Sch.1
s.85, applied: SI 2014/909 Art.27, Art.32, SI
2014/941 Sch.1, SI 2014/1052 Art.30, SI
2014/1599 Art.22, SI 2014/1796 Art.22,
Art.23, SI 2014/1821 Art.7, SI 2014/1873
Art.30, SI 2014/2269 Art.25, Art.28, SI
2014/2384 Art.48, SI 2014/2434 Art.24, SI
2014/2441 Art.30, SI 2014/2637 Art.26,
Art.31, SI 2014/2935 Art.39, SI 2014/2950
Art.26, SI 2014/3102 Art.29, SI 2014/3106
Sch.1, SI 2014/3107 Sch.1, SI 2014/3108
Sch.1, SI 2014/3109 Sch.1, SI 2014/3310
Sch.1, SI 2014/3311 Sch.1, SI 2014/3328
Art.23, SI 2014/3331 Art.22
s.86, applied: SI 2014/3102 Art.3, SI
2014/3105 Sch.1, SI 2014/3310 Sch.1, SI
2014/3311 Sch.1
s.86, referred to: SI 2014/909 Art.12, SI
2014/941 Sch.1, SI 2014/1052 Art.13, SI
2014/2027 Art.4, SI 2014/2269 Art.8, SI
2014/2441 Art.13, SI 2014/2637 Art.8, SI
2014/3105 Sch.1, SI 2014/3106 Sch.1, SI
2014/3107 Sch.1, SI 2014/3108 Sch.1, SI
2014/3109 Sch.1, SI 2014/3110 Sch.1, SI
2014/3112 Sch.1, SI 2014/3310 Sch.1
s.87, applied: SI 2014/909 Art.10, SI
2014/1052 Art.10, SI 2014/2027 Art.4, SI
2014/2269 Art.8, SI 2014/2441 Art.16, SI
2014/2637 Art.8, SI 2014/3310 Sch.1, SI
2014/3311 Sch.1
s.88, applied: SI 2014/3105 Sch.1, SI
2014/3108 Sch.1, SI 2014/3109 Sch.1, SI
2014/3110 Sch.1, SI 2014/3112 Sch.1, SI
2014/3310 Sch.1, SI 2014/3311 Sch.1
s.88, referred to: SI 2014/3106 Sch.1, SI
2014/3107 Sch.1
s.88, varied: SI 2014/3105 Sch.1, SI
2014/3106 Sch.1, SI 2014/3107 Sch.1, SI
2014/3108 Sch.1, SI 2014/3109 Sch.1, SI
2014/3110 Sch.1, SI 2014/3112 Sch.1

s.90, applied: SI 2014/3105 Sch.1, SI
2014/3108 Sch.1, SI 2014/3109 Sch.1, SI
2014/3110 Sch.1, SI 2014/3112 Sch.1, SI
2014/3311 Sch.1
s.90, varied: SI 2014/466 Sch.1, SI 2014/941
Sch.1
s.93, applied: SI 2014/3105 Sch.1, SI
2014/3108 Sch.1, SI 2014/3109 Sch.1, SI
2014/3110 Sch.1, SI 2014/3112 Sch.1, SI
2014/3310 Sch.1, SI 2014/3311 Sch.1
s.93, referred to: SI 2014/3106 Sch.1, SI
2014/3107 Sch.1
s.93, varied: SI 2014/3105 Sch.1, SI
2014/3106 Sch.1, SI 2014/3107 Sch.1, SI
2014/3108 Sch.1, SI 2014/3109 Sch.1, SI
2014/3110 Sch.1, SI 2014/3112 Sch.1
s.96, applied: SI 2014/941 Sch.1, SI
2014/3109 Sch.1, SI 2014/3310 Sch.1, SI
2014/3311 Sch.1
s.96, referred to: SI 2014/466 Sch.1
s.98, applied: SI 2014/941 Sch.1, SI
2014/3106 Sch.1, SI 2014/3110 Sch.1
s.98, referred to: SI 2014/3105 Sch.1, SI
2014/3112 Sch.1
s.99, applied: SI 2014/466 Sch.1, SI
2014/941 Sch.1, SI 2014/3105 Sch.1, SI
2014/3109 Sch.1, SI 2014/3110 Sch.1, SI
2014/3112 Sch.1, SI 2014/3310 Sch.1, SI
2014/3311 Sch.1
s.105, varied: SI 2014/3105 Sch.1, SI
2014/3106 Sch.1, SI 2014/3107 Sch.1, SI
2014/3110 Sch.1, SI 2014/3112 Sch.1
s.106, applied: SI 2014/3328 Art.14
s.112A, applied: SSI 2014/58 Reg.3
s.112A, referred to: SSI 2014/58 Reg.3
s.112A, enabling: SSI 2014/58
s.134, enabling: SSI 2014/56
s.163, enabling: SSI 2014/58
s.163A, applied: SSI 2014/56, SSI 2014/58
Sch.3A, disapplied: SI 2014/909 Art.12, SI
2014/2027 Art.4, SI 2014/2269 Art.8, SI
2014/2384 Sch.19 para.4, SI 2014/2637
Art.8, SI 2014/3102 Art.3
Sch.3A, varied: SI 2014/3105 Sch.1, SI
2014/3106 Sch.1, SI 2014/3107 Sch.1, SI
2014/3108 Sch.1, SI 2014/3109 Sch.1, SI
2014/3110 Sch.1, SI 2014/3112 Sch.1
Sch.3A para.2, applied: SI 2014/2384 Sch.19
para.4
Sch.3A para.3, applied: SI 2014/2384 Sch.19
para.4

Sch.3A para.3, disapplied: SI 2014/2384
Sch.19 para.4
Sch.3A para.5, disapplied: SI 2014/2384
Sch.19 para.4
Sch.4, applied: SI 2014/466 Sch.1, SI
2014/941 Sch.1, SI 2014/3106 Sch.1, SI
2014/3107 Sch.1, SI 2014/3108 Sch.1, SI
2014/3109 Sch.1, SI 2014/3310 Sch.1, SI
2014/3311 Sch.1
23. Children and Young Persons (Protection from Tobacco) Act 1991
s.5, amended: 2014 c.6 s.93
25. Criminal Procedure (Insanity and Unfitness to Plead) Act 1991
s.1, applied: SI 2014/1610 r.38_14
28. Natural Heritage (Scotland) Act 1991
s.7, amended: 2014 asp 3 Sch.3 para.41
s.24, amended: 2014 asp 3 Sch.3 para.24
Sch.1 para.17, amended: 2014 asp 3 Sch.3
para.41
31. Finance Act 1991
s.116, applied: SI 2014/9 Reg.3
s.116, enabling: SI 2014/9
s.117, enabling: SI 2014/9
40. Road Traffic Act 1991
s.49, applied: SI 2014/3105 Sch.1, SI
2014/3110 Sch.1, SI 2014/3112 Sch.1, SI
2014/3310 Sch.1, SI 2014/3311 Sch.1
s.66, applied: SSI 2014/84 Art.4, SSI
2014/85 Reg.2, SSI 2014/86 Reg.4, SSI
2014/169 Art.4, SSI 2014/171 Reg.4
s.66, referred to: SSI 2014/170 Reg.2
s.66, varied: SSI 2014/84 Sch.2 para.1, SSI
2014/169 Sch.2 para.1
s.69, applied: SSI 2014/84 Art.4, SSI
2014/85 Reg.2, SSI 2014/169 Art.4
s.69, referred to: SSI 2014/170 Reg.2
s.69, varied: SSI 2014/84 Sch.2 para.2, SSI
2014/169 Sch.2 para.2
s.71, applied: SSI 2014/86 Reg.4, SSI
2014/171 Reg.4
s.71, varied: SSI 2014/84 Sch.2 para.3, SSI
2014/169 Sch.2 para.3
s.72, applied: 2014 asp 10 Sch.1 para.13, SSI
2014/86 Reg.14, SSI 2014/171 Reg.3,
Reg.14
s.72, referred to: SSI 2014/86 Reg.3
s.73, applied: 2014 asp 10 Sch.1 para.13, SSI
2014/84 Art.6, SSI 2014/86 Reg.6, Reg.9,
SSI 2014/169 Art.6, SSI 2014/171 Reg.6,
Reg.9

s.73, varied: SSI 2014/84 Sch.2 para.4, SSI
2014/169 Sch.2 para.4
s.73, enabling: SSI 2014/86, SSI 2014/171
s.74, varied: SSI 2014/84 Sch.2 para.5, SSI
2014/169 Sch.2 para.5
s.79, applied: SSI 2014/84 Art.4, SSI
2014/169 Art.4
s.82, applied: SSI 2014/84 Art.4, SSI
2014/169 Art.4
s.82, varied: SSI 2014/84 Sch.2 para.6, SSI
2014/169 Sch.2 para.6
Sch.3 para.1, applied: SSI 2014/84, SSI
2014/169
Sch.3 para.1, enabling: SSI 2014/84, SSI
2014/169
Sch.3 para.2, applied: SSI 2014/84, SSI
2014/169
Sch.3 para.2, enabling: SSI 2014/84, SSI
2014/169
Sch.3 para.3, enabling: SSI 2014/84, SSI
2014/169
Sch.6, applied: SSI 2014/84 Art.4, SSI
2014/169 Art.4
Sch.6 para.1, varied: SSI 2014/84 Sch.2
para.7, SSI 2014/169 Sch.2 para.7
Sch.6 para.2, applied: SSI 2014/86 Reg.4,
SSI 2014/171 Reg.4
Sch.6 para.2, varied: SSI 2014/84 Sch.2
para.7, SSI 2014/169 Sch.2 para.7
Sch.6 para.3, varied: SSI 2014/84 Sch.2
para.7, SSI 2014/169 Sch.2 para.7
Sch.6 para.4, varied: SSI 2014/84 Sch.2
para.7, SSI 2014/169 Sch.2 para.7
Sch.6 para.5, applied: SSI 2014/86 Reg.14,
SSI 2014/171 Reg.3, Reg.14
Sch.6 para.5, referred to: SSI 2014/86 Reg.3
Sch.6 para.5, varied: SSI 2014/84 Sch.2
para.7, SSI 2014/169 Sch.2 para.7
Sch.6 para.6, varied: SSI 2014/84 Sch.2
para.7, SSI 2014/169 Sch.2 para.7
Sch.6 para.7, varied: SSI 2014/84 Sch.2
para.7, SSI 2014/169 Sch.2 para.7
Sch.6 para.8, varied: SSI 2014/84 Sch.2
para.7, SSI 2014/169 Sch.2 para.7
45. Coal Mining Subsidence Act 1991
Pt III., see *Hicks v Coal Authority* [2014]
R.V.R. 340 (UT (Lands)), PR Francis FRICS
s.1, see *Hicks v Coal Authority* [2014]
R.V.R. 340 (UT (Lands)), PR Francis FRICS

s.2, see *Newbold v Coal Authority* [2013] EWCA Civ 584, [2014] 1 W.L.R. 1288 (CA (Civ Div)), Longmore LJ

s.3, see *Newbold v Coal Authority* [2013] EWCA Civ 584, [2014] 1 W.L.R. 1288 (CA (Civ Div)), Longmore LJ

s.38, see *Hicks v Coal Authority* [2014] R.V.R. 340 (UT (Lands)), PR Francis FRICS

s.40, see *Hicks v Coal Authority* [2014] R.V.R. 340 (UT (Lands)), PR Francis FRICS

46. Atomic Weapons Establishment Act 1991
Sch.1 para.10D, added: SI 2014/469 Sch.2 para.14

48. Child Support Act 1991
applied: SI 2014/612 Reg.3, Reg.5, SI 2014/614 Reg.7, SSI 2014/290 Reg.3
referred to: SI 2014/612 Reg.13
s.1, applied: SI 2014/840 Sch.1
s.3, amended: 2014 c.6 Sch.2 para.52
s.3, referred to: SI 2014/612 Reg.5
s.4, applied: SI 2014/614 Reg.1, Reg.4, Reg.6, Reg.7, SI 2014/1635 Art.3
s.7, applied: SI 2014/614 Reg.1, Reg.4, Reg.6, Reg.7, SI 2014/1635 Art.3
s.11, applied: SI 2014/612 Reg.3
s.16, enabling: SI 2014/1386
s.20, applied: SI 2014/840 r.5
s.28A, see *Hakki v Secretary of State for Work and Pensions* [2014] EWCA Civ 530, [2014] B.T.C. 22 (CA (Civ Div)), Longmore LJ
s.28E, enabling: SI 2014/1386
s.28I, see *Hakki v Secretary of State for Work and Pensions* [2014] EWCA Civ 530, [2014] B.T.C. 22 (CA (Civ Div)), Longmore LJ
s.29, applied: SI 2014/612 Reg.7
s.29, enabling: SI 2014/1386
s.31, referred to: SI 2014/614 Reg.7
s.32, enabling: SI 2014/1386
s.32A, referred to: SI 2014/614 Reg.7
s.32L, applied: SI 2014/840 Sch.1
s.32M, applied: SI 2014/840 Sch.1
s.33, see *Child Maintenance and Enforcement Commission v Wilson* 2014 S.L.T. 46 (IH (Ex Div)), Lord Menzies; see *Secretary of State for Work & Pensions, The Child Support Agency v Anderson* 2014 G.W.D. 17-306 (Sh Ct (Lothian) (Edinburgh)), Sheriff Principal M M Stephen
s.34, enabling: SI 2014/1386

s.39A, disapplied: SI 2014/612 Reg.13
s.40, disapplied: SI 2014/612 Reg.13
s.40A, disapplied: SI 2014/612 Reg.13
s.40B, disapplied: SI 2014/612 Reg.13
s.42, enabling: SI 2014/884, SI 2014/1386
s.43, enabling: SI 2014/612
s.43A, enabling: SI 2014/1386, SI 2014/1621
s.51, enabling: SI 2014/612, SI 2014/1386, SI 2014/1621
s.52, applied: SI 2014/612
s.52, enabling: SI 2014/1386, SI 2014/1621
s.54, enabling: SI 2014/1386
Sch.1, applied: SI 2014/840 Sch.1
Sch.1 Part I para.4, enabling: SI 2014/884
Sch.1 Part I para.6, amended: SI 2014/560
Sch.1 para.21, SI 2014/3229 Sch.5 para.8
Sch.1 Part I para.6, repealed (in part): SI 2014/560 Sch.1 para.21, SI 2014/3229 Sch.5 para.8
Sch.1 Part I para.10C, amended: SI 2014/560 Sch.1 para.21, SI 2014/3229 Sch.5 para.8
Sch.1 Part I para.10C, repealed (in part): SI 2014/560 Sch.1 para.21, SI 2014/3229 Sch.5 para.8
Sch.1 Part II para.11, enabling: SI 2014/1386

53. Criminal Justice Act 1991
see *R. (on the application of Whiston) v Secretary of State for Justice* [2012] EWCA Civ 1374, [2014] Q.B. 306 (CA (Civ Div)), Pill, L.J.
Part II, applied: SI 2014/1652 Sch.1
s.20A, applied: SI 2014/1610 r.37_10, r.38_16
s.53, applied: SI 2014/1610 r.14_1

55. Agricultural Holdings (Scotland) Act 1991
see *Curran v Angus Estates Tealing Ltd* 2014 S.L.T. 49 (IH (1 Div)), The Lord President (Gill)
applied: 2014 asp 18 s.94
s.26, repealed (in part): 2014 asp 3 Sch.3 para.25

56. Water Industry Act 1991
see *Fish Legal v Information Commissioner (C-279/12)* [2014] Q.B. 521 (ECJ (Grand Chamber)), Judge Skouris (President); see *Manchester Ship Canal Co Ltd v United Utilities Water Plc* [2014] UKSC 40, [2014] 1 W.L.R. 2576 (SC), Lord Neuberger PSC

applied: 2014 c.21 s.52, Sch.11 para.7,
Sch.11 para.8, 2014 c.25 Sch.1, SI
2014/1599 Sch.9 para.4, SI 2014/1873
Art.20, SI 2014/2269 Art.14, SI 2014/2306
Art.4, SI 2014/2434 Sch.8 para.4, SI
2014/2441 Art.18, SI 2014/2907 Art.4, SI
2014/2935 Sch.9 para.102
referred to: 2014 c.5 Sch.1 para.1, 2014 c.21
s.3, Sch.11 para.8, Sch.11 para.11
Part II c.I, applied: 2014 c.21 s.55
Part II c.IA, applied: 2014 c.21 s.49, s.55
Part II c.IA, substituted: 2014 c.21 Sch.7
para.9
Part III c.I, amended: 2014 c.21 Sch.7
para.46
Part III c.II, amended: 2014 c.21 Sch.7
para.62
Part III c.IIB, added: 2014 c.21 s.12
Part III c.III, amended: 2014 c.21 Sch.7
para.66
Part IV c.I, amended: 2014 c.21 Sch.7
para.84
Part IV c.IIA, added: 2014 c.21 Sch.4
Part V c.I, applied: 2014 c.21 s.45
s.2, amended: 2014 c.21 s.22, s.23, s.24,
Sch.5 para.2, Sch.7 para.3, SI 2014/892
Sch.1 para.74
s.2, applied: 2014 c.21 s.50
s.2, referred to: 2014 c.21 s.50
s.2, repealed (in part): 2014 c.21 Sch.5
para.2, Sch.7 para.3
s.2, varied: SI 2014/3320 Art.3
s.2A, amended: 2014 c.21 Sch.7 para.4
s.2A, referred to: 2014 c.21 Sch.7 para.132,
Sch.12 para.1
s.2A, substituted: 2014 c.21 s.24
s.2B, amended: 2014 c.21 Sch.5 para.3,
Sch.7 para.5
s.2B, referred to: 2014 c.21 Sch.12 para.1
s.6, amended: 2014 c.21 Sch.7 para.6
s.8, amended: 2014 c.21 s.13
s.10, amended: 2014 c.21 Sch.7 para.7
s.12, amended: 2014 c.21 Sch.7 para.8
s.12, applied: SI 2014/559
s.14B, amended: SI 2014/892 Sch.1 para.75
s.14B, applied: SI 2014/559
s.14B, referred to: SI 2014/892 Sch.2 para.2
s.16B, amended: SI 2014/892 Sch.1 para.76
s.16B, applied: SI 2014/559
s.16B, referred to: SI 2014/892 Sch.2 para.2
s.17, amended: SI 2014/892 Sch.1 para.77

s.17A, amended: 2014 c.21 Sch.5 para.4
s.17A, referred to: 2014 c.21 s.3
s.17A, repealed (in part): 2014 c.21 Sch.5
para.4
s.17A, substituted: 2014 c.21 s.1
s.17AA, amended: 2014 c.21 Sch.5 para.5
s.17AA, repealed (in part): 2014 c.21 Sch.5
para.5
s.17B, amended: 2014 c.21 s.2, Sch.5 para.6,
Sch.7 para.10
s.17B, applied: 2014 c.21 Sch.11 para.7,
Sch.12 para.4
s.17B, repealed (in part): 2014 c.21 Sch.5
para.6, Sch.7 para.10
s.17BA, added: 2014 c.21 s.4
s.17BA, amended: 2014 c.21 Sch.5 para.7
s.17BA, applied: 2014 c.21 Sch.12 para.4
s.17BB, amended: 2014 c.21 Sch.5 para.8
s.17C, amended: 2014 c.21 Sch.5 para.9,
Sch.7 para.11
s.17D, amended: 2014 c.21 Sch.7 para.12
s.17D, referred to: 2014 c.21 Sch.11 para.6
s.17D, repealed (in part): 2014 c.21 Sch.5
para.10, Sch.7 para.12
s.17DA, added: 2014 c.21 Sch.7 para.13
s.17DA, repealed (in part): 2014 c.21 Sch.5
para.11
s.17E, amended: 2014 c.21 Sch.5 para.12,
Sch.7 para.14
s.17E, repealed (in part): 2014 c.21 Sch.5
para.12
s.17F, amended: 2014 c.21 s.25, Sch.7
para.15
s.17F, repealed (in part): 2014 c.21 s.25,
Sch.7 para.15
s.17FA, added: 2014 c.21 s.6
s.17FA, amended: 2014 c.21 Sch.5 para.13
s.17G, amended: 2014 c.21 Sch.5 para.14,
Sch.7 para.16
s.17H, amended: 2014 c.21 Sch.5 para.15,
Sch.7 para.17
s.17H, repealed (in part): 2014 c.21 Sch.5
para.15, Sch.7 para.17
s.17HA, added: 2014 c.21 Sch.7 para.18
s.17HA, amended: 2014 c.21 Sch.5 para.16
s.17I, amended: 2014 c.21 Sch.5 para.17,
Sch.7 para.19
s.17I, applied: 2014 c.21 Sch.11 para.3
s.17J, amended: 2014 c.21 Sch.5 para.18,
Sch.7 para.20

s.17K, amended: 2014 c.21 Sch.5 para.19,
Sch.7 para.21
s.17M, amended: SI 2014/892 Sch.1 para.78
s.17M, applied: SI 2014/559
s.17M, referred to: SI 2014/892 Sch.2 para.2
s.17N, amended: 2014 c.21 Sch.5 para.20,
Sch.7 para.22
s.17O, amended: 2014 c.21 Sch.5 para.21,
Sch.7 para.23
s.17P, amended: 2014 c.21 Sch.5 para.22,
Sch.7 para.24
s.17Q, amended: SI 2014/892 Sch.1 para.79
s.17Q, applied: SI 2014/559
s.17Q, referred to: SI 2014/892 Sch.2 para.2
s.17R, amended: 2014 c.21 Sch.7 para.25, SI
2014/892 Sch.1 para.80
s.18, amended: 2014 c.21 Sch.7 para.26
s.18, applied: 2014 c.21 s.47
s.19, amended: 2014 c.21 Sch.7 para.27
s.20, amended: 2014 c.21 Sch.7 para.28
s.21, amended: 2014 c.21 Sch.7 para.29
s.22, amended: 2014 c.21 Sch.7 para.30
s.22A, amended: 2014 c.21 Sch.7 para.31
s.22C, amended: 2014 c.21 s.26, Sch.7
para.32
s.22E, amended: 2014 c.21 Sch.7 para.33
s.22F, amended: 2014 c.21 Sch.7 para.34
s.23, amended: 2014 c.21 Sch.5 para.23,
Sch.7 para.35
s.23, referred to: 2014 c.21 s.46
s.24, amended: 2014 c.21 Sch.5 para.24,
Sch.7 para.36
s.25, amended: 2014 c.21 Sch.7 para.37
s.26, amended: 2014 c.21 Sch.7 para.38
s.27, amended: 2014 c.21 Sch.7 para.39, SI
2014/892 Sch.1 para.81
s.27A, amended: 2014 c.21 Sch.7 para.40
s.27C, amended: 2014 c.21 Sch.5 para.25,
Sch.7 para.41
s.27C, repealed (in part): 2014 c.21 Sch.5
para.25
s.27E, amended: 2014 c.21 Sch.7 para.42, SI
2014/892 Sch.1 para.82
s.27H, amended: 2014 c.21 Sch.7 para.43
s.27K, amended: 2014 c.21 Sch.7 para.44
s.29, amended: 2014 c.21 Sch.7 para.45
s.29A, amended: SI 2014/892 Sch.1 para.83
s.31, amended: SI 2014/892 Sch.1 para.84
s.32, amended: 2014 c.21 s.14, SI 2014/892
Sch.1 para.85

s.32, applied: SI 2014/549 Art.3, SI
2014/892 Art.3
s.33, amended: 2014 c.21 s.15, SI 2014/892
Sch.1 para.86
s.33A, added: 2014 c.21 s.14
s.33D, added: 2014 c.21 s.14
s.35, amended: SI 2014/892 Sch.1 para.87
s.37, applied: 2014 c.21 s.61
s.37A, amended: 2014 c.21 s.27, s.28, Sch.7
para.47
s.37AA, added: 2014 c.21 s.27
s.37C, amended: 2014 c.21 Sch.7 para.48
s.37D, amended: 2014 c.21 s.27, s.28, Sch.7
para.49
s.38A, amended: 2014 c.21 s.29
s.38B, amended: 2014 c.21 Sch.7 para.50
s.38ZA, added: 2014 c.21 s.29
s.38ZA, amended: 2014 c.21 Sch.5 para.26
s.39A, amended: 2014 c.21 Sch.7 para.51
s.39B, amended: 2014 c.21 s.28, Sch.7
para.52
s.39C, amended: 2014 c.21 Sch.7 para.53
s.39D, added: 2014 c.21 s.28
s.39ZA, added: 2014 c.21 s.29
s.40, substituted: 2014 c.21 s.8
s.40A, varied: 2014 c.21 s.8
s.40I, referred to: 2014 c.21 Sch.12 para.1
s.42, amended: 2014 c.21 s.18
s.42, repealed (in part): 2014 c.21 s.18,
Sch.7 para.54
s.43, repealed: 2014 c.21 Sch.7 para.55
s.45, amended: 2014 c.21 s.18
s.46, amended: 2014 c.21 s.18
s.46, repealed (in part): 2014 c.21 s.18
s.47, amended: 2014 c.21 s.18, Sch.7 para.56
s.48, repealed: 2014 c.21 Sch.7 para.57
s.51A, amended: 2014 c.21 s.10
s.51A, repealed (in part): 2014 c.21 s.10
s.51B, substituted: 2014 c.21 s.10
s.51E, amended: 2014 c.21 s.10
s.52, amended: 2014 c.21 Sch.5 para.27,
Sch.7 para.58
s.52, repealed (in part): 2014 c.21 Sch.5
para.27
s.55, amended: 2014 c.21 Sch.5 para.28,
Sch.7 para.59
s.61, amended: 2014 c.21 Sch.7 para.60
s.63, amended: 2014 c.21 Sch.7 para.61
s.63AA, amended: 2014 c.21 Sch.7 para.63
s.63AA, applied: 2014 c.21 s.43
s.63AB, amended: 2014 c.21 Sch.7 para.64

s.63AB, applied: 2014 c.21 s.43
s.63AC, amended: 2014 c.21 Sch.5 para.29,
Sch.7 para.65
s.63AC, applied: 2014 c.21 s.46
s.63AC, substituted: 2014 c.21 s.31
s.66A, amended: 2014 c.21 Sch.5 para.30
s.66A, referred to: 2014 c.21 Sch.11 para.10
s.66A, repealed (in part): 2014 c.21 Sch.5
para.30
s.66A, substituted: 2014 c.21 Sch.2 para.1
s.66AA, amended: 2014 c.21 Sch.5 para.31
s.66AA, repealed (in part): 2014 c.21 Sch.5
para.31
s.66B, amended: 2014 c.21 Sch.5 para.32
s.66B, applied: 2014 c.21 Sch.11 para.7,
Sch.11 para.8
s.66B, repealed (in part): 2014 c.21 Sch.5
para.32
s.66C, amended: 2014 c.21 Sch.5 para.33
s.66C, repealed (in part): 2014 c.21 Sch.5
para.33
s.66CA, added: 2014 c.21 Sch.2 para.2
s.66D, amended: SI 2014/892 Sch.1 para.88
s.66D, applied: 2014 c.21 Sch.11 para.7,
Sch.11 para.10
s.66D, referred to: 2014 c.21 Sch.11 para.8,
Sch.11 para.9, Sch.11 para.10
s.66D, substituted: 2014 c.21 Sch.2 para.3
s.66DA, added: 2014 c.21 Sch.2 para.4
s.66E, amended: 2014 c.21 Sch.5 para.34
s.66E, applied: 2014 c.21 Sch.11 para.7, SI
2014/3320 Art.3
s.66E, referred to: 2014 c.21 Sch.11 para.8,
Sch.11 para.10
s.66E, substituted: 2014 c.21 Sch.2 para.5
s.66E, varied: SI 2014/3320 Art.3
s.66EA, amended: 2014 c.21 Sch.5 para.35
s.66F, referred to: 2014 c.21 Sch.11 para.10
s.66F, repealed: 2014 c.21 Sch.2 para.6
s.66G, amended: 2014 c.21 Sch.2 para.7
s.66G, repealed (in part): 2014 c.21 Sch.5
para.36
s.66H, amended: 2014 c.21 Sch.2 para.8
s.66H, repealed (in part): 2014 c.21 Sch.5
para.37
s.66I, amended: 2014 c.21 Sch.2 para.9
s.68, amended: 2014 c.21 Sch.5 para.38,
Sch.7 para.67
s.69, amended: 2014 c.21 Sch.7 para.68
s.71, applied: 2014 c.21 Sch.8 para.30
s.72, amended: 2014 c.21 Sch.7 para.69

s.73, amended: 2014 c.21 Sch.7 para.70
s.74, amended: 2014 c.21 Sch.7 para.71
s.75, amended: 2014 c.21 Sch.7 para.72
s.76, amended: 2014 c.21 Sch.7 para.73
s.78, amended: 2014 c.21 Sch.7 para.74
s.86, amended: 2014 c.21 Sch.7 para.75
s.86, applied: 2014 c.21 s.51
s.86ZA, added: 2014 c.21 s.40
s.86ZA, applied: 2014 c.21 Sch.12 para.1
s.87, amended: 2014 c.21 Sch.7 para.76
s.87C, amended: 2014 c.21 Sch.7 para.77
s.90, amended: 2014 c.21 Sch.7 para.78
s.93, amended: 2014 c.21 Sch.7 para.79
s.93A, amended: 2014 c.21 Sch.7 para.80
s.93B, amended: 2014 c.21 Sch.7 para.81
s.93C, amended: 2014 c.21 Sch.7 para.82
s.93D, amended: 2014 c.21 Sch.7 para.83
s.95A, amended: 2014 c.21 s.30
s.95B, amended: 2014 c.21 Sch.7 para.85
s.95ZA, added: 2014 c.21 s.30
s.95ZA, amended: 2014 c.21 Sch.5 para.39
s.96A, amended: 2014 c.21 Sch.7 para.86
s.96ZA, added: 2014 c.21 s.30
s.96ZA, amended: 2014 c.21 Sch.5 para.40
s.99, amended: 2014 c.21 s.19
s.99, repealed (in part): 2014 c.21 s.19,
Sch.7 para.87
s.100, repealed: 2014 c.21 Sch.7 para.88
s.101A, amended: 2014 c.21 s.41
s.101B, amended: 2014 c.21 s.19, Sch.7
para.89
s.102, amended: 2014 c.21 Sch.7 para.90
s.104, amended: 2014 c.21 s.11
s.104, repealed (in part): 2014 c.21 s.11,
Sch.7 para.91
s.105, amended: 2014 c.21 Sch.7 para.92
s.105, repealed (in part): 2014 c.21 Sch.7
para.92
s.105C, amended: 2014 c.21 Sch.7 para.93
s.105ZA, added: 2014 c.21 s.11
s.106, applied: SI 2014/909 Art.18, SI
2014/1052 Art.17, SI 2014/1599 Art.13, SI
2014/1796 Art.17, SI 2014/1873 Art.20, SI
2014/2027 Art.13, SI 2014/2269 Art.15, SI
2014/2384 Art.19, SI 2014/2434 Art.14, SI
2014/2441 Art.18, SI 2014/2637 Art.16, SI
2014/2846 Art.10, SI 2014/2935 Art.20, SI
2014/2950 Art.15, SI 2014/3102 Art.16, SI
2014/3331 Art.12
s.106, disapplied: SI 2014/2384 Sch.19
para.5

s.106B, amended: 2014 c.21 Sch.7 para.94
s.107, amended: 2014 c.21 s.19, Sch.7
para.95
s.110A, referred to: 2014 c.21 s.9
s.110A, substituted: 2014 c.21 s.9
s.110B, varied: 2014 c.21 s.9
s.110J, referred to: 2014 c.21 Sch.12 para.1
s.110K, added: 2014 c.21 s.32
s.110K, applied: 2014 c.21 s.43
s.110L, applied: 2014 c.21 s.46
s.113, amended: 2014 c.21 Sch.7 para.96
s.114A, added: 2014 c.21 s.21
s.116, see *Manchester Ship Canal Co Ltd v
United Utilities Water Plc* [2014] UKSC 40,
[2014] 1 W.L.R. 2576 (SC), Lord Neuberger
PSC
s.117, amended: 2014 c.21 Sch.7 para.97
s.117G, amended: 2014 c.21 Sch.5 para.41
s.117G, applied: 2014 c.21 Sch.5 para.41
s.117K, amended: 2014 c.21 Sch.5 para.42
s.117L, amended: 2014 c.21 Sch.5 para.43
s.117M, amended: 2014 c.21 Sch.5 para.44
s.117N, amended: 2014 c.21 Sch.5 para.45
s.117O, amended: 2014 c.21 Sch.5 para.46
s.117P, amended: 2014 c.21 Sch.5 para.47
s.117Q, amended: 2014 c.21 Sch.5 para.48
s.117S, amended: 2014 c.21 Sch.5 para.49
s.142, amended: 2014 c.21 s.33
s.143, amended: 2014 c.21 s.16
s.143, applied: 2014 c.21 s.43
s.143B, added: 2014 c.21 s.16
s.144C, enabling: SI 2014/3156
s.144ZA, added: 2014 c.21 s.17
s.144ZE, added: 2014 c.21 s.38
s.144ZE, varied: SI 2014/3320 Art.3
s.146, amended: 2014 c.21 s.19, Sch.7
para.98
s.147, amended: 2014 c.21 Sch.7 para.99
s.148, amended: 2014 c.21 Sch.7 para.100
s.150, amended: 2014 c.21 Sch.7 para.101
s.152, amended: 2014 c.21 Sch.7 para.102
s.154A, amended: 2014 c.21 Sch.7 para.103
s.158, amended: 2014 c.21 s.21, Sch.5
para.50, Sch.7 para.104
s.159, see *Manchester Ship Canal Co Ltd v
United Utilities Water Plc* [2014] UKSC 40,
[2014] 1 W.L.R. 2576 (SC), Lord Neuberger
PSC
s.162, amended: 2014 c.21 Sch.7 para.105
s.163, amended: 2014 c.21 Sch.7 para.106
s.164, amended: 2014 c.21 Sch.7 para.107

s.169, referred to: 2014 c.21 Sch.8 para.20
s.174, amended: 2014 c.21 Sch.7 para.108
s.175, amended: 2014 c.21 Sch.7 para.109
s.179, amended: 2014 c.21 Sch.7 para.110
s.185, amended: 2014 c.21 s.20
s.192A, amended: 2014 c.21 s.24
s.192B, amended: SI 2014/892 Sch.1 para.89
s.195, amended: 2014 c.21 s.33, s.34, s.35,
Sch.5 para.51, Sch.7 para.111, SI 2014/892
Sch.1 para.90
s.195, applied: 2014 c.21 s.46
s.195, repealed (in part): 2014 c.21 Sch.7
para.111
s.195A, amended: 2014 c.21 Sch.7 para.112
s.201, amended: 2014 c.21 Sch.7 para.113,
SI 2014/892 Sch.1 para.91
s.202, amended: 2014 c.21 Sch.7 para.114
s.203, amended: 2014 c.21 s.36
s.205, amended: 2014 c.21 Sch.7 para.115
s.206, amended: 2014 c.21 Sch.7 para.116,
SI 2014/892 Sch.1 para.92
s.207A, added: 2014 c.21 s.37
s.207D, added: 2014 c.21 s.39
s.207D, amended: 2014 c.21 Sch.5 para.52
s.207D, applied: 2014 c.21 Sch.12 para.1
s.208, amended: 2014 c.21 Sch.7 para.117
s.211, amended: 2014 c.21 Sch.7 para.118
s.213, amended: 2014 c.21 s.37, Sch.7
para.119
s.213, repealed (in part): 2014 c.21 Sch.5
para.53
s.213, enabling: SI 2014/3156
s.219, amended: 2014 c.21 Sch.7 para.120
Sch.1A para.9, amended: 2014 c.21 Sch.7
para.121
Sch.2, referred to: 2014 c.21 s.46
Sch.2A, added: 2014 c.21 Sch.1
Sch.2A, applied: 2014 c.21 Sch.11 para.6
Sch.2B, added: 2014 c.21 Sch.3
Sch.2 para.1, amended: 2014 c.21 Sch.7
para.122
Sch.2 para.2, amended: 2014 c.21 Sch.7
para.122
Sch.2A para.1, repealed: 2014 c.21 Sch.5
para.54
Sch.2A para.6, repealed: 2014 c.21 Sch.5
para.54
Sch.2A para.7, referred to: 2014 c.21 s.3
Sch.2A para.9, amended: 2014 c.21 Sch.5
para.54

Sch.2A para.10, amended: 2014 c.21 Sch.5
para.54
Sch.4ZA, applied: SI 2014/549 Sch.2 para.3,
Sch.2 para.4, Sch.2 para.5
Sch.4ZA para.1, applied: SI 2014/559
Sch.4ZA para.2, amended: SI 2014/892
Sch.1 para.93
Sch.4ZA para.2A, added: SI 2014/892 Sch.1
para.93
Sch.4ZA para.3, amended: SI 2014/892
Sch.1 para.93
Sch.4ZA para.4, amended: SI 2014/892
Sch.1 para.93
Sch.4ZA para.5, amended: SI 2014/892
Sch.1 para.93
Sch.4ZA para.6, amended: SI 2014/892
Sch.1 para.93
Sch.4ZA para.7, amended: SI 2014/892
Sch.1 para.93
Sch.8 para.2, amended: 2014 c.21 Sch.7
para.123
Sch.15 Part I, amended: SI 2014/631 Sch.1
para.6, SI 2014/892 Sch.1 para.94
Sch.15 Part II, amended: SI 2014/892 Sch.1
para.94
Sch.16, added: 2014 c.21 Sch.6

57. Water Resources Act 1991
applied: SI 2014/1796 Art.17, SI 2014/2027
Art.13, SI 2014/2269 Art.15, SI 2014/2384
Art.19, SI 2014/2637 Art.16
Part II c.II, applied: 2014 c.21 Sch.8 para.30
s.24, applied: SI 2014/3223 Sch.1 para.2
s.24, disapplied: SI 2014/3102 Art.17, SI
2014/3263 Sch.2 para.2
s.48A, applied: SI 2014/3102 Art.17
s.48A, disapplied: SI 2014/3102 Art.17
s.61, amended: 2014 c.21 s.58
s.61A, repealed: 2014 c.21 s.58
s.109, applied: 2014 c.21 Sch.8 para.30, SI
2014/17 Art.17, SI 2014/3102 Art.4
s.109, disapplied: SI 2014/3331 Art.30
s.113, amended: 2014 c.21 s.59
s.134, amended: 2014 c.21 Sch.10 para.6
s.134, repealed (in part): 2014 c.21 Sch.10
para.6
s.135, amended: 2014 c.21 Sch.10 para.7
s.137, amended: 2014 c.21 Sch.10 para.8
s.138, amended: 2014 c.21 Sch.10 para.9
s.143, amended: 2014 c.21 Sch.10 para.10
s.145, amended: 2014 c.21 Sch.10 para.11
s.166, amended: 2014 c.21 Sch.10 para.12

s.193, substituted: 2014 c.21 s.59
s.195, repealed: 2014 c.21 s.60
s.203, amended: 2014 c.21 Sch.7 para.125
s.204, amended: 2014 c.21 Sch.7 para.126,
SI 2014/892 Sch.1 para.96
s.221, amended: 2014 c.21 s.59, Sch.10
para.13
s.221, applied: 2014 c.21 s.61
s.221, repealed (in part): 2014 c.21 Sch.10
para.13
Sch.15 para.3, amended: 2014 c.21 Sch.10
para.14
Sch.23 para.7, amended: 2014 c.21 s.60
Sch.24 Part I, amended: SI 2014/892 Sch.1
para.97
Sch.24 Part II, amended: SI 2014/892 Sch.1
para.97
Sch.25 para.5, applied: 2014 c.21 Sch.8
para.30
Sch.25 para.5, disapplied: SI 2014/3331
Art.30
Sch.26 para.7, amended: 2014 c.21 Sch.10
para.15

59. Land Drainage Act 1991
applied: SI 2014/17 Art.17
s.1, amended: 2014 c.21 Sch.10 para.4
s.2, amended: 2014 c.21 Sch.9 para.2
s.3, amended: 2014 c.21 Sch.9 para.3
s.3, applied: SI 2014/1030, SI 2014/3194
s.3, referred to: SI 2014/1030, SI 2014/3194
s.3, enabling: SI 2014/1030, SI 2014/3194
s.23, applied: SI 2014/1796 Sch.2 para.20,
SI 2014/3102 Art.4
s.23, disapplied: SI 2014/2935 Art.4, SI
2014/3331 Art.30
s.25, applied: SI 2014/3331 Sch.1 para.13
s.38, amended: 2014 c.21 Sch.9 para.4
s.39, amended: 2014 c.21 Sch.9 para.5
s.48, amended: 2014 c.21 Sch.9 para.6
s.58, amended: 2014 c.21 Sch.9 para.7
s.65, amended: 2014 c.21 s.86
s.66, amended: 2014 c.21 s.86
s.66, disapplied: SI 2014/3331 Art.30
s.66A, added: 2014 c.21 s.86
Sch.1, applied: SI 2014/1030 Sch.1
Sch.3 para.1, applied: SI 2014/1030 Sch.1
Sch.3 para.2, applied: SI 2014/1030, SI
2014/3194
Sch.3 para.2, referred to: SI 2014/1030
Sch.3 para.4, amended: 2014 c.21 s.85
Sch.3 para.4, applied: SI 2014/1030 Sch.1

Sch.3 para.5, amended: 2014 c.21 s.85
Sch.3 para.5, applied: SI 2014/1030 Sch.1
Sch.5 para.1, amended: 2014 c.21 Sch.9
para.8

62. Armed Forces Act 1991
s.17, amended: 2014 c.6 s.9, Sch.2 para.54
s.18, amended: 2014 c.6 s.9, Sch.2 para.55
s.20, amended: 2014 c.6 s.9, Sch.2 para.56
s.22A, amended: 2014 c.6 s.9, Sch.2 para.57
s.23, amended: 2014 c.6 Sch.2 para.58

65. Dangerous Dogs Act 1991
s.1, amended: 2014 c.12 s.107
s.3, see *Criminal Injuries Compensation Authority v First-Tier Tribunal (Social Entitlement Chamber)* [2014] EWCA Civ 65, [2014] P.I.Q.R. P10 (CA (Civ Div)), Moore-Bick LJ; see *McLaughlin v Harvie* [2014] HCJAC 98, 2014 S.L.T. 961 (HCJ), Lady Paton; see *R. v Robinson-Pierre (Symieon)* [2013] EWCA Crim 2396, [2014] 1 W.L.R. 2638 (CA (Crim Div)), Pitchford LJ
s.3, amended: 2014 c.12 s.106
s.3, repealed (in part): 2014 c.12 s.106
s.4, amended: 2014 c.12 s.106, s.107
s.4, applied: SI 2014/1610 r.42_6, r.76_1, r.76_7
s.4A, amended: 2014 c.12 s.106
s.4B, amended: 2014 c.12 s.107
s.5, amended: 2014 c.12 s.106
s.10, see *McLaughlin v Harvie* [2014] HCJAC 98, 2014 S.L.T. 961 (HCJ), Lady Paton
s.10, amended: 2014 c.12 s.106

1992

3. Severn Bridges Act 1992
s.9, enabling: SI 2014/3313

4. Social Security Contributions and Benefits Act 1992
applied: 2014 c.7 s.1, SI 2014/368 Art.2, SI 2014/1964 Sch.1 para.12, Sch.1 para.33, Sch.1 para.44, SI 2014/3134 Sch.1 para.10
referred to: 2014 c.19 s.8
Part I, applied: 2014 c.7 s.1
Part I, referred to: SI 2014/475
Part II, applied: 2014 c.19 s.1, SI 2014/618 Reg.2
Part II, amended: 2014 c.19 Sch.16 para.7

Part IX, applied: SI 2014/3037 Reg.25
Part XI, applied: SI 2014/3051 Reg.26
Part XII, applied: SI 2014/3050 Reg.7, Reg.23, SI 2014/3051 Reg.14
Part XIIZA, amended: 2014 c.6 Sch.7 para.10
Part XIIZA, applied: SI 2014/3050 Reg.7, Reg.23
Part XIIZA, substituted: 2014 c.6 Sch.7 para.11
Part XIIZA, varied: 2014 c.6 s.126
Part XIIZA, substituted: 2014 c.6 Sch.7 para.17
Part XIIZA, substituted: 2014 c.6 Sch.7 para.18
Part XIIZC, added: 2014 c.6 s.119
Part XIIZC, applied: SI 2014/1640 Art.8, SI 2014/3050 Reg.7, Reg.11, Reg.27, SI 2014/3051 Reg.32, Reg.33, Reg.39, Reg.48, SI 2014/3093 Reg.3, SI 2014/3134 Reg.4, Reg.5, Reg.6, Reg.8, Reg.9, Reg.10, Sch.2 para.2
s.1, amended: 2014 c.6 Sch.7 para.7, 2014 c.19 Sch.12 para.3, Sch.13 para.49, Sch.15 para.2
s.1, applied: SI 2014/3050 Reg.36, SI 2014/3051 Reg.29, SI 2014/3134 Reg.6
s.1, varied: 2014 c.6 s.126
s.2, amended: 2014 c.7 s.15
s.2, enabling: SI 2014/635
s.3, enabling: SI 2014/608, SI 2014/3228
s.4, amended: 2014 c.6 Sch.7 para.8
s.4, repealed (in part): 2014 c.6 Sch.7 para.8
s.4, varied: 2014 c.6 s.126
s.4A, applied: 2014 c.7 s.2
s.4AA, added: 2014 c.7 s.14
s.4AA, enabling: SI 2014/3159
s.4B, amended: 2014 c.7 s.14
s.4B, applied: SI 2014/3051 Reg.32
s.4C, amended: 2014 c.6 Sch.7 para.9, 2014 c.19 Sch.13 para.50
s.4C, varied: 2014 c.6 s.126
s.5, applied: SI 2014/3051 Reg.30, Reg.31
s.5, enabling: SI 2014/569
s.6, see *Forde & McHugh Ltd v Revenue and Customs Commissioners* [2014] UKSC 14, [2014] 1 W.L.R. 810 (SC), Lord Neuberger PSC
s.6, applied: SI 2014/3134 Reg.6
s.7, amended: 2014 c.7 Sch.2 para.2
s.7, enabling: SI 2014/635

s.8, repealed (in part): 2014 c.19 Sch.13
para.51
s.9, amended: 2014 c.7 s.9
s.9, repealed (in part): 2014 c.19 Sch.13
para.52
s.9A, added: 2014 c.7 s.9
s.10, amended: 2014 c.7 s.14
s.10A, applied: SI 2014/3051 Reg.32
s.11, amended: SI 2014/475 Art.2
s.12ZA, applied: SI 2014/1640 Art.17,
Art.19
s.13, amended: 2014 c.19 Sch.12 para.4, SI
2014/475 Art.3
s.14A, added: 2014 c.19 Sch.15 para.3
s.14A, amended: SI 2014/2746 Reg.2
s.14A, enabling: SI 2014/3240
s.14B, enabling: SI 2014/2746
s.14C, enabling: SI 2014/2746
s.15, amended: SI 2014/475 Art.4
s.18, amended: SI 2014/475 Art.4
s.18A, added: 2014 c.7 s.13
s.18A, enabling: SI 2014/3196
s.19B, added: 2014 c.19 Sch.12 para.5
s.20, amended: 2014 c.19 Sch.13 para.53,
Sch.16 para.3
s.20, repealed (in part): 2014 c.19 Sch.16
para.3
s.21, amended: 2014 c.19 Sch.11 para.3,
Sch.16 para.4, SI 2014/606 Reg.2
s.21, repealed (in part): 2014 c.19 Sch.16
para.4
s.22, amended: 2014 c.19 Sch.12 para.6,
Sch.16 para.5
s.22, applied: 2014 c.19 s.31, Sch.1 para.3
s.22, referred to: 2014 c.19 s.2, s.4
s.23A, amended: 2014 c.19 Sch.12 para.58,
Sch.16 para.6
s.23A, repealed (in part): 2014 c.19 Sch.16
para.6
s.35, amended: 2014 c.6 s.120, SI 2014/606
Reg.2
s.35, applied: SI 2014/606 Reg.1, SI
2014/3050 Reg.5, Reg.7, Reg.23, Sch.1
para.1, Sch.1 para.2, SI 2014/3051 Reg.5,
Reg.10, Sch.1 para.1, Sch.1 para.2, Sch.1
para.4, Sch.1 para.5
s.35, referred to: SI 2014/3050 Reg.36
s.35, enabling: SI 2014/884, SI 2014/3053
s.35A, amended: SI 2014/606 Reg.2
s.35A, applied: SI 2014/3050 Reg.6, SI
2014/3051 Reg.10, Reg.29

s.35B, added: SI 2014/606 Reg.2
s.35B, applied: SI 2014/884
s.35B, enabling: SI 2014/884
s.36, amended: SI 2014/560 Sch.1 para.22,
SI 2014/3229 Sch.4 para.2
s.36, repealed: 2014 c.19 Sch.16 para.8
s.36A, repealed: 2014 c.19 Sch.16 para.9
s.37, amended: 2014 c.19 Sch.16 para.10, SI
2014/560 Sch.1 para.22, SI 2014/3229 Sch.4
para.2
s.38, amended: 2014 c.19 Sch.16 para.11, SI
2014/560 Sch.1 para.22, SI 2014/3229 Sch.4
para.2
s.39A, amended: 2014 c.19 Sch.16 para.12,
SI 2014/560 Sch.1 para.22, SI 2014/3229
Sch.4 para.2
s.39B, amended: SI 2014/560 Sch.1 para.22,
SI 2014/3229 Sch.4 para.2
s.39B, repealed: 2014 c.19 Sch.16 para.13
s.39C, amended: 2014 c.19 Sch.12 para.93,
Sch.16 para.14
s.39C, repealed (in part): 2014 c.19 Sch.16
para.14
s.43, amended: 2014 c.19 Sch.11 para.4,
Sch.15 para.5
s.44, amended: 2014 c.19 Sch.12 para.55,
Sch.15 para.6, SI 2014/516 Art.4
s.44, applied: 2014 c.19 Sch.5 para.2, Sch.5
para.3
s.44, referred to: 2014 c.19 Sch.7 para.3
s.44C, enabling: SI 2014/591
s.45, amended: 2014 c.19 Sch.15 para.7
s.45, applied: SI 2014/3240 Reg.4
s.45, referred to: 2014 c.19 Sch.1 para.3,
Sch.1 para.5
s.45, enabling: SI 2014/3240
s.45B, disapplied: 2014 c.19 Sch.1 para.3
s.46, amended: 2014 c.19 Sch.12 para.59
s.47, amended: SI 2014/3213 Art.2
s.47, applied: SI 2014/516 Art.6
s.48, amended: 2014 c.19 Sch.12 para.56, SI
2014/3229 Sch.4 para.2
s.48, applied: 2014 c.19 Sch.5 para.2, Sch.5
para.3
s.48A, amended: SI 2014/3229 Sch.4 para.2
s.48A, applied: 2014 c.19 Sch.5 para.2,
Sch.5 para.3, SI 2014/3229 Art.8, Art.12
s.48A, disapplied: SI 2014/3229 Art.8
s.48A, substituted: 2014 c.19 Sch.12 para.60
s.48B, amended: 2014 c.19 Sch.12 para.61,
Sch.16 para.15, SI 2014/3229 Sch.4 para.2

s.48B, applied: 2014 c.19 Sch.3 para.2,
Sch.3 para.4, Sch.5 para.2, Sch.5 para.3, SI
2014/3229 Art.9
s.48B, disapplied: SI 2014/3229 Art.9
s.48BB, amended: 2014 c.19 Sch.12 para.62,
Sch.16 para.16
s.48BB, applied: 2014 c.19 Sch.3 para.2,
Sch.3 para.3, Sch.5 para.2, Sch.5 para.3
s.48BB, disapplied: 2014 c.19 Sch.3 para.3
s.48C, amended: 2014 c.19 Sch.12 para.63
s.48C, applied: SI 2014/516 Art.6
s.51, amended: SI 2014/3229 Sch.4 para.2
s.51, disapplied: SI 2014/3229 Art.10
s.51, substituted: 2014 c.19 Sch.12 para.64
s.51ZA, added: 2014 c.19 Sch.12 para.65
s.52, amended: 2014 c.19 Sch.12 para.66,
Sch.15 para.8
s.55A, amended: 2014 c.19 Sch.11 para.5
s.55A, applied: SI 2014/516 Art.4
s.55AA, added: 2014 c.19 Sch.11 para.6
s.55B, amended: 2014 c.19 Sch.11 para.7
s.60, repealed (in part): 2014 c.19 Sch.16
para.17
s.61ZA, added: 2014 c.19 Sch.15 para.9
s.62, amended: SI 2014/3229 Sch.4 para.2
s.62, enabling: SI 2014/76
s.63, amended: 2014 c.19 Sch.12 para.79,
Sch.12 para.85
s.70, enabling: SI 2014/904
s.71, applied: SI 2014/3219 Sch.1 para.1
s.77, applied: SI 2014/3037 Reg.25
s.78, amended: 2014 c.19 Sch.12 para.80,
Sch.12 para.84
s.78, repealed (in part): 2014 c.19 Sch.12
para.80
s.79, amended: 2014 c.19 Sch.12 para.85
s.80, amended: SI 2014/516 Art.7
s.83, applied: SI 2014/3229 Art.11
s.84, applied: SI 2014/3229 Art.11
s.90, enabling: SI 2014/618
s.94, applied: 2014 c.19 s.31
s.108, applied: 2014 c.19 s.31
s.113, enabling: SI 2014/618, SI 2014/881
s.117, enabling: SI 2014/634
s.120, amended: 2014 c.7 s.12
s.120, enabling: SI 2014/572
s.122, amended: 2014 c.7 s.9, 2014 c.19
Sch.12 para.7, Sch.15 para.10
s.122, repealed (in part): SI 2014/560 Sch.1
para.22, SI 2014/3229 Sch.4 para.2
s.122, enabling: SI 2014/618

s.123, enabling: SI 2014/212, SI 2014/213,
SI 2014/539, SI 2014/591, SI 2014/902, SI
2014/1913, SI 2014/3117
s.126, amended: SI 2014/516 Art.16
s.130A, enabling: SI 2014/212, SI 2014/213
s.135, enabling: SI 2014/213, SI 2014/902,
SI 2014/2888
s.136, enabling: SI 2014/213, SI 2014/591,
SI 2014/1913, SI 2014/2888, SI 2014/3117
s.136A, enabling: SI 2014/591, SI
2014/2888
s.137, amended: SI 2014/560 Sch.1 para.22,
SI 2014/3229 Sch.4 para.2
s.137, repealed (in part): SI 2014/560 Sch.1
para.22, SI 2014/3229 Sch.4 para.2
s.137, enabling: SI 2014/212, SI 2014/213,
SI 2014/539, SI 2014/591, SI 2014/902, SI
2014/1913, SI 2014/2888, SI 2014/3117
s.138, enabling: SI 2014/2687, SI 2014/3270
s.142, enabling: SI 2014/1231, SI 2014/2924
s.146, enabling: SI 2014/1511
s.150, amended: 2014 c.19 Sch.12 para.86
s.151, applied: SI 2014/3051 Reg.32
s.157, amended: SI 2014/147 Art.3
s.159A, enabling: SI 2014/897
s.163, amended: 2014 c.7 Sch.2 para.3
s.163, varied: SI 2014/3159 Reg.3
s.165, amended: 2014 c.6 s.120
s.165, applied: SI 2014/3050 Reg.5, Reg.6,
Sch.1 para.1, Sch.1 para.2, SI 2014/3051
Reg.4, Reg.5, Reg.10, Sch.1 para.1, Sch.1
para.2, Sch.1 para.4, Sch.1 para.5, SI
2014/3054 Reg.7
s.165, enabling: SI 2014/3054
s.167, applied: SI 2014/2929 Reg.3
s.171, amended: 2014 c.7 Sch.2 para.4
s.171, varied: SI 2014/3159 Reg.3
s.171ZA, varied: 2014 c.6 s.120
s.171ZA, amended: 2014 c.6 Sch.7 para.12
s.171ZA, varied: 2014 c.6 s.126, SI
2014/2866 Sch.1
s.171ZB, varied: 2014 c.6 s.126
s.171ZB, amended: 2014 c.6 s.121, Sch.7
para.13
s.171ZB, applied: SI 2014/2934 Reg.26
s.171ZB, varied: 2014 c.6 s.126, SI
2014/2866 Sch.1
s.171ZB, enabling: SI 2014/2934
s.171ZC, varied: 2014 c.6 s.126
s.171ZC, enabling: SI 2014/2862

s.171ZC, amended: 2014 c.6 s.123, Sch.7 para.14

s.171ZC, varied: 2014 c.6 s.126

s.171ZC, enabling: SI 2014/2862, SI 2014/2934

s.171ZD, varied: 2014 c.6 s.126

s.171ZD, amended: 2014 c.6 Sch.7 para.15

s.171ZD, varied: 2014 c.6 s.126

s.171ZD, enabling: SI 2014/2934

s.171ZE, varied: 2014 c.6 s.126

s.171ZE, amended: 2014 c.6 s.120, s.121, s.123, Sch.7 para.16

s.171ZE, varied: 2014 c.6 s.126, SI 2014/2866 Sch.1

s.171ZE, enabling: SI 2014/2934

s.171ZEA, repealed: 2014 c.6 s.125

s.171ZED, varied: 2014 c.6 s.126

s.171ZF, amended: 2014 c.6 Sch.7 para.19

s.171ZF, varied: 2014 c.6 s.126

s.171ZG, repealed (in part): 2014 c.6 Sch.7 para.20

s.171ZG, varied: 2014 c.6 s.126

s.171ZG, enabling: SI 2014/2934

s.171ZJ, amended: 2014 c.6 s.121, Sch.7 para.21, 2014 c.7 Sch.2 para.5

s.171ZJ, varied: 2014 c.6 s.126, SI 2014/3159 Reg.3

s.171ZJ, enabling: SI 2014/2934

s.171ZK, amended: 2014 c.6 s.122

s.171ZK, substituted: 2014 c.6 s.122

s.171ZK, enabling: SI 2014/2866

s.171ZL, amended: 2014 c.6 s.121

s.171ZL, applied: SI 2014/2934 Reg.26

s.171ZL, varied: SI 2014/2866 Sch.2

s.171ZL, enabling: SI 2014/2934

s.171ZM, enabling: SI 2014/2934

s.171ZN, amended: 2014 c.6 s.120, s.121, s.124

s.171ZN, applied: SI 2014/3050 Reg.21, Reg.22, Sch.1 para.6, Sch.1 para.7, SI 2014/3051 Reg.17, Reg.18, Reg.22, Sch.1 para.7, Sch.1 para.8, Sch.1 para.9, Sch.1 para.10, Sch.1 para.11, SI 2014/3054 Reg.12

s.171ZN, referred to: SI 2014/1640 Art.13

s.171ZN, repealed (in part): 2014 c.6 s.124

s.171ZN, varied: SI 2014/2866 Sch.2

s.171ZN, enabling: SI 2014/2934, SI 2014/3054

s.171ZP, enabling: SI 2014/2934

s.171ZS, amended: 2014 c.6 s.121, 2014 c.7 Sch.2 para.6

s.171ZS, varied: SI 2014/3159 Reg.3

s.171ZS, enabling: SI 2014/2934

s.171ZT, amended: 2014 c.6 s.122

s.171ZT, substituted: 2014 c.6 s.122

s.171ZT, enabling: SI 2014/2866

s.171ZU, applied: SI 2014/3051 Reg.34, Reg.35, Reg.36, Reg.37, Reg.38, SI 2014/3134 Reg.7

s.171ZU, enabling: SI 2014/3051

s.171ZV, applied: SI 2014/3134 Reg.7

s.171ZV, varied: SI 2014/2866 Sch.3

s.171ZV, enabling: SI 2014/3051, SI 2014/3093, SI 2014/3097

s.171ZW, applied: SI 2014/2929 Reg.9, Reg.11

s.171ZW, enabling: SI 2014/3051, SI 2014/3093, SI 2014/3097

s.171ZX, applied: SI 2014/3051 Reg.7, Reg.45, Reg.46

s.171ZX, enabling: SI 2014/3051, SI 2014/3093, SI 2014/3097

s.171ZY, applied: SI 2014/3051 Reg.12, Reg.13, Reg.24, Reg.25, Reg.30, Reg.31, Reg.35, Reg.36, Reg.42

s.171ZY, enabling: SI 2014/3051, SI 2014/3093, SI 2014/3097

s.171ZZ1, applied: SI 2014/3051 Reg.41

s.171ZZ1, enabling: SI 2014/3051, SI 2014/3093, SI 2014/3097

s.171ZZ3, enabling: SI 2014/3134

s.171ZZ4, applied: SI 2014/3051 Reg.32, Reg.33, Reg.40

s.171ZZ4, enabling: SI 2014/3051, SI 2014/3093, SI 2014/3097, SI 2014/3134

s.171ZZ5, enabling: SI 2014/2857, SI 2014/2866

s.175, applied: 2014 c.7 s.5

s.175, enabling: SI 2014/76, SI 2014/212, SI 2014/213, SI 2014/539, SI 2014/569, SI 2014/572, SI 2014/591, SI 2014/608, SI 2014/618, SI 2014/634, SI 2014/635, SI 2014/881, SI 2014/884, SI 2014/902, SI 2014/904, SI 2014/1231, SI 2014/1511, SI 2014/1913, SI 2014/2397, SI 2014/2687, SI 2014/2888, SI 2014/2924, SI 2014/2934, SI 2014/3051, SI 2014/3053, SI 2014/3054, SI 2014/3093, SI 2014/3097, SI 2014/3117, SI 2014/3159, SI 2014/3196, SI 2014/3270

s.176, amended: 2014 c.6 s.119, s.123, s.124, Sch.7 para.22, 2014 c.7 s.9, s.13, 2014 c.19 Sch.15 para.11

s.176, applied: SI 2014/569, SI 2014/897, SI
2014/3051, SI 2014/3093, SI 2014/3097, SI
2014/3159, SI 2014/3196
Sch.1, amended: 2014 c.19 Sch.15 para.12
Sch.1 para.1, repealed (in part): 2014 c.19
Sch.13 para.54
Sch.1 para.6, amended: SI 2014/1283 Sch.1
para.1
Sch.1 para.6, applied: 2014 c.7 s.4
Sch.1 para.6, enabling: SI 2014/608, SI
2014/1016, SI 2014/2397
Sch.1 para.8, amended: 2014 c.7 s.7
Sch.1 para.8, applied: 2014 c.7 s.7
Sch.1 para.8, enabling: SI 2014/3240
Sch.2 para.3, repealed (in part): 2014 c.7
s.17
Sch.2 para.9, repealed: 2014 c.7 s.17
Sch.3 Part I para.4, repealed: 2014 c.19
Sch.16 para.18
Sch.3 Part I para.5, amended: 2014 c.19
Sch.12 para.67
Sch.3 Part I para.5A, amended: 2014 c.19
Sch.12 para.67, SI 2014/3229 Sch.4 para.2
Sch.3 Part I para.5A, applied: SI 2014/3229
Art.12
Sch.3 Part II para.7, repealed: 2014 c.19
Sch.16 para.18
Sch.3 Part II para.9, repealed: 2014 c.19
Sch.16 para.18
Sch.4 Part I, amended: 2014 c.19 Sch.12
para.68
Sch.4 Part I, referred to: 2014 c.19 Sch.7
para.2, SI 2014/516 Art.3
Sch.4 Part I, substituted: SI 2014/516 Sch.1
Sch.4 Part II, repealed: 2014 c.19 Sch.16
para.19
Sch.4 Part II, substituted: SI 2014/516 Sch.1
Sch.4 Part III, amended: 2014 c.19 Sch.12
para.81, SI 2014/828 Art.2
Sch.4 Part III, applied: SI 2014/516 Art.3
Sch.4 Part III, referred to: SI 2014/516 Art.3
Sch.4 Part III, repealed: 2014 c.19 Sch.12
para.81
Sch.4 Part III, substituted: SI 2014/516
Sch.1
Sch.4 Part IV, applied: SI 2014/516 Art.3
Sch.4 Part IV, substituted: SI 2014/516
Sch.1
Sch.4 Part V, applied: SI 2014/516 Art.3
Sch.4 Part V, substituted: SI 2014/516 Sch.1

Sch.4A Part I para.1, amended: 2014 c.19
Sch.12 para.69
Sch.4B Part V para.13, amended: SI
2014/369 Art.2
Sch.5, applied: 2014 c.19 s.21, SI 2014/516
Art.4
Sch.5 para.1, applied: 2014 c.19 Sch.5 para.2
Sch.5 para.2A, applied: 2014 c.19 Sch.5
para.2
Sch.5 para.4, amended: 2014 c.19 Sch.12
para.94
Sch.5 para.4, applied: 2014 c.19 Sch.5
para.2, Sch.5 para.3
Sch.5 para.4, varied: 2014 c.19 Sch.5 para.2,
Sch.5 para.3
Sch.5 para.5, amended: SI 2014/560 Sch.3
para.4, SI 2014/3168 Sch.1 para.11, SI
2014/3229 Sch.4 para.2
Sch.5 para.5, disapplied: SI 2014/3229 Sch.2
para.6
Sch.5 para.5A, amended: SI 2014/560 Sch.3
para.4, SI 2014/3168 Sch.1 para.11, SI
2014/3229 Sch.4 para.2
Sch.5 para.5A, disapplied: SI 2014/3229
Sch.2 para.6
Sch.5 para.6, amended: SI 2014/560 Sch.3
para.4, SI 2014/3229 Sch.4 para.2
Sch.5 para.6, disapplied: SI 2014/3229 Sch.2
para.6
Sch.5 para.6A, amended: SI 2014/560 Sch.3
para.4, SI 2014/3168 Sch.1 para.11, SI
2014/3229 Sch.4 para.2
Sch.5 para.7, amended: SI 2014/3168 Sch.1
para.11, SI 2014/3229 Sch.4 para.2
Sch.5 para.7A, applied: SI 2014/516 Art.4
Sch.5 para.7B, applied: 2014 c.19 s.8
Sch.5 para.7ZA, added: 2014 c.19 Sch.12
para.94
Sch.5A para.2, applied: SI 2014/516 Art.4
Sch.7 Part I para.3, amended: SI 2014/3213
Art.3
Sch.7 Part I para.4, amended: SI 2014/560
Sch.1 para.22, SI 2014/3229 Sch.4 para.2
Sch.7 Part V para.13, applied: SI 2014/516
Art.6
Sch.7 Part V para.13, varied: SI 2014/516
Art.4
Sch.7 Part VI para.15, amended: SI
2014/560 Sch.1 para.22, SI 2014/3229 Sch.4
para.2
Sch.9 para.3, enabling: SI 2014/1231

5. Social Security Administration Act 1992
applied: SI 2014/3280 Art.4, Art.5
Part VII, added: SI 2014/2888 Reg.9
s.1, amended: 2014 c.19 Sch.12 para.9,
Sch.16 para.21
s.1, applied: 2014 c.19 s.17
s.1, enabling: SI 2014/2887
s.2A, amended: 2014 c.19 Sch.16 para.22
s.2A, applied: SI 2014/1097 Reg.2
s.2A, enabling: SI 2014/1097
s.2D, enabling: SI 2014/1097
s.2E, enabling: SI 2014/1097
s.2G, enabling: SI 2014/1097
s.2H, enabling: SI 2014/1097
s.3, amended: 2014 c.19 Sch.16 para.23
s.3, repealed (in part): 2014 c.19 Sch.16
para.23
s.5, amended: 2014 c.6 Sch.7 para.24, 2014
c.19 Sch.12 para.10, Sch.16 para.24
s.5, varied: 2014 c.6 s.126
s.5, enabling: SI 2014/213, SI 2014/591, SI
2014/597, SI 2014/612, SI 2014/618, SI
2014/2888, SI 2014/2934, SI 2014/3051, SI
2014/3093, SI 2014/3097
s.15A, amended: SI 2014/560 Sch.1 para.23,
SI 2014/3229 Sch.5 para.9
s.15A, applied: SI 2014/485
s.15A, repealed (in part): SI 2014/560 Sch.1
para.23, SI 2014/3229 Sch.5 para.9
s.15A, enabling: SI 2014/485
s.64, applied: SI 2014/1230 Reg.24
s.71, amended: 2014 c.19 Sch.12 para.11,
Sch.16 para.25
s.71, applied: SI 2014/1230 Reg.24
s.71ZB, applied: SI 2014/3280 Art.4
s.71ZB, varied: SI 2014/3280 Art.4
s.72, applied: SI 2014/1230 Reg.24
s.73, amended: 2014 c.19 Sch.12 para.12
s.73, applied: SI 2014/1230 Reg.24
s.104, applied: SI 2014/1230 Reg.24
s.110ZA, amended: 2014 c.7 s.7
s.111A, see *Fraser v Deveney* [2014]
HCJAC 3, 2014 S.C.L. 242 (HCJ), Lord
Drummond Young; see *Ryan v Murphy*
[2014] HCJAC 106, 2014 S.L.T. 1027
(HCJ), Lord Brodie
s.115A, enabling: SI 2014/591
s.121C, see *O'Rorke v Revenue and Customs
Commissioners* [2014] S.T.C. 279 (UT
(Tax)), Hildyard J
s.121C, amended: SI 2014/1283 Sch.1 para.2

s.121DA, amended: 2014 c.19 Sch.12
para.13, Sch.16 para.26
s.122AA, amended: 2014 c.6 Sch.7 para.25
s.122AA, varied: 2014 c.6 s.126
s.122B, amended: 2014 c.19 Sch.12 para.14,
Sch.16 para.27
s.123, amended: 2014 c.2 Sch.12 para.28
s.123, repealed (in part): 2014 c.2 Sch.12
para.28
s.124, amended: 2014 c.19 Sch.12 para.15,
Sch.16 para.28, SI 2014/3168 Sch.1 para.12
s.125, amended: 2014 c.19 Sch.12 para.16,
Sch.16 para.29
s.130, enabling: SI 2014/55
s.133A, added: SI 2014/2888 Reg.9
s.139A, applied: 2014 c.2 s.49, Sch.12
para.85
s.139BA, repealed: 2014 c.2 Sch.12 para.29
s.139D, amended: 2014 c.2 s.37
s.140B, enabling: SI 2014/1667
s.140C, enabling: SI 2014/1667
s.140F, enabling: SI 2014/1667
s.141, applied: SI 2014/475, SI 2014/634
s.141, enabling: SI 2014/475
s.142, enabling: SI 2014/475
s.148, applied: SI 2014/10, SI 2014/367
s.148, enabling: SI 2014/367
s.148A, applied: SI 2014/368
s.148A, enabling: SI 2014/368
s.148AA, applied: SI 2014/369
s.148AA, enabling: SI 2014/369
s.148AC, added: 2014 c.19 Sch.12 para.17
s.148AC, applied: 2014 c.19 Sch.1 para.6
s.148AD, added: 2014 c.19 Sch.11 para.8
s.150, amended: 2014 c.6 Sch.7 para.26,
2014 c.19 Sch.12 para.18, Sch.12 para.70,
Sch.13 para.56, Sch.16 para.30, SI
2014/2888 Reg.7
s.150, applied: 2014 c.19 s.17, Sch.1 para.3,
SI 2014/384, SI 2014/516 Art.4, SI
2014/618, SI 2014/668, SI 2014/828, SI
2014/838, SI 2014/1230 Reg.36
s.150, referred to: SI 2014/384, SI 2014/668,
SI 2014/828, SI 2014/838
s.150, enabling: SI 2014/516, SI 2014/828
s.150A, amended: 2014 c.19 Sch.12 para.19,
Sch.12 para.82, SI 2014/2888 Reg.7
s.150A, applied: 2014 c.19 Sch.1 para.3, SI
2014/618
s.150A, enabling: SI 2014/516
s.151, amended: 2014 c.19 Sch.12 para.20

s.151, applied: SI 2014/668
s.151, enabling: SI 2014/516
s.151A, added: 2014 c.19 Sch.12 para.21
s.151A, applied: 2014 c.19 s.9, Sch.2 para.4,
Sch.4 para.5, Sch.4 para.6, Sch.9 para.5,
Sch.9 para.6
s.155, applied: SI 2014/618 Reg.2
s.155, disapplied: SI 2014/881 Reg.2
s.155, enabling: SI 2014/618, SI 2014/881
s.155A, amended: 2014 c.19 Sch.12 para.22
s.162, amended: 2014 c.19 Sch.15 para.13,
SI 2014/992 Art.5
s.163, amended: 2014 c.6 Sch.7 para.27,
2014 c.19 Sch.12 para.23, Sch.16 para.31
s.163, varied: 2014 c.6 s.126
s.165, amended: 2014 c.6 Sch.7 para.28,
2014 c.7 s.19
s.165, repealed (in part): 2014 c.6 Sch.7
para.28
s.165, varied: 2014 c.6 s.126
s.170, amended: 2014 c.19 Sch.12 para.24,
Sch.16 para.32
s.172, applied: SI 2014/1097, SI 2014/1626,
SI 2014/2309
s.173, applied: SI 2014/212, SI 2014/213, SI
2014/591, SI 2014/771, SI 2014/902, SI
2014/2735, SI 2014/2887, SI 2014/3270
s.176, applied: SI 2014/212, SI 2014/213, SI
2014/591, SI 2014/771, SI 2014/1626, SI
2014/1667, SI 2014/2888
s.179, amended: 2014 c.19 Sch.12 para.25,
Sch.16 para.33
s.187, amended: 2014 c.19 Sch.12 para.26,
Sch.16 para.34
s.189, applied: SI 2014/1667
s.189, enabling: SI 2014/213, SI 2014/367,
SI 2014/368, SI 2014/369, SI 2014/485, SI
2014/516, SI 2014/591, SI 2014/597, SI
2014/612, SI 2014/618, SI 2014/828, SI
2014/881, SI 2014/1097, SI 2014/1456, SI
2014/1667
s.190, amended: 2014 c.19 Sch.12 para.27
s.190, applied: SI 2014/475, SI 2014/668, SI
2014/828
s.190, enabling: SI 2014/881
s.191, amended: 2014 c.19 Sch.12 para.28,
Sch.13 para.57, Sch.16 para.35, SI
2014/2888 Reg.7
s.191, referred to: SSI 2014/225 Reg.6
s.191, enabling: SI 2014/591, SI 2014/618,
SI 2014/881, SI 2014/1097

Sch.4 Part V para.2, referred to: SI
2014/1230 Reg.24
**7. Social Security Contributions and Benefits
(Northern Ireland) Act 1992**
applied: 2014 c.7 s.1
Part I, applied: 2014 c.7 s.1
s.1, amended: 2014 c.19 Sch.15 para.16
s.1, varied: 2014 c.6 s.126
s.2, amended: 2014 c.7 s.15
s.2, enabling: SI 2014/635
s.3, enabling: SI 2014/608, SI 2014/3228
s.4A, applied: 2014 c.7 s.2
s.4AA, added: 2014 c.7 s.14
s.4AA, enabling: SI 2014/3159
s.4B, amended: 2014 c.7 s.14
s.4C, varied: 2014 c.6 s.126
s.5, enabling: SI 2014/569
s.7, amended: 2014 c.7 Sch.2 para.8
s.7, enabling: SI 2014/635
s.9, amended: 2014 c.7 s.9
s.9A, added: 2014 c.7 s.9
s.10, amended: 2014 c.7 s.14
s.11, amended: SI 2014/475 Art.2
s.13, amended: SI 2014/475 Art.3
s.14A, added: 2014 c.19 Sch.15 para.17
s.14A, amended: SI 2014/2746 Reg.3
s.14A, enabling: SI 2014/3240
s.14B, enabling: SI 2014/2746
s.14C, enabling: SI 2014/2746
s.15, amended: SI 2014/475 Art.4
s.18, amended: SI 2014/475 Art.4
s.18A, added: 2014 c.7 s.13
s.18A, enabling: SI 2014/3196
s.113, enabling: SI 2014/881
s.117, enabling: SI 2014/634
s.121, amended: 2014 c.7 s.9, 2014 c.19
Sch.15 para.19
s.138, enabling: SI 2014/1231, SI 2014/2924
s.142, enabling: SI 2014/1511
s.155A, enabling: SI 2014/897
s.159, amended: 2014 c.7 Sch.2 para.9
s.159, varied: SI 2014/3159 Reg.4
s.167, amended: 2014 c.7 Sch.2 para.10
s.167, varied: SI 2014/3159 Reg.4
s.167ZJ, amended: 2014 c.7 Sch.2 para.11
s.167ZJ, varied: SI 2014/3159 Reg.4
s.167ZS, amended: 2014 c.7 Sch.2 para.12
s.167ZS, varied: SI 2014/3159 Reg.4
s.171, enabling: SI 2014/569, SI 2014/608,
SI 2014/634, SI 2014/635, SI 2014/881, SI

2014/1231, SI 2014/1511, SI 2014/2397, SI
2014/2924, SI 2014/3159, SI 2014/3196
s.172, amended: 2014 c.7 s.9, s.13, s.18,
2014 c.19 Sch.15 para.20
s.172, applied: SI 2014/569, SI 2014/897, SI
2014/3159, SI 2014/3196
Sch.1, amended: 2014 c.19 Sch.15 para.21
Sch.1 para.6, amended: SI 2014/1283 Sch.1
para.3
Sch.1 para.6, applied: 2014 c.7 s.4
Sch.1 para.6, enabling: SI 2014/608, SI
2014/1016, SI 2014/2397
Sch.1 para.8, amended: 2014 c.7 s.7
Sch.1 para.8, applied: 2014 c.7 s.7
Sch.1 para.8, enabling: SI 2014/3240
Sch.2, repealed: 2014 c.7 s.17
Sch.4 Part III, amended: SI 2014/838 Art.2
Sch.9 para.3, enabling: SI 2014/1231

8. Social Security Administration (Northern Ireland) Act 1992

s.104ZA, amended: 2014 c.7 s.7
s.115B, amended: SI 2014/1283 Sch.1 para.4
s.117, amended: 2014 c.2 Sch.12 para.30
s.117, repealed (in part): 2014 c.2 Sch.12
para.30
s.129, applied: SI 2014/475, SI 2014/634
s.129, enabling: SI 2014/475
s.132, applied: SI 2014/384, SI 2014/838
s.132, enabling: SI 2014/384, SI 2014/838
s.135, disapplied: SI 2014/881 Reg.2
s.135, enabling: SI 2014/881
s.142, amended: 2014 c.19 Sch.15 para.22,
SI 2014/992 Art.6
s.145, amended: 2014 c.7 s.19
s.165, amended: 2014 c.7 s.18
s.165, enabling: SI 2014/838, SI 2014/881
s.166, applied: SI 2014/475, SI 2014/838
s.167, enabling: SI 2014/881

12. Taxation of Chargeable Gains Act 1992

applied: SI 2014/1120 Art.2
Part VI c.IV, amended: 2014 c.14 Sch.4
para.51
s.2A, see *Stolkin v Revenue and Customs
Commissioners* [2014] UKUT 165 (TCC),
[2014] S.T.C. 2672 (UT (Tax)), David
Richards J
s.3, amended: 2014 c.26 s.8, s.9
s.3, disapplied: 2014 c.26 s.8, s.9
s.4, amended: 2014 c.26 Sch.38 para.15,
2014 c.29 s.9

s.4A, amended: 2014 c.26 Sch.38 para.15,
2014 c.29 s.9
s.12, amended: 2014 c.26 s.59
s.35, see *Blum v Revenue and Customs*
[2014] R.V.R. 137 (UT (Lands)), PR Francis
FRICS
s.44, see *Lord Howard of Henderskelfe's
Executors v Revenue and Customs
Commissioners* [2014] EWCA Civ 278,
[2014] 1 W.L.R. 3902 (CA (Civ Div)),
Rimer LJ
s.45, see *Lord Howard of Henderskelfe's
Executors v Revenue and Customs
Commissioners* [2014] EWCA Civ 278,
[2014] 1 W.L.R. 3902 (CA (Civ Div)),
Rimer LJ
s.48, see *Revenue and Customs
Commissioners v Morrison* [2014] S.T.C.
574 (UT (Tax)), Lord Glennie
s.49, see *Revenue and Customs
Commissioners v Morrison* [2014] CSIH 113
(IH (1 Div)), The Lord President (Gill); see
*Revenue and Customs Commissioners v
Morrison* [2014] S.T.C. 574 (UT (Tax)),
Lord Glennie
s.55, see *Blum v Revenue and Customs*
[2014] R.V.R. 137 (UT (Lands)), PR Francis
FRICS
s.59B, added: 2014 c.26 Sch.17 para.17
s.60, see *Wagstaff v Revenue and Customs
Commissioners* [2014] UKFTT 43 (TC),
[2014] W.T.L.R. 547 (FTT (Tax)), Judge
Malcolm Gammie QC
s.61, amended: SI 2014/605 Art.20
s.72, amended: 2014 c.26 s.60
s.73, amended: 2014 c.26 s.60
s.87, see *Bowring v Revenue and Customs
Commissioners* [2014] S.F.T.D. 347 (FTT
(Tax)), Judge Barbara Mosedale
s.91, see *Bowring v Revenue and Customs
Commissioners* [2014] S.F.T.D. 347 (FTT
(Tax)), Judge Barbara Mosedale
s.97, see *Bowring v Revenue and Customs
Commissioners* [2014] S.F.T.D. 347 (FTT
(Tax)), Judge Barbara Mosedale
s.104, amended: 2014 c.26 Sch.37 para.18
s.105A, amended: 2014 c.26 Sch.8 para.122
s.105B, amended: 2014 c.26 Sch.8 para.123
s.116, see *DMWSHNZ Ltd v Revenue and
Customs Commissioners* [2014] UKUT 98
(TCC), [2014] S.T.C. 1440 (UT (Tax)), Rose

J; see *Hancock v Revenue and Customs Commissioners* [2014] UKFTT 695 (TC), [2014] S.F.T.D. 1163 (FTT (Tax)), Judge Roger Berner
s.117, see *Hancock v Revenue and Customs Commissioners* [2014] UKFTT 695 (TC), [2014] S.F.T.D. 1163 (FTT (Tax)), Judge Roger Berner
s.119A, amended: 2014 c.26 Sch.9 para.23
s.119B, amended: 2014 c.26 Sch.9 para.24
s.126, see *Hancock v Revenue and Customs Commissioners* [2014] UKFTT 695 (TC), [2014] S.F.T.D. 1163 (FTT (Tax)), Judge Roger Berner
s.127, see *DMWSHNZ Ltd v Revenue and Customs Commissioners* [2014] UKUT 98 (TCC), [2014] S.T.C. 1440 (UT (Tax)), Rose J; see *Hancock v Revenue and Customs Commissioners* [2014] UKFTT 695 (TC), [2014] S.F.T.D. 1163 (FTT (Tax)), Judge Roger Berner
s.130, see *DMWSHNZ Ltd v Revenue and Customs Commissioners* [2014] UKUT 98 (TCC), [2014] S.T.C. 1440 (UT (Tax)), Rose J; see *Hancock v Revenue and Customs Commissioners* [2014] UKFTT 695 (TC), [2014] S.F.T.D. 1163 (FTT (Tax)), Judge Roger Berner
s.132, see *Hancock v Revenue and Customs Commissioners* [2014] UKFTT 695 (TC), [2014] S.F.T.D. 1163 (FTT (Tax)), Judge Roger Berner
s.135, see *DMWSHNZ Ltd v Revenue and Customs Commissioners* [2014] UKUT 98 (TCC), [2014] S.T.C. 1440 (UT (Tax)), Rose J
s.140E, amended: 2014 c.14 Sch.4 para.47
s.140F, amended: 2014 c.14 Sch.4 para.48
s.140G, amended: 2014 c.14 Sch.4 para.49
s.144ZB, amended: 2014 c.26 Sch.9 para.25
s.149A, amended: 2014 c.26 Sch.9 para.26
s.149AA, amended: 2014 c.26 Sch.9 para.27
s.150G, amended: 2014 c.26 s.55
s.151, enabling: SI 2014/654, SI 2014/1450
s.155, amended: 2014 c.26 s.61
s.156ZB, amended: 2014 c.26 s.62
s.170, amended: 2014 c.14 Sch.4 para.50
s.171, see *DMWSHNZ Ltd v Revenue and Customs Commissioners* [2014] UKUT 98 (TCC), [2014] S.T.C. 1440 (UT (Tax)), Rose J; see *Iliffe News & Media Ltd v Revenue*

and Customs Commissioners [2014] F.S.R. 6 (FTT (Tax)), Judge John Walters Q.C.
s.171A, see *DMWSHNZ Ltd v Revenue and Customs Commissioners* [2014] UKUT 98 (TCC), [2014] S.T.C. 1440 (UT (Tax)), Rose J
s.184G, amended: 2014 c.26 s.63
s.184H, amended: 2014 c.26 s.63
s.198J, added: 2014 c.26 s.71
s.217D, amended: 2014 c.14 Sch.4 para.52, 2014 c.26 Sch.39 para.1
s.223, amended: 2014 c.26 s.58
s.223, repealed (in part): 2014 c.26 s.58
s.225, see *Wagstaff v Revenue and Customs Commissioners* [2014] UKFTT 43 (TC), [2014] W.T.L.R. 547 (FTT (Tax)), Judge Malcolm Gammie QC
s.225E, added: 2014 c.26 s.58
s.236A, amended: 2014 c.26 Sch.8 para.34
s.236H, added: 2014 c.26 Sch.37 para.1
s.236H, varied: 2014 c.26 Sch.37 para.3
s.236L, applied: 2014 c.26 Sch.37 para.4
s.236N, varied: 2014 c.26 Sch.37 para.3
s.236O, varied: 2014 c.26 Sch.37 para.3
s.236P, varied: 2014 c.26 Sch.37 para.3
s.236Q, varied: 2014 c.26 Sch.37 para.3
s.236R, varied: 2014 c.26 Sch.37 para.3
s.238A, amended: 2014 c.26 Sch.8 para.35, Sch.8 para.124, Sch.8 para.184
s.255A, added: 2014 c.26 Sch.12 para.2
s.261B, see *Acornwood LLP v Revenue and Customs Commissioners* [2014] UKFTT 416 (TC), [2014] S.F.T.D. 694 (FTT (Tax)), Judge Colin Bishopp
s.261B, applied: 2014 c.26 s.253
s.263B, see *Barnes v Revenue and Customs Commissioners* [2014] EWCA Civ 31, [2014] B.T.C. 5 (CA (Civ Div)), McFarlane LJ
s.288, amended: 2014 c.26 Sch.9 para.28
Sch.A1 para.3, see *Stolkin v Revenue and Customs Commissioners* [2014] UKUT 165 (TCC), [2014] S.T.C. 2672 (UT (Tax)), David Richards J
Sch.A1 para.9, see *Stolkin v Revenue and Customs Commissioners* [2014] UKUT 165 (TCC), [2014] S.T.C. 2672 (UT (Tax)), David Richards J
Sch.1 para.1, see *Stolkin v Revenue and Customs Commissioners* [2014] UKUT 165

(TCC), [2014] S.T.C. 2672 (UT (Tax)),
David Richards J

Sch.5B, see *Stolkin v Revenue and Customs
Commissioners* [2014] UKUT 165 (TCC),
[2014] S.T.C. 2672 (UT (Tax)), David
Richards J

Sch.5BB para.1, amended: 2014 c.26 s.55

Sch.5B para.1, see *Harvey's Jersey Cream
Ltd v Revenue and Customs Commissioners*
[2014] S.F.T.D. 599 (FTT (Tax)), Judge
Charles Hellier

Sch.7C, amended: 2014 c.26 Sch.8 para.37

Sch.7D, amended: 2014 c.26 Sch.8 para.40

Sch.7AC Part II para.15A, amended: 2014
c.26 s.72

Sch.7AC Part IV para.26, amended: 2014
c.14 Sch.4 para.53

Sch.7C para.2, amended: 2014 c.26 Sch.8
para.38

Sch.7D Part 1, amended: 2014 c.26 Sch.8
para.41

Sch.7D Part 1 para.1, amended: 2014 c.26
Sch.8 para.42

Sch.7D Part 1 para.2, amended: 2014 c.26
Sch.8 para.43

Sch.7D Part 2, amended: 2014 c.26 Sch.8
para.126

Sch.7D Part 2 para.9, amended: 2014 c.26
Sch.8 para.127

Sch.7D Part 2 para.10, amended: 2014 c.26
Sch.8 para.128

Sch.7D Part 3, amended: 2014 c.26 Sch.8
para.186

Sch.7D Part 3 para.11, amended: 2014 c.26
Sch.8 para.187

Sch.7D Part 3 para.12, amended: 2014 c.26
Sch.8 para.188

Sch.7D Part 3 para.13, amended: 2014 c.26
Sch.8 para.189

Sch.8B, added: 2014 c.26 Sch.12 para.3

Sch.9 Part I para.1, enabling: SI 2014/1120

13. Further and Higher Education Act 1992

s.16, applied: SI 2014/2067

s.16, enabling: SI 2014/2067

s.16A, applied: SI 2014/2067

s.17, enabling: SI 2014/2067

s.20, enabling: SI 2014/2068

s.21, enabling: SI 2014/2068

s.27, applied: SI 2014/2126 Reg.3, Reg.4

s.27, enabling: SI 2014/2126

s.27B, applied: SI 2014/2126 Reg.5

s.27B, enabling: SI 2014/2126

s.69, enabling: SI 2014/1464

s.79, applied: SI 2014/2179 Reg.2

s.79, enabling: SI 2014/2179

s.85A, applied: SI 2014/1132 Sch.7 para.10,
SI 2014/2709 Sch.2 para.10

s.89, enabling: SI 2014/1464, SI 2014/2126

s.90, applied: SI 2014/512 Sch.1 para.14

s.91, applied: SI 2014/512 Sch.1 para.14

Sch.4, enabling: SI 2014/2068

14. Local Government Finance Act 1992

Part I c.IVZA, enabling: SI 2014/35

s.3, enabling: SI 2014/2653

s.6, see *Orme v Charnwood BC* [2014]
R.V.R. 273 (VT), Graham Zellick Q.C.
(President); see *Percival v Ealing LBC*
[2014] R.V.R. 271 (VT), Graham Zellick
Q.C. (President)

s.11, see *Orme v Charnwood BC* [2014]
R.V.R. 273 (VT), Graham Zellick Q.C.
(President); see *Percival v Ealing LBC*
[2014] R.V.R. 271 (VT), Graham Zellick
Q.C. (President)

s.11B, see *K v Wolverhampton City Council*
[2014] R.V.R. 160 (VT), Graham Zellick
Q.C. (President)

s.13A, see *SC v East Riding of Yorkshire
Council* [2014] R.A. 279 (VT), Graham
Zellick Q.C. (President)

s.13A, applied: SI 2014/66, SI 2014/825, SI
2014/3312 Reg.3

s.13A, enabling: SI 2014/66, SI 2014/825

s.14A, enabling: SI 2014/825

s.14B, enabling: SI 2014/825

s.14C, enabling: SI 2014/825

s.14D, applied: SI 2014/825

s.14D, enabling: SI 2014/825

s.16, see *SC v East Riding of Yorkshire
Council* [2014] R.A. 279 (VT), Graham
Zellick Q.C. (President); see *Yang v Official
Receiver* [2013] EWHC 3577 (Ch), [2014]
B.P.I.R. 826 (Ch D (Manchester)), Judge
Hodge Q.C.

s.31A, see *R. (on the application of Buck) v
Doncaster MBC* [2013] EWCA Civ 1190,
[2014] P.T.S.R. 111 (CA (Civ Div)), Master
of the Rolls

s.31A, amended: SI 2014/389 Art.2

s.41, enabling: SI 2014/35

s.42A, amended: SI 2014/389 Art.3

s.52ZC, varied: 2014 c.2 s.41

s.52ZG, amended: 2014 c.2 s.41
s.52ZH, amended: 2014 c.2 s.41
s.52ZK, amended: 2014 c.2 s.41
s.52ZO, amended: 2014 c.2 s.41
s.52ZQ, applied: SI 2014/925
s.52ZQ, enabling: SI 2014/925
s.52ZX, amended: 2014 c.2 s.41
s.52ZX, applied: 2014 c.2 s.41
s.52ZX, repealed (in part): 2014 c.2 s.41
s.66, see *K v Wolverhampton City Council*
[2014] R.V.R. 160 (VT), Graham Zellick
Q.C. (President)
s.79, applied: SSI 2014/3 Art.7
s.80, enabling: SSI 2014/35
s.81, applied: SSI 2014/3 Art.10
s.113, enabling: SI 2014/35, SI 2014/122, SI
2014/129, SI 2014/448, SI 2014/825, SI
2014/925, SI 2014/2653, SI 2014/3312, SSI
2014/35, SSI 2014/37
Sch.1 para.4, see *R. (on the application of
Earl) v Winchester City Council* [2014]
EWHC 195 (Admin), [2014] E.L.R. 225
(QBD (Admin)), Thirlwall J
Sch.1 para.4, enabling: SSI 2014/37
Sch.1 para.5, applied: 2014 c.22 Sch.3
para.11, SI 2014/2359 Art.6
Sch.1A para.2, enabling: SI 2014/448, SI
2014/3312
Sch.1B para.6, applied: SI 2014/825 Reg.3,
SI 2014/856 Art.3
Sch.1B para.6, enabling: SI 2014/66, SI
2014/825
Sch.2 para.1, enabling: SI 2014/122, SI
2014/129, SSI 2014/35
Sch.2 para.2, enabling: SI 2014/122, SI
2014/129
Sch.2 para.4, enabling: SI 2014/129
Sch.2 para.5, enabling: SI 2014/129
Sch.2 para.8, enabling: SI 2014/129
Sch.2 para.9, enabling: SI 2014/129
Sch.2 para.10, enabling: SI 2014/129
Sch.12 Part I para.1, enabling: SSI 2014/36,
SSI 2014/74
Sch.12 Part I para.2, applied: SSI 2014/36,
SSI 2014/74
Sch.12 Part II para.9, applied: SSI 2014/36
Art.3
Sch.12 Part II para.9, enabling: SSI 2014/36
Sch.13 para.13, repealed: 2014 c.14 Sch.7
31. Firearms (Amendment) Act 1992
applied: SI 2014/1638 Reg.5

34. Sexual Offences (Amendment) Act 1992
s.1, applied: SI 2014/1610 r.16_1, r.37_2
35. Timeshare Act 1992
see *Link Financial Ltd v Wilson* [2014]
EWHC 252 (Ch), [2014] C.T.L.C. 145 (Ch
D), David Railton QC
**37. Further and Higher Education (Scotland)
Act 1992**
Part I, applied: SSI 2014/22 Art.2, SSI
2014/164 Sch.2 Part 1, SSI 2014/217 Sch.1
para.6, SSI 2014/250 Art.2, SSI 2014/292
Sch.1 para.6
s.3, enabling: SSI 2014/52, SSI 2014/250
s.5, applied: SSI 2014/52
s.24, amended: SSI 2014/21 Art.3
s.25, applied: SSI 2014/52
s.25, enabling: SSI 2014/52
s.44, applied: SSI 2014/217 Sch.1 para.3,
SSI 2014/292 Sch.1 para.3
s.45, enabling: SSI 2014/268
s.60, enabling: SSI 2014/52, SSI 2014/250
Sch.2 para.3, varied: SSI 2014/250 Art.5
Sch.2 para.5, varied: SSI 2014/250 Art.5
Sch.2 para.5A, amended: SSI 2014/21 Art.3
Sch.2 para.5B, amended: SSI 2014/21 Art.3
Sch.2 para.5C, varied: SSI 2014/250 Art.5
Sch.2 para.5D, varied: SSI 2014/250 Art.5
40. Friendly Societies Act 1992
applied: SI 2014/2418 Sch.1
s.83, repealed: 2014 c.14 Sch.7
Sch.12, see *Speechley v Allott* [2014] EWCA
Civ 230, [2014] L.L.R. 817 (CA (Civ Div)),
Sullivan LJ
42. Transport and Works Act 1992
applied: SI 2014/310 Art.18
s.1, enabling: SI 2014/310, SI 2014/1604, SI
2014/1821, SI 2014/2027, SI 2014/3102
s.3, enabling: SI 2014/3102
s.5, enabling: SI 2014/310, SI 2014/1604, SI
2014/1821, SI 2014/2027, SI 2014/3102
s.11, applied: SI 2014/3102
Sch.1 para.1, enabling: SI 2014/310, SI
2014/1604, SI 2014/2027, SI 2014/3102
Sch.1 para.2, enabling: SI 2014/310, SI
2014/2027, SI 2014/3102
Sch.1 para.3, enabling: SI 2014/310, SI
2014/1821, SI 2014/2027, SI 2014/3102
Sch.1 para.4, enabling: SI 2014/310, SI
2014/1821, SI 2014/2027, SI 2014/3102
Sch.1 para.5, enabling: SI 2014/310, SI
2014/1821, SI 2014/3102

Sch.1 para.7, enabling: SI 2014/310, SI
2014/1821, SI 2014/2027, SI 2014/3102
Sch.1 para.8, enabling: SI 2014/310, SI
2014/1604, SI 2014/1821, SI 2014/2027, SI
2014/3102
Sch.1 para.10, enabling: SI 2014/310, SI
2014/2027, SI 2014/3102
Sch.1 para.11, enabling: SI 2014/310, SI
2014/1821, SI 2014/2027, SI 2014/3102
Sch.1 para.15, enabling: SI 2014/310, SI
2014/1604, SI 2014/3102
Sch.1 para.16, enabling: SI 2014/310, SI
2014/1821, SI 2014/2027, SI 2014/3102
Sch.1 para.17, enabling: SI 2014/1604, SI
2014/3102

48. Finance (No.2) Act 1992

s.42, see *R. (on the application of de Silva) v
Revenue and Customs Commissioners*
[2014] UKUT 170 (TCC), [2014] S.T.C.
2088 (UT (Tax)), Sales J

**52. Trade Union and Labour Relations
(Consolidation) Act 1992**

applied: SI 2014/1139 Reg.4
Part IV c.II, applied: SI 2014/3352 Sch.2
para.30
s.5, see *North Essex Partnership NHS
Foundation Trust v Bone* [2014] EWCA Civ
652, [2014] 3 All E.R. 964 (CA (Civ Div)),
Jackson LJ
s.6, see *North Essex Partnership NHS
Foundation Trust v Bone* [2014] EWCA Civ
652, [2014] 3 All E.R. 964 (CA (Civ Div)),
Jackson LJ
s.8, see *North Essex Partnership NHS
Foundation Trust v Bone* [2014] EWCA Civ
652, [2014] 3 All E.R. 964 (CA (Civ Div)),
Jackson LJ
s.10, amended: 2014 c.14 Sch.4 para.54
s.24, amended: 2014 c.4 s.43
s.24A, amended: 2014 c.4 s.41, s.42
s.24B, added: 2014 c.4 s.43
s.24ZA, added: 2014 c.4 s.40
s.24ZB, added: 2014 c.4 s.41
s.24ZH, added: 2014 c.4 s.42
s.25, amended: 2014 c.4 s.43
s.26, amended: 2014 c.4 s.43
s.38, amended: SI 2014/560 Sch.1 para.24,
SI 2014/3229 Sch.5 para.10
s.44, amended: 2014 c.4 s.40, s.41
s.45D, amended: 2014 c.4 s.43
s.67, applied: SI 2014/382 Art.4

s.70C, applied: SI 2014/382 Art.4
s.118, amended: 2014 c.4 s.40
s.137, applied: SI 2014/382 Art.4
s.138, applied: SI 2014/382 Art.4
s.139, applied: SI 2014/382 Art.4
s.145A, applied: SI 2014/382 Art.4
s.145E, amended: SI 2014/382 Sch.1
s.145E, applied: SI 2014/382 Art.4
s.146, see *North Essex Partnership NHS
Foundation Trust v Bone* [2014] EWCA Civ
652, [2014] 3 All E.R. 964 (CA (Civ Div)),
Jackson LJ; see *Smith v Carillion (JM) Ltd*
[2014] I.R.L.R. 344 (EAT), Slade J
s.156, amended: SI 2014/382 Sch.1
s.159, applied: SI 2014/382 Art.4
s.161, applied: SI 2014/254 Reg.3
s.168, applied: SI 2014/3352 Sch.2 para.30
s.170, applied: SI 2014/3352 Sch.2 para.30
s.176, amended: SI 2014/382 Sch.1
s.176, applied: SI 2014/382 Art.4
s.178, see *R. (on the application of Boots
Management Services Ltd) v Central
Arbitration Committee* [2014] EWHC 2930
(Admin), [2014] I.R.L.R. 887 (QBD
(Admin)), Sir Brian Keith; see *R. (on the
application of Boots Management Services
Ltd) v Central Arbitration Committee* [2014]
EWHC 65 (Admin), [2014] I.R.L.R. 278
(QBD (Admin)), Keith J
s.188, see *United States v Nolan* [2014]
EWCA Civ 71, [2014] I.C.R. 685 (CA (Civ
Div)), Moore-Bick LJ; see *University
College Union v University of Stirling*
[2014] CSIH 5, 2014 S.C. 414 (IH (Ex
Div)), Lord Brodie; see *USDAW v Ethel
Austin Ltd (In Administration)* [2014] 1
C.M.L.R. 23 (EAT), Judge McMullen QC;
see *USDAW v Ethel Austin Ltd (In
Administration)* [2014] EWCA Civ 142,
[2014] 2 C.M.L.R. 45 (CA (Civ Div)),
Maurice Kay LJ
s.189, see *United States v Nolan* [2014]
EWCA Civ 71, [2014] I.C.R. 685 (CA (Civ
Div)), Moore-Bick LJ
s.189, amended: SI 2014/431 Sch.1 para.1
s.189, applied: SI 2014/3051 Reg.32
s.195, see *University College Union v
University of Stirling* [2014] CSIH 5, 2014
S.C. 414 (IH (Ex Div)), Lord Brodie
s.196, referred to: SI 2014/3352 Sch.2
para.30

s.198A, added: SI 2014/16 Reg.3

s.199, applied: SI 2014/1665

s.200, applied: SI 2014/1665

s.200, enabling: SI 2014/1665

s.207, see *Roberts v GB Oils Ltd* [2014] I.C.R. 462 (EAT), Jeffrey Burke Q.C.

s.220, applied: 2014 c.12 s.36

s.256, amended: 2014 c.4 s.43

s.299, amended: 2014 c.4 s.41, SI 2014/16 Reg.3

Sch.A1, see *R. (on the application of Boots Management Services Ltd) v Central Arbitration Committee* [2014] EWHC 2930 (Admin), [2014] I.R.L.R. 887 (QBD (Admin)), Sir Brian Keith

Sch.A1 Pt I, see *R. (on the application of Boots Management Services Ltd) v Central Arbitration Committee* [2014] EWHC 2930 (Admin), [2014] I.R.L.R. 887 (QBD (Admin)), Sir Brian Keith

Sch.A1 Pt IV, see *R. (on the application of Boots Management Services Ltd) v Central Arbitration Committee* [2014] EWHC 2930 (Admin), [2014] I.R.L.R. 887 (QBD (Admin)), Sir Brian Keith

Sch.A1 Pt VI, see *R. (on the application of Boots Management Services Ltd) v Central Arbitration Committee* [2014] EWHC 2930 (Admin), [2014] I.R.L.R. 887 (QBD (Admin)), Sir Brian Keith

Sch.A1 Pt VIII, see *R. (on the application of Boots Management Services Ltd) v Central Arbitration Committee* [2014] EWHC 2930 (Admin), [2014] I.R.L.R. 887 (QBD (Admin)), Sir Brian Keith

Sch.A1 Pt I para.3, see *R. (on the application of Boots Management Services Ltd) v Central Arbitration Committee* [2014] EWHC 2930 (Admin), [2014] I.R.L.R. 887 (QBD (Admin)), Sir Brian Keith; see *R. (on the application of Boots Management Services Ltd) v Central Arbitration Committee* [2014] EWHC 65 (Admin), [2014] I.R.L.R. 278 (QBD (Admin)), Keith J

Sch.A1 Pt I para.35, see *R. (on the application of Boots Management Services Ltd) v Central Arbitration Committee* [2014] EWHC 2930 (Admin), [2014] I.R.L.R. 887 (QBD (Admin)), Sir Brian Keith; see *R. (on the application of Boots Management Services Ltd) v Central Arbitration*

Committee [2014] EWHC 65 (Admin), [2014] I.R.L.R. 278 (QBD (Admin)), Keith J

Sch.A1 para.134, see *R. (on the application of Boots Management Services Ltd) v Central Arbitration Committee* [2014] EWHC 2930 (Admin), [2014] I.R.L.R. 887 (QBD (Admin)), Sir Brian Keith; see *R. (on the application of Boots Management Services Ltd) v Central Arbitration Committee* [2014] EWHC 65 (Admin), [2014] I.R.L.R. 278 (QBD (Admin)), Keith J

53. Tribunals and Inquiries Act 1992

s.14, amended: SI 2014/631 Sch.2 para.3, SI 2014/892 Sch.1 para.98

s.14, repealed (in part): SI 2014/892 Sch.1 para.98

Sch.1 Part I, amended: SI 2014/631 Sch.2 para.3, SI 2014/3248 Sch.3 Part 2

Sch.1 Part I, referred to: SSI 2014/84 Art.6, SSI 2014/169 Art.6

1993

3. Social Security Act 1993

s.2, amended: 2014 c.19 Sch.12 para.29, Sch.16 para.36

s.2, applied: 2014 c.25 Sch.1, SI 2014/475, SI 2014/475 Art.5

s.2, enabling: SI 2014/475

6. Bankruptcy (Scotland) Act 1993

Sch.1 para.31, repealed: 2014 asp 11 Sch.4

8. Judicial Pensions and Retirement Act 1993

s.9A, enabling: SI 2014/483

s.26, amended: 2014 asp 10 Sch.9 para.11

s.26, applied: 2014 asp 10 Sch.7 para.9, Sch.7 para.10

s.26, repealed (in part): SI 2014/3248 Sch.3 Part 2

s.26, enabling: SSI 2014/155

s.27, repealed (in part): SSI 2014/155 Art.2

s.29, enabling: SI 2014/483, SSI 2014/155

s.30, amended: 2014 asp 10 Sch.9 para.11

Sch.5, amended: 2014 asp 10 Sch.9 para.11, 2014 asp 18 Sch.5 para.8, SSI 2014/155 Art.2

9. Prisoners and Criminal Proceedings (Scotland) Act 1993

s.1, applied: SI 2014/2871 Sch.1

s.2, see *Chalmers (Robert Davidson) v HM Advocate* [2014] HCJAC 24, 2014 J.C. 220

(HCJ), The Lord Justice General (Gill); see
Dutch v Parole Board for Scotland 2014
S.L.T. 285 (OH), Lord Burns

11. Clean Air Act 1993

Part III, applied: SI 2014/491, SI 2014/491
Reg.2, SI 2014/684 Reg.2, SI 2014/2366
Reg.2, SSI 2014/317 Reg.2
s.1, disapplied: SI 2014/3318 Reg.2
s.1, enabling: SI 2014/3318
s.6, referred to: SI 2014/3318 Reg.3
s.7, enabling: SI 2014/3318
s.14, applied: SI 2014/3318 Reg.4
s.14, enabling: SI 2014/3318
s.20, amended: 2014 asp 3 s.50
s.20, applied: SI 2014/504 Art.2, SI
2014/694 Art.2
s.20, disapplied: SI 2014/2404 Art.2
s.20, referred to: SSI 2014/316 Art.3
s.20, enabling: SI 2014/491, SI 2014/684, SI
2014/2366, SSI 2014/317
s.21, amended: 2014 asp 3 s.50
s.21, substituted: 2014 asp 3 s.50
s.21, enabling: SI 2014/504, SI 2014/694, SI
2014/2404, SSI 2014/316
s.29, amended: 2014 asp 3 s.50
s.31, amended: 2014 asp 3 Sch.3 para.4
s.33, amended: 2014 asp 3 Sch.3 para.4
s.35, amended: 2014 asp 3 Sch.3 para.4
s.35, applied: SI 2014/3318 Reg.9
s.36, amended: 2014 asp 3 Sch.3 para.4
s.36, applied: SI 2014/3318 Reg.8
s.36, disapplied: SI 2014/3318 Reg.10
s.36, enabling: SI 2014/3318
s.37, applied: SI 2014/3318, SI 2014/3318
Reg.8, Reg.9
s.37, enabling: SI 2014/3318
s.38, applied: SI 2014/3318
s.38, enabling: SI 2014/3318
s.41A, amended: 2014 asp 3 Sch.3 para.4
s.42, amended: 2014 asp 3 Sch.3 para.26
s.59, applied: SI 2014/3318 Reg.8
s.63, enabling: SI 2014/3318

12. Radioactive Substances Act 1993

referred to: SSI 2014/324 Sch.1 para.7
varied: 2014 c.20 Sch.1 para.5
s.32, applied: SSI 2014/319 Sch.1 para.3,
Sch.2 para.5, Sch.3 para.3
s.33, applied: SSI 2014/319 Sch.2 para.5
s.34A, applied: SSI 2014/319 Sch.2 para.5
s.40, amended: 2014 asp 3 Sch.3 para.42
s.46, amended: 2014 asp 3 Sch.3 para.42

Sch.3 Part II para.11, repealed (in part):
2014 asp 3 Sch.3 para.27
Sch.3 Part II para.16, amended: 2014 asp 3
Sch.3 para.27

21. Osteopaths Act 1993

s.6, applied: SI 2014/598 Sch.1
s.6, enabling: SI 2014/598
s.35, applied: SI 2014/598, SI 2014/598
Sch.1
s.35, enabling: SI 2014/598
s.36, applied: SI 2014/598
s.37, applied: SI 2014/1887 Sch.3 para.10,
Sch.3 para.15
s.37, disapplied: SI 2014/1887 Sch.3 para.10
s.37, substituted: SI 2014/1887 Sch.1 para.9

23. Asylum and Immigration Appeals Act 1993

applied: SI 2014/2604 Sch.1 para.2

26. Bail (Amendment) Act 1993

s.1, applied: SI 2014/1610 r.19_9

28. Leasehold Reform, Housing and Urban Development Act 1993

see *Cravecrest Ltd v Sixth Duke of
Westminster* [2013] EWCA Civ 731, [2014]
Ch. 301 (CA (Civ Div)), Sir Terence
Etherton C; see *Westbrook Dolphin Square
Ltd v Friends Life Ltd* [2014] EWHC 2433
(Ch), [2014] L. & T.R. 28 (Ch D), Mann J
Pt I., see *Padmore v Barry and Peggy High
Foundation* [2014] R.V.R. 237 (UT
(Lands)), Martin Rodger Q.C.
s.1, see *Regent Wealth Ltd v Wiggins* [2014]
EWCA Civ 1078, [2014] H.L.R. 45 (CA
(Civ Div)), Moore-Bick LJ
s.2, see *Regent Wealth Ltd v Wiggins* [2014]
EWCA Civ 1078, [2014] H.L.R. 45 (CA
(Civ Div)), Moore-Bick LJ
s.5, see *Westbrook Dolphin Square Ltd v
Friends Life Ltd* [2014] EWHC 2433 (Ch),
[2014] L. & T.R. 28 (Ch D), Mann J
s.13, see *Regent Wealth Ltd v Wiggins*
[2014] EWCA Civ 1078, [2014] H.L.R. 45
(CA (Civ Div)), Moore-Bick LJ; see
*Westbrook Dolphin Square Ltd v Friends
Life Ltd* [2014] EWHC 2433 (Ch), [2014] L.
& T.R. 28 (Ch D), Mann J
s.19, see *Regent Wealth Ltd v Wiggins*
[2014] EWCA Civ 1078, [2014] H.L.R. 45
(CA (Civ Div)), Moore-Bick LJ
s.21, see *Westbrook Dolphin Square Ltd v
Friends Life Ltd* [2014] EWHC 2433 (Ch),
[2014] L. & T.R. 28 (Ch D), Mann J

s.42, see *Bolton v Godwin-Austen* [2014]
EWCA Civ 27, [2014] H.L.R. 15 (CA (Civ
Div)), Goldring LJ; see *Burchell v Raj
Properties Ltd* [2014] L. & T.R. 3 (UT
(Lands)), Martin Rodger Q.C.
s.45, see *Bolton v Godwin-Austen* [2014]
EWCA Civ 27, [2014] H.L.R. 15 (CA (Civ
Div)), Goldring LJ
s.48, see *Bolton v Godwin-Austen* [2014]
EWCA Civ 27, [2014] H.L.R. 15 (CA (Civ
Div)), Goldring LJ; see *Voyvoda v
Grosvenor West End Properties* [2014] L. &
T.R. 10 (UT (Lands)), Jeremy Sullivan QC
s.49, see *Bolton v Godwin-Austen* [2014]
EWCA Civ 27, [2014] H.L.R. 15 (CA (Civ
Div)), Goldring LJ
s.56, see *Bolton v Godwin-Austen* [2014]
EWCA Civ 27, [2014] H.L.R. 15 (CA (Civ
Div)), Goldring LJ
s.57, see *Bolton v Godwin-Austen* [2014]
EWCA Civ 27, [2014] H.L.R. 15 (CA (Civ
Div)), Goldring LJ; see *Burchell v Raj
Properties Ltd* [2014] L. & T.R. 3 (UT
(Lands)), Martin Rodger Q.C.
s.97, see *Regent Wealth Ltd v Wiggins*
[2014] EWCA Civ 1078, [2014] H.L.R. 45
(CA (Civ Div)), Moore-Bick LJ
s.99, amended: 2014 c.10 s.1
s.156, repealed: 2014 asp 14 Sch.2 para.7
Sch.3 Pt III para.15, see *Regent Wealth Ltd v
Wiggins* [2014] EWCA Civ 1078, [2014]
H.L.R. 45 (CA (Civ Div)), Moore-Bick LJ
Sch.6, see *Cravecrest Ltd v Sixth Duke of
Westminster* [2013] EWCA Civ 731, [2014]
Ch. 301 (CA (Civ Div)), Sir Terence
Etherton C
Sch.6 Pt II para.3, see *Cravecrest Ltd v Sixth
Duke of Westminster* [2013] EWCA Civ
731, [2014] Ch. 301 (CA (Civ Div)), Sir
Terence Etherton C; see *Padmore v Barry
and Peggy High Foundation* [2014] R.V.R.
237 (UT (Lands)), Martin Rodger Q.C.
Sch.6 Pt II para.4, see *Padmore v Barry and
Peggy High Foundation* [2014] R.V.R. 237
(UT (Lands)), Martin Rodger Q.C.

34. Finance Act 1993
Part II c.III, referred to: SI 2014/3133
s.179B, amended: SI 2014/3133 Reg.3
s.182, enabling: SI 2014/3133
s.184, amended: SI 2014/3133 Reg.4
Sch.20A, substituted: SI 2014/3133 Reg.5

Sch.20A Part IA, added: SI 2014/3133 Reg.5
Sch.20A Part III para.9, amended: SI
2014/3133 Reg.5
Sch.20A Part III para.9A, added: SI
2014/3133 Reg.5
Sch.20A Part III para.10, amended: SI
2014/3133 Reg.5
Sch.20A Part III para.11, amended: SI
2014/3133 Reg.5

38. Welsh Language Act 1993
s.22, applied: SI 2014/1610 r.37_13, r.3_26
s.26, enabling: SI 2014/704, SI 2014/918, SI
2014/919
s.28, repealed: 2014 c.14 Sch.7

39. National Lottery etc Act 1993
s.5, applied: SI 2014/1510 Reg.2

43. Railways Act 1993
applied: SI 2014/1604 Art.5
Part I, applied: SI 2014/909 Art.34, SI
2014/1599 Sch.9 para.19, SI 2014/1796
Art.24, SI 2014/1873 Sch.12 para.19, SI
2014/2027 Art.31, SI 2014/2384 Sch.16
para.18, SI 2014/2434 Sch.8 para.17, SI
2014/3328 Sch.9 para.19, SI 2014/3331
Sch.12 para.28
s.4, amended: SI 2014/892 Sch.1 para.100
s.7, enabling: SI 2014/3244
s.13B, amended: SI 2014/892 Sch.1 para.101
s.13B, applied: SI 2014/559
s.13B, referred to: SI 2014/892 Sch.2 para.2
s.15C, amended: SI 2014/892 Sch.1 para.102
s.15C, applied: SI 2014/559
s.15C, referred to: SI 2014/892 Sch.2 para.2
s.16, amended: SI 2014/892 Sch.1 para.103
s.22, amended: SI 2014/892 Sch.1 para.104
s.24, enabling: SI 2014/3244
s.67, amended: SI 2014/892 Sch.1 para.105
s.67, substituted: SI 2014/892 Sch.1
para.105
s.69, amended: SI 2014/892 Sch.1 para.106
s.71, amended: SI 2014/892 Sch.1 para.107
s.72, amended: SI 2014/892 Sch.1 para.108
s.122, disapplied: SI 2014/310 Art.25
s.122, referred to: SI 2014/2027 Art.28
s.143, enabling: SI 2014/3244
s.145, amended: SI 2014/892 Sch.1 para.109
s.145, repealed (in part): SI 2014/892 Sch.1
para.109
s.153, enabling: SI 2014/3244
Sch.4A para.10A, amended: SI 2014/892
Sch.1 para.111

Sch.4A para.10A, applied: SI 2014/559
Sch.4A para.10A, referred to: SI 2014/892
Sch.2 para.2
Sch.4A para.15, amended: SI 2014/892
Sch.1 para.112
Sch.4A para.15, applied: SI 2014/559
Sch.4A para.15, referred to: SI 2014/892
Sch.2 para.2

44. Crofters (Scotland) Act 1993
applied: 2014 asp 10 Sch.1 para.13
s.19, amended: 2014 asp 14 s.92

45. Scottish Land Court Act 1993
Sch.1 para.3, substituted: 2014 asp 18 s.126
Sch.1 para.6, applied: SSI 2014/229 Sch.1
Sch.1 para.12, enabling: SSI 2014/229
Sch.1 para.18, substituted: 2014 asp 18 s.126

46. Health Service Commissioners Act 1993
applied: SI 2014/3090 Art.5, SI 2014/3218
Art.4

48. Pension Schemes Act 1993
applied: SI 2014/1964 Reg.120, Reg.164, SI
2014/2336 Reg.66, SI 2014/2848 Reg.83,
Reg.166, SSI 2014/164 Reg.47, Reg.75, SSI
2014/290 Reg.3
Part III, amended: 2014 c.19 Sch.13 para.3
Part III, applied: SI 2014/367 Art.2, SI
2014/1964 Reg.142, Reg.164, SI 2014/2848
Reg.133, Reg.166
Part III, varied: SI 2014/1711 Reg.7
Part III c.I, substituted: 2014 c.19 Sch.13
para.4
Part III c.I, repealed: 2014 c.19 Sch.13
para.8
Part III c.I, substituted: 2014 c.19 Sch.13
para.12
Part III c.I, amended: 2014 c.19 Sch.13
para.23
Part III c.II, substituted: 2014 c.19 Sch.13
para.26
Part III c.II, repealed: 2014 c.19 Sch.13
para.28
Part IV, applied: SI 2014/512 Reg.200,
Reg.204
Part IV c.III, applied: SSI 2014/164 Reg.86
Part IV c.IV, applied: SI 2014/512 Reg.197,
SI 2014/1964 Reg.140, SI 2014/2336
Reg.99, SI 2014/2848 Reg.131, SSI
2014/164 Reg.94, Reg.96, SSI 2014/217
Reg.191, SSI 2014/292 Reg.191
Part IV c.IV, referred to: SI 2014/1964
Reg.140, SI 2014/2336 Reg.99

Part IV c.V, applied: SI 2014/512 Reg.197,
SI 2014/1964 Reg.140, SI 2014/2336
Reg.96, Reg.99, SI 2014/2848 Reg.131
Part IV c.V, disapplied: SSI 2014/292
Reg.191
Part IV c.V, referred to: SI 2014/1964
Reg.140, SSI 2014/217 Reg.191
Part IVA, applied: SI 2014/1711 Reg.76
Part IVA c.II, applied: SI 2014/1964
Reg.132
Part V, disapplied: SI 2014/1711 Reg.56
Part X, applied: SI 2014/2336 Reg.57,
Reg.63, Reg.123
s.7, repealed: 2014 c.19 Sch.13 para.5
s.7A, added: 2014 c.19 Sch.13 para.6
s.8, amended: 2014 c.19 Sch.13 para.2,
Sch.13 para.7, SI 2014/3229 Sch.5 para.11
s.8, applied: SSI 2014/164 Reg.49
s.9, applied: SI 2014/1711 Reg.7, SI
2014/1964 Reg.164, SI 2014/2848 Reg.166
s.9, repealed: 2014 c.19 Sch.13 para.9
s.11, repealed: 2014 c.19 Sch.13 para.9
s.12A, repealed: 2014 c.19 Sch.13 para.11
s.12E, added: 2014 c.19 Sch.13 para.13
s.13, amended: 2014 c.19 Sch.13 para.14
s.14, amended: 2014 c.19 Sch.13 para.15
s.14, applied: SI 2014/512 Reg.223, SI
2014/1964 Reg.84, Reg.86, Reg.164,
Reg.165, Reg.167, Reg.168, Reg.174, SI
2014/2336 Reg.121, SI 2014/2848 Reg.72,
Reg.171, Reg.174, Reg.175, SSI 2014/164
Reg.49, SSI 2014/217 Reg.213, SSI
2014/292 Reg.213
s.15, amended: SI 2014/516 Art.5
s.15, applied: SI 2014/1964 Reg.164, SI
2014/2848 Reg.166
s.16, amended: 2014 c.19 Sch.13 para.16
s.17, amended: 2014 c.19 Sch.13 para.17, SI
2014/3229 Sch.5 para.11
s.17, applied: SI 2014/512 Reg.223, SI
2014/1964 Reg.120, Reg.165, Reg.166,
Reg.174, SI 2014/2336 Reg.66, SI
2014/2848 Reg.83, Reg.171, Reg.172, SSI
2014/217 Reg.213, SSI 2014/292 Reg.213
s.17, repealed (in part): SI 2014/560 Sch.1
para.25
s.19, applied: SSI 2014/164 Reg.98
s.19, enabling: SI 2014/540
s.20, amended: 2014 c.19 Sch.13 para.18
s.23, repealed (in part): 2014 c.19 Sch.13
para.19

s.24A, substituted: 2014 c.19 Sch.13 para.20
s.24D, amended: SI 2014/3229 Sch.5
para.11
s.25, amended: 2014 c.19 Sch.13 para.21
s.31, amended: 2014 c.19 Sch.13 para.2
s.34, repealed: 2014 c.19 Sch.13 para.22
s.37, amended: 2014 c.19 Sch.13 para.24, SI
2014/3229 Sch.5 para.11
s.37A, added: 2014 c.19 Sch.13 para.25
s.40, amended: 2014 c.19 Sch.13 para.27
s.40, repealed (in part): 2014 c.19 Sch.13
para.27
s.41, applied: 2014 c.19 Sch.14 para.7,
Sch.14 para.8
s.41, referred to: 2014 c.19 s.24
s.41, repealed: 2014 c.19 Sch.13 para.29
s.42, repealed: 2014 c.19 Sch.13 para.30
s.42A, amended: 2014 c.19 Sch.13 para.2
s.43, amended: 2014 c.19 Sch.13 para.2
s.45, amended: 2014 c.19 Sch.13 para.2
s.46, amended: 2014 c.19 Sch.12 para.71, SI
2014/3213 Art.4
s.46, disapplied: 2014 c.19 Sch.1 para.5
s.46A, repealed: 2014 c.19 Sch.12 para.95
s.47, amended: SI 2014/3229 Sch.5 para.11
s.48A, amended: 2014 c.19 Sch.13 para.31
s.48A, applied: 2014 c.19 Sch.1 para.3
s.48A, disapplied: 2014 c.19 Sch.1 para.5
s.48A, referred to: 2014 c.19 s.6
s.49, repealed: 2014 c.19 Sch.13 para.32
s.50, repealed: 2014 c.19 Sch.13 para.33
s.51, amended: 2014 c.19 Sch.13 para.34
s.52, substituted: 2014 c.19 Sch.13 para.35
s.53, repealed (in part): 2014 c.19 Sch.13
para.36
s.55, applied: SSI 2014/164 Reg.18, Reg.95
s.55, repealed: 2014 c.19 Sch.13 para.37
s.61, applied: SI 2014/512 Reg.191, SSI
2014/164 Reg.18, SSI 2014/217 Reg.185,
SSI 2014/292 Reg.185
s.63, applied: SSI 2014/217 Reg.185
s.71, amended: 2014 c.19 s.36
s.73, applied: SI 2014/1964 Reg.155,
Reg.156
s.74, enabling: SI 2014/1711
s.77, see *LPA Umbrella Trust, Re* [2014]
EWHC 1378 (Ch), [2014] Pens. L.R. 319
(Ch D), Rose J
s.84, amended: SI 2014/3229 Sch.5 para.11
s.84, varied: SI 2014/1711 Reg.25
s.87, amended: 2014 c.19 Sch.13 para.38

s.93A, applied: SI 2014/1711 Reg.30,
Reg.31, SI 2014/2336 Reg.100
s.93A, disapplied: SI 2014/1711 Reg.31
s.94, amended: 2014 c.19 Sch.17 para.20,
Sch.18 para.9
s.94, applied: SI 2014/1711 Reg.30
s.95, applied: SI 2014/512 Reg.203, SI
2014/2336 Reg.101, SI 2014/2848 Reg.133,
SSI 2014/217 Reg.197
s.95, referred to: SI 2014/1711 Reg.30, SI
2014/1964 Reg.142, SI 2014/2336 Reg.103,
SSI 2014/292 Reg.197
s.96, amended: 2014 c.19 Sch.13 para.39
s.96, applied: SI 2014/1711 Reg.30, SI
2014/1964 Reg.142, SI 2014/2336 Reg.103,
SI 2014/2848 Reg.133
s.97, applied: SI 2014/1964 Reg.146, SI
2014/2336 Reg.102, SI 2014/2848 Reg.137
s.97, enabling: SI 2014/1711
s.99, amended: SI 2014/3229 Sch.5 para.11
s.99, applied: SI 2014/1711 Reg.30
s.100, applied: SI 2014/1711 Reg.30, SI
2014/2336 Reg.101
s.101AA, amended: 2014 c.19 s.36
s.101AA, applied: SI 2014/1711 Reg.56
s.101AB, applied: SI 2014/1711 Reg.34
s.101AD, applied: SI 2014/1711 Reg.34
s.101AF, enabling: SI 2014/1711
s.101AI, amended: 2014 c.19 Sch.17
para.20, Sch.18 para.9
s.101I, enabling: SI 2014/1711
s.101L, enabling: SI 2014/1711
s.109, amended: 2014 c.19 Sch.13 para.40
s.109, applied: SI 2014/515, SI 2014/515
Art.2
s.109, enabling: SI 2014/515
s.113, amended: 2014 c.19 s.44
s.113, enabling: SI 2014/1711
s.123, amended: 2014 c.19 s.42
s.124, amended: 2014 c.19 s.42
s.151, see *NHS Business Services Authority v
Wheeler* [2014] EWHC 2155 (Ch), [2014]
Pens. L.R. 639 (Ch D), Jonathan Gaunt QC
s.153, enabling: SI 2014/1711
s.156, amended: 2014 c.19 Sch.13 para.2
s.161, amended: 2014 c.19 s.42
s.165, amended: 2014 c.19 s.42
s.169, applied: SI 2014/512 Reg.200,
Reg.204
s.171, repealed (in part): 2014 c.19 Sch.13
para.41

s.175, referred to: 2014 c.19 Sch.17 para.18
s.178, amended: 2014 c.19 Sch.13 para.42
s.181, amended: 2014 c.7 Sch.2 para.13,
2014 c.19 Sch.13 para.2, Sch.13 para.43
s.181, enabling: SI 2014/1711
s.181A, repealed: 2014 c.19 Sch.13 para.44
s.182, enabling: SI 2014/540, SI 2014/1711
s.183, enabling: SI 2014/1711
s.185, applied: SI 2014/540, SI 2014/1711
s.185, repealed (in part): 2014 c.19 Sch.13
para.45
Sch.2 Part I para.1, repealed: 2014 c.19
Sch.13 para.46
Sch.2 Part I para.5, amended: 2014 c.19
Sch.13 para.46
Sch.2 Part I para.6, repealed: 2014 c.19
Sch.13 para.46
Sch.3 para.1, amended: SI 2014/3229 Sch.5
para.11
Sch.3 para.2, applied: SI 2014/3078 Art.2
Sch.3 para.2, enabling: SI 2014/3078
Sch.4 para.2, amended: 2014 c.19 Sch.13
para.47
Sch.4 para.3, amended: 2014 c.19 Sch.13
para.47
Sch.4 para.4, repealed (in part): 2014 c.19
Sch.13 para.47

49. Pension Schemes (Northern Ireland) Act 1993
s.176, amended: 2014 c.7 Sch.2 para.14

1994

9. Finance Act 1994
Part I c.II, applied: 2014 c.26 s.170, s.171
s.9, applied: 2014 c.26 s.175
s.12, amended: 2014 c.26 Sch.28 para.16
s.12, applied: 2014 c.26 s.167, s.180
s.13A, referred to: 2014 c.26 s.182
s.13A, repealed (in part): 2014 c.26 Sch.28
para.17
s.14, applied: 2014 c.26 s.182
s.15A, applied: 2014 c.26 s.172, Sch.27
para.2, Sch.27 para.4, Sch.27 para.6, Sch.27
para.7
s.15C, applied: 2014 c.26 s.172, Sch.27
para.2, Sch.27 para.4, Sch.27 para.6, Sch.27
para.7
s.16, amended: SI 2014/1264 Art.2

s.16, applied: 2014 c.26 s.172, Sch.27
para.2, Sch.27 para.4, Sch.27 para.5, Sch.27
para.6, Sch.27 para.7
s.28, see *Ryanair Ltd v Revenue and
Customs Commissioners* [2014] EWCA Civ
410, [2014] S.T.I. 1725 (CA (Civ Div)),
Lord Dyson MR
s.30, see *Ryanair Ltd v Revenue and
Customs Commissioners* [2014] EWCA Civ
410, [2014] S.T.I. 1725 (CA (Civ Div)),
Lord Dyson MR
s.30, amended: 2014 c.26 s.78, s.79
s.30, repealed (in part): 2014 c.26 s.79
s.30A, amended: 2014 c.26 s.79
s.30A, repealed (in part): 2014 c.26 s.79
s.31, see *Ryanair Ltd v Revenue and
Customs Commissioners* [2014] EWCA Civ
410, [2014] S.T.I. 1725 (CA (Civ Div)),
Lord Dyson MR
s.59G, amended: SI 2014/1264 Art.3
s.71, enabling: SI 2014/2856
Sch.5 para.2, amended: 2014 c.26 Sch.21
para.9
Sch.5 para.6, amended: 2014 c.26 Sch.28
para.18
Sch.5 para.6, repealed (in part): 2014 c.26
Sch.28 para.18
Sch.5A Part 2, repealed: 2014 c.26 s.79
Sch.5A Part 3, amended: 2014 c.26 s.80
Sch.7A Part I para.7A, added: SI 2014/2856
Art.2
Sch.7A Part II para.16A, amended: SI
2014/2856 Art.3

13. Intelligence Services Act 1994
s.5, applied: SI 2014/3103 Art.2, SI
2014/3103(1)

17. Chiropractors Act 1994
s.20, see *Professional Standards Authority v
General Chiropractic Council* [2014]
EWHC 2190 (Admin), [2014] Med. L.R.
363 (QBD (Admin)), Lang J
s.37, substituted: SI 2014/1887 Sch.1
para.10

19. Local Government (Wales) Act 1994
Sch.16 para.42, repealed (in part): SI
2014/3266 Sch.2 para.2

21. Coal Industry Act 1994
Commencement Orders: SI 2014/888 Art.2,
Sch.1
s.19, applied: SI 2014/2672 Sch.1 para.41
s.59, amended: SI 2014/892 Sch.1 para.113

s.59, repealed (in part): SI 2014/892 Sch.1
para.113
s.67, enabling: SI 2014/683
s.68, enabling: SI 2014/888

22. Vehicle Excise and Registration Act 1994
applied: 2014 c.26 Sch.18 para.12, Sch.18
para.13, Sch.18 para.15, Sch.18 para.17,
Sch.18 para.18
s.3, amended: 2014 c.26 s.87
s.4, amended: 2014 c.26 s.88, s.89
s.7, repealed (in part): 2014 c.26 Sch.19
para.2
s.7, enabling: SI 2014/2358
s.7A, amended: 2014 c.26 Sch.19 para.3
s.7A, repealed (in part): 2014 c.26 Sch.19
para.3
s.10, repealed: 2014 c.26 Sch.19 para.4
s.10, enabling: SI 2014/2358
s.11, enabling: SI 2014/2358
s.13, amended: 2014 c.26 s.89
s.13, repealed (in part): 2014 c.26 Sch.18
para.10
s.14, amended: 2014 c.26 Sch.19 para.5
s.14, repealed (in part): 2014 c.26 Sch.19
para.5
s.14, enabling: SI 2014/2358
s.15, repealed (in part): 2014 c.26 Sch.18
para.10
s.19, amended: 2014 c.26 Sch.19 para.6
s.19A, amended: 2014 c.26 s.89
s.19B, amended: 2014 c.26 s.89
s.21, applied: SI 2014/3178 Art.4
s.22, repealed (in part): 2014 c.26 Sch.19
para.7
s.22, enabling: SI 2014/2358, SI 2014/2676
s.23, enabling: SI 2014/2358
s.26, enabling: SI 2014/2358
s.27, enabling: SI 2014/2358
s.29, amended: 2014 c.26 Sch.19 para.8
s.29, repealed (in part): 2014 c.26 Sch.19
para.8
s.31, amended: 2014 c.26 Sch.19 para.9
s.31A, amended: 2014 c.26 Sch.19 para.10
s.31A, repealed (in part): 2014 c.26 Sch.19
para.10
s.31B, amended: 2014 c.26 Sch.19 para.11
s.31C, amended: 2014 c.26 Sch.19 para.12
s.33, applied: 2014 c.26 s.84
s.33, repealed: 2014 c.26 Sch.19 para.13
s.33, enabling: SI 2014/2358
s.33A, repealed: 2014 c.26 Sch.19 para.14

s.35, repealed: 2014 c.26 Sch.19 para.15
s.35A, amended: 2014 c.26 s.89, Sch.19
para.16
s.35A, repealed (in part): 2014 c.26 Sch.19
para.16
s.35A, substituted: 2014 c.26 s.89
s.36, amended: 2014 c.26 s.89, Sch.19
para.17
s.44, repealed (in part): 2014 c.26 Sch.19
para.18
s.45, amended: 2014 c.26 Sch.18 para.3
s.57, enabling: SI 2014/480, SI 2014/2116,
SI 2014/2358, SI 2014/2676
s.58, amended: 2014 c.26 Sch.19 para.19
s.60A, amended: 2014 c.26 s.90
s.61, amended: 2014 c.26 s.90
s.61B, repealed: 2014 c.26 Sch.18 para.2
s.61B, enabling: SI 2014/480, SI 2014/2116
s.62, amended: 2014 c.26 Sch.19 para.20
Sch.1 Part I para.1, amended: 2014 c.26 s.81
Sch.1 Part IA para.1B, amended: 2014 c.26
s.81
Sch.1 Part IB para.1J, amended: 2014 c.26
s.81
Sch.1 Part II para.2, amended: 2014 c.26
s.81
Sch.1 Part III para.3, amended: 2014 c.26
Sch.18 para.4
Sch.1 Part III para.3, repealed (in part): 2014
c.26 Sch.18 para.3, Sch.18 para.4
Sch.1 Part IV para.4, repealed (in part): 2014
c.26 Sch.18 para.3
Sch.1 Part V para.5, repealed (in part): 2014
c.26 Sch.18 para.3
Sch.1 Part VI para.6, amended: 2014 c.26
s.83, Sch.18 para.5
Sch.1 Part VI para.6, repealed (in part): 2014
c.26 Sch.18 para.5
Sch.1 Part VII para.7, amended: 2014 c.26
Sch.18 para.6
Sch.1 Part VII para.7, repealed (in part):
2014 c.26 Sch.18 para.3
Sch.1 Part VIII, substituted: 2014 c.26 s.83
Sch.1 Part VIII para.9, amended: 2014 c.26
s.83, Sch.18 para.10
Sch.1 Part VIII para.9, repealed (in part):
2014 c.26 Sch.18 para.10
Sch.1 Part VIII para.9A, repealed: 2014 c.26
Sch.18 para.7
Sch.1 Part VIII para.10, substituted: 2014
c.26 s.82

Sch.1 Part VIII para.11, amended: 2014 c.26
s.83, Sch.18 para.10
Sch.1 Part VIII para.11, applied: SI
2014/326 Reg.2
Sch.1 Part VIII para.11, repealed (in part):
2014 c.26 Sch.18 para.10
Sch.1 Part VIII para.11A, repealed: 2014
c.26 Sch.18 para.8
Sch.1 Part VIII para.11C, amended: 2014
c.26 s.83, Sch.18 para.9
Sch.1 Part VIII para.11C, repealed (in part):
2014 c.26 Sch.18 para.9
Sch.1 Part VIII para.11D, repealed: 2014
c.26 s.83
Sch.2 para.1A, amended: 2014 c.26 s.84,
s.85
Sch.2 para.22, amended: 2014 c.26 Sch.18
para.3
Sch.2 para.22, repealed (in part): 2014 c.26
Sch.18 para.3
Sch.2A para.1, enabling: SI 2014/2358
Sch.2A para.3, enabling: SI 2014/2358
Sch.2A para.5, enabling: SI 2014/2358
Sch.4 para.8, amended: 2014 c.26 s.89,
Sch.18 para.10

23. Value Added Tax Act 1994

see *288 Group Ltd v Revenue and Customs
Commissioners* [2014] S.F.T.D. 592 (FTT
(Tax)), Judge Barbara Mosedale; see *Bratt
Auto Services Ltd v Revenue and Customs
Commissioners* [2014] UKFTT 676 (TC),
[2014] S.F.T.D. 1120 (FTT (Tax)), Judge
Roger Berner; see *Colaingrove Ltd v
Revenue and Customs Commissioners*
[2014] UKUT 132 (TCC), [2014] S.T.C.
1457 (UT (Tax)), Rose J; see *Marlow
Gardner & Cooke Ltd Directors Pension
Scheme v Revenue and Customs
Commissioners* [2006] EWHC 1612 (Ch),
[2006] S.T.C. 2014 (Ch D), Mann J; see
*Mercedes-Benz Financial Services UK Ltd v
Revenue and Customs Commissioners*
[2014] UKUT 200 (TCC), [2014] S.T.C.
2558 (UT (Tax)), Nugee J; see *Westinsure
Group Ltd v Revenue and Customs
Commissioners* [2014] UKUT 452 (TCC),
[2014] B.V.C. 540 (UT (Tax)), Nugee J
applied: 2014 c.4 s.2, s.23
para.2, see *Marlow Gardner & Cooke Ltd
Directors Pension Scheme v Revenue and
Customs Commissioners* [2006] EWHC

1612 (Ch), [2006] S.T.C. 2014 (Ch D),
Mann J
para.3, see *Marlow Gardner & Cooke Ltd
Directors Pension Scheme v Revenue and
Customs Commissioners* [2006] EWHC
1612 (Ch), [2006] S.T.C. 2014 (Ch D),
Mann J
s.3, see *GB Housley Ltd v Revenue and
Customs Commissioners* [2014] UKUT 320
(TCC), [2014] S.T.C. 2733 (UT (Tax)),
Warren J
s.3A, amended: 2014 c.26 Sch.22 para.2,
Sch.22 para.12
s.7A, applied: 2014 c.26 s.105
s.7A, enabling: SI 2014/2726
s.9, amended: 2014 c.26 s.104
s.9A, applied: SI 2014/1458 Art.5
s.23A, amended: 2014 c.26 Sch.28 para.19
s.25, see *AR Communications & Electronics
Ltd, Petitioners* [2014] CSOH 125, 2014
S.L.T. 949 (OH), Lord Burns
s.25, enabling: SI 2014/1497
s.29A, see *Pinevale Ltd v Revenue and
Customs Commissioners* [2014] UKUT 202
(TCC), [2014] S.T.C. 2217 (UT (Tax)),
David Richards J
s.30, enabling: SI 2014/1111
s.31, enabling: SI 2014/3185
s.33, see *Currie v Revenue and Customs
Commissioners* [2014] UKFTT 882 (TC)
(FTT (Tax)), Judge Anne Redston; see
*Suffolk Constabulary v Revenue and
Customs Commissioners* [2014] UKFTT 517
(TC), [2014] S.T.I. 2162 (FTT (Tax)), Judge
John Brooks
s.33, applied: SI 2014/1112 Art.2
s.33, enabling: SI 2014/1112
s.33A, enabling: SI 2014/2858
s.35, see *Revenue and Customs
Commissioners v Patel* [2014] UKUT 361
(TCC) (UT (Tax)), Judge Colin Bishopp
s.36, enabling: SI 2014/2430
s.37, enabling: SI 2014/2364
s.39, enabling: SI 2014/2430
s.41, amended: 2014 c.26 s.107
s.43, see *Taylor Clark Leisure Plc v Revenue
and Customs Commissioners* [2014] UKUT
396 (TCC), [2014] B.V.C. 536 (UT (Tax)),
Lord Doherty

s.43B, see *Copthorn Holdings Ltd v Revenue and Customs Commissioners* [2014] S.F.T.D. 1 (FTT (Tax)), Judge John Clark
s.47, amended: 2014 c.26 s.106
s.55A, applied: SI 2014/1458 Art.3
s.55A, enabling: SI 2014/1458
s.61, see *Butt v Revenue and Customs Commissioners* [2014] UKFTT 490 (TC), [2014] S.T.I. 2097 (FTT (Tax)), Judge Jennifer Blewitt
s.76, amended: 2014 c.26 Sch.22 para.13
s.76A, added: 2014 c.26 Sch.22 para.14
s.77, amended: 2014 c.26 Sch.22 para.15
s.78, see *Littlewoods Retail Ltd v Revenue and Customs Commissioners* [2014] EWHC 868 (Ch), [2014] S.T.C. 1761 (Ch D), Henderson J
s.79, see *Our Communications Ltd v Revenue and Customs Commissioners* [2014] S.T.C. 608 (UT (Tax)), Arnold J
s.80, see *Bratt Auto Services Ltd v Revenue and Customs Commissioners* [2014] UKFTT 676 (TC), [2014] S.F.T.D. 1120 (FTT (Tax)), Judge Roger Berner; see *Isle of Wight Council v Revenue and Customs Commissioners* [2014] UKUT 446 (TCC), [2014] B.V.C. 538 (UT (Tax)), Proudman J; see *Iveco Ltd v Revenue and Customs Commissioners* [2014] S.F.T.D. 661 (FTT (Tax)), Judge Roger Berner; see *Leeds City Council v Revenue and Customs Commissioners* [2014] S.T.C. 789 (UT (Tax)), Judge Colin Bishopp; see *Littlewoods Retail Ltd v Revenue and Customs Commissioners* [2014] EWHC 868 (Ch), [2014] S.T.C. 1761 (Ch D), Henderson J; see *Taylor Clark Leisure Plc v Revenue and Customs Commissioners* [2014] UKUT 396 (TCC), [2014] B.V.C. 536 (UT (Tax)), Lord Doherty
s.80, amended: 2014 c.26 Sch.22 para.16
s.80, enabling: SI 2014/2430
s.80A, enabling: SI 2014/2430
s.81, see *Birmingham Hippodrome Theatre Trust Ltd v Revenue and Customs Commissioners* [2014] EWCA Civ 684, [2014] 1 W.L.R. 3867 (CA (Civ Div)), Lewison LJ
s.83, see *Iveco Ltd v Revenue and Customs Commissioners* [2014] S.F.T.D. 661 (FTT (Tax)), Judge Roger Berner; see *Suffolk*

Constabulary v Revenue and Customs Commissioners [2014] UKFTT 517 (TC), [2014] S.T.I. 2162 (FTT (Tax)), Judge John Brooks
s.83G, amended: SI 2014/1264 Art.4
s.84, amended: 2014 c.26 Sch.22 para.17
s.85A, see *288 Group Ltd v Revenue and Customs Commissioners* [2014] S.F.T.D. 592 (FTT (Tax)), Judge Barbara Mosedale
s.85B, see *288 Group Ltd v Revenue and Customs Commissioners* [2014] S.F.T.D. 592 (FTT (Tax)), Judge Barbara Mosedale
s.96, enabling: SI 2014/1111, SI 2014/3185
s.97A, disapplied: 2014 c.26 s.105
Sch.1 para.1, amended: SI 2014/703 Art.3
Sch.1 para.4, amended: SI 2014/703 Art.3
Sch.1 para.15, enabling: SI 2014/703
Sch.1A para.12, amended: 2014 c.26 Sch.22 para.18
Sch.3B, amended: 2014 c.26 Sch.22 para.5
Sch.3BA, added: 2014 c.26 Sch.22 para.1
Sch.3 para.1, amended: SI 2014/703 Art.4
Sch.3 para.2, amended: SI 2014/703 Art.4
Sch.3 para.9, enabling: SI 2014/703
Sch.3BA Part 2 para.5, enabling: SI 2014/2430
Sch.3BA Part 2 para.6, enabling: SI 2014/2430
Sch.3BA Part 3 para.10, enabling: SI 2014/2430
Sch.3BA Part 4 para.17, enabling: SI 2014/2430
Sch.3BA Part 4 para.19, enabling: SI 2014/2430
Sch.3BA Part 4 para.23, enabling: SI 2014/2430
Sch.3BA Part 4 para.30, enabling: SI 2014/2430
Sch.3BA Part 4 para.31, enabling: SI 2014/2430
Sch.3BA Part 4 para.32, enabling: SI 2014/2430
Sch.3B Part 1, amended: 2014 c.26 Sch.22 para.6
Sch.3B Part 1 para.2, amended: 2014 c.26 Sch.22 para.6
Sch.3B Part 1 para.3, substituted: 2014 c.26 Sch.22 para.4
Sch.3B Part 1 para.4, amended: 2014 c.26 Sch.22 para.6

Sch.3B Part 1 para.4, enabling: SI 2014/2430

Sch.3B Part 1 para.5, repealed: 2014 c.26 Sch.22 para.6

Sch.3B Part 1 para.7, amended: 2014 c.26 Sch.22 para.6

Sch.3B Part 1 para.7, repealed (in part): 2014 c.26 Sch.22 para.6

Sch.3B Part 1 para.7, enabling: SI 2014/2430

Sch.3B Part 1 para.8, amended: 2014 c.26 Sch.22 para.6

Sch.3B Part 1 para.8, repealed (in part): 2014 c.26 Sch.22 para.6

Sch.3B Part 1 para.9, repealed: 2014 c.26 Sch.22 para.6

Sch.3B Part 2, amended: 2014 c.26 Sch.22 para.7

Sch.3B Part 2 para.10, amended: 2014 c.26 Sch.22 para.7

Sch.3B Part 2 para.10, repealed (in part): 2014 c.26 Sch.22 para.7

Sch.3B Part 2 para.11, amended: 2014 c.26 Sch.22 para.7

Sch.3B Part 2 para.11, repealed (in part): 2014 c.26 Sch.22 para.7

Sch.3B Part 2 para.12, amended: 2014 c.26 Sch.22 para.7

Sch.3B Part 2 para.12, enabling: SI 2014/2430

Sch.3B Part 2 para.13, amended: 2014 c.26 Sch.22 para.7

Sch.3B Part 2 para.15, amended: 2014 c.26 Sch.22 para.7

Sch.3B Part 2 para.15A, added: 2014 c.26 Sch.22 para.7

Sch.3B Part 3, substituted: 2014 c.26 Sch.22 para.8

Sch.3B Part 3 para.16C, enabling: SI 2014/2430

Sch.3B Part 3 para.16J, enabling: SI 2014/2430

Sch.3B Part 3 para.16K, enabling: SI 2014/2430

Sch.3B Part 3 para.16L, enabling: SI 2014/2430

Sch.3B Part 4, amended: 2014 c.26 Sch.22 para.9

Sch.3B Part 4 para.17, substituted: 2014 c.26 Sch.22 para.9

Sch.3B Part 4 para.18, amended: 2014 c.26 Sch.22 para.9

Sch.3B Part 4 para.18A, added: 2014 c.26 Sch.22 para.9

Sch.3B Part 4 para.20, amended: 2014 c.26 Sch.22 para.9

Sch.3B Part 4 para.21, repealed: 2014 c.26 Sch.22 para.9

Sch.3B Part 5 para.23, amended: 2014 c.26 Sch.22 para.10

Sch.3B Part 5 para.23, repealed (in part): 2014 c.26 Sch.22 para.10

Sch.4A Part 3 para.15, substituted: SI 2014/2726 Art.3

Sch.4A Part 3 para.16, amended: SI 2014/2726 Art.4

Sch.4A Part 3 para.16, repealed (in part): SI 2014/2726 Art.4

Sch.6 Pt 2 para.2, see *Avon Cosmetics Ltd v Revenue and Customs Commissioners* [2014] UKFTT 172 (TC), [2014] S.F.T.D. 852 (FTT (Tax)), Judge Howard M Nowlan

Sch.6 Part 2 para.4, substituted: 2014 c.26 s.108

Sch.7A, see *Pinevale Ltd v Revenue and Customs Commissioners* [2014] UKUT 202 (TCC), [2014] S.T.C. 2217 (UT (Tax)), David Richards J

Sch.7A Pt II Group 2, see *Pinevale Ltd v Revenue and Customs Commissioners* [2014] UKUT 202 (TCC), [2014] S.T.C. 2217 (UT (Tax)), David Richards J

Sch.8, see *McCarthy and Stone (Developments) Ltd v Revenue and Customs Commissioners* [2014] S.F.T.D. 625 (FTT (Tax)), Judge Charles Hellier; see *Pinevale Ltd v Revenue and Customs Commissioners* [2014] UKUT 202 (TCC), [2014] S.T.C. 2217 (UT (Tax)), David Richards J; see *Roger Skinner Ltd v Revenue and Customs Commissioners* [2014] UKUT 204 (TCC), [2014] S.T.C. 2335 (UT (Tax)), Newey J

Sch.8 Part II, amended: SI 2014/1111 Art.2

Sch.8 Pt II Group 1, see *Sub One Ltd (t/a Subway) v Revenue and Customs Commissioners* [2014] EWCA Civ 773, [2014] S.T.C. 2508 (CA (Civ Div)), Rimer LJ

Sch.8 Group 5, see *Capernwray Missionary Fellowship of Torchbearers v Revenue and Customs Commissioners* [2014] UKFTT 626

(TC), [2014] S.F.T.D. 1051 (FTT (Tax)),
Judge Charles Hellier; see *Shields v
Revenue and Customs Commissioners*
[2014] UKUT 453 (TCC), [2014] B.V.C.
541 (UT (Tax)), Judge Greg Sinfield
Sch.8 Pt II Group 5, see *Colchester v
Revenue and Customs Commissioners*
[2014] UKUT 83 (TCC), [2014] S.T.C. 2078
(UT (Tax)), Judge Greg Sinfield; see
*Longridge on the Thames v Revenue and
Customs Commissioners* [2014] UKUT 504
(TCC), [2014] B.V.C. 546 (UT (Tax)), Rose
J; see *Shields v Revenue and Customs
Commissioners* [2014] UKUT 453 (TCC),
[2014] B.V.C. 541 (UT (Tax)), Judge Greg
Sinfield
Sch.8 Pt II Group 9, see *Colaingrove Ltd v
Revenue and Customs Commissioners*
[2014] UKUT 132 (TCC), [2014] S.T.C.
1457 (UT (Tax)), Rose J
Sch.9, see *McCarthy and Stone
(Developments) Ltd v Revenue and Customs
Commissioners* [2014] S.F.T.D. 625 (FTT
(Tax)), Judge Charles Hellier
Sch.9 Part II, amended: 2014 c.6 Sch.3
para.66, SI 2014/3185 Art.2
Sch.9 Part II, repealed (in part): SI
2014/3185 Art.2
Sch.9 Pt II Group 1, see *Finnamore (t/a
Hanbidge Storage Services) v Revenue and
Customs Commissioners* [2014] UKUT 336
(TCC), [2014] S.T.C. 2754 (UT (Tax)),
Warren J
Sch.9 Pt II Group 4, see *Revenue and
Customs Commissioners v Rank Group Plc*
[2013] EWCA Civ 1289, [2014] S.T.C. 470
(CA (Civ Div)), Rimer LJ
Sch.9 Group 6, see *Finance and Business
Training Ltd v Revenue and Customs
Commissioners* [2014] S.T.C. 900 (UT
(Tax)), Morgan J; see *London College of
Computing Ltd v Revenue and Customs
Commissioners* [2014] S.T.C. 404 (UT
(Tax)), Judge Colin Bishopp
Sch.9 Pt II Group 6, see *Finance and
Business Training Ltd v Revenue and
Customs Commissioners* [2014] S.T.C. 900
(UT (Tax)), Morgan J
Sch.9 Group 12, see *Loughborough
Students' Union v Revenue and Customs*

Commissioners [2014] S.T.C. 357 (UT
(Tax)), Judge Greg Sinfield
Sch.9 Pt II Group 13, see *Loughborough
Students' Union v Revenue and Customs
Commissioners* [2014] S.T.C. 357 (UT
(Tax)), Judge Greg Sinfield
Sch.11 para.2, enabling: SI 2014/548, SI
2014/1497

26. Trade Marks Act 1994
see *Iliffe News & Media Ltd v Revenue and
Customs Commissioners* [2014] F.S.R. 6
(FTT (Tax)), Judge John Walters Q.C.
s.3, see *Comic Enterprises Ltd v Twentieth
Century Fox Film Corp* [2014] EWHC 185
(Ch), [2014] E.T.M.R. 46 (Ch D), Roger
Wyand QC; see *Hendrick v Knight* [2014]
E.T.M.R. 58 (App Person), Geoffrey Hobbs
Q.C.; see *IPC Media Ltd v Media 10 Ltd*
[2013] EWHC 3796 (IPEC), [2014] F.S.R.
25 (IPEC), John Baldwin, Q.C.; see
*National Guild of Removers and Storers Ltd
v Milner (t/a Intransit Removals and
Storage)* [2014] EWHC 670 (IPEC), [2014]
F.S.R. 38 (IPEC), Judge Hacon; see *Societe
des Produits Nestle SA v Cadbury UK Ltd*
[2014] EWHC 16 (Ch), [2014] E.T.M.R. 17
(Ch D), Arnold J; see *Thomas Pink Ltd v
Victoria's Secret UK Ltd* [2014] EWHC
2631 (Ch), [2014] E.T.M.R. 57 (Ch D),
Birss J
s.5, see *Hendrick v Knight* [2014] E.T.M.R.
58 (App Person), Geoffrey Hobbs Q.C.; see
IPC Media Ltd v Media 10 Ltd [2013]
EWHC 3796 (IPEC), [2014] F.S.R. 25
(IPEC), John Baldwin, Q.C.; see *Thomas
Pink Ltd v Victoria's Secret UK Ltd* [2014]
EWHC 2631 (Ch), [2014] E.T.M.R. 57 (Ch
D), Birss J
s.10, see *Comic Enterprises Ltd v Twentieth
Century Fox Film Corp* [2014] EWHC 185
(Ch), [2014] E.T.M.R. 46 (Ch D), Roger
Wyand QC; see *Hearst Holdings Inc v
AVELA Inc* [2014] EWHC 439 (Ch), [2014]
E.T.M.R. 34 (Ch D), Birss J; see *IPC Media
Ltd v Media 10 Ltd* [2013] EWHC 3796
(IPEC), [2014] F.S.R. 25 (IPEC), John
Baldwin, Q.C.; see *Thomas Pink Ltd v
Victoria's Secret UK Ltd* [2014] EWHC
2631 (Ch), [2014] E.T.M.R. 57 (Ch D),
Birss J

s.11, see *Hearst Holdings Inc v AVELA Inc*
[2014] EWHC 439 (Ch), [2014] E.T.M.R.
34 (Ch D), Birss J
s.24, see *Iliffe News & Media Ltd v Revenue
and Customs Commissioners* [2014] F.S.R. 6
(FTT (Tax)), Judge John Walters Q.C.
s.46, see *Comic Enterprises Ltd v Twentieth
Century Fox Film Corp* [2014] EWHC 185
(Ch), [2014] E.T.M.R. 46 (Ch D), Roger
Wyand QC; see *Healey Sports Cars
Switzerland Ltd v Jensen Cars Ltd* [2014]
EWHC 24 (Pat), [2014] E.T.M.R. 18 (Ch D
(Patents Ct)), Henry Carr QC; see *Quasar
Manufacturing Ltd v Ricotti* [2014] R.P.C.
25 (App Person), Daniel Alexander QC; see
Thomas Pink Ltd v Victoria's Secret UK Ltd
[2014] EWHC 2631 (Ch), [2014] E.T.M.R.
57 (Ch D), Birss J
s.47, see *Comic Enterprises Ltd v Twentieth
Century Fox Film Corp* [2014] EWHC 185
(Ch), [2014] E.T.M.R. 46 (Ch D), Roger
Wyand QC
s.76, see *Hendrick v Knight* [2014] E.T.M.R.
58 (App Person), Geoffrey Hobbs Q.C.
s.83, applied: SI 2014/3238 Sch.4 para.8
s.83A, applied: SI 2014/3238 Art.11, Art.12,
Sch.3 para.2, Sch.3 para.5, Sch.4 para.2

33. Criminal Justice and Public Order Act 1994
s.25, referred to: SI 2014/1610 r.19_17
s.35, see *R. v D* [2013] EWCA Crim 465,
[2014] 1 W.L.R. 525 (CA (Crim Div)),
Treacy LJ
s.35, applied: SI 2014/1610 r.38_9, r.37_3
s.60, see *R. (on the application of Roberts) v
Commissioner of Police of the Metropolis*
[2014] EWCA Civ 69, [2014] 1 W.L.R.
3299 (CA (Civ Div)), Maurice Kay LJ
s.68, see *Richardson v DPP* [2014] UKSC 8,
[2014] A.C. 635 (SC), Lady Hale DPSC

37. Drug Trafficking Act 1994
see *R. (on the application of Gibson) v
Secretary of State for Justice* [2013] EWHC
2481 (Admin), [2014] 1 W.L.R. 2658 (QBD
(Admin)), Judge Gosnell; see *R. v Okedare
(Charles)* [2014] EWCA Crim 1173, [2014]
1 W.L.R. 4088 (CA (Crim Div)), Elias LJ;
see *R. v Y* [2012] EWCA Crim 2437, [2013]
1 W.L.R. 2014 (CA (Crim Div)), Sir John
Thomas PQBD
s.2, applied: SI 2014/3141 Reg.20
s.3, applied: SI 2014/1610 r.56_2

s.5, see *R. v Y* [2012] EWCA Crim 2437,
[2013] 1 W.L.R. 2014 (CA (Crim Div)), Sir
John Thomas PQBD
s.10, applied: SI 2014/1610 r.56_5
s.11, applied: SI 2014/1610 r.56_1
s.13, applied: SI 2014/1610 r.56_3
s.19, see *R. v Okedare (Charles)* [2014]
EWCA Crim 1173, [2014] 1 W.L.R. 4088
(CA (Crim Div)), Elias LJ
s.22, applied: SI 2014/1610 r.56_6
s.26, applied: SI 2014/3141 Reg.19
s.55, applied: SI 2014/1610 r.56_4
s.60, amended: SI 2014/834 Sch.2 para.9

39. Local Government etc (Scotland) Act 1994
s.2, applied: SSI 2014/296 Reg.3
s.29, applied: 2014 asp 10 Sch.1 para.13, SSI
2014/3 Art.9, Art.10
s.40, applied: SSI 2014/164 Sch.2 Part 1
s.128, applied: SSI 2014/164 Sch.2 Part 1
s.153, enabling: SSI 2014/30
Sch.13 para.95, repealed (in part): 2014 asp
3 Sch.3 para.28
Sch.13 para.152, repealed (in part): 2014 asp
14 Sch.2 para.8

40. Deregulation and Contracting Out Act 1994
s.69, enabling: SI 2014/856
s.70, applied: SI 2014/829, SI 2014/856
s.70, enabling: SI 2014/829, SI 2014/856
s.77, applied: SI 2014/829, SI 2014/856
s.77, enabling: SI 2014/829, SI 2014/856
Sch.15, applied: 2014 c.23 s.79

1995

4. Finance Act 1995
see *Stolkin v Revenue and Customs
Commissioners* [2014] UKUT 165 (TCC),
[2014] S.T.C. 2672 (UT (Tax)), David
Richards J
s.152, applied: 2014 c.26 s.114
s.152, enabling: SI 2014/1932

7. Requirements of Writing (Scotland) Act 1995
applied: 2014 c.14 s.52, s.55
s.1, see *Gyle Shopping Centre General
Partners Ltd v Marks & Spencer Plc* [2014]
CSOH 122, 2014 G.W.D. 26-527 (OH),
Lord Tyre
s.1, repealed (in part): SSI 2014/190 Art.3

s.1, see *Gyle Shopping Centre General Partners Ltd v Marks & Spencer Plc* [2014] CSOH 122, 2014 G.W.D. 26-527 (OH), Lord Tyre

s.1, applied: SSI 2014/83 Reg.2

s.9B, enabling: SSI 2014/83

s.9C, applied: SSI 2014/83 Reg.3

s.9C, enabling: SSI 2014/83

s.9E, applied: SSI 2014/347

s.9E, enabling: SSI 2014/83, SSI 2014/347

s.9G, applied: SSI 2014/347

s.9G, enabling: SSI 2014/347

Sch.4 Part 1 para.1, amended: SSI 2014/346 Art.2

Sch.4 Part 2 para.42, repealed: 2014 c.14 Sch.7

8. Agricultural Tenancies Act 1995

s.37, varied: SI 2014/2708 Art.5

12. Carers (Recognition and Services) Act 1995

s.1, applied: SI 2014/829 Sch.1 para.14

18. Jobseekers Act 1995

applied: SI 2014/1230 Reg.32

s.1, referred to: SI 2014/3117 Reg.14, SSI 2014/225 Reg.6

s.1, enabling: SI 2014/884

s.2, referred to: SI 2014/147 Sch.4 para.1

s.3, applied: SI 2014/147 Sch.1 para.1, Sch.4 para.1

s.4, referred to: SI 2014/147 Sch.4 para.1

s.4, enabling: SI 2014/902, SI 2014/2735, SI 2014/2888

s.6, enabling: SI 2014/884, SI 2014/1623

s.6H, enabling: SI 2014/597

s.6J, enabling: SI 2014/597

s.6K, enabling: SI 2014/597

s.12, enabling: SI 2014/591, SI 2014/597, SI 2014/1913, SI 2014/3117

s.16, applied: SI 2014/147 Sch.1 para.1, Sch.3 para.1, Sch.4 para.1

s.17A, see *R. (on the application of Reilly) v Secretary of State for Work and Pensions* [2014] A.C. 453 (SC), Lord Neuberger PSC

s.17A, applied: SI 2014/1913 Reg.3, SI 2014/3117 Reg.3

s.17A, enabling: SI 2014/1913, SI 2014/3117

s.19, applied: SI 2014/1230 Reg.32, Reg.33

s.19A, applied: SI 2014/1230 Reg.32

s.20E, enabling: SI 2014/1913, SI 2014/3117

s.21, enabling: SI 2014/2309

s.23, varied: SI 2014/605 Art.21

s.29, enabling: SI 2014/1913, SI 2014/3117

s.35, amended: SI 2014/560 Sch.1 para.26, SI 2014/3229 Sch.5 para.12

s.35, applied: SI 2014/3051 Reg.36

s.35, repealed (in part): SI 2014/560 Sch.1 para.26, SI 2014/3229 Sch.5 para.12

s.35, enabling: SI 2014/591, SI 2014/597, SI 2014/902, SI 2014/1623, SI 2014/1913, SI 2014/2309, SI 2014/2735, SI 2014/2888, SI 2014/3117

s.36, enabling: SI 2014/591, SI 2014/597, SI 2014/902, SI 2014/1623, SI 2014/1913, SI 2014/2309, SI 2014/2735, SI 2014/2888, SI 2014/3117

s.37, applied: SI 2014/1913, SI 2014/3117

Sch.1 para.3, enabling: SI 2014/884

Sch.1 para.4, applied: SI 2014/2309 Reg.4

Sch.1 para.4, enabling: SI 2014/2309

Sch.1 para.10, enabling: SI 2014/2309

21. Merchant Shipping Act 1995

applied: SI 2014/3102 Art.14

Part IX, applied: SI 2014/2933 Art.6, SSI 2014/224 Art.7

s.24, amended: SI 2014/1614 Reg.2

s.25, enabling: SI 2014/1614

s.26, enabling: SI 2014/1614

s.27, enabling: SI 2014/1614

s.32, amended: SI 2014/1614 Reg.2

s.32, enabling: SI 2014/1614

s.35, amended: SI 2014/1614 Reg.2

s.36, enabling: SI 2014/1614

s.47, enabling: SI 2014/1614

s.62, applied: SI 2014/1613 Reg.38, Reg.39

s.63, applied: SI 2014/1613 Reg.38

s.70, amended: SI 2014/1614 Reg.2

s.73, enabling: SI 2014/1614

s.77, enabling: SI 2014/1614

s.78, enabling: SI 2014/1614

s.85, enabling: SI 2014/308, SI 2014/1512, SI 2014/1613, SI 2014/1614, SI 2014/1616, SI 2014/3306

s.86, applied: SI 2014/1613, SI 2014/1614, SI 2014/1616, SI 2014/3306

s.86, referred to: SI 2014/1512

s.86, enabling: SI 2014/308, SI 2014/1613, SI 2014/1616, SI 2014/3306

s.128, enabling: SI 2014/3076, SI 2014/3306

s.136A, amended: 2014 asp 3 Sch.3 para.6

s.145, varied: SI 2014/1512 Reg.14, SI 2014/1613 Reg.56

s.147, enabling: SI 2014/499

s.183, applied: SI 2014/1361

s.183, enabling: SI 2014/1361

s.184, applied: SI 2014/1361

s.184, enabling: SI 2014/1361

s.185, see *Cosmotrade SA v Kairos Shipping Ltd* [2014] EWCA Civ 217, [2014] 1 W.L.R. 3883 (CA (Civ Div)), Rimer LJ

s.190, see *Owners of the Stolt Kestrel v Owners of the Niyazi S* [2014] EWHC 1731 (Admlty), [2014] 2 Lloyd's Rep. 483 (QBD (Admlty)), Hamblen J

s.205, enabling: SI 2014/527

s.252, applied: SI 2014/2935 Sch.9 para.22

s.258, varied: SI 2014/1613 Reg.54

s.259, varied: SI 2014/1613 Reg.54

s.260, varied: SI 2014/1613 Reg.54

s.261, varied: SI 2014/1613 Reg.54

s.284, applied: SI 2014/1512 Reg.14

s.284, referred to: SI 2014/1512 Reg.14, SI 2014/1613 Reg.58

s.284, varied: SI 2014/1613 Reg.58

s.306, applied: SI 2014/1614

Sch.6 Part I, substituted: SI 2014/1361 Sch.1

Sch.6 Part II para.4, amended: SI 2014/1361 Art.2

Sch.6 Part II para.9A, added: SI 2014/1361 Art.2

Sch.6 Part II para.10, enabling: SI 2014/1355

Sch.6 Part II para.11, enabling: SI 2014/1438

Sch.7 Part II para.13, enabling: SI 2014/1355

23. Goods Vehicles (Licensing of Operators) Act 1995

s.45, enabling: SI 2014/2119

s.57, applied: SI 2014/2119

s.57, enabling: SI 2014/2119

s.58, enabling: SI 2014/2119

25. Environment Act 1995

Part I, applied: SSI 2014/258 Sch.1 para.8

s.6, amended: 2014 c.21 Sch.10 para.16

s.20, applied: SSI 2014/164 Sch.2 Part 1

s.20A, added: 2014 asp 3 s.51

s.21, amended: 2014 asp 3 Sch.3 para.29

s.21, repealed (in part): 2014 asp 3 Sch.3 para.29

s.23, repealed (in part): 2014 asp 3 Sch.3 para.29

s.27, amended: 2014 asp 3 Sch.3 para.43

s.27, applied: SSI 2014/319 Sch.2 para.6

s.30, amended: 2014 asp 3 Sch.3 para.43

s.31, amended: 2014 asp 3 Sch.3 para.14

s.32, repealed (in part): 2014 asp 3 Sch.3 para.14

s.33, amended: 2014 asp 3 Sch.3 para.14

s.33, repealed (in part): 2014 asp 3 Sch.3 para.14

s.34, repealed (in part): 2014 asp 3 Sch.3 para.14

s.36, repealed (in part): 2014 asp 3 Sch.3 para.14

s.37, amended: 2014 asp 3 Sch.3 para.43

s.38, amended: 2014 asp 3 Sch.3 para.43

s.39, amended: 2014 asp 3 Sch.3 para.14

s.40, amended: 2014 asp 3 Sch.3 para.43

s.40, applied: SI 2014/861 Reg.23

s.41, amended: SI 2014/861 Reg.22

s.41, applied: SI 2014/861 Reg.23, SSI 2014/258 Sch.1 para.2, Sch.1 para.8

s.43, substituted: 2014 asp 3 Sch.3 para.43

s.48, applied: 2014 asp 6 Sch.3

s.51, amended: 2014 asp 16 Sch.4 para.2

s.53, amended: 2014 asp 3 Sch.3 para.43

s.56, amended: 2014 asp 3 Sch.3 para.5

s.56, repealed (in part): 2014 asp 3 Sch.3 para.29

s.61, see *Lake District National Park Authority v Grace (Valuation Officer)* [2014] R.A. 81 (VT), A Clark

s.63, enabling: SI 2014/571

s.81, amended: 2014 asp 3 Sch.3 para.14

s.84, amended: 2014 asp 3 s.49

s.84, repealed (in part): 2014 asp 3 s.49

s.87, amended: 2014 asp 3 Sch.3 para.43

s.91, amended: 2014 asp 3 Sch.3 para.29

s.93, applied: SI 2014/2890

s.93, referred to: SI 2014/2890

s.93, enabling: SI 2014/2890

s.94, enabling: SI 2014/2890

s.108, see *R. (on the application of Allensway Recycling Ltd) v Environment Agency* [2014] EWHC 1638 (Admin), [2014] 1 W.L.R. 3753 (QBD (Admin)), Blair J

s.108, amended: 2014 asp 3 s.46, Sch.3 para.5, Sch.3 para.43

s.108, referred to: 2014 asp 3 Sch.2 para.17, 2014 c.21 Sch.8 para.20

s.108, repealed (in part): 2014 asp 3 s.46

s.108A, added: 2014 asp 3 s.46

s.110, amended: 2014 asp 3 Sch.3 para.29

s.110, applied: SSI 2014/319 Sch.2 para.6
s.110, referred to: 2014 asp 3 Sch.3 para.30
s.113, amended: 2014 asp 3 Sch.3 para.43,
2014 asp 16 Sch.4 para.2
s.114, amended: 2014 asp 3 Sch.3 para.5
s.114, repealed (in part): 2014 asp 3 Sch.3
para.29
s.122, amended: 2014 asp 3 Sch.3 para.43
Sch.6 para.15, amended: 2014 asp 3 Sch.3
para.43
Sch.7 para.1, enabling: SI 2014/571
Sch.7 para.2, applied: SI 2014/571
Sch.7 para.2, enabling: SI 2014/571
Sch.11 para.1, amended: 2014 asp 3 Sch.3
para.29
Sch.11 para.4, amended: 2014 asp 3 Sch.3
para.29
Sch.11 para.5, amended: 2014 asp 3 Sch.3
para.43
Sch.18, see *R. (on the application of
Allensway Recycling Ltd) v Environment
Agency* [2014] EWHC 1638 (Admin),
[2014] 1 W.L.R. 3753 (QBD (Admin)), Blair
J
Sch.18 para.2, amended: 2014 asp 3 s.46
Sch.18 para.3, amended: 2014 asp 3 s.46
Sch.20 para.4, repealed (in part): 2014 asp 3
Sch.3 para.29
Sch.22 para.1, repealed (in part): 2014 asp 3
Sch.3 para.29
Sch.22 para.29, amended: 2014 asp 3 Sch.3
para.29
Sch.22 para.29, repealed (in part): 2014 asp
3 Sch.3 para.29
Sch.22 para.93, repealed (in part): 2014 asp
3 Sch.3 para.29
Sch.22 para.96, repealed (in part): 2014 asp
3 Sch.3 para.29
Sch.23 Part I para.4, repealed (in part): 2014
asp 3 Sch.3 para.29
Sch.23 Part I para.6, repealed (in part): 2014
asp 3 Sch.3 para.29
Sch.23 Part I para.8, repealed (in part): 2014
asp 3 Sch.3 para.29
Sch.23 Part I para.18, repealed (in part):
2014 asp 3 Sch.3 para.29

26. Pensions Act 1995
s.3A, added: 2014 c.19 s.46
s.4, amended: 2014 c.19 s.46
s.6, amended: 2014 c.19 Sch.19 para.2
s.7, amended: 2014 c.19 Sch.19 para.3

s.9, amended: 2014 c.19 Sch.19 para.4
s.10, applied: 2014 c.19 s.34, Sch.14
para.14, SI 2014/1711 Reg.23, Reg.46,
Reg.49
s.10, enabling: SI 2014/1711
s.29, applied: SI 2014/1711 Reg.8
s.37, applied: SI 2014/1711 Reg.37, Reg.38
s.37, referred to: SI 2014/1711 Reg.38
s.37, enabling: SI 2014/1711
s.47, applied: SI 2014/1711 Reg.40
s.47, disapplied: SI 2014/1711 Reg.40
s.47, enabling: SI 2014/540, SI 2014/1711
s.49, referred to: SSI 2014/164 Reg.67
s.49, enabling: SI 2014/3138
s.50, applied: SI 2014/2848 Reg.148,
Reg.163
s.51, amended: 2014 c.19 Sch.13 para.59
s.51, applied: SI 2014/1711 Reg.26
s.51, disapplied: SI 2014/1711 Reg.26
s.54, amended: 2014 c.19 Sch.13 para.60
s.67, see *Arcadia Group Ltd v Arcadia
Group Pension Trust Ltd* [2014] EWHC
2683 (Ch), [2014] B.T.C. 40 (Ch D), Newey
J
s.67, applied: SI 2014/1711 Reg.8
s.67, referred to: SI 2014/1711 Reg.8
s.67A, applied: 2014 c.19 Sch.14 para.3
s.67A, varied: SI 2014/1711 Reg.8, Reg.9
s.67B, referred to: SI 2014/1711 Reg.8
s.67C, applied: SI 2014/1711 Reg.8
s.69, substituted: 2014 c.19 Sch.13 para.61
s.70, repealed (in part): 2014 c.19 Sch.13
para.62
s.71, amended: 2014 c.19 Sch.13 para.63
s.72, amended: 2014 c.19 Sch.13 para.64
s.73, applied: 2014 c.19 Sch.20 para.15, SI
2014/1711 Reg.10, Reg.11, Reg.15
s.73, varied: SI 2014/1711 Reg.11, Reg.13,
Reg.14, Reg.15, Reg.16
s.73, enabling: SI 2014/1711
s.73A, applied: 2014 c.19 Sch.20 para.15
s.75, see *Storm Funding Ltd (In
Administration), Re* [2013] EWHC 4019
(Ch), [2014] Bus. L.R. 454 (Ch D
(Companies Ct)), David Richards J
s.75, applied: SI 2014/1711 Reg.19, Reg.20,
Reg.21, Reg.22, Reg.23, Reg.24, Reg.43
s.75, disapplied: SI 2014/1711 Reg.20
s.75, varied: SI 2014/1711 Reg.21, Reg.22,
Reg.24
s.75, enabling: SI 2014/1711

s.76, applied: SI 2014/1711 Reg.37

s.87, applied: SI 2014/1711 Reg.68

s.89, enabling: SI 2014/540

s.91, see *LPA Umbrella Trust, Re* [2014] EWHC 1378 (Ch), [2014] Pens. L.R. 319 (Ch D), Rose J

s.91, applied: SI 2014/512 Reg.180, Reg.195, SI 2014/1964 Reg.168, SI 2014/2848 Reg.175

s.91, disapplied: SSI 2014/217 Reg.189, SSI 2014/292 Reg.189

s.93, applied: SI 2014/2336 Reg.121

s.120, applied: SI 2014/540, SI 2014/1711, SI 2014/3138

s.124, amended: SI 2014/560 Sch.1 para.27, SI 2014/3229 Sch.5 para.13

s.124, applied: SI 2014/1964 Reg.168, SI 2014/2848 Reg.175

s.124, enabling: SI 2014/540, SI 2014/1711, SI 2014/3138

s.128, amended: 2014 c.19 Sch.12 para.72

s.136, repealed (in part): 2014 c.19 Sch.13 para.65

s.137, repealed (in part): 2014 c.19 Sch.13 para.65

s.148, repealed: 2014 c.19 Sch.13 para.65

s.174, enabling: SI 2014/540, SI 2014/1711, SI 2014/3138

Sch.4, applied: SI 2014/525 Reg.24, SSI 2014/233 Reg.24

Sch.4 Part I para.1, amended: 2014 c.19 s.26, Sch.12 para.30

Sch.4 Part II para.3, repealed (in part): 2014 c.19 Sch.12 para.73

27. Geneva Conventions (Amendment) Act 1995

referred to: SI 2014/2706 Art.2

30. Landlord and Tenant (Covenants) Act 1995

see *Pavilion Property Trustees Ltd v Permira Advisers LLP* [2014] EWHC 145 (Ch), [2014] 1 P. & C.R. 21 (Ch D), Morgan J

s.1, see *Pavilion Property Trustees Ltd v Permira Advisers LLP* [2014] EWHC 145 (Ch), [2014] 1 P. & C.R. 21 (Ch D), Morgan J

s.5, see *Pavilion Property Trustees Ltd v Permira Advisers LLP* [2014] EWHC 145 (Ch), [2014] 1 P. & C.R. 21 (Ch D), Morgan J

s.11, see *Pavilion Property Trustees Ltd v Permira Advisers LLP* [2014] EWHC 145 (Ch), [2014] 1 P. & C.R. 21 (Ch D), Morgan J

s.19, see *Schroder Exempt Property Unit Trust v Birmingham City Council* [2014] EWHC 2207 (Admin), [2014] B.C.C. 690 (QBD (Admin)), Hickinbottom J

s.24, see *Pavilion Property Trustees Ltd v Permira Advisers LLP* [2014] EWHC 145 (Ch), [2014] 1 P. & C.R. 21 (Ch D), Morgan J

s.25, see *Pavilion Property Trustees Ltd v Permira Advisers LLP* [2014] EWHC 145 (Ch), [2014] 1 P. & C.R. 21 (Ch D), Morgan J

35. Criminal Appeal Act 1995

s.9, applied: SI 2014/1610 r.68_1

s.11, applied: SI 2014/1610 r.63_1

s.13, applied: SI 2014/1610 r.63_1, r.68_1

s.22, amended: 2014 c.20 s.44

s.22, repealed (in part): SI 2014/834 Sch.2 para.10

36. Children (Scotland) Act 1995

applied: SSI 2014/193 Art.3, SSI 2014/360 Art.2

Part I, referred to: 2014 asp 8 s.70

Part II, applied: 2014 asp 8 s.37

Part II c.1, applied: 2014 asp 8 s.37

s.1, see *Midlothian Council v M* 2014 S.C. 168 (IH (Ex Div)), Lord Clarke

s.2, see *Midlothian Council v M* 2014 S.C. 168 (IH (Ex Div)), Lord Clarke

s.7, applied: 2014 asp 8 s.71

s.17, applied: SSI 2014/116 Art.1

s.17, referred to: 2014 asp 9 Sch.1 Part 1

s.17, enabling: SSI 2014/310

s.19, referred to: 2014 asp 9 Sch.1 Part 1

s.19, repealed: 2014 asp 8 Sch.5 para.4

s.22, applied: 2014 asp 8 s.68, SSI 2014/25 Reg.3A, SSI 2014/32 Art.4, SSI 2014/65 Reg.3

s.23A, added: 2014 asp 8 s.95

s.26A, added: 2014 asp 8 s.67

s.27, amended: 2014 asp 8 s.55

s.29, amended: 2014 asp 8 s.66, s.67

s.29, referred to: 2014 asp 9 Sch.1 Part 1

s.30, amended: 2014 asp 8 s.66

s.30, repealed (in part): 2014 asp 8 s.66

s.36, referred to: 2014 asp 9 Sch.1 Part 1

s.38, referred to: 2014 asp 9 Sch.1 Part 1

s.44, amended: 2014 asp 8 Sch.5 para.4
s.44, repealed (in part): 2014 asp 8 Sch.5
para.4
s.51, see *Contempt of court proceedings in respect of M and L* 2014 S.L.T. (Sh Ct) 21
(Sh Ct (Lothian) (Edinburgh)), Sheriff K E C
Mackie; see *D, Appellant* 2014 Fam. L.R.
66 (Sh Ct (Tayside) (Falkirk)), Sheriff K J
McGowan
s.52, see *D, Appellant* 2014 Fam. L.R. 66
(Sh Ct (Tayside) (Falkirk)), Sheriff K J
McGowan; see *S v Locality Reporter Manager* [2014] CSIH 70, 2014 Fam. L.R.
109 (IH (Ex Div)), Lady Smith
s.70, see *Contempt of court proceedings in respect of M and L* 2014 S.L.T. (Sh Ct) 21
(Sh Ct (Lothian) (Edinburgh)), Sheriff K E C
Mackie
s.76, referred to: 2014 asp 9 Sch.1 Part 1
s.93, applied: 2014 asp 8 s.37
s.103, enabling: SSI 2014/310

38. Civil Evidence Act 1995
applied: SI 2014/1610 r.62_11
s.1, applied: SI 2014/1610 r.50_1
s.1, referred to: SI 2014/1610 r.62_11,
r.50_1
s.2, applied: SI 2014/1610 r.62_11, r.50_6
s.2, disapplied: SI 2014/1610 r.61_8
s.3, applied: SI 2014/1610 r.50_7, r.62_14
s.5, applied: SI 2014/1610 r.50_8, r.62_15
s.6, applied: SI 2014/1610 r.50_8, r.62_15
s.13, referred to: SI 2014/1610 r.62_11,
r.50_1

39. Criminal Law (Consolidation) (Scotland) Act 1995
Part II, applied: SSI 2014/5 Art.2
s.18, enabling: SSI 2014/5, SSI 2014/374
s.27, applied: SI 2014/2418 Sch.1
s.44, applied: 2014 c.4 s.10
s.47, see *Smith v Shanks* [2014] HCJAC 25,
2014 S.L.T. 626 (HCJ), Lady Smith
s.49, see *Hill (Brian) v HM Advocate* [2014]
HCJAC 117, 2014 S.L.T. 1061 (HCJ), The
Lord Justice Clerk (Carloway); see *HM Advocate v Small (Darren)* 2014 S.L.T. (Sh
Ct) 49 (Sh Ct (Tayside) (Dundee)), Sheriff K
J McGowan; see *Whitham (James) v HM Advocate* 2014 S.L.T. 51 (HCJ), Lady Paton

42. Private International Law (Miscellaneous Provisions) Act 1995
s.9, see *Cox v Ergo Versicherung AG
(formerly Victoria)* [2014] UKSC 22, [2014]
A.C. 1379 (SC), Lord Neuberger PSC
s.11, see *Cox v Ergo Versicherung AG
(formerly Victoria)* [2014] UKSC 22, [2014]
A.C. 1379 (SC), Lord Neuberger PSC
s.12, see *Cox v Ergo Versicherung AG
(formerly Victoria)* [2014] UKSC 22, [2014]
A.C. 1379 (SC), Lord Neuberger PSC
s.14, see *Cox v Ergo Versicherung AG
(formerly Victoria)* [2014] UKSC 22, [2014]
A.C. 1379 (SC), Lord Neuberger PSC
s.15, see *Cox v Ergo Versicherung AG
(formerly Victoria)* [2014] UKSC 22, [2014]
A.C. 1379 (SC), Lord Neuberger PSC

43. Proceeds of Crime (Scotland) Act 1995
s.1, applied: SI 2014/3141 Reg.22
s.28, applied: SI 2014/3141 Reg.21

45. Gas Act 1995
Sch.5 Part II para.17, enabling: SI 2014/528

46. Criminal Procedure (Scotland) Act 1995
see *Griffith (Javaughn) v HM Advocate* 2014
J.C. 141 (HCJ), Lord Eassie; see *Menni
(Nasserdine) v HM Advocate* [2014] HCJAC
54, 2014 J.C. 258 (HCJ), The Lord Justice
General (Gill)
applied: 2014 asp 8 s.37, 2014 asp 18 s.45
referred to: 2014 asp 18 s.118
Part XZA, added: 2014 asp 18 s.119
s.6, amended: 2014 asp 18 Sch.5 para.39
s.7, repealed (in part): 2014 asp 18 Sch.5
para.39
s.14, see *HM Advocate v Sinclair (Angus
Robertson)* [2014] HCJAC 131, 2014 S.L.T.
1092 (HCJ), The Lord Justice Clerk
(Carloway); see *L v HM Advocate* [2014]
HCJAC 35, 2014 J.C. 199 (HCJ), Lord
Brodie; see *Sabiu v Wyllie* 2014 S.C.C.R. 59
(HCJ), The Lord Justice Clerk (Carloway)
s.14, applied: SSI 2014/159 Reg.2
s.19A, see *HM Advocate v Sinclair (Angus
Robertson)* [2014] HCJAC 131, 2014 S.L.T.
1092 (HCJ), The Lord Justice Clerk
(Carloway)
s.19AA, amended: 2014 c.12 Sch.11 para.51
s.19AB, amended: 2014 c.12 Sch.11 para.52
s.19C, see *HM Advocate v Sinclair (Angus
Robertson)* [2014] HCJAC 131, 2014 S.L.T.

1092 (HCJ), The Lord Justice Clerk
(Carloway)
s.24, applied: SSI 2014/337 Sch.1 para.1,
Sch.2 para.8
s.30, applied: SSI 2014/337 Sch.1 para.5
s.32, amended: 2014 asp 18 s.122
s.41, referred to: SSI 2014/337 Sch.2 para.7
s.43, applied: SSI 2014/337 Sch.2 para.16
s.44, amended: 2014 asp 8 Sch.5 para.5
s.44A, added: 2014 asp 8 s.91
s.47, amended: 2014 asp 1 s.15
s.50, applied: 2014 asp 18 Sch.2 para.2
s.51, applied: SSI 2014/337 Sch.2 para.18
s.51, referred to: 2014 asp 9 Sch.1 Part 1
s.57A, amended: 2014 asp 8 Sch.5 para.5
s.62, see *Speirs (Allan) v HM Advocate* 2014
S.C.L. 58 (HCJ), The Lord Justice Clerk
(Carloway)
s.65, see *Akhtar v Murphy* [2014] HCJAC
80, 2014 S.L.T. 923 (HCJ), Lord Eassie; see
Collins (Kenneth) v HM Advocate 2014
S.L.T. 704 (HCJ), Lord Eassie; see *HM
Advocate v Thomson (Stuart Rae)* [2014]
HCJ 107, 2014 S.C.L. 825 (HCJ), Lord
Turnbull; see *M v HM Advocate* [2014]
HCJAC 91, 2014 S.C.L. 695 (HCJ), Lady
Paton
s.66, see *Newlands (John) v HM Advocate*
2014 J.C. 183 (HCJ), Lady Smith
s.70, applied: SI 2014/195 Reg.15, SI
2014/3085 Reg.23
s.71, see *HM Advocate v Small (Darren)*
2014 S.L.T. (Sh Ct) 49 (Sh Ct (Tayside)
(Dundee)), Sheriff K J McGowan
s.71, amended: 2014 asp 1 s.11
s.72, amended: 2014 asp 1 s.11
s.76, see *HM Advocate v McAllister (Jason)*
[2014] HCJ 111, 2014 S.L.T. 1023 (HCJ),
Lord Boyd of Duncansby
s.76, applied: 2014 asp 18 s.45
s.79, see *Blance (Andrew) v HM Advocate*
2014 S.C.L. 13 (HCJ), Lady Smith; see *HM
Advocate v McCrossan (Darryl)* 2014 J.C.
161 (HCJ), Lady Paton
s.85, amended: 2014 asp 18 Sch.5 para.44
s.96, see *Kilpatrick (William James) v HM
Advocate* [2014] HCJAC 73, 2014 S.C.C.R.
509 (HCJ), The Lord Justice Clerk
(Carloway)
s.97, see *Lauchlan (William Hugh) v HM
Advocate* [2014] HCJAC 62, 2014 S.L.T.

813 (HCJ), The Lord Justice Clerk
(Carloway)
s.106, see *Young (Thomas Ross) v HM
Advocate* [2014] HCJAC 113, 2014 S.L.T.
1037 (HCJ), Lord Eassie
s.108, amended: 2014 asp 3 s.44
s.136, applied: SI 2014/195 Reg.13, SI
2014/507 Reg.13, SI 2014/587 Reg.13, SI
2014/1826 Reg.13, SI 2014/1827 Reg.13, SI
2014/2054 Reg.7, SI 2014/3349 Reg.13
s.136, disapplied: SI 2014/1615 Reg.9
s.143, applied: SI 2014/195 Reg.15, SI
2014/3085 Reg.23
s.148, amended: SSI 2014/242 r.2
s.160, see *Kalyanjee (Ashok) v HM Advocate*
[2014] HCJAC 44, 2014 J.C. 233 (HCJ),
The Lord Justice Clerk (Carloway)
s.173, amended: 2014 asp 18 Sch.3 para.2
s.174, amended: 2014 asp 18 Sch.3 para.3
s.175, amended: 2014 asp 3 s.44, 2014 asp
18 Sch.3 para.4
s.175A, added: 2014 asp 18 s.120
s.176, amended: 2014 asp 18 Sch.3 para.5
s.177, amended: 2014 asp 18 Sch.3 para.6
s.178, amended: 2014 asp 18 Sch.3 para.7
s.179, amended: 2014 asp 18 Sch.3 para.8
s.180, amended: 2014 asp 18 Sch.3 para.9
s.181, amended: 2014 asp 18 Sch.3 para.10
s.182, amended: 2014 asp 18 Sch.3 para.11
s.183, amended: 2014 asp 18 Sch.3 para.12
s.184, amended: 2014 asp 18 Sch.3 para.13
s.185, amended: 2014 asp 18 Sch.3 para.14
s.186, amended: 2014 asp 18 Sch.3 para.15
s.187, amended: 2014 asp 18 Sch.3 para.16
s.188, amended: 2014 asp 18 Sch.3 para.17
s.189, amended: 2014 asp 18 Sch.3 para.18
s.190, amended: 2014 asp 18 Sch.3 para.19
s.191, amended: 2014 asp 18 Sch.3 para.20,
Sch.3 para.21
s.191A, amended: 2014 asp 18 Sch.3 para.21
s.191B, amended: 2014 asp 18 Sch.3 para.22
s.192, amended: 2014 asp 18 Sch.3 para.23
s.193A, amended: 2014 asp 18 Sch.3 para.24
s.194B, amended: 2014 asp 18 s.121
s.194C, see *Carberry (Frank) v HM
Advocate* 2014 J.C. 56 (HCJ), The Lord
Justice Clerk (Carloway)
s.194ZA, repealed: 2014 asp 18 Sch.3
para.25

s.195, see *O'Leary (Thomas) v HM Advocate*
[2014] HCJAC 45, 2014 S.L.T. 711 (HCJ),
The Lord Justice Clerk (Carloway)
s.203, referred to: 2014 asp 9 Sch.1 Part 1
s.204, see *Hughes (Barry) v HM Advocate*
[2014] HCJAC 74, 2014 S.C.C.R. 506
(HCJ), The Lord Justice Clerk (Carloway)
s.207, see *Muirhead (Warren) v HM
Advocate* [2014] HCJAC 90, 2014 S.C.L.
702 (HCJ), Lady Paton
s.209, see *Hughes (Christopher) v HM
Advocate* [2014] HCJAC 18, 2014 S.C.L.
363 (HCJ), Lady Clark of Calton
s.210, amended: 2014 c.12 s.172
s.210, repealed (in part): 2014 c.12 s.172
s.210A, see *Dutch v Parole Board for
Scotland* 2014 S.L.T. 285 (OH), Lord Burns
s.210A, applied: 2014 asp 14 s.34
s.210B, see *Ferguson (James Douglas) v
HM Advocate* [2014] HCJAC 19, 2014
S.L.T. 431 (HCJ), The Lord Justice Clerk
(Carloway)
s.210C, see *O'Leary (Thomas) v HM
Advocate* [2014] HCJAC 45, 2014 S.L.T.
711 (HCJ), The Lord Justice Clerk
(Carloway)
s.210E, see *Ferguson (James Douglas) v
HM Advocate* [2014] HCJAC 19, 2014
S.L.T. 431 (HCJ), The Lord Justice Clerk
(Carloway); see *O'Leary (Thomas) v HM
Advocate* [2014] HCJAC 45, 2014 S.L.T.
711 (HCJ), The Lord Justice Clerk
(Carloway)
s.210F, see *Ferguson (James Douglas) v HM
Advocate* [2014] HCJAC 19, 2014 S.L.T.
431 (HCJ), The Lord Justice Clerk
(Carloway)
s.223E, amended: SSI 2014/322 Art.3
s.223FA, added: SSI 2014/322 Art.4
s.223G, repealed: SSI 2014/322 Art.5
s.223H, amended: SSI 2014/322 Art.6, SSI
2014/336 Art.3
s.223H, repealed (in part): SSI 2014/322
Art.6
s.223I, amended: SSI 2014/322 Art.7
s.223T, amended: SSI 2014/336 Art.4
s.227, applied: SI 2014/2871 Sch.1
s.227ZC, see *Murphy v Cameron* 2014
S.L.T. (Sh Ct) 90 (Sh Ct (Grampian)
(Peterhead)), Sheriff P Mann

s.227ZD, see *Murphy v Cameron* 2014
S.L.T. (Sh Ct) 90 (Sh Ct (Grampian)
(Peterhead)), Sheriff P Mann
s.234B, applied: SI 2014/2871 Sch.1
s.234B, referred to: 2014 asp 9 Sch.1 Part 1
s.245A, see *Whitham (James) v HM
Advocate* 2014 S.L.T. 51 (HCJ), Lady Paton
s.245A, referred to: 2014 asp 9 Sch.1 Part 1
s.245A, repealed (in part): 2014 asp 18 Sch.5
para.39
s.246, see *HM Advocate v H* [2014] HCJAC
36, 2014 J.C. 195 (HCJ), The Lord Justice
Clerk (Carloway)
s.247, see *HM Advocate v H* [2014] HCJAC
36, 2014 J.C. 195 (HCJ), The Lord Justice
Clerk (Carloway)
s.248C, amended: 2014 asp 18 Sch.5 para.39
s.249, amended: 2014 asp 1 s.24, 2014 asp 3
Sch.3 para.12, 2014 asp 18 Sch.5 para.39
s.249, varied: 2014 asp 3 s.34
s.253A, added: 2014 asp 1 s.25
s.253F, added: 2014 asp 1 s.26
s.253G, added: 2014 asp 1 s.26
s.253H, added: 2014 asp 1 s.26
s.260, see *Croal (Brian) v HM Advocate*
[2014] HCJAC 34, 2014 S.C.L. 423 (HCJ),
The Lord Justice Clerk (Carloway); see
Matulewicz v Brown [2014] HCJAC 7, 2014
S.C.C.R. 154 (HCJ), Lord Drummond
Young
s.266, see *Griffith (Javaughn) v HM
Advocate* 2014 J.C. 141 (HCJ), Lord Eassie;
see *Griffith (Javaughn) v HM Advocate*
2014 S.C.L. 39 (HCJ), Lord Eassie
s.268, see *Webster (Malcolm John) v HM
Advocate* 2014 S.C.L. 256 (HCJ), Lord
Eassie
s.271, amended: 2014 asp 1 s.10, s.11
s.271, repealed (in part): 2014 asp 1 s.10
s.271A, amended: 2014 asp 1 s.11, s.12,
s.13, s.14
s.271B, amended: 2014 asp 1 s.14
s.271BA, added: 2014 asp 1 s.16
s.271C, amended: 2014 asp 1 s.11, s.16, s.17
s.271D, amended: 2014 asp 1 s.14, s.18
s.271E, amended: 2014 asp 1 s.11
s.271F, amended: 2014 asp 1 s.11, s.20
s.271H, amended: 2014 asp 1 s.20, s.21
s.271H, repealed (in part): 2014 asp 1 s.21
s.271HA, added: 2014 asp 1 s.19
s.271HB, added: 2014 asp 1 s.20

s.271R, see *Griffiths v R* 2014 S.C.L. 61 (Sh
Ct (Tayside) (Dundee)), Sheriff A N Brown
s.274, see *Branney (Leslie McPherson) v
HM Advocate* [2014] HCJAC 78, 2014
S.C.L. 728 (HCJ), Lady Smith
s.275, see *HM Advocate v W* [2014] HCJAC
47, 2014 S.C.C.R. 361 (HCJ), The Lord
Justice Clerk (Carloway)
s.277, amended: 2014 asp 3 Sch.3 para.31
s.280, amended: 2014 asp 3 Sch.3 para.31
s.288E, amended: 2014 asp 1 s.11
s.288ZB, see *O'Leary (Thomas) v HM
Advocate* [2014] HCJAC 45, 2014 S.L.T.
711 (HCJ), The Lord Justice Clerk
(Carloway)
s.293, applied: SSI 2014/319 Sch.1 para.4,
Sch.2 para.7, Sch.3 para.4, Sch.4 para.4
s.299, see *Murphy v B* [2014] HCJAC 82,
2014 S.C.L. 648 (HCJ), Lord Brodie
s.300A, see *Newlands (John) v HM
Advocate* 2014 J.C. 183 (HCJ), Lady Smith
s.302, applied: 2014 asp 3 s.22, s.25, s.27,
s.28
s.302A, applied: 2014 asp 3 s.22, s.25, s.27,
s.28
s.302B, applied: 2014 asp 3 s.22, s.25, s.27,
s.28
s.302ZA, applied: 2014 asp 3 s.22, s.25,
s.27, s.28
s.303ZA, applied: 2014 asp 3 s.28
s.304, amended: 2014 asp 18 Sch.5 para.15
s.304, applied: 2014 asp 18 Sch.2 para.2
s.305, enabling: SSI 2014/162, SSI
2014/242, SSI 2014/349
s.307, amended: 2014 asp 18 Sch.3 para.26,
Sch.5 para.39
Sch.1, see *S v Locality Reporter Manager*
[2014] CSIH 70, 2014 Fam. L.R. 109 (IH
(Ex Div)), Lady Smith
Sch.9, amended: 2014 asp 3 Sch.3 para.31
Sch.12 Part I para.4, amended: SSI 2014/322
Art.8
Sch.12 Part I para.5A, added: SSI 2014/322
Art.8
Sch.12 Part I para.6, substituted: SSI
2014/336 Art.5
Sch.12 Part III para.47, amended: SSI
2014/322 Art.8

50. Disability Discrimination Act 1995
see *Finnigan v Chief Constable of
Northumbria* [2013] EWCA Civ 1191,

[2014] 1 W.L.R. 445 (CA (Civ Div)), Lord
Dyson MR; see *Gallop v Newport City
Council* [2013] EWCA Civ 1583, [2014]
I.R.L.R. 211 (CA (Civ Div)), Longmore LJ;
see *Secretary of State for Work and
Pensions v Higgins* [2014] I.C.R. 341
(EAT), Judge David Richardson
Part VA, applied: SI 2014/466 Sch.1, SI
2014/3310 Sch.1, SI 2014/3311 Sch.1
s.1, see *Gallop v Newport City Council*
[2013] EWCA Civ 1583, [2014] I.R.L.R.
211 (CA (Civ Div)), Longmore LJ
s.3B, see *Environment Agency v Donnelly*
[2014] Eq. L.R. 13 (EAT), Judge J Burke
Q.C.
s.21B, see *Finnigan v Chief Constable of
Northumbria* [2013] EWCA Civ 1191,
[2014] 1 W.L.R. 445 (CA (Civ Div)), Lord
Dyson MR
s.21E, see *Finnigan v Chief Constable of
Northumbria* [2013] EWCA Civ 1191,
[2014] 1 W.L.R. 445 (CA (Civ Div)), Lord
Dyson MR
s.49A, see *Huzrat v Hounslow LBC* [2013]
EWCA Civ 1865, [2014] H.L.R. 17 (CA
(Civ Div)), Moses LJ
Sch.1, see *Gallop v Newport City Council*
[2013] EWCA Civ 1583, [2014] I.R.L.R.
211 (CA (Civ Div)), Longmore LJ

1996

6. Chemical Weapons Act 1996
s.30A, amended: SI 2014/834 Sch.2 para.11
8. Finance Act 1996
see *Greene King Plc v Revenue and Customs
Commissioners* [2014] UKUT 178 (TCC),
[2014] S.T.C. 2439 (UT (Tax)), Mann J
Pt IV., see *Versteegh Ltd v Revenue and
Customs Commissioners* [2014] S.F.T.D.
547 (FTT (Tax)), Judge Roger Berner
s.40, see *Patersons of Greenoakhill Ltd v
Revenue and Customs Commissioners*
[2014] UKUT 225 (TCC), [2014] S.T.C.
2178 (UT (Tax)), Rose J
s.40, amended: 2014 c.29 s.19
s.42, amended: 2014 c.26 s.100
s.51, enabling: SI 2014/707
s.53, enabling: SI 2014/707
s.54G, amended: SI 2014/1264 Art.5

s.64, see *Patersons of Greenoakhill Ltd v
Revenue and Customs Commissioners*
[2014] UKUT 225 (TCC), [2014] S.T.C.
2178 (UT (Tax)), Rose J
s.80, see *Shop Direct Group v Revenue and
Customs Commissioners* [2014] EWCA Civ
255, [2014] S.T.C. 1383 (CA (Civ Div)),
Rimer LJ; see *Versteegh Ltd v Revenue and
Customs Commissioners* [2014] S.F.T.D.
547 (FTT (Tax)), Judge Roger Berner
s.84, see *Vocalspruce Ltd v Revenue and
Customs Commissioners* [2014] EWCA Civ
1302, [2014] B.T.C. 50 (CA (Civ Div)),
Gross LJ
s.85, see *Versteegh Ltd v Revenue and
Customs Commissioners* [2014] S.F.T.D.
547 (FTT (Tax)), Judge Roger Berner
s.100, see *Shop Direct Group v Revenue and
Customs Commissioners* [2014] EWCA Civ
255, [2014] S.T.C. 1383 (CA (Civ Div)),
Rimer LJ
Sch.9 para.12, see *Vocalspruce Ltd v
Revenue and Customs Commissioners*
[2014] EWCA Civ 1302, [2014] B.T.C. 50
(CA (Civ Div)), Gross LJ
Sch.9 para.13, see *Iliffe News & Media Ltd v
Revenue and Customs Commissioners*
[2014] F.S.R. 6 (FTT (Tax)), Judge John
Walters Q.C.; see *Versteegh Ltd v Revenue
and Customs Commissioners* [2014]
S.F.T.D. 547 (FTT (Tax)), Judge Roger
Berner
Sch.13, see *Pike v Revenue and Customs
Commissioners* [2014] EWCA Civ 824,
[2014] S.T.C. 2549 (CA (Civ Div)), Rimer
LJ
Sch.13 para.3, see *Pike v Revenue and
Customs Commissioners* [2014] EWCA Civ
824, [2014] S.T.C. 2549 (CA (Civ Div)),
Rimer LJ

14. Reserve Forces Act 1996
applied: SI 2014/512 Reg.26, SI 2014/1964
Reg.27, SSI 2014/217 Reg.25, SSI 2014/292
Reg.25
Part I, applied: 2014 c.5 Sch.2 para.1, Sch.3
para.1, 2014 c.25 Sch.1
Part III, applied: 2014 c.5 Sch.2 para.1,
Sch.3 para.1, 2014 c.25 Sch.1
Part VIII, amended: 2014 c.20 Sch.7 para.2
s.1, amended: 2014 c.20 s.44
s.1, referred to: SI 2014/3352 Sch.2 para.30

s.2, amended: 2014 c.20 s.44
s.12, amended: 2014 c.20 s.44
s.20, amended: 2014 c.20 s.44
s.28, amended: 2014 c.20 s.45
s.53, applied: SI 2014/2410 Reg.2
s.54, amended: 2014 c.20 s.45
s.55, applied: SI 2014/2410 Reg.2
s.56, amended: 2014 c.20 s.45
s.57, amended: 2014 c.20 s.45
s.57, applied: SI 2014/2410 Reg.2
s.57A, amended: 2014 c.20 s.45
s.61, applied: SI 2014/2410 Reg.2
s.64, substituted: 2014 c.20 s.45
s.83, amended: 2014 c.20 Sch.7 para.3
s.84, amended: 2014 c.20 Sch.7 para.3
s.84A, added: 2014 c.20 s.46
s.84A, enabling: SI 2014/2410
s.85, amended: 2014 c.20 Sch.7 para.4,
Sch.7 para.5
s.85, applied: SI 2014/2410
s.86, amended: 2014 c.20 Sch.7 para.6
s.87, amended: 2014 c.20 Sch.7 para.7
s.89, amended: 2014 c.20 Sch.7 para.8
s.110, applied: SI 2014/531 Sch.1
s.113, amended: 2014 c.20 s.44
s.113A, added: 2014 c.20 s.47
s.129, amended: 2014 c.20 Sch.6 para.2,
Sch.6 para.3
s.132, applied: 2014 c.20 s.49
Sch.9, amended: 2014 c.20 Sch.6 para.5
Sch.9 Part I, amended: 2014 c.20 Sch.6
para.4
Sch.9 Part I para.1, amended: 2014 c.20
Sch.6 para.4
Sch.9 Part I para.4, amended: 2014 c.20
Sch.6 para.4
Sch.9 Part II, amended: 2014 c.20 Sch.6
para.4
Sch.9 Part II para.6, amended: 2014 c.20
Sch.6 para.4
Sch.9 Part II para.12A, added: 2014 c.20
Sch.6 para.4
Sch.9 Part II para.19, amended: 2014 c.20
Sch.7 para.9
Sch.9 Part III, added: 2014 c.20 Sch.6 para.4
Sch.10 para.19, amended: 2014 c.20 s.44

**15. National Health Service (Residual
Liabilities) Act 1996**
s.2, amended: 2014 asp 9 s.64

16. Police Act 1996
Part IIIA, added: 2014 c.12 s.132

Pt I s.25, see *Leeds United Football Club Ltd
v Chief Constable of West Yorkshire* [2013]
EWCA Civ 115, [2014] Q.B. 168 (CA (Civ
Div)), Lord Dyson MR
s.2, applied: SI 2014/1638 Reg.13, SI
2014/2418 Sch.1
s.36, amended: 2014 c.12 Sch.11 para.87
s.39A, amended: 2014 c.12 s.124
s.40C, added: 2014 c.12 s.126
s.46, amended: 2014 c.12 s.142
s.47, amended: 2014 c.12 s.142
s.50, amended: 2014 c.12 s.123
s.50, applied: SI 2014/2372, SI 2014/2373
s.50, enabling: SI 2014/2372, SI 2014/2373,
SI 2014/2403, SI 2014/3347
s.51, amended: 2014 c.12 s.123
s.51, enabling: SI 2014/2403, SI 2014/3347
s.52, amended: 2014 c.12 s.133
s.52A, added: 2014 c.12 s.133
s.53, applied: SI 2014/395
s.53, enabling: SI 2014/395
s.53A, amended: 2014 c.12 s.123
s.53A, repealed (in part): 2014 c.12 s.123
s.53E, added: 2014 c.12 s.125
s.61, applied: 2014 c.12 s.131
s.61, repealed (in part): 2014 c.12 s.131
s.63, amended: 2014 c.12 s.123, s.133
s.63, applied: SI 2014/2403, SI 2014/2406,
SI 2014/3347
s.84, enabling: SI 2014/2403
s.92, amended: 2014 c.12 s.142
s.93, see *R. v Zinga (Munaf Ahmed)* [2014]
EWCA Crim 52, [2014] 1 W.L.R. 2228 (CA
(Crim Div)), Lord Thomas LCJ
s.95A, added: 2014 c.12 s.127
s.97, amended: 2014 c.12 Sch.11 para.88
s.100A, added: 2014 c.12 s.128
s.100B, added: 2014 c.12 s.129
s.101, referred to: SI 2014/2936 Sch.2 para.6
s.105, amended: 2014 c.12 Sch.11 para.89
Sch.4B, added: 2014 c.12 Sch.7
Sch.4A para.2, repealed (in part): 2014 c.2
Sch.12 para.31
Sch.4A para.3, repealed (in part): 2014 c.2
Sch.12 para.31
Sch.4A para.4, repealed (in part): 2014 c.2
Sch.12 para.31
Sch.4A para.6, amended: 2014 c.2 Sch.12
para.31
Sch.7 Part II para.28, repealed: 2014 c.12
Sch.11 para.102

17. Employment Tribunals Act 1996
see *Ladak v DRC Locums Ltd* [2014]
I.R.L.R. 851 (EAT), Judge David
Richardson
applied: SI 2014/1139 Reg.4
s.7, enabling: SI 2014/271, SI 2014/611, SI
2014/787
s.18, amended: SI 2014/308 Sch.1 para.1, SI
2014/431 Art.2
s.18, applied: SI 2014/253 Art.5
s.18, enabling: SI 2014/431
s.18A, applied: SI 2014/254 Reg.3, SI
2014/271 Reg.11, SI 2014/853 Art.3
s.18A, enabling: SI 2014/254, SI 2014/847
s.21, amended: SI 2014/308 Sch.1 para.1
s.41, enabling: SI 2014/254, SI 2014/271, SI
2014/431, SI 2014/611, SI 2014/787, SI
2014/847

18. Employment Rights Act 1996
see *Benkharbouche v Embassy of Sudan*
[2014] 1 C.M.L.R. 40 (EAT), Langstaff J;
see *Powell v OMV Exploration &
Production Ltd* [2014] I.C.R. 63 (EAT),
Langstaff J; see *R. (on the application of
United Road Transport Union) v Secretary
of State for Transport* [2013] EWCA Civ
962, [2014] R.T.R. 9 (CA (Civ Div)),
Jackson LJ
applied: SI 2014/1139 Reg.4, SI 2014/3050
Reg.45, SI 2014/3051 Reg.4, Reg.5, Reg.17,
Reg.18, Reg.32
referred to: 2014 c.6 s.134
Part VIII, applied: SI 2014/512 Reg.189, SI
2014/3050 Reg.7, Reg.23, Reg.41, SSI
2014/217 Reg.183, SSI 2014/292 Reg.183
Part VIII c.IB, added: 2014 c.6 s.117
Part VIII c.IB, referred to: SI 2014/3092
Reg.3
Part X, applied: SI 2014/254 Reg.3, SI
2014/1139 Reg.4, SI 2014/3050 Reg.42,
Reg.43
Part XIV c.II, applied: SI 2014/3050 Reg.44
Pt X., see *Manchester College v Hazel*
[2014] EWCA Civ 72, [2014] I.C.R. 989
(CA (Civ Div)), Moore-Bick LJ
Pt X s.98A, see *D v Royal Bank of Scotland*
[2014] I.R.L.R. 25 (IH (Ex Div)), Lady
Paton
Pt X s.103A, see *Blackbay Ventures Ltd (t/a
Chemistree) v Gahir* [2014] I.C.R. 747
(EAT), Judge Serota QC; see *Panayiotou v*

Kernaghan [2014] I.R.L.R. 500 (EAT), Lewis J

s.1, see *Davies v Haringey LBC* [2014] EWHC 3393 (QB), [2014] B.L.G.R. 743 (QBD), Supperstone J

s.3, repealed (in part): 2014 c.19 Sch.13 para.67

s.11, see *Davies v Haringey LBC* [2014] EWHC 3393 (QB), [2014] B.L.G.R. 743 (QBD), Supperstone J

s.11, amended: SI 2014/431 Sch.1 para.3

s.11, repealed (in part): 2014 c.19 Sch.13 para.68

s.13, see *Cleeve Link Ltd v Bryla* [2014] I.C.R. 264 (EAT), Judge Hand Q.C.

s.14, see *Whittlestone v BJP Home Support Ltd* [2014] I.C.R. 275 (EAT), Langstaff J

s.23, see *Abercrombie v Aga Rangemaster Ltd* [2013] EWCA Civ 1148, [2014] 1 All E.R. 1101 (CA (Civ Div)), Sir Terence Etherton C

s.23, amended: SI 2014/3322 Reg.2

s.27, amended: 2014 c.6 Sch.7 para.30

s.27, varied: 2014 c.6 s.126

s.28, see *Abercrombie v Aga Rangemaster Ltd* [2013] EWCA Civ 1148, [2014] 1 All E.R. 1101 (CA (Civ Div)), Sir Terence Etherton C

s.28, applied: SI 2014/382 Art.4

s.31, amended: SI 2014/382 Sch.1

s.34, see *Abercrombie v Aga Rangemaster Ltd* [2013] EWCA Civ 1148, [2014] 1 All E.R. 1101 (CA (Civ Div)), Sir Terence Etherton C

s.43B, see *Blackbay Ventures Ltd (t/a Chemistree) v Gahir* [2014] I.C.R. 747 (EAT), Judge Serota QC; see *Gebremariam v Ethiopian Airlines Enterprise (t/a Ethiopian Airlines)* [2014] I.R.L.R. 354 (EAT), Jeffrey Burke Q.C.; see *Millbank Financial Services Ltd v Crawford* [2014] I.R.L.R. 18 (EAT), Judge David Richardson; see *Norbrook Laboratories (GB) Ltd v Shaw* [2014] I.C.R. 540 (EAT), Slade J; see *Panayiotou v Kernaghan* [2014] I.R.L.R. 500 (EAT), Lewis J

s.43F, applied: SI 2014/2418 Art.3

s.43F, enabling: SI 2014/596, SI 2014/2418

s.43K, see *Keppel Seghers UK Ltd v Hinds* [2014] I.C.R. 1105 (EAT), Judge Eady QC

s.44, see *Smith v Carillion (JM) Ltd* [2014] I.R.L.R. 344 (EAT), Slade J

s.45A, amended: SI 2014/308 Sch.1 para.2

s.47B, see *Blackbay Ventures Ltd (t/a Chemistree) v Gahir* [2014] I.C.R. 747 (EAT), Judge Serota QC; see *Panayiotou v Kernaghan* [2014] I.R.L.R. 500 (EAT), Lewis J

s.47C, amended: 2014 c.6 s.127, s.128, s.129, Sch.7 para.31

s.47C, applied: SI 2014/3050 Reg.42

s.47C, enabling: SI 2014/2112, SI 2014/3050, SI 2014/3092, SI 2014/3096

s.47E, repealed (in part): 2014 c.6 s.132

s.48, see *Blackbay Ventures Ltd (t/a Chemistree) v Gahir* [2014] I.C.R. 747 (EAT), Judge Serota QC

s.48, amended: 2014 c.6 s.129

s.49, amended: 2014 c.6 s.129

s.49, applied: SI 2014/382 Art.4

s.50, applied: SI 2014/3352 Sch.2 para.30

s.55, applied: SI 2014/3352 Sch.2 para.30

s.57, amended: 2014 c.6 s.130

s.57ZC, amended: 2014 c.6 s.130

s.57ZE, added: 2014 c.6 s.127

s.57ZJ, added: 2014 c.6 s.128

s.62, see *Turullols v Revenue and Customs Commissioners* [2014] UKFTT 672 (TC), [2014] S.F.T.D. 1099 (FTT (Tax)), Judge Kevin Poole

s.63J, applied: SI 2014/382 Art.4

s.71, applied: SI 2014/3050 Reg.4, Reg.5, Reg.6, Sch.1 para.1, Sch.1 para.2

s.71, enabling: SI 2014/3221

s.71, amended: 2014 c.6 s.118

s.71, applied: SI 2014/3053 Reg.5, SI 2014/3054 Reg.7

s.71, enabling: SI 2014/3052, SI 2014/3221

s.73, applied: SI 2014/3050 Reg.4, Reg.5, Reg.6, Sch.1 para.1, Sch.1 para.2

s.73, amended: 2014 c.6 s.118

s.73, enabling: SI 2014/3052

s.75, enabling: SI 2014/3052

s.75A, amended: 2014 c.6 s.118, s.121, s.122

s.75A, applied: SI 2014/3050 Reg.20, Reg.21, Reg.22, Sch.1 para.6, Sch.1 para.7, SI 2014/3095 Reg.2

s.75A, enabling: SI 2014/2112, SI 2014/3052, SI 2014/3092, SI 2014/3095, SI 2014/3096, SI 2014/3206

s.75B, amended: 2014 c.6 s.118, s.122

s.75B, applied: SI 2014/3050 Reg.20,
Reg.21, Reg.22, Sch.1 para.6, Sch.1 para.7
s.75B, enabling: SI 2014/3052, SI
2014/3092, SI 2014/3095, SI 2014/3096
s.75C, enabling: SI 2014/3096
s.75D, amended: 2014 c.6 s.122
s.75D, enabling: SI 2014/2112, SI
2014/3052, SI 2014/3092, SI 2014/3096, SI
2014/3206, SSI 2014/217
s.75E, enabling: SI 2014/3050
s.75F, enabling: SI 2014/3050
s.75G, varied: SI 2014/3091 Sch.1, SI
2014/3095 Sch.1
s.75G, enabling: SI 2014/3050, SI
2014/3092, SI 2014/3096
s.75H, varied: SI 2014/3091 Sch.1, SI
2014/3095 Sch.1
s.75H, enabling: SI 2014/3050, SI
2014/3091, SI 2014/3092, SI 2014/3095, SI
2014/3096
s.75I, applied: SI 2014/3050 Reg.38
s.75I, enabling: SI 2014/3050, SI 2014/3092,
SI 2014/3096
s.75J, enabling: SI 2014/3050, SI 2014/3092,
SI 2014/3096
s.75K, enabling: SI 2014/3050, SI
2014/3092, SI 2014/3096
s.76, enabling: SI 2014/3221
s.77, enabling: SI 2014/3221
s.80A, amended: 2014 c.6 s.118, Sch.7
para.32
s.80A, varied: SI 2014/3095 Sch.2
s.80A, enabling: SI 2014/2112, SI
2014/3096
s.80AA, repealed: 2014 c.6 s.125
s.80B, amended: 2014 c.6 s.118, s.121,
s.122, s.128, Sch.7 para.33
s.80B, varied: SI 2014/3095 Sch.2
s.80B, enabling: SI 2014/2112, SI
2014/3092, SI 2014/3095, SI 2014/3096, SI
2014/3206
s.80BB, repealed: 2014 c.6 s.125
s.80C, amended: 2014 c.6 Sch.7 para.34
s.80C, repealed (in part): 2014 c.6 Sch.7
para.34
s.80C, enabling: SI 2014/2112, SI 2014/3096
s.80D, amended: 2014 c.6 Sch.7 para.35
s.80D, enabling: SI 2014/2112, SI
2014/3096
s.80E, amended: 2014 c.6 Sch.7 para.36

s.80E, repealed (in part): 2014 c.6 Sch.7
para.36
s.80E, enabling: SI 2014/3096
s.80F, amended: 2014 c.6 s.131
s.80F, applied: SI 2014/1665 Art.3
s.80F, repealed (in part): 2014 c.6 s.131
s.80F, enabling: SI 2014/1398
s.80G, amended: 2014 c.6 s.132
s.80G, repealed (in part): 2014 c.6 s.132
s.80G, enabling: SI 2014/1398
s.80H, amended: 2014 c.6 s.133
s.80H, applied: SI 2014/1398 Reg.6
s.80H, repealed (in part): 2014 c.6 s.132
s.80H, enabling: SI 2014/1398
s.80I, amended: 2014 c.6 s.132
s.80I, applied: SI 2014/382 Art.4, SI
2014/1398 Reg.6
s.80I, enabling: SI 2014/1398
s.88, amended: 2014 c.6 Sch.7 para.37
s.88, varied: 2014 c.6 s.126
s.89, amended: 2014 c.6 Sch.7 para.38
s.89, varied: 2014 c.6 s.126
s.94, disapplied: SI 2014/1139 Reg.4
s.95, see *Aberdeen City Council v McNeill*
2014 S.C. 335 (IH (Ex Div)), Lord Eassie;
see *Cockram v Air Products Plc* [2014]
I.C.R. 1065 (EAT), Simler J; see
Manchester College v Hazel [2014] EWCA
Civ 72, [2014] I.C.R. 989 (CA (Civ Div)),
Moore-Bick LJ
s.97, see *Gebremariam v Ethiopian Airlines
Enterprise (t/a Ethiopian Airlines)* [2014]
I.R.L.R. 354 (EAT), Jeffrey Burke Q.C.
s.97, applied: SI 2014/2112 Reg.14, SI
2014/3050 Reg.2
s.97, referred to: 2014 c.20 s.48, SI 2014/382
Art.4
s.98, see *D v Royal Bank of Scotland* [2014]
I.R.L.R. 25 (IH (Ex Div)), Lady Paton; see
Docherty v SW Global Resourcing Ltd 2014
S.C. 180 (IH (1 Div)), The Lord President
(Gill); see *Manchester College v Hazel*
[2014] EWCA Civ 72, [2014] I.C.R. 989
(CA (Civ Div)), Moore-Bick LJ; see *RR
Donnelley Global Document Solutions
Group Ltd v Besagni* [2014] I.C.R. 1008
(EAT), Slade J; see *Secretary of State for
Work and Pensions v Higgins* [2014] I.C.R.
341 (EAT), Judge David Richardson; see *Z
v A* [2014] I.R.L.R. 244 (EAT), Langstaff J
s.98, applied: SI 2014/1139 Reg.4

s.99, amended: 2014 c.6 s.127, s.128, Sch.7
para.39
s.99, applied: SI 2014/3050 Reg.43
s.99, enabling: SI 2014/2112, SI 2014/3092,
SI 2014/3096
s.101A, amended: SI 2014/308 Sch.1 para.2
s.104, amended: SI 2014/308 Sch.1 para.2
s.104C, repealed (in part): 2014 c.6 s.132
s.106, amended: 2014 c.6 Sch.7 para.40
s.108, amended: 2014 c.20 s.48
s.112, applied: SI 2014/382 Art.4
s.114, see *British Airways Plc v Valencia*
[2014] I.R.L.R. 683 (EAT), Simler J
s.114, applied: SI 2014/382 Art.4
s.115, see *British Airways Plc v Valencia*
[2014] I.R.L.R. 683 (EAT), Simler J
s.115, applied: SI 2014/382 Art.4
s.116, see *British Airways Plc v Valencia*
[2014] I.R.L.R. 683 (EAT), Simler J; see
Manchester College v Hazel [2014] EWCA
Civ 72, [2014] I.C.R. 989 (CA (Civ Div)),
Moore-Bick LJ
s.117, see *Manchester College v Hazel*
[2014] EWCA Civ 72, [2014] I.C.R. 989
(CA (Civ Div)), Moore-Bick LJ
s.117, applied: SI 2014/382 Art.4
s.120, amended: SI 2014/382 Sch.1
s.122, see *Frith Accountants Ltd v Law*
[2014] I.C.R. 805 (EAT), Langstaff J; see
Steen v ASP Packaging Ltd [2014] I.C.R. 56
(EAT), Langstaff J
s.123, see *Frith Accountants Ltd v Law*
[2014] I.C.R. 805 (EAT), Langstaff J; see
Steen v ASP Packaging Ltd [2014] I.C.R. 56
(EAT), Langstaff J
s.124, amended: SI 2014/382 Sch.1
s.128, see *Turullols v Revenue and Customs
Commissioners* [2014] UKFTT 672 (TC),
[2014] S.F.T.D. 1099 (FTT (Tax)), Judge
Kevin Poole
s.128, applied: SI 2014/254 Reg.3
s.130, see *Turullols v Revenue and Customs
Commissioners* [2014] UKFTT 672 (TC),
[2014] S.F.T.D. 1099 (FTT (Tax)), Judge
Kevin Poole
s.135, applied: SI 2014/382 Art.4, SI
2014/1139 Reg.4
s.135, referred to: SI 2014/382 Art.4
s.139, applied: SI 2014/1139 Reg.4
s.153, applied: SI 2014/382 Art.4
s.153, referred to: SI 2014/382 Art.4

s.182, applied: SI 2014/382 Art.4
s.185, applied: SI 2014/382 Art.4
s.186, amended: SI 2014/382 Sch.1
s.192, amended: 2014 c.20 s.48
s.199, amended: SI 2014/1614 Reg.3
s.200, see *Redbridge LBC v Dhinsa* [2014]
EWCA Civ 178, [2014] I.C.R. 834 (CA (Civ
Div)), Longmore LJ
s.203, see *Portnykh v Nomura International
Plc* [2014] I.R.L.R. 251 (EAT), Judge Hand
Q.C.
s.203, amended: SI 2014/431 Sch.1 para.4
s.203, repealed (in part): SI 2014/431 Sch.1
para.4
s.225, amended: 2014 c.6 s.127, s.128
s.227, amended: SI 2014/382 Sch.1
s.230, see *Bates van Winkelhof v Clyde & Co
LLP* [2014] UKSC 32, [2014] 1 W.L.R.
2047 (SC), Lord Neuberger PSC; see
Windle v Secretary of State for Justice
[2014] I.R.L.R. 914 (EAT), Judge Peter
Clark
s.230, amended: 2014 c.6 Sch.7 para.41
s.235, amended: 2014 c.6 s.128, Sch.7
para.42
s.236, amended: 2014 c.6 s.117, Sch.7
para.43
s.236, applied: SI 2014/3091, SI 2014/3092,
SI 2014/3095, SI 2014/3096, SI 2014/3206,
SI 2014/3221
s.236, enabling: SI 2014/1398, SI
2014/2418, SI 2014/3095

23. Arbitration Act 1996
see *Hurley Palmer Flatt Ltd v Barclays Bank
Plc* [2014] EWHC 3042 (TCC), [2014]
B.L.R. 713 (QBD (TCC)), Ramsey J; see *S
v S (Arbitral Award: Approval)* [2014]
EWHC 7 (Fam), [2014] 1 W.L.R. 2299
(Fam Div), Sir James Munby PFD
s.6, see *Kruppa v Benedetti* [2014] EWHC
1887 (Comm), [2014] 2 All E.R. (Comm)
617 (QBD (Comm)), Cooke J
s.9, see *Assaubayev v Michael Wilson and
Partners Ltd* [2014] EWCA Civ 1491,
[2014] 6 Costs L.R. 1058 (CA (Civ Div)),
Aikens LJ; see *Assaubayev v Michael
Wilson and Partners Ltd* [2014] EWHC 821
(QB), [2014] 3 Costs L.O. 446 (QBD),
Walker J; see *Kruppa v Benedetti* [2014]
EWHC 1887 (Comm), [2014] 2 All E.R.
(Comm) 617 (QBD (Comm)), Cooke J; see

Pitalia v NHS Commissioning Board [2014] EWCA Civ 474, (2014) 138 B.M.L.R. 89 (CA (Civ Div)), Aikens LJ

s.18, see *British American Insurance (Kenya) Ltd v Matelec SAL* [2013] EWHC 3278 (Comm), [2014] Lloyd's Rep. I.R. 287 (QBD (Comm)), Walker J; see *Man Enterprise SAL v Al-Waddan Hotel Ltd* [2013] EWHC 2356 (TCC), [2014] 1 Lloyd's Rep. 217 (QBD (TCC)), Ramsey J

s.33, see *Brockton Capital LLP v Atlantic-Pacific Capital Inc* [2014] EWHC 1459 (Comm), [2014] 2 Lloyd's Rep. 275 (QBD (Comm)), Field J

s.44, see *Barnwell Enterprises Ltd v ECP Africa FII Investments LLC* [2013] EWHC 2517 (Comm), [2014] 1 Lloyd's Rep. 171 (QBD (Comm)), Hamblen J; see *Doosan Babcock Ltd v Comercializadora de Equipos y Materiales Mabe Lda (formerly Mabe Chile Lda)* [2013] EWHC 3010 (TCC), [2014] 1 Lloyd's Rep. 464 (QBD (TCC)), Edwards-Stuart J

s.49, see *Societe pour la Recherche, la Production, le Transport, la Transformation et la Commercialisation des Hydrocarbures SpA (Sonatrach) v Statoil Natural Gas LLC (Statoil)* [2014] EWHC 875 (Comm), [2014] 2 All E.R. (Comm) 857 (QBD (Comm)), Flaux J

s.66, see *Honeywell International (Middle East) Ltd v Meydan Group LLP* [2014] B.L.R. 599 (QBD (TCC)), Ramsey J; see *London Steam Ship Owners Mutual Insurance Association Ltd v Spain (The Prestige)* [2013] EWHC 2840 (Comm), [2014] 1 All E.R. (Comm) 300 (QBD (Comm)), Walker J; see *London Steam Ship Owners Mutual Insurance Association Ltd v Spain (The Prestige)* [2013] EWHC 3188 (Comm), [2014] 1 Lloyd's Rep. 309 (QBD (Comm)), Hamblen J; see *Societe pour la Recherche, la Production, le Transport, la Transformation et la Commercialisation des Hydrocarbures SpA (Sonatrach) v Statoil Natural Gas LLC (Statoil)* [2014] EWHC 875 (Comm), [2014] 2 All E.R. (Comm) 857 (QBD (Comm)), Flaux J

s.67, see *A Ltd v B Ltd* [2014] EWHC 1870 (Comm), [2014] 2 Lloyd's Rep. 393 (QBD (Comm)), Andrew Smith J; see *Central*

Trading & Exports Ltd v Fioralba Shipping Co [2014] EWHC 2397 (Comm), [2014] 2 Lloyd's Rep. 449 (QBD (Comm)), Males J; see *Interprods Ltd v De La Rue International Ltd* [2014] EWHC 68 (Comm), [2014] 1 Lloyd's Rep. 540 (QBD (Comm)), Teare J; see *London Steam Ship Owners Mutual Insurance Association Ltd v Spain (The Prestige)* [2013] EWHC 2840 (Comm), [2014] 1 All E.R. (Comm) 300 (QBD (Comm)), Walker J; see *London Steam Ship Owners Mutual Insurance Association Ltd v Spain (The Prestige)* [2013] EWHC 3188 (Comm), [2014] 1 Lloyd's Rep. 309 (QBD (Comm)), Hamblen J; see *Sun United Maritime Ltd v Kasteli Marine Inc* [2014] EWHC 1476 (Comm), [2014] 2 Lloyd's Rep. 386 (QBD (Comm)), Hamblen J

s.68, see *A Ltd v B Ltd* [2014] EWHC 1870 (Comm), [2014] 2 Lloyd's Rep. 393 (QBD (Comm)), Andrew Smith J; see *Brockton Capital LLP v Atlantic-Pacific Capital Inc* [2014] EWHC 1459 (Comm), [2014] 2 Lloyd's Rep. 275 (QBD (Comm)), Field J; see *Flame SA v Glory Wealth Shipping Pte Ltd* [2013] EWHC 3153 (Comm), [2014] Q.B. 1080 (QBD (Comm)), Teare J; see *Interprods Ltd v De La Rue International Ltd* [2014] EWHC 68 (Comm), [2014] 1 Lloyd's Rep. 540 (QBD (Comm)), Teare J; see *Primera Maritime (Hellas) Ltd v Jiangsu Eastern Heavy Industry Co Ltd* [2013] EWHC 3066 (Comm), [2014] 1 All E.R. (Comm) 813 (QBD (Comm)), Flaux J; see *Societe pour la Recherche, la Production, le Transport, la Transformation et la Commercialisation des Hydrocarbures SpA (Sonatrach) v Statoil Natural Gas LLC (Statoil)* [2014] EWHC 875 (Comm), [2014] 2 All E.R. (Comm) 857 (QBD (Comm)), Flaux J

s.69, see *A Ltd v B Ltd* [2014] EWHC 1870 (Comm), [2014] 2 Lloyd's Rep. 393 (QBD (Comm)), Andrew Smith J; see *Flame SA v Glory Wealth Shipping Pte Ltd* [2013] EWHC 3153 (Comm), [2014] Q.B. 1080 (QBD (Comm)), Teare J; see *Geden Operations Ltd v Dry Bulk Handy Holdings Inc (The Bulk Uruguay)* [2014] EWHC 885 (Comm), [2014] 2 All E.R. (Comm) 196 (QBD (Comm)), Popplewell J; see *Sun*

United Maritime Ltd v Kasteli Marine Inc
[2014] EWHC 1476 (Comm), [2014] 2
Lloyd's Rep. 386 (QBD (Comm)), Hamblen
J
s.70, see *A Ltd v B Ltd* [2014] EWHC 1870
(Comm), [2014] 2 Lloyd's Rep. 393 (QBD
(Comm)), Andrew Smith J; see *Konkola
Copper Mines Plc v U&M Mining Zambia
Ltd* [2014] EWHC 2146 (Comm), [2014] 2
Lloyd's Rep. 507 (QBD (Comm)), Eder J;
see *London Steam Ship Owners Mutual
Insurance Association Ltd v Spain (The
Prestige)* [2013] EWHC 2840 (Comm),
[2014] 1 All E.R. (Comm) 300 (QBD
(Comm)), Walker J
s.72, see *London Steam Ship Owners Mutual
Insurance Association Ltd v Spain (The
Prestige)* [2013] EWHC 2840 (Comm),
[2014] 1 All E.R. (Comm) 300 (QBD
(Comm)), Walker J; see *London Steam Ship
Owners Mutual Insurance Association Ltd v
Spain (The Prestige)* [2013] EWHC 3188
(Comm), [2014] 1 Lloyd's Rep. 309 (QBD
(Comm)), Hamblen J
s.73, see *A Ltd v B Ltd* [2014] EWHC 1870
(Comm), [2014] 2 Lloyd's Rep. 393 (QBD
(Comm)), Andrew Smith J; see *Habas Sinai
Ve Tibbi Gazlar Istihsal Endustrisi v VSC
Steel Co Ltd* [2013] EWHC 4071 (Comm),
[2014] 1 Lloyd's Rep. 479 (QBD (Comm)),
Hamblen J
s.82, see *A Ltd v B Ltd* [2014] EWHC 1870
(Comm), [2014] 2 Lloyd's Rep. 393 (QBD
(Comm)), Andrew Smith J
s.94, referred to: 2014 c.1 s.16
s.100, see *Diag Human SE v Czech Republic*
[2014] EWHC 1639 (Comm), [2014] 2
Lloyd's Rep. 283 (QBD (Comm)), Eder J
s.101, see *Honeywell International (Middle
East) Ltd v Meydan Group LLP* [2014]
B.L.R. 599 (QBD (TCC)), Ramsey J; see
*Honeywell International Middle East Ltd v
Meydan Group LLC* [2014] EWHC 1344
(TCC), [2014] 2 Lloyd's Rep. 133 (QBD
(TCC)), Ramsey J; see *IPCO (Nigeria) Ltd
v Nigerian National Petroleum Corp* [2014]
EWHC 576 (Comm), [2014] 1 Lloyd's Rep.
625 (QBD (Comm)), Field J; see *Travis
Coal Restructured Holdings LLC v Essar
Global Fund Ltd* [2014] EWHC 2510

(Comm), [2014] 2 Lloyd's Rep. 494 (QBD
(Comm)), Blair J
s.102, see *Rainstorm Pictures Inc v
Lombard-Knight* [2014] EWCA Civ 356,
[2014] Bus. L.R. 1196 (CA (Civ Div)),
Tomlinson LJ
s.103, see *Diag Human SE v Czech Republic*
[2014] EWHC 1639 (Comm), [2014] 2
Lloyd's Rep. 283 (QBD (Comm)), Eder J;
see *Honeywell International (Middle East)
Ltd v Meydan Group LLP* [2014] B.L.R. 599
(QBD (TCC)), Ramsey J; see *Honeywell
International Middle East Ltd v Meydan
Group LLC* [2014] EWHC 1344 (TCC),
[2014] 2 Lloyd's Rep. 133 (QBD (TCC)),
Ramsey J; see *IPCO (Nigeria) Ltd v
Nigerian National Petroleum Corp* [2014]
EWHC 576 (Comm), [2014] 1 Lloyd's Rep.
625 (QBD (Comm)), Field J; see *Rainstorm
Pictures Inc v Lombard-Knight* [2014]
EWCA Civ 356, [2014] Bus. L.R. 1196 (CA
(Civ Div)), Tomlinson LJ; see *Travis Coal
Restructured Holdings LLC v Essar Global
Fund Ltd* [2014] EWHC 2510 (Comm),
[2014] 2 Lloyd's Rep. 494 (QBD (Comm)),
Blair J
Sch.3 para.20, repealed: 2014 c.14 Sch.7

**25. Criminal Procedure and Investigations Act
1996**

see *R. (on the application of Nunn) v Chief
Constable of Suffolk* [2014] UKSC 37,
[2014] 3 W.L.R. 77 (SC), Lord Neuberger
JSC
applied: SI 2014/1610 r.22_1, r.22_5,
r.29_19, r.22_9
disapplied: SI 2014/1610 r.22_9
referred to: SI 2014/1610 r.2_3
Part I, applied: SI 2014/1610 r.3_26, r.22_9
s.1, applied: SI 2014/1610 r.22_9
s.2, referred to: SI 2014/1610 r.22_9
s.3, see *DPP v Gowing* [2013] EWHC 4614
(Admin), (2014) 178 J.P. 181 (DC), Beatson
LJ; see *R. (on the application of Nunn) v
Chief Constable of Suffolk* [2014] UKSC 37,
[2014] 3 W.L.R. 77 (SC), Lord Neuberger
JSC
s.3, applied: SI 2014/1610 r.36_2, r.22_2,
r.22_3, r.22_9
s.5, applied: SI 2014/1610 r.22_4

s.6A, see *Joseph Hill & Co Solicitors, Re*
[2013] EWCA Crim 775, [2014] 1 W.L.R.
786 (CA (Crim Div)), Leveson LJ
s.6A, applied: SI 2014/1610 r.22_9
s.6C, applied: SI 2014/1610 r.22_4, r.22_9
s.6E, applied: SI 2014/1610 r.22_9
s.7, applied: SI 2014/1610 r.22_3, r.22_9
s.7A, see *R. (on the application of Nunn) v
Chief Constable of Suffolk* [2014] UKSC 37,
[2014] 3 W.L.R. 77 (SC), Lord Neuberger
JSC
s.7A, applied: SI 2014/1610 r.22_3, r.22_9
s.8, applied: SI 2014/1610 r.22_5
s.11, applied: SI 2014/1610 r.22_9, r.3_5
s.14, applied: SI 2014/1610 r.22_6
s.15, applied: SI 2014/1610 r.22_6
s.16, applied: SI 2014/1610 r.22_3
s.17, applied: SI 2014/1610 r.62_9, r.22_7,
r.22_8
s.18, applied: SI 2014/1610 r.5_8
s.19, applied: SI 2014/1610 r.22_3, r.22_6,
r.22_7, r.62_16
s.19, enabling: SI 2014/1610
s.20, applied: SI 2014/1610 r.33_3, r.3_5
s.20, enabling: SI 2014/1610
s.29, see *R. v R* [2013] EWCA Crim 708,
[2014] 1 Cr. App. R. 5 (CA (Crim Div)),
Treacy LJ; see *R. v Y* [2012] EWCA Crim
2437, [2013] 1 W.L.R. 2014 (CA (Crim
Div)), Sir John Thomas PQBD
s.29, applied: SI 2014/1610 r.3_14
s.30, applied: SI 2014/1610 r.3_18
s.31, see *R. v Y* [2012] EWCA Crim 2437,
[2013] 1 W.L.R. 2014 (CA (Crim Div)), Sir
John Thomas PQBD
s.31, applied: SI 2014/1610 r.35_3, r.36_2,
r.34_3, r.33_6, r.35_4, r.3_14
s.34, applied: SI 2014/1610 r.3_14
s.35, see *R. v R* [2013] EWCA Crim 708,
[2014] 1 Cr. App. R. 5 (CA (Crim Div)),
Treacy LJ
s.35, applied: SI 2014/1610 r.74_1, r.66_1,
r.66_4
s.37, see *Guardian News and Media Ltd v
AB* Times, June 18, 2014 (CA (Crim Div)),
Gross LJ
s.37, applied: SI 2014/1610 r.16_1
s.40, see *R. v R* [2013] EWCA Crim 708,
[2014] 1 Cr. App. R. 5 (CA (Crim Div)),
Treacy LJ

s.40, applied: SI 2014/1610 r.35_3, r.36_2,
r.34_3, r.3_13, r.33_6, r.35_4
s.41, applied: SI 2014/1610 r.16_1
s.54, applied: SI 2014/1610 r.40_1, r.40_4,
r.40_5, r.40_6, r.40_7, r.40_8
s.54, referred to: SI 2014/1610 r.40_2,
r.40_3, r.40_6
s.58, applied: SI 2014/1610 r.16_1, r.69_1
27. Family Law Act 1996
Commencement Orders: 2014 c.6 s.18
Part IV, applied: SI 2014/840 r.16
Part IVA, applied: SI 2014/840 r.16
Pt IV., see *Practice Guidance (Fam Ct:
Duration of Ex Parte (Without Notice)
Orders)* [2014] 3 F.C.R. 402 (Fam Ct), Sir
James Munby PFD
s.1, amended: 2014 c.6 s.18
s.1, repealed (in part): 2014 c.6 s.18
s.2, repealed: 2014 c.6 s.18
s.23, repealed: 2014 c.6 s.18
s.33, applied: SI 2014/840 r.16, SI
2014/1610 r.19_17
s.63, repealed (in part): 2014 c.6 s.18
s.63C, see *Bedfordshire Constabulary v RU*
[2013] EWHC 2350 (Fam), [2014] Fam. 69
(Fam Div), Holman J
s.63CA, added: 2014 c.12 s.120
s.63CA, amended: 2014 c.12 s.120
s.63E, amended: 2014 c.12 s.120
s.63G, repealed (in part): 2014 c.12 s.120
s.63H, applied: SI 2014/949 Art.10
s.63H, repealed: 2014 c.12 s.120
s.63I, repealed: 2014 c.12 s.120
s.63J, amended: 2014 c.12 s.120
s.63J, repealed (in part): 2014 c.12 s.120
s.63K, amended: 2014 c.12 s.120
s.63L, repealed (in part): 2014 c.12 s.120
s.64, repealed (in part): 2014 c.6 s.18
s.65, amended: 2014 c.6 s.18
Sch.8 Part I para.1, repealed: 2014 c.6 s.18
Sch.8 Part I para.5, repealed: 2014 c.6 s.18
Sch.8 Part I para.16, repealed (in part): 2014
c.6 s.18
Sch.8 Part I para.16A, repealed: 2014 c.6
s.18
Sch.8 Part I para.17, repealed: 2014 c.6 s.18
Sch.8 Part I para.25A, repealed: 2014 c.6
s.18
Sch.8 Part I para.26, repealed: 2014 c.6 s.18
Sch.8 Part I para.43A, repealed: 2014 c.6
s.18

Sch.9 para.1, repealed: 2014 c.6 s.18
Sch.9 para.4, amended: 2014 c.6 s.18
Sch.10, amended: 2014 c.6 s.18

30. Community Care (Direct Payments) Act 1996

s.4, repealed: SSI 2014/90 Sch.1 Part 1

31. Defamation Act 1996

s.2, see *Murray v Associated Newspapers Ltd* [2014] EWHC 1170 (QB), [2014] E.M.L.R. 23 (QBD), Tugendhat J
s.3, see *Murray v Associated Newspapers Ltd* [2014] EWHC 1170 (QB), [2014] E.M.L.R. 23 (QBD), Tugendhat J
Sch.1 Part II para.11, amended: 2014 c.29 s.4

37. Noise Act 1996

s.12, repealed (in part): 2014 c.2 Sch.12 para.33
s.14, amended: 2014 c.2 Sch.12 para.34

40. Party Wall etc Act 1996

s.1, applied: SI 2014/2384 Sch.19 para.6
s.1, disapplied: SI 2014/2384 Sch.19 para.6
s.2, disapplied: SI 2014/2384 Sch.19 para.6
s.6, disapplied: SI 2014/2384 Sch.19 para.6

49. Asylum and Immigration Act 1996

applied: SI 2014/2604 Sch.1 para.2

52. Housing Act 1996

see *Hines v Lambeth LBC* [2014] EWCA Civ 660, [2014] 1 W.L.R. 4112 (CA (Civ Div)), Sullivan LJ; see *Southend-on-Sea BC v Armour* [2014] EWCA Civ 231, [2014] H.L.R. 23 (CA (Civ Div)), Sullivan LJ
applied: 2014 c.23 s.23
Part I, applied: 2014 c.14 s.118, SI 2014/1763 Reg.7, SI 2014/2418 Sch.1
Part I c.I, applied: SI 2014/928 Sch.4 para.1
Part VI, applied: 2014 c.22 Sch.3 para.2, SI 2014/2603 Reg.3, Reg.4, Reg.8
Part VII, applied: SI 2014/2603 Reg.5, Reg.6, Reg.8
Pt V., see *Birmingham City Council v James* [2013] EWCA Civ 552, [2014] 1 W.L.R. 23 (CA (Civ Div)), Maurice Kay LJ
Pt VII., see *Birmingham City Council v Balog* [2013] EWCA Civ 1582, [2014] H.L.R. 14 (CA (Civ Div)), Sullivan LJ; see *Haile v Waltham Forest LBC* [2014] EWCA Civ 792, [2014] P.T.S.R. 1376 (CA (Civ Div)), Jackson LJ; see *Kanu v Southwark LBC* [2014] EWCA Civ 1085, [2014] P.T.S.R. 1197 (CA (Civ Div)), Aikens LJ;

see *P v Ealing LBC* [2013] EWCA Civ 1579, [2014] H.L.R. 5 (CA (Civ Div)), Arden LJ; see *Tachie v Welwyn Hatfield BC* [2013] EWHC 3972 (QB), [2014] P.T.S.R. 662 (QBD), Jay J; see *Viackiene v Tower Hamlets LBC* [2013] EWCA Civ 1764, [2014] H.L.R. 13 (CA (Civ Div)), Hallett LJ
s.1A, amended: 2014 c.14 Sch.4 para.57
s.2, amended: 2014 c.14 Sch.4 para.58
s.3, amended: 2014 c.14 Sch.4 para.56
s.4, amended: 2014 c.14 Sch.4 para.56
s.6, amended: 2014 c.14 Sch.4 para.56
s.22, applied: 2014 c.14 s.24
s.41, amended: 2014 c.14 Sch.4 para.56
s.44, amended: 2014 c.14 Sch.4 para.56, SI 2014/3486 Art.29
s.45, amended: 2014 c.14 Sch.4 para.56
s.48, amended: 2014 c.14 Sch.4 para.56, Sch.4 para.59
s.57, amended: 2014 c.14 Sch.4 para.56, Sch.4 para.60
s.59, amended: 2014 c.14 Sch.4 para.56, Sch.4 para.61
s.60, amended: 2014 c.14 Sch.4 para.56, Sch.4 para.62
s.61, amended: 2014 c.14 Sch.4 para.63
s.64, amended: 2014 c.14 Sch.4 para.56, Sch.4 para.64
s.122, enabling: SI 2014/3126
s.128, see *Southend-on-Sea BC v Armour* [2014] EWCA Civ 231, [2014] H.L.R. 23 (CA (Civ Div)), Sullivan LJ
s.153A, see *Swan Housing Association Ltd v Gill* [2013] EWCA Civ 1566, [2014] H.L.R. 18 (CA (Civ Div)), Richards LJ
s.153A, repealed: 2014 c.12 Sch.11 para.22
s.159, disapplied: 2014 c.22 Sch.3 para.2
s.160, applied: 2014 c.22 Sch.3 para.2
s.160, disapplied: 2014 c.22 Sch.3 para.2
s.160A, enabling: SI 2014/2603
s.160ZA, enabling: SI 2014/435
s.172, enabling: SI 2014/435, SI 2014/2603
s.175, applied: 2014 c.22 Sch.3 para.7
s.182, see *Birmingham City Council v Balog* [2013] EWCA Civ 1582, [2014] H.L.R. 14 (CA (Civ Div)), Sullivan LJ
s.184, see *Farah v Hillingdon LBC* [2014] EWCA Civ 359, [2014] H.L.R. 24 (CA (Civ Div)), Longmore LJ; see *P v Ealing LBC* [2013] EWCA Civ 1579, [2014] H.L.R. 5 (CA (Civ Div)), Arden LJ; see *R. (on the*

application of N) v Lewisham LBC [2014] UKSC 62, [2014] 3 W.L.R. 1548 (SC), Lord Neuberger PSC

s.185, see *Hines v Lambeth LBC* [2014] EWCA Civ 660, [2014] 1 W.L.R. 4112 (CA (Civ Div)), Sullivan LJ

s.185, enabling: SI 2014/435, SI 2014/2603

s.188, see *R. (on the application of N) v Lewisham LBC* [2013] EWCA Civ 804, [2014] 2 W.L.R. 719 (CA (Civ Div)), Moses LJ; see *R. (on the application of N) v Lewisham LBC* [2014] UKSC 62, [2014] 3 W.L.R. 1548 (SC), Lord Neuberger PSC

s.189, see *Kanu v Southwark LBC* [2014] EWCA Civ 1085, [2014] P.T.S.R. 1197 (CA (Civ Div)), Aikens LJ

s.190, see *Haile v Waltham Forest LBC* [2014] EWCA Civ 792, [2014] P.T.S.R. 1376 (CA (Civ Div)), Jackson LJ; see *Huzrat v Hounslow LBC* [2013] EWCA Civ 1865, [2014] H.L.R. 17 (CA (Civ Div)), Moses LJ; see *R. (on the application of N) v Lewisham LBC* [2013] EWCA Civ 804, [2014] 2 W.L.R. 719 (CA (Civ Div)), Moses LJ

s.191, see *Birmingham City Council v Balog* [2013] EWCA Civ 1582, [2014] H.L.R. 14 (CA (Civ Div)), Sullivan LJ; see *Chishimba v Kensington and Chelsea RLBC* [2013] EWCA Civ 786, [2014] P.T.S.R. 49 (CA (Civ Div)), Richards LJ; see *Huzrat v Hounslow LBC* [2013] EWCA Civ 1865, [2014] H.L.R. 17 (CA (Civ Div)), Moses LJ; see *Noel v Hillingdon LBC* [2013] EWCA Civ 1602, [2014] H.L.R. 10 (CA (Civ Div)), Richards LJ; see *Viackiene v Tower Hamlets LBC* [2013] EWCA Civ 1764, [2014] H.L.R. 13 (CA (Civ Div)), Hallett LJ

s.193, see *Akerman-Livingstone v Aster Communities Ltd (formerly Flourish Homes Ltd)* [2014] EWCA Civ 1081, [2014] 1 W.L.R. 3980 (CA (Civ Div)), Arden LJ; see *Chishimba v Kensington and Chelsea RLBC* [2013] EWCA Civ 786, [2014] P.T.S.R. 49 (CA (Civ Div)), Richards LJ; see *Haile v Waltham Forest LBC* [2014] EWCA Civ 792, [2014] P.T.S.R. 1376 (CA (Civ Div)), Jackson LJ; see *Kanu v Southwark LBC* [2014] EWCA Civ 1085, [2014] P.T.S.R. 1197 (CA (Civ Div)), Aikens LJ; see *Mohamoud v Birmingham City Council*

[2014] EWCA Civ 227, [2014] H.L.R. 22 (CA (Civ Div)), Moore-Bick LJ; see *NJ v Wandsworth LBC* [2013] EWCA Civ 1373, [2014] P.T.S.R. 497 (CA (Civ Div)), Lewison LJ; see *R. (on the application of N) v Lewisham LBC* [2013] EWCA Civ 804, [2014] 2 W.L.R. 719 (CA (Civ Div)), Moses LJ; see *Solihull MBC v Khan* [2014] EWCA Civ 41, [2014] H.L.R. 33 (CA (Civ Div)), Rafferty LJ

s.198, see *NJ v Wandsworth LBC* [2013] EWCA Civ 1373, [2014] P.T.S.R. 497 (CA (Civ Div)), Lewison LJ

s.199, see *NJ v Wandsworth LBC* [2013] EWCA Civ 1373, [2014] P.T.S.R. 497 (CA (Civ Div)), Lewison LJ

s.202, see *Birmingham City Council v Balog* [2013] EWCA Civ 1582, [2014] H.L.R. 14 (CA (Civ Div)), Sullivan LJ; see *Farah v Hillingdon LBC* [2014] EWCA Civ 359, [2014] H.L.R. 24 (CA (Civ Div)), Longmore LJ; see *Kanu v Southwark LBC* [2014] EWCA Civ 1085, [2014] P.T.S.R. 1197 (CA (Civ Div)), Aikens LJ; see *NJ v Wandsworth LBC* [2013] EWCA Civ 1373, [2014] P.T.S.R. 497 (CA (Civ Div)), Lewison LJ; see *P v Ealing LBC* [2013] EWCA Civ 1579, [2014] H.L.R. 5 (CA (Civ Div)), Arden LJ; see *R. (on the application of N) v Lewisham LBC* [2014] UKSC 62, [2014] 3 W.L.R. 1548 (SC), Lord Neuberger PSC; see *Slattery v Basildon BC* [2014] EWCA Civ 30, [2014] H.L.R. 16 (CA (Civ Div)), Sullivan LJ; see *Tachie v Welwyn Hatfield BC* [2013] EWHC 3972 (QB), [2014] P.T.S.R. 662 (QBD), Jay J

s.204, see *Bhatia Best Ltd v Lord Chancellor* [2014] EWHC 746 (QB), [2014] 1 W.L.R. 3487 (QBD), Silber J; see *Hines v Lambeth LBC* [2014] EWCA Civ 660, [2014] 1 W.L.R. 4112 (CA (Civ Div)), Sullivan LJ; see *P v Ealing LBC* [2013] EWCA Civ 1579, [2014] H.L.R. 5 (CA (Civ Div)), Arden LJ; see *Tachie v Welwyn Hatfield BC* [2013] EWHC 3972 (QB), [2014] P.T.S.R. 662 (QBD), Jay J

s.215, enabling: SI 2014/435, SI 2014/2603

s.218A, amended: 2014 c.12 Sch.11 para.23

Sch.1 Part I para.1, amended: 2014 c.14 Sch.4 para.56

Sch.1 Part I para.2, amended: 2014 c.14
Sch.4 para.56
Sch.1 Part I para.3, amended: 2014 c.14
Sch.4 para.56
Sch.1 Part II, amended: 2014 c.14 Sch.4
para.65
Sch.1 Part II para.8, amended: 2014 c.14
Sch.4 para.56
Sch.1 Part II para.9, amended: 2014 c.14
Sch.4 para.56, Sch.4 para.65
Sch.1 Part II para.12, amended: 2014 c.14
Sch.4 para.56, Sch.4 para.65
Sch.1 Part II para.13, amended: 2014 c.14
Sch.4 para.65
Sch.1 Part II para.14, amended: 2014 c.14
Sch.4 para.56, Sch.4 para.65
Sch.1 Part II para.15, amended: 2014 c.14
Sch.4 para.56, Sch.4 para.65
Sch.1 Part II para.15H, amended: 2014 c.14
Sch.4 para.56, Sch.4 para.65
Sch.1 Part III, amended: 2014 c.14 Sch.4
para.65
Sch.1 Part III para.17, amended: 2014 c.14
Sch.4 para.65
Sch.2, applied: SI 2014/2359 Art.6
Sch.19 Pt VII, see *Ajilore v Hackney LBC*
[2014] EWCA Civ 1273, [2014] H.L.R. 46
(CA (Civ Div)), Gloster LJ; see *NJ v
Wandsworth LBC* [2013] EWCA Civ 1373,
[2014] P.T.S.R. 497 (CA (Civ Div)),
Lewison LJ

**53. Housing Grants, Construction and
Regeneration Act 1996**

see *Joint Administrators of Connaught
Partnerships Ltd v Perth and Kinross
Council* 2014 S.L.T. 608 (OH), Lord
Malcolm
s.3, enabling: SI 2014/1829
s.30, referred to: SI 2014/3117
s.30, enabling: SI 2014/1829, SI 2014/1913,
SI 2014/3117
s.107, see *Glendalough Associated SA v
Harris Calnan Construction Co Ltd* [2013]
EWHC 3142 (TCC), [2014] 1 W.L.R. 1751
(QBD (TCC)), Edwards-Stuart J
s.108, see *Hurley Palmer Flatt Ltd v
Barclays Bank Plc* [2014] EWHC 3042
(TCC), [2014] B.L.R. 713 (QBD (TCC)),
Ramsey J; see *Twintec Ltd v
Volkerfitzpatrick Ltd* [2014] EWHC 10

(TCC), [2014] B.L.R. 150 (QBD (TCC)),
Edwards-Stuart J
s.146, enabling: SI 2014/1829, SI
2014/1913, SI 2014/3117

55. Broadcasting Act 1996
Part I, applied: SI 2014/774 Sch.1 para.1
Part II, applied: SI 2014/774 Sch.1 para.1
s.101B, repealed (in part): SI 2014/1184
Reg.2

56. Education Act 1996
applied: 2014 c.6 s.76, s.83, SI 2014/2128
r.38
varied: 2014 c.6 s.100
Part IV c.I, amended: 2014 c.6 Sch.3 para.9
Part IV c.I, applied: SI 2014/2270 Art.4,
Art.8, Art.9, Art.10, Art.11
Part IV c.I, amended: 2014 c.6 Sch.3 para.30
Part VI c.II, applied: SI 2014/3352 Sch.1
para.11
Part X c.VA, applied: SI 2014/2270 Art.30
Pt IV., see *WH v Warrington BC* [2014]
EWCA Civ 398, [2014] 3 All E.R. 747 (CA
(Civ Div)), Lord Dyson MR
s.4, see *TB v Essex CC* [2014] E.L.R. 46 (UT
(AAC)), Judge Lane
s.6, amended: 2014 c.6 Sch.3 para.2
s.6, repealed (in part): 2014 c.6 Sch.3 para.2
s.8, applied: SI 2014/3283 Sch.1 para.2
s.9, see *FS v Bromley LBC* [2014] E.L.R. 1
(UT (AAC)), Judge Levenson; see *SM v
Hackney Learning Trust* [2014] EWCA Civ
397, [2014] P.T.S.R. 826 (CA (Civ Div)),
Lord Dyson MR; see *WH v Warrington BC*
[2014] EWCA Civ 398, [2014] 3 All E.R.
747 (CA (Civ Div)), Lord Dyson MR
s.10, see *R. (on the application of Tigere) v
Secretary of State for Business, Innovation
and Skills* [2014] EWCA Civ 1216, [2014]
H.R.L.R. 26 (CA (Civ Div)), Laws LJ
s.13, amended: 2014 c.6 Sch.3 para.3
s.13, applied: SI 2014/3352 Sch.2 para.8
s.13, repealed (in part): 2014 c.6 Sch.3
para.3
s.13A, amended: 2014 c.6 Sch.3 para.4
s.15, applied: SI 2014/512 Sch.1 para.21,
Sch.1 para.30
s.15A, amended: 2014 c.6 Sch.3 para.6
s.15B, amended: 2014 c.6 Sch.3 para.7
s.15ZA, amended: 2014 c.6 Sch.3 para.5

s.15ZA, applied: SI 2014/863 Sch.2 para.4,
SI 2014/865 Sch.2 para.3, SI 2014/1012
Sch.2 para.3, SI 2014/3352 Sch.1 para.18
s.15ZB, applied: SI 2014/863 Sch.2 para.4
s.15ZC, applied: SI 2014/863 Sch.2 para.4,
SI 2014/3352 Sch.1 para.18
s.17A, applied: SI 2014/863 Sch.2 para.4, SI
2014/865 Sch.2 para.3, SI 2014/1012 Sch.2
para.3
s.18, applied: SI 2014/3352 Sch.2 para.7
s.18A, amended: 2014 c.6 Sch.3 para.8
s.18A, applied: SI 2014/863 Sch.2 para.4, SI
2014/865 Sch.2 para.3, SI 2014/1012 Sch.2
para.3
s.19, see *SG v Bromley LBC* [2014] E.L.R.
190 (UT (AAC)), Judge SM Lane; see *TB v
Essex CC* [2014] E.L.R. 46 (UT (AAC)),
Judge Lane
s.19, applied: SI 2014/3352 Sch.2 para.21
s.19, enabling: SI 2014/3216
s.21, enabling: SI 2014/2677
s.29, applied: 2014 c.6 s.76
s.30, enabling: SI 2014/2677
s.32, applied: SI 2014/1836, SI 2014/2235,
SI 2014/2237, SI 2014/2238
s.131, enabling: SI 2014/2677
s.210, enabling: SI 2014/2677
s.311A, added: 2014 c.6 Sch.3 para.10
s.312, amended: 2014 c.6 Sch.3 para.11
s.313, see *Manchester City Council v JW*
[2014] UKUT 168 (AAC), [2014] E.L.R.
304 (UT (AAC)), Judge Michael Mark
s.313, amended: 2014 c.6 Sch.3 para.12
s.313, repealed (in part): 2014 c.6 Sch.3
para.12
s.314, amended: 2014 c.6 Sch.3 para.13
s.316, see *TB v Essex CC* [2014] E.L.R. 46
(UT (AAC)), Judge Lane
s.316A, amended: 2014 c.6 Sch.3 para.14
s.316A, repealed (in part): 2014 c.6 Sch.3
para.14
s.317, amended: 2014 c.6 Sch.3 para.15
s.317, repealed (in part): 2014 c.6 Sch.3
para.15
s.318, amended: 2014 c.6 Sch.3 para.16
s.318, repealed (in part): 2014 c.6 Sch.3
para.16
s.319, see *TB v Essex CC* [2014] E.L.R. 46
(UT (AAC)), Judge Lane
s.320, applied: SI 2014/3352 Sch.2 para.22
s.321, applied: SI 2014/3352 Sch.1 para.2

s.323, applied: SI 2014/2270 Art.3, Art.5,
Art.6, Art.7, Art.8, Art.23
s.324, see *K v A Local Authority* [2014]
E.L.R. 295 (UT (AAC)), Michael Fordham
QC; see *Manchester City Council v JW*
[2014] UKUT 168 (AAC), [2014] E.L.R.
304 (UT (AAC)), Judge Michael Mark; see
SM v Hackney Learning Trust [2014]
EWCA Civ 397, [2014] P.T.S.R. 826 (CA
(Civ Div)), Lord Dyson MR
s.324, applied: SI 2014/2270 Art.4, Art.8,
Art.11
s.325, applied: SI 2014/2270 Art.5, Art.6,
Art.7, Art.9
s.326, amended: 2014 c.6 Sch.3 para.17
s.326, applied: SI 2014/2270 Art.16
s.326, disapplied: SI 2014/2270 Art.19
s.326A, amended: 2014 c.6 Sch.3 para.18
s.326A, repealed (in part): 2014 c.6 Sch.3
para.18
s.328, applied: SI 2014/2270 Art.23
s.328, disapplied: SI 2014/2270 Art.19
s.328A, repealed: 2014 c.6 Sch.3 para.19
s.329, applied: SI 2014/2270 Art.3, Art.6,
Art.8
s.329A, amended: 2014 c.6 Sch.3 para.20
s.329A, applied: SI 2014/2270 Art.6, Art.8,
Art.23
s.329A, disapplied: SI 2014/2270 Art.19
s.329A, repealed (in part): 2014 c.6 Sch.3
para.20
s.329A, varied: 2014 c.6 Sch.3 para.20
s.331, applied: SI 2014/2270 Art.3, Art.4,
Art.5, Art.6, Art.7, Art.11
s.332A, repealed: 2014 c.6 Sch.3 para.24
s.332AA, amended: 2014 c.6 Sch.3 para.25
s.332B, repealed: 2014 c.6 Sch.3 para.26
s.332BA, amended: 2014 c.6 Sch.3 para.27
s.332BB, amended: 2014 c.6 Sch.3 para.28
s.332C, repealed: 2014 c.6 Sch.3 para.29
s.332ZA, amended: 2014 c.6 Sch.3 para.21
s.332ZB, amended: 2014 c.6 Sch.3 para.22
s.332ZC, amended: 2014 c.6 Sch.3 para.23
s.333, amended: 2014 c.6 Sch.3 para.31
s.333, repealed (in part): 2014 c.6 Sch.3
para.31
s.335, amended: 2014 c.6 Sch.3 para.32
s.336, amended: 2014 c.6 Sch.3 para.33
s.336, repealed (in part): 2014 c.6 Sch.3
para.33
s.336A, amended: 2014 c.6 Sch.3 para.35

s.336A, repealed (in part): 2014 c.6 Sch.3
para.35
s.336ZB, amended: 2014 c.6 Sch.3 para.34
s.337, substituted: 2014 c.6 Sch.3 para.36
s.342, amended: 2014 c.6 Sch.3 para.37
s.348, amended: 2014 c.6 Sch.3 para.38
s.390, applied: SI 2014/3352 Sch.1 para.24
s.408, applied: 2014 c.6 s.76, SI 2014/1998
s.408, enabling: SI 2014/1998
s.438, amended: 2014 c.6 Sch.3 para.39
s.439, applied: SI 2014/1132 Reg.63
s.440, amended: 2014 c.6 Sch.3 para.40
s.441, amended: 2014 c.6 Sch.3 para.41
s.442, amended: 2014 c.6 Sch.3 para.42
s.458, applied: SI 2014/3352 Sch.2 para.13
s.463, amended: 2014 c.6 Sch.3 para.43
s.470, applied: SI 2014/1132 Sch.7 para.9,
SI 2014/2365 Reg.5, SI 2014/2709 Sch.2
para.9
s.471, applied: SI 2014/2365 Reg.5
s.483A, amended: 2014 c.6 Sch.3 para.44
s.485, enabling: SI 2014/80
s.496, applied: SI 2014/178 Art.3, SI
2014/1530 Reg.17
s.497A, amended: 2014 c.6 s.101
s.497A, applied: SI 2014/512 Sch.1 para.3
s.507A, applied: SI 2014/512 Sch.1 para.21,
SI 2014/3352 Sch.1 para.19
s.507B, see *Hunt v North Somerset Council*
[2013] EWCA Civ 1320, [2014] B.L.G.R. 1
(CA (Civ Div)), Moore-Bick LJ
s.507B, amended: 2014 c.6 Sch.3 para.45
s.508, applied: SI 2014/512 Sch.1 para.30
s.508A, applied: SI 2014/3352 Sch.1 para.10
s.508F, amended: 2014 c.6 Sch.3 para.46
s.508I, amended: 2014 c.6 Sch.3 para.47
s.509AB, amended: 2014 c.6 Sch.3 para.48
s.509AC, amended: 2014 c.6 Sch.3 para.49
s.510, applied: SI 2014/3352 Sch.1 para.10
s.512B, added: 2014 c.6 s.106
s.512ZB, amended: 2014 c.6 s.106
s.514, applied: SI 2014/3352 Sch.2 para.13
s.514A, amended: 2014 c.6 Sch.3 para.50
s.514A, applied: SI 2014/863 Sch.2 para.4,
SI 2014/865 Sch.2 para.3, SI 2014/1012
Sch.2 para.3
s.514A, repealed (in part): 2014 c.6 Sch.3
para.50
s.517, amended: 2014 c.6 Sch.3 para.51
s.518, applied: SI 2014/3352 Sch.1 para.10
s.519, applied: SI 2014/3352 Sch.5 para.14

s.532A, amended: 2014 c.6 Sch.3 para.52
s.532A, repealed (in part): 2014 c.6 Sch.3
para.52
s.532B, amended: 2014 c.6 Sch.3 para.53
s.532B, enabling: SI 2014/166
s.532C, enabling: SI 2014/166
s.537, applied: 2014 c.6 s.76
s.537, enabling: SI 2014/2677
s.537A, applied: 2014 c.6 s.76
s.537B, applied: 2014 c.6 s.76
s.538, applied: 2014 c.6 s.76
s.547, applied: SI 2014/1132 Sch.7 para.10,
SI 2014/2709 Sch.2 para.10
s.554, applied: SI 2014/699(1), SI 2014/2295
s.554, enabling: SI 2014/699, SI 2014/942,
SI 2014/1836, SI 2014/2006, SI 2014/2235,
SI 2014/2236, SI 2014/2237, SI 2014/2238,
SI 2014/2295, SI 2014/2631, SI 2014/2719,
SI 2014/3246, SI 2014/3247
s.555, applied: SI 2014/699(4), SI
2014/3247(4), SI 2014/3246(4), SI
2014/1836, SI 2014/2006, SI 2014/2235, SI
2014/2236, SI 2014/2237, SI 2014/2238, SI
2014/2295, SI 2014/2631, SI 2014/2719
s.556, enabling: SI 2014/699, SI 2014/942,
SI 2014/1836, SI 2014/2006, SI 2014/2235,
SI 2014/2236, SI 2014/2237, SI 2014/2238,
SI 2014/2295, SI 2014/2631, SI 2014/2719,
SI 2014/3246, SI 2014/3247
s.560A, amended: 2014 c.6 Sch.3 para.54
s.560A, applied: SI 2014/863 Sch.2 para.4,
SI 2014/865 Sch.2 para.3, SI 2014/1012
Sch.2 para.3
s.562, referred to: 2014 c.6 s.48
s.562C, amended: 2014 c.6 Sch.3 para.55
s.562D, amended: 2014 c.6 Sch.3 para.56
s.562G, amended: 2014 c.6 Sch.3 para.57
s.562H, amended: 2014 c.6 Sch.3 para.58
s.562H, repealed (in part): 2014 c.6 Sch.3
para.58
s.562J, referred to: 2014 c.6 s.70
s.568, applied: SI 2014/166
s.568, enabling: SI 2014/166
s.569, enabling: SI 2014/1609, SI
2014/1998, SI 2014/2677, SI 2014/2709, SI
2014/3216
s.573, see *WH v Warrington BC* [2014]
EWCA Civ 398, [2014] 3 All E.R. 747 (CA
(Civ Div)), Lord Dyson MR
s.578, amended: 2014 c.6 s.140
s.578, applied: 2014 c.6 s.140

s.579, amended: 2014 c.6 Sch.3 para.59
s.579, applied: SI 2014/3219 Sch.1 para.2
s.580, amended: 2014 c.6 Sch.3 para.60
Sch.1 para.3, enabling: SI 2014/1609, SI 2014/2677, SI 2014/2709
Sch.1 para.6, applied: SI 2014/2709 Reg.22
Sch.1 para.6, enabling: SI 2014/2709
Sch.1 para.15, enabling: SI 2014/2709
Sch.27 para.3, see *FS v Bromley LBC* [2014] E.L.R. 1 (UT (AAC)), Judge Levenson; see *SM v Hackney Learning Trust* [2014] EWCA Civ 397, [2014] P.T.S.R. 826 (CA (Civ Div)), Lord Dyson MR; see *WH v Warrington BC* [2014] EWCA Civ 398, [2014] 3 All E.R. 747 (CA (Civ Div)), Lord Dyson MR
Sch.27 para.8, see *SM v Hackney Learning Trust* [2014] EWCA Civ 397, [2014] P.T.S.R. 826 (CA (Civ Div)), Lord Dyson MR
Sch.27 para.8, applied: SI 2014/2270 Art.16
Sch.27 para.11, applied: SI 2014/2270 Art.10, Art.26
Sch.31, applied: SI 2014/3352 Sch.1 para.24
Sch.35B para.15, amended: 2014 c.6 Sch.3 para.61
Sch.36A para.2, amended: 2014 c.6 Sch.3 para.62
Sch.37 Part I para.11, repealed: 2014 asp 8 Sch.5 para.6

61. Channel Tunnel Rail Link Act 1996
s.9, enabling: SI 2014/1332, SI 2014/1333
s.21, amended: SI 2014/892 Sch.1 para.114
s.34, enabling: SI 2014/1332
Sch.6 Part I para.1, enabling: SI 2014/1332
Sch.6 Part IV para.32, enabling: SI 2014/1333
Sch.6 Part IV para.36, enabling: SI 2014/1333
Sch.6 Part IV para.37, enabling: SI 2014/1333

62. Theft (Amendment) Act 1996
see *R. v White (Anthony Alan)* [2014] EWCA Crim 714, [2014] 2 Cr. App. R. 14 (CA (Crim Div)), Sir Brian Leveson PQBD

1997

5. Firearms (Amendment) Act 1997
applied: SI 2014/1638 Reg.5

s.1, amended: 2014 c.12 s.108
s.2, amended: 2014 c.12 s.109
s.7, amended: 2014 c.12 s.109
s.8, amended: 2014 c.12 s.109

8. Town and Country Planning (Scotland) Act 1997
see *Archid Architecture and Interior Design v Dundee City Council* 2014 S.L.T. 81 (OH), Lord Glennie
applied: SSI 2014/224 Sch.1 para.1
s.27, applied: SSI 2014/300 Art.2
s.30, enabling: SSI 2014/142, SSI 2014/184, SSI 2014/300
s.31, enabling: SSI 2014/142, SSI 2014/184, SSI 2014/300
s.47, see *Caroll v Scottish Borders Council* [2014] CSOH 6, 2014 S.C.L.R. 532 (OH), Lord Armstrong
s.57, see *Sustainable Shetland v Scottish Ministers* [2014] CSIH 60, 2014 S.L.T. 806 (IH (1 Div)), The Lord President (Gill)
s.150, see *Archid Architecture and Interior Design v Dundee City Council* 2014 S.L.T. 81 (OH), Lord Glennie
s.173, enabling: SSI 2014/53
s.182, enabling: SSI 2014/139, SSI 2014/249
s.186, enabling: SSI 2014/139
s.239, see *Caroll v Scottish Borders Council* [2014] CSOH 6, 2014 S.C.L.R. 532 (OH), Lord Armstrong; see *Carroll v Scottish Borders Council* [2014] CSOH 30, 2014 S.L.T. 659 (OH), Lord Drummond Young
s.252, amended: 2014 asp 3 s.55
s.252, repealed (in part): 2014 asp 3 s.55
s.252, enabling: SSI 2014/214, SSI 2014/301
s.275, amended: 2014 asp 3 Sch.3 para.32
s.275, enabling: SSI 2014/139, SSI 2014/142, SSI 2014/184, SSI 2014/300
Sch.15 para.26, see *Aberdeen City Council v Morrison* 2014 S.L.T. (Lands Tr) 113 (Lands Tr (Scot)), R Smith QC
Sch.15 para.27, see *Aberdeen City Council v Morrison* 2014 S.L.T. (Lands Tr) 113 (Lands Tr (Scot)), R Smith QC

9. Planning (Listed Buildings and Conservation Areas) (Scotland) Act 1997
referred to: 2014 asp 19 s.16
s.1, amended: 2014 asp 19 s.22, Sch.3 para.2
s.1A, added: 2014 asp 19 Sch.3 para.3
s.2, repealed: 2014 asp 19 Sch.3 para.4
s.3, amended: 2014 asp 19 Sch.3 para.5

s.5A, amended: 2014 asp 19 Sch.3 para.6
s.5B, added: 2014 asp 19 Sch.3 para.18
s.7, amended: 2014 asp 19 Sch.3 para.8
s.7, repealed (in part): 2014 asp 19 Sch.3 para.8
s.9, amended: 2014 asp 19 Sch.3 para.9
s.12, amended: 2014 asp 19 s.23
s.13, amended: 2014 asp 19 s.23
s.13, repealed (in part): 2014 asp 19 s.23
s.14, amended: 2014 asp 19 s.23
s.19, amended: 2014 asp 19 Sch.3 para.19
s.20, amended: 2014 asp 19 Sch.3 para.20
s.22, amended: 2014 asp 19 Sch.3 para.10
s.23, amended: 2014 asp 19 Sch.3 para.11
s.26, amended: 2014 asp 19 Sch.3 para.25
s.37, amended: 2014 asp 19 Sch.3 para.21
s.57, amended: 2014 asp 19 Sch.3 para.22
s.61, amended: 2014 asp 19 Sch.3 para.13
s.62, amended: 2014 asp 19 Sch.3 para.14
s.66, amended: 2014 asp 19 s.24
s.73, amended: 2014 asp 19 Sch.3 para.26
s.76, amended: 2014 asp 19 Sch.3 para.27
Sch.1 para.2, amended: 2014 asp 19 Sch.3 para.15
Sch.1 para.3, repealed: 2014 asp 19 Sch.3 para.16
Sch.2 para.1, amended: 2014 asp 19 Sch.3 para.28
Sch.3 para.1, amended: 2014 asp 19 Sch.3 para.23
Sch.3 para.2, amended: 2014 asp 19 Sch.3 para.23
Sch.3 para.3, amended: 2014 asp 19 Sch.3 para.23
Sch.3 para.5, repealed (in part): 2014 asp 19 Sch.3 para.23

10. Planning (Hazardous Substances) (Scotland) Act 1997
s.3, enabling: SSI 2014/51
s.5, amended: SI 2014/469 Sch.2 para.16
s.7, amended: SI 2014/469 Sch.2 para.17
s.8, amended: SI 2014/469 Sch.2 para.18
s.16, amended: SI 2014/469 Sch.2 para.19
s.28, amended: SI 2014/469 Sch.2 para.20
s.38, amended: SI 2014/469 Sch.2 para.20

11. Planning (Consequential Provisions) (Scotland) Act 1997
Sch.2 para.23, repealed (in part): 2014 asp 3 Sch.3 para.33

12. Civil Procedure Act 1997
s.1, amended: 2014 c.12 s.174

s.1, applied: SI 2014/482, SI 2014/610, SI 2014/1233, SI 2014/2044, SI 2014/2948, SI 2014/3299
s.1, enabling: SI 2014/407, SI 2014/610, SI 2014/867
s.2, applied: SI 2014/482, SI 2014/610, SI 2014/867, SI 2014/1233, SI 2014/2044, SI 2014/2948, SI 2014/3299
s.2, enabling: SI 2014/407, SI 2014/482, SI 2014/610, SI 2014/867, SI 2014/1233, SI 2014/2044, SI 2014/2948, SI 2014/3299
s.7, applied: SI 2014/840 Sch.2

16. Finance Act 1997
s.10, see *Aspinalls Club Ltd v Revenue and Customs Commissioners* [2013] EWCA Civ 1464, [2014] 2 W.L.R. 1574 (CA (Civ Div)), Moses LJ
s.11, see *Aspinalls Club Ltd v Revenue and Customs Commissioners* [2013] EWCA Civ 1464, [2014] 2 W.L.R. 1574 (CA (Civ Div)), Moses LJ
s.11, amended: 2014 c.26 s.121
s.12, enabling: SI 2014/1930
s.39, see *Revenue and Customs Commissioners v British Telecommunications Plc* [2014] EWCA Civ 433, [2014] S.T.C. 1926 (CA (Civ Div)), Rimer LJ
Sch.1 Part II para.12, amended: 2014 c.26 Sch.28 para.20
Sch.1 Part II para.16, amended: 2014 c.26 Sch.28 para.20

20. British Nationality (Hong Kong) Act 1997
applied: SI 2014/581 Sch.4 para.2, SI 2014/922 Sch.4 para.2

22. Architects Act 1997
s.25, amended: SI 2014/4 Art.2
Sch.1 Part I para.2, applied: SI 2014/4 Art.4
Sch.1 Part I para.3, applied: SI 2014/4 Art.4
Sch.1 Part I para.4, amended: SI 2014/4 Art.2
Sch.1 Part I para.5, amended: SI 2014/4 Art.2
Sch.1 Part IV para.24, enabling: SI 2014/4

27. Social Security (Recovery of Benefits) Act 1997
s.1, amended: 2014 c.1 Sch.1 para.2
s.1A, amended: 2014 c.1 Sch.1 para.17
s.1A, enabling: SI 2014/1456
s.6, applied: SI 2014/916 Reg.26
s.8A, added: 2014 c.1 Sch.1 para.3

s.9, amended: 2014 c.1 Sch.1 para.8

s.10, amended: 2014 c.1 Sch.1 para.4

s.11, amended: 2014 c.1 Sch.1 para.5, Sch.1 para.8

s.13, amended: 2014 c.1 Sch.1 para.6, Sch.1 para.8

s.14, amended: 2014 c.1 Sch.1 para.8

s.14, enabling: SI 2014/1456

s.19, amended: 2014 c.1 Sch.1 para.8

s.19, enabling: SI 2014/1456

s.20, amended: 2014 c.1 Sch.1 para.8

s.21, amended: 2014 c.1 Sch.1 para.8

s.21, enabling: SI 2014/1456

s.23, amended: 2014 c.1 Sch.1 para.19

s.23, enabling: SI 2014/1456

s.29, amended: 2014 c.1 Sch.1 para.7

s.29, enabling: SI 2014/1456

s.30, enabling: SI 2014/1456

Sch.1 Part I para.4, enabling: SI 2014/1456

28. Merchant Shipping and Maritime Security Act 1997

s.30, enabling: SI 2014/265

29. Local Government and Rating Act 1997

Sch.2 para.3, applied: SSI 2014/30 Reg.3

Sch.2 para.4, applied: SSI 2014/30 Reg.5

40. Protection from Harassment Act 1997

see *Grant v Hayes* [2014] EWHC 2646 (Ch), [2014] B.P.I.R. 1455 (Ch D), Nugee J

s.1, see *Grant v Hayes* [2014] EWHC 2646 (Ch), [2014] B.P.I.R. 1455 (Ch D), Nugee J

s.3, see *Grant v Hayes* [2014] EWHC 2646 (Ch), [2014] B.P.I.R. 1455 (Ch D), Nugee J; see *Hayes v Hayes* [2014] EWHC 2694 (Ch), [2014] Bus. L.R. 1238 (Ch D), Nugee J

s.5, see *R. v McDermott (David Steven)* [2013] EWCA Crim 1807, [2014] 1 Cr. App. R. (S.) 81 (CA (Crim Div)), Davis LJ

s.5, applied: SI 2014/1610 r.50_1, SI 2014/3300 Reg.17

s.5, varied: SI 2014/3300 Reg.13

s.5A, see *R. v McDermott (Stephen Paul)* [2013] EWCA Crim 607, [2014] 1 Cr. App. R. (S.) 1 (CA (Crim Div)), Laws LJ

s.5A, applied: SI 2014/1610 r.50_1

s.8, see *Vaickuviene v J Sainsbury Plc* 2014 S.C. 147 (IH (2 Div)), The Lord Justice Clerk (Carloway)

s.8, applied: 2014 asp 18 Sch.1 para.2

43. Crime (Sentences) Act 1997

applied: 2014 c.11 s.23

Part II c.II, applied: SI 2014/1652 Sch.1, SI 2014/2871 Sch.1

s.28, see *R. (on the application of Kaiyam) v Secretary of State for Justice* [2014] UKSC 66 (SC), Lord Neuberger PSC

s.30, see *Attorney General's Reference (No.69 of 2013)* [2014] EWCA Crim 188, [2014] 1 W.L.R. 3964 (CA (Crim Div)), Lord Thomas LCJ

Sch.1, applied: 2014 c.11 s.23

Sch.1 Part II para.6, amended: 2014 c.11 Sch.3 para.2

Sch.1 Part II para.8, amended: 2014 c.11 s.13, Sch.3 para.3

Sch.1 Part II para.8A, added: 2014 c.11 Sch.3 para.4

Sch.1 Part II para.9, amended: 2014 c.11 s.13, Sch.3 para.5

Sch.1 Part II para.9, repealed (in part): 2014 c.11 Sch.3 para.5

Sch.1 Part II para.15, amended: 2014 c.11 Sch.3 para.6

Sch.1 Part III para.19, applied: 2014 c.11 s.23

Sch.1 Part III para.19A, added: 2014 c.11 Sch.3 para.7

Sch.1 Part III para.20, amended: 2014 c.11 Sch.3 para.8

44. Education Act 1997

s.19, enabling: SI 2014/2677

s.32ZA, amended: 2014 c.29 s.4

s.54, enabling: SI 2014/2677

48. Crime and Punishment (Scotland) Act 1997

s.16, see *Dutch v Parole Board for Scotland* 2014 S.L.T. 285 (OH), Lord Burns

s.30, amended: 2014 asp 3 Sch.3 para.34

s.30, repealed (in part): 2014 asp 3 Sch.3 para.34

50. Police Act 1997

Commencement Orders: SI 2014/237 Art.2

applied: SI 2014/2871 Reg.3

Part III, applied: SI 2014/3103 Art.2, SI 2014/3103(1)

s.91, amended: 2014 c.12 s.150

s.93, amended: SI 2014/892 Sch.1 para.116

s.94, amended: SI 2014/892 Sch.1 para.117

s.112, applied: 2014 asp 14 s.35, SI 2014/1610 r.5_9

s.112, enabling: SI 2014/239

s.113A, see *R. (on the application of T) v
Chief Constable of Greater Manchester*
[2014] UKSC 35 (SC), Lord Neuberger JSC
s.113A, applied: SI 2014/1610 r.5_9, SI
2014/2936 Sch.3 para.2
s.113A, enabling: SI 2014/100
s.113B, see *R. (on the application of T) v
Chief Constable of Greater Manchester*
[2014] UKSC 35 (SC), Lord Neuberger JSC
s.113B, applied: SI 2014/1132 Sch.7
para.13, SI 2014/2709 Sch.2 para.11, SI
2014/2824 Reg.2, SI 2014/2871 Reg.3,
Reg.5, SI 2014/2889 Reg.2, SI 2014/2936
Sch.3 para.3, SI 2014/3283 Reg.2, Sch.1
para.20
s.113B, enabling: SI 2014/955, SI 2014/2122
s.113BA, applied: SI 2014/2824 Reg.2, SI
2014/2889 Reg.2
s.113BB, applied: SI 2014/2824 Reg.2, SI
2014/2889 Reg.2
s.113CA, amended: 2014 c.12 Sch.11
para.53
s.113CB, amended: 2014 c.12 Sch.11
para.54
s.120, referred to: SI 2014/3283 Reg.2
s.125, amended: 2014 c.12 s.151
s.125, enabling: SI 2014/239, SI 2014/955,
SI 2014/2122
s.126, applied: SI 2014/1920 Reg.18
s.135, enabling: SI 2014/237
s.137, amended: 2014 c.12 Sch.11 para.90

51. Sex Offenders Act 1997
s.1, see *R. (on the application of Hamill) v
Chelmsford Magistrates' Court* [2014]
EWHC 2799 (Admin), (2014) 178 J.P. 401
(QBD (Admin)), Aikens LJ

54. Road Traffic Reduction Act 1997
s.2, applied: SI 2014/865 Art.11

57. Appropriation (No.2) Act 1997
Sch.B, varied: SI 2014/2708 Art.5

64. Firearms (Amendment) (No.2) Act 1997
applied: SI 2014/1638 Reg.5

65. Local Government (Contracts) Act 1997
s.8, amended: 2014 c.2 Sch.12 para.35
s.8, repealed (in part): 2014 c.2 Sch.12
para.35

66. Plant Varieties Act 1997
s.7, applied: 2014 c.18 s.21

**68. Special Immigration Appeals Commission
Act 1997**
s.2, amended: 2014 c.22 Sch.9 para.2, Sch.9
para.26
s.2, applied: SI 2014/922 Sch.1 para.1
s.2, repealed (in part): 2014 c.22 Sch.9
para.26
s.2B, amended: 2014 c.22 Sch.9 para.26
s.2C, see *R. (on the application of Ignaoua)
v Secretary of State for the Home
Department* [2013] EWCA Civ 1498, [2014]
1 W.L.R. 651 (CA (Civ Div)), Lord Dyson
MR
s.2E, added: 2014 c.22 s.18
s.5, amended: 2014 c.22 Sch.9 para.10
s.6A, amended: 2014 c.22 Sch.9 para.26
s.7, amended: 2014 c.22 Sch.9 para.26
Sch.3 para.4, amended: 2014 c.22 Sch.9
para.10

1998

11. Bank of England Act 1998
s.2AA, amended: SI 2014/894 Reg.36
s.9C, applied: SI 2014/3348 Art.9
s.9H, amended: SI 2014/894 Reg.36
s.9I, amended: SI 2014/894 Reg.36
s.9Q, amended: SI 2014/894 Reg.36
s.9U, amended: SI 2014/894 Reg.36
s.19, applied: SI 2014/3354 Reg.11

14. Social Security Act 1998
applied: SI 2014/618 Reg.2
Part I c.II, applied: 2014 c.28 s.59
s.2, amended: 2014 c.19 Sch.12 para.32,
Sch.16 para.38
s.3, amended: 2014 c.1 Sch.1 para.21
s.3, applied: SI 2014/1892 Art.2
s.8, amended: 2014 c.19 Sch.12 para.33,
Sch.16 para.39
s.8, applied: SI 2014/881 Reg.2
s.9, applied: 2014 c.28 s.37, SI 2014/1230
Reg.6, Reg.13, Reg.14, SI 2014/1452 Art.3
s.9, enabling: SI 2014/1097
s.10, enabling: SI 2014/597, SI 2014/1097
s.11, amended: 2014 c.19 Sch.12 para.34,
Sch.16 para.40
s.12, amended: SI 2014/886 Art.4
s.27, amended: 2014 c.19 Sch.12 para.35,
Sch.16 para.41

s.28, amended: 2014 c.19 Sch.12 para.36,
Sch.16 para.42
s.79, enabling: SI 2014/213, SI 2014/597
s.84, enabling: SI 2014/597, SI 2014/1097
Sch.3 Part I para.6C, added: 2014 c.19
Sch.12 para.37

17. Petroleum Act 1998

referred to: SI 2014/615 Reg.3, SI
2014/2555 Art.3
s.3, applied: SI 2014/1686 Sch.3 para.2
s.4, applied: SI 2014/1686 Reg.2
s.4, enabling: SI 2014/1686
s.5C, amended: SI 2014/834 Sch.2 para.12
s.24, enabling: SI 2014/430
s.25, applied: SI 2014/430
s.27, applied: SI 2014/422
s.27, enabling: SI 2014/422

18. Audit Commission Act 1998

applied: 2014 c.2 Sch.2 para.29, SI
2014/1629 Reg.3, SI 2014/2418 Sch.1
referred to: 2014 c.2 s.1
repealed: 2014 c.2 s.1
s.1, amended: 2014 c.2 Sch.1 para.2
s.2, applied: 2014 c.2 Sch.2 para.29
s.4, referred to: 2014 c.2 Sch.6 para.8
s.11, disapplied: SI 2014/864 Art.8
s.16, applied: 2014 c.2 s.27
s.30, disapplied: SI 2014/864 Art.8
s.53, referred to: SI 2014/2418 Sch.1
Sch.1 para.5, applied: 2014 c.2 Sch.1 para.5
Sch.1 para.7, applied: 2014 c.2 Sch.1 para.5
Sch.1 para.11, applied: 2014 c.2 Sch.1 para.3
Sch.1 para.14, applied: 2014 c.2 Sch.1 para.4
Sch.2 para.4, disapplied: SI 2014/864 Art.8
Sch.4 para.4, applied: 2014 c.2 Sch.2
para.29, SI 2014/1629 Reg.3
Sch.4 para.7, applied: 2014 c.2 Sch.2
para.29, SI 2014/1629 Reg.3

**20. Late Payment of Commercial Debts
(Interest) Act 1998**

see *National Museums and Galleries on
Merseyside Board of Trustees v AEW
Architects and Designers Ltd* [2013] EWHC
3025 (TCC), [2014] 1 Costs L.O. 39 (QBD
(TCC)), Akenhead J

29. Data Protection Act 1998

see *AB v A Chief Constable* [2014] EWHC
1965 (QB), [2014] I.R.L.R. 700 (QBD),
Cranston J; see *Hussain v King Edward VII
Hospital* [2013] EWCA Civ 1863, (2014)
136 B.M.L.R. 54 (CA (Civ Div)), Longmore

LJ; see *Oakley Smith v Information Officer*
[2013] EWHC 2485 (Ch), [2014] Ch. 426
(Ch D (Companies Ct)), David Richards J;
see *Weller v Associated Newspapers Ltd*
[2014] EWHC 1163 (QB), [2014] E.M.L.R.
24 (QBD), Dingemans J
applied: 2014 c.22 Sch.6 para.6, 2014 c.2
Sch.9 para.3, 2014 c.12 Sch.4 para.7, SI
2014/507 Sch.1 para.6, SI 2014/587 Sch.1
para.6, SI 2014/693 Sch.1 para.6, SI
2014/1610 r.5_8, SI 2014/1825 Art.3, SI
2014/1826 Sch.1 para.6, SI 2014/1827 Sch.1
para.6, SI 2014/2054 Sch.1 para.6, SI
2014/2833 Reg.20, SI 2014/3349 Sch.1
para.6
disapplied: SI 2014/3141 Reg.50
s.1, see *Oakley Smith v Information Officer*
[2013] EWHC 2485 (Ch), [2014] Ch. 426
(Ch D (Companies Ct)), David Richards J
s.4, see *AB v A Chief Constable* [2014]
EWHC 1965 (QB), [2014] I.R.L.R. 700
(QBD), Cranston J; see *Vidal-Hall v Google
Inc* [2014] EWHC 13 (QB), [2014] 1 W.L.R.
4155 (QBD), Tugendhat J
s.5, amended: SI 2014/3141 Reg.52
s.7, see *Oakley Smith v Information Officer*
[2013] EWHC 2485 (Ch), [2014] Ch. 426
(Ch D (Companies Ct)), David Richards J
s.7, varied: SI 2014/3141 Reg.44
s.8, varied: SI 2014/3141 Reg.44
s.31, amended: SI 2014/892 Sch.1 para.118
s.34, applied: SI 2014/1610 r.5_8
s.40, varied: SI 2014/3141 Reg.51
s.41A, applied: SI 2014/3282 Art.2
s.41A, enabling: SI 2014/3282
s.42, varied: SI 2014/3141 Reg.51
s.47, varied: SI 2014/3141 Reg.51
s.48, varied: SI 2014/3141 Reg.51
s.51, see *Central London Community
Healthcare NHS Trust v Information
Commissioner* (2014) 136 B.M.L.R. 61 (UT
(AAC)), Judge Nicholas Wikeley
s.51, varied: SI 2014/3141 Reg.51
s.54, amended: SI 2014/3141 Reg.52
s.54, applied: SI 2014/3141 Reg.50
s.54A, varied: SI 2014/3141 Reg.51
s.55A, see *Central London Community
Healthcare NHS Trust v Information
Commissioner* (2014) 136 B.M.L.R. 61 (UT
(AAC)), Judge Nicholas Wikeley
s.55A, varied: SI 2014/3141 Reg.51

s.58, varied: SI 2014/3141 Reg.51
s.60, varied: SI 2014/3141 Reg.51
s.63, varied: SI 2014/3141 Reg.51
s.64, varied: SI 2014/3141 Reg.51
s.67, applied: SI 2014/3282
s.70, amended: 2014 c.29 s.4
Sch.2, see *AB v A Chief Constable* [2014]
EWHC 1965 (QB), [2014] I.R.L.R. 700
(QBD), Cranston J
Sch.3, see *AB v A Chief Constable* [2014]
EWHC 1965 (QB), [2014] I.R.L.R. 700
(QBD), Cranston J
Sch.3, applied: SI 2014/3141 Reg.33
Sch.3 para.8, disapplied: SI 2014/3141
Reg.33

30. Teaching and Higher Education Act 1998
see *R. (on the application of Guildhall
College) v Secretary of State for Business,
Innovation and Skills* [2013] EWHC 3257
(Admin), [2014] E.L.R. 10 (QBD (Admin)),
Cranston J
s.3, applied: SI 2014/2365 Reg.5
s.22, applied: SI 2014/1314 Reg.5, Reg.7, SI
2014/2929 Reg.4, SI 2014/3037 Reg.7, SI
2014/3352 Sch.1 para.12
s.22, enabling: SI 2014/290, SI 2014/651, SI
2014/1314, SI 2014/1712, SI 2014/1766, SI
2014/1895, SI 2014/2765, SI 2014/3037
s.42, enabling: SI 2014/290, SI 2014/651, SI
2014/1314, SI 2014/1712, SI 2014/1766, SI
2014/1895, SI 2014/2765, SI 2014/3037
s.43, enabling: SI 2014/1895, SI 2014/3037
Sch.2, applied: SI 2014/2365 Reg.5

31. School Standards and Framework Act 1998
see *TB v Essex CC* [2014] E.L.R. 46 (UT
(AAC)), Judge Lane
applied: 2014 c.6 s.83
Part II c.IV, applied: SI 2014/1132 Reg.77,
SI 2014/3352 Sch.1 para.20
s.1, referred to: 2014 c.6 s.43
s.45A, applied: SI 2014/3352 Reg.4, Reg.6
s.45A, enabling: SI 2014/3352
s.45AA, enabling: SI 2014/3352
s.47, applied: SI 2014/3352 Reg.24
s.47, enabling: SI 2014/3352
s.47A, applied: SI 2014/3352 Sch.2 para.2
s.47A, enabling: SI 2014/3352
s.47ZA, enabling: SI 2014/3352
s.48, applied: SI 2014/1132 Reg.63, Reg.82,
Reg.89, SI 2014/3352 Reg.26, Sch.1 para.20
s.48, enabling: SI 2014/3352

s.49, applied: SI 2014/3352 Sch.5 para.9
s.49, enabling: SI 2014/3352
s.50, applied: SI 2014/1132 Reg.82, Reg.89,
SI 2014/3352 Sch.5 para.13
s.50, varied: SI 2014/1132 Reg.78
s.63, applied: SI 2014/1132 Reg.63
s.69, applied: SI 2014/1132 Reg.6, Reg.9,
Reg.10, Reg.11, Reg.12, Reg.43, Reg.44,
Reg.46
s.69, enabling: SI 2014/1024, SI 2014/2320,
SI 2014/2342, SI 2014/3261, SI 2014/3361
s.78, applied: SI 2014/1132 Reg.77
s.88, applied: SI 2014/1132 Reg.63
s.88C, applied: SI 2014/3352 Sch.2 para.1
s.88C, enabling: SI 2014/2886
s.88E, enabling: SI 2014/2886
s.88F, enabling: SI 2014/2886
s.88H, enabling: SI 2014/2886
s.88K, enabling: SI 2014/2886
s.88M, enabling: SI 2014/2886
s.89, applied: SI 2014/1132 Reg.63
s.90, applied: SI 2014/1132 Reg.63
s.92, enabling: SI 2014/2886
s.94, applied: SI 2014/1132 Reg.63
s.95, applied: SI 2014/1132 Reg.63
s.97, applied: SI 2014/1132 Reg.63
s.98, amended: 2014 c.6 Sch.3 para.68
s.100, enabling: SI 2014/2886
s.102, enabling: SI 2014/2886
s.114A, enabling: SI 2014/1603, SI
2014/1855, SI 2014/3001
s.118, see *R. (on the application of West) v
Rhondda Cynon Taff CBC* [2014] EWHC
2134 (Admin), [2014] E.L.R. 396 (QBD
(Admin)), Supperstone J
s.122, enabling: SI 2014/1212
s.123, amended: 2014 c.6 Sch.3 para.69
s.124B, applied: SI 2014/1024, SI
2014/2320, SI 2014/2342, SI 2014/3361
s.138, enabling: SI 2014/1212, SI
2014/1603, SI 2014/1855, SI 2014/2886, SI
2014/3001, SI 2014/3261, SI 2014/3352
Sch.14 para.2A, applied: SI 2014/3352
Reg.27
Sch.14 para.2B, enabling: SI 2014/3352
Sch.22 Part AI paraA.23, amended: 2014 c.6
Sch.3 para.70
Sch.26 para.6B, enabling: SI 2014/1212
Sch.30 para.75, repealed (in part): 2014 c.6
Sch.3 para.16

Sch.30 para.225, repealed: 2014 c.2 Sch.1 Part 2

32. Police (Northern Ireland) Act 1998
s.25, amended: 2014 c.12 s.134
s.25A, added: 2014 c.12 s.134
s.34, repealed: 2014 c.12 Sch.11 para.102
s.60ZB, added: 2014 c.22 s.64

33. Landmines Act 1998
s.21, amended: SI 2014/834 Sch.2 para.13

36. Finance Act 1998
see *Stolkin v Revenue and Customs Commissioners* [2014] UKUT 165 (TCC), [2014] S.T.C. 2672 (UT (Tax)), David Richards J
Sch.18, see *Marks & Spencer Plc v Revenue and Customs Commissioners* [2014] UKSC 11, [2014] 1 W.L.R. 711 (SC), Lord Neuberger PSC
Sch.18 Part II para.8, amended: 2014 c.26 Sch.1 para.6
Sch.18 Part II para.10, amended: 2014 c.26 Sch.4 para.4
Sch.18 Part IV para.34, applied: 2014 c.26 s.208
Sch.18 Part V para.46, amended: 2014 c.26 s.277
Sch.18 Part VI para.52, amended: 2014 c.26 Sch.4 para.5
Sch.18 Pt IV para.32, see *Bristol & West Plc v Revenue and Customs Commissioners* [2014] UKUT 73 (TCC), [2014] S.T.C. 1048 (UT (Tax)), Peter Smith J
Sch.18 Pt IV para.34, see *Bristol & West Plc v Revenue and Customs Commissioners* [2014] UKUT 73 (TCC), [2014] S.T.C. 1048 (UT (Tax)), Peter Smith J
Sch.18 Pt VIII para.69, see *Marks & Spencer Plc v Revenue and Customs Commissioners* [2014] UKSC 11, [2014] 1 W.L.R. 711 (SC), Lord Neuberger PSC
Sch.18 Pt VIII para.70, see *Marks & Spencer Plc v Revenue and Customs Commissioners* [2014] UKSC 11, [2014] 1 W.L.R. 711 (SC), Lord Neuberger PSC
Sch.18 Pt VIII para.73, see *Marks & Spencer Plc v Revenue and Customs Commissioners* [2014] UKSC 11, [2014] 1 W.L.R. 711 (SC), Lord Neuberger PSC
Sch.18 Pt VIII para.74, see *R (on the application of GMGRM North Ltd) v Ritchie* [2014] EWCA Civ 844, [2014] B.T.C. 32

(CA (Civ Div)), Sir Stanley Burnton; see *R. (on the application of Bampton Property Group Ltd) v King* [2012] EWCA Civ 1744, [2014] S.T.C. 56 (CA (Civ Div)), Rix LJ
Sch.18 Part IXD, substituted: 2014 c.26 Sch.4 para.6
Sch.18 Part IXD para.83S, amended: 2014 c.26 Sch.4 para.6

37. Crime and Disorder Act 1998
applied: SI 2014/840 Sch.1, SI 2014/1610 r.5_9
s.1, see *Birmingham City Council v James* [2013] EWCA Civ 552, [2014] 1 W.L.R. 23 (CA (Civ Div)), Maurice Kay LJ
s.1, amended: 2014 c.12 Sch.11 para.24
s.1, repealed: 2014 c.12 Sch.11 para.24
s.1A, amended: 2014 c.12 Sch.11 para.24
s.1AA, applied: 2014 c.12 s.33
s.1C, applied: 2014 c.12 s.33, SI 2014/1610 r.50_1
s.1C, repealed: 2014 c.12 Sch.11 para.24
s.1CA, repealed: 2014 c.12 Sch.11 para.24
s.1D, applied: SI 2014/1610 r.50_1
s.1D, repealed (in part): 2014 c.12 Sch.11 para.24, Sch.11 para.24
s.1I, applied: SI 2014/1610 r.50_3
s.1I, repealed (in part): 2014 c.12 Sch.11 para.24
s.1J, repealed (in part): 2014 c.12 Sch.11 para.24
s.1K, repealed (in part): 2014 c.12 Sch.11 para.24
s.4, repealed: 2014 c.12 Sch.11 para.24
s.8, amended: 2014 c.12 Sch.11 para.25, Sch.11 para.55
s.8, applied: SI 2014/1610 r.50_1
s.8A, applied: SI 2014/1610 r.50_2
s.8A, repealed: 2014 c.12 Sch.11 para.24
s.9, amended: 2014 c.12 Sch.11 para.26
s.9, applied: SI 2014/1610 r.50_1, r.50_2
s.9, repealed (in part): 2014 c.12 Sch.11 para.26
s.10, applied: SI 2014/1610 r.63_1
s.18, amended: 2014 c.12 Sch.11 para.27
s.18, repealed (in part): 2014 c.12 Sch.11 para.27
s.38, amended: 2014 c.11 Sch.3 para.9, 2014 c.12 Sch.11 para.28
s.40, repealed (in part): 2014 c.12 Sch.11 para.50
s.47, applied: SI 2014/1610 r.37_1

s.50A, applied: SI 2014/1610 r.9_1, r.9_2
s.51, applied: SI 2014/1610 r.8_1, r.9_3,
r.3_1, r.9_5, r.9_7, r.9_14, r.14_1
s.51A, applied: SI 2014/1610 r.38_1, r.9_1
s.51B, applied: SI 2014/1610 r.9_6
s.51B, repealed (in part): SI 2014/834 Sch.2
para.15
s.51D, applied: SI 2014/1610 r.9_3, r.9_5,
r.14_1
s.51E, applied: SI 2014/1610 r.9_7
s.52, applied: SI 2014/1610 r.9_2
s.52A, applied: SI 2014/1610 r.16_1
s.57A, applied: SI 2014/1610 r.19_2, r.9_2
s.57D, applied: SI 2014/1610 r.37_10,
r.38_16
s.66A, applied: 2014 c.12 s.102
s.66BA, added: 2014 c.12 s.103
s.66H, repealed (in part): SI 2014/834 Sch.2
para.16
s.114, amended: 2014 c.12 Sch.11 para.29
s.115, applied: SI 2014/1610 r.5_9
Sch.3 para.1, applied: SI 2014/1610 r.14_1
Sch.3 para.2, applied: SI 2014/1610 r.9_16
Sch.3 para.3, applied: SI 2014/1610 r.16_1
Sch.3 para.4, applied: SI 2014/1610 Part 28,
r.28_1, r.28_3

38. Government of Wales Act 1998
s.145B, amended: SI 2014/77 Art.2

39. National Minimum Wage Act 1998
s.1, enabling: SI 2014/2485
s.2, enabling: SI 2014/2485
s.3, enabling: SI 2014/546, SI 2014/2485, SI
2014/2832
s.19A, amended: SI 2014/547 Reg.2
s.19A, enabling: SI 2014/547
s.24, applied: SI 2014/382 Art.4
s.49, amended: SI 2014/431 Sch.1 para.5
s.51, applied: SI 2014/546, SI 2014/547, SI
2014/2832
s.51, enabling: SI 2014/546, SI 2014/2485,
SI 2014/2832

41. Competition Act 1998
see *Dahabshiil Transfer Services Ltd v
Barclays Bank Plc* [2013] EWHC 3379
(Ch), [2014] U.K.C.L.R. 215 (Ch D),
Henderson J
applied: 2014 c.21 s.50, SI 2014/458 Sch.1
para.3, Sch.1 para.8
Part I, applied: SI 2014/458
s.2, see *Deutsche Bank AG v Unitech Global
Ltd* [2013] EWHC 2793 (Comm), [2014] 2

All E.R. (Comm) 268 (QBD (Comm)),
Teare J; see *Lindum Construction Co Ltd v
Office of Fair Trading* [2014] EWHC 1613
(Ch), [2014] Bus. L.R. 681 (Ch D), Morgan
J; see *Martin Retail Group Ltd v Crawley
BC* [2014] L. & T.R. 17 (CC (Central
London)), Judge Dight; see *Somerfield
Stores Ltd v Office of Fair Trading* [2014]
EWCA Civ 400, [2014] U.K.C.L.R. 1215
(CA (Civ Div)), Laws LJ
s.9, see *Martin Retail Group Ltd v Crawley
BC* [2014] L. & T.R. 17 (CC (Central
London)), Judge Dight
s.9, applied: SI 2014/458 Sch.1 para.10,
Sch.1 para.15
s.10, applied: SI 2014/458 Sch.1 para.15
s.18, see *Arriva The Shires Ltd v London
Luton Airport Operations Ltd* [2014] EWHC
64 (Ch), [2014] U.K.C.L.R. 313 (Ch D),
Rose J; see *Infederation Ltd v Google Inc*
[2013] EWHC 2295 (Ch), [2014] 1 All E.R.
325 (Ch D), Roth J
s.26, applied: SI 2014/458 Sch.1 para.4
s.26A, applied: SI 2014/458 Sch.1 para.4
s.27, applied: SI 2014/536 Reg.10
s.28, applied: SI 2014/458
s.31, applied: SI 2014/536 Reg.8, Reg.9
s.31A, applied: SI 2014/536 Reg.9
s.32, applied: SI 2014/458 Sch.1 para.12
s.35, applied: SI 2014/458 Sch.1 para.13, SI
2014/536 Reg.9
s.36, applied: SI 2014/458 Sch.1 para.11,
Sch.1 para.12
s.37, see *Lindum Construction Co Ltd v
Office of Fair Trading* [2014] EWHC 1613
(Ch), [2014] Bus. L.R. 681 (Ch D), Morgan
J
s.40A, applied: SI 2014/536 Reg.9, SI
2014/559, SI 2014/559 Art.4
s.40A, enabling: SI 2014/559
s.44, applied: 2014 c.23 s.92
s.45, disapplied: SI 2014/549 Art.3
s.46, see *Lindum Construction Co Ltd v
Office of Fair Trading* [2014] EWHC 1613
(Ch), [2014] Bus. L.R. 681 (Ch D), Morgan
J
s.47, see *WH Newson Holding Ltd v IMI Plc*
[2013] EWCA Civ 1377, [2014] 1 All E.R.
1132 (CA (Civ Div)), Arden LJ
s.47A, see *Deutsche Bahn AG v Morgan
Advanced Materials Plc (formerly Morgan*

Crucible Co Plc) [2013] EWCA Civ 1484, [2014] C.P. Rep. 10 (CA (Civ Div)), Richards LJ; see *Deutsche Bahn AG v Morgan Crucible Co Plc* [2014] UKSC 24, [2014] 2 All E.R. 785 (SC), Lord Neuberger JSC; see *WH Newson Holding Ltd v IMI Plc* [2013] EWCA Civ 1377, [2014] 1 All E.R. 1132 (CA (Civ Div)), Arden LJ; see *WH Newson Holding Ltd v IMI Plc* [2013] EWHC 3788 (Ch), [2014] U.K.C.L.R. 306 (Ch D), Rose J

s.50, applied: SI 2014/458 Sch.1 para.17

s.51, applied: SI 2014/458

s.51, enabling: SI 2014/458

s.54, applied: SI 2014/458

s.54, enabling: SI 2014/536

s.59, referred to: SI 2014/458 Sch.1 para.1

s.65E, applied: SI 2014/458 Sch.1 para.4

s.71, enabling: SI 2014/458, SI 2014/536

s.75A, applied: SI 2014/458

s.75A, enabling: SI 2014/458

Sch.1 Part I para.1, applied: SI 2014/458 Sch.1 para.17

Sch.1 Part I para.4, applied: SI 2014/458 Sch.1 para.17

Sch.3 para.9, applied: SI 2014/458 Sch.1 para.17

Sch.7 Part I para.12, varied: SI 2014/416 Sch.1 para.2

Sch.7 Part I para.12A, varied: SI 2014/416 Sch.1 para.2

Sch.9, applied: SI 2014/458

42. Human Rights Act 1998

see *DW (A Child) (Termination of Parental Responsibility), Re* [2014] EWCA Civ 315, [2014] 3 F.C.R. 314 (CA (Civ Div)), Arden LJ; see *Griffith (Javaughn) v HM Advocate* 2014 S.C.L. 39 (HCJ), Lord Eassie; see *Press Association v Newcastle Upon Tyne Hospitals Foundation Trust* [2014] EWCOP 6, [2014] C.O.P.L.R. 502 (CP), Peter Jackson J; see *R. (on the application of AB) v Secretary of State for the Home Department* [2013] EWHC 3453 (Admin), [2014] 2 C.M.L.R. 22 (QBD (Admin)), Mostyn J; see *R. (on the application of Eastenders Cash & Carry Plc) v Revenue and Customs Commissioners* [2014] UKSC 34, [2014] 2 W.L.R. 1580 (SC), Lord Neuberger PSC; see *R. (on the application of HC) v Secretary of State for the Home*

Department [2013] EWHC 982 (Admin), [2014] 1 W.L.R. 1234 (DC), Moses LJ; see *R. (on the application of Lord Carlile of Berriew QC) v Secretary of State for the Home Department* [2014] UKSC 60, [2014] 3 W.L.R. 1404 (SC), Lord Neuberger PSC; see *R. (on the application of Nicklinson) v Ministry of Justice* [2013] EWCA Civ 961, [2014] 2 All E.R. 32 (CA (Civ Div)), Lord Judge LCJ; see *R. (on the application of Revenue and Customs Commissioners) v HM Coroner for Liverpool* [2014] EWHC 1586 (Admin), [2014] 3 W.L.R. 1660 (DC), Gross LJ; see *TN (Afghanistan) v Secretary of State for the Home Department* [2013] EWCA Civ 1609, [2014] 1 W.L.R. 2095 (CA (Civ Div)), Maurice Kay LJ

applied: SI 2014/840 Sch.2, SI 2014/1610 r.65_12, r.17_28, SI 2014/3141 Reg.9, Reg.14, Sch.1 para.4, Sch.1 para.5, Sch.1 para.10, Sch.2 para.5, Sch.2 para.10

s.2, see *Moohan, Petitioner* [2014] CSIH 56, 2014 S.L.T. 755 (IH (1 Div)), The Lord President (Gill); see *R. (on the application of Hicks) v Commissioner of Police of the Metropolis* [2014] EWCA Civ 3, [2014] 1 W.L.R. 2152 (CA (Civ Div)), Maurice Kay LJ

s.3, see *Al-Malki v Reyes* [2014] I.C.R. 135 (EAT), Langstaff J; see *Benkharbouche v Embassy of Sudan* [2014] 1 C.M.L.R. 40 (EAT), Langstaff J; see *Blackburn (t/a Cornish Moorland Honey) v Revenue and Customs Commissioners* [2014] S.F.T.D. 195 (FTT (Tax)), Barbara Mosedale (Tribunal Judge); see *Dutch v Parole Board for Scotland* 2014 S.L.T. 285 (OH), Lord Burns; see *Mba v Merton LBC* [2013] EWCA Civ 1562, [2014] 1 W.L.R. 1501 (CA (Civ Div)), Maurice Kay LJ; see *Pallet Route Solutions Ltd v Morris* [2014] I.C.R. 394 (EAT), Langstaff J; see *R. (on the application of Barclay) v Secretary of State for Justice* [2014] UKSC 54, [2014] 3 W.L.R. 1142 (SC), Lord Neuberger JSC; see *R. (on the application of Boots Management Services Ltd) v Central Arbitration Committee* [2014] EWHC 65 (Admin), [2014] I.R.L.R. 278 (QBD (Admin)), Keith J; see *Revenue and Customs Commissioners*

v Bosher [2014] S.T.C. 617 (UT (Tax)),
Warren J
s.4, see *R. (on the application of Barclay) v
Secretary of State for Justice* [2014] UKSC
54, [2014] 3 W.L.R. 1142 (SC), Lord
Neuberger JSC; see *Speirs (Allan) v HM
Advocate* 2014 S.C.L. 58 (HCJ), The Lord
Justice Clerk (Carloway)
s.4, applied: SI 2014/1610 r.17_28, r.65_12
s.6, see *A (A Child) (Intractable Contact
Dispute: Human Rights Violations), Re*
[2013] EWCA Civ 1104, [2014] 1 F.L.R.
1185 (CA (Civ Div)), Aikens LJ; see *AJA v
Commissioner of Police of the Metropolis*
[2013] EWCA Civ 1342, [2014] 1 W.L.R.
285 (CA (Civ Div)), Lord Dyson MR; see *G
(A Child) (Care Proceedings: Welfare
Evaluation), Re* [2013] EWCA Civ 965,
[2014] 1 F.L.R. 670 (CA (Civ Div)),
Longmore LJ; see *O'Leary (Thomas) v HM
Advocate* [2014] HCJAC 45, 2014 S.L.T.
711 (HCJ), The Lord Justice Clerk
(Carloway); see *R. (on the application of
MM (Lebanon)) v Secretary of State for the
Home Department* [2013] EWHC 1900
(Admin), [2014] 1 W.L.R. 2306 (QBD
(Admin)), Blake J; see *Sarjantson v Chief
Constable of Humberside* [2013] EWCA Civ
1252, [2014] Q.B. 411 (CA (Civ Div)), Lord
Dyson MR; see *Speirs (Allan) v HM
Advocate* 2014 S.C.L. 58 (HCJ), The Lord
Justice Clerk (Carloway)
s.6, applied: 2014 c.12 s.54, s.89, 2014 c.23
s.73, SI 2014/2013 Reg.15, SI 2014/2043
Reg.85
s.7, see *ACCG v MN* [2013] EWHC 3859
(COP), [2014] C.O.P.L.R. 11 (CP), Eleanor
King J; see *Bedford v Bedfordshire CC*
[2013] EWHC 1717 (QB), [2014] P.T.S.R.
351 (QBD), Jay J
s.8, see *E (A Child) (Care Order: Change of
Care Plan), Re* [2014] EWFC 6, [2014] 3
W.L.R. 1733 (Fam Ct), Baker J
s.12, see *Ashworth v Royal National Theatre*
[2014] EWHC 1176 (QB), [2014] 4 All E.R.
238 (QBD), Cranston J; see *BBC, Re* [2014]
UKSC 25, [2014] 2 W.L.R. 1243 (SC), Lady
Hale DPSC; see *R. v Marine A* [2013]
EWCA Crim 2367, [2014] 1 W.L.R. 3326
(CMAC), Lord Thomas LCJ; see

Volkswagen AG v Garcia [2013] EWHC
1832 (Ch), [2014] F.S.R. 12 (Ch D), Birss J
s.21, amended: 2014 c.29 s.4

46. Scotland Act 1998
see *Moohan, Petitioner* 2014 S.L.T. 213
(OH), Lord Glennie
applied: 2014 asp 8 s.3
Part IVA, referred to: 2014 asp 6 Sch.1,
2014 c.29
Part IVA c.2, referred to: 2014 c.29 s.14
s.30, enabling: SI 2014/1559
s.35, see *Moohan, Petitioner* [2014] CSIH
56, 2014 S.L.T. 755 (IH (1 Div)), The Lord
President (Gill); see *Moohan, Petitioner*
2014 S.L.T. 213 (OH), Lord Glennie
s.53, applied: SI 2014/2753 Art.2
s.58, see *Moohan, Petitioner* [2014] CSIH
56, 2014 S.L.T. 755 (IH (1 Div)), The Lord
President (Gill); see *Moohan, Petitioner*
2014 S.L.T. 213 (OH), Lord Glennie
s.63, enabling: SI 2014/2918
s.65, applied: 2014 asp 6 s.5, s.6
s.80A, applied: SI 2014/2418 Sch.1
s.80C, amended: 2014 c.26 Sch.38 para.16
s.80D, amended: 2014 c.29 s.11
s.80DA, added: 2014 c.29 s.11
s.80E, amended: 2014 c.29 s.11
s.80F, amended: 2014 c.29 s.11
s.80G, amended: 2014 c.26 Sch.38 para.16
s.80G, repealed (in part): 2014 c.26 Sch.38
para.16
s.80HA, added: 2014 c.26 s.297
s.88, applied: SI 2014/791, SI 2014/1924
s.93, applied: SI 2014/1892 Art.2
s.93, enabling: SI 2014/1892
s.95, applied: 2014 asp 18 s.3, s.4
s.101, see *Joint Liquidators of the Scottish
Coal Co Ltd, Noters* 2014 S.C. 372 (IH (2
Div)), The Lord Justice Clerk (Carloway)
s.104, enabling: SI 2014/513, SI 2014/2747,
SI 2014/3061, SI 2014/3168, SI 2014/3229,
SI 2014/3294
s.106, applied: SI 2014/2753
s.106, enabling: SI 2014/2753
s.110, amended: 2014 c.26 Sch.38 para.16
s.112, enabling: SI 2014/513, SI 2014/2747,
SI 2014/2753, SI 2014/3061, SI 2014/3168,
SI 2014/3229, SI 2014/3294
s.113, enabling: SI 2014/513, SI 2014/1892,
SI 2014/2747, SI 2014/2918, SI 2014/3061,
SI 2014/3168, SI 2014/3229, SI 2014/3294

s.114, enabling: SI 2014/3294
s.115, applied: SI 2014/1559, SI 2014/2918,
SI 2014/3168
s.117, applied: SI 2014/2918 Art.3
s.124, enabling: SI 2014/2918
Sch.1 para.1, applied: SI 2014/501 Art.2
Sch.1 para.2, applied: SI 2014/501 Art.3
Sch.1 para.3, applied: SI 2014/501
Sch.1 para.6, applied: SI 2014/501
Sch.1 para.6, enabling: SI 2014/501
Sch.5 Part II paraC.2, amended: 2014 c.14
Sch.4 para.66
Sch.5 Part II paraJ.4, amended: SI
2014/1559 Art.5
Sch.5 Part II paraC.5, amended: SI
2014/1559 Art.2
Sch.5 Part II paraC.7, amended: SI
2014/1559 Art.3
Sch.5 Part II paraC.8, amended: SI
2014/1559 Art.4
Sch.7 para.1, amended: 2014 c.26 Sch.38
para.16
Sch.7 para.1, applied: SI 2014/1559, SI
2014/2918, SI 2014/3168, SI 2014/3229, SI
2014/3294

47. Northern Ireland Act 1998
applied: 2014 c.25 Sch.1
referred to: 2014 c.5 Sch.1 para.1
s.4, amended: 2014 c.13 s.10, s.11
s.7A, added: 2014 c.13 s.6
s.14, amended: 2014 c.13 s.6
s.28, applied: SI 2014/469 Art.5
s.31, amended: 2014 c.13 s.7
s.34, amended: 2014 c.13 s.23
s.34, enabling: SI 2014/1804
s.37, amended: 2014 c.13 s.3
s.47, amended: 2014 c.13 s.3
s.53, amended: 2014 c.13 s.6
s.69C, amended: 2014 c.22 Sch.9 para.11
s.75, amended: 2014 c.13 s.22
s.84, amended: 2014 c.13 s.23
s.84, applied: SI 2014/270, SI 2014/1116, SI
2014/1880
s.84, enabling: SI 2014/270, SI 2014/1116,
SI 2014/1880
s.87, enabling: SI 2014/1423
s.96, applied: SI 2014/1804
Sch.2 para.10C, added: 2014 c.28 s.68
Sch.2 para.12, substituted: 2014 c.13 s.12
Sch.2 para.21, amended: 2014 c.13 s.10
Sch.2 para.22, amended: 2014 c.13 s.11

Sch.3 para.7A, added: 2014 c.13 s.6
Sch.3 para.16, amended: 2014 c.13 s.10
Sch.3 para.41A, added: 2014 c.13 s.12
Sch.3 para.42, amended: 2014 c.13 s.11
Sch.4A Part 1A para.3B, substituted: 2014
c.13 s.8
Sch.4A Part 1A para.3C, substituted: 2014
c.13 s.8
Sch.4A Part 1A para.3D, amended: 2014
c.13 s.8
Sch.4A Part 1A para.3E, added: 2014 c.13
s.9
Sch.9 para.4, amended: 2014 c.13 s.22

1999

**2. Social Security Contributions (Transfer of
Functions, etc.) Act 1999**
s.8, amended: 2014 c.6 Sch.7 para.45, 2014
c.7 s.6
s.8, applied: SI 2014/3051 Reg.44, Reg.45
s.8, varied: 2014 c.6 s.126
s.8, enabling: SI 2014/2929
s.11, amended: 2014 c.6 Sch.7 para.46
s.11, varied: 2014 c.6 s.126
s.14, amended: 2014 c.6 Sch.7 para.47
s.14, varied: 2014 c.6 s.126
s.25, enabling: SI 2014/2929

8. Health Act 1999
s.31, applied: SI 2014/3352 Sch.1 para.7
s.60, enabling: SI 2014/1101, SI 2014/1887,
SI 2014/3272
s.62, applied: SI 2014/1101, SI 2014/1887,
SI 2014/3272
s.62, enabling: SI 2014/1101, SI 2014/1887,
SI 2014/3272
Sch.3, enabling: SI 2014/1101, SI
2014/1887, SI 2014/3272
Sch.3 para.9, applied: SI 2014/1101, SI
2014/1887, SI 2014/3272
Sch.3 para.9, referred to: SI 2014/1101, SI
2014/1887, SI 2014/3272

14. Protection of Children Act 1999
s.1, applied: SI 2014/1132 Sch.7 para.9, SI
2014/2709 Sch.2 para.9

16. Finance Act 1999
s.123, amended: 2014 c.26 s.114
s.132, varied: 2014 c.6 Sch.7 para.48
s.132, enabling: SI 2014/489, SI 2014/548,
SI 2014/1497

s.133, enabling: SI 2014/472, SI 2014/548, SI 2014/1497

Sch.13, applied: 2014 c.26 Sch.24 para.5

Sch.19 Part II, repealed: 2014 c.26 s.114

Sch.19 Part II para.2, applied: 2014 c.26 s.114, SI 2014/1932 Reg.1

22. Access to Justice Act 1999

see *Coventry v Lawrence* [2014] UKSC 46 (SC), Lord Neuberger PSC; see *Herridge v Parker* [2014] Lloyd's Rep. I.R. 177 (CC (Cardiff)), Recorder James Thom QC

s.6, enabling: SI 2014/1818, SI 2014/2864

s.11, see *Simpson (t/a Harrow Solicitors and Advocates) v Godson* [2013] EWCA Civ 1339, [2014] 1 Costs L.O. 77 (CA (Civ Div)), Moore-Bick LJ

s.11, applied: SI 2014/1610 r.61_22

s.22, see *JG (A Child) v Legal Services Commission* [2014] EWCA Civ 656, [2014] 5 Costs L.O. 708 (CA (Civ Div)), Richards LJ

s.25, enabling: SI 2014/1818

s.54, see *A (A Patient) (Court of Protection: Appeal), Re* [2013] EWCA Civ 1661, [2014] 1 W.L.R. 3773 (CA (Civ Div)), Moses LJ; see *C (Children) (Transcripts: Permission to Appeal), Re* [2013] EWCA Civ 1158, [2014] 2 F.L.R. 147 (CA (Civ Div)), Sir James Munby PFD

s.54, enabling: SI 2014/667

s.56, applied: SI 2014/602

s.56, enabling: SI 2014/602

Sch.2 para.2, amended: SI 2014/1773 Art.3

Sch.2 para.2, repealed (in part): SI 2014/1773 Art.3

Sch.4 para.50, repealed: 2014 c.6 s.18

23. Youth Justice and Criminal Evidence Act 1999

applied: SI 2014/1610 r.29_15, r.50_3, r.29_17

Part II c.I, applied: 2014 c.12 s.16, s.31

s.16, applied: SI 2014/1610 r.29_26

s.17, varied: 2014 c.12 s.16, s.31

s.19, applied: 2014 c.12 s.16, s.31, SI 2014/1610 r.29_1, r.38_11, r.37_4, r.16_6, r.29_19, r.36_6, r.29_26

s.20, applied: SI 2014/1610 r.29_1, r.5_4, r.29_4, r.29_11, r.29_12

s.21, applied: SI 2014/1610 r.29_9, r.29_13, r.29_26

s.21, varied: 2014 c.12 s.16, s.31

s.22A, varied: 2014 c.12 s.16, s.31

s.23, applied: SI 2014/1610 r.29_1

s.24, applied: SI 2014/1610 r.29_1, r.29_26

s.25, applied: SI 2014/1610 r.29_1

s.26, applied: SI 2014/1610 r.29_1

s.27, applied: SI 2014/1610 r.29_1

s.27, varied: 2014 c.12 s.16, s.31

s.28, applied: SI 2014/1610 r.29_26

s.29, applied: SI 2014/1610 r.29_1

s.30, applied: SI 2014/1610 r.29_1

s.32, varied: 2014 c.12 s.16, s.31

s.33A, applied: SI 2014/1610 r.5_4, r.29_1, r.29_4, r.29_15, r.29_16, r.29_26

s.33BA, applied: SI 2014/1610 r.29_1, r.29_15, r.3_9, r.29_26

s.33BB, applied: SI 2014/1610 r.5_4, r.29_4, r.29_16

s.34, applied: SI 2014/1610 Part 36, r.37_4, r.31_1, r.31_2, r.31_3, r.38_11

s.36, applied: SI 2014/1610 r.31_4

s.38, applied: SI 2014/1610 r.31_2, r.31_3

s.41, see *R. v All-Hilly (Salaam David)* [2014] EWCA Crim 1614, [2014] 2 Cr. App. R. 33 (CA (Crim Div)), Treacy LJ; see *R. v P* [2013] EWCA Crim 2331, [2014] 1 W.L.R. 3058 (CA (Crim Div)), McCombe LJ

s.41, applied: SI 2014/1610 Part 36, r.36_1, r.36_3

s.45, see *R. (on the application of JC) v Central Criminal Court* [2014] EWHC 1041 (Admin), [2014] 1 W.L.R. 3697 (DC), Sir Brian Leveson PQBD

s.45, applied: 2014 c.12 s.30

s.46, see *R. (on the application of JC) v Central Criminal Court* [2014] EWHC 1041 (Admin), [2014] 1 W.L.R. 3697 (DC), Sir Brian Leveson PQBD; see *R. v ITN News* [2013] EWCA Crim 773, [2014] 1 W.L.R. 199 (CA (Crim Div)), Lord Judge LCJ

s.46, applied: SI 2014/1610 r.16_1, r.29_19, r.37_2, r.16_4

s.47, applied: 2014 c.12 s.16, s.31, SI 2014/1610 r.37_2, r.16_1

s.49, applied: 2014 c.12 s.16, s.31

s.53, applied: SI 2014/1610 r.38_11, r.37_4

s.55, applied: SI 2014/1610 r.38_11, r.37_4

24. Pollution Prevention and Control Act 1999

s.1, amended: 2014 asp 3 Sch.3 para.7

s.1, repealed (in part): 2014 asp 3 Sch.3 para.7

s.2, amended: 2014 c.21 s.62
s.2, applied: 2014 c.21 s.62, SI 2014/255, SI
2014/656, SI 2014/2852, SI 2014/3125, SSI
2014/258 Sch.1 para.1, SSI 2014/267
s.2, enabling: SI 2014/255, SI 2014/656, SI
2014/2852, SI 2014/3125, SSI 2014/267
s.7, enabling: SI 2014/2852, SI 2014/3125
Sch.1, enabling: SI 2014/255, SI 2014/656,
SI 2014/2852, SI 2014/3125, SSI 2014/267
Sch.3, amended: 2014 asp 3 Sch.3 para.36

26. Employment Relations Act 1999
s.10, see *Roberts v GB Oils Ltd* [2014]
I.C.R. 462 (EAT), Jeffrey Burke Q.C.
s.11, see *Roberts v GB Oils Ltd* [2014]
I.C.R. 462 (EAT), Jeffrey Burke Q.C.
s.11, applied: SI 2014/382 Art.4
s.14, amended: SI 2014/431 Sch.1 para.6
s.34, enabling: SI 2014/382
s.38, enabling: SI 2014/16, SI 2014/1139

27. Local Government Act 1999
Part I, applied: 2014 c.2 Sch.11 para.1,
Sch.11 para.2, SI 2014/3352 Sch.1 para.20
s.1, applied: 2014 c.2 Sch.9 para.2, SI
2014/512 Sch.1 para.6
s.10, substituted: 2014 c.2 Sch.10 para.2
s.11, amended: 2014 c.2 Sch.10 para.3
s.12, substituted: 2014 c.2 Sch.10 para.4
s.13, amended: 2014 c.2 Sch.10 para.5
s.13, repealed (in part): 2014 c.2 Sch.10
para.5, Sch.10 para.11
s.15, amended: 2014 c.2 Sch.10 para.6, 2014
c.6 s.101
s.15, applied: SI 2014/512 Sch.1 para.3
s.15, repealed (in part): 2014 c.2 Sch.10
para.6
s.22, repealed (in part): 2014 c.2 Sch.1 Part
2, Sch.10 para.7
s.23, amended: 2014 c.2 Sch.12 para.36
s.23, repealed (in part): 2014 c.2 Sch.12
para.36
s.25, amended: 2014 c.2 Sch.10 para.8
s.26, repealed (in part): 2014 c.2 Sch.10
para.9
s.33, repealed (in part): 2014 c.2 Sch.10
para.10

28. Food Standards Act 1999
s.22, amended: 2014 c.29 s.4

29. Greater London Authority Act 1999
applied: 2014 c.5 Sch.1 para.1, 2014 c.25
Sch.1

s.7, repealed (in part): 2014 c.2 Sch.12
para.38
s.9, amended: 2014 c.2 Sch.12 para.39
s.14, repealed (in part): 2014 c.2 Sch.12
para.40
s.21, repealed (in part): 2014 c.2 Sch.12
para.41
s.34A, amended: 2014 c.14 Sch.4 para.67
s.54, disapplied: 2014 c.2 Sch.7 para.7
s.58, applied: 2014 c.2 s.40
s.86, amended: SI 2014/389 Art.5
s.86, repealed (in part): SI 2014/389 Art.5
s.102, repealed (in part): SI 2014/389 Art.6
s.125, amended: 2014 c.2 Sch.12 para.42
s.125, repealed (in part): 2014 c.2 Sch.12
para.42
s.133, repealed: 2014 c.2 Sch.1 Part 2
s.134, amended: 2014 c.2 Sch.12 para.43
s.163, applied: SI 2014/3102 Art.41
s.207, applied: SI 2014/3102 Art.41
s.235, amended: SI 2014/892 Sch.1 para.119
s.235, repealed (in part): SI 2014/892 Sch.1
para.119
s.408, repealed (in part): SI 2014/3184 Sch.1
para.13
Sch.6 para.3, amended: SI 2014/3308 Reg.2
Sch.6 para.9ZA, added: SI 2014/389 Art.7
Sch.6 para.10, enabling: SI 2014/3308
Sch.8, repealed: 2014 c.2 Sch.1 Part 2
Sch.27 para.92, repealed (in part): 2014 c.12
Sch.11 para.102

30. Welfare Reform and Pensions Act 1999
see *X (Application for Income Payments
Order), Re* [2014] B.P.I.R. 1081 (Ch D),
District Judge Smith
Part IV, applied: SI 2014/1711 Reg.76
s.23, applied: SI 2014/1711 Reg.76
s.23, enabling: SI 2014/1711
s.26, enabling: SI 2014/1711
s.28, amended: 2014 c.6 s.18
s.28, repealed (in part): 2014 c.6 s.18
s.29, applied: SI 2014/2848 Reg.21, SI
2014/3138 Reg.4, SSI 2014/164 Reg.8
s.29, referred to: 2014 c.26 Sch.6 para.1
s.30, enabling: SI 2014/1711
s.31, applied: SI 2014/1964 Reg.95, SI
2014/2336 Reg.50, Reg.85, SI 2014/2848
Reg.91
s.47, amended: 2014 c.19 Sch.11 para.10,
Sch.15 para.14
s.48, amended: 2014 c.19 Sch.11 para.11

s.48, repealed (in part): 2014 c.6 s.18
s.49, amended: 2014 c.19 Sch.11 para.12
s.49A, added: 2014 c.19 Sch.11 para.13
s.51, substituted: 2014 c.19 Sch.11 para.14
s.83, applied: SI 2014/1711
s.83, enabling: SI 2014/1711
Sch.12 Part I para.64, repealed: 2014 c.6
s.18

**31. Contracts (Rights of Third Parties) Act
1999**

see *Starlight Shipping Co v Allianz Marine
& Aviation Versicherungs AG* [2014]
EWHC 3068 (Comm), [2014] 2 Lloyd's Rep.
579 (QBD (Comm)), Flaux J
s.1, see *Hurley Palmer Flatt Ltd v Barclays
Bank Plc* [2014] EWHC 3042 (TCC), [2014]
B.L.R. 713 (QBD (TCC)), Ramsey J; see
*San Evans Maritime Inc v Aigaion Insurance
Co SA* [2014] EWHC 163 (Comm), [2014] 2
Lloyd's Rep. 265 (QBD (Comm)), Teare J;
see *Starlight Shipping Co v Allianz Marine
& Aviation Versicherungs AG* [2014]
EWHC 3068 (Comm), [2014] 2 Lloyd's Rep.
579 (QBD (Comm)), Flaux J
s.8, see *Hurley Palmer Flatt Ltd v Barclays
Bank Plc* [2014] EWHC 3042 (TCC), [2014]
B.L.R. 713 (QBD (TCC)), Ramsey J

33. Immigration and Asylum Act 1999

applied: 2014 c.22 s.62, SI 2014/2604 Sch.1
para.2
Part VI, applied: SI 2014/3352 Reg.16
s.4, see *Mensah v Salford City Council*
[2014] EWHC 3537 (Admin), (2014) 17
C.C.L. Rep. 492 (QBD (Admin)), Lewis J
s.4, applied: 2014 c.22 Sch.3 para.8
s.10, see *Patel v Secretary of State for the
Home Department* [2014] A.C. 651 (SC),
Lord Mance JSC; see *R. (on the application
of George) v Secretary of State for the Home
Department* [2014] UKSC 28, [2014] 1
W.L.R. 1831 (SC), Lord Neuberger PSC; see
*R. (on the application of Thapa) v Secretary
of State for the Home Department* [2014]
EWHC 659 (Admin), [2014] 1 W.L.R. 4138
(QBD (Admin)), Helen Mountfield QC
s.10, amended: 2014 c.22 Sch.1 para.2
s.10, applied: SI 2014/2816 Reg.4
s.10, substituted: 2014 c.22 s.1
s.10, enabling: SI 2014/2816
s.23, repealed: 2014 c.22 Sch.9 para.28
s.24, amended: 2014 c.22 s.55, s.56

s.24, applied: 2014 c.22 Sch.6 para.3
s.24, referred to: 2014 c.22 s.62
s.24, enabling: SI 2014/1660
s.24A, amended: 2014 c.22 s.55, s.56
s.24A, enabling: SI 2014/1660
s.31, see *R. v Mateta (Koshi Pitshou)* [2013]
EWCA Crim 1372, [2014] 1 W.L.R. 1516
(CA (Crim Div)), Leveson LJ; see *SXH v
Crown Prosecution Service* [2014] EWCA
Civ 90, [2014] 1 W.L.R. 3238 (CA (Civ
Div)), Pitchford LJ
s.41, enabling: SI 2014/1513, SI 2014/2702
s.84, amended: 2014 c.22 Sch.7 para.2,
Sch.7 para.5
s.84, applied: 2014 c.22 Sch.9 para.67, SI
2014/2604 r.10
s.84, repealed (in part): 2014 c.22 Sch.7
para.2
s.85, applied: 2014 c.22 Sch.9 para.67
s.85, repealed (in part): 2014 c.22 Sch.7
para.2
s.87, amended: 2014 c.22 Sch.7 para.4,
Sch.7 para.5
s.87, repealed (in part): 2014 c.22 Sch.7
para.2
s.88, repealed (in part): 2014 c.22 Sch.7
para.2
s.89, amended: 2014 c.22 Sch.7 para.7
s.89, repealed (in part): 2014 c.22 Sch.7
para.2
s.95, applied: 2014 c.22 Sch.3 para.8, 2014
c.23 s.21
s.95, referred to: 2014 c.23 s.21
s.98, applied: 2014 c.22 Sch.3 para.8
s.115, applied: 2014 c.23 s.21
s.115, enabling: SI 2014/902
s.141, amended: 2014 c.22 Sch.9 para.29
s.141, repealed (in part): 2014 c.22 Sch.9
para.29
s.141, varied: SI 2014/1704 Art.8
s.143, repealed: 2014 c.22 Sch.9 para.17
s.143, varied: SI 2014/1704 Art.8
s.144, amended: 2014 c.22 Sch.2 para.2,
Sch.9 para.17
s.144A, added: 2014 c.22 s.14
s.146, amended: 2014 c.22 Sch.1 para.5
s.147, amended: 2014 c.22 s.6
s.155, amended: 2014 c.22 s.6
s.157A, added: 2014 c.22 s.6
s.166, repealed (in part): 2014 c.22 Sch.9
para.17

s.167, varied: SI 2014/1704 Art.8

Sch.5 Part I para.4A, added: 2014 c.22 Sch.7 para.6

Sch.5 Part I para.5, amended: 2014 c.22 Sch.7 para.7

Sch.5 Part I para.5, disapplied: 2014 c.22 Sch.9 para.69

Sch.5 Part I para.5, referred to: 2014 c.22 Sch.9 para.68

Sch.5 Part I para.6, repealed (in part): 2014 c.22 Sch.7 para.2

Sch.5 Part I para.7, repealed: 2014 c.22 Sch.7 para.8

Sch.5 Part I para.9, amended: 2014 c.22 Sch.7 para.4, Sch.7 para.7

Sch.5 Part I para.9, referred to: 2014 c.22 Sch.9 para.68

Sch.5 Part I para.9, repealed (in part): 2014 c.22 Sch.7 para.2, Sch.7 para.4

Sch.5 Part I para.10A, added: 2014 c.22 Sch.7 para.8

Sch.5 Part I para.10A, applied: 2014 c.22 Sch.9 para.69

Sch.6 para.3, amended: 2014 c.22 Sch.7 para.4

Sch.6 para.3, repealed (in part): 2014 c.22 Sch.7 para.4

Sch.6 para.4A, added: 2014 c.22 Sch.7 para.4

Sch.6 para.4B, added: 2014 c.22 Sch.7 para.5

Sch.6 para.5, amended: 2014 c.22 Sch.7 para.3

Sch.6 para.5, enabling: SI 2014/2847

Sch.6 para.6, repealed (in part): 2014 c.22 Sch.7 para.2

Sch.11 para.3, amended: 2014 c.22 Sch.9 para.12

Sch.11 para.4, amended: 2014 c.22 Sch.9 para.12

Sch.11 para.5, amended: 2014 c.22 Sch.9 para.12

Sch.12 para.4, amended: 2014 c.22 Sch.9 para.12

Sch.12 para.8, amended: 2014 c.22 Sch.9 para.12

34. House of Lords Act 1999

s.1, applied: 2014 c.24 s.4

s.2, applied: 2014 c.24 s.4

2000

vii. London Local Authorities Act 2000

s.33, see *Keep Streets Live Campaign Ltd v Camden LBC* [2014] EWHC 607 (Admin), [2014] B.L.G.R. 286 (QBD (Admin)), Patterson J

Pt V., see *Keep Streets Live Campaign Ltd v Camden LBC* [2014] EWHC 607 (Admin), [2014] B.L.G.R. 286 (QBD (Admin)), Patterson J

1. Northern Ireland Act 2000

applied: 2014 c.25 Sch.1

referred to: 2014 c.5 Sch.1 para.1

2. Representation of the People Act 2000

Sch.1 para.7, repealed: 2014 c.13 s.14

5. Nuclear Safeguards Act 2000

s.2, applied: SI 2014/469 Sch.4 para.20

s.4, applied: SI 2014/469 Sch.4 para.25

6. Powers of Criminal Courts (Sentencing) Act 2000

applied: SI 2014/1610 r.55_2, r.42_5

referred to: 2014 c.11 s.7

s.1, applied: SI 2014/1610 r.37_10, r.38_16, r.63_2

s.1C, applied: SI 2014/1610 r.42_10

s.3, see *R. v de Brito (Paulo Aguiar)* [2013] EWCA Crim 1134, [2014] 1 Cr. App. R. (S.) 38 (CA (Crim Div)), Keith J

s.3, applied: SI 2014/1610 r.37_10, r.42_10, r.9_11

s.3B, applied: SI 2014/1610 r.9_7

s.3C, applied: SI 2014/1610 r.9_11

s.4, applied: SI 2014/1610 r.9_8

s.4A, applied: SI 2014/1610 r.9_7

s.6, see *R. v de Brito (Paulo Aguiar)* [2013] EWCA Crim 1134, [2014] 1 Cr. App. R. (S.) 38 (CA (Crim Div)), Keith J; see *R. v Jepson (Matthew Joseph)* [2013] EWCA Crim 1362, [2014] 1 Cr. App. R. (S.) 43 (CA (Crim Div)), Moore-Bick LJ

s.6, applied: SI 2014/1610 r.37_10, r.42_10, r.9_7, r.9_8, r.9_11

s.7, see *R. v Jepson (Matthew Joseph)* [2013] EWCA Crim 1362, [2014] 1 Cr. App. R. (S.) 43 (CA (Crim Div)), Moore-Bick LJ

s.8, applied: SI 2014/1610 r.37_10, r.42_10

s.9, applied: SI 2014/1610 r.37_1, r.42_10

s.10, applied: SI 2014/1610 r.42_10

s.11, applied: SI 2014/1610 r.33_1, r.42_8

s.12, applied: 2014 c.12 s.30

s.13, applied: SI 2014/1610 r.42_10

s.14, see *HM Advocate v H* [2014] HCJAC 36, 2014 J.C. 195 (HCJ), The Lord Justice Clerk (Carloway)

s.41, applied: SI 2014/1610 r.76_2, SI 2014/1652 Sch.1, SI 2014/2871 Sch.1

s.51, applied: SI 2014/1652 Sch.1, SI 2014/2871 Sch.1

s.52, applied: SI 2014/1652 Sch.1, SI 2014/2871 Sch.1

s.66, applied: SI 2014/512 Sch.1 para.17

s.73, applied: SI 2014/1610 r.42_1

s.82A, see *Attorney General's Reference (No.27 of 2013)* [2014] EWCA Crim 334, [2014] 1 W.L.R. 4209 (CA (Crim Div)), Lord Thomas LCJ; see *R. v Leacock (Mark)* [2013] EWCA Crim 1994, [2014] 2 Cr. App. R. (S.) 12 (CA (Crim Div)), Lord Thomas LCJ

s.82A, applied: SI 2014/1610 r.68_1

s.83, see *R. v Henry (Derek Nicholas)* [2013] EWCA Crim 1415, [2014] 1 Cr. App. R. (S.) 55 (CA (Crim Div)), Leveson LJ

s.83, applied: SI 2014/1610 r.38_2

s.85, see *R. (on the application of Minter) v Chief Constable of Hampshire* [2013] EWCA Civ 697, [2014] 1 W.L.R. 179 (CA (Civ Div)), Laws LJ

s.89, applied: SI 2014/1610 r.62_5, r.62_9

s.91, see *R. (on the application of BH (A Child)) v Llandudno Youth Court* [2014] EWHC 1833 (Admin), (2014) 178 J.P. 305 (QBD (Admin)), Andrews J; see *R. v K* [2013] EWCA Crim 649, [2014] 1 Cr. App. R. (S.) 5 (CA (Crim Div)), McCombe LJ; see *R. v Walsh (Anthony)* [2014] EWCA Crim 1155, [2014] 2 Cr. App. R. (S.) 59 (CA (Crim Div)), Beatson LJ

s.101, amended: 2014 c.11 s.6

s.103, amended: 2014 c.11 s.6, Sch.3 para.11

s.103, repealed (in part): 2014 c.11 Sch.3 para.11

s.106B, added: 2014 c.11 s.6

s.107, amended: 2014 c.11 Sch.3 para.12

s.108, applied: SI 2014/1610 r.62_5, r.62_9

s.110, see *R. v Gallone (Paulo)* [2014] EWCA Crim 1140, [2014] 2 Cr. App. R. (S.) 57 (CA (Crim Div)), Beatson LJ; see *R. v Goodale (Gavin)* [2013] EWCA Crim 1144, [2014] 1 Cr. App. R. (S.) 37 (CA (Crim Div)), Elias LJ

s.130, see *R. v Carrington (Marion)* [2014] EWCA Crim 325, [2014] 2 Cr. App. R. (S.) 41 (CA (Crim Div)), Aikens LJ

s.130, applied: SI 2014/1610 r.42_1, r.42_5

s.137, see *R. v Bailey (Wayne)* [2013] EWCA Crim 1551, [2014] 1 Cr. App. R. (S.) 59 (CA (Crim Div)), Leveson LJ

s.140, applied: SI 2014/1610 r.42_10, r.56_5

s.146, applied: SI 2014/1610 r.55_2

s.147, applied: SI 2014/1610 r.55_2

s.148, applied: SI 2014/1610 r.42_7

s.155, see *R. v Catchpole (Scott Jamie)* [2014] EWCA Crim 1037, [2014] 2 Cr. App. R. (S.) 66 (CA (Crim Div)), Treacy LJ; see *R. v Hoggard (Barrie)* [2013] EWCA Crim 1024, [2014] 1 Cr. App. R. (S.) 42 (CA (Crim Div)), Hughes LJ; see *R. v Leacock (Mark)* [2013] EWCA Crim 1994, [2014] 2 Cr. App. R. (S.) 12 (CA (Crim Div)), Lord Thomas LCJ

s.155, applied: SI 2014/1610 r.42_4

s.155, enabling: SI 2014/1610

Sch.3, applied: SI 2014/1610 r.44_1

Sch.3 Part III para.10, applied: SI 2014/1610 r.63_1

Sch.5, applied: SI 2014/1610 r.44_1

Sch.7, applied: SI 2014/1610 r.44_1

Sch.9 para.192, repealed: 2014 c.12 Sch.11 para.50

7. Electronic Communications Act 2000

s.7, applied: SI 2014/1610 r.5_3

s.8, enabling: SI 2014/184, SI 2014/1602

s.9, enabling: SI 2014/184

s.15, applied: SSI 2014/4 Reg.2, SSI 2014/347 Reg.1

s.15, referred to: SSI 2014/122 Art.2, SSI 2014/325 Reg.2, SSI 2014/338 Reg.2

8. Financial Services and Markets Act 2000

see *O'Neil v Gale* [2013] EWCA Civ 1554, [2014] Lloyd's Rep. F.C. 202 (CA (Civ Div)), Laws LJ

applied: 2014 c.21 s.79, s.81, SI 2014/208 Art.8, SI 2014/366 Art.20, SI 2014/1825 Art.3, SI 2014/2080 Art.14, SI 2014/2879 Reg.5, SI 2014/3085 Reg.3, SI 2014/3348 Art.15, Art.21, Art.23, Art.29, Art.56, Art.67, Art.90, Art.217, SSI 2014/164 Sch.2 para.7

referred to: 2014 c.21 s.79, s.81, 2014 c.22 s.41

Part IV, applied: SSI 2014/164 Sch.2 para.7

Part IVA, applied: SI 2014/208 Art.2, SI 2014/366 Art.4, SI 2014/894 Reg.22, Reg.30, SI 2014/1960 Art.11, Art.12
Part VI, applied: SI 2014/2418 Sch.1
Part IX, applied: SI 2014/894 Reg.4, SI 2014/2879 Reg.5
Part IX, varied: SI 2014/3348 Art.67
Part XI, applied: SI 2014/3085 Reg.11, Reg.14
Part XI, varied: SI 2014/3085 Reg.14
Part XIV, applied: SI 2014/2879 Reg.5, SI 2014/3085 Reg.28
Part XV, applied: SI 2014/3348 Art.183
Part XVIII, referred to: SI 2014/2418 Sch.1
Part XXV, varied: SI 2014/3085 Reg.29
Part XXVI, applied: SI 2014/3085 Reg.26
s.2, applied: SI 2014/229 Sch.5 para.3
s.3M, amended: SI 2014/3329 Art.113
s.19, see *O'Neil v Gale* [2013] EWCA Civ 1554, [2014] Lloyd's Rep. F.C. 202 (CA (Civ Div)), Laws LJ
s.19, applied: SI 2014/366 Art.15, Art.17
s.22, applied: 2014 c.26 s.128, SI 2014/826 Reg.4, SI 2014/899 Reg.4
s.22, referred to: SI 2014/2418 Sch.1
s.22, enabling: SI 2014/366, SI 2014/1292, SI 2014/1313, SI 2014/1448, SI 2014/1740
s.22A, applied: SI 2014/2418 Sch.1
s.23, see *O'Neil v Gale* [2013] EWCA Civ 1554, [2014] Lloyd's Rep. F.C. 202 (CA (Civ Div)), Laws LJ
s.23, applied: SI 2014/334 Art.2
s.23, enabling: SI 2014/334
s.23A, applied: SI 2014/334
s.26, applied: SI 2014/208 Art.2
s.28A, applied: SI 2014/208 Art.2
s.31, applied: SI 2014/2418 Sch.1
s.38, enabling: SI 2014/506
s.39, enabling: SI 2014/206
s.55U, applied: SI 2014/208 Art.2, SI 2014/366 Art.4
s.59, applied: SI 2014/3085 Reg.19
s.59, referred to: SI 2014/3085 Reg.19
s.63A, applied: SI 2014/3085 Reg.19
s.63A, referred to: SI 2014/3085 Reg.19
s.66, applied: SI 2014/3085 Reg.28
s.69, applied: SI 2014/3085 Reg.28
s.77, amended: SI 2014/3329 Art.114
s.78, amended: SI 2014/3329 Art.115
s.86, amended: SI 2014/3293 Reg.2

s.87A, repealed (in part): SI 2014/3293 Reg.2
s.87FA, added: SI 2014/3293 Reg.3
s.87FB, added: SI 2014/3293 Reg.3
s.87K, amended: SI 2014/3293 Reg.2
s.87L, amended: SI 2014/3293 Reg.2
s.89C, amended: SI 2014/3293 Reg.4
s.89C, repealed (in part): SI 2014/3293 Reg.4
s.89L, applied: SI 2014/3348 Art.41
s.103, amended: SI 2014/3293 Reg.5
s.103, varied: SI 2014/1261 Reg.2
s.111, see *Insurance Co of the State of Pennsylvania v Equitas Insurance Ltd* [2013] EWHC 3713 (Comm), [2014] Lloyd's Rep. I.R. 195 (QBD (Comm)), Field J
s.118, see *7722656 Canada Inc (formerly Swift Trade Inc) v Financial Services Authority* [2013] EWCA Civ 1662, [2014] Lloyd's Rep. F.C. 207 (CA (Civ Div)), Longmore LJ; see *Hannam v Financial Conduct Authority* [2014] UKUT 233 (TCC), [2014] Lloyd's Rep. F.C. 704 (UT (Tax)), Warren J
s.118, amended: SI 2014/3081 Reg.2
s.118A, amended: SI 2014/3081 Reg.2
s.118C, see *Hannam v Financial Conduct Authority* [2014] UKUT 233 (TCC), [2014] Lloyd's Rep. F.C. 704 (UT (Tax)), Warren J
s.133, amended: SI 2014/3329 Art.116
s.133, applied: SI 2014/2879 Reg.5
s.133, varied: SI 2014/3085 Reg.30
s.133A, varied: SI 2014/3085 Reg.30
s.133B, varied: SI 2014/3085 Reg.30
s.137FA, added: 2014 c.19 s.44
s.137J, amended: SI 2014/3348 Sch.3 para.2
s.137K, amended: SI 2014/3348 Sch.3 para.3
s.137K, substituted: SI 2014/3348 Sch.3 para.3
s.137M, repealed: SI 2014/3348 Sch.3 para.4
s.137N, amended: SI 2014/3348 Sch.3 para.5
s.138D, see *Bate v Aviva Insurance UK Ltd* [2014] EWCA Civ 334, [2014] Lloyd's Rep. I.R. 527 (CA (Civ Div)), Maurice Kay LJ
s.138K, amended: 2014 c.14 Sch.4 para.69
s.140A, amended: SI 2014/892 Sch.1 para.121

s.140A, repealed (in part): SI 2014/892
Sch.1 para.121

s.140B, amended: SI 2014/892 Sch.1
para.122

s.140B, repealed (in part): SI 2014/892
Sch.1 para.122

s.140C, amended: SI 2014/892 Sch.1
para.123

s.140D, amended: SI 2014/892 Sch.1
para.124

s.140D, applied: SI 2014/559, SI 2014/892
Sch.2 para.3, Sch.2 para.4

s.140D, substituted: SI 2014/892 Sch.1
para.124

s.140E, substituted: SI 2014/892 Sch.1
para.125

s.140F, amended: SI 2014/892 Sch.1
para.126

s.140H, amended: SI 2014/892 Sch.1
para.127

s.142A, enabling: SI 2014/1960

s.142B, enabling: SI 2014/1960

s.142D, enabling: SI 2014/2080

s.142E, enabling: SI 2014/2080

s.142F, enabling: SI 2014/1960, SI
2014/2080

s.142Z, applied: SI 2014/1960, SI 2014/2080

s.150, see *Bate v Aviva Insurance UK Ltd*
[2014] EWCA Civ 334, [2014] Lloyd's Rep.
I.R. 527 (CA (Civ Div)), Maurice Kay LJ;
see *Green v Royal Bank of Scotland Plc*
[2013] EWCA Civ 1197, [2014] Bus. L.R.
168 (CA (Civ Div)), Richards LJ

s.165, varied: SI 2014/3085 Reg.14

s.166, varied: SI 2014/3085 Reg.14

s.166A, varied: SI 2014/3085 Reg.14

s.167, varied: SI 2014/3085 Reg.14

s.168, varied: SI 2014/3085 Reg.14

s.170, varied: SI 2014/3085 Reg.14

s.171, varied: SI 2014/3085 Reg.14

s.172, varied: SI 2014/3085 Reg.14

s.174, varied: SI 2014/3085 Reg.14

s.175, varied: SI 2014/3085 Reg.14

s.176, varied: SI 2014/3085 Reg.14

s.187A, amended: SI 2014/3329 Art.117

s.189, amended: SI 2014/3329 Art.118

s.190, amended: SI 2014/3329 Art.119

s.192B, enabling: SI 2014/3348

s.192JB, amended: SI 2014/3329 Art.120

s.192K, amended: SI 2014/3329 Art.121

s.192L, amended: SI 2014/3329 Art.122

s.210, applied: SI 2014/2879 Reg.5, SI
2014/3085 Reg.28

s.212, applied: SI 2014/378 Art.2, SI
2014/3330 Reg.9

s.213, applied: SI 2014/916 Sch.2, SI
2014/3330 Reg.9

s.215, applied: SI 2014/229 Art.5

s.225, see *Clark v In Focus Asset
Management & Tax Solutions Ltd* [2014]
EWCA Civ 118, [2014] 1 W.L.R. 2502 (CA
(Civ Div)), Arden LJ

s.228, see *Clark v In Focus Asset
Management & Tax Solutions Ltd* [2014]
EWCA Civ 118, [2014] 1 W.L.R. 2502 (CA
(Civ Div)), Arden LJ

s.234H, amended: SI 2014/892 Sch.1
para.128

s.235, see *Financial Conduct Authority v
Capital Alternatives Ltd* [2014] EWHC 144
(Ch), [2014] 3 All E.R. 780 (Ch D),
Nicholas Strauss QC

s.286, applied: SI 2014/1828 Art.5

s.313, amended: SI 2014/892 Sch.1 para.129

s.327, applied: SI 2014/366 Art.15, Art.17

s.348, see *Tchenguiz v Director of the
Serious Fraud Office* [2013] EWHC 2128
(QB), [2014] 1 W.L.R. 1476 (QBD), Eder J

s.348, applied: SI 2014/3348 Art.17, Art.41,
Art.56, Art.85, Art.166, Art.184, Art.188,
Art.225

s.348, varied: SI 2014/3085 Reg.12

s.349, enabling: SI 2014/883

s.352, varied: SI 2014/3085 Reg.12

s.355, amended: 2014 c.14 Sch.4 para.70

s.356, applied: SI 2014/229 Art.6

s.359, applied: SI 2014/229 Art.7

s.359, disapplied: SI 2014/229 Art.10

s.361, applied: SI 2014/229 Art.8

s.362, applied: SI 2014/229 Art.9

s.362, disapplied: SI 2014/229 Art.10

s.362A, applied: SI 2014/229 Art.9

s.387, applied: SI 2014/2879 Reg.5

s.387, varied: SI 2014/3085 Reg.29

s.388, applied: SI 2014/2879 Reg.5

s.388, varied: SI 2014/3085 Reg.29

s.390, varied: SI 2014/3085 Reg.29

s.391, amended: SI 2014/2879 Reg.6

s.391, applied: SI 2014/2879 Reg.5

s.391, varied: SI 2014/3085 Reg.29

s.393, applied: SI 2014/2879 Reg.5, SI
2014/3085 Reg.26

s.393, varied: SI 2014/3085 Reg.29
s.395, varied: SI 2014/3085 Reg.29
s.397, see *Financial Conduct Authority v
Capital Alternatives Ltd* [2014] EWHC 144
(Ch), [2014] 3 All E.R. 780 (Ch D),
Nicholas Strauss QC
s.399, amended: SI 2014/892 Sch.1 para.130
s.409, enabling: SI 2014/1292, SI 2014/1313
s.417, amended: 2014 c.14 Sch.4 para.71, SI
2014/892 Sch.1 para.131, SI 2014/2879
Reg.6
s.417, applied: SI 2014/3348 Art.67, Art.217
s.418, amended: SI 2014/1292 Art.2
s.419, enabling: SI 2014/3340
s.426, enabling: SI 2014/208, SI 2014/376,
SI 2014/506, SI 2014/835, SI 2014/1446, SI
2014/2632
s.427, amended: SI 2014/892 Sch.1 para.132
s.428, enabling: SI 2014/334, SI 2014/366,
SI 2014/883, SI 2014/1292, SI 2014/1313,
SI 2014/1960, SI 2014/3340
s.429, applied: SI 2014/3340
Sch.1ZA Part 3 para.19, varied: SI
2014/3085 Reg.6
Sch.1ZA Part 3 para.20, applied: SI
2014/3085 Reg.6
Sch.1ZA Part 3 para.23, varied: SI
2014/3085 Reg.7
Sch.1ZA Part 4 para.25, varied: SI
2014/3085 Reg.8
Sch.2, applied: SI 2014/826 Reg.4, SI
2014/899 Reg.4
Sch.2 Part III para.25, enabling: SI
2014/366, SI 2014/1292, SI 2014/1313, SI
2014/1448, SI 2014/1740
Sch.3 Part I para.5, applied: SI 2014/3348
Art.222
Sch.3 Part I para.5, referred to: SSI 2014/164
Sch.2 para.7
Sch.3 Part II para.12, applied: SI 2014/3348
Art.222, SSI 2014/164 Sch.2 para.7
Sch.3 Part II para.15, applied: SSI 2014/164
Sch.2 para.7
Sch.3 Part II para.15, referred to: SI
2014/208 Art.8
Sch.6 Part 1B para.2C, amended: SI
2014/366 Art.5
Sch.6 Part 1B para.2D, amended: SI
2014/366 Art.5
Sch.6 Part 1B para.2F, amended: SI
2014/366 Art.5

Sch.6 Part 1B para.2G, amended: SI
2014/366 Art.5
Sch.11A Part II para.7, amended: 2014 c.14
Sch.4 para.72
Sch.17 Part II para.4, applied: SI 2014/882
Sch.1
Sch.17 Part II para.5, applied: SI 2014/882
Sch.1
Sch.17A Part 2 para.11, amended: SI
2014/2879 Reg.6
Sch.17A Part 2 para.23, amended: SI
2014/2879 Reg.6
Sch.18 Part IV, repealed: 2014 c.14 Sch.7

**10. Crown Prosecution Service Inspectorate Act
2000**
s.2, amended: 2014 c.12 s.149
s.2, repealed (in part): SI 2014/834 Sch.2
para.17
Sch.1 para.2, repealed (in part): 2014 c.2
Sch.12 para.44
Sch.1 para.4, repealed (in part): 2014 c.2
Sch.12 para.44
Sch.1 para.6, amended: 2014 c.2 Sch.12
para.44

11. Terrorism Act 2000
applied: 2014 c.5 Sch.1 para.1, 2014 c.25
Sch.1, SI 2014/1610 r.6_1, r.6_9, r.6_10, SI
2014/1838
s.1, see *R. (on the application of Miranda) v
Secretary of State for the Home Department*
[2014] EWHC 255 (Admin), [2014] 1
W.L.R. 3140 (DC), Laws LJ; see *R. v Gul
(Mohammed)* [2014] A.C. 1260 (SC), Lord
Neuberger JSC
s.3, applied: SI 2014/1612, SI 2014/2210
s.3, enabling: SI 2014/927, SI 2014/1612, SI
2014/1624, SI 2014/2210, SI 2014/3189
s.17, see *Menni (Nasserdine) v HM Advocate*
[2014] HCJAC 54, 2014 J.C. 258 (HCJ),
The Lord Justice General (Gill); see *Menni
(Nasserdine) v HM Advocate* 2014 S.C.L.
191 (HCJ), The Lord Justice General (Gill)
s.40, see *R. (on the application of Miranda)
v Secretary of State for the Home
Department* [2014] EWHC 255 (Admin),
[2014] 1 W.L.R. 3140 (DC), Laws LJ
s.44, see *Beghal v DPP* [2013] EWHC 2573
(Admin), [2014] Q.B. 607 (DC), Gross LJ
s.58, see *Guardian News and Media Ltd v
AB* Times, June 18, 2014 (CA (Crim Div)),
Gross LJ

s.117, see *R. v Gul (Mohammed)* [2014] A.C. 1260 (SC), Lord Neuberger JSC

s.123, applied: SI 2014/927, SI 2014/1624, SI 2014/1838, SI 2014/3189

s.123, enabling: SI 2014/1838

Sch.2, amended: SI 2014/927 Art.2, SI 2014/1624 Art.2, SI 2014/3189 Art.2

Sch.2, applied: SI 2014/927, SI 2014/2210

Sch.2, disapplied: SI 2014/1612 Art.2

Sch.2, referred to: SI 2014/1612, SI 2014/1612 Art.2, SI 2014/2210 Art.2, SI 2014/3189

Sch.3A Part I para.2, amended: 2014 c.14 Sch.4 para.73

Sch.3A Part II para.4, repealed (in part): SI 2014/892 Sch.1 para.148

Sch.4 Part I para.11D, applied: SI 2014/3141 Reg.8

Sch.4 Part II para.25D, applied: SI 2014/3141 Sch.1 para.4

Sch.4 Part III para.41D, applied: SI 2014/3141 Sch.2 para.4

Sch.5 Part I para.4, applied: SI 2014/1610 r.6_7

Sch.5 Part I para.5, applied: SI 2014/1610 r.6_1, r.6_13

Sch.5 Part I para.10, applied: SI 2014/1610 r.6_1, r.6_13

Sch.5 Part I para.10, enabling: SI 2014/1610

Sch.5 Part I para.13, applied: SI 2014/1610 r.6_1, r.6_8, r.6_13

Sch.5 Part I para.14, applied: SI 2014/1610 r.6_13

Sch.6, applied: SI 2014/1610 r.6_9

Sch.6A, applied: SI 2014/1610 r.6_10

Sch.6 para.1, applied: SI 2014/1610 r.6_1, r.6_13

Sch.6 para.4, applied: SI 2014/1610 r.6_1

Sch.6 para.4, enabling: SI 2014/1610

Sch.6A para.2, applied: SI 2014/1610 r.6_1, r.6_13

Sch.6A para.4, applied: SI 2014/1610 r.6_1

Sch.6A para.5, applied: SI 2014/1610 r.6_1

Sch.6A para.5, enabling: SI 2014/1610

Sch.6A para.6, applied: SI 2014/1610 r.6_13

Sch.7, see *Beghal v DPP* [2013] EWHC 2573 (Admin), [2014] Q.B. 607 (DC), Gross LJ; see *R. (on the application of Elosta) v Commissioner of Police of the Metropolis* [2013] EWHC 3397 (Admin), [2014] 1 W.L.R. 239 (QBD (Admin)), Bean J; see *R.*

(on the application of Miranda) v Secretary of State for the Home Department [2014] EWHC 255 (Admin), [2014] 1 W.L.R. 3140 (DC), Laws LJ; see *R. v Gul (Mohammed)* [2014] A.C. 1260 (SC), Lord Neuberger JSC

Sch.7, applied: SI 2014/1838 Art.3

Sch.7 para.1, amended: 2014 c.12 Sch.9 para.1

Sch.7 para.1A, added: 2014 c.12 Sch.9 para.1

Sch.7 para.1A, applied: SI 2014/1838

Sch.7 para.2, see *R. (on the application of Miranda) v Secretary of State for the Home Department* [2014] EWHC 255 (Admin), [2014] 1 W.L.R. 3140 (DC), Laws LJ

Sch.7 para.6, amended: 2014 c.12 Sch.9 para.7

Sch.7 para.6, repealed (in part): 2014 c.12 Sch.9 para.2

Sch.7 para.6A, added: 2014 c.12 Sch.9 para.2

Sch.7 para.8, amended: 2014 c.12 Sch.9 para.3

Sch.7 para.11A, added: 2014 c.12 Sch.9 para.4

Sch.8, applied: SI 2014/1610 r.6_35

Sch.8 Part I para.1, amended: 2014 c.12 Sch.9 para.5

Sch.8 Part I para.2, amended: 2014 c.12 Sch.9 para.5

Sch.8 Part I para.6, amended: 2014 c.12 Sch.9 para.5

Sch.8 Part I para.7, amended: 2014 c.12 Sch.9 para.5

Sch.8 Part I para.7A, added: 2014 c.12 Sch.9 para.5

Sch.8 Part I para.8, amended: 2014 c.12 Sch.9 para.5

Sch.8 Part I para.9, amended: 2014 c.12 Sch.9 para.5

Sch.8 Part IA para.20K, added: 2014 c.12 Sch.9 para.7

Sch.8 Part IA para.20K, applied: SI 2014/1838

Sch.8 Part IA para.20L, added: 2014 c.12 Sch.9 para.7

Sch.8 Part I para.10, amended: 2014 c.12 Sch.9 para.6

Sch.8 Part I para.16, amended: 2014 c.12 Sch.9 para.5

Sch.8 Part I para.16A, added: 2014 c.12
Sch.9 para.5
Sch.8 Part I para.17, amended: 2014 c.12
Sch.9 para.5
Sch.8 Part I para.18, amended: 2014 c.12
Sch.9 para.5
Sch.8 Part I para.20A, applied: SI 2014/1610
r.6_35
Sch.8 Part I para.20B, amended: 2014 c.12
Sch.11 para.125
Sch.8 Part I para.20B, applied: SI 2014/1610
r.6_1, r.6_35, r.6_36
Sch.8 Part I para.20G, applied: SI 2014/1610
r.6_1, r.6_35
Sch.8 Part I para.20I, amended: 2014 c.12
s.146
Sch.8 Part I para.20J, amended: 2014 c.12
Sch.11 para.125
Sch.8 Pt I para.7, see *R. (on the application of Elosta) v Commissioner of Police of the Metropolis* [2013] EWHC 3397 (Admin), [2014] 1 W.L.R. 239 (QBD (Admin)), Bean J
Sch.14 para.1, amended: 2014 c.12 Sch.9 para.8
Sch.14 para.6, applied: SI 2014/1838
Sch.14 para.6A, added: 2014 c.12 Sch.9 para.8
Sch.14 para.7, applied: SI 2014/1838
Sch.14 para.7, enabling: SI 2014/1838

12. Limited Liability Partnerships Act 2000
applied: SI 2014/1893 Art.23
s.4, see *Bates van Winkelhof v Clyde & Co LLP* [2014] UKSC 32, [2014] 1 W.L.R. 2047 (SC), Lord Neuberger PSC
s.15, enabling: SI 2014/3209
s.17, applied: SI 2014/3209
s.17, enabling: SI 2014/3209
s.18, referred to: SI 2014/2833 Reg.7, Reg.18

14. Care Standards Act 2000
applied: SI 2014/1795 Reg.22, SI 2014/2418 Sch.1, SI 2014/2936 Sch.2 para.2
Part II, applied: 2014 c.23 s.50, s.73, SI 2014/2418 Sch.1
s.1, see *Liverpool City Council v SG* [2014] EWCOP 10, [2014] C.O.P.L.R. 585 (CP), Holman J
s.4, applied: SI 2014/1920 Reg.19
s.8, referred to: SI 2014/2418 Sch.1
s.14A, amended: 2014 c.6 s.102

s.15, amended: 2014 c.6 s.102
s.16, enabling: SI 2014/410, SI 2014/670
s.20B, amended: 2014 c.6 s.102
s.22, amended: 2014 c.6 s.103
s.23, amended: 2014 c.6 s.104
s.72B, amended: 2014 c.29 s.4
s.73, amended: 2014 c.29 s.4
s.75A, amended: 2014 c.29 s.4
s.118, enabling: SI 2014/410, SI 2014/670
Sch.2B para.1, amended: 2014 c.29 s.4

16. Carers and Disabled Children Act 2000
s.1, applied: SI 2014/829 Sch.1 para.15
s.2, applied: SI 2014/829 Sch.1 para.16
s.4, applied: SI 2014/829 Sch.1 para.17
s.6A, applied: SI 2014/829 Sch.1 para.18

17. Finance Act 2000
Sch.6 Part II para.12A, added: 2014 c.26 Sch.20 para.2
Sch.6 Part II para.12A, amended: 2014 c.26 Sch.20 para.12
Sch.6 Part II para.13A, amended: 2014 c.26 Sch.20 para.13
Sch.6 Part II para.18, applied: 2014 c.26 Sch.20 para.9
Sch.6 Part II para.18, enabling: SI 2014/844
Sch.6 Part II para.22, applied: 2014 c.26 Sch.20 para.8
Sch.6 Part IV para.42, amended: 2014 c.26 s.96, Sch.20 para.3
Sch.6 Part IV para.42, repealed (in part): 2014 c.26 Sch.20 para.3
Sch.6 Part IV para.42A, amended: 2014 c.26 s.97, s.98
Sch.6 Part IV para.43A, repealed: 2014 c.26 Sch.20 para.4
Sch.6 Part IV para.43B, repealed (in part): 2014 c.26 Sch.20 para.5
Sch.6 Part IV para.50, enabling: SI 2014/1318
Sch.6 Part IV para.52D, enabling: SI 2014/2872
Sch.6 Part VI para.62, repealed (in part): 2014 c.26 Sch.20 para.6
Sch.6 Part VIII para.101, amended: 2014 c.26 Sch.20 para.7
Sch.6 Part VIII para.101, repealed (in part): 2014 c.26 Sch.20 para.7
Sch.6 Part X para.120, referred to: SI 2014/1643 Reg.16
Sch.6 Part XI para.121G, amended: SI 2014/1264 Art.6

Sch.6 Part XIII para.146, amended: 2014
c.26 Sch.20 para.14
Sch.6 Part XIII para.146, applied: SI
2014/844
Sch.6 Part XIII para.146, enabling: SI
2014/1318, SI 2014/2872
Sch.15 Part III para.22A, amended: 2014 c.6
Sch.7 para.49
Sch.22 Part IV para.29, enabling: SI
2014/2394
Sch.22 Part IV para.31, enabling: SI
2014/2394
Sch.22 Part IV para.36, enabling: SI
2014/2394
Sch.22 Part VII para.57, amended: 2014 c.26
Sch.1 para.7

19. Child Support, Pensions and Social Security Act 2000

Commencement Orders: SI 2014/1263 Art.2
s.1, applied: SI 2014/560 Sch.1 para.21
s.42, amended: 2014 c.19 Sch.12 para.38,
Sch.13 para.70
s.70, applied: SI 2014/2918 Art.2
s.70, disapplied: SI 2014/2918 Art.4
s.70, enabling: SI 2014/1667, SSI 2014/298
s.86, enabling: SI 2014/1263
Sch.1, applied: SI 2014/560 Sch.1 para.21
Sch.5 Part II, repealed: 2014 c.19 Sch.13
para.71
Sch.7, applied: SI 2014/1230 Reg.13
Sch.7 para.4, enabling: SI 2014/213
Sch.7 para.20, enabling: SI 2014/213
Sch.7 para.23, enabling: SI 2014/213

20. Government Resources and Accounts Act 2000

s.2, applied: 2014 c.25 s.5
s.4A, applied: SI 2014/531, SI 2014/3314
s.4A, enabling: SI 2014/531, SI 2014/3314
s.5, applied: SI 2014/416 Sch.1 para.2
s.9, applied: SI 2014/1627 Reg.9
s.10, applied: SI 2014/2234, SI 2014/2234
Art.2
s.10, enabling: SI 2014/2234

21. Learning and Skills Act 2000

Pt I., see *R. (on the application of S) v
Suffolk CC* [2014] EWHC 2780 (Admin),
[2014] E.L.R. 413 (QBD (Admin)), Mark
Ockelton
s.35, amended: 2014 c.6 Sch.3 para.72
s.41, amended: 2014 c.6 Sch.3 para.73
s.77, enabling: SI 2014/1212

s.80, enabling: SI 2014/1212
s.139A, see *R. (on the application of S) v
Suffolk CC* [2014] EWHC 2780 (Admin),
[2014] E.L.R. 413 (QBD (Admin)), Mark
Ockelton
s.139A, applied: SI 2014/2270 Art.27,
Art.28
s.139A, repealed: 2014 c.6 Sch.3 para.74
s.139B, applied: SI 2014/2270 Art.27
s.139B, referred to: SI 2014/2270 Art.28
s.150, enabling: SI 2014/1212
s.152, enabling: SI 2014/1212

22. Local Government Act 2000

see *R. (on the application of Buck) v
Doncaster MBC* [2013] EWCA Civ 1190,
[2014] P.T.S.R. 111 (CA (Civ Div)), Master
of the Rolls
Part III, applied: 2014 c.2 Sch.11 para.2
s.2, applied: 2014 c.14 s.24
s.9FG, applied: SI 2014/863 Sch.1 para.4, SI
2014/864 Sch.1 para.4, SI 2014/865 Sch.1
para.4
s.9FG, referred to: SI 2014/1012 Sch.1
para.4
s.9GA, applied: SI 2014/863 Sch.1 para.4, SI
2014/864 Sch.1 para.4, SI 2014/865 Sch.1
para.4, SI 2014/1012 Sch.1 para.4
s.9HB, enabling: SI 2014/2172
s.9HE, applied: SI 2014/370, SI 2014/920
s.9HE, enabling: SI 2014/370, SI 2014/920
s.9MG, enabling: SI 2014/920, SI 2014/924
s.13, enabling: SI 2014/3362
s.44, applied: SI 2014/370, SI 2014/920
s.44, enabling: SI 2014/370, SI 2014/920
s.49, referred to: SI 2014/2418 Sch.1
s.69, see *Heesom v Public Services
Ombudsman for Wales* [2014] EWHC 1504
(Admin), [2014] 4 All E.R. 269 (QBD
(Admin)), Hickinbottom J
s.79, see *Heesom v Public Services
Ombudsman for Wales* [2014] EWHC 1504
(Admin), [2014] 4 All E.R. 269 (QBD
(Admin)), Hickinbottom J
s.87, enabling: SI 2014/3033
s.91, repealed (in part): 2014 c.2 Sch.1 Part 2
s.105, applied: SI 2014/370, SI 2014/920, SI
2014/924
s.105, enabling: SI 2014/370, SI 2014/920,
SI 2014/924, SI 2014/2172, SI 2014/3033,
SI 2014/3362
s.106, enabling: SI 2014/3033, SI 2014/3362

Sch.5 para.30, repealed: 2014 c.2 Sch.1 Part 2

23. Regulation of Investigatory Powers Act 2000

see *Complaint of Surveillance, Re* [2014] 2 All E.R. 576 (IPT), Mummery, L.J.; see *Menni (Nasserdine) v HM Advocate* [2014] HCJAC 54, 2014 J.C. 258 (HCJ), The Lord Justice General (Gill); see *R. v Mahmood (Asad)* [2013] EWCA Crim 2356, [2014] 1 Cr. App. R. 31 (CA (Crim Div)), Fulford LJ applied: SI 2014/1610 r.6_1

Part I, applied: 2014 c.2 Sch.9 para.3, 2014 c.22 Sch.6 para.6, SI 2014/507 Sch.1 para.6, SI 2014/587 Sch.1 para.6, SI 2014/693 Sch.1 para.6, SI 2014/1826 Sch.1 para.6, SI 2014/1827 Sch.1 para.6, SI 2014/2054 Sch.1 para.6, SI 2014/3349 Sch.1 para.6

Part I, disapplied: 2014 c.12 Sch.4 para.7

Part I c.II, applied: 2014 c.27 s.1, SI 2014/2042 Reg.15

Part II, applied: SI 2014/3119(1), SI 2014/3103 Art.2, SI 2014/3103(1), SI 2014/3119 Art.2

Pt II., see *AJA v Commissioner of Police of the Metropolis* [2013] EWCA Civ 1342, [2014] 1 W.L.R. 285 (CA (Civ Div)), Lord Dyson MR; see *Complaint of Surveillance, Re* [2014] 2 All E.R. 576 (IPT), Mummery, L.J.

s.1, see *R. v Coulson (Andrew)* [2013] EWCA Crim 1026, [2014] 1 W.L.R. 1119 (CA (Crim Div)), Lord Judge LCJ

s.2, see *R. v Coulson (Andrew)* [2013] EWCA Crim 1026, [2014] 1 W.L.R. 1119 (CA (Crim Div)), Lord Judge LCJ

s.2, amended: 2014 c.27 s.5

s.2, repealed (in part): 2014 c.27 s.5

s.4, see *R. v Mahmood (Asad)* [2013] EWCA Crim 2356, [2014] 1 Cr. App. R. 31 (CA (Crim Div)), Fulford LJ

s.4, amended: 2014 c.29 s.4

s.5, amended: 2014 c.27 s.3

s.11, amended: 2014 c.27 s.4

s.11, repealed (in part): 2014 c.27 s.4

s.12, amended: 2014 c.27 s.4

s.12, repealed (in part): 2014 c.27 s.4

s.17, applied: SI 2014/1610 r.22_9

s.21, applied: SI 2014/826 Reg.4, SI 2014/899 Reg.4

s.21, referred to: SI 2014/1610 r.6_27

s.22, amended: 2014 c.27 s.3, s.4

s.22, applied: 2014 c.27 s.1, SI 2014/1610 r.6_27

s.22, repealed (in part): 2014 c.27 s.4

s.23A, applied: SI 2014/1610 r.6_1, r.6_27, r.6_28

s.23B, applied: SI 2014/1610 r.6_27, r.6_28

s.26, see *AJA v Commissioner of Police of the Metropolis* [2013] EWCA Civ 1342, [2014] 1 W.L.R. 285 (CA (Civ Div)), Lord Dyson MR

s.26, referred to: SI 2014/1610 r.6_27

s.27, see *AJA v Commissioner of Police of the Metropolis* [2013] EWCA Civ 1342, [2014] 1 W.L.R. 285 (CA (Civ Div)), Lord Dyson MR

s.28, applied: SI 2014/467 Art.4, SI 2014/1610 r.6_27

s.29, applied: SI 2014/1610 r.6_27

s.30, enabling: SI 2014/467

s.32, amended: SI 2014/892 Sch.1 para.134

s.32A, applied: SI 2014/1610 r.6_1, r.6_27, r.6_28

s.32B, applied: SI 2014/1610 r.6_27, r.6_28

s.33, amended: SI 2014/892 Sch.1 para.135

s.34, amended: SI 2014/892 Sch.1 para.136

s.35, amended: SI 2014/892 Sch.1 para.137

s.36, amended: SI 2014/892 Sch.1 para.138

s.37, amended: SI 2014/892 Sch.1 para.139

s.40, amended: SI 2014/892 Sch.1 para.140

s.43, applied: SI 2014/1610 r.6_27

s.46, amended: SI 2014/892 Sch.1 para.141

s.46, enabling: SI 2014/467

s.48, see *Complaint of Surveillance, Re* [2014] 2 All E.R. 576 (IPT), Mummery, L.J.

s.48, amended: SI 2014/892 Sch.1 para.142

s.58, amended: 2014 c.27 s.6

s.65, see *AJA v Commissioner of Police of the Metropolis* [2013] EWCA Civ 1342, [2014] 1 W.L.R. 285 (CA (Civ Div)), Lord Dyson MR

s.71, applied: 2014 c.27 s.2, SI 2014/3103, SI 2014/3103(1), SI 2014/3119, SI 2014/3103(2), SI 2014/3119(1), SI 2014/3119(2)

s.71, varied: SI 2014/2042 Reg.10

s.71, enabling: SI 2014/3103, SI 2014/3119

s.72, varied: SI 2014/2042 Reg.10

s.78, enabling: SI 2014/467

Sch.1 Part I, amended: 2014 c.29 s.4

Sch.1 Part I para.16, amended: 2014 c.29 s.4

Sch.1 Part I para.20B, substituted: SI
2014/892 Sch.1 para.143
26. Postal Services Act 2000
applied: SI 2014/631 Art.3
referred to: SI 2014/2269 Art.14, SI
2014/2306 Art.4, SI 2014/2469 Art.4, SI
2014/3384 Art.4
s.93, amended: SI 2014/631 Sch.1 para.7
s.102, amended: SI 2014/631 Sch.1 para.7
s.125, amended: SI 2014/631 Sch.1 para.7
s.125, referred to: SSI 2014/226 Reg.3,
Reg.5, SSI 2014/269 Art.7, SSI 2014/378
Art.4
27. Utilities Act 2000
applied: 2014 c.25 Sch.1, SI 2014/631 Art.3
referred to: 2014 c.5 Sch.1 para.1
s.3, amended: SI 2014/631 Sch.1 para.8
s.3, repealed (in part): SI 2014/631 Sch.1
para.8
s.4, amended: SI 2014/631 Sch.1 para.8
s.5, amended: SI 2014/631 Sch.1 para.8
s.7, repealed: SI 2014/631 Sch.1 para.8
s.8, amended: SI 2014/631 Sch.1 para.8, SI
2014/892 Sch.1 para.145
s.8, applied: SI 2014/631 Sch.1 para.28
s.8, repealed (in part): SI 2014/631 Sch.1
para.8
s.103, amended: SI 2014/631 Sch.1 para.8
s.103, applied: SI 2014/3219, SI 2014/3231
s.103, enabling: SI 2014/3219, SI 2014/3231
s.103A, amended: SI 2014/631 Sch.1 para.8
s.103A, applied: SI 2014/3219
s.103A, enabling: SI 2014/3219
s.105, amended: SI 2014/469 Sch.2 para.21,
SI 2014/631 Sch.1 para.8, SI 2014/892 Sch.1
para.146
s.105, repealed (in part): SI 2014/892 Sch.1
para.146
s.106, amended: SI 2014/631 Sch.1 para.8
29. Trustee Act 2000
s.3, applied: SI 2014/3234 Art.3
**31. Warm Homes and Energy Conservation Act
2000**
applied: SI 2014/631 Art.3
s.1A, applied: SI 2014/3220, SI 2014/3220
Reg.2
s.1A, enabling: SI 2014/3220
s.2, amended: SI 2014/631 Sch.1 para.9
s.4, amended: SI 2014/631 Sch.1 para.9
32. Police (Northern Ireland) Act 2000
s.41, amended: 2014 c.12 s.134

s.49, amended: 2014 c.12 Sch.11 para.91
Sch.6 para.12, repealed (in part): 2014 c.12
Sch.11 para.102
35. Children (Leaving Care) Act 2000
see *R. (on the application of GE (Eritrea)) v
Secretary of State for the Home Department*
[2013] EWHC 2186 (Admin), [2014]
P.T.S.R. 124 (QBD), CMG Ockelton (Vice
President)
36. Freedom of Information Act 2000
see *Browning v Information Commissioner*
[2014] EWCA Civ 1050, [2014] 1 W.L.R.
3848 (CA (Civ Div)), Maurice Kay LJ; see
Kennedy v Information Commissioner
[2014] UKSC 20, [2014] 2 W.L.R. 808 (SC),
Lord Neuberger JSC; see *R. (on the
application of Evans) v Attorney General*
[2014] EWCA Civ 254, [2014] Q.B. 855
(CA (Civ Div)), Lord Dyson MR
applied: 2014 c.2 Sch.11 para.3, 2014 c.20
Sch.5 para.5, SI 2014/469 Sch.4 para.21, SI
2014/1794 Reg.11, SI 2014/2012 Reg.12
s.1, see *R. (on the application of Evans) v
Attorney General* [2014] EWCA Civ 254,
[2014] Q.B. 855 (CA (Civ Div)), Lord
Dyson MR
s.2, see *Kennedy v Information
Commissioner* [2014] UKSC 20, [2014] 2
W.L.R. 808 (SC), Lord Neuberger JSC
s.4, amended: 2014 c.29 s.4
s.5, applied: SI 2014/2009 Art.3
s.7, amended: 2014 c.29 s.4
s.22A, added: 2014 c.18 s.20
s.28, amended: 2014 c.29 s.4
s.32, see *Kennedy v Information
Commissioner* [2014] UKSC 20, [2014] 2
W.L.R. 808 (SC), Lord Neuberger JSC
s.35, amended: 2014 c.29 s.4
s.36, amended: 2014 c.29 s.4
s.40, see *Foster v Information Commissioner*
(2014) 136 B.M.L.R. 193 (FTT (GRC)),
Judge Christopher Ryan
s.53, see *R. (on the application of Evans) v
Attorney General* [2014] EWCA Civ 254,
[2014] Q.B. 855 (CA (Civ Div)), Lord
Dyson MR
s.53, amended: 2014 c.29 s.4
s.63, see *Kennedy v Information
Commissioner* [2014] UKSC 20, [2014] 2
W.L.R. 808 (SC), Lord Neuberger JSC

s.78, see *Kennedy v Information Commissioner* [2014] UKSC 20, [2014] 2 W.L.R. 808 (SC), Lord Neuberger JSC
s.81, amended: 2014 c.29 s.4
s.84, amended: 2014 c.29 s.4
Sch.1 Part I para.5A, amended: 2014 c.29 s.4
Sch.1 Part II para.28, disapplied: SI 2014/864 Art.8
Sch.1 Part III, amended: 2014 c.23 Sch.5 para.34
Sch.1 Part VI, amended: 2014 c.2 Sch.12 para.45, 2014 c.4 Sch.2 para.13, 2014 c.12 Sch.11 para.92, Sch.11 para.102, 2014 c.20 Sch.4 para.21, 2014 c.21 Sch.10 para.17, 2014 c.23 Sch.7 para.26, SI 2014/631 Sch.1 para.10, SI 2014/892 Sch.1 para.147, SI 2014/1068 Art.3, SI 2014/1924 Sch.1, SI 2014/3184 Sch.1 para.14

37. Countryside and Rights of Way Act 2000
s.3A, enabling: SI 2014/846, SI 2014/851, SI 2014/3128
s.86, applied: 2014 c.2 Sch.2 para.18
Sch.13 para.8, repealed: 2014 c.2 Sch.1 Part 2

38. Transport Act 2000
Part II, applied: SI 2014/865 Art.8, SI 2014/1012 Art.8
s.12B, amended: SI 2014/892 Sch.1 para.150
s.12B, applied: SI 2014/559
s.12B, referred to: SI 2014/892 Sch.2 para.2
s.18, amended: SI 2014/892 Sch.1 para.151
s.18, referred to: SI 2014/892 Sch.2 para.2
s.19, amended: SI 2014/892 Sch.1 para.152
s.85, amended: SI 2014/892 Sch.1 para.153
s.86, amended: SI 2014/892 Sch.1 para.154
s.89, amended: SI 2014/892 Sch.1 para.155
s.90, amended: SI 2014/892 Sch.1 para.156
s.91, amended: SI 2014/892 Sch.1 para.157
s.108, applied: SI 2014/1012 Sch.1 para.3, SI 2014/2178 Art.3
s.108, varied: SI 2014/2178 Art.3
s.113A, enabling: SI 2014/2178
s.162, disapplied: SI 2014/864 Art.8
s.163, enabling: SI 2014/81
s.173, enabling: SI 2014/81
s.197, enabling: SI 2014/81
s.247, enabling: SI 2014/3217
Sch.9 para.3, amended: SI 2014/892 Sch.1 para.158
Sch.9 para.3, repealed (in part): SI 2014/892 Sch.1 para.158

Sch.9 para.5, amended: SI 2014/892 Sch.1 para.158

41. Political Parties, Elections and Referendums Act 2000
applied: 2014 c.4 s.47
referred to: 2014 c.4 s.33
Part VI, applied: 2014 c.4 s.39
Part VI c.II, amended: 2014 c.4 s.30
Part VI c.II, added: 2014 c.4 s.30
Part VII, applied: 2014 c.29 Sch.1 para.6, Sch.1 para.15
s.7, applied: SI 2014/270, SI 2014/450, SI 2014/492, SI 2014/494, SI 2014/920, SI 2014/921, SI 2014/923, SI 2014/1116, SI 2014/1234, SI 2014/1250, SI 2014/1803, SI 2014/1804, SI 2014/1805, SI 2014/1808, SI 2014/1880, SI 2014/1963, SI 2014/2764, SI 2014/3124, SI 2014/3161
s.12, enabling: SI 2014/556
s.13, applied: SI 2014/510 Art.2
s.13, enabling: SI 2014/510
s.24, applied: SI 2014/2764 Reg.2
s.26, amended: 2014 c.14 Sch.4 para.75
s.50, see *Robson (Deceased), Re* [2014] EWHC 295 (Ch), [2014] Ch. 470 (Ch D), Richard Sheldon Q.C.
s.54, see *Robson (Deceased), Re* [2014] EWHC 295 (Ch), [2014] Ch. 470 (Ch D), Richard Sheldon Q.C.
s.54, amended: 2014 c.14 Sch.4 para.76
s.56, see *Robson (Deceased), Re* [2014] EWHC 295 (Ch), [2014] Ch. 470 (Ch D), Richard Sheldon Q.C.
s.65, applied: SI 2014/1806 Reg.2
s.65, enabling: SI 2014/1806
s.71E, amended: 2014 c.13 s.1
s.71Z4, amended: 2014 c.13 s.2
s.79, amended: 2014 c.4 s.30
s.80, amended: 2014 c.4 s.30
s.85, amended: 2014 c.4 s.26, s.32
s.85, referred to: 2014 c.4 s.35
s.85, repealed (in part): 2014 c.4 s.26
s.87, amended: 2014 c.4 s.30
s.87, repealed (in part): 2014 c.4 s.26
s.88, amended: 2014 c.4 s.32
s.90, amended: 2014 c.4 s.35
s.94, amended: 2014 c.4 s.26, s.27, s.28, s.29, s.30, s.35
s.94A, added: 2014 c.4 s.27
s.95A, added: 2014 c.4 s.33
s.95A, applied: 2014 c.4 s.33

s.95C, applied: 2014 c.4 s.33
s.96, amended: 2014 c.4 s.29, s.34
s.96A, added: 2014 c.4 s.35
s.97, amended: 2014 c.4 s.35
s.98, amended: 2014 c.4 s.35
s.98, applied: 2014 c.4 s.35
s.99, amended: 2014 c.4 s.27
s.99A, added: 2014 c.4 s.35
s.99A, applied: 2014 c.4 s.35
s.100, amended: 2014 c.4 s.35
s.104, applied: 2014 c.29 Sch.1 para.4
s.143, amended: 2014 c.4 s.26
s.143A, added: 2014 c.4 s.26
s.145, amended: 2014 c.4 s.38
s.149, amended: 2014 c.4 s.33
s.155, amended: 2014 c.4 s.31, s.33
s.156, amended: 2014 c.4 s.26
s.156, applied: SI 2014/335, SI 2014/2448
s.156, enabling: SI 2014/510
s.160, applied: SI 2014/2764 Reg.2
Sch.1 para.3, amended: 2014 c.4 s.33
Sch.6 para.2, applied: SI 2014/1806 Reg.2
Sch.6 para.2, enabling: SI 2014/1806
Sch.6 para.2A, amended: 2014 c.14 Sch.4 para.77
Sch.6 para.3, applied: SI 2014/1806 Reg.2
Sch.6 para.3, enabling: SI 2014/1806
Sch.6A para.2, applied: SI 2014/1806 Reg.2
Sch.6A para.2, enabling: SI 2014/1806
Sch.6A para.2A, amended: 2014 c.14 Sch.4 para.78
Sch.6A para.3, applied: SI 2014/1806 Reg.2
Sch.6A para.3, enabling: SI 2014/1806
Sch.7 Part III para.10, applied: SI 2014/1806 Reg.2
Sch.7 Part III para.10, enabling: SI 2014/1806
Sch.8A, added: 2014 c.4 Sch.3
Sch.9 Part II para.3, varied: 2014 c.4 s.46
Sch.9 Part III para.11, applied: 2014 c.4 s.46
Sch.9 Part III para.11, varied: 2014 c.4 s.46
Sch.10 Part I para.2A, added: 2014 c.4 s.29
Sch.10 Part II para.3, amended: 2014 c.4 s.28, s.29
Sch.10 Part II para.3, varied: 2014 c.4 s.46
Sch.10 Part III para.9, amended: 2014 c.4 s.29
Sch.10 Part III para.10, amended: 2014 c.4 s.29
Sch.10 Part III para.11, amended: 2014 c.4 s.29

Sch.10 Part III para.11, applied: 2014 c.4 s.46
Sch.10 Part III para.11, varied: 2014 c.4 s.46
Sch.11A, added: 2014 c.4 Sch.4
Sch.11 Part III, amended: 2014 c.4 s.33
Sch.11 Part III, referred to: 2014 c.4 s.33
Sch.11 Part III para.10, applied: SI 2014/1806 Reg.2
Sch.11 Part III para.10, enabling: SI 2014/1806
Sch.15 Part III para.10, applied: SI 2014/1806 Reg.2
Sch.15 Part III para.10, enabling: SI 2014/1806
Sch.19C Part I para.1, enabling: SI 2014/335, SI 2014/2448
Sch.19C Part II para.5, enabling: SI 2014/335, SI 2014/2448
Sch.19C Part III para.10, enabling: SI 2014/2448
Sch.19C Part IV para.15, enabling: SI 2014/2448
Sch.19C Part V para.16, enabling: SI 2014/335, SI 2014/2448
Sch.19C Part V para.17, applied: SI 2014/335, SI 2014/2448
Sch.19C Part V para.18, enabling: SI 2014/335
Sch.20, amended: 2014 c.4 s.30, s.33, s.35

43. Criminal Justice and Court Services Act 2000

s.28, applied: SI 2014/1132 Sch.7 para.9, SI 2014/2709 Sch.2 para.9
s.36, amended: 2014 c.6 Sch.5 para.9
s.64, amended: 2014 c.11 s.11, Sch.3 para.13
s.64, applied: SI 2014/2871 Sch.1
s.64A, added: 2014 c.11 s.12
s.70, amended: 2014 c.11 s.11
Sch.1A para.2, repealed (in part): 2014 c.2 Sch.12 para.46
Sch.1A para.3, repealed (in part): 2014 c.2 Sch.12 para.46
Sch.1A para.4, repealed (in part): 2014 c.2 Sch.12 para.46
Sch.1A para.6, amended: 2014 c.2 Sch.12 para.46

2001

2. Capital Allowances Act 2001

s.5, referred to: 2014 c.26 Sch.15 para.6

s.45A, enabling: SI 2014/1868

s.45D, amended: 2014 c.26 s.64

s.45DA, amended: 2014 c.26 s.64

s.45DB, amended: 2014 c.26 Sch.13 para.2

s.45E, amended: 2014 c.26 s.64

s.45H, enabling: SI 2014/1869

s.45K, amended: 2014 c.26 s.64, Sch.13 para.3

s.45K, applied: SI 2014/3183 Art.2

s.45K, enabling: SI 2014/3183

s.45M, amended: 2014 c.26 Sch.13 para.4

s.45M, repealed (in part): 2014 c.26 Sch.13 para.4

s.45N, amended: 2014 c.26 Sch.13 para.5

s.51A, applied: 2014 c.26 Sch.2 para.1, Sch.2 para.2, Sch.2 para.3, Sch.2 para.4, Sch.2 para.5

s.51A, varied: 2014 c.26 s.10

s.51M, referred to: 2014 c.26 Sch.2 para.5

s.99, amended: 2014 c.26 Sch.1 para.8

s.99, applied: 2014 c.26 Sch.1 para.22

s.99, repealed (in part): 2014 c.26 Sch.1 para.8

s.109, see *Revenue and Customs Commissioners v Lloyds TSB Equipment Leasing (No.1) Ltd* [2014] S.T.C. 191 (UT (Tax)), Newey J

s.110, see *Revenue and Customs Commissioners v Lloyds TSB Equipment Leasing (No.1) Ltd* [2014] S.T.C. 191 (UT (Tax)), Newey J

s.123, see *Revenue and Customs Commissioners v Lloyds TSB Equipment Leasing (No.1) Ltd* [2014] EWCA Civ 1062, [2014] S.T.C. 2770 (CA (Civ Div)), Rimer LJ; see *Revenue and Customs Commissioners v Lloyds TSB Equipment Leasing (No.1) Ltd* [2014] S.T.C. 191 (UT (Tax)), Newey J

s.160, substituted: 2014 c.26 s.67

s.161, amended: 2014 c.26 s.67

s.161, repealed (in part): 2014 c.26 s.67

s.212T, amended: 2014 c.26 Sch.13 para.6

s.212U, amended: 2014 c.26 Sch.13 para.7

s.281, see *Thomson v Revenue and Customs Commissioners* [2014] UKUT 360 (TCC), [2014] B.T.C. 524 (UT (Tax)), Lord Tyre

s.360B, amended: 2014 c.26 s.66

s.360B, enabling: SI 2014/1687

s.360BA, added: 2014 c.26 s.66

s.360C, enabling: SI 2014/1687

s.360D, enabling: SI 2014/1687

s.360L, substituted: 2014 c.26 s.66

s.360L, varied: 2014 c.26 s.66

s.360M, amended: 2014 c.26 s.66

s.394, amended: 2014 c.26 s.67

s.396, amended: 2014 c.26 s.68

s.398, amended: 2014 c.26 s.68

s.399, amended: 2014 c.26 s.67

s.431A, added: 2014 c.26 s.67

s.437, see *Vaccine Research LP v Revenue and Customs Commissioners* [2014] UKUT 389 (TCC), [2014] B.T.C. 525 (UT (Tax)), Sales J

Sch.A1 Part 1 para.11, amended: 2014 c.26 Sch.4 para.7

Sch.1 Part 2, amended: 2014 c.26 Sch.1 para.9

7. Elections Act 2001

Sch.Part 1 para.4, amended: SI 2014/1116 Art.9

Sch.Part 1 para.5, amended: SI 2014/1116 Art.9

Sch.Part 1 para.10A, added: SI 2014/1116 Art.9

Sch.Part 2 para.19, amended: SI 2014/1116 Art.9

Sch.Part 2 para.24A, added: SI 2014/1116 Art.9

Sch.Part 2 para.29, amended: SI 2014/1116 Art.9

9. Finance Act 2001

Part 2, referred to: 2014 c.26 s.95

s.17, amended: 2014 c.26 s.94

s.17, repealed (in part): 2014 c.26 s.94

s.18, amended: 2014 c.26 s.94

s.19, see *Northumbrian Water Ltd v Revenue and Customs Commissioners* [2014] S.F.T.D. 316 (FTT (Tax)), Judge Swami Raghavan

s.19, amended: 2014 c.26 s.94

s.22, amended: 2014 c.26 s.94

s.24, enabling: SI 2014/836

s.40G, amended: SI 2014/1264 Art.7

s.45, enabling: SI 2014/836

s.48, see *Northumbrian Water Ltd v Revenue and Customs Commissioners* [2014]

S.F.T.D. 316 (FTT (Tax)), Judge Swami
Raghavan
s.93, repealed: 2014 c.26 s.114

10. Special Educational Needs and Disability Act 2001
s.2, repealed: 2014 c.6 Sch.3 para.24
s.3, repealed: 2014 c.6 Sch.3 para.26

11. Social Security Fraud Act 2001
s.6A, amended: 2014 c.19 Sch.12 para.40,
Sch.16 para.44
s.6B, applied: SI 2014/1230 Reg.35, Reg.36
s.7, applied: SI 2014/1230 Reg.35, Reg.36
s.8, applied: SI 2014/1230 Reg.35
s.9, applied: SI 2014/1230 Reg.35
s.10, amended: 2014 c.19 Sch.12 para.41,
Sch.16 para.45

16. Criminal Justice and Police Act 2001
s.1, amended: SI 2014/1365 Art.2
s.1, enabling: SI 2014/1365
s.3, enabling: SI 2014/1383
s.8, applied: SI 2014/1610 r.52_6
s.10A, applied: SI 2014/1365
s.12, repealed: 2014 c.12 Sch.11 para.30
s.13, applied: 2014 c.12 s.75
s.33, applied: SI 2014/1610 r.42_1
s.35, applied: SI 2014/1610 r.42_6
s.50, see *R. (on the application of S) v Chief
Constable of the British Transport Police*
[2013] EWHC 2189 (Admin), [2014] 1
W.L.R. 1647 (QBD (Admin)), Aikens LJ
s.59, see *Lees v Solihull Magistrates' Court*
[2013] EWHC 3779 (Admin), [2014]
Lloyd's Rep. F.C. 233 (DC), Treacy LJ; see
*R. (on the application of Panesar) v Central
Criminal Court* [2014] EWHC 2821
(Admin), [2014] Lloyd's Rep. F.C. 662
(DC), Lord Thomas LCJ; see *R. (on the
application of Van der Pijl) v Secretary of
State for the Home Department* [2014]
EWHC 281 (Admin), [2014] Lloyd's Rep.
F.C. 362 (QBD (Admin)), Collins J
s.97, amended: 2014 c.12 s.123
s.97, repealed (in part): 2014 c.12 s.123
Sch.1 Part 1 para.27, repealed: 2014 c.26
Sch.28 para.21

17. International Criminal Court Act 2001
see *R. (on the application of Khan) v
Secretary of State for Foreign and
Commonwealth Affairs* [2014] EWCA Civ
24, [2014] 1 W.L.R. 872 (CA (Civ Div)),
Lord Dyson MR

s.23, applied: SI 2014/2706 Art.2
s.44, applied: SI 2014/2706 Art.2
s.44, varied: SI 2014/2706 Sch.1 para.1
s.45, varied: SI 2014/2706 Sch.1 para.2
s.52, see *R. (on the application of Khan) v
Secretary of State for Foreign and
Commonwealth Affairs* [2014] EWCA Civ
24, [2014] 1 W.L.R. 872 (CA (Civ Div)),
Lord Dyson MR
s.70, applied: SI 2014/2706 Art.2
s.70, varied: SI 2014/2706 Sch.1 para.3
s.79, enabling: SI 2014/2706
s.83, applied: SI 2014/2706 Art.2
Sch.10, varied: SI 2014/2706 Sch.1 para.4

24. Anti-terrorism, Crime and Security Act 2001
applied: SI 2014/469 Sch.1 para.1
s.17, referred to: 2014 c.2 Sch.11 para.2
s.36, repealed: 2014 c.22 Sch.9 para.18
s.53, amended: SI 2014/834 Sch.2 para.18
s.77, applied: SI 2014/526
s.77, varied: SI 2014/469 Art.7
s.77, enabling: SI 2014/526
s.102, applied: 2014 c.27 s.1, SI 2014/2042
Reg.15
Sch.4 Part 1 para.41, repealed: 2014 c.2
Sch.12 para.48
Sch.4 Part 1 para.53F, added: 2014 c.2
Sch.12 para.48
Sch.7 para.9, repealed: 2014 c.12 s.112

2002

1. International Development Act 2002
s.1, amended: 2014 c.9 s.1
s.3, substituted: 2014 c.9 s.1
s.11, applied: SI 2014/2456, SI 2014/2457,
SI 2014/3055, SI 2014/3055 Art.3, SI
2014/3056
s.11, referred to: SI 2014/3055
s.11, enabling: SI 2014/2456, SI 2014/2457,
SI 2014/3055, SI 2014/3056

8. British Overseas Territories Act 2002
applied: SI 2014/511 Reg.5

9. Land Registration Act 2002
see *Nugent v Nugent* [2013] EWHC 4095
(Ch), [2014] 3 W.L.R. 59 (Ch D (Bristol)),
Morgan J
s.23, see *Helman v John Lyon Free
Grammar School* [2014] EWCA Civ 17,

[2014] 1 W.L.R. 2451 (CA (Civ Div)),
Arden LJ
s.24, see *Helman v John Lyon Free
Grammar School* [2014] EWCA Civ 17,
[2014] 1 W.L.R. 2451 (CA (Civ Div)),
Arden LJ
s.27, see *Helman v John Lyon Free
Grammar School* [2014] EWCA Civ 17,
[2014] 1 W.L.R. 2451 (CA (Civ Div)),
Arden LJ
s.29, see *Blemain Finance Ltd v Cugley*
[2014] B.P.I.R. 20 (CC (Bristol)), Recorder
Stead; see *Hotel Company 42 The Calls Ltd,
Re* [2013] EWHC 3925 (Ch), [2014] B.C.C.
136 (Ch D), Judge Purle Q.C.; see *Lictor
Anstalt v Mir Steel UK Ltd* [2014] EWHC
3316 (CH), [2014] 6 Costs L.O. 918 (Ch D),
Asplin J; see *North East Property Buyers
Litigation, Re* [2014] UKSC 52, [2014] 3
W.L.R. 1163 (SC), Lady Hale JSC
s.30, see *Hotel Company 42 The Calls Ltd,
Re* [2013] EWHC 3925 (Ch), [2014] B.C.C.
136 (Ch D), Judge Purle Q.C.
s.32, see *Hotel Company 42 The Calls Ltd,
Re* [2013] EWHC 3925 (Ch), [2014] B.C.C.
136 (Ch D), Judge Purle Q.C.
s.36, see *Bank of Scotland Plc v Joseph*
[2014] EWCA Civ 28, [2014] 1 P. & C.R.
18 (CA (Civ Div)), Patten LJ
s.58, see *Blemain Finance Ltd v Cugley*
[2014] B.P.I.R. 20 (CC (Bristol)), Recorder
Stead; see *Helman v John Lyon Free
Grammar School* [2014] EWCA Civ 17,
[2014] 1 W.L.R. 2451 (CA (Civ Div)),
Arden LJ
s.77, see *Bank of Scotland Plc v Joseph*
[2014] EWCA Civ 28, [2014] 1 P. & C.R.
18 (CA (Civ Div)), Patten LJ
s.86, see *Blemain Finance Ltd v Cugley*
[2014] B.P.I.R. 20 (CC (Bristol)), Recorder
Stead; see *Helman v John Lyon Free
Grammar School* [2014] EWCA Civ 17,
[2014] 1 W.L.R. 2451 (CA (Civ Div)),
Arden LJ
s.91, amended: 2014 c.14 Sch.4 para.80
s.132, see *North East Property Buyers
Litigation, Re* [2014] UKSC 52, [2014] 3
W.L.R. 1163 (SC), Lady Hale JSC
Sch.3 para.2, see *Blemain Finance Ltd v
Cugley* [2014] B.P.I.R. 20 (CC (Bristol)),
Recorder Stead; see *Credit and Mercantile*

Plc v Kaymuu Ltd [2014] EWHC 1746 (Ch),
[2014] B.P.I.R. 1127 (Ch D), Tim Kerr QC;
see *North East Property Buyers Litigation,
Re* [2014] UKSC 52, [2014] 3 W.L.R. 1163
(SC), Lady Hale JSC
Sch.4 para.5, see *Walker v Burton* [2013]
EWCA Civ 1228, [2014] 1 P. & C.R. 9 (CA
(Civ Div)), Mummery, L.J.
Sch.4 para.6, see *Walker v Burton* [2013]
EWCA Civ 1228, [2014] 1 P. & C.R. 9 (CA
(Civ Div)), Mummery, L.J.
Sch.6, see *R. (on the application of Best) v
Chief Land Registrar* [2014] EWHC 1370
(Admin), [2014] 3 All E.R. 637 (QBD
(Admin)), Ouseley J

**13. Electoral Fraud (Northern Ireland) Act
2002**

s.6, repealed: 2014 c.13 s.20

**15. Commonhold and Leasehold Reform Act
2002**

see *Fairhold Mercury Ltd v HQ (Block 1)
Action Management Co Ltd* [2014] L. &
T.R. 5 (UT (Lands)), Martin Rodger Q.C.
Part 2, applied: SI 2014/2359 Art.6
s.73, see *Danescroft RTM Co Ltd v Inspired
Holdings Ltd* [2014] L. & T.R. 4 (LVT), I
Mohabir; see *Fairhold Mercury Ltd v HQ
(Block 1) Action Management Co Ltd* [2014]
L. & T.R. 5 (UT (Lands)), Martin Rodger
Q.C.
s.74, see *Fairhold Mercury Ltd v HQ (Block
1) Action Management Co Ltd* [2014] L. &
T.R. 5 (UT (Lands)), Martin Rodger Q.C.
s.79, see *R. (on the application of O Twelve
Baytree Ltd) v Rent Assessment Panel* [2014]
EWHC 1229 (Admin), [2014] 3 All E.R. 732
(QBD (Admin)), Lewis J
s.80, see *Danescroft RTM Co Ltd v Inspired
Holdings Ltd* [2014] L. & T.R. 4 (LVT), I
Mohabir
s.84, see *Fairhold (Yorkshire) Ltd v Trinity
Wharf (SE16) RTM Co Ltd* [2014] L. & T.R.
6 (UT (Lands)), Sir Keith Lindblom P; see
*R. (on the application of O Twelve Baytree
Ltd) v Rent Assessment Panel* [2014] EWHC
1229 (Admin), [2014] 3 All E.R. 732 (QBD
(Admin)), Lewis J
s.88, see *R. (on the application of O Twelve
Baytree Ltd) v Rent Assessment Panel* [2014]
EWHC 1229 (Admin), [2014] 3 All E.R. 732
(QBD (Admin)), Lewis J

s.108, varied: SI 2014/2708 Art.5
s.168, see *Cussens v Realreed Ltd* [2013] EWHC 1229 (QB), [2014] 1 W.L.R. 275 (QBD), Andrew Smith J
s.172, varied: SI 2014/2708 Art.5
Sch.11 Pt 1 para.1, see *Christoforou v Standard Apartments Ltd* [2014] L. & T.R. 12 (UT (Lands)), Martin Rodger Q.C.
Sch.11 Pt 1 para.2, see *Christoforou v Standard Apartments Ltd* [2014] L. & T.R. 12 (UT (Lands)), Martin Rodger Q.C.
Sch.11 Pt 1 para.5, see *Christoforou v Standard Apartments Ltd* [2014] L. & T.R. 12 (UT (Lands)), Martin Rodger Q.C.
Sch.12 para.1, enabling: SI 2014/287
Sch.12 para.9, enabling: SI 2014/287
Sch.12 para.10, see *Christoforou v Standard Apartments Ltd* [2014] L. & T.R. 12 (UT (Lands)), Martin Rodger Q.C.

16. State Pension Credit Act 2002
applied: SI 2014/1230 Reg.5, SSI 2014/225 Reg.6
s.1, enabling: SI 2014/902
s.2, enabling: SI 2014/2888
s.3, amended: 2014 c.19 Sch.12 para.89
s.3ZA, added: 2014 c.19 Sch.12 para.90
s.6, amended: 2014 c.19 s.28
s.7, amended: 2014 c.19 Sch.12 para.43
s.9, amended: 2014 c.19 s.29
s.9, applied: 2014 c.19 s.28
s.15, enabling: SI 2014/591, SI 2014/2888
s.16, amended: 2014 c.19 Sch.11 para.15, Sch.12 para.44
s.17, amended: SI 2014/560 Sch.1 para.28, SI 2014/3229 Sch.5 para.14
s.17, repealed (in part): SI 2014/560 Sch.1 para.28, SI 2014/3229 Sch.5 para.14
s.17, enabling: SI 2014/591, SI 2014/902, SI 2014/2888
s.19, enabling: SI 2014/591, SI 2014/902

17. National Health Service Reform and Health Care Professions Act 2002
s.29, see *Professional Standards Authority v General Chiropractic Council* [2014] EWHC 2190 (Admin), [2014] Med. L.R. 363 (QBD (Admin)), Lang J

20. Industrial and Provident Societies Act 2002
repealed: 2014 c.14 Sch.7

21. Tax Credits Act 2002
Commencement Orders: SI 2014/1848 Art.2

applied: SI 2014/1230 Reg.12A, Reg.7, Reg.8, Reg.37, SSI 2014/225 Reg.6
Part 1, applied: SI 2014/3037 Reg.25, SI 2014/3219 Sch.1 para.1
s.2, applied: SI 2014/3280 Art.3
s.3, enabling: SI 2014/1511
s.7, varied: SI 2014/1230 Sch.1 para.2
s.7, enabling: SI 2014/658, SI 2014/845, SI 2014/2924
s.8, enabling: SI 2014/1231, SI 2014/2924
s.9, enabling: SI 2014/845, SI 2014/2924
s.11, enabling: SI 2014/658, SI 2014/845, SI 2014/2924
s.12, applied: SI 2014/2319 Reg.3
s.12, enabling: SI 2014/2924
s.13, enabling: SI 2014/845
s.14, applied: SI 2014/1230 Reg.11
s.17, applied: SI 2014/1230 Reg.11
s.17, varied: SI 2014/1230 Sch.1 para.3
s.18, amended: SI 2014/886 Art.2
s.18, applied: SI 2014/1230 Reg.11
s.18, varied: SI 2014/1230 Sch.1 para.4
s.19, amended: SI 2014/886 Art.2
s.19, applied: SI 2014/1230 Reg.13
s.19, varied: SI 2014/1230 Sch.1 para.5
s.20, amended: SI 2014/886 Art.2
s.20, varied: SI 2014/1230 Sch.1 para.6
s.21, varied: SI 2014/1230 Sch.1 para.7
s.21A, added: SI 2014/886 Art.2
s.21A, applied: 2014 c.28 s.30, s.35
s.23, amended: SI 2014/886 Art.2
s.23, varied: SI 2014/1230 Sch.1 para.8
s.24, applied: SI 2014/1230 Reg.11
s.28, amended: SI 2014/886 Art.2
s.28, varied: SI 2014/1230 Reg.12
s.29, varied: SI 2014/1230 Reg.12
s.30, amended: SI 2014/886 Art.2
s.30, varied: SI 2014/1230 Sch.1 para.9
s.31, amended: SI 2014/886 Art.2
s.37, applied: SI 2014/3280 Art.2
s.38, amended: SI 2014/886 Art.2
s.38, applied: 2014 c.28 s.30, s.36
s.38, varied: SI 2014/1230 Sch.1 para.10
s.39, amended: SI 2014/886 Art.2
s.39, referred to: SI 2014/885 Art.2
s.39, repealed (in part): SI 2014/886 Art.2
s.39A, added: SI 2014/885 Art.2
s.39A, applied: SI 2014/885 Art.2
s.41, applied: SI 2014/384
s.41, referred to: SI 2014/384, SI 2014/845
s.42, enabling: SI 2014/658

s.48, varied: SI 2014/1230 Reg.12
s.61, enabling: SI 2014/1848
s.62, enabling: SI 2014/1848
s.63, enabling: SI 2014/1933
s.65, enabling: SI 2014/658, SI 2014/845, SI 2014/1231, SI 2014/1511, SI 2014/1933, SI 2014/2924
s.66, applied: SI 2014/845
s.67, enabling: SI 2014/658, SI 2014/845, SI 2014/1231, SI 2014/2924
Sch.2, varied: SI 2014/1230 Reg.12

22. Employment Act 2002
s.7, amended: 2014 c.6 Sch.7 para.51
s.7, applied: SI 2014/2929 Reg.3, Reg.7
s.7, varied: 2014 c.6 s.126
s.7, enabling: SI 2014/2929
s.8, amended: 2014 c.6 Sch.7 para.52
s.8, varied: 2014 c.6 s.126
s.8, enabling: SI 2014/2929, SI 2014/2934
s.10, amended: 2014 c.6 Sch.7 para.53
s.10, varied: 2014 c.6 s.126
s.10, enabling: SI 2014/2929
s.11, amended: 2014 c.6 Sch.7 para.54
s.11, varied: 2014 c.6 s.126
s.12, amended: 2014 c.6 Sch.7 para.55
s.12, varied: 2014 c.6 s.126
s.13, amended: 2014 c.6 Sch.7 para.56
s.13, referred to: SI 2014/1640 Art.19
s.13, varied: 2014 c.6 s.126, SI 2014/1640 Art.19
s.14, amended: 2014 c.6 Sch.7 para.57
s.14, varied: 2014 c.6 s.126
s.15, amended: 2014 c.6 Sch.7 para.58, 2014 c.19 Sch.13 para.72
s.15, repealed (in part): 2014 c.6 Sch.7 para.58
s.15, varied: 2014 c.6 s.126
s.38, applied: SI 2014/382 Art.4
s.51, enabling: SI 2014/2929, SI 2014/2934
s.55, amended: 2014 c.6 Sch.7 para.59
s.55, varied: 2014 c.6 s.126

23. Finance Act 2002
s.83, see *Bristol & West Plc v Revenue and Customs Commissioners* [2014] UKUT 73 (TCC), [2014] S.T.C. 1048 (UT (Tax)), Peter Smith J
s.135, enabling: SI 2014/1497
s.136, enabling: SI 2014/472, SI 2014/1497
Sch.26 Pt 6 para.28, see *Bristol & West Plc v Revenue and Customs Commissioners*

[2014] UKUT 73 (TCC), [2014] S.T.C. 1048 (UT (Tax)), Peter Smith J
Sch.29, see *Iliffe News & Media Ltd v Revenue and Customs Commissioners* [2014] F.S.R. 6 (FTT (Tax)), Judge John Walters Q.C.
Sch.29 Pt 5 para.28, see *Bristol & West Plc v Revenue and Customs Commissioners* [2014] UKUT 73 (TCC), [2014] S.T.C. 1048 (UT (Tax)), Peter Smith J
Sch.29 para.111, see *Iliffe News & Media Ltd v Revenue and Customs Commissioners* [2014] F.S.R. 6 (FTT (Tax)), Judge John Walters Q.C.

24. European Parliamentary Elections Act 2002
s.6, enabling: SI 2014/923, SI 2014/1803
s.7, applied: SI 2014/704
s.7, enabling: SI 2014/923, SI 2014/1803
s.8, see *R. (on the application of Chester) v Secretary of State for Justice* [2014] A.C. 271 (SC), Lady Hale JSC; see *Teshome v Lord President of the Council* [2014] EWHC 1468 (Admin), [2014] 3 C.M.L.R. 28 (QBD (Admin)), Moses LJ
s.13, applied: SI 2014/923, SI 2014/1803

26. Justice (Northern Ireland) Act 2002
Sch.1, referred to: SI 2014/1919 Reg.21

28. Export Control Act 2002
s.1, enabling: SI 2014/702, SI 2014/1069, SI 2014/2357, SI 2014/2932
s.2, enabling: SI 2014/1069, SI 2014/2357, SI 2014/2932
s.3, enabling: SI 2014/2357, SI 2014/2932
s.4, enabling: SI 2014/702, SI 2014/1069, SI 2014/2357, SI 2014/2932
s.5, enabling: SI 2014/702, SI 2014/1069, SI 2014/2357, SI 2014/2932
s.7, enabling: SI 2014/702, SI 2014/1069, SI 2014/2357, SI 2014/2932
s.11, applied: SI 2014/2357 Art.1

29. Proceeds of Crime Act 2002
see *HM Advocate v McAllister (Jason)* [2014] HCJ 111, 2014 S.L.T. 1023 (HCJ), Lord Boyd of Duncansby; see *Hughes (Barry) v HM Advocate* [2014] HCJAC 74, 2014 S.C.C.R. 506 (HCJ), The Lord Justice Clerk (Carloway); see *R. (on the application of Gibson) v Secretary of State for Justice* [2013] EWHC 2481 (Admin), [2014] 1 W.L.R. 2658 (QBD (Admin)), Judge Gosnell; see *R. v Ahmad (Shakeel)* [2014]

UKSC 36, [2014] 3 W.L.R. 23 (SC), Lord Neuberger JSC; see *R. v Boughton-Fox (Christopher)* [2014] EWCA Crim 227, [2014] Lloyd's Rep. F.C. 343 (CA (Crim Div)), Pitchford LJ; see *R. v Elsayed (Shearif Stephen)* [2014] EWCA Crim 333, [2014] 1 W.L.R. 3916 (CA (Civ Div)), Davis LJ; see *R. v Fields (Michael)* [2013] EWCA Crim 2042, [2014] 2 W.L.R. 233 (CA (Crim Div)), Davis LJ; see *R. v Odamo (Sunday Adeddayo)* [2013] EWCA Crim 1275, [2014] 1 Cr. App. R. (S.) 44 (CA (Crim Div)), Treacy LJ; see *R. v Okedare (Charles)* [2014] EWCA Crim 1173, [2014] 1 W.L.R. 4088 (CA (Crim Div)), Elias LJ; see *R. v Wright (Robert)* [2014] EWCA Crim 382, [2014] 1 W.L.R. 2913 (CA (Crim Div)), Treacy LJ; see *R. v Zinga (Munaf Ahmed)* [2014] EWCA Crim 52, [2014] 1 W.L.R. 2228 (CA (Crim Div)), Lord Thomas LCJ
applied: 2014 asp 6 Sch.1, SI 2014/1610 r.6_1, r.58_1, SI 2014/1893 Art.5, SI 2014/3101 Art.3
Part 2, applied: SI 2014/882 Reg.4, SI 2014/1610 r.71_1, r.71_2, r.71_4, r.71_5, r.57_2, r.71_8, r.57_3, r.76_1, r.71_9, r.57_8, r.57_9, r.71_10, r.57_14, SI 2014/1893 Art.19, Art.26, Art.31, SI 2014/3141 Reg.10, Reg.15
Part 3, applied: SI 2014/3141 Sch.1 para.6, Sch.1 para.11
Part 4, applied: SI 2014/1893 Art.19, Art.26, Art.31, SI 2014/3141 Sch.2 para.6, Sch.2 para.11
Part 5, applied: SI 2014/882 Reg.5
Part 5, referred to: SI 2014/2418 Sch.1
Part 8, applied: SI 2014/1610 r.6_1
Part 8, referred to: SI 2014/2418 Sch.1
Part 8 c.2, applied: SI 2014/1893 Art.35
Pt 2., see *R. v Padda (Gurpreet Singh)* [2013] EWCA Crim 2330, [2014] 1 W.L.R. 1920 (CA (Crim Div)), Rafferty LJ
Pt 5., see *Scottish Ministers v Ellis* [2014] CSOH 10, 2014 S.C.L.R. 434 (OH), Lord Burns; see *Scottish Ministers v M* [2014] CSOH 131, 2014 S.L.T. 929 (OH), Lord Jones
s.2A, amended: SI 2014/834 Sch.2 para.20
s.2A, repealed (in part): SI 2014/834 Sch.2 para.20

s.2C, amended: SI 2014/834 Sch.2 para.21
s.2C, repealed (in part): SI 2014/834 Sch.2 para.21
s.6, see *R. v Bestel (Jean Pierre)* [2013] EWCA Crim 1305, [2014] 1 W.L.R. 457 (CA (Crim Div)), Pitchford LJ; see *R. v Fields (Michael)* [2013] EWCA Crim 2042, [2014] 2 W.L.R. 233 (CA (Crim Div)), Davis LJ; see *R. v King (Scott)* [2014] EWCA Crim 621, [2014] 2 Cr. App. R. (S.) 54 (CA (Crim Div)), Fulford LJ; see *R. v Morgan (Christopher Lynn)* [2013] EWCA Crim 1307, [2014] 1 W.L.R. 3450 (CA (Crim Div)), Aikens LJ; see *R. v Okedare (Charles)* [2014] EWCA Crim 1173, [2014] 1 W.L.R. 4088 (CA (Crim Div)), Elias LJ; see *R. v Onuigbo (aka Okoronkwo) (Unoamaka)* [2014] EWCA Crim 65, [2014] Lloyd's Rep. F.C. 302 (CA (Crim Div)), Pitchford LJ; see *R. v Zinga (Munaf Ahmed)* [2014] EWCA Crim 52, [2014] 1 W.L.R. 2228 (CA (Crim Div)), Lord Thomas LCJ
s.6, applied: SI 2014/1610 r.58_7, SI 2014/3141 Reg.20
s.8, see *R. v Chahal (Bhabdeep Singh)* [2014] EWCA Crim 101, [2014] 2 Cr. App. R. (S.) 35 (CA (Crim Div)), Davis LJ
s.9, see *R. v Smith (Kim)* [2013] EWCA Crim 502, [2014] 1 W.L.R. 898 (CA (Crim Div)), Laws LJ
s.10, see *R. v Ernest (Sam)* [2014] EWCA Crim 1312, [2014] Lloyd's Rep. F.C. 595 (CA (Crim Div)), Davis LJ; see *R. v Harvey (Jack Frederick)* [2013] EWCA Crim 1104, [2014] 1 W.L.R. 124 (CA (Crim Div)), Jackson LJ; see *R. v Morgan (Christopher Lynn)* [2013] EWCA Crim 1307, [2014] 1 W.L.R. 3450 (CA (Crim Div)), Aikens LJ
s.12, disapplied: SI 2014/3141 Reg.15
s.14, see *R. v Johal (Jaswinder Singh)* [2013] EWCA Crim 647, [2014] 1 W.L.R. 146 (CA (Crim Div)), Elias LJ
s.14, applied: SI 2014/1610 r.58_2
s.16, see *R. v Zinga (Munaf Ahmed)* [2014] EWCA Crim 52, [2014] 1 W.L.R. 2228 (CA (Crim Div)), Lord Thomas LCJ
s.16, applied: SI 2014/1610 r.58_1
s.17, applied: SI 2014/1610 r.58_1
s.18, applied: SI 2014/1610 r.58_1
s.19, applied: SI 2014/1610 r.58_3

s.21, see *R. v Chahal (Bhabdeep Singh)* [2014] EWCA Crim 101, [2014] 2 Cr. App. R. (S.) 35 (CA (Crim Div)), Davis LJ

s.22, see *R. v John (Leon)* [2014] EWCA Crim 1240, [2014] 2 Cr. App. R. (S.) 73 (CA (Crim Div)), McCombe LJ; see *R. v Padda (Gurpreet Singh)* [2013] EWCA Crim 2330, [2014] 1 W.L.R. 1920 (CA (Crim Div)), Rafferty LJ

s.22, applied: SI 2014/1610 r.58_4

s.23, see *R. v Bestel (Jean Pierre)* [2013] EWCA Crim 1305, [2014] 1 W.L.R. 457 (CA (Crim Div)), Pitchford LJ

s.23, applied: SI 2014/1610 r.58_5

s.24, applied: SI 2014/1610 r.58_6

s.25, applied: SI 2014/1610 r.58_6

s.28, see *R. v Okedare (Charles)* [2014] EWCA Crim 1173, [2014] 1 W.L.R. 4088 (CA (Crim Div)), Elias LJ

s.28, applied: SI 2014/1610 r.58_7, r.58_8, r.58_11

s.29, applied: SI 2014/1610 r.58_7, r.58_11

s.30, applied: SI 2014/1610 r.58_8

s.31, applied: SI 2014/1610 r.71_8, r.72_1, r.72_3

s.35, disapplied: SI 2014/3141 Reg.15

s.38, disapplied: SI 2014/3141 Reg.15

s.39, applied: SI 2014/1610 r.58_9

s.40, see *R. (on the application of Mills) v Sussex Police* [2014] EWHC 2523 (Admin), [2014] 2 Cr. App. R. 34 (QBD (Admin)), Elias LJ; see *R. v Zinga (Munaf Ahmed)* [2014] EWCA Crim 52, [2014] 1 W.L.R. 2228 (CA (Crim Div)), Lord Thomas LCJ

s.41, see *Crown Prosecution Service v Eastenders Group* [2014] UKSC 26 (SC), Lady Hale DPSC; see *Director of the Serious Fraud Office v O'Brien* [2014] UKSC 23, [2014] A.C. 1246 (SC), Lord Mance JSC; see *R. v Boughton-Fox (Christopher)* [2014] EWCA Crim 227, [2014] Lloyd's Rep. F.C. 343 (CA (Crim Div)), Pitchford LJ

s.41, applied: SI 2014/1610 r.59_1, r.59_2, r.59_3, r.59_5, SI 2014/3141 Reg.19

s.42, applied: SI 2014/1610 r.59_1, r.61_14, r.59_3, r.59_4, r.59_5

s.43, applied: SI 2014/1610 r.73_1, r.73_2, r.73_3, r.73_4, r.73_5, r.73_6, r.73_7

s.48, see *Crown Prosecution Service v Eastenders Group* [2014] UKSC 26 (SC), Lady Hale DPSC

s.48, applied: SI 2014/1610 r.60_1, r.60_5, r.60_6, r.60_7, r.60_8

s.49, applied: SI 2014/1610 r.60_2, r.60_6

s.50, applied: SI 2014/1610 r.58_4, r.60_1, r.58_5, r.60_5, r.60_6, r.60_7, r.58_6, r.60_8

s.51, applied: SI 2014/1610 r.60_2

s.55, applied: SI 2014/1610 r.60_1, r.60_5, r.60_6

s.55, repealed (in part): SI 2014/834 Sch.2 para.22

s.58, applied: SI 2014/1610 r.61_1

s.59, applied: SI 2014/1610 r.61_1

s.62, applied: SI 2014/1610 r.60_3

s.63, applied: SI 2014/1610 r.60_3

s.65, applied: SI 2014/1610 r.73_1, r.73_2, r.73_3, r.73_4, r.73_5, r.73_6, r.73_7

s.67, applied: SI 2014/1610 r.58_12

s.68, applied: SI 2014/1610 r.60_1, r.59_1, r.59_4, r.60_2

s.72, see *R. v Zinga (Munaf Ahmed)* [2014] EWCA Crim 52, [2014] 1 W.L.R. 2228 (CA (Crim Div)), Lord Thomas LCJ

s.72, applied: SI 2014/1610 r.58_10

s.72, repealed (in part): SI 2014/834 Sch.2 para.23

s.73, applied: SI 2014/1610 r.58_11

s.75, see *R. v Odamo (Sunday Adeddayo)* [2013] EWCA Crim 1275, [2014] 1 Cr. App. R. (S.) 44 (CA (Crim Div)), Treacy LJ

s.76, see *R. v Ahmad (Shakeel)* [2014] UKSC 36, [2014] 3 W.L.R. 23 (SC), Lord Neuberger JSC; see *R. v Louca (Anastasis)* [2013] EWCA Crim 2090, [2014] 2 Cr. App. R. (S.) 9 (CA (Crim Div)), Sir Brian Leveson PQBD; see *R. v Morgan (Christopher Lynn)* [2013] EWCA Crim 1307, [2014] 1 W.L.R. 3450 (CA (Crim Div)), Aikens LJ; see *R. v Sale (Peter John)* [2013] EWCA Crim 1306, [2014] 1 W.L.R. 663 (CA (Crim Div)), Treacy LJ; see *R. v Wright (Robert)* [2014] EWCA Crim 382, [2014] 1 W.L.R. 2913 (CA (Crim Div)), Treacy LJ

s.77, see *R. v Smith (Kim)* [2013] EWCA Crim 502, [2014] 1 W.L.R. 898 (CA (Crim Div)), Laws LJ

s.79, see *R. v Elsayed (Shearif Stephen)* [2014] EWCA Crim 333, [2014] 1 W.L.R.

3916 (CA (Civ Div)), Davis LJ; see *R. v Fields (Michael)* [2013] EWCA Crim 2042, [2014] 2 W.L.R. 233 (CA (Crim Div)), Davis LJ; see *R. v Smith (Kim)* [2013] EWCA Crim 502, [2014] 1 W.L.R. 898 (CA (Crim Div)), Laws LJ

s.80, see *R. v Elsayed (Shearif Stephen)* [2014] EWCA Crim 333, [2014] 1 W.L.R. 3916 (CA (Civ Div)), Davis LJ

s.81, see *R. v Smith (Kim)* [2013] EWCA Crim 502, [2014] 1 W.L.R. 898 (CA (Crim Div)), Laws LJ

s.84, see *R. v Morgan (Christopher Lynn)* [2013] EWCA Crim 1307, [2014] 1 W.L.R. 3450 (CA (Crim Div)), Aikens LJ

s.85, see *R. v Okedare (Charles)* [2014] EWCA Crim 1173, [2014] 1 W.L.R. 4088 (CA (Crim Div)), Elias LJ

s.85, applied: SI 2014/1610 r.72_3

s.91, enabling: SI 2014/1610

s.92, see *HM Advocate v McAllister (Jason)* [2014] HCJ 112, 2014 S.C.L. 807 (HCJ), Lord Boyd of Duncansby

s.92, applied: SI 2014/3141 Reg.22

s.96, see *HM Advocate v McAllister (Jason)* [2014] HCJ 112, 2014 S.C.L. 807 (HCJ), Lord Boyd of Duncansby

s.101, see *HM Advocate v McAllister (Jason)* [2014] HCJ 112, 2014 S.C.L. 807 (HCJ), Lord Boyd of Duncansby

s.117, disapplied: SI 2014/3141 Sch.1 para.11

s.120, applied: SI 2014/3141 Reg.21

s.127R, applied: SI 2014/3101 Art.3

s.130, see *R. v Zinga (Munaf Ahmed)* [2014] EWCA Crim 52, [2014] 1 W.L.R. 2228 (CA (Crim Div)), Lord Thomas LCJ

s.142, enabling: SSI 2014/187

s.156, see *R. v Mackle (Plunkett Jude)* [2014] UKSC 5, [2014] A.C. 678 (SC), Lord Neuberger JSC

s.156, applied: SI 2014/3141 Reg.24

s.158, see *R. v Mackle (Plunkett Jude)* [2014] UKSC 5, [2014] A.C. 678 (SC), Lord Neuberger JSC

s.162, disapplied: SI 2014/3141 Sch.2 para.11

s.185, disapplied: SI 2014/3141 Sch.2 para.11

s.187, disapplied: SI 2014/3141 Sch.2 para.11

s.190, applied: SI 2014/3141 Reg.23

s.266, see *Scottish Ministers v Ellis* [2014] CSOH 10, 2014 S.C.L.R. 434 (OH), Lord Burns; see *Scottish Ministers v Mirza* [2014] CSIH 103 (IH (Ex Div)), Lady Clark of Calton; see *Scottish Ministers v Stirton* 2014 S.C. 218 (IH (2 Div)), The Lord Justice Clerk (Carloway)

s.298, see *Fletcher v Chief Constable of Leicestershire* [2013] EWHC 3357 (Admin), [2014] Lloyd's Rep. F.C. 60 (QBD (Admin)), Lewis J

s.302, applied: SI 2014/1610 r.58_10

s.302A, amended: SI 2014/834 Sch.2 para.24

s.316, amended: SI 2014/834 Sch.2 para.25

s.316, referred to: SI 2014/1610 r.6_1

s.317, see *Fenech v Serious Organised Crime Agency* [2014] Lloyd's Rep. F.C. 68 (FTT (Tax)), Judge David Demack

s.323, amended: 2014 c.6 Sch.7 para.60

s.323, referred to: SI 2014/1640 Art.19

s.323, repealed (in part): 2014 c.6 Sch.7 para.60

s.323, varied: 2014 c.6 s.126, SI 2014/1640 Art.19

s.327, see *Fletcher v Chief Constable of Leicestershire* [2013] EWHC 3357 (Admin), [2014] Lloyd's Rep. F.C. 60 (QBD (Admin)), Lewis J; see *McAughey (Charles Gray) v HM Advocate* 2014 S.C.L. 165 (HCJ), Lord Menzies; see *R. v Onuigbo (aka Okoronkwo) (Unoamaka)* [2014] EWCA Crim 65, [2014] Lloyd's Rep. F.C. 302 (CA (Crim Div)), Pitchford LJ; see *R. v Pace (Martin Edward)* [2014] EWCA Crim 186, [2014] 1 W.L.R. 2867 (CA (Crim Div)), Davis LJ; see *R. v Rogers (Bradley David)* [2014] EWCA Crim 1680, [2014] 2 Cr. App. R. 32 (CA (Crim Div)), Treacy LJ; see *Sweeney v Westminster Magistrates' Court* [2014] EWHC 2068 (Admin), (2014) 178 J.P. 336 (DC), Pitchford LJ

s.328, see *R. v Onuigbo (aka Okoronkwo) (Unoamaka)* [2014] EWCA Crim 65, [2014] Lloyd's Rep. F.C. 302 (CA (Crim Div)), Pitchford LJ; see *Sweeney v Westminster Magistrates' Court* [2014] EWHC 2068 (Admin), (2014) 178 J.P. 336 (DC), Pitchford LJ

s.329, see *Sweeney v Westminster Magistrates' Court* [2014] EWHC 2068 (Admin), (2014) 178 J.P. 336 (DC), Pitchford LJ

s.333A, applied: SI 2014/1893 Art.5

s.340, see *R. v Pace (Martin Edward)* [2014] EWCA Crim 186, [2014] 1 W.L.R. 2867 (CA (Crim Div)), Davis LJ; see *R. v Rogers (Bradley David)* [2014] EWCA Crim 1680, [2014] 2 Cr. App. R. 32 (CA (Crim Div)), Treacy LJ

s.341, applied: SI 2014/1610 r.6_1

s.342, applied: SI 2014/1610 r.6_22

s.343, applied: SI 2014/1610 r.6_1

s.345, applied: SI 2014/1610 r.6_1, r.6_15, r.6_22

s.347, applied: SI 2014/1610 r.6_1, r.6_16

s.348, applied: SI 2014/1610 r.6_3

s.351, applied: SI 2014/1610 r.6_1, r.6_22

s.351, enabling: SI 2014/1610

s.352, see *R. (on the application of Golfrate Property Management Ltd) v Southwark Crown Court* [2014] EWHC 840 (Admin), [2014] 2 Cr. App. R. 12 (QBD (Admin)), Lord Thomas LCJ; see *R. (on the application of Mills) v Sussex Police* [2014] EWHC 2523 (Admin), [2014] 2 Cr. App. R. 34 (QBD (Admin)), Elias LJ

s.352, amended: SI 2014/834 Sch.2 para.26

s.353, see *R. (on the application of Mills) v Sussex Police* [2014] EWHC 2523 (Admin), [2014] 2 Cr. App. R. 34 (QBD (Admin)), Elias LJ

s.357, amended: SI 2014/834 Sch.2 para.27

s.357, applied: SI 2014/1610 r.6_1, r.6_17, SI 2014/3207 Art.2

s.357, enabling: SI 2014/3207

s.359, applied: SI 2014/1610 r.6_22, SI 2014/1893 Art.19

s.361, applied: SI 2014/1610 r.6_3, r.6_17

s.362, applied: SI 2014/1610 r.6_1

s.362, enabling: SI 2014/1610

s.363, applied: SI 2014/1610 r.6_1, r.6_18

s.366, applied: SI 2014/1610 r.6_22, SI 2014/1893 Art.26

s.368, applied: SI 2014/1610 r.6_18

s.369, applied: SI 2014/1610 r.6_1

s.369, enabling: SI 2014/1610

s.370, applied: SI 2014/1610 r.6_1, r.6_19, r.6_22

s.374, applied: SI 2014/1610 r.6_19

s.375, applied: SI 2014/1610 r.6_1, r.6_22

s.375, enabling: SI 2014/1610

s.377, applied: SI 2014/1610 r.6_14

s.377A, amended: SI 2014/834 Sch.2 para.28

s.377A, applied: SI 2014/1610 r.6_14

s.378, see *R. v Zinga (Munaf Ahmed)* [2014] EWCA Crim 52, [2014] 1 W.L.R. 2228 (CA (Crim Div)), Lord Thomas LCJ

s.391, see *Scottish Ministers v M* [2014] CSOH 131, 2014 S.L.T. 929 (OH), Lord Jones

s.396, see *Scottish Ministers v M* [2014] CSOH 131, 2014 S.L.T. 929 (OH), Lord Jones

s.438, amended: SI 2014/834 Sch.2 para.29

s.439, repealed (in part): SI 2014/834 Sch.2 para.30

s.441, amended: SI 2014/834 Sch.2 para.31

s.441, enabling: SSI 2014/49

s.444, amended: SI 2014/834 Sch.2 para.32

s.444, repealed (in part): SI 2014/834 Sch.2 para.32

s.445, amended: SI 2014/834 Sch.2 para.33

s.445, enabling: SI 2014/1893

s.451, amended: SI 2014/834 Sch.2 para.34

s.453, enabling: SI 2014/467

s.459, applied: SSI 2014/49, SSI 2014/187

s.459, enabling: SI 2014/467, SI 2014/1893

s.460, amended: SI 2014/834 Sch.2 para.35

Sch.4 para.9AA, added: SSI 2014/187 Art.3

Sch.9 Part 1 para.2, amended: 2014 c.14

Sch.4 para.81

Sch.9 Part 2 para.4, repealed (in part): SI 2014/892 Sch.1 para.159

30. Police Reform Act 2002

see *R. (on the application of the Chief Constable of West Yorkshire) v Independent Police Complaints Commission* [2013] EWHC 2698 (Admin), [2014] P.T.S.R. 242 (QBD (Admin)), Judge Jeremy Richardson QC

s.10, see *R. (on the application of the Chief Constable of West Yorkshire) v Independent Police Complaints Commission* [2013] EWHC 2698 (Admin), [2014] P.T.S.R. 242 (QBD (Admin)), Judge Jeremy Richardson QC

s.12, amended: 2014 c.12 s.135

s.12, referred to: SI 2014/2418 Sch.1

s.24, applied: SI 2014/2406

s.26BA, added: 2014 c.12 s.130
s.29, amended: 2014 c.12 Sch.11 para.93
s.29, enabling: SI 2014/2406
s.39, repealed (in part): 2014 c.12 Sch.11 para.94
s.50, amended: 2014 c.12 Sch.11 para.31
s.61, repealed: 2014 c.12 Sch.11 para.50
Sch.3 Part 3 para.19, amended: 2014 c.12 s.136, Sch.11 para.95
Sch.3 Part 3 para.19, enabling: SI 2014/2402
Sch.3 Part 3 para.19ZA, added: 2014 c.12 s.137
Sch.3 Part 3 para.20A, amended: 2014 c.12 Sch.11 para.95
Sch.3 Part 3 para.20C, amended: 2014 c.12 Sch.11 para.95
Sch.3 Part 3 para.20H, amended: 2014 c.12 Sch.11 para.95
Sch.3 Part 3 para.23, amended: 2014 c.12 Sch.11 para.95
Sch.3 Part 3 para.24A, amended: 2014 c.12 Sch.11 para.95
Sch.3 Part 3 para.24C, amended: 2014 c.12 s.138, Sch.11 para.95
Sch.3 Part 3 para.24C, repealed (in part): 2014 c.12 Sch.11 para.95
Sch.3 Part 3 para.27, amended: 2014 c.12 s.138, Sch.11 para.95
Sch.3 Part 3 para.28A, added: 2014 c.12 s.139
Sch.3 Part 3 para.28A, enabling: SI 2014/2406
Sch.4 Part 1 para.1, amended: 2014 c.12 s.53, s.69, Sch.10 para.2, Sch.10 para.3, Sch.11 para.102
Sch.4 Part 1 para.1, repealed (in part): 2014 c.12 Sch.11 para.32
Sch.4 Part 1 para.1ZB, added: 2014 c.12 s.53
Sch.4 Part 1 para.2, amended: 2014 c.12 s.40
Sch.4 Part 1 para.2B, added: 2014 c.12 Sch.10 para.4
Sch.4 Part 1 para.3B, added: 2014 c.12 Sch.10 para.5
Sch.4 Part 1 para.4A, substituted: 2014 c.12 s.40
Sch.4 Part 1 para.5, substituted: 2014 c.12 s.69
Sch.4 Part 1 para.11A, amended: 2014 c.12 Sch.10 para.6
Sch.5 para.1, repealed (in part): 2014 c.12 Sch.11 para.33

32. Education Act 2002
s.12, applied: SI 2014/3352 Sch.1 para.20
s.12, enabling: SI 2014/2923
s.19, see *TB v Essex CC* [2014] E.L.R. 46 (UT (AAC)), Judge Lane
s.19, enabling: SI 2014/1132, SI 2014/1257, SI 2014/1609, SI 2014/1959, SI 2014/2225
s.20, see *TB v Essex CC* [2014] E.L.R. 46 (UT (AAC)), Judge Lane
s.20, enabling: SI 2014/1132, SI 2014/1257, SI 2014/1959
s.21, enabling: SI 2014/1257, SI 2014/1609, SI 2014/1959, SI 2014/2677
s.24, applied: SI 2014/3352 Reg.22
s.24, enabling: SI 2014/1257, SI 2014/1959, SI 2014/3352
s.25, enabling: SI 2014/1257, SI 2014/1959
s.27, applied: SI 2014/3352 Sch.1 para.20, Sch.5 para.25
s.28, amended: 2014 c.6 s.88
s.28, repealed (in part): 2014 c.6 s.88
s.29, applied: SI 2014/2709 Reg.22
s.30, enabling: SI 2014/2677
s.31, applied: SI 2014/2709 Reg.22
s.32A, applied: SI 2014/1249 Sch.1
s.32A, enabling: SI 2014/1249
s.32B, enabling: SI 2014/1462
s.34, enabling: SI 2014/1132, SI 2014/1257, SI 2014/1609, SI 2014/1959
s.35, enabling: SI 2014/798, SI 2014/1132, SI 2014/1257, SI 2014/1609, SI 2014/1959
s.36, enabling: SI 2014/798, SI 2014/1132, SI 2014/1257, SI 2014/1609, SI 2014/1959
s.44, applied: SI 2014/3352 Sch.1 para.20
s.52, see *R. (on the application of CR) v Independent Review Panel of Lambeth LBC* [2014] EWHC 2461 (Admin), [2014] E.L.R. 359 (QBD (Admin)), Collins J
s.52, applied: SI 2014/1132 Reg.68
s.87, applied: SI 2014/3352 Sch.1 para.23
s.87, enabling: SI 2014/1867, SI 2014/1941, SI 2014/3285
s.91, enabling: SI 2014/1866, SI 2014/3286
s.92, amended: 2014 c.6 Sch.3 para.77
s.94, amended: 2014 c.6 Sch.3 para.78
s.96, applied: SI 2014/1866, SI 2014/1867, SI 2014/1941, SI 2014/3285, SI 2014/3286
s.102, applied: SI 2014/1999 Art.2
s.102, enabling: SI 2014/1996
s.103, applied: SI 2014/1999 Art.2
s.108, enabling: SI 2014/1996, SI 2014/1999

s.116A, enabling: SI 2014/42
s.116D, enabling: SI 2014/42
s.117, applied: SI 2014/1996
s.120, applied: SI 2014/2045
s.121, applied: SI 2014/2045
s.122, enabling: SI 2014/1063, SI 2014/2045
s.123, enabling: SI 2014/2045
s.124, enabling: SI 2014/2045
s.125, applied: SI 2014/2045
s.126, applied: SI 2014/1063, SI 2014/2045
s.131, applied: SI 2014/2677
s.131, enabling: SI 2014/2677
s.132, enabling: SI 2014/2697
s.135A, applied: SI 2014/1530 Reg.49
s.141B, see *O v Secretary of State for
Education* [2014] EWHC 22 (Admin),
[2014] E.L.R. 232 (QBD (Admin)), Stephen
Morris QC
s.141B, applied: SI 2014/2365 Reg.5
s.141F, applied: SI 2014/1610 r.16_1, r.16_5
s.142, applied: SI 2014/512 Reg.111, SI
2014/1132 Sch.7 para.9, SI 2014/1977
Reg.8, SI 2014/2365 Reg.5, SI 2014/2709
Sch.2 para.9, SI 2014/3283 Sch.1 para.18,
Sch.1 para.20, Sch.1 para.21
s.145, enabling: SI 2014/2697
s.157, enabling: SI 2014/2374
s.158, referred to: 2014 c.6 s.41, SI
2014/2379 Art.3
s.161, applied: SI 2014/512 Sch.1 para.2
s.162A, applied: SI 2014/2379 Art.3
s.167A, applied: SI 2014/1132 Sch.7 para.9,
SI 2014/2709 Sch.2 para.9
s.175, applied: SI 2014/3352 Sch.1 para.6
s.194, repealed (in part): 2014 c.6 Sch.3
para.16
s.210, enabling: SI 2014/42, SI 2014/1063,
SI 2014/1132, SI 2014/1249, SI 2014/1257,
SI 2014/1462, SI 2014/1609, SI 2014/1685,
SI 2014/1867, SI 2014/1941, SI 2014/1959,
SI 2014/1996, SI 2014/1999, SI 2014/2225,
SI 2014/2374, SI 2014/2677, SI 2014/2697,
SI 2014/2923, SI 2014/3285
s.214, enabling: SI 2014/1132
Sch.2 Part 2 para.7, applied: SI 2014/1132
Reg.67
Sch.11A, enabling: SI 2014/1685

**33. Copyright (Visually Impaired Persons) Act
2002**

repealed: SI 2014/1384 Sch.1 para.8

38. Adoption and Children Act 2002
Commencement Orders: SI 2014/1961 Art.2
see *A (Placement Order: Imposition of
Conditions on Adoption), Re* [2013] EWCA
Civ 1611, [2014] 1 W.L.R. 2139 (CA (Civ
Div)), Laws LJ; see *A County Council v M*
[2013] EWHC 1501 (Fam), [2014] 1 F.L.R.
881 (Fam Div), Peter Jackson J; see *E (A
Child) (Adoption Order: Proportionality of
Outcome to Circumstances), Re* [2013]
EWCA Civ 1614, [2014] 2 F.L.R. 514 (CA
(Civ Div)), Laws LJ
applied: SI 2014/1795 Reg.9
s.1, see *A County Council v M* [2013]
EWHC 1501 (Fam), [2014] 1 F.L.R. 881
(Fam Div), Peter Jackson J; see *C (A Child)
(Placement for Adoption: Judicial
Approach), Re* [2013] EWCA Civ 1257,
[2014] 1 W.L.R. 2247 (CA (Civ Div)),
Patten LJ; see *G (A Child) (Non-relative
Carer: Joinder to Adoption Proceedings), Re*
[2014] EWCA Civ 432, [2014] 3 W.L.R.
1719 (CA (Civ Div)), Sullivan LJ; see *HA
(Capacity to Change), Re* [2013] EWHC
3634 (Fam), [2014] 2 F.L.R. 540 (Fam Div),
Baker J; see *J v G (Parental Orders)* [2013]
EWHC 1432 (Fam), [2014] 1 F.L.R. 297
(Fam Div), Theis J; see *P (A Child)
(Enforced Caesarean: Adoption), Re* [2014]
EWHC 1146 (Fam), [2014] 2 F.L.R. 426
(Fam Div), Sir James Munby PFD
s.1, amended: 2014 c.6 s.3, s.9
s.2, applied: SI 2014/1795 Reg.9, SI
2014/2672 Sch.1 para.25, Sch.2 para.30, SI
2014/3037 Reg.25
s.3, applied: SI 2014/2672 Sch.2 para.30
s.3A, added: 2014 c.6 s.4
s.3A, disapplied: 2014 c.6 s.4
s.4, applied: SI 2014/1957 Reg.4, SI
2014/3037 Reg.25
s.4A, added: 2014 c.6 s.5
s.4B, added: 2014 c.6 s.6
s.4B, enabling: SI 2014/1563
s.9, enabling: SI 2014/567, SI 2014/1556, SI
2014/2696
s.18, applied: SI 2014/1795 Reg.9
s.21, see *A (Placement Order: Imposition of
Conditions on Adoption), Re* [2013] EWCA
Civ 1611, [2014] 1 W.L.R. 2139 (CA (Civ
Div)), Laws LJ
s.21, applied: SI 2014/840 Sch.1

s.23, applied: SI 2014/840 Sch.1

s.24, see *G (A Child) (Non-relative Carer: Joinder to Adoption Proceedings), Re* [2014] EWCA Civ 432, [2014] 3 W.L.R. 1719 (CA (Civ Div)), Sullivan LJ

s.24, applied: SI 2014/840 Sch.1

s.26, amended: 2014 c.6 Sch.2 para.60

s.26, applied: SI 2014/840 Sch.1

s.26, repealed (in part): 2014 c.6 s.9

s.27, applied: SI 2014/840 Sch.1

s.28, see *A (A Child) (Adoption: Placement Outside Jurisdiction), Re* [2013] EWHC 578 (Fam), [2014] Fam. 1 (Fam Div), Pauffley J; see *RO v A Local Authority* [2014] EWHC 97 (Fam), [2014] 2 F.L.R. 1007 (Fam Div), Keehan J

s.28, amended: 2014 c.6 Sch.2 para.61

s.28, applied: SI 2014/840 Sch.1

s.29, see *G (A Child) (Non-relative Carer: Joinder to Adoption Proceedings), Re* [2014] EWCA Civ 432, [2014] 3 W.L.R. 1719 (CA (Civ Div)), Sullivan LJ

s.29, amended: 2014 c.6 Sch.2 para.62

s.30, applied: SI 2014/1795 Reg.9

s.31, applied: SI 2014/3051 Sch.1 para.12

s.32, amended: 2014 c.6 Sch.2 para.63

s.35, amended: 2014 c.6 Sch.2 para.64

s.35, referred to: 2014 c.6 s.13

s.36, applied: SI 2014/1795 Reg.9

s.41, applied: SI 2014/840 r.16

s.42, see *IH (A Child) (Permission to Apply for Adoption), Re* [2013] EWHC 1235 (Fam), [2014] 1 F.L.R. 70 (Fam Div), Pauffley J; see *MW (A Child) (Leave to Apply for Adoption), Re* [2014] EWHC 385 (Fam), [2014] 2 F.L.R. 978 (Fam Div (Leeds)), Holman J

s.46, see *N v B (Adoption by Grandmother)* [2013] EWHC 820 (Fam), [2014] 1 F.L.R. 369 (Fam Div), Theis J

s.46, applied: SI 2014/840 Sch.1, SI 2014/3352 Reg.16

s.47, see *B-S (Children) (Adoption: Leave to Oppose), Re* [2013] EWCA Civ 1146, [2014] 1 W.L.R. 563 (CA (Civ Div)), Lord Dyson MR; see *D (A Child) (Leave to Oppose Making of Adoption Order), Re* [2013] EWCA Civ 1480, [2014] 2 F.L.R. 866 (CA (Civ Div)), Moses LJ; see *G (A Child) (Non-relative Carer: Joinder to Adoption Proceedings), Re* [2014] EWCA

Civ 432, [2014] 3 W.L.R. 1719 (CA (Civ Div)), Sullivan LJ; see *L (A Child) (Leave to Oppose Making of Adoption Order), Re* [2013] EWCA Civ 1481, [2014] 2 F.L.R. 913 (CA (Civ Div)), Moses LJ; see *W (A Child) (Adoption Order: Leave to Oppose), Re* [2013] EWCA Civ 1177, [2014] 1 W.L.R. 1993 (CA (Civ Div)), Sir James Munby PFD

s.51A, added: 2014 c.6 s.9

s.51A, applied: SI 2014/840 Sch.1

s.51A, disapplied: SI 2014/1042 Art.3

s.51B, referred to: SI 2014/603 Sch.1

s.52, see *A (Placement Order: Imposition of Conditions on Adoption), Re* [2013] EWCA Civ 1611, [2014] 1 W.L.R. 2139 (CA (Civ Div)), Laws LJ; see *E (A Child) (Adoption Order: Proportionality of Outcome to Circumstances), Re* [2013] EWCA Civ 1614, [2014] 2 F.L.R. 514 (CA (Civ Div)), Laws LJ; see *Kent CC v IS* [2013] EWHC 2308 (Fam), [2014] 1 F.L.R. 787 (Fam Div), Theis J; see *P (A Child) (Adoption: Step-parent), Re* [2014] EWCA Civ 1174, [2014] 3 F.C.R. 193 (CA (Civ Div)), Moore-Bick LJ

s.55, applied: SI 2014/840 Sch.1

s.60, applied: SI 2014/840 Sch.1

s.66, applied: SI 2014/840 Sch.1

s.69, amended: 2014 c.16 s.4

s.71, applied: SI 2014/2672 Sch.1 para.25

s.79, applied: SI 2014/840 Sch.1

s.87, applied: SI 2014/840 Sch.1

s.94, applied: 2014 c.6 s.13

s.96, amended: 2014 c.6 s.9

s.98, amended: 2014 c.6 s.1

s.98, enabling: SI 2014/2696

s.109, amended: 2014 c.6 s.14

s.121, repealed (in part): 2014 c.6 s.15

s.125, amended: 2014 c.6 s.7, Sch.1 para.2

s.125, repealed (in part): 2014 c.6 Sch.1 para.11

s.125, enabling: SI 2014/1492

s.126, amended: 2014 c.6 Sch.1 para.3

s.126, applied: SI 2014/1957 Reg.3

s.126, repealed (in part): 2014 c.6 Sch.1 para.3

s.127, amended: 2014 c.6 Sch.1 para.4

s.127, repealed (in part): 2014 c.6 Sch.1 para.4

s.128, amended: 2014 c.6 s.7, Sch.1 para.5

s.128, enabling: SI 2014/1492

s.128A, added: 2014 c.6 s.7

s.128A, applied: SI 2014/1957, SI
2014/1957 Reg.5

s.128A, enabling: SI 2014/1957

s.129, amended: 2014 c.6 s.7, Sch.1 para.6

s.129, repealed (in part): 2014 c.6 Sch.1
para.6

s.129, enabling: SI 2014/1492

s.130, repealed: 2014 c.6 Sch.1 para.7

s.131, amended: 2014 c.6 Sch.1 para.8

s.131, repealed (in part): 2014 c.6 Sch.1
para.8

s.140, amended: 2014 c.6 s.4, s.7

s.140, enabling: SI 2014/567, SI 2014/1492,
SI 2014/1556, SI 2014/1563, SI 2014/1957,
SI 2014/2696

s.142, amended: 2014 c.6 Sch.1 para.9

s.142, enabling: SI 2014/567

s.143, applied: SI 2014/1610 r.4_3

s.144, amended: 2014 c.6 Sch.1 para.10

s.148, enabling: SI 2014/1961 Art.2

s.149, repealed (in part): 2014 c.6 Sch.1
para.11

Sch.1 para.4, applied: SI 2014/840 Sch.1

Sch.6, amended: 2014 c.6 Sch.2 para.65

39. Commonwealth Act 2002

see *Commonwealth Institute (In Members'
Voluntary Liquidation), Re* [2014] EWHC
2218 (Ch), [2014] W.T.L.R. 1621 (Ch D
(Companies Ct)), David Richards J

40. Enterprise Act 2002

applied: 2014 c.21 s.50

s.2, disapplied: SI 2014/549 Art.3

s.4, varied: SI 2014/416 Sch.1 para.2

s.8A, amended: SI 2014/892 Sch.1 para.2

s.22, see *Global Radio Holdings Ltd v
Competition Commission* [2014] Comp.
A.R. 51 (CAT), Newey J

s.22, applied: SI 2014/534 Art.12

s.22, varied: SI 2014/416 Sch.1 para.2

s.23, see *Global Radio Holdings Ltd v
Competition Commission* [2014] Comp.
A.R. 51 (CAT), Newey J; see *Groupe
Eurotunnel SA v Competition Commission*
[2014] Comp. A.R. 77 (CAT), Marcus Smith
QC

s.26, see *Groupe Eurotunnel SA v
Competition Commission* [2014] Comp.
A.R. 77 (CAT), Marcus Smith QC

s.31, applied: SI 2014/549 Sch.2 para.4, SI
2014/891 Art.22

s.33, applied: SI 2014/534 Art.12

s.33, varied: SI 2014/416 Sch.1 para.2

s.45, varied: SI 2014/416 Sch.1 para.2

s.62, varied: SI 2014/416 Sch.1 para.2

s.68, enabling: SI 2014/891

s.71, applied: SI 2014/549 Sch.2 para.5

s.71, varied: SI 2014/416 Sch.1 para.5

s.73, applied: 2014 c.23 s.92

s.80, varied: SI 2014/416 Sch.1 para.5

s.86, see *Akzo Nobel NV v Competition
Commission* [2014] EWCA Civ 482, [2014]
Bus. L.R. 802 (CA (Civ Div)), Richards LJ

s.91, enabling: SI 2014/558

s.94A, applied: SI 2014/533 Art.2, Art.3,
Sch.1 para.5

s.94A, enabling: SI 2014/533

s.96, applied: SI 2014/534 Art.12

s.97, varied: SI 2014/416 Sch.1 para.6

s.98, varied: SI 2014/416 Sch.1 para.6

s.99, applied: SI 2014/534 Art.12

s.109, amended: SI 2014/892 Sch.1 para.3

s.109, applied: SI 2014/549 Sch.2 para.3,
Sch.2 para.6, Sch.2 para.7, SI 2014/891
Art.22, SI 2014/892 Sch.2 para.1, Sch.2
para.2

s.109, referred to: SI 2014/549 Sch.2 para.6

s.109, varied: SI 2014/416 Sch.1 para.10

s.110B, varied: SI 2014/416 Sch.1 para.6

s.111, applied: SI 2014/559, SI 2014/559
Art.2

s.111, enabling: SI 2014/559

s.112, applied: SI 2014/536 Reg.9

s.117, applied: 2014 c.23 s.92

s.121, enabling: SI 2014/534

s.124, applied: SI 2014/891

s.124, enabling: SI 2014/533, SI 2014/534,
SI 2014/559, SI 2014/891

s.127, see *Groupe Eurotunnel SA v
Competition Commission* [2014] Comp.
A.R. 77 (CAT), Marcus Smith QC

s.129, see *Akzo Nobel NV v Competition
Commission* [2014] EWCA Civ 482, [2014]
Bus. L.R. 802 (CA (Civ Div)), Richards LJ;
see *Groupe Eurotunnel SA v Competition
Commission* [2014] Comp. A.R. 77 (CAT),
Marcus Smith QC

s.130A, applied: SI 2014/416 Sch.1 para.1

s.131, varied: SI 2014/416 Sch.1 para.2

s.132, varied: SI 2014/416 Sch.1 para.2

s.139, varied: SI 2014/416 Sch.1 para.9,
Sch.1 para.16
s.140A, varied: SI 2014/416 Sch.1 para.16
s.166, enabling: SI 2014/558
s.168, amended: 2014 c.21 Sch.7 para.129
s.174, applied: SI 2014/892 Sch.2 para.3,
Sch.2 para.4
s.174C, varied: SI 2014/416 Sch.1 para.10
s.174D, applied: SI 2014/559, SI 2014/559
Art.3
s.174D, enabling: SI 2014/559
s.175, applied: SI 2014/892 Sch.2 para.3
s.188A, applied: SI 2014/535 Art.2
s.188A, enabling: SI 2014/535
s.192, applied: SI 2014/458 Sch.1 para.10
s.205, amended: SI 2014/892 Sch.1 para.4
s.206, amended: SI 2014/892 Sch.1 para.5
s.210, enabling: SI 2014/2908
s.212, applied: SI 2014/2908 Art.4
s.212, enabling: SI 2014/2908
s.213, amended: SI 2014/892 Sch.1 para.6
s.214, amended: SI 2014/892 Sch.1 para.7
s.215, amended: SI 2014/892 Sch.1 para.8
s.216, amended: SI 2014/892 Sch.1 para.9
s.219, amended: SI 2014/892 Sch.1 para.10
s.220, amended: SI 2014/892 Sch.1 para.11
s.224, amended: SI 2014/892 Sch.1 para.12
s.225, amended: SI 2014/892 Sch.1 para.13
s.229, amended: SI 2014/892 Sch.1 para.14
s.230, amended: SI 2014/892 Sch.1 para.15
s.230, repealed (in part): SI 2014/892 Sch.1
para.15
s.231, amended: SI 2014/631 Sch.2 para.4,
SI 2014/892 Sch.1 para.16
s.241, enabling: SI 2014/2807
s.249, amended: 2014 c.21 Sch.7 para.130
s.255, repealed (in part): 2014 c.14 Sch.7
s.255, enabling: SI 2014/229
s.259, see *Thomas v Edmondson* [2014]
EWHC 1494 (Ch), [2014] 3 All E.R. 976
(Ch D), Asplin J
s.277, applied: 2014 c.14 s.118
Sch.7 para.1, varied: SI 2014/416 Sch.1
para.5
Sch.13 Part 1 para.9F, added: SI 2014/2908
Art.3
Sch.14, amended: SI 2014/892 Sch.1 para.17
Sch.15, amended: SI 2014/469 Sch.2
para.22, SI 2014/892 Sch.1 para.17, SI
2014/2807 Art.2

Sch.24 para.1, repealed: SI 2014/892 Sch.1
para.18
Sch.24 para.3, repealed: SI 2014/892 Sch.1
para.18
Sch.24 para.15, amended: SI 2014/892 Sch.1
para.18
Sch.24 para.16, amended: SI 2014/892 Sch.1
para.18
Sch.24 para.17, amended: SI 2014/892 Sch.1
para.18
Sch.24 para.18, amended: SI 2014/892 Sch.1
para.18

**41. Nationality, Immigration and Asylum Act
2002**
see *SM (Withdrawal of Appealed Decision:
Effect: Pakistan)* [2014] UKUT 64 (IAC),
[2014] Imm. A.R. 662 (UT (IAC)), Judge
Peter Lane
applied: SI 2014/2604 r.19, Sch.1 para.2
Part 5, substituted: 2014 c.22 Sch.9 para.33
Part 5A, added: 2014 c.22 s.19
s.36, amended: 2014 c.6 Sch.3 para.79
s.44, referred to: 2014 c.23 s.21
s.44, varied: 2014 c.23 s.21
s.62, see *R. (on the application of JB
(Jamaica)) v Secretary of State for the Home
Department* [2013] EWCA Civ 666, [2014]
1 W.L.R. 836 (CA (Civ Div)), Pill, L.J.
s.62, amended: 2014 c.22 Sch.9 para.3,
Sch.9 para.13
s.62, repealed (in part): 2014 c.22 Sch.9
para.3
s.72, amended: 2014 c.22 Sch.9 para.31
s.73, repealed (in part): 2014 c.22 Sch.9
para.7
s.74, repealed: 2014 c.22 Sch.9 para.7
s.75, repealed (in part): 2014 c.22 Sch.9
para.7
s.76, see *R. (on the application of George) v
Secretary of State for the Home Department*
[2014] UKSC 28, [2014] 1 W.L.R. 1831
(SC), Lord Neuberger PSC
s.76, amended: 2014 c.22 Sch.9 para.3
s.76, repealed (in part): 2014 c.22 Sch.9
para.3, Sch.9 para.7
s.78A, added: 2014 c.22 s.2
s.79, amended: 2014 c.22 Sch.9 para.32
s.82, see *Ahmadi (S.47 Decision: Validity:
Sapkota: Afghanistan), Re* [2013] EWCA
Civ 512, [2014] 1 W.L.R. 401 (CA (Civ
Div)), Sullivan LJ; see *AS (Afghanistan) v*

Secretary of State for the Home Department
[2013] EWCA Civ 1469, [2014] Imm. A.R.
513 (CA (Civ Div)), Longmore LJ; see
*Greenwood (Automatic Deportation: Order
of Events), Re* [2014] UKUT 342 (IAC),
[2014] Imm. A.R. 1288 (UT (IAC)), CMG
Ockelton (Vice President); see *R. (on the
application of Khan) v Secretary of State for
the Home Department* [2014] EWCA Civ
88, [2014] 1 W.L.R. 3173 (CA (Civ Div)),
Moore-Bick LJ; see *R. (on the application
of Pryor) v Secretary of State for the Home
Department* [2013] EWHC 2853 (Admin),
[2014] Imm. A.R. 341 (QBD (Admin)),
Jeremy Baker J; see *R. (on the application
of Thapa) v Secretary of State for the Home
Department* [2014] EWHC 659 (Admin),
[2014] 1 W.L.R. 4138 (QBD (Admin)),
Helen Mountfield QC; see *Rahman v
Secretary of State for the Home Department*
[2014] EWCA Civ 11, [2014] 1 W.L.R.
3574 (CA (Civ Div)), Richards LJ; see *SM
(Withdrawal of Appealed Decision: Effect:
Pakistan)* [2014] UKUT 64 (IAC), [2014]
Imm. A.R. 662 (UT (IAC)), Judge Peter
Lane; see *Virk v Secretary of State for the
Home Department* [2013] EWCA Civ 652,
[2014] Imm. A.R. 95 (CA (Civ Div)),
Leveson LJ
s.82, applied: SI 2014/922 Sch.1 para.1, SI
2014/2768 Reg.3, SI 2014/2771 Art.11
s.82, substituted: 2014 c.22 s.15
s.83, see *MS (Uganda) v Secretary of State
for the Home Department* [2014] EWCA Civ
50, [2014] 1 W.L.R. 2766 (CA (Civ Div)),
Elias LJ; see *TN (Afghanistan) v Secretary
of State for the Home Department* [2013]
EWCA Civ 1609, [2014] 1 W.L.R. 2095
(CA (Civ Div)), Maurice Kay LJ
s.83, applied: SI 2014/2771 Art.11
s.83, repealed: 2014 c.22 s.15
s.83A, see *MS (Uganda) v Secretary of State
for the Home Department* [2014] EWCA Civ
50, [2014] 1 W.L.R. 2766 (CA (Civ Div)),
Elias LJ
s.84, see *Qongwane v Secretary of State for
the Home Department* [2014] EWCA Civ
957, [2014] Imm. A.R. 1179 (CA (Civ Div)),
Lewison LJ
s.84, substituted: 2014 c.22 s.15

s.85, see *Patel v Secretary of State for the
Home Department* [2014] A.C. 651 (SC),
Lord Mance JSC
s.85, amended: 2014 c.22 s.15, Sch.9 para.34
s.85A, see *Patel v Secretary of State for the
Home Department* [2014] A.C. 651 (SC),
Lord Mance JSC; see *Rahman v Secretary
of State for the Home Department* [2014]
EWCA Civ 11, [2014] 1 W.L.R. 3574 (CA
(Civ Div)), Richards LJ
s.85A, applied: SI 2014/2604 r.14
s.85A, repealed: 2014 c.22 Sch.9 para.35
s.86, see *Greenwood (Automatic
Deportation: Order of Events), Re* [2014]
UKUT 342 (IAC), [2014] Imm. A.R. 1288
(UT (IAC)), CMG Ockelton (Vice
President); see *Qongwane v Secretary of
State for the Home Department* [2014]
EWCA Civ 957, [2014] Imm. A.R. 1179
(CA (Civ Div)), Lewison LJ; see *Rahman v
Secretary of State for the Home Department*
[2014] EWCA Civ 11, [2014] 1 W.L.R.
3574 (CA (Civ Div)), Richards LJ; see *SM
(Withdrawal of Appealed Decision: Effect:
Pakistan)* [2014] UKUT 64 (IAC), [2014]
Imm. A.R. 662 (UT (IAC)), Judge Peter
Lane
s.86, amended: 2014 c.22 Sch.9 para.36
s.86, repealed (in part): 2014 c.22 Sch.9
para.36
s.87, see *SM (Withdrawal of Appealed
Decision: Effect: Pakistan)* [2014] UKUT 64
(IAC), [2014] Imm. A.R. 662 (UT (IAC)),
Judge Peter Lane
s.87, repealed: 2014 c.22 Sch.9 para.37
s.90, repealed: 2014 c.22 Sch.9 para.37
s.92, see *R. (on the application of EM
(Eritrea)) v Secretary of State for the Home
Department* [2014] UKSC 12, [2014] A.C.
1321 (SC), Lord Neuberger PSC
s.92, substituted: 2014 c.22 s.17
s.92, varied: SI 2014/1820 Art.4, SI
2014/2771 Art.15
s.94, see *R. (on the application of JB
(Jamaica)) v Secretary of State for the Home
Department* [2013] EWCA Civ 666, [2014]
1 W.L.R. 836 (CA (Civ Div)), Pill, L.J.
s.94, amended: 2014 c.22 Sch.9 para.38
s.94, repealed (in part): 2014 c.22 Sch.9
para.38
s.94A, amended: 2014 c.22 Sch.9 para.39

s.94B, added: 2014 c.22 s.17
s.95, repealed: 2014 c.22 Sch.9 para.40
s.96, see *R. (on the application of Khan) v
Secretary of State for the Home Department*
[2014] EWCA Civ 88, [2014] 1 W.L.R.
3173 (CA (Civ Div)), Moore-Bick LJ; see
*SK (Namibia) v Secretary of State for the
Home Department* [2014] CSOH 52, 2014
S.L.T. 587 (OH), Lord Stewart
s.96, amended: 2014 c.22 Sch.9 para.41
s.96, referred to: SI 2014/2771 Art.11
s.97, see *R. (on the application of Ignaoua) v
Secretary of State for the Home Department*
[2013] EWCA Civ 1498, [2014] 1 W.L.R.
651 (CA (Civ Div)), Lord Dyson MR
s.97, amended: 2014 c.22 Sch.9 para.42
s.97, applied: SI 2014/2604 r.18
s.97A, amended: 2014 c.22 Sch.9 para.43
s.97A, repealed (in part): 2014 c.22 Sch.9
para.43
s.97B, repealed: 2014 c.22 Sch.9 para.44
s.98, applied: SI 2014/2604 r.18
s.98, repealed: 2014 c.22 Sch.9 para.45
s.99, see *R. (on the application of Ignaoua) v
Secretary of State for the Home Department*
[2013] EWCA Civ 1498, [2014] 1 W.L.R.
651 (CA (Civ Div)), Lord Dyson MR
s.99, amended: 2014 c.22 Sch.9 para.46
s.99, applied: SI 2014/2604 Sch.1 para.9
s.104, see *SM (Withdrawal of Appealed
Decision: Effect: Pakistan)* [2014] UKUT 64
(IAC), [2014] Imm. A.R. 662 (UT (IAC)),
Judge Peter Lane
s.104, amended: 2014 c.22 Sch.9 para.47
s.104, applied: SI 2014/2604 r.16, Sch.1
para.9, SI 2014/3037 Reg.6
s.104, repealed (in part): 2014 c.22 Sch.9
para.47
s.105, amended: 2014 c.22 Sch.9 para.48
s.105, enabling: SI 2014/2768
s.106, amended: 2014 c.22 Sch.9 para.49
s.106, enabling: SI 2014/2604
s.107, amended: 2014 c.22 Sch.9 para.50
s.108, amended: 2014 c.22 Sch.9 para.51
s.108, applied: SI 2014/2604 r.27
s.109, enabling: SI 2014/1976
s.112, amended: 2014 c.22 Sch.9 para.52
s.112, repealed (in part): 2014 c.22 Sch.9
para.52
s.112, enabling: SI 2014/2768
s.113, amended: 2014 c.22 Sch.9 para.53

s.113, repealed (in part): 2014 c.22 Sch.9
para.53
s.115, repealed: 2014 c.22 Sch.9 para.54
s.117D, applied: SI 2014/2928 Art.2
s.117D, referred to: SI 2014/2771 Art.10
s.120, see *Patel v Secretary of State for the
Home Department* [2014] A.C. 651 (SC),
Lord Mance JSC
s.120, substituted: 2014 c.22 Sch.9 para.55
s.126, amended: 2014 c.22 s.8, s.14, Sch.2
para.3, Sch.9 para.19
s.126, repealed (in part): 2014 c.22 Sch.9
para.19
s.127, amended: 2014 c.22 Sch.2 para.4
s.127, repealed (in part): 2014 c.22 Sch.2
para.4
Sch.3 para.7, see *Mensah v Salford City
Council* [2014] EWHC 3537 (Admin),
(2014) 17 C.C.L. Rep. 492 (QBD (Admin)),
Lewis J
Sch.7 para.27, repealed: 2014 c.22 Sch.9
para.60

2003

1. Income Tax (Earnings and Pensions) Act
2003

Part 2 c.5A, substituted: 2014 c.26 Sch.9
para.5
Part 3 c.2, applied: SI 2014/3159 Reg.3,
Reg.4
Part 4 c.10A, added: 2014 c.26 Sch.37 para.5
Part 7 c.6, amended: 2014 c.26 Sch.8 para.2
Part 7 c.7, amended: 2014 c.26 Sch.8 para.98
Part 7 c.8, amended: 2014 c.26 Sch.8
para.159
Part 9, referred to: 2014 c.30 s.4
Pt 3., see *Reed Employment Plc v Revenue
and Customs Commissioners* [2014] UKUT
160 (TCC), [2014] S.T.C. 1982 (UT (Tax)),
Proudman J
Pt 7., see *Metso Paper Bender Forrest Ltd v
Revenue and Customs Commissioners*
[2014] S.F.T.D. 529 (FTT (Tax)), Lady
Mitting; see *Tower Radio Ltd v Revenue
and Customs Commissioners* [2014]
S.F.T.D. 377 (FTT (Tax)), Judge Peter
Kempster; see *UBS AG v Revenue and
Customs Commissioners* [2014] EWCA Civ

452, [2014] S.T.C. 2278 (CA (Civ Div)),
Rimer LJ
Pt 7 s.425, see *UBS AG v Revenue and*
Customs Commissioners [2014] EWCA Civ
452, [2014] S.T.C. 2278 (CA (Civ Div)),
Rimer LJ
Pt 7 s.426, see *UBS AG v Revenue and*
Customs Commissioners [2014] EWCA Civ
452, [2014] S.T.C. 2278 (CA (Civ Div)),
Rimer LJ
Pt 7 s.429, see *UBS AG v Revenue and*
Customs Commissioners [2014] EWCA Civ
452, [2014] S.T.C. 2278 (CA (Civ Div)),
Rimer LJ
s.6, amended: 2014 c.26 Sch.9 para.3
s.10, amended: 2014 c.26 Sch.9 para.4
s.11, see *Martin v Revenue and Customs*
Commissioners [2014] UKUT 429 (TCC),
[2014] B.T.C. 527 (UT (Tax)), Warren J
s.23, amended: 2014 c.26 Sch.3 para.2
s.24A, added: 2014 c.26 Sch.3 para.3
s.41C, amended: 2014 c.26 Sch.3 para.4
s.44, substituted: 2014 c.26 s.16
s.45, amended: 2014 c.26 s.16
s.46, amended: 2014 c.26 s.16
s.46A, added: 2014 c.26 s.16
s.47, repealed (in part): 2014 c.26 s.16
s.54, amended: 2014 c.26 Sch.17 para.5
s.62, see *Apollo Fuels Ltd v Revenue and*
Customs Commissioners [2014] UKUT 95
(TCC), [2014] B.T.C. 510 (UT (Tax)), Rose
J
s.65, see *Reed Employment Plc v Revenue*
and Customs Commissioners [2014] UKUT
160 (TCC), [2014] S.T.C. 1982 (UT (Tax)),
Proudman J
s.72, amended: SI 2014/211 Art.3
s.114, see *Apollo Fuels Ltd v Revenue and*
Customs Commissioners [2014] UKUT 95
(TCC), [2014] B.T.C. 510 (UT (Tax)), Rose
J
s.114, repealed (in part): 2014 c.26 s.23
s.133, amended: 2014 c.26 s.24
s.133, repealed (in part): 2014 c.26 s.24
s.139, amended: 2014 c.26 s.24
s.139, repealed (in part): 2014 c.26 s.24
s.140, amended: 2014 c.26 s.24
s.140, repealed (in part): 2014 c.26 s.24
s.141, repealed: 2014 c.26 s.24
s.142, amended: 2014 c.26 s.24
s.144, amended: 2014 c.26 s.25

s.150, amended: SI 2014/2896 Art.2
s.155, amended: SI 2014/2896 Art.3
s.158, amended: 2014 c.26 s.25
s.161, amended: SI 2014/2896 Art.4
s.170, amended: 2014 c.26 s.24
s.170, enabling: SI 2014/2896
s.175, see *Leeds Design Innovation Centre*
Ltd v Revenue and Customs Commissioners
[2014] UKFTT 9 (TC), [2014] S.F.T.D. 681
(FTT (Tax)), Judge Rachel Short
s.180, amended: 2014 c.26 s.22
s.181, enabling: SI 2014/496
s.222, amended: 2014 c.26 s.19, s.21
s.227, amended: 2014 c.26 Sch.8 para.45,
Sch.8 para.130, Sch.8 para.191
s.229, see *Apollo Fuels Ltd v Revenue and*
Customs Commissioners [2014] UKUT 95
(TCC), [2014] B.T.C. 510 (UT (Tax)), Rose
J
s.241A, added: SI 2014/211 Art.2
s.266, amended: 2014 c.26 s.12
s.270A, amended: 2014 c.28 s.63
s.270AA, added: 2014 c.28 s.63
s.291, amended: 2014 c.29 s.4
s.293B, amended: 2014 c.29 s.4
s.294, amended: 2014 c.29 s.4
s.312E, applied: 2014 c.26 Sch.37 para.4
s.318A, amended: 2014 c.28 s.64
s.318AZA, added: 2014 c.28 s.64
s.318B, amended: 2014 c.28 s.64
s.320C, added: 2014 c.26 s.12
s.320C, applied: SI 2014/3227 Reg.3
s.320C, enabling: SI 2014/3227
s.340A, added: SI 2014/211 Art.2
s.343, amended: SI 2014/859 Art.2
s.343, enabling: SI 2014/859
s.386, see *McWhinnie v Revenue and*
Customs Commissioners [2014] Pens. L.R. 1
(FTT (Tax)), Judge Malachy Cornwell-
Kelly; see *Revenue and Customs*
Commissioners v Dhanak [2014] UKUT 68
(TCC), [2014] S.T.C. 1525 (UT (Tax)),
David Richards J
s.392, see *Revenue and Customs*
Commissioners v Dhanak [2014] UKUT 68
(TCC), [2014] S.T.C. 1525 (UT (Tax)),
David Richards J
s.395B, added: SI 2014/211 Art.5
s.401, see *Harding v Revenue and Customs*
Commissioners [2014] S.T.C. 891 (UT
(Tax)), Judge Colin Bishopp

s.401, amended: SI 2014/211 Art.5

s.403, see *Turullols v Revenue and Customs Commissioners* [2014] UKFTT 672 (TC), [2014] S.F.T.D. 1099 (FTT (Tax)), Judge Kevin Poole

s.414A, added: SI 2014/211 Art.5

s.417, amended: 2014 c.26 Sch.8 para.46, Sch.8 para.131, Sch.8 para.192

s.418, amended: 2014 c.26 Sch.9 para.7

s.421D, amended: 2014 c.26 Sch.9 para.35

s.421E, repealed: 2014 c.26 Sch.9 para.8

s.421J, amended: 2014 c.26 Sch.8 para.227

s.421J, repealed (in part): 2014 c.26 Sch.8 para.227

s.421JA, added: 2014 c.26 Sch.8 para.228

s.421JB, added: 2014 c.26 Sch.8 para.228

s.421K, amended: 2014 c.26 Sch.8 para.229

s.421L, amended: 2014 c.26 s.21, Sch.8 para.230

s.423, see *Tower Radio Ltd v Revenue and Customs Commissioners* [2014] S.F.T.D. 377 (FTT (Tax)), Judge Peter Kempster; see *UBS AG v Revenue and Customs Commissioners* [2014] EWCA Civ 452, [2014] S.T.C. 2278 (CA (Civ Div)), Rimer LJ

s.425, amended: 2014 c.26 Sch.9 para.9

s.428, amended: 2014 c.26 Sch.9 para.10

s.430, amended: 2014 c.26 Sch.9 para.11

s.430A, added: 2014 c.26 Sch.9 para.36

s.431, amended: 2014 c.26 Sch.9 para.12

s.431A, amended: 2014 c.26 Sch.8 para.47, Sch.8 para.132, Sch.8 para.193

s.446T, amended: 2014 c.26 Sch.9 para.13

s.446U, amended: 2014 c.26 Sch.9 para.37

s.471, see *Metso Paper Bender Forrest Ltd v Revenue and Customs Commissioners* [2014] S.F.T.D. 529 (FTT (Tax)), Lady Mitting

s.473, amended: 2014 c.26 Sch.8 para.133, Sch.8 para.194

s.474, repealed: 2014 c.26 Sch.9 para.14

s.475, amended: 2014 c.26 Sch.8 para.195

s.476, amended: 2014 c.26 Sch.8 para.134, Sch.8 para.196

s.480, amended: 2014 c.26 Sch.8 para.197, Sch.9 para.15

s.488, amended: 2014 c.26 Sch.8 para.3

s.488, repealed (in part): 2014 c.26 Sch.8 para.3

s.489, amended: 2014 c.26 Sch.8 para.4

s.498, amended: 2014 c.26 Sch.8 para.5

s.500, amended: 2014 c.26 Sch.8 para.6

s.503, amended: 2014 c.26 Sch.8 para.7

s.506, amended: 2014 c.26 Sch.8 para.8

s.509, amended: 2014 c.26 Sch.8 para.9

s.510, amended: 2014 c.26 Sch.8 para.10

s.511, amended: 2014 c.26 Sch.8 para.11

s.515, amended: 2014 c.26 Sch.8 para.12

s.516, amended: 2014 c.26 Sch.8 para.99

s.516, repealed (in part): 2014 c.26 Sch.8 para.99

s.517, amended: 2014 c.26 Sch.8 para.100

s.519, amended: 2014 c.26 Sch.8 para.101

s.521, amended: 2014 c.26 Sch.8 para.160

s.521, repealed (in part): 2014 c.26 Sch.8 para.160

s.522, amended: 2014 c.26 Sch.8 para.161

s.524, amended: 2014 c.26 Sch.8 para.162

s.539, amended: 2014 c.26 Sch.8 para.198

s.540, amended: 2014 c.26 Sch.9 para.16

s.540, repealed (in part): 2014 c.26 Sch.9 para.16

s.549, amended: 2014 c.26 Sch.8 para.48, Sch.8 para.135, Sch.8 para.199

s.554E, amended: 2014 c.26 Sch.8 para.49, Sch.8 para.136, Sch.8 para.200

s.554L, amended: 2014 c.26 Sch.9 para.18

s.554M, amended: 2014 c.26 Sch.9 para.19

s.554N, amended: 2014 c.26 Sch.9 para.20, Sch.9 para.38

s.554Z9, amended: 2014 c.26 Sch.3 para.5

s.573, amended: 2014 c.30 Sch.2 para.25

s.574, amended: 2014 c.30 Sch.2 para.25

s.576A, amended: 2014 c.30 Sch.1 para.83, Sch.1 para.84

s.576A, repealed (in part): 2014 c.30 Sch.1 para.84

s.577, amended: 2014 c.19 Sch.12 para.45, Sch.12 para.74

s.579A, amended: 2014 c.30 Sch.2 para.25

s.579CA, amended: 2014 c.30 Sch.1 para.81, Sch.1 para.82

s.579CA, repealed (in part): 2014 c.30 Sch.1 para.82

s.579CZA, added: 2014 c.30 Sch.2 para.25

s.579D, amended: 2014 c.30 Sch.2 para.25

s.636A, amended: 2014 c.26 Sch.5 para.5, 2014 c.30 Sch.1 para.31, Sch.1 para.62, Sch.2 para.19

s.636A, repealed (in part): 2014 c.30 Sch.2 para.19

s.639, referred to: SI 2014/1230 Reg.24
s.660, amended: 2014 c.6 Sch.7 para.62,
2014 c.19 Sch.16 para.47
s.660, varied: 2014 c.6 s.126
s.677, amended: 2014 c.19 Sch.16 para.48,
SI 2014/606 Reg.3
s.684, amended: SI 2014/992 Art.7, SI
2014/2438 Art.2
s.684, enabling: SI 2014/472, SI 2014/1017,
SI 2014/2396, SI 2014/2438, SI 2014/2689
s.688, amended: 2014 c.26 s.16, s.17
s.688, applied: 2014 c.26 s.17
s.689, amended: 2014 c.26 s.20, s.21
s.689A, added: 2014 c.26 s.21
s.689A, amended: 2014 c.26 s.21
s.690, amended: 2014 c.26 s.21
s.697, amended: 2014 c.26 Sch.8 para.137,
Sch.8 para.201
s.700A, amended: 2014 c.26 Sch.9 para.21
s.701, amended: 2014 c.26 Sch.8 para.138,
Sch.8 para.202
s.710, amended: 2014 c.26 s.21
s.715, enabling: SI 2014/584
s.716B, added: 2014 c.26 s.18
s.717, amended: 2014 c.26 Sch.37 para.6,
Sch.3 para.6, 2014 c.28 s.63, s.64
Sch.1 Part 2, amended: 2014 c.26 Sch.37
para.7
Sch.2, amended: 2014 c.26 Sch.8 para.14
Sch.2, referred to: 2014 c.26 Sch.8 para.91
Sch.2 Part 1 para.1, amended: 2014 c.26
Sch.8 para.15, Sch.8 para.16
Sch.2 Part 2 para.6, amended: 2014 c.26
Sch.8 para.17
Sch.2 Part 2 para.6, substituted: 2014 c.26
Sch.8 para.18
Sch.2 Part 2 para.7, amended: 2014 c.26
Sch.8 para.19
Sch.2 Part 2 para.7, repealed (in part): 2014
c.26 Sch.8 para.19
Sch.2 Part 3 para.18, amended: 2014 c.26
Sch.8 para.20
Sch.2 Part 3 para.18A, amended: 2014 c.26
Sch.8 para.21
Sch.2 Part 4 para.27, amended: 2014 c.26
Sch.37 para.19
Sch.2 Part 4 para.28, amended: 2014 c.14
Sch.4 para.82
Sch.2 Part 5 para.35, amended: 2014 c.26
s.49, s.50

Sch.2 Part 5 para.37, amended: 2014 c.26
Sch.8 para.22
Sch.2 Part 6 para.43, amended: 2014 c.26
Sch.8 para.23
Sch.2 Part 6 para.46, amended: 2014 c.26
s.49, s.50
Sch.2 Part 6 para.56, amended: 2014 c.26
Sch.8 para.24, Sch.8 para.25
Sch.2 Part 7 para.60, amended: 2014 c.26
s.50
Sch.2 Part 8 para.65, substituted: 2014 c.26
Sch.8 para.26
Sch.2 Part 9 para.71A, amended: 2014 c.26
Sch.8 para.27
Sch.2 Part 10, substituted: 2014 c.26 Sch.8
para.28
Sch.2 Part 10 para.81A, varied: 2014 c.26
Sch.8 para.94
Sch.2 Part 10 para.81B, referred to: 2014
c.26 Sch.8 para.92
Sch.2 Part 11 para.89, repealed (in part):
2014 c.26 Sch.8 para.29
Sch.2 Part 11 para.90, amended: 2014 c.26
Sch.8 para.30
Sch.2 Part 11 para.93, amended: 2014 c.26
Sch.8 para.31
Sch.2 Part 11 para.93, applied: 2014 c.26
Sch.8 para.96
Sch.2 Part 11 para.100, amended: 2014 c.26
Sch.8 para.32
Sch.3, amended: 2014 c.26 Sch.8 para.103
Sch.3, referred to: 2014 c.26 Sch.8 para.148
Sch.3 Part 1 para.1, amended: 2014 c.26
Sch.8 para.104, Sch.8 para.105
Sch.3 Part 2, amended: 2014 c.26 Sch.8
para.106
Sch.3 Part 2 para.4, amended: 2014 c.26
Sch.8 para.107
Sch.3 Part 2 para.5, substituted: 2014 c.26
Sch.8 para.108
Sch.3 Part 4 para.17, amended: 2014 c.26
Sch.8 para.109
Sch.3 Part 4 para.19, amended: 2014 c.26
Sch.37 para.20
Sch.3 Part 5 para.25, amended: 2014 c.26
Sch.8 para.110, SI 2014/402 Art.2
Sch.3 Part 5 para.25, enabling: SI 2014/402
Sch.3 Part 6 para.28, amended: 2014 c.26
Sch.8 para.111
Sch.3 Part 6 para.28, referred to: 2014 c.26
Sch.8 para.151

Sch.3 Part 6 para.28, repealed (in part): 2014 c.26 Sch.8 para.111

Sch.3 Part 6 para.32, amended: 2014 c.26 Sch.8 para.112

Sch.3 Part 6 para.34, amended: 2014 c.26 Sch.8 para.113

Sch.3 Part 6 para.34, referred to: 2014 c.26 Sch.8 para.153

Sch.3 Part 6 para.34, repealed (in part): 2014 c.26 Sch.8 para.113

Sch.3 Part 6 para.37, amended: 2014 c.26 Sch.8 para.114

Sch.3 Part 6 para.37, referred to: 2014 c.26 Sch.8 para.154

Sch.3 Part 7 para.38, amended: 2014 c.26 Sch.8 para.115

Sch.3 Part 7 para.39, amended: 2014 c.26 Sch.8 para.116

Sch.3 Part 8, substituted: 2014 c.26 Sch.8 para.117

Sch.3 Part 8 para.40A, varied: 2014 c.26 Sch.8 para.155

Sch.3 Part 8 para.40B, referred to: 2014 c.26 Sch.8 para.149

Sch.3 Part 9 para.45, amended: 2014 c.26 Sch.8 para.118

Sch.3 Part 9 para.45, applied: 2014 c.26 Sch.8 para.157

Sch.3 Part 9 para.47A, added: 2014 c.26 Sch.8 para.119

Sch.3 Part 9 para.49, amended: 2014 c.26 Sch.8 para.120

Sch.4, amended: 2014 c.26 Sch.8 para.164

Sch.4, referred to: 2014 c.26 Sch.8 para.206

Sch.4 Part 1 para.1, amended: 2014 c.26 Sch.8 para.165, Sch.8 para.166

Sch.4 Part 2, amended: 2014 c.26 Sch.8 para.167

Sch.4 Part 2 para.4, amended: 2014 c.26 Sch.8 para.168

Sch.4 Part 2 para.5, substituted: 2014 c.26 Sch.8 para.169

Sch.4 Part 2 para.6, amended: 2014 c.26 Sch.8 para.170

Sch.4 Part 3 para.11, amended: 2014 c.26 Sch.8 para.50

Sch.4 Part 4 para.15, amended: 2014 c.26 Sch.8 para.171

Sch.4 Part 4 para.17, amended: 2014 c.26 Sch.37 para.21

Sch.4 Part 5 para.21, amended: 2014 c.26 Sch.8 para.172

Sch.4 Part 5 para.21A, added: 2014 c.26 Sch.8 para.173

Sch.4 Part 5 para.22, amended: 2014 c.26 Sch.8 para.174

Sch.4 Part 5 para.22, applied: 2014 c.26 Sch.8 para.210

Sch.4 Part 5 para.22, repealed (in part): 2014 c.26 Sch.8 para.174

Sch.4 Part 5 para.25, amended: 2014 c.26 Sch.8 para.175

Sch.4 Part 5 para.25, applied: 2014 c.26 Sch.8 para.211

Sch.4 Part 5 para.25A, amended: 2014 c.26 Sch.8 para.176

Sch.4 Part 5 para.25A, applied: 2014 c.26 Sch.8 para.212

Sch.4 Part 6 para.26, amended: 2014 c.26 Sch.8 para.177

Sch.4 Part 6 para.27, amended: 2014 c.26 Sch.8 para.178

Sch.4 Part 7, substituted: 2014 c.26 Sch.8 para.179

Sch.4 Part 7 para.28A, applied: 2014 c.26 Sch.8 para.213

Sch.4 Part 7 para.28A, varied: 2014 c.26 Sch.8 para.213

Sch.4 Part 7 para.28F, referred to: 2014 c.26 Sch.8 para.213

Sch.4 Part 7 para.28F, varied: 2014 c.26 Sch.8 para.213

Sch.4 Part 7 para.28I, referred to: 2014 c.26 Sch.8 para.213

Sch.4 Part 7 para.29, applied: 2014 c.26 Sch.8 para.213

Sch.4 Part 7 para.32, applied: 2014 c.26 Sch.8 para.213

Sch.4 Part 8 para.33, amended: 2014 c.26 Sch.8 para.180

Sch.4 Part 8 para.33, applied: 2014 c.26 Sch.8 para.215

Sch.4 Part 8 para.35ZA, added: 2014 c.26 Sch.8 para.181

Sch.4 Part 8 para.37, amended: 2014 c.26 Sch.8 para.182

Sch.5 Part 2 para.5, amended: 2014 c.26 Sch.8 para.203

Sch.5 Part 3 para.9, amended: 2014 c.26 Sch.37 para.22

Sch.5 Part 3 para.12A, amended: 2014 c.6
Sch.7 para.63
Sch.5 Part 4 para.26, amended: 2014 c.6
Sch.7 para.63
Sch.5 Part 4 para.30, amended: 2014 c.26
Sch.8 para.51
Sch.5 Part 7 para.44, amended: 2014 c.26
Sch.8 para.217
Sch.5 Part 7 para.44, repealed (in part): 2014
c.26 Sch.8 para.217
Sch.5 Part 8 para.52, substituted: 2014 c.26
Sch.8 para.218
Sch.5 Part 8 para.53, amended: 2014 c.26
Sch.8 para.219
Sch.5 Part 8 para.57A, added: 2014 c.26
Sch.8 para.220

5. Community Care (Delayed Discharges etc.) Act 2003

s.4, applied: SI 2014/829 Sch.1 para.19

7. European Parliament (Representation) Act 2003

s.17, applied: SI 2014/1803
s.17, enabling: SI 2014/1803
s.18, applied: SI 2014/1803
s.18, enabling: SI 2014/1803

14. Finance Act 2003

see *DV3 RS Limited Partnership v Revenue and Customs Commissioners* [2013] EWCA Civ 907, [2014] 1 W.L.R. 1136 (CA (Civ Div)), Maurice Kay LJ
applied: SSI 2014/377 Art.3, Art.4
Part 4, applied: 2014 c.29 s.15
Part 4, referred to: 2014 c.29 s.16
s.26, applied: 2014 c.26 s.102
s.29, applied: 2014 c.26 s.102
s.33F, amended: SI 2014/1264 Art.8
s.43, see *DV3 RS Limited Partnership v Revenue and Customs Commissioners* [2013] EWCA Civ 907, [2014] 1 W.L.R. 1136 (CA (Civ Div)), Maurice Kay LJ
s.44, see *DV3 RS Limited Partnership v Revenue and Customs Commissioners* [2013] EWCA Civ 907, [2014] 1 W.L.R. 1136 (CA (Civ Div)), Maurice Kay LJ
s.44, applied: SSI 2014/377 Art.3, Art.4
s.45, see *DV3 RS Limited Partnership v Revenue and Customs Commissioners* [2013] EWCA Civ 907, [2014] 1 W.L.R. 1136 (CA (Civ Div)), Maurice Kay LJ; see *R. (on the application of St Matthews (West) Ltd) v HM Treasury* [2014] EWHC 1848

(Admin), [2014] S.T.C. 2350 (QBD (Admin)), Andrews J
s.48, amended: 2014 c.29 s.16, Sch.2 para.3
s.48A, added: 2014 c.29 Sch.2 para.4
s.50, see *DV3 RS Limited Partnership v Revenue and Customs Commissioners* [2013] EWCA Civ 907, [2014] 1 W.L.R. 1136 (CA (Civ Div)), Maurice Kay LJ
s.60, amended: 2014 c.29 Sch.2 para.5
s.72, applied: SSI 2014/377 Art.5
s.72, referred to: SSI 2014/377 Art.5
s.72A, applied: SSI 2014/377 Art.5
s.72A, referred to: SSI 2014/377 Art.5
s.73, amended: 2014 c.29 Sch.2 para.6
s.74, amended: 2014 c.26 s.112
s.107, amended: 2014 c.29 s.4
s.117, amended: 2014 c.29 Sch.2 para.8
s.121, amended: 2014 c.29 Sch.2 para.9
Sch.4 para.1, see *DV3 RS Limited Partnership v Revenue and Customs Commissioners* [2013] EWCA Civ 907, [2014] 1 W.L.R. 1136 (CA (Civ Div)), Maurice Kay LJ
Sch.4A para.1, amended: 2014 c.26 s.111
Sch.4A para.4, amended: 2014 c.26 s.111
Sch.4A para.6, amended: 2014 c.26 s.111
Sch.5, applied: SSI 2014/377 Art.10
Sch.7 Part 1 para.2B, amended: 2014 c.29 Sch.2 para.10
Sch.8 para.1, amended: 2014 c.26 Sch.23 para.2
Sch.8 para.3A, added: 2014 c.26 Sch.23 para.3
Sch.8 para.4, amended: 2014 c.26 Sch.23 para.4
Sch.9 para.7, amended: 2014 c.29 Sch.2 para.11
Sch.10 Pt 3 para.12, see *Portland Gas Storage Ltd v Revenue and Customs Commissioners* [2014] UKUT 270 (TCC), [2014] S.T.C. 2589 (UT (Tax)), Judge Timothy Herrington
Sch.10 Pt 3 para.23, see *Portland Gas Storage Ltd v Revenue and Customs Commissioners* [2014] UKUT 270 (TCC), [2014] S.T.C. 2589 (UT (Tax)), Judge Timothy Herrington
Sch.10 Part 5 para.31, amended: 2014 c.26 s.277
Sch.10 Part 7 para.35, applied: 2014 c.26 s.208

Sch.10 Pt 7 para.35, see *Portland Gas
Storage Ltd v Revenue and Customs
Commissioners* [2014] UKUT 270 (TCC),
[2014] S.T.C. 2589 (UT (Tax)), Judge
Timothy Herrington
Sch.10 Part 7 para.39, amended: 2014 c.26
s.224
Sch.10 Part 7 para.39, applied: 2014 c.26
s.227
Sch.10 Part 7 para.40, amended: 2014 c.26
s.224
Sch.10 Part 7 para.43, amended: 2014 c.26
s.225
Sch.10 Part 7 para.45, amended: 2014 c.29
Sch.2 para.12
Sch.15, see *DV3 RS Limited Partnership v
Revenue and Customs Commissioners*
[2013] EWCA Civ 907, [2014] 1 W.L.R.
1136 (CA (Civ Div)), Maurice Kay LJ
Sch.15 Pt 3 para.10, see *DV3 RS Limited
Partnership v Revenue and Customs
Commissioners* [2013] EWCA Civ 907,
[2014] 1 W.L.R. 1136 (CA (Civ Div)),
Maurice Kay LJ
Sch.15 Part 3 para.17, applied: SSI 2014/377
Art.7
Sch.15 Part 3 para.17, referred to: SSI
2014/377 Art.7
Sch.15 Part 3 para.17A, applied: SSI
2014/377 Art.8
Sch.15 Part 3 para.17A, referred to: SSI
2014/377 Art.8
Sch.17A, applied: SSI 2014/377 Art.12,
Art.13
Sch.17A para.11, applied: SSI 2014/377
Art.11
Sch.17A para.11, referred to: SSI 2014/377
Art.11
Sch.17A para.12A, see *Portland Gas
Storage Ltd v Revenue and Customs
Commissioners* [2014] UKUT 270 (TCC),
[2014] S.T.C. 2589 (UT (Tax)), Judge
Timothy Herrington
Sch.23, see *Metso Paper Bender Forrest Ltd
v Revenue and Customs Commissioners*
[2014] S.F.T.D. 529 (FTT (Tax)), Lady
Mitting
Sch.23 Pt 1 para.1, see *Metso Paper Bender
Forrest Ltd v Revenue and Customs
Commissioners* [2014] S.F.T.D. 529 (FTT
(Tax)), Lady Mitting

Sch.24 para.1, see *Scotts Atlantic
Management Ltd v Revenue and Customs
Commissioners* [2014] S.F.T.D. 210 (FTT
(Tax)), Judge Howard M Nowlan
**15. Co-operatives and Community Benefit
Societies Act 2003**
repealed: 2014 c.14 Sch.7
17. Licensing Act 2003
see *R. (on the application of Extreme Oyster)
v Guildford BC* [2013] EWHC 2174
(Admin), [2014] P.T.S.R. 325 (QBD
(Admin)), Turner J; see *R. (on the
application of Star Oyster Ltd) v Guildford
Borough Council* [2014] EWHC 1412
(Admin), [2014] L.L.R. 768 (QBD
(Admin)), Jay J
Part 5, applied: 2014 c.12 s.62
s.16, see *R. (on the application of Extreme
Oyster) v Guildford BC* [2013] EWHC 2174
(Admin), [2014] P.T.S.R. 325 (QBD
(Admin)), Turner J
s.18, see *R. (on the application of Extreme
Oyster) v Guildford BC* [2013] EWHC 2174
(Admin), [2014] P.T.S.R. 325 (QBD
(Admin)), Turner J
s.19, applied: SI 2014/1252 Art.2
s.19A, applied: SI 2014/1252, SI 2014/2440
s.19A, enabling: SI 2014/1252, SI
2014/2440
s.34, see *R. (on the application of Star
Oyster Ltd) v Guildford Borough Council*
[2014] EWHC 1412 (Admin), [2014] L.L.R.
768 (QBD (Admin)), Jay J
s.35, see *R. (on the application of Star
Oyster Ltd) v Guildford Borough Council*
[2014] EWHC 1412 (Admin), [2014] L.L.R.
768 (QBD (Admin)), Jay J
s.41A, see *R. (on the application of Star
Oyster Ltd) v Guildford Borough Council*
[2014] EWHC 1412 (Admin), [2014] L.L.R.
768 (QBD (Admin)), Jay J
s.41B, see *R. (on the application of Star
Oyster Ltd) v Guildford Borough Council*
[2014] EWHC 1412 (Admin), [2014] L.L.R.
768 (QBD (Admin)), Jay J
s.47, see *R. (on the application of Bednash)
v Westminster City Council* [2014] EWHC
2160 (Admin), [2014] L.L.R. 755 (DC),
Moses LJ
s.51, see *R. (on the application of D&D Bar
Services Ltd) v Romford Magistrates' Court*

[2014] EWHC 344 (Admin), [2014] L.L.R. 761 (QBD (Admin)), Judge Blackett
s.64, amended: 2014 c.14 Sch.4 para.84
s.65, amended: 2014 c.14 Sch.4 para.85
s.73A, applied: SI 2014/1252 Art.2
s.73B, applied: SI 2014/1252, SI 2014/2440
s.73B, enabling: SI 2014/1252, SI 2014/2440
s.100, enabling: SI 2014/1371, SI 2014/2417
s.133, enabling: SI 2014/3284
s.155, repealed (in part): 2014 c.12 Sch.11 para.50
s.159, referred to: SI 2014/2440 Art.3
s.161, applied: 2014 c.12 s.93
s.161, repealed: 2014 c.12 Sch.11 para.34
s.165, applied: 2014 c.12 s.93
s.167, amended: 2014 c.12 Sch.11 para.35
s.168, amended: 2014 c.12 Sch.11 para.36
s.169, repealed: 2014 c.12 Sch.11 para.37
s.170, amended: 2014 c.12 Sch.11 para.38
s.170, repealed (in part): 2014 c.12 Sch.11 para.38
s.171, amended: 2014 c.12 Sch.11 para.39
s.172, applied: SI 2014/1294
s.172, enabling: SI 2014/1294
s.177A, amended: SI 2014/3253 Art.2
s.183, enabling: SI 2014/2341
s.193, enabling: SI 2014/1371, SI 2014/2341, SI 2014/2417, SI 2014/3284
s.197, applied: SI 2014/1252, SI 2014/1294, SI 2014/2440
s.197, enabling: SI 2014/1252, SI 2014/1294, SI 2014/1371, SI 2014/2341, SI 2014/2417, SI 2014/2440, SI 2014/3284
Sch.1 Part 2 para.7, amended: SI 2014/3253 Art.3
Sch.1 Part 2 para.12A, substituted: SI 2014/3253 Art.3
Sch.1 Part 2 para.12B, amended: SI 2014/3253 Art.3
Sch.1 Part 2 para.12D, added: SI 2014/3253 Art.3
Sch.1 Part 2 para.12ZA, added: SI 2014/3253 Art.3
Sch.1 Part 3 para.19, added: SI 2014/3253 Art.4
Sch.3, amended: 2014 c.12 Sch.11 para.40
Sch.6 para.121, repealed: 2014 c.12 Sch.11 para.50

21. Communications Act 2003
applied: SI 2014/631 Art.3, SI 2014/774 Sch.3 para.1, Sch.4 para.1, Sch.8 Part 2, Sch.9 Part 2
referred to: SI 2014/1059 Art.3, SI 2014/2694 Art.4, SI 2014/2938 Art.4
s.17, amended: SI 2014/631 Sch.1 para.11
s.127, see *I v Dunn* [2014] HCJAC 9, 2014 S.C.L. 281 (HCJ), The Lord Justice Clerk (Carloway)
s.277, applied: SI 2014/3137
s.277, enabling: SI 2014/3137
s.309, applied: SI 2014/3137
s.309, enabling: SI 2014/3137
s.316, see *British Sky Broadcasting Ltd v Office of Communications* [2014] EWCA Civ 133, [2014] 4 All E.R. 673 (CA (Civ Div)), Arden LJ
s.319, see *R. (on the application of London Christian Radio Ltd) v Radio Advertising Clearance Centre* [2013] EWCA Civ 1495, [2014] 1 W.L.R. 307 (CA (Civ Div)), Lord Dyson MR
s.320, see *R. (on the application of London Christian Radio Ltd) v Radio Advertising Clearance Centre* [2013] EWCA Civ 1495, [2014] 1 W.L.R. 307 (CA (Civ Div)), Lord Dyson MR
s.321, see *R. (on the application of London Christian Radio Ltd) v Radio Advertising Clearance Centre* [2013] EWCA Civ 1495, [2014] 1 W.L.R. 307 (CA (Civ Div)), Lord Dyson MR
s.368B, amended: SI 2014/2916 Reg.3
s.368E, amended: SI 2014/2916 Reg.2
s.370, amended: SI 2014/892 Sch.1 para.161
s.371, amended: SI 2014/892 Sch.1 para.162
s.388, repealed: SI 2014/892 Sch.1 para.163
s.393, amended: SI 2014/892 Sch.1 para.164
s.393, applied: SI 2014/1825, SI 2014/1825 Art.2, Art.3
s.393, repealed (in part): SI 2014/892 Sch.1 para.164
s.393, enabling: SI 2014/1825
Sch.11 para.4, amended: SI 2014/892 Sch.1 para.165
Sch.11 para.5, amended: SI 2014/892 Sch.1 para.165
Sch.11 para.6, amended: SI 2014/892 Sch.1 para.165
Sch.12 Part 1 para.1, applied: SI 2014/3137

Sch.12 Part 1 para.1, enabling: SI 2014/3137
Sch.12 Part 2 para.7, applied: SI 2014/3137
Sch.12 Part 2 para.7, enabling: SI 2014/3137

22. Fireworks Act 2003
s.14, amended: SI 2014/1638 Sch.13 para.7

26. Local Government Act 2003
s.11, enabling: SI 2014/481
s.21, amended: 2014 c.2 Sch.12 para.50
s.21, applied: SI 2014/3362 Reg.3, Reg.4
s.21, repealed (in part): 2014 c.2 Sch.12 para.50
s.21, enabling: SI 2014/481, SI 2014/1375, SI 2014/3362
s.22, amended: 2014 c.2 Sch.12 para.51
s.23, applied: SI 2014/3362 Reg.3
s.23, enabling: SI 2014/3362
s.24, amended: 2014 c.2 Sch.12 para.52
s.24, enabling: SI 2014/481, SI 2014/3362
s.31, applied: SI 2014/3362 Reg.8
s.42, enabling: SI 2014/3199
s.43, applied: SI 2014/3204 Sch.3 para.1
s.43, varied: SI 2014/3204 Sch.5 para.1
s.44, applied: SI 2014/3204 Reg.18, Reg.19
s.44, varied: SI 2014/3204 Sch.5 para.1
s.46, applied: SI 2014/3204 Reg.18, Reg.19
s.46, varied: SI 2014/3204 Sch.5 para.1
s.47, applied: SI 2014/3204 Reg.18, Reg.19
s.51, varied: SI 2014/3204 Sch.5 para.1
s.53, varied: SI 2014/3204 Sch.5 para.1
s.55, enabling: SI 2014/3199
s.99, repealed: 2014 c.2 Sch.12 para.53
s.100, amended: 2014 c.2 Sch.12 para.54
s.100, repealed (in part): 2014 c.2 Sch.12 para.54
s.107, repealed: 2014 c.2 Sch.1 Part 2
s.108, repealed: 2014 c.2 Sch.1 Part 2
s.110, repealed: 2014 c.2 Sch.1 Part 2
s.111, repealed: 2014 c.2 Sch.1 Part 2
s.123, enabling: SI 2014/481, SI 2014/1375, SI 2014/3199, SI 2014/3362
Sch.5, applied: SI 2014/3204 Reg.22
Sch.7 para.65, repealed: 2014 c.2 Sch.1 Part 2

27. Dealing in Cultural Objects (Offences) Act 2003
s.4, amended: SI 2014/834 Sch.2 para.36

32. Crime (International Co-operation) Act 2003
Commencement Orders: SI 2014/3192 Art.2
see *R. (on the application of Omar) v Secretary of State for Foreign and*

Commonwealth Affairs [2013] EWCA Civ 118, [2014] Q.B. 112 (CA (Civ Div)), Lord Judge LCJ; see *R. (on the application of Secretary of State for the Home Department) v Southwark Crown Court* [2013] EWHC 4366 (Admin), [2014] 1 W.L.R. 2529 (QBD (Admin)), Moses LJ
s.3, applied: SI 2014/1610 r.4_4, r.32_1
s.4, applied: SI 2014/1610 r.32_2
s.7, applied: SI 2014/1610 r.32_3
s.8, applied: SI 2014/1610 r.32_3
s.13, see *R. (on the application of Secretary of State for the Home Department) v Southwark Crown Court* [2013] EWHC 4366 (Admin), [2014] 1 W.L.R. 2529 (QBD (Admin)), Moses LJ
s.15, see *R. (on the application of Secretary of State for the Home Department) v Southwark Crown Court* [2013] EWHC 4366 (Admin), [2014] 1 W.L.R. 2529 (QBD (Admin)), Moses LJ
s.15, applied: SI 2014/1610 r.32_4, r.32_5
s.16, see *R. (on the application of Secretary of State for the Home Department) v Southwark Crown Court* [2013] EWHC 4366 (Admin), [2014] 1 W.L.R. 2529 (QBD (Admin)), Moses LJ
s.21, applied: SI 2014/1610 r.32_10
s.30, applied: SI 2014/1610 r.32_6, r.32_7
s.30, referred to: SI 2014/1610 r.32_6
s.31, applied: SI 2014/1610 r.32_6, r.32_8
s.31, referred to: SI 2014/1610 r.32_6
s.56, applied: SI 2014/1610 r.55_5
s.57, applied: SI 2014/1610 r.55_5
s.57, disapplied: SI 2014/1610 r.55_5
s.59, applied: SI 2014/1610 r.55_5
s.60, applied: SI 2014/1610 r.55_5
s.63, applied: SI 2014/1610 r.55_5
s.94, enabling: SI 2014/3192
Sch.1, applied: SI 2014/1610 r.32_4, r.32_5
Sch.1 para.6, applied: SI 2014/1610 r.32_5
Sch.2 Part 1, applied: SI 2014/1610 r.32_6, r.32_7
Sch.2 Part 2, applied: SI 2014/1610 r.32_8

33. Waste and Emissions Trading Act 2003
s.13, applied: SSI 2014/319 Sch.2 para.10

37. Water Act 2003
applied: 2014 c.5 Sch.1 para.1, 2014 c.25 Sch.1
referred to: 2014 c.5 Sch.1 para.1
Part 1, applied: 2014 c.21 Sch.8 para.30

s.40, repealed: 2014 c.21 Sch.7 para.132

s.52, amended: 2014 c.21 Sch.7 para.133

s.58, amended: 2014 c.21 Sch.7 para.134

38. Anti-social Behaviour Act 2003

Part 1, repealed: 2014 c.12 Sch.11 para.41

Part 1A, repealed: 2014 c.12 Sch.11 para.41

Part 4, applied: 2014 c.12 s.42

Part 4, repealed: 2014 c.12 Sch.11 para.41

s.1, applied: 2014 c.12 s.93

s.1, varied: SI 2014/1704 Art.4

s.2, applied: 2014 c.12 s.93

s.5, varied: SI 2014/1704 Art.4

s.9, varied: SI 2014/1704 Art.4

s.11, varied: SI 2014/1704 Art.4

s.11A, applied: 2014 c.12 s.93

s.11B, applied: 2014 c.12 s.93

s.13, repealed: 2014 c.12 Sch.11 para.50

s.14, repealed (in part): 2014 c.12 Sch.11 para.50

s.30, applied: 2014 c.12 s.42

s.40, applied: 2014 c.12 s.93

s.40, repealed: 2014 c.12 Sch.11 para.41

s.48, applied: 2014 c.12 s.58

s.48, repealed: 2014 c.12 Sch.11 para.41

s.56, repealed (in part): 2014 c.12 Sch.11 para.50

s.85, repealed (in part): 2014 c.12 Sch.11 para.50

s.86, repealed (in part): 2014 c.12 Sch.11 para.50

39. Courts Act 2003

applied: SI 2014/1610 r.6_1, r.52_1, r.2_1

Part 4, applied: SI 2014/786 Art.4

s.1, referred to: 2014 c.12 s.180

s.3, applied: SI 2014/1610 r.3_25, r.37_13

s.8, applied: SI 2014/322, SI 2014/1899, SI 2014/2867

s.8, enabling: SI 2014/322, SI 2014/1899, SI 2014/2867

s.9, applied: SI 2014/1610 r.63_10

s.10, applied: SI 2014/1919 Reg.6

s.18, applied: SI 2014/840 r.11

s.19, enabling: SI 2014/842

s.20, applied: SI 2014/842

s.28, applied: SI 2014/1610 r.9_4, r.19_3, r.37_14

s.66, applied: SI 2014/1610 r.6_1

s.68, amended: 2014 c.12 s.174

s.69, applied: SI 2014/1610

s.72, applied: SI 2014/1610

s.75, referred to: 2014 c.6 s.10, s.13

s.75, enabling: SI 2014/524, SI 2014/667, SI 2014/843, SI 2014/3296

s.76, enabling: SI 2014/524, SI 2014/667, SI 2014/843, SI 2014/3296

s.79, applied: SI 2014/667, SI 2014/843, SI 2014/3296

s.92, applied: 2014 c.12 s.180, SI 2014/590, SI 2014/874, SI 2014/875, SI 2014/876, SI 2014/877, SI 2014/1610 r.17_31, SI 2014/1834, SI 2014/2059

s.92, enabling: SI 2014/590, SI 2014/874, SI 2014/875, SI 2014/876, SI 2014/877, SI 2014/1834, SI 2014/2059

s.98, applied: 2014 c.22 s.31

s.108, enabling: SI 2014/322, SI 2014/875, SI 2014/877, SI 2014/1899, SI 2014/2867

Sch.5, applied: SI 2014/1610 r.52_1, r.76_1

Sch.5 Pt 4, see *R. (on the application of Lawson) v Westminster Magistrates' Court* [2013] EWHC 2434 (Admin), [2014] 1 W.L.R. 2085 (DC), Treacy LJ

Sch.5 Part 4 para.12, applied: SI 2014/1610 r.52_2, r.52_4

Sch.5 Part 6 para.22, applied: SI 2014/1610 r.52_4

Sch.5 Part 6 para.23, applied: SI 2014/1610 r.52_4

Sch.5 Part 8 para.31, applied: SI 2014/1610 r.52_4

Sch.5 Part 8 para.32, applied: SI 2014/1610 r.52_4

Sch.5 Part 9 para.37, applied: SI 2014/1610 r.52_4

Sch.5 Pt 9 para.42, see *R. (on the application of Lawson) v Westminster Magistrates' Court* [2013] EWHC 2434 (Admin), [2014] 1 W.L.R. 2085 (DC), Treacy LJ

41. Extradition Act 2003

see *Edwards v United States* [2013] EWHC 1906 (Admin), [2014] 1 W.L.R. 1532 (QBD (Admin)), Laws LJ

applied: 2014 c.12 s.156, s.157, s.158, SI 2014/1610 r.17_1, r.17_17, SI 2014/3141 Sch.6 para.8

Part 1, applied: SI 2014/1610, SI 2014/1610 r.17_1, r.17_2, r.76_1, r.17_3, r.17_4, r.17_5, r.17_15, r.17_16, r.17_19, r.17_20, r.17_23, r.17_29, r.76_4, r.76_5, SSI 2014/337 Sch.2 para.7

Part 2, applied: SI 2014/1610, SI 2014/1610
r.76_5, r.17_1, r.17_3, r.17_4, r.17_8,
r.17_10, r.17_16, r.17_19, r.17_23
Pt 1., see *Director of the Serious Fraud
Office v O'Brien* [2014] UKSC 23, [2014]
A.C. 1246 (SC), Lord Mance JSC; see
Lithuania v Bucnys [2014] A.C. 480 (SC),
Lord Mance JSC
Pt 2., see *Director of the Serious Fraud
Office v O'Brien* [2014] UKSC 23, [2014]
A.C. 1246 (SC), Lord Mance JSC
Pt 3., see *Director of the Serious Fraud
Office v O'Brien* [2014] UKSC 23, [2014]
A.C. 1246 (SC), Lord Mance JSC
s.2, see *Lithuania v Bucnys* [2014] A.C. 480
(SC), Lord Mance JSC
s.2, amended: 2014 c.12 s.157
s.4, applied: SI 2014/1610 r.17_5, r.17_16
s.6, applied: SI 2014/1610 r.17_5, r.17_16
s.8, amended: 2014 c.12 s.155
s.8, applied: SI 2014/1610 r.17_16
s.8A, applied: SI 2014/1610 r.17_3
s.9, applied: SI 2014/1610 r.17_3
s.10, applied: SI 2014/1610 r.17_6
s.11, amended: 2014 c.12 s.156, s.157,
Sch.11 para.104
s.11, applied: 2014 c.12 s.156, s.157, s.158
s.11, repealed (in part): 2014 c.12 s.158
s.12A, added: 2014 c.12 s.156
s.16, repealed: 2014 c.12 s.158
s.20, applied: SI 2014/1610 r.17_6
s.21, amended: 2014 c.12 Sch.11 para.105
s.21, substituted: 2014 c.12 Sch.11 para.105
s.21A, added: 2014 c.12 s.157
s.21A, applied: 2014 c.12 s.157
s.21B, added: 2014 c.12 s.159
s.21B, applied: SI 2014/1610 r.17_3, r.17_6
s.22, applied: SI 2014/1610 r.17_3
s.25, applied: SI 2014/1610 r.17_3, r.17_6
s.26, amended: 2014 c.12 s.160, Sch.11
para.106
s.26, applied: SI 2014/1610, SI 2014/1610
r.17_19
s.28, amended: 2014 c.12 s.160, Sch.11
para.107
s.28, applied: SI 2014/1610, SI 2014/1610
r.17_19
s.31, applied: SI 2014/1610 r.17_23
s.32, applied: SI 2014/1610 r.17_1, r.17_25
s.33A, applied: SI 2014/1610 r.17_26
s.35, amended: 2014 c.12 Sch.11 para.108

s.35, applied: SI 2014/1610 r.17_16
s.36, amended: 2014 c.12 Sch.11 para.109
s.36, applied: SI 2014/1610 r.17_16, r.17_24
s.36A, applied: SI 2014/1610 r.17_6,
r.17_23
s.36A, enabling: SI 2014/1610
s.36AA, added: 2014 c.12 s.161
s.36B, applied: SI 2014/1610 r.17_6, r.17_23
s.36B, enabling: SI 2014/1610
s.37, applied: SI 2014/1610 r.17_16
s.39, amended: 2014 c.12 s.162
s.39, repealed (in part): 2014 c.12 s.162
s.40, amended: 2014 c.12 Sch.11 para.121
s.41, applied: SI 2014/1610 r.17_7
s.44, applied: SI 2014/1610 r.17_3
s.45, applied: SI 2014/1610 r.17_5
s.45, repealed (in part): 2014 c.12 s.163
s.46, applied: SI 2014/1610 r.17_16
s.47, applied: SI 2014/1610 r.17_16
s.60, applied: SI 2014/1610 r.76_1, r.76_5
s.61, applied: SI 2014/1610 r.76_4
s.62A, applied: SI 2014/1610 r.76_4
s.64, see *Jama v Germany* [2013] EWHC
3276 (Admin), [2014] 1 W.L.R. 1843 (DC),
Richards LJ
s.64, applied: SI 2014/1610 r.17_6
s.64, substituted: 2014 c.12 s.164
s.66, amended: 2014 c.12 s.164, Sch.11
para.110
s.67, applied: SI 2014/1610 r.17_2
s.70, see *South Africa v Dewani* [2014]
EWHC 153 (Admin), [2014] 1 W.L.R. 3220
(DC), Lord Thomas LCJ
s.70, applied: SI 2014/1610 r.17_8
s.70, repealed (in part): 2014 c.12 Sch.11
para.121
s.72, applied: SI 2014/1610 r.17_9, r.17_16
s.73, applied: SI 2014/1610 r.17_10
s.74, applied: SI 2014/1610 r.17_11, r.17_16
s.75, applied: SI 2014/1610 r.17_9, r.17_16
s.76, applied: SI 2014/1610 r.17_12, r.17_16
s.76A, applied: SI 2014/1610 r.17_3
s.77, see *R. (on the application of B) v
Westminster Magistrates' Court* [2014]
UKSC 59, [2014] 3 W.L.R. 1336 (SC), Lord
Neuberger PSC
s.77, applied: SI 2014/1610 r.17_3
s.78, applied: SI 2014/1610 r.17_13
s.81, see *R. (on the application of B) v
Westminster Magistrates' Court* [2014]

UKSC 59, [2014] 3 W.L.R. 1336 (SC), Lord
Neuberger PSC
s.84, see *R. (on the application of B) v
Westminster Magistrates' Court* [2014]
UKSC 59, [2014] 3 W.L.R. 1336 (SC), Lord
Neuberger PSC
s.84, applied: SI 2014/1610 r.17_13, r.17_15
s.86, applied: SI 2014/1610 r.17_15
s.88, applied: SI 2014/1610 r.17_3
s.91, see *Ghana v Gambrah* [2014] EWHC
1569 (Admin), [2014] 1 W.L.R. 4464 (DC),
Moses LJ; see *South Africa v Dewani*
[2014] EWHC 153 (Admin), [2014] 1
W.L.R. 3220 (DC), Lord Thomas LCJ
s.91, applied: SI 2014/1610 r.17_3, r.17_13
s.93, amended: 2014 c.12 s.162
s.103, amended: 2014 c.12 s.160, Sch.11
para.111
s.103, applied: SI 2014/1610, SI 2014/1610
r.17_13, r.17_19, r.17_23
s.105, amended: 2014 c.12 s.160, Sch.11
para.112
s.105, applied: SI 2014/1610, SI 2014/1610
r.17_19, r.17_29
s.106, applied: SI 2014/1610 r.17_29
s.108, amended: 2014 c.12 s.160, Sch.11
para.113
s.108, applied: SI 2014/1610, SI 2014/1610
r.17_19
s.110, amended: 2014 c.12 s.160, Sch.11
para.114
s.110, applied: SI 2014/1610
s.113, applied: SI 2014/1610 r.17_23
s.114, applied: SI 2014/1610 r.17_1, r.17_25
s.115A, applied: SI 2014/1610 r.17_26
s.117, amended: 2014 c.12 Sch.11 para.115
s.117, applied: SI 2014/1610 r.17_16
s.118, amended: 2014 c.12 Sch.11 para.116
s.118, applied: SI 2014/1610 r.17_16,
r.17_24
s.118A, applied: SI 2014/1610 r.17_13,
r.17_23
s.118A, enabling: SI 2014/1610
s.118AA, added: 2014 c.12 s.161
s.118B, enabling: SI 2014/1610
s.121, amended: 2014 c.12 s.162
s.121, repealed (in part): 2014 c.12 s.162
s.122, applied: SI 2014/1610 r.17_14
s.127, applied: SI 2014/1610 r.17_9, r.17_11
s.128, repealed (in part): 2014 c.12 s.163
s.133, applied: SI 2014/1610 r.76_1, r.76_5

s.134, applied: SI 2014/1610 r.76_4
s.135A, applied: SI 2014/1610 r.76_4
s.137, amended: 2014 c.12 s.164
s.137, applied: SI 2014/1610 r.17_8,
r.17_10, r.17_13
s.137, repealed (in part): 2014 c.12 Sch.11
para.117
s.138, amended: 2014 c.12 s.164
s.138, repealed (in part): 2014 c.12 Sch.11
para.118
s.139, applied: SI 2014/1610 r.17_2
s.142, amended: 2014 c.12 s.165
s.142, applied: SI 2014/3141 Reg.98
s.148, see *Director of the Serious Fraud
Office v O'Brien* [2014] UKSC 23, [2014]
A.C. 1246 (SC), Lord Mance JSC
s.150, amended: 2014 c.12 s.166
s.151A, see *Director of the Serious Fraud
Office v O'Brien* [2014] UKSC 23, [2014]
A.C. 1246 (SC), Lord Mance JSC
s.151A, amended: 2014 c.12 s.166
s.151B, added: 2014 c.12 s.166
s.153D, repealed (in part): 2014 c.12 Sch.11
para.121
s.157, amended: 2014 c.12 s.174
s.160, amended: 2014 c.12 s.174
s.177, applied: 2014 c.12 s.184
s.180, amended: 2014 c.12 s.167
s.180, applied: SI 2014/1610 r.17_16
s.181, amended: 2014 c.12 s.167
s.181, applied: SI 2014/1610 r.17_16
s.187, applied: SI 2014/1610 r.17_16
s.189A, added: 2014 c.12 s.168
s.193, substituted: 2014 c.12 s.169
s.197, amended: 2014 c.12 Sch.11 para.119
s.202, applied: SI 2014/1610 r.17_15
s.204, amended: 2014 c.12 s.170, Sch.11
para.120
s.204, repealed (in part): 2014 c.12 Sch.11
para.120
s.205, applied: SI 2014/1610 r.17_15
s.206A, applied: SI 2014/1610 r.17_3
s.210, enabling: SSI 2014/242
s.212, see *Lithuania v Bucnys* [2014] A.C.
480 (SC), Lord Mance JSC
s.216, amended: 2014 c.12 Sch.11 para.121
s.222, applied: 2014 c.12 s.184
s.223, amended: 2014 c.12 Sch.11 para.122
s.226, amended: 2014 c.12 Sch.11 para.123
Sch.1 Part 1 para.3, amended: 2014 c.12
Sch.11 para.124

42. Sexual Offences Act 2003
see *HM Advocate v H* [2014] HCJAC 36,
2014 J.C. 195 (HCJ), The Lord Justice Clerk
(Carloway); see *R. v Stocker (Keith
Anthony)* [2013] EWCA Crim 1993, [2014]
1 Cr. App. R. 18 (CA (Crim Div)), Hallett
LJ; see *Young v Brown* 2014 J.C. 4 (HCJ),
The Lord Justice Clerk (Gill)
Part 2, applied: SI 2014/1610 r.42_3
Part 2, referred to: 2014 c.12 s.181
Part 2, amended: 2014 c.12 Sch.11 para.59
Part 2, amended: 2014 c.12 Sch.11 para.64
Part 2, amended: 2014 c.12 Sch.11 para.69
Pt 2., see *R. (on the application of Hamill) v
Chelmsford Magistrates' Court* [2014]
EWHC 2799 (Admin), (2014) 178 J.P. 401
(QBD (Admin)), Aikens LJ; see *R. (on the
application of Minter) v Chief Constable of
Hampshire* [2013] EWCA Civ 697, [2014] 1
W.L.R. 179 (CA (Civ Div)), Laws LJ
s.1, see *R. (on the application of F) v DPP*
[2013] EWHC 945 (Admin), [2014] Q.B.
581 (DC), Lord Judge LCJ
s.1, applied: 2014 c.12 s.116
s.3, see *R. v A* [2014] EWCA Crim 299,
[2014] 1 W.L.R. 2469 (CA (Crim Div)),
Macur LJ
s.5, applied: 2014 c.12 s.116
s.8, see *R. (on the application of BH (A
Child)) v Llandudno Youth Court* [2014]
EWHC 1833 (Admin), (2014) 178 J.P. 305
(QBD (Admin)), Andrews J
s.9, applied: 2014 c.12 s.116
s.16, applied: 2014 c.12 s.116
s.25, applied: 2014 c.12 s.116
s.30, see *R. v A* [2014] EWCA Crim 299,
[2014] 1 W.L.R. 2469 (CA (Crim Div)),
Macur LJ
s.30, applied: 2014 c.12 s.116
s.31, see *R. v A* [2014] EWCA Crim 299,
[2014] 1 W.L.R. 2469 (CA (Crim Div)),
Macur LJ
s.32, see *R. v A* [2014] EWCA Crim 299,
[2014] 1 W.L.R. 2469 (CA (Crim Div)),
Macur LJ
s.33, see *R. v A* [2014] EWCA Crim 299,
[2014] 1 W.L.R. 2469 (CA (Crim Div)),
Macur LJ
s.47, applied: 2014 c.12 s.116
s.59A, applied: 2014 c.12 s.116
s.61, applied: 2014 c.12 s.116

s.66, see *R. v Hardy (James)* [2013] EWCA
Crim 2125, [2014] 1 Cr. App. R. (S.) 70 (CA
(Crim Div)), Laws LJ
s.66, applied: 2014 c.12 s.116
s.74, see *R. (on the application of F) v DPP*
[2013] EWHC 945 (Admin), [2014] Q.B.
581 (DC), Lord Judge LCJ; see *R. v A*
[2014] EWCA Crim 299, [2014] 1 W.L.R.
2469 (CA (Crim Div)), Macur LJ
s.75, see *R. v A* [2014] EWCA Crim 299,
[2014] 1 W.L.R. 2469 (CA (Crim Div)),
Macur LJ
s.76, see *R. v A* [2014] EWCA Crim 299,
[2014] 1 W.L.R. 2469 (CA (Crim Div)),
Macur LJ
s.80, see *Speirs (Allan) v HM Advocate* 2014
S.C.L. 58 (HCJ), The Lord Justice Clerk
(Carloway)
s.82, see *R. (on the application of Minter) v
Chief Constable of Hampshire* [2013]
EWCA Civ 697, [2014] 1 W.L.R. 179 (CA
(Civ Div)), Laws LJ
s.87, applied: SSI 2014/147 Reg.2
s.87, enabling: SSI 2014/147
s.88, amended: 2014 c.12 Sch.11 para.56
s.89, amended: 2014 c.12 Sch.11 para.57
s.91, see *R. v Day (Adrian Harold)* [2013]
EWCA Crim 1648, [2014] 1 Cr. App. R. (S.)
72 (CA (Crim Div)), Lloyd Jones LJ
s.91A, see *R. (on the application of Minter)
v Chief Constable of Hampshire* [2013]
EWCA Civ 697, [2014] 1 W.L.R. 179 (CA
(Civ Div)), Laws LJ
s.91A, amended: 2014 c.12 Sch.11 para.58
s.91B, see *R. (on the application of Hamill)
v Chelmsford Magistrates' Court* [2014]
EWHC 2799 (Admin), (2014) 178 J.P. 401
(QBD (Admin)), Aikens LJ
s.91D, see *R. (on the application of Hamill)
v Chelmsford Magistrates' Court* [2014]
EWHC 2799 (Admin), (2014) 178 J.P. 401
(QBD (Admin)), Aikens LJ
s.91F, see *R. (on the application of Minter) v
Chief Constable of Hampshire* [2013]
EWCA Civ 697, [2014] 1 W.L.R. 179 (CA
(Civ Div)), Laws LJ
s.103A, added: 2014 c.12 Sch.5 para.2
s.103A, applied: SI 2014/1610 r.50_1
s.104, see *A v Murphy* [2014] HCJAC 96,
2014 S.C.L. 784 (HCJ), Lady Paton
s.104, applied: SI 2014/1610 r.50_1

s.104, referred to: 2014 c.12 s.114
s.104, repealed (in part): 2014 c.12 Sch.5 para.3
s.107, applied: SI 2014/1610 r.50_3
s.108, see *R. v Spencer (Adam Kenneth)* [2013] EWCA Crim 2286, [2014] 2 Cr. App. R. (S.) 18 (CA (Crim Div)), Davis LJ
s.108, amended: 2014 c.12 Sch.11 para.60
s.109, amended: 2014 c.12 Sch.11 para.61
s.110, see *R. v Spencer (Adam Kenneth)* [2013] EWCA Crim 2286, [2014] 2 Cr. App. R. (S.) 18 (CA (Crim Div)), Davis LJ
s.110, amended: 2014 c.12 Sch.11 para.62
s.110, substituted: 2014 c.12 Sch.11 para.62
s.112, see *Chief Constable of the Police Service of Scotland v R* [2014] CSIH 8, 2014 S.C. 448 (IH (2 Div)), The Lord Justice Clerk (Carloway)
s.113, amended: 2014 c.12 Sch.11 para.63
s.117A, amended: 2014 c.12 Sch.11 para.65
s.117A, substituted: 2014 c.12 Sch.11 para.65
s.117B, amended: 2014 c.12 Sch.11 para.66
s.119, amended: 2014 c.12 Sch.11 para.67
s.119, substituted: 2014 c.12 Sch.11 para.67
s.122, amended: 2014 c.12 Sch.11 para.68
s.122A, added: 2014 c.12 Sch.5 para.4
s.123, amended: 2014 c.12 Sch.11 para.70
s.123, referred to: 2014 c.12 s.114
s.123, repealed (in part): 2014 c.12 Sch.5 para.5, Sch.11 para.70
s.125, amended: 2014 c.12 Sch.11 para.71
s.126, amended: 2014 c.12 Sch.11 para.72
s.127, amended: 2014 c.12 Sch.11 para.73
s.128, amended: 2014 c.12 Sch.11 para.74
s.129, amended: 2014 c.12 Sch.11 para.75
s.133, amended: 2014 c.12 Sch.11 para.76
s.136, amended: 2014 c.12 Sch.11 para.77
s.136, referred to: 2014 c.12 s.181
s.136A, amended: 2014 c.12 Sch.6 para.2
s.136B, amended: 2014 c.12 Sch.6 para.3
s.136BA, added: 2014 c.12 Sch.6 para.4
s.136BA, applied: 2014 c.12 s.115
s.136C, amended: 2014 c.12 Sch.6 para.5
s.136D, amended: 2014 c.12 Sch.6 para.6
s.136D, applied: 2014 c.12 s.115
s.136H, amended: 2014 c.12 Sch.6 para.7
s.136I, amended: 2014 c.12 Sch.6 para.8
s.136J, amended: 2014 c.12 Sch.6 para.9
s.136O, amended: 2014 c.12 Sch.6 para.10
s.136R, amended: 2014 c.12 Sch.6 para.11

s.136ZA, added: 2014 c.12 Sch.5 para.6
s.137, amended: 2014 c.12 Sch.5 para.7
s.138, enabling: SSI 2014/147
s.142, amended: 2014 c.12 s.113
s.142, referred to: 2014 c.12 s.181
Sch.3, applied: SI 2014/1610 r.42_3
Sch.3 para.36, referred to: 2014 asp 1 s.8, s.9
Sch.3 para.40, see *Thompson v Dunn* 2014 J.C. 16 (HCJ), The Lord Justice Clerk (Gill); see *Young v Brown* 2014 J.C. 4 (HCJ), The Lord Justice Clerk (Gill)
Sch.3 para.60, see *Akdeniz v Cameron* 2014 J.C. 13 (HCJ), The Lord Justice Clerk (Gill); see *Halcrow v Shanks* 2014 J.C. 1 (HCJ), The Lord Justice Clerk (Gill); see *Hay (Ian Morris) v HM Advocate* 2014 J.C. 19 (HCJ), The Lord Justice Clerk (Gill); see *Heatherall v McGowan* 2014 J.C. 8 (HCJ), The Lord Justice Clerk (Gill); see *Thompson v Dunn* 2014 J.C. 16 (HCJ), The Lord Justice Clerk (Gill); see *Young v Brown* 2014 J.C. 4 (HCJ), The Lord Justice Clerk (Gill)
Sch.5 para.103E, applied: 2014 c.12 s.114
Sch.5 para.103I, applied: 2014 c.12 s.114
Sch.5 para.122D, applied: 2014 c.12 s.114
Sch.5 para.122H, applied: 2014 c.12 s.114
Sch.6 para.38, repealed (in part): 2014 c.12 Sch.11 para.50

43. Health and Social Care (Community Health and Standards) Act 2003

Commencement Orders: SI 2014/1793 Art.2
applied: SI 2014/2418 Sch.1
Part 2 c.4, applied: 2014 c.2 Sch.11 para.2
s.95, repealed (in part): 2014 c.2 Sch.12 para.56
s.114, enabling: SI 2014/1794
s.115, enabling: SI 2014/1794
s.148, referred to: SI 2014/2418 Sch.1
s.148, repealed (in part): 2014 c.2 Sch.12 para.57
s.153, enabling: SI 2014/204, SSI 2014/57
s.168, enabling: SSI 2014/57
s.195, applied: SI 2014/204
s.195, enabling: SI 2014/204, SI 2014/1794, SSI 2014/57
s.199, enabling: SI 2014/1793
Sch.9 para.12, repealed: 2014 c.2 Sch.1 Part 2

44. Criminal Justice Act 2003
Commencement Orders: 2014 c.12 s.181,
2014 c.14 s.151, Sch.7, 2014 c.12 Sch.11
para.50; SI 2014/633 Art.2
see *Attorney General's Reference (No.27 of
2013)* [2014] EWCA Crim 334, [2014] 1
W.L.R. 4209 (CA (Crim Div)), Lord
Thomas LCJ; see *R. v Bailey (Wayne)*
[2013] EWCA Crim 1551, [2014] 1 Cr. App.
R. (S.) 59 (CA (Crim Div)), Leveson LJ; see
R. v Powell (Carl Michael) [2014] EWCA
Crim 642, [2014] 1 W.L.R. 2757 (CA (Crim
Div)), Jackson LJ
applied: 2014 c.11 s.23, SI 2014/1610
r.41_10, r.29_26
referred to: 2014 c.11 s.7
Part 9, applied: SI 2014/1610 r.74_1
Part 10, applied: SI 2014/1610 r.41_11
Part 12, applied: SI 2014/1610 r.42_2,
r.33_1
Part 12 c.6, amended: 2014 c.11 Sch.3
para.15
Part 12 c.6, applied: 2014 c.11 Sch.7 para.2,
SI 2014/1652 Sch.1, SI 2014/2871 Sch.1
Part 12 c.6, amended: 2014 c.11 Sch.3
para.19
Pt 12., see *R. v Saunders (Red)* [2013]
EWCA Crim 1027, [2014] 1 Cr. App. R. (S.)
45 (CA (Crim Div)), Lord Judge LCJ
Pt 12 s.225, see *Attorney General's
Reference (No.27 of 2013)* [2014] EWCA
Crim 334, [2014] 1 W.L.R. 4209 (CA (Crim
Div)), Lord Thomas LCJ; see *R. v Cheshire
(John)* [2014] EWCA Crim 627, [2014] 2
Cr. App. R. (S.) 53 (CA (Crim Div)),
Pitchford LJ; see *R. v Curwen (David John)*
[2014] EWCA Crim 1046, [2014] 2 Cr. App.
R. (S.) 52 (CA (Crim Div)), Sir Brian
Leveson PQBD; see *R. v Fort (Jamie
Daniel)* [2013] EWCA Crim 2332, [2014] 2
Cr. App. R. (S.) 24 (CA (Crim Div)), Aikens
LJ; see *R. v Saunders (Red)* [2013] EWCA
Crim 1027, [2014] 1 Cr. App. R. (S.) 45 (CA
(Crim Div)), Lord Judge LCJ
s.8, applied: SI 2014/1610 r.3_1
s.16, applied: SI 2014/1610 r.19_8
s.22, applied: 2014 c.12 s.102
s.23ZA, added: 2014 c.12 s.103
s.27, repealed (in part): SI 2014/834 Sch.2
para.38

s.29, applied: SI 2014/1610 r.7_1, r.37_8,
r.2_4
s.29, repealed (in part): SI 2014/834 Sch.2
para.39
s.30, applied: SI 2014/1610 r.7_2, r.7_4
s.30, enabling: SI 2014/1610
s.44, applied: SI 2014/1610 r.38_6, r.3_14,
r.38_15
s.45, applied: SI 2014/1610 r.3_14
s.46, applied: SI 2014/1610 r.38_6, r.38_15
s.47, applied: SI 2014/1610 r.74_1, r.66_1,
r.66_4
s.49, applied: SI 2014/1610 r.65_1
s.51, applied: SI 2014/1610 r.38_11, r.37_4,
r.29_1, r.29_4, r.29_24, r.29_26
s.52, applied: SI 2014/1610 r.29_4, r.29_25
s.57, applied: SI 2014/1610 r.67_1, r.67_4,
r.67_5
s.58, applied: SI 2014/1610 r.67_1, r.67_2
s.59, applied: SI 2014/1610 r.67_1, r.67_6
s.66, see *R. v Crawley (Scott)* [2014] EWCA
Crim 1028, [2014] 2 Cr. App. R. 16 (CA
(Crim Div)), Sir Brian Leveson PQBD
s.71, applied: SI 2014/1610 r.16_1
s.73, applied: SI 2014/1610 r.67_9
s.76, applied: SI 2014/1610 r.41_1
s.77, applied: SI 2014/1610 r.41_13, r.3_1,
r.41_14, r.14_1, r.41_15
s.80, applied: SI 2014/1610 r.41_3, r.41_4,
r.41_10, r.41_11
s.82, applied: SI 2014/1610 r.16_1, r.41_8,
r.41_9
s.88, applied: SI 2014/1610 r.41_5
s.89, applied: SI 2014/1610 r.41_6
s.90, applied: SI 2014/1610 r.41_7
s.98, applied: SI 2014/1610 r.35_1
s.100, see *R. v All-Hilly (Salaam David)*
[2014] EWCA Crim 1614, [2014] 2 Cr. App.
R. 33 (CA (Crim Div)), Treacy LJ
s.100, applied: SI 2014/1610 r.35_1
s.101, see *R. v Golds (Mark Richard)* [2014]
EWCA Crim 748, [2014] 4 All E.R. 64 (CA
(Crim Div)), Elias LJ; see *R. v Lewis
(Jermaine Nathaniel)* [2014] EWCA Crim
48, [2014] 2 Cr. App. R. (S.) 27 (CA (Crim
Div)), Sir Brian Leveson PQBD; see *R. v M*
[2014] EWCA Crim 1523, [2014] 2 Cr. App.
R. 29 (CA (Crim Div)), Pitchford LJ; see *R.
v Powell (Carl Michael)* [2014] EWCA
Crim 642, [2014] 1 W.L.R. 2757 (CA (Crim
Div)), Jackson LJ

s.101, applied: SI 2014/1610 r.35_1

s.102, applied: SI 2014/1610 r.35_1

s.103, see *R. v Powell (Carl Michael)* [2014]
EWCA Crim 642, [2014] 1 W.L.R. 2757
(CA (Crim Div)), Jackson LJ

s.107, applied: SI 2014/1610 r.35_5

s.110, applied: SI 2014/1610 r.35_5

s.111, applied: SI 2014/1610 r.35_4

s.114, see *R. v R* [2013] EWCA Crim 708,
[2014] 1 Cr. App. R. 5 (CA (Crim Div)),
Treacy LJ

s.114, applied: SI 2014/1610 r.34_1, r.34_2

s.116, see *R. v Ferdinand (Sean)* [2014]
EWCA Crim 1243, [2014] 2 Cr. App. R. 23
(CA (Crim Div)), Pitchford LJ

s.116, applied: SI 2014/1610 r.29_19, r.34_2

s.117, applied: SI 2014/1610 r.34_2, r.35_2

s.119, applied: SI 2014/1610 r.38_12

s.121, applied: SI 2014/1610 r.34_2

s.127, applied: SI 2014/1610 r.34_2, r.33_4

s.131, see *R. v R* [2013] EWCA Crim 708,
[2014] 1 Cr. App. R. 5 (CA (Crim Div)),
Treacy LJ

s.132, applied: SI 2014/1610 r.34_2, r.34_4,
r.3_5

s.132, enabling: SI 2014/1610

s.133, applied: SI 2014/1610 r.27_4

s.139, applied: SI 2014/1610 r.38_11, r.37_4

s.142, see *R. v Martin (Lewys Stephen)*
[2013] EWCA Crim 1420, [2014] 1 Cr. App.
R. (S.) 63 (CA (Crim Div)), Leveson LJ

s.142A, see *R. v Gomes Monteiro (Juranir
Silvertre)* [2014] EWCA Crim 747, [2014] 2
Cr. App. R. (S.) 62 (CA (Crim Div)), Lord
Thomas LCJ

s.143, see *Attorney General's Reference
(Nos 7 and 8 of 2013)* [2013] EWCA Crim
709, [2014] 1 Cr. App. R. (S.) 26 (CA (Crim
Div)), Pitchford LJ; see *R. v Howe (Kevin
James)* [2014] EWCA Crim 114, [2014] 2
Cr. App. R. (S.) 38 (CA (Crim Div)), Lord
Thomas LCJ; see *R. v Kovvali (Bala
Subrahmanyam)* [2013] EWCA Crim 1056,
[2014] 1 Cr. App. R. (S.) 33 (CA (Crim
Div)), Pitchford LJ; see *R. v Martin (Lewys
Stephen)* [2013] EWCA Crim 1420, [2014] 1
Cr. App. R. (S.) 63 (CA (Crim Div)),
Leveson LJ; see *R. v Pyranha Mouldings
Ltd* [2014] EWCA Crim 533, [2014] 2 Cr.
App. R. (S.) 43 (CA (Crim Div)), Elias LJ

s.143, applied: SI 2014/1610 r.37_10,
r.38_16

s.154, applied: 2014 c.1 s.9, 2014 c.26 s.174

s.154, referred to: 2014 c.12 s.121, 2014
c.20 Sch.5 para.2, Sch.5 para.6, 2014 c.21
Sch.8 para.37, SI 2014/2357 Art.11

s.156, applied: SI 2014/1610 r.37_10,
r.38_16

s.157, applied: SI 2014/1610 r.42_8

s.158, applied: SI 2014/1610 r.37_10,
r.38_16

s.159, applied: SI 2014/1610 r.37_10,
r.38_16

s.161A, see *R. v Bailey (Wayne)* [2013]
EWCA Crim 1551, [2014] 1 Cr. App. R. (S.)
59 (CA (Crim Div)), Leveson LJ

s.161A, enabling: SI 2014/2120

s.161B, enabling: SI 2014/2120

s.162, applied: SI 2014/1610 r.37_10,
r.38_16

s.164, see *R. v Sellafield Ltd* [2014] EWCA
Crim 49, [2014] Env. L.R. 19 (CA (Crim
Div)), Lord Thomas LCJ

s.164, applied: SI 2014/1610 r.37_10,
r.38_16

s.165, amended: 2014 c.12 s.179

s.165, applied: SI 2014/1610 r.52_5

s.172, applied: SI 2014/1610 r.37_10,
r.38_16

s.174, applied: SI 2014/1610 r.5_4, r.37_10,
r.38_16, r.42_1

s.174, enabling: SI 2014/1610

s.177, amended: 2014 c.11 s.15, Sch.5 para.2

s.177, applied: SI 2014/1652 Sch.1

s.177, referred to: SI 2014/1610 r.42_2, SI
2014/2871 Sch.1

s.177, repealed (in part): 2014 c.11 Sch.5
para.2

s.189, applied: SI 2014/1610 r.42_2,
r.42_10, SI 2014/1652 Sch.1

s.189, referred to: SI 2014/2871 Sch.1

s.190, amended: 2014 c.11 s.15, Sch.5 para.3

s.190, applied: SI 2014/1610 r.42_2

s.190, repealed (in part): 2014 c.11 Sch.5
para.3

s.191, amended: 2014 c.11 Sch.4 para.2

s.192, amended: 2014 c.11 Sch.4 para.3

s.197, substituted: 2014 c.11 s.14

s.198, amended: 2014 c.11 Sch.4 para.11

s.198, repealed (in part): 2014 c.11 Sch.4
para.11

s.200A, added: 2014 c.11 s.15

s.201, repealed: 2014 c.11 s.15

s.202, see *R. v Price (Jamie)* [2013] EWCA Crim 1283, [2014] 1 Cr. App. R. (S.) 36 (CA (Crim Div)), Elias LJ

s.202, repealed (in part): 2014 c.11 s.16

s.207, applied: SI 2014/1610 r.42_8

s.209, referred to: SI 2014/1652 Sch.1, SI 2014/2871 Sch.1

s.210, amended: 2014 c.11 Sch.4 para.4

s.211, amended: 2014 c.11 Sch.4 para.5

s.212, referred to: SI 2014/1652 Sch.1, SI 2014/2871 Sch.1

s.212A, applied: SI 2014/1787 Art.2

s.212A, enabling: SI 2014/1787

s.213, repealed: 2014 c.11 s.15

s.214, amended: 2014 c.11 s.17

s.215, applied: SI 2014/1610 r.42_2

s.215, enabling: SI 2014/163, SI 2014/669

s.218, amended: 2014 c.11 s.17

s.218, repealed (in part): 2014 c.11 Sch.5 para.4

s.219, amended: 2014 c.11 Sch.4 para.12

s.219, applied: SI 2014/1610 r.42_2, r.42_10

s.220, repealed (in part): 2014 c.11 s.18

s.220A, added: 2014 c.11 s.18

s.222, amended: 2014 c.11 Sch.5 para.5

s.224A, see *Attorney General's Reference (No.27 of 2013)* [2014] EWCA Crim 334, [2014] 1 W.L.R. 4209 (CA (Crim Div)), Lord Thomas LCJ; see *R. v Saunders (Red)* [2013] EWCA Crim 1027, [2014] 1 Cr. App. R. (S.) 45 (CA (Crim Div)), Lord Judge LCJ

s.226A, see *Attorney General's Reference (No.27 of 2013)* [2014] EWCA Crim 334, [2014] 1 W.L.R. 4209 (CA (Crim Div)), Lord Thomas LCJ

s.226A, amended: 2014 c.11 s.8

s.226B, amended: 2014 c.11 s.8

s.227, see *R. v Saunders (Red)* [2013] EWCA Crim 1027, [2014] 1 Cr. App. R. (S.) 45 (CA (Crim Div)), Lord Judge LCJ

s.229, applied: SI 2014/1977 Reg.2

s.237, amended: 2014 c.11 s.2

s.239, enabling: SI 2014/240

s.240, see *R. v Leacock (Mark)* [2013] EWCA Crim 1994, [2014] 2 Cr. App. R. (S.) 12 (CA (Crim Div)), Lord Thomas LCJ

s.240A, see *R. v Hoggard (Barrie)* [2013] EWCA Crim 1024, [2014] 1 Cr. App. R. (S.) 42 (CA (Crim Div)), Hughes LJ; see *R. v*

Leacock (Mark) [2013] EWCA Crim 1994, [2014] 2 Cr. App. R. (S.) 12 (CA (Crim Div)), Lord Thomas LCJ

s.240A, amended: 2014 c.11 s.9

s.240ZA, amended: 2014 c.11 s.9

s.243A, amended: 2014 c.11 s.1, Sch.3 para.16, Sch.3 para.17

s.244, amended: 2014 c.11 s.9, Sch.3 para.18

s.246, see *R. (on the application of Whiston) v Secretary of State for Justice* [2012] EWCA Civ 1374, [2014] Q.B. 306 (CA (Civ Div)), Pill, L.J.; see *R. (on the application of Whiston) v Secretary of State for Justice* [2014] UKSC 39, [2014] 3 W.L.R. 436 (SC), Lord Neuberger PSC

s.249, amended: 2014 c.11 s.5

s.250, amended: 2014 c.11 s.12

s.250, repealed (in part): 2014 c.11 s.5

s.253, enabling: SI 2014/163, SI 2014/669

s.255, see *R. (on the application of Whiston) v Secretary of State for Justice* [2012] EWCA Civ 1374, [2014] Q.B. 306 (CA (Civ Div)), Pill, L.J.; see *R. (on the application of Whiston) v Secretary of State for Justice* [2014] UKSC 39, [2014] 3 W.L.R. 436 (SC), Lord Neuberger PSC

s.255, amended: 2014 c.11 s.9

s.255A, amended: 2014 c.11 s.9

s.255A, repealed (in part): 2014 c.11 s.9

s.255B, amended: 2014 c.11 s.9

s.256AA, added: 2014 c.11 s.2

s.256AA, applied: SI 2014/2871 Sch.1

s.256AB, added: 2014 c.11 Sch.1 para.1

s.256AB, referred to: 2014 c.11 s.2

s.256AC, added: 2014 c.11 s.3

s.256B, substituted: 2014 c.11 Sch.3 para.20

s.256B, amended: 2014 c.11 s.4

s.256B, repealed (in part): 2014 c.11 s.4

s.256C, amended: 2014 c.11 Sch.3 para.21, Sch.3 para.22

s.256D, added: 2014 c.11 Sch.1 para.2

s.256D, referred to: 2014 c.11 s.2

s.258, applied: SI 2014/1610 r.62_5, r.62_9

s.264, amended: 2014 c.11 s.5

s.264B, added: 2014 c.11 s.5

s.268, amended: 2014 c.11 Sch.3 para.23

s.269, see *Attorney General's Reference (No.69 of 2013)* [2014] EWCA Crim 188, [2014] 1 W.L.R. 3964 (CA (Crim Div)), Lord Thomas LCJ; see *R. v Leacock (Mark)* [2013] EWCA Crim 1994, [2014] 2 Cr. App.

R. (S.) 12 (CA (Crim Div)), Lord Thomas
LCJ
s.269, applied: SI 2014/1610 r.68_1
s.274, applied: SI 2014/1610 r.68_1, r.68_2
s.280, referred to: SI 2014/574 Reg.8
s.281, applied: 2014 c.20 Sch.7 para.11
s.281, referred to: 2014 c.12 s.86, 2014 c.20
Sch.7 para.11, 2014 c.21 Sch.8 para.37
s.302, amended: 2014 c.11 Sch.3 para.24
s.305, amended: 2014 c.11 Sch.5 para.6
s.322, repealed: 2014 c.12 Sch.11 para.50
s.330, amended: 2014 c.11 Sch.3 para.25,
Sch.4 para.13
s.330, enabling: SI 2014/163, SI 2014/669,
SI 2014/1787, SI 2014/2120
s.336, enabling: SI 2014/633
s.338, applied: 2014 c.11 s.23
Sch.3, applied: SI 2014/1610 r.14_1
Sch.8, applied: SI 2014/1610 r.44_1
Sch.8 Part 1 para.1A, added: 2014 c.11
Sch.4 para.6
Sch.8 Part 2 para.5, amended: 2014 c.11
Sch.4 para.6
Sch.8 Part 2 para.6, amended: 2014 c.11
Sch.4 para.6
Sch.8 Part 2 para.6A, added: 2014 c.11
Sch.4 para.6
Sch.8 Part 2 para.9, applied: SI 2014/1610
r.63_1
Sch.8 Part 2 para.9, repealed (in part): 2014
c.11 s.18
Sch.8 Part 3 para.13, amended: 2014 c.11
Sch.4 para.6
Sch.8 Part 3 para.13, applied: SI 2014/1610
r.63_1
Sch.8 Part 3 para.14, amended: 2014 c.11
Sch.4 para.6
Sch.8 Part 4 para.16, substituted: 2014 c.11
s.18
Sch.8 Part 4 para.17, amended: 2014 c.11
Sch.4 para.6
Sch.8 Part 4 para.18, amended: 2014 c.11
Sch.4 para.6
Sch.8 Part 4 para.19, amended: 2014 c.11
Sch.4 para.6
Sch.8 Part 4 para.19A, amended: 2014 c.11
Sch.4 para.6
Sch.8 Part 4 para.20, amended: 2014 c.11
Sch.4 para.6

Sch.8 Pt 5 para.22, see *R. v de Brito (Paulo
Aguiar)* [2013] EWCA Crim 1134, [2014] 1
Cr. App. R. (S.) 38 (CA (Crim Div)), Keith J
Sch.8 Part 6 para.24, amended: 2014 c.11
s.18, Sch.4 para.6
Sch.8 Part 6 para.25A, amended: 2014 c.11
Sch.4 para.14
Sch.8 Part 6 para.27, amended: 2014 c.11
Sch.4 para.14
Sch.9 Part 1 para.1, amended: 2014 c.11
Sch.5 para.7
Sch.9 Part 1 para.2, repealed (in part): 2014
c.11 s.16, Sch.5 para.7
Sch.9 Part 2 para.3, amended: 2014 c.11
Sch.5 para.7
Sch.9 Part 2 para.4, repealed (in part): 2014
c.11 s.16, Sch.5 para.7
Sch.12, applied: SI 2014/1610 r.44_1,
r.42_10
Sch.12 Part 1 para.1A, added: 2014 c.11
Sch.4 para.7
Sch.12 Part 2 para.4, amended: 2014 c.11
Sch.4 para.7
Sch.12 Part 2 para.5, amended: 2014 c.11
Sch.4 para.7
Sch.12 Part 2 para.5A, added: 2014 c.11
Sch.4 para.7
Sch.12 Part 2 para.8, applied: SI 2014/1610
r.42_1
Sch.12 Part 2 para.8, repealed (in part): 2014
c.11 s.18
Sch.12 Pt 2 para.8, see *R. v Prime (Timothy
James)* [2013] EWCA Crim 2525, [2014] 2
Cr. App. R. (S.) 19 (CA (Crim Div)),
Jackson LJ
Sch.12 Part 3 para.13, amended: 2014 c.11
Sch.4 para.7
Sch.12 Part 3 para.14, substituted: 2014 c.11
s.18
Sch.12 Part 3 para.15, amended: 2014 c.11
Sch.4 para.7
Sch.12 Part 3 para.16, amended: 2014 c.11
Sch.4 para.7
Sch.12 Part 3 para.17, amended: 2014 c.11
Sch.4 para.7
Sch.12 Part 3 para.18, amended: 2014 c.11
Sch.4 para.7
Sch.12 Part 3 para.19, amended: 2014 c.11
s.18, Sch.4 para.7
Sch.12 Part 3 para.22, amended: 2014 c.11
Sch.4 para.15

Sch.13 Part 1 para.1, amended: 2014 c.11
Sch.5 para.8
Sch.13 Part 1 para.4, repealed (in part): 2014
c.11 s.16, Sch.5 para.8
Sch.13 Part 2 para.6, amended: 2014 c.11
Sch.5 para.8
Sch.13 Part 2 para.9, repealed (in part): 2014
c.11 s.16, Sch.5 para.8
Sch.14, amended: 2014 c.11 s.17, Sch.5
para.9
Sch.15B, see *R. v Saunders (Red)* [2013]
EWCA Crim 1027, [2014] 1 Cr. App. R. (S.)
45 (CA (Crim Div)), Lord Judge LCJ
Sch.19A, added: 2014 c.11 Sch.2
Sch.19A, referred to: 2014 c.11 s.3
Sch.20B Part 2 para.22, amended: 2014 c.11
s.5
Sch.20B Part 3 para.33, amended: 2014 c.11
s.5
Sch.21, see *Attorney General's Reference
(No.34 of 2014)* [2014] EWCA Crim 1394,
[2014] 2 Cr. App. R. (S.) 84 (CA (Crim
Div)), Treacy LJ; see *Attorney General's
Reference (No.69 of 2013)* [2014] EWCA
Crim 188, [2014] 1 W.L.R. 3964 (CA (Crim
Div)), Lord Thomas LCJ; see *R. v
Edgington (Nicola Caroline)* [2013] EWCA
Crim 2185, [2014] 1 Cr. App. R. 24 (CA
(Crim Div)), Treacy LJ
Sch.21 para.5, see *R. v Minto (David)* [2014]
EWCA Crim 297, [2014] 2 Cr. App. R. (S.)
36 (CA (Crim Div)), Macur LJ
Sch.21 para.5A, see *R. v Beckford (Kyle)*
[2014] EWCA Crim 1299, [2014] 2 Cr. App.
R. (S.) 34 (CA (Crim Div)), Laws LJ
Sch.21 para.10, see *R. v Minto (David)*
[2014] EWCA Crim 297, [2014] 2 Cr. App.
R. (S.) 36 (CA (Crim Div)), Macur LJ
Sch.22 para.14, applied: SI 2014/1610
r.68_1, r.68_2, r.74_1
Sch.25 para.60, repealed: 2014 c.14 Sch.7
Sch.26 para.59, repealed: 2014 c.12 Sch.11
para.50
Sch.31 para.3B, added: 2014 c.11 s.18
Sch.31 para.4, amended: 2014 c.11 s.18

2004

**5. Planning and Compulsory Purchase Act
2004**

see *R. (on the application of Cherkley
Campaign Ltd) v Mole Valley DC* [2013]
EWHC 2582 (Admin), [2014] 1 P. & C.R.
12 (QBD (Admin)), Haddon-Cave J; see *R.
(on the application of Cherkley Campaign
Ltd) v Mole Valley DC* [2014] EWCA Civ
567, Times, May 22, 2014 (CA (Civ Div)),
Richards LJ
s.38, see *R. (on the application of Corbett) v
Cornwall Council* [2013] EWHC 3958
(Admin), [2014] P.T.S.R. 727 (QBD
(Admin)), Lewis J; see *R. (on the
application of HS2 Action Alliance Ltd) v
Secretary of State for Transport* [2014]
EWHC 2759 (Admin), [2014] P.T.S.R. 1334
(QBD (Admin)), Lindblom J; see *R. (on the
application of Lloyds Pharmacy Ltd) v Leeds
City Council* [2013] EWHC 4031 (Admin),
[2014] J.P.L. 758 (QBD (Admin)), Judge
Behrens; see *UK Coal Mining Ltd v
Secretary of State for Communities and
Local Government* [2013] EWHC 2142
(Admin), [2014] J.P.L. 14 (QBD (Admin)),
Judge Cooke QC
s.38A, enabling: SI 2014/333
s.39, see *Scrivens v Secretary of State for
Communities and Local Government* [2013]
EWHC 3549 (Admin), [2014] J.P.L. 521
(QBD (Admin)), Collins J
s.56, amended: SI 2014/1770 Art.3
s.56, repealed (in part): SI 2014/1770 Art.3
s.113, see *R. (on the application of IM
Properties Development Ltd) v Lichfield DC*
[2014] EWHC 2440 (Admin), [2014]
P.T.S.R. 1484 (QBD (Birmingham)),
Patterson J
Sch.8 para.17, enabling: SI 2014/692
Sch.8 para.18, enabling: SI 2014/692

6. Child Trust Funds Act 2004
s.3, enabling: SI 2014/649, SI 2014/1453
s.5, enabling: SI 2014/1453
s.7, enabling: SI 2014/1453
s.12, enabling: SI 2014/649, SI 2014/1453
s.13, enabling: SI 2014/1453
s.15, enabling: SI 2014/1453
s.28, enabling: SI 2014/649, SI 2014/1453

7. Gender Recognition Act 2004
applied: SI 2014/3061 Sch.1 para.12, Sch.2
para.10, SI 2014/3229 Art.8, Art.9, Art.10
s.1, applied: SI 2014/840 Sch.1
s.2, amended: 2014 asp 5 Sch.2 para.14, SI
2014/3229 Sch.5 para.15
s.3, amended: 2014 asp 5 Sch.2 para.3, Sch.2
para.16, SI 2014/3229 Sch.5 para.15
s.3C, added: 2014 asp 5 Sch.2 para.15
s.3C, referred to: SSI 2014/212 Sch.1
s.3D, added: 2014 asp 5 Sch.2 para.17
s.3D, referred to: SSI 2014/212 Sch.1
s.3E, added: SI 2014/3229 Sch.5 para.15
s.4, see *MB v Secretary of State for Work
and Pensions* [2014] EWCA Civ 1112,
[2014] I.C.R. 1129 (CA (Civ Div)), Maurice
Kay LJ
s.4, amended: 2014 asp 5 Sch.2 para.4
s.4, repealed (in part): 2014 asp 5 Sch.2
para.4
s.4A, applied: SI 2014/3181 Reg.4
s.4C, added: 2014 asp 5 Sch.2 para.5
s.4C, varied: SI 2014/3229 Art.15, SSI
2014/361 Reg.8
s.4F, varied: SI 2014/3229 Art.15, SSI
2014/361 Reg.8
s.5, amended: 2014 asp 5 Sch.2 para.6
s.5C, added: 2014 asp 5 Sch.2 para.7
s.5D, referred to: SSI 2014/212 Sch.1
s.7, enabling: SI 2014/590
s.7, amended: 2014 asp 5 Sch.2 para.19
s.8, applied: SI 2014/840 Sch.1
s.8, amended: 2014 asp 5 Sch.2 para.8, SI
2014/3229 Sch.5 para.15
s.8, applied: SI 2014/840 r.7, Sch.1
s.9, see *MB v Secretary of State for Work
and Pensions* [2014] EWCA Civ 1112,
[2014] I.C.R. 1129 (CA (Civ Div)), Maurice
Kay LJ
s.10, amended: 2014 asp 5 Sch.2 para.9
s.11C, added: 2014 asp 5 Sch.2 para.10, SI
2014/3229 Sch.5 para.15
s.11D, added: 2014 asp 5 Sch.2 para.11
s.21, amended: SI 2014/3229 Sch.5 para.15
s.21, repealed (in part): 2014 asp 5 Sch.2
para.12
s.22, amended: 2014 asp 5 Sch.2 para.19
s.23, varied: 2014 c.19 Sch.12 para.47
s.24, amended: 2014 asp 5 Sch.2 para.19
s.25, amended: 2014 asp 5 Sch.2 para.2
s.25, applied: 2014 asp 5 s.30

Sch.1, applied: SI 2014/840 Sch.1
Sch.1 para.4, amended: 2014 asp 5 Sch.2
para.18
Sch.3 Part 2 para.19, amended: 2014 asp 5
Sch.2 para.9
Sch.3 Part 2 para.20A, added: 2014 asp 5
Sch.2 para.9
Sch.3 Part 2 para.20A, referred to: SSI
2014/212 Sch.1
Sch.5 Part 2 para.6A, added: 2014 c.19
Sch.12 para.48
Sch.5 Part 2 para.7, amended: 2014 c.19
Sch.12 para.48
Sch.5 Part 2 para.8, amended: 2014 c.19
Sch.12 para.76
Sch.5 Part 2 para.9, amended: 2014 c.19
Sch.11 para.16
Sch.5 Part 2 para.10, amended: 2014 c.19
Sch.12 para.48
Sch.5 Part 2 para.11, repealed: 2014 c.19
Sch.12 para.83

8. Higher Education Act 2004
applied: SI 2014/3109 Sch.1
s.28, enabling: SI 2014/2071
s.47, enabling: SI 2014/2071

10. Age-Related Payments Act 2004
s.2, applied: SI 2014/2672 Sch.2 para.31
s.7, applied: SI 2014/2672 Sch.2 para.35

12. Finance Act 2004
see *Palmer v Royal Bank of Scotland Plc*
[2014] I.C.R. 1288 (EAT), Langstaff J
applied: SI 2014/1964 Reg.125, SSI
2014/164 Reg.17, Reg.18, Reg.25, Reg.26,
Reg.28, Reg.85
Part 4, applied: 2014 c.30 s.4, SI 2014/512
Reg.183, SI 2014/1964 Reg.84, Reg.97,
Reg.142, Reg.170, Reg.175, SI 2014/2336
Reg.59, Reg.103, Reg.117, Reg.129, SI
2014/2848 Reg.71, Reg.109, Reg.133,
Reg.177, SSI 2014/217 Reg.177, Reg.194,
Reg.198, SSI 2014/292 Reg.177, Reg.194,
Reg.198
Part 4, referred to: 2014 c.26 Sch.6 para.1,
Sch.6 para.6
Part 7, disapplied: 2014 c.26 Sch.35 para.13
Part 7, referred to: 2014 c.26 Sch.34 para.5
Pt 5., see *LPA Umbrella Trust, Re* [2014]
EWHC 1378 (Ch), [2014] Pens. L.R. 319
(Ch D), Rose J
s.59, amended: 2014 c.29 s.4
s.61, applied: SI 2014/2929 Reg.4

s.73, enabling: SI 2014/472
s.107, see *Prudential Assurance Co Ltd v Revenue and Customs Commissioners* [2013] EWHC 3249 (Ch), [2014] S.T.C. 1236 (Ch D), Henderson J
s.153, amended: 2014 c.26 Sch.7 para.2
s.153A, added: 2014 c.26 Sch.7 para.3
s.156A, added: 2014 c.26 Sch.7 para.4
s.158, amended: 2014 c.26 Sch.7 para.6
s.159A, added: 2014 c.26 Sch.7 para.7
s.160, applied: SI 2014/512 Reg.183, SI 2014/1964 Reg.175
s.160, referred to: SSI 2014/292 Reg.177
s.164, amended: 2014 c.30 Sch.1 para.85
s.164, applied: SSI 2014/164 Reg.33
s.165, amended: 2014 c.26 s.41, 2014 c.30 Sch.1 para.1, Sch.1 para.32, Sch.1 para.41
s.165, applied: 2014 c.30 Sch.1 para.76, Sch.1 para.77
s.165, repealed (in part): 2014 c.30 Sch.1 para.32
s.166, amended: 2014 c.26 Sch.5 para.2, Sch.5 para.5, Sch.5 para.13, 2014 c.30 Sch.1 para.54, Sch.1 para.55
s.166, applied: SSI 2014/164 Reg.33
s.167, amended: 2014 c.26 s.41, 2014 c.30 Sch.1 para.6, Sch.1 para.32, Sch.2 para.2
s.167, applied: SI 2014/1964 Reg.90, Reg.119, SI 2014/2336 Reg.61, Reg.64, SI 2014/2848 Reg.75, Reg.104
s.167, repealed (in part): 2014 c.30 Sch.1 para.32
s.168, amended: 2014 c.30 Sch.1 para.7
s.168, applied: SSI 2014/164 Reg.33
s.169, amended: 2014 c.26 Sch.7 para.23, 2014 c.30 Sch.1 para.8, Sch.1 para.92, Sch.2 para.4
s.169, applied: 2014 c.30 Sch.1 para.34, SI 2014/1964 Reg.142, SSI 2014/164 Reg.94
s.169, referred to: SSI 2014/292 Reg.194, Reg.198
s.169, enabling: SI 2014/1449
s.172, amended: 2014 c.30 Sch.2 para.5
s.172A, amended: 2014 c.26 Sch.7 para.10, 2014 c.30 Sch.2 para.6, Sch.2 para.7, Sch.2 para.8, Sch.2 para.9, Sch.2 para.10
s.172A, repealed (in part): 2014 c.26 Sch.7 para.10
s.172B, amended: 2014 c.30 Sch.1 para.9, Sch.1 para.10, Sch.2 para.11, Sch.2 para.12

s.182, amended: 2014 c.30 Sch.1 para.11, Sch.1 para.12, Sch.2 para.13
s.185J, added: 2014 c.26 Sch.5 para.3
s.188, amended: 2014 c.26 Sch.7 para.13
s.188, applied: SI 2014/3037 Sch.2 para.3, Sch.2 para.4
s.189, amended: 2014 c.26 Sch.17 para.18
s.195, amended: 2014 c.26 Sch.8 para.52, Sch.8 para.139
s.205, applied: SI 2014/512 Reg.191, SI 2014/1964 Reg.139, SI 2014/2336 Reg.96, SI 2014/2848 Reg.116, SSI 2014/217 Reg.185, SSI 2014/292 Reg.185
s.205A, amended: 2014 c.30 s.2
s.206, amended: 2014 c.30 s.2, Sch.1 para.13, Sch.2 para.17
s.206, applied: SI 2014/1964 Reg.125, SSI 2014/164 Reg.17
s.207, amended: 2014 c.26 Sch.7 para.11
s.211, amended: 2014 c.30 Sch.1 para.14
s.212, amended: 2014 c.30 Sch.1 para.15
s.212, applied: 2014 c.26 Sch.6 para.4
s.214, applied: SI 2014/512 Reg.182, SI 2014/1964 Reg.171, SI 2014/2848 Reg.178, SSI 2014/217 Reg.176, SSI 2014/292 Reg.176
s.216, amended: 2014 c.30 Sch.1 para.16, Sch.2 para.21
s.216, referred to: SI 2014/1964 Reg.171, Reg.172, SI 2014/2336 Reg.118, SI 2014/2848 Reg.178, Reg.179
s.217, amended: 2014 c.30 Sch.2 para.22
s.218, applied: SSI 2014/164 Reg.48
s.219, amended: 2014 c.26 Sch.6 para.10, 2014 c.30 Sch.2 para.23
s.227, amended: 2014 c.30 Sch.1 para.63, Sch.1 para.66
s.227, applied: SI 2014/512 Reg.182, SI 2014/2336 Reg.119, SSI 2014/217 Reg.176, SSI 2014/292 Reg.176
s.227A, repealed: 2014 c.30 Sch.1 para.66
s.227B, added: 2014 c.30 Sch.1 para.65
s.227ZA, added: 2014 c.30 Sch.1 para.64
s.228, applied: SSI 2014/164 Reg.54
s.228A, amended: 2014 c.30 Sch.1 para.67
s.237B, amended: 2014 c.30 Sch.1 para.68
s.237B, applied: SI 2014/525 Reg.16, SI 2014/1964 Reg.174, SI 2014/2848 Reg.181, SSI 2014/164 Reg.84, SSI 2014/233 Reg.16, SSI 2014/292 Reg.176

s.238A, applied: SI 2014/512 Reg.182, SSI
2014/217 Reg.176
s.239, amended: 2014 c.26 Sch.5 para.12
s.241, applied: SI 2014/1964 Reg.97
s.251, amended: 2014 c.30 Sch.1 para.93
s.251, enabling: SI 2014/1842, SI 2014/1843
s.255, amended: 2014 c.26 Sch.7 para.17
s.255, enabling: SI 2014/1928
s.257, amended: 2014 c.26 Sch.7 para.23
s.261, amended: 2014 c.26 Sch.7 para.23
s.264, amended: 2014 c.26 Sch.7 para.23
s.266A, amended: 2014 c.26 Sch.7 para.14
s.266B, amended: 2014 c.26 Sch.7 para.15
s.268, amended: 2014 c.26 Sch.5 para.12
s.270, amended: 2014 c.26 Sch.7 para.9
s.272, amended: 2014 c.26 Sch.7 para.18
s.272A, added: 2014 c.26 Sch.7 para.19
s.273, amended: 2014 c.26 Sch.7 para.20
s.273A, amended: 2014 c.30 Sch.1 para.17
s.273A, applied: 2014 c.30 Sch.1 para.30
s.273B, added: 2014 c.30 Sch.1 para.79
s.273ZA, applied: SI 2014/1928 Reg.1
s.274, amended: 2014 c.26 Sch.7 para.21
s.275, applied: SSI 2014/164 Reg.17
s.280, amended: 2014 c.26 Sch.5 para.5,
2014 c.30 Sch.1 para.18, Sch.1 para.56,
Sch.2 para.14, Sch.2 para.18
s.282, amended: 2014 c.26 Sch.5 para.14
s.282, applied: 2014 c.30 s.4
s.282, enabling: SI 2014/1449, SI 2014/1843
s.283, applied: 2014 c.30 Sch.1 para.69
s.308, applied: 2014 c.26 Sch.34 para.5
s.309, applied: 2014 c.26 Sch.34 para.5
s.310, applied: 2014 c.26 s.284, Sch.34
para.5
s.310A, added: 2014 c.26 s.284
s.312, applied: 2014 c.26 s.227
s.312, disapplied: 2014 c.26 s.227
s.313ZA, applied: 2014 c.26 Sch.34 para.5
s.316, amended: 2014 c.26 s.284
s.318, amended: 2014 c.26 s.284
s.320, see *Prudential Assurance Co Ltd v
Revenue and Customs Commissioners*
[2013] EWHC 3249 (Ch), [2014] S.T.C.
1236 (Ch D), Henderson J; see *Test
Claimants in the FII Group Litigation v
Inland Revenue Commissioners (C-362/12)*
[2014] A.C. 1161 (ECJ (3rd Chamber)),
Judge Ilesic (President)
Sch.28 Part 1 para.1, referred to: SI
2014/2336 Reg.58

Sch.28 Part 1 para.3, amended: 2014 c.30
Sch.1 para.37, Sch.1 para.43, Sch.1 para.44
Sch.28 Part 1 para.6, amended: 2014 c.30
Sch.1 para.38, Sch.1 para.45, Sch.1 para.46
Sch.28 Part 1 para.7, amended: 2014 c.30
Sch.1 para.19
Sch.28 Part 1 para.8, amended: 2014 c.30
Sch.1 para.2
Sch.28 Part 1 para.8A, added: 2014 c.30
Sch.1 para.3
Sch.28 Part 1 para.8D, added: 2014 c.30
Sch.1 para.3
Sch.28 Part 1 para.10, repealed (in part):
2014 c.30 Sch.1 para.32
Sch.28 Part 1 para.10A, repealed (in part):
2014 c.30 Sch.1 para.32
Sch.28 Part 1 para.14A, amended: 2014 c.26
s.41
Sch.28 Part 1 para.14A, repealed: 2014 c.30
Sch.1 para.32
Sch.28 Part 2 para.15, applied: SI 2014/1964
Reg.87, Reg.89, SI 2014/2336 Reg.63, SI
2014/2848 Reg.72, Reg.74
Sch.28 Part 2 para.17, amended: 2014 c.30
Sch.1 para.39, Sch.1 para.47, Sch.1 para.48,
Sch.1 para.49
Sch.28 Part 2 para.20, amended: 2014 c.30
Sch.1 para.40, Sch.1 para.50, Sch.1 para.51
Sch.28 Part 2 para.21, amended: 2014 c.30
Sch.1 para.20
Sch.28 Part 2 para.22, amended: 2014 c.30
Sch.1 para.21
Sch.28 Part 2 para.22A, added: 2014 c.30
Sch.1 para.4
Sch.28 Part 2 para.22D, added: 2014 c.30
Sch.1 para.4
Sch.28 Part 2 para.24, repealed (in part):
2014 c.30 Sch.1 para.32
Sch.28 Part 2 para.24A, repealed (in part):
2014 c.30 Sch.1 para.32
Sch.28 Part 2 para.24C, amended: 2014 c.26
s.41
Sch.28 Part 2 para.24C, repealed: 2014 c.30
Sch.1 para.32
Sch.28 Part 2 para.27A, added: 2014 c.30
Sch.2 para.3
Sch.29 Part 1 para.1A, added: 2014 c.26
Sch.5 para.1
Sch.29 Part 1 para.1B, added: 2014 c.26
Sch.5 para.2

Sch.29 Part 1 para.3, amended: 2014 c.26
Sch.5 para.4, 2014 c.30 Sch.1 para.22
Sch.29 Part 1 para.3A, amended: 2014 c.30
Sch.1 para.70
Sch.29 Part 1 para.3A, disapplied: SI
2014/512 Reg.167, SSI 2014/217 Reg.161,
SSI 2014/292 Reg.161
Sch.29 Part 1 para.4A, added: 2014 c.30
Sch.1 para.57
Sch.29 Part 1 para.7, amended: 2014 c.26
s.42, 2014 c.30 Sch.1 para.71
Sch.29 Part 1 para.7, applied: SSI 2014/164
Reg.79
Sch.29 Part 1 para.7, referred to: SI
2014/512 Reg.174, SSI 2014/217 Reg.168,
SSI 2014/292 Reg.168
Sch.29 Part 1 para.8, amended: 2014 c.26
s.42
Sch.29 Part 1 para.8, repealed (in part): 2014
c.26 s.42
Sch.29 Part 1 para.11A, added: 2014 c.26
Sch.5 para.5
Sch.29 Part 1 para.12, amended: 2014 c.30
Sch.1 para.58, Sch.1 para.59, Sch.1 para.60
Sch.29 Part 2 para.14, applied: SI 2014/1964
Reg.125
Sch.29 Part 2 para.15, amended: 2014 c.30
Sch.2 para.19
Sch.29 Part 2 para.15, repealed (in part):
2014 c.30 Sch.2 para.19
Sch.29 Part 2 para.17, amended: 2014 c.30
Sch.1 para.23
Sch.29 Part 2 para.17A, added: 2014 c.30
Sch.1 para.24
Sch.29 Part 2 para.18, amended: 2014 c.30
Sch.1 para.25, Sch.2 para.15
Sch.29 Part 2 para.20, amended: 2014 c.30
Sch.1 para.74
Sch.29 Part 2 para.20, referred to: SSI
2014/217 Reg.168, SSI 2014/292 Reg.168
Sch.29 Part 2 para.21, repealed: 2014 c.30
Sch.1 para.75
Sch.32 para.1, amended: 2014 c.30 Sch.2
para.24
Sch.32 para.4, amended: 2014 c.30 Sch.1
para.26
Sch.32 para.7, amended: 2014 c.30 Sch.1
para.76
Sch.32 para.14B, added: 2014 c.30 Sch.2
para.24

Sch.32 para.15, amended: 2014 c.30 Sch.1
para.61
Sch.32 para.16, amended: 2014 c.30 Sch.2
para.19
Sch.32 para.17, amended: 2014 c.30 Sch.1
para.27
Sch.33 para.5, amended: 2014 c.30 Sch.1
para.94
Sch.34, applied: 2014 c.30 Sch.1 para.33
Sch.34 para.1, amended: 2014 c.30 Sch.1
para.95
Sch.34 para.4A, repealed: 2014 c.30 Sch.1
para.32
Sch.34 para.5A, added: 2014 c.30 Sch.1
para.95
Sch.34 para.6, amended: 2014 c.30 Sch.1
para.95
Sch.34 para.7, amended: 2014 c.30 Sch.1
para.95
Sch.34 para.9ZA, added: 2014 c.30 Sch.1
para.95
Sch.34 para.10, amended: 2014 c.26 s.45
Sch.34 para.11, amended: 2014 c.26 s.45,
2014 c.30 Sch.1 para.95
Sch.34 para.12, amended: 2014 c.30 Sch.1
para.95
Sch.34 para.13, applied: 2014 c.26 Sch.6
para.6
Sch.34 para.14, applied: 2014 c.26 Sch.6
para.3, Sch.6 para.5
Sch.34 para.19, amended: 2014 c.30 Sch.1
para.95
Sch.35 para.46, repealed: 2014 c.26 s.114
Sch.36, applied: SSI 2014/164 Reg.48
Sch.36 Part 2 para.7, applied: SI 2014/1842
Reg.4
Sch.36 Part 2 para.7, referred to: 2014 c.26
Sch.6 para.1
Sch.36 Part 2 para.12, applied: 2014 c.26
Sch.6 para.1
Sch.36 Part 2 para.20, amended: 2014 c.30
Sch.1 para.28, Sch.1 para.77
Sch.36 Part 2 para.20, applied: 2014 c.26
Sch.6 para.2
Sch.36 Part 2 para.20, referred to: 2014 c.26
Sch.6 para.2, 2014 c.30 Sch.1 para.77
Sch.36 Part 3 para.22, amended: 2014 c.26
Sch.5 para.7
Sch.36 Part 3 para.23, amended: 2014 c.26
Sch.5 para.7

Sch.36 Part 3 para.23ZA, added: 2014 c.30
Sch.1 para.78
Sch.36 Part 3 para.29, amended: 2014 c.26
Sch.5 para.8, 2014 c.30 Sch.1 para.29
Sch.36 Part 3 para.31, amended: 2014 c.26
Sch.5 para.9
Sch.36 Part 3 para.34, amended: 2014 c.26
Sch.5 para.10

15. Carers (Equal Opportunities) Act 2004
s.3, applied: SI 2014/829 Sch.1 para.20

18. Traffic Management Act 2004
applied: SI 2014/3105 Sch.1, SI 2014/3106
Sch.1, SI 2014/3107 Sch.1, SI 2014/3110
Sch.1, SI 2014/3112 Sch.1, SI 2014/3310
Sch.1, SI 2014/3311 Sch.1
referred to: SI 2014/941 Sch.1
Part 3, applied: SI 2014/466 Sch.1, SI
2014/941 Sch.1, SI 2014/3105 Sch.1, SI
2014/3106 Sch.1, SI 2014/3107 Sch.1, SI
2014/3108 Sch.1, SI 2014/3109 Sch.1, SI
2014/3110 Sch.1, SI 2014/3112 Sch.1, SI
2014/3310 Sch.1, SI 2014/3311 Sch.1
s.16, applied: SI 2014/466 Sch.1, SI
2014/3102 Sch.8 para.23, SI 2014/3310
Sch.1, SI 2014/3311 Sch.1
s.32, applied: SI 2014/466 Sch.1, SI
2014/3310 Sch.1, SI 2014/3311 Sch.1
s.33, applied: SI 2014/941 Sch.1
s.34, applied: SI 2014/466, SI 2014/941, SI
2014/941 Sch.1, SI 2014/2460, SI
2014/2462, SI 2014/3105, SI 2014/3106, SI
2014/3107, SI 2014/3108, SI 2014/3109, SI
2014/3110, SI 2014/3112, SI 2014/3310, SI
2014/3311
s.34, enabling: SI 2014/466, SI 2014/941, SI
2014/2460, SI 2014/2462, SI 2014/3105, SI
2014/3106, SI 2014/3107, SI 2014/3108, SI
2014/3109, SI 2014/3110, SI 2014/3112, SI
2014/3310, SI 2014/3311
s.36, applied: SI 2014/941 Sch.1
s.37, applied: SI 2014/941 Sch.1
s.39, enabling: SI 2014/466, SI 2014/2460,
SI 2014/2462, SI 2014/3105, SI 2014/3106,
SI 2014/3107, SI 2014/3108, SI 2014/3109,
SI 2014/3110, SI 2014/3112, SI 2014/3310,
SI 2014/3311
s.89, enabling: SI 2014/3205
s.95, repealed (in part): 2014 c.2 Sch.12
para.123

Sch.7, applied: SI 2014/909 Art.38, SI
2014/1052 Art.41, SI 2014/2269 Art.37, SI
2014/2384 Art.18, SI 2014/2637 Art.15
Sch.8 Part 2 para.8, applied: SI 2014/2722,
SI 2014/3205
Sch.8 Part 2 para.8, enabling: SI 2014/2722,
SI 2014/3205
Sch.8 Part 2 para.9, enabling: SI 2014/2725
Sch.8 Part 2 para.10, applied: SI 2014/2725
Sch.8 Part 2 para.10, enabling: SI 2014/2725
Sch.10 para.3, applied: SI 2014/2722, SI
2014/3205
Sch.10 para.3, enabling: SI 2014/2722, SI
2014/3205

19. Asylum and Immigration (Treatment of Claimants, etc.) Act 2004
applied: SI 2014/2604 Sch.1 para.2
s.4, applied: 2014 asp 1 s.8
s.8, amended: 2014 c.22 Sch.9 para.4
s.14, amended: SI 2014/3229 Sch.5 para.16
s.14, repealed (in part): SI 2014/3229 Sch.5
para.16
s.15, repealed (in part): 2014 c.22 Sch.9
para.60
s.19, amended: 2014 c.22 s.58
s.26, repealed (in part): 2014 c.22 Sch.9
para.60
s.27, repealed (in part): 2014 c.22 Sch.9
para.60
s.28, repealed: 2014 c.22 Sch.9 para.60
s.31, repealed: 2014 c.22 Sch.9 para.60
s.35, amended: 2014 c.22 Sch.2 para.5
s.36, applied: SI 2014/2604 r.38
s.42, amended: 2014 c.22 Sch.9 para.73
s.42, applied: SI 2014/922
s.42, repealed (in part): 2014 c.22 Sch.9
para.73
Sch.2 Part 1 para.18, repealed (in part): 2014
c.22 Sch.9 para.60
Sch.2 Part 1 para.19, repealed: 2014 c.22
Sch.9 para.60
Sch.3 Part 1 para.1, amended: 2014 c.22
Sch.9 para.56
Sch.3 Part 2 para.5, amended: 2014 c.22
Sch.9 para.56
Sch.3 Part 2 para.5, repealed (in part): 2014
c.22 Sch.9 para.56
Sch.3 Pt 2 para.5, see *R. (on the application
of EM (Eritrea)) v Secretary of State for the
Home Department* [2014] UKSC 12, [2014]
A.C. 1321 (SC), Lord Neuberger PSC

Sch.3 Part 3 para.10, amended: 2014 c.22
Sch.9 para.56
Sch.3 Part 3 para.10, repealed (in part): 2014
c.22 Sch.9 para.56
Sch.3 Part 4 para.15, amended: 2014 c.22
Sch.9 para.56
Sch.3 Part 4 para.15, repealed (in part): 2014
c.22 Sch.9 para.56
Sch.3 Part 5 para.19, amended: 2014 c.22
Sch.9 para.56
Sch.3 Part 5 para.19, repealed (in part): 2014
c.22 Sch.9 para.56

20. Energy Act 2004
Commencement Orders: SI 2014/1460 Art.2
s.39, enabling: SI 2014/1391
s.105, applied: SI 2014/1599 Art.36, Sch.1
para.9, SI 2014/1873 Art.10, Sch.1 para.8,
Sch.13 para.22, Sch.14 para.14, SI
2014/2594 Art.8, Sch.1 para.8, SI 2014/2950
Art.36, Sch.1 para.14, Sch.10 para.14, SI
2014/3331 Art.33, Sch.1 para.10
s.106, applied: SI 2014/1599 Sch.10 para.4,
Sch.11 para.4, SI 2014/1873 Sch.13 para.4,
Sch.14 para.4, SI 2014/2594 Sch.2 para.4,
Sch.3 para.4, SI 2014/2950 Sch.9 para.4,
Sch.10 para.4, SI 2014/3331 Sch.8 para.3
s.108, applied: SI 2014/1599 Sch.11 para.4,
SI 2014/1873 Sch.13 para.4, Sch.14 para.4,
SI 2014/2594 Sch.2 para.4, Sch.3 para.4, SI
2014/2950 Sch.9 para.4, Sch.10 para.4, SI
2014/3331 Sch.8 para.3
s.173, applied: SI 2014/1293, SI 2014/1293
Art.1, Art.2, Art.3, Art.4, Art.14
s.173, enabling: SI 2014/1293
s.198, enabling: SI 2014/1460

21. Fire and Rescue Services Act 2004
s.2, applied: 2014 c.2 s.40, Sch.2 para.22
s.4, applied: 2014 c.2 s.40, Sch.2 para.22
s.5B, amended: 2014 c.14 Sch.4 para.86
s.21, applied: SI 2014/3317
s.21, enabling: SI 2014/3317
s.34, applied: SI 2014/445, SI 2014/447, SI
2014/523, SI 2014/3256, SSI 2014/60, SSI
2014/109, SSI 2014/110, SSI 2014/149
s.34, enabling: SI 2014/445, SI 2014/447, SI
2014/523, SI 2014/3256, SSI 2014/60, SSI
2014/109, SSI 2014/110, SSI 2014/149
s.60, enabling: SI 2014/445, SI 2014/447, SI
2014/523, SI 2014/3256, SSI 2014/60, SSI
2014/109, SSI 2014/110, SSI 2014/149
s.62, enabling: SI 2014/523, SI 2014/3256

Sch.1 para.19, repealed: 2014 c.14 Sch.7
Sch.1 para.88, repealed: 2014 c.2 Sch.1 Part
2
Sch.1 para.102, repealed: 2014 c.2 Sch.12
para.123

23. Public Audit (Wales) Act 2004
applied: 2014 c.2 Sch.11 para.2
Part 2 c.1, applied: SI 2014/2704 Art.3
s.22, applied: SI 2014/3362 Reg.25
s.23, applied: SI 2014/3362 Reg.10, Reg.15
s.29, applied: SI 2014/3362 Reg.13, Reg.18
s.30, applied: SI 2014/3362 Reg.12, Reg.17,
Reg.21, Reg.22
s.31, applied: SI 2014/3362 Reg.21, Reg.25
s.33, applied: SI 2014/3362 Reg.10, Reg.15
s.37, applied: SI 2014/3362 Reg.28
s.38, applied: SI 2014/3362 Reg.1
s.39, applied: SI 2014/3362
s.39, enabling: SI 2014/3362
s.43, repealed: 2014 c.2 Sch.12 para.60
s.57, repealed: 2014 c.2 Sch.12 para.61
s.58, enabling: SI 2014/3362
s.62, amended: 2014 c.2 Sch.12 para.62
s.62, repealed (in part): 2014 c.2 Sch.12
para.62
s.64D, amended: 2014 c.2 Sch.12 para.63
s.68, amended: SI 2014/77 Art.3
s.68, substituted: SI 2014/77 Art.3
s.69, repealed: 2014 c.2 Sch.12 para.64
Sch.1 para.14, repealed: 2014 c.2 Sch.12
para.123
Sch.2 para.9, repealed (in part): 2014 c.2
Sch.12 para.123
Sch.2 para.20, repealed (in part): 2014 c.2
Sch.12 para.123
Sch.2 para.21, repealed: 2014 c.2 Sch.1 Part
2
Sch.2 para.32, repealed: 2014 c.2 Sch.1 Part
2
Sch.3 para.1, amended: SI 2014/77 Art.3
Sch.3 para.1, repealed (in part): 2014 c.2
Sch.12 para.65
Sch.3 para.2, amended: 2014 c.2 Sch.12
para.65, SI 2014/77 Art.3
Sch.3 para.2, repealed (in part): 2014 c.2
Sch.12 para.65
Sch.3 para.4, amended: SI 2014/77 Art.3
Sch.3 para.5, amended: SI 2014/77 Art.3

**25. Horserace Betting and Olympic Lottery Act
2004**
Part 2, applied: 2014 c.17 s.2

s.26, enabling: SI 2014/1510
s.36, enabling: SI 2014/1510
27. Companies (Audit, Investigations and Community Enterprise) Act 2004
Part 2, applied: 2014 c.14 s.115, s.135
s.15D, amended: 2014 c.14 Sch.4 para.88
s.16, amended: 2014 c.2 Sch.12 para.67, 2014 c.19 s.47
s.30, enabling: SI 2014/2483
s.34, enabling: SI 2014/2483
s.53, amended: 2014 c.14 Sch.4 para.89
s.56, amended: 2014 c.14 Sch.4 para.90
s.62, applied: SI 2014/2483
s.62, enabling: SI 2014/2483
28. Domestic Violence, Crime and Victims Act 2004
s.5, see *R. v Hopkinson (Jessica Marie)* [2013] EWCA Crim 795, [2014] 1 Cr. App. R. 3 (CA (Crim Div)), Lord Judge LCJ
s.5, applied: SI 2014/1610 r.38_9
s.6, applied: SI 2014/1610 r.38_9
s.17, applied: SI 2014/1610 r.38_6, r.3_14, r.38_15
s.18, applied: SI 2014/1610 r.3_14
Sch.9 para.20A, added: SI 2014/469 Sch.2 para.23
30. Human Tissue Act 2004
s.32, amended: SI 2014/1459 Reg.12
31. Children Act 2004
s.2, substituted: 2014 c.6 s.107
s.2D, added: 2014 c.6 s.108
s.2E, added: 2014 c.6 s.109
s.2F, added: 2014 c.6 s.110
s.3, amended: 2014 c.6 Sch.5 para.1
s.3, applied: SI 2014/1492 Reg.6
s.3, repealed (in part): 2014 c.6 Sch.5 para.1
s.4, repealed (in part): 2014 c.6 Sch.5 para.2
s.5, amended: 2014 c.6 Sch.5 para.3
s.5, repealed (in part): 2014 c.6 Sch.5 para.2
s.6, amended: 2014 c.6 Sch.5 para.4
s.6, repealed (in part): 2014 c.6 Sch.5 para.2
s.7, amended: 2014 c.6 Sch.5 para.5
s.7, repealed (in part): 2014 c.6 Sch.5 para.2
s.7A, added: 2014 c.6 s.111
s.7B, added: 2014 c.6 s.112
s.8, amended: 2014 c.6 s.113
s.8, repealed (in part): 2014 c.6 s.113
s.8A, added: 2014 c.6 s.114
s.9, substituted: 2014 c.6 Sch.5 para.6
s.10, amended: 2014 c.6 Sch.3 para.80
s.10, applied: SI 2014/2407 Reg.3

s.11, see *Huzrat v Hounslow LBC* [2013] EWCA Civ 1865, [2014] H.L.R. 17 (CA (Civ Div)), Moses LJ; see *R. (on the application of HC) v Secretary of State for the Home Department* [2013] EWHC 982 (Admin), [2014] 1 W.L.R. 1234 (DC), Moses LJ
s.12C, applied: SI 2014/2407 Reg.3
s.15A, applied: SI 2014/2418 Sch.1
s.17A, applied: SI 2014/2407 Reg.3
s.20, applied: SI 2014/2418 Sch.1
s.20, repealed (in part): 2014 c.2 Sch.12 para.68
s.65, see *R. (on the application of HC) v Secretary of State for the Home Department* [2013] EWHC 982 (Admin), [2014] 1 W.L.R. 1234 (DC), Moses LJ
Sch.1 para.3, amended: 2014 c.6 Sch.5 para.7
Sch.1 para.3A, added: 2014 c.6 Sch.5 para.8
Sch.1 para.5, amended: 2014 c.6 Sch.5 para.9
Sch.1 para.5, repealed (in part): 2014 c.6 Sch.5 para.9
Sch.2 para.8, repealed: 2014 c.12 Sch.11 para.50
32. Armed Forces (Pensions and Compensation) Act 2004
s.1, enabling: SI 2014/412, SI 2014/2958
s.10, enabling: SI 2014/2958
33. Civil Partnership Act 2004
applied: 2014 asp 5 s.30, SI 2014/93 Art.4, SI 2014/1132 Sch.10 para.1, SSI 2014/287 Art.5
Part 5, applied: SSI 2014/287 Art.5
s.1, amended: 2014 asp 5 s.11
s.8, amended: 2014 c.22 Sch.4 para.19
s.8, applied: 2014 c.22 Sch.9 para.66
s.8A, added: 2014 c.22 Sch.4 para.20
s.9, substituted: 2014 c.22 Sch.4 para.21
s.11, amended: 2014 c.22 Sch.4 para.22
s.12, amended: 2014 c.22 Sch.4 para.23
s.12A, added: 2014 c.22 Sch.4 para.24
s.12A, applied: 2014 c.22 s.48, s.61, Sch.6 para.1, Sch.6 para.2
s.14, amended: 2014 c.22 Sch.4 para.26
s.14, applied: 2014 c.22 s.48
s.14A, added: 2014 c.22 Sch.4 para.26
s.15, amended: 2014 c.22 Sch.4 para.26
s.16, amended: 2014 c.22 Sch.4 para.26
s.30A, added: 2014 c.22 Sch.4 para.27

s.34, enabling: SI 2014/1789
s.36, amended: 2014 c.22 Sch.4 para.28
s.37, referred to: SI 2014/603 Sch.1
s.40, amended: 2014 c.6 s.17
s.42, referred to: SI 2014/603 Sch.1
s.44, referred to: SI 2014/603 Sch.1
s.52, amended: 2014 c.22 Sch.4 para.29
s.56, repealed (in part): 2014 c.6 s.17
s.63, repealed: 2014 c.6 s.17
s.85, amended: 2014 asp 5 s.24
s.86, amended: 2014 asp 5 s.24
s.87, amended: 2014 asp 5 s.24
s.88, amended: 2014 asp 5 s.24, s.25
s.88, enabling: SSI 2014/306
s.89, amended: 2014 asp 5 s.24
s.90, amended: 2014 asp 5 s.24
s.91, amended: 2014 asp 5 s.24
s.92, amended: 2014 asp 5 s.24
s.93, amended: 2014 asp 5 s.24
s.93, repealed (in part): 2014 asp 5 s.24
s.93, substituted: 2014 asp 5 s.24
s.93A, added: 2014 asp 5 s.24
s.94, amended: 2014 asp 5 s.24
s.94A, added: 2014 asp 5 s.24
s.94A, applied: SSI 2014/303, SSI 2014/303
Reg.2
s.94A, referred to: SSI 2014/212 Sch.1
s.94A, enabling: SSI 2014/303
s.94B, referred to: SSI 2014/212 Sch.1
s.94E, referred to: SSI 2014/212 Sch.1
s.95, amended: 2014 asp 5 s.24
s.95A, amended: 2014 asp 5 s.24
s.95ZA, added: 2014 asp 5 s.24
s.95ZA, referred to: SSI 2014/212 Sch.1
s.95ZA, enabling: SSI 2014/306
s.96, amended: 2014 asp 5 s.24
s.97, amended: 2014 asp 5 s.24
s.100, amended: 2014 asp 5 s.24, s.28
s.103, applied: 2014 asp 5 s.11, SSI
2014/287 Art.5
s.104, applied: 2014 asp 18 Sch.1 para.2, SSI
2014/287 Art.5
s.113, applied: 2014 asp 18 Sch.1 para.2
s.126, amended: 2014 asp 5 s.24
s.126, applied: SSI 2014/306
s.135, amended: 2014 asp 5 s.24
s.210, applied: 2014 asp 5 s.11
s.211, applied: 2014 asp 5 s.11
s.212, amended: SI 2014/560 Sch.1 para.29
s.214, amended: 2014 asp 5 s.26
s.241, enabling: SI 2014/1107

s.244, enabling: SI 2014/1107
s.258, enabling: SI 2014/1789
s.259, applied: SI 2014/3168, SI 2014/3229
s.259, enabling: SI 2014/107, SI 2014/560,
SI 2014/3061, SI 2014/3168, SI 2014/3229
Sch.2 Part 1 para.1, amended: 2014 c.6
Sch.2 para.66
Sch.2 Part 1 para.2, amended: 2014 c.6
Sch.2 para.66
Sch.2 Part 1 para.2A, added: 2014 c.6 Sch.2
para.66
Sch.2 Part 2 para.5, amended: SI 2014/560
Sch.1 para.29
Sch.2 Part 3 para.11, added: SI 2014/560
Sch.1 para.29
Sch.3A, added: 2014 c.22 Sch.4 para.25
Sch.5 Part 1, applied: SI 2014/3037 Sch.2
para.1
Sch.5 Part 6, applied: SI 2014/3037 Sch.2
para.1
Sch.5 Part 11 para.60, amended: 2014 c.16
Sch.3 para.5
Sch.6, applied: SI 2014/840 Sch.1
Sch.7, applied: SI 2014/840 Sch.1
Sch.7 Part 1 para.4, applied: SI 2014/840
Sch.1
Sch.7 Part 1 para.9, applied: SI 2014/840
Sch.1
Sch.10, substituted: 2014 asp 5 s.24
Sch.20, amended: 2014 asp 5 s.26
Sch.23 Part 1 paraA.1, added: 2014 c.22 s.58
Sch.23 Part 1 para.1, amended: 2014 c.22
s.58
Sch.23 Part 2 para.3, substituted: 2014 c.22
s.58
Sch.23 Part 3 para.8, substituted: 2014 c.22
s.58
Sch.23 Part 4 para.12, substituted: 2014 c.22
s.58
Sch.24 Part 3 para.25, repealed (in part):
2014 c.19 Sch.12 para.75
Sch.24 Part 3 para.28, repealed (in part):
2014 c.19 Sch.12 para.75
Sch.27 para.24, repealed: 2014 c.14 Sch.7

34. Housing Act 2004
see *Simon v Denbighshire CC* [2014] J.P.L.
268 (UT (Lands)), Martin Rodger Q.C.
s.11, see *Odeniran v Southend on Sea BC*
[2013] EWHC 3888 (Admin), [2014] H.L.R.
11 (QBD (Admin)), Collins J

s.12, see *Odeniran v Southend on Sea BC*
[2013] EWHC 3888 (Admin), [2014] H.L.R.
11 (QBD (Admin)), Collins J
s.13, see *Odeniran v Southend on Sea BC*
[2013] EWHC 3888 (Admin), [2014] H.L.R.
11 (QBD (Admin)), Collins J
s.55, see *Bristol City Council v Digs
(Bristol) Ltd* [2014] EWHC 869 (Admin),
[2014] H.L.R. 30 (QBD (Admin)), Burnett J
s.231A, amended: SI 2014/1900 Sch.1
para.13
s.231B, amended: SI 2014/1900 Sch.1
para.14
s.231C, amended: SI 2014/1900 Sch.1
para.15
s.231D, amended: SI 2014/1900 Sch.1
para.16
s.250, applied: SI 2014/2553
s.250, enabling: SI 2014/286, SI 2014/2553
Sch.1 Pt 2 para.6, see *Simon v Denbighshire
CC* [2014] J.P.L. 268 (UT (Lands)), Martin
Rodger Q.C.
Sch.13, enabling: SI 2014/286, SI 2014/2553
Sch.14 para.2B, amended: 2014 c.14 Sch.4
para.91

35. Pensions Act 2004
Commencement Orders: SI 2014/1636 Art.2
see *Granada UK Rental & Retail Ltd v
Pensions Regulator* [2014] Pens. L.R. 17
(UT (Tax)), Judge Timothy Herrington; see
LPA Umbrella Trust, Re [2014] EWHC
1378 (Ch), [2014] Pens. L.R. 319 (Ch D),
Rose J; see *Storm Funding Ltd (In
Administration), Re* [2013] EWHC 4019
(Ch), [2014] Bus. L.R. 454 (Ch D
(Companies Ct)), David Richards J
applied: SSI 2014/164 Reg.17
referred to: 2014 c.19 s.45
Part 2, applied: SI 2014/1711 Reg.43,
Reg.44, Reg.52, Reg.54, Reg.55, Reg.56
Part 2, varied: SI 2014/1711 Reg.53, Reg.57
Part 2 c.3, applied: 2014 c.19 Sch.20
para.14, Sch.20 para.15
Part 3, applied: SI 2014/1711 Reg.38,
Reg.64
Part 3, disapplied: SI 2014/1711 Reg.63
Part 3, referred to: SI 2014/1711 Reg.62
Part 3, varied: SI 2014/1711 Reg.62, Reg.64
s.5, amended: 2014 c.19 s.48
s.10, amended: 2014 c.19 Sch.19 para.6

s.47, see *Storm Funding Ltd (In
Administration), Re* [2013] EWHC 4019
(Ch), [2014] Bus. L.R. 454 (Ch D
(Companies Ct)), David Richards J
s.48, see *Storm Funding Ltd (In
Administration), Re* [2013] EWHC 4019
(Ch), [2014] Bus. L.R. 454 (Ch D
(Companies Ct)), David Richards J
s.63, amended: 2014 c.19 s.49
s.66, amended: 2014 c.19 Sch.19 para.7
s.72, amended: 2014 c.19 s.41
s.91, enabling: SI 2014/1926
s.96, amended: 2014 c.19 Sch.19 para.8
s.97, amended: 2014 c.19 Sch.19 para.9
s.103, see *Granada UK Rental & Retail Ltd
v Pensions Regulator* [2014] Pens. L.R. 17
(UT (Tax)), Judge Timothy Herrington
s.117, enabling: SI 2014/1711
s.121, enabling: SI 2014/1664
s.126, applied: 2014 c.19 Sch.20 para.17
s.126, enabling: SI 2014/1711
s.127, see *Olympic Airlines SA, Re* [2013]
EWCA Civ 643, [2014] 1 W.L.R. 1401 (CA
(Civ Div)), Moore-Bick LJ
s.134, applied: SI 2014/1711 Reg.44
s.135, referred to: SI 2014/1711 Reg.72
s.135, enabling: SI 2014/1711
s.138, applied: 2014 c.19 Sch.20 para.14
s.138, enabling: SI 2014/1711
s.143, applied: SI 2014/1711 Reg.44
s.144, applied: SI 2014/1711 Reg.44
s.146, enabling: SI 2014/1711
s.149, applied: SI 2014/1711 Reg.15
s.151, applied: SI 2014/1711 Reg.44
s.152, applied: SI 2014/1711 Reg.44
s.153, applied: SI 2014/1711 Reg.16,
Reg.52, Reg.55
s.154, applied: SI 2014/1711 Reg.15
s.154, referred to: SI 2014/1711 Reg.16
s.156, applied: SI 2014/1711 Reg.44
s.158, applied: SI 2014/1711 Reg.44, Reg.55
s.160, applied: SI 2014/1711 Reg.44
s.161, enabling: SI 2014/1711
s.162, applied: 2014 c.19 Sch.20 para.13
s.170, applied: SI 2014/1711 Reg.53
s.175, see *West of England Ship Owners
Insurance Services Ltd Retirement Benefits
Scheme, Re* [2014] EWHC 20 (Ch), [2014]
Pens. L.R. 167 (Ch D (Companies Ct)),
Andrew Spink, Q.C.
s.177, applied: SI 2014/10 Art.3

s.178, applied: SI 2014/10, SI 2014/10 Art.2
s.178, enabling: SI 2014/10
s.179, applied: SI 2014/1711 Reg.45,
Reg.46, Reg.47, Reg.49
s.179, enabling: SI 2014/1711
s.181, see *West of England Ship Owners*
Insurance Services Ltd Retirement Benefits
Scheme, Re [2014] EWHC 20 (Ch), [2014]
Pens. L.R. 167 (Ch D (Companies Ct)),
Andrew Spink, Q.C.
s.181, applied: SI 2014/1711 Reg.47
s.181A, applied: SI 2014/1711 Reg.47
s.189, applied: SI 2014/1711 Reg.50
s.189, enabling: SI 2014/1711
s.190, enabling: SI 2014/1711
s.207, see *West of England Ship Owners*
Insurance Services Ltd Retirement Benefits
Scheme, Re [2014] EWHC 20 (Ch), [2014]
Pens. L.R. 167 (Ch D (Companies Ct)),
Andrew Spink, Q.C.
s.207, enabling: SI 2014/1711
s.217, see *West of England Ship Owners*
Insurance Services Ltd Retirement Benefits
Scheme, Re [2014] EWHC 20 (Ch), [2014]
Pens. L.R. 167 (Ch D (Companies Ct)),
Andrew Spink, Q.C.
s.223, applied: SI 2014/1711 Reg.69
s.224, applied: SI 2014/1711 Reg.23,
Reg.65, Reg.67, Reg.69
s.225, applied: SI 2014/1711 Reg.69
s.226, applied: SI 2014/1711 Reg.69
s.227, applied: SI 2014/1711 Reg.68, Reg.69
s.232, enabling: SI 2014/1711
s.256, amended: 2014 c.19 Sch.17 para.21,
Sch.18 para.10
s.258, amended: 2014 c.19 Sch.13 para.73
s.258, enabling: SI 2014/540
s.286, applied: SI 2014/1711 Reg.70
s.286, varied: SI 2014/1711 Reg.72
s.286, enabling: SI 2014/837
s.287, applied: SI 2014/1711 Reg.77
s.288, applied: SI 2014/1711 Reg.77
s.289, applied: SI 2014/1711 Reg.77
s.292A, repealed: 2014 c.19 s.38
s.299, disapplied: SI 2014/3229 Sch.2 para.6
s.315, enabling: SI 2014/10, SI 2014/540, SI
2014/837, SI 2014/1636, SI 2014/1664, SI
2014/1711
s.316, amended: 2014 c.19 Sch.20 para.5
s.316, applied: SI 2014/837

s.317, applied: SI 2014/540, SI 2014/837, SI
2014/1664, SI 2014/1711
s.318, enabling: SI 2014/540, SI 2014/837,
SI 2014/1664, SI 2014/1711
s.322, enabling: SI 2014/1636
Sch.2 Part 2 para.5A, added: 2014 c.19
Sch.19 para.10
Sch.2 Part 2 para.9, amended: 2014 c.19
Sch.19 para.10
Sch.5 Part 3, applied: SI 2014/1711 Reg.43,
Reg.52, Reg.54, Reg.55, Reg.56
Sch.5 Part 3, varied: SI 2014/1711 Reg.53,
Reg.57
Sch.7, applied: 2014 c.19 Sch.20 para.12, SI
2014/1711 Reg.43, Reg.52, Reg.54, Reg.55,
Reg.56
Sch.7, varied: SI 2014/1711 Reg.53, Reg.57
Sch.7 para.3, applied: 2014 c.19 Sch.20
para.8, SI 2014/1711 Reg.59
Sch.7 para.4, applied: 2014 c.19 Sch.20
para.10
Sch.7 para.5, applied: SI 2014/1711 Reg.59
Sch.7 para.11, applied: 2014 c.19 Sch.20
para.8
Sch.7 para.12, enabling: SI 2014/1711
Sch.7 para.13, applied: 2014 c.19 Sch.20
para.10
Sch.7 para.15, applied: 2014 c.19 Sch.20
para.8
Sch.7 para.17, enabling: SI 2014/1711
Sch.7 para.18, applied: 2014 c.19 Sch.20
para.10
Sch.7 para.20, enabling: SI 2014/1711
Sch.7 para.24, amended: 2014 c.19 Sch.20
para.6
Sch.7 para.25, applied: 2014 c.19 Sch.20
para.11
Sch.7 para.25A, applied: 2014 c.19 Sch.20
para.11
Sch.7 para.25E, applied: 2014 c.19 Sch.20
para.12
Sch.7 para.26, amended: 2014 c.19 s.51,
Sch.20 para.2, Sch.20 para.6
Sch.7 para.26, applied: 2014 c.19 Sch.20
para.8, Sch.20 para.12, SI 2014/10 Art.4
Sch.7 para.26, enabling: SI 2014/10
Sch.7 para.26A, added: 2014 c.19 Sch.20
para.3
Sch.7 para.26A, referred to: 2014 c.19
Sch.20 para.22

Sch.7 para.26A, varied: 2014 c.19 Sch.20
para.8, Sch.20 para.12
Sch.7 para.27, amended: 2014 c.19 Sch.20
para.6
Sch.7 para.27, enabling: SI 2014/10

2005

4. Constitutional Reform Act 2005
s.40, see *Bank Mellat v HM Treasury* [2014]
A.C. 700 (SC), Lord Neuberger PSC
s.40, repealed (in part): 2014 asp 18 Sch.5
para.33
s.52, applied: SI 2014/590
s.52, enabling: SI 2014/590
s.54, applied: SI 2014/590
s.85, enabling: SI 2014/2040
s.108, applied: SI 2014/1919 Reg.17
s.110, varied: SI 2014/1919 Reg.22
s.111, applied: SI 2014/1919 Reg.19, Reg.23
s.113, applied: SI 2014/1919 Reg.19
s.113, varied: SI 2014/1919 Reg.22
s.115, enabling: SI 2014/1919
s.116, enabling: SI 2014/1919
s.117, enabling: SI 2014/1919
s.118, applied: SI 2014/1919 Reg.3
s.120, enabling: SI 2014/1919
s.121, enabling: SI 2014/1919
Sch.1 Part 1 para.2, applied: SI 2014/840, SI
2014/3297
Sch.1 Part 2 para.22, repealed: 2014 c.6 s.18
Sch.7 para.4, amended: 2014 c.14 Sch.7,
2014 c.18 s.10
Sch.14 Part 3, amended: SI 2014/2040 Art.2,
SI 2014/3248 Sch.3 Part 2

**5. Income Tax (Trading and Other Income)
Act 2005**
Part 4, applied: SI 2014/1506 Reg.12
Part 4 c.3, amended: 2014 c.26 Sch.8 para.55
Part 4 c.4, amended: 2014 c.26 Sch.8 para.61
Part 6 c.9, amended: 2014 c.26 Sch.8 para.66
s.34, see *Revenue and Customs
Commissioners v Healy* [2014] S.T.C. 384
(UT (Tax)), Judge Timothy Herrington; see
*Vaccine Research LP v Revenue and
Customs Commissioners* [2014] UKUT 389
(TCC), [2014] B.T.C. 525 (UT (Tax)), Sales
J
s.54, amended: SI 2014/1283 Sch.1 para.5
s.94A, amended: 2014 c.26 Sch.8 para.140

s.94A, applied: 2014 c.26 Sch.8 para.156,
Sch.8 para.214
s.94A, repealed (in part): 2014 c.26 Sch.8
para.140
s.94AA, added: 2014 c.26 Sch.17 para.3
s.272, amended: 2014 c.26 Sch.17 para.3
s.367, amended: 2014 c.14 Sch.4 para.93
s.369, amended: 2014 c.14 Sch.4 para.93, SI
2014/992 Art.8
s.379, amended: 2014 c.14 Sch.4 para.94
s.379, substituted: 2014 c.14 Sch.4 para.94
s.382, amended: 2014 c.26 Sch.8 para.54
s.392, amended: 2014 c.26 Sch.8 para.56
s.394, amended: 2014 c.26 Sch.8 para.57
s.395, amended: 2014 c.26 Sch.8 para.58
s.396, amended: 2014 c.26 Sch.8 para.59
s.405, amended: 2014 c.26 Sch.8 para.62
s.407, amended: 2014 c.26 Sch.8 para.63
s.408, amended: 2014 c.26 Sch.8 para.64
s.483, amended: 2014 c.14 Sch.4 para.95
s.609, see *Eclipse Film Partners No.35 LLP
v Revenue and Customs Commissioners*
[2014] S.T.C. 1114 (UT (Tax)), Sales J
s.628, amended: SI 2014/3062 Art.2
s.694, enabling: SI 2014/654, SI 2014/1450
s.695, enabling: SI 2014/654, SI 2014/1450
s.695A, enabling: SI 2014/654
s.696, enabling: SI 2014/654
s.699, enabling: SI 2014/1450
s.701, enabling: SI 2014/654, SI 2014/1450
s.703, amended: 2014 c.26 Sch.8 para.141
s.744, amended: 2014 c.6 Sch.2 para.68
s.749, amended: SI 2014/992 Art.8
s.770, amended: 2014 c.26 Sch.8 para.67
s.806, amended: 2014 c.6 Sch.2 para.69
s.850, amended: 2014 c.26 Sch.17 para.7
s.850C, added: 2014 c.26 Sch.17 para.7
s.850D, added: 2014 c.26 Sch.17 para.7
s.863A, added: 2014 c.26 Sch.17 para.1
s.863A, applied: SI 2014/3159 Reg.3, Reg.4
s.863A, enabling: SI 2014/3159
s.863B, referred to: SI 2014/3159 Reg.3,
Reg.4
s.863G, applied: SI 2014/3159 Reg.3, Reg.4
s.863G, referred to: SI 2014/3159 Reg.3,
Reg.4
s.863G, enabling: SI 2014/3159
s.863H, added: 2014 c.26 Sch.17 para.15
7. Finance Act 2005
see *Leeds Design Innovation Centre Ltd v
Revenue and Customs Commissioners*

[2014] UKFTT 9 (TC), [2014] S.F.T.D. 681
(FTT (Tax)), Judge Rachel Short
s.83, applied: SI 2014/1831 Art.3
s.97, repealed (in part): 2014 c.26 s.114
Sch.1A para.1, amended: 2014 c.26 s.291
Sch.1A para.3, amended: 2014 c.26 s.291
Sch.1A para.4, amended: 2014 c.26 s.291

9. Mental Capacity Act 2005
see *A Local Authority v K* [2013] EWHC
242 (COP), [2014] 1 F.C.R. 209 (CP), Cobb
J; see *A Local Authority v P* [2014] EWHC
87 (COP), [2014] 2 F.L.R. 1051 (CP), Baker
J; see *A Local Authority v SY* [2013] EWHC
3485 (COP), [2014] C.O.P.L.R. 1 (CP),
Keehan J; see *A London Borough v G*
[2014] EWHC 485 (COP), [2014]
C.O.P.L.R. 292 (CP), Russell J; see *AB
(Revocation of Enduring Power of Attorney),
Re* [2014] EWCOP 12, [2014] W.T.L.R.
1303 (CP), Senior Judge Denzil Lush; see
Cheshire West and Chester Council v P
[2014] UKSC 19, [2014] A.C. 896 (SC),
Lord Neuberger PSC; see *M (An Adult)
(Capacity: Consent to Sexual Relations), Re*
[2014] EWCA Civ 37, [2014] 3 W.L.R. 409
(CA (Civ Div)), Sir Brian Leveson PQBD;
see *Meek, Re* [2014] EWCOP 1, [2014]
C.O.P.L.R. 535 (CP), Judge Hodge Q.C.; see
NHS Trust v FG [2014] EWCOP 30, [2014]
C.O.P.L.R. 598 (CP), Keehan J; see *O
(Court of Protection: Jurisdiction), Re*
[2013] EWHC 3932 (COP), [2014] Fam.
197 (CP), Sir James Munby PFD; see
*Practice Guidance (CP: Deprivation of
Liberty: Guidance for Providers of
Children's Homes and Residential Special
Schools)* [2014] C.O.P.L.R. 243 (CP), Sir
James Munby PFD; see *Westminster City
Council v Sykes* (2014) 17 C.C.L. Rep. 139
(CP), District Judge Eldergill
applied: 2014 c.6 s.80, 2014 c.14 s.36, 2014
c.23 s.18, s.32, s.47, s.80, SI 2014/1652
Reg.5, Reg.16, SI 2014/1794 Reg.9, SI
2014/2871 Reg.5, Reg.7, SI 2014/2936
Reg.8, Reg.9, Reg.11
referred to: 2014 c.23 s.80
Pt 1., see *M (An Adult) (Capacity: Consent
to Sexual Relations), Re* [2014] EWCA Civ
37, [2014] 3 W.L.R. 409 (CA (Civ Div)), Sir
Brian Leveson PQBD

s.1, see *AA (Compulsorily Detained Patient:
Elective Caesarean), Re* [2012] EWHC 4378
(COP), [2014] 2 F.L.R. 237 (CP), Mostyn J;
see *Fischer v Diffley* [2013] EWHC 4567
(Ch), [2014] C.O.P.L.R. 212 (Ch D), Judge
Dight; see *G (An Adult) (Costs), Re* [2014]
EWCOP 5, [2014] C.O.P.L.R. 432 (CP), Sir
James Munby PFD; see *Lewis v Lewis*
[2014] EWCA Civ 412, [2014] W.T.L.R.
1021 (CA (Civ Div)), Richards LJ; see
Meek, Re [2014] EWCOP 1, [2014]
C.O.P.L.R. 535 (CP), Judge Hodge Q.C.; see
*RB (A Patient) v Brighton and Hove City
Council* [2014] EWCA Civ 561, [2014]
C.O.P.L.R. 629 (CA (Civ Div)), Arden LJ
s.2, see *A Local Authority v TZ* [2014]
EWHC 973 (COP), [2014] C.O.P.L.R. 159
(CP), Baker J; see *A London Borough v G*
[2014] EWHC 485 (COP), [2014]
C.O.P.L.R. 292 (CP), Russell J; see *Fischer
v Diffley* [2013] EWHC 4567 (Ch), [2014]
C.O.P.L.R. 212 (Ch D), Judge Dight; see *G
(An Adult), Re* [2014] EWCOP 1361, [2014]
C.O.P.L.R. 416 (CP), Sir James Munby
PFD; see *Islington LBC v QR* [2014]
EWCOP 26, (2014) 17 C.C.L. Rep. 344
(CP), District Judge Batten; see *R. v A*
[2014] EWCA Crim 299, [2014] 1 W.L.R.
2469 (CA (Crim Div)), Macur LJ; see *York
City Council v C* [2013] EWCA Civ 478,
[2014] Fam. 10 (CA (Civ Div)), Richards LJ
s.2, applied: SI 2014/2843 Reg.7, SI
2014/2936 Reg.8
s.3, see *A Local Authority v TZ* [2014]
EWHC 973 (COP), [2014] C.O.P.L.R. 159
(CP), Baker J; see *A London Borough v G*
[2014] EWHC 485 (COP), [2014]
C.O.P.L.R. 292 (CP), Russell J; see *G (An
Adult), Re* [2014] EWCOP 1361, [2014]
C.O.P.L.R. 416 (CP), Sir James Munby
PFD; see *M (An Adult) (Capacity: Consent
to Sexual Relations), Re* [2014] EWCA Civ
37, [2014] 3 W.L.R. 409 (CA (Civ Div)), Sir
Brian Leveson PQBD; see *R. v A* [2014]
EWCA Crim 299, [2014] 1 W.L.R. 2469
(CA (Crim Div)), Macur LJ; see *RB (A
Patient) v Brighton and Hove City Council*
[2014] EWCA Civ 561, [2014] C.O.P.L.R.
629 (CA (Civ Div)), Arden LJ; see *York
City Council v C* [2013] EWCA Civ 478,
[2014] Fam. 10 (CA (Civ Div)), Richards LJ

s.4, see *A NHS Foundation Trust v X* [2014]
EWCOP 35, (2014) 140 B.M.L.R. 41 (CP),
Cobb J; see *AK (Gift Application), Re*
[2014] C.O.P.L.R. 180 (CP), Senior Judge
Denzil Lush; see *G (An Adult) (Costs), Re*
[2014] EWCOP 5, [2014] C.O.P.L.R. 432
(CP), Sir James Munby PFD; see *M (Best
Interests: Deprivation of Liberty), Re* [2013]
EWHC 3456 (COP), [2014] C.O.P.L.R. 35
(CP), Peter Jackson J; see *NHS Trust v FG*
[2014] EWCOP 30, [2014] C.O.P.L.R. 598
(CP), Keehan J; see *NHS v VT* [2014]
C.O.P.L.R. 44 (CP), Hayden J; see *RB (A
Patient) v Brighton and Hove City Council*
[2014] EWCA Civ 561, [2014] C.O.P.L.R.
629 (CA (Civ Div)), Arden LJ; see *UF v X
County Council* [2014] EWCOP 18, (2014)
17 C.C.L. Rep. 445 (CP), Cobb J
s.4, applied: SI 2014/2936 Reg.14
s.5, applied: SI 2014/2936 Reg.11
s.7, see *Aster Healthcare Ltd v Shafi* [2014]
EWHC 77 (QB), [2014] 3 All E.R. 283
(QBD), Andrews J; see *Blankley v Central
Manchester and Manchester Children's
University Hospitals NHS Trust* [2014]
EWHC 168 (QB), [2014] 1 W.L.R. 2683
(QBD), Phillips J
s.9, see *E, Re* [2014] EWCOP 27, [2014]
Med. L.R. 417 (CP), Senior Judge Denzil
Lush
s.12, see *DP (Revocation of Lasting Power
of Attorney), Re* [2014] C.O.P.L.R. 188
(CP), Senior Judge Denzil Lush
s.15, see *A v M* [2013] EWHC 4020 (COP),
[2014] C.O.P.L.R. 114 (CP), Parker J
s.16, see *ACCG v MN* [2013] EWHC 3859
(COP), [2014] C.O.P.L.R. 11 (CP), Eleanor
King J
s.16, applied: 2014 c.23 s.80
s.16A, see *An NHS Trust v A* [2013] EWHC
2442 (COP), [2014] Fam. 161 (CP), Baker J
s.17, see *PB v RB* [2014] C.O.P.L.R. 481
(CP), Judge Altman
s.18, see *A Local Authority v P* [2014]
EWHC 87 (COP), [2014] 2 F.L.R. 1051
(CP), Baker J
s.20, see *PB v RB* [2014] C.O.P.L.R. 481
(CP), Judge Altman
s.21A, see *A (A Patient) (Court of
Protection: Appeal), Re* [2013] EWCA Civ
1661, [2014] 1 W.L.R. 3773 (CA (Civ Div)),

Moses LJ; see *UF v X County Council*
[2014] EWCOP 18, (2014) 17 C.C.L. Rep.
445 (CP), Cobb J; see *UF, Re* [2013]
EWHC 4289 (COP), [2014] C.O.P.L.R. 93
(CP), Charles J; see *X (Deprivation of
Liberty), Re* [2014] EWCOP 25, [2014]
C.O.P.L.R. 674 (CP), Sir James Munby PFD
s.22, see *DP (Revocation of Lasting Power
of Attorney), Re* [2014] C.O.P.L.R. 188
(CP), Senior Judge Denzil Lush; see *OB, Re*
[2014] EWCOP 28, [2014] W.T.L.R. 1705
(CP), Senior Judge Denzil Lush
s.23, see *OB, Re* [2014] EWCOP 28, [2014]
W.T.L.R. 1705 (CP), Senior Judge Denzil
Lush
s.24, see *Nottinghamshire Healthcare NHS
Trust v RC* [2014] EWCOP 1317, [2014]
C.O.P.L.R. 468 (CP), Mostyn J
s.25, see *E, Re* [2014] EWCOP 27, [2014]
Med. L.R. 417 (CP), Senior Judge Denzil
Lush
s.26, see *E, Re* [2014] EWCOP 27, [2014]
Med. L.R. 417 (CP), Senior Judge Denzil
Lush
s.27, see *M (An Adult) (Capacity: Consent to
Sexual Relations), Re* [2014] EWCA Civ 37,
[2014] 3 W.L.R. 409 (CA (Civ Div)), Sir
Brian Leveson PQBD
s.27, applied: SI 2014/1530 Reg.65
s.27, disapplied: 2014 c.6 s.80
s.44, see *R. v A* [2014] EWCA Crim 299,
[2014] 1 W.L.R. 2469 (CA (Crim Div)),
Macur LJ; see *R. v Kenyon (Lindsay)* [2013]
EWCA Crim 2123, [2014] 1 Cr. App. R. (S.)
71 (CA (Crim Div)), Laws LJ
s.46, see *A (A Patient) (Court of Protection:
Appeal), Re* [2013] EWCA Civ 1661, [2014]
1 W.L.R. 3773 (CA (Civ Div)), Moses LJ;
see *A Local Authority v K* [2013] EWHC
242 (COP), [2014] 1 F.C.R. 209 (CP), Cobb
J
s.53, see *A (A Patient) (Court of Protection:
Appeal), Re* [2013] EWCA Civ 1661, [2014]
1 W.L.R. 3773 (CA (Civ Div)), Moses LJ
s.54, applied: 2014 c.12 s.180, SI 2014/590
s.54, enabling: SI 2014/590
s.58, applied: 2014 c.12 s.180
s.64, see *Cheshire West and Chester Council
v P* [2014] UKSC 19, [2014] A.C. 896 (SC),
Lord Neuberger PSC

Sch.A1, see *A (A Patient) (Court of Protection: Appeal), Re* [2013] EWCA Civ 1661, [2014] 1 W.L.R. 3773 (CA (Civ Div)), Moses LJ; see *Practice Guidance (CP: Deprivation of Liberty: Guidance for Providers of Children's Homes and Residential Special Schools)* [2014] C.O.P.L.R. 243 (CP), Sir James Munby PFD; see *RB (A Patient) v Brighton and Hove City Council* [2014] EWCA Civ 561, [2014] C.O.P.L.R. 629 (CA (Civ Div)), Arden LJ; see *Westminster City Council v Sykes* (2014) 17 C.C.L. Rep. 139 (CP), District Judge Eldergill

Sch.A1 Pt 1 para.2, see *UF, Re* [2013] EWHC 4289 (COP), [2014] C.O.P.L.R. 93 (CP), Charles J

Sch.A1 Pt 3 para.15, see *RB (A Patient) v Brighton and Hove City Council* [2014] EWCA Civ 561, [2014] C.O.P.L.R. 629 (CA (Civ Div)), Arden LJ

Sch.A1 Pt 10, see *UF, Re* [2013] EWHC 4289 (COP), [2014] C.O.P.L.R. 93 (CP), Charles J

Sch.A1 Part 13 para.185, amended: SI 2014/560 Sch.1 para.30

Sch.4 Pt 1 para.3, see *AB (Revocation of Enduring Power of Attorney), Re* [2014] EWCOP 12, [2014] W.T.L.R. 1303 (CP), Senior Judge Denzil Lush

Sch.4 Pt 5 para.16, see *AB (Revocation of Enduring Power of Attorney), Re* [2014] EWCOP 12, [2014] W.T.L.R. 1303 (CP), Senior Judge Denzil Lush

Sch.6 para.11, repealed: 2014 c.14 Sch.7

10. Public Services Ombudsman (Wales) Act 2005

applied: SI 2014/1794 Reg.11
s.16, amended: 2014 c.29 s.4
s.24, amended: 2014 c.29 s.4
s.29, amended: 2014 c.29 s.4
s.30, amended: 2014 c.29 s.4
Sch.1 para.7, amended: 2014 c.29 s.4
Sch.1 para.14, amended: 2014 c.29 s.4
Sch.2 para.1, amended: 2014 c.29 s.4
Sch.3, amended: 2014 c.21 Sch.10 para.18
Sch.6 para.59, repealed: 2014 c.2 Sch.1 Part 2

11. Commissioners for Revenue and Customs Act 2005

referred to: SI 2014/2418 Sch.1

s.5, applied: SI 2014/3294 Art.4
s.15, amended: 2014 c.29 s.7
s.15, substituted: 2014 c.29 s.7
s.17, amended: 2014 c.29 s.7
s.18, see *R. (on the application of Ingenious Media Holdings Plc) v Revenue and Customs Commissioners* [2013] EWHC 3258 (Admin), [2014] S.T.C. 673 (QBD (Admin)), Sales J; see *R. (on the application of Privacy International) v Revenue and Customs Commissioners* [2014] EWHC 1475 (Admin), [2014] B.T.C. 25 (QBD (Admin)), Green J; see *R. (on the application of Revenue and Customs Commissioners) v HM Coroner for Liverpool* [2014] EWHC 1586 (Admin), [2014] 3 W.L.R. 1660 (DC), Gross LJ
s.18, amended: 2014 c.29 s.7, SI 2014/3294 Art.4
s.18, applied: 2014 c.26 s.287
s.18, referred to: 2014 c.28 s.27
s.18, repealed (in part): SI 2014/3294 Art.4
s.19, amended: SI 2014/834 Sch.1 para.6, SI 2014/3294 Art.4
s.19, applied: 2014 c.21 s.69, 2014 c.28 s.28
s.20, see *R. (on the application of Revenue and Customs Commissioners) v HM Coroner for Liverpool* [2014] EWHC 1586 (Admin), [2014] 3 W.L.R. 1660 (DC), Gross LJ
s.20, applied: 2014 c.28 s.28
s.20, referred to: 2014 c.21 s.69
s.21, amended: SI 2014/834 Sch.1 para.7
s.29, amended: SI 2014/834 Sch.1 para.8
s.34, repealed: SI 2014/834 Sch.1 para.9
s.38, applied: SI 2014/834 Art.5, Art.6, Art.7
s.40, amended: 2014 c.29 s.7, SI 2014/834 Sch.1 para.10
s.40, applied: SI 2014/834 Art.9
s.40, repealed (in part): SI 2014/834 Sch.1 para.10
s.41, repealed: SI 2014/834 Sch.1 para.11
s.42, repealed: SI 2014/834 Sch.1 para.12
s.49, repealed: SI 2014/834 Sch.1 para.13
s.51, amended: 2014 c.29 s.7
Sch.1 para.26, amended: 2014 c.6 Sch.7 para.64
Sch.1 para.26, referred to: SI 2014/1640 Art.19
Sch.1 para.26, varied: SI 2014/1640 Art.19
Sch.1 para.26A, repealed: 2014 c.6 Sch.7 para.64

Sch.1 para.26B, added: 2014 c.6 Sch.7
para.64
Sch.3, repealed: SI 2014/834 Sch.1 para.14
Sch.4 para.30, repealed: SI 2014/834 Sch.1
para.15
Sch.4 para.41, repealed: SI 2014/834 Sch.1
para.15
Sch.4 para.69, repealed: SI 2014/834 Sch.1
para.15
Sch.4 para.77, repealed: SI 2014/834 Sch.1
para.15
Sch.4 para.97, repealed: SI 2014/834 Sch.1
para.15

12. Inquiries Act 2005

see *Kennedy v Information Commissioner*
[2014] UKSC 20, [2014] 2 W.L.R. 808 (SC),
Lord Neuberger JSC
applied: SI 2014/1492 Reg.6
s.1, see *R. (on the application of Litvinenko)
v Secretary of State for the Home
Department* [2014] EWHC 194 (Admin),
[2014] H.R.L.R. 6 (DC), Richards LJ

14. Railways Act 2005

s.33, disapplied: SI 2014/864 Art.8
s.38, enabling: SI 2014/3244

**15. Serious Organised Crime and Police Act
2005**

s.33, see *Tchenguiz v Director of the Serious
Fraud Office* [2013] EWHC 2128 (QB),
[2014] 1 W.L.R. 1476 (QBD), Eder J
s.60, amended: SI 2014/834 Sch.2 para.41
s.60, repealed (in part): SI 2014/834 Sch.2
para.41
s.71, repealed (in part): SI 2014/834 Sch.2
para.42
s.73, see *R. v Hankin (Thomas David)* [2013]
EWCA Crim 749, [2014] 1 Cr. App. R. (S.)
7 (CA (Crim Div)), Roderick Evans J
s.73, applied: SI 2014/1610 r.42_1, r.42_11
s.74, applied: SI 2014/1610 r.74_1, r.68_1
s.75, applied: SI 2014/1610 r.16_1
s.82, amended: 2014 c.12 s.178
s.82, repealed (in part): 2014 c.12 s.178
s.91, repealed: 2014 c.12 s.178
s.93, repealed (in part): 2014 c.12 s.178
s.128, enabling: SI 2014/411, SI 2014/2263
s.139, repealed (in part): 2014 c.12 Sch.11
para.50
s.140, repealed (in part): 2014 c.12 Sch.11
para.50
s.141, repealed: 2014 c.12 Sch.11 para.50

s.172, repealed (in part): 2014 c.12 s.178
Sch.4 para.111, repealed: 2014 c.2 Sch.1
Part 2
Sch.5, repealed: 2014 c.12 s.178
Sch.5 para.12, amended: SI 2014/834 Sch.2
para.43
Sch.7 Part 1 para.36, repealed: 2014 c.12
Sch.11 para.50
Sch.10 Part 1 para.3, repealed (in part): 2014
c.12 Sch.11 para.50

**16. Clean Neighbourhoods and Environment
Act 2005**

Part 6 c.1, applied: 2014 c.12 s.75
s.2, repealed: 2014 c.12 Sch.11 para.50
s.20, repealed (in part): 2014 c.12 Sch.11
para.50
s.21, repealed: 2014 c.12 Sch.11 para.50
s.31, repealed: 2014 c.12 Sch.11 para.50
s.55, repealed: 2014 c.12 Sch.11 para.42
s.66, repealed: 2014 c.12 Sch.11 para.42
Sch.4 para.7, repealed: 2014 c.12 Sch.11
para.50
Sch.4 para.13, repealed: 2014 c.12 Sch.11
para.50
Sch.4 para.16, repealed: 2014 c.12 Sch.11
para.50

17. Drugs Act 2005

s.20, repealed: 2014 c.12 Sch.11 para.50
Sch.1 para.7, repealed: 2014 c.12 Sch.11
para.50

18. Education Act 2005

Part 1, applied: SI 2014/699 Sch.1 para.3, SI
2014/1836 Sch.1 para.2, SI 2014/2006 Sch.1
para.3, SI 2014/2235 Sch.1 para.2, SI
2014/2236 Sch.1 para.2, SI 2014/2237 Sch.1
para.2, SI 2014/2238 Sch.1 para.2, SI
2014/2295 Sch.1 para.3, SI 2014/2631 Sch.1
para.3, SI 2014/2719 Sch.1 para.3, SI
2014/3246 Sch.1 para.3, SI 2014/3247 Sch.1
para.3
s.5, applied: SI 2014/3352 Reg.1, Sch.2
para.9
s.10, applied: SI 2014/1530 Reg.17
s.19, enabling: SI 2014/2922
s.28, applied: SI 2014/2677 Reg.6
s.28, enabling: SI 2014/1212
s.39, enabling: SI 2014/1212
s.42, enabling: SI 2014/1212
s.50, enabling: SI 2014/1212
s.55, enabling: SI 2014/1212
s.56, enabling: SI 2014/1212

s.57, enabling: SI 2014/1212
s.120, enabling: SI 2014/1212
Sch.4 para.6, enabling: SI 2014/1212
Sch.6 para.2, enabling: SI 2014/1212
Sch.6 para.3, enabling: SI 2014/1212
Sch.14 para.18, repealed: 2014 c.2 Sch.1
Part 2

19. Gambling Act 2005
see *Aspinalls Club Ltd v Revenue and
Customs Commissioners* [2013] EWCA Civ
1464, [2014] 2 W.L.R. 1574 (CA (Civ Div)),
Moses LJ
applied: 2014 c.17 s.1, s.2, s.5, SI 2014/1641
Art.4
s.33, amended: 2014 c.17 s.1
s.36, amended: 2014 c.17 s.1
s.67, amended: 2014 c.26 Sch.28 para.23
s.80, disapplied: SI 2014/1641 Art.4
s.100, applied: SI 2014/1641 Art.5, Art.6,
Art.7
s.104, disapplied: SI 2014/1641 Art.4
s.110, varied: SI 2014/1641 Art.4
s.111, disapplied: SI 2014/1641 Art.4
s.112, disapplied: SI 2014/1641 Art.4
s.118, amended: 2014 c.26 Sch.28 para.24
s.118, applied: 2014 c.26 Sch.27 para.3
s.118A, added: 2014 c.26 Sch.28 para.25
s.119, amended: 2014 c.26 Sch.28 para.26
s.119, applied: 2014 c.26 Sch.27 para.6
s.236, enabling: SI 2014/45
s.331, repealed: 2014 c.17 s.3
s.332, repealed (in part): 2014 c.17 s.3
s.333, amended: 2014 c.17 s.3, s.4
s.333, repealed (in part): 2014 c.17 s.3, s.4
s.355, applied: SI 2014/45
s.355, enabling: SI 2014/45
s.361, repealed (in part): 2014 c.17 s.3
Sch.6 Part 2, amended: SI 2014/892 Sch.1
para.166

22. Finance (No.2) Act 2005
s.3, see *Reed Employment Ltd v Revenue and
Customs Commissioners* [2014] EWCA Civ
32, [2014] S.T.C. 1026 (CA (Civ Div)),
Arden LJ
s.8, amended: 2014 c.19 Sch.12 para.50
s.9, amended: 2014 c.19 Sch.12 para.51
s.17, applied: 2014 c.26 s.114
s.17, enabling: SI 2014/518, SI 2014/685, SI
2014/1932
s.18, enabling: SI 2014/685

2006

3. Equality Act 2006
s.39, enabling: SI 2014/406
Sch.1 Part 2 para.21, repealed (in part): SI
2014/406 Art.3
Sch.1 Part 2 para.22, repealed (in part): SI
2014/406 Art.3
Sch.1 Part 2 para.29, repealed (in part): SI
2014/406 Art.3
Sch.1 Part 2 para.30, repealed (in part): SI
2014/406 Art.3
Sch.1 Part 5, repealed: SI 2014/406 Art.3
Sch.1 Part 5 para.49, applied: SI 2014/406
Art.2
Sch.1 Part 5 para.60, applied: SI 2014/406

5. Transport (Wales) Act 2006
s.8, enabling: SI 2014/595
s.9, enabling: SI 2014/595

11. Terrorism Act 2006
s.2, see *R. v Gul (Mohammed)* [2014] A.C.
1260 (SC), Lord Neuberger JSC
s.5, see *Guardian News and Media Ltd v AB*
Times, June 18, 2014 (CA (Crim Div)),
Gross LJ

**12. London Olympic Games and Paralympic
Games Act 2006**
s.3, repealed: SI 2014/3184 Sch.1 para.2
s.4, repealed: SI 2014/3184 Sch.1 para.2
s.5, repealed: SI 2014/3184 Sch.1 para.2
s.6, repealed: SI 2014/3184 Sch.1 para.2
s.7, repealed: SI 2014/3184 Sch.1 para.2
s.8, repealed: SI 2014/3184 Sch.1 para.2
s.9, applied: SI 2014/3184
s.9, enabling: SI 2014/3184
s.20, repealed (in part): SI 2014/3184 Sch.1
para.3
s.22, amended: SI 2014/3184 Sch.1 para.4
s.22, repealed (in part): SI 2014/3184 Sch.1
para.4
s.23, repealed: SI 2014/3184 Sch.1 para.2
s.25, repealed (in part): SI 2014/3184 Sch.1
para.2
s.26, amended: SI 2014/3184 Sch.1 para.5
s.26, repealed (in part): SI 2014/3184 Sch.1
para.5
s.28, amended: SI 2014/3184 Sch.1 para.6
s.28, repealed (in part): SI 2014/3184 Sch.1
para.6
s.29, repealed: SI 2014/3184 Sch.1 para.2
s.31A, repealed: SI 2014/3184 Sch.1 para.2

s.31B, repealed: SI 2014/3184 Sch.1 para.2

s.31C, repealed: SI 2014/3184 Sch.1 para.2

s.31D, repealed: SI 2014/3184 Sch.1 para.2

s.31E, repealed: SI 2014/3184 Sch.1 para.2

s.37, amended: SI 2014/3184 Sch.1 para.7

s.37, repealed (in part): SI 2014/3184 Sch.1 para.7

s.41, repealed (in part): SI 2014/3184 Sch.1 para.2

Sch.1, repealed: SI 2014/3184 Sch.1 para.2

Sch.1 Part 2 para.18, applied: SI 2014/3184 Art.4, Art.5

Sch.2, repealed: SI 2014/3184 Sch.1 para.2

13. Immigration, Asylum and Nationality Act 2006

Commencement Orders: 2014 c.22 Sch.9 para.57, para.60

applied: SI 2014/2604 Sch.1 para.2

s.1, repealed: 2014 c.22 Sch.9 para.60

s.11, repealed (in part): 2014 c.22 Sch.9 para.60

s.12, amended: 2014 c.22 Sch.9 para.57

s.13, repealed: 2014 c.22 Sch.9 para.57

s.15, amended: 2014 c.22 Sch.9 para.61

s.15, applied: SI 2014/1262 Art.2, SI 2014/1820 Art.6

s.15, enabling: SI 2014/1183, SI 2014/1262

s.17, amended: 2014 c.22 s.44

s.18, amended: 2014 c.22 s.45

s.19, applied: SI 2014/1183, SI 2014/1183 Art.10

s.19, enabling: SI 2014/1183

s.20, applied: SI 2014/1262

s.20, enabling: SI 2014/1183, SI 2014/1262

s.23, applied: SI 2014/1183, SI 2014/1183 Art.11

s.23, referred to: SI 2014/1183

s.23, enabling: SI 2014/1183

s.25, enabling: SI 2014/1183

s.47, see *Ahmadi (S.47 Decision: Validity: Sapkota: Afghanistan), Re* [2013] EWCA Civ 512, [2014] 1 W.L.R. 401 (CA (Civ Div)), Sullivan LJ; see *Patel v Secretary of State for the Home Department* [2014] A.C. 651 (SC), Lord Mance JSC; see *Rahman v Secretary of State for the Home Department* [2014] EWCA Civ 11, [2014] 1 W.L.R. 3574 (CA (Civ Div)), Richards LJ

s.47, amended: 2014 c.22 Sch.1 para.2

s.47, repealed (in part): 2014 c.22 Sch.9 para.5, Sch.9 para.60

s.48, repealed: 2014 c.22 Sch.9 para.7

s.51, repealed: 2014 c.22 Sch.9 para.74

s.51, enabling: SI 2014/205, SI 2014/581, SI 2014/922, SI 2014/2398

s.52, applied: SI 2014/205

s.52, enabling: SI 2014/205, SI 2014/581, SI 2014/922, SI 2014/2398

s.55, amended: 2014 c.22 Sch.9 para.57

s.57, repealed (in part): 2014 c.22 Sch.9 para.60

Sch.1 para.2, repealed: 2014 c.22 Sch.9 para.60

Sch.1 para.10, repealed: 2014 c.22 Sch.9 para.60

Sch.1 para.11, repealed: 2014 c.22 Sch.9 para.57, Sch.9 para.60

Sch.1 para.13, repealed: 2014 c.22 Sch.9 para.60

Sch.1 para.14, repealed (in part): 2014 c.22 Sch.9 para.60

Sch.2 para.6, repealed: 2014 c.22 Sch.9 para.76

15. Identity Cards Act 2006

s.7, applied: SI 2014/3263 Sch.3 para.1

s.25, see *R. v Mateta (Koshi Pitshou)* [2013] EWCA Crim 1372, [2014] 1 W.L.R. 1516 (CA (Crim Div)), Leveson LJ; see *SXH v Crown Prosecution Service* [2014] EWCA Civ 90, [2014] 1 W.L.R. 3238 (CA (Civ Div)), Pitchford LJ

16. Natural Environment and Rural Communities Act 2006

Sch.7 para.11, repealed: SI 2014/1924 Sch.1

18. Work and Families Act 2006

s.3, repealed: 2014 c.6 Sch.7 para.66

s.9, varied: 2014 c.6 s.126

s.11, repealed (in part): 2014 c.6 Sch.7 para.67

s.11, varied: 2014 c.6 s.126

Sch.1 para.1, repealed (in part): 2014 c.6 Sch.7 para.68

Sch.1 para.1, varied: 2014 c.6 s.126

Sch.1 para.2, varied: 2014 c.6 s.126

Sch.1 para.3, varied: 2014 c.6 s.126

Sch.1 para.4, varied: 2014 c.6 s.126

Sch.1 para.5, varied: 2014 c.6 s.126

Sch.1 para.11, repealed: 2014 c.6 Sch.7 para.68

Sch.1 para.12, varied: 2014 c.6 s.126

Sch.1 para.13, varied: 2014 c.6 s.126

Sch.1 para.14, varied: 2014 c.6 s.126

Sch.1 para.15, varied: 2014 c.6 s.126
Sch.1 para.16, varied: 2014 c.6 s.126
Sch.1 para.17, repealed: 2014 c.6 Sch.7
para.68
Sch.1 para.18, varied: 2014 c.6 s.126
Sch.1 para.19, repealed: 2014 c.6 Sch.7
para.68
Sch.1 para.19, varied: 2014 c.6 s.126
Sch.1 para.20, varied: 2014 c.6 s.126
Sch.1 para.22, repealed: 2014 c.6 Sch.7
para.68
Sch.1 para.24, varied: 2014 c.6 s.126
Sch.1 para.25, varied: 2014 c.6 s.126
Sch.1 para.27, varied: 2014 c.6 s.126
Sch.1 para.28, varied: 2014 c.6 s.126
Sch.1 para.29, varied: 2014 c.6 s.126
Sch.1 para.38, repealed (in part): 2014 c.6
Sch.7 para.68
Sch.1 para.39, varied: 2014 c.6 s.126
Sch.1 para.40, varied: 2014 c.6 s.126
Sch.1 para.45, varied: 2014 c.6 s.126
Sch.1 para.46, varied: 2014 c.6 s.126
Sch.1 para.47, varied: 2014 c.6 s.126
Sch.1 para.48, varied: 2014 c.6 s.126
Sch.1 para.49, repealed: 2014 c.6 Sch.7
para.68
Sch.1 para.50, varied: 2014 c.6 s.126
Sch.1 para.51, varied: 2014 c.6 s.126
Sch.1 para.52, varied: 2014 c.6 s.126
Sch.1 para.53, varied: 2014 c.6 s.126
Sch.1 para.54, varied: 2014 c.6 s.126
Sch.1 para.55, varied: 2014 c.6 s.126
Sch.1 para.56, varied: 2014 c.6 s.126
Sch.1 para.57, repealed (in part): 2014 c.6
Sch.7 para.68
Sch.1 para.58, varied: 2014 c.6 s.126
Sch.1 para.59, varied: 2014 c.6 s.126
Sch.1 para.60, varied: 2014 c.6 s.126

20. Children and Adoption Act 2006
Sch.2 para.12, repealed: 2014 c.6 s.18

21. Childcare Act 2006
Part 3, applied: 2014 c.6 s.100, SI 2014/1132
Sch.7 para.9, SI 2014/1920 Sch.1 para.1,
Sch.1 para.2, SI 2014/1922 Reg.13, SI
2014/2709 Sch.2 para.9
Part 3 c.2, applied: SI 2014/1920 Sch.1
para.14, Sch.1 para.16, Sch.2 para.5, SI
2014/1922 Reg.3, Reg.5, Reg.6, Reg.10,
Reg.13, Reg.14, SI 2014/2319 Reg.4
Part 3 c.2A, added: 2014 c.6 Sch.4 para.13

Part 3 c.3, applied: SI 2014/1920 Sch.1
para.15, Sch.1 para.17, Sch.2 para.5, SI
2014/1922 Reg.3, Reg.5, Reg.6, Reg.10,
Reg.13, Reg.14, SI 2014/2319 Reg.4
Part 3 c.3A, added: 2014 c.6 Sch.4 para.26
Part 3 c.4, applied: SI 2014/1920 Sch.2
para.5, SI 2014/1922 Reg.3, Reg.5, Reg.6,
Reg.14
Part 3 c.5, amended: 2014 c.6 Sch.4 para.43
s.1, applied: SI 2014/840 Sch.1
s.7, applied: SI 2014/2147 Reg.2, Reg.3,
Reg.4, Reg.5, Reg.8, SI 2014/3283 Sch.1
para.32
s.7, enabling: SI 2014/1705, SI 2014/2147
s.7A, added: 2014 c.6 s.87
s.7A, enabling: SI 2014/2147
s.9A, added: 2014 c.6 s.87
s.9A, enabling: SI 2014/2147
s.11, repealed: 2014 c.6 s.86
s.12, enabling: SI 2014/1921
s.13, enabling: SI 2014/2319
s.18, see *R. (on the application of West) v
Rhondda Cynon Taff CBC* [2014] EWHC
2134 (Admin), [2014] E.L.R. 396 (QBD
(Admin)), Supperstone J
s.22, see *R. (on the application of West) v
Rhondda Cynon Taff CBC* [2014] EWHC
2134 (Admin), [2014] E.L.R. 396 (QBD
(Admin)), Supperstone J
s.32, amended: 2014 c.6 Sch.4 para.2
s.33, amended: 2014 c.6 Sch.4 para.4
s.33, enabling: SI 2014/913
s.34, amended: 2014 c.6 Sch.4 para.5
s.34, enabling: SI 2014/913
s.35, amended: 2014 c.6 Sch.4 para.6
s.35, applied: SI 2014/1920 Sch.1 para.12
s.35, enabling: SI 2014/912, SI 2014/1921
s.36, amended: 2014 c.6 Sch.4 para.7
s.36, enabling: SI 2014/912, SI 2014/1921
s.37, amended: 2014 c.6 Sch.4 para.8
s.37, applied: SI 2014/1922 Reg.13
s.37A, added: 2014 c.6 Sch.4 para.9
s.37A, enabling: SI 2014/1921
s.38, amended: 2014 c.6 Sch.4 para.10
s.39, applied: SI 2014/1920 Sch.2 para.16,
SI 2014/2319 Reg.3
s.39, enabling: SI 2014/912, SI 2014/913
s.40, applied: SI 2014/2147 Reg.2
s.42, applied: SI 2014/913
s.42, enabling: SI 2014/913
s.43, applied: SI 2014/912

s.43, enabling: SI 2014/912
s.44, amended: 2014 c.6 Sch.4 para.11
s.44, enabling: SI 2014/912, SI 2014/913
s.49, amended: 2014 c.6 s.85, Sch.4 para.12
s.51A, applied: SI 2014/1920 Reg.3, Reg.4, Reg.7
s.51A, enabling: SI 2014/1920
s.51B, applied: SI 2014/1920 Reg.5, Reg.11
s.51B, enabling: SI 2014/1920
s.51C, applied: 2014 c.6 s.137, SI 2014/1920 Reg.5
s.51D, enabling: SI 2014/1920
s.51F, applied: 2014 c.6 s.137
s.52, amended: 2014 c.6 Sch.4 para.15
s.52, enabling: SI 2014/913
s.53, amended: 2014 c.6 Sch.4 para.16
s.53, enabling: SI 2014/913
s.54, amended: 2014 c.6 Sch.4 para.17
s.54, applied: SI 2014/1920 Sch.1 para.13
s.54, enabling: SI 2014/912, SI 2014/1921
s.55, amended: 2014 c.6 Sch.4 para.18
s.55, enabling: SI 2014/912, SI 2014/1921
s.56, amended: 2014 c.6 Sch.4 para.19
s.56, applied: SI 2014/1922 Reg.14
s.56A, added: 2014 c.6 Sch.4 para.20
s.56A, enabling: SI 2014/1921
s.57, amended: 2014 c.6 Sch.4 para.21
s.57A, added: 2014 c.6 Sch.4 para.22
s.58, amended: 2014 c.6 Sch.4 para.23
s.59, amended: 2014 c.6 Sch.4 para.24
s.59, applied: SI 2014/912, SI 2014/1920 Sch.2 para.16, SI 2014/1921
s.59, enabling: SI 2014/912, SI 2014/1921
s.60, amended: 2014 c.6 Sch.4 para.25
s.61A, applied: SI 2014/1920 Reg.3, Reg.4, Reg.8
s.61A, enabling: SI 2014/1920
s.61B, applied: SI 2014/1920 Reg.5
s.61B, enabling: SI 2014/1920
s.61D, applied: 2014 c.6 s.137, SI 2014/1920 Reg.5
s.61E, enabling: SI 2014/1920
s.61G, applied: 2014 c.6 s.137
s.64, applied: SI 2014/1922 Reg.13, Reg.14
s.65, amended: 2014 c.6 Sch.4 para.28
s.65A, added: 2014 c.6 Sch.4 para.29
s.65A, enabling: SI 2014/1921
s.66, amended: 2014 c.6 Sch.4 para.30
s.67, amended: 2014 c.6 Sch.4 para.31
s.67, applied: SI 2014/912, SI 2014/1920 Sch.2 para.16, SI 2014/1921

s.67, enabling: SI 2014/912, SI 2014/1921
s.68, amended: 2014 c.6 Sch.4 para.33
s.69, amended: 2014 c.6 Sch.4 para.34
s.69, enabling: SI 2014/1921
s.69A, added: 2014 c.6 Sch.4 para.35
s.69A, applied: 2014 c.6 s.137
s.69A, enabling: SI 2014/1922
s.69B, added: 2014 c.6 Sch.4 para.36
s.69B, enabling: SI 2014/1922
s.69C, applied: 2014 c.6 s.137
s.70, amended: 2014 c.6 Sch.4 para.37
s.70A, added: 2014 c.6 Sch.4 para.38
s.71, amended: 2014 c.6 Sch.4 para.39
s.72, amended: 2014 c.6 Sch.4 para.40
s.73, amended: 2014 c.6 Sch.4 para.41
s.74, amended: 2014 c.6 Sch.4 para.42
s.75, amended: 2014 c.6 Sch.4 para.44
s.75, applied: SI 2014/1922 Reg.3, Reg.13, Reg.14
s.75, enabling: SI 2014/1921
s.76, amended: 2014 c.6 Sch.4 para.45
s.76A, added: 2014 c.6 Sch.4 para.46
s.76A, enabling: SI 2014/1921
s.76B, applied: 2014 c.6 s.137
s.77, amended: 2014 c.6 Sch.4 para.47
s.78, amended: 2014 c.6 Sch.4 para.48
s.78A, added: 2014 c.6 Sch.4 para.49
s.79, amended: 2014 c.6 Sch.4 para.50
s.79, applied: SI 2014/840 r.16
s.80, applied: SI 2014/840 Sch.1
s.82, amended: 2014 c.6 Sch.4 para.51
s.83, amended: 2014 c.6 Sch.4 para.52
s.83, enabling: SI 2014/1921
s.83A, added: 2014 c.6 Sch.4 para.53
s.83A, amended: 2014 c.28 s.29
s.83A, applied: SI 2014/1920 Reg.14, Reg.15
s.83A, referred to: SI 2014/1920 Reg.14, Reg.15
s.83A, enabling: SI 2014/1920
s.84, amended: 2014 c.6 Sch.4 para.54
s.84, enabling: SI 2014/1921
s.84A, added: 2014 c.6 Sch.4 para.55
s.84A, applied: SI 2014/1920 Reg.16, Reg.17, Reg.20
s.84A, enabling: SI 2014/1920
s.85, amended: 2014 c.6 Sch.4 para.56
s.87, amended: 2014 c.6 Sch.4 para.57
s.89, amended: 2014 c.6 Sch.4 para.58
s.89, enabling: SI 2014/1920
s.90, amended: 2014 c.6 Sch.4 para.59

s.90, enabling: SI 2014/1921
s.92, enabling: SI 2014/1920
s.93, amended: 2014 c.6 Sch.4 para.60
s.94, amended: 2014 c.6 Sch.4 para.61
s.98, amended: 2014 c.6 Sch.4 para.62
s.99, amended: 2014 c.6 Sch.4 para.63
s.99, enabling: SI 2014/3197
s.104, enabling: SI 2014/912, SI 2014/913,
SI 2014/1705, SI 2014/1921, SI 2014/1922,
SI 2014/2147, SI 2014/2319, SI 2014/3197
Sch.1, applied: SI 2014/840 Sch.1
Sch.2 para.21, repealed: 2014 c.6 Sch.3
para.16
Sch.2 para.22, repealed (in part): 2014 c.6
Sch.3 para.20

22. Electoral Administration Act 2006
Commencement Orders: SI 2014/1809 Art.2
s.10, applied: SI 2014/1116 Art.1, SI
2014/1880 Art.1
s.63, amended: 2014 c.13 s.2
s.63, applied: 2014 c.13 s.26
s.77, enabling: SI 2014/1809
s.78, amended: 2014 c.13 s.18, SI 2014/1116
Art.2

25. Finance Act 2006
s.173, applied: SI 2014/1356, SI 2014/1357,
SI 2014/1358, SI 2014/1359, SI 2014/1360,
SI 2014/1875, SI 2014/1876, SI 2014/1879,
SI 2014/1881, SI 2014/3274, SI 2014/3275
s.173, enabling: SI 2014/1356, SI
2014/1357, SI 2014/1358, SI 2014/1359, SI
2014/1360, SI 2014/1875, SI 2014/1876, SI
2014/1879, SI 2014/1881, SI 2014/3274, SI
2014/3275

26. Commons Act 2006
Commencement Orders: SI 2014/3026 Art.3
see *Church Commissioners for England v
Hampshire CC* [2014] EWCA Civ 634,
[2014] 1 W.L.R. 4555 (CA (Civ Div)),
Arden LJ
applied: SI 2014/3038 Reg.3, Reg.49
Part 1, applied: SI 2014/3102 Art.4
Part 1, disapplied: SI 2014/3038 Reg.5,
Reg.10
Part 2, applied: SI 2014/3038 Reg.46
s.1, referred to: SI 2014/3038 Sch.8 para.3
s.3, enabling: SI 2014/3038
s.4, applied: SI 2014/3038 Reg.5
s.5, applied: SI 2014/3038 Reg.5, Reg.10
s.6, applied: SI 2014/3038 Reg.35, Sch.4
para.1, Sch.5, Sch.6, Sch.7 para.2

s.7, applied: SI 2014/3038 Reg.35, Sch.4
para.2, Sch.4 para.3
s.8, applied: SI 2014/3038 Reg.17, Reg.26,
Sch.4 para.2, Sch.4 para.3, Sch.4 para.5,
Sch.4 para.7, Sch.4 para.8, Sch.4 para.12,
Sch.4 para.13
s.8, enabling: SI 2014/3038
s.9, applied: SI 2014/219 Art.3
s.9, enabling: SI 2014/219
s.10, applied: SI 2014/3038 Sch.4 para.4,
Sch.5, Sch.6, Sch.7 para.2
s.11, applied: SI 2014/3038 Sch.4 para.3,
Sch.4 para.5
s.11, referred to: SI 2014/3038 Sch.4 para.5
s.11, enabling: SI 2014/3038
s.12, applied: SI 2014/3038 Sch.4 para.6
s.13, applied: SI 2014/3038 Sch.4 para.3,
Sch.4 para.7
s.14, enabling: SI 2014/3038
s.15, see *Church Commissioners for
England v Hampshire CC* [2013] EWHC
1933 (Admin), [2014] A.C.D. 21 (QBD
(Admin)), Collins J; see *Church
Commissioners for England v Hampshire
CC* [2014] EWCA Civ 634, [2014] 1 W.L.R.
4555 (CA (Civ Div)), Arden LJ; see *R. (on
the application of Barkas) v North Yorkshire
CC* [2014] UKSC 31, [2014] 2 W.L.R. 1360
(SC), Lord Neuberger PSC; see *R. (on the
application of Newhaven Port and
Properties Ltd) v East Sussex CC* [2013]
EWCA Civ 276, [2014] Q.B. 186 (CA (Civ
Div)), Richards LJ; see *R. (on the
application of Newhaven Port and
Properties Ltd) v Secretary of State for the
Environment, Food and Rural Affairs* [2013]
EWCA Civ 673, [2014] Q.B. 282 (CA (Civ
Div)), Lloyd LJ
s.15, applied: SI 2014/257 Art.4, SI
2014/3038 Reg.19, Reg.21, Reg.54, Sch.4
para.9, Sch.4 para.10, Sch.5, Sch.6, Sch.7
para.2
s.15C, applied: SI 2014/257 Art.4
s.15C, enabling: SI 2014/257
s.16, applied: SI 2014/3038 Reg.48
s.17, applied: SI 2014/3038 Reg.7, Reg.48
s.17, enabling: SI 2014/3038
s.19, applied: SI 2014/3026 Art.3, SI
2014/3038 Reg.1, Reg.21, Reg.26, Sch.4
para.11, Sch.5, Sch.6, Sch.7 para.2, Sch.8
para.1, Sch.8 para.2

s.19, referred to: SI 2014/3038 Sch.4 para.11

s.20, applied: SI 2014/3038 Reg.52

s.20, referred to: SI 2014/3038 Reg.53

s.20, enabling: SI 2014/3038

s.21, referred to: SI 2014/3038 Reg.53

s.21, enabling: SI 2014/3038

s.24, enabling: SI 2014/3038

s.56, enabling: SI 2014/3026

s.59, enabling: SI 2014/219, SI 2014/257, SI 2014/3026, SI 2014/3038

s.61, varied: SI 2014/3026 Art.4

s.61, enabling: SI 2014/219

Sch.1, applied: SI 2014/3038 Sch.7 para.2

Sch.1A, amended: SI 2014/257 Art.3

Sch.1A, referred to: SI 2014/257 Art.4

Sch.1 para.1, applied: SI 2014/3038 Reg.45, Sch.4 para.3, Sch.4 para.12, Sch.6

Sch.1 para.1, referred to: SI 2014/3038 Reg.45, Sch.4 para.12

Sch.1 para.1, enabling: SI 2014/3038

Sch.1 para.2, enabling: SI 2014/219

Sch.1 para.3, applied: SI 2014/3038 Sch.4 para.3, Sch.4 para.13, Sch.6

Sch.2, applied: SI 2014/3038 Reg.1, Reg.18, Reg.21, Reg.37, Sch.4 para.14, Sch.7 para.2, SI 2014/3102 Art.4

Sch.2 para.2, applied: SI 2014/3038 Sch.4 para.14, Sch.5, Sch.6

Sch.2 para.2, referred to: SI 2014/3038 Sch.4 para.14

Sch.2 para.2, enabling: SI 2014/3038

Sch.2 para.3, applied: SI 2014/3038 Sch.4 para.14

Sch.2 para.3, referred to: SI 2014/3038 Sch.4 para.14

Sch.2 para.3, enabling: SI 2014/3038

Sch.2 para.4, applied: SI 2014/3038 Reg.26, Sch.4 para.14

Sch.2 para.4, referred to: SI 2014/3038 Sch.4 para.14

Sch.2 para.4, enabling: SI 2014/3038

Sch.2 para.5, referred to: SI 2014/3038 Sch.4 para.14

Sch.2 para.5, enabling: SI 2014/3038

Sch.2 para.6, applied: SI 2014/3026 Art.3, SI 2014/3038 Reg.1, Sch.8 para.1, Sch.8 para.2

Sch.2 para.6, referred to: SI 2014/3038 Sch.4 para.14

Sch.2 para.6, enabling: SI 2014/3038

Sch.2 para.7, referred to: SI 2014/3038 Sch.4 para.14

Sch.2 para.7, enabling: SI 2014/3038

Sch.2 para.8, referred to: SI 2014/3038 Sch.4 para.14

Sch.2 para.8, enabling: SI 2014/3038

Sch.2 para.9, referred to: SI 2014/3038 Sch.4 para.14

Sch.2 para.9, enabling: SI 2014/3038

Sch.2 para.10, enabling: SI 2014/3038

Sch.3, applied: SI 2014/3038 Reg.41, Reg.42

Sch.3, referred to: SI 2014/3038 Reg.39

Sch.3 para.2, applied: SI 2014/3038 Reg.17, Reg.18, Reg.26, Reg.38, Reg.41, Sch.4 para.15, Sch.4 para.16, Sch.4 para.17, Sch.4 para.18, Sch.4 para.19, Sch.4 para.20, Sch.4 para.21, Sch.5, Sch.6

Sch.3 para.2, referred to: SI 2014/3038 Reg.42

Sch.3 para.2, enabling: SI 2014/3038

Sch.3 para.3, applied: SI 2014/3038 Reg.42

Sch.3 para.3, disapplied: SI 2014/3038 Reg.42

Sch.3 para.4, applied: SI 2014/3038 Reg.17, Reg.26, Reg.41, Sch.6

Sch.3 para.4, enabling: SI 2014/3038

Sch.3 para.5, enabling: SI 2014/3038

Sch.3 para.8, applied: SI 2014/3038 Reg.47

Sch.3 para.8, enabling: SI 2014/3038

28. Health Act 2006

Part 1 c.1, varied: 2014 c.6 s.91

s.5, amended: 2014 c.6 s.95

s.6, applied: 2014 c.6 s.91

s.7, applied: 2014 c.6 s.91

s.9, amended: 2014 c.6 s.95

s.9, varied: 2014 c.6 s.91

s.10, amended: 2014 c.6 s.95

s.11, disapplied: 2014 c.6 s.91

s.11, varied: 2014 c.6 s.91

s.79, amended: 2014 c.6 s.95

Sch.1, varied: 2014 c.6 s.91

Sch.1 para.17, added: 2014 c.6 s.95

Sch.2, varied: 2014 c.6 s.91

Sch.2 para.10, disapplied: 2014 c.6 s.91

Sch.8 para.39, repealed: 2014 c.2 Sch.1 Part 2

29. Compensation Act 2006

applied: SI 2014/3316 Sch.1 para.1, Sch.1 para.2, Sch.1 para.3, Sch.1 para.4

Part 2, applied: SI 2014/3307 Art.4

s.5, applied: SI 2014/3316 Reg.4

s.9, enabling: SI 2014/3239

s.15, amended: SI 2014/892 Sch.1 para.170

s.15, enabling: SI 2014/3239
Sch.1 para.1, enabling: SI 2014/3239
Sch.1 para.2, enabling: SI 2014/3239
Sch.1 para.8, enabling: SI 2014/3239
Sch.1 para.9, enabling: SI 2014/3239
Sch.1 para.10, enabling: SI 2014/3239
Sch.1 para.11, enabling: SI 2014/3239
Sch.1 para.13, enabling: SI 2014/3239
Sch.1 para.14, enabling: SI 2014/3239
Sch.1 para.16, enabling: SI 2014/3239

30. Commissioner for Older People (Wales) Act 2006

s.2, amended: 2014 c.29 s.4
s.4, amended: 2014 c.29 s.4
s.6, amended: 2014 c.29 s.4
s.7, amended: 2014 c.29 s.4
s.15, amended: 2014 c.29 s.4
s.28, amended: 2014 c.29 s.4

31. International Development (Reporting and Transparency) Act 2006

s.4, amended: 2014 c.9 s.2

32. Government of Wales Act 2006

Part 2, amended: 2014 c.29 s.4
Part 4A c.1, added: 2014 c.29 s.6
Part 4A c.2, added: 2014 c.29 s.8
Part 4A c.3, added: 2014 c.29 s.15
Part 4A c.4, added: 2014 c.29 s.18
s.3, amended: 2014 c.29 s.1
s.7, amended: 2014 c.29 s.2
s.9, amended: 2014 c.29 s.2
s.11, amended: 2014 c.29 s.2
s.16, amended: 2014 c.29 s.3
s.17A, added: 2014 c.29 s.3
s.37, amended: 2014 c.29 s.4
s.45, amended: 2014 c.29 s.4
s.46, amended: 2014 c.29 s.5
s.48, applied: 2014 c.29 s.13
s.52, amended: 2014 c.29 s.4
s.59, enabling: SI 2014/1890
s.63, applied: SI 2014/1924
s.83, amended: 2014 c.29 s.4
s.89, amended: 2014 c.29 s.4
s.90, amended: 2014 c.29 s.4
s.108, see *Attorney General for England and Wales v Counsel General for Wales* [2014] UKSC 43, [2014] 1 W.L.R. 2622 (SC), Lord Neuberger PSC
s.108, amended: 2014 c.29 s.6
s.111, amended: 2014 c.29 s.6
s.116A, amended: 2014 c.29 s.8
s.116D, referred to: 2014 c.29 s.14

s.116L, applied: 2014 c.29 s.15
s.116M, added: 2014 c.29 s.17
s.116N, applied: 2014 c.29 s.18
s.118, applied: 2014 c.29 s.23
s.121, amended: 2014 c.29 s.20
s.121, applied: 2014 c.29 s.21
s.122, amended: 2014 c.29 s.20
s.122A, added: 2014 c.29 s.20
s.122A, applied: 2014 c.29 s.21
s.129, amended: 2014 c.29 s.4
s.131, applied: 2014 c.29 s.21
s.133, amended: 2014 c.29 s.4
s.146, amended: 2014 c.29 s.4
s.147, amended: 2014 c.29 s.4
s.148, amended: 2014 c.29 s.4
s.155A, added: 2014 c.29 s.10
s.158, amended: 2014 c.29 s.6
s.159, amended: 2014 c.29 s.4, s.6
Sch.2 para.3, amended: 2014 c.29 s.4
Sch.3 Part 3 para.12, amended: 2014 c.29 s.4
Sch.7, see *Attorney General for England and Wales v Counsel General for Wales* [2014] UKSC 43, [2014] 1 W.L.R. 2622 (SC), Lord Neuberger PSC
Sch.7 Part 1 para.4, amended: 2014 c.29 s.6
Sch.7 Part 1 para.12, amended: 2014 c.12
Sch.11 para.43
Sch.7 Part 1 para.13, amended: 2014 c.29 s.22
Sch.7 Part 1 para.14, amended: 2014 c.29 s.4
Sch.7 Part 1 para.16A, added: 2014 c.29 s.6
Sch.7 Part 1 para.19, amended: 2014 c.21
Sch.7 para.135
Sch.7 Part 2 para.2, amended: 2014 c.29 s.4
Sch.7 Part 2 para.4A, added: 2014 c.29 s.7
Sch.7 Part 2 para.5, amended: 2014 c.29 s.22
Sch.7 Part 3 para.7A, added: 2014 c.29 s.7
Sch.10 para.3, amended: 2014 c.29 s.4
Sch.10 para.20, amended: 2014 c.29 s.4
Sch.10 para.29, amended: 2014 c.29 s.4
Sch.10 para.31, amended: 2014 c.29 s.4
Sch.10 para.34, amended: 2014 c.29 s.4
Sch.10 para.35, amended: 2014 c.29 s.4
Sch.10 para.36, amended: 2014 c.29 s.4
Sch.10 para.37, amended: 2014 c.29 s.4
Sch.10 para.39, amended: 2014 c.29 s.4
Sch.10 para.40, amended: 2014 c.29 s.4
Sch.10 para.45, amended: 2014 c.29 s.4
Sch.10 para.56, amended: 2014 c.29 s.4
Sch.10 para.63, amended: 2014 c.29 s.4
Sch.10 para.64, amended: 2014 c.29 s.4

Sch.10 para.65, amended: 2014 c.29 s.4
Sch.10 para.69, amended: 2014 c.29 s.4
Sch.10 para.70, amended: 2014 c.29 s.4
Sch.10 para.73, amended: 2014 c.29 s.4
Sch.10 para.76, amended: 2014 c.29 s.4
Sch.10 para.79, amended: 2014 c.29 s.4
Sch.10 para.80, amended: 2014 c.29 s.4
Sch.10 para.86, amended: 2014 c.29 s.4
Sch.10 para.87, amended: 2014 c.29 s.4
Sch.10 para.88, amended: 2014 c.29 s.4
Sch.11 para.30, applied: SI 2014/1515
Sch.11 para.42A, amended: 2014 c.29 s.4
Sch.11 para.43, amended: 2014 c.29 s.4
Sch.11 para.63, amended: 2014 c.29 s.4

33. Northern Ireland (Miscellaneous Provisions) Act 2006

s.1, enabling: SI 2014/1116, SI 2014/1880
s.7, repealed: 2014 c.13 s.20
s.14, substituted: 2014 c.13 s.1
s.15A, added: 2014 c.13 s.1
Sch.1, amended: 2014 c.13 s.1
Sch.4 Part 1 para.7, repealed (in part): 2014 c.13 s.16

35. Fraud Act 2006

see *R. v Pennock (Angela)* [2014] EWCA Crim 598, [2014] 2 Cr. App. R. 10 (CA (Crim Div)), Aikens LJ
s.1, see *R. v Augunas (Darius)* [2013] EWCA Crim 2046, [2014] 1 Cr. App. R. 17 (CA (Crim Div)), McCombe LJ; see *R. v White (Anthony Alan)* [2014] EWCA Crim 714, [2014] 2 Cr. App. R. 14 (CA (Crim Div)), Sir Brian Leveson PQBD
s.2, see *R. v White (Anthony Alan)* [2014] EWCA Crim 714, [2014] 2 Cr. App. R. 14 (CA (Crim Div)), Sir Brian Leveson PQBD
s.3, see *R. v White (Anthony Alan)* [2014] EWCA Crim 714, [2014] 2 Cr. App. R. 14 (CA (Crim Div)), Sir Brian Leveson PQBD
s.6, see *R. v Augunas (Darius)* [2013] EWCA Crim 2046, [2014] 1 Cr. App. R. 17 (CA (Crim Div)), McCombe LJ; see *R. v Sakalauskas (Gytis)* [2013] EWCA Crim 2278, [2014] 1 W.L.R. 1204 (CA (Crim Div)), Goldring LJ

36. Wireless Telegraphy Act 2006

s.8, applied: SI 2014/953 Reg.4
s.8, enabling: SI 2014/953, SI 2014/1484
s.12, enabling: SI 2014/1295
s.13, enabling: SI 2014/1295
s.29, enabling: SI 2014/774

s.111, amended: SI 2014/892 Sch.1 para.171
s.111, repealed (in part): SI 2014/892 Sch.1 para.171
s.122, applied: SI 2014/774, SI 2014/953, SI 2014/1295, SI 2014/1484
s.122, enabling: SI 2014/1295

38. Violent Crime Reduction Act 2006

s.1, repealed: 2014 c.12 Sch.11 para.44
s.6, applied: 2014 c.12 s.33, SI 2014/1610 r.50_1, r.50_2
s.6, repealed: 2014 c.12 Sch.11 para.44
s.8, repealed (in part): 2014 c.12 Sch.11 para.44, Sch.11 para.50
s.9, repealed (in part): 2014 c.12 Sch.11 para.44, Sch.11 para.44
s.10, applied: SI 2014/1610 r.63_1
s.10, repealed (in part): 2014 c.12 Sch.11 para.44
s.26, repealed: 2014 c.12 Sch.11 para.50
s.27, applied: 2014 c.12 s.42
s.27, repealed: 2014 c.12 Sch.11 para.45
s.56, repealed (in part): 2014 c.12 Sch.11 para.80
s.59, repealed (in part): 2014 c.12 Sch.11 para.50

40. Education and Inspections Act 2006

Commencement Orders: SI 2014/2380 Art.2
Part 2, applied: SI 2014/3352 Sch.1 para.10
Part 8 c.4, applied: 2014 c.2 Sch.11 para.2
s.15, enabling: SI 2014/2650
s.16, amended: 2014 c.6 Sch.3 para.81
s.60, see *R. (on the application of Uplands Junior School Governing Body) v Leicester City Council* [2013] EWHC 4128 (Admin), [2014] E.L.R. 143 (QBD (Admin)), Thirlwall J
s.60, applied: SI 2014/3352 Sch.1 para.9
s.60A, applied: SI 2014/3352 Sch.1 para.9
s.63, applied: SI 2014/3352 Sch.1 para.9
s.64, applied: SI 2014/3352 Sch.1 para.9
s.65, applied: SI 2014/3352 Sch.1 para.9
s.66, applied: SI 2014/3352 Sch.1 para.9
s.69, see *R. (on the application of Warren Comprehensive School) v Secretary of State for Education* [2014] EWHC 2252 (Admin), [2014] E.L.R. 530 (QBD (Admin)), Supperstone J
s.88, applied: SI 2014/1132 Reg.63, SI 2014/2709 Reg.22
s.100, enabling: SI 2014/3216

s.114, enabling: SI 2014/261, SI 2014/498, SI 2014/1103, SI 2014/1354, SI 2014/1560, SI 2014/1877, SI 2014/2921

s.117, amended: 2014 c.6 s.116

s.117, referred to: SI 2014/2418 Sch.1

s.118, applied: SI 2014/2418 Sch.1

s.119, amended: 2014 c.6 s.116

s.120, repealed: 2014 c.6 s.116

s.135, referred to: SI 2014/2418 Sch.1

s.140, applied: SI 2014/1530 Reg.17

s.143, applied: SI 2014/2418 Sch.1

s.155, enabling: SI 2014/410, SI 2014/670

s.166, applied: SI 2014/2068 Sch.2 para.4

s.181, enabling: SI 2014/410, SI 2014/670, SI 2014/3216

s.188, enabling: SI 2014/2380

Sch.2, applied: SI 2014/3352 Sch.1 para.10

Sch.6, see *R. (on the application of Warren Comprehensive School) v Secretary of State for Education* [2014] EWHC 2252 (Admin), [2014] E.L.R. 530 (QBD (Admin)), Supperstone J

Sch.13 para.1, amended: 2014 c.2 Sch.12 para.69

Sch.13 para.1, repealed (in part): 2014 c.2 Sch.12 para.69

Sch.13 para.8, amended: 2014 c.2 Sch.12 para.69

Sch.13 para.10, amended: 2014 c.2 Sch.12 para.69

Sch.14 para.26, repealed: 2014 c.2 Sch.1 Part 2

Sch.14 para.30, repealed: 2014 c.2 Sch.1 Part 2

41. National Health Service Act 2006

see *Coombs v Dorset NHS Primary Care Trust* [2013] EWCA Civ 471, [2014] 1 W.L.R. 111 (CA (Civ Div)), Rix LJ

applied: 2014 c.2 Sch.11 para.2, 2014 c.23 s.6, s.22, Sch.3 para.2, Sch.6 para.2, SI 2014/512 Sch.1 para.19, SI 2014/2871 Reg.10, SI 2014/2936 Sch.1 para.10, Sch.2 para.7, Sch.2 para.8

referred to: 2014 c.23 s.6, Sch.1 para.1

Part 6, applied: SI 2014/2936 Sch.2 para.7

Part 7, applied: SI 2014/2936 Sch.2 para.8

s.1, see *R. (on the application of A) v Secretary of State for Health* [2014] EWHC 1364 (Admin), [2014] Med. L.R. 246 (QBD (Admin)), King J

s.1F, amended: 2014 c.23 s.97

s.1F, applied: 2014 c.23 s.97

s.1G, applied: 2014 c.23 s.105

s.1H, applied: 2014 c.23 s.105

s.1H, referred to: 2014 c.23 s.101, Sch.5 para.15

s.3, see *R. (on the application of A) v Secretary of State for Health* [2014] EWHC 1364 (Admin), [2014] Med. L.R. 246 (QBD (Admin)), King J; see *R. (on the application of Whapples) v Birmingham CrossCity Clinical Commissioning Group* [2014] EWHC 2647 (Admin), [2014] P.T.S.R. 1413 (QBD (Admin)), Sales J

s.3, applied: 2014 c.2 s.44, 2014 c.6 s.28, SI 2014/2821 Reg.2

s.3, referred to: SI 2014/3099 Reg.2

s.3B, applied: SI 2014/91, SI 2014/452

s.3B, enabling: SI 2014/91, SI 2014/452

s.4, applied: SI 2014/512 Sch.1 para.18

s.6E, enabling: SI 2014/1611

s.9, see *NHS Commissioning Board (NHS England) v Bargain Dentist.Com* [2014] EWHC 1994 (QB), [2014] Med. L.R. 301 (QBD), Elisabeth Laing J; see *Pitalia v NHS Commissioning Board* [2014] EWCA Civ 474, (2014) 138 B.M.L.R. 89 (CA (Civ Div)), Aikens LJ

s.9, amended: 2014 c.23 Sch.5 para.16

s.12, applied: SI 2014/512 Sch.1 para.19

s.12A, applied: 2014 c.6 s.49, SI 2014/2871 Reg.10

s.13A, applied: 2014 c.23 s.101, SI 2014/3487

s.13A, enabling: SI 2014/3487

s.13M, amended: 2014 c.23 s.97

s.13N, amended: 2014 c.23 s.3

s.13Q, amended: 2014 c.23 s.120

s.14D, applied: SI 2014/531 Sch.1, SI 2014/3282 Sch.1 para.2

s.14Z, amended: 2014 c.23 s.97

s.14Z1, amended: 2014 c.23 s.3

s.14Z2, amended: 2014 c.23 s.120

s.14Z3, amended: SI 2014/2436 Art.2

s.14Z9, amended: SI 2014/2436 Art.3

s.14Z9, substituted: SI 2014/2436 Art.3

s.25, applied: 2014 c.2 Sch.2 para.24B, 2014 c.23 s.111, SI 2014/358, SI 2014/360, SI 2014/531 Sch.1, SI 2014/1903, SI 2014/1904, SI 2014/2459, SI 2014/2524, SI 2014/2844, SI 2014/3282 Sch.1 para.5

s.25, enabling: SI 2014/358, SI 2014/360, SI
2014/588, SI 2014/784, SI 2014/1597, SI
2014/1903, SI 2014/1904, SI 2014/2459, SI
2014/2524, SI 2014/2844
s.27, enabling: SI 2014/792
s.28, applied: SI 2014/3282 Sch.1 para.3
s.28, enabling: SI 2014/413
s.30, applied: SI 2014/531 Sch.1
s.51, applied: SI 2014/531 Sch.1
s.65D, amended: 2014 c.23 s.84
s.65DA, amended: 2014 c.23 s.85
s.65F, see *R. (on the application of
Lewisham LBC) v Secretary of State for
Health* [2013] EWCA Civ 1409, [2014] 1
W.L.R. 514 (CA (Civ Div)), Lord Dyson
MR
s.65F, amended: 2014 c.23 s.85, s.120
s.65G, amended: 2014 c.23 s.85, s.120
s.65H, amended: 2014 c.23 s.85, s.120
s.65H, repealed (in part): 2014 c.23 s.120
s.65I, see *R. (on the application of Lewisham
LBC) v Secretary of State for Health* [2013]
EWCA Civ 1409, [2014] 1 W.L.R. 514 (CA
(Civ Div)), Lord Dyson MR
s.65K, see *R. (on the application of
Lewisham LBC) v Secretary of State for
Health* [2013] EWCA Civ 1409, [2014] 1
W.L.R. 514 (CA (Civ Div)), Lord Dyson
MR
s.65KB, amended: 2014 c.23 s.85
s.65KB, referred to: SI 2014/2849
s.65KD, amended: 2014 c.23 s.85
s.65LA, enabling: SI 2014/2849
s.65N, amended: 2014 c.23 s.84, s.120
s.65O, substituted: 2014 c.23 s.120
s.71, amended: 2014 c.23 Sch.5 para.24,
Sch.7 para.18
s.71, applied: SI 2014/931, SI 2014/932, SI
2014/933
s.71, enabling: SI 2014/931, SI 2014/932, SI
2014/933
s.72, amended: 2014 c.23 Sch.5 para.15
s.73A, referred to: 2014 c.23 s.6
s.75, applied: 2014 c.23 s.22, SI 2014/3352
Sch.1 para.7
s.83, applied: SI 2014/1788 Sch.1
s.84, applied: SI 2014/1788 Sch.1, SI
2014/3282 Sch.1 para.8
s.84, enabling: SI 2014/2721
s.85, enabling: SI 2014/465
s.88, enabling: SI 2014/1625

s.89, enabling: SI 2014/465, SI 2014/2721
s.92, applied: SI 2014/1788 Sch.1, SI
2014/3282 Sch.1 para.8
s.94, enabling: SI 2014/465, SI 2014/2721
s.104, enabling: SI 2014/443
s.109, enabling: SI 2014/443
s.115, enabling: SI 2014/418, SI 2014/545,
SI 2014/2667
s.116, enabling: SI 2014/418, SI 2014/545,
SI 2014/2667
s.121, enabling: SI 2014/418
s.126, enabling: SI 2014/417
s.129, enabling: SI 2014/417
s.169, enabling: SI 2014/443
s.172, enabling: SI 2014/545
s.175, enabling: SI 2014/1534
s.176, enabling: SI 2014/545
s.178, enabling: SI 2014/545
s.179, enabling: SI 2014/418, SI 2014/545
s.180, enabling: SI 2014/418, SI 2014/545,
SI 2014/2667
s.181, enabling: SI 2014/418, SI 2014/2667
s.182, enabling: SI 2014/418, SI 2014/545,
SI 2014/2667
s.183, enabling: SI 2014/545, SI 2014/2667
s.184, enabling: SI 2014/2667
s.187, enabling: SI 2014/3099
s.188, enabling: SI 2014/418
s.212, referred to: 2014 c.2 s.3
s.213, referred to: SI 2014/1387
s.213, enabling: SI 2014/230, SI 2014/1387,
SI 2014/1390
s.217, enabling: SI 2014/196, SI 2014/230,
SI 2014/1387, SI 2014/1390
s.223B, amended: 2014 c.23 s.121
s.223GA, added: 2014 c.23 s.121
s.242, see *R. (on the application of Ealing
LBC) v NHS England* [2013] EWHC 3255
(Admin), (2014) 135 B.M.L.R. 128 (QBD
(Admin)), Mitting J
s.242, amended: 2014 c.23 s.120
s.247C, amended: 2014 c.23 Sch.5 para.13
s.251, applied: 2014 c.23 Sch.7 para.8
s.254, applied: SI 2014/829 Sch.1 para.21,
SI 2014/2936 Sch.1 para.10
s.258, applied: 2014 c.23 s.97
s.272, enabling: SI 2014/91, SI 2014/196, SI
2014/230, SI 2014/358, SI 2014/360, SI
2014/413, SI 2014/417, SI 2014/418, SI
2014/443, SI 2014/452, SI 2014/465, SI
2014/545, SI 2014/588, SI 2014/784, SI

2014/931, SI 2014/932, SI 2014/933, SI
2014/1387, SI 2014/1390, SI 2014/1534, SI
2014/1597, SI 2014/1611, SI 2014/1625, SI
2014/1903, SI 2014/1904, SI 2014/1905, SI
2014/2459, SI 2014/2524, SI 2014/2667, SI
2014/2721, SI 2014/2844, SI 2014/2849, SI
2014/3099, SI 2014/3487
s.273, enabling: SI 2014/358, SI 2014/360,
SI 2014/443, SI 2014/588, SI 2014/1597, SI
2014/1903, SI 2014/1904, SI 2014/1905, SI
2014/2459, SI 2014/2844
s.275, see *R. (on the application of Muaza) v
Secretary of State for the Home Department*
[2013] EWCA Civ 1561, [2014] 1 W.L.R.
1870 (CA (Civ Div)), Lewison LJ
Sch.1A Part 2 para.17, amended: 2014 c.2
Sch.12 para.71
Sch.4 Part 1 para.4, enabling: SI 2014/784
Sch.4 Part 1 para.5, applied: SI 2014/2524
Art.4
Sch.4 Part 1 para.5, enabling: SI 2014/2459,
SI 2014/2524
Sch.4 Part 1 para.7, enabling: SI 2014/2524
Sch.4 Part 1 para.10, applied: 2014 c.2 Sch.2
para.24B, Sch.13 para.1, Sch.13 para.3
Sch.4 Part 1 para.10, enabling: SI 2014/196,
SI 2014/1905
Sch.4 Part 1 para.12, amended: 2014 c.2
Sch.12 para.76
Sch.4 Part 3 para.28, applied: SI 2014/588,
SI 2014/1597, SI 2014/2524
Sch.4 Part 3 para.28, enabling: SI
2014/1597, SI 2014/2524
Sch.5 para.1, applied: SI 2014/792
Sch.5 para.1, enabling: SI 2014/792
Sch.6 para.3, enabling: SI 2014/413
Sch.6 para.4, applied: SI 2014/413
Sch.7 para.23, amended: 2014 c.2 Sch.12
para.73
Sch.7 para.23, repealed (in part): 2014 c.2
Sch.12 para.73
Sch.7 para.24, amended: 2014 c.2 Sch.12
para.74
Sch.7 para.24, repealed (in part): 2014 c.2
Sch.12 para.74
Sch.12 para.3, enabling: SI 2014/417
Sch.15, applied: SI 2014/3090 Art.4
Sch.15 para.4, amended: 2014 c.2 Sch.12
para.75
Sch.15 para.4, repealed (in part): 2014 c.2
Sch.12 para.75

Sch.20, applied: SI 2014/829 Sch.1 para.21,
SI 2014/2936 Sch.1 para.10
Sch.20 para.2, applied: SI 2014/512 Sch.1
para.19
42. National Health Service (Wales) Act 2006
applied: SI 2014/512 Sch.1 para.19, SI
2014/3249 Sch.1
referred to: 2014 c.23 Sch.1 para.1
s.4, applied: SI 2014/512 Sch.1 para.18
s.10, applied: SI 2014/512 Sch.1 para.19
s.11, applied: SI 2014/3282 Sch.1 para.4
s.11, enabling: SI 2014/566
s.12, enabling: SI 2014/566
s.13, enabling: SI 2014/566
s.18, applied: SI 2014/3282 Sch.1 para.5
s.22, applied: SI 2014/3282 Sch.1 para.3
s.33, applied: SI 2014/1794 Reg.9, Reg.10
s.42, applied: SI 2014/3282 Sch.1 para.8
s.46, enabling: SI 2014/109
s.47, enabling: SI 2014/2291
s.50, applied: SI 2014/3282 Sch.1 para.8
s.61, enabling: SI 2014/872
s.66, enabling: SI 2014/872
s.71, enabling: SI 2014/460, SI 2014/2015
s.76, enabling: SI 2014/2015
s.80, enabling: SI 2014/2291
s.83, enabling: SI 2014/2291
s.86, enabling: SI 2014/2291
s.124, enabling: SI 2014/1622
s.125, enabling: SI 2014/461
s.128, enabling: SI 2014/460, SI 2014/462,
SI 2014/2015
s.129, enabling: SI 2014/460, SI 2014/462,
SI 2014/2015
s.130, enabling: SI 2014/460, SI 2014/462,
SI 2014/1099
s.131, enabling: SI 2014/460, SI 2014/1099
s.132, enabling: SI 2014/1099
s.182, applied: SI 2014/3282 Sch.1 para.7
s.203, enabling: SI 2014/109, SI 2014/460,
SI 2014/461, SI 2014/462, SI 2014/566, SI
2014/872, SI 2014/1099, SI 2014/1622, SI
2014/2015, SI 2014/2291
Sch.2 Part 1 para.4, enabling: SI 2014/566
Sch.3 Part 1 para.12, amended: 2014 c.2
Sch.12 para.77
Sch.16 para.2, applied: SI 2014/512 Sch.1
para.19

43. National Health Service (Consequential Provisions) Act 2006

    Sch.1 para.186, repealed: 2014 c.2 Sch.1 Part 2

45. Animal Welfare Act 2006

    s.4, see *R. (on the application of Gray) v Aylesbury Crown Court* [2013] EWHC 500 (Admin), [2014] 1 W.L.R. 818 (QBD (Admin)), Toulson, L.J.

    s.9, see *R. (on the application of Gray) v Aylesbury Crown Court* [2013] EWHC 500 (Admin), [2014] 1 W.L.R. 818 (QBD (Admin)), Toulson, L.J.

    s.13, applied: SI 2014/3266, SI 2014/3266 Reg.4, Reg.5, Reg.6

    s.13, enabling: SI 2014/3266

    s.18, see *R. (on the application of Gray) v Aylesbury Crown Court* [2013] EWHC 500 (Admin), [2014] 1 W.L.R. 818 (QBD (Admin)), Toulson, L.J.

    s.23, applied: SI 2014/3266 Reg.23

    s.34, applied: SI 2014/3266 Reg.10, Reg.24

    s.42, applied: SI 2014/3266 Reg.24

    s.61, applied: SI 2014/3266

    Sch.1 Part 1, enabling: SI 2014/3266

    Sch.1 Part 3, enabling: SI 2014/3266

46. Companies Act 2006

    see *Glasgow City Council v Fox Cross Claimants* [2014] CSIH 27, 2014 S.C. 610 (IH (Ex Div)), Lord Brodie; see *HLC Environmental Projects Ltd, Re* [2013] EWHC 2876 (Ch), [2014] B.C.C. 337 (Ch D (Companies Ct)), John Randall QC; see *Liberty Mercian Ltd v Cuddy Civil Engineering Ltd* [2013] EWHC 2688 (TCC), [2014] 1 All E.R. (Comm) 761 (QBD (TCC)), Ramsey J

    applied: 2014 asp 14 s.30, 2014 asp 19 Sch.1 para.12, 2014 c.1 s.7, 2014 c.4 s.25, 2014 c.21 s.65, SI 2014/1643 Sch.1 para.7, SI 2014/1893 Art.23, SI 2014/3140 Reg.6, SI 2014/3348 Art.217, Art.220, Sch.4 para.25, SSI 2014/268 Art.10, Art.17

    referred to: SSI 2014/268 Art.8

    Part 1, applied: 2014 c.14 s.115, s.135

    Part 5, referred to: 2014 c.14 s.135

    Part 26, referred to: SI 2014/229 Sch.1 para.1

    Part 31, applied: SI 2014/512 Sch.1 para.2, Sch.1 para.3, Sch.1 para.8

    Part 31, referred to: 2014 c.14 s.135

    Part 42, applied: 2014 c.2 s.18, s.44, Sch.5 para.1, Sch.5 para.2, Sch.11 para.2, 2014 c.14 s.91, SI 2014/1627 Reg.2, Reg.9, SI 2014/2009 Art.2

    Part 42, referred to: 2014 c.2 Sch.5 para.2

    Part 42, varied: 2014 c.2 Sch.5 para.2

    Part 42 c.1, varied: 2014 c.2 Sch.5 para.3

    Part 42 c.3, varied: 2014 c.2 Sch.5 para.3

    Part 42 c.5, varied: 2014 c.2 Sch.5 para.3

    Part 45, applied: 2014 c.14 s.115, s.135

    Pt 26., see *Apcoa Parking (UK) Ltd, Re* [2014] EWHC 997 (Ch), [2014] 4 All E.R. 150 (Ch D), Hildyard J; see *Apcoa Parking Holdings GmbH, Re* [2014] EWHC 1867 (Ch), [2014] B.C.C. 538 (Ch D), Hildyard J; see *Magyar Telecom BV, Re* [2013] EWHC 3800 (Ch), [2014] B.C.C. 448 (Ch D), Richards J; see *Zodiac Pool Solutions SAS, Re* [2014] EWHC 2365 (Ch), [2014] B.C.C. 569 (Ch D (Companies Ct)), Morgan J

    Pt 9., see *Eckerle v Wickeder Westfalenstahl GmbH* [2013] EWHC 68 (Ch), [2014] Ch. 196 (Ch D), Norris J

    s.54, amended: 2014 c.29 s.4

    s.55, applied: SI 2014/3140 Reg.3, Reg.4, Reg.5, Reg.6

    s.55, referred to: SI 2014/3140 Reg.2

    s.55, enabling: SI 2014/3140

    s.56, enabling: SI 2014/3140

    s.58, see *Fairhold Mercury Ltd v HQ (Block 1) Action Management Co Ltd* [2014] L. & T.R. 5 (UT (Lands)), Martin Rodger Q.C.

    s.59, see *Fairhold Mercury Ltd v HQ (Block 1) Action Management Co Ltd* [2014] L. & T.R. 5 (UT (Lands)), Martin Rodger Q.C.

    s.64, see *Fairhold Mercury Ltd v HQ (Block 1) Action Management Co Ltd* [2014] L. & T.R. 5 (UT (Lands)), Martin Rodger Q.C.

    s.88, referred to: SI 2014/3140 Reg.2, Reg.6

    s.98, see *Eckerle v Wickeder Westfalenstahl GmbH* [2013] EWHC 68 (Ch), [2014] Ch. 196 (Ch D), Norris J

    s.116, see *Burry & Knight Ltd, Re* [2014] EWCA Civ 604, [2014] 1 W.L.R. 4046 (CA (Civ Div)), Arden LJ

    s.117, see *Burry & Knight Ltd, Re* [2014] EWCA Civ 604, [2014] 1 W.L.R. 4046 (CA (Civ Div)), Arden LJ

    s.140, amended: 2014 c.19 Sch.13 para.75

s.145, see *Eckerle v Wickeder Westfalenstahl GmbH* [2013] EWHC 68 (Ch), [2014] Ch. 196 (Ch D), Norris J
s.145, varied: SI 2014/3348 Sch.4 para.2
s.153, varied: SI 2014/3348 Sch.4 para.3
s.161, see *Macnabs LLP v Fordlane Ltd* 2014 S.L.T. (Sh Ct) 80 (Sh Ct (Tayside) (Dundee)), Sheriff Principal R A Dunlop, QC
s.171, see *Campbell v Peter Gordon Joiners Ltd* 2014 S.L.T. 178 (OH), Lord Glennie
s.171, applied: SSI 2014/268 Art.16
s.172, see *Bilta (UK) Ltd (In Liquidation) v Nazir* [2013] EWCA Civ 968, [2014] Ch. 52 (CA (Civ Div)), Lord Dyson MR; see *HLC Environmental Projects Ltd, Re* [2013] EWHC 2876 (Ch), [2014] B.C.C. 337 (Ch D (Companies Ct)), John Randall QC; see *Richmond Pharmacology Ltd v Chester Overseas Ltd* [2014] EWHC 2692 (Ch), [2014] Bus. L.R. 1110 (Ch D), Stephen Jourdan QC
s.174, see *Richmond Pharmacology Ltd v Chester Overseas Ltd* [2014] EWHC 2692 (Ch), [2014] Bus. L.R. 1110 (Ch D), Stephen Jourdan QC
s.175, see *Richmond Pharmacology Ltd v Chester Overseas Ltd* [2014] EWHC 2692 (Ch), [2014] Bus. L.R. 1110 (Ch D), Stephen Jourdan QC; see *Sharma v Sharma* [2013] EWCA Civ 1287, [2014] B.C.C. 73 (CA (Civ Div)), Jackson LJ
s.177, see *Campbell v Peter Gordon Joiners Ltd* 2014 S.L.T. 178 (OH), Lord Glennie
s.190, see *Smithton Ltd (formerly Hobart Capital Markets Ltd) v Naggar* [2013] EWHC 1961 (Ch), [2014] 1 B.C.L.C. 602 (Ch D), Rose J
s.239, see *Bilta (UK) Ltd (In Liquidation) v Nazir* [2013] EWCA Civ 968, [2014] Ch. 52 (CA (Civ Div)), Lord Dyson MR
s.252, varied: 2014 c.14 s.49
s.282, varied: SI 2014/3348 Sch.4 para.4
s.283, varied: SI 2014/3348 Sch.4 para.5
s.284, varied: SI 2014/3348 Sch.4 para.6
s.303, varied: SI 2014/3348 Sch.4 para.7
s.307, varied: SI 2014/3348 Sch.4 para.8
s.307A, varied: SI 2014/3348 Sch.4 para.9
s.311, varied: SI 2014/3348 Sch.4 para.10
s.311A, varied: SI 2014/3348 Sch.4 para.11
s.319A, varied: SI 2014/3348 Sch.4 para.11

s.327, varied: SI 2014/3348 Sch.4 para.12
s.330, varied: SI 2014/3348 Sch.4 para.13
s.333A, varied: SI 2014/3348 Sch.4 para.14
s.334, varied: SI 2014/3348 Sch.4 para.15
s.336, varied: SI 2014/3348 Sch.4 para.16
s.337, varied: SI 2014/3348 Sch.4 para.17
s.338, varied: SI 2014/3348 Sch.4 para.18
s.338A, varied: SI 2014/3348 Sch.4 para.18
s.341, varied: SI 2014/3348 Sch.4 para.19
s.352, varied: SI 2014/3348 Sch.4 para.20
s.360, varied: SI 2014/3348 Sch.4 para.21
s.360A, varied: SI 2014/3348 Sch.4 para.22
s.360B, varied: SI 2014/3348 Sch.4 para.23
s.394, applied: SI 2014/1643 Sch.1 para.5, Sch.1 para.6
s.395, applied: SI 2014/1643 Sch.1 para.6
s.461, amended: 2014 c.14 Sch.4 para.100
s.468, enabling: SI 2014/3209
s.473, applied: SI 2014/3209
s.474, varied: SI 2014/1643 Sch.1 para.4, SI 2014/2410 Sch.1 para.3
s.550, varied: SI 2014/3348 Sch.4 para.26
s.551, varied: SI 2014/3348 Sch.4 para.27
s.561, varied: SI 2014/3348 Sch.4 para.28
s.568, varied: SI 2014/3348 Sch.4 para.28
s.569, varied: SI 2014/3348 Sch.4 para.29
s.570, varied: SI 2014/3348 Sch.4 para.30
s.571, varied: SI 2014/3348 Sch.4 para.31
s.586, varied: SI 2014/3348 Sch.4 para.32
s.593, varied: SI 2014/3348 Sch.4 para.33
s.617, varied: SI 2014/3348 Sch.4 para.34
s.618, varied: SI 2014/3348 Sch.4 para.35
s.646, see *Vodafone Group Plc, Re* [2014] EWHC 1357 (Ch), [2014] B.C.C. 554 (Ch D (Companies Ct)), Henderson J
s.656, varied: SI 2014/3348 Sch.4 para.36
s.673, repealed (in part): 2014 c.19 Sch.13 para.76
s.793, see *Eclairs Group Ltd v JKX Oil & Gas Plc* [2013] EWHC 2631 (Ch), [2014] Bus. L.R. 18 (Ch D), Mann J; see *Eclairs Group Ltd v JKX Oil & Gas Plc* [2014] EWCA Civ 640, [2014] 4 All E.R. 463 (CA (Civ Div)), Longmore LJ
s.859A, applied: SI 2014/3344 Art.3
s.859C, applied: SI 2014/3344 Art.3
s.859K, varied: SI 2014/3344 Art.3
s.859L, varied: SI 2014/3344 Art.3
s.859O, varied: SI 2014/3344 Art.3

s.889, see *Stemcor (SEA) Pte Ltd, Re* [2014]
EWHC 1096 (Ch), [2014] 2 B.C.L.C. 373
(Ch D (Companies Ct)), Birss J
s.895, see *Icopal AS, Re* [2013] EWHC 3469
(Ch), [2014] 2 All E.R. (Comm) 1183 (Ch
D), Proudman J; see *Magyar Telecom BV,
Re* [2013] EWHC 3800 (Ch), [2014] B.C.C.
448 (Ch D), Richards J; see *Zlomrex
International Finance SA, Re* [2013] EWHC
3866 (Ch), [2014] B.C.C. 440 (Ch D
(Companies Ct)), Mann J
s.895, varied: SI 2014/229 Sch.2 para.3
s.896, see *Vietnam Shipbuilding Industry
Group, Re* [2013] EWHC 2476 (Ch), [2014]
B.C.C. 433 (Ch D), David Richards J
s.899, see *Icopal AS, Re* [2013] EWHC 3469
(Ch), [2014] 2 All E.R. (Comm) 1183 (Ch
D), Proudman J; see *Magyar Telecom BV,
Re* [2013] EWHC 3800 (Ch), [2014] B.C.C.
448 (Ch D), Richards J
s.899, applied: SI 2014/229 Sch.2 para.7
s.899, varied: SI 2014/229 Sch.2 para.4
s.900, see *TSB Nuclear Energy Investment
UK Ltd, Re* [2014] EWHC 1272 (Ch),
[2014] B.C.C. 531 (Ch D), Henderson J
s.900, applied: SI 2014/229 Sch.2 para.7
s.900, varied: SI 2014/229 Sch.2 para.5
s.901, applied: SI 2014/229 Sch.2 para.7
s.901, varied: SI 2014/229 Sch.2 para.6
s.902, varied: SI 2014/3348 Sch.4 para.24
s.943, varied: SI 2014/3348 Art.219
s.994, see *Apex Global Management Ltd v Fi
Call Ltd* [2013] EWCA Civ 642, [2014] 1
W.L.R. 492 (CA (Civ Div)), Maurice Kay
LJ; see *Apex Global Management Ltd v Fi
Call Ltd* [2013] EWHC 1652 (Ch), [2014]
B.C.C. 286 (Ch D), Vos J; see *Batesons
Hotels (1958), Re* [2013] EWHC 2530 (Ch),
[2014] 1 B.C.L.C. 507 (Ch D (Manchester)),
Judge Hodge Q.C.; see *Coroin Ltd, Re*
[2013] EWCA Civ 781, [2014] B.C.C. 14
(CA (Civ Div)), Arden LJ; see *Graham v
Every* [2014] EWCA Civ 191, [2014] B.C.C.
376 (CA (Civ Div)), Arden LJ; see *I Fit
Global Ltd, Re* [2013] EWHC 2090 (Ch),
[2014] 2 B.C.L.C. 116 (Ch D (Companies
Ct)), Roth J; see *Sunrise Radio Ltd, Re*
[2013] EWCA Civ 667, [2014] 1 B.C.L.C.
427 (CA (Civ Div)), Laws LJ

s.996, see *Apex Global Management Ltd v Fi
Call Ltd* [2013] EWHC 1652 (Ch), [2014]
B.C.C. 286 (Ch D), Vos J
s.1000, amended: SI 2014/1602 Art.2
s.1002, amended: SI 2014/1602 Art.2
s.1012, see *Keene v Wellcom London Ltd*
[2014] EWHC 134 (Ch), [2014] W.T.L.R.
1011 (Ch D), Peter Smith J
s.1044, referred to: SI 2014/3140 Reg.6
s.1059A, amended: SI 2014/1557 Art.3
s.1069, applied: SI 2014/3209
s.1069, enabling: SI 2014/3209
s.1074, see *Registrar of Companies v
Swarbrick* [2014] EWHC 1466 (Ch), [2014]
Bus. L.R. 625 (Ch D), Richard Spearman
QC
s.1076, see *Registrar of Companies v
Swarbrick* [2014] EWHC 1466 (Ch), [2014]
Bus. L.R. 625 (Ch D), Richard Spearman
QC
s.1078, amended: SI 2014/1557 Art.4, SI
2014/3209 Reg.20
s.1079A, added: SI 2014/1557 Art.5
s.1080, see *Registrar of Companies v
Swarbrick* [2014] EWHC 1466 (Ch), [2014]
Bus. L.R. 625 (Ch D), Richard Spearman
QC
s.1081, see *Registrar of Companies v
Swarbrick* [2014] EWHC 1466 (Ch), [2014]
Bus. L.R. 625 (Ch D), Richard Spearman
QC
s.1094, see *Registrar of Companies v
Swarbrick* [2014] EWHC 1466 (Ch), [2014]
Bus. L.R. 625 (Ch D), Richard Spearman
QC
s.1099, amended: 2014 c.14 Sch.4 para.101
s.1105, applied: SI 2014/3209 Reg.15
s.1105, enabling: SI 2014/3209
s.1139, applied: SI 2014/1610 r.4_4
s.1157, see *Madoff Securities International
Ltd (In Liquidation) v Raven* [2013] EWHC
3147 (Comm), [2014] Lloyd's Rep. F.C. 95
(QBD (Comm)), Popplewell J
s.1159, applied: 2014 asp 2 s.38, SI
2014/2257 Reg.4
s.1159, referred to: SI 2014/1641 Art.3
s.1161, applied: 2014 c.26 s.256, SI
2014/533 Art.2
s.1162, applied: SI 2014/533 Art.2, SI
2014/1643 Reg.17
s.1162, disapplied: SI 2014/533 Art.2

s.1168, referred to: SI 2014/2068 Sch.1
para.10, Sch.1 para.19
s.1194, applied: SI 2014/3140 Reg.3, Reg.5,
Reg.6
s.1194, enabling: SI 2014/3140
s.1195, enabling: SI 2014/3140
s.1212, applied: SI 2014/1958 Reg.14
s.1212, varied: 2014 c.2 Sch.5 para.4
s.1214, applied: 2014 c.2 s.7, 2014 c.14 s.92,
SI 2014/2009 Art.2
s.1214, varied: 2014 c.2 Sch.5 para.5
s.1215, applied: SI 2014/1710 Reg.3
s.1215, varied: 2014 c.2 Sch.5 para.6
s.1216, varied: 2014 c.2 Sch.5 para.7
s.1217, varied: 2014 c.2 Sch.5 para.8
s.1219, applied: SI 2014/1627 Reg.2, SI
2014/2009 Art.2
s.1219, varied: 2014 c.2 Sch.5 para.9
s.1219, enabling: SI 2014/1627
s.1220, varied: 2014 c.2 Sch.5 para.3
s.1223, applied: SI 2014/2009 Art.7
s.1223A, varied: 2014 c.2 Sch.5 para.3
s.1224, applied: SI 2014/2009 Art.2
s.1224A, referred to: 2014 c.2 Sch.5 para.3
s.1224A, varied: 2014 c.2 Sch.5 para.3
s.1224ZA, applied: SI 2014/2009 Art.2
s.1224ZA, varied: 2014 c.2 Sch.5 para.10
s.1225, varied: 2014 c.2 Sch.5 para.11
s.1225C, varied: 2014 c.2 Sch.5 para.12
s.1225D, applied: SI 2014/2009 Art.8
s.1225E, applied: SI 2014/2009 Art.8
s.1225F, varied: 2014 c.2 Sch.5 para.13
s.1226, referred to: SI 2014/2418 Sch.1
s.1239, applied: 2014 c.2 Sch.6 para.1, SI
2014/2009 Art.2
s.1239, varied: 2014 c.2 Sch.5 para.14
s.1240, varied: 2014 c.2 Sch.5 para.15
s.1248, varied: 2014 c.2 Sch.5 para.16
s.1249, varied: 2014 c.2 Sch.5 para.17
s.1250, varied: 2014 c.2 Sch.5 para.18
s.1251, applied: SI 2014/1710 Reg.8
s.1251, varied: 2014 c.2 Sch.5 para.19
s.1251A, varied: 2014 c.2 Sch.5 para.20
s.1252, applied: 2014 c.2 Sch.6 para.1,
Sch.11 para.1, SI 2014/1710 Reg.7, Reg.8,
SI 2014/2009
s.1252, varied: 2014 c.2 Sch.5 para.21
s.1252, enabling: SI 2014/2009
s.1253, varied: 2014 c.2 Sch.5 para.22
s.1253, enabling: SI 2014/2009
s.1253A, varied: 2014 c.2 Sch.5 para.3

s.1254, applied: SI 2014/2009 Art.2
s.1254, varied: 2014 c.2 Sch.5 para.23
s.1256, varied: 2014 c.2 Sch.5 para.24, SI
2014/2009 Art.9
s.1257, varied: 2014 c.2 Sch.5 para.25
s.1261, applied: SI 2014/2009 Art.2
s.1261, referred to: SI 2014/2418 Sch.1
s.1261, varied: 2014 c.2 Sch.5 para.26
s.1262, varied: 2014 c.2 Sch.5 para.27
s.1263, applied: SI 2014/2009 Art.2
s.1264, varied: 2014 c.2 Sch.5 para.3
s.1288, applied: 2014 c.2 Sch.5 para.1
s.1290, applied: SI 2014/2009, SI 2014/3209
s.1292, applied: 2014 c.2 Sch.5 para.1, SI
2014/3209
s.1292, enabling: SI 2014/1627, SI
2014/3140
Sch.2 Part 2 para.25, amended: SI 2014/892
Sch.1 para.168
Sch.2 Part 2 para.25, repealed (in part): SI
2014/631 Sch.2 para.5
Sch.2 Part 2 para.26, repealed: SI 2014/892
Sch.1 para.168
Sch.2 Part 2 para.36A, added: SI 2014/631
Sch.2 para.5
Sch.2 Part 2 para.37, amended: 2014 c.14
Sch.4 para.102
Sch.7, applied: 2014 c.26 s.256
Sch.8, applied: 2014 c.4 s.4
Sch.10 Part 1 para.4, varied: 2014 c.2 Sch.5
para.28
Sch.10 Part 2 para.6, varied: 2014 c.2 Sch.5
para.28
Sch.10 Part 2 para.7, varied: 2014 c.2 Sch.5
para.28
Sch.10 Part 2 para.7A, varied: 2014 c.2
Sch.5 para.28
Sch.10 Part 2 para.10A, varied: 2014 c.2
Sch.5 para.28
Sch.10 Part 2 para.10B, varied: 2014 c.2
Sch.5 para.28
Sch.10 Part 2 para.13, applied: SI 2014/1627
Reg.12, SI 2014/2009 Art.2, Art.4
Sch.10 Part 2 para.13, referred to: SI
2014/2418 Sch.1
Sch.10 Part 2 para.13, varied: 2014 c.2 Sch.5
para.28
Sch.10 Part 2 para.13, enabling: SI
2014/1627
Sch.10 Part 2 para.16A, varied: 2014 c.2
Sch.5 para.28

Sch.10 Part 2 para.20A, varied: 2014 c.2
Sch.5 para.28
Sch.10 Part 3 para.22A, varied: 2014 c.2
Sch.5 para.28
Sch.10 Part 3 para.23, applied: 2014 c.2
Sch.11 para.1
Sch.10 Part 3 para.23, varied: 2014 c.2 Sch.5
para.28
Sch.10 Part 3 para.23A, varied: 2014 c.2
Sch.5 para.28
Sch.10 Part 3 para.24, applied: 2014 c.2
Sch.11 para.1
Sch.10 Part 3 para.24, referred to: SI
2014/2418 Sch.1
Sch.10 Part 3 para.24, varied: 2014 c.2 Sch.5
para.28
Sch.10 Part 3 para.25, varied: 2014 c.2 Sch.5
para.28
Sch.10 Part 3 para.26, varied: 2014 c.2 Sch.5
para.28
Sch.10 Part 3 para.27, varied: 2014 c.2 Sch.5
para.28
Sch.11, varied: 2014 c.2 Sch.5 para.3
Sch.11A, varied: 2014 c.2 Sch.5 para.3
Sch.11A Part 1 para.17A, added: 2014 c.2
Sch.12 para.78
Sch.11A Part 2 para.39, amended: SI
2014/892 Sch.1 para.169
Sch.11A Part 2 para.39, repealed (in part): SI
2014/631 Sch.2 para.5
Sch.11A Part 2 para.40, repealed: SI
2014/892 Sch.1 para.169
Sch.11A Part 2 para.51A, added: SI
2014/631 Sch.2 para.5
Sch.11A Part 2 para.52, amended: 2014 c.14
Sch.4 para.103
Sch.12, varied: 2014 c.2 Sch.5 para.3
Sch.13 para.7, enabling: SI 2014/2009
Sch.13 para.9, varied: 2014 c.2 Sch.5
para.29
Sch.13 para.10, varied: 2014 c.2 Sch.5
para.29
Sch.13 para.11, enabling: SI 2014/2009
Sch.14, varied: 2014 c.2 Sch.5 para.3

47. Safeguarding Vulnerable Groups Act 2006
s.2, applied: SI 2014/512 Reg.111, SI
2014/2936 Sch.4 para.5
s.3, applied: SI 2014/512 Reg.111, SI
2014/1132 Sch.7 para.9, SI 2014/2365
Reg.5, SI 2014/2709 Sch.2 para.9, SI

2014/3283 Sch.1 para.18, Sch.1 para.20,
Sch.1 para.21
s.30A, referred to: SI 2014/2936 Sch.3
para.2
s.59, amended: 2014 c.22 Sch.9 para.14
Sch.3 Part 1 para.1, applied: SI 2014/1610
r.42_3
Sch.3 Part 2 para.7, applied: SI 2014/1610
r.42_3
Sch.3 Part 3 para.24, applied: SI 2014/1610
r.42_3
Sch.4 Part 1, applied: SI 2014/3283 Reg.2,
Sch.1 para.18, Sch.1 para.20

48. Police and Justice Act 2006
s.26, repealed: 2014 c.12 Sch.11 para.50
Sch.3 para.3, amended: 2014 c.12 s.133
Sch.4 para.3, repealed: 2014 c.12 Sch.11
para.102
Sch.4 para.10, repealed: 2014 c.12 Sch.11
para.102
Sch.14 para.12, repealed (in part): 2014 c.12
Sch.11 para.50
Sch.14 para.13, repealed (in part): 2014 c.12
Sch.11 para.50
Sch.14 para.15, repealed: 2014 c.12 Sch.11
para.50
Sch.14 para.32, repealed: 2014 c.12 Sch.11
para.50

49. Road Safety Act 2006
Sch.3 para.9, amended: 2014 c.22 Sch.9
para.64

50. Charities Act 2006
Sch.8 para.47, repealed: 2014 c.14 Sch.7

**51. Legislative and Regulatory Reform Act
2006**
Part 1, applied: SI 2014/580, SI 2014/1190,
SI 2014/1997, SI 2014/2436
s.1, enabling: SI 2014/542, SI 2014/580, SI
2014/1997, SI 2014/2436, SI 2014/3253
s.2, enabling: SI 2014/542
s.3, applied: SI 2014/542, SI 2014/580, SI
2014/1997, SI 2014/2436
s.3, referred to: SI 2014/3253
s.4, amended: 2014 c.29 s.4
s.11, applied: SI 2014/580
s.13, applied: SI 2014/542, SI 2014/580, SI
2014/1997, SI 2014/2436, SI 2014/3253
s.14, applied: SI 2014/542, SI 2014/580, SI
2014/1997, SI 2014/2436, SI 2014/3253

s.15, applied: SI 2014/542, SI 2014/580, SI 2014/1190, SI 2014/1997, SI 2014/2436, SI 2014/3253

s.16, applied: SI 2014/1190

s.16, referred to: SI 2014/580

s.17, applied: SI 2014/542, SI 2014/1997, SI 2014/2436, SI 2014/3253

s.22, applied: SI 2014/929

s.23, applied: SI 2014/929

s.23, enabling: SI 2014/929

s.24, applied: SI 2014/860

s.24, enabling: SI 2014/860

s.27, amended: 2014 c.29 s.4

s.31, repealed (in part): 2014 c.2 Sch.12 para.123

52. Armed Forces Act 2006

applied: SI 2014/1777 Art.2, SI 2014/1882, SI 2014/1977 Reg.2

s.15, see *R. v Price (Patrick David)* [2014] EWCA Crim 229, [2014] 1 W.L.R. 3501 (CA (Crim Div)), Pitchford LJ

s.44, referred to: 2014 c.20 s.49

s.74, enabling: SI 2014/934

s.84, amended: 2014 c.12 s.176

s.92, enabling: SI 2014/934

s.183, amended: 2014 c.11 Sch.6 para.4, Sch.6 para.8

s.183, repealed (in part): 2014 c.11 Sch.6 para.4

s.205, amended: 2014 c.11 Sch.6 para.9

s.211, applied: 2014 c.11 Sch.7 para.2

s.213, amended: 2014 c.11 Sch.6 para.2

s.246, amended: 2014 c.11 Sch.6 para.3

s.328, enabling: SI 2014/3068

s.329, amended: 2014 c.20 s.44

s.329, enabling: SI 2014/3068

s.343B, amended: 2014 c.29 s.4

s.374, amended: 2014 c.20 s.44

s.376, applied: SI 2014/1977 Reg.2

s.382, enabling: SI 2014/1882

s.384, applied: 2014 c.20 s.49

s.384, referred to: 2014 c.12 s.184

s.385, disapplied: 2014 c.11 s.23

Sch.3A Part 2 para.13, repealed (in part): 2014 c.12 Sch.11 para.81

Sch.5 Part 1 para.1, amended: 2014 c.11 Sch.6 para.5, Sch.6 para.10

Sch.5 Part 1 para.2, repealed: 2014 c.11 Sch.6 para.5

Sch.5 Part 1 para.2A, added: 2014 c.11 Sch.6 para.5

Sch.5 Part 2 para.10, amended: 2014 c.11 Sch.6 para.6, Sch.6 para.11

Sch.5 Part 2 para.12, substituted: 2014 c.11 Sch.6 para.6

Sch.7 Part 1 para.1, amended: 2014 c.11 Sch.6 para.7

Sch.7 Part 2 para.4, repealed: 2014 c.11 Sch.6 para.7

Sch.7 Part 2 para.4A, added: 2014 c.11 Sch.6 para.7

Sch.11 para.9, amended: 2014 c.20 s.44

2007

3. Income Tax Act 2007

Part 3 c.3, amended: 2014 c.26 s.11

Part 3 c.3A, added: 2014 c.26 s.11

Part 4, applied: 2014 c.26 s.253

Part 5B, added: 2014 c.26 Sch.11 para.1

Part 8 c.1, amended: 2014 c.26 s.13

Part 13 c.5AA, added: 2014 c.26 Sch.17 para.24

Part 13 c.5D, added: 2014 c.26 Sch.17 para.25

s.2, amended: 2014 c.26 Sch.11 para.4

s.6, amended: 2014 c.26 Sch.38 para.2, 2014 c.29 s.9

s.6, repealed (in part): 2014 c.26 Sch.38 para.2

s.6A, added: 2014 c.26 Sch.38 para.3

s.6B, added: 2014 c.29 s.9

s.7, amended: 2014 c.26 s.3

s.10, amended: 2014 c.26 s.1, Sch.38 para.4, 2014 c.29 s.9

s.10, referred to: 2014 c.26 s.1, s.2

s.10, repealed (in part): 2014 c.26 Sch.38 para.4

s.11A, added: 2014 c.26 Sch.38 para.5

s.11B, added: 2014 c.29 s.9

s.12, amended: 2014 c.26 s.3

s.13, amended: 2014 c.26 Sch.38 para.6, 2014 c.29 s.9

s.16, amended: 2014 c.26 Sch.38 para.7, 2014 c.29 s.9

s.21, amended: 2014 c.26 s.4

s.21, disapplied: 2014 c.26 s.1, s.2, s.3

s.23, amended: 2014 c.26 Sch.17 para.19

s.24A, amended: 2014 c.26 Sch.11 para.5

s.26, amended: 2014 c.26 s.11, Sch.11 para.6

s.27, amended: 2014 c.26 Sch.11 para.7

s.29, amended: 2014 c.26 Sch.11 para.8

s.31, amended: 2014 c.26 s.11

s.32, amended: 2014 c.26 Sch.11 para.9

s.33, amended: 2014 c.26 s.11

s.34, amended: 2014 c.26 s.2

s.35, amended: 2014 c.26 s.1, s.2

s.35, referred to: 2014 c.26 s.1, s.2

s.36, repealed: 2014 c.26 s.2

s.37, amended: SI 2014/3273 Art.2

s.38, amended: SI 2014/3273 Art.2

s.43, amended: SI 2014/3273 Art.2

s.45, amended: 2014 c.26 s.2, SI 2014/3273 Art.2

s.46, amended: 2014 c.26 s.2, SI 2014/3273 Art.2

s.56, amended: 2014 c.26 s.11

s.57, amended: 2014 c.26 s.2, s.4

s.57, disapplied: 2014 c.26 s.1, s.2

s.57, enabling: SI 2014/3273

s.64, see *Acornwood LLP v Revenue and Customs Commissioners* [2014] UKFTT 416 (TC), [2014] S.F.T.D. 694 (FTT (Tax)), Judge Colin Bishopp

s.71, see *Acornwood LLP v Revenue and Customs Commissioners* [2014] UKFTT 416 (TC), [2014] S.F.T.D. 694 (FTT (Tax)), Judge Colin Bishopp

s.72, see *Acornwood LLP v Revenue and Customs Commissioners* [2014] UKFTT 416 (TC), [2014] S.F.T.D. 694 (FTT (Tax)), Judge Colin Bishopp

s.102, amended: 2014 c.26 Sch.17 para.8

s.103B, see *Acornwood LLP v Revenue and Customs Commissioners* [2014] UKFTT 416 (TC), [2014] S.F.T.D. 694 (FTT (Tax)), Judge Colin Bishopp

s.103C, see *Acornwood LLP v Revenue and Customs Commissioners* [2014] UKFTT 416 (TC), [2014] S.F.T.D. 694 (FTT (Tax)), Judge Colin Bishopp

s.116A, added: 2014 c.26 Sch.17 para.8

s.117, amended: 2014 c.26 Sch.17 para.9

s.127C, added: 2014 c.26 Sch.17 para.9

s.128, see *Martin v Revenue and Customs Commissioners* [2014] UKUT 429 (TCC), [2014] B.T.C. 527 (UT (Tax)), Warren J

s.151, amended: 2014 c.14 Sch.4 para.105

s.186A, amended: 2014 c.6 Sch.7 para.70

s.192, amended: 2014 c.26 s.56

s.198A, amended: 2014 c.14 Sch.4 para.106, 2014 c.26 s.56

s.198B, added: 2014 c.26 s.56

s.257A, amended: 2014 c.26 s.54

s.257A, repealed (in part): 2014 c.26 s.54

s.257DJ, amended: 2014 c.6 Sch.7 para.71

s.257JD, applied: SI 2014/3066 Reg.7, Reg.8, Reg.10

s.257JE, enabling: SI 2014/3066

s.257JF, applied: SI 2014/3066 Reg.4, Reg.8, Reg.10

s.257JF, enabling: SI 2014/3066

s.264A, added: 2014 c.26 Sch.10 para.2

s.270, amended: 2014 c.26 Sch.10 para.1

s.272, enabling: SI 2014/1929

s.281, amended: 2014 c.26 Sch.10 para.3

s.281, referred to: 2014 c.26 Sch.10 para.3

s.284, amended: 2014 c.26 Sch.10 para.5

s.284, enabling: SI 2014/1929

s.297A, amended: 2014 c.6 Sch.7 para.72

s.303, amended: 2014 c.26 s.56

s.309A, amended: 2014 c.14 Sch.4 para.107, 2014 c.26 s.56

s.309B, added: 2014 c.26 s.56

s.322, amended: 2014 c.26 Sch.10 para.4

s.330A, added: 2014 c.26 Sch.10 para.5

s.383, amended: 2014 c.26 s.13

s.392, amended: 2014 c.26 s.13, Sch.11 para.10

s.393A, added: 2014 c.26 s.13

s.397, amended: 2014 c.26 s.14

s.416, amended: 2014 c.26 Sch.11 para.11

s.462, amended: 2014 c.26 Sch.8 para.69

s.479, amended: 2014 c.26 Sch.8 para.70

s.488, amended: 2014 c.26 Sch.8 para.71

s.489, amended: 2014 c.26 Sch.8 para.72

s.490, amended: 2014 c.26 Sch.8 para.73

s.720, see *Fisher v Revenue and Customs Commissioners* [2014] UKFTT 804 (TC), [2014] S.F.T.D. 1341 (FTT (Tax)), Judge Swami Raghavan

s.809AZF, amended: 2014 c.26 Sch.17 para.23

s.809AZF, repealed (in part): 2014 c.26 Sch.17 para.23

s.809B, applied: 2014 c.28 s.10

s.809E, applied: 2014 c.28 s.10

s.809G, amended: 2014 c.26 s.11

s.809H, amended: 2014 c.26 Sch.38 para.8, 2014 c.29 s.9

s.809K, amended: 2014 c.26 Sch.9 para.29

s.828B, amended: 2014 c.26 Sch.38 para.9, 2014 c.29 s.9

s.852, amended: 2014 c.26 s.3
s.853, amended: 2014 c.14 Sch.4 para.108
s.874, amended: 2014 c.14 Sch.4 para.109
s.887, amended: 2014 c.14 Sch.4 para.110
s.887, substituted: 2014 c.14 Sch.4 para.110
s.966, disapplied: 2014 c.26 s.47
s.989, amended: 2014 c.26 Sch.38 para.10,
2014 c.29 s.9
s.989, applied: SI 2014/1506 Reg.9
s.991, amended: 2014 c.14 Sch.4 para.111
s.991, applied: 2014 c.26 s.285
s.993, applied: 2014 c.7 Sch.1 para.8, SI
2014/685 Reg.3
s.993, varied: 2014 c.7 Sch.1 para.8
s.1014, amended: 2014 c.26 Sch.11 para.12
s.1014, disapplied: 2014 c.26 s.12, Sch.37
para.22, 2014 c.30 s.4
s.1022, amended: 2014 c.26 Sch.11 para.13
Sch.4, amended: 2014 c.14 Sch.4 para.112,
2014 c.26 Sch.38 para.11, 2014 c.29 s.9

5. Welfare Reform Act 2007
Part 1, applied: SI 2014/1230 Reg.21, SSI
2014/225 Reg.6
s.2, applied: SI 2014/1230 Reg.19, Reg.21
s.4, applied: SI 2014/1230 Reg.19, Reg.21
s.4, enabling: SI 2014/902, SI 2014/2888
s.11E, enabling: SI 2014/1097
s.11H, enabling: SI 2014/597
s.11J, enabling: SI 2014/597
s.13, see *Secretary of State for Work and
Pensions v Brade* [2014] CSIH 39, 2014
S.C. 742 (IH (Ex Div)), Lady Smith
s.13, enabling: SI 2014/1097
s.17, enabling: SI 2014/591, SI 2014/597
s.20, amended: 2014 c.6 Sch.7 para.73
s.22, enabling: SI 2014/2309
s.24, see *Secretary of State for Work and
Pensions v Brade* [2014] CSIH 39, 2014
S.C. 742 (IH (Ex Div)), Lady Smith
s.24, enabling: SI 2014/591, SI 2014/597, SI
2014/902, SI 2014/1097, SI 2014/2309, SI
2014/2888
s.25, enabling: SI 2014/591, SI 2014/597, SI
2014/902, SI 2014/1097, SI 2014/2309, SI
2014/2888
Sch.1 Part 2 para.6, amended: SI 2014/560
Sch.1 para.32, SI 2014/3229 Sch.5 para.17
Sch.1 Part 2 para.6, repealed (in part): SI
2014/560 Sch.1 para.32, SI 2014/3229 Sch.5
para.17
Sch.2 para.1, enabling: SI 2014/884

Sch.2 para.2, applied: SI 2014/2309 Reg.4
Sch.2 para.2, enabling: SI 2014/2309, SI
2014/2888

**6. Justice and Security (Northern Ireland) Act
2007**
applied: 2014 c.5 Sch.1 para.1, 2014 c.25
Sch.1

11. Finance Act 2007
see *Aspinalls Club Ltd v Revenue and
Customs Commissioners* [2013] EWCA Civ
1464, [2014] 2 W.L.R. 1574 (CA (Civ Div)),
Moses LJ
s.11, see *Aspinalls Club Ltd v Revenue and
Customs Commissioners* [2013] EWCA Civ
1464, [2014] 2 W.L.R. 1574 (CA (Civ Div)),
Moses LJ
s.107, amended: 2014 c.26 s.299
Sch.19 para.28, repealed (in part): 2014 c.30
Sch.2 para.19
Sch.24, see *Harding v Revenue and Customs
Commissioners* [2014] S.T.C. 891 (UT
(Tax)), Judge Colin Bishopp
Sch.24, disapplied: 2014 c.26 Sch.35 para.13
Sch.24 Part 1, applied: 2014 c.26 s.276
Sch.24 Part 1 para.1, amended: 2014 c.26
Sch.22 para.19
Sch.24 Pt 1 para.1, see *Harding v Revenue
and Customs Commissioners* [2014] S.T.C.
891 (UT (Tax)), Judge Colin Bishopp
Sch.24 Part 1 para.3, applied: 2014 c.26
s.276
Sch.24 Part 2 para.12, amended: 2014 c.26
Sch.33 para.3
Sch.24 Part 5 para.28, amended: 2014 c.26
Sch.4 para.8

12. Mental Health Act 2007
Sch.1 Part 2 para.21, repealed: 2014 c.12
Sch.11 para.50

**15. Tribunals, Courts and Enforcement Act
2007**
Commencement Orders: SI 2014/768 Art.2
see *Gilchrist v Revenue and Customs
Commissioners* [2014] UKUT 169 (TCC)
(UT (Tax)), David Richards J; see *SM
(Withdrawal of Appealed Decision: Effect:
Pakistan)* [2014] UKUT 64 (IAC), [2014]
Imm. A.R. 662 (UT (IAC)), Judge Peter
Lane
applied: SI 2014/1610 r.52_1
referred to: SI 2014/2604 r.4
Part 3, applied: SI 2014/600 Art.3

s.7, enabling: SI 2014/1901
s.9, enabling: SI 2014/2604
s.10, see *Samuda v Secretary of State for Work and Pensions* [2014] EWCA Civ 1, [2014] 3 All E.R. 201 (CA (Civ Div)), Lewison LJ
s.11, see *Fairford Group Ltd Plc (In Liquidation) v Revenue and Customs Commissioners* [2014] UKUT 329 (TCC), [2014] B.V.C. 529 (UT (Tax)), Simon J; see *M, Petitioner* [2014] CSOH 28, 2014 S.L.T. 483 (OH), Lord Glennie; see *Samuda v Secretary of State for Work and Pensions* [2014] EWCA Civ 1, [2014] 3 All E.R. 201 (CA (Civ Div)), Lewison LJ; see *Singh v Secretary of State for the Home Department* [2014] EWCA Civ 438, [2014] 1 W.L.R. 3585 (CA (Civ Div)), Arden LJ; see *Virk v Secretary of State for the Home Department* [2013] EWCA Civ 652, [2014] Imm. A.R. 95 (CA (Civ Div)), Leveson LJ
s.11, applied: 2014 c.26 s.172
s.11, disapplied: 2014 c.26 s.256, s.266
s.12, see *General Healthcare Group Ltd v Revenue and Customs Commissioners* [2014] UKFTT 353 (TC), [2014] S.F.T.D. 1026 (FTT (Tax)), Judge Roger Berner; see *SM (Withdrawal of Appealed Decision: Effect: Pakistan)* [2014] UKUT 64 (IAC), [2014] Imm. A.R. 662 (UT (IAC)), Judge Peter Lane
s.13, see *Samuda v Secretary of State for Work and Pensions* [2014] EWCA Civ 1, [2014] 3 All E.R. 201 (CA (Civ Div)), Lewison LJ
s.13, applied: 2014 c.26 s.172
s.13, disapplied: 2014 c.26 s.256, s.266
s.14, see *SA (Sri Lanka) v Secretary of State for the Home Department* [2014] EWCA Civ 683, [2014] Imm. A.R. 1133 (CA (Civ Div)), Laws LJ; see *Virk v Secretary of State for the Home Department* [2013] EWCA Civ 652, [2014] Imm. A.R. 95 (CA (Civ Div)), Leveson LJ
s.22, see *Browning v Information Commissioner* [2014] EWCA Civ 1050, [2014] 1 W.L.R. 3848 (CA (Civ Div)), Maurice Kay LJ
s.22, enabling: SI 2014/514, SI 2014/2128, SI 2014/2604

s.25, see *Universal Enterprises (EU) Ltd v Revenue and Customs Commissioners* [2014] S.T.C. 1515 (UT (Tax)), Judge Colin Bishopp
s.25, applied: SI 2014/2604 r.6
s.29, see *Bedale Golf Club Ltd v Revenue and Customs Commissioners* [2014] UKUT 99 (TCC), [2014] B.V.C. 512 (UT (Tax)), Newey J; see *Dickinson v Network Rail Infrastructure Ltd* [2014] UKUT 372 (LC) (UT (Lands)), Sir Keith Lindblom P; see *Eclipse Film Partners No.35 LLP v Revenue and Customs Commissioners* [2014] EWCA Civ 184, [2014] C.P. Rep. 26 (CA (Civ Div)), Moses LJ
s.29, applied: SI 2014/2604 r.9
s.29, enabling: SI 2014/514, SI 2014/2604
s.30, enabling: SI 2014/1900
s.31, applied: SI 2014/602 Art.2
s.31, enabling: SI 2014/1900
s.39, referred to: 2014 c.12 s.180, SI 2014/786 Art.2
s.42, applied: 2014 c.12 s.180, SI 2014/182, SI 2014/590, SI 2014/878, SI 2014/1900
s.42, enabling: SI 2014/182, SI 2014/590, SI 2014/878, SI 2014/1900
s.49, applied: SI 2014/1900
s.49, enabling: SI 2014/590
s.51, applied: SI 2014/2898
s.51, enabling: SI 2014/2898
s.64, applied: SI 2014/421 Reg.3, Reg.4, Reg.14
s.64, enabling: SI 2014/421
s.66, applied: SI 2014/600 Art.3
s.78, applied: SI 2014/1 Reg.17
s.90, enabling: SI 2014/1, SI 2014/421
s.95, amended: SI 2014/605 Art.23
s.97, amended: 2014 c.29 s.4
s.104, amended: SI 2014/605 Art.24
s.143, repealed: 2014 c.18 s.10
s.145, enabling: SI 2014/600
s.148, enabling: SI 2014/768
Sch.2 para.1, applied: SI 2014/602 Art.2
Sch.3 para.1, applied: SI 2014/602 Art.2
Sch.3 para.7, applied: SI 2014/602 Art.2
Sch.5, enabling: SI 2014/514, SI 2014/2128, SI 2014/2604
Sch.5 Pt 1 para.7, see *Browning v Information Commissioner* [2014] EWCA Civ 1050, [2014] 1 W.L.R. 3848 (CA (Civ Div)), Maurice Kay LJ

Sch.5 Pt 1 para.11, see *Browning v Information Commissioner* [2014] EWCA Civ 1050, [2014] 1 W.L.R. 3848 (CA (Civ Div)), Maurice Kay LJ

Sch.5 Pt 1 para.16, see *Browning v Information Commissioner* [2014] EWCA Civ 1050, [2014] 1 W.L.R. 3848 (CA (Civ Div)), Maurice Kay LJ

Sch.5 Part 2 para.22, enabling: SI 2014/1505

Sch.5 Part 3 para.28, applied: SI 2014/514, SI 2014/1505, SI 2014/2128, SI 2014/2604

Sch.6 Part 4, amended: SI 2014/3248 Sch.3 Part 2

Sch.12, applied: SI 2014/3204 Sch.4 para.13, Sch.4 para.14

Sch.12 Part 2 para.13, enabling: SI 2014/1

Sch.12 Part 2 para.42, enabling: SI 2014/1

Sch.12 Part 2 para.50, enabling: SI 2014/1

Sch.12 Part 2 para.62, enabling: SI 2014/1

17. Consumers, Estate Agents and Redress Act 2007

applied: SI 2014/631 Art.3, Art.4

Part 1, substituted: SI 2014/631 Sch.1 para.12

Part 1, amended: SI 2014/631 Sch.1 para.12

s.1, substituted: SI 2014/631 Sch.1 para.12

s.2, repealed: SI 2014/631 Sch.1 para.12

s.4, amended: 2014 c.21 Sch.7 para.137, SI 2014/631 Sch.1 para.12

s.5, amended: SI 2014/631 Sch.1 para.12

s.5, repealed (in part): SI 2014/631 Sch.1 para.12

s.6, amended: SI 2014/631 Sch.1 para.12

s.6, repealed (in part): SI 2014/631 Sch.1 para.12

s.6A, added: SI 2014/631 Sch.1 para.12

s.7, repealed: SI 2014/631 Sch.1 para.12

s.7A, repealed: SI 2014/631 Sch.1 para.12

s.8, amended: SI 2014/631 Sch.1 para.12

s.9, amended: SI 2014/631 Sch.1 para.12

s.10, amended: SI 2014/631 Sch.1 para.12

s.11, amended: SI 2014/631 Sch.1 para.12

s.12, amended: SI 2014/631 Sch.1 para.12

s.13, amended: SI 2014/631 Sch.1 para.12

s.14, amended: SI 2014/631 Sch.1 para.12

s.15, amended: SI 2014/631 Sch.1 para.12

s.16, amended: SI 2014/631 Sch.1 para.12

s.17, amended: SI 2014/631 Sch.1 para.12

s.18, amended: SI 2014/631 Sch.1 para.12

s.19, amended: SI 2014/631 Sch.1 para.12

s.19A, amended: SI 2014/631 Sch.1 para.12

s.20, repealed: SI 2014/631 Sch.1 para.12

s.20A, repealed: SI 2014/631 Sch.1 para.12

s.21, repealed: SI 2014/631 Sch.1 para.12

s.24, amended: SI 2014/631 Sch.1 para.12, SI 2014/892 Sch.1 para.173

s.25, amended: 2014 c.21 Sch.7 para.138, SI 2014/631 Sch.1 para.12

s.26, amended: SI 2014/631 Sch.1 para.12

s.27, amended: SI 2014/631 Sch.1 para.12, SI 2014/892 Sch.1 para.174

s.28, amended: SI 2014/631 Sch.1 para.12

s.29, amended: SI 2014/631 Sch.1 para.12

s.31, amended: SI 2014/631 Sch.1 para.12

s.32, amended: SI 2014/631 Sch.1 para.12

s.33, amended: 2014 c.21 Sch.7 para.139, SI 2014/631 Sch.1 para.12

s.35, amended: SI 2014/631 Sch.1 para.12

s.35, repealed (in part): SI 2014/631 Sch.1 para.12

s.36, amended: SI 2014/631 Sch.1 para.12

s.37, amended: SI 2014/631 Sch.1 para.12

s.37, substituted: SI 2014/631 Sch.1 para.12

s.38, repealed: SI 2014/631 Sch.1 para.12

s.40A, added: SI 2014/631 Sch.1 para.12

s.41, amended: 2014 c.21 Sch.7 para.140, SI 2014/631 Sch.1 para.12

s.42, amended: 2014 c.21 Sch.7 para.141

s.43, amended: SI 2014/631 Sch.1 para.12

s.45, amended: SI 2014/631 Sch.1 para.12

s.47, applied: SI 2014/2378

s.47, enabling: SI 2014/2378

s.49, amended: SI 2014/631 Sch.1 para.12

s.52, amended: 2014 c.21 Sch.7 para.142

s.62, amended: SI 2014/631 Sch.1 para.12

s.62, repealed (in part): SI 2014/631 Sch.1 para.12

s.65, amended: SI 2014/631 Sch.1 para.12

s.65, repealed (in part): SI 2014/631 Sch.1 para.12

Sch.1, repealed: SI 2014/631 Sch.1 para.12

Sch.4 para.5, amended: SI 2014/631 Sch.1 para.12

Sch.4 para.8, amended: SI 2014/631 Sch.1 para.12

Sch.4 para.12, amended: SI 2014/631 Sch.1 para.12

18. Statistics and Registration Service Act 2007

s.6, amended: 2014 c.29 s.4

s.42, amended: SI 2014/560 Sch.1 para.33, SI 2014/3168 Sch.1 para.13

19. Corporate Manslaughter and Corporate Homicide Act 2007

    s.2, amended: 2014 c.22 Sch.9 para.15
    Sch.1, amended: 2014 c.29 s.4, SI 2014/834
    Sch.2 para.44

21. Offender Management Act 2007

    s.3, amended: 2014 c.11 s.10
    s.3, applied: SI 2014/1198 Reg.3
    s.4, amended: 2014 c.11 Sch.4 para.8
    s.5, applied: SI 2014/531 Sch.1
    s.5, enabling: SI 2014/2704
    s.13, enabling: SI 2014/1198
    s.36, enabling: SI 2014/1198, SI 2014/2704

22. Pensions Act 2007

    s.15, amended: 2014 c.19 Sch.13 para.78
    s.27, amended: 2014 c.19 Sch.13 para.79
    Sch.1 Part 8 para.44, repealed: 2014 c.19 Sch.12 para.91
    Sch.4 Part 3 para.61, amended: 2014 c.19 Sch.13 para.80
    Sch.4 Part 3 para.62, amended: 2014 c.19 Sch.13 para.80
    Sch.4 Part 3 para.65, amended: 2014 c.19 Sch.13 para.80
    Sch.4 Part 3 para.66, amended: 2014 c.19 Sch.13 para.80
    Sch.4 Part 3 para.67, amended: 2014 c.19 Sch.13 para.80

26. Building Societies (Funding) and Mutual Societies (Transfers) Act 2007

    Commencement Orders: SI 2014/2796 Art.2
    s.3, amended: 2014 c.14 Sch.4 para.114
    s.4, amended: 2014 c.14 Sch.4 para.115
    s.6, enabling: SI 2014/2796

27. Serious Crime Act 2007

    s.8, applied: SI 2014/1610 r.50_3
    s.8, repealed (in part): SI 2014/834 Sch.2 para.46
    s.9, applied: SI 2014/1610 r.68_1
    s.10, repealed (in part): SI 2014/834 Sch.2 para.47
    s.19, applied: SI 2014/1610 r.50_1
    s.24, applied: SI 2014/1610 r.68_1, r.74_1, r.68_3, r.68_4
    s.27, amended: 2014 c.14 Sch.4 para.116, SI 2014/834 Sch.2 para.48
    s.43, amended: SI 2014/834 Sch.2 para.49
    s.44, see *R. (on the application of Khan) v Secretary of State for Foreign and Commonwealth Affairs* [2014] EWCA Civ 24, [2014] 1 W.L.R. 872 (CA (Civ Div)), Lord Dyson MR
    s.45, see *R. v Hall (Clifford)* [2013] EWCA Crim 2499, [2014] 2 Cr. App. R. (S.) 20 (CA (Crim Div)), Jackson LJ; see *R. v Woodford (Anthony Graham)* [2013] EWCA Crim 1098, [2014] 1 Cr. App. R. (S.) 32 (CA (Crim Div)), Fulford LJ
    s.46, see *R. (on the application of Khan) v Secretary of State for Foreign and Commonwealth Affairs* [2014] EWCA Civ 24, [2014] 1 W.L.R. 872 (CA (Civ Div)), Lord Dyson MR; see *R. v Hall (Clifford)* [2013] EWCA Crim 2499, [2014] 2 Cr. App. R. (S.) 20 (CA (Crim Div)), Jackson LJ; see *R. v Sadique (Omar)* [2013] EWCA Crim 1150, [2014] 1 W.L.R. 986 (CA (Crim Div)), Lord Judge LCJ
    s.58, see *R. v Hall (Clifford)* [2013] EWCA Crim 2499, [2014] 2 Cr. App. R. (S.) 20 (CA (Crim Div)), Jackson LJ; see *R. v Sadique (Omar)* [2013] EWCA Crim 1150, [2014] 1 W.L.R. 986 (CA (Crim Div)), Lord Judge LCJ; see *R. v Woodford (Anthony Graham)* [2013] EWCA Crim 1098, [2014] 1 Cr. App. R. (S.) 32 (CA (Crim Div)), Fulford LJ
    s.68, applied: SI 2014/1608 Art.2
    s.68, enabling: SI 2014/1608
    s.70, amended: SI 2014/834 Sch.2 para.50
    s.84, repealed (in part): SI 2014/834 Sch.2 para.51
    Sch.2 para.2, applied: SI 2014/1610 r.50_3
    Sch.2 para.5A, added: SI 2014/834 Sch.2 para.52
    Sch.2 para.6, amended: SI 2014/834 Sch.2 para.52
    Sch.2 para.6, repealed: SI 2014/834 Sch.2 para.52
    Sch.2 para.7, applied: SI 2014/1610 r.50_3
    Sch.2 para.13, applied: SI 2014/1610 r.50_3
    Sch.7 Part 1, repealed: 2014 c.2 Sch.1 Part 2
    Sch.8 Part 6 para.135, repealed (in part): SI 2014/834 Sch.2 para.53
    Sch.8 Part 7 para.165, repealed: SI 2014/834 Sch.2 para.53
    Sch.8 Part 7 para.168, repealed: SI 2014/834 Sch.2 para.53
    Sch.13 para.9, repealed (in part): 2014 c.2 Sch.12 para.79

28. Local Government and Public Involvement in Health Act 2007

applied: 2014 c.5 Sch.1 para.1, 2014 c.25 Sch.1

s.92, applied: SI 2014/1308, SI 2014/1335, SI 2014/2562

s.92, enabling: SI 2014/1308, SI 2014/1335, SI 2014/2562

s.104, amended: SI 2014/469 Sch.2 para.24

s.116, applied: 2014 c.23 s.106

s.116A, applied: 2014 c.23 s.106

s.116B, applied: 2014 c.6 s.26, s.27

s.145, repealed: 2014 c.2 Sch.1 Part 2

s.148, referred to: 2014 c.2 Sch.12 para.85

s.148, repealed: 2014 c.2 Sch.12 para.81

s.149, repealed: 2014 c.2 Sch.1 Part 2

s.151, repealed (in part): 2014 c.2 Sch.1 Part 2

s.153, repealed: 2014 c.2 Sch.1 Part 2

s.155, repealed (in part): 2014 c.2 Sch.1 Part 2

s.157, repealed: 2014 c.2 Sch.1 Part 2

s.158, repealed: 2014 c.2 Sch.12 para.123

s.159, repealed: 2014 c.2 Sch.1 Part 2

s.201, repealed (in part): 2014 c.2 Sch.1 Part 2

s.207, applied: 2014 c.2 Sch.2 para.25

s.212, amended: 2014 c.2 Sch.12 para.82

s.214, amended: 2014 c.2 Sch.12 para.83

s.214, repealed (in part): 2014 c.2 Sch.12 para.83

Sch.9, repealed: 2014 c.2 Sch.1 Part 2

Sch.10, referred to: 2014 c.2 Sch.12 para.85

Sch.10, repealed: 2014 c.2 Sch.12 para.84

Sch.11, repealed: 2014 c.2 Sch.1 Part 2

Sch.13 Part 2 para.52, repealed: 2014 c.2 Sch.1 Part 2

Sch.14 para.5, repealed (in part): 2014 c.2 Sch.12 para.123

29. Legal Services Act 2007

Commencement Orders: SI 2014/3307 Art.2

see *Bentine v Bentine* [2013] EWHC 3098 (Ch), [2014] 1 All E.R. 983 (Ch D), Proudman J

applied: SI 2014/3235 Reg.2

Part 5, applied: SI 2014/1897 Art.4, SI 2014/1898 Art.4, SI 2014/3238 Art.6, Art.13

s.3, see *R. (on the application of Lumsdon) v Legal Services Board* [2014] EWCA Civ 1276, [2014] H.R.L.R. 29 (CA (Civ Div)), Lord Dyson MR

s.13, applied: SI 2014/1610 r.2_4

s.14, see *Assaubayev v Michael Wilson and Partners Ltd* [2014] EWHC 821 (QB), [2014] 3 Costs L.O. 446 (QBD), Walker J

s.18, applied: SI 2014/2359 Art.6

s.57, amended: SI 2014/892 Sch.1 para.176

s.57, applied: SI 2014/559, SI 2014/892 Sch.2 para.3, Sch.2 para.4

s.59, varied: SI 2014/416 Sch.1 para.2

s.60, amended: SI 2014/892 Sch.1 para.177

s.60, applied: SI 2014/559

s.60, referred to: SI 2014/892 Sch.2 para.2

s.64, applied: SI 2014/3234 Art.4

s.64, enabling: SI 2014/3234, SI 2014/3236, SI 2014/3238

s.69, applied: SI 2014/3234, SI 2014/3236, SI 2014/3238

s.69, enabling: SI 2014/3234, SI 2014/3236, SI 2014/3238

s.70, applied: SI 2014/3234, SI 2014/3236, SI 2014/3238

s.80, applied: SI 2014/1897, SI 2014/1898

s.80, enabling: SI 2014/1897, SI 2014/1898

s.81, applied: SI 2014/1897, SI 2014/1898

s.96, varied: SI 2014/1897 Sch.1 para.1, SI 2014/1898 Sch.1 para.1

s.99, referred to: SI 2014/3238 Sch.1 para.2

s.125, varied: SI 2014/3307 Art.3

s.128, applied: SI 2014/3307 Art.4

s.137, see *Layard Horsfall Ltd v Legal Ombudsman* [2013] EWHC 4137 (QB), [2014] 2 Costs L.O. 277 (QBD (Admin)), Phillips J

s.161, amended: SI 2014/3307 Art.5

s.161, referred to: SI 2014/3307 Art.4

s.173, applied: SI 2014/1185

s.173, enabling: SI 2014/1185

s.174, enabling: SI 2014/1185

s.174A, enabling: SI 2014/3316

s.176, applied: SI 2014/3238 Sch.1 para.2, Sch.2 para.3, Sch.3 para.2, Sch.4 para.3

s.194, amended: SI 2014/605 Art.25

s.204, enabling: SI 2014/1185, SI 2014/1897, SI 2014/1898, SI 2014/3234, SI 2014/3236, SI 2014/3238, SI 2014/3316

s.205, applied: SI 2014/1185

s.206, applied: SI 2014/1872, SI 2014/1897, SI 2014/1898, SI 2014/2937, SI 2014/3234, SI 2014/3236, SI 2014/3238, SI 2014/3316

s.208, enabling: SI 2014/3307

s.211, enabling: SI 2014/3307

Sch.4 Part 2 para.3, applied: SI 2014/1872, SI 2014/2937

Sch.4 Part 2 para.3, enabling: SI 2014/1872

Sch.4 Part 2 para.5, applied: SI 2014/1872, SI 2014/2937

Sch.4 Part 2 para.9, applied: SI 2014/1872, SI 2014/2937

Sch.4 Part 2 para.11, applied: SI 2014/1872, SI 2014/2937

Sch.4 Part 2 para.16, applied: SI 2014/1872

Sch.4 Part 2 para.17, enabling: SI 2014/2937

Sch.10 Part 1, applied: SI 2014/1897 Art.2, SI 2014/3238 Art.2

Sch.10 Part 1 para.1, applied: SI 2014/1925, SI 2014/3077

Sch.10 Part 1 para.1, referred to: SI 2014/1925

Sch.10 Part 1 para.14, applied: SI 2014/3077

Sch.10 Part 1 para.15, referred to: SI 2014/1925

Sch.10 Part 1 para.15, enabling: SI 2014/1925, SI 2014/3077

Sch.13 Part 2 para.18, varied: SI 2014/1897 Sch.1 para.2, SI 2014/1898 Sch.1 para.2

Sch.13 Part 2 para.20, varied: SI 2014/1897 Sch.1 para.2, SI 2014/1898 Sch.1 para.2

Sch.13 Part 3 para.29, varied: SI 2014/1897 Sch.1 para.2, SI 2014/1898 Sch.1 para.2

Sch.13 Part 3 para.32, varied: SI 2014/1897 Sch.1 para.2, SI 2014/1898 Sch.1 para.2

Sch.13 Part 3 para.34, varied: SI 2014/1897 Sch.1 para.2, SI 2014/1898 Sch.1 para.2

Sch.13 Part 3 para.37, varied: SI 2014/1897 Sch.1 para.2, SI 2014/1898 Sch.1 para.2

Sch.13 Part 5 para.47, varied: SI 2014/1897 Sch.1 para.2, SI 2014/1898 Sch.1 para.2

Sch.13 Part 5 para.48, varied: SI 2014/1897 Sch.1 para.2, SI 2014/1898 Sch.1 para.2

Sch.13 Part 5 para.50, varied: SI 2014/1897 Sch.1 para.2, SI 2014/1898 Sch.1 para.2

Sch.14, applied: SI 2014/3238 Sch.2 para.12, Sch.4 para.12

Sch.14, referred to: SI 2014/3238 Sch.2 para.12, Sch.4 para.12

Sch.14, varied: SI 2014/3234 Art.5, SI 2014/3236 Art.3

Sch.14 para.1, varied: SI 2014/3236 Art.3, SI 2014/3238 Sch.2 para.12, Sch.4 para.12

Sch.14 para.18, varied: SI 2014/3238 Sch.2 para.12, Sch.4 para.12

30. UK Borders Act 2007

see *R. (on the application of George) v Secretary of State for the Home Department* [2014] UKSC 28, [2014] 1 W.L.R. 1831 (SC), Lord Neuberger PSC

applied: SI 2014/2604 Sch.1 para.2

s.5, applied: SI 2014/3181 Sch.1 para.1

s.7, amended: 2014 c.22 s.11

s.8, substituted: 2014 c.22 s.14

s.15, amended: 2014 c.22 s.12, Sch.9 para.75

s.15, repealed (in part): 2014 c.22 s.12

s.17, amended: 2014 c.22 Sch.9 para.58

s.19, repealed: 2014 c.22 Sch.9 para.60

s.20, repealed: 2014 c.22 Sch.9 para.76

s.32, see *Attorney General's Reference (No.41 of 2013)* [2013] EWCA Crim 1729, [2014] 1 Cr. App. R. (S.) 80 (CA (Crim Div)), Pitchford LJ; see *Greenwood (Automatic Deportation: Order of Events), Re* [2014] UKUT 342 (IAC), [2014] Imm. A.R. 1288 (UT (IAC)), CMG Ockelton (Vice President); see *MF (Nigeria) v Secretary of State for the Home Department* [2013] EWCA Civ 1192, [2014] 1 W.L.R. 544 (CA (Civ Div)), Lord Dyson MR; see *R. (on the application of Akpinar) v Upper Tribunal (Immigration and Asylum Chamber)* [2014] EWCA Civ 937, Times, July 17, 2014 (CA (Civ Div)), Maurice Kay LJ; see *R. (on the application of Nouazli) v Secretary of State for the Home Department* [2013] EWCA Civ 1608, [2014] 1 W.L.R. 3313 (CA (Civ Div)), Moore-Bick LJ; see *SS (Nigeria) v Secretary of State for the Home Department* [2013] EWCA Civ 550, [2014] 1 W.L.R. 998 (CA (Civ Div)), Laws LJ

s.33, see *Attorney General's Reference (No.41 of 2013)* [2013] EWCA Crim 1729, [2014] 1 Cr. App. R. (S.) 80 (CA (Crim Div)), Pitchford LJ; see *Greenwood (Automatic Deportation: Order of Events), Re* [2014] UKUT 342 (IAC), [2014] Imm. A.R. 1288 (UT (IAC)), CMG Ockelton (Vice President); see *R. (on the application of Akpinar) v Upper Tribunal (Immigration and Asylum Chamber)* [2014] EWCA Civ 937, Times, July 17, 2014 (CA (Civ Div)), Maurice Kay LJ; see *R. (on the application of Nouazli) v Secretary of State for the Home Department* [2013] EWCA Civ 1608, [2014]

1 W.L.R. 3313 (CA (Civ Div)), Moore-Bick LJ

s.34, see *Greenwood (Automatic Deportation: Order of Events), Re* [2014] UKUT 342 (IAC), [2014] Imm. A.R. 1288 (UT (IAC)), CMG Ockelton (Vice President)

s.35, repealed (in part): 2014 c.22 Sch.9 para.60

s.36, see *R. (on the application of Nouazli) v Secretary of State for the Home Department* [2013] EWCA Civ 1608, [2014] 1 W.L.R. 3313 (CA (Civ Div)), Moore-Bick LJ

s.40, amended: SI 2014/834 Sch.2 para.55

s.41, amended: SI 2014/834 Sch.2 para.56

s.41A, amended: SI 2014/834 Sch.2 para.57

s.41B, amended: SI 2014/834 Sch.2 para.58

s.42, amended: SI 2014/834 Sch.2 para.59

s.48, amended: 2014 c.22 Sch.9 para.16

s.56A, see *HHG (Iraq) v Secretary of State for the Home Department* [2014] CSOH 48, 2014 S.L.T. 693 (OH), Lord Boyd of Duncansby

s.61, amended: 2014 c.22 s.73

2008

4. Criminal Justice and Immigration Act 2008

applied: SI 2014/1610 r.44_1

Part 1, applied: SI 2014/1610 r.42_2

s.1, applied: SI 2014/1610 r.42_2, r.42_8

s.7, referred to: SI 2014/1610 r.42_2

s.21, see *R. v Leacock (Mark)* [2013] EWCA Crim 1994, [2014] 2 Cr. App. R. (S.) 12 (CA (Crim Div)), Lord Thomas LCJ

s.76, see *R. v Oye (Seun)* [2013] EWCA Crim 1725, [2014] 1 W.L.R. 3354 (CA (Crim Div)), Davis LJ

s.81, amended: SI 2014/3141 Sch.3 para.2

s.83, amended: SI 2014/3141 Sch.3 para.3

s.84, amended: SI 2014/3141 Sch.3 para.4

s.84, applied: SI 2014/1610 r.52_10

s.85, amended: SI 2014/3141 Sch.3 para.5

s.85, repealed (in part): SI 2014/3141 Sch.3 para.5

s.86, amended: SI 2014/3141 Sch.3 para.6

s.87, amended: SI 2014/3141 Sch.3 para.7

s.88, amended: SI 2014/3141 Sch.3 para.8

s.89, amended: SI 2014/3141 Sch.3 para.9

s.90, amended: SI 2014/3141 Sch.3 para.10

s.90A, amended: SI 2014/3141 Sch.3 para.11

s.91, amended: SI 2014/3141 Sch.3 para.12

s.91, applied: SI 2014/1610 r.52_10

s.92, amended: SI 2014/3141 Sch.3 para.13

s.98, amended: 2014 c.12 s.119

s.99, amended: 2014 c.12 s.119

s.118, repealed: 2014 c.12 Sch.11 para.50

s.123, repealed: 2014 c.12 Sch.11 para.50

s.147, amended: 2014 c.12 s.119, SI 2014/3141 Sch.3 para.14

s.147, enabling: SI 2014/163

s.152, amended: SI 2014/3141 Sch.3 para.15

Sch.1 Part 2 para.22, applied: SI 2014/1652 Sch.1

Sch.1 Part 2 para.23, applied: SI 2014/1652 Sch.1

Sch.1 Part 2 para.24, applied: SI 2014/1652 Sch.1

Sch.1 Part 2 para.26, applied: 2014 c.12 Sch.2 para.6

Sch.1 Part 2 para.26, enabling: SI 2014/163

Sch.1 Part 4 para.34, applied: SI 2014/1610 r.42_2, r.42_10

Sch.2, applied: SI 2014/1610 r.44_1

Sch.19, applied: SI 2014/1610 r.52_10

Sch.19 Part 1 paraA.1, added: SI 2014/3141 Sch.3 para.16

Sch.19 Part 1 para.2A, added: SI 2014/3141 Sch.3 para.16

Sch.19 Part 1 para.3, repealed (in part): SI 2014/3141 Sch.3 para.16

Sch.19 Part 1 para.3A, added: SI 2014/3141 Sch.3 para.16

Sch.19 Part 1 para.4, repealed (in part): SI 2014/3141 Sch.3 para.16

Sch.19 Part 1 para.5A, added: SI 2014/3141 Sch.3 para.16

Sch.19 Part 1 para.6, substituted: SI 2014/3141 Sch.3 para.16

Sch.19 Part 3 para.47, amended: SI 2014/3141 Sch.3 para.16

Sch.20, repealed: 2014 c.12 Sch.11 para.50

6. Child Maintenance and Other Payments Act 2008

Commencement Orders: SI 2014/576 Art.2; SI 2014/1635 Art.2

s.6, applied: SI 2014/614 Reg.5

s.6, enabling: SI 2014/612, SI 2014/614

s.46, enabling: SI 2014/868

s.47, amended: 2014 c.1 Sch.2 para.2

s.53, applied: SI 2014/868
s.53, enabling: SI 2014/868
s.55, applied: SI 2014/612, SI 2014/614
s.55, enabling: SI 2014/612, SI 2014/614, SI 2014/1386
s.62, enabling: SI 2014/576, SI 2014/1635
Sch.5 para.1, applied: SI 2014/614 Reg.3, Reg.4, Reg.5, Reg.8
Sch.5 para.1, referred to: SI 2014/614 Reg.8
Sch.5 para.2, enabling: SI 2014/614, SI 2014/1386
Sch.5 para.3, enabling: SI 2014/614
Sch.5 para.5, applied: SI 2014/614 Reg.6
Sch.5 para.5, enabling: SI 2014/614, SI 2014/1386
Sch.5 para.6, enabling: SI 2014/614
Sch.5 para.7, enabling: SI 2014/614

9. Finance Act 2008
Commencement Orders: SI 2014/906 Art.2, Art.3
s.21, enabling: SI 2014/495, SI 2014/3262
s.121, see *Taylor Clark Leisure Plc v Revenue and Customs Commissioners* [2014] UKUT 396 (TCC), [2014] B.V.C. 536 (UT (Tax)), Lord Doherty
s.124, applied: SI 2014/885, SI 2014/886, SI 2014/1264
s.124, enabling: SI 2014/885, SI 2014/886, SI 2014/1264
s.128, see *Cloburn Quarry Co Ltd v Revenue and Customs Commissioners* [2014] S.T.C. 1073 (OH), Lord Burns
s.129, enabling: SI 2014/906
s.130, see *R. (on the application of Rouse) v Revenue and Customs Commissioners* [2014] S.T.C. 230 (UT (Tax)), Warren J
s.130, applied: 2014 c.28 s.67
s.157, enabling: SI 2014/1327
s.160, applied: SI 2014/211
s.160, enabling: SI 2014/211
Sch.36, see *Patel v Revenue and Customs Commissioners* [2014] UKFTT 167 (TC), [2014] W.T.L.R. 1183 (FTT (Tax)), Judge Greg Sinfield
Sch.36 Part 1, applied: SI 2014/1842 Reg.11
Sch.36 Part 1 para.1, applied: 2014 c.26 Sch.34 para.10
Sch.36 Pt 1 para.1, see *Behague v Revenue and Customs Commissioners* [2014] W.T.L.R. 187 (FTT (Tax)), Judge Barbara Mosedale

Sch.36 Pt 1 para.2, see *R. (on the application of Derrin Brother Properties Ltd) v Revenue and Customs Commissioners* [2014] EWHC 1152 (Admin), [2014] S.T.C. 2238 (QBD (Admin)), Simler J
Sch.36 Part 1 para.5, applied: 2014 c.26 Sch.34 para.10
Sch.36 Pt 4 para.18, see *Patel v Revenue and Customs Commissioners* [2014] UKFTT 167 (TC), [2014] W.T.L.R. 1183 (FTT (Tax)), Judge Greg Sinfield
Sch.41 para.1, amended: 2014 c.26 Sch.28 para.27
Sch.41 para.15, amended: 2014 c.26 Sch.33 para.4
Sch.46 para.3, enabling: SI 2014/1327
Sch.46 para.5, enabling: SI 2014/1327
Sch.46 para.6, enabling: SI 2014/1327
Sch.46 para.7, enabling: SI 2014/1327
Sch.46 para.9, enabling: SI 2014/1327
Sch.46 para.10, enabling: SI 2014/1327
Sch.46 para.11, enabling: SI 2014/1327
Sch.46 para.12, enabling: SI 2014/1327

11. Special Educational Needs (Information) Act 2008
s.1, repealed: 2014 c.6 Sch.3 para.29

13. Regulatory Enforcement and Sanctions Act 2008
s.12, amended: SI 2014/892 Sch.1 para.179
s.28, enabling: SI 2014/573, SI 2014/3070
s.29, enabling: SI 2014/573
s.73, amended: SI 2014/892 Sch.1 para.180
Sch.3, amended: SI 2014/1637 Sch.4 Part 1
Sch.5, amended: SI 2014/892 Sch.1 para.181
Sch.6, amended: SI 2014/1637 Sch.4 Part 1, SI 2014/1639 Sch.3 Part 1

14. Health and Social Care Act 2008
Commencement Orders: SI 2014/3251 Art.2
Part 1, applied: 2014 c.23 s.57, SI 2014/2418 Sch.1, SI 2014/2936 Reg.24
Part 1 c.2, applied: 2014 c.23 s.48
Part 1 c.6, applied: 2014 c.23 s.57
s.8, applied: SI 2014/2936 Reg.3
s.8, referred to: SI 2014/2418 Sch.1
s.8, enabling: SI 2014/2936
s.10, applied: SI 2014/2936 Sch.5
s.17, applied: 2014 c.23 s.57
s.19, amended: 2014 c.23 s.86
s.19, applied: 2014 c.23 s.86
s.20, amended: 2014 c.23 s.81, s.95
s.20, applied: SI 2014/2936

s.20, enabling: SI 2014/2936
s.21, applied: SI 2014/2936 Reg.21
s.23, applied: SI 2014/2936 Reg.21
s.26, amended: 2014 c.23 s.87
s.28, amended: 2014 c.23 s.87
s.29, amended: 2014 c.23 s.82
s.29, applied: SI 2014/2936 Reg.26
s.29A, added: 2014 c.23 s.82
s.32, amended: 2014 c.23 s.82
s.33, applied: SI 2014/2936 Sch.5
s.34, applied: SI 2014/2936 Sch.5
s.35, enabling: SI 2014/2936
s.39, amended: 2014 c.23 s.82
s.46, applied: SI 2014/1788 Reg.2
s.46, substituted: 2014 c.23 s.91
s.46, enabling: SI 2014/1788
s.47, repealed: 2014 c.23 s.91
s.48, amended: 2014 c.23 s.91
s.48, repealed (in part): 2014 c.23 s.90, s.91
s.49, repealed: 2014 c.23 s.91
s.50, amended: 2014 c.23 s.91
s.51, amended: 2014 c.23 s.91
s.54, amended: 2014 c.23 s.90
s.55, repealed (in part): 2014 c.23 s.90
s.56, repealed: 2014 c.2 Sch.12 para.87
s.57, amended: 2014 c.23 s.90
s.61, repealed (in part): 2014 c.23 s.90
s.63, applied: SI 2014/2936 Sch.5
s.64, applied: 2014 c.23 s.92, SI 2014/2936
Sch.5
s.65, applied: SI 2014/2936 Sch.5
s.70, amended: 2014 c.23 s.91
s.72, amended: 2014 c.23 s.91
s.83, repealed (in part): 2014 c.23 s.90
s.86, applied: SI 2014/2936 Reg.24
s.86, enabling: SI 2014/2936
s.87, enabling: SI 2014/2936
s.88, amended: 2014 c.23 s.82
s.89, amended: 2014 c.23 s.82
s.89, applied: SI 2014/2936 Reg.24
s.93, applied: SI 2014/2936 Reg.24
s.94, applied: SI 2014/2936 Reg.24
s.161, enabling: SI 2014/1788, SI 2014/2936
s.162, applied: SI 2014/2936
s.170, enabling: SI 2014/3251
Sch.1, amended: 2014 c.23 s.88
Sch.1 para.3, amended: 2014 c.23 s.88
Sch.1 para.3A, added: 2014 c.23 s.89
Sch.1 para.4, amended: 2014 c.23 s.88
Sch.1 para.5, amended: 2014 c.23 s.88

Sch.1 para.5, repealed (in part): 2014 c.23
s.88
Sch.4 Part 1 para.1, amended: 2014 c.2
Sch.12 para.88
Sch.4 Part 1 para.1, repealed (in part): 2014
c.2 Sch.12 para.88
Sch.4 Part 2 para.5, amended: 2014 c.23 s.90
Sch.4 Part 2 para.5, repealed (in part): 2014
c.23 s.90
Sch.4 Part 2 para.9, amended: 2014 c.2
Sch.12 para.88
Sch.5 Part 3 para.64, repealed: 2014 c.2
Sch.1 Part 2

17. Housing and Regeneration Act 2008
Part 2, applied: 2014 c.2 Sch.11 para.2, SI
2014/2418 Sch.1
s.61, amended: 2014 c.14 Sch.4 para.122
s.62, amended: 2014 c.14 Sch.4 para.123
s.79, amended: 2014 c.14 Sch.4 para.122,
Sch.4 para.124
s.106A, repealed: 2014 c.2 Sch.12 para.90
s.120, amended: 2014 c.14 Sch.4 para.122
s.122, amended: 2014 c.14 Sch.4 para.123
s.128, amended: 2014 c.2 Sch.12 para.91
s.134, amended: 2014 c.14 Sch.4 para.122,
Sch.4 para.123, Sch.4 para.125
s.144, amended: 2014 c.14 Sch.4 para.122
s.145, amended: 2014 c.14 Sch.4 para.122
s.152, amended: SI 2014/3486 Art.30
s.153, amended: 2014 c.14 Sch.4 para.122
s.154, amended: 2014 c.14 Sch.4 para.122
s.157, amended: 2014 c.14 Sch.4 para.122,
Sch.4 para.123, Sch.4 para.126
s.161, amended: 2014 c.14 Sch.4 para.122,
Sch.4 para.123, Sch.4 para.127
s.163, amended: 2014 c.14 Sch.4 para.122,
Sch.4 para.123, Sch.4 para.128
s.164, amended: 2014 c.14 Sch.4 para.122,
Sch.4 para.123, Sch.4 para.129
s.165, amended: 2014 c.14 Sch.4 para.122,
Sch.4 para.123, Sch.4 para.130
s.166, amended: 2014 c.14 Sch.4 para.122
s.167, amended: 2014 c.14 Sch.4 para.122,
Sch.4 para.131
s.167, repealed (in part): 2014 c.14 Sch.4
para.131
s.196, repealed (in part): 2014 c.2 Sch.12
para.92
s.197, repealed (in part): 2014 c.2 Sch.12
para.93

s.201, repealed (in part): 2014 c.2 Sch.12 para.94

s.210A, amended: 2014 c.2 Sch.12 para.95

s.210A, repealed (in part): 2014 c.2 Sch.12 para.95

s.212, amended: 2014 c.14 Sch.4 para.122, Sch.4 para.123, Sch.4 para.132

s.249, amended: 2014 c.2 Sch.12 para.96

s.255, amended: 2014 c.14 Sch.4 para.122, Sch.4 para.123, Sch.4 para.133

s.270, amended: 2014 c.14 Sch.4 para.123, Sch.4 para.134

s.271, amended: 2014 c.14 Sch.4 para.122, Sch.4 para.135

s.275, amended: 2014 c.14 Sch.4 para.122, Sch.4 para.136, SI 2014/3486 Art.30

s.276, amended: 2014 c.14 Sch.4 para.123, Sch.4 para.137, SI 2014/3486 Art.30

Sch.9 para.20, repealed: 2014 c.2 Sch.1 Part 2

18. Crossrail Act 2008

see *GPE (Hanover Square) Ltd v Transport for London* [2014] R.V.R. 77 (UT (Lands)), George Bartlett QC

applied: SI 2014/310 Art.18, Art.20, Sch.6 para.2

referred to: SI 2014/310 Sch.6 para.2

s.8, applied: SI 2014/310 Sch.6 para.1

s.8, referred to: SI 2014/310 Sch.6 para.4

s.10, applied: SI 2014/310 Sch.6 para.4

s.10, referred to: SI 2014/310 Sch.6 para.3

s.12, applied: SI 2014/310 Sch.6 para.4

s.12, enabling: SI 2014/1382

s.15, applied: SI 2014/310 Sch.6 para.1

s.20, applied: SI 2014/310 Sch.6 para.1, Sch.6 para.4

s.39, enabling: SI 2014/1367

s.48, enabling: SI 2014/310

s.54, applied: SI 2014/310 Sch.6 para.4

Sch.2 para.6, applied: SI 2014/310 Art.6

Sch.2 para.8, applied: SI 2014/310 Sch.6 para.1

Sch.2 para.9, applied: SI 2014/310 Art.27

Sch.3 para.1, applied: SI 2014/310 Art.5, Sch.6 para.1

Sch.3 para.1, referred to: SI 2014/310 Sch.6 para.3

Sch.3 para.5, applied: SI 2014/310 Art.6, Sch.6 para.1

Sch.3 para.6, applied: SI 2014/310 Sch.6 para.1

Sch.3 para.14, applied: SI 2014/310 Sch.6 para.1

Sch.3 para.14, referred to: SI 2014/310 Sch.6 para.3

Sch.3 para.15, applied: SI 2014/310 Sch.6 para.1

Sch.7, applied: SI 2014/310 Sch.6 para.3, Sch.6 para.4

Sch.7 Part 1 para.1, enabling: SI 2014/1367

Sch.7 Part 2, applied: SI 2014/310 Sch.6 para.1

Sch.7 Part 2 para.3, applied: SI 2014/310 Sch.6 para.1

Sch.7 Part 2 para.7, disapplied: SI 2014/310 Sch.6 para.3

Sch.7 Part 2 para.11, referred to: SI 2014/310 Sch.6 para.3

Sch.7 Part 4 para.28, applied: SI 2014/310 Sch.6 para.1

Sch.7 Part 4 para.30, applied: SI 2014/310 Sch.6 para.4

Sch.7 Part 4 para.30, enabling: SI 2014/1382

Sch.7 Part 4 para.34, applied: SI 2014/310 Sch.6 para.4

Sch.7 Part 4 para.34, enabling: SI 2014/1382

Sch.7 Part 4 para.35, enabling: SI 2014/1382

Sch.14 para.14, applied: SI 2014/310 Sch.6 para.1

Sch.17 Part 1, applied: SI 2014/310 Sch.6 para.1

Sch.17 Part 1 para.18, applied: SI 2014/310 Sch.6 para.3

Sch.17 Part 2 para.13, applied: SI 2014/310 Sch.6 para.3

Sch.17 Part 4, applied: SI 2014/310 Sch.6 para.1

Sch.17 Part 4 para.4, referred to: SI 2014/310 Sch.6 para.3

Sch.17 Part 4 para.6, applied: SI 2014/310 Sch.6 para.3

20. Health and Safety (Offences) Act 2008

Sch.3 para.1, repealed: SI 2014/1639 Sch.3 Part 1

22. Human Fertilisation and Embryology Act 2008

see *M v F (Legal Paternity)* [2013] EWHC 1901 (Fam), [2014] 1 F.L.R. 352 (Fam Div), Peter Jackson J; see *P-M (Parental Order: Payments to Surrogacy Agency), Re* [2013] EWHC 2328 (Fam), [2014] 1 F.L.R. 725 (Fam Div), Theis J

s.35, see *M v F (Legal Paternity)* [2013]
EWHC 1901 (Fam), [2014] 1 F.L.R. 352
(Fam Div), Peter Jackson J
s.35, amended: SI 2014/3229 Sch.5 para.18
s.40, amended: SI 2014/3229 Sch.5 para.18
s.42, see *G (Children) (Shared Residence
Order: Biological Non-Birth Mother), Re*
[2014] EWCA Civ 336, [2014] 2 F.L.R. 897
(CA (Civ Div)), Moses LJ
s.42, amended: SI 2014/3229 Sch.5 para.18
s.42, applied: SI 2014/511 Reg.7
s.43, see *G (Children) (Shared Residence
Order: Biological Non-Birth Mother), Re*
[2014] EWCA Civ 336, [2014] 2 F.L.R. 897
(CA (Civ Div)), Moses LJ
s.46, amended: SI 2014/3229 Sch.5 para.18
s.54, see *C (A Child) (Parental Order), Re*
[2013] EWHC 2408 (Fam), [2014] 1 F.L.R.
757 (Fam Div), Theis J; see *C (A Child)
(Parental Order), Re* [2013] EWHC 2413
(Fam), [2014] 1 F.L.R. 654 (Fam Div), Theis
J; see *J v G (Parental Orders)* [2013]
EWHC 1432 (Fam), [2014] 1 F.L.R. 297
(Fam Div), Theis J; see *P-M (Parental
Order: Payments to Surrogacy Agency), Re*
[2013] EWHC 2328 (Fam), [2014] 1 F.L.R.
725 (Fam Div), Theis J
s.54, applied: SI 2014/840 Sch.1
s.64, enabling: SI 2014/560

23. Children and Young Persons Act 2008
Part 1, applied: SI 2014/2407 Reg.4
s.1, applied: SI 2014/2407 Reg.3, Reg.4
s.1, enabling: SI 2014/2407
s.40, enabling: SI 2014/2407

25. Education and Skills Act 2008
Commencement Orders: SI 2014/2379 Art.2,
Art.3; SI 2014/3364 Art.2, Art.3, Art.4, Art.5
Part 4, applied: SI 2014/3283 Reg.3
Part 4 c.1, referred to: 2014 c.6 s.41
s.4, amended: 2014 c.6 Sch.3 para.83
s.4, repealed (in part): 2014 c.6 Sch.3
para.83
s.17, amended: 2014 c.6 Sch.3 para.84
s.47, amended: 2014 c.6 Sch.3 para.85
s.47, repealed (in part): 2014 c.6 Sch.3
para.85
s.78, amended: 2014 c.6 Sch.3 para.86
s.80, repealed: 2014 c.6 Sch.3 para.75
s.94, enabling: SI 2014/3283
s.95, applied: SI 2014/2379 Art.3
s.95, referred to: 2014 c.6 s.41

s.99, applied: SI 2014/512 Sch.1 para.2
s.100, applied: SI 2014/3283 Sch.1 para.32
s.105, applied: SI 2014/3283 Sch.1 para.32
s.106, applied: SI 2014/1530 Reg.59, SI
2014/2158 Reg.2
s.106, varied: SI 2014/2379 Art.3
s.106, enabling: SI 2014/2158
s.107, applied: SI 2014/2158 Reg.2
s.108, applied: SI 2014/3283 Sch.1 para.32
s.109, applied: SI 2014/2379 Art.3, SI
2014/3283 Sch.1 para.33
s.112, applied: SI 2014/3283 Sch.1 para.32
s.116, applied: SI 2014/3283 Sch.1 para.32
s.119, applied: SI 2014/3283 Sch.1 para.32
s.120, applied: SI 2014/3283 Sch.1 para.32
s.123, applied: SI 2014/3283 Sch.1 para.32
s.128, applied: SI 2014/1977 Reg.8, SI
2014/3283 Sch.1 para.18, Sch.1 para.20,
Sch.1 para.21
s.128, varied: SI 2014/2379 Art.3
s.128, enabling: SI 2014/1977
s.129, applied: SI 2014/1977 Reg.6, Reg.7
s.129, enabling: SI 2014/1977
s.132, amended: 2014 c.6 Sch.3 para.87
s.138, varied: SI 2014/2379 Art.3
s.141, applied: SI 2014/1977 Reg.8
s.141, enabling: SI 2014/1977
s.166, enabling: SI 2014/1977, SI 2014/3283
s.173, enabling: SI 2014/2379, SI 2014/3364
Sch.1 Part 2 para.76, repealed: 2014 c.6
Sch.3 para.75

26. Local Transport Act 2008
Part 5, applied: SI 2014/863 Art.8, SI
2014/865 Art.10, SI 2014/1012 Art.10
s.82, applied: SI 2014/863, SI 2014/864, SI
2014/865, SI 2014/1012
s.84, enabling: SI 2014/863, SI 2014/864, SI
2014/865, SI 2014/1012
s.91, enabling: SI 2014/863, SI 2014/864, SI
2014/865, SI 2014/1012
s.93, enabling: SI 2014/863, SI 2014/864, SI
2014/865, SI 2014/1012
s.94, applied: SI 2014/863, SI 2014/864, SI
2014/865, SI 2014/1012
s.102C, amended: 2014 c.14 Sch.4 para.138
Sch.4 Part 4 para.61, repealed: 2014 c.2
Sch.1 Part 2

27. Climate Change Act 2008
s.44, enabling: SI 2014/502
s.46, enabling: SI 2014/502
s.48, applied: SI 2014/502

s.77, enabling: SI 2014/2291

s.90, enabling: SI 2014/502, SI 2014/2291

Sch.2, enabling: SI 2014/502

Sch.3 Part 3 para.9, enabling: SI 2014/502

Sch.3 Part 3 para.10, applied: SI 2014/502

Sch.6 Part 1 para.3, enabling: SI 2014/2291

28. Counter-Terrorism Act 2008

see *Bank Mellat v HM Treasury* [2014] A.C. 700 (SC), Lord Neuberger PSC

applied: 2014 c.25 Sch.1

Part 4, applied: SI 2014/1610 r.42_3

s.18D, amended: 2014 c.12 Sch.11 para.126

s.18E, amended: 2014 c.12 Sch.11 para.126

s.42, applied: SI 2014/1610 r.68_1, r.63_1

s.45, see *Bank Mellat v HM Treasury* [2014] A.C. 700 (SC), Lord Neuberger PSC

Sch.7, see *Bank Mellat v HM Treasury* [2014] A.C. 700 (SC), Lord Neuberger PSC

Sch.7 Part 2 para.6, amended: 2014 c.14 Sch.4 para.139

Sch.7 Pt 3 para.13, see *Bank Mellat v HM Treasury* [2014] A.C. 700 (SC), Lord Neuberger JSC

Sch.7 Part 7 para.33, repealed (in part): SI 2014/834 Sch.2 para.60

29. Planning Act 2008

Commencement Orders: SI 2014/1769 Art.2; SI 2014/2780 Art.2

see *R. (on the application of Gate) v Secretary of State for Transport* [2013] EWHC 2937 (Admin), [2014] J.P.L. 383 (QBD (Admin)), Turner J

applied: SI 2014/2434 Sch.8 para.4, SI 2014/2935 Sch.9 para.35, SI 2014/3301, SI 2014/3328 Art.3, SI 2014/3331 Art.32

referred to: SI 2014/1599 Art.38, SI 2014/2594 Art.11

Part 4, applied: SI 2014/2434

Part 6 c.2, applied: SI 2014/2935

Part 6 c.3, applied: SI 2014/909, SI 2014/1052, SI 2014/1796, SI 2014/2594

Part 6 c.4, applied: SI 2014/1052, SI 2014/1599, SI 2014/1796, SI 2014/1873, SI 2014/2269, SI 2014/2384, SI 2014/2637, SI 2014/2846, SI 2014/2935, SI 2014/3331

s.7, enabling: SI 2014/692

s.14, applied: SI 2014/2441 Sch.1 Part 1, SI 2014/3328 Sch.1 Part 1

s.14, referred to: SI 2014/1599 Sch.1 para.1, SI 2014/1873 Sch.1 para.1, SI 2014/2269 Sch.1, SI 2014/2384 Sch.1 Part 1, SI

2014/2434 Sch.1 Part 1, SI 2014/2594 Sch.1 para.1, SI 2014/2846 Sch.1, SI 2014/2950 Sch.1 para.1, SI 2014/3331 Sch.1 para.1

s.21, applied: SI 2014/3328 Art.5, Sch.1 Part 1

s.22, see *R. (on the application of Gate) v Secretary of State for Transport* [2013] EWHC 2937 (Admin), [2014] J.P.L. 383 (QBD (Admin)), Turner J

s.22, referred to: SI 2014/2269 Sch.1

s.29, referred to: SI 2014/2384 Sch.1 Part 1

s.32, applied: SI 2014/2384 Sch.15 para.3

s.33, see *R. (on the application of Gate) v Secretary of State for Transport* [2013] EWHC 2937 (Admin), [2014] J.P.L. 383 (QBD (Admin)), Turner J

s.37, applied: SI 2014/909, SI 2014/1599, SI 2014/1796, SI 2014/2269, SI 2014/2384, SI 2014/2637, SI 2014/2935, SI 2014/3328

s.37, enabling: SI 2014/2381

s.74, applied: SI 2014/1599, SI 2014/1873, SI 2014/2384, SI 2014/2434, SI 2014/2935

s.83, applied: SI 2014/909, SI 2014/1052, SI 2014/1796, SI 2014/2269, SI 2014/2594, SI 2014/2846, SI 2014/3328

s.103, applied: SI 2014/1599 Art.35

s.103, enabling: SI 2014/2384

s.104, referred to: SI 2014/3328

s.106, applied: SI 2014/3331 Sch.10 para.3, Sch.11 para.3

s.108, applied: SI 2014/3331 Sch.10 para.3, Sch.11 para.3

s.114, applied: SI 2014/1599, SI 2014/2434

s.114, enabling: SI 2014/1052, SI 2014/1599, SI 2014/1796, SI 2014/1873, SI 2014/2269, SI 2014/2384, SI 2014/2434, SI 2014/2441, SI 2014/2594, SI 2014/2637, SI 2014/2846, SI 2014/2935, SI 2014/2950, SI 2014/3328, SI 2014/3331

s.115, applied: SI 2014/1796 Sch.1 Part 2, SI 2014/1873 Sch.1 para.1, Sch.13 para.2, SI 2014/2269 Sch.1, SI 2014/2384 Sch.1 Part 1, SI 2014/2594 Sch.1 para.1, Sch.2 para.2, Sch.3 para.2, SI 2014/2637 Sch.1, SI 2014/2950 Sch.1 para.1, Sch.9 para.2, Sch.10 para.2, SI 2014/3328 Sch.1 Part 1, SI 2014/3331 Sch.1 para.1

s.115, enabling: SI 2014/909, SI 2014/1052, SI 2014/1599, SI 2014/1796, SI 2014/1873, SI 2014/2269, SI 2014/2384, SI 2014/2434, SI 2014/2441, SI 2014/2594, SI 2014/2637,

SI 2014/2846, SI 2014/2935, SI 2014/2950, SI 2014/3331
s.117, applied: SI 2014/909, SI 2014/1796, SI 2014/2384
s.119, enabling: SI 2014/3301
s.120, applied: SI 2014/1599, SI 2014/2434
s.120, enabling: SI 2014/909, SI 2014/1052, SI 2014/1599, SI 2014/1796, SI 2014/1873, SI 2014/2269, SI 2014/2384, SI 2014/2434, SI 2014/2441, SI 2014/2594, SI 2014/2637, SI 2014/2846, SI 2014/2935, SI 2014/2950, SI 2014/3328, SI 2014/3331
s.122, applied: SI 2014/2935
s.122, enabling: SI 2014/909, SI 2014/1796, SI 2014/2269, SI 2014/2384, SI 2014/2637, SI 2014/2935, SI 2014/2950
s.123, enabling: SI 2014/2384
s.125, applied: SI 2014/909 Art.24, Art.26, Art.28, Art.29, Art.30, SI 2014/1052 Art.31, Art.32, SI 2014/1599 Art.19, Art.21, Art.23, Art.24, SI 2014/1796 Art.21, SI 2014/1873 Art.27, Art.31, Art.32, SI 2014/2269 Art.26, SI 2014/2384 Art.35, Art.36, SI 2014/2434 Art.21, Art.23, Art.25, Art.26, SI 2014/2441 Art.25, SI 2014/2637 Art.23, Art.27, Art.28, SI 2014/2935 Art.36, Art.38, Art.40, SI 2014/2950 Art.23, Art.25, Art.27, Art.28, SI 2014/3328 Art.21, Art.24, Art.25, SI 2014/3331 Art.23, Art.24
s.131, applied: SI 2014/3038 Sch.4 para.8
s.132, enabling: SI 2014/2950
s.134, applied: SI 2014/2384 Art.28, SI 2014/2434 Art.16, SI 2014/2935 Art.30
s.138, applied: SI 2014/1052 Art.26, SI 2014/1599 Art.18, SI 2014/1873 Art.26, SI 2014/2269 Art.21, SI 2014/2384 Art.46, SI 2014/2434 Art.18, SI 2014/2441 Art.24, SI 2014/2637 Art.30, SI 2014/2935 Art.35, SI 2014/2950 Art.22, SI 2014/3331 Art.18
s.138, disapplied: SI 2014/909 Art.23, SI 2014/3328 Art.20
s.138, referred to: SI 2014/2637 Art.22
s.149A, applied: SI 2014/1599, SI 2014/2434, SI 2014/2555 Sch.1, Sch.2
s.149A, enabling: SI 2014/1599, SI 2014/1873, SI 2014/2434, SI 2014/2594, SI 2014/2950, SI 2014/3331
s.150, applied: SI 2014/2384 Art.55
s.152, applied: SI 2014/909 Art.23, Art.28, Art.29, Art.30, SI 2014/1052 Art.31, SI 2014/1599 Art.18, Art.24, SI 2014/1873

Art.26, Art.31, Art.32, SI 2014/2269 Art.16, Art.21, Art.26, SI 2014/2384 Art.33, SI 2014/2441 Art.24, SI 2014/2637 Art.17, Art.27, Art.28, SI 2014/2935 Art.21, Art.40, Art.41, SI 2014/2950 Art.16, Art.22, Art.27, SI 2014/3328 Art.19, Art.24, Art.25, SI 2014/3331 Art.18
s.156, referred to: SI 2014/2846 Art.7
s.158, applied: SI 2014/2384 Art.33, SI 2014/2441 Art.9
s.158, disapplied: SI 2014/1796 Art.9
s.158, referred to: SI 2014/3328 Art.19
s.203, applied: SI 2014/1770, SI 2014/2773
s.203, enabling: SI 2014/1770, SI 2014/2773
s.205, enabling: SI 2014/385
s.208, disapplied: SI 2014/2384 Sch.19 para.7
s.208, enabling: SI 2014/385
s.209, enabling: SI 2014/385
s.211, see *R. (on the application of Fox Strategic Land and Property Ltd) v Chorley BC* [2014] EWHC 1179 (Admin), [2014] J.P.L. 1152 (QBD (Admin)), Lindblom J
s.211, enabling: SI 2014/385
s.215, enabling: SI 2014/385
s.217, enabling: SI 2014/385
s.218, enabling: SI 2014/385
s.220, enabling: SI 2014/385
s.222, applied: SI 2014/385
s.222, enabling: SI 2014/385
s.223, enabling: SI 2014/385
s.232, enabling: SI 2014/692, SI 2014/2381
s.241, enabling: SI 2014/1769, SI 2014/2780
Sch.4, enabling: SI 2014/3301
Sch.4 para.1, applied: SI 2014/3301
Sch.4 para.1, referred to: SI 2014/3301
Sch.5 Part 1 para.1, enabling: SI 2014/909, SI 2014/1796, SI 2014/2269, SI 2014/2637, SI 2014/2935
Sch.5 Part 1 para.2, enabling: SI 2014/909, SI 2014/1796, SI 2014/2269, SI 2014/2637, SI 2014/2935
Sch.5 Part 1 para.3, enabling: SI 2014/909, SI 2014/1796, SI 2014/2269, SI 2014/2637, SI 2014/2935
Sch.5 Part 1 para.8, enabling: SI 2014/2637
Sch.5 Part 1 para.10, enabling: SI 2014/909, SI 2014/1796, SI 2014/2269, SI 2014/2637, SI 2014/2935

Sch.5 Part 1 para.11, enabling: SI 2014/909,
SI 2014/1796, SI 2014/2269, SI 2014/2637,
SI 2014/2935
Sch.5 Part 1 para.12, enabling: SI 2014/909,
SI 2014/1796, SI 2014/2269, SI 2014/2637,
SI 2014/2935
Sch.5 Part 1 para.13, enabling: SI 2014/909,
SI 2014/1796, SI 2014/2269, SI 2014/2637,
SI 2014/2935
Sch.5 Part 1 para.14, enabling: SI 2014/909,
SI 2014/1796, SI 2014/2269, SI 2014/2637,
SI 2014/2935
Sch.5 Part 1 para.15, enabling: SI 2014/909,
SI 2014/1796, SI 2014/2269, SI 2014/2637,
SI 2014/2935
Sch.5 Part 1 para.16, enabling: SI 2014/909,
SI 2014/1796, SI 2014/2269, SI 2014/2637,
SI 2014/2935
Sch.5 Part 1 para.17, enabling: SI 2014/909,
SI 2014/1796, SI 2014/2269, SI 2014/2637,
SI 2014/2935
Sch.5 Part 1 para.18, enabling: SI 2014/1796
Sch.5 Part 1 para.19, enabling: SI 2014/2269
Sch.5 Part 1 para.24, enabling: SI 2014/909,
SI 2014/2637, SI 2014/2935
Sch.5 Part 1 para.26, enabling: SI 2014/909,
SI 2014/2269, SI 2014/2637, SI 2014/2935
Sch.5 Part 1 para.30A, enabling: SI
2014/2935
Sch.5 Part 1 para.30B, enabling: SI
2014/2935
Sch.5 Part 1 para.31, enabling: SI 2014/2935
Sch.5 Part 1 para.32, enabling: SI 2014/2935
Sch.5 Part 1 para.32B, enabling: SI
2014/2935
Sch.5 Part 1 para.33, enabling: SI
2014/1796, SI 2014/2637, SI 2014/2935
Sch.5 Part 1 para.34, enabling: SI
2014/1796, SI 2014/2935
Sch.5 Part 1 para.36, enabling: SI 2014/909,
SI 2014/1796, SI 2014/2269, SI 2014/2637,
SI 2014/2935
Sch.5 Part 1 para.37, enabling: SI 2014/909,
SI 2014/1796, SI 2014/2269, SI 2014/2637,
SI 2014/2935

30. Pensions Act 2008
Commencement Orders: 2014 c.19 Sch.12
para.96; SI 2014/463 Art.2
Part 1, applied: 2014 c.19 Sch.18 para.1
Part 1 c.1, applied: SI 2014/2418 Sch.1

Part 3 c.1, applied: 2014 c.19 Sch.20
para.22, SI 2014/1711 Reg.43, Reg.52,
Reg.54, Reg.55, Reg.56
Part 3 c.1, varied: SI 2014/1711 Reg.53,
Reg.57
s.3, amended: SI 2014/623 Art.2
s.3, applied: SI 2014/512 Reg.15, SI
2014/623 Art.3
s.3, referred to: SI 2014/623
s.5, amended: 2014 c.19 s.37, SI 2014/623
Art.2
s.5, applied: SI 2014/623 Art.3, SI
2014/1964 Reg.22, SI 2014/2848 Reg.13
s.5, referred to: SI 2014/623
s.5, repealed (in part): 2014 c.19 s.38
s.10, amended: 2014 c.19 s.38
s.13, amended: 2014 c.6 Sch.7 para.74, SI
2014/623 Art.2
s.13, applied: SI 2014/623 Art.3
s.13, referred to: SI 2014/623
s.13, varied: 2014 c.6 s.126
s.14, applied: SI 2014/623
s.14, enabling: SI 2014/623
s.15A, enabling: SI 2014/623
s.16, amended: 2014 c.19 Sch.18 para.11
s.16, repealed (in part): 2014 c.19 Sch.18
para.11
s.16, enabling: SI 2014/715
s.21, substituted: 2014 c.19 Sch.13 para.82
s.22, amended: 2014 c.19 Sch.13 para.83
s.23A, added: 2014 c.19 s.39
s.24, amended: 2014 c.19 s.39
s.28, amended: 2014 c.19 s.39
s.28, enabling: SI 2014/715
s.29, amended: 2014 c.19 s.39
s.30, amended: 2014 c.19 s.37, s.39, s.40
s.30, disapplied: 2014 c.19 s.40
s.30, varied: 2014 c.19 s.40
s.40, amended: 2014 c.19 s.41
s.50, applied: SI 2014/2418 Sch.1
s.54, applied: SI 2014/2418 Sch.1
s.87A, added: 2014 c.19 s.38
s.99, applied: SSI 2014/200 Sch.1 para.13
s.99, enabling: SI 2014/715
s.102, repealed: 2014 c.19 Sch.12 para.96
s.103, repealed: 2014 c.19 Sch.12 para.96
s.105, repealed (in part): 2014 c.19 s.29
s.143, applied: SI 2014/623, SI 2014/715
s.144, enabling: SI 2014/623, SI 2014/715
s.149, enabling: SI 2014/463
Sch.3, repealed: 2014 c.19 Sch.12 para.96

Sch.4 para.4, repealed (in part): 2014 c.19
Sch.12 para.96
Sch.4 para.6, repealed (in part): 2014 c.19
Sch.12 para.96
Sch.4 para.7, repealed (in part): 2014 c.19
Sch.12 para.96
Sch.4 para.8, repealed (in part): 2014 c.19
Sch.12 para.96
Sch.4 para.9, repealed (in part): 2014 c.19
Sch.12 para.96
Sch.4 para.10, repealed: 2014 c.19 Sch.12
para.96
Sch.4 para.13, repealed: 2014 c.19 Sch.12
para.96
Sch.5, applied: SI 2014/1711 Reg.43,
Reg.52, Reg.54, Reg.55, Reg.56
Sch.5, varied: SI 2014/1711 Reg.53, Reg.57
Sch.5 Part 4 para.18, amended: 2014 c.19
Sch.20 para.7
Sch.5 Part 4 para.18, applied: 2014 c.19
Sch.20 para.22

32. Energy Act 2008
Commencement Orders: SI 2014/1461 Art.2
Part 1, referred to: SI 2014/615 Reg.3, SI
2014/2555 Art.3
Part 4, referred to: SI 2014/615 Reg.3, SI
2014/2555 Art.3
s.43, enabling: SI 2014/1601, SI 2014/2865
s.100, applied: SI 2014/928, SI 2014/1413
s.100, referred to: SI 2014/2418 Sch.1
s.100, enabling: SI 2014/928, SI 2014/1413
s.104, enabling: SI 2014/928, SI 2014/1413,
SI 2014/1601, SI 2014/2865
s.105, applied: SI 2014/928, SI 2014/1413
s.110, enabling: SI 2014/1461

2009

1. Banking Act 2009
applied: SI 2014/3330 Reg.8, SI 2014/3348
Art.170, Art.177, SI 2014/3350 Art.6
referred to: SI 2014/3348 Art.157
Part 1, applied: SI 2014/3348 Art.41,
Art.188, Art.216
Part 1 c.4, added: SI 2014/3329 Art.97
Part 1 c.6, added: SI 2014/3329 Art.103
Part 6, applied: SI 2014/2418 Sch.1
s.1, amended: SI 2014/3329 Art.4
s.1, referred to: SI 2014/3348 Art.155,
Art.157

s.1, substituted: SI 2014/3329 Art.3
s.3, amended: SI 2014/3329 Art.5
s.3A, added: SI 2014/3329 Art.6
s.3A, applied: SI 2014/3348 Art.122,
Art.134, Art.141
s.4, amended: SI 2014/3329 Art.8
s.4, substituted: SI 2014/3329 Art.7
s.5, amended: SI 2014/3329 Art.9
s.6A, added: SI 2014/3329 Art.10
s.6E, added: SI 2014/3329 Art.11
s.6E, applied: SI 2014/3348 Art.158
s.7, amended: SI 2014/3329 Art.12
s.7A, added: SI 2014/3329 Art.13
s.8, substituted: SI 2014/3329 Art.14
s.8A, repealed: SI 2014/3329 Art.16
s.8ZA, added: SI 2014/3329 Art.15
s.9, amended: SI 2014/3329 Art.17
s.11, applied: SI 2014/1828 Art.2, SI
2014/3330 Reg.3
s.12, amended: SI 2014/3329 Art.18
s.12, applied: SI 2014/1828 Art.2, SI
2014/3330 Reg.3, SI 2014/3350 Art.6
s.12A, amended: SI 2014/3329 Art.20
s.12A, applied: SI 2014/3330 Reg.3, SI
2014/3348 Art.159, Art.163
s.12AA, added: SI 2014/3329 Art.21
s.12B, repealed: SI 2014/3329 Art.22
s.12ZA, added: SI 2014/3329 Art.19
s.13, amended: SI 2014/3329 Art.23
s.13, applied: SI 2014/1828 Art.2
s.17, amended: SI 2014/3329 Art.24
s.18, amended: SI 2014/3329 Art.25
s.19, amended: SI 2014/3329 Art.26
s.20, amended: SI 2014/3329 Art.27
s.22, repealed: SI 2014/3329 Art.28
s.24, amended: SI 2014/3329 Art.29
s.25, amended: SI 2014/3329 Art.30
s.26, amended: SI 2014/3329 Art.31
s.29A, added: SI 2014/3329 Art.32
s.30, amended: SI 2014/3329 Art.33
s.31, amended: SI 2014/3329 Art.34
s.33, amended: SI 2014/3329 Art.35
s.34, applied: SI 2014/1828 Art.7
s.36A, amended: SI 2014/3329 Art.36
s.38, repealed: SI 2014/3329 Art.37
s.38, applied: SI 2014/1828 Art.6
s.39, amended: SI 2014/3329 Art.38
s.39, applied: SI 2014/1828 Art.2, Art.5
s.39B, added: SI 2014/3329 Art.39
s.41, amended: SI 2014/3329 Art.40
s.41A, amended: SI 2014/3329 Art.41

s.42, amended: SI 2014/3329 Art.42

s.42, applied: SI 2014/1828 Art.2

s.42, referred to: SI 2014/3350 Art.6

s.43, amended: SI 2014/3329 Art.43

s.44, amended: SI 2014/3329 Art.44

s.44, applied: SI 2014/1828 Art.8

s.44A, amended: SI 2014/3329 Art.45

s.44B, amended: SI 2014/3329 Art.46

s.44B, applied: SI 2014/3330 Reg.3, SI 2014/3350 Art.6

s.45, applied: SI 2014/1828 Art.2

s.46, applied: SI 2014/1828 Art.8

s.47, amended: SI 2014/3329 Art.47

s.47, applied: SI 2014/1831, SI 2014/3350

s.47, enabling: SI 2014/1828, SI 2014/1831, SI 2014/3350

s.48, applied: SI 2014/3348 Art.123, Art.158, SI 2014/3350

s.48, enabling: SI 2014/1828, SI 2014/3350

s.48B, amended: SI 2014/3329 Art.48

s.48B, repealed (in part): SI 2014/3329 Art.48

s.48B, applied: SI 2014/3348 Art.186

s.48C, amended: SI 2014/3329 Art.49

s.48D, repealed (in part): SI 2014/3329 Art.50

s.48H, amended: SI 2014/3329 Art.51

s.48I, repealed: SI 2014/3329 Art.52

s.48L, amended: SI 2014/3329 Art.53

s.48L, applied: SI 2014/3348 Art.186

s.48M, repealed: SI 2014/3329 Art.54

s.48N, amended: SI 2014/3329 Art.55

s.48O, amended: SI 2014/3329 Art.56

s.48P, applied: SI 2014/3350

s.48P, enabling: SI 2014/3350

s.48T, amended: SI 2014/3329 Art.57

s.48U, amended: SI 2014/3329 Art.58

s.48V, amended: SI 2014/3329 Art.59

s.48W, amended: SI 2014/3329 Art.60

s.48X, added: SI 2014/3329 Art.61

s.48X, applied: SI 2014/3348 Art.158

s.48Z, added: SI 2014/3329 Art.62

s.52, amended: SI 2014/3329 Art.63

s.53, amended: SI 2014/3329 Art.64

s.54, amended: SI 2014/3329 Art.65

s.57, applied: SI 2014/3330 Reg.8

s.58, amended: SI 2014/3329 Art.66

s.60, amended: SI 2014/3329 Art.67

s.60, applied: SI 2014/1830

s.60, enabling: SI 2014/1830

s.60A, enabling: SI 2014/3330

s.60A, applied: SI 2014/3330

s.60A, enabling: SI 2014/3330

s.60B, amended: SI 2014/3329 Art.68

s.62A, added: SI 2014/3329 Art.69

s.62B, added: SI 2014/3329 Art.70

s.63, amended: SI 2014/3329 Art.71

s.64, amended: SI 2014/3329 Art.72

s.65, amended: SI 2014/3329 Art.73

s.66, amended: SI 2014/3329 Art.74

s.67, amended: SI 2014/3329 Art.75

s.68, amended: SI 2014/3329 Art.76

s.70A, added: SI 2014/3329 Art.77

s.71, amended: SI 2014/3329 Art.78

s.72, repealed: SI 2014/3329 Art.79

s.73, amended: SI 2014/3329 Art.80

s.74, amended: SI 2014/3329 Art.81

s.76, amended: SI 2014/3329 Art.82

s.77, amended: SI 2014/3329 Art.83

s.78, amended: SI 2014/3329 Art.84

s.78A, added: SI 2014/3329 Art.85

s.79, amended: SI 2014/3329 Art.86

s.80, amended: SI 2014/3329 Art.87

s.81A, amended: SI 2014/3329 Art.88

s.81AA, added: SI 2014/3329 Art.89

s.81B, amended: SI 2014/3329 Art.90

s.81BA, amended: SI 2014/3329 Art.92

s.81C, amended: SI 2014/3329 Art.93

s.81CA, amended: SI 2014/3329 Art.94

s.81CA, substituted: SI 2014/3329 Art.7

s.81D, amended: SI 2014/3329 Art.95

s.81D, applied: SI 2014/1831, SI 2014/1831 Art.3

s.81D, enabling: SI 2014/1831

s.81ZBA, added: SI 2014/3329 Art.91

s.83, amended: SI 2014/3329 Art.96

s.83A, amended: SI 2014/3329 Art.99

s.83A, substituted: SI 2014/3329 Art.98

s.84, amended: SI 2014/3344 Art.2

s.84, applied: SI 2014/3330 Reg.12

s.84A, added: SI 2014/3344 Art.2

s.84A, applied: SI 2014/3344 Art.3

s.85, amended: SI 2014/3329 Art.100

s.89A, amended: SI 2014/3329 Art.101

s.89A, applied: SI 2014/3350 Art.2

s.89B, amended: SI 2014/3329 Art.102

s.89H, applied: SI 2014/3330 Reg.3, SI 2014/3348 Art.197

s.96, amended: SI 2014/3329 Art.104

s.120, amended: SI 2014/3329 Art.105

s.120, repealed (in part): SI 2014/3329 Art.105

Part 6, applied: SI 2014/863 Art.8, SI
2014/865 Art.10, SI 2014/866 Art.2, SI
2014/1012 Art.10
s.23, amended: SI 2014/469 Sch.2 para.25
s.36, amended: 2014 c.2 Sch.12 para.98,
2014 c.14 Sch.4 para.149
s.36, repealed (in part): 2014 c.2 Sch.12
para.98
s.37, repealed (in part): 2014 c.2 Sch.12
para.99
s.38, amended: 2014 c.2 Sch.12 para.100
s.38, repealed (in part): 2014 c.2 Sch.12
para.100
s.39, amended: 2014 c.2 Sch.12 para.101
s.40, amended: 2014 c.2 Sch.12 para.102,
2014 c.14 Sch.4 para.149, Sch.4 para.150
s.41, amended: 2014 c.2 Sch.12 para.103
s.42, amended: 2014 c.2 Sch.12 para.104
s.42, repealed (in part): 2014 c.2 Sch.12
para.104
s.43, amended: 2014 c.2 Sch.12 para.105,
2014 c.14 Sch.4 para.149, Sch.4 para.151
s.44, amended: 2014 c.2 Sch.12 para.106,
2014 c.14 Sch.4 para.149, Sch.4 para.152
s.45, amended: 2014 c.2 Sch.12 para.107
s.46, repealed (in part): 2014 c.2 Sch.12
para.108
s.48, amended: 2014 c.14 Sch.4 para.149
s.50, amended: 2014 c.2 Sch.12 para.109
s.50, repealed (in part): 2014 c.2 Sch.12
para.109
s.51, amended: 2014 c.2 Sch.12 para.110
s.52, repealed: 2014 c.2 Sch.12 para.111
s.53, amended: 2014 c.2 Sch.12 para.112
s.53, repealed (in part): 2014 c.2 Sch.12
para.112
s.54, amended: 2014 c.2 Sch.12 para.113,
2014 c.14 Sch.4 para.149, Sch.4 para.153
s.58, applied: SI 2014/18, SI 2014/19, SI
2014/20, SI 2014/21, SI 2014/22, SI
2014/23, SI 2014/24, SI 2014/25, SI
2014/26, SI 2014/27, SI 2014/243, SI
2014/455, SI 2014/456, SI 2014/1187, SI
2014/1188, SI 2014/1189, SI 2014/1334, SI
2014/1906, SI 2014/1907, SI 2014/1908, SI
2014/1909, SI 2014/1910, SI 2014/1911, SI
2014/3057, SI 2014/3058, SI 2014/3059, SI
2014/3060, SI 2014/3287, SI 2014/3288, SI
2014/3289, SI 2014/3290, SI 2014/3291, SI
2014/3334, SI 2014/3335, SI 2014/3336, SI
2014/3338, SI 2014/3339, SI 2014/3341

s.59, enabling: SI 2014/18, SI 2014/19, SI
2014/20, SI 2014/21, SI 2014/22, SI
2014/23, SI 2014/24, SI 2014/25, SI
2014/26, SI 2014/27, SI 2014/243, SI
2014/455, SI 2014/456, SI 2014/1187, SI
2014/1188, SI 2014/1189, SI 2014/1334, SI
2014/1906, SI 2014/1907, SI 2014/1908, SI
2014/1909, SI 2014/1910, SI 2014/1911, SI
2014/3057, SI 2014/3058, SI 2014/3059, SI
2014/3060, SI 2014/3287, SI 2014/3288, SI
2014/3289, SI 2014/3290, SI 2014/3291, SI
2014/3334, SI 2014/3335, SI 2014/3336, SI
2014/3338, SI 2014/3339, SI 2014/3341
s.69, applied: SI 2014/865 Sch.2 para.4, SI
2014/1012 Sch.2 para.4
s.88, applied: 2014 c.2 Sch.2 para.27
s.103, enabling: SI 2014/863, SI 2014/864,
SI 2014/865, SI 2014/1012
s.104, enabling: SI 2014/863, SI 2014/864,
SI 2014/865, SI 2014/1012
s.105, enabling: SI 2014/863, SI 2014/864,
SI 2014/865, SI 2014/1012
s.109, applied: SI 2014/863, SI 2014/864, SI
2014/865, SI 2014/1012
s.113B, amended: 2014 c.14 Sch.4 para.154
s.114, enabling: SI 2014/863, SI 2014/864,
SI 2014/865, SI 2014/866, SI 2014/1012
s.115, applied: SI 2014/865 Art.8
s.115, enabling: SI 2014/863, SI 2014/864,
SI 2014/865, SI 2014/866, SI 2014/1012
s.116, enabling: SI 2014/863, SI 2014/864,
SI 2014/865, SI 2014/866, SI 2014/1012
s.117, applied: SI 2014/863, SI 2014/864, SI
2014/865, SI 2014/866, SI 2014/1012
Sch.6 para.89, repealed: 2014 c.2 Sch.1 Part
2

21. Health Act 2009
s.2, amended: 2014 c.23 s.99
**22. Apprenticeships, Skills, Children and
Learning Act 2009**
applied: SI 2014/2418 Sch.1
varied: SI 2014/1012 Art.16
s.32, applied: SI 2014/1530 Sch.2 para.8
s.83, amended: 2014 c.6 Sch.3 para.89
s.83, repealed (in part): 2014 c.6 Sch.3
para.89
s.86, amended: 2014 c.6 Sch.3 para.90
s.87, amended: 2014 c.6 Sch.3 para.91
s.101, amended: 2014 c.6 Sch.3 para.92
s.115, amended: 2014 c.6 Sch.3 para.93

s.120A, added: SI 2014/3329 Art.106
s.145A, amended: SI 2014/3329 Art.107
s.228, applied: SI 2014/3348 Art.221
s.230, enabling: SI 2014/3348
s.244, amended: SI 2014/3329 Art.108
s.244, applied: SI 2014/3348 Art.186
s.256A, amended: SI 2014/3329 Art.109
s.258A, applied: SI 2014/1832, SI
2014/1832 Art.2, SI 2014/3348 Art.221
s.258A, enabling: SI 2014/1832
s.259, amended: SI 2014/3329 Art.110
s.259, enabling: SI 2014/1828, SI
2014/1831, SI 2014/3330, SI 2014/3350
s.261, amended: SI 2014/3329 Art.111
2. Appropriation Act 2009
Sch.2 Part 2, varied: SI 2014/2708 Art.5
02. Local Government (Wales) Measure 2009
s.38, amended: SI 2014/1713 Art.2
s.38, applied: SI 2014/1713
s.38, enabling: SI 2014/1713
s.50, applied: SI 2014/1713
**03. Healthy Eating in Schools (Wales) Measure
2009**
s.4, enabling: SI 2014/2303, SI 2014/3087
s.10, enabling: SI 2014/2303, SI 2014/3087
3. Northern Ireland Act 2009
applied: 2014 c.25 Sch.1
referred to: 2014 c.5 Sch.1 para.1
4. Corporation Tax Act 2009
Part 3 c.9, amended: 2014 c.14 Sch.4
para.143
Part 6 c.5, amended: 2014 c.14 Sch.4
para.143
Part 7, applied: 2014 c.26 s.29
Part 11 c.1, substituted: 2014 c.26 Sch.8
para.82
Part 15B c.3, amended: 2014 c.26 s.34
Part 15C, added: 2014 c.26 Sch.4 para.1
Part 15C, applied: 2014 c.26 Sch.4 para.17
s.92A, added: 2014 c.26 Sch.17 para.4
s.104BA, amended: 2014 c.26 Sch.4 para.9
s.104N, amended: 2014 c.26 Sch.1 para.10
s.132, amended: 2014 c.14 Sch.4 para.141,
Sch.4 para.143
s.155, amended: 2014 c.29 s.4
s.210, amended: 2014 c.26 Sch.17 para.4
s.302, amended: 2014 c.14 Sch.4 para.143
s.310, enabling: SI 2014/3188
s.319, enabling: SI 2014/3187
s.322, amended: 2014 c.26 s.26, SI
2014/3329 Art.123

s.328, enabling: SI 2014/3188
s.345, amended: 2014 c.26 s.28
s.345, repealed (in part): 2014 c.26 s.28
s.346, amended: 2014 c.26 s.28
s.346, repealed (in part): 2014 c.26 s.28
s.431, amended: 2014 c.14 Sch.4 para.142
s.439, amended: 2014 c.14 Sch.4 para.142
s.465, amended: 2014 c.14 Sch.4 para.144,
2014 c.26 s.27
s.465A, enabling: SI 2014/3325
s.477, amended: 2014 c.14 Sch.4 para.143
s.490, amended: 2014 c.26 s.27
s.490, repealed (in part): 2014 c.26 s.27
s.492, substituted: 2014 c.26 s.27
s.495, amended: 2014 c.26 s.27
s.495, repealed (in part): 2014 c.26 s.27
s.499, amended: 2014 c.14 Sch.4 para.141,
Sch.4 para.145
s.500, amended: 2014 c.14 Sch.4 para.141
s.598, enabling: SI 2014/3187, SI 2014/3188
s.606, enabling: SI 2014/3188
s.631, amended: 2014 c.26 s.28
s.631, repealed (in part): 2014 c.26 s.28
s.632, amended: 2014 c.26 s.28
s.632, repealed (in part): 2014 c.26 s.28
s.682, amended: 2014 c.14 Sch.4 para.142
s.688, amended: 2014 c.14 Sch.4 para.142
s.695A, added: 2014 c.26 s.29
s.695A, disapplied: 2014 c.26 s.29
s.695A, varied: 2014 c.26 s.29
s.710, varied: SI 2014/685 Reg.3
s.764, amended: 2014 c.14 Sch.4 para.141
s.773, amended: 2014 c.14 Sch.4 para.141
s.808C, added: 2014 c.26 Sch.4 para.10
s.821, amended: 2014 c.14 Sch.4 para.142
s.823, amended: 2014 c.14 Sch.4 para.142
s.826, amended: 2014 c.14 Sch.4 para.141
s.870A, added: 2014 c.26 s.62
s.983, amended: 2014 c.26 Sch.8 para.75
s.987, amended: 2014 c.26 Sch.8 para.76
s.987, applied: 2014 c.26 Sch.8 para.95
s.987, repealed (in part): 2014 c.26 Sch.8
para.76
s.988, amended: 2014 c.26 Sch.8 para.77
s.989, amended: 2014 c.26 Sch.8 para.78
s.994, amended: 2014 c.26 Sch.8 para.79
s.995, amended: 2014 c.26 Sch.8 para.80
s.997, amended: 2014 c.26 Sch.8 para.81
s.998, amended: 2014 c.26 Sch.8 para.83
s.999, amended: 2014 c.26 Sch.8 para.142

s.999, applied: 2014 c.26 Sch.8 para.156,
Sch.8 para.214
s.999, repealed (in part): 2014 c.26 Sch.8
para.142
s.1002, amended: 2014 c.26 Sch.9 para.40
s.1005, amended: 2014 c.26 Sch.9 para.41
s.1007A, added: 2014 c.26 Sch.9 para.42
s.1015A, added: 2014 c.26 Sch.9 para.43
s.1016, amended: 2014 c.26 Sch.9 para.44
s.1017, repealed (in part): 2014 c.26 Sch.9
para.31
s.1025, repealed (in part): 2014 c.26 Sch.9
para.32
s.1025A, added: 2014 c.26 Sch.9 para.45
s.1030A, added: 2014 c.26 Sch.9 para.46
s.1032, repealed (in part): 2014 c.26 Sch.9
para.33
s.1040ZA, amended: 2014 c.26 Sch.4
para.11
s.1058, amended: 2014 c.26 s.31
s.1114, amended: 2014 c.26 Sch.1 para.11
s.1198, amended: 2014 c.26 s.32
s.1202, amended: 2014 c.26 s.32
s.1207, amended: SI 2014/834 Sch.2 para.62
s.1216A, amended: 2014 c.26 s.33
s.1216B, amended: 2014 c.26 s.33
s.1216CN, amended: SI 2014/834 Sch.2
para.63
s.1217A, amended: 2014 c.26 s.34
s.1217AE, amended: 2014 c.26 s.34
s.1217B, amended: 2014 c.26 s.34
s.1217C, amended: 2014 c.26 s.34
s.1217CB, applied: SI 2014/1958, SI
2014/1958 Reg.4
s.1217CB, enabling: SI 2014/1958
s.1217CC, applied: SI 2014/1958 Reg.12
s.1217CC, enabling: SI 2014/1958
s.1217CE, amended: 2014 c.26 s.34
s.1217CE, substituted: 2014 c.26 s.34
s.1217CF, amended: 2014 c.26 s.34
s.1217CG, amended: 2014 c.26 s.34
s.1217CN, amended: SI 2014/834 Sch.2
para.64
s.1217EB, amended: 2014 c.26 s.34
s.1217EB, substituted: 2014 c.26 s.34
s.1224, amended: 2014 c.26 Sch.17 para.4
s.1227A, added: 2014 c.26 Sch.17 para.4
s.1262, amended: 2014 c.26 Sch.17 para.10
s.1264A, added: 2014 c.26 Sch.17 para.10
s.1273A, added: 2014 c.26 Sch.17 para.2
s.1292, amended: 2014 c.26 Sch.37 para.23

s.1303, amended: SI 2014/1283 Sch.1 para.6
s.1305A, added: 2014 c.26 s.30
s.1310, amended: 2014 c.26 Sch.4 para.12
s.1310, applied: SI 2014/3325
s.1319, amended: 2014 c.14 Sch.4 para.142
Sch.1 Part 1 para.163, amended: 2014 c.14
Sch.4 para.141, Sch.4 para.143
Sch.3 Part 1, amended: 2014 c.14 Sch.4
para.141
Sch.4, amended: 2014 c.14 Sch.4 para.146,
2014 c.26 s.34, Sch.1 para.12, Sch.4 para.13

**04. National Assembly for Wales Commissioner
for Standards Measure 2009**
s.1, amended: 2014 c.29 s.4
s.20, amended: 2014 c.29 s.4

05. Education (Wales) Measure 2009
s.17, enabling: SI 2014/3267
s.24, enabling: SI 2014/3267

7. Business Rate Supplements Act 2009
Commencement Orders: SI 2014/1860 Art.2;
SI 2014/3200 Art.2
s.29, applied: SI 2014/3204
s.29, enabling: SI 2014/3204
s.32, enabling: SI 2014/1860, SI 2014/3200
Sch.2, applied: SI 2014/3204 Reg.22
Sch.2 para.2, applied: SI 2014/3204 Reg.3
Sch.2 para.2, enabling: SI 2014/3204
Sch.2 para.3, applied: SI 2014/3204 Reg.18,
Reg.19, Sch.3 para.1
Sch.2 para.4, applied: SI 2014/3204 Sch.4
para.12, Sch.4 para.13
Sch.2 para.5, applied: SI 2014/3204 Reg.10
Sch.2 para.5, enabling: SI 2014/3204
Sch.2 para.7, applied: SI 2014/3204 Reg.14
Sch.2 para.7, varied: SI 2014/3204 Sch.5
para.2
Sch.2 para.7, enabling: SI 2014/3204
Sch.2 para.8, enabling: SI 2014/3204
Sch.2 para.10, enabling: SI 2014/3204

9. Appropriation (No.2) Act 2009
Sch.2 Part 4, amended: 2014 c.29 s.4
Sch.2 Part 47, varied: SI 2014/2708 Art.5

10. Finance Act 2009
Commencement Orders: SI 2014/992 Art.3;
SI 2014/2395 Art.2; SI 2014/3269 Art.3,
Art.4; SI 2014/3324 Art.3; SI 2014/3346
Art.2
s.12, applied: SI 2014/1327 Reg.9
s.31, see *DMWSHNZ Ltd v Revenue and
Customs Commissioners* [2014] UKUT 98

(TCC), [2014] S.T.C. 1440 (UT (Tax)), Rose
J
s.94, applied: 2014 c.26 Sch.34 para.2
s.101, amended: 2014 c.26 Sch.22 para.20
s.101, applied: 2014 c.26 s.176
s.101, referred to: 2014 c.26 s.176
s.102, applied: 2014 c.7 s.4
s.104, applied: 2014 c.26 s.176
s.104, enabling: SI 2014/992, SI 2014/1283,
SI 2014/3269, SI 2014/3324, SI 2014/3346
s.106, enabling: SI 2014/2395, SI
2014/3269, SI 2014/3346
s.107, enabling: SI 2014/3269, SI 2014/3346
s.108, amended: 2014 c.26 Sch.22 para.20
s.124, amended: 2014 c.14 Sch.4 para.147
Sch.54A para.2, amended: 2014 c.26 Sch.4
para.14
Sch.55 para.1, amended: 2014 c.26 Sch.21
para.7, Sch.28 para.29
Sch.55 para.4, see *Revenue and Customs
Commissioners v Donaldson* [2014] UKUT
536 (TCC), [2014] B.T.C. 531 (UT (Tax)),
Warren J
Sch.55 para.5, applied: 2014 c.26 s.212
Sch.55 para.6, applied: 2014 c.26 s.212
Sch.55 para.6C, enabling: SI 2014/2396
Sch.55 para.17, amended: 2014 c.26 Sch.33
para.5
Sch.55 para.18, see *Revenue and Customs
Commissioners v Donaldson* [2014] UKUT
536 (TCC), [2014] B.T.C. 531 (UT (Tax)),
Warren J
Sch.56 para.1, amended: 2014 c.26 Sch.21
para.8, Sch.28 para.30
Sch.56 para.6, enabling: SI 2014/472
Sch.56 para.9, applied: 2014 c.26 s.226
Sch.56 para.11, disapplied: 2014 c.26 s.226
Sch.61 Part 1 para.1, amended: 2014 c.29
Sch.2 para.7, Sch.2 para.14
Sch.61 Part 3 para.5, amended: 2014 c.29
Sch.2 para.15
Sch.61 Part 3 para.5, applied: SI 2014/1327
Reg.3, SSI 2014/377 Art.6
Sch.61 Part 3 para.5, referred to: SSI
2014/377 Art.6
Sch.61 Part 3 para.6, amended: 2014 c.29
Sch.2 para.15
Sch.61 Part 3 para.8, referred to: SSI
2014/377 Art.6
Sch.61 Part 3 para.11, amended: 2014 c.29
Sch.2 para.15

Sch.61 Part 3 para.12, ame
Sch.2 para.15
Sch.61 Part 3 para.18, amen
Sch.2 para.15
Sch.61 Part 3 para.19, amend
Sch.2 para.15

**11. Borders, Citizenship and Imm
2009**
Commencement Orders: SI 201
s.15, amended: SI 2014/834 Sch
s.18, amended: SI 2014/834 Sch.
s.29, enabling: SI 2014/907
s.31, applied: SI 2014/834 Art.8
s.31, repealed: SI 2014/834 Sch.2
s.37, repealed (in part): SI 2014/83
para.69
s.37, enabling: SI 2014/907
s.39, amended: 2014 c.8 s.1
s.51, repealed (in part): 2014 c.22 Sch
para.60
s.54A, added: 2014 c.22 s.3
s.55, see *R. (on the application of B) v
Secretary of State for the Home Depart
[2014] EWCA Civ 854, [2014] 1 W.L.R.
4188 (CA (Civ Div)), Lord Dyson MR; se
R. (on the application of NS) v Secretary
State for the Home Department* [2014]
EWHC 1971 (Admin), [2014] Imm. A.R.
1153 (QBD (Admin)), Kenneth Parker J; se
*R. (on the application of Tigere) v Secretary
of State for Business, Innovation and Skills*
[2014] EWCA Civ 1216, [2014] H.R.L.R.
26 (CA (Civ Div)), Laws LJ; see *SM
(Withdrawal of Appealed Decision: Effect:
Pakistan)* [2014] UKUT 64 (IAC), [2014]
Imm. A.R. 662 (UT (IAC)), Judge Peter
Lane
s.58, applied: SI 2014/2634
s.58, enabling: SI 2014/2634

12. Political Parties and Elections Act 2009
referred to: 2014 c.4 s.33
s.1, repealed (in part): 2014 c.4 s.38

13. Parliamentary Standards Act 2009
s.4, applied: 2014 c.4 Sch.1 para.5
s.5, applied: 2014 c.4 Sch.1 para.5

**20. Local Democracy, Economic Development
and Construction Act 2009**
applied: 2014 c.5 Sch.1 para.1, 2014 c.25
Sch.1

s.115, repealed (in part): 2014 c.6 Sch.3
para.93
s.129, amended: 2014 c.6 Sch.3 para.94
s.129, repealed (in part): 2014 c.6 Sch.3
para.94
Sch.12 para.17, amended: 2014 c.29 s.4
23. Marine and Coastal Access Act 2009
Commencement Orders: SI 2014/3088 Art.2
applied: SI 2014/1599 Art.2, Art.29, Sch.11
para.10, SI 2014/2950 Art.37
Part 4, applied: SI 2014/2384 Art.50, SI
2014/2935 Art.44, SI 2014/3102 Art.14, SI
2014/3331 Art.35
Part 4 c.1, applied: SI 2014/1599 Art.29, SI
2014/1873 Art.11, SI 2014/2594 Art.9, SI
2014/2950 Art.37
Part 4 c.3, applied: SI 2014/2935 Sch.8
para.13, SI 2014/3102 Art.4
Part 8 c.2, applied: SI 2014/3102 Art.4
s.14, amended: 2014 c.29 s.4
s.41, applied: SI 2014/3306 Reg.2
s.59, amended: 2014 c.29 s.4
s.60, amended: 2014 c.29 s.4
s.65, applied: SI 2014/3102 Art.4
s.66, applied: SI 2014/1599 Sch.10 para.2,
Sch.11 para.2, SI 2014/1873 Sch.13 para.2,
Sch.14 para.2, SI 2014/2384 Sch.15 para.3,
SI 2014/2434 Art.36, Sch.7 para.3, SI
2014/2594 Sch.2 para.2, Sch.3 para.2, SI
2014/2950 Sch.9 para.2, Sch.10 para.2, SI
2014/3331 Sch.8 para.2, Sch.9 para.2,
Sch.10 para.2, Sch.11 para.2
s.66, referred to: SI 2014/2555 Sch.1
s.67, applied: SI 2014/615 Reg.4
s.67, enabling: SI 2014/615, SI 2014/950
s.71, applied: SI 2014/3102 Art.4
s.72, applied: SI 2014/1599 Sch.10 para.5,
Sch.11 para.5, SI 2014/1873 Sch.13 para.5,
Sch.14 para.5, SI 2014/2555 Art.5, Art.8,
Art.10, SI 2014/2594 Sch.2 para.5, Sch.3
para.5, SI 2014/2950 Sch.9 para.2, Sch.10
para.2, SI 2014/3331 Sch.9 para.2, Sch.10
para.2, Sch.11 para.2
s.74, applied: SI 2014/2384 Sch.15 para.3
s.113, applied: SI 2014/615, SI 2014/615
Reg.3, SI 2014/950, SI 2014/2555 Art.3
s.232, enabling: SI 2014/3303
s.246, applied: SI 2014/3102 Sch.8 para.84
s.263, applied: SI 2014/3102 Art.4
s.300, applied: SI 2014/1940 Art.2
s.300, enabling: SI 2014/1940

s.316, applied: SI 2014/3303
s.316, enabling: SI 2014/615, SI 2014/950,
SI 2014/3088, SI 2014/3303
s.324, enabling: SI 2014/3088
24. Welfare Reform Act 2009
s.8, applied: SI 2014/1097
s.45, amended: 2014 c.29 s.4
Sch.6 Part 1 para.2, amended: SI 2014/560
Sch.1 para.34
25. Coroners and Justice Act 2009
applied: SI 2014/1610 r.6_1
Part 7, applied: SI 2014/1610 r.6_1
s.52, see *R. v Williams (Dean)* [2013]
EWCA Crim 2749, [2014] 1 Cr. App. R. 23
(CA (Crim Div)), Laws LJ
s.54, see *R. v Asmelash (Dawit)* [2013]
EWCA Crim 157, [2014] Q.B. 103 (CA
(Crim Div)), Lord Judge LCJ; see *R. v
Dawes (Carlos)* [2013] EWCA Crim 322,
[2014] 1 W.L.R. 947 (CA (Crim Div)), Lord
Judge LCJ
s.55, see *R. v Dawes (Carlos)* [2013] EWCA
Crim 322, [2014] 1 W.L.R. 947 (CA (Crim
Div)), Lord Judge LCJ
s.76, applied: SI 2014/1610 r.6_1
s.77, applied: SI 2014/1610 r.6_24
s.77, repealed (in part): SI 2014/834 Sch.2
para.71
s.78, applied: SI 2014/1610 r.6_24
s.79, applied: SI 2014/1610 r.6_1, r.6_26
s.80, applied: SI 2014/1610 r.6_1, r.6_25,
r.6_26
s.80, repealed (in part): SI 2014/834 Sch.2
para.72
s.81, repealed (in part): SI 2014/834 Sch.2
para.73
s.86, applied: SI 2014/1610 r.29_1, r.16_6,
r.29_26
s.87, see *R. (on the application of B) v
Westminster Magistrates' Court* [2014]
UKSC 59, [2014] 3 W.L.R. 1336 (SC), Lord
Neuberger PSC
s.88, applied: SI 2014/1610 r.29_19, r.29_26
s.88, referred to: SI 2014/1610 r.29_22
s.91, applied: SI 2014/1610 r.29_1, r.29_21
s.115, applied: SI 2014/1610 r.19_1, r.19_10
s.120, applied: SI 2014/1610 r.37_10,
r.38_16
s.122, applied: SI 2014/1610 r.9_10
s.125, see *R. v Dyer (Richard)* [2013]
EWCA Crim 2114, [2014] 2 Cr. App. R. (S.)

11 (CA (Crim Div)), Sir Brian Leveson
PQBD
s.125, applied: SI 2014/1610 r.42_1
s.148, enabling: SI 2014/786
s.176, applied: SI 2014/786
s.176, enabling: SI 2014/786
Sch.2 para.2, enabling: SI 2014/3157
Sch.3 Part 4 para.14, enabling: SI 2014/1919
Sch.5, see *R. (on the application of Revenue
and Customs Commissioners) v HM Coroner
for Liverpool* [2014] EWHC 1586 (Admin),
[2014] 3 W.L.R. 1660 (DC), Gross LJ
Sch.20 Part 2 para.7, amended: 2014 c.29 s.4
Sch.21 Part 6 para.72, repealed: 2014 c.12
Sch.11 para.50

26. Policing and Crime Act 2009

Commencement Orders: SI 2014/3101 Art.2,
Art.3
Pt 4., see *Birmingham City Council v James*
[2013] EWCA Civ 552, [2014] 1 W.L.R. 23
(CA (Civ Div)), Maurice Kay LJ
s.12, repealed (in part): 2014 c.12 Sch.11
para.102
s.27, see *R. (on the application of Bridgerow
Ltd) v Cheshire West and Chester BC* [2014]
EWHC 1187 (Admin), [2014] B.L.G.R. 485
(QBD (Admin)), Stuart-Smith J; see *R. (on
the application of Thompson) v Oxford City
Council* [2014] EWCA Civ 94, [2014] 1
W.L.R. 1811 (CA (Civ Div)), Lord Dyson
MR
s.31, repealed: 2014 c.12 Sch.11 para.50
s.34, see *Birmingham City Council v James*
[2013] EWCA Civ 552, [2014] 1 W.L.R. 23
(CA (Civ Div)), Maurice Kay LJ
s.57, applied: SI 2014/3101
s.116, applied: SI 2014/3101
s.116, enabling: SI 2014/3101

2010

01. Children and Families (Wales) Measure 2010

Commencement Orders: SI 2014/373 Art.2;
SI 2014/1606 Art.2
Part 2, applied: SI 2014/1132 Sch.7 para.9
s.34, applied: SI 2014/840 Sch.1
s.74, enabling: SI 2014/373
s.75, enabling: SI 2014/373, SI 2014/1606
Sch.1 para.14, amended: 2014 c.29 s.4

02. Social Care Charges (Wales) Measure 2010

s.2, enabling: SI 2014/666
s.7, enabling: SI 2014/666
s.12, enabling: SI 2014/666
s.17, enabling: SI 2014/666

4. Corporation Tax Act 2010

Part 3, applied: 2014 c.26 s.6
Part 3, repealed: 2014 c.26 Sch.1 para.4
Part 6 c.2A, added: 2014 c.26 s.35
Part 8 c.3A, added: 2014 c.26 Sch.1 para.5
Part 8 c.5A, added: 2014 c.26 Sch.14 para.1
Part 8 c.8, added: 2014 c.26 Sch.15 para.3
Part 8ZA, added: 2014 c.26 Sch.16 para.4
Part 8ZA, applied: 2014 c.26 Sch.16 para.9
Part 10 c.2, applied: 2014 c.7 Sch.1 para.4,
Sch.1 para.5
Part 13 c.9, amended: 2014 c.26 s.35
Part 16 c.1A, added: 2014 c.26 Sch.17
para.28
Part 16 c.4, added: 2014 c.26 Sch.17 para.29
Part 22 c.4, applied: 2014 c.26 Sch.16 para.8
Part 23 c.3, amended: 2014 c.14 Sch.4
para.165
s.1, amended: 2014 c.26 Sch.16 para.2,
Sch.1 para.2
s.1, repealed (in part): 2014 c.26 Sch.1
para.2
s.3, substituted: 2014 c.26 Sch.1 para.3
s.25, referred to: 2014 c.26 Sch.1 para.22
s.45, applied: 2014 c.26 Sch.16 para.9
s.47, amended: 2014 c.14 Sch.4 para.156
s.47, substituted: 2014 c.14 Sch.4 para.157
s.90, amended: 2014 c.14 Sch.4 para.158
s.122, applied: 2014 c.26 s.160
s.151, amended: 2014 c.14 Sch.4 para.159
s.169, amended: 2014 c.26 s.40
s.188, amended: 2014 c.26 s.40
s.189, amended: 2014 c.26 s.35
s.192, amended: 2014 c.26 s.35
s.200, amended: 2014 c.26 s.35
s.202, amended: 2014 c.26 s.35
s.202A, added: 2014 c.26 s.35
s.270, amended: 2014 c.26 Sch.14 para.2,
Sch.1 para.5, Sch.15 para.5
s.285A, added: 2014 c.26 Sch.16 para.3
s.333, amended: 2014 c.26 Sch.15 para.5
s.333, repealed (in part): 2014 c.26 Sch.15
para.5
s.352, amended: 2014 c.26 Sch.15 para.4
s.352, referred to: 2014 c.26 Sch.15 para.7
s.356AA, amended: 2014 c.26 Sch.15 para.5

s.356C, referred to: 2014 c.26 Sch.15 para.7
s.356D, applied: 2014 c.26 Sch.15 para.9
s.356DA, applied: 2014 c.26 Sch.15 para.9
s.356DA, varied: 2014 c.26 Sch.15 para.9
s.356EB, varied: 2014 c.26 Sch.15 para.10
s.356GB, applied: 2014 c.26 Sch.15 para.10
s.356L, applied: 2014 c.26 Sch.16 para.7,
Sch.16 para.9
s.356M, applied: 2014 c.26 Sch.16 para.9
s.357, substituted: 2014 c.26 Sch.15 para.2
s.357CG, amended: 2014 c.26 Sch.4 para.15
s.357CL, amended: 2014 c.26 Sch.1 para.13
s.357CL, applied: 2014 c.26 Sch.1 para.22
s.357CL, repealed (in part): 2014 c.26 Sch.1
para.13
s.357CM, amended: 2014 c.26 Sch.1 para.13
s.357CM, repealed (in part): 2014 c.26 Sch.1
para.13
s.439, applied: 2014 c.7 Sch.1 para.4, Sch.1
para.5
s.442, amended: 2014 c.14 Sch.4 para.156
s.450, applied: SI 2014/3274 Sch.1 Part 2
s.450, varied: 2014 c.7 Sch.1 para.2
s.451, applied: 2014 c.7 Sch.1 para.3
s.453, applied: 2014 c.7 Sch.1 para.5
s.458, applied: 2014 c.26 Sch.30 para.2
s.523, applied: SI 2014/518 Reg.1
s.524, applied: SI 2014/518 Reg.1
s.528, amended: SI 2014/518 Reg.2
s.528, enabling: SI 2014/518
s.534, repealed (in part): 2014 c.26 Sch.1
para.14
s.535, repealed (in part): 2014 c.26 Sch.1
para.14
s.543, repealed (in part): 2014 c.26 Sch.1
para.14
s.544, amended: SI 2014/518 Reg.2
s.544, enabling: SI 2014/518
s.551, repealed (in part): 2014 c.26 Sch.1
para.14
s.552, amended: 2014 c.26 Sch.1 para.14
s.564, repealed (in part): 2014 c.26 Sch.1
para.14
s.614, amended: 2014 c.26 Sch.1 para.15
s.618, amended: 2014 c.26 Sch.1 para.15
s.622A, enabling: SI 2014/685
s.627, amended: 2014 c.26 Sch.1 para.15
s.628, amended: 2014 c.26 Sch.1 para.15
s.630, amended: 2014 c.26 Sch.1 para.15
s.645, amended: 2014 c.14 Sch.4 para.160
s.653, amended: 2014 c.14 Sch.4 para.161

s.654, amended: 2014 c.14 Sch.4 para.162
s.661E, added: 2014 c.26 s.35
s.662, amended: SI 2014/3327 Art.2
s.662, applied: SI 2014/3327 Art.1
s.662, enabling: SI 2014/3327
s.663, amended: SI 2014/3327 Art.3
s.663, applied: SI 2014/3327 Art.1
s.663, enabling: SI 2014/3327
s.664, amended: 2014 c.26 s.35
s.665A, amended: 2014 c.26 s.35
s.688, amended: 2014 c.26 s.37
s.723, amended: 2014 c.26 s.37
s.724A, added: 2014 c.26 s.37
s.726, amended: 2014 c.26 s.37
s.730B, amended: 2014 c.26 s.38
s.756, amended: 2014 c.26 Sch.17 para.27
s.756, repealed (in part): 2014 c.26 Sch.17
para.27
s.964, applied: 2014 c.26 Sch.16 para.8
s.1001, amended: 2014 c.14 Sch.4 para.163
s.1029, amended: 2014 c.14 Sch.4 para.164
s.1055, amended: 2014 c.14 Sch.4 para.156,
Sch.4 para.166
s.1056, amended: 2014 c.14 Sch.4 para.156,
Sch.4 para.167
s.1119, amended: 2014 c.14 Sch.4 para.168,
2014 c.26 Sch.1 para.16
s.1120, amended: 2014 c.14 Sch.4 para.169
s.1122, applied: SI 2014/520 Reg.3, SI
2014/685 Reg.3, SI 2014/1506 Reg.6, Reg.7,
SI 2014/2388 Art.13, SI 2014/3274 Sch.1
Part 2
s.1124, applied: SI 2014/3274 Sch.1 Part 2
s.1172, applied: 2014 c.26 s.27, s.294
Sch.1 Part 2 para.704, amended: 2014 c.14
Sch.4 para.156
Sch.4, amended: 2014 c.14 Sch.4 para.170,
2014 c.26 Sch.14 para.3, Sch.15 para.5,
Sch.16 para.5, Sch.1 para.17

**04. National Assembly for Wales
(Remuneration) Measure 2010**
s.5, applied: SI 2014/1004
s.5, enabling: SI 2014/1004
Sch.1 para.1, amended: 2014 c.29 s.4, SI
2014/1004 Art.2
Sch.1 para.1, repealed (in part): SI
2014/1004 Art.2

5. Appropriation Act 2010
Sch.2 Part 2, amended: 2014 c.29 s.4
Sch.2 Part 2, varied: SI 2014/2708 Art.5

7. Co-operative and Community Benefit Societies and Credit Unions Act 2010

    Commencement Orders: 2014 c.14 Sch.7; SI 2014/183 Art.2, Art.3

    s.1, repealed: 2014 c.14 Sch.7

    s.2, repealed: 2014 c.14 Sch.7

    s.4, applied: SI 2014/574

    s.4, repealed: 2014 c.14 Sch.7

    s.4, enabling: SI 2014/574

    s.6, enabling: SI 2014/574, SI 2014/1815

    s.7, applied: SI 2014/1815

    s.7, enabling: SI 2014/574

    s.8, enabling: SI 2014/183

8. Taxation (International and Other Provisions) Act 2010

    Part 8, amended: 2014 c.26 s.289

    s.1, amended: 2014 c.26 s.289

    s.2, enabling: SI 2014/1874, SI 2014/1875, SI 2014/1876, SI 2014/1879, SI 2014/1881, SI 2014/3274, SI 2014/3275

    s.5, applied: SI 2014/1874, SI 2014/1875, SI 2014/1876, SI 2014/1879, SI 2014/1881, SI 2014/3274, SI 2014/3275

    s.34, amended: 2014 c.26 s.292

    s.42, amended: 2014 c.26 s.292

    s.49B, added: 2014 c.26 s.292

    s.112, amended: 2014 c.26 s.292

    s.118, amended: 2014 c.14 Sch.4 para.171

    s.174, amended: 2014 c.26 s.75

    s.174A, added: 2014 c.26 s.75

    s.187A, added: 2014 c.26 s.75

    s.345, amended: 2014 c.26 s.39

    s.353A, amended: 2014 c.26 s.39

    s.354, enabling: SI 2014/685, SI 2014/1931

    s.363A, amended: 2014 c.26 s.289

    s.363A, substituted: 2014 c.26 s.289

    s.371IH, amended: 2014 c.26 s.293, s.294

    s.371RE, amended: SI 2014/3237 Reg.2

    s.371RF, enabling: SI 2014/3237

9. Child Poverty Act 2010

    s.6, applied: SI 2014/3232 Reg.2

    s.6, enabling: SI 2014/3232

    s.28, applied: SI 2014/3232

13. Finance Act 2010

    Sch.1 Part 3 para.44, amended: 2014 c.14 Sch.4 para.172

    Sch.6 Part 1 para.2, enabling: SI 2014/1807

    Sch.6 Part 2 para.15, repealed (in part): 2014 c.26 s.114

15. Equality Act 2010

    see *C (A Child) (Care Proceedings: Deaf Parent), Re* [2014] EWCA Civ 128, [2014] 1 W.L.R. 2495 (CA (Civ Div)), Rimer LJ; see *CalMac Ferries Ltd v Wallace* [2014] I.C.R. 453 (EAT (SC)), Langstaff J; see *Campbell v Thomas Cook Tour Operations Ltd* [2014] Eq. L.R. 108 (CC (Sheffield)), District Judge Bellamy; see *Cary v Commissioner of Police of the Metropolis* [2014] EWCA Civ 987, [2014] C.P. Rep. 42 (CA (Civ Div)), Arden LJ; see *Gayhurst Community School v ER* [2014] E.L.R. 103 (UT (AAC)), Judge Edward Jacobs; see *Griffiths v Secretary of State for Work and Pensions* [2014] Eq. L.R. 545 (EAT), Recorder Luba Q.C.; see *Hutchison 3G UK Ltd v Edwards* [2014] Eq. L.R. 525 (EAT), Judge Eady QC; see *Kapenova v Department of Health* [2014] I.C.R. 884 (EAT), Slade J; see *M v Fife Council* 2014 S.L.T. (Sh Ct) 147 (Sh Ct (Tayside) (Kirkcaldy)), Sheriff J H Williamson; see *MM v Secretary of State for Work and Pensions* [2013] EWCA Civ 1565, [2014] 1 W.L.R. 1716 (CA (Civ Div)), Maurice Kay LJ; see *R. (on the application of Howard) v Official Receiver* [2013] EWHC 1839 (Admin), [2014] Q.B. 930 (QBD (Admin)), Stadlen J; see *R. (on the application of Rotherham MBC) v Secretary of State for Business, Innovation and Skills* [2014] EWHC 232 (Admin), [2014] B.L.G.R. 389 (QBD (Admin)), Stewart J; see *Rowstock Ltd v Jessemey* [2014] EWCA Civ 185, [2014] 1 W.L.R. 3615 (CA (Civ Div)), Maurice Kay LJ; see *Secretary of State for Work and Pensions v Higgins* [2014] I.C.R. 341 (EAT), Judge David Richardson; see *Taiwo v Olaigbe* [2014] EWCA Civ 279, [2014] 1 W.L.R. 3636 (CA (Civ Div)), Maurice Kay LJ; see *Warner v Armfield Retail & Leisure Ltd* [2014] I.C.R. 239 (EAT), Judge David Richardson

    applied: 2014 c.6 s.83, SI 2014/941 Sch.1, SI 2014/1183, SI 2014/2128 r.38, SI 2014/2874, SI 2014/3283 Sch.1 para.2, Sch.1 para.5, SI 2014/3352 Sch.1 para.20

    referred to: 2014 c.22 s.33

    Part 6, applied: SI 2014/3283 Sch.1 para.3

    Part 6 c.1, referred to: 2014 c.6 s.58, s.59

    Part 10, referred to: 2014 asp 14 s.34

Pt 8., see *Rowstock Ltd v Jessemey* [2014] EWCA Civ 185, [2014] 1 W.L.R. 3615 (CA (Civ Div)), Maurice Kay LJ
s.2, amended: 2014 c.29 s.4
s.4, applied: SI 2014/2936 Reg.13
s.6, see *Hutchison 3G UK Ltd v Edwards* [2014] Eq. L.R. 525 (EAT), Judge Eady QC; see *R. (on the application of Howard) v Official Receiver* [2013] EWHC 1839 (Admin), [2014] Q.B. 930 (QBD (Admin)), Stadlen J
s.6, applied: SI 2014/2147 Reg.8, SI 2014/2319 Reg.3
s.13, see *Heron v Sefton MBC* [2014] Eq. L.R. 130 (EAT), Mitting J; see *Lyons v DWP Jobcentre Plus* [2014] I.C.R. 668 (EAT), Cox J; see *Taiwo v Olaigbe* [2014] EWCA Civ 279, [2014] 1 W.L.R. 3636 (CA (Civ Div)), Maurice Kay LJ
s.15, see *Akerman-Livingstone v Aster Communities Ltd (formerly Flourish Homes Ltd)* [2014] EWCA Civ 1081, [2014] 1 W.L.R. 3980 (CA (Civ Div)), Arden LJ; see *City Facilities Management (UK) Ltd v Ling* [2014] Eq. L.R. 399 (EAT), Judge Eady QC; see *Hamnett v Essex CC* [2014] EWHC 246 (Admin), [2014] 1 W.L.R. 2562 (Admin)), Singh J; see *SN v Nottinghamshire CC* [2014] UKUT 2 (AAC), [2014] E.L.R. 286 (UT (AAC)), Judge Ward
s.18, see *Commissioner of Police of the Metropolis v Keohane* [2014] I.C.R. 1073 (EAT), Langstaff J; see *Lyons v DWP Jobcentre Plus* [2014] I.C.R. 668 (EAT), Cox J
s.19, see *Essop v Home Office (UK Border Agency)* [2014] I.C.R. 871 (EAT), Langstaff J; see *R. (on the application of Bapio Action Ltd) v Royal College of General Practitioners* [2014] EWHC 1416 (Admin), [2014] Eq. L.R. 409 (QBD (Admin)), Mitting J; see *Smith-Twigger v Abbey Protection Group Ltd* [2014] I.C.R. D33 (EAT), Langstaff J
s.20, see *City Facilities Management (UK) Ltd v Ling* [2014] Eq. L.R. 399 (EAT), Judge Eady QC; see *Hainsworth v Ministry of Defence* [2014] EWCA Civ 763, [2014] 3 C.M.L.R. 43 (CA (Civ Div)), Laws LJ; see *Hamnett v Essex CC* [2014] EWHC 246

(Admin), [2014] 1 W.L.R. 2562 (QBD (Admin)), Singh J; see *Secretary of State for Work and Pensions v Higgins* [2014] I.C.R. 341 (EAT), Judge David Richardson
s.21, see *MM v Secretary of State for Work and Pensions* [2013] EWCA Civ 1565, [2014] 1 W.L.R. 1716 (CA (Civ Div)), Maurice Kay LJ
s.23, see *Innospec Ltd v Walker* [2014] I.C.R. 645 (EAT), Langstaff J; see *Palmer v Royal Bank of Scotland Plc* [2014] I.C.R. 1288 (EAT), Langstaff J
s.29, see *Crown Prosecution Service v Fraser* [2014] Eq. L.R. 535 (EAT), Cox J; see *Hamnett v Essex CC* [2014] EWHC 246 (Admin), [2014] 1 W.L.R. 2562 (Admin)), Singh J
s.35, see *Swan Housing Association Ltd v Gill* [2013] EWCA Civ 1566, [2014] H.L.R. 18 (CA (Civ Div)), Richards LJ
s.39, see *Heron v Sefton MBC* [2014] Eq. L.R. 130 (EAT), Mitting J; see *Rowstock Ltd v Jessemey* [2014] EWCA Civ 185, [2014] 1 W.L.R. 3615 (CA (Civ Div)), Maurice Kay LJ
s.40, see *Wijesundera v Heathrow 3PL Logistics Ltd* [2014] I.C.R. 523 (EAT), Langstaff J
s.65, see *CalMac Ferries Ltd v Wallace* [2014] I.C.R. 453 (EAT (SC)), Langstaff J
s.66, see *CalMac Ferries Ltd v Wallace* [2014] I.C.R. 453 (EAT (SC)), Langstaff J
s.67, amended: SI 2014/560 Sch.1 para.35, SI 2014/3229 Sch.5 para.19
s.69, see *CalMac Ferries Ltd v Wallace* [2014] I.C.R. 453 (EAT (SC)), Langstaff J
s.80, repealed (in part): SI 2014/560 Sch.1 para.35, SI 2014/3229 Sch.5 para.19
s.83, see *Windle v Secretary of State for Justice* [2014] I.R.L.R. 914 (EAT), Judge Peter Clark
s.108, see *Rowstock Ltd v Jessemey* [2014] EWCA Civ 185, [2014] 1 W.L.R. 3615 (CA (Civ Div)), Maurice Kay LJ
s.110, amended: SI 2014/3229 Sch.5 para.19
s.113, see *Hamnett v Essex CC* [2014] EWHC 246 (Admin), [2014] 1 W.L.R. 2562 (QBD (Admin)), Singh J
s.115, amended: 2014 c.22 Sch.9 para.59
s.136, see *Akerman-Livingstone v Aster Communities Ltd (formerly Flourish Homes*

Ltd) [2014] EWCA Civ 1081, [2014] 1 W.L.R. 3980 (CA (Civ Div)), Arden LJ

s.139A, applied: SI 2014/2559

s.139A, enabling: SI 2014/2559

s.149, see *Hamnett v Essex CC* [2014] EWHC 246 (Admin), [2014] 1 W.L.R. 2562 (QBD (Admin)), Singh J; see *Hunt v North Somerset Council* [2013] EWCA Civ 1320, [2014] B.L.G.R. 1 (CA (Civ Div)), Moore-Bick LJ; see *Kanu v Southwark LBC* [2014] EWCA Civ 1085, [2014] P.T.S.R. 1197 (CA (Civ Div)), Aikens LJ; see *R. (on the application of Bapio Action Ltd) v Royal College of General Practitioners* [2014] EWHC 1416 (Admin), [2014] Eq. L.R. 409 (QBD (Admin)), Mitting J; see *R. (on the application of Bracking) v Secretary of State for Work and Pensions* [2013] EWCA Civ 1345, [2014] Eq. L.R. 60 (CA (Civ Div)), Elias LJ; see *R. (on the application of Core Issues Trust) v Transport for London* [2014] EWCA Civ 34, [2014] P.T.S.R. 785 (CA (Civ Div)), Lord Dyson MR; see *R. (on the application of Flatley) v Hywel Dda University Local Health Board* [2014] EWHC 2258 (Admin), (2014) 140 B.M.L.R. 1 (QBD (Admin)), Hickinbottom J; see *R. (on the application of Howard) v Official Receiver* [2013] EWHC 1839 (Admin), [2014] Q.B. 930 (QBD (Admin)), Stadlen J; see *R. (on the application of LH) v Shropshire Council* [2014] EWCA Civ 404, [2014] P.T.S.R. 1052 (CA (Civ Div)), Longmore LJ; see *R. (on the application of MA) v Secretary of State for Work and Pensions* [2014] EWCA Civ 13, [2014] P.T.S.R. 584 (CA (Civ Div)), Lord Dyson MR; see *R. (on the application of Rotherham MBC) v Secretary of State for Business, Innovation and Skills* [2014] EWHC 232 (Admin), [2014] B.L.G.R. 389 (QBD (Admin)), Stewart J; see *R. (on the application of Unison) v Lord Chancellor* [2014] EWHC 218 (Admin), [2014] I.C.R. 498 (DC), Moses LJ; see *R. (on the application of West) v Rhondda Cynon Taff CBC* [2014] EWHC 2134 (Admin), [2014] E.L.R. 396 (QBD (Admin)), Supperstone J; see *Robson v Salford City Council* [2014] EWHC 3481 (Admin), (2014) 17 C.C.L. Rep. 474 (QBD (Admin)), Judge Stephen

Davies; see *Swan Housing Association Ltd v Gill* [2013] EWCA Civ 1566, [2014] H.L.R. 18 (CA (Civ Div)), Richards LJ

s.149, referred to: SI 2014/2936 Reg.10

s.157, amended: 2014 c.29 s.4

s.183, applied: SI 2014/2660

s.183, enabling: SI 2014/2660, SI 2014/3244

s.184, applied: SI 2014/2660, SI 2014/3244

s.207, enabling: SI 2014/2559, SI 2014/2660

s.208, applied: SI 2014/2559

s.212, amended: 2014 c.29 s.4

s.212, enabling: SI 2014/1711

Sch.1, see *Hutchison 3G UK Ltd v Edwards* [2014] Eq. L.R. 525 (EAT), Judge Eady QC; see *R. (on the application of Howard) v Official Receiver* [2013] EWHC 1839 (Admin), [2014] Q.B. 930 (QBD (Admin)), Stadlen J

Sch.2 para.2, see *MM v Secretary of State for Work and Pensions* [2013] EWCA Civ 1565, [2014] 1 W.L.R. 1716 (CA (Civ Div)), Maurice Kay LJ

Sch.3 Part 1 para.2, amended: 2014 c.29 s.4

Sch.3 Pt 1 para.3, see *Crown Prosecution Service v Fraser* [2014] Eq. L.R. 535 (EAT), Cox J

Sch.3 Part 6B, added: SI 2014/3229 Sch.5 para.19

Sch.3 Part 6ZA, amended: SI 2014/3229 Sch.5 para.19

Sch.3 Part 6 para.25, amended: SI 2014/3229 Sch.5 para.19

Sch.6 para.2, amended: 2014 c.29 s.4

Sch.7 Part 2 para.5, enabling: SI 2014/1711

Sch.8 Pt 2 para.5, see *Hainsworth v Ministry of Defence* [2014] EWCA Civ 763, [2014] 3 C.M.L.R. 43 (CA (Civ Div)), Laws LJ

Sch.9 Pt 3 para.18, see *Innospec Ltd v Walker* [2014] I.C.R. 645 (EAT), Langstaff J

Sch.10 para.1, applied: SI 2014/1530 Sch.2 para.7

Sch.17, applied: 2014 c.6 s.58, s.59

Sch.17 Part 2 para.3, amended: 2014 c.6 s.60

Sch.18 para.3, see *R. (on the application of Howard) v Official Receiver* [2013] EWHC 1839 (Admin), [2014] Q.B. 930 (QBD (Admin)), Stadlen J

Sch.19 Part 1, amended: 2014 c.12 Sch.11 para.96, 2014 c.23 Sch.5 para.35, Sch.7 para.27, 2014 c.2 Sch.12 para.114, SI

2014/892 Sch.1 para.182, SI 2014/3184
Sch.1 para.15
Sch.19 Part 2, amended: 2014 c.29 s.4
Sch.22 para.1, see *Heron v Sefton MBC*
[2014] Eq. L.R. 130 (EAT), Mitting J
Sch.22 para.1, amended: 2014 c.29 s.4
Sch.23 para.2, amended: SI 2014/3229 Sch.5
para.19

17. Crime and Security Act 2010
Commencement Orders: SI 2014/478 Art.2
s.40, repealed: 2014 c.12 Sch.11 para.46
s.59, enabling: SI 2014/478

23. Bribery Act 2010
s.10, amended: SI 2014/834 Sch.2 para.74
s.10, repealed (in part): SI 2014/834 Sch.2
para.74

24. Digital Economy Act 2010
Commencement Orders: SI 2014/1659 Art.2
s.43, repealed (in part): SI 2014/1372 Sch.1
para.12
s.47, enabling: SI 2014/1659

25. Constitutional Reform and Governance Act 2010
Commencement Orders: SI 2014/3245 Art.2;
SI 2014/3249 Art.2
s.5, amended: 2014 c.29 s.4
s.7, amended: 2014 c.29 s.4
s.8, amended: 2014 c.29 s.4
s.15, amended: 2014 c.29 s.4
s.16, amended: 2014 c.29 s.4
s.45, applied: SI 2014/3249 Art.2
s.45, enabling: SI 2014/3249
s.52, enabling: SI 2014/3245
Sch.2 Part 1 para.15, amended: 2014 c.29 s.4

26. Children, Schools and Families Act 2010
s.2, repealed: 2014 c.6 Sch.3 para.19

27. Energy Act 2010
s.9, enabling: SI 2014/695
s.14, applied: SI 2014/695
s.31, applied: SI 2014/695
s.31, enabling: SI 2014/695

29. Flood and Water Management Act 2010
Commencement Orders: SI 2014/3155 Art.2
s.6, amended: 2014 c.21 Sch.7 para.144
s.28, amended: 2014 c.29 s.4
s.30, disapplied: SI 2014/2384 Sch.19
para.11
s.35, amended: 2014 c.21 Sch.7 para.145
s.42, amended: 2014 c.21 Sch.7 para.146
s.42, repealed (in part): 2014 c.21 Sch.7
para.146

s.44, amended: 2014 c.21 Sch.7 para.147
s.49, enabling: SI 2014/3155
Sch.1, disapplied: SI 2014/2384 Sch.19
para.11
Sch.3, applied: SI 2014/1796 Sch.2 para.20
Sch.3 para.12, amended: 2014 c.21 s.88
Sch.3 para.19A, added: 2014 c.21 s.21

30. Appropriation (No.3) Act 2010
Sch.2 Part 5, amended: 2014 c.29 s.4
Sch.2 Part 46, varied: SI 2014/2708 Art.5

31. Finance (No.2) Act 2010
Sch.4 para.3, amended: 2014 c.29 s.4

32. Academies Act 2010
s.1, applied: SI 2014/512 Sch.1 para.10, SI
2014/531 Sch.1
s.1, repealed (in part): 2014 c.6 Sch.3
para.95
s.1C, applied: SI 2014/3352 Sch.2 para.25
s.4, see *R. (on the application of Warren*
Comprehensive School) v Secretary of State
for Education [2014] EWHC 2252 (Admin),
[2014] E.L.R. 530 (QBD (Admin)),
Supperstone J
s.4, applied: SI 2014/3352 Reg.1
s.10A, applied: SI 2014/3352 Sch.2 para.13

33. Finance (No.3) Act 2010
Sch.10 para.2, amended: 2014 c.26 Sch.22
para.21
Sch.10 para.7, amended: 2014 c.26 Sch.22
para.21
Sch.11 para.2, amended: 2014 c.26 Sch.22
para.22
Sch.11 para.7, amended: 2014 c.26 Sch.22
para.22

38. Terrorist Asset-Freezing etc Act 2010
s.23, amended: 2014 c.29 s.4

40. Identity Documents Act 2010
s.4, see *Guardian News and Media Ltd v AB*
Times, June 18, 2014 (CA (Crim Div)),
Gross LJ; see *R. v Mateta (Koshi Pitshou)*
[2013] EWCA Crim 1372, [2014] 1 W.L.R.
1516 (CA (Crim Div)), Leveson LJ
s.4, applied: 2014 c.12 Sch.8 para.6
s.6, applied: 2014 c.12 Sch.8 para.6

41. Loans to Ireland Act 2010
applied: 2014 c.5 Sch.1 para.1, 2014 c.25
Sch.1

2011

01. Welsh Language (Wales) Measure 2011
s.22, amended: 2014 c.29 s.4
Sch.6, amended: SI 2014/892 Sch.1 para.259
Sch.11 Part 4 para.13, amended: 2014 c.29
s.4
Sch.12 para.1, amended: 2014 c.29 s.4
2. Appropriation Act 2011
Sch.2 Part 2, amended: 2014 c.29 s.4
**4. Budget Responsibility and National Audit
Act 2011**
s.4, applied: SI 2014/2671 Reg.9
04. Local Government (Wales) Measure 2011
Commencement Orders: SI 2014/453 Art.2
s.178, enabling: SI 2014/453
05. Housing (Wales) Measure 2011
applied: SI 2014/2418 Sch.1
5. Postal Services Act 2011
applied: SI 2014/500 Art.2, SI 2014/531
Sch.1, SI 2014/631 Art.3
Part 2, applied: SI 2014/500 Art.2
Part 3, applied: SI 2014/3204 Sch.2 para.10
s.16, applied: SI 2014/500 Art.2
s.17, amended: SI 2014/500 Art.5
s.17, applied: SI 2014/500 Art.2
s.20, amended: SI 2014/500 Art.5
s.20, applied: SI 2014/500 Art.2
s.21, amended: SI 2014/500 Art.5
s.24, amended: SI 2014/500 Art.5
s.24, applied: SI 2014/500 Art.2
s.25, amended: SI 2014/500 Art.5
s.25, applied: SI 2014/500 Art.2
s.26, amended: SI 2014/500 Art.5
s.51, amended: SI 2014/631 Sch.1 para.13,
SI 2014/892 Sch.1 para.185
s.51, applied: SI 2014/631 Sch.1 para.28
s.56, amended: SI 2014/631 Sch.1 para.13,
SI 2014/892 Sch.1 para.186
s.57, amended: SI 2014/631 Sch.1 para.13
s.60, applied: SI 2014/559
s.61, amended: SI 2014/631 Sch.1 para.13
s.65, amended: SI 2014/631 Sch.1 para.13
s.89, amended: SI 2014/500 Art.5
s.91, amended: SI 2014/500 Art.5
s.91, applied: SI 2014/500 Art.2
Sch.5 para.1, amended: SI 2014/631 Sch.1
para.13
Sch.5 para.1, repealed (in part): SI 2014/631
Sch.1 para.13

Sch.7 para.1, amended: SI 2014/631 Sch.1
para.13
07. Education (Wales) Measure 2011
Commencement Orders: SI 2014/1066 Art.2
Part 2 c.1, applied: SI 2014/1133 Art.2
s.6, enabling: SI 2014/1132
s.10, applied: SI 2014/1132 Reg.4
s.10, enabling: SI 2014/1132
s.11, applied: SI 2014/1132 Reg.4, Reg.9,
Reg.11, SI 2014/1133 Art.2
s.11, enabling: SI 2014/1132
s.12, enabling: SI 2014/1132
s.13, enabling: SI 2014/1132
s.14, enabling: SI 2014/1132
s.15, enabling: SI 2014/1133
s.18, enabling: SI 2014/1132, SI 2014/1609
s.22, enabling: SI 2014/2225
s.32, enabling: SI 2014/1132, SI 2014/1133,
SI 2014/1609, SI 2014/2225
s.33, enabling: SI 2014/1066
**10. Supply and Appropriation (Main
Estimates) Act 2011**
referred to: 2014 c.5 s.7
s.6, referred to: 2014 c.5 s.7
Sch.1, amended: 2014 c.29 s.4
Sch.1, referred to: 2014 c.5 s.7, Sch.3 para.1
11. Finance Act 2011
Sch.16 Part 1 para.1, repealed (in part): 2014
c.30 Sch.1 para.32
Sch.16 Part 1 para.8, repealed (in part): 2014
c.30 Sch.1 para.32
Sch.16 Part 1 para.10, repealed: 2014 c.30
Sch.1 para.32
Sch.16 Part 1 para.11, repealed (in part):
2014 c.30 Sch.1 para.32
Sch.16 Part 1 para.18, repealed (in part):
2014 c.30 Sch.1 para.32
Sch.16 Part 1 para.20, repealed: 2014 c.30
Sch.1 para.32
Sch.16 Part 1 para.35, repealed (in part):
2014 c.30 Sch.2 para.19
Sch.16 Part 1 para.41, repealed (in part):
2014 c.30 Sch.2 para.17
Sch.16 Part 1 para.42, repealed (in part):
2014 c.30 Sch.2 para.19
Sch.16 Part 1 para.45, repealed: 2014 c.30
Sch.1 para.66
Sch.16 Part 2 para.81, repealed (in part):
2014 c.30 Sch.1 para.32
Sch.16 Part 3 para.87, amended: 2014 c.30
Sch.1 para.52

Sch.16 Part 3 para.95, amended: 2014 c.30
Sch.1 para.52
Sch.18 Part 1 para.4, repealed (in part): 2014
c.26 s.42
Sch.18 Part 1 para.6, repealed (in part): 2014
c.30 Sch.1 para.74
Sch.18 Part 1 para.7, repealed: 2014 c.30
Sch.1 para.75
Sch.18 Part 2 para.14, applied: 2014 c.26
Sch.6 para.1
Sch.19 Part 2 para.6, amended: 2014 c.26
s.119
Sch.19 Part 2 para.7, amended: 2014 c.26
s.119
Sch.19 Part 3 para.11, applied: 2014 c.26
s.285
Sch.19 Part 4 para.15, amended: 2014 c.26
Sch.26 para.2
Sch.19 Part 4 para.17, amended: 2014 c.26
Sch.26 para.3
Sch.19 Part 4 para.19, amended: 2014 c.26
Sch.26 para.4
Sch.19 Part 4 para.19, applied: 2014 c.26
s.285
Sch.19 Part 4 para.21, amended: 2014 c.26
Sch.26 para.5
Sch.19 Part 4 para.27, amended: 2014 c.26
Sch.26 para.6
Sch.19 Part 4 para.29, amended: 2014 c.26
Sch.26 para.8
Sch.19 Part 4 para.29, repealed (in part):
2014 c.26 Sch.26 para.8
Sch.19 Part 4 para.30, amended: 2014 c.26
Sch.26 para.9
Sch.19 Part 4 para.38A, added: 2014 c.26
Sch.26 para.10
Sch.19 Part 8 para.73, amended: 2014 c.14
Sch.4 para.173
Sch.19 Part 8 para.75, amended: 2014 c.26
Sch.26 para.11
Sch.19 Part 8 para.76A, added: 2014 c.26
Sch.26 para.11
Sch.19 Part 8 para.77, amended: 2014 c.26
Sch.26 para.11
Sch.19 Part 8 para.78, applied: 2014 c.26
s.285
Sch.19 Part 8 para.80, applied: 2014 c.26
s.285
Sch.19 Part 9 para.81, amended: 2014 c.26
Sch.26 para.12

Sch.25 para.5, amended: SI 2014/834 Sch.2
para.75

12. European Union Act 2011
s.8, applied: 2014 c.3, s.1

**13. Police Reform and Social Responsibility Act
2011**

Part 3, amended: 2014 c.12 s.153
s.7, amended: 2014 c.12 Sch.11 para.97
s.9, repealed: 2014 c.12 Sch.11 para.98
s.18, amended: 2014 c.2 Sch.12 para.116
s.19, amended: 2014 c.2 Sch.12 para.117
s.24, repealed (in part): 2014 c.12 Sch.11
para.102
s.31, applied: SI 2014/2418 Sch.1
s.42, amended: 2014 c.12 s.140
s.42, applied: SI 2014/2376, SI 2014/2376
Reg.2, Reg.3
s.42, enabling: SI 2014/2376
s.51, applied: SI 2014/1963 Art.6
s.58, amended: SI 2014/268 Art.4
s.58, applied: SI 2014/268 Art.2
s.58, enabling: SI 2014/921, SI 2014/1963
s.142A, added: 2014 c.12 s.153
s.143, amended: 2014 c.12 s.153
s.144, amended: 2014 c.12 s.153
s.145, amended: 2014 c.12 s.153
s.146, amended: 2014 c.12 s.153
s.147, amended: 2014 c.12 s.153
s.148, amended: 2014 c.12 s.153
s.149, amended: 2014 c.12 s.153
s.154, amended: SI 2014/268 Art.4
s.154, applied: SI 2014/921, SI 2014/1963
s.154, enabling: SI 2014/921, SI 2014/1963
Sch.2 para.4, referred to: SI 2014/1638
Reg.2, Reg.3, Sch.11 para.9
Sch.2 para.7, repealed (in part): 2014 c.12
Sch.11 para.99
Sch.2 para.7A, added: 2014 c.12 s.141
Sch.4 para.4, referred to: SI 2014/1638
Reg.3
Sch.4 para.4, repealed (in part): 2014 c.12
Sch.11 para.100
Sch.4 para.4A, added: 2014 c.12 s.141
Sch.8 Part 1 para.2, amended: 2014 c.12
s.140
Sch.8 Part 1 para.2, applied: SI 2014/2376,
SI 2014/2376 Reg.2, Reg.3
Sch.8 Part 1 para.2, enabling: SI 2014/2376
Sch.16 Part 1 para.30, repealed (in part):
2014 c.12 Sch.11 para.102

Sch.16 Part 1 para.35, repealed (in part):
2014 c.12 Sch.11 para.102
Sch.16 Part 1 para.38, repealed: 2014 c.12
Sch.11 para.102
Sch.16 Part 3 para.226, repealed: 2014 c.2
Sch.1 Part 2
Sch.16 Part 3 para.307, repealed: 2014 c.12
Sch.11 para.50

14. Fixed-term Parliaments Act 2011
s.5, repealed: 2014 c.29 s.1

16. Energy Act 2011
s.1, enabling: SI 2014/2020
s.30, enabling: SI 2014/436, SI 2014/1850
s.40, applied: SI 2014/436, SI 2014/1850, SI
2014/2020
s.74, enabling: SI 2014/880

18. Armed Forces Act 2011
Commencement Orders: SI 2014/1444 Art.3
s.2, amended: 2014 c.29 s.4
s.17, repealed: 2014 c.12 Sch.11 para.82
s.28, repealed: 2014 c.20 s.45
s.32, enabling: SI 2014/1444
Sch.4 para.3, repealed (in part): 2014 c.12
Sch.11 para.82

19. Pensions Act 2011
Commencement Orders: 2014 c.19 s.23,
2014 c.19 Sch.12 para.97; SI 2014/1683
Art.2
applied: SI 2014/1711 Reg.47
Part 4, applied: SI 2014/1711 Reg.41
Part 4, disapplied: SI 2014/1711 Reg.6
Part 4, referred to: SI 2014/1711 Reg.44
s.2, repealed (in part): 2014 c.19 Sch.12
para.97
s.3, repealed: 2014 c.19 Sch.12 para.97
s.10, repealed: 2014 c.19 Sch.18 para.12
s.18, repealed: 2014 c.19 s.38
s.29, applied: SI 2014/1711 Reg.23
s.30, enabling: SI 2014/1711
s.31, enabling: SI 2014/1711, SI 2014/1954
s.33, applied: SI 2014/1954
s.33, enabling: SI 2014/1711, SI 2014/1954
s.38, enabling: SI 2014/1683
Sch.2, repealed: 2014 c.19 Sch.12 para.97
Sch.3, repealed: 2014 c.19 Sch.12 para.97

20. Localism Act 2011
see *R. (on the application of Daws Hill
Neighbourhood Forum) v Wycombe DC*
[2014] EWCA Civ 228, [2014] 1 W.L.R.
1362 (CA (Civ Div)), Lord Dyson MR
applied: SI 2014/2418 Sch.1

referred to: 2014 c.5 Sch.1 para.1
s.1, applied: 2014 c.14 s.24, SI 2014/863
Sch.2 para.1, SI 2014/864 Sch.3 para.1, SI
2014/865 Sch.2 para.1, SI 2014/1012 Sch.2
para.1, SI 2014/1190
s.4, amended: 2014 c.14 Sch.4 para.175
s.5, applied: SI 2014/1190
s.5, enabling: SI 2014/1190
s.6, applied: SI 2014/1190
s.7, applied: SI 2014/1190
s.25, see *R. (on the application of IM
Properties Development Ltd) v Lichfield DC*
[2014] EWHC 2440 (Admin), [2014]
P.T.S.R. 1484 (QBD (Birmingham)),
Patterson J
s.52, amended: 2014 c.29 s.4
s.62, amended: 2014 c.29 s.4
s.81, see *Draper v Lincolnshire CC* [2014]
EWHC 2388 (Admin), [2014] B.L.G.R. 673
(QBD (Admin)), Collins J
s.155, repealed (in part): 2014 c.12 Sch.11
para.50
s.185, repealed (in part): 2014 c.14 Sch.7
s.190, amended: 2014 c.14 Sch.4 para.176
s.191, amended: 2014 c.14 Sch.4 para.177
s.200, amended: 2014 c.14 Sch.4 para.178
s.200, repealed (in part): SI 2014/3184 Sch.1
para.16
s.216, amended: 2014 c.14 Sch.4 para.179
s.235, applied: SI 2014/389
s.235, enabling: SI 2014/389
s.236, enabling: SI 2014/389
Sch.14 para.4A, added: 2014 c.12 s.100
Sch.14 para.5A, added: 2014 c.12 s.100
Sch.14 para.6, amended: 2014 c.12 Sch.11
para.47
Sch.14 para.6A, added: 2014 c.12 Sch.11
para.48
Sch.17 para.10, repealed (in part): 2014 c.2
Sch.12 para.123
Sch.20 para.3, repealed: 2014 c.2 Sch.1 Part
2
Sch.22 para.51, repealed (in part): SI
2014/3184 Sch.1 para.16

21. Education Act 2011
Sch.5 para.13, repealed: 2014 c.2 Sch.1 Part
2

**22. London Olympic Games and Paralympic
Games (Amendment) Act 2011**
s.1, repealed (in part): SI 2014/3184 Sch.1
para.17

s.2, repealed (in part): SI 2014/3184 Sch.1 para.17

24. Public Bodies Act 2011
s.1, enabling: SI 2014/631, SI 2014/1068, SI 2014/1924
s.2, enabling: SI 2014/834
s.4, applied: SI 2014/2555
s.4, enabling: SI 2014/2555
s.5, enabling: SI 2014/631
s.6, applied: SI 2014/631
s.6, enabling: SI 2014/631, SI 2014/834, SI 2014/1068, SI 2014/1924, SI 2014/2555
s.8, applied: SI 2014/631(a), SI 2014/834, SI 2014/1068, SI 2014/1924, SI 2014/2555
s.8, referred to: SI 2014/834, SI 2014/1924, SI 2014/2555
s.9, amended: 2014 c.29 s.4
s.9, applied: SI 2014/631, SI 2014/1068, SI 2014/1924
s.10, applied: SI 2014/631, SI 2014/834, SI 2014/1068, SI 2014/1924
s.11, applied: SI 2014/631, SI 2014/834, SI 2014/1068, SI 2014/1924, SI 2014/2555
s.11, referred to: SI 2014/834, SI 2014/1068, SI 2014/2555
s.14, repealed (in part): 2014 c.21 s.40
s.21, applied: SI 2014/631
s.23, enabling: SI 2014/834
s.24, enabling: SI 2014/834, SI 2014/1924
s.35, enabling: SI 2014/834, SI 2014/1068, SI 2014/1924
s.36, amended: 2014 c.14 Sch.4 para.180, 2014 c.29 s.4
s.36, repealed (in part): 2014 c.14 Sch.7
Sch.1, amended: SI 2014/631 Sch.1 para.14, SI 2014/1068 Art.3, SI 2014/1924 Sch.1
Sch.1, referred to: SI 2014/631 Art.3
Sch.2, amended: SI 2014/892 Sch.1 para.183
Sch.4, amended: 2014 c.21 s.40
Sch.5, amended: SI 2014/631 Sch.2 para.6
Sch.5, referred to: SI 2014/631 Art.5

25. Charities Act 2011
see *Kennedy v Information Commissioner* [2014] UKSC 20, [2014] 2 W.L.R. 808 (SC), Lord Neuberger JSC
applied: SI 2014/1132 Reg.49
s.30, enabling: SI 2014/242
s.115, see *Rosenzweig v NMC Recordings Ltd* [2013] EWHC 3792 (Ch), [2014] P.T.S.R. 261 (Ch D), Norris J
s.141, referred to: SI 2014/1960 Art.5

s.149, amended: 2014 c.2 Sch.12 para.119
s.149, applied: SI 2014/531 Sch.1
s.149, repealed (in part): 2014 c.2 Sch.12 para.119
s.151, amended: 2014 c.2 Sch.12 para.120
s.152, amended: 2014 c.2 Sch.12 para.121
s.154, amended: 2014 c.2 Sch.12 para.122
s.185, applied: SI 2014/2068 Sch.1 para.9
s.189, applied: SI 2014/2068 Sch.1 para.9
s.229, amended: 2014 c.14 Sch.4 para.182
Sch.3 para.26, amended: 2014 c.14 Sch.4 para.183
Sch.3 para.27, amended: 2014 c.14 Sch.4 para.183
Sch.7 Part 2 para.14, repealed: 2014 c.14 Sch.7
Sch.7 Part 2 para.16, repealed: 2014 c.14 Sch.7
Sch.9 para.5, repealed: 2014 c.14 Sch.7
Sch.9 para.27, repealed: 2014 c.14 Sch.7

2012

1. Supply and Appropriation (Anticipation and Adjustments) Act 2012
applied: 2014 c.5 s.7
disapplied: 2014 c.5 Sch.2 para.1
Sch.1, amended: 2014 c.29 s.4
Sch.1, referred to: 2014 c.5 Sch.3 para.1

3. Public Services (Social Value) Act 2012
s.1, amended: 2014 c.29 s.4

5. Welfare Reform Act 2012
Commencement Orders: SI 2014/209 Art.3, Art.4, Art.6, Sch.1 Part 1, 2; SI 2014/1452 Art.3; SI 2014/1583 Art.3, Art.4, Sch.1; SI 2014/1635 Art.4; SI 2014/2321 Art.3, Art.4, Art.6, Sch.1, Sch.1 Part 1, Sch.1; SI 2014/3094 Art.3, Art.4
see *R. (on the application of JS) v Secretary of State for Work and Pensions* [2013] EWHC 3350 (QB), [2014] P.T.S.R. 23 (QBD (Admin)), Elias LJ
Part 1, applied: SI 2014/3037 Reg.25, SSI 2014/225 Reg.6
Part 4, applied: SI 2014/3219 Sch.1 para.1
s.4, applied: SI 2014/1230 Reg.12A, Reg.7, Reg.8
s.4, referred to: SI 2014/1230 Reg.12A, Reg.7, Reg.8, Reg.12
s.4, enabling: SI 2014/2887

s.7, enabling: SI 2014/2887

s.8, enabling: SI 2014/2887, SI 2014/2888

s.9, enabling: SI 2014/597, SI 2014/2887

s.10, enabling: SI 2014/597, SI 2014/2887, SI 2014/2888

s.11, enabling: SI 2014/597, SI 2014/771, SI 2014/2887, SI 2014/2888

s.12, enabling: SI 2014/597, SI 2014/884, SI 2014/2887

s.18, enabling: SI 2014/597

s.19, applied: SI 2014/1230 Reg.19, Reg.21, Reg.23, Reg.26

s.19, enabling: SI 2014/2887, SI 2014/2888

s.20, enabling: SI 2014/1097

s.21, applied: SI 2014/1230 Reg.19, Reg.21, Reg.23, Reg.24, Reg.26

s.21, enabling: SI 2014/1097

s.22, enabling: SI 2014/597, SI 2014/2888

s.24, enabling: SI 2014/597

s.26, applied: SI 2014/1230 Reg.32

s.26, enabling: SI 2014/597

s.27, applied: SI 2014/1230 Reg.30, Reg.32

s.27, enabling: SI 2014/597

s.28, enabling: SI 2014/597

s.30, enabling: SI 2014/902

s.32, enabling: SI 2014/2887, SI 2014/2888

s.37, enabling: SI 2014/597

s.39, amended: SI 2014/560 Sch.1 para.36, SI 2014/3229 Sch.5 para.20

s.39, repealed (in part): SI 2014/560 Sch.1 para.36, SI 2014/3229 Sch.5 para.20

s.40, enabling: SI 2014/597, SI 2014/902, SI 2014/1097, SI 2014/2888

s.42, enabling: SI 2014/597, SI 2014/771, SI 2014/902, SI 2014/1097, SI 2014/1230, SI 2014/1626, SI 2014/2887, SI 2014/2888

s.63, repealed (in part): 2014 c.6 Sch.7 para.75

s.63, varied: 2014 c.6 s.126

s.82, referred to: 2014 c.23 s.19

s.96, amended: 2014 c.19 Sch.12 para.52, 2014 c.29 s.4

s.96, enabling: SI 2014/771, SI 2014/884

s.97, enabling: SI 2014/771, SI 2014/884

s.126, enabling: SI 2014/3280

s.127, amended: 2014 c.28 s.27, SI 2014/606 Reg.4

s.131, amended: 2014 c.29 s.4

s.150, applied: SI 2014/1230 Reg.6, Reg.10, Reg.18, Reg.19, Reg.20, Reg.29, Reg.30, Reg.32, Reg.35

s.150, enabling: SI 2014/209, SI 2014/1452, SI 2014/1583, SI 2014/1635, SI 2014/1661, SI 2014/1923, SI 2014/2321, SI 2014/3067, SI 2014/3094

Sch.1 para.2, enabling: SI 2014/884

Sch.1 para.3, enabling: SI 2014/2887

Sch.1 para.4, enabling: SI 2014/884, SI 2014/2888

Sch.1 para.7, enabling: SI 2014/902

Sch.6 para.1, enabling: SI 2014/1230, SI 2014/1626

Sch.6 para.3, enabling: SI 2014/1230

Sch.6 para.4, enabling: SI 2014/1230

Sch.6 para.5, enabling: SI 2014/1230, SI 2014/1626

Sch.6 para.6, enabling: SI 2014/1230, SI 2014/1626

7. Health and Social Care Act 2012

Commencement Orders: SI 2014/39 Art.2; SI 2014/1454 Art.2

s.72, amended: SI 2014/892 Sch.1 para.188

s.73, amended: SI 2014/892 Sch.1 para.189

s.74, amended: SI 2014/892 Sch.1 para.190

s.75, enabling: SI 2014/1611

s.79, amended: SI 2014/892 Sch.1 para.191

s.80, amended: SI 2014/892 Sch.1 para.192

s.97, amended: SI 2014/892 Sch.1 para.193

s.102, amended: SI 2014/892 Sch.1 para.194

s.111, amended: 2014 c.23 s.83

s.124, amended: SI 2014/39 Art.3

s.125, amended: SI 2014/39 Art.3

s.155, repealed (in part): 2014 c.2 Sch.12 para.123

s.179, applied: 2014 c.2 Sch.13 para.1

s.179, referred to: 2014 c.2 Sch.12 para.76

s.194, applied: SI 2014/1530 Reg.54

s.253, amended: 2014 c.23 s.122

s.261, amended: 2014 c.23 s.122

s.262A, added: 2014 c.23 s.122

s.290, amended: 2014 c.23 Sch.5 para.15

s.290, applied: 2014 c.23 s.111

s.293, repealed (in part): 2014 c.23 s.90, s.91

s.304, enabling: SI 2014/39

s.306, enabling: SI 2014/39, SI 2014/1454

Sch.5 para.157, repealed: 2014 c.23 s.91

Sch.5 para.159, repealed: 2014 c.23 s.91

Sch.5 para.163, repealed: 2014 c.23 s.91

Sch.10 para.10, amended: SI 2014/892 Sch.1 para.195

Sch.10 para.10, applied: SI 2014/559

Sch.10 para.10, referred to: SI 2014/892
Sch.2 para.2
Sch.12 para.10, applied: SI 2014/559
Sch.14 Part 1 para.4A, added: 2014 c.23 s.120
Sch.14 Part 1 para.15, amended: 2014 c.23 s.85, s.120
Sch.14 Part 1 para.16, substituted: 2014 c.23 s.120
Sch.14 Part 1 para.17, amended: 2014 c.23 s.120
Sch.14 Part 1 para.24, amended: 2014 c.23 s.84, s.120
Sch.14 Part 1 para.24A, added: 2014 c.23 s.120
Sch.14 Part 1 para.35, amended: 2014 c.23 s.120

9. Protection of Freedoms Act 2012
Commencement Orders: SI 2014/3315 Art.2
s.20, referred to: SI 2014/198
s.22, applied: SI 2014/198
s.22, enabling: SI 2014/198
s.64, applied: SI 2014/3283 Reg.2
s.116, enabling: SI 2014/831
s.120, enabling: SI 2014/3315
Sch.1 Part 7 para.8, amended: 2014 c.13 s.24
Sch.8 para.8, enabling: SI 2014/238

10. Legal Aid, Sentencing and Punishment of Offenders Act 2012
Commencement Orders: SI 2014/423 Art.2, Art.3, Art.4; SI 2014/1291 Art.2; SI 2014/1777 Art.2, Art.3
see *Attorney General's Reference (No.27 of 2013)* [2014] EWCA Crim 334, [2014] 1 W.L.R. 4209 (CA (Crim Div)), Lord Thomas LCJ; see *Bhatia Best Ltd v Lord Chancellor* [2014] EWHC 746 (QB), [2014] 1 W.L.R. 3487 (QBD), Silber J; see *C (A Child) (Prohibited Steps Order: Procedural Irregularity), Re* [2013] EWCA Civ 1412, [2014] 1 W.L.R. 2182 (CA (Civ Div)), Sullivan LJ; see *King's Lynn and West Norfolk Council v Bunning* [2013] EWHC 3390 (QB), [2014] 2 All E.R. 1095 (QBD), Blake J; see *R. (on the application of Public Law Project) v Secretary of State for Justice* [2014] EWHC 2365 (Admin), [2014] H.R.L.R. 24 (QBD (Admin)), Moses LJ; see *R. v Bush (Liam)* [2013] EWCA Crim 1164, [2014] 1 Cr. App. R. (S.) 40 (CA (Crim Div)), Fulford LJ; see *R. v Docherty (Shaun*

Kevin) [2014] EWCA Crim 1197, [2014] 2 Cr. App. R. (S.) 76 (CA (Crim Div)), Treacy LJ; see *R. v Leacock (Mark)* [2013] EWCA Crim 1994, [2014] 2 Cr. App. R. (S.) 12 (CA (Crim Div)), Lord Thomas LCJ; see *Rubin v Rubin* [2014] EWHC 611 (Fam), [2014] 1 W.L.R. 3289 (Fam Div), Mostyn J
applied: 2014 c.25 Sch.1
referred to: 2014 c.5 Sch.1 para.1
Part 1, applied: SI 2014/131
Part 3 c.3, applied: SI 2014/3141 Reg.91
s.2, enabling: SI 2014/7, SI 2014/415, SI 2014/586, SI 2014/607, SI 2014/1389, SI 2014/1824, SI 2014/2422
s.4, see *Bhatia Best Ltd v Lord Chancellor* [2014] EWHC 746 (QB), [2014] 1 W.L.R. 3487 (QBD), Silber J
s.9, see *R. (on the application of Public Law Project) v Secretary of State for Justice* [2014] EWHC 2365 (Admin), [2014] H.R.L.R. 24 (QBD (Admin)), Moses LJ
s.9, enabling: SI 2014/3305
s.10, see *R. (on the application of Public Law Project) v Secretary of State for Justice* [2014] EWHC 2365 (Admin), [2014] H.R.L.R. 24 (QBD (Admin)), Moses LJ
s.10, applied: SI 2014/131 Reg.5, SI 2014/607 Reg.5, SI 2014/814 Reg.6, SI 2014/1562 Reg.4, SI 2014/2701 Reg.4
s.11, applied: SI 2014/131
s.12, enabling: SI 2014/814, SI 2014/1824
s.14, see *King's Lynn and West Norfolk Council v Bunning* [2013] EWHC 3390 (QB), [2014] 2 All E.R. 1095 (QBD), Blake J
s.14, applied: SI 2014/1610 r.17_26, r.74_3, r.62_5
s.16, see *King's Lynn and West Norfolk Council v Bunning* [2013] EWHC 3390 (QB), [2014] 2 All E.R. 1095 (QBD), Blake J
s.16, applied: SI 2014/1610 r.17_26, r.74_3, SI 2014/2422 Reg.3
s.19, see *King's Lynn and West Norfolk Council v Bunning* [2013] EWHC 3390 (QB), [2014] 2 All E.R. 1095 (QBD), Blake J
s.19, applied: SI 2014/1610 r.17_26, r.74_3
s.21, enabling: SI 2014/812, SI 2014/2701
s.22, enabling: SI 2014/901
s.25, enabling: SI 2014/1824

s.30, see *JG (A Child) v Legal Services Commission* [2014] EWCA Civ 656, [2014] 5 Costs L.O. 708 (CA (Civ Div)), Richards LJ

s.33, applied: SI 2014/1610 r.5_8

s.41, see *R. (on the application of Public Law Project) v Secretary of State for Justice* [2014] EWHC 2365 (Admin), [2014] H.R.L.R. 24 (QBD (Admin)), Moses LJ

s.41, applied: SI 2014/131, SI 2014/901, SI 2014/3305

s.41, enabling: SI 2014/7, SI 2014/131, SI 2014/415, SI 2014/586, SI 2014/607, SI 2014/812, SI 2014/814, SI 2014/1389, SI 2014/1562, SI 2014/1824, SI 2014/2422, SI 2014/2701, SI 2014/3305

s.59, applied: SI 2014/3235 Reg.2

s.59, enabling: SI 2014/3235

s.60, applied: SI 2014/3235

s.75, see *R. v Price (Jamie)* [2013] EWCA Crim 1283, [2014] 1 Cr. App. R. (S.) 36 (CA (Crim Div)), Elias LJ

s.77, enabling: SI 2014/1777

s.85, applied: 2014 c.1 s.9, 2014 c.4 s.12, s.30, s.33, s.35, s.36, 2014 c.6 s.137, 2014 c.20 Sch.5 para.2, Sch.5 para.6, Sch.7 para.12, SI 2014/3178 Art.7, SI 2014/3209 Reg.16, Reg.17, Reg.18, SI 2014/3303 Reg.14

s.85, referred to: 2014 c.4 s.33, s.35, s.36, 2014 c.6 s.137, 2014 c.20 Sch.5 para.2, Sch.5 para.6, Sch.7 para.12, 2014 c.26 s.173, s.174, s.280, SI 2014/2936 Reg.23

s.85, varied: 2014 c.4 s.30, s.33, s.35, s.36, 2014 c.6 s.137

s.91, applied: SI 2014/1610 r.18_4, r.19_2, SI 2014/3141 Reg.91

s.93, applied: SI 2014/1610 r.18_4, r.19_2

s.102, applied: SI 2014/1610 r.19_2, r.18_4

s.103, enabling: SI 2014/562, SI 2014/981, SI 2014/2931, SSI 2014/298

s.122, see *R. v Saunders (Red)* [2013] EWCA Crim 1027, [2014] 1 Cr. App. R. (S.) 45 (CA (Crim Div)), Lord Judge LCJ

s.123, see *R. v Saunders (Red)* [2013] EWCA Crim 1027, [2014] 1 Cr. App. R. (S.) 45 (CA (Crim Div)), Lord Judge LCJ

s.124, see *R. v Saunders (Red)* [2013] EWCA Crim 1027, [2014] 1 Cr. App. R. (S.) 45 (CA (Crim Div)), Lord Judge LCJ

s.140, see *HHG (Iraq) v Secretary of State for the Home Department* [2014] CSOH 48, 2014 S.L.T. 693 (OH), Lord Boyd of Duncansby

s.141, see *HHG (Iraq) v Secretary of State for the Home Department* [2014] CSOH 48, 2014 S.L.T. 693 (OH), Lord Boyd of Duncansby

s.141, enabling: SI 2014/423

s.144, see *R. (on the application of Best) v Chief Land Registrar* [2014] EWHC 1370 (Admin), [2014] 3 All E.R. 637 (QBD (Admin)), Ouseley J

s.151, enabling: SI 2014/423, SI 2014/1291

Sch.1 Pt 1, see *R. (on the application of Public Law Project) v Secretary of State for Justice* [2014] EWHC 2365 (Admin), [2014] H.R.L.R. 24 (QBD (Admin)), Moses LJ

Sch.1 Part 1 para.2, amended: 2014 c.6 Sch.3 para.96

Sch.1 Part 1 para.6, applied: SI 2014/1562 Reg.2

Sch.1 Part 1 para.6, enabling: SI 2014/1562

Sch.1 Part 1 para.12, amended: 2014 c.6 s.9

Sch.1 Part 1 para.13, amended: 2014 c.6 s.9, Sch.2 para.70

Sch.1 Part 1 para.19, repealed (in part): 2014 c.22 Sch.9 para.6

Sch.1 Pt 1 para.19, see *Bhatia Best Ltd v Lord Chancellor* [2014] EWHC 746 (QB), [2014] 1 W.L.R. 3487 (QBD), Silber J

Sch.1 Part 1 para.36, amended: 2014 c.12 Sch.11 para.49

Sch.1 Part 3 para.5A, added: SI 2014/605 Art.26

Sch.1 Part 3 para.6, amended: SI 2014/3305 Art.2

Sch.1 Part 3 para.7, amended: 2014 c.12 Sch.11 para.49, SI 2014/605 Art.26, SI 2014/3305 Art.2

Sch.1 Part 3 para.17, amended: SI 2014/3305 Art.2

Sch.3 para.3, enabling: SI 2014/131

Sch.5 Part 1 para.43, repealed: 2014 c.6 s.18

Sch.5 Part 2, amended: 2014 c.6 s.18

11. Scotland Act 2012

Commencement Orders: SI 2014/3250 Art.2

s.24, repealed (in part): SI 2014/3294 Art.4

s.25, applied: 2014 c.29 s.14

s.26, repealed: 2014 c.26 Sch.38 para.17

s.44, enabling: SI 2014/3241, SI 2014/3250

Sch.2 para.1, repealed (in part): 2014 c.26
Sch.38 para.17
Sch.3 Part 1 para.31, repealed (in part): 2014
c.29 Sch.2 para.16

**13. Supply and Appropriation (Main
Estimates) Act 2012**
referred to: 2014 c.5 s.5
Sch.1, amended: 2014 c.29 s.4
Sch.1, applied: 2014 c.5 s.5
Sch.1, referred to: 2014 c.5 s.5

14. Finance Act 2012
s.102, repealed (in part): 2014 c.26 Sch.1
para.18
s.217, enabling: SI 2014/911
s.221, amended: 2014 c.26 s.295
Sch.7 Part 1 para.24, repealed (in part): 2014
c.14 Sch.7
Sch.8 para.22, repealed (in part): 2014 c.14
Sch.7
Sch.14, referred to: 2014 c.26 s.118
Sch.14 Part 5 para.32A, added: 2014 c.26
s.118
Sch.24 Part 1 para.3, amended: 2014 c.26
Sch.28 para.31
Sch.24 Part 1 para.5, amended: SI 2014/47
Art.3
Sch.24 Part 1 para.5, substituted: 2014 c.26
s.124
Sch.24 Part 1 para.5, enabling: SI 2014/47
Sch.24 Part 1 para.6, amended: 2014 c.26
s.124
Sch.24 Part 1 para.9, substituted: 2014 c.26
s.124
Sch.24 Part 1 para.37, amended: 2014 c.26
Sch.28 para.31
Sch.24 Part 1 para.38, amended: 2014 c.26
Sch.28 para.31
Sch.38 Part 2 para.4, applied: 2014 c.26
Sch.34 para.4

17. Local Government Finance Act 2012
see *SC v East Riding of Yorkshire Council*
[2014] R.A. 279 (VT), Graham Zellick Q.C.
(President)
s.20, enabling: SI 2014/939
Sch.3 Part 2 para.31, repealed: 2014 c.2
Sch.1 Part 2

**18. Mental Health (Approval Functions) Act
2012**
applied: 2014 c.23 s.92

19. Civil Aviation Act 2012
Commencement Orders: SI 2014/262 Art.2,
Art.3
s.60, amended: SI 2014/892 Sch.1 para.197
s.61, amended: SI 2014/892 Sch.1 para.198
s.62, amended: SI 2014/892 Sch.1 para.199
s.63, amended: SI 2014/892 Sch.1 para.200
s.64, amended: SI 2014/892 Sch.1 para.201
s.65, amended: SI 2014/892 Sch.1 para.202
s.110, enabling: SI 2014/262
Sch.6 para.4, amended: SI 2014/892 Sch.1
para.203
Sch.6 para.5, amended: SI 2014/469 Sch.2
para.26

**20. Prisons (Interference with Wireless
Telegraphy) Act 2012**
Commencement Orders: SSI 2014/34 Art.2
s.5, enabling: SSI 2014/34

21. Financial Services Act 2012
Commencement Orders: SI 2014/1447 Art.2;
SI 2014/1847 Art.2; SI 2014/3323 Art.2
applied: 2014 c.21 s.79, s.81
referred to: 2014 c.21 s.79, s.81
Part 6, applied: SI 2014/506 Art.7
s.61, amended: SI 2014/3329 Art.124
s.68, referred to: SI 2014/882 Sch.1
s.69, applied: SI 2014/882 Sch.1
s.85, applied: SI 2014/1195 Art.2
s.85, enabling: SI 2014/1195
s.107, applied: SI 2014/366 Art.20
s.115, enabling: SI 2014/2371
s.118, enabling: SI 2014/366, SI 2014/2371
s.122, enabling: SI 2014/1447, SI
2014/1847, SI 2014/3323
Sch.21 Part 2, applied: SI 2014/208 Art.8

2013

**3. Prevention of Social Housing Fraud Act
2013**
s.7, applied: SI 2014/826 Reg.4
s.7, referred to: SI 2014/899 Reg.4
s.7, enabling: SI 2014/826, SI 2014/899
s.8, enabling: SI 2014/826, SI 2014/899
s.9, applied: SI 2014/826, SI 2014/899
s.9, enabling: SI 2014/899

**5. European Union (Croatian Accession and
Irish Protocol) Act 2013**
s.4, enabling: SI 2014/530

6. Electoral Registration and Administration Act 2013

Commencement Orders: SI 2014/336 Art.2; SI 2014/414 Art.2, Art.3, Art.4, Art.5; SI 2014/2439 Art.2

s.10, applied: SI 2014/3178

s.10, enabling: SI 2014/3178

s.11, applied: SI 2014/449

s.11, enabling: SI 2014/449, SI 2014/3178

s.25, enabling: SI 2014/336, SI 2014/414, SI 2014/2439

s.27, applied: SI 2014/336

s.27, enabling: SI 2014/336, SI 2014/414, SI 2014/2439

Sch.2, applied: SI 2014/3178 Art.2

Sch.4 para.9, repealed (in part): SI 2014/1116 Art.4

Sch.4 para.10, repealed (in part): SI 2014/1116 Art.4

7. HGV Road User Levy Act 2013

Commencement Orders: SI 2014/175 Art.2; SI 2014/797 Art.2

disapplied: SI 2014/800 Art.2

s.3, enabling: SI 2014/800

s.8, enabling: SI 2014/326

s.14A, added: 2014 c.26 s.93

s.21, enabling: SI 2014/175, SI 2014/797

Sch.1 para.2, amended: 2014 c.26 s.82

Sch.1 para.4, amended: 2014 c.26 s.92

Sch.1 para.5, amended: 2014 c.26 s.92

12. Supply and Appropriation (Anticipation and Adjustments) Act 2013

applied: 2014 c.5 s.5, s.7

referred to: 2014 c.5 s.3, Sch.3 para.1

Sch.1, referred to: 2014 c.5 s.3, Sch.1 para.1, Sch.2 para.1

Sch.1 para.1, amended: 2014 c.29 s.4

13. Presumption of Death Act 2013

Commencement Orders: SI 2014/1810 Art.2

s.9, applied: SI 2014/2044

s.22, enabling: SI 2014/1810

Sch.1 para.1, applied: SI 2014/2387 Reg.2, Reg.3

Sch.1 para.1, enabling: SI 2014/2387

Sch.1 para.2, enabling: SI 2014/2387

Sch.1 para.6, enabling: SI 2014/2386

14. Mobile Homes Act 2013

Commencement Orders: SI 2014/816 Art.2, Art.4, Art.5

applied: SI 2014/5 Reg.15

s.8, amended: SI 2014/1900 Sch.1 para.17

s.15, enabling: SI 2014/816

16. Welfare Benefits Up-rating Act 2013

s.1, amended: SI 2014/2888 Reg.7

s.1, enabling: SI 2014/147, SI 2014/384

s.2, enabling: SI 2014/384

18. Justice and Security Act 2013

s.6, see *CF v Security Service* [2013] EWHC 3402 (QB), [2014] 1 W.L.R. 1699 (QBD), Irwin J

s.15, see *R. (on the application of Ignaoua) v Secretary of State for the Home Department* [2013] EWCA Civ 1498, [2014] 1 W.L.R. 651 (CA (Civ Div)), Lord Dyson MR

Sch.3 Pt 2 para.4, see *R. (on the application of Ignaoua) v Secretary of State for the Home Department* [2013] EWCA Civ 1498, [2014] 1 W.L.R. 651 (CA (Civ Div)), Lord Dyson MR

19. Groceries Code Adjudicator Act 2013

s.13, amended: SI 2014/892 Sch.1 para.205

s.14, amended: SI 2014/892 Sch.1 para.206

s.15, amended: SI 2014/892 Sch.1 para.207

s.15, repealed (in part): SI 2014/892 Sch.1 para.207

Sch.1 para.17, amended: SI 2014/892 Sch.1 para.208

22. Crime and Courts Act 2013

Commencement Orders: SI 2014/258 Art.2; SI 2014/830 Art.2; SI 2014/954 Art.2, Art.3; SI 2014/3098 Art.2, Art.3; SI 2014/3268 Art.2

see *Chelmsford County Court v Ramet* [2014] EWHC 56 (Fam), [2014] 2 F.L.R. 1081 (Fam Div), Sir James Munby PFD

Part 1, applied: SI 2014/1704 Art.3, Art.4, Art.7, Art.8

s.32, applied: SI 2014/1610 r.16_1

s.49, referred to: SI 2014/3098

s.51, repealed (in part): 2014 c.22 Sch.9 para.7, Sch.9 para.60

s.52, repealed: 2014 c.22 Sch.9 para.60

s.58, applied: SI 2014/605, SI 2014/1773

s.58, enabling: SI 2014/605, SI 2014/879

s.59, enabling: SI 2014/605, SI 2014/820, SI 2014/879, SI 2014/1773

s.60, enabling: SI 2014/820, SI 2014/954, SI 2014/956

s.61, amended: 2014 c.14 Sch.7

s.61, applied: SI 2014/3098

s.61, repealed (in part): 2014 c.14 Sch.7

s.61, enabling: SI 2014/258, SI 2014/830, SI
2014/954, SI 2014/3098, SI 2014/3268
Sch.5 Part 8 para.27, enabling: SI 2014/1704
Sch.8 Part 1 para.7, enabling: SI 2014/1704
Sch.8 Part 1 para.12, repealed: SI 2014/834
Sch.2 para.76
Sch.9 Part 3 para.52, amended: 2014 c.14
Sch.7
Sch.9 Part 3 para.62, repealed: 2014 c.2
Sch.1 Part 2
Sch.9 Part 3 para.91, repealed: 2014 c.14
Sch.7
Sch.17, applied: SI 2014/1610 r.12_1
Sch.17 Part 1 para.2, applied: SI 2014/1610
r.3_1, r.12_4, r.12_7
Sch.17 Part 1 para.5, applied: SI 2014/1610
r.12_3
Sch.17 Part 1 para.6, applied: SI 2014/1610
r.12_1, r.12_2, r.12_3
Sch.17 Part 1 para.7, applied: SI 2014/1610
r.12_2, r.12_3
Sch.17 Part 1 para.8, applied: SI 2014/1610
r.12_2, r.12_4
Sch.17 Part 1 para.9, applied: SI 2014/1610
r.12_5, r.12_7
Sch.17 Part 1 para.10, applied: SI 2014/1610
r.12_2, r.12_6
Sch.17 Part 1 para.11, applied: SI 2014/1610
r.12_8
Sch.17 Part 1 para.12, applied: SI 2014/1610
r.12_9
Sch.17 Part 1 para.13, applied: SI 2014/1610
r.12_4
Sch.17 Part 2, referred to: SI 2014/1610
r.12_3
Sch.19, referred to: SI 2014/3098

**24. Enterprise and Regulatory Reform Act
2013**
Commencement Orders: SI 2014/253 Art.2,
Art.3, Art.5; SI 2014/416 Art.2, Art.3; SI
2014/824 Art.2; SI 2014/2481 Art.2, Art.4
see *Attorney General for England and Wales
v Counsel General for Wales* [2014] UKSC
43, [2014] 1 W.L.R. 2622 (SC), Lord
Neuberger PSC
applied: SI 2014/891 Art.23, SI 2014/892
Art.3
Part 3, applied: SI 2014/892 Art.3
s.27, applied: SI 2014/416 Sch.1 para.2, SI
2014/549 Art.3, SI 2014/892 Art.3
s.28, applied: SI 2014/458

s.29, applied: SI 2014/892 Sch.2 para.1
s.29, disapplied: SI 2014/549 Sch.2 para.6
s.36, applied: SI 2014/892 Sch.2 para.3
s.78, enabling: SI 2014/434
s.83, applied: SI 2014/2359, SI 2014/2359
Art.4
s.83, enabling: SI 2014/2359
s.84, applied: SI 2014/2359, SI 2014/2359
Art.6
s.84, enabling: SI 2014/2359
s.85, enabling: SI 2014/2359
s.88, applied: SI 2014/2359
s.88, enabling: SI 2014/2359
s.99, applied: SI 2014/892
s.99, enabling: SI 2014/386, SI 2014/549, SI
2014/553, SI 2014/853, SI 2014/892
s.100, enabling: SI 2014/253, SI 2014/416,
SI 2014/2481
s.103, enabling: SI 2014/253, SI 2014/416,
SI 2014/824, SI 2014/2481
Sch.4, applied: 2014 c.21 Sch.11 para.2, SI
2014/891 Art.20
Sch.4 Part 3, applied: SI 2014/549 Art.3, SI
2014/891 Art.20, SI 2014/892 Art.3
Sch.5 Part 3, referred to: SI 2014/549 Art.3
Sch.11, applied: SI 2014/892 Sch.2 para.3

25. Public Service Pensions Act 2013
Commencement Orders: SI 2014/433 Art.2,
Art.3, Art.4, Art.5; SI 2014/839 Art.2, Art.3,
Art.4, Art.5, Art.6, Art.7; SI 2014/1912
Art.2, Art.3
applied: SI 2014/1627 Reg.12, SSI 2014/164
Reg.61
s.1, applied: 2014 c.2 s.20, s.44, Sch.2
para.11, SI 2014/1627 Reg.12, SI 2014/1964
Sch.2 para.2, Sch.2 para.37, SI 2014/2848
Sch.2 para.2
s.1, enabling: SI 2014/512, SI 2014/1146, SI
2014/1964, SI 2014/2328, SI 2014/2336, SI
2014/2652, SI 2014/2848, SSI 2014/164,
SSI 2014/217, SSI 2014/233, SSI 2014/292
s.2, enabling: SI 2014/512, SI 2014/1964, SI
2014/2336, SI 2014/2652, SI 2014/2848
s.3, applied: SI 2014/512, SI 2014/1146, SI
2014/2328, SI 2014/2336, SI 2014/2652, SI
2014/2848, SSI 2014/217, SSI 2014/292
s.3, enabling: SI 2014/512, SI 2014/1146, SI
2014/1964, SI 2014/2336, SI 2014/2652, SI
2014/2848
s.4, applied: SI 2014/1964, SI 2014/2848

s.4, enabling: SI 2014/512, SI 2014/1964, SI 2014/2336, SI 2014/2652, SI 2014/2848
s.5, applied: SI 2014/1964, SSI 2014/217 Reg.12, SSI 2014/292 Reg.12
s.5, enabling: SI 2014/512, SI 2014/2336, SI 2014/2652
s.7, applied: SSI 2014/217 Reg.12, SSI 2014/292 Reg.12
s.7, enabling: SI 2014/512, SI 2014/2336, SI 2014/2652
s.8, applied: SI 2014/1964
s.8, enabling: SI 2014/512, SI 2014/2336, SI 2014/2652, SI 2014/2848
s.9, applied: SI 2014/2848 Reg.165
s.11, applied: SI 2014/1964 Reg.158, SI 2014/2336 Reg.113
s.11, enabling: SI 2014/2336, SI 2014/2652
s.12, applied: SI 2014/1964, SI 2014/1964 Reg.159, SI 2014/2336 Reg.114
s.12, enabling: SI 2014/575, SI 2014/2336, SI 2014/2652
s.13, enabling: SI 2014/2336
s.14, applied: SI 2014/512 Reg.221, SI 2014/1964 Reg.179, SI 2014/2336 Reg.133, SI 2014/2848 Reg.183, SSI 2014/164 Reg.87, SSI 2014/217 Reg.211, SSI 2014/292 Reg.211
s.14, enabling: SI 2014/512, SI 2014/2336
s.16, applied: SI 2014/512 Reg.219, SI 2014/3138 Reg.3
s.16, enabling: SI 2014/3138
s.18, amended: 2014 c.19 s.52
s.18, applied: SI 2014/1964, SI 2014/1964 Sch.2 para.9, Sch.2 para.27, SI 2014/2848 Sch.2 para.9, Sch.2 para.10, Sch.2 para.21
s.18, disapplied: SI 2014/1964 Sch.2 para.10, Sch.2 para.20, SI 2014/2848 Sch.2 para.16, SSI 2014/217 Sch.3 para.7, Sch.3 para.10, SSI 2014/292 Sch.3 para.7, Sch.3 para.10
s.18, referred to: SI 2014/1964 Sch.2 para.14, Sch.2 para.15, Sch.2 para.23, Sch.2 para.24
s.18, enabling: SI 2014/512, SI 2014/2336, SI 2014/2652, SI 2014/2848
s.21, applied: SI 2014/512, SI 2014/1146, SI 2014/2328, SI 2014/2336, SI 2014/2652, SI 2014/2848, SSI 2014/164, SSI 2014/217, SSI 2014/233, SSI 2014/292
s.25, applied: SI 2014/1964, SI 2014/1964 Reg.3

s.25, enabling: SI 2014/2336
s.31, applied: SI 2014/1964 Sch.2 para.14, Sch.2 para.15, Sch.2 para.23, Sch.2 para.24
s.37, enabling: SI 2014/512, SI 2014/2336, SI 2014/2652
s.41, enabling: SI 2014/433, SI 2014/839, SI 2014/1912
Sch.1 para.1, enabling: SI 2014/2336
Sch.1 para.4, enabling: SI 2014/512, SI 2014/2652
Sch.2 para.1, applied: SI 2014/1964
Sch.2 para.1, enabling: SI 2014/2336
Sch.2 para.4, enabling: SI 2014/512, SI 2014/2652, SSI 2014/217, SSI 2014/292
Sch.2 para.6, enabling: SI 2014/2848
Sch.3, applied: SI 2014/1964
Sch.3, enabling: SI 2014/512, SI 2014/2336, SI 2014/2652, SI 2014/2848
Sch.5 para.1, enabling: SI 2014/2336
Sch.5 para.18, enabling: SI 2014/512, SI 2014/2652
Sch.5 para.25, referred to: SI 2014/2336 Reg.71
Sch.6 para.1, enabling: SI 2014/2336
Sch.6 para.6, enabling: SI 2014/512
Sch.7, referred to: SI 2014/1964 Sch.2 para.40, SSI 2014/217 Sch.3 para.21, SSI 2014/292 Sch.3 para.21
Sch.7 para.1, applied: SI 2014/1964
Sch.7 para.1, enabling: SI 2014/512, SI 2014/2336, SI 2014/2652
Sch.7 para.2, applied: SI 2014/1964
Sch.7 para.2, enabling: SI 2014/512, SI 2014/2336, SI 2014/2652
Sch.7 para.3, applied: SI 2014/1964 Sch.2 para.40
Sch.7 para.5, applied: SI 2014/1964
Sch.7 para.5, enabling: SI 2014/512, SI 2014/2652
Sch.10, referred to: SI 2014/1964 Reg.3

26. Defamation Act 2013
s.1, see *Cooke v MGN Ltd* [2014] EWHC 2831 (QB), [2014] E.M.L.R. 31 (QBD), Bean J
s.9, amended: SI 2014/2947 Sch.4 para.7
s.11, see *Yeo v Times Newspapers Ltd* [2014] EWHC 2853 (QB), [2014] 5 Costs L.O. 823 (QBD), Warby J
27. Growth and Infrastructure Act 2013
Commencement Orders: SI 2014/1531 Art.2
s.33, enabling: SI 2014/1532

s.35, enabling: SI 2014/1531

28. Supply and Appropriation (Main Estimates) Act 2013

Sch.1, amended: 2014 c.29 s.4

29. Finance Act 2013

Commencement Orders: SI 2014/1962 Art.2
Part 5, applied: 2014 c.7 s.10
Part 5, disapplied: 2014 c.7 s.11
Part 5, varied: 2014 c.7 s.10
s.6, amended: 2014 c.26 Sch.1 para.19
s.6, repealed (in part): 2014 c.26 Sch.1
para.19
s.7, amended: 2014 c.26 Sch.2 para.6
s.7, referred to: 2014 c.26 Sch.2 para.2
s.10, amended: 2014 c.29 s.4
s.10, referred to: 2014 c.26 Sch.2 para.2
s.23, repealed (in part): 2014 c.26 s.24
s.50, repealed (in part): 2014 c.26 s.41
s.94, amended: 2014 c.26 s.109, s.110
s.97, applied: 2014 c.26 s.231
s.99, amended: 2014 c.26 s.109, s.110
s.101, applied: SI 2014/854 Art.2
s.101, enabling: SI 2014/854
s.159, varied: 2014 c.26 s.109
s.163, varied: 2014 c.26 s.109
s.203, repealed: 2014 c.26 s.119
s.206, varied: 2014 c.7 s.10
s.207, applied: 2014 c.7 s.10
s.207, varied: 2014 c.7 s.10
s.209, applied: 2014 c.7 s.10
s.210, applied: 2014 c.7 s.10
s.217, enabling: SI 2014/585, SI 2014/685
s.219, enabling: SI 2014/3062
s.222, applied: SI 2014/520 Reg.2, Reg.19,
SI 2014/1506 Reg.2, Reg.28
s.222, enabling: SI 2014/520, SI 2014/1506
s.235, applied: SI 2014/520 Reg.2, SI
2014/1506 Reg.2
Sch.1 para.1, amended: 2014 c.26 Sch.2
para.7
Sch.1 para.4, repealed: 2014 c.26 Sch.2
para.7
Sch.1 para.5, amended: 2014 c.26 Sch.2
para.7
Sch.17 Part 2 para.2, enabling: SI 2014/1962
Sch.17 Part 2 para.3, enabling: SI 2014/1962
Sch.22 Part 1 para.1, applied: 2014 c.26
Sch.6 para.1
Sch.22 Part 2 para.8, repealed (in part): 2014
c.26 s.42

Sch.25 Part 2 para.19, repealed: 2014 c.26
Sch.1 para.20
Sch.33 Part 5 para.25, amended: 2014 c.26
s.277
Sch.33 Part 7 para.35, applied: 2014 c.26
s.208
Sch.33 Part 7 para.48, amended: 2014 c.26
s.224
Sch.33 Part 7 para.48, applied: 2014 c.26
s.227
Sch.33 Part 7 para.49, amended: 2014 c.26
s.224
Sch.33 Part 7 para.53, amended: 2014 c.26
s.225
Sch.43, applied: 2014 c.26 Sch.34 para.7
Sch.43 para.10, applied: 2014 c.26 Sch.32
para.3, Sch.34 para.7
Sch.43 para.11, applied: 2014 c.26 s.287,
Sch.32 para.3, Sch.34 para.7
Sch.43 para.12, applied: 2014 c.7 s.10, 2014
c.26 s.287

30. Marriage (Same Sex Couples) Act 2013

Commencement Orders: 2014 c.19 s.23,
2014 c.19 Sch.12 para.77; SI 2014/93 Art.2,
Art.3, Art.4, Art.5; SI 2014/1662 Art.2,
Art.3; SI 2014/3169 Art.2
see *MB v Secretary of State for Work and
Pensions* [2014] EWCA Civ 1112, [2014]
I.C.R. 1129 (CA (Civ Div)), Maurice Kay LJ
s.1, applied: SI 2014/3265 Art.9
s.9, applied: SI 2014/3181 Reg.18, SI
2014/3229 Art.12
s.9, enabling: SI 2014/3181
s.10, applied: SI 2014/93 Art.4
s.11, applied: SI 2014/560 Sch.2 para.4
s.11, disapplied: SI 2014/560 Sch.2 para.1,
Sch.2 para.2, Sch.2 para.3, Sch.2 para.5, SI
2014/3168 Art.3
s.13, enabling: SI 2014/1110, SI 2014/3265
s.17, enabling: SI 2014/107, SI 2014/560, SI
2014/3061, SI 2014/3168
s.18, applied: SI 2014/3061, SI 2014/3168,
SI 2014/3181
s.18, enabling: SI 2014/93, SI 2014/107, SI
2014/560, SI 2014/3168, SI 2014/3181
s.21, enabling: SI 2014/93, SI 2014/1662, SI
2014/3169
Sch.2 Part 1 para.1, enabling: SI 2014/560,
SI 2014/3168
Sch.3 Part 1 para.1, applied: SI 2014/560
Sch.2 para.4

Sch.3 Part 1 para.1, disapplied: SI
2014/3168 Art.3
Sch.4 Part 5 para.11, repealed: 2014 c.19
Sch.12 para.77
Sch.4 Part 5 para.14, applied: SI 2014/76
Sch.4 Part 5 para.16, repealed: 2014 c.19
Sch.12 para.77
Sch.4 Part 7 para.27, enabling: SI 2014/560,
SI 2014/3168
Sch.6 Part 1 para.1, applied: SI 2014/1110
Art.3, SI 2014/3265 Art.3
Sch.6 Part 1 para.1, referred to: SI
2014/1110 Art.2, SI 2014/3265 Art.2
Sch.6 Part 1 para.1, enabling: SI 2014/1110,
SI 2014/3265
Sch.6 Part 1 para.2, applied: SI 2014/1110
Art.13, SI 2014/3265 Art.13
Sch.6 Part 1 para.2, enabling: SI 2014/1110,
SI 2014/3265
Sch.6 Part 2 para.7, enabling: SI 2014/1110,
SI 2014/3265
Sch.6 Part 3 para.8, applied: SI 2014/1108
Art.3, Art.4, Art.6
Sch.6 Part 3 para.8, referred to: SI
2014/1108 Art.7
Sch.6 Part 3 para.8, enabling: SI 2014/1108
Sch.6 Part 3 para.9, enabling: SI 2014/1108
Sch.6 Part 3 para.12, applied: SI 2014/1108
Art.10
Sch.6 Part 4 para.13, applied: SI 2014/1108,
SI 2014/1110, SI 2014/3265
Sch.6 Part 4 para.13, enabling: SI
2014/1110, SI 2014/3265
Sch.6 Part 4 para.14, enabling: SI
2014/1108, SI 2014/1110, SI 2014/3265
Sch.7 Part 2 para.29, repealed (in part): SI
2014/3229 Sch.5 para.21

32. Energy Act 2013
Commencement Orders: SI 2014/251 Art.2,
Art.3, Art.4
applied: SI 2014/469 Art.4, Sch.4 para.6,
Sch.4 para.18, Sch.4 para.26
disapplied: SI 2014/469 Sch.4 para.26
referred to: SI 2014/469 Sch.4 para.13
Part 2, applied: SI 2014/2043 Reg.78
Part 2 c.2, applied: SI 2014/2511 Reg.16
s.5, referred to: SI 2014/2010, SI 2014/2011,
SI 2014/2012, SI 2014/2043, SI 2014/2043
Reg.12, SI 2014/3354
s.6, applied: SI 2014/2010, SI 2014/2011, SI
2014/2012

s.6, enabling: SI 2014/2010, SI 2014/2011,
SI 2014/2012, SI 2014/2013, SI 2014/2014
s.7, applied: SI 2014/1709 Art.2, SI
2014/2014 Reg.2, Sch.1 para.9, Sch.1
para.19, Sch.1 para.22, Sch.1 para.28
s.7, enabling: SI 2014/1709
s.9, enabling: SI 2014/2014
s.10, applied: SI 2014/2011 Reg.57, Reg.58,
Reg.59, Reg.60
s.10, enabling: SI 2014/2010, SI 2014/2011
s.11, applied: SI 2014/2012 Reg.3, Reg.4
s.11, enabling: SI 2014/2012
s.12, enabling: SI 2014/2011, SI 2014/2013
s.13, applied: SI 2014/2013 Reg.15
s.13, enabling: SI 2014/2011
s.14, enabling: SI 2014/2012
s.15, enabling: SI 2014/2012
s.16, enabling: SI 2014/2012, SI 2014/2013
s.17, applied: SI 2014/2014 Reg.2
s.17, enabling: SI 2014/2014
s.18, enabling: SI 2014/2014
s.19, enabling: SI 2014/2011, SI 2014/2012,
SI 2014/2013, SI 2014/2014
s.21, enabling: SI 2014/2014
s.22, enabling: SI 2014/2014
s.24, referred to: SI 2014/2010, SI
2014/2011, SI 2014/2012
s.26, applied: SI 2014/2014 Reg.2
s.27, applied: SI 2014/2043 Reg.3
s.27, enabling: SI 2014/2043, SI 2014/3354
s.28, applied: SI 2014/2043 Reg.3
s.28, enabling: SI 2014/2043, SI 2014/3354
s.29, enabling: SI 2014/2043
s.30, enabling: SI 2014/2043, SI 2014/3354
s.31, enabling: SI 2014/2043, SI 2014/3354
s.32, enabling: SI 2014/2043, SI 2014/3354
s.33, applied: SI 2014/2043 Reg.66
s.33, enabling: SI 2014/2043, SI 2014/3354
s.34, enabling: SI 2014/2043
s.36, enabling: SI 2014/2043, SI 2014/3354
s.38, enabling: SI 2014/2043
s.40, applied: SI 2014/2043, SI 2014/3354
s.40, referred to: SI 2014/2043, SI
2014/3354
s.40, enabling: SI 2014/2043, SI 2014/3354
s.51, applied: SI 2014/2511, SI 2014/2511
Reg.31
s.51, enabling: SI 2014/2511
s.54, applied: SI 2014/2511 Reg.31
s.58, applied: SI 2014/2434 Sch.1 para.38
s.63, enabling: SI 2014/2013, SI 2014/2043

s.68, applied: SI 2014/2418 Sch.1
s.70, applied: SI 2014/526 Reg.2
s.70, enabling: SI 2014/526
s.74, applied: SI 2014/469 Sch.1 para.1,
Sch.1 para.2
s.75, varied: SI 2014/469 Art.7
s.81, applied: SI 2014/1638, SI 2014/1639
s.84, applied: SI 2014/469 Sch.4 para.9
s.85, applied: SI 2014/469 Sch.1 para.7,
Sch.4 para.10
s.85, varied: SI 2014/469 Art.7
s.86, applied: SI 2014/469 Sch.4 para.10
s.90, applied: SI 2014/469 Art.5
s.97, applied: SI 2014/469 Sch.1 para.4,
Sch.1 para.5, Sch.4 para.20
s.97, varied: SI 2014/469 Art.7, Sch.1 para.5
s.98, applied: SI 2014/469 Sch.1 para.4
s.99, applied: SI 2014/469 Sch.1 para.1
s.99, varied: SI 2014/469 Art.7
s.101, applied: SI 2014/469 Sch.1 para.8
s.102, applied: SI 2014/469 Sch.1 para.1
s.102, varied: SI 2014/469 Art.7
s.103, varied: SI 2014/469 Art.7
s.104, applied: SI 2014/469 Sch.1 para.1
s.104, varied: SI 2014/469 Art.7
s.105, applied: SI 2014/469 Sch.1 para.4
s.105, varied: SI 2014/469 Art.7, Sch.1
para.5
s.113, enabling: SI 2014/468, SI 2014/469
s.114, enabling: SI 2014/469
s.116, enabling: SI 2014/469
s.156, enabling: SI 2014/251
Sch.2, applied: SI 2014/2511 Reg.16
Sch.2 Part 4 para.16, applied: SI 2014/2014
Reg.2, SI 2014/2511 Reg.16
Sch.2 Part 4 para.16, enabling: SI 2014/2014
Sch.8, applied: SI 2014/469 Sch.1 para.5
Sch.8 Part 1 para.2, applied: SI 2014/469
Sch.1 para.4
Sch.8 Part 2 para.4, applied: SI 2014/469
Sch.4 para.14, Sch.4 para.15
Sch.8 Part 2 para.6, applied: SI 2014/469
Sch.4 para.16
Sch.8 Part 2 para.6, enabling: SI 2014/468
Sch.8 Part 2 para.7, varied: SI 2014/469
Art.7
Sch.8 Part 3, applied: SI 2014/469 Sch.1
para.4
Sch.8 Part 3 para.15, applied: SI 2014/469
Sch.1 para.4

Sch.8 Part 3 para.17, applied: SI 2014/469
Sch.1 para.4
Sch.8 Part 3 para.17, varied: SI 2014/469
Art.7, Sch.1 para.5
Sch.8 Part 3 para.18, applied: SI 2014/469
Sch.1 para.4
Sch.8 Part 3 para.18, varied: SI 2014/469
Art.7, Sch.1 para.5
Sch.8 Part 3 para.19, applied: SI 2014/469
Sch.1 para.4
Sch.8 Part 3 para.19, varied: SI 2014/469
Art.7, Sch.1 para.5
Sch.9, applied: SI 2014/469 Sch.4 para.21
Sch.9 Part 1 para.1, referred to: SI 2014/469
Sch.4 para.21
Sch.9 Part 2 para.2, applied: SI 2014/469
Sch.1 para.4
Sch.9 Part 2 para.3, applied: SI 2014/469
Sch.1 para.4
Sch.9 Part 2 para.3, varied: SI 2014/469
Sch.1 para.5
Sch.9 Part 2 para.4, applied: SI 2014/469
Sch.1 para.4
Sch.9 Part 2 para.6, varied: SI 2014/469
Art.7
Sch.9 Part 3 para.10, applied: SI 2014/469
Sch.1 para.4
Sch.9 Part 3 para.11, applied: SI 2014/469
Sch.1 para.4
Sch.9 Part 3 para.12, applied: SI 2014/469
Sch.1 para.4
Sch.9 Part 3 para.13, applied: SI 2014/469
Sch.1 para.4
Sch.9 Part 3 para.14, applied: SI 2014/469
Sch.1 para.4
Sch.9 Part 3 para.15, applied: SI 2014/469
Sch.1 para.4
Sch.9 Part 3 para.16, referred to: SI
2014/469 Sch.4 para.21
Sch.10 para.3, disapplied: SI 2014/469 Sch.1
para.4, Sch.1 para.5
Sch.10 para.12, disapplied: SI 2014/469
Sch.1 para.4, Sch.1 para.5
Sch.10 para.13, applied: SI 2014/469 Sch.1
para.4, Sch.4 para.19
Sch.10 para.13, varied: SI 2014/469 Art.7,
Sch.1 para.5
Sch.11, applied: SI 2014/469 Sch.4 para.13,
Sch.4 para.21
Sch.12, applied: SI 2014/469 Sch.4 para.12,
Sch.4 para.22, Sch.4 para.23

Sch.12 Part 5 para.50, repealed (in part): SI
2014/1638 Sch.13 para.8, Sch.14 Part 1

**33. Financial Services (Banking Reform) Act
2013**

Commencement Orders: SI 2014/377 Art.2,
Sch.1 Part 1, 2; SI 2014/772 Art.2; SI
2014/785 Art.2; SI 2014/823 Art.2; SI
2014/1819 Art.2; SI 2014/2458 Art.2, Art.3;
SI 2014/3160 Art.2
applied: SI 2014/1825 Art.3
s.17, amended: SI 2014/3348 Sch.3 para.6
s.17, enabling: SI 2014/3344
s.41, applied: SI 2014/2418 Sch.1
s.92, enabling: SI 2014/882
s.142, enabling: SI 2014/882, SI 2014/3344
s.146, enabling: SI 2014/378
s.148, enabling: SI 2014/377, SI 2014/772,
SI 2014/785, SI 2014/823, SI 2014/1819, SI
2014/2458, SI 2014/3160

2014

1. Mesothelioma Act 2014

Commencement Orders: SI 2014/459 Art.2,
Art.3, Art.4
Royal Assent, January 30, 2014
s.1, enabling: SI 2014/916, SI 2014/917
s.2, applied: SI 2014/916 Reg.4, Reg.5,
Reg.6, Reg.8, Reg.9, Reg.12, Reg.16,
Reg.20, Reg.26, Sch.1 para.2
s.3, see *Yates v Revenue and Customs
Commissioners* [2014] EWHC 2311 (QB),
[2014] P.I.Q.R. P24 (QBD), Master
McCloud
s.3, applied: SI 2014/916 Reg.15, Sch.1
para.6
s.3, referred to: SI 2014/916 Reg.16
s.10, applied: SI 2014/916 Reg.26
s.13, enabling: SI 2014/2904
s.17, applied: SI 2014/916
s.17, enabling: SI 2014/916, SI 2014/2904
s.18, applied: SI 2014/916 Reg.7
s.19, enabling: SI 2014/459
Sch.1 Part 2 para.17, applied: SI 2014/1456

2. Local Audit and Accountability Act 2014

Commencement Orders: SI 2014/900 Art.2;
SI 2014/940 Art.2; SI 2014/1596 Art.2; SI
2014/3319 Art.2
Royal Assent, January 30, 2014
applied: SI 2014/1628 Reg.3

s.10, applied: SI 2014/3224 Reg.7
s.10, enabling: SI 2014/3224
s.12, applied: SI 2014/1710 Reg.9
s.14, enabling: SI 2014/1628
s.16, enabling: SI 2014/1710
s.40, enabling: SI 2014/2095
s.43, applied: SI 2014/2845
s.43, disapplied: SI 2014/2095
s.43, enabling: SI 2014/1710, SI 2014/2095
s.46, enabling: SI 2014/231, SI 2014/2845
s.49, enabling: SI 2014/900, SI 2014/940, SI
2014/1596, SI 2014/3319
Sch.4 para.1, applied: SI 2014/3224 Reg.10
Sch.4 para.2, amended: SI 2014/2845 Reg.2
Sch.4 para.2, enabling: SI 2014/2845
Sch.4 para.4, enabling: SI 2014/3224
Sch.4 para.5, enabling: SI 2014/3224
Sch.4 para.8, substituted: SI 2014/2845
Reg.2
Sch.5, applied: SI 2014/1627 Reg.2, Reg.12,
SI 2014/2009 Art.1
Sch.5 para.9, applied: SI 2014/1627
Sch.5 para.28, applied: SI 2014/1627, SI
2014/2418 Sch.1
Sch.7 para.5, varied: SI 2014/1629 Reg.2
Sch.7 para.5, enabling: SI 2014/1629

3. European Union (Approvals) Act 2014

Royal Assent, January 30, 2014

**4. Transparency of Lobbying, Non-Party
Campaigning and Trade Union Administration
Act 2014**

Commencement Orders: SI 2014/1236 Art.2
Royal Assent, January 30, 2014
s.45, enabling: SI 2014/1236
Sch.1 Part 1 para.1, amended: 2014 c.29 s.4

**5. Supply and Appropriation (Anticipation and
Adjustments) Act 2014**

Royal Assent, March 13, 2014
s.1, applied: 2014 c.25 s.3
s.4, applied: SI 2014/3229 Sch.2 para.3
s.10, applied: SI 2014/3229 Art.12, Art.14
s.11, applied: SI 2014/3229 Art.14
Sch.1 Part 2 para.1, amended: 2014 c.29 s.4

6. Children and Families Act 2014

Commencement Orders: SI 2014/793 Art.2;
SI 2014/889 Art.4A, Art.3, Art.4, Art.5,
Art.6, Art.7; SI 2014/1640 Art.3, Art.4,
Art.5, Art.6, Art.7, Art.15; SI 2014/2270
Art.27, Art.28, Art.29; SI 2014/2609 Art.2;
SI 2014/2749 Art.3, Art.4
Royal Assent, March 13, 2014

see *S (Parenting Assessment), Re* [2014] 2
F.L.R. 575 (CC (Bournemouth)), Sir James
Munby PFD
applied: SI 2014/1530 Reg.17, SI 2014/1640
Art.9, SI 2014/2270 Art.20
Part 3, applied: SI 2014/2270 Art.5, Art.6,
Art.7, Art.21, Art.22, Art.27
Part 3, referred to: SI 2014/1530 Reg.63
Part 3, varied: SI 2014/2270 Art.23
s.9, disapplied: SI 2014/1042 Art.4
s.10, enabling: SI 2014/843
s.13, see *S (Parenting Assessment), Re*
[2014] 2 F.L.R. 575 (CC (Bournemouth)),
Sir James Munby PFD
s.13, referred to: SI 2014/603 Sch.1
s.14, see *S (Parenting Assessment), Re*
[2014] 2 F.L.R. 575 (CC (Bournemouth)),
Sir James Munby PFD
s.17, applied: SI 2014/1042 Art.11
s.19, applied: SI 2014/1530 Sch.3 Part 1
s.20, applied: SI 2014/2147 Reg.8, SI
2014/2319 Reg.3
s.22, applied: SI 2014/3352 Sch.1 para.2
s.24, applied: SI 2014/1530 Reg.3, Reg.4,
Reg.5, Reg.10, Reg.13
s.27, applied: SI 2014/1530 Sch.3 Part 1
s.30, applied: SI 2014/1530 Sch.2 para.16,
Sch.3 Part 1
s.30, enabling: SI 2014/1530
s.31, applied: SI 2014/1530 Reg.8
s.31, varied: SI 2014/2270 Art.20
s.32, applied: SI 2014/1530 Sch.1 para.11,
Sch.2 para.15, Sch.3 Part 1, SI 2014/3352
Sch.1 para.5
s.33, applied: SI 2014/1530 Reg.22, Reg.27,
Sch.3 Part 2
s.34, applied: SI 2014/1530 Sch.3 Part 2
s.34, enabling: SI 2014/1530
s.36, applied: SI 2014/1530 Reg.3, Reg.4,
Reg.5, Reg.10, Reg.13, Reg.48, Sch.3 Part 2,
SI 2014/2270 Art.3, Art.5, Art.7, Art.8,
Art.27, Art.28, SI 2014/3352 Sch.1 para.2
s.36, disapplied: SI 2014/2270 Art.3
s.36, enabling: SI 2014/1530
s.37, enabling: SI 2014/1530
s.38, applied: SI 2014/1530 Reg.22, Reg.27,
SI 2014/1652 Reg.4
s.39, applied: SI 2014/1530 Reg.14, Reg.22,
Reg.27, Sch.3 Part 2
s.40, applied: SI 2014/1530 Reg.14, Reg.27,
Sch.3 Part 2

s.41, applied: SI 2014/1530 Reg.20, Reg.58,
Sch.2 para.1, Sch.2 para.3, Sch.2 para.20
s.41, enabling: SI 2014/1530
s.42, applied: SI 2014/1530 Sch.3 Part 2
s.44, applied: SI 2014/1530 Reg.15, Reg.24,
Reg.43, Sch.3 Part 2, SI 2014/1652 Reg.4,
Reg.11, SI 2014/2270 Art.23, SI 2014/3352
Sch.1 para.2
s.44, varied: SI 2014/2270 Art.21
s.44, enabling: SI 2014/1530, SI 2014/2096
s.45, enabling: SI 2014/1530
s.46, applied: SI 2014/1530 Reg.46
s.46, enabling: SI 2014/1530
s.47, enabling: SI 2014/1530
s.49, applied: SI 2014/1530 Sch.3 Part 2
s.49, enabling: SI 2014/1652, SI 2014/2096
s.51, applied: SI 2014/1530 Reg.14, Reg.20,
Reg.21, Reg.22, Reg.25, Reg.43, Sch.3 Part
2, SI 2014/2270 Art.8, Art.22, Art.25
s.51, enabling: SI 2014/1530
s.52, applied: SI 2014/1530 Sch.3 Part 2
s.53, applied: SI 2014/1530 Reg.32, Sch.2
para.22, Sch.3 Part 2
s.54, applied: SI 2014/1530 Sch.3 Part 2
s.55, applied: SI 2014/1530 Reg.32, Reg.34,
Reg.39, Sch.3 Part 2
s.56, applied: SI 2014/1530 Sch.3 Part 2
s.56, enabling: SI 2014/1530
s.57, applied: SI 2014/1530 Sch.2 para.23,
Sch.3 Part 2
s.61, applied: SI 2014/1530 Sch.3 Part 2
s.62, applied: SI 2014/3352 Sch.2 para.22
s.63, applied: SI 2014/3352 Sch.2 para.22
s.67, applied: SI 2014/1530 Reg.49, Reg.50
s.67, enabling: SI 2014/1530
s.68, applied: SI 2014/1530 Sch.3 Part 2
s.69, applied: SI 2014/1530 Reg.51, Sch.2
para.6
s.69, enabling: SI 2014/1530
s.70, applied: SI 2014/1530 Sch.3 Part 2
s.78, enabling: SI 2014/2254
s.80, applied: SI 2014/1652 Reg.16
s.80, enabling: SI 2014/1530
s.81, applied: SI 2014/2270 Art.4, Art.8,
Art.9, Art.10, Art.11
s.119, applied: SI 2014/2857, SI 2014/2866,
SI 2014/2934, SI 2014/3051, SI 2014/3093,
SI 2014/3097, SI 2014/3134
s.120, applied: SI 2014/3053, SI 2014/3054
s.122, applied: SI 2014/2866
s.123, applied: SI 2014/2862

s.123, disapplied: SI 2014/1640 Art.9
s.124, applied: SI 2014/1640 Art.13
s.125, applied: SI 2014/1640 Art.17, Art.19
s.125, disapplied: SI 2014/1640 Art.14
s.126, applied: SI 2014/1640 Art.8
s.126, disapplied: SI 2014/1640 Art.15
s.130, applied: SI 2014/1640 Art.11
s.131, disapplied: SI 2014/1640 Art.10
s.135, applied: SI 2014/1652
s.135, enabling: SI 2014/3255
s.136, enabling: SI 2014/852, SI 2014/2103, SI 2014/3255
s.137, enabling: SI 2014/1042, SI 2014/1640, SI 2014/2270, SI 2014/2749
s.139, enabling: SI 2014/793, SI 2014/889, SI 2014/1134, SI 2014/1640, SI 2014/2609, SI 2014/2749
Sch.3, applied: SI 2014/2270 Art.4, Art.8, Art.9, Art.10, Art.11, Art.27, Art.30
Sch.7, applied: SI 2014/1640 Art.8, Art.19
Sch.7, disapplied: SI 2014/1640 Art.16
Sch.7 para.5, applied: SI 2014/1640 Art.8, Art.17
Sch.7 para.5, disapplied: SI 2014/1640 Art.18
Sch.7 para.40, disapplied: SI 2014/1640 Art.12
Sch.7 para.48, applied: SI 2014/1640 Art.8
Sch.7 para.51, disapplied: SI 2014/1640 Art.9
Sch.7 para.53, disapplied: SI 2014/1640 Art.12
Sch.7 para.56, applied: SI 2014/1640 Art.19
Sch.7 para.57, applied: SI 2014/1640 Art.19
Sch.7 para.58, applied: SI 2014/1640 Art.19
Sch.7 para.59, applied: SI 2014/1640 Art.8
Sch.7 para.59, disapplied: SI 2014/1640 Art.18
Sch.7 para.60, applied: SI 2014/1640 Art.8, Art.19
Sch.7 para.60, disapplied: SI 2014/1640 Art.18
Sch.7 para.64, applied: SI 2014/1640 Art.19
Sch.7 para.68, applied: SI 2014/1640 Art.8
Sch.7 para.73, disapplied: SI 2014/1640 Art.9

7. National Insurance Contributions Act 2014
Royal Assent, March 13, 2014

8. Citizenship (Armed Forces) Act 2014
Royal Assent, March 13, 2014

9. International Development (Gender Equality) Act 2014
Royal Assent, March 13, 2014

10. Leasehold Reform (Amendment) Act 2014
Royal Assent, March 13, 2014

11. Offender Rehabilitation Act 2014
Commencement Orders: SI 2014/1287 Art.2
Royal Assent, March 13, 2014
s.22, enabling: SI 2014/1287

12. Anti-social Behaviour, Crime and Policing Act 2014
Commencement Orders: SI 2014/630 Art.2, Art.3; SI 2014/949 Art.2, Art.3, Art.4, Art.5, Art.6, Art.7, Art.8, Art.9, Art.10, Sch.1 para.2, para.3, para.4, para.5, para.6, para.7, para.8, para.9, para.10, para.11, para.12, para.13, para.14, para.15, para.16, para.17, para.18, para.19, para.20, para.21, para.22, para.23; SI 2014/1226 Art.2; SI 2014/1241 Art.2; SI 2014/1916 Art.2, Art.3, Art.4; SI 2014/2125 Art.2, Art.3, Art.4; SI 2014/2454 Art.2, Art.3, Art.4; SI 2014/2590 Art.5A, Art.2, Art.3; SI 2014/2754 Art.3, Art.5; SI 2014/2830 Art.2, Art.2
Royal Assent, March 13, 2014
s.22, applied: SI 2014/1610 r.50_1
s.31, applied: SI 2014/1610 r.50_3
s.59, enabling: SI 2014/2591
s.60, enabling: SI 2014/2591
s.61, enabling: SI 2014/2591
s.94, referred to: SI 2014/2830 Art.3
s.99, applied: SI 2014/949 Art.7
s.102, amended: SI 2014/2590 Art.5A
s.104, amended: SI 2014/949 Art.8
s.106, referred to: SI 2014/949 Art.9
s.120, disapplied: SI 2014/949 Art.10
s.181, enabling: SI 2014/2522
s.182, applied: SI 2014/2522
s.185, enabling: SI 2014/630, SI 2014/949, SI 2014/1226, SI 2014/1241, SI 2014/1916, SI 2014/2125, SI 2014/2454, SI 2014/2590, SI 2014/2754, SI 2014/2830, SSI 2014/221

13. Northern Ireland (Miscellaneous Provisions) Act 2014
Commencement Orders: SI 2014/2613 Art.2
Royal Assent, March 13, 2014
s.28, enabling: SI 2014/2613

14. Co-operative and Community Benefit Societies Act 2014
Royal Assent, May 14, 2014

applied: SI 2014/229 Sch.1 para.1, SI
2014/2418 Sch.1, SSI 2014/296 Reg.4
referred to: SI 2014/229 Sch.1 para.3
s.30, applied: SI 2014/229 Sch.1 para.1
s.111, varied: SI 2014/229 Art.13
s.113, varied: SI 2014/229 Art.14
s.118, enabling: SI 2014/1822
s.126, varied: SI 2014/229 Art.15
Sch.4 Part 2 para.47, amended: 2014 c.26
Sch.39 para.3
Sch.4 Part 2 para.48, amended: 2014 c.26
Sch.39 para.4
Sch.4 Part 2 para.49, amended: 2014 c.26
Sch.39 para.5
Sch.4 Part 2 para.50, amended: 2014 c.26
Sch.39 para.6
Sch.4 Part 2 para.53, amended: 2014 c.26
Sch.39 para.7
Sch.4 Part 2 para.82, amended: 2014 c.26
Sch.39 para.8
Sch.4 Part 2 para.94, amended: 2014 c.26
Sch.39 para.9
Sch.4 Part 2 para.105, amended: 2014 c.26
Sch.39 para.10
Sch.4 Part 2 para.110, amended: 2014 c.26
Sch.39 para.11
Sch.4 Part 2 para.158, amended: 2014 c.26
Sch.39 para.12
Sch.4 Part 2 para.168, amended: 2014 c.26
Sch.39 para.13
Sch.4 Part 2 para.171, amended: 2014 c.26
Sch.39 para.14

15. Deep Sea Mining Act 2014
Royal Assent, May 14, 2014

16. Inheritance and Trustees Powers Act 2014
Royal Assent, May 14, 2014
s.12, enabling: SI 2014/2039

17. Gambling (Licensing and Advertising) Act 2014
Commencement Orders: SI 2014/2444 Art.2;
SI 2014/2646 Art.2
Royal Assent, May 14, 2014
s.1, enabling: SI 2014/1641, SI 2014/1675,
SI 2014/2665
s.6, enabling: SI 2014/2444, SI 2014/2646

18. Intellectual Property Act 2014
Commencement Orders: SI 2014/1715 Art.3;
SI 2014/2069 Art.2; SI 2014/2330 Art.3,
Art.4, Art.5, Art.6, Art.7, Art.8, Sch.1
Royal Assent, May 14, 2014
s.13, amended: SI 2014/2329 Reg.3

s.23, enabling: SI 2014/2330
s.24, enabling: SI 2014/1715, SI 2014/2069,
SI 2014/2330

19. Pensions Act 2014
Commencement Orders: SI 2014/2377 Art.2;
SI 2014/2727 Art.2
Royal Assent, May 14, 2014
s.45, enabling: SI 2014/2939
s.53, enabling: SI 2014/3213
s.54, applied: SI 2014/3213
s.54, enabling: SI 2014/2939
s.56, enabling: SI 2014/1965, SI 2014/2377,
SI 2014/2727

20. Defence Reform Act 2014
Commencement Orders: SI 2014/1751 Art.3,
Art.4; SI 2014/2370 Art.3, Art.4; SI
2014/3162 Art.3
Royal Assent, May 14, 2014
applied: SI 2014/3337 Reg.5
Part 2, applied: SI 2014/3337 Reg.54,
Reg.63
s.14, applied: SI 2014/3337 Reg.5, Reg.6,
Reg.7, Reg.20
s.14, referred to: SI 2014/3337 Reg.5
s.14, enabling: SI 2014/3337
s.15, enabling: SI 2014/3337
s.16, applied: SI 2014/3337 Reg.15
s.16, varied: SI 2014/3337 Reg.64
s.16, enabling: SI 2014/3337
s.17, varied: SI 2014/3337 Reg.64
s.17, enabling: SI 2014/3337
s.18, applied: SI 2014/3337 Reg.23
s.18, varied: SI 2014/3337 Reg.64
s.18, enabling: SI 2014/3337
s.19, applied: SI 2014/3337 Reg.11
s.20, applied: SI 2014/3337 Reg.16, Reg.19,
Reg.23
s.20, referred to: SI 2014/3337 Reg.10
s.21, applied: SI 2014/3337 Reg.16
s.21, disapplied: SI 2014/3337 Reg.64
s.21, enabling: SI 2014/3337
s.23, applied: SI 2014/3337 Reg.21
s.23, enabling: SI 2014/3337
s.24, enabling: SI 2014/3337
s.25, applied: SI 2014/3337 Reg.31
s.25, enabling: SI 2014/3337
s.26, applied: SI 2014/3337 Reg.56
s.26, referred to: SI 2014/3337 Reg.46
s.27, enabling: SI 2014/3337
s.28, applied: SI 2014/3337 Reg.58, Reg.59,
Reg.60

s.28, referred to: SI 2014/3337 Reg.58
s.28, enabling: SI 2014/3337
s.29, applied: SI 2014/3337 Reg.58
s.29, enabling: SI 2014/3337
s.30, enabling: SI 2014/3337
s.31, applied: SI 2014/3337 Reg.48, Reg.49, Reg.50
s.31, enabling: SI 2014/3337
s.32, applied: SI 2014/3337 Reg.49
s.32, enabling: SI 2014/3337
s.33, applied: SI 2014/3337 Reg.50
s.33, enabling: SI 2014/3337
s.35, applied: SI 2014/3337 Reg.51, Reg.52, Reg.53, Reg.55
s.35, varied: SI 2014/3337 Reg.64
s.35, enabling: SI 2014/3337
s.36, applied: SI 2014/3337 Reg.56
s.37, applied: SI 2014/3337 Reg.56
s.38, enabling: SI 2014/3337
s.41, enabling: SI 2014/3337
s.42, enabling: SI 2014/3337
s.43, varied: SI 2014/3337 Reg.64
s.43, enabling: SI 2014/3337
s.50, enabling: SI 2014/1751, SI 2014/2370, SI 2014/3162
Sch.5 para.1, applied: SI 2014/3337 Reg.56
Sch.5 para.1, enabling: SI 2014/3337

21. Water Act 2014
Commencement Orders: SI 2014/1823 Art.2, Art.3; SI 2014/3320 Art.2, Art.4
Royal Assent, May 14, 2014
s.1, referred to: SI 2014/3320 Art.3
s.23, referred to: SI 2014/3320 Art.3
s.38, applied: SI 2014/3320 Art.3
s.38, referred to: SI 2014/3320 Art.3
s.91, enabling: SI 2014/3320
s.94, enabling: SI 2014/1823, SI 2014/3320
Sch.2 para.5, referred to: SI 2014/3320 Art.3
Sch.12, enabling: SI 2014/3320

22. Immigration Act 2014
Commencement Orders: SI 2014/1820 Art.2, Art.3, Art.5, Art.6; SI 2014/1943 Art.2; SI 2014/2771 Art.2, Art.3, Art.4, Art.5, Art.6, Art.7, Art.8, Art.9, Art.10, Art.11, Art.13
Royal Assent, May 14, 2014
applied: SI 2014/2604 Sch.1 para.2
Part 3 c.1, applied: SI 2014/2873 Art.3, Art.4, Art.5, SI 2014/2874
s.7, applied: SI 2014/2604 r.39
s.15, applied: SI 2014/2768 Reg.3
s.21, applied: SI 2014/2874 Art.4

s.23, applied: SI 2014/2874 Art.10
s.24, applied: SI 2014/2874 Art.3, Art.8, Art.9
s.24, varied: SI 2014/2873 Sch.1 para.1, Sch.1 para.3
s.24, enabling: SI 2014/2874
s.25, applied: SI 2014/2874 Art.10
s.26, applied: SI 2014/2874 Art.3, Art.8, Art.9
s.26, varied: SI 2014/2873 Sch.1 para.2, Sch.1 para.4
s.26, enabling: SI 2014/2874
s.29, applied: SI 2014/2874 Art.11, Art.12
s.29, enabling: SI 2014/2874
s.32, applied: SI 2014/2874, SI 2014/2874 Art.13
s.32, enabling: SI 2014/2874
s.33, applied: SI 2014/2874, SI 2014/2874 Art.14
s.33, enabling: SI 2014/2874
s.34, enabling: SI 2014/2874
s.35, applied: SI 2014/2771 Art.12
s.35, enabling: SI 2014/2771
s.37, enabling: SI 2014/2873, SI 2014/2874
s.40, amended: SI 2014/3074 Art.2
s.40, applied: SI 2014/1798 Art.2, SI 2014/3085 Reg.11
s.40, disapplied: SI 2014/3086 Art.2
s.40, enabling: SI 2014/1798, SI 2014/3086
s.41, enabling: SI 2014/3085
s.43, applied: SI 2014/3085 Reg.11
s.43, enabling: SI 2014/3074
s.68, applied: SI 2014/1820 Art.7
s.70, varied: SI 2014/1820 Art.7
s.73, enabling: SI 2014/1820, SI 2014/2038, SI 2014/2771, SI 2014/2928
s.74, applied: SI 2014/3074, SI 2014/3085, SI 2014/3086
s.75, enabling: SI 2014/1820, SI 2014/1943, SI 2014/2771
Sch.3 para.6, amended: 2014 c.29 s.4
Sch.9 Part 4 para.26, applied: SI 2014/2928 Art.3
Sch.9 Part 11, referred to: SI 2014/2771 Art.13

23. Care Act 2014
Commencement Orders: SI 2014/1714 Art.2, Art.3, Art.4; SI 2014/2473 Art.2, Art.3, Art.4, Art.5, Art.6, Art.7; SI 2014/3186 Art.2
Royal Assent, May 14, 2014

applied: SI 2014/2672 Reg.16, Reg.17, Sch.1 para.33, Sch.2 para.4
Part 1, applied: SI 2014/2821 Reg.3, SI 2014/2824 Reg.5, Reg.7, SI 2014/2829 Reg.1, Reg.2, SI 2014/2889 Reg.5, Reg.7
s.1, applied: SI 2014/2824 Reg.5, SI 2014/2889 Reg.5
s.2, applied: SI 2014/2673 Reg.3, Reg.5
s.2, enabling: SI 2014/2673
s.4, applied: SI 2014/1530 Sch.2 para.13
s.9, applied: SI 2014/2821 Reg.3
s.12, enabling: SI 2014/2827
s.14, applied: SI 2014/2671 Reg.2, Reg.5, Reg.6, Reg.11, SI 2014/2672 Reg.3, Reg.4, Reg.5, Reg.6, Reg.7, SI 2014/2840 Reg.2
s.14, enabling: SI 2014/2672
s.17, applied: SI 2014/2671 Reg.2, SI 2014/2672 Reg.9, Reg.11
s.17, varied: SI 2014/2473 Art.7
s.17, enabling: SI 2014/2672
s.18, applied: SI 2014/2670 Reg.2, SI 2014/2671 Reg.2, Reg.3, SI 2014/2672 Reg.2, Reg.3, Reg.4, Reg.5, Reg.8, SI 2014/2823 Reg.7, Reg.9
s.19, applied: SI 2014/2671 Reg.2, Reg.3
s.20, applied: SI 2014/2672 Reg.5
s.22, applied: SI 2014/2821 Reg.2
s.22, enabling: SI 2014/2821
s.26, enabling: SI 2014/2840
s.30, applied: SI 2014/2670 Reg.5, SI 2014/2671 Reg.5, Reg.6, Reg.11
s.30, enabling: SI 2014/2670
s.31, applied: SI 2014/2672 Sch.1 para.5, SI 2014/2871 Reg.7
s.32, applied: SI 2014/2871 Reg.3, Reg.4, Reg.5, Reg.7
s.32, disapplied: SI 2014/2871 Reg.9
s.33, applied: SI 2014/2871 Reg.7, Reg.8
s.33, enabling: SI 2014/2871
s.34, enabling: SI 2014/2671
s.35, enabling: SI 2014/2671
s.37, applied: SI 2014/2825 Reg.2, SI 2014/2829 Reg.1
s.38, applied: SI 2014/2825 Reg.2
s.38, enabling: SI 2014/2825
s.39, applied: SI 2014/2828 Reg.2
s.39, enabling: SI 2014/2828, SI 2014/2839, SI 2014/2843
s.40, applied: SI 2014/2829 Reg.7
s.40, enabling: SI 2014/2829

s.48, applied: SI 2014/2829 Reg.1, Reg.5, Reg.6, SI 2014/2843 Reg.1, Reg.5
s.49, applied: SI 2014/2843 Reg.7
s.50, applied: SI 2014/2843 Reg.5, Reg.7
s.51, applied: SI 2014/2843 Reg.5, Reg.7
s.55, applied: SI 2014/2822 Reg.4
s.55, enabling: SI 2014/2822
s.65, enabling: SI 2014/2827
s.67, applied: SI 2014/2824 Reg.2, Reg.4, Reg.6, Reg.7, SI 2014/2889 Reg.2, Reg.4, Reg.6, Reg.7
s.67, disapplied: SI 2014/2824 Reg.4, SI 2014/2889 Reg.4
s.67, referred to: SI 2014/2824 Reg.3, Reg.4, SI 2014/2889 Reg.3
s.67, enabling: SI 2014/2824, SI 2014/2889
s.75, enabling: SI 2014/2871
s.77, applied: SI 2014/2854 Reg.2
s.77, enabling: SI 2014/2854
s.88, enabling: SI 2014/2825
s.96, enabling: SI 2014/3218
s.104, enabling: SI 2014/3215
s.105, enabling: SI 2014/3215
s.109, disapplied: SI 2014/3090 Art.4
s.109, enabling: SI 2014/3090
s.118, enabling: SI 2014/3090, SI 2014/3218
s.124, enabling: SI 2014/2473
s.125, enabling: SI 2014/2670, SI 2014/2671, SI 2014/2672, SI 2014/2673, SI 2014/2821, SI 2014/2822, SI 2014/2823, SI 2014/2824, SI 2014/2827, SI 2014/2828, SI 2014/2829, SI 2014/2839, SI 2014/2840, SI 2014/2843, SI 2014/2871, SI 2014/2889, SI 2014/3090, SI 2014/3215, SI 2014/3218
s.127, disapplied: SI 2014/2473
s.127, enabling: SI 2014/1714, SI 2014/2473, SI 2014/3186
Sch.1 para.1, enabling: SI 2014/2839
Sch.1 para.2, enabling: SI 2014/2839
Sch.1 para.4, enabling: SI 2014/2839
Sch.1 para.5, enabling: SI 2014/2843
Sch.1 para.11, applied: SI 2014/2839, SI 2014/2843
Sch.3 para.1, applied: SI 2014/2823 Reg.2, Reg.3
Sch.3 para.2, applied: SI 2014/2823 Reg.2, Reg.6, Reg.8
Sch.3 para.2, enabling: SI 2014/2823
Sch.3 para.3, referred to: SI 2014/2823 Reg.4

Sch.3 para.4, applied: SI 2014/2823 Reg.9,
Reg.10, Reg.12
Sch.3 para.4, enabling: SI 2014/2823
Sch.3 para.6, enabling: SI 2014/2823
Sch.3 para.8, enabling: SI 2014/2823
Sch.5 Part 1 para.2, enabling: SI 2014/3215
Sch.6 para.2, enabling: SI 2014/3215
24. House of Lords Reform Act 2014
Royal Assent, May 14, 2014
25. Supply and Appropriation (Main Estimates) Act 2014
Royal Assent, July 17, 2014
Sch.1, amended: 2014 c.29 s.4
26. Finance Act 2014
Commencement Orders: SI 2014/2228 Art.2
Royal Assent, July 17, 2014
Part 3, applied: SI 2014/2257 Reg.7
s.12, enabling: SI 2014/3226
s.32, enabling: SI 2014/2880
s.114, enabling: SI 2014/1932
s.126, applied: SI 2014/2912 Reg.5
s.141, applied: SI 2014/2912 Reg.3
s.142, applied: SI 2014/2912 Reg.4
s.151, applied: SI 2014/2912 Reg.4
s.162, applied: SI 2014/2912 Reg.4
s.163, enabling: SI 2014/2257
s.164, applied: SI 2014/2257 Reg.3, Reg.4,
Reg.5, Reg.6, SI 2014/2912 Reg.2, Reg.3
s.164, enabling: SI 2014/2257, SI 2014/2912
s.165, applied: SI 2014/2912 Reg.3
s.166, enabling: SI 2014/2912
s.167, enabling: SI 2014/2912
s.168, enabling: SI 2014/2257, SI 2014/2912
s.169, enabling: SI 2014/2912
s.171, applied: SI 2014/2257 Reg.3
s.189, enabling: SI 2014/2257, SI 2014/2912
s.194, enabling: SI 2014/2257, SI 2014/2912
Sch.4 Part 3 para.16, enabling: SI 2014/2228
Sch.6 Part 1 para.1, applied: SI 2014/1842
Reg.5, Reg.11
Sch.6 Part 2 para.8, enabling: SI 2014/1842
Sch.6 Part 2 para.9, enabling: SI 2014/1842
Sch.37 Part 4 para.22, enabling: SI
2014/2461
27. Data Retention and Investigatory Powers Act 2014
Royal Assent, July 17, 2014
s.1, applied: SI 2014/2042 Reg.8, Reg.9,
Reg.13, Reg.14, Reg.15
s.1, enabling: SI 2014/2042

s.2, applied: SI 2014/2042, SI 2014/2042
Reg.14
s.2, enabling: SI 2014/2042
28. Childcare Payments Act 2014
Royal Assent, December 17, 2014
29. Wales Act 2014
Royal Assent, December 17, 2014
30. Taxation of Pensions Act 2014
Royal Assent, December 17, 2014

CURRENT LAW

STATUTORY INSTRUMENT CITATOR 2014

The Statutory Instrument Citator covers the period 2014 and is up to date to February 13, 2015 (Orders and Acts received).It comprises in a single table:

(i) Statutory Instruments made between January 1, 2014 and February 13, 2015;
(ii) Amendments, modifications and repeals made to existing Statutory Instruments during this period;
(iii) Statutory Instruments judicially considered during this period;
(iv) Statutory Instruments made under the powers of any Statutory Instrument issued during this period.

The material is arranged in numerical order under the relevant year.

Definitions of legislative effects:

"added" : new provisions are inserted by subsequent legislation

"amended" : text of legislation is modified by subsequent legislation

"applied" : brought to bear, or exercised by subsequent legislation

"consolidated" : used where previous legislation in the same subject area is brought together in subsequent legislation, with or without amendments

"disapplied" : an exception made to the application of an earlier enactment

"enabling" : giving power for the relevant SI to be made

"referred to" : direction from other legislation without specific effect or application

"repealed" : rescinded by subsequent legislation

"restored" : reinstated by subsequent legislation (where previously repealed/ revoked)

"substituted" : text of provision is completely replaced by subsequent legislation

"varied" : provisions modified in relation to their application to specified areas or circumstances, however the text itself remains unchanged

STATUTORY INSTRUMENT CITATOR 2014

340

STATUTORY INSTRUMENTS ISSUED BY THE SCOTTISH PARLIAMENT

2000

54. National Health Service (Clinical Negligence and Other Risks Indemnity Scheme) (Scotland) Regulations 2000
disapplied: SSI 2014/344 Sch.1, Sch.2
59. Disabled Persons (Badges for Motor Vehicles) (Scotland) Regulations 2000
Reg.4, amended: SSI 2014/145 Reg.3
Reg.6, amended: SSI 2014/145 Reg.4
95. Environmental Protection (Disposal of Polychlorinated Biphenyls and other Dangerous Substances) (Scotland) Regulations 2000
Reg.13, applied: SSI 2014/319 Sch.1 para.6, Sch.2 para.9, Sch.3 para.6
96. Designation of Nitrate Vulnerable Zones (Scotland) Regulations 2000
Reg.2, amended: SSI 2014/373 Reg.5
Reg.3, revoked: SSI 2014/373 Reg.5
169. Sulphur Content of Liquid Fuels (Scotland) Regulations 2000
Sch.1, applied: SSI 2014/258 Reg.8
309. Food Irradiation Provisions (Scotland) Regulations 2000
revoked: SSI 2014/312 Sch.4 Part 1

2001

38. Coffee Extracts and Chicory Extracts (Scotland) Regulations 2001
Reg.2, amended: SSI 2014/312 Sch.5 para.6
Reg.5, amended: SSI 2014/312 Sch.5 para.6
Reg.6, revoked: SSI 2014/312 Sch.5 para.6
Reg.11, revoked (in part): SSI 2014/312 Sch.4 Part 1
151. Western Isles Salmon Fishery District Designation Order 2001
Art.2, applied: SSI 2014/327 Sch.1
Art.4, applied: SSI 2014/327 Sch.1
Sch.1, applied: SSI 2014/327 Sch.1
Sch.3, applied: SSI 2014/327 Sch.1
163. Fees in the Registers of Scotland Amendment Order 2001
revoked: SSI 2014/188 Sch.2
207. Water Supply (Water Quality) (Scotland) Regulations 2001
revoked: SSI 2014/364 Reg.50

Reg.3, applied: SSI 2014/364 Reg.51
Reg.20, applied: SSI 2014/364 Reg.52
223. St Mary's Music School (Aided Places) (Scotland) Regulations 2001
Sch.1 Part I para.1, amended: SSI 2014/143 Reg.3
Sch.1 Part II para.4, amended: SSI 2014/143 Reg.3
Sch.1 Part III para.10, amended: SSI 2014/143 Reg.3
Sch.1 Part III para.13, amended: SSI 2014/143 Reg.3
Sch.1 Part III para.14, amended: SSI 2014/143 Reg.3
Sch.1 Part IV para.17, amended: SSI 2014/143 Reg.3
Sch.1 Part IV para.18, amended: SSI 2014/143 Reg.3
Sch.1 Part IV para.24, amended: SSI 2014/143 Reg.3
238. Water Supply (Water Quality) (Scotland) Amendment Regulations 2001
revoked: SSI 2014/364 Reg.50
302. Health Boards (Membership and Procedure) (Scotland) Regulations 2001
disapplied: SSI 2014/344 Sch.1, Sch.2

2002

90. Provision of School Education for Children under School Age (Prescribed Children) (Scotland) Order 2002
revoked: SSI 2014/196 Art.4
95. Adults with Incapacity (Supervision of Welfare Guardians etc by Local Authorities) (Scotland) Regulations 2002
Reg.2, amended: SSI 2014/123 Reg.3, Reg.4
Reg.2A, added: SSI 2014/123 Reg.5
Reg.2A, amended: SSI 2014/157 Reg.2
Reg.3, amended: SSI 2014/123 Reg.6
Reg.3A, added: SSI 2014/123 Reg.7
Sch.1, added: SSI 2014/123 Reg.8
132. Act of Sederunt (Summary Cause Rules) 2002
Sch.1 Appendix, amended: SSI 2014/152 r.4
Sch.1 Part 6 para.6_A4, amended: SSI 2014/291 r.4

Sch.1 Part 18 para.18_2A, added: SSI
2014/152 r.4
Sch.1 Part 18 para.18_4, amended: SSI
2014/152 r.4
Sch.1 Part 34 para.34_7, amended: SSI
2014/152 r.4
Sch.1 Part 34 para.34_7, revoked (in part):
SSI 2014/152 r.4
Sch.1 Part 34 para.34_8, amended: SSI
2014/152 r.4

133. Act of Sederunt (Small Claim Rules) 2002
Sch.1 Part 7 para.7_A4, amended: SSI
2014/291 r.5

138. Mull Salmon Fishery District Designation
(Scotland) Order 2002
Art.2, applied: SSI 2014/327 Sch.1
Sch.1, applied: SSI 2014/327 Sch.1

260. Marriage (Approval of Places) (Scotland)
Regulations 2002
revoked: SSI 2014/287 Art.6

265. Community Care (Additional Payments)
(Scotland) Regulations 2002
Reg.2, applied: SSI 2014/345 Sch.1 Part 2

276. Designation of Nitrate Vulnerable Zones
(Scotland) Regulations 2002
Reg.2, amended: SSI 2014/373 Reg.5
Reg.3, revoked: SSI 2014/373 Reg.5
Reg.6, revoked (in part): SSI 2014/373
Reg.5

303. Community Care (Personal Care and
Nursing Care) (Scotland) Regulations 2002
Reg.2, amended: SSI 2014/91 Reg.2

317. Housing (Right to Buy) (Houses Liable to
Demolition) (Scotland) Order 2002
revoked: 2014 asp 14 s.1

494. Civil Legal Aid (Scotland) Regulations
2002
Reg.33, amended: SSI 2014/90 Sch.1 Part 3
Sch.2 para.5, amended: SSI 2014/90 Sch.1
Part 3
Sch.3 para.8, amended: SSI 2014/90 Sch.1
Part 3

533. Community Care (Joint Working etc.)
(Scotland) Regulations 2002
Sch.1, added: SSI 2014/66 Reg.3
Sch.1, amended: SSI 2014/66 Reg.3, SSI
2014/90 Sch.1 Part 3
Sch.3, amended: SSI 2014/90 Sch.1 Part 3
Sch.5 para.1, amended: SSI 2014/66 Reg.4,
SSI 2014/90 Sch.1 Part 3

546. Designation of Nitrate Vulnerable Zones
(Scotland) (No.2) Regulations 2002
revoked: SSI 2014/373 Reg.5

2003

93. Proceeds of Crime Act 2002 (Disclosure of
Information to and by Lord Advocate and
Scottish Ministers) Order 2003
Art.3, amended: SSI 2014/49 Art.2

135. Ethical Standards in Public Life etc
(Scotland) Act 2000 (Register of Interests)
Regulations 2003
Reg.4, amended: SSI 2014/50 Reg.3
Reg.4A, added: SSI 2014/50 Reg.4
Reg.5, amended: SSI 2014/50 Reg.5
Reg.6, amended: SSI 2014/50 Reg.6
Sch.1, amended: SSI 2014/50 Reg.7

176. Council Tax (Discounts) (Scotland)
Consolidation and Amendment Order 2003
Art.6, amended: SSI 2014/37 Art.3, Art.4

179. Advice and Assistance (Assistance by Way
of Representation) (Scotland) Regulations 2003
Reg.6, amended: SSI 2014/366 Reg.12

210. Proceeds of Crime Act 2002
(Commencement No 6, Transitional Provisions
and Savings) (Scotland) Order 2003
Art.3, applied: SI 2014/3141 Reg.22
Art.4, applied: SI 2014/3141 Reg.21
Art.7, applied: SI 2014/3141 Reg.21, Reg.22

235. Landfill (Scotland) Regulations 2003
referred to: SSI 2014/324 Sch.1 para.10
Reg.19, applied: SSI 2014/319 Sch.1 para.7,
Sch.2 para.12, Sch.3 para.7

243. Community Care (Direct Payments)
(Scotland) Regulations 2003
revoked: SSI 2014/90 Sch.1 Part 2

278. Food Supplements (Scotland) Regulations
2003
Reg.2, amended: SSI 2014/312 Sch.5 para.7
Reg.6, amended: SSI 2014/312 Sch.5 para.7
Reg.7, amended: SSI 2014/312 Sch.5 para.7

291. Cocoa and Chocolate Products (Scotland)
Regulations 2003
Reg.2, amended: SSI 2014/312 Sch.5 para.9
Reg.5, amended: SSI 2014/312 Sch.5 para.9
Reg.6, amended: SSI 2014/312 Sch.5 para.9
Reg.7, amended: SSI 2014/312 Sch.5 para.9
Reg.7, revoked (in part): SSI 2014/312 Sch.5
para.9

Reg.12, revoked (in part): SSI 2014/312
Sch.4 Part 1

**294. Agricultural Holdings (Relevant Date and
Relevant Period) (Scotland) Order 2003**
revoked: SSI 2014/98 Art.2

**331. Water Industry (Scotland) Act 2002
(Consequential Provisions) Order 2003**
Sch.1 Part II para.10, revoked: SSI 2014/364
Reg.50
Sch.1 Part II para.13, revoked: SSI 2014/364
Reg.50

**344. National Health Service (Compensation for
Premature Retirement) (Scotland) Regulations
2003**
Reg.13, amended: SSI 2014/293 Sch.1
para.6

**415. Road Works (Inspection Fees) (Scotland)
Regulations 2003**
Reg.3, amended: SSI 2014/56 Reg.2

**426. Classical Swine Fever (Scotland) Order
2003**
revoked: SI 2014/1894 Sch.5

**527. Specified Sugar Products (Scotland)
Regulations 2003**
Reg.2, amended: SSI 2014/312 Sch.5 para.8
Reg.5, amended: SSI 2014/312 Sch.5 para.8
Reg.11, revoked (in part): SSI 2014/312
Sch.4 Part 1
Sch.2, amended: SSI 2014/312 Sch.5 para.8

**531. Control of Pollution (Silage, Slurry and
Agricultural Fuel Oil) (Scotland) Regulations
2003**
Reg.2, applied: SSI 2014/319 Sch.4 para.6
Reg.3, applied: SSI 2014/319 Sch.4 para.6
Reg.6, applied: SSI 2014/319 Sch.4 para.6
Reg.11, applied: SSI 2014/319 Sch.1 para.8,
Sch.2 para.13, Sch.3 para.8, Sch.4 para.6

569. Honey (Scotland) Regulations 2003
Reg.5, amended: SSI 2014/312 Sch.5
para.10
Reg.7, revoked: SSI 2014/312 Sch.5 para.10

**578. Food Labelling Amendment (Scotland)
Regulations 2003**
revoked: SSI 2014/312 Sch.4 Part 1

586. African Swine Fever (Scotland) Order 2003
revoked: SI 2014/1894 Sch.5

**615. Wester Ross Salmon Fishery District
Designation Order 2003**
Art.2, applied: SSI 2014/327 Sch.1
Sch.1, applied: SSI 2014/327 Sch.1

2004

6. Meat Products (Scotland) Regulations 2004
revoked: SSI 2014/289 Reg.8

**8. Processed Cereal-based Foods and Baby
Foods for Infants and Young Children
(Scotland) Regulations 2004**
applied: SSI 2014/289 Reg.3
Reg.8, amended: SSI 2014/312 Sch.5
para.11

**111. Potatoes Originating in Egypt (Scotland)
Regulations 2004**
Reg.6, applied: SSI 2014/338 Reg.6
Reg.6, revoked: SSI 2014/338 Reg.6

**114. National Health Service (Primary Medical
Services Performers Lists) (Scotland)
Regulations 2004**
disapplied: SSI 2014/344 Sch.1, Sch.2

**115. National Health Service (General Medical
Services Contracts) (Scotland) Regulations 2004**
Reg.2, amended: SSI 2014/73 Reg.3
Sch.5 Part 3 para.44, amended: SSI 2014/73
Reg.4, SSI 2014/148 Reg.11
Sch.5 Part 4 para.58, amended: SSI 2014/73
Reg.4
Sch.5 Part 9 para.112, amended: SI
2014/1887 Sch.2 para.3
Sch.5 Part 9 para.113, amended: SI
2014/1887 Sch.2 para.3

**116. National Health Service (Primary Medical
Services Section 17C Agreements) (Scotland)
Regulations 2004**
disapplied: SSI 2014/344 Sch.1, Sch.2
Reg.2, amended: SSI 2014/73 Reg.6
Sch.1 Part 3 para.15, amended: SSI 2014/73
Reg.7, SSI 2014/148 Reg.13
Sch.1 Part 4 para.28, amended: SSI 2014/73
Reg.7
Sch.1 Part 9 para.76, amended: SI
2014/1887 Sch.2 para.4
Sch.1 Part 9 para.77, amended: SI
2014/1887 Sch.2 para.4

**219. Town and Country Planning (Fees for
Applications and Deemed Applications)
(Scotland) Regulations 2004**
Reg.1, referred to: SSI 2014/214 Reg.3
Reg.12, amended: SSI 2014/214 Reg.2
Reg.13, amended: SSI 2014/214 Reg.2, SSI
2014/301 Reg.2
Reg.14, amended: SSI 2014/214 Reg.2

Sch.1 Part II para.4, amended: SSI 2014/214 Reg.2
Sch.1 Part II para.5, amended: SSI 2014/214 Reg.2
Sch.1 Part II para.6, amended: SSI 2014/214 Reg.2
Sch.1 Part II para.7, amended: SSI 2014/214 Reg.2
Sch.1 Part III, amended: SSI 2014/214 Sch.1
Sch.1 Part III para.14, amended: SSI 2014/214 Reg.2

230. Community Right to Buy (Register of Community Interests in Land Charges) (Scotland) Regulations 2004
applied: SSI 2014/188 Art.6
revoked: SSI 2014/188 Sch.2

269. Food Labelling Amendment (Scotland) Regulations 2004
revoked: SSI 2014/312 Sch.4 Part 1

317. Oil and Fibre Plant Seed (Scotland) Regulations 2004
referred to: SSI 2014/167 Reg.4

318. Register of Sasines (Application Procedure) Rules 2004
r.2, substituted: SSI 2014/190 Art.7
r.5, amended: SSI 2014/190 Art.7
r.6, amended: SSI 2014/190 Art.7
Sch.1, added: SSI 2014/190 Sch.1
Sch.1, amended: SSI 2014/190 Art.7
Sch.1, substituted: SSI 2014/190 Art.7

406. Building (Scotland) Regulations 2004
Sch.1 para.1, substituted: SI 2014/1638 Sch.13 para.20
Sch.5 Part 6 para.6_1, amended: SSI 2014/219 Reg.2
Sch.5 Part 6 para.6_9, amended: SSI 2014/219 Reg.2

426. Controlled Waste (Fixed Penalty Notices) (Scotland) Order 2004
revoked: SSI 2014/320 Art.3

427. Litter (Fixed Penalty Notices) (Scotland) Order 2004
revoked: SSI 2014/321 Art.3

472. Food Labelling Amendment (No.2) (Scotland) Regulations 2004
revoked: SSI 2014/312 Sch.4 Part 1

477. Title Conditions (Scotland) Act 2003 (Rural Housing Bodies) Order 2004
Sch.1, amended: SSI 2014/130 Art.2, SSI 2014/220 Art.2

489. Homeless Persons (Unsuitable Accommodation) (Scotland) Order 2004
revoked: SSI 2014/243 Art.8

496. Agricultural Holdings (Fees) (Scotland) Order 2004
applied: SSI 2014/188 Art.6
revoked: SSI 2014/188 Sch.2

507. Fees in the Registers of Scotland Amendment Order 2004
revoked: SSI 2014/188 Sch.2

520. Environmental Information (Scotland) Regulations 2004
Reg.10, applied: SI 2014/1663 Reg.28
Reg.11, applied: SI 2014/1663 Reg.28

2005

1. Food Labelling (Added Phytosterols or Phytostanols) (Scotland) Regulations 2005
revoked: SSI 2014/312 Sch.4 Part 1

114. Community Care (Direct Payments) (Scotland) Amendment Regulations 2005
revoked: SSI 2014/90 Sch.1 Part 2

127. Non-Domestic Rating (Valuation of Utilities) (Scotland) Order 2005
Art.7A, amended: SSI 2014/64 Art.2

216. Plant Health (Import Inspection Fees) (Scotland) Regulations 2005
revoked: SSI 2014/338 Reg.6
Reg.4, applied: SSI 2014/338 Reg.6

222. Food Labelling Amendment (Scotland) Regulations 2005
revoked: SSI 2014/312 Sch.4 Part 1

275. Right to Purchase (Prescribed Persons) (Scotland) Amendment Order 2005
revoked: 2014 asp 14 s.1

318. Regulation of Care (Social Service Workers) (Scotland) Order 2005
Art.1, amended: SSI 2014/129 Art.2
Art.2, amended: SSI 2014/129 Art.2

328. Cereal Seed (Scotland) Regulations 2005
referred to: SSI 2014/167 Reg.4

329. Fodder Plant Seed (Scotland) Regulations 2005
referred to: SSI 2014/167 Reg.4

393. Teachers Superannuation (Scotland) Regulations 2005
applied: SSI 2014/217 Sch.1 para.4, Sch.3 para.34, Sch.3 para.35, Sch.3 para.39, Sch.3 para.40, SSI 2014/292 Sch.1 para.4, Sch.3

para.34, Sch.3 para.35, Sch.3 para.39, Sch.3
para.40
Part B regB.2, amended: SSI 2014/69 Reg.4
Part B regB.2, revoked (in part): SSI
2014/69 Reg.4
Part B regB.5, applied: SSI 2014/217 Sch.1
para.2, SSI 2014/292 Sch.1 para.2
Part B regB.6, amended: SSI 2014/69 Reg.5
Part B regB.7, applied: SSI 2014/292 Reg.18
Part B regB.7, substituted: SSI 2014/69
Reg.6
Part B regB.8, substituted: SSI 2014/69
Reg.7
Part E regE.10A, amended: SSI 2014/69
Reg.3
Part E regE.10A, applied: SSI 2014/217
Sch.3 para.28, SSI 2014/292 Sch.3 para.28
Part E regE.17, applied: SSI 2014/217 Sch.3
para.30, SSI 2014/292 Sch.3 para.30
Part E regE.17, varied: SSI 2014/217 Sch.3
para.29, SSI 2014/292 Sch.3 para.29
Part E regE.18, amended: SSI 2014/69
Reg.11
Part E regE.21, applied: SSI 2014/217 Sch.3
para.31, SSI 2014/292 Sch.3 para.31
Part E regE.21, substituted: SSI 2014/69
Reg.12
Part E regE.21A, added: SSI 2014/69 Reg.13
Part E regE.24, amended: SSI 2014/69
Reg.3, Reg.14
Part E regE.24, applied: SSI 2014/217 Sch.3
para.41, SSI 2014/292 Sch.3 para.41
Part E regE.24, varied: SSI 2014/217 Sch.3
para.47, SSI 2014/292 Sch.3 para.47
Part E regE.26A, varied: SSI 2014/217 Sch.3
para.47, SSI 2014/292 Sch.3 para.47
Part E regE.27, varied: SSI 2014/217 Sch.3
para.47, SSI 2014/292 Sch.3 para.47
Part E regE.28, applied: SSI 2014/217 Sch.3
para.33, SSI 2014/292 Sch.3 para.33, Sch.3
para.38
Part E regE.29, amended: SSI 2014/69 Reg.3
Part E regE.29, applied: SSI 2014/217 Sch.3
para.38
Part E regE.31, applied: SSI 2014/217 Sch.3
para.32, Sch.3 para.37, SSI 2014/292 Sch.3
para.32
Part E regE.31, disapplied: SSI 2014/292
Sch.3 para.37
Part E regE.34, amended: SSI 2014/69 Reg.3

Part E regE.36, applied: SSI 2014/217 Sch.3
para.23, Sch.3 para.25, Sch.3 para.26, Sch.3
para.32, Sch.3 para.36, Sch.3 para.37, Sch.3
para.42, SSI 2014/292 Sch.3 para.23, Sch.3
para.25, Sch.3 para.26, Sch.3 para.32, Sch.3
para.36, Sch.3 para.37, Sch.3 para.42
Part E regE.38, amended: SSI 2014/293
Sch.1 para.7
Part E regE.6, amended: SSI 2014/69 Reg.3
Part E regE.8, amended: SSI 2014/69 Reg.10
Part E regE.8, applied: SSI 2014/217 Sch.3
para.41, Sch.3 para.42, SSI 2014/292 Sch.3
para.41, Sch.3 para.42
Part H regH.2, revoked: SSI 2014/69 Reg.16
Part H regH.2A, added: SSI 2014/69 Reg.17
Part H regH.3, amended: SSI 2014/69
Reg.18
Part H regH.3, revoked (in part): SSI
2014/69 Reg.18
Part H regH.5, revoked: SSI 2014/69 Reg.19
Part H regH.6, amended: SSI 2014/69
Reg.20
Part J regJ.4, amended: SSI 2014/69 Reg.3
Part J regJ.6B, substituted: SSI 2014/69
Reg.21
Part C regC.1, amended: SSI 2014/69 Reg.3
Part C regC.1, applied: SSI 2014/217 Sch.3
para.49, SSI 2014/292 Sch.3 para.49
Part C regC.11, applied: SSI 2014/217 Sch.3
para.48, SSI 2014/292 Sch.3 para.48
Part C regC.15, substituted: SSI 2014/69
Reg.9
Part C regC.2, amended: SSI 2014/69 Reg.3
Part C regC.3, amended: SSI 2014/44 Reg.2
Part C regC.4, revoked: SSI 2014/69 Reg.8
Part C regC.4B, applied: SSI 2014/217 Sch.3
para.24, SSI 2014/292 Sch.3 para.24
Part C regC.9, applied: SSI 2014/217 Sch.3
para.51, SSI 2014/292 Sch.3 para.51
Part D regD.1, amended: SSI 2014/69 Reg.3
Reg.G2, amended: SSI 2014/69 Reg.15
Sch.1, amended: SSI 2014/69 Reg.22
Sch.2 para.14, applied: SSI 2014/217 Sch.1
para.16, SSI 2014/292 Sch.1 para.16
Sch.6, applied: SSI 2014/217 Sch.3 para.34,
Sch.3 para.35, Sch.3 para.39, Sch.3 para.40,
SSI 2014/292 Sch.3 para.34, Sch.3 para.35,
Sch.3 para.39, Sch.3 para.40

458. Registration of Civil Partnerships (Prescription of Forms, Publicisation and Errors) (Scotland) Regulations 2005
    Reg.6A, added: SSI 2014/306 Reg.2
    Sch.1, amended: SSI 2014/306 Sch.1
    Sch.3A, added: SSI 2014/306 Sch.2
464. Mental Health (Safety and Security) (Scotland) Regulations 2005
    disapplied: SSI 2014/344 Sch.2
467. Mental Health (Cross border transfer patients subject to detention requirement or otherwise in hospital) (Scotland) Regulations 2005
    disapplied: SSI 2014/344 Sch.2
468. Mental Health (Use of Telephones) (Scotland) Regulations 2005
    disapplied: SSI 2014/344 Sch.2
487. Argyll Salmon Fishery District Designation Order 2005
    Art.2, applied: SSI 2014/327 Sch.1
580. Fees in the Registers of Scotland Amendment Order 2005
    revoked: SSI 2014/188 Sch.2
613. Plant Health (Scotland) Order 2005
    Art.12, applied: SSI 2014/338 Reg.3
    Art.19B, amended: SSI 2014/140 Art.3
    Sch.1 Part B, amended: SSI 2014/140 Art.4
657. Marriage (Approval of Places) (Scotland) Amendment Regulations 2005
    revoked: SSI 2014/287 Art.6

2006

3. Food Hygiene (Scotland) Regulations 2006
    Reg.2, amended: SSI 2014/213 Reg.2
    Reg.32A, revoked: SSI 2014/118 Reg.2
    Sch.1, amended: SSI 2014/118 Reg.2, SSI 2014/213 Reg.2
    Sch.2, amended: SSI 2014/213 Reg.2
    Sch.3 para.2, revoked: SSI 2014/213 Reg.2
    Sch.3 para.14, amended: SSI 2014/213 Reg.2
    Sch.3 para.14, revoked (in part): SSI 2014/213 Reg.2
    Sch.4 para.4, amended: SSI 2014/312 Sch.5 para.12
    Sch.6A, revoked: SSI 2014/118 Reg.2
    Sch.7 para.12, revoked: SSI 2014/312 Sch.4 Part 1

44. Foot-and-Mouth Disease (Scotland) Order 2006
    applied: SI 2014/1894 Reg.4
135. National Health Service (General Ophthalmic Services) (Scotland) Regulations 2006
    disapplied: SSI 2014/344 Sch.1, Sch.2
209. Private Water Supplies (Scotland) Regulations 2006
    Reg.37, revoked (in part): SSI 2014/364 Reg.50
218. Charities Accounts (Scotland) Regulations 2006
    Reg.1, amended: SSI 2014/295 Reg.3, SSI 2014/335 Reg.3
    Reg.1, referred to: SI 2014/1960 Art.5
    Reg.14, amended: SSI 2014/295 Reg.4, SSI 2014/335 Reg.4
310. Approval of Research on Organs No Longer Required for Procurator Fiscal Purposes (Specified Persons) (Scotland) Order 2006
    Art.1, amended: 2014 c.23 Sch.8 para.7
313. Seed (Registration, Licensing and Enforcement) (Scotland) Regulations 2006
    referred to: SSI 2014/167 Reg.5
330. National Health Service (Discipline Committees) (Scotland) Regulations 2006
    disapplied: SSI 2014/344 Sch.1, Sch.2
333. Education (Student Loans for Tuition Fees) (Scotland) Regulations 2006
    Reg.12, amended: SSI 2014/293 Sch.1 para.8
338. Firefighters Compensation Scheme (Scotland) Order 2006
    Sch.1, added: SSI 2014/109 Sch.1 para.1, Sch.1 para.2, Sch.1 para.7, Sch.1 para.9, Sch.1 para.10, Sch.1 para.11
    Sch.1, amended: SSI 2014/109 Sch.1 para.1, Sch.1 para.2, Sch.1 para.3, Sch.1 para.4, Sch.1 para.5, Sch.1 para.6, Sch.1 para.7, Sch.1 para.8, Sch.1 para.9, Sch.1 para.10, Sch.1 para.11
    Sch.1, applied: SSI 2014/109 Art.3
    Sch.1, revoked: SSI 2014/109 Sch.1 para.7, Sch.1 para.8
    Sch.1, substituted: SSI 2014/109 Sch.1 para.1, Sch.1 para.7
447. Northern Salmon Fishery District Designation Order 2006
    Art.2, applied: SSI 2014/327 Sch.1
    Sch.1, applied: SSI 2014/327 Sch.1

573. Marriage (Approval of Places) (Scotland) Amendment Regulations 2006
revoked: SSI 2014/287 Art.6

582. Environmental Impact Assessment (Agriculture) (Scotland) Regulations 2006
applied: SSI 2014/325 Sch.1 para.6

588. Personal Injuries (NHS Charges) (Amounts) (Scotland) Regulations 2006
Reg.2F, amended: SSI 2014/57 Reg.2
Reg.2G, added: SSI 2014/57 Reg.2
Reg.3, amended: SSI 2014/57 Reg.2
Reg.6, amended: SSI 2014/57 Reg.2

600. Fees in the Registers of Scotland Amendment Order 2006
revoked: SSI 2014/188 Sch.2

2007

27. Sulphur Content of Liquid Fuels (Scotland) Regulations 2007
applied: SSI 2014/258 Reg.8
revoked: SSI 2014/258 Reg.8
Sch.1, applied: SSI 2014/258 Reg.8

138. Plant Health (Import Inspection Fees) (Scotland) Amendment Regulations 2007
revoked: SSI 2014/338 Reg.6

147. Tuberculosis (Scotland) Order 2007
Art.2, amended: SSI 2014/71 Art.2
Art.2A, added: SSI 2014/71 Art.2
Art.6, amended: SSI 2014/71 Art.2
Art.8, amended: SSI 2014/71 Art.2
Art.10, amended: SSI 2014/71 Art.2
Art.11, substituted: SSI 2014/71 Art.2
Art.20, amended: SSI 2014/71 Art.2
Art.21, amended: SSI 2014/71 Art.2
Art.22, amended: SSI 2014/71 Art.2
Art.23, amended: SSI 2014/71 Art.2

154. Education (Student Loans) (Scotland) Regulations 2007
Reg.15, amended: SSI 2014/293 Sch.1 para.9

199. Firefighters Pension Scheme (Scotland) Order 2007
Sch.1, added: SSI 2014/110 Sch.1 para.1, Sch.1 para.2, Sch.1 para.3, Sch.1 para.4, Sch.1 para.5, Sch.1 para.6, Sch.1 para.9, Sch.1 para.10, Sch.1 para.11, Sch.1 para.12, Sch.1 para.13, Sch.1 para.15, Sch.1 para.16, Sch.1 para.17

Sch.1, amended: SSI 2014/60 Art.3, SSI 2014/110 Sch.1 para.1, Sch.1 para.2, Sch.1 para.3, Sch.1 para.4, Sch.1 para.5, Sch.1 para.6, Sch.1 para.7, Sch.1 para.8, Sch.1 para.9, Sch.1 para.10, Sch.1 para.11, Sch.1 para.12, SSI 2014/149 Art.3, Art.4, Art.5
Sch.1, substituted: SSI 2014/110 Sch.1 para.3, Sch.1 para.14

201. Police Pensions (Scotland) Regulations 2007
Reg.7, amended: SSI 2014/62 Reg.3

325. Addition of Vitamins, Minerals and Other Substances (Scotland) Regulations 2007
Reg.4, amended: SSI 2014/312 Sch.5 para.13

354. Reciprocal Enforcement of Maintenance Orders (United States of America) (Scotland) Order 2007
Sch.2, amended: SI 2014/879 Art.120

360. Act of Sederunt (Rules of the Court of Session Amendment No 7) (Devolution Issues) 2007
r.2, amended: 2014 c.29 s.4

361. Act of Adjournal (Criminal Procedure Rules Amendment No 4) (Devolution Issues) 2007
r.2, amended: 2014 c.29 s.4

362. Act of Sederunt (Proceedings for Determination of Devolution Issues Rules) Amendment 2007
r.2, amended: 2014 c.29 s.4

383. Nutrition and Health Claims (Scotland) Regulations 2007
Reg.5, amended: SSI 2014/312 Sch.5 para.14
Reg.8, revoked: SSI 2014/312 Sch.4 Part 1

396. Provision of School Education for Children under School Age (Prescribed Children) (Scotland) Amendment Order 2007
revoked: SSI 2014/196 Art.4

458. Community Care (Direct Payments) (Scotland) Amendment Regulations 2007
revoked: SSI 2014/90 Sch.1 Part 2

483. Natural Mineral Water, Spring Water and Bottled Drinking Water (Scotland) (No.2) Regulations 2007
Reg.2, amended: SSI 2014/312 Sch.5 para.15
Reg.4, applied: SSI 2014/364 Reg.1

499. Plant Health (Import Inspection Fees) (Scotland) Amendment (No.2) Regulations 2007
revoked: SSI 2014/338 Reg.6

549. Infant Formula and Follow-on Formula (Scotland) Regulations 2007
Reg.2, amended: SSI 2014/12 Reg.2
Reg.8, amended: SSI 2014/12 Reg.2
Reg.9, substituted: SSI 2014/12 Reg.2
Reg.15, amended: SSI 2014/12 Reg.2
Reg.16, amended: SSI 2014/12 Reg.2

2008

16. Scottish Road Works Register (Prescribed Fees and Amounts) Regulations 2008
Reg.3, amended: SSI 2014/58 Reg.5

81. Bankruptcy (Scotland) Act 1985 (Low Income, Low Asset Debtors etc.) Regulations 2008
revoked: SSI 2014/296 Reg.10
Reg.4, applied: SSI 2014/296 Reg.11

82. Bankruptcy (Scotland) Regulations 2008
Reg.3, revoked: SSI 2014/225 Reg.23
Reg.9, revoked: SSI 2014/225 Reg.23
Sch.1, revoked: SSI 2014/225 Reg.23

97. Meat Products (Scotland) Amendment Regulations 2008
revoked: SSI 2014/289 Reg.8

100. Rural Development Contracts (Rural Priorities) (Scotland) Regulations 2008
Sch.1, amended: SSI 2014/373 Reg.4

115. Bankruptcy and Diligence etc (Scotland) Act 2007 (Commencement No 3, Savings and Transitionals) Order 2008
Art.5, amended: SSI 2014/173 Art.3
Art.6, amended: SSI 2014/173 Art.3

128. Sexual Offences Act 2003 (Prescribed Police Stations) (Scotland) Regulations 2008
revoked: SSI 2014/147 Sch.2

158. Products of Animal Origin (Disease Control) (Scotland) Order 2008
applied: SI 2014/1894 Reg.30
Art.4, amended: SI 2014/1894 Reg.43
Sch.1 para.1, amended: SI 2014/1894 Reg.43
Sch.1 para.3, revoked: SI 2014/1894 Reg.43
Sch.1 para.5, revoked: SI 2014/1894 Reg.43

159. Rural Development Contracts (Land Managers Options) (Scotland) Regulations 2008
Sch.1, amended: SSI 2014/373 Reg.4

180. Food Labelling (Declaration of Allergens) (Scotland) Regulations 2008
revoked: SSI 2014/312 Sch.4 Part 1

219. Diseases of Animals (Approved Disinfectants) (Scotland) Order 2008
applied: SI 2014/1894 Reg.15

228. Local Government Pension Scheme (Administration) (Scotland) Regulations 2008
applied: SSI 2014/233 Reg.3, Reg.14, Reg.17, Reg.22, Reg.24
revoked: SSI 2014/233 Sch.1
varied: SSI 2014/233 Reg.24
Reg.3, applied: SSI 2014/233 Reg.5
Reg.6, applied: SSI 2014/233 Reg.5
Reg.9, applied: SSI 2014/233 Reg.5
Reg.10, amended: SSI 2014/23 Reg.3
Reg.10, revoked (in part): SSI 2014/23 Reg.3
Reg.11, applied: SSI 2014/233 Reg.5
Reg.13, applied: SSI 2014/233 Sch.2 para.6
Reg.14, applied: SSI 2014/233 Reg.10
Reg.15, amended: SI 2014/3255 Art.19
Reg.15, revoked (in part): SI 2014/3255 Art.19
Reg.20, applied: SSI 2014/233 Reg.11, Reg.15
Reg.21B, applied: SSI 2014/233 Reg.17
Reg.23, amended: SSI 2014/23 Reg.4
Reg.35, amended: SI 2014/3255 Art.19
Reg.36, applied: SSI 2014/233 Reg.24
Reg.41, applied: SSI 2014/233 Reg.10
Reg.43, applied: SSI 2014/233 Reg.1
Reg.49, amended: SSI 2014/293 Sch.1 para.10
Reg.64, applied: SSI 2014/233 Reg.3
Reg.79, applied: SSI 2014/233 Sch.2 para.4
Reg.82, applied: SSI 2014/233 Reg.10
Sch.1, amended: SSI 2014/23 Reg.5
Sch.2, referred to: SSI 2014/233 Reg.5
Sch.4 Part I para.2B, applied: SSI 2014/233 Reg.19

229. Local Government Pension Scheme (Transitional Provisions) (Scotland) Regulations 2008
applied: SSI 2014/233 Reg.3, Reg.17, Reg.22, Reg.24
revoked: SSI 2014/233 Sch.1
varied: SSI 2014/233 Reg.24
Reg.3, applied: SSI 2014/233 Sch.2 para.6
Reg.3, disapplied: SSI 2014/233 Reg.3
Reg.4, applied: SSI 2014/233 Sch.2 para.6

230. Local Government Pension Scheme (Benefits, Membership and Contributions) (Scotland) Regulations 2008
    applied: SSI 2014/233 Reg.3, Reg.14, Reg.17, Reg.22, Reg.24
    revoked: SSI 2014/233 Sch.1
    varied: SSI 2014/233 Reg.24
    Reg.5, referred to: SSI 2014/233 Reg.14
    Reg.9, applied: SSI 2014/233 Reg.1, Reg.4, Reg.8, Reg.10, Reg.17
    Reg.12, applied: SSI 2014/233 Sch.2 para.4
    Reg.13, applied: SSI 2014/233 Reg.3, Reg.11
    Reg.14, applied: SSI 2014/233 Reg.11, Reg.15
    Reg.14A, applied: SSI 2014/233 Reg.17
    Reg.16A, applied: SSI 2014/233 Reg.24
    Reg.18, applied: SSI 2014/233 Sch.2 para.4, Sch.2 para.5
    Reg.19, applied: SSI 2014/233 Reg.24
    Reg.20, applied: SSI 2014/233 Reg.4, Reg.12, Reg.17
    Reg.25, applied: SSI 2014/233 Reg.17
    Reg.26, applied: SSI 2014/233 Reg.17
    Reg.30, applied: SSI 2014/233 Sch.2 para.1
    Reg.32, applied: SSI 2014/233 Reg.17
    Reg.35, amended: SSI 2014/23 Reg.6
    Reg.35, applied: SSI 2014/233 Reg.17
    Reg.38, applied: SSI 2014/233 Reg.24
    Sch.1 Part 001 para.1, applied: SSI 2014/233 Reg.4, Reg.8, Reg.10, Reg.17
    Sch.1 Part 001 para.1, referred to: SSI 2014/233 Reg.14
    Sch.1 Part 002 para.7, applied: SSI 2014/233 Reg.17

235. Graduate Endowment (Scotland) Regulations 2008
    Reg.12, amended: SSI 2014/293 Sch.1 para.11

298. Action Programme for Nitrate Vulnerable Zones (Scotland) Regulations 2008
    Reg.3, amended: SSI 2014/373 Reg.4

306. Adult Support and Protection (Scotland) Act 2007 (Restriction on the Authorisation of Council Officers) Order 2008
    Art.3, applied: SSI 2014/282 Sch.1

312. National Health Service (Functions of the Common Services Agency) (Scotland) Order 2008
    Art.2, amended: SSI 2014/100 Art.2

334. Bankruptcy (Scotland) Amendment Regulations 2008
    revoked: SSI 2014/225 Reg.23

356. Mental Health (England and Wales Cross-border transfer patients subject to requirements other than detention) (Scotland) Regulations 2008
    disapplied: SSI 2014/344 Sch.2

361. Whiteness Marina Harbour Revision Order 2008
    revoked: SSI 2014/224 Art.1

386. Book of Scottish Connections Regulations 2008
    Sch.7, amended: SSI 2014/306 Sch.3

395. Eggs and Chicks (Scotland) (No.2) Regulations 2008
    Reg.2, amended: SSI 2014/312 Sch.5 para.16
    Reg.15, amended: SSI 2014/312 Sch.5 para.16
    Reg.15A, amended: SSI 2014/312 Sch.5 para.16
    Sch.2 Part 2, amended: SSI 2014/312 Sch.5 para.16

399. Pre-release Access to Official Statistics (Scotland) Order 2008
    Sch.1 para.2, amended: 2014 c.29 s.4

400. Provision of School Lunches (Disapplication of the Requirement to Charge) (Scotland) Order 2008
    revoked: SSI 2014/315 Art.2

2009

8. Plant Health (Import Inspection Fees) (Scotland) Amendment Regulations 2009
    revoked: SSI 2014/338 Reg.6

45. Specified Animal Pathogens (Scotland) Order 2009
    applied: SI 2014/1894 Reg.4

93. Local Government Pension Scheme Amendment (Scotland) Regulations 2009
    revoked: SSI 2014/233 Sch.1

140. Renewables Obligation (Scotland) Order 2009
    applied: SSI 2014/94 Art.27
    Part 5, amended: SSI 2014/94 Art.8
    Art.2, amended: SSI 2014/94 Art.3
    Art.3, amended: SSI 2014/94 Art.4
    Art.17AB, substituted: SSI 2014/94 Art.5

Art.21A, added: SSI 2014/94 Art.6
Art.22C, amended: SSI 2014/94 Art.7
Art.23A, added: SSI 2014/94 Art.8
Art.24, amended: SSI 2014/94 Art.9
Art.24, revoked (in part): SSI 2014/94 Art.9
Art.25, substituted: SSI 2014/94 Art.10
Art.26, amended: SSI 2014/94 Art.11
Art.30B, amended: SSI 2014/94 Art.12
Art.30C, added: SSI 2014/94 Art.13
Art.30C, applied: SI 2014/2388 Art.9
Art.30D, applied: SI 2014/2388 Art.10
Art.41, amended: SSI 2014/94 Art.14
Art.53, amended: SSI 2014/94 Art.15
Art.54, amended: SSI 2014/94 Art.16
Art.54A, amended: SSI 2014/94 Art.17
Art.54B, added: SSI 2014/94 Art.18
Art.57, amended: SSI 2014/94 Art.19
Art.58, substituted: SSI 2014/94 Art.20
Art.58A, amended: SSI 2014/94 Art.22
Art.58B, added: SSI 2014/94 Art.23
Art.58ZA, amended: SSI 2014/94 Art.21
Art.60, amended: SSI 2014/94 Art.24
Sch.A2 para.3, amended: SSI 2014/94
Art.25
Sch.2 Part 1, referred to: SI 2014/2388
Art.11
Sch.3A para.2, amended: SSI 2014/94
Art.26

154. Adoption Agencies (Scotland) Regulations 2009
Reg.8, applied: SI 2014/2934 Reg.3, SI 2014/3050 Reg.3, SI 2014/3051 Reg.2, SI 2014/3134 Reg.2
Reg.13, amended: SSI 2014/112 Sch.1 para.1
Reg.21, amended: SSI 2014/112 Sch.1 para.1
Reg.22, amended: SSI 2014/112 Sch.1 para.1
Reg.23, amended: SSI 2014/112 Sch.1 para.1
Sch.1 Part II para.10, amended: SSI 2014/112 Sch.1 para.1
Sch.8, amended: SSI 2014/112 Sch.1 para.1

166. National Health Service (Appointment of Consultants) (Scotland) Regulations 2009
disapplied: SSI 2014/344 Sch.1

169. Adoption and Children (Scotland) Act 2007 (Supervision Requirement Reports in Applications for Permanence Orders) Regulations 2009
revoked: SSI 2014/113 Reg.4

171. Fees in the Registers of Scotland Amendment Order 2009
revoked: SSI 2014/188 Sch.2

173. Swine Vesicular Disease (Scotland) Order 2009
revoked: SI 2014/1894 Sch.5

183. National Health Service (Pharmaceutical Services) (Scotland) Regulations 2009
disapplied: SSI 2014/344 Sch.1, Sch.2
referred to: SSI 2014/148 Reg.14
Reg.2, amended: SSI 2014/73 Reg.9, SSI 2014/148 Reg.3
Reg.5, amended: SSI 2014/148 Reg.4
Reg.5, revoked (in part): SSI 2014/148 Reg.4
Reg.5A, added: SSI 2014/148 Reg.5
Reg.5A, applied: SSI 2014/148 Reg.14
Reg.15, amended: SSI 2014/148 Reg.6
Sch.1 para.4, amended: SSI 2014/73 Reg.10
Sch.2, amended: SSI 2014/148 Sch.1
Sch.3 para.1, amended: SSI 2014/148 Reg.8
Sch.3 para.1A, added: SSI 2014/148 Reg.8
Sch.3 para.2, revoked: SSI 2014/148 Reg.8
Sch.3 para.3, substituted: SSI 2014/148 Reg.8
Sch.3 para.4, amended: SSI 2014/148 Reg.8
Sch.3 para.5, amended: SSI 2014/148 Reg.8
Sch.3 para.5, applied: 2014 asp 10 Sch.1 para.13
Sch.3 para.6, amended: SSI 2014/148 Reg.8
Sch.4 Part I para.5A, added: SSI 2014/148 Reg.9
Sch.4 Part I para.6, amended: SSI 2014/148 Reg.9

187. Local Government (Discretionary Payments and Injury Benefits) (Scotland) Amendment Regulations 2009
revoked: SSI 2014/233 Sch.1

210. Looked After Children (Scotland) Regulations 2009
Reg.20, amended: SSI 2014/310 Reg.2
Reg.22, amended: SSI 2014/310 Reg.2
Reg.27, amended: SSI 2014/310 Reg.2
Reg.27A, added: SSI 2014/310 Reg.2
Reg.45, amended: SSI 2014/112 Sch.1 para.2

Sch.4 para.6, amended: SSI 2014/112 Sch.1 para.2

232. Brucellosis (Scotland) Order 2009
Art.7, amended: SSI 2014/63 Art.2, SSI 2014/72 Art.3

266. Environmental Liability (Scotland) Regulations 2009
Reg.10, applied: SSI 2014/319 Sch.1 para.10, Sch.2 para.15, Sch.3 para.10
Reg.11, applied: SSI 2014/319 Sch.2 para.15
Reg.12, applied: SSI 2014/319 Sch.1 para.10, Sch.2 para.15, Sch.3 para.10
Reg.18, applied: SSI 2014/319 Sch.2 para.15

284. Act of Sederunt (Sheriff Court Rules Amendment) (Adoption and Children (Scotland) Act 2007) 2009
Sch.1, amended: SSI 2014/302 r.8

305. Plant Health (Import Inspection Fees) (Scotland) Amendment (No.2) Regulations 2009
revoked: SSI 2014/338 Reg.6

328. Food Labelling (Nutrition Information) (Scotland) Regulations 2009
revoked: SSI 2014/312 Sch.4 Part 1

366. A9 Trunk Road (Kincraig to Dalraddy) (Side Roads) Order 2009
revoked: SSI 2014/246 Art.4

376. Rural Payments (Appeals) (Scotland) Regulations 2009
Sch.1 para.9A, added: SSI 2014/325 Reg.9
Sch.1 para.13A, amended: SSI 2014/7 Reg.7

435. Food Enzymes (Scotland) Regulations 2009
Reg.7, revoked: SSI 2014/312 Sch.4 Part 1

436. Food Additives (Scotland) Regulations 2009
Reg.18, revoked (in part): SSI 2014/289 Reg.8

446. Official Feed and Food Controls (Scotland) Regulations 2009
Reg.2, amended: SSI 2014/213 Reg.3
Sch.1, amended: SSI 2014/213 Reg.3

2010

95. Water Quality (Scotland) Regulations 2010
Reg.7, revoked: SSI 2014/364 Reg.50

145. Additional Support for Learning (Sources of Information) (Scotland) Order 2010
Art.2, amended: SSI 2014/103 Art.2

148. Beet Seed (Scotland) (No.2) Regulations 2010
referred to: SSI 2014/167 Reg.4

199. Sports Grounds and Sporting Events (Designation) (Scotland) Order 2010
revoked: SSI 2014/5 Sch.3

208. National Health Service (General Dental Services) (Scotland) Regulations 2010
disapplied: SSI 2014/344 Sch.1

233. Local Government Pension Scheme (Management and Investment of Funds) (Scotland) Regulations 2010
Reg.4, applied: SSI 2014/164 Reg.67
Reg.12, applied: SSI 2014/164 Reg.55, Reg.56

234. Local Government Pension Scheme Amendment (Scotland) Regulations 2010
revoked: SSI 2014/233 Sch.1

271. Smoke Control Areas (Authorised Fuels) (Scotland) Regulations 2010
revoked: SSI 2014/317 Reg.3

272. Smoke Control Areas (Exempt Fireplaces) (Scotland) Order 2010
revoked: SSI 2014/316 Art.4

273. Less Favoured Area Support Scheme (Scotland) Regulations 2010
Reg.2, amended: SSI 2014/7 Reg.3
Reg.3, amended: SSI 2014/7 Reg.4
Reg.10, amended: SSI 2014/7 Reg.5
Sch.5 Part I, amended: SSI 2014/7 Reg.6
Sch.5 Part II, amended: SSI 2014/7 Reg.6

350. Regulation of Investigatory Powers (Prescription of Offices, etc and Specification of Public Authorities) (Scotland) Order 2010
Art.1, amended: SSI 2014/339 Art.12
Art.1A, added: SSI 2014/339 Art.12
Art.2A, added: SSI 2014/339 Art.12
Sch.1, amended: SSI 2014/339 Art.12, Art.13
Sch.1A, added: SSI 2014/339 Art.12

367. Bankruptcy (Scotland) Amendment Regulations 2010
Reg.3, revoked: SSI 2014/225 Reg.23
Sch.1, revoked: SSI 2014/225 Reg.23

397. Bankruptcy (Certificate for Sequestration) (Scotland) Regulations 2010
Reg.3, revoked: SSI 2014/296 Reg.7
Reg.4, revoked: SSI 2014/296 Reg.7
Reg.5, amended: SSI 2014/296 Reg.7
Sch.1, amended: SSI 2014/296 Sch.1

404. Fees in the Registers of Scotland Amendment Order 2010
revoked: SSI 2014/188 Sch.2

405. Plant Health (Import Inspection Fees) (Scotland) Amendment Regulations 2010
revoked: SSI 2014/338 Reg.6

434. Town and Country Planning (Tree Preservation Order and Trees in Conservation Areas) (Scotland) Regulations 2010
Reg.8, amended: SSI 2014/53 Reg.2

435. Waste Information (Scotland) Regulations 2010
Reg.6, applied: SSI 2014/319 Sch.2 para.19

439. Flavourings in Food (Scotland) Regulations 2010
Reg.7, revoked: SSI 2014/312 Sch.4 Part 1

446. Protection of Vulnerable Groups (Scotland) Act 2007 (Miscellaneous Provisions) Order 2010
Art.16A, added: SSI 2014/33 Art.2

450. Eggs and Chicks (Scotland) Amendment Regulations 2010
Reg.2, amended: SSI 2014/312 Sch.5 para.17
Reg.19, revoked: SSI 2014/312 Sch.4 Part 1

2011

55. National Health Service (Free Prescriptions and Charges for Drugs and Appliances) (Scotland) Regulations 2011
disapplied: SSI 2014/344 Sch.2
Reg.3, amended: SSI 2014/115 Reg.2

64. Local Authority Accounts (Scotland) Amendment Regulations 2011
revoked: SSI 2014/200 Reg.4

84. Drinking Milk (Scotland) Regulations 2011
Reg.8, revoked: SSI 2014/312 Sch.4 Part 1

97. Right to Purchase (Application Form) (Scotland) Order 2011
revoked: 2014 asp 14 s.1

117. National Health Service Superannuation Scheme (Scotland) Regulations 2011
Part A regA.2, amended: SSI 2014/154 Reg.3
Part B regB.4, amended: SSI 2014/154 Reg.4
Part E regE.7, amended: SSI 2014/154 Reg.8
Part F regF.2, amended: SSI 2014/154 Reg.9
Part r regR.7, amended: SSI 2014/154 Reg.10
Part T regT.11, added: SSI 2014/154 Reg.12
Part T regT.3, amended: SSI 2014/154 Reg.11

Part T regT.4, amended: SSI 2014/293 Sch.1 para.12
Part U regU.3, substituted: SSI 2014/154 Reg.13
Part C regC.1, amended: SSI 2014/154 Reg.5
Part D regD.1, amended: SSI 2014/43 Reg.3, SSI 2014/154 Reg.6
Part D regD.3, added: SSI 2014/154 Reg.7
Sch.1 Part II para.8, amended: SSI 2014/154 Reg.14
Sch.1 Part II para.10, amended: SSI 2014/154 Reg.14
Sch.1 Part IV para.14, amended: SSI 2014/43 Reg.4, SSI 2014/154 Reg.14

139. Town and Country Planning (Environmental Impact Assessment) (Scotland) Regulations 2011
Reg.2, amended: SI 2014/469 Sch.3 para.202
Reg.14, amended: SI 2014/469 Sch.3 para.202
Reg.15, amended: SI 2014/469 Sch.3 para.202
Reg.19, amended: SI 2014/469 Sch.3 para.202

141. Debt Arrangement Scheme (Scotland) Regulations 2011
Reg.2, amended: SSI 2014/294 Reg.4
Reg.7, amended: SSI 2014/294 Reg.5
Reg.8A, added: SSI 2014/294 Reg.5
Reg.9, amended: SSI 2014/294 Reg.6
Reg.9, applied: SSI 2014/294 Reg.23
Reg.12, amended: SSI 2014/294 Reg.7, Reg.8
Reg.12A, added: SSI 2014/294 Reg.7
Reg.19, amended: SSI 2014/294 Reg.9
Reg.20, amended: SSI 2014/294 Reg.8, Reg.10, Reg.11, Reg.21
Reg.20, applied: SSI 2014/294 Reg.23
Reg.21, amended: SSI 2014/294 Reg.12
Reg.22, amended: SSI 2014/294 Reg.12
Reg.22A, added: SSI 2014/294 Reg.13
Reg.23, amended: SSI 2014/294 Reg.14
Reg.24, amended: SSI 2014/294 Reg.8
Reg.25, amended: SSI 2014/294 Reg.8
Reg.27, amended: SSI 2014/294 Reg.15
Reg.29, amended: SSI 2014/294 Reg.21
Reg.30, applied: SSI 2014/294 Reg.23
Reg.30, revoked (in part): SSI 2014/294 Reg.22

Reg.33, amended: SSI 2014/294 Reg.16
Reg.36, amended: SSI 2014/294 Reg.17,
Reg.21
Reg.36, revoked (in part): SSI 2014/294
Reg.17
Reg.37, amended: SSI 2014/294 Reg.17
Reg.40A, amended: SSI 2014/294 Reg.18
Reg.41, amended: SSI 2014/294 Reg.18,
Reg.21
Reg.42, amended: SSI 2014/294 Reg.19
Reg.44A, amended: SSI 2014/294 Reg.18
Reg.45, revoked: SSI 2014/294 Reg.22
Reg.46A, amended: SSI 2014/294 Reg.20
Sch.A1, added: SSI 2014/294 Sch.1
Sch.1, amended: SSI 2014/294 Sch.2
Sch.3, amended: SSI 2014/294 Reg.6
Sch.3, referred to: SSI 2014/294 Reg.23

146. Disclosure (Persons engaged in the Investigation and Reporting of Crime or Sudden Deaths) (Scotland) Regulations 2011
    Sch.1, amended: SI 2014/469 Sch.3 para.203

147. Radioactive Substances Exemption (Scotland) Order 2011
    referred to: SSI 2014/324 Sch.1 para.14

152. Food Labelling (Declaration of Allergens) (Scotland) Regulations 2011
    revoked: SSI 2014/312 Sch.4 Part 1

209. Water Environment (Controlled Activities) (Scotland) Regulations 2011
    applied: SSI 2014/325 Sch.1 para.3
    referred to: SSI 2014/324 Sch.1 para.15
    Part II, applied: SSI 2014/325 Sch.1 para.2
    Reg.3, referred to: SSI 2014/323 Sch.1 para.2
    Reg.32, applied: SSI 2014/325 Sch.1 para.3
    Reg.44, applied: SSI 2014/319 Sch.1 para.11, Sch.2 para.20, Sch.3 para.11, Sch.4 para.7
    Sch.4 Part 2, amended: SSI 2014/373 Reg.4

211. Public Services Reform (Scotland) Act 2010 (Consequential Modifications) Order 2011
    Sch.2 Part 2 para.16, revoked: SSI 2014/188 Sch.2

228. Waste Management Licensing (Scotland) Regulations 2011
    referred to: SSI 2014/324 Sch.1 para.16
    Reg.19, applied: SSI 2014/319 Sch.2 para.21
    Reg.28, applied: SSI 2014/319 Sch.2 para.21
    Reg.30, applied: SSI 2014/319 Sch.2 para.21
    Sch.4 Part 1 para.12, applied: SSI 2014/4 Reg.3, SSI 2014/319 Sch.2 para.21

Sch.4 Part 1 para.14, applied: SSI 2014/319 Sch.2 para.21

311. Plant Health (Import Inspection Fees) (Scotland) Amendment Regulations 2011
    revoked: SSI 2014/338 Reg.6

331. Prisons and Young Offenders Institutions (Scotland) Rules 2011
    Sch.2, amended: SSI 2014/26 r.2

349. Local Government Pension Scheme (Miscellaneous Amendments) (Scotland) Regulations 2011
    revoked: SSI 2014/233 Sch.1

413. Seed (Fees) (Scotland) Regulations 2011
    revoked: SSI 2014/167 Reg.7

415. Common Agricultural Policy Schemes (Cross-Compliance) (Scotland) Regulations 2011
    revoked: SSI 2014/325 Reg.10
    Sch.1 Part V para.19, amended: SSI 2014/6 Reg.2
    Sch.1 Part V para.21, added: SSI 2014/6 Reg.2

2012

4. Sea Fish (Prohibited Methods of Fishing) (Firth of Clyde) Order 2012
    revoked: SSI 2014/2 Art.5

36. Patient Rights (Complaints Procedure and Consequential Provisions) (Scotland) Regulations 2012
    disapplied: SSI 2014/344 Sch.2

50. Sexual Offences Act 2003 (Prescribed Police Stations) (Scotland) Amendment Regulations 2012
    revoked: SSI 2014/147 Sch.2

87. National Health Service (Charges to Overseas Visitors) (Scotland) Amendment Regulations 2012
    revoked: SSI 2014/70 Reg.3

88. Public Contracts (Scotland) Regulations 2012
    Reg.6, referred to: 2014 asp 12 s.4

110. Patient Rights (Treatment Time Guarantee) (Scotland) Regulations 2012
    Reg.1, amended: SSI 2014/93 Reg.2
    Reg.4, amended: SSI 2014/93 Reg.2
    Reg.4A, added: SSI 2014/93 Reg.2
    Reg.7, revoked (in part): SSI 2014/93 Reg.2

111. Evidence in Civil Partnership and Divorce Actions (Scotland) Order 2012

    Art.2, varied: 2014 asp 5 s.27

118. Bankruptcy Fees etc (Scotland) Regulations 2012

    applied: SSI 2014/227 Reg.13

    revoked: SSI 2014/227 Reg.14

164. Sports Grounds and Sporting Events (Designation) (Scotland) Amendment Order 2012

    revoked: SSI 2014/5 Sch.3

177. Trade in Animals and Related Products (Scotland) Regulations 2012

    Reg.3, substituted: SI 2014/3158 Sch.1 para.17

    Reg.9, applied: SI 2014/1894 Reg.4

236. Local Government Pension Scheme (Administration) (Scotland) Amendment Regulations 2012

    revoked: SSI 2014/233 Sch.1

250. Road Works (Inspection Fees) (Scotland) Amendment Regulations 2012

    revoked: SSI 2014/56 Reg.3

295. Crofting Register (Fees) (Scotland) Order 2012

    applied: SSI 2014/188 Art.6

    revoked: SSI 2014/188 Sch.2

297. Crofting Register (Transfer of Ownership) (Scotland) Regulations 2012

    Reg.2, amended: SSI 2014/190 Art.8

    Reg.2, revoked (in part): SSI 2014/190 Art.8

    Reg.3, amended: SSI 2014/190 Art.8

    Reg.3, revoked (in part): SSI 2014/190 Art.8

303. Council Tax Reduction (Scotland) Regulations 2012

    Reg.2, amended: SI 2014/3255 Art.23

    Reg.2, varied: 2014 c.6 s.126

    Reg.6, amended: SI 2014/3255 Art.23

    Reg.28, amended: SI 2014/3255 Art.23

    Reg.28, varied: 2014 c.6 s.126

    Reg.34, amended: SI 2014/3255 Art.23

    Reg.35, amended: SI 2014/3255 Art.23

    Reg.67, amended: SSI 2014/35 Reg.3

    Sch.1 Part 1 para.1, amended: SSI 2014/35 Reg.4

    Sch.1 Part 1 para.3, amended: SSI 2014/35 Reg.4

    Sch.1 Part 2 para.4, amended: SSI 2014/35 Reg.4

    Sch.1 Part 4 para.17, amended: SSI 2014/35 Reg.4

    Sch.1 Part 5 para.23, amended: SSI 2014/35 Reg.4

    Sch.1 Part 5 para.24, amended: SSI 2014/35 Reg.4

    Sch.2 para.1, amended: SSI 2014/35 Reg.5

    Sch.4 para.57, amended: SSI 2014/90 Sch.1 Part 3

    Sch.5 para.62, amended: SSI 2014/90 Sch.1 Part 3

318. Materials and Articles in Contact with Food (Scotland) Regulations 2012

    Reg.29, revoked: SSI 2014/312 Sch.4 Part 1

319. Council Tax Reduction (State Pension Credit) (Scotland) Regulations 2012

    Reg.2, amended: SI 2014/3255 Art.24

    Reg.2, varied: 2014 c.6 s.126

    Reg.6, amended: SI 2014/3255 Art.24

    Reg.27, amended: SI 2014/3255 Art.24

    Reg.27, varied: 2014 c.6 s.126

    Reg.29, amended: SI 2014/3255 Art.24

    Reg.29, varied: 2014 c.6 s.126

    Reg.32, amended: SI 2014/3255 Art.24

    Reg.32, varied: 2014 c.6 s.126

    Reg.33, amended: SI 2014/3255 Art.24

    Reg.33, varied: 2014 c.6 s.126

    Reg.48, amended: SSI 2014/35 Reg.7

    Sch.1 Part 1 para.2, amended: SSI 2014/35 Reg.8

    Sch.1 Part 1 para.3, amended: SSI 2014/35 Reg.8

    Sch.1 Part 2 para.4, amended: SSI 2014/35 Reg.8

    Sch.1 Part 4 para.13, amended: SSI 2014/35 Reg.8

    Sch.4 Part 1 para.29, amended: SSI 2014/90 Sch.1 Part 3

    Sch.5 para.1, amended: SSI 2014/35 Reg.9

328. Crofting Register (Fees) (Scotland) Amendment Order 2012

    revoked: SSI 2014/188 Sch.2

347. Local Government Pension Scheme (Miscellaneous Amendments) (Scotland) Regulations 2012

    revoked: SSI 2014/233 Sch.1

353. Non-Domestic Rates (Levying) (Scotland) (No.3) Regulations 2012

    revoked: SSI 2014/30 Reg.6

360. Pollution Prevention and Control (Scotland) Regulations 2012

    applied: SSI 2014/4 Reg.3

    referred to: SSI 2014/324 Sch.1 para.17

Reg.3, amended: SSI 2014/267 Reg.4
Reg.10, amended: SSI 2014/267 Reg.5
Reg.20A, added: SSI 2014/267 Reg.6
Reg.34, substituted: SSI 2014/267 Reg.7
Reg.48, amended: SSI 2014/267 Reg.8
Reg.67, amended: SSI 2014/267 Reg.9
Reg.67, applied: SSI 2014/319 Sch.1
para.13, Sch.2 para.23, Sch.3 para.13, Sch.4
para.8
Sch.1A, added: SSI 2014/267 Sch.1
Sch.1 Part 1, added: SSI 2014/267 Reg.10
Sch.1 Part 1, amended: SSI 2014/267 Reg.10
Sch.1 Part 2 para.2, amended: SSI 2014/267
Reg.10
Sch.4 Part 2 para.13, amended: SI 2014/469
Sch.3 para.206
Sch.4 Part 2 para.13A, added: SI 2014/469
Sch.3 para.206
Sch.4 Part 2 para.20, amended: SSI
2014/267 Reg.12
Sch.7 Part 1 para.2, amended: SSI 2014/267
Reg.13
Sch.7 Part 2 para.4, amended: SSI 2014/267
Reg.13
Sch.10 Part 1 para.3, amended: SSI
2014/267 Reg.14
Sch.10 Part 1 para.5, amended: SSI
2014/267 Reg.14
Sch.10 Part 2 para.7, amended: SSI
2014/267 Reg.14
Sch.10 Part 3 para.11, amended: SSI
2014/267 Reg.14
Sch.10 Part 3 para.13, amended: SSI
2014/267 Reg.14

2013

**4. Sports Grounds and Sporting Events
(Designation) (Scotland) Amendment Order
2013**
revoked: SSI 2014/5 Sch.3
**8. Scottish Road Works Register (Prescribed
Fees) Regulations 2013**
revoked: SSI 2014/58 Reg.4
**28. A9 and A82 Trunk Roads (Kessock Bridge)
(Temporary Prohibitions on Use and Speed
Limits) Order 2013**
revoked: SSI 2014/198 Art.3

**34. Non-Domestic Rates (Levying) (Scotland)
Amendment Regulations 2013**
revoked: SSI 2014/30 Reg.6
35. Police Service of Scotland Regulations 2013
Reg.2, amended: SSI 2014/68 Sch.2 para.2
Reg.11, amended: SSI 2014/67 Reg.48
Reg.18, amended: SSI 2014/1 Reg.2
Reg.18, applied: SSI 2014/1 Reg.3
**40. National Assistance (Sums for Personal
Requirements) (Scotland) Regulations 2013**
revoked: SSI 2014/39 Reg.3
**41. National Assistance (Assessment of
Resources) Amendment (Scotland) Regulations
2013**
revoked: SSI 2014/38 Reg.5
**44. Local Government Finance (Scotland)
Order 2013**
Art.2, revoked: SSI 2014/36 Art.5
Sch.1, amended: SSI 2014/36 Art.5
**48. Council Tax Reduction (Scotland)
Amendment Regulations 2013**
Reg.3, varied: 2014 c.6 s.126
**50. Rehabilitation of Offenders Act 1974
(Exclusions and Exceptions) (Scotland) Order
2013**
Sch.1 para.10, substituted: SI 2014/1638
Sch.13 para.30
Sch.1 para.10A, added: SI 2014/1942
Reg.18
Sch.3 para.3, amended: SI 2014/1638 Sch.13
para.30, SI 2014/1942 Reg.18
Sch.4 Part 3 para.4, amended: SI 2014/1638
Sch.13 para.30
**59. Fees in the Registers of Scotland
(Consequential Provisions) Amendment Order
2013**
revoked: SSI 2014/188 Sch.2
**60. Police Service of Scotland (Conduct)
Regulations 2013**
Reg.1, revoked: SSI 2014/68 Reg.4
Reg.24, applied: SSI 2014/68 Reg.22
Sch.1, revoked: SSI 2014/68 Reg.4
**61. Police Service of Scotland (Performance)
Regulations 2013**
Reg.1, revoked: SSI 2014/67 Reg.4
Reg.5, applied: SSI 2014/67 Reg.4
**62. Police Service of Scotland (Senior Officers)
(Conduct) Regulations 2013**
Reg.2, amended: SSI 2014/68 Sch.2 para.1
Reg.4, amended: SSI 2014/68 Sch.2 para.1
Reg.5, amended: SSI 2014/68 Sch.2 para.1

Reg.6, amended: SSI 2014/68 Sch.2 para.1

Reg.16, amended: SSI 2014/68 Sch.2 para.1

Reg.20, amended: SSI 2014/68 Sch.2 para.1

Reg.23, amended: SSI 2014/68 Sch.2 para.1

Reg.25, amended: SSI 2014/68 Sch.2 para.1

Reg.26, amended: SSI 2014/68 Sch.2 para.1

63. Police Appeals Tribunals (Scotland) Rules 2013

r.2, amended: SSI 2014/67 Reg.47, SSI 2014/68 Sch.2 para.3

108. Community Care (Personal Care and Nursing Care) (Scotland) Amendment Regulations 2013

revoked: SSI 2014/91 Reg.3

119. Police and Fire Reform (Scotland) Act 2012 (Consequential Modifications and Savings) Order 2013

Sch.1 Part 2 para.22, revoked: SSI 2014/200 Reg.4

Sch.1 Part 2 para.32, revoked: SSI 2014/147 Sch.2

137. Welfare Reform (Consequential Amendments) (Scotland) (No.2) Regulations 2013

Reg.18, revoked: SSI 2014/296 Reg.10

148. Home Energy Assistance Scheme (Scotland) Regulations 2013

Reg.4, amended: SSI 2014/40 Reg.3

Reg.6, amended: SSI 2014/40 Reg.4

155. Town and Country Planning (Development Management Procedure) (Scotland) Regulations 2013

Sch.5, amended: SI 2014/469 Sch.3 para.209

Sch.5 para.3, amended: SI 2014/469 Sch.3 para.209

Sch.5 para.3A, added: SI 2014/469 Sch.3 para.209

174. National Health Service Superannuation Scheme (2008 Section) (Scotland) Regulations 2013

Reg.1, amended: SSI 2014/154 Reg.18

Reg.1, amended: SSI 2014/154 Reg.25

Reg.2, amended: SSI 2014/154 Reg.16

Reg.2, amended: SSI 2014/43 Reg.6, SSI 2014/154 Reg.20

Reg.2, amended: SSI 2014/43 Reg.8, SSI 2014/154 Reg.27

Reg.4, amended: SSI 2014/43 Reg.7, SSI 2014/154 Reg.21

Reg.6, amended: SSI 2014/154 Reg.19

Reg.6, amended: SSI 2014/154 Reg.22

Reg.6, amended: SSI 2014/154 Reg.26

Reg.6, amended: SSI 2014/154 Reg.28

Reg.10A, added: SSI 2014/154 Reg.23

Reg.10A, added: SSI 2014/154 Reg.29

Reg.13A, added: SSI 2014/154 Reg.17

Reg.14, amended: SSI 2014/154 Reg.24

177. European Union (Amendments in respect of the Accession of Croatia) (Scotland) Regulations 2013

Sch.1 para.9, revoked: SSI 2014/364 Reg.50

194. Children's Hearings (Scotland) Act 2011 (Rules of Procedure in Children's Hearings) Rules 2013

Part 4 r.13, applied: SSI 2014/113 Reg.3

200. Children's Legal Assistance (Scotland) Regulations 2013

Sch.2 para.8, amended: SSI 2014/90 Sch.1 Part 3

220. Public Services Reform (Functions of the Common Services Agency for the Scottish Health Service) (Scotland) Order 2013

revoked: 2014 asp 9 s.71

225. Debt Arrangement Scheme (Scotland) Amendment Regulations 2013

Reg.7, revoked: SSI 2014/294 Reg.6

227. Registration of Social Workers and Social Service Workers in Care Services (Scotland) Regulations 2013

Reg.5, amended: SSI 2014/192 Reg.2

Sch.1, amended: SSI 2014/192 Reg.2

229. Sports Grounds and Sporting Events (Designation) (Scotland) Amendment (No.2) Order 2013

revoked: SSI 2014/5 Sch.3

248. M898/A898 Trunk Road (Erskine Bridge) (Temporary Prohibition of Traffic and 40mph Speed Restriction) (No.2) Order 2013

revoked: SSI 2014/204 Art.5

266. Food Additives, Flavourings, Enzymes and Extraction Solvents (Scotland) Regulations 2013

Reg.18, revoked (in part): SSI 2014/312 Sch.4 Part 1

291. Act of Sederunt (Commissary Business) 2013

Sch.4 Part 1, amended: SSI 2014/265 Art.2

305. Fruit Juices and Fruit Nectars (Scotland) Regulations 2013

Reg.15, amended: SSI 2014/312 Sch.5 para.18

307. Animal By-Products (Enforcement) (Scotland) Regulations 2013
  applied: SI 2014/1894 Reg.30, Sch.3 para.3, Sch.3 para.13

318. Protected Trust Deeds (Scotland) Regulations 2013
  Reg.2, amended: SSI 2014/290 Reg.7
  Reg.7, amended: SSI 2014/290 Reg.7
  Reg.8, amended: SSI 2014/290 Reg.7
  Reg.10, amended: SSI 2014/290 Reg.7
  Reg.11, amended: SSI 2014/290 Reg.7
  Reg.19, amended: SSI 2014/290 Reg.10
  Reg.21, amended: SSI 2014/290 Reg.8
  Reg.23, amended: SSI 2014/290 Reg.8, Reg.9, Reg.10
  Reg.24, amended: SSI 2014/290 Reg.8, Reg.10
  Reg.24, applied: SSI 2014/227 Reg.11
  Reg.25, applied: SSI 2014/227 Reg.8
  Sch.1, amended: SSI 2014/290 Reg.10, Sch.1

2014

5. Sports Grounds and Sporting Events (Designation) (Scotland) Order 2014
  Sch.1, amended: SSI 2014/374 Art.2

6. Common Agricultural Policy Schemes (Cross-Compliance) (Scotland) Amendment Regulations 2014
  revoked: SSI 2014/325 Reg.10

21. Post-16 Education (Scotland) Act 2013 (Commencement No 3 and Transitory and Savings Provisions) Order 2014
  Sch.2, amended: SSI 2014/52 Art.7

23. Local Government Pension Scheme (Miscellaneous Amendments) (Scotland) Regulations 2014
  revoked: SSI 2014/233 Sch.1

25. Self-directed Support (Direct Payments) (Scotland) Regulations 2014
  Reg.3, amended: SSI 2014/65 Reg.4
  Reg.3A, added: SSI 2014/65 Reg.4

36. Local Government Finance (Scotland) Order 2014
  Sch.1, substituted: SSI 2014/74 Sch.1
  Sch.2, substituted: SSI 2014/74 Sch.2

63. Brucellosis (Scotland) Amendment Order 2014
  Art.2, revoked (in part): SSI 2014/72 Art.2

67. Police Service of Scotland (Performance) Regulations 2014
  applied: SSI 2014/68 Reg.26, Reg.27

83. Electronic Documents (Scotland) Regulations 2014
  applied: SSI 2014/150 Reg.7
  Reg.1, amended: SSI 2014/347 Reg.9
  Reg.5, added: SSI 2014/347 Reg.9

84. Road Traffic (Permitted Parking Area and Special Parking Area) (Argyll and Bute Council) Designation Order 2014
  referred to: SSI 2014/86 Reg.2

99. Act of Sederunt (Fitness for Judicial Office Tribunal Rules) 2014
  revoked: SSI 2014/102 r.16

110. Firefighters&rsquo Pension Scheme (Scotland) Amendment (No.2) Order 2014
  Sch.1 para.1, amended: SSI 2014/149 Art.7
  Sch.1 para.1, revoked (in part): SSI 2014/149 Art.7
  Sch.1 para.12, amended: SSI 2014/149 Art.8

142. Town and Country Planning (General Permitted Development) (Scotland) Amendment Order 2014
  Sch.1, substituted: SSI 2014/184 Art.2

150. Land Register Rules etc (Scotland) Regulations 2014
  Reg.7, amended: SSI 2014/347 Reg.8
  Sch.1 Part 4, amended: SSI 2014/346 Art.5

156. A90 Trunk Road (Temporary Northbound Slip Road to Ferrytoll Roundabout) (Temporary Prohibition of Overtaking and Temporary Speed Restrictions) Order 2014
  revoked: SSI 2014/228 Art.10

164. Local Government Pension Scheme (Scotland) Regulations 2014
  applied: SSI 2014/233 Reg.4, Reg.12, Reg.14, Reg.17, Reg.19, Reg.24
  Reg.2, applied: SSI 2014/233 Reg.3
  Reg.3, applied: SSI 2014/233 Reg.5, Reg.7
  Reg.3, disapplied: SSI 2014/233 Reg.5
  Reg.9, applied: SSI 2014/233 Reg.4, Sch.2 para.4
  Reg.11, referred to: SSI 2014/233 Reg.8
  Reg.16, applied: SSI 2014/233 Reg.4, Reg.8, Reg.11, Sch.2 para.4
  Reg.17, applied: SSI 2014/233 Reg.4, Reg.11, Reg.15
  Reg.17, disapplied: SSI 2014/233 Reg.15
  Reg.18, applied: SSI 2014/233 Reg.14
  Reg.20, applied: SSI 2014/233 Reg.8

Reg.20, disapplied: SSI 2014/233 Reg.8
Reg.21, applied: SSI 2014/233 Reg.8
Reg.21, referred to: SSI 2014/233 Reg.8
Reg.22, applied: SSI 2014/233 Sch.2 para.6
Reg.29, applied: SSI 2014/233 Reg.4,
Reg.11, Sch.2 para.1, Sch.2 para.5
Reg.30, applied: SSI 2014/233 Reg.4,
Reg.11
Reg.31, referred to: SSI 2014/233 Sch.2
para.4
Reg.32, applied: SSI 2014/233 Reg.13
Reg.34, applied: SSI 2014/233 Reg.11
Reg.36, applied: SSI 2014/233 Reg.11
Reg.37, applied: SSI 2014/233 Reg.4,
Reg.12
Reg.38, applied: SSI 2014/233 Reg.17
Reg.39, applied: SSI 2014/233 Reg.17
Reg.58, applied: SSI 2014/233 Sch.2 para.2
Reg.68, applied: SSI 2014/233 Reg.22
Reg.70, applied: SSI 2014/233 Reg.23
Reg.82, amended: SSI 2014/293 Sch.1
para.13
Reg.93, applied: SSI 2014/233 Reg.1
Sch.1, referred to: SSI 2014/233 Reg.3
Sch.1, varied: SSI 2014/233 Reg.17
188. Registers of Scotland (Fees) Order 2014
Sch.1 Part 1 para.1, amended: SSI 2014/346
Art.6

212. Marriage and Civil Partnership (Scotland) Act 2014 (Commencement No 2 and Saving Provisions) Order 2014
Art.3, amended: SSI 2014/218 Art.2
Sch.1, substituted: SSI 2014/218 Sch.1
217. Teachers Pension Scheme (Scotland) Regulations 2014
revoked: SSI 2014/292 Reg.215
Reg.1, revoked: SSI 2014/292 Reg.215
260. South Arran Marine Conservation Order 2014
Art.2, amended: SSI 2014/297 Art.2
Art.4, amended: SSI 2014/297 Art.2
Art.5, amended: SSI 2014/297 Art.2
290. Common Financial Tool etc (Scotland) Regulations 2014
applied: SSI 2014/296 Reg.4
295. Charities Accounts (Scotland) Amendment Regulations 2014
revoked: SSI 2014/335 Reg.5
327. Conservation of Salmon (Annual Close Time and Catch and Release) (Scotland) Regulations 2014
Sch.1, amended: SSI 2014/357 Reg.2
359. Victims and Witnesses (Scotland) Act 2014 (Commencement No 3 and Transitional Provision) Order 2014
varied: 2014 asp 1 s.34

STATUTORY RULES ISSUED BY THE UK PARLIAMENT

1898

248. Compressed Acetylene in admixture with oil-gas-Order (No.5) 1898
revoked: SI 2014/1639 Sch.3 Part 2

1905

1128. Compressed Acetylene in admixture with oil-gas-Order 1905
revoked: SI 2014/1639 Sch.3 Part 2

1919

809. Compressed Acetylene in Porous Substances-Order (No.9) 1919
revoked: SI 2014/1639 Sch.3 Part 2

1922

184. Government of Ireland (Companies, Societies, etc.) Order 1922
Art.22, disapplied: 2014 c.14 s.142

1924

1129. Order of the Secretary of State (No.11) dated September 20, 1924 Making Byelaws as to the Conveyance of Explosives on Roads, and in Certain Special Cases 1924
revoked: SI 2014/1638 Sch.14 Part 2

1926

823. Picric acid and picrates etc-Order in Council (No.26) 1926
  revoked: SI 2014/1638 Sch.14 Part 2

1929

952. Petroleum-spirit (Motor Vehicles etc.) Regulations 1929
  applied: SI 2014/1637 Reg.22
  revoked: SI 2014/1637 Sch.4 Part 1
  Reg.2, applied: SI 2014/1637 Reg.22, Sch.2 para.6
  Reg.4, applied: SI 2014/1637 Reg.22, Sch.2 para.6
993. Petroleum (Mixtures) Order 1929
  revoked: SI 2014/1637 Sch.4 Part 1

1931

1140. Asbestos Industry Regulations 1931
  see *McDonald v Department for Communities and Local Government* [2013] EWCA Civ 1346, [2014] P.I.Q.R. P7 (CA (Civ Div)), Dyson LJ; see *McDonald v Department for Communities and Local Government* [2014] UKSC 53, [2014] 3 W.L.R. 1197 (SC), Lord Neuberger PSC
  Reg.2, see *McDonald v Department for Communities and Local Government* [2013] EWCA Civ 1346, [2014] P.I.Q.R. P7 (CA (Civ Div)), Dyson LJ; see *McDonald v Department for Communities and Local Government* [2014] UKSC 53, [2014] 3 W.L.R. 1197 (SC), Lord Neuberger PSC

1934

1346. London Cab Order 1934
  Art.20, amended: SI 2014/107 Sch.1 para.1

1937

54. Acetylene, Restrictions-Order in Council 1937
  applied: SI 2014/1639 Reg.15

  revoked: SI 2014/1639 Sch.3 Part 2

1938

610. Factories Act (Docks, Building and Engineering Construction etc.) Modification Regulations 1938
  revoked: SI 2014/486 Sch.1

1944

500. War Pensions (Coastguards) Scheme 1944
  disapplied: SI 2014/3229 Sch.2 para.6
  referred to: SI 2014/3061 Sch.1 para.12, Sch.2 para.10
  varied: SI 2014/3061 Sch.2 para.10

1947

805. Compressed Acetylene Order 1947
  revoked: SI 2014/1639 Sch.3 Part 2

1948

707. Factories Act, 1937 (Extension of Section 46) Regulations 1948
  revoked: SI 2014/486 Sch.1
1411. Civil Aviation (Births, Deaths and Missing Persons) Regulations 1948
  disapplied: SI 2014/3229 Sch.2 para.6
2361. Airways Corporations (General Staff Pensions) Regulations 1948
  disapplied: SI 2014/3229 Sch.2 para.6

1949

917. Coal Industry (Superannuation Scheme) (Winding Up, No 1) Regulations 1949
  revoked: SI 2014/1986 Sch.1

1950

792. Town and Country Planning (Churches, Places of Religious Worship and Burial Grounds) Regulations 1950
  disapplied: SI 2014/2384 Art.23
915. Schools (Scotland) Code, 1950
  Reg.5, see *Educational Institute of Scotland v Glasgow City Council* [2014] CSIH 13, 2014 S.C. 457 (IH (Ex Div)), Lady Paton

1951

393. Coal Industry (Superannuation Scheme) (Winding Up, No 2) Regulations 1951
  revoked: SI 2014/1986 Sch.1
527. Airways Corporations (Pilots Pensions) Regulations 1951
  disapplied: SI 2014/3229 Sch.2 para.6
2010. Coal Industry (Superannuation Scheme) (Winding Up, No 3) Regulations 1951
  revoked: SI 2014/1986 Sch.1

1952

1869. Marriage (Authorised Persons) Regulations 1952
  Reg.2, amended: SI 2014/107 Sch.1 para.2, SI 2014/3061 Sch.1 para.1
  Reg.4, amended: SI 2014/107 Sch.1 para.2
  Reg.15, amended: SI 2014/107 Sch.1 para.2
  Reg.16, amended: SI 2014/107 Sch.1 para.2
  Reg.17, amended: SI 2014/107 Sch.1 para.2
  Reg.18, amended: SI 2014/107 Sch.1 para.2
  Reg.19, amended: SI 2014/107 Sch.1 para.2
  Reg.20, amended: SI 2014/107 Sch.1 para.2
  Reg.21, amended: SI 2014/107 Sch.1 para.2
2018. Coal Industry (Superannuation Scheme) (Winding Up, No 4) Regulations 1952
  revoked: SI 2014/1986 Sch.1

1953

845. Coal Industry (Superannuation Scheme) (Winding Up, No 5) Regulations 1953
  revoked: SI 2014/1986 Sch.1

1296. Airways Corporations (Radio, Navigating and Engineer Officers Pensions) Regulations 1953
  disapplied: SI 2014/3229 Sch.2 para.6

1954

155. Coal Industry (Superannuation Scheme) (Winding Up, No 6) Regulations 1954
  revoked: SI 2014/1986 Sch.1
219. Foreign Compensation (Hungary) (Registration) Order 1954
  varied: SI 2014/2708 Art.5
221. Foreign Compensation (Roumania) (Registration) Order 1954
  varied: SI 2014/2708 Art.5
970. Coal Industry (Superannuation Scheme) (Winding Up, No 7) Regulations 1954
  revoked: SI 2014/1986 Sch.1

1955

281. Coal Industry (Superannuation Scheme) (Winding Up, No 8) Regulations 1955
  revoked: SI 2014/1986 Sch.1
1345. Coal Industry (Superannuation Scheme) (Winding Up, No 9) Regulations 1955
  revoked: SI 2014/1986 Sch.1

1956

248. Coal Industry (Superannuation Scheme) (Winding Up, No 10) Regulations 1956
  revoked: SI 2014/1986 Sch.1
1943. Stratified Ironstone, Shale and Fireclay Mines (Explosives) Regulations 1956
  applied: SI 2014/1638 Reg.47

1957

87. Airways Corporations (General Staff, Pilots and Officers Pensions) (Amendment) Regulations 1957
  disapplied: SI 2014/3229 Sch.2 para.6
156. Coal Industry (Superannuation Scheme) (Winding Up, No 11) Regulations 1957
  revoked: SI 2014/1986 Sch.1

859. Petroleum (Liquid Methane) Order 1957
revoked: SI 2014/1637 Sch.4 Part 1

1958

878. Dark Smoke (Permitted Periods) (Vessels) Regulations 1958
revoked (in part): SI 2014/3318 Sch.4

1959

406. Service Departments Registers Order, 1959
Art.1, amended: SI 2014/3061 Sch.1 para.2
Art.3, amended: SI 2014/3061 Sch.1 para.2
2258. Miscellaneous Mines (Explosives) Regulations 1959
applied: SI 2014/1638 Reg.47

1960

105. Movement of Animals (Records) Order 1960
applied: SI 2014/2337 Art.10
250. Cycle Racing on Highways Regulations 1960
Reg.5, varied: SI 2014/887 Reg.3

1962

2715. British Transport Reorganisation (Pensions of Employees) (No.2) Order 1962
disapplied: SI 2014/3229 Sch.2 para.6
referred to: SI 2014/3061 Sch.1 para.12,
Sch.2 para.10
varied: SI 2014/3061 Sch.2 para.10

1963

614. Consular Conventions (Spanish State) Order 1963
varied: SI 2014/2708 Art.5
615. Consular Conventions (Income Tax) (Kingdom of Denmark) Order 1963
varied: SI 2014/2708 Art.5

815. Meadow Bank Mine (Explosives) Special Regulations 1963
applied: SI 2014/3248 Reg.73
Reg.4, referred to: SI 2014/3248 Reg.73
Reg.4, varied: SI 2014/3248 Reg.73
Reg.6, referred to: SI 2014/3248 Reg.73
Reg.6, varied: SI 2014/3248 Reg.73
Reg.9, referred to: SI 2014/3248 Reg.73
Reg.9, varied: SI 2014/3248 Reg.73
1108. Air Corporations (General Staff, Pilots and Officers Pensions) (Amendment) (No.2) Regulations 1963
disapplied: SI 2014/3229 Sch.2 para.6

1964

1171. Artificial Insemination of Pigs (Scotland) Regulations 1964
Reg.8, amended: SI 2014/1894 Reg.43
1172. Artificial Insemination of Pigs (England and Wales) Regulations 1964
Reg.7, amended: SI 2014/1894 Reg.43
1755. Ecclesiastical Jurisdiction (Discipline) Rules 1964
r.49., applied: SI 2014/895 Sch.2 para.4

1965

620. Probation (Compensation) Regulations 1965
Reg.24, amended: SI 2014/107 Sch.1 para.3
Reg.25, amended: SI 2014/107 Sch.1 para.3
Reg.26, amended: SI 2014/107 Sch.1 para.3
1776. Rules of the Supreme Court (Revision) 1965
see *Chandra v Brooke North (A Firm)*
[2013] EWCA Civ 1559, [2014] T.C.L.R. 1
(CA (Civ Div)), Laws LJ
Ord.20 r.5, see *Chandra v Brooke North (A Firm)* [2013] EWCA Civ 1559, [2014]
T.C.L.R. 1 (CA (Civ Div)), Laws LJ
1824. Nuclear Installations (Dangerous Occurrences) Regulations 1965
Reg.4, substituted: SI 2014/469 Sch.3
para.29

1967

739. Air Corporations (General Staff, Pilots and Officers Pensions) (Amendment) Regulations 1967
　　disapplied: SI 2014/3229 Sch.2 para.6
1194. County Court (Records of Proceedings) Regulations 1967
　　Sch.1, amended: SI 2014/879 Art.2
1353. Trunk Roads (40 m.p.h Speed Limit) (No.1) (Wales) Order 1967
　　varied: SI 2014/128 Art.6
1889. Harbour Reorganisation (Compensation to Employees) Regulations 1967
　　disapplied: SI 2014/3229 Sch.2 para.6
　　referred to: SI 2014/3061 Sch.1 para.12, Sch.2 para.10
　　Reg.28, varied: SI 2014/3061 Sch.2 para.10
　　Reg.32, varied: SI 2014/3061 Sch.2 para.10
　　Reg.39, varied: SI 2014/3061 Sch.2 para.10
　　Sch.1, varied: SI 2014/3061 Sch.2 para.10

1968

1728. Children (Performances) Regulations 1968
　　revoked (in part): SI 2014/3309 Sch.1, SSI 2014/372 Reg.32
2049. Registration of Births, Deaths and Marriages Regulations 1968
　　Reg.11, amended: SI 2014/3061 Sch.1 para.3

1969

411. Clean Air (Height of Chimneys) (Exemption) Regulations 1969
　　revoked (in part): SI 2014/3318 Sch.4
592. Civil Aviation Act 1949 (Overseas Territories) Order 1969
　　applied: SI 2014/2925, SI 2014/2926, SI 2014/3281
745. Trunk Roads (50 M.P.H.Speed Limit) (Wales) (No.1) Order 1969
　　varied: SI 2014/3420 Art.7
1037. Co-operative and Community Benefit Societies (Group Accounts) Regulations 1969
　　amended: SI 2014/1815 Sch.1 para.1
　　Reg.1, amended: SI 2014/1815 Sch.1 para.1

1262. Clean Air (Arrestment Plant) (Exemption) Regulations 1969
　　revoked (in part): SI 2014/3318 Sch.4
1263. Clean Air (Emission of Dark Smoke) (Exemption) Regulations 1969
　　Sch.1, amended: SI 2014/1638 Sch.13 para.9
1576. London Holyhead Trunk Road (Prohibition of Waiting) (Clearways) Order 1969
　　varied: SI 2014/2469 Art.7

1970

104. Swansea-Manchester Trunk Road (Prohibition of Waiting) (Clearways) Order 1970
　　Sch.1, varied: SI 2014/2269 Art.14
187. British Transport (Compensation to Employees) Regulations 1970
　　disapplied: SI 2014/3229 Sch.2 para.6
　　referred to: SI 2014/3061 Sch.1 para.12, Sch.2 para.10
　　Reg.27, varied: SI 2014/3061 Sch.2 para.10
　　Reg.32, varied: SI 2014/3061 Sch.2 para.10
　　Reg.35, varied: SI 2014/3061 Sch.2 para.10
　　Sch.2, varied: SI 2014/3061 Sch.2 para.10
484. Valuation Roll Amendment (Scotland) Order 1970
　　varied: SI 2014/2708 Art.5
1539. Foreign Marriage Order 1970
　　revoked (in part): SI 2014/1110 Art.17
　　Art.6, applied: SI 2014/3061 Sch.4 para.1
　　Art.7, applied: SI 2014/3061 Sch.4 para.2
2019. London Transport (Compensation to Employees) Regulations 1970
　　referred to: SI 2014/3061 Sch.1 para.12

1971

218. Lands Tribunal for Scotland Rules 1971
　　Sch.2, amended: SSI 2014/24 Sch.1
230. London Authorities (Parks and Open Spaces) (Miscellaneous Property) Order 1971
　　see *Redbridge LBC v Dhinsa* [2014] EWCA Civ 178, [2014] I.C.R. 834 (CA (Civ Div)), Longmore LJ
531. Diseases of Animals (Extension of Definitions) Order 1971
　　revoked: SSI 2014/63 Art.3

809. Magistrates Courts (Attachment of Earnings) Rules 1971

    r.4, revoked: SI 2014/879 Art.4

    r.6, amended: SI 2014/879 Art.5

    r.6, revoked (in part): SI 2014/879 Art.5

    r.8, revoked: SI 2014/879 Art.6

    r.9, amended: SI 2014/879 Art.7

    r.13, revoked (in part): SI 2014/879 Art.8

    r.14, amended: SI 2014/879 Art.9

    r.15, amended: SI 2014/879 Art.10

    r.18, amended: SI 2014/879 Art.11

    r.18, revoked (in part): SI 2014/879 Art.11

    r.19, revoked: SI 2014/879 Art.12

    r.23, amended: SI 2014/879 Art.13

    r.23, revoked (in part): SI 2014/879 Art.13

1377. Mines and Quarries (Tips) Regulations 1971

    applied: SI 2014/3248 Reg.65

    Reg.2, applied: SI 2014/3248 Reg.72

    Reg.8, applied: SI 2014/3248 Reg.65

    Reg.9, applied: SI 2014/3248 Reg.72

    Reg.10, applied: SI 2014/3248 Reg.71

    Reg.12, applied: SI 2014/3248 Reg.72

    Reg.18, applied: SI 2014/3248 Reg.72

1861. Blood Tests (Evidence of Paternity) Regulations 1971

    Sch.1, amended: SI 2014/879 Art.14

1991. Magistrates Courts (Blood Tests) Rules 1971

    revoked: SI 2014/879 Sch.1

2008. Courts (Compensation to Officers) Regulations 1971

    Reg.26, amended: SI 2014/107 Sch.1 para.4

    Reg.27, amended: SI 2014/107 Sch.1 para.4

    Reg.28, amended: SI 2014/107 Sch.1 para.4

    Reg.33, amended: SI 2014/107 Sch.1 para.4

    Reg.36, amended: SI 2014/107 Sch.1 para.4

2084. Indictments (Procedure) Rules 1971

    r.6., applied: SI 2014/1610 r.3_1, r.14_1

1972

632. Transport Holding Company (Compensation to Employees) Regulations 1972

    disapplied: SI 2014/3229 Sch.2 para.6

    referred to: SI 2014/3061 Sch.1 para.12, Sch.2 para.10

    Reg.27, varied: SI 2014/3061 Sch.2 para.10

    Reg.32, varied: SI 2014/3061 Sch.2 para.10

    Reg.35, varied: SI 2014/3061 Sch.2 para.10

    Sch.1, varied: SI 2014/3061 Sch.2 para.10

765. Premium Savings Bonds Regulations 1972

    Reg.5, amended: SI 2014/1182 Reg.2

963. Employers Liability (Defective Equipment and Compulsory Insurance) (Northern Ireland) Order 1972

    Art.7, applied: 2014 c.1 s.18

1265. Health and Personal Social Services (Northern Ireland) Order 1972

    applied: 2014 c.23 Sch.1 para.4

    disapplied: 2014 c.23 Sch.1 para.1, Sch.1 para.2, Sch.1 para.3

    referred to: 2014 c.23 Sch.1 para.1

    Part IV, applied: SI 2014/3282 Sch.1 para.12

    Art.15, applied: 2014 c.23 s.49, s.50, s.73, Sch.1 para.4

    Art.36, amended: 2014 c.23 Sch.1 para.5

1298. Pensions Increase (Annual Review) Order 1972

    referred to: SI 2014/668 Sch.1

1610. Immigration (Control of Entry through Republic of Ireland) Order 1972

    Art.2, amended: SI 2014/2475 Art.3

    Art.2, revoked (in part): SI 2014/2475 Art.3

    Art.3, amended: SI 2014/2475 Art.3

    Art.3A, added: SI 2014/2475 Art.3

    Art.4, amended: SI 2014/2475 Art.3

    Art.4, revoked (in part): SI 2014/2475 Art.3

    Sch.1, added: SI 2014/2475 Sch.1

1635. Merchant Shipping (Maintenance of Seamen's Dependants) Regulations 1972

    Reg.4, amended: SI 2014/107 Sch.1 para.5, SI 2014/3229 Sch.6 para.1

1698. Merchant Shipping (Seamen's Allotments) Regulations 1972

    Reg.2, substituted: SI 2014/1614 Reg.4

    Reg.3, amended: SI 2014/1614 Reg.4

    Reg.6, added: SI 2014/1614 Reg.4

1700. Merchant Shipping (Seamen's Wages and Accounts) Regulations 1972

    Reg.1, amended: SI 2014/1614 Reg.5

    Reg.2, revoked: SI 2014/1614 Reg.5

    Reg.4, amended: SI 2014/1614 Reg.5

    Reg.5, amended: SI 2014/1614 Reg.5

    Reg.5, revoked (in part): SI 2014/1614 Reg.5

    Reg.8, amended: SI 2014/1614 Reg.5

    Sch.1, revoked: SI 2014/1614 Reg.5

1973

798. Misuse of Drugs (Safe Custody) Regulations 1973
Sch.1 para.3, amended: SI 2014/1275 Reg.7

1370. Pensions Increase (Annual Review) Order 1973
referred to: SI 2014/668 Sch.1

1642. Dairy Herd Conversion Premium Regulations 1973
revoked: SI 2014/1902 Sch.1

1729. West Yorkshire Passenger Transport Area (Establishment of Executive) Order 1973
revoked: SI 2014/864 Art.8

1974

460. Town and Country Planning (Development Plans) Order 1974
revoked (in part): SI 2014/683 Sch.1

502. Motorways Traffic (Speed Limit) Regulations 1974
Reg.3, applied: SI 2014/158 Art.4
Reg.3, disapplied: SI 2014/176 Art.10
Reg.3, varied: SI 2014/158 Art.4, SI 2014/1317 Art.4, SI 2014/1515 Art.6, SI 2014/1595 Art.12

812. Local Government Superannuation (Scotland) Regulations 1974
applied: SSI 2014/233 Reg.3, Reg.17, Reg.22, Reg.24
varied: SSI 2014/233 Reg.24

1373. Pensions Increase (Annual Review) Order 1974
referred to: SI 2014/668 Sch.1

1885. Explosives Acts 1875 and 1923 etc (Repeals and Modifications) Regulations 1974
Reg.2, revoked (in part): SI 2014/1638 Sch.14 Part 2
Reg.3, revoked: SI 2014/1638 Sch.14 Part 2
Sch.1, amended: SI 2014/1638 Sch.14 Part 2
Sch.2 para.1, revoked: SI 2014/1638 Sch.14 Part 2
Sch.2 para.5, revoked: SI 2014/1638 Sch.13 para.10
Sch.2 para.6, revoked: SI 2014/1638 Sch.14 Part 2
Sch.3, revoked: SI 2014/1638 Sch.14 Part 2

1942. Petroleum (Regulation) Acts 1928 and 1936 (Repeals and Modifications) Regulations 1974
revoked: SI 2014/1637 Sch.4 Part 1

1943. Offices, Shops and Railway Premises Act 1963 (Repeals and Modifications) Regulations 1974
revoked: SI 2014/486 Sch.1

2013. Mines and Quarries Acts 1954 to 1971 (Repeals and Modifications) Regulations 1974
Reg.2, revoked (in part): SI 2014/3248 Sch.4 Part 2
Reg.3, revoked (in part): SI 2014/3248 Sch.4 Part 2
Reg.7, revoked (in part): SI 2014/3248 Sch.4 Part 2
Sch.1, revoked (in part): SI 2014/3248 Sch.4 Part 2
Sch.2 Part I para.1, revoked (in part): SI 2014/3248 Sch.4 Part 2
Sch.2 Part I para.4, revoked (in part): SI 2014/3248 Sch.4 Part 2
Sch.2 Part I para.12, revoked (in part): SI 2014/3248 Sch.4 Part 2
Sch.2 Part I para.16, revoked (in part): SI 2014/3248 Sch.4 Part 2
Sch.2 Part I para.19, revoked (in part): SI 2014/3248 Sch.4 Part 2

2040. Health and Safety Licensing Appeals (Hearings Procedure) Rules 1974
applied: SI 2014/1637 Reg.11, Reg.15
referred to: SI 2014/1637 Reg.11, Reg.15

2056. Nuclear Installations Act 1965 etc (Repeals and Modifications) Regulations 1974
Reg.2, revoked (in part): SI 2014/469 Sch.3 para.210

2068. Health and Safety Licensing Appeals (Hearings Procedure) (Scotland) Rules 1974
referred to: SI 2014/1637 Reg.11, Reg.15

2160. Fuel and Electricity (Heating) (Control) Order 1974
revoked: SI 2014/1509 Art.2

2166. Explosives Acts 1875 and 1923 etc (Repeals and Modifications) (Amendment) Regulations 1974
revoked: SI 2014/1638 Sch.14 Part 2

2211. Rabies (Importation of Dogs, Cats and Other Mammals) Order 1974
Art.2, amended: SI 2014/3158 Sch.1 para.2
Art.4, amended: SI 2014/3158 Sch.1 para.3
Art.5, amended: SI 2014/3158 Sch.1 para.4

Art.6, amended: SI 2014/3158 Sch.1 para.5
Art.8, amended: SI 2014/3158 Sch.1 para.6
Art.12, amended: SI 2014/3158 Sch.1 para.7
Art.13, amended: SI 2014/3158 Sch.1 para.8
Art.14, amended: SI 2014/3158 Sch.1 para.9
Art.16, amended: SI 2014/3158 Sch.1
para.10
Art.17, amended: SI 2014/3158 Sch.1
para.11

1975

335. Health and Safety Inquiries (Procedure) Regulations 1975

applied: SI 2014/469 Sch.1 para.7
disapplied: SI 2014/469 Sch.1 para.7
Reg.2, amended: SI 2014/469 Sch.3
para.165
Reg.3, amended: SI 2014/469 Sch.3
para.166
Reg.4, amended: SI 2014/469 Sch.3
para.167
Reg.5, amended: SI 2014/469 Sch.3
para.168
Reg.5A, added: SI 2014/469 Sch.3 para.169
Reg.6, amended: SI 2014/469 Sch.3
para.170
Reg.7, amended: SI 2014/469 Sch.3
para.171
Reg.8, amended: SI 2014/469 Sch.3
para.172
Reg.9, amended: SI 2014/469 Sch.3
para.173
Reg.10, amended: SI 2014/469 Sch.3
para.174
Reg.11, substituted: SI 2014/469 Sch.3
para.175
Reg.12, added: SI 2014/469 Sch.3 para.176

438. Trunk Roads (Restricted Roads) (Kirkcudbrightshire) Order 1975

Sch.1, revoked: SSI 2014/247 Art.3

556. Social Security (Credits) Regulations 1975

Reg.8B, applied: SI 2014/1230 Reg.21,
Reg.26, Reg.27
Reg.8C, amended: SI 2014/3061 Sch.1
para.4
Reg.9C, amended: SI 2014/3255 Art.2
Sch.1 para.3, amended: SI 2014/3061 Sch.1
para.4

Sch.1 para.3, revoked (in part): SI
2014/3061 Sch.1 para.4

563. Social Security Benefit (Persons Abroad) Regulations 1975

Reg.5, applied: SI 2014/618 Reg.3, SI
2014/881 Reg.3

1011. Offices, Shops and Railway Premises Act 1963 (Repeals) Regulations 1975

revoked: SI 2014/486 Sch.1

1012. Factories Act 1961 (Repeals) Regulations 1975

revoked: SI 2014/486 Sch.1

1023. Rehabilitation of Offenders Act 1974 (Exceptions) Order 1975

applied: SI 2014/1977 Reg.5
see *R. (on the application of T) v Chief
Constable of Greater Manchester* [2014]
UKSC 35 (SC), Lord Neuberger JSC
Art.2, amended: SI 2014/1707 Art.3
Art.2A, applied: SI 2014/1920 Sch.1 para.20
Art.3, amended: SI 2014/1707 Art.4, SI
2014/1942 Reg.17
Art.3ZA, amended: SI 2014/1942 Reg.17
Art.4, amended: SI 2014/1707 Art.5
Sch.1 Part I para.16, substituted: SI
2014/1707 Art.6
Sch.1 Part II para.9, substituted: SI
2014/1707 Art.6
Sch.1 Part II para.14B, added: SI 2014/1707
Art.6
Sch.1 Part II para.14D, added: SI 2014/1707
Art.6
Sch.1 Part II para.18A, revoked: SI
2014/834 Sch.3 para.1
Sch.1 Part III para.8, amended: SI
2014/1638 Sch.13 para.11
Sch.1 Part III para.14, added: SI 2014/1707
Art.6
Sch.1 Part IV, amended: SI 2014/1707 Art.6
Sch.2 para.3, amended: SI 2014/1638 Sch.13
para.11
Sch.2 para.6, added: SI 2014/1942 Reg.17
Sch.3 para.13, substituted: SI 2014/1638
Sch.13 para.11
Sch.3 para.17A, added: SI 2014/1707 Art.7
Sch.3 para.19A, added: SI 2014/1942
Reg.17

1102. Mines and Quarries Acts 1954 to 1971 (Repeals and Modifications) Regulations 1975

revoked (in part): SI 2014/3248 Sch.4 Part 1

**1287. Land Compensation (Scotland)
Development Order 1975**
    Art.4, see *Network Rail Infrastructure Ltd v
Scottish Ministers* 2014 S.C. 15 (IH (2 Div)),
The Lord Justice Clerk (Carloway)
**1384. Pensions Increase (Annual Review) Order
1975**
    referred to: SI 2014/668 Sch.1

1976

**409. Social Security (Invalid Care Allowance)
Regulations 1976**
    Reg.8, amended: SI 2014/904 Reg.2
**516. Sale of Goods for Mothers and Children
(Designation and Charging) Regulations 1976**
    disapplied: SI 2014/3099 Reg.3
**1356. Pensions Increase (Annual Review) Order
1976**
    referred to: SI 2014/668 Sch.1
**2004. Factories Act 1961 etc (Repeals)
Regulations 1976**
    revoked: SI 2014/486 Sch.1
**2005. Offices, Shops and Railway Premises Act
1963 etc (Repeals) Regulations 1976**
    revoked: SI 2014/486 Sch.1
**2012. National Savings Stock Register
Regulations 1976**
    Reg.28, amended: SI 2014/3214 Reg.2
**2063. Mines and Quarries (Metrication)
Regulations 1976**
    revoked (in part): SI 2014/3248 Sch.4 Part 1

1977

**17. Control of Atmospheric Pollution (Appeals)
Regulations 1977**
    revoked (in part): SI 2014/3318 Sch.4
**18. Control of Atmospheric Pollution
(Exempted Premises) Regulations 1977**
    revoked (in part): SI 2014/3318 Sch.4
**19. Control of Atmospheric Pollution (Research
and Publicity) Regulations 1977**
    revoked (in part): SI 2014/3318 Sch.4
**343. Social Security Benefit (Dependency)
Regulations 1977**
    Sch.2 Part I para.2B, amended: SI 2014/618
Reg.4

    Sch.2 Part I para.2C, amended: SI 2014/107
    Sch.1 para.6, SI 2014/3229 Sch.6 para.2
**500. Safety Representatives and Safety
Committees Regulations 1977**
    applied: SI 2014/3352 Sch.2 para.30
    Reg.2, amended: SI 2014/469 Sch.3 para.31
    Reg.2, applied: SI 2014/3248 Reg.18
    Reg.4, amended: SI 2014/469 Sch.3 para.32
    Reg.4A, amended: SI 2014/469 Sch.3
    para.33
    Reg.5, amended: SI 2014/469 Sch.3 para.34,
    SI 2014/3248 Sch.5 para.4
    Reg.6, amended: SI 2014/469 Sch.3 para.35
    Reg.7, amended: SI 2014/469 Sch.3 para.36
    Reg.11, amended: SI 2014/431 Sch.1 para.8
    Reg.12, added: SI 2014/431 Sch.1 para.9
**913. Coal Mines (Precautions against
Inflammable Dust) Amendment Regulations
1977**
    revoked: SI 2014/3248 Sch.4 Part 1
**1210. National Savings Bank (Investment
Deposits) (Limits) Order 1977**
    Art.3B, revoked: SI 2014/484 Art.2
    Art.4, amended: SI 2014/484 Art.2
**1304. Non-Marketing of Milk and Milk Products
and the Dairy Herd Conversion Premiums
Regulations 1977**
    revoked: SI 2014/1902 Sch.1
**1316. Vehicle and Driving Licences
(Compensation to Officers) Regulations 1977**
    disapplied: SI 2014/3229 Sch.2 para.6
    referred to: SI 2014/3061 Sch.1 para.12,
    Sch.2 para.10
    Reg.12, varied: SI 2014/3061 Sch.2 para.10
    Reg.23, varied: SI 2014/3061 Sch.2 para.10
    Reg.30, varied: SI 2014/3061 Sch.2 para.10
    Reg.33, varied: SI 2014/3061 Sch.2 para.10
    Sch.1, varied: SI 2014/3061 Sch.2 para.10
**1360. Teachers Superannuation (Scotland)
Regulations 1977**
    Sch.1 para.4, applied: SSI 2014/217 Sch.1
    para.16, SSI 2014/292 Sch.1 para.16
    Sch.1 para.5, applied: SSI 2014/292 Sch.1
    para.17
    Sch.1 para.5, referred to: SSI 2014/217
    Sch.1 para.17
**1387. Pensions Increase (Annual Review) Order
1977**
    referred to: SI 2014/668 Sch.1

1670. Marriage (Prescription of Religious Bodies) (Scotland) Regulations 1977
    referred to: SSI 2014/212 Art.3
    revoked: SSI 2014/304 Reg.1

2157. Rates (Northern Ireland) Order 1977
    Art.42, applied: 2014 c.22 Sch.3 para.11

1978

393. Social Security (Graduated Retirement Benefit) (No.2) Regulations 1978
    Reg.3, amended: SI 2014/76 Reg.3, SI 2014/3229 Sch.6 para.3
    Sch.2, varied: SI 2014/516 Art.8

795. Merchant Shipping (Crew Accommodation) Regulations 1978
    Sch.6, referred to: SI 2014/1613 Reg.30

1039. Health and Safety at Work (Northern Ireland) Order 1978
    applied: SI 2014/469 Sch.4 para.20, Sch.4 para.21
    Part I, applied: SI 2014/469 Sch.4 para.20, Sch.4 para.21
    Part 2, applied: SI 2014/469 Sch.4 para.20, Sch.4 para.21
    Part II, applied: SI 2014/469 Sch.4 para.20, Sch.4 para.21
    Part III, applied: SI 2014/469 Sch.4 para.20, Sch.4 para.21
    Part IV, applied: SI 2014/469 Sch.4 para.20, Sch.4 para.21
    Art., applied: SI 2014/469 Sch.4 para.20, Sch.4 para.21
    Art.1, applied: SI 2014/469 Sch.4 para.20, Sch.4 para.21
    Art.2, applied: SI 2014/469 Sch.4 para.20, Sch.4 para.21
    Art.3, applied: SI 2014/469 Sch.4 para.20, Sch.4 para.21
    Art.4, applied: SI 2014/469 Sch.4 para.20, Sch.4 para.21
    Art.(5), applied: SI 2014/469 Sch.4 para.20, Sch.4 para.21
    Art.5, applied: SI 2014/469 Sch.4 para.20, Sch.4 para.21
    Art.6, applied: SI 2014/469 Sch.4 para.20, Sch.4 para.21
    Art.6(b), applied: SI 2014/469 Sch.4 para.20, Sch.4 para.21

Art.6, applied: SI 2014/469 Sch.4 para.20, Sch.4 para.21
Art.7, applied: SI 2014/469 Sch.4 para.20, Sch.4 para.21
Art.8, applied: SI 2014/469 Sch.4 para.20, Sch.4 para.21
Art.9, applied: SI 2014/469 Sch.4 para.20, Sch.4 para.21
Art.12, applied: SI 2014/469 Sch.4 para.20, Sch.4 para.21
Art.13, applied: SI 2014/469 Sch.4 para.20, Sch.4 para.21
Art.15, applied: SI 2014/469 Sch.4 para.20, Sch.4 para.21
Art.16, applied: SI 2014/469 Sch.4 para.20, Sch.4 para.21
Art.17, applied: SI 2014/469 Sch.4 para.20, Sch.4 para.21
Art.17(4), applied: SI 2014/469 Sch.4 para.20, Sch.4 para.21
Art.17(5), applied: SI 2014/469 Sch.4 para.20, Sch.4 para.21
Art.17(6), applied: SI 2014/469 Sch.4 para.20, Sch.4 para.21
Art.18, applied: SI 2014/469 Sch.4 para.20, Sch.4 para.21
Art.20, applied: SI 2014/469 Sch.4 para.20, Sch.4 para.21
Art.21, applied: SI 2014/469 Sch.4 para.20, Sch.4 para.21
Art.22, applied: SI 2014/469 Sch.4 para.20, Sch.4 para.21
Art.23, applied: SI 2014/469 Sch.4 para.20, Sch.4 para.21
Art.24, applied: SI 2014/469 Sch.4 para.20, Sch.4 para.21
Art.25, applied: SI 2014/469 Sch.4 para.20, Sch.4 para.21
Art.26, applied: SI 2014/469 Sch.4 para.20, Sch.4 para.21
Art.27, applied: SI 2014/469 Sch.4 para.20, Sch.4 para.21
Art.27A, applied: SI 2014/469 Sch.4 para.20, Sch.4 para.21
Art.28, applied: SI 2014/469 Sch.4 para.20, Sch.4 para.21
Art.29, applied: SI 2014/469 Sch.4 para.20, Sch.4 para.21
Art.29A, applied: SI 2014/469 Sch.4 para.20, Sch.4 para.21

Art.30, applied: SI 2014/469 Sch.4 para.20, Sch.4 para.21

Art.31, applied: SI 2014/469 Sch.4 para.20, Sch.4 para.21

Art.32, applied: SI 2014/469 Sch.4 para.20, Sch.4 para.21

Art.33, applied: SI 2014/469 Sch.4 para.20, Sch.4 para.21

Art.34, applied: SI 2014/469 Sch.4 para.20, Sch.4 para.21

Art.34A, applied: SI 2014/469 Sch.4 para.20, Sch.4 para.21

Art.35, applied: SI 2014/469 Sch.4 para.20, Sch.4 para.21

Art.36, applied: SI 2014/469 Sch.4 para.20, Sch.4 para.21

Art.37, applied: SI 2014/469 Sch.4 para.20, Sch.4 para.21

Art.38, applied: SI 2014/469 Sch.4 para.20, Sch.4 para.21

Art.39, applied: SI 2014/469 Sch.4 para.20, Sch.4 para.21

Art.40, applied: SI 2014/469 Sch.4 para.20, Sch.4 para.21

Art.40(2), applied: SI 2014/469 Sch.4 para.20, Sch.4 para.21

Art.40(4), applied: SI 2014/469 Sch.4 para.20, Sch.4 para.21

Art.43, applied: SI 2014/469 Sch.4 para.20, Sch.4 para.21

Art.44, applied: SI 2014/469 Sch.4 para.20, Sch.4 para.21

Art.45, applied: SI 2014/469 Sch.4 para.20, Sch.4 para.21

Art.46, applied: SI 2014/469 Sch.4 para.20, Sch.4 para.21

Art.46(1), applied: SI 2014/469 Sch.4 para.20, Sch.4 para.21

Art.47A, applied: SI 2014/469 Sch.4 para.20, Sch.4 para.21

Art.48, applied: SI 2014/469 Sch.4 para.20, Sch.4 para.21

Art.49, applied: SI 2014/469 Sch.4 para.20, Sch.4 para.21

Art.51, applied: SI 2014/469 Sch.4 para.20, Sch.4 para.21

Art.53, applied: SI 2014/469 Sch.4 para.20, Sch.4 para.21

Art.(54, applied: SI 2014/469 Sch.4 para.20, Sch.4 para.21

Art.54, applied: SI 2014/469 Sch.4 para.20, Sch.4 para.21

Art.54(5), applied: SI 2014/469 Sch.4 para.20, Sch.4 para.21

Art.(55, applied: SI 2014/469 Sch.4 para.20, Sch.4 para.21

Art.55, applied: SI 2014/469 Sch.4 para.20, Sch.4 para.21

Art.55(2), applied: SI 2014/469 Sch.4 para.20, Sch.4 para.21

Art.56, applied: SI 2014/469 Sch.4 para.20, Sch.4 para.21

Art.71, applied: SI 2014/469 Sch.4 para.20, Sch.4 para.21

Art.105, applied: SI 2014/469 Sch.4 para.20, Sch.4 para.21

Art.409, applied: SI 2014/469 Sch.4 para.20, Sch.4 para.21

para., applied: SI 2014/469 Sch.4 para.20, Sch.4 para.21

para(.13)., applied: SI 2014/469 Sch.4 para.20, Sch.4 para.21

para(.15)., applied: SI 2014/469 Sch.4 para.20, Sch.4 para.21

para(.2)., applied: SI 2014/469 Sch.4 para.20, Sch.4 para.21

para(.6)., applied: SI 2014/469 Sch.4 para.20, Sch.4 para.21

para.1(1)., applied: SI 2014/469 Sch.4 para.20, Sch.4 para.21

Reg.3, applied: SI 2014/469 Sch.4 para.20, Sch.4 para.21

Reg.35, applied: SI 2014/469 Sch.4 para.20, Sch.4 para.21

Reg.36, applied: SI 2014/469 Sch.4 para.20, Sch.4 para.21

Reg.37, applied: SI 2014/469 Sch.4 para.20, Sch.4 para.21

s.2, applied: SI 2014/469 Sch.4 para.20, Sch.4 para.21

s.5, applied: SI 2014/469 Sch.4 para.20, Sch.4 para.21

s.27, applied: SI 2014/469 Sch.4 para.20, Sch.4 para.21

s.46, applied: SI 2014/469 Sch.4 para.20, Sch.4 para.21

s.55, applied: SI 2014/469 Sch.4 para.20, Sch.4 para.21

Sch.1, applied: SI 2014/469 Sch.4 para.20, Sch.4 para.21

Sch.2, applied: SI 2014/469 Sch.4 para.20,
Sch.4 para.21
Sch.3, applied: SI 2014/469 Sch.4 para.20,
Sch.4 para.21
Sch.3A, applied: SI 2014/469 Sch.4 para.20,
Sch.4 para.21
Sch.4, applied: SI 2014/469 Sch.4 para.20,
Sch.4 para.21
Sch.5, applied: SI 2014/469 Sch.4 para.20,
Sch.4 para.21
Sch.6, applied: SI 2014/469 Sch.4 para.20,
Sch.4 para.21
Sch.7, applied: SI 2014/469 Sch.4 para.20,
Sch.4 para.21

**1045. Matrimonial Causes (Northern Ireland)
Order 1978**
Art.35A, see *Official Receiver for Northern
Ireland v Gallagher* [2014] NICh 6, [2014]
B.P.I.R. 918 (Ch D (NI)), Deeny J

**1211. Pensions Increase (Annual Review) Order
1978**
referred to: SI 2014/668 Sch.1

**1555. Trunk Road (Llandybie, Dyfed) (Speed
Limits) Order 1978**
revoked: SI 2014/2893 Art.3

**1648. Coal and Other Mines (Metrication)
Regulations 1978**
revoked (in part): SI 2014/3248 Sch.4 Part 1

**1689. Social Security (Categorisation of Earners)
Regulations 1978**
applied: SI 2014/3051 Reg.33
see *ITV Services Ltd v Revenue and Customs
Commissioners* [2013] EWCA Civ 867,
[2014] S.T.C. 325 (CA (Civ Div)), Sir James
Munby PFD
Reg.1, amended: SI 2014/635 Reg.2
Sch.1 Part I, revoked: SI 2014/635 Reg.2
Sch.1 Part I, substituted: SI 2014/635 Reg.2
Sch.3, amended: SI 2014/635 Reg.2
Sch.3, revoked: SI 2014/635 Reg.2
Sch.3, substituted: SI 2014/635 Reg.2

**1723. Compressed Acetylene (Importation)
Regulations 1978**
revoked: SI 2014/1639 Sch.3 Part 2

**1815. Daw Mill Mine (Refuge Holes) Regulations
1978**
revoked: SI 2014/3248 Sch.4 Part 1

1979

72. Isles of Scilly (Functions) Order 1979
Art.3, amended: SI 2014/1637 Sch.4 para.5,
SI 2014/1638 Sch.13 para.12

**97. Merchant Shipping (Repatriation)
Regulations 1979**
Reg.2, amended: SI 2014/1614 Reg.6
Reg.11, revoked: SI 2014/1614 Reg.6

**318. Mines (Precautions Against Inrushes)
Regulations 1979**
revoked (in part): SI 2014/3248 Sch.4 Part 1
Reg.6, applied: SI 2014/3248 Reg.71

**427. Petroleum (Consolidation) Act 1928
(Enforcement) Regulations 1979**
revoked: SI 2014/1637 Sch.4 Part 1

**521. European Assembly Election Petition Rules
1979**
r.5, amended: SI 2014/1129 r.2

**643. Social Security (Widow's Benefit,
Retirement Pensions and Other Benefits)
(Transitional) Regulations 1979**
Reg.7, amended: SI 2014/3061 Sch.1 para.5

**907. Transfer of Functions (Arts and Libraries)
Order 1979**
Art.1, varied: SI 2014/2708 Art.5
Art.6, varied: SI 2014/2708 Art.5

**912. International Oil Pollution Compensation
Fund (Immunities and Privileges) Order 1979**
Art.6, see *Assuranceforeningen Gard
Gjensidig v International Oil Pollution
Compensation Fund 1971* [2014] EWHC
1394 (Comm), [2014] 2 Lloyd's Rep. 219
(QBD (Comm)), Hamblen J

**925. Pneumoconiosis, etc., (Workers
Compensation) (Northern Ireland) Order 1979**
Art.3, amended: 2014 c.1 Sch.2 para.4
Art.4, amended: 2014 c.1 Sch.2 para.5

1047. Pensions Increase (Review) Order 1979
referred to: SI 2014/668 Sch.1
Art.2, amended: SI 2014/560 Sch.3 para.3,
SI 2014/3229 Sch.3 para.2
Art.2, disapplied: SI 2014/3229 Sch.2 para.6

**1378. Explosives Act 1875 (Exemptions)
Regulations 1979**
applied: SI 2014/1639 Reg.15
revoked: SI 2014/1639 Sch.3 Part 2

**1577. Merchant Shipping (Returns of Births and
Deaths) Regulations 1979**
Reg.11, amended: SI 2014/107 Sch.1 para.7,
SI 2014/3229 Sch.6 para.4

1714. Perjury (Northern Ireland) Order 1979
  Art.10, applied: 2014 c.4 s.10, SI 2014/1893
  Art.19

1980

124. Non-Marketing of Milk and Milk Products and the Dairy Herd Conversion Premiums (Amendment) Regulations 1980
  revoked: SI 2014/1902 Sch.1
146. African Swine Fever (Compensation) Order 1980
  revoked: SI 2014/1894 Sch.5
397. County Courts (Northern Ireland) Order 1980
  Part III, applied: SI 2014/3298 Reg.3
  Art.47A, added: 2014 c.13 Sch.1 para.3
  Art.60, applied: SI 2014/3298 Reg.3
657. National Freight Corporation (Central Trust) (Amendment) Order 1980
  disapplied: SI 2014/3229 Sch.2 para.6
709. Double Taxation Relief (Taxes on Income) (Canada) Order 1980
  Sch.1, added: SI 2014/3274 Sch.1 Part 1
  Sch.1, referred to: SI 2014/3274 Art.2
  Sch.1, revoked: SI 2014/3274 Sch.1 Part 1
  Sch.1, substituted: SI 2014/3274 Sch.1 Part 1
942. Coal and Other Mines (Fire and Rescue) (Amendment) Regulations 1980
  revoked (in part): SI 2014/3248 Sch.4 Part 1
1013. Fuel and Electricity (Heating) (Control) (Amendment) Order 1980
  revoked: SI 2014/1509 Art.2
1092. Carriage of Passengers and their Luggage by Sea (Interim Provisions) Order 1980
  revoked: SI 2014/1361 Art.4
1125. Carriage of Passengers and their Luggage by Sea (Interim Provisions) (Notice) Order 1980
  revoked: SI 2014/1438 Art.2
1302. Pensions Increase (Review) Order 1980
  referred to: SI 2014/668 Sch.1
  Art.2, amended: SI 2014/560 Sch.3 para.3, SI 2014/3229 Sch.3 para.2
  Art.2, disapplied: SI 2014/3229 Sch.2 para.6
1394. Non-Marketing of Milk and Milk Products and the Dairy Herd Conversion Premiums (Amendment) (No.2) Regulations 1980
  revoked: SI 2014/1902 Sch.1

1981

154. Road Traffic (Northern Ireland) Order 1981
  Art.5, amended: 2014 c.22 Sch.9 para.62
  Art.5, revoked (in part): 2014 c.22 Sch.9 para.62
  Art.13, amended: 2014 c.22 s.46
  Art.13A, added: 2014 c.22 s.46
  Art.15, amended: 2014 c.22 s.47
  Art.16, amended: 2014 c.22 s.47
156. Housing (Northern Ireland) Order 1981
  Part II, applied: 2014 c.22 Sch.3 para.2
207. Transfer of Functions (Arts, Libraries and National Heritage) Order 1981
  Art.1, varied: SI 2014/2708 Art.5
  Sch.2 para.4, varied: SI 2014/2708 Art.5
226. Judgments Enforcement (Northern Ireland) Order 1981
  Art.22, applied: 2014 c.22 s.31
  Art.23, applied: 2014 c.22 s.31
  Art.116, applied: 2014 c.22 s.31
228. Legal Aid, Advice and Assistance (Northern Ireland) Order 1981
  Art.36, see *Brownlee's Application for Judicial Review, Re* [2014] UKSC 4, [2014] N.I. 188 (SC), Lord Neuberger PSC
  Art.37, see *Brownlee's Application for Judicial Review, Re* [2014] UKSC 4, [2014] N.I. 188 (SC), Lord Neuberger PSC
257. Public Service Vehicles (Conditions of Fitness, Equipment, Use and Certification) Regulations 1981
  Reg.46, amended: SI 2014/480 Reg.2
394. Industrial and Provident Societies (Increase in Deposit-taking Limits) Order 1981
  revoked: 2014 c.14 Sch.7
  Art.4, applied: 2014 c.14 Sch.3 para.8
395. Industrial and Provident Societies (Increase in Shareholding Limit) Order 1981
  revoked: SI 2014/210 Art.4
  Art.4, applied: 2014 c.14 Sch.3 para.6
552. Magistrates Courts Rules 1981
  r.2., amended: SI 2014/600 Sch.1 para.1, SI 2014/879 Art.16
  r.2., revoked (in part): SI 2014/879 Art.16
  r.3., revoked: SI 2014/879 Art.17
  r.38., revoked: SI 2014/879 Art.17
  r.39., revoked (in part): SI 2014/879 Art.17
  r.41., revoked: SI 2014/879 Art.17
  r.43., revoked: SI 2014/879 Art.17

r.46., amended: SI 2014/600 Sch.1 para.1
r.51., amended: SI 2014/879 Art.18
r.53., amended: SI 2014/600 Sch.1 para.1
r.54., amended: SI 2014/600 Sch.1 para.1
r.54., revoked (in part): SI 2014/600 Sch.1
para.1
r.55., amended: SI 2014/600 Sch.1 para.1
r.59., revoked: SI 2014/879 Art.19
r.60., revoked (in part): SI 2014/879 Art.19
r.61., revoked: SI 2014/879 Art.19
r.63., revoked (in part): SI 2014/879 Art.19
r.65., amended: SI 2014/600 Sch.1 para.1
r.69., revoked: SI 2014/879 Art.19
r.101B., added: SI 2014/879 Art.20
r.105., revoked: SI 2014/879 Art.21
r.109., amended: SI 2014/600 Sch.1 para.1
r.114., revoked: SI 2014/879 Art.21

612. Prevention of Oil Pollution (Convention Countries) Order 1981
revoked: SI 2014/499 Art.2

750. Submarine Pipe-lines (Electricity Generating Stations) Regulations 1981
revoked: SI 2014/430 Reg.2

834. Ministerial and other Salaries Order 1981
Sch.1 Part I, varied: SI 2014/2708 Art.5

839. Employment (Miscellaneous Provisions) (Northern Ireland) Order 1981
Art.7B, applied: SI 2014/1615 Reg.12
Art.11, referred to: SI 2014/1615 Reg.2

917. Health and Safety (First-Aid) Regulations 1981
Reg.2, amended: SI 2014/3248 Sch.5 para.5
Reg.8, substituted: SI 2014/3248 Sch.5
para.5

1076. Merchant Shipping (Certification of Ships Cooks) Regulations 1981
applied: SI 2014/1613 Reg.39
revoked: SI 2014/1614 Reg.15
Reg.8, applied: SI 2014/1613 Reg.39
Reg.9, applied: SI 2014/1613 Reg.39

1086. Education (Schools and Further Education) Regulations 1981
Reg.5, amended: SI 2014/2103 Art.2

1123. County Courts Jurisdiction Order 1981
revoked: SI 2014/503 Art.2

1217. Pensions Increase (Review) Order 1981
referred to: SI 2014/668 Sch.1
Art.2, amended: SI 2014/560 Sch.3 para.3,
SI 2014/3229 Sch.3 para.2
Art.2, disapplied: SI 2014/3229 Sch.2 para.6

1519. Estate Agents (Entry and Inspection) Regulations 1981
revoked: SI 2014/631 Sch.2 para.8

1675. Magistrates Courts (Northern Ireland) Order 1981
applied: SI 2014/195 Reg.10
Art.13, amended: 2014 c.13 Sch.1 para.4
Art.13A, added: 2014 c.13 Sch.1 para.4
Art.19, disapplied: SI 2014/1615 Reg.9
Art.47, varied: SI 2014/3141 Reg.110
Art.49, applied: SI 2014/3141 Reg.110
Art.88, amended: SI 2014/3298 Reg.6
Sch.4, applied: SI 2014/195 Reg.15, SI
2014/3085 Reg.23, SI 2014/3263 Reg.26

1686. Companies (Inspectors Reports) (Fees) Regulations 1981
applied: SI 2014/574 Reg.2

1694. Motor Vehicles (Tests) Regulations 1981
Reg.3, amended: SI 2014/480 Reg.3
Reg.7, amended: SI 2014/480 Reg.3
Reg.7A, amended: SI 2014/480 Reg.3
Reg.8A, amended: SI 2014/480 Reg.3
Reg.8B, amended: SI 2014/480 Reg.3
Reg.8C, amended: SI 2014/480 Reg.3
Reg.8D, amended: SI 2014/480 Reg.3
Reg.8E, amended: SI 2014/480 Reg.3
Reg.20, amended: SI 2014/2114 Reg.3
Reg.21, amended: SI 2014/480 Reg.3
Reg.23, amended: SI 2014/480 Reg.3

1829. Control of Noise (Code of Practice on Noise from Audible Intruder Alarms) Order 1981
revoked (in part): SI 2014/2123 Art.2

1982

209. Commons (Schemes) Regulations 1982
Reg.4, varied: SI 2014/2708 Art.5

217. Poisons List Order 1982
Sch.1 Part II, amended: SI 2014/1942
Reg.15

218. Poisons Rules 1982
Sch.4 Part II, amended: SI 2014/1942
Reg.16

630. Petroleum-Spirit (Plastic Containers) Regulations 1982
revoked: SI 2014/1637 Sch.4 Part 1
Reg.3, applied: SI 2014/1637 Reg.22, Sch.2
para.6

Sch.1, applied: SI 2014/1637 Reg.22, Sch.2
para.6

**719. Public Lending Right Scheme 1982
(Commencement) Order 1982**

Part II para.4, amended: SI 2014/1457 para.1

Part II para.6, amended: SI 2014/1457 para.2

Part III para.14A, amended: SI 2014/1457
para.5

Part III para.17, amended: SI 2014/1457
para.6

Part III para.9A, amended: SI 2014/1457
para.3

Part III para.9B, added: SI 2014/1457 para.4

Part III para.9B, substituted: SI 2014/1945
Sch.1 para.1

Part IV para.39, amended: SI 2014/1457
para.7

Appendix 1., referred to: SI 2014/1945

**817. Town and Country Planning
(Telecommunication Networks) (Railway
Operational Land) Special Development Order
1982**

revoked (in part): SI 2014/683 Sch.1

**894. Statutory Sick Pay (General) Regulations
1982**

Reg.13, revoked: SI 2014/55 Reg.2

Reg.17, amended: SI 2014/3255 Art.3

**1070. British Protectorates, Protected States and
Protected Persons Order 1982**

Art.11, applied: SI 2014/581 Sch.4 para.2

**1080. Agricultural Marketing (Northern
Ireland) Order 1982**

Art.23, amended: SI 2014/892 Sch.1
para.210

Art.29, amended: SI 2014/892 Sch.1
para.210

Art.42, amended: SI 2014/892 Sch.1
para.210

**1123. Registration of Overseas Births and
Deaths Regulations 1982**

revoked: SI 2014/511 Reg.17

**1163. Motorways Traffic (England and Wales)
Regulations 1982**

Reg.5, amended: SI 2014/3065 Art.4

Reg.5, disapplied: SI 2014/948 Art.8, SI
2014/971 Art.7, SI 2014/3394 Art.5

Reg.5, varied: SI 2014/50 Art.9, SI 2014/57
Art.7, SI 2014/61 Art.6, SI 2014/62 Art.5, SI
2014/64 Art.4, SI 2014/83 Art.7, SI
2014/115 Art.8, SI 2014/151 Art.5, SI
2014/153 Art.4, SI 2014/169 Art.9, SI

2014/187 Art.7, SI 2014/199 Art.5, SI
2014/200 Art.7, SI 2014/225 Art.6, SI
2014/246 Art.6, SI 2014/284 Art.8, SI
2014/292 Art.4, SI 2014/298 Art.7, SI
2014/304 Art.7, SI 2014/317 Art.5, SI
2014/328 Art.7, SI 2014/339 Art.7, SI
2014/351 Art.4, SI 2014/394 Art.7, SI
2014/397 Art.10, SI 2014/401 Art.3, SI
2014/428 Art.5, SI 2014/621 Art.7, SI
2014/653 Art.7, SI 2014/657 Art.7, SI
2014/661 Art.7, SI 2014/671 Art.6, SI
2014/678 Art.4, SI 2014/716 Art.7, SI
2014/718 Art.6, SI 2014/721 Art.7, SI
2014/739 Art.7, SI 2014/751 Art.4, SI
2014/757 Art.7, SI 2014/764 Art.5, SI
2014/948 Art.8, SI 2014/971 Art.7, SI
2014/993 Art.13, SI 2014/1010 Art.7, SI
2014/1021 Art.6, SI 2014/1084 Art.7, SI
2014/1096 Art.7, SI 2014/1104 Art.7, SI
2014/1138 Art.8, SI 2014/1145 Art.5, SI
2014/1147 Art.5, SI 2014/1155 Art.9, SI
2014/1162 Art.6, SI 2014/1163 Art.5, SI
2014/1164 Art.17, SI 2014/1174 Art.9, SI
2014/1224 Art.3, SI 2014/1225 Art.6, SI
2014/1305 Art.7, SI 2014/1311 Art.4, SI
2014/1428 Art.7, SI 2014/1467 Art.5, SI
2014/1472 Art.5, SI 2014/1490 Art.7, SI
2014/1595 Art.13, SI 2014/1630 Art.7, SI
2014/1633 Art.4, SI 2014/1642 Art.7, SI
2014/1644 Art.5, SI 2014/1654 Art.9, SI
2014/1679 Art.3, SI 2014/1681 Art.6, SI
2014/1688 Art.8, SI 2014/1689 Art.9, SI
2014/1726 Art.7, SI 2014/1733 Art.7, SI
2014/1744 Art.3, SI 2014/1757 Art.7, SI
2014/1783 Art.6, SI 2014/1784 Art.6, SI
2014/1845 Art.7, SI 2014/1853 Art.5, SI
2014/1856 Art.11, SI 2014/1861 Art.5, SI
2014/1947 Art.9, SI 2014/1956 Art.8, SI
2014/1978 Art.5, SI 2014/1982 Art.7, SI
2014/1984 Art.5, SI 2014/1987 Art.4, SI
2014/1988 Art.5, SI 2014/2001 Art.8, SI
2014/2004 Art.7, SI 2014/2005 Art.5, SI
2014/2022 Art.8, SI 2014/2024 Art.7, SI
2014/2032 Art.8, SI 2014/2052 Art.7, SI
2014/2064 Art.5, SI 2014/2066 Art.7, SI
2014/2089 Art.9, SI 2014/2091 Art.3, SI
2014/2099 Art.5, SI 2014/2155 Art.5, SI
2014/2157 Art.4, SI 2014/2163 Art.7, SI
2014/2183 Art.7, SI 2014/2217 Art.5, SI
2014/2219 Art.7, SI 2014/2244 Art.6, SI
2014/2285 Art.3, SI 2014/2313 Art.4, SI

2014/2331 Art.7, SI 2014/2334 Art.5, SI
2014/2335 Art.5, SI 2014/2348 Art.4, SI
2014/2360 Art.7, SI 2014/2412 Art.8, SI
2014/2433 Art.5, SI 2014/2447 Art.6, SI
2014/2449 Art.6, SI 2014/2470 Art.5, SI
2014/2514 Art.6, SI 2014/2536 Art.8, SI
2014/2537 Art.7, SI 2014/2546 Art.3, SI
2014/2583 Art.4, SI 2014/2593 Art.5, SI
2014/2599 Art.6, SI 2014/2601 Art.3, SI
2014/2615 Art.7, SI 2014/2684 Art.7, SI
2014/2695 Art.5, SI 2014/2733 Art.8, SI
2014/2784 Art.3, SI 2014/2791 Art.9, SI
2014/2805 Art.5, SI 2014/2814 Art.3, SI
2014/2826 Art.6, SI 2014/2834 Art.8, SI
2014/2870 Art.10, SI 2014/2951 Art.5, SI
2014/2952 Art.3, SI 2014/2965 Art.4, SI
2014/2972 Art.7, SI 2014/2980 Art.6, SI
2014/2984 Art.9, SI 2014/2985 Art.9, SI
2014/2992 Art.7, SI 2014/3006 Art.5, SI
2014/3010 Art.7, SI 2014/3013 Art.7, SI
2014/3016 Art.8, SI 2014/3023 Art.7, SI
2014/3028 Art.3, SI 2014/3032 Art.7, SI
2014/3042 Art.6, SI 2014/3047 Art.7, SI
2014/3069 Art.5, SI 2014/3170 Art.4, SI
2014/3175 Art.9, SI 2014/3353 Art.3, SI
2014/3406 Art.9, SI 2014/3410 Art.3, SI
2014/3419 Art.6, SI 2014/3438 Art.6, SI
2014/3454 Art.8, SI 2014/3481 Art.5
Reg.6, varied: SI 2014/50 Art.9, SI 2014/169
Art.9, SI 2014/304 Art.7, SI 2014/1174
Art.9, SI 2014/1595 Art.11
Reg.9, amended: SI 2014/3065 Art.4
Reg.9, disapplied: SI 2014/948 Art.8, SI
2014/971 Art.7, SI 2014/3394 Art.5
Reg.9, varied: SI 2014/50 Art.9, SI 2014/57
Art.7, SI 2014/61 Art.6, SI 2014/62 Art.5, SI
2014/64 Art.4, SI 2014/83 Art.7, SI
2014/115 Art.8, SI 2014/151 Art.5, SI
2014/153 Art.4, SI 2014/169 Art.9, SI
2014/187 Art.7, SI 2014/199 Art.5, SI
2014/200 Art.7, SI 2014/225 Art.6, SI
2014/246 Art.6, SI 2014/284 Art.8, SI
2014/292 Art.4, SI 2014/298 Art.7, SI
2014/304 Art.7, SI 2014/317 Art.5, SI
2014/328 Art.7, SI 2014/339 Art.7, SI
2014/351 Art.4, SI 2014/394 Art.7, SI
2014/397 Art.10, SI 2014/401 Art.3, SI
2014/428 Art.5, SI 2014/621 Art.7, SI
2014/653 Art.7, SI 2014/657 Art.7, SI
2014/661 Art.7, SI 2014/671 Art.6, SI
2014/678 Art.4, SI 2014/716 Art.7, SI

2014/718 Art.6, SI 2014/721 Art.7, SI
2014/739 Art.7, SI 2014/751 Art.4, SI
2014/757 Art.7, SI 2014/764 Art.5, SI
2014/948 Art.8, SI 2014/971 Art.7, SI
2014/993 Art.13, SI 2014/1010 Art.7, SI
2014/1021 Art.6, SI 2014/1084 Art.7, SI
2014/1096 Art.7, SI 2014/1104 Art.7, SI
2014/1138 Art.8, SI 2014/1145 Art.5, SI
2014/1147 Art.5, SI 2014/1155 Art.9, SI
2014/1162 Art.6, SI 2014/1163 Art.5, SI
2014/1164 Art.17, SI 2014/1174 Art.9, SI
2014/1224 Art.3, SI 2014/1225 Art.6, SI
2014/1305 Art.7, SI 2014/1311 Art.4, SI
2014/1428 Art.7, SI 2014/1467 Art.5, SI
2014/1472 Art.5, SI 2014/1490 Art.7, SI
2014/1595 Art.13, SI 2014/1630 Art.7, SI
2014/1633 Art.4, SI 2014/1642 Art.7, SI
2014/1644 Art.5, SI 2014/1654 Art.9, SI
2014/1679 Art.3, SI 2014/1681 Art.6, SI
2014/1688 Art.8, SI 2014/1689 Art.9, SI
2014/1726 Art.7, SI 2014/1733 Art.7, SI
2014/1744 Art.3, SI 2014/1757 Art.7, SI
2014/1783 Art.6, SI 2014/1784 Art.6, SI
2014/1845 Art.7, SI 2014/1853 Art.5, SI
2014/1856 Art.11, SI 2014/1861 Art.5, SI
2014/1947 Art.9, SI 2014/1956 Art.8, SI
2014/1978 Art.5, SI 2014/1982 Art.7, SI
2014/1984 Art.5, SI 2014/1987 Art.4, SI
2014/1988 Art.5, SI 2014/2001 Art.8, SI
2014/2004 Art.7, SI 2014/2005 Art.5, SI
2014/2022 Art.8, SI 2014/2024 Art.7, SI
2014/2032 Art.8, SI 2014/2052 Art.7, SI
2014/2064 Art.5, SI 2014/2066 Art.7, SI
2014/2089 Art.9, SI 2014/2091 Art.3, SI
2014/2099 Art.5, SI 2014/2155 Art.5, SI
2014/2157 Art.4, SI 2014/2163 Art.7, SI
2014/2183 Art.7, SI 2014/2217 Art.5, SI
2014/2219 Art.7, SI 2014/2244 Art.6, SI
2014/2285 Art.3, SI 2014/2313 Art.4, SI
2014/2331 Art.7, SI 2014/2334 Art.5, SI
2014/2335 Art.5, SI 2014/2348 Art.4, SI
2014/2360 Art.7, SI 2014/2412 Art.8, SI
2014/2433 Art.5, SI 2014/2447 Art.6, SI
2014/2449 Art.6, SI 2014/2470 Art.5, SI
2014/2514 Art.6, SI 2014/2536 Art.8, SI
2014/2537 Art.7, SI 2014/2546 Art.3, SI
2014/2583 Art.4, SI 2014/2593 Art.5, SI
2014/2599 Art.6, SI 2014/2601 Art.3, SI
2014/2615 Art.7, SI 2014/2684 Art.7, SI
2014/2695 Art.5, SI 2014/2733 Art.8, SI
2014/2784 Art.3, SI 2014/2791 Art.9, SI

2014/2805 Art.5, SI 2014/2814 Art.3, SI
2014/2826 Art.6, SI 2014/2834 Art.8, SI
2014/2870 Art.10, SI 2014/2951 Art.5, SI
2014/2952 Art.3, SI 2014/2965 Art.4, SI
2014/2972 Art.7, SI 2014/2980 Art.6, SI
2014/2984 Art.9, SI 2014/2985 Art.9, SI
2014/2992 Art.7, SI 2014/3006 Art.5, SI
2014/3010 Art.7, SI 2014/3013 Art.7, SI
2014/3016 Art.8, SI 2014/3023 Art.7, SI
2014/3028 Art.3, SI 2014/3032 Art.7, SI
2014/3042 Art.6, SI 2014/3047 Art.7, SI
2014/3069 Art.5, SI 2014/3170 Art.4, SI
2014/3175 Art.9, SI 2014/3353 Art.3, SI
2014/3406 Art.9, SI 2014/3410 Art.3, SI
2014/3419 Art.6, SI 2014/3438 Art.6, SI
2014/3454 Art.8, SI 2014/3481 Art.5
Reg.16, enabled: SI 2014/57, SI 2014/61, SI
2014/64, SI 2014/83, SI 2014/115, SI
2014/153, SI 2014/187, SI 2014/199, SI
2014/200, SI 2014/225, SI 2014/246, SI
2014/284, SI 2014/292, SI 2014/317, SI
2014/328, SI 2014/339, SI 2014/346, SI
2014/351, SI 2014/401, SI 2014/420, SI
2014/428, SI 2014/621, SI 2014/653, SI
2014/657, SI 2014/661, SI 2014/671, SI
2014/678, SI 2014/716, SI 2014/721, SI
2014/739, SI 2014/751, SI 2014/757, SI
2014/948, SI 2014/971, SI 2014/993, SI
2014/1010, SI 2014/1021, SI 2014/1084, SI
2014/1104, SI 2014/1138, SI 2014/1155, SI
2014/1162, SI 2014/1163, SI 2014/1164, SI
2014/1225, SI 2014/1305, SI 2014/1311, SI
2014/1467, SI 2014/1472, SI 2014/1490, SI
2014/1630, SI 2014/1633, SI 2014/1642, SI
2014/1644, SI 2014/1679, SI 2014/1688, SI
2014/1689, SI 2014/1726, SI 2014/1733, SI
2014/1744, SI 2014/1784, SI 2014/1845, SI
2014/1853, SI 2014/1856, SI 2014/1956, SI
2014/1982, SI 2014/1987, SI 2014/2001, SI
2014/2004, SI 2014/2005, SI 2014/2024, SI
2014/2052, SI 2014/2064, SI 2014/2066, SI
2014/2089, SI 2014/2091, SI 2014/2099, SI
2014/2155, SI 2014/2157, SI 2014/2183, SI
2014/2244, SI 2014/2313, SI 2014/2331, SI
2014/2348, SI 2014/2360, SI 2014/2433, SI
2014/2447, SI 2014/2449, SI 2014/2470, SI
2014/2514, SI 2014/2583, SI 2014/2601, SI
2014/2615, SI 2014/2684, SI 2014/2733, SI
2014/2791, SI 2014/2805, SI 2014/2814, SI
2014/2834, SI 2014/2870, SI 2014/2952, SI
2014/2965, SI 2014/2972, SI 2014/2980, SI

2014/2984, SI 2014/2985, SI 2014/2992, SI
2014/3006, SI 2014/3010, SI 2014/3013, SI
2014/3016, SI 2014/3028, SI 2014/3032, SI
2014/3042, SI 2014/3065, SI 2014/3069, SI
2014/3170, SI 2014/3175, SI 2014/3406, SI
2014/3410, SI 2014/3419, SI 2014/3438, SI
2014/3481

1178. Pensions Increase (Review) Order 1982
referred to: SI 2014/668 Sch.1
Art.2, amended: SI 2014/560 Sch.3 para.3,
SI 2014/3229 Sch.3 para.2
Art.2, disapplied: SI 2014/3229 Sch.2 para.6

1474. Rent Book (Forms of Notice) Regulations 1982
Sch.1 Part I, amended: SI 2014/493 Reg.2
Sch.1 Part II, amended: SI 2014/493 Reg.2
Sch.1 Part III, amended: SI 2014/493 Reg.2
Sch.1 Part IV, amended: SI 2014/493 Reg.2

1983

366. Agricultural Marketing Act 1983 (Commencement) Order 1983
revoked: SI 2014/1924 Sch.1

686. Personal Injuries (Civilians) Scheme 1983
Sch.3, substituted: SI 2014/444 Sch.1
Sch.4, substituted: SI 2014/444 Sch.2

713. Civil Courts Order 1983
revoked: SI 2014/820 Art.2
Art.6, applied: SI 2014/820 Art.3
Art.10, applied: SI 2014/820 Art.3
Art.10, referred to: SI 2014/820 Art.3
Sch.3, applied: SI 2014/820 Art.3
Sch.3, referred to: SI 2014/820 Art.3

748. Mobile Homes (Commissions) Order 1983
applied: SI 2014/11 Art.4

764. Dogs (Northern Ireland) Order 1983
Art.33A, applied: SI 2014/3266 Reg.10

879. Transfer of Functions (Arts, Libraries and National Heritage) Order 1983
Art.3, varied: SI 2014/2708 Art.5

994. Miscellaneous Mines (Metrication) Regulations 1983
revoked (in part): SI 2014/3248 Sch.4 Part 1

1106. Merchant Shipping (Prevention of Oil Pollution) Order 1983
Art.3, enabled: SI 2014/3306

1128. Ministerial and other Salaries Order 1983
Sch.1, varied: SI 2014/2708 Art.5

1264. Pensions Increase (Review) Order 1983
  referred to: SI 2014/668 Sch.1
  Art.2, amended: SI 2014/560 Sch.3 para.3,
  SI 2014/3229 Sch.3 para.2
  Art.2, disapplied: SI 2014/3229 Sch.2 para.6
1460. Trunk Road (A483) (Builth Wells, Powys)
(One Way Traffic) Order 1983
  Art.3, varied: SI 2014/2757 Art.7
  Art.4, varied: SI 2014/2464 Art.4
1561. Consumer Credit (Enforcement, Default
and Termination Notices) Regulations 1983
  Sch.2 para.10A, amended: SI 2014/366 Art.6
1771. Trunk Road (A5) (Llanfairpwllgwyngyll,
Gwynedd) (Prohibition of Foot Passengers)
Order 1983
  revoked: SI 2014/2927 Art.5
1772. Trunk Road (A5) (Llanfairpwllgwyngyll,
Gwynedd) (50 mph Speed Limit) Order 1983
  varied: SI 2014/1549 Art.10
1932. Trunk Road (A5) (Bangor By-Pass,
Gwynedd) (Prohibition of Foot Passengers)
Order 1983
  revoked: SI 2014/2927 Art.5

1984

297. Civil Courts (Amendment) Order 1984
  revoked: SI 2014/820 Sch.1
467. Town and Country Planning (Control of
Advertisements) (Scotland) Regulations 1984
  Reg.24, applied: SSI 2014/139 Reg.3
  Reg.26A, added: SSI 2014/139 Reg.2
  Sch.4, amended: SSI 2014/249 Reg.2
510. Explosives Act 1875 etc (Metrication and
Miscellaneous Amendment) Regulations 1984
  Reg.1, revoked (in part): SI 2014/1639 Sch.3
  Part 2
  Reg.3, revoked: SI 2014/1639 Sch.3 Part 2
  Sch.2, revoked: SI 2014/1639 Sch.3 Part 2
552. Coroners Rules 1984
  r.28, see *R. (on the application of Cooper) v*
  HM Coroner for North East Kent [2014]
  EWHC 586 (Admin), (2014) 178 J.P. 505
  (QBD (Admin)), Mitting J
690. Trunk Road (A470) (Llandinam, Powys)
(40 MPH Speed Limit) Order 1984
  revoked: SI 2014/348 Art.4
746. Value Added Tax (Imported Goods) Relief
Order 1984
  Sch.2 Part 8, amended: SI 2014/2364 Art.2

1075. Civil Courts (Amendment No 2) Order
1984
  revoked: SI 2014/820 Sch.1
1307. Pensions Increase (Review) Order 1984
  referred to: SI 2014/668 Sch.1
  Art.2, amended: SI 2014/560 Sch.3 para.3,
  SI 2014/3229 Sch.3 para.2
  Art.2, disapplied: SI 2014/3229 Sch.2 para.6
1315. Weights and Measures Act 1963 (Cheese,
Fish, Fresh Fruits and Vegetables, Meat and
Poultry) Order 1984
  Art.2, amended: SI 2014/2975 Reg.14
  Art.2, substituted: SI 2014/2975 Reg.14
  Art.4, amended: SI 2014/2975 Reg.15
  Art.5, amended: SI 2014/2975 Reg.16
1719. Special Road (A55) (Llanddulas to Colwyn
Bay) Regulations 1984
  varied: SI 2014/915 Art.13
1814. Transfer of Functions (Arts, Libraries and
National Heritage) Order 1984
  Art.1, varied: SI 2014/2708 Art.5
1822. General Consumer Council (Northern
Ireland) Order 1984
  Sch.1, added: SI 2014/631 Sch.1 para.21
  Sch.1, amended: SI 2014/631 Sch.1 para.21
1984. Family Law (Miscellaneous Provisions)
(Northern Ireland) Order 1984
  Art.18, applied: SI 2014/1110 Art.14, SI
  2014/3265 Art.16

1985

166. Transfer of Functions (British Museum
(Natural History)) Order 1985
  Art.2, varied: SI 2014/2708 Art.5
201. Public Lending Right (Increase of Limit)
Order 1985
  varied: SI 2014/2708 Art.5
267. Local Authority Accounts (Scotland)
Regulations 1985
  revoked: SSI 2014/200 Reg.4
454. Local Elections (Northern Ireland) Order
1985
  Art.6, amended: SI 2014/1116 Art.7
  Sch.2, added: SI 2014/1116 Art.7
  Sch.2, amended: SI 2014/1116 Art.7, SI
  2014/1880 Art.4
  Sch.2, substituted: SI 2014/1116 Art.7, SI
  2014/1880 Art.4

511. Civil Courts (Amendment) Order 1985
revoked: SI 2014/820 Sch.1

539. Trunk Roads (A470/A483) (Builth Wells, Powys) (Traffic Regulation) Order 1985
Art.5, varied: SI 2014/2757 Art.8

824. Special Road Order (Colwyn Bay to Glan Conwy) Regulations 1985
varied: SI 2014/915 Art.12
Reg.13, varied: SI 2014/2892 Art.8

960. Films Co-Production Agreements Order 1985
Sch.1, substituted: SI 2014/1561 Art.2

1205. Credit Unions (Northern Ireland) Order 1985
applied: SI 2014/2418 Sch.1

1574. Registration of Overseas Births and Deaths (Amendment) Regulations 1985
revoked: SI 2014/511 Reg.17

1575. Pensions Increase (Review) Order 1985
referred to: SI 2014/668 Sch.1
Art.2, amended: SI 2014/560 Sch.3 para.3, SI 2014/3229 Sch.3 para.2
Art.2, disapplied: SI 2014/3229 Sch.2 para.6

1581. Public Lending Right Scheme 1982 (Amendment) Order 1985
varied: SI 2014/2708 Art.5

1986

17. Trunk Road (A55/A494) (Ewloe Interchange, Clwyd) (De-restriction) Order 1986
varied: SI 2014/915 Art.16

183. Removal and Disposal of Vehicles Regulations 1986
Reg.5C, amended: SI 2014/1388 Reg.2

595. Mental Health (Northern Ireland) Order 1986
Art.3, applied: SI 2014/2843 Reg.7

600. Transfer of Functions (Arts, Libraries and National Heritage) Order 1986
Art.1, varied: SI 2014/2708 Art.5

754. Civil Courts (Amendment) Order 1986
revoked: SI 2014/820 Sch.1

975. National Health Service (General Ophthalmic Services) Regulations 1986
Reg.13, amended: SI 2014/460 Reg.3

1078. Road Vehicles (Construction and Use) Regulations 1986
see *DPP v Issler* [2014] EWHC 669 (Admin), [2014] 1 W.L.R. 3686 (DC), Rafferty LJ
Reg.37, see *DPP v Issler* [2014] EWHC 669 (Admin), [2014] 1 W.L.R. 3686 (DC), Rafferty LJ
Reg.80, amended: SI 2014/264 Reg.2
Sch.7B Part I para.7, amended: SI 2014/1862 Reg.2

1116. Pensions Increase (Review) Order 1986
referred to: SI 2014/668 Sch.1
Art.2, amended: SI 2014/560 Sch.3 para.3, SI 2014/3229 Sch.3 para.2
Art.2, disapplied: SI 2014/3229 Sch.2 para.6

1335. Costs in Criminal Cases (General) Regulations 1986
Part II, applied: SI 2014/1610 r.76_1
Part III, applied: SI 2014/1610 r.76_4
Reg.3, applied: SI 2014/1610 r.76_1, r.76_8
Reg.3, see *R. (on the application of Singh) v Ealing Magistrates' Court* [2014] EWHC 1443 (Admin), (2014) 178 J.P. 253 (QBD (Admin)), Beatson LJ
Reg.3B, applied: SI 2014/1610 r.63_1
Reg.3C, applied: SI 2014/1610 r.63_1, r.68_1
Reg.3D, applied: SI 2014/1610 r.76_1
Reg.3F, applied: SI 2014/1610 r.63_1, r.76_1, r.76_10, r.68_1
Reg.3H, applied: SI 2014/1610 r.63_1, r.68_1
Reg.3I, applied: SI 2014/1610 r.76_1
Reg.4A, applied: SI 2014/1610 r.76_4
Reg.7, applied: SI 2014/1610 r.76_4
Reg.14, applied: SI 2014/1610 r.76_4, r.76_5

1361. Civil Courts (Amendment No.2) Order 1986
revoked: SI 2014/820 Sch.1

1442. Registration of Marriages Regulations 1986
Reg.5, amended: SI 2014/107 Sch.1 para.8
Reg.11, amended: SI 2014/3061 Sch.1 para.6
Reg.12, amended: SI 2014/107 Sch.1 para.8
Sch.1, amended: SI 2014/107 Sch.1 para.8

1510. Control of Pesticides Regulations 1986
applied: SI 2014/3223 Sch.1 para.1

1596. Agriculture Act 1986 (Commencement No.3) Order 1986
 revoked: SI 2014/1924 Sch.1
1629. Public Service Vehicles (Traffic Commissioners Publication and Inquiries) Regulations 1986
 Reg.3, amended: SI 2014/3142 Reg.2
 Reg.3, revoked (in part): SI 2014/3142 Reg.2
1648. Tyne and Wear Passenger Transport Executive (Exclusion of Bus Operating Powers) Order 1986
 revoked (in part): SI 2014/1364 Sch.1
1649. Greater Manchester Passenger Transport Executive (Exclusion of Bus Operating Powers) Order 1986
 revoked (in part): SI 2014/1364 Sch.1
1650. Merseyside Passenger Transport Executive (Exclusion of Bus Operating Powers) Order 1986
 revoked (in part): SI 2014/1364 Sch.1
1651. South Yorkshire Passenger Transport Executive (Exclusion of Bus Operating Powers) Order 1986
 revoked (in part): SI 2014/1364 Sch.1
1652. West Midlands Passenger Transport Executive (Exclusion of Bus Operating Powers) Order 1986
 revoked (in part): SI 2014/1364 Sch.1
1653. West Yorkshire Passenger Transport Executive (Exclusion of Bus Operating Powers) Order 1986
 revoked (in part): SI 2014/1364 Sch.1
1711. Stamp Duty Reserve Tax Regulations 1986
 Reg.2, amended: SI 2014/1932 Reg.2
 Reg.2, revoked (in part): SI 2014/1932 Reg.2
 Reg.2A, revoked: SI 2014/1932 Reg.2
 Reg.3, amended: SI 2014/1932 Reg.2
 Reg.4, amended: SI 2014/1932 Reg.2
 Reg.4, revoked (in part): SI 2014/1932 Reg.2
 Reg.4B, revoked: SI 2014/1932 Reg.2
 Reg.6, amended: SI 2014/1932 Reg.2
 Reg.7, amended: SI 2014/1932 Reg.2
 Reg.7, revoked (in part): SI 2014/1932 Reg.2
 Reg.12, amended: SI 2014/1932 Reg.2
 Reg.13, amended: SI 2014/1932 Reg.2
 Reg.14, amended: SI 2014/1932 Reg.2
 Sch.1 Part I, amended: SI 2014/1932 Reg.2
 Sch.1 Part II, amended: SI 2014/1932 Reg.2

1915. Insolvency (Scotland) Rules 1986
 applied: SSI 2014/114 r.29
 Part I, applied: SI 2014/229 Art.11
 Part 001 r.0.2, amended: SSI 2014/114 r.3, r.26
 Part I r.1.6, varied: SI 2014/229 Sch.4 para.39
 Part I r.1.40, varied: SI 2014/229 Sch.4 para.40
 Part 2, applied: SI 2014/229 Art.11
 Part 2 r.2.10, varied: SI 2014/229 Sch.4 para.41
 Part 2 r.2.22, varied: SI 2014/229 Sch.4 para.42
 Part 2 r.2.23, varied: SI 2014/229 Sch.4 para.43
 Part 2 r.2.27, varied: SI 2014/229 Sch.4 para.44, Sch.4 para.45
 Part 2 r.2.27A, varied: SI 2014/229 Sch.4 para.44
 Part 2 r.2.28, varied: SI 2014/229 Sch.4 para.44, Sch.4 para.46
 Part 2 r.2.29, varied: SI 2014/229 Sch.4 para.47
 Part 2 r.2.34, varied: SI 2014/229 Sch.4 para.48
 Part 2 r.2.35, varied: SI 2014/229 Sch.4 para.44, Sch.4 para.49
 Part 2 r.2.40, varied: SI 2014/229 Sch.4 para.50
 Part 2 r.2.41, amended: SSI 2014/114 r.4
 Part 2 r.2.41, varied: SI 2014/229 Sch.4 para.51
 Part 2 r.2.41A, amended: SSI 2014/114 r.5
 Part 2 r.2.41A, varied: SI 2014/229 Sch.4 para.50
 Part 2 r.2.45, varied: SI 2014/229 Sch.4 para.52
 Part 2 r.2.50, varied: SI 2014/229 Sch.4 para.53
 Part 2 r.2.53, varied: SI 2014/229 Sch.4 para.54
 Part 2 r.2.56, varied: SI 2014/229 Sch.4 para.54
 Part 3 r.3.2, amended: SSI 2014/114 r.24
 Part 3 r.3.2A, added: SSI 2014/114 r.24
 Part 3 r.3.9A, added: SSI 2014/114 r.26
 Part 4 r.4.5, amended: SSI 2014/114 r.6
 Part 4 r.4.7, amended: SSI 2014/114 r.25
 Part 4 r.4.8, amended: SSI 2014/114 r.25
 Part 4 r.4.8A, added: SSI 2014/114 r.25

Part 4 r.4.15, amended: SSI 2014/114 r.7

Part 4 r.4.16, substituted: SSI 2014/114 r.8

Part 4 r.4.22, revoked (in part): SSI 2014/114 r.9

Part 4 r.4.22A, added: SSI 2014/114 r.10

Part 4 r.4.26A, added: SSI 2014/114 r.11

Part 4 r.4.32, substituted: SSI 2014/114 r.12

Part 4 r.4.42, amended: SSI 2014/114 r.13

Part 4 r.4.45, amended: SSI 2014/114 r.14

Part 4 r.4.48, amended: SSI 2014/114 r.15

Part 4 r.4.50, substituted: SSI 2014/114 r.16

Part 4 r.4.59, substituted: SSI 2014/114 r.17

Part 4 r.4.68, substituted: SSI 2014/114 r.18

Part 4 r.4.75A, added: SSI 2014/114 r.26

Part 4 r.4.76, amended: SSI 2014/114 r.19

Part 4 r.4.83, amended: SSI 2014/114 r.20

Part 4 r.4.83, revoked (in part): SSI 2014/114 r.20

Part 7, applied: SI 2014/229 Art.11

Part 7 r.7.6, varied: SI 2014/229 Sch.4 para.55

Part 7 r.7.7, varied: SI 2014/229 Sch.4 para.56

Part 7 r.7.9, amended: SSI 2014/114 r.21

Part 7 r.7.12, varied: SI 2014/229 Sch.4 para.57

Part 7 r.7.21, amended: SSI 2014/114 r.26

Part 7 r.7.21A, amended: SSI 2014/114 r.27

Part 7 r.7.21B, amended: SSI 2014/114 r.27

Part 7 r.7.30, varied: SI 2014/229 Sch.4 para.58

Part 7 r.7.30A, amended: SSI 2014/114 r.26

Part 7 r.7.30B, amended: SSI 2014/114 r.26

Part 7 r.7.30C, added: SSI 2014/114 r.26

Part 7 r.7.32, substituted: SSI 2014/114 r.22

Sch.1 para.4, amended: SSI 2014/114 r.25

Sch.1 para.4A, added: SSI 2014/114 r.25

Sch.1 para.10, amended: SSI 2014/114 r.23

Sch.1 para.10, substituted: SSI 2014/114 r.23

Sch.1 para.29A, added: SSI 2014/114 r.23

Sch.1 para.32A, added: SSI 2014/114 r.26

Sch.2 para.6, amended: SSI 2014/114 r.10

Sch.2 para.7A, added: SSI 2014/114 r.11

Sch.2 para.15, added: SSI 2014/114 r.26

Sch.5, amended: SSI 2014/114 Sch.1

1925. Insolvency Rules 1986

see *Games Station Ltd, Re* [2014] EWCA Civ 180, [2014] 3 W.L.R. 901 (CA (Civ Div)), Patten LJ; see *Hayes v Hayes* [2014] EWHC 2694 (Ch), [2014] Bus. L.R. 1238

(Ch D), Nugee J; see *Salliss v Hunt* [2014] EWHC 229 (Ch), [2014] 1 W.L.R. 2402 (Ch D), Sir Terence Etherton C

Part 1, applied: SI 2014/229 Art.11

Part 1 r.1.6, varied: SI 2014/229 Sch.4 para.7

Part 1 r.1.48, varied: SI 2014/229 Sch.4 para.8

Part 2, applied: SI 2014/229 Art.11

Part 2 r.2.16, varied: SI 2014/229 Sch.4 para.9

Part 2 r.2.30, varied: SI 2014/229 Sch.4 para.10

Part 2 r.2.31, varied: SI 2014/229 Sch.4 para.11

Part 2 r.2.34, varied: SI 2014/229 Sch.4 para.12

Part 2 r.2.35, varied: SI 2014/229 Sch.4 para.12, Sch.4 para.13

Part 2 r.2.36, varied: SI 2014/229 Sch.4 para.12

Part 2 r.2.37, varied: SI 2014/229 Sch.4 para.14

Part 2 r.2.43, varied: SI 2014/229 Sch.4 para.12, Sch.4 para.15

Part 2 r.2.45, varied: SI 2014/229 Sch.4 para.16

Part 2 r.2.46, varied: SI 2014/229 Sch.4 para.12

Part 2 r.2.47, varied: SI 2014/229 Sch.4 para.17

Part 2 r.2.48, varied: SI 2014/229 Sch.4 para.18

Part 2 r.2.49, varied: SI 2014/229 Sch.4 para.19

Part 2 r.2.68, varied: SI 2014/229 Sch.4 para.20

Part 2 r.2.69, varied: SI 2014/229 Sch.4 para.21

Part 2 r.2.85, varied: SI 2014/229 Sch.4 para.22

Part 2 r.2.95, varied: SI 2014/229 Sch.4 para.23

Part 2 r.2.97, varied: SI 2014/229 Sch.4 para.24

Part 2 r.2.98, varied: SI 2014/229 Sch.4 para.25

Part 2 r.2.99, varied: SI 2014/229 Sch.4 para.26

Part 2 r.2.100, varied: SI 2014/229 Sch.4 para.27

Part 2 r.2.103, varied: SI 2014/229 Sch.4
para.28
Part 2 r.2.112, varied: SI 2014/229 Sch.4
para.29
Part 2 r.2.113, varied: SI 2014/229 Sch.4
para.30
Part 2 r.2.120, varied: SI 2014/229 Sch.4
para.31
Part 2 r.2.122, varied: SI 2014/229 Sch.4
para.32
Part 2 r.2.125, varied: SI 2014/229 Sch.4
para.32
Part 2 r.2.132, applied: SI 2014/2839 Reg.4
Part 5A r.5A.2, amended: SI 2014/879
Art.22
Part 5A r.5A.21, amended: SI 2014/817
Sch.2 para.1
Part 6 r.6.4, amended: SI 2014/817 Sch.2
para.2
Part 6 r.6.9A, amended: SI 2014/817 Sch.2
para.3
Part 6 r.6.40A, amended: SI 2014/817 Sch.2
para.4
Part 7, applied: SI 2014/229 Art.11
Part 7 r.7.10C, amended: SI 2014/817 Sch.2
para.5
Part 7 r.7.11, amended: SI 2014/817 Sch.2
para.6
Part 7 r.7.12, amended: SI 2014/817 Sch.2
para.7
Part 7 r.7.13, amended: SI 2014/817 Sch.2
para.8
Part 7 r.7.14, amended: SI 2014/817 Sch.2
para.9
Part 7 r.7.15, amended: SI 2014/817 Sch.2
para.10
Part 7 r.7.16, amended: SI 2014/817 Sch.2
para.11
Part 7 r.7.19, amended: SI 2014/817 Sch.2
para.12
Part 7 r.7.21, amended: SI 2014/817 Sch.2
para.13
Part 7 r.7.24, revoked: SI 2014/817 Sch.2
para.14
Part 7 r.7.35, amended: SI 2014/817 Sch.2
para.15
Part 7 r.7.47, amended: SI 2014/817 Sch.2
para.16
Part 7 r.7.52, amended: SI 2014/817 Sch.2
para.17
Part 12 r.12.3, amended: SI 2014/879 Art.22

Part 12A r.12A.21, varied: SI 2014/229
Sch.4 para.33
Part 12A r.12A.28, amended: SI 2014/817
Sch.2 para.18
Part 12A r.12A.30, varied: SI 2014/229
Sch.4 para.34
Part 12A r.12A.33, amended: SI 2014/817
Sch.2 para.19
Part 13 r.13.13, varied: SI 2014/229 Sch.4
para.35
Pt 2., see *Registrar of Companies v
Swarbrick* [2014] EWHC 1466 (Ch), [2014]
Bus. L.R. 625 (Ch D), Richard Spearman
QC
Pt 5 r.5.17, see *Davis v Price* [2014] EWCA
Civ 26, [2014] 1 W.L.R. 2129 (CA (Civ
Div)), Arden LJ
Pt 5 r.5.21, see *Cahillane v National Asset
Loan Management Ltd* [2014] EWHC 1992
(Ch), [2014] B.P.I.R. 1093 (Ch D), Judge
Pelling QC; see *Davis v Price* [2014]
EWCA Civ 26, [2014] 1 W.L.R. 2129 (CA
(Civ Div)), Arden LJ
r.2.33A, see *Registrar of Companies v
Swarbrick* [2014] EWHC 1466 (Ch), [2014]
Bus. L.R. 625 (Ch D), Richard Spearman
QC
r.2.67, see *Bloom v Pensions Regulator*
[2014] A.C. 209 (SC), Lord Neuberger JSC;
see *Laverty v British Gas Trading Ltd*
[2014] EWHC 2721 (Ch), [2014] B.C.C. 701
(Ch D (Companies Ct)), Sir Terence
Etherton C; see *Portsmouth City Football
Club Ltd (In Liquidation), Re* [2013] EWCA
Civ 916, [2014] 1 All E.R. 12 (CA (Civ
Div)), Mummery, L.J.
r.2.78, see *Lehman Brothers International
(Europe) (In Administration), Re* [2014]
EWHC 1687 (Ch), [2014] Bus. L.R. 1186
(Ch D (Companies Ct)), David Richards J
r.2.106, see *Maxwell v Brookes* [2014]
B.P.I.R. 1395 (Ch D (Companies Ct)),
Registrar Jones
r.4.90, see *FG Skerritt Ltd v Caledonian
Building Systems Ltd* [2013] EWHC 1898
(TCC), [2014] B.P.I.R. 393 (QBD (TCC)),
Ramsey J
r.4.218, see *Portsmouth City Football Club
Ltd (In Liquidation), Re* [2013] EWCA Civ
916, [2014] 1 All E.R. 12 (CA (Civ Div)),
Mummery, L.J.

r.6.3, see *Yang v Official Receiver* [2013] EWHC 3577 (Ch), [2014] B.P.I.R. 826 (Ch D (Manchester)), Judge Hodge Q.C.

r.6.5, see *Cahillane v National Asset Loan Management Ltd* [2014] EWHC 1992 (Ch), [2014] B.P.I.R. 1093 (Ch D), Judge Pelling QC

r.6.14, see *Yang v Official Receiver* [2013] EWHC 3577 (Ch), [2014] B.P.I.R. 826 (Ch D (Manchester)), Judge Hodge Q.C.

r.6.25, see *Rightmatch Ltd v Meisels* [2014] B.P.I.R. 733 (Ch D), Registrar Jones

r.6.93, see *Cahillane v National Asset Loan Management Ltd* [2014] EWHC 1992 (Ch), [2014] B.P.I.R. 1093 (Ch D), Judge Pelling QC

r.6.141, see *Salliss v Hunt* [2014] EWHC 229 (Ch), [2014] 1 W.L.R. 2402 (Ch D), Sir Terence Etherton C

r.6.185, see *Hunt v Conwy CBC* [2013] EWHC 1154 (Ch), [2014] 1 W.L.R. 254 (Ch D), Sir William Blackburne

r.7.51, see *Hayes v Hayes* [2014] EWHC 2694 (Ch), [2014] Bus. L.R. 1238 (Ch D), Nugee J

r.12.2, see *Bloom v Pensions Regulator* [2014] A.C. 209 (SC), Lord Neuberger JSC

r.12.3, see *Bloom v Pensions Regulator* [2014] A.C. 209 (SC), Lord Neuberger JSC; see *Hellard v Chadwick* [2014] B.P.I.R. 163 (Ch D), Registrar Barber; see *Laverty v British Gas Trading Ltd* [2014] EWHC 2721 (Ch), [2014] B.C.C. 701 (Ch D (Companies Ct)), Sir Terence Etherton C

r.12.9, see *Lehman Brothers International (Europe) (In Administration), Re* [2014] EWHC 1687 (Ch), [2014] Bus. L.R. 1186 (Ch D (Companies Ct)), David Richards J

r.13.12, see *Bloom v Pensions Regulator* [2014] A.C. 209 (SC), Lord Neuberger JSC; see *Kaye v South Oxfordshire DC* [2013] EWHC 4165 (Ch), [2014] 2 All E.R. 1019 (Ch D (Manchester)), Judge Hodge Q.C.; see *Laverty v British Gas Trading Ltd* [2014] EWHC 2721 (Ch), [2014] B.C.C. 701 (Ch D (Companies Ct)), Sir Terence Etherton C
Sch.2, amended: SI 2014/817 Sch.2 para.20
Sch.2, substituted: SI 2014/817 Sch.2 para.20
Sch.4, amended: SI 2014/817 Sch.2 para.21, Sch.2 para.22, Sch.2 para.23, Sch.2 para.24,

Sch.2 para.25, Sch.2 para.26, Sch.2 para.27, Sch.2 para.28, Sch.2 para.29, Sch.2 para.30, Sch.2 para.31, Sch.2 para.32
Sch.4, substituted: SI 2014/817 Sch.2 para.22

1960. Statutory Maternity Pay (General) Regulations 1986
Reg.6, amended: SI 2014/147 Art.4
Reg.11, amended: SI 2014/3255 Art.4
Reg.20, amended: SI 2014/3255 Art.4

2194. Housing (Right to Buy) (Prescribed Forms) Regulations 1986
Sch.1, amended: SI 2014/1797 Sch.1

2207. Civil Courts (Amendment No 3) Order 1986
revoked: SI 2014/820 Sch.1

2211. Charitable Deductions (Approved Schemes) Regulations 1986
Reg.2, amended: SI 2014/584 Reg.3
Reg.3, amended: SI 2014/584 Reg.4
Reg.4A, substituted: SI 2014/584 Reg.5
Reg.9, amended: SI 2014/584 Reg.6
Reg.11, amended: SI 2014/584 Reg.7
Reg.11, revoked (in part): SI 2014/584 Reg.7

2224. Limitation of Liability for Maritime Claims (Parties to Convention) Order 1986
revoked: SI 2014/1355 Art.2

2297. Act of Sederunt (Sheriff Court Company Insolvency Rules) 1986
Part IV r.25, amended: SSI 2014/119 r.3
Part V r.31AA, added: SSI 2014/119 r.3

1987

37. Dangerous Substances in Harbour Areas Regulations 1987
Part IX, disapplied: SI 2014/1638 Reg.3
Reg.2, amended: SI 2014/469 Sch.3 para.38, SI 2014/1637 Sch.4 para.6
Reg.5, amended: SI 2014/1637 Sch.4 para.6
Reg.29, amended: SI 2014/1637 Sch.4 para.6
Reg.33, amended: SI 2014/1638 Sch.13 para.13
Reg.35, amended: SI 2014/469 Sch.3 para.39
Reg.36, amended: SI 2014/469 Sch.3 para.40
Reg.36, applied: SI 2014/1638 Reg.2

Reg.36A, added: SI 2014/469 Sch.3 para.41
Reg.41, amended: SI 2014/469 Sch.3
para.42
Reg.44, amended: SI 2014/469 Sch.3
para.43
Reg.47, revoked (in part): SI 2014/1637
Sch.4 Part 1
Sch.7 para.1, amended: SI 2014/469 Sch.3
para.44
Sch.7 para.2, amended: SI 2014/469 Sch.3
para.44
Sch.7 para.3, amended: SI 2014/469 Sch.3
para.44
Sch.7 para.4, amended: SI 2014/469 Sch.3
para.44
Sch.7 para.5, amended: SI 2014/469 Sch.3
para.44

52. Health and Safety (Explosives and Petroleum Fees) (Modification) Regulations 1987
revoked: SI 2014/1637 Sch.4 Part 1

130. Pensions Increase (Review) Order 1987
referred to: SI 2014/668 Sch.1
Art.2, amended: SI 2014/560 Sch.3 para.3,
SI 2014/3229 Sch.3 para.2
Art.2, disapplied: SI 2014/3229 Sch.2 para.6

257. Police Pensions Regulations 1987
Reg.1, amended: SI 2014/79 Reg.5, SI
2014/3061 Sch.1 para.13
Reg.2, amended: SI 2014/381 Reg.2, SSI
2014/62 Reg.2
Reg.6, amended: SI 2014/79 Reg.4
Reg.12, amended: SI 2014/79 Reg.3
Sch.CPart I para.1, amended: SI 2014/79
Reg.6, SI 2014/3061 Sch.1 para.13
Sch.CPart III para.1, amended: SI 2014/79
Reg.7, SI 2014/3061 Sch.1 para.13
Sch.CPart V para.1, amended: SI 2014/79
Reg.9
Sch.CPart V para.1A, amended: SI 2014/79
Reg.9
Sch.CPart V para.1B, added: SI 2014/3061
Sch.1 para.13
Sch.CPart I para.3, amended: SI 2014/79
Reg.6
Sch.CPart III para.3, amended: SI 2014/79
Reg.7
Sch.CPart IV para.4, amended: SI 2014/79
Reg.8
Sch.CPart IV para.5, amended: SI 2014/79
Reg.8

Sch.CPart IV para.5A, added: SI 2014/3061
Sch.1 para.13
Sch.CPart IV para.6, amended: SI 2014/79
Reg.8

299. Prosecution of Offences (Custody Time Limits) Regulations 1987
applied: SI 2014/1610 r.3_26
Reg.4, applied: SI 2014/1610 r.19_16
Reg.7, applied: SI 2014/1610 r.19_16

375. Judicial Pensions (Widows and Children's Benefits) Regulations 1987
disapplied: SI 2014/3229 Sch.2 para.6
Reg.2, amended: SI 2014/288 Reg.2
Reg.4, amended: SI 2014/288 Reg.2
Reg.5, amended: SI 2014/288 Reg.2
Reg.6, amended: SI 2014/288 Reg.2

416. Social Security (Maternity Allowance) Regulations 1987
Reg.1, amended: SI 2014/884 Reg.2
Reg.2, applied: SI 2014/3053 Reg.5
Reg.2, substituted: SI 2014/884 Reg.2
Reg.3, amended: SI 2014/884 Reg.2

470. Merchant Shipping (Prevention and Control of Pollution) Order 1987
Art.3, enabled: SI 2014/3306

670. Carriage of Passengers and their Luggage by Sea (Domestic Carriage) Order 1987
applied: SI 2014/1361 Art.3

764. Town and Country Planning (Use Classes) Order 1987
see *Hannan v Newham LBC* [2014] EWHC
1424 (Admin), [2014] J.P.L. 1101 (QBD
(Admin)), Ouseley J; see *Royal London
Mutual Insurance Society Ltd v Secretary of
State for Communities and Local
Government* [2013] EWHC 3597 (Admin),
[2014] J.P.L. 458 (QBD (Admin)), Patterson
J

908. Milk (Cessation of Production) (England and Wales) Scheme 1987
Art.22, varied: SI 2014/2708 Art.5

931. Carriage of Passengers and their Luggage by Sea (Parties to Convention) Order 1987
revoked: SI 2014/1355 Art.2

1538. Weights and Measures (Quantity Marking and Abbreviations of Units) Regulations 1987
Reg.2, amended: SI 2014/2975 Reg.18

1783. Olive Oil (Marketing Standards) Regulations 1987
revoked: SI 2014/195 Reg.20

1836. Ministerial and other Salaries Order 1987
Sch.1 Part I, varied: SI 2014/2708 Art.5
1850. Local Government Superannuation (Scotland) Regulations 1987
applied: SSI 2014/233 Reg.3, Reg.17, Reg.22, Reg.24
varied: SSI 2014/233 Reg.24
1967. Income Support (General) Regulations 1987
applied: SI 2014/1230 Reg.7
Reg.2, amended: SI 2014/107 Sch.1 para.9, SI 2014/591 Reg.2, SI 2014/3229 Sch.6 para.5, SI 2014/3255 Art.5
Reg.5, amended: SI 2014/3255 Art.5
Reg.21AA, amended: SI 2014/902 Reg.2
Reg.22A, applied: SI 2014/516 Sch.4
Reg.35, amended: SI 2014/591 Reg.2, SI 2014/3255 Art.5
Reg.37, applied: SI 2014/2672 Reg.14
Reg.41, applied: SI 2014/2672 Reg.16
Reg.42, amended: SI 2014/591 Reg.2
Reg.42, applied: SI 2014/2672 Reg.17
Reg.50, applied: SI 2014/2672 Reg.21
Reg.51, applied: SI 2014/2672 Reg.22
Sch.1B para.1, applied: SI 2014/1097 Reg.2
Sch.1B para.14B, amended: SI 2014/3255 Art.5
Sch.1B para.14B, varied: 2014 c.6 s.126
Sch.2 Part I para.1, applied: SI 2014/1097 Reg.8
Sch.2 Part I para.1, referred to: SI 2014/147 Art.6
Sch.2 Part I para.2, substituted: SI 2014/516 Sch.2
Sch.2 Part II para.3, amended: SI 2014/516 Art.14
Sch.2 Part III para.12, amended: SI 2014/2888 Reg.3
Sch.2 Part III para.13, amended: SI 2014/2888 Reg.3
Sch.2 Part III para.14, amended: SI 2014/591 Reg.2, SI 2014/2888 Reg.3
Sch.2 Part IV para.15, substituted: SI 2014/516 Sch.3
Sch.3, applied: SI 2014/2672 Sch.1 para.3
Sch.3 para.5, applied: SI 2014/516 Sch.4
Sch.3 para.6, applied: SI 2014/516 Sch.4, SI 2014/1230 Reg.29
Sch.3 para.7, applied: SI 2014/516 Sch.4
Sch.3 para.8, applied: SI 2014/516 Sch.4, SI 2014/1230 Reg.29

Sch.3 para.10, applied: SI 2014/516 Sch.4
Sch.3 para.11, applied: SI 2014/516 Sch.4
Sch.3 para.12, amended: SI 2014/591 Reg.2
Sch.3 para.12, applied: SI 2014/516 Sch.4
Sch.3 para.14, applied: SI 2014/1230 Reg.29
Sch.3 para.15, applied: SI 2014/1230 Reg.29
Sch.3 para.18, amended: SI 2014/516 Art.14, SI 2014/2888 Reg.3
Sch.7, applied: SI 2014/516 Sch.4
Sch.9 para.2A, amended: SI 2014/591 Reg.2
Sch.9 para.3, applied: SI 2014/2672 Sch.1 para.7
Sch.9 para.4, amended: SI 2014/3255 Art.5
Sch.9 para.4A, amended: SI 2014/3255 Art.5
Sch.9 para.4A, applied: SI 2014/2672 Sch.1 para.7
Sch.9 para.5, applied: SI 2014/2672 Sch.1 para.3
Sch.9 para.8, applied: SI 2014/2672 Sch.1 para.10
Sch.9 para.8, referred to: SI 2014/2672 Sch.1 para.17
Sch.9 para.10, applied: SI 2014/2672 Sch.1 para.13
Sch.9 para.13, applied: SI 2014/2672 Sch.1 para.14
Sch.9 para.16, applied: SI 2014/2672 Sch.1 para.17
Sch.9 para.16, referred to: SI 2014/2672 Sch.1 para.17
Sch.9 para.17, applied: SI 2014/2672 Sch.1 para.20
Sch.9 para.23, applied: SI 2014/2672 Sch.1 para.23
Sch.9 para.24, applied: SI 2014/2672 Sch.1 para.24
Sch.9 para.25, amended: SI 2014/852 Art.2
Sch.9 para.26, applied: SI 2014/2672 Sch.1 para.26
Sch.9 para.28, applied: SI 2014/2672 Sch.1 para.26
Sch.9 para.31, applied: SI 2014/2672 Sch.1 para.28
Sch.9 para.33, applied: SI 2014/2672 Sch.1 para.30
Sch.9 para.36, referred to: SI 2014/2672 Sch.1 para.17
Sch.9 para.39, applied: SI 2014/2672 Sch.1 para.31
Sch.9 para.40, applied: SI 2014/2672 Sch.1 para.32

Sch.9 para.43, applied: SI 2014/2672 Sch.1 para.32

Sch.9 para.46, applied: SI 2014/2672 Sch.1 para.3

Sch.9 para.48, applied: SI 2014/2672 Sch.1 para.32

Sch.9 para.53, applied: SI 2014/2672 Sch.1 para.34

Sch.9 para.54, applied: SI 2014/2672 Sch.1 para.35

Sch.9 para.58, amended: SI 2014/513 Sch.1 para.1

Sch.9 para.79, added: SI 2014/2103 Art.3

Sch.10, varied: SI 2014/2672 Reg.22

Sch.10 para.2, applied: SI 2014/2672 Sch.2 para.4

Sch.10 para.3, applied: SI 2014/2672 Sch.2 para.7

Sch.10 para.4, applied: SI 2014/2672 Sch.2 para.4

Sch.10 para.5, applied: SI 2014/2672 Sch.2 para.8

Sch.10 para.6, varied: SI 2014/2672 Sch.2 para.9

Sch.10 para.7, varied: SI 2014/2672 Sch.2 para.10

Sch.10 para.8, applied: SI 2014/2672 Sch.2 para.12

Sch.10 para.11, applied: SI 2014/2672 Sch.2 para.14

Sch.10 para.12, applied: SI 2014/2672 Sch.2 para.15

Sch.10 para.12A, applied: SI 2014/2672 Sch.2 para.16

Sch.10 para.13, applied: SI 2014/2672 Sch.2 para.17

Sch.10 para.15, applied: SI 2014/2672 Sch.2 para.19

Sch.10 para.18, applied: SI 2014/2672 Sch.2 para.19

Sch.10 para.21, applied: SI 2014/2672 Sch.2 para.21

Sch.10 para.27, applied: SI 2014/2672 Sch.2 para.22

Sch.10 para.29, applied: SI 2014/2672 Sch.2 para.23

Sch.10 para.34, applied: SI 2014/2672 Sch.2 para.23

Sch.10 para.36, applied: SI 2014/2672 Sch.2 para.23

Sch.10 para.44, applied: SI 2014/2672 Reg.22, Sch.2 para.25

Sch.10 para.45, applied: SI 2014/2672 Reg.22, Sch.2 para.25

Sch.10 para.61, applied: SI 2014/2672 Sch.2 para.26

Sch.10 para.64, applied: SI 2014/2672 Sch.2 para.27

Sch.10 para.67, amended: SI 2014/513 Sch.1 para.1

Sch.10 para.71, added: SI 2014/2103 Art.3

1968. Social Security (Claims and Payments) Regulations 1987

applied: SI 2014/1230 Reg.6, SI 2014/1452 Art.3, SI 2014/3067 Art.2

referred to: SI 2014/1452 Art.3

Reg.2, amended: SI 2014/107 Sch.1 para.10, SI 2014/3229 Sch.6 para.6

Reg.4, amended: SI 2014/591 Reg.3

Reg.6, applied: SI 2014/1230 Reg.6, SI 2014/1452 Art.3, SI 2014/3094 Art.6

Reg.21, amended: SI 2014/2888 Reg.5

Reg.33, applied: SI 2014/1230 Reg.16

Reg.35, applied: SI 2014/1230 Reg.18

Sch.9, applied: SI 2014/1230 Reg.18

Sch.9 para.4, amended: SI 2014/618 Reg.5

Sch.9A para.7, amended: SI 2014/485 Reg.2

Sch.9B para.1, amended: SI 2014/612 Reg.14

Sch.9B para.2, amended: SI 2014/612 Reg.14

Sch.9B para.3, amended: SI 2014/612 Reg.14

Sch.9B para.4, amended: SI 2014/612 Reg.14

Sch.9B para.5, amended: SI 2014/612 Reg.14

Sch.9B para.6, amended: SI 2014/612 Reg.14

1969. Income Support (Transitional) Regulations 1987

Reg.15, varied: SI 2014/516 Art.15

1971. Housing Benefit (General) Regulations 1987

Reg.7A, applied: SI 2014/2603 Reg.5

Sch.1B, applied: SI 2014/2672 Sch.2 para.28

Sch.1B, referred to: SI 2014/2672 Sch.1 para.36

1973. Family Credit (General) Regulations 1987

Sch.2 para.57, amended: SI 2014/513 Sch.1 para.2

2023. Insolvent Companies (Disqualification of Unfit Directors) Proceedings Rules 1987
r.1, amended: SI 2014/549 Sch.1 para.24
2024. Non-Contentious Probate Rules 1987
r.32, amended: SI 2014/852 Art.3
2053. Double Taxation Relief (Taxes on Income) (Belgium) Order 1987
Sch.1, referred to: SI 2014/1875 Art.2
2088. Registration of Births and Deaths Regulations 1987
Reg.9, amended: SI 2014/107 Sch.1 para.11, SI 2014/3061 Sch.1 para.7
Reg.19, amended: SI 2014/107 Sch.1 para.11
Reg.42, amended: SI 2014/107 Sch.1 para.11
2197. Civil Jurisdiction (Offshore Activities) Order 1987
Art.1, referred to: SI 2014/1686 Sch.3 para.20
2244. Secretary of State's Traffic Orders (Procedure) (Scotland) Regulations 1987
applied: SSI 2014/247
Part II, applied: SSI 2014/96, SSI 2014/97, SSI 2014/125, SSI 2014/126, SSI 2014/198, SSI 2014/204, SSI 2014/222, SSI 2014/269, SSI 2014/378

1988

217. Pensions Increase (Review) Order 1988
referred to: SI 2014/668 Sch.1
Art.2, amended: SI 2014/560 Sch.3 para.3, SI 2014/3229 Sch.3 para.2
Art.2, disapplied: SI 2014/3229 Sch.2 para.6
370. International Carriage of Dangerous Goods by Road (Fees) Regulations 1988
Reg.2, revoked (in part): SI 2014/2117 Reg.2
Reg.3, substituted: SI 2014/2117 Reg.2
Reg.4, amended: SI 2014/2117 Reg.2
Reg.5, substituted: SI 2014/2117 Reg.2
Reg.11, revoked: SI 2014/2117 Reg.2
643. Department of Transport (Fees) Order 1988
applied: SI 2014/1816
Sch.1, referred to: SI 2014/2117
Sch.2 para.1, referred to: SI 2014/2117

664. Social Security (Payments on account, Overpayments and Recovery) Regulations 1988
applied: SI 2014/1230 Reg.10
668. Pneumoconiosis etc (Workers Compensation) (Payment of Claims) Regulations 1988
Reg.5, amended: SI 2014/869 Reg.2
Reg.6, amended: SI 2014/869 Reg.2
Reg.8, amended: SI 2014/869 Reg.2
Sch.1, substituted: SI 2014/869 Reg.2
784. Veterinary Surgeons (Agreement with the Republic of Ireland) Order 1988
applied: SI 2014/3493 Sch.1
900. Urban Development Corporations (Appropriate Ministers) Order 1988
revoked (in part): SI 2014/683 Sch.1
994. Esk Salmon Fishery District Designation Order 1988
Art.2, applied: SSI 2014/327 Sch.1
Art.4, applied: SSI 2014/327 Sch.1
Sch.1, applied: SSI 2014/327 Sch.1
1001. Cereals Co-responsibility Levy Regulations 1988
revoked: SI 2014/1902 Sch.1
1155. Trunk Road (Great Yarmouth Western Bypass) (Prohibition of Right Turns) Order 1988
disapplied: SI 2014/1571 Art.5
varied: SI 2014/1571 Art.5
1267. Cereals Co-responsibility Levy (Certified Seed Exemption) Regulations 1988
revoked: SI 2014/1902 Sch.1
1352. Set-Aside Regulations 1988
revoked: SI 2014/3263 Sch.5
1418. Judicial Pensions (Preservation of Benefits) Order 1988
Art.9, amended: SI 2014/107 Sch.1 para.12, SI 2014/3229 Sch.6 para.7
1420. Judicial Pensions (Requisite Benefits) Order 1988
Art.4, amended: SI 2014/107 Sch.1 para.13, SI 2014/3229 Sch.6 para.8
Art.7, amended: SI 2014/107 Sch.1 para.13, SI 2014/3229 Sch.6 para.8
Art.9, amended: SI 2014/107 Sch.1 para.13, SI 2014/3229 Sch.6 para.8
Art.9, substituted: SI 2014/107 Sch.1 para.13, SI 2014/3229 Sch.6 para.8
Art.10, revoked (in part): SI 2014/107 Sch.1 para.13, SI 2014/3229 Sch.6 para.8
Art.11, amended: SI 2014/107 Sch.1 para.13, SI 2014/3229 Sch.6 para.8

Art.12, amended: SI 2014/107 Sch.1 para.13, SI 2014/3229 Sch.6 para.8
Art.13, substituted: SI 2014/107 Sch.1 para.13, SI 2014/3229 Sch.6 para.8

1478. Goods Vehicles (Plating and Testing) Regulations 1988
Reg.3, amended: SI 2014/480 Reg.4
Reg.12, amended: SI 2014/2115 Reg.3
Reg.16, amended: SI 2014/2115 Reg.4
Reg.25, amended: SI 2014/2115 Reg.5
Reg.34, amended: SI 2014/2115 Reg.5, Reg.6
Reg.34, revoked (in part): SI 2014/2115 Reg.6
Reg.37B, amended: SI 2014/2115 Reg.5

1724. Social Fund Cold Weather Payments (General) Regulations 1988
Sch.1, substituted: SI 2014/2687 Sch.1
Sch.2, substituted: SI 2014/2687 Sch.2

1729. Mines (Safety of Exit) Regulations 1988
revoked (in part): SI 2014/3248 Sch.4 Part 1

1788. Fees for Inquiries (Standard Daily Amount) Regulations 1988
revoked (in part): SI 2014/692 Sch.1

1990. Housing (Northern Ireland) Order 1988
Art.2, applied: 2014 c.22 Sch.3 para.2
Art.3, applied: 2014 c.22 Sch.3 para.7

2039. Weights and Measures (Intoxicating Liquor) Order 1988
Art.6, amended: SI 2014/2975 Reg.34

2040. Weights and Measures (Miscellaneous Foods) Order 1988
Art.2, amended: SI 2014/2975 Reg.20
Art.2, substituted: SI 2014/2975 Reg.20
Art.3, substituted: SI 2014/2975 Reg.21
Art.4, amended: SI 2014/2975 Reg.22
Art.5, amended: SI 2014/2975 Reg.23
Art.7, substituted: SI 2014/2975 Reg.24
Art.8, amended: SI 2014/2975 Reg.25
Art.9, amended: SI 2014/2975 Reg.26
Art.11, amended: SI 2014/2975 Reg.27
Art.12, substituted: SI 2014/2975 Reg.28
Art.14, amended: SI 2014/2975 Reg.29
Art.17, amended: SI 2014/2975 Reg.30
Art.18, amended: SI 2014/2975 Reg.31
Sch.1, substituted: SI 2014/2975 Sch.1

2050. Distress for Rent Rules 1988
applied: SI 2014/421 Reg.14
revoked: SI 2014/600 Sch.1 Part 2
Appendix 1 para.2., applied: SI 2014/600 Art.4

2165. Civil Courts (Amendment) Order 1988
revoked: SI 2014/820 Sch.1

2253. Ministerial and other Salaries Order 1988
Sch.1 Part I, varied: SI 2014/2708 Art.5

2256. Church of England Pensions Regulations 1988
Reg.2, amended: SI 2014/3061 Sch.3 para.5

1989

102. Merchant Shipping (Provisions and Water) Regulations 1989
Reg.2, amended: SI 2014/1614 Reg.7
Reg.3, amended: SI 2014/1614 Reg.7
Reg.3, revoked (in part): SI 2014/1614 Reg.7
Reg.9, revoked: SI 2014/1614 Reg.7

106. Civil Courts (Amendment) Order 1989
revoked: SI 2014/820 Sch.1

107. Civil Courts (Amendment No.2) Order 1989
revoked: SI 2014/820 Sch.1

247. Heathrow Airport-London Noise Insulation Grants Scheme 1989
revoked: SI 2014/3233 Art.2

248. Gatwick Airport-London Noise Insulation Grants Scheme 1989
revoked: SI 2014/3233 Art.2

306. National Health Service (Charges to Overseas Visitors) Regulations 1989
Reg.1, amended: SI 2014/1622 Reg.2
Reg.5, amended: SI 2014/1622 Reg.2
Sch.3i, revoked (in part): SI 2014/1622 Reg.2
Sch.4, added: SI 2014/1622 Reg.2

364. National Health Service (Charges to Overseas Visitors) (Scotland) Regulations 1989
disapplied: SSI 2014/344 Sch.2
Reg.3, amended: SSI 2014/70 Reg.2
Reg.5, amended: SSI 2014/70 Reg.2
Reg.5, revoked (in part): SSI 2014/70 Reg.2
Sch.1, amended: SSI 2014/70 Reg.2
Sch.2, amended: SSI 2014/70 Reg.2

433. Grant-aided Colleges (Scotland) Grant Regulations 1989
applied: SSI 2014/52 Art.4

477. Pensions Increase (Review) Order 1989
referred to: SI 2014/668 Sch.1
Art.2, amended: SI 2014/560 Sch.3 para.3, SI 2014/3229 Sch.3 para.2

Art.2, disapplied: SI 2014/3229 Sch.2 para.6

576. Cereals Co-responsibility Levy (Amendment) Regulations 1989
revoked: SI 2014/1902 Sch.1

635. Electricity at Work Regulations 1989
Reg.2, amended: SI 2014/3248 Sch.4 Part 2
Reg.3, amended: SI 2014/3248 Sch.5 para.6
Reg.17, revoked (in part): SI 2014/3248 Sch.4 Part 2
Reg.29, amended: SI 2014/3248 Sch.5 para.6
Sch.1, revoked (in part): SI 2014/3248 Sch.4 Part 2

638. European Economic Interest Grouping Regulations 1989
Reg.2, revoked (in part): SI 2014/2382 Reg.3
Reg.4, amended: SI 2014/2382 Reg.4
Reg.5, amended: SI 2014/2382 Reg.5
Reg.9, amended: SI 2014/2382 Reg.6
Reg.12, amended: SI 2014/2382 Reg.7
Reg.12A, amended: SI 2014/2382 Reg.8
Reg.13, substituted: SI 2014/2382 Reg.9
Sch.2, revoked: SI 2014/2382 Reg.10

878. Tuberculosis (Deer) Order 1989
applied: SI 2014/2337 Art.20
revoked (in part): SI 2014/2337 Art.19

914. Civil Courts (Amendment No 3) Order 1989
revoked: SI 2014/820 Sch.1

1013. Copyright (Sub-titling of Broadcasts and Cable Programmes) (Designated Body) Order 1989
revoked: SI 2014/1384 Sch.1 para.8

1042. Set-Aside (Amendment) Regulations 1989
revoked: SI 2014/3263 Sch.5

1058. Non-Domestic Rating (Collection and Enforcement) (Local Lists) Regulations 1989
applied: SI 2014/600 Art.4
see *Kaye v South Oxfordshire DC* [2013] EWHC 4165 (Ch), [2014] 2 All E.R. 1019 (Ch D (Manchester)), Judge Hodge Q.C.
Part III, applied: SI 2014/3204 Sch.4 para.13
Reg.2, amended: SI 2014/379 Reg.2
Reg.7, amended: SI 2014/479 Reg.3
Reg.10, amended: SI 2014/600 Sch.1 para.2
Reg.10, varied: SI 2014/3204 Sch.4 para.9
Reg.11, applied: SI 2014/3204 Sch.4 para.13
Reg.11, disapplied: SI 2014/3204 Sch.4 para.9

Reg.12, applied: SI 2014/3204 Sch.4 para.10, Sch.4 para.13
Reg.12, varied: SI 2014/3204 Sch.4 para.9
Reg.13, referred to: SI 2014/3204 Sch.4 para.14
Reg.14, substituted: SI 2014/600 Sch.1 para.2
Reg.15, revoked: SI 2014/600 Sch.1 para.2
Reg.16, amended: SI 2014/600 Sch.1 para.2
Reg.16, applied: SI 2014/3204 Sch.4 para.10, Sch.4 para.13, Sch.4 para.14
Reg.18, applied: SI 2014/3204 Sch.4 para.14
Reg.19, amended: SI 2014/600 Sch.1 para.2
Reg.20, applied: SI 2014/3204 Sch.4 para.10
Reg.20, varied: SI 2014/3204 Sch.4 para.9
Reg.21, amended: SI 2014/600 Sch.1 para.2
Reg.21, varied: SI 2014/3204 Sch.4 para.9
Reg.22, varied: SI 2014/3204 Sch.4 para.9
Reg.23, applied: SI 2014/3204 Sch.4 para.10
Reg.23, varied: SI 2014/3204 Sch.4 para.9
Reg.24, amended: SI 2014/600 Sch.1 para.2
Sch.1 Part I para.1, amended: SI 2014/479 Reg.3
Sch.3, applied: SI 2014/3204 Sch.4 para.13
Sch.3, revoked: SI 2014/600 Sch.1 para.2, Sch.1 Part 2
Sch.3 para.1, applied: SI 2014/600 Art.4
Sch.4, varied: SI 2014/3204 Sch.4 para.9

1067. Copyright (Application of Provisions relating to Educational Establishments to Teachers) (No.2) Order 1989
Art.2, amended: SI 2014/1372 Sch.1 para.13

1263. Sludge (Use in Agriculture) Regulations 1989
referred to: SSI 2014/324 Sch.1 para.5
Reg.3, applied: SSI 2014/319 Sch.4 para.1
Reg.9, applied: SSI 2014/319 Sch.1 para.1, Sch.2 para.2, Sch.3 para.1, Sch.4 para.1

1297. Taxes (Interest Rate) Regulations 1989
Reg.5, amended: SI 2014/496 Reg.2

1316. Tuberculosis (Deer) Notice of Intended Slaughter and Compensation Order 1989
revoked (in part): SI 2014/2338 Art.6

1490. Civil Legal Aid (Scotland) (Fees) Regulations 1989
Sch.5, amended: SSI 2014/257 Reg.3

1491. Criminal Legal Aid (Scotland) (Fees) Regulations 1989
see *HM Advocate v McCrossan (Darryl)* 2014 J.C. 161 (HCJ), Lady Paton
Sch.1 para.3AA, added: SSI 2014/257 Reg.4

1499. Annual Close Time (River Dee (Aberdeenshire) Salmon Fishery District) Order 1989
    Art.2, applied: SSI 2014/327 Sch.1
    Sch.1, applied: SSI 2014/327 Sch.1

1598. A6(M) Motorway (Stockport North-South Bypass) and Connecting Roads Scheme 1989
    revoked: SI 2014/1043 Art.2

1599. A6 Trunk Road (Hazel Grove Diversion) Order 1989
    revoked: SI 2014/1045 Art.2

1796. Road Vehicles Lighting Regulations 1989
    Reg.3, see *DPP v Issler* [2014] EWHC 669 (Admin), [2014] 1 W.L.R. 3686 (DC), Rafferty LJ
    Reg.11, amended: SI 2014/480 Reg.5
    Reg.16, see *DPP v Issler* [2014] EWHC 669 (Admin), [2014] 1 W.L.R. 3686 (DC), Rafferty LJ
    Sch.17 Part II, amended: SI 2014/480 Reg.5
    Sch.18 Part II, amended: SI 2014/480 Reg.5

1812. Aberdeen-Inverness Trunk Road (A96) (Forres Bypass) (40 mph Speed Limit) Order 1989
    revoked: SSI 2014/222 Art.3

1823. Cereals Co-responsibility Levy (Amendment) (No.2) Regulations 1989
    revoked: SI 2014/1902 Sch.1

1958. A55 Trunk Road (Penmaenmawr, Gwynedd) (Derestriction) Order 1989
    disapplied: SI 2014/3377 Art.14
    varied: SI 2014/827 Art.14, SI 2014/915 Art.10

2158. Trunk Road (A55) (Llanfairfechan, Gwynedd) (Derestriction) Order 1989
    disapplied: SI 2014/3377 Art.13
    varied: SI 2014/827 Art.13, SI 2014/915 Art.6

2260. Non-Domestic Rating (Collection and Enforcement) (Central Lists) Regulations 1989
    Reg.7, amended: SI 2014/479 Reg.2
    Sch.1 Part I para.1, amended: SI 2014/479 Reg.2

2404. Companies (Northern Ireland) Order 1989
    Part II, applied: SI 2014/1132 Sch.7 para.7, SI 2014/2709 Sch.2 para.7

2405. Insolvency (Northern Ireland) Order 1989
    Part II, applied: SI 2014/882 Reg.5, SI 2014/3486 Art.3
    Part VIII, applied: SI 2014/3486 Art.3
    Part IX, applied: SI 2014/882 Reg.5

    Art.17, amended: SI 2014/3486 Art.16
    Art.149, amended: SI 2014/3486 Art.17
    Art.149, revoked (in part): SI 2014/3486 Art.17
    Art.232, amended: SI 2014/3486 Art.18
    Art.257, see *Official Receiver for Northern Ireland v Gallagher* [2014] NICh 6, [2014] B.P.I.R. 918 (Ch D (NI)), Deeny J
    Art.279B, applied: SI 2014/1610 r.60_4
    Art.300, amended: SI 2014/3486 Art.19
    Art.300, revoked (in part): SI 2014/3486 Art.19
    Art.346, amended: SI 2014/3486 Art.20
    Sch.A1 para.41, amended: SI 2014/3486 Art.21
    Sch.B1, referred to: SI 2014/229 Art.10
    Sch.B1 para.19, applied: SI 2014/3486 Art.3
    Sch.B1 para.30, applied: SI 2014/3486 Art.3
    Sch.B1 para.74, amended: SI 2014/3486 Art.22
    Sch.4 para.18, added: SI 2014/3486 Art.23

2416. Ministerial and other Salaries Order 1989
    Sch.1 Part I, varied: SI 2014/2708 Art.5

1990

145. Non-Domestic Rating (Collection and Enforcement) (Miscellaneous Provisions) Regulations 1990
    Reg.4, amended: SI 2014/600 Sch.1 para.2
    Reg.5, amended: SI 2014/600 Sch.1 para.2

247. Health and Personal Social Services(Special Agencies)(Northern Ireland) Order 1990
    Art.3, applied: SI 2014/3282 Sch.1 para.11

263. Electricity (Non-Fossil Fuel Sources) (England and Wales) Order 1990
    Sch.2, amended: SI 2014/469 Sch.3 para.177

304. Dangerous Substances (Notification and Marking of Sites) Regulations 1990
    Reg.8, substituted: SI 2014/469 Sch.3 para.45
    Sch.1 para.2, amended: SI 2014/1637 Sch.4 para.7
    Sch.1 para.4, substituted: SI 2014/1637 Sch.4 para.7

324. Caithness Salmon Fishery District Designation Order 1990
    Art.2, applied: SSI 2014/327 Sch.1
    Sch.1, applied: SSI 2014/327 Sch.1
    Sch.2, applied: SSI 2014/327 Sch.1

483. Pensions Increase (Review) Order 1990
referred to: SI 2014/668 Sch.1
Art.2, amended: SI 2014/560 Sch.3 para.3,
SI 2014/3229 Sch.3 para.2
Art.2, disapplied: SI 2014/3229 Sch.2 para.6

598. Foreign Marriage (Amendment) Order 1990
revoked (in part): SI 2014/1110 Art.17

776. Local Government Finance (Repeals, Savings and Consequential Amendments) Order 1990
Sch.3 Part I para.9, revoked: 2014 c.14 Sch.7

1095. Trunk Road (A55) (Travellers Inn, Clwyd) (Derestriction) Order 1990
varied: SI 2014/915 Art.15

1380. Health and Safety (Training for Employment) Regulations 1990
varied: SI 2014/1663 Reg.30

1504. Companies (No.2) (Northern Ireland) Order 1990
Art.104, amended: SI 2014/2947 Sch.4
para.3

1519. Planning (Listed Buildings and Conservation Areas) Regulations 1990
Reg.5A, amended: SI 2014/1532 Art.10

1553. Local Government (Committees and Political Groups) Regulations 1990
Reg.16A, amended: SI 2014/476 Reg.2
Reg.16AA, added: SI 2014/476 Reg.2

1586. Special Road (Glan Conwy to Conwy Morfa) Regulations 1990
varied: SI 2014/915 Art.11
Reg.13, varied: SI 2014/2892 Art.9

1715. EEC Merger Control (Distinct Market Investigations) Regulations 1990
Reg.2, amended: SI 2014/549 Sch.1 para.1
Reg.3, substituted: SI 2014/549 Sch.1 para.1

1716. Set-Aside (Amendment) Regulations 1990
revoked: SI 2014/3263 Sch.5

1854. Annual Close Time (Rivers Irvine and Garnock Salmon Fishery District) Order 1990
Art.2, applied: SSI 2014/327 Sch.1
Sch.1, applied: SSI 2014/327 Sch.1

2020. Annual Close Time (River Tay Salmon Fishery District) Order 1990
Art.2, applied: SSI 2014/327 Sch.1
Sch.1, applied: SSI 2014/327 Sch.1

2024. National Health Service Trusts (Membership and Procedure) Regulations 1990
Reg.1, amended: SI 2014/1815 Sch.1 para.2
Reg.11, amended: SI 2014/784 Reg.2

Reg.11, revoked (in part): SI 2014/3090
Sch.1 para.1

2027. Fees for Inquiries (Standard Daily Amount) Regulations 1990
revoked (in part): SI 2014/692 Sch.1

2145. Civil Aviation Act 1982 (Jersey) Order 1990
applied: SI 2014/2713

2174. Trunk Road (A46) (Coventry Eastern Bypass) (60 MPH and De-restriction) Order 1990
revoked: SI 2014/136 Art.7

2519. Social Work (Representations Procedure) (Scotland) Order 1990
see *McCue v Glasgow City Council* [2014] CSOH 124, 2014 S.L.T. 891 (OH), Lord Jones

2595. Merchant Shipping (Prevention and Control of Pollution) Order 1990
Art.3, enabled: SI 2014/3306

2596. Ministerial and other Salaries Order 1990
Sch.1 Part I, varied: SI 2014/2708 Art.5

2615. Quick-frozen Foodstuffs Regulations 1990
Reg.2, amended: SSI 2014/312 Sch.5 para.1
Reg.5, amended: SSI 2014/312 Sch.5 para.1
Sch.1 para.2, amended: SSI 2014/312 Sch.5
para.1

1991

167. Occupational Pension Schemes (Preservation of Benefit) Regulations 1991
Reg.10, amended: SI 2014/1711 Reg.27
Reg.14, revoked: SI 2014/1711 Reg.27
Reg.14A, substituted: SI 2014/1711 Reg.27

168. Occupational Pension Schemes (Revaluation) Regulations 1991
Reg.4, amended: SI 2014/1711 Reg.28

194. Health and Personal Social Services (Northern Ireland) Order 1991
Art.10, applied: SI 2014/3282 Sch.1 para.10

507. Environmental Protection (Applications, Appeals and Registers) Regulations 1991
Reg.4, amended: SI 2014/469 Sch.3
para.178

684. Pensions Increase (Review) Order 1991
referred to: SI 2014/668 Sch.1
Art.6, substituted: SI 2014/107 Sch.1
para.56, SI 2014/3229 Sch.6 para.35

724. High Court and County Courts Jurisdiction Order 1991
 amended: SI 2014/821 Art.2
 Art.1A, amended: SI 2014/821 Art.2
 Art.2, amended: SI 2014/821 Art.2
 Art.2, revoked (in part): SI 2014/821 Art.2
 Art.3, amended: SI 2014/821 Art.2
 Art.4, amended: SI 2014/821 Art.2
 Art.4A, amended: SI 2014/821 Art.2
 Art.6A, amended: SI 2014/821 Art.2
 Art.6B, amended: SI 2014/821 Art.2
 Art.6C, added: SI 2014/821 Art.2
 Art.6G, added: SI 2014/2947 Sch.4 para.4
 Art.8, amended: SI 2014/821 Art.2
 Art.8A, amended: SI 2014/821 Art.2
 Art.8B, amended: SI 2014/821 Art.2
 Art.11, amended: SI 2014/821 Art.2
 Sch.1, amended: SI 2014/821 Art.2
 Sch.1 Part I, amended: SI 2014/821 Art.2
 Sch.1 Part II, amended: SI 2014/821 Art.2

755. European Communities (Designation) (No.2) Order 1991
 Sch.1, amended: SI 2014/2705 Art.6

875. Buying Agency Trading Fund Order 1991
 Art.3, amended: SI 2014/561 Art.2

893. Placement of Children with Parents etc Regulations 1991
 Reg.1, amended: SI 2014/852 Art.4
 Reg.8, amended: SI 2014/852 Art.4

1184. County Courts (Interest on Judgment Debts) Order 1991
 applied: SI 2014/2604 r.9
 Art.1, amended: SI 2014/1773 Art.5
 Art.2, amended: SI 2014/1773 Art.6
 Art.4, amended: SI 2014/1773 Art.7
 Art.5, amended: SI 2014/1773 Art.8

1220. Planning (Northern Ireland) Order 1991
 Art.111, applied: SI 2014/1643 Sch.4 para.13
 Art.127, varied: SI 2014/1643 Sch.4 para.15

1222. County Court Remedies Regulations 1991
 revoked: SI 2014/982 Reg.2
 Reg.3, revoked (in part): SI 2014/879 Art.23

1247. Family Proceedings Rules 1991
 see *Sharbatly v Shagroon* [2013] EWHC 3756 (Fam), [2014] 2 F.L.R. 209 (Fam Div), Parker J

1325. Litter Control Areas Order 1991
 Art.2, amended: SI 2014/3302 Sch.1 para.5

1397. Act of Sederunt (Messengers-at-Arms and Sheriff Officers Rules) 1991
 Part II r.3, revoked (in part): SSI 2014/29 r.2
 Part III r.7, revoked (in part): SSI 2014/29 r.2
 Part III r.8, revoked (in part): SSI 2014/29 r.2

1408. Broadcasting (Independent Productions) Order 1991
 Art.3, amended: SI 2014/3137 Art.3, Art.5, Art.6, Art.7
 Art.3, revoked (in part): SI 2014/3137 Art.4

1478. Parental Responsibility Agreement Regulations 1991
 Sch.1, amended: SI 2014/879 Art.24

1531. Control of Explosives Regulations 1991
 applied: SI 2014/1638 Reg.47
 revoked: SI 2014/1638 Sch.14 Part 2
 Reg.2, amended: SI 2014/469 Sch.3 para.47
 Reg.3, amended: SI 2014/469 Sch.3 para.48
 Reg.4, applied: SI 2014/1638 Reg.47
 Reg.11, amended: SI 2014/469 Sch.3 para.49
 Reg.13, amended: SI 2014/469 Sch.3 para.50
 Reg.15, substituted: SI 2014/469 Sch.3 para.51

1714. Genetically Modified Organisms (Northern Ireland) Order 1991
 Art.8, applied: SI 2014/1663 Reg.3

1809. Civil Courts (Amendment) Order 1991
 revoked: SI 2014/820 Sch.1

1993. Set-Aside (Amendment) Regulations 1991
 revoked: SI 2014/3263 Sch.5

1997. Companies Act 1989 (Eligibility for Appointment as Company Auditor) (Consequential Amendments) Regulations 1991
 Sch.1 para.48, revoked: SI 2014/1924 Sch.1

2144. Merchant Shipping (Crew Agreements, Lists of Crew and Discharge of Seamen) Regulations 1991
 Reg.2, amended: SI 2014/1614 Reg.8
 Reg.3, substituted: SI 2014/1614 Reg.8
 Reg.13, revoked: SI 2014/1614 Reg.8
 Reg.14, amended: SI 2014/1614 Reg.8
 Reg.14, revoked (in part): SI 2014/1614 Reg.8
 Reg.16, amended: SI 2014/1614 Reg.8
 Reg.19, substituted: SI 2014/1614 Reg.8
 Reg.20, amended: SI 2014/1614 Reg.8
 Reg.21, amended: SI 2014/1614 Reg.8

Reg.23, revoked: SI 2014/1614 Reg.8
Reg.25, applied: SI 2014/1613 Reg.12
Reg.26, amended: SI 2014/1614 Reg.8

2211. Civil Courts (Amendment No 2) Order 1991
revoked: SI 2014/820 Sch.1

2271. Skye Salmon Fishery District Designation Order 1991
Art.2, applied: SSI 2014/327 Sch.1
Sch.1, applied: SSI 2014/327 Sch.1

2340. Ealing Hospital National Health Service Trust (Establishment) Order 1991
revoked: SI 2014/2524 Art.8

2509. Coal Mining Subsidence (Notices and Claims) Regulations 1991
Sch.1, see *Newbold v Coal Authority* [2013] EWCA Civ 584, [2014] 1 W.L.R. 1288 (CA (Civ Div)), Longmore LJ

2731. Judicial Pensions (Widowers and Children's Benefits) Regulations 1991
disapplied: SI 2014/3229 Sch.2 para.6
Reg.2, amended: SI 2014/288 Reg.3
Reg.4, amended: SI 2014/288 Reg.3
Reg.5, amended: SI 2014/288 Reg.3
Reg.6, amended: SI 2014/288 Reg.3

2749. Simple Pressure Vessels (Safety) Regulations 1991
Sch.5 para.1, amended: SI 2014/469 Sch.3 para.52
Sch.5 para.9, amended: SI 2014/469 Sch.3 para.52

2839. Environmental Protection (Duty of Care) Regulations 1991
revoked (in part): SSI 2014/4 Reg.7

2847. Trunk Road (A470) (Newbridge-On-Wye, Powys) (Restricted Roads) Order 1991
revoked: SI 2014/3116 Art.3
varied: SI 2014/241 Art.4

2848. A483 Trunk Road (Ruabon and Newbridge by-pass, Ruabon, Clwyd) (Derestriction) Order 1991
varied: SI 2014/810 Art.9

2886. Ministerial and other Salaries Order 1991
Sch.1 Part I, varied: SI 2014/2708 Art.5

2887. Disability Working Allowance (General) Regulations 1991
Sch.3 para.55, amended: SI 2014/513 Sch.1 para.3

2890. Social Security (Disability Living Allowance) Regulations 1991
Reg.4, amended: SI 2014/516 Art.9

1992

129. Firemen's Pension Scheme Order 1992
Part AI para.1, amended: SI 2014/446 Art.2
Part AI para.2, amended: SI 2014/446 Art.2
Part AI para.3, amended: SI 2014/446 Art.2, SI 2014/522 Art.3
Part I, amended: SI 2014/446 Art.2, SSI 2014/108 Art.3
Part 1A para.1, amended: SSI 2014/108 Art.5
Part 1A para.2, amended: SSI 2014/108 Art.5
Part 1A para.3, amended: SSI 2014/59 Art.3
Part III para.1, added: SI 2014/560 Sch.3 para.17
Part III para.1, amended: SI 2014/3061 Sch.1 para.11
Part III para.2, added: SI 2014/560 Sch.3 para.17
Part III para.3, added: SI 2014/3061 Sch.1 para.11
Part IV para.2, amended: SI 2014/446 Art.2, SSI 2014/108 Art.4
Part IV para.7, added: SI 2014/446 Art.2, SSI 2014/108 Art.4
Sch.2 para.G1, see *Stokes v Oxfordshire CC* [2014] EWHC 2177 (Ch), [2014] Pens. L.R. 631 (Ch D), Barling J

198. Pensions Increase (Review) Order 1992
referred to: SI 2014/668 Sch.1
Art.6, substituted: SI 2014/107 Sch.1
para.56, SI 2014/3229 Sch.6 para.35

223. Town and Country Planning (General Permitted Development) (Scotland) Order 1992
Art.2, amended: SSI 2014/142 Art.2
Art.3, amended: SSI 2014/142 Art.2
Art.3, applied: SSI 2014/224 Sch.1 para.1
Sch.1 Part 2A, added: SSI 2014/142 Sch.1
Sch.1 Part 4 para.15, amended: SSI 2014/142 Art.2
Sch.1 Part 6 para.18, amended: SSI 2014/142 Art.2, SSI 2014/300 Art.3
Sch.1 Part 7 para.22, amended: SSI 2014/142 Art.2, SSI 2014/300 Art.3
Sch.1 Part 8 para.25, substituted: SSI 2014/142 Art.2
Sch.1 Part 8 para.26, amended: SSI 2014/142 Art.2
Sch.1 Part 11 para.29, applied: SSI 2014/224 Sch.1 para.1

Sch.1 Part 12 para.30, substituted: SSI
2014/142 Art.2
Sch.1 Part 12 para.33, amended: SSI
2014/142 Art.2
Sch.1 Part 13 para.35, applied: SSI 2014/224
Sch.1 para.1
Sch.1 Part 15 para.54, amended: SSI
2014/142 Art.2
Sch.1 Part 20 para.67, amended: SSI
2014/142 Art.2
Sch.1 Part 20 para.67, revoked (in part): SSI
2014/142 Art.2

231. Electricity (Northern Ireland) Order 1992
Art.9, applied: SI 2014/1458 Art.5
Art.15, amended: SI 2014/892 Sch.1
para.212
Art.15B, amended: SI 2014/892 Sch.1
para.213
Art.15B, applied: SI 2014/559
Art.15B, referred to: SI 2014/892 Sch.2
para.2
Art.17A, amended: SI 2014/892 Sch.1
para.214
Art.17A, referred to: SI 2014/892 Sch.2
para.2
Art.18, amended: SI 2014/892 Sch.1
para.215
Art.46, amended: SI 2014/892 Sch.1
para.216
Art.50, amended: SI 2014/892 Sch.1
para.216
Sch.6 para.3, applied: SI 2014/1458 Art.5

314. Common Agricultural Policy (Protection of Community Arrangements) Regulations 1992
applied: SI 2014/3263 Reg.35
revoked: SI 2014/3263 Sch.5

460. HIV Testing Kits and Services Regulations 1992
revoked (in part): SI 2014/256 Reg.3, SI
2014/451 Reg.2, SSI 2014/42 Reg.2

549. Council Tax (Chargeable Dwellings) Order 1992
Art.2, amended: SI 2014/2653 Art.3
Art.3, see *Kelderman v Valuation Office Agency* [2014] EWHC 1592 (Admin),
[2014] R.V.R. 323 (QBD (Admin)), Nicol J
Art.3, amended: SI 2014/2653 Art.3
Art.3B, added: SI 2014/2653 Art.3

558. Council Tax (Exempt Dwellings) Order 1992
Art.3, see *A2Dominion Housing Group Ltd v Hammersmith and Fulham LBC* [2014]
R.V.R. 268 (VT), Graham Zellick Q.C.
(President); see *RQ v Bromley LBC* [2014]
R.V.R. 163 (VT), Graham Zellick Q.C.
(President)

593. Civil Courts (Amendment) Order 1992
revoked: SI 2014/820 Sch.1

613. Council Tax (Administration and Enforcement) Regulations 1992
applied: SI 2014/600 Art.4
Reg.1, amended: SI 2014/129 Reg.3
Reg.9, amended: SI 2014/129 Reg.4
Reg.10, amended: SI 2014/129 Reg.5
Reg.11, amended: SI 2014/129 Reg.6
Reg.15, amended: SI 2014/129 Reg.7
Reg.16, amended: SI 2014/129 Reg.8
Reg.20, amended: SI 2014/129 Reg.9
Reg.32, amended: SI 2014/600 Sch.1 para.3
Reg.34, see *Yang v Official Receiver* [2013]
EWHC 3577 (Ch), [2014] B.P.I.R. 826 (Ch
D (Manchester)), Judge Hodge Q.C.
Reg.37, amended: SI 2014/600 Sch.1 para.3
Reg.37, revoked (in part): SI 2014/600 Sch.1
para.3
Reg.45, substituted: SI 2014/600 Sch.1
para.3
Reg.45A, revoked: SI 2014/600 Sch.1
para.3, Sch.1 Part 2
Reg.47, amended: SI 2014/600 Sch.1 para.3
Reg.49, see *Yang v Official Receiver* [2013]
EWHC 3577 (Ch), [2014] B.P.I.R. 826 (Ch
D (Manchester)), Judge Hodge Q.C.
Reg.52, amended: SI 2014/600 Sch.1 para.3
Reg.53, amended: SI 2014/600 Sch.1 para.3
Reg.54, amended: SI 2014/600 Sch.1 para.3
Reg.57, see *Yang v Official Receiver* [2013]
EWHC 3577 (Ch), [2014] B.P.I.R. 826 (Ch
D (Manchester)), Judge Hodge Q.C.
Reg.58, amended: SI 2014/600 Sch.1 para.3
Sch.5, revoked: SI 2014/600 Sch.1 para.3,
Sch.1 Part 2
Sch.5 para.1, applied: SI 2014/600 Art.4

656. Planning (Hazardous Substances) Regulations 1992
applied: SI 2014/375 Reg.3
Reg.10, amended: SI 2014/469 Sch.3
para.180

Reg.11, amended: SI 2014/469 Sch.3
para.181
Sch.1 Part A, amended: SI 2014/162 Reg.3,
SI 2014/375 Reg.2, SI 2014/469 Sch.3
para.182, SI 2014/1638 Sch.13 para.14
Sch.1 Part B, amended: SI 2014/469 Sch.3
para.182, SI 2014/1638 Sch.13 para.14
**695. Oilseeds Producers (Support System)
Regulations 1992**
revoked: SI 2014/1902 Sch.1
**1190. Gas Transit (EEC Requirements)
Regulations 1992**
revoked: SI 2014/529 Reg.2
Reg.1, applied: SI 2014/529 Reg.3
Reg.2, applied: SI 2014/529 Reg.3
Reg.5, applied: SI 2014/529 Reg.3
Reg.6, applied: SI 2014/529 Reg.3
**1228. Legal Aid in Contempt of Court
Proceedings (Scotland) (Fees) Regulations 1992**
Sch.1 para.5A, added: SSI 2014/257 Reg.5
**1296. Transfer of Functions (Science) Order
1992**
Art.1, varied: SI 2014/2708 Art.5
Sch.1 para.1, varied: SI 2014/2708 Art.5
Sch.1 para.2, varied: SI 2014/2708 Art.5
Sch.1 para.5, varied: SI 2014/2708 Art.5
Sch.1 para.6, varied: SI 2014/2708 Art.5
Sch.1 para.7, varied: SI 2014/2708 Art.5
Sch.1 para.8, varied: SI 2014/2708 Art.5
**1302. Serbia and Montenegro (United Nations
Sanctions) Order 1992**
revoked: SI 2014/2711 Sch.1
**1304. Serbia and Montenegro (United Nations
Prohibition of Flights) Order 1992**
revoked: SI 2014/2711 Sch.1
**1332. Council Tax (Administration and
Enforcement) (Scotland) Regulations 1992**
Reg.17, applied: SSI 2014/3 Art.6
Reg.20, applied: SSI 2014/3 Art.8
Reg.27, applied: SSI 2014/3 Art.8
Sch.1, applied: SSI 2014/3 Art.8
**1345. Civil Courts (Amendment No 2) Order
1992**
revoked: SI 2014/820 Sch.1
**1691. Street Works (Maintenance) Regulations
1992**
applied: SI 2014/3105 Sch.1, SI 2014/3110
Sch.1, SI 2014/3112 Sch.1
**1810. Civil Courts (Amendment No 3) Order
1992**
revoked: SI 2014/820 Sch.1

**1811. Health and Safety (Miscellaneous
Provisions) (Metrication etc.) Regulations 1992**
Sch.1 Part I, amended: SI 2014/1637 Sch.4
Part 1
**1815. Child Support (Maintenance Assessments
and Special Cases) Regulations 1992**
see *Hakki v Secretary of State for Work and
Pensions* [2014] EWCA Civ 530, [2014]
B.T.C. 22 (CA (Civ Div)), Longmore LJ
Reg.1, amended: SI 2014/107 Sch.1 para.14,
SI 2014/3229 Sch.6 para.9
Reg.26, applied: SI 2014/614 Reg.4
Reg.27A, amended: SI 2014/1386 Reg.3
Reg.28, applied: SI 2014/614 Reg.4
Sch.1 Part I para.1, amended: SI 2014/3255
Art.6
Sch.2 para.48C, amended: SI 2014/513
Sch.1 para.4
Sch.4, amended: SI 2014/884 Reg.3
**1989. Child Support (Collection and
Enforcement) Regulations 1992**
applied: SI 2014/600 Art.4
Reg.1, amended: SI 2014/1386 Reg.2
Reg.2, amended: SI 2014/1386 Reg.2
Reg.3, amended: SI 2014/107 Sch.1 para.15,
SI 2014/1386 Reg.2, SI 2014/3229 Sch.6
para.10
Reg.4, amended: SI 2014/1386 Reg.2
Reg.7, amended: SI 2014/1386 Reg.2
Reg.17, amended: SI 2014/1386 Reg.2
Reg.20, amended: SI 2014/1386 Reg.2
Reg.25AB, amended: SI 2014/879 Art.25
Reg.25AB, applied: SI 2014/840 r.5
Reg.27, amended: SI 2014/1386 Reg.2
Reg.30, substituted: SI 2014/600 Sch.1
para.4
Reg.31, revoked (in part): SI 2014/600 Sch.1
para.4
Sch.1, amended: SI 2014/1386 Reg.2
Sch.2, revoked (in part): SI 2014/600 Sch.1
para.4
Sch.2 para.1, applied: SI 2014/600 Art.4
**2071. Magistrates Courts (Children and Young
Persons) Rules 1992**
Part III r.13., amended: SI 2014/879 Art.26
**2559. North Staffordshire Hospital Centre
National Health Service Trust (Establishment)
Order 1992**
Art.1, amended: SI 2014/2844 Art.2
Art.2, amended: SI 2014/2844 Art.3
Art.5, substituted: SI 2014/2844 Art.4

Art.6, revoked: SI 2014/2844 Art.6

2590. Olive Oil (Marketing Standards) (Amendment) Regulations 1992
revoked: SI 2014/195 Reg.20

2645. Child Support (Maintenance Arrangements and Jurisdiction) Regulations 1992
Reg.5, amended: SI 2014/879 Art.27
Reg.6, amended: SI 2014/879 Art.27

2656. Scottish Land Court Rules 1992
revoked: SSI 2014/229 Art.2

2673. Civil Aviation (Personnel Licences) Order 1992
revoked: SI 2014/3225 Reg.2

2789. Transport Levying Bodies Regulations 1992
applied: SI 2014/863 Art.9, SI 2014/864 Art.9

2790. Statistics of Trade (Customs and Excise) Regulations 1992
Reg.3, amended: SI 2014/3135 Reg.2

2870. European Communities (Designation) (No.4) Order 1992
Sch.1, amended: SI 2014/1362 Sch.1

2966. Personal Protective Equipment at Work Regulations 1992
see *Kennedy v Cordia (Services) LLP* [2014] CSIH 76, 2014 S.L.T. 984 (IH (Ex Div)), Lady Smith
Reg.4, see *Kennedy v Cordia (Services) LLP* [2014] CSIH 76, 2014 S.L.T. 984 (IH (Ex Div)), Lady Smith; see *McPake v SRCL Ltd* 2014 S.C.L.R. 199 (OH), Lord Stewart

2977. National Assistance (Assessment of Resources) Regulations 1992
see *Aster Healthcare Ltd v Shafi* [2014] EWHC 77 (QB), [2014] 3 All E.R. 283 (QBD), Andrews J; see *R. (on the application of Walford) v Worcestershire CC* [2014] EWHC 234 (Admin), [2014] 3 All E.R. 128 (QBD (Admin)), Supperstone J
Reg.20, amended: SSI 2014/38 Reg.2
Reg.20A, amended: SI 2014/666 Reg.4
Reg.28, amended: SSI 2014/38 Reg.3
Sch.3 Part I para.17, amended: SI 2014/852 Art.5
Sch.3 Part I para.28G, amended: SSI 2014/38 Reg.4
Sch.3 Part I para.28I, amended: SSI 2014/90 Sch.1 Part 3

Sch.4 para.2, see *R. (on the application of Walford) v Worcestershire CC* [2014] EWHC 234 (Admin), [2014] 3 All E.R. 128 (QBD (Admin)), Supperstone J
Sch.4 para.23, amended: SSI 2014/90 Sch.1 Part 3

3004. Workplace (Health, Safety and Welfare) Regulations 1992
Reg.3, substituted: SI 2014/3248 Sch.5 para.7

3071. Civil Courts (Amendment No 4) Order 1992
revoked: SI 2014/820 Sch.1

3122. Value Added Tax (Cars) Order 1992
see *Pendragon Plc v Revenue and Customs Commissioners* [2013] EWCA Civ 868, [2014] S.T.C. 844 (CA (Civ Div)), Lloyd LJ

3159. Specified Diseases (Notification and Slaughter) Order 1992
Art.2, amended: SSI 2014/151 Art.2

3238. Non-Domestic Rating Contributions (Wales) Regulations 1992
Sch.1 para.3, substituted: SI 2014/3193 Reg.2
Sch.4, substituted: SI 2014/3193 Sch.1

3239. Billing Authorities (Anticipation of Precepts) Regulations 1992
Reg.1, amended: SI 2014/35 Reg.2

3288. Package Travel, Package Holidays and Package Tours Regulations 1992
see *Japp v Virgin Holidays Ltd* [2013] EWCA Civ 1371, [2014] P.I.Q.R. P8 (CA (Civ Div)), Richards LJ

1993

12. Wildlife and Countryside (Definitive Maps and Statements) Regulations 1993
Reg.2, see *R. (on the application of Trail Riders' Fellowship) v Dorset CC* [2013] EWCA Civ 553, [2014] 3 All E.R. 429 (CA (Civ Div)), Maurice Kay LJ

74. Copyright (Recording for Archives of Designated Class of Broadcasts and Cable Programmes) (Designated Bodies) Order 1993
revoked: SI 2014/1372 Reg.8

208. Coal and Other Safety-Lamp Mines (Explosives) Regulations 1993
revoked (in part): SI 2014/3248 Sch.4 Part 1

Reg.2, amended: SI 2014/1638 Sch.13
para.15

226. District Electoral Areas (Northern Ireland) Order 1993
revoked: SI 2014/270 Art.3

255. Council Tax (Demand Notices) (Wales) Regulations 1993
Sch.1 para.8A, amended: SI 2014/122 Reg.3

302. Mines (Shafts and Winding) Regulations 1993
revoked (in part): SI 2014/3248 Sch.4 Part 1

323. Town and Country Planning (Hazardous Substances) (Scotland) Regulations 1993
applied: SSI 2014/51 Reg.3
Reg.11, amended: SI 2014/469 Sch.3
para.184
Reg.12, amended: SI 2014/469 Sch.3
para.185
Reg.21, applied: SSI 2014/51 Reg.3
Sch.1 Part A, amended: SI 2014/469 Sch.3
para.186, SI 2014/1638 Sch.13 para.16, SSI
2014/51 Reg.2
Sch.1 Part B, amended: SI 2014/469 Sch.3
para.186, SI 2014/1638 Sch.13 para.16

355. Council Tax (Alteration of Lists and Appeals) (Scotland) Regulations 1993
Part IV, applied: SSI 2014/3 Art.10

584. Child Support (Northern Ireland Reciprocal Arrangements) Regulations 1993
Reg.2, amended: SI 2014/1423 Reg.2
Sch.1D, added: SI 2014/1423 Sch.1

592. Social Security (Northern Ireland) Order 1993
Art.4, applied: SI 2014/475, SI 2014/475
Art.6
Art.4, enabled: SI 2014/475

593. Reciprocal Enforcement of Maintenance Orders (Hague Convention Countries) Order 1993
Sch.2 para.3, amended: SI 2014/879 Art.30
Sch.2 para.5, revoked: SI 2014/879 Art.31
Sch.2 para.8, revoked (in part): SI 2014/879
Art.32
Sch.2 para.9, revoked (in part): SI 2014/879
Art.32
Sch.2 para.21, amended: SI 2014/879 Art.34
Sch.3, added: SI 2014/879 Art.36, Art.43
Sch.3, amended: SI 2014/879 Art.36, Art.38,
Art.40, Art.41, Art.42, Art.43, Art.44
Sch.3, revoked: SI 2014/879 Art.36, Art.37,
Art.38, Art.39, Art.41

594. Reciprocal Enforcement of Maintenance Orders (Republic of Ireland) Order 1993
Sch.1 para.5, revoked (in part): SI 2014/879
Art.47
Sch.1 para.8, revoked (in part): SI 2014/879
Art.48
Sch.1 para.19, amended: SI 2014/879 Art.49
Sch.2, added: SI 2014/879 Art.51, Art.57
Sch.2, amended: SI 2014/879 Art.51, Art.53,
Art.54, Art.55, Art.56, Art.57, Art.58
Sch.2, revoked (in part): SI 2014/879 Art.51,
Art.52, Art.53, Art.55

779. Pensions Increase (Review) Order 1993
referred to: SI 2014/668 Sch.1
Art.6, substituted: SI 2014/107 Sch.1
para.56, SI 2014/3229 Sch.6 para.35

987. Retention of Registration Marks Regulations 1993
Reg.4, amended: SI 2014/2358 Sch.3 para.3
Reg.4, revoked (in part): SI 2014/2358 Sch.3
para.3
Reg.10, amended: SI 2014/2358 Sch.3
para.4

1188. Serbia and Montenegro (United Nations Sanctions) Order 1993
revoked: SI 2014/2711 Sch.1

1366. Crop Residues (Burning) Regulations 1993
Reg.4, disapplied: SI 2014/3263 Sch.2
para.2
Reg.5, disapplied: SI 2014/3263 Sch.2
para.2
Sch.1, referred to: SI 2014/3223 Sch.1 para.8

1572. House of Commons Disqualification Order 1993
Sch.1 Part 1 para.2, amended: SI 2014/1924
Sch.1
Sch.1 Part 2 para.4, amended: SI 2014/1924
Sch.1

1607. Swanage Light Railway (Extension) Order 1993
applied: SI 2014/1604 Sch.1

1625. Right to Purchase (Prescribed Persons) (Scotland) Order 1993
revoked: 2014 asp 14 s.1

1787. United Nations Arms Embargoes (Liberia, Somalia and the Former Yugoslavia) Order 1993
revoked: SI 2014/2711 Sch.1

1809. Civil Courts (Amendment) Order 1993
revoked: SI 2014/820 Sch.1

1813. Channel Tunnel (International Arrangements) Order 1993
Sch.4 para.1, amended: SI 2014/1814 Art.2
1897. Management and Administration of Safety and Health at Mines Regulations 1993
revoked (in part): SI 2014/3248 Sch.4 Part 1
Reg.7, applied: SI 2014/3248 Reg.6
Reg.11, applied: SI 2014/3248 Reg.71
Reg.27, applied: SI 2014/3248 Reg.71
1956. Act of Sederunt (Sheriff Court Ordinary Cause Rules) 1993
Sch.1, see *Lamb v Wray* 2014 S.L.T. (Sh Ct) 2 (Sh Ct (Lothian) (Edinburgh)), Sheriff K E C Mackie
2008. Vegetable Seeds Regulations 1993
referred to: SSI 2014/167 Reg.4
2010. Tuberculosis (Deer) (Amendment) Order 1993
revoked (in part): SI 2014/2337 Art.19
2072. Enforcement of Road Traffic Debts (Certificated Bailiffs) Regulations 1993
revoked: SI 2014/600 Sch.1 Part 2
Sch.1 para.1, applied: SI 2014/600 Art.4
Sch.1 para.3, applied: SI 2014/600 Art.4
2073. Enforcement of Road Traffic Debts Order 1993
applied: SI 2014/600 Art.4
Art.1, amended: SI 2014/600 Sch.1 para.5
Art.2, amended: SI 2014/600 Sch.1 para.5
Art.3, amended: SI 2014/600 Sch.1 para.5
Art.4, amended: SI 2014/600 Sch.1 para.5
Art.5, amended: SI 2014/600 Sch.1 para.5
Art.7, amended: SI 2014/600 Sch.1 para.5
Art.7, revoked (in part): SI 2014/600 Sch.1 para.5
Art.9, revoked: SI 2014/600 Sch.1 para.5, Sch.1 Part 2
2152. A55 Trunk Road (Bodelwyddan &mdash St Asaph, Clwyd) (Derestriction) Order 1993
varied: SI 2014/915 Art.14
2331. Coal Mines (Owner's Operating Rules) Regulations 1993
revoked (in part): SI 2014/3248 Sch.4 Part 1
2407. Leasehold Reform (Collective Enfranchisement and Lease Renewal) Regulations 1993
Sch.2 para.7, see *Bolton v Godwin-Austen* [2014] EWCA Civ 27, [2014] H.L.R. 15 (CA (Civ Div)), Goldring LJ

2714. Placing on the Market and Supervision of Transfers of Explosives Regulations 1993
applied: SI 2014/1638 Reg.47
revoked: SI 2014/1638 Sch.14 Part 2
Reg.3, amended: SI 2014/469 Sch.3 para.54
Reg.9, amended: SI 2014/469 Sch.3 para.55
2854. Employment Appeal Tribunal Rules 1993
r.34, see *Horizon Security Services Ltd v Ndeze* [2014] I.R.L.R. 854 (EAT), Judge Eady QC
r.34A, see *Horizon Security Services Ltd v Ndeze* [2014] I.R.L.R. 854 (EAT), Judge Eady QC
3053. Commercial Agents (Council Directive) Regulations 1993
see *Fern Computer Consultancy Ltd v Intergraph Cadworx & Analysis Solutions Inc* [2014] EWHC 2908 (Ch), [2014] Bus. L.R. 1397 (Ch D), Mann J
Reg.17, see *Shearman (t/a Charles Shearman Agencies) v Hunter Boot Ltd* [2014] EWHC 47 (QB), [2014] 1 All E.R. (Comm) 689 (QBD (Merc) (London)), Judge Mackie QC; see *Thinc Group Ltd v Kingdom* [2013] EWCA Civ 1306, [2014] C.P. Rep. 8 (CA (Civ Div), Arden LJ
3080. Act of Sederunt (Fees of Solicitors in the Sheriff Court) (Amendment and Further Provisions) 1993
Sch.1 Part 1, substituted: SSI 2014/14 Sch.1
Sch.1 Part 1, added: SSI 2014/14 Sch.9
Sch.1 Part 1, amended: SSI 2014/14 Sch.8
Sch.1 Part 1, substituted: SSI 2014/14 Sch.3, Sch.4, Sch.5, Sch.6, Sch.7
Sch.1 Part 1 para.1, amended: SSI 2014/14 Sch.2
Sch.1 Part 1 para.2, amended: SSI 2014/14 Sch.2
Sch.1 Part 1 para.3, amended: SSI 2014/14 Sch.2
Sch.1 para.14, amended: SSI 2014/14 Art.2
Sch.1 para.15, added: SSI 2014/14 Art.2
3120. Civil Courts (Amendment No 2) Order 1993
revoked: SI 2014/820 Sch.1
3270. A483 Trunk Road (Wrexham Road, Eccleston, Chester) (Prohibition of Use of Gap in Central Reservation) Order 1993
revoked: SI 2014/2946 Art.3

1994

192. Trunk Road (A55) (Pen-y-clip Section, Gwynedd) (One Way Traffic) Order 1994
　　disapplied: SI 2014/3377 Art.10
　　varied: SI 2014/827 Art.10

236. Distraint by Collectors (Fees, Costs and Charges) Regulations 1994
　　revoked (in part): SI 2014/600 Sch.1 Part 2

341. Industrial and Provident Societies (Increase in Shareholding Limit) Order 1994
　　revoked: SI 2014/210 Art.4

515. A282 Trunk Road (Dartford Tunnels and Approaches) (One Way Traffic and Weight Restriction) Order 1994
　　revoked: SI 2014/2518 Art.5
　　varied: SI 2014/2333 Art.5, SI 2014/3458 Art.7

611. Research Councils (Transfer of Property etc.) Order 1994
　　varied: SI 2014/2708 Art.5

642. Fees for Inquiries (Standard Daily Amount) Regulations 1994
　　revoked (in part): SI 2014/692 Sch.1

706. Civil Courts (Amendment) Order 1994
　　revoked: SI 2014/820 Sch.1

776. Pensions Increase (Review) Order 1994
　　referred to: SI 2014/668 Sch.1
　　Art.6, substituted: SI 2014/107 Sch.1
　　para.56, SI 2014/3229 Sch.6 para.35

790. A55 Trunk Road (Pen-y-clip Section, Gwynedd) (Derestriction) Order 1994
　　disapplied: SI 2014/3377 Art.11
　　varied: SI 2014/827 Art.11, SI 2014/915 Art.8

1056. Waste Management Licensing Regulations 1994
　　Reg.17, see *Doonin Plant Ltd v HM Advocate* [2014] HCJAC 26, 2014 J.C. 207 (HCJ), The Lord Justice Clerk (Carloway)

1323. Haiti (United Nations Sanctions) Order 1994
　　revoked: SI 2014/2711 Sch.1

1405. Channel Tunnel (Miscellaneous Provisions) Order 1994
　　Art.2, amended: SI 2014/409 Art.3
　　Art.3, amended: SI 2014/409 Art.3
　　Sch.1, amended: SI 2014/409 Art.3
　　Sch.2 Part III, amended: SI 2014/409 Art.3
　　Sch.2 Part III, substituted: SI 2014/409 Art.3
　　Sch.2 Part IV, added: SI 2014/409 Art.3

1433. Railways Pension Scheme Order 1994
　　disapplied: SI 2014/3229 Sch.2 para.6

1438. Bail (Amendment) Act 1993 (Prescription of Prosecuting Authorities) Order 1994
　　Sch.1, amended: SI 2014/834 Sch.3 para.2

1443. Act of Sederunt (Rules of the Court of Session 1994) 1994
　　see *Scottish Ministers v Mirza* [2014] CSIH 103 (IH (Ex Div)), Lady Clark of Calton
　　Appendix 1., added: SSI 2014/302 r.4
　　Appendix 1., amended: SSI 2014/152 r.2, SSI 2014/291 Sch.1, SSI 2014/302 r.4, SSI 2014/371 Sch.1
　　Appendix 1., revoked: SSI 2014/302 r.4
　　Appendix 1., substituted: SSI 2014/302 r.4
　　Sch.2, see *MacDonald v Aberdeenshire Council* 2014 S.C. 114 (IH (Ex Div)), Lady Paton; see *McLaughlin v Morrison* 2014 S.L.T. 111 (OH), Lord Jones; see *Smith v Greater Glasgow & Clyde NHS Health Board* 2014 S.L.T. 137 (OH), Lord Jones
　　Sch.2 para.1.3, see *Scottish Ministers v Mirza* [2014] CSIH 103 (IH (Ex Div)), Lady Clark of Calton
　　Sch.2 para.2.1, see *Little Cumbrae Estate Ltd v Rolyat1 Ltd* [2014] CSOH 163, 2014 S.L.T. 1118 (OH), Lord Woolman
　　Sch.2 Part 2 para.4_2, amended: SSI 2014/371 r.2
　　Sch.2 Part 3 para.14A_4, amended: SSI 2014/291 r.2
　　Sch.2 Part 3 para.35_3, amended: SSI 2014/152 r.2
　　Sch.2 Part 3 para.35_3A, amended: SSI 2014/152 r.2
　　Sch.2 Part 3 para.35_3A, revoked (in part): SSI 2014/152 r.2
　　Sch.2 Part 3 para.35_3A, substituted: SSI 2014/152 r.2
　　Sch.2 Part 3 para.35_8, amended: SSI 2014/152 r.2
　　Sch.2 Part 3 para.41_52, amended: SSI 2014/201 r.2
　　Sch.2 Pt 3 para.41.57, see *R, Applicant* [2014] CSIH 44, 2014 G.W.D. 17-326 (IH), Lord Drummond Young
　　Sch.2 Part 3 para.42_16, amended: SSI 2014/15 r.3, Sch.1, Sch.2, Sch.3, Sch.4, Sch.5, Sch.6, Sch.7, Sch.8

Sch.2 Pt 4 para.43.1, see *Moran v Freyssinet Ltd* [2014] CSOH 173 (OH), Lord Boyd of Duncansby

Sch.2 Part 4 para.43_6, amended: SSI 2014/152 r.2

Sch.2 Part 4 para.43_6, revoked (in part): SSI 2014/152 r.2

Sch.2 Pt 4 para.43.6, see *Smith v Greater Glasgow & Clyde NHS Health Board* 2014 S.L.T. 137 (OH), Lord Jones

Sch.2 Part 4 para.43_8, amended: SSI 2014/152 r.2

Sch.2 Pt 4 para.43.8, see *Smith v Greater Glasgow & Clyde NHS Health Board* 2014 S.L.T. 137 (OH), Lord Jones

Sch.2 Pt 4 para.43.9, see *Moran v Freyssinet Ltd* [2014] CSOH 173 (OH), Lord Boyd of Duncansby

Sch.2 Part 4 para.47_9, amended: SSI 2014/291 r.2

Sch.2 Part 4 para.49_1, amended: SSI 2014/302 r.2

Sch.2 Part 4 para.49_6A, added: SSI 2014/302 r.2

Sch.2 Part 4 para.49_28, amended: SSI 2014/302 r.2

Sch.2 Part 4 para.49_91, amended: SSI 2014/302 r.2

Sch.2 Part 4 para.58A_5, amended: SSI 2014/152 r.2

Sch.2 Part 5, added: SSI 2014/291 r.2

Sch.2 Part 5, added: SSI 2014/371 r.2

Sch.2 Part 5 para.74_28, amended: SSI 2014/119 r.2

Sch.2 Part 5 para.74_32A, substituted: SSI 2014/119 r.2

Sch.2 Part 5 para.85A_1, amended: SSI 2014/371 r.2

Sch.2 Part 5 para.85_1, amended: SSI 2014/371 r.2

Sch.2 Part 5 para.85_1, substituted: SSI 2014/371 r.2

Sch.2 Part 5 para.85_5, amended: SSI 2014/371 r.2

Sch.2 Part 5 para.91_3, added: SSI 2014/302 r.3

Sch.2 para.19.1, see *McLaughlin v Morrison* 2014 S.L.T. 111 (OH), Lord Jones

Sch.2 para.19.2, see *Little Cumbrae Estate Ltd v Rolyat1 Ltd* [2014] CSOH 163, 2014 S.L.T. 1118 (OH), Lord Woolman

Sch.2 para.21.2, see *McLaughlin v Morrison* 2014 S.L.T. 111 (OH), Lord Jones

Sch.2 para.38.1, see *Scottish Ministers v Mirza* [2014] CSIH 103 (IH (Ex Div)), Lady Clark of Calton

Sch.2 para.38.2, see *Scottish Ministers v Mirza* [2014] CSIH 103 (IH (Ex Div)), Lady Clark of Calton

Sch.2 para.49.7, see *Moran v Freyssinet Ltd* [2014] CSOH 173 (OH), Lord Boyd of Duncansby

Sch.2 para.58A_1, see *Carroll v Scottish Borders Council* [2014] CSOH 30, 2014 S.L.T. 659 (OH), Lord Drummond Young

Sch.2 para.58A_3, see *Carroll v Scottish Borders Council* [2014] CSOH 30, 2014 S.L.T. 659 (OH), Lord Drummond Young

Sch.2 para.58A_4, see *McGinty v Scottish Ministers* 2014 S.C. 81 (IH (Ex Div)), Lord Clarke

Sch.2 para.58A_5, see *Carroll v Scottish Borders Council* [2014] CSOH 30, 2014 S.L.T. 659 (OH), Lord Drummond Young

Sch.2 para.58.3, see *McCue v Glasgow City Council* [2014] CSOH 124, 2014 S.L.T. 891 (OH), Lord Jones

Sch.2 para.58.4, see *Carroll v Scottish Borders Council* [2014] CSOH 30, 2014 S.L.T. 659 (OH), Lord Drummond Young

Sch.2 para.58.8, see *Hendrick v Chief Constable of Strathclyde* [2014] CSIH 75, 2014 S.L.T. 955 (IH (Ex Div)), Lady Paton

Sch.2 para.58.9, see *SA (Nigeria) v Secretary of State for the Home Department* 2014 S.C. 1 (IH (2 Div)), The Lord Justice Clerk (Carloway)

Sch.2 para.58.12, see *G v Watson* [2014] CSIH 81, 2014 S.L.T. 1030 (IH (Ex Div)), Lord Eassie

Sch.2 para.65.3, see *Scotch Whisky Association v Lord Advocate* [2014] CSIH 38, 2014 G.W.D. 17-309 (IH (Ex Div)), Lord Eassie

1519. Traffic Signs Regulations and General Directions 1994

applied: SI 2014/3102 Sch.8 para.27

1536. Civil Courts (Amendment No 2) Order 1994

revoked: SI 2014/820 Sch.1

1623. Employment Tribunals Extension of Jurisdiction (England and Wales) Order 1994
>   Art.7, amended: SI 2014/431 Sch.1 para.11
>   Art.8B, added: SI 2014/431 Sch.1 para.12

1624. Employment Tribunals Extension of Jurisdiction (Scotland) Order 1994
>   Art.7, amended: SI 2014/431 Sch.1 para.14
>   Art.8B, added: SI 2014/431 Sch.1 para.15

1637. United Nations Arms Embargoes (Amendment) (Rwanda) Order 1994
>   revoked: SI 2014/2711 Sch.1

1733. Civil Aviation (Personnel Licences) Order 1992 (Amendment) Regulations 1994
>   revoked: SI 2014/3225 Reg.2

1821. Air Passenger Duty (Connected Flights) Order 1994
>   see *Ryanair Ltd v Revenue and Customs Commissioners* [2014] EWCA Civ 410, [2014] S.T.I. 1725 (CA (Civ Div)), Lord Dyson MR
>   Art.2, see *Ryanair Ltd v Revenue and Customs Commissioners* [2014] EWCA Civ 410, [2014] S.T.I. 1725 (CA (Civ Div)), Lord Dyson MR
>   Art.3, see *Ryanair Ltd v Revenue and Customs Commissioners* [2014] EWCA Civ 410, [2014] S.T.I. 1725 (CA (Civ Div)), Lord Dyson MR
>   Sch.1 para.1, see *Ryanair Ltd v Revenue and Customs Commissioners* [2014] EWCA Civ 410, [2014] S.T.I. 1725 (CA (Civ Div)), Lord Dyson MR

1899. Wills and Administration Proceedings (Northern Ireland) Order 1994
>   Art.35, see *Muckian v Hoey* [2014] NICh 11, [2014] W.T.L.R. 1255 (Ch D (NI)), Deeny J

2005. Railway Pensions (Transfer and Miscellaneous Provisions) Order 1994
>   disapplied: SI 2014/3229 Sch.2 para.6

2097. Right to Purchase (Prescribed Persons) (Scotland) Amendment Order 1994
>   revoked: 2014 asp 14 s.1

2229. Railways Act 1993 (Consequential Modifications) (No.3) Order 1994
>   revoked: SI 2014/3244 Sch.2

2421. Insolvent Partnerships Order 1994
>   applied: SI 2014/3204 Sch.4 para.14
>   Art.7, applied: SI 2014/3204 Sch.4 para.14
>   Art.8, applied: SI 2014/3204 Sch.4 para.14
>   Sch.1 Part I, amended: SI 2014/3486 Art.12

Sch.1 Part I, substituted: SI 2014/3486 Art.12
>   Sch.2 para.25, amended: SI 2014/3486 Art.13
>   Sch.2 para.25, substituted: SI 2014/3486 Art.13
>   Sch.4 Part I, applied: SI 2014/3204 Sch.4 para.14
>   Sch.4 Part II para.23, amended: SI 2014/3486 Art.14
>   Sch.4 Part II para.23, substituted: SI 2014/3486 Art.14
>   Sch.7 para.21, amended: SI 2014/3486 Art.15
>   Sch.7 para.21, substituted: SI 2014/3486 Art.15

2567. Coal Industry Act 1994 (Consequential Modifications of Subordinate Legislation) Order 1994
>   Sch.1, amended: SI 2014/683 Sch.1

2576. British Coal Staff Superannuation Scheme (Modification) Regulations 1994
>   disapplied: SI 2014/3229 Sch.2 para.6

2577. Mineworkers Pension Scheme (Modification) Regulations 1994
>   disapplied: SI 2014/3229 Sch.2 para.6

2626. Civil Courts (Amendment No 3) Order 1994
>   revoked: SI 2014/820 Sch.1

2673. Former Yugoslavia (United Nations Sanctions) Order 1994
>   revoked: SI 2014/2711 Sch.1

2716. Conservation (Natural Habitats, &c.) Regulations 1994
>   Reg.48, applied: SSI 2014/224 Art.33
>   Reg.60, applied: SSI 2014/224 Art.33
>   Reg.60, disapplied: SSI 2014/224 Art.33

2893. Civil Courts (Amendment No 4) Order 1994
>   revoked: SI 2014/820 Sch.1

2924. Teachers Superannuation (Additional Voluntary Contributions) Regulations 1994
>   applied: SI 2014/512 Reg.4, Sch.1 para.2, Sch.1 para.3, Sch.1 para.8

2946. Social Security (Incapacity Benefit) Regulations 1994
>   Reg.10, amended: SI 2014/516 Art.11

2973. Industry-Wide Coal Staff Superannuation Scheme Regulations 1994
>   disapplied: SI 2014/3229 Sch.2 para.6

2974. Industry-Wide Mineworkers Pension Scheme Regulations 1994
  disapplied: SI 2014/3229 Sch.2 para.6
3019. A470 Trunk Road (Conway Road, Glan Conwy, Gwynedd) (Prohibition of Waiting) Order 1994
  revoked: SI 2014/1059 Art.6
3047. Court of Protection (Enduring Powers of Attorney) Rules 1994
  varied: SI 2014/915 Art.5
3087. A55 Trunk Road (Abergwyngregyn, Gwynedd) (Derestriction) Order 1994
  disapplied: SI 2014/3377 Art.15
  varied: SI 2014/827 Art.15
3178. Pathfinder National Health Service Trust (Establishment) Order 1994
  Art.1, amended: SI 2014/2459 Art.2
  Art.3, substituted: SI 2014/2459 Art.3
  Art.4, amended: SI 2014/2459 Art.4
  Art.5, substituted: SI 2014/2459 Art.5
  Art.6, revoked: SI 2014/2459 Art.6
  Art.7, revoked: SI 2014/2459 Art.6
3200. Non-Domestic Rating (Unoccupied Property) (Scotland) Regulations 1994
  Reg.1, amended: SSI 2014/31 Reg.3
  Reg.4, amended: SSI 2014/31 Reg.4
3260. Electrical Equipment (Safety) Regulations 1994
  Reg.11, amended: SI 2014/469 Sch.3 para.57
  Reg.17, amended: SI 2014/469 Sch.3 para.58

1995

184. Surplus Food Regulations 1995
  revoked: SI 2014/1902 Sch.1
239. Non-Domestic Rating (Telecommunications and Canals) (Scotland) Order 1995
  Art.2, see *Assessor for Tayside Valuation Joint Board v Hutchison 3G (UK) Ltd* [2014] CSIH 40, 2014 S.L.T. 699 (LVAC), The Lord President (Gill)
300. National Health Service Pension Scheme Regulations 1995
  Reg.1, amended: SI 2014/570 Reg.5
  Reg.1, amended: SI 2014/570 Reg.6, SI 2014/1607 Reg.4
  Reg.1, amended: SI 2014/570 Reg.10

Reg.2, amended: SI 2014/78 Reg.3, SI 2014/570 Reg.3, SI 2014/1607 Reg.3
Reg.2, amended: SI 2014/570 Reg.7
Reg.2A, amended: SI 2014/570 Reg.12
Reg.3, amended: SI 2014/570 Reg.4
Reg.3, added: SI 2014/570 Reg.8
Reg.3, amended: SI 2014/1607 Reg.5
Reg.3, substituted: SI 2014/570 Reg.15
Reg.3A, amended: SI 2014/570 Reg.9
Reg.4, added: SI 2014/78 Reg.4
Reg.4, amended: SI 2014/3061 Sch.1 para.14
Reg.8, amended: SI 2014/570 Reg.13
Reg.9, revoked (in part): SI 2014/78 Reg.5
Reg.9, added: SI 2014/570 Reg.14
Reg.9, amended: SI 2014/1607 Reg.6
Reg.13, revoked (in part): SI 2014/78 Reg.6
Reg.16, amended: SI 2014/78 Reg.7
Reg.17, amended: SI 2014/78 Reg.8
s.art S Reg.2, amended: SI 2014/570 Reg.11
Sch.2B, added: SI 2014/570 Reg.17
Sch.2 para.1, amended: SI 2014/570 Reg.16
Sch.2 para.2, amended: SI 2014/570 Reg.16
Sch.2 para.3, amended: SI 2014/570 Reg.16
Sch.2 para.5, revoked (in part): SI 2014/570 Reg.16
Sch.2 para.6, amended: SI 2014/570 Reg.16
Sch.2 para.10, amended: SI 2014/570 Reg.16, SI 2014/1607 Reg.7
Sch.2 para.23, amended: SI 2014/570 Reg.16, SI 2014/1607 Reg.7
310. Social Security (Incapacity Benefit) (Transitional) Regulations 1995
  Reg.18, amended: SI 2014/516 Art.12
418. Town and Country Planning (General Permitted Development) Order 1995
  Art.1, amended: SI 2014/564 Art.2
  Art.3, applied: SI 2014/1761 Reg.5, SI 2014/2933 Art.16, SI 2014/2935 Art.11
  Art.3, varied: SI 2014/2933 Sch.1 para.1
  Art.4, applied: SI 2014/593 Reg.3, SI 2014/1761 Reg.5, SI 2014/2693 Reg.3
  Art.5, applied: SI 2014/593 Reg.4, Reg.6, SI 2014/2693 Reg.4, Reg.6
  Art.6, applied: SI 2014/593 Reg.6, SI 2014/2693 Reg.6
  Sch.2, referred to: SI 2014/1761 Reg.5
  Sch.2 Part 1, applied: SI 2014/593 Reg.2, SI 2014/2693 Reg.2
  Sch.2 Part 1, added: SI 2014/564 Art.3
  Sch.2 Part 1, amended: SI 2014/564 Art.3

Sch.2 Part 1 paraA.1, amended: SI 2014/564 Art.3

Sch.2 Part 1 paraB.1, amended: SI 2014/564 Art.3

Sch.2 Part 1 paraC.1, amended: SI 2014/564 Art.3

Sch.2 Part 1 paraD.1, amended: SI 2014/564 Art.3

Sch.2 Part 1 paraE.1, amended: SI 2014/564 Art.3

Sch.2 Part 1 paraH.1, amended: SI 2014/564 Art.3

Sch.2 Part 1 paraB.2, amended: SI 2014/564 Art.3

Sch.2 Part 1 paraA.4, amended: SI 2014/564 Art.3

Sch.2 Part 1 paraB.4, added: SI 2014/564 Art.3

Sch.2 Part 2 paraA.2, substituted: SI 2014/564 Art.4

Sch.2 Part 3, amended: SI 2014/564 Art.5

Sch.2 Part 3, added: SI 2014/564 Art.5

Sch.2 Part 3 paraK, amended: SI 2014/564 Art.5

Sch.2 Part 3, added: SI 2014/564 Art.5

Sch.2 Part 3 paraN, amended: SI 2014/564 Art.5

Sch.2 Part 3 paraO, amended: SI 2014/469 Sch.3 para.188, SI 2014/564 Art.5

Sch.2 Part 3 paraB.1, amended: SI 2014/592 Art.2

Sch.2 Part 3 paraM.1, amended: SI 2014/564 Art.5

Sch.2 Part 3 paraK.2, amended: SI 2014/564 Art.5

Sch.2 Part 3 paraM.2, amended: SI 2014/564 Art.5

Sch.2 Part 3 paraM.3, amended: SI 2014/564 Art.5

Sch.2 Part 4 paraE, amended: SI 2014/469 Sch.3 para.189

Sch.2 Part 6 paraA.1, amended: SI 2014/564 Art.6

Sch.2 Part 6 paraB.2, amended: SI 2014/564 Art.6

Sch.2 Pt 6 para.A2, see *R. (on the application of Evans) v Cornwall Council* [2013] EWHC 4109 (Admin), [2014] P.T.S.R. 556 (QBD (Admin)), Judge Birtles

Sch.2 Part 8, applied: SI 2014/593 Reg.2, SI 2014/2693 Reg.2

Sch.2 Part 8, substituted: SI 2014/592 Art.2

Sch.2 Part 8, applied: SI 2014/2693 Reg.2

Sch.2 Part 11, applied: SI 2014/2933 Art.16

Sch.2 Part 11, varied: SI 2014/2933 Sch.1 para.1

Sch.2 Part 17, applied: SI 2014/2933 Art.16, SI 2014/2935 Art.11

Sch.2 Part 17, varied: SI 2014/2933 Sch.1 para.1

Sch.2 Part 24, applied: SI 2014/2693 Reg.2

Sch.2 Part 24 paraA, amended: SI 2014/2692 Art.2

Sch.2 Part 24 paraA.1, amended: SI 2014/2692 Art.2

Sch.2 Part 24 paraA.2, amended: SI 2014/2692 Art.2

Sch.2 Part 24 paraA.3, amended: SI 2014/2692 Art.2

Sch.2 Part 24 paraA.4, amended: SI 2014/2692 Art.2

Sch.2 Part 24 paraA.4A, added: SI 2014/2692 Art.2

Sch.2 Part 32, applied: SI 2014/593 Reg.2, SI 2014/2693 Reg.2

Sch.2 Part 32, substituted: SI 2014/592 Art.2

Sch.2 Part 32 paraC, substituted: SI 2014/564 Art.7

Sch.2 Part 40, applied: SI 2014/593 Reg.2, SI 2014/2693 Reg.2

Sch.2 Part 41, added: SI 2014/592 Art.2

Sch.2 Part 41, applied: SI 2014/593 Reg.2, SI 2014/2693 Reg.2

Sch.2 Part 42, applied: SI 2014/593 Reg.2, SI 2014/2693 Reg.2

Sch.2 Part 43, applied: SI 2014/593 Reg.2, SI 2014/2693 Reg.2

419. Town and Country Planning (General Development Procedure) Order 1995

see *Elliott v Secretary of State for Communities and Local Government* [2013] EWCA Civ 703, [2014] Env. L.R. 1 (CA (Civ Div)), Laws LJ

Art.1, see *Elliott v Secretary of State for Communities and Local Government* [2013] EWCA Civ 703, [2014] Env. L.R. 1 (CA (Civ Div)), Laws LJ

Art.26, see *Sanger v Newham LBC* [2014] EWHC 1922 (Admin), [2014] 2 Cr. App. R. 27 (DC), Sir Brian Leveson PQBD

512. Statutory Sick Pay Percentage Threshold Order 1995
revoked: SI 2014/897 Art.2

572. Valuation Appeal Committee (Procedure in Appeals under the Valuation Acts) (Scotland) Regulations 1995
Reg.5, see *BAE Systems Surface Ships Ltd v Assessor for Glasgow* 2014 S.L.T. (Lands Tr) 2 (Lands Tr (Scot)), J N Wright, QC; see *Danzan 2003 Trust v Assessor for Lothian* 2014 S.L.T. (Lands Tr) 4 (Lands Tr (Scot)), J N Wright, QC; see *DSM Nutritional Products v Assessor for Ayrshire Valuation Joint Board* 2014 S.L.T. (Lands Tr) 7 (Lands Tr (Scot)), J N Wright, QC; see *Historic Scotland Executive Agency v Highland and Western Isles Valuation Joint Board Assessor* 2014 S.L.T. (Lands Tr) 50 (Lands Tr (Scot)), J N Wright, QC; see *Ministry of Defence v Assessor for Fife Council* 2014 S.L.T. (Lands Tr) 34 (Lands Tr (Scot)), J N Wright, QC; see *Ministry of Defence v Grampian Assessor* 2014 S.L.T. (Lands Tr) 44 (Lands Tr (Scot)), J N Wright, QC; see *NHS Greater Glasgow and Clyde v Assessor for Renfrewshire* 2014 S.L.T. (Lands Tr) 52 (Lands Tr (Scot)), J N Wright, QC; see *Opal Glen Properties Ltd v Central Scotland Valuation Joint Board Assessor* 2014 S.L.T. (Lands Tr) 22 (Lands Tr (Scot)), Lord McGhie; see *WAP Fyfe v Assessor for Fife Council* 2014 S.L.T. (Lands Tr) 10 (Lands Tr (Scot)), J N Wright, QC
Reg.10, see *Marks & Spencer Plc v Assessor for Highland and Western Isles Valuation Joint Board* 2014 S.L.T. 241 (LVAC), The Lord President (Gill)

614. Animal By-Products (Identification) Regulations 1995
revoked: SI 2014/517 Reg.28

630. Research Councils (Transfer of Property etc) Order 1995
varied: SI 2014/2708 Art.5

708. Pensions Increase (Review) Order 1995
referred to: SI 2014/668 Sch.1
Art.6, substituted: SI 2014/107 Sch.1
para.56, SI 2014/3229 Sch.6 para.35

731. Welfare of Animals (Slaughter or Killing) Regulations 1995
applied: SI 2014/951 Reg.8, Reg.10, Reg.16, SI 2014/1240 Reg.8, Reg.10, Reg.16

revoked (in part): SI 2014/951 Reg.46, SI 2014/1240 Reg.47
Sch.12 Part II para.3, applied: SI 2014/951 Sch.3 para.3, SI 2014/1240 Sch.3 para.3

738. Offshore Installations and Pipeline Works (Management and Administration) Regulations 1995
Reg.3, disapplied: SI 2014/1638 Reg.3

849. Local Authorities (Companies) Order 1995
Art.1, amended: SI 2014/1815 Sch.1 para.3

866. National Health Service (Injury Benefits) Regulations 1995
Reg.2, amended: SI 2014/78 Reg.25
Reg.2B, added: SI 2014/78 Reg.26

1019. Local Government Pension Scheme Regulations 1995
revoked: SI 2014/525 Sch.1

1268. Value Added Tax (Special Provisions) Order 1995
see *Pendragon Plc v Revenue and Customs Commissioners* [2013] EWCA Civ 868, [2014] S.T.C. 844 (CA (Civ Div)), Lloyd LJ

1803. Merchant Shipping (Ships Doctors) Regulations 1995
revoked: SI 2014/1614 Reg.15

1897. Civil Courts (Amendment) Order 1995
revoked: SI 2014/820 Sch.1

1945. Fees in the Registers of Scotland Order 1995
applied: SSI 2014/188 Art.6
revoked: SSI 2014/188 Sch.2
Sch.1 Part III paraA, amended: SI 2014/1815 Sch.1 para.4
Sch.1 Part III paraA, substituted: SI 2014/1815 Sch.1 para.4

1979. Venture Capital Trust Regulations 1995
Reg.2, amended: SI 2014/1929 Reg.2
Reg.9, amended: SI 2014/1929 Reg.2
Reg.24, amended: SI 2014/1929 Reg.2
Reg.25, amended: SI 2014/1929 Reg.2

2005. Mines Miscellaneous Health and Safety Provisions Regulations 1995
revoked (in part): SI 2014/3248 Sch.4 Part 1
Reg.4, applied: SI 2014/3248 Reg.71

2151. Distraint by Collectors (Fees, Costs and Charges) (Amendment) Regulations 1995
revoked (in part): SI 2014/600 Sch.1 Part 2

2261. Royal Scottish Academy of Music and Drama (Scotland) Order of Council 1995
applied: SSI 2014/268 Art.22
revoked: SSI 2014/268 Art.21

2297. A483 Trunk Road (Derwydd, Llandybie, Dyfed) (De-Restriction) Order 1995
revoked: SI 2014/1065 Art.2
2417. A282 Trunk Road (Dartford West Tunnel and Essex Viaduct) (Weight Restriction) Order 1995
revoked: SI 2014/2518 Art.5
2498. Merchant Shipping (Reporting Requirements for Ships Carrying Dangerous or Polluting Goods) Regulations 1995
Reg.3, amended: SI 2014/3306 Sch.2 para.1
2518. Value Added Tax Regulations 1995
see *Revenue and Customs Commissioners v GMAC UK Plc (C-589/12)* [2014] S.T.C. 2603 (ECJ (2nd Chamber)), Judge Silva de Lapuerta (President)
Part XXVI, added: SI 2014/2430 Reg.9
Part XXVI, substituted: SI 2014/2430 Reg.10
Part XXVII, added: SI 2014/2430 Reg.11
Reg.4B, amended: SI 2014/548 Reg.3
Reg.13, see *GB Housley Ltd v Revenue and Customs Commissioners* [2014] UKUT 320 (TCC), [2014] S.T.C. 2733 (UT (Tax)), Warren J
Reg.23A, amended: SI 2014/1497 Reg.3
Reg.25, applied: SI 2014/1497 Reg.2
Reg.25A, amended: SI 2014/1497 Reg.4
Reg.25A, see *Blackburn (t/a Cornish Moorland Honey) v Revenue and Customs Commissioners* [2014] S.F.T.D. 195 (FTT (Tax)), Barbara Mosedale (Tribunal Judge)
Reg.29, see *GB Housley Ltd v Revenue and Customs Commissioners* [2014] UKUT 320 (TCC), [2014] S.T.C. 2733 (UT (Tax)), Warren J; see *Our Communications Ltd v Revenue and Customs Commissioners* [2014] S.T.C. 608 (UT (Tax)), Arnold J
Reg.32, see *Iveco Ltd v Revenue and Customs Commissioners* [2014] S.F.T.D. 661 (FTT (Tax)), Judge Roger Berner
Reg.37, see *Bratt Auto Services Ltd v Revenue and Customs Commissioners* [2014] UKFTT 676 (TC), [2014] S.F.T.D. 1120 (FTT (Tax)), Judge Roger Berner
Reg.38, see *Iveco Ltd v Revenue and Customs Commissioners* [2014] S.F.T.D. 661 (FTT (Tax)), Judge Roger Berner
Reg.38ZA, added: SI 2014/548 Reg.4
Reg.43A, amended: SI 2014/2430 Reg.3

Reg.90, see *Esporta Ltd v Revenue and Customs Commissioners* [2014] EWCA Civ 155, [2014] S.T.C. 1548 (CA (Civ Div)), Arden LJ
Reg.101, see *Chard Bowling Club v Customs and Excise Commissioners* [1998] B.V.C. 2014 (V&DTr), Malcolm JF Palmer (Chairman)
Reg.148A, amended: SI 2014/548 Reg.5
Reg.148A, revoked (in part): SI 2014/548 Reg.5
Reg.165, amended: SI 2014/2430 Reg.4
Reg.166, amended: SI 2014/2430 Reg.5
Reg.166AA, added: SI 2014/2430 Reg.5
Reg.168, amended: SI 2014/2430 Reg.6
Reg.171, amended: SI 2014/2430 Reg.7
Reg.171A, added: SI 2014/2430 Reg.7
Reg.173B, amended: SI 2014/2430 Reg.8
Reg.173E, amended: SI 2014/2430 Reg.8
Reg.173L, amended: SI 2014/2430 Reg.8
Reg.201, see *Revenue and Customs Commissioners v Patel* [2014] UKUT 361 (TCC) (UT (Tax)), Judge Colin Bishopp
Reg.218, substituted: SI 2014/2430 Reg.10
2587. Collective Redundancies and Transfer of Undertakings (Protection of Employment) (Amendment) Regulations 1995
see *United States v Nolan* [2014] EWCA Civ 71, [2014] I.C.R. 685 (CA (Civ Div)), Moore-Bick LJ
2644. Statutory Nuisance (Appeals) Regulations 1995
Reg.2, see *North Lincolnshire CC v Act Fast North Lincolnshire (CIC)* [2013] EWHC 2890 (Admin), [2014] Env. L.R. 7 (QBD (Admin)), Judge Behrens
2652. Marketing of Vegetable Plant Material Regulations 1995
Reg.2, amended: SI 2014/487 Reg.2, SI 2014/519 Reg.3, SSI 2014/111 Reg.3
Reg.3, amended: SI 2014/487 Reg.2, SI 2014/519 Reg.3, SSI 2014/111 Reg.4
Reg.5, amended: SI 2014/487 Reg.2, SI 2014/519 Reg.3, SSI 2014/111 Reg.5
Reg.14, added: SSI 2014/111 Reg.6
2709. Reciprocal Enforcement of Maintenance Orders (United States of America) Order 1995
Sch.2 para.4, revoked (in part): SI 2014/879 Art.61
Sch.2 para.8, amended: SI 2014/879 Art.62
Sch.2 para.16, amended: SI 2014/879 Art.63

Sch.2 para.17, amended: SI 2014/879 Art.64
Sch.3, added: SI 2014/879 Art.72
Sch.3, amended: SI 2014/879 Art.67, Art.68,
Art.69, Art.70, Art.71, Art.72, Art.73
Sch.3, revoked (in part): SI 2014/879 Art.66,
Art.67, Art.68, Art.70

2716. Other Fuel Substitutes (Rates of Excise Duty etc) Order 1995
Art.3, amended: SI 2014/470 Art.4
Art.3, substituted: SI 2014/470 Art.3
Art.5, amended: SI 2014/470 Art.5

2800. National Health Service Litigation Authority (Establishment and Constitution) Order 1995
Art.1, amended: SI 2014/3090 Sch.1 para.1

2801. National Health Service Litigation Authority Regulations 1995
Reg.14, amended: SI 2014/1815 Sch.1
para.5

2814. Teachers Superannuation (Additional Voluntary Contributions) (Scotland) Regulations 1995
applied: SSI 2014/217 Sch.1 para.2, SSI
2014/292 Sch.1 para.2
Reg.5, amended: SSI 2014/69 Reg.24
Reg.11, amended: SSI 2014/69 Reg.25
Reg.12, amended: SSI 2014/69 Reg.26

2870. Escape and Rescue from Mines Regulations 1995
revoked (in part): SI 2014/3248 Sch.4 Part 1

2880. Sale of Registration Marks Regulations 1995
Sch.1 para.9, amended: SI 2014/2358 Sch.3
para.1

2909. Public Service Vehicles (Operators Licences) (Fees) Regulations 1995
Sch.1, amended: SI 2014/2118 Reg.2

2923. Health and Safety Information for Employees (Modifications and Repeals) Regulations 1995
Sch.1 Part I, amended: SI 2014/1637 Sch.4
Part 1

2985. Transfer of Functions (Science) Order 1995
Art.3, varied: SI 2014/2708 Art.5
Art.4, varied: SI 2014/2708 Art.5
Art.5, varied: SI 2014/2708 Art.5
Sch.1 para.1, varied: SI 2014/2708 Art.5
Sch.1 para.4, varied: SI 2014/2708 Art.5
Sch.1 para.5, varied: SI 2014/2708 Art.5
Sch.1 para.6, varied: SI 2014/2708 Art.5

3000. Goods Vehicles (Licensing of Operators) (Fees) Regulations 1995
Sch.1 Part I, amended: SI 2014/2119 Reg.2

3173. Civil Courts (Amendment) (No.2) Order 1995
revoked: SI 2014/820 Sch.1

3183. Occupational Pension Schemes (Equal Treatment) Regulations 1995
Reg.15, varied: SI 2014/1711 Reg.73

3213. Pensions (Northern Ireland) Order 1995
Art.75, see *Pensions Regulator v Desmond*
[2014] Pens. L.R. 9 (CA (NI)), Morgan LCJ

1996

24. Town and Country Planning (Costs of Inquiries etc.) (Standard Daily Amount) Regulations 1996
revoked (in part): SI 2014/692 Sch.1

68. Civil Courts (Amendment) Order 1996
revoked: SI 2014/820 Sch.1

90. London Ambulance Service National Health Service Trust (Establishment) Order 1996
Art.1, amended: SI 2014/1904 Art.2
Art.3, amended: SI 2014/1904 Art.3
Art.4, amended: SI 2014/1904 Art.4
Art.5, substituted: SI 2014/1904 Art.5
Art.6, revoked: SI 2014/1904 Art.6
Art.7, revoked: SI 2014/1904 Art.6

180. Charities (Exception from Registration) Regulations 1996
Reg.4, amended: SI 2014/242 Reg.2

192. Equipment and Protective Systems Intended for Use in Potentially Explosive Atmospheres Regulations 1996
Reg.2, amended: SI 2014/469 Sch.3 para.60
Reg.14, amended: SI 2014/469 Sch.3
para.61
Reg.15, amended: SI 2014/469 Sch.3
para.62
Reg.20, revoked (in part): SI 2014/3248
Sch.4 Part 2
Sch.14 para.1, amended: SI 2014/469 Sch.3
para.63
Sch.14 para.2, amended: SI 2014/469 Sch.3
para.63
Sch.14 para.4, amended: SI 2014/469 Sch.3
para.63
Sch.14 para.6, amended: SI 2014/469 Sch.3
para.63

Sch.14 para.7, amended: SI 2014/469 Sch.3
para.63
207. Jobseeker's Allowance Regulations 1996
applied: SI 2014/3117 Reg.7, Reg.12
Reg.1, amended: SI 2014/107 Sch.1 para.16,
SI 2014/591 Reg.4, SI 2014/2735 Reg.2, SI
2014/3229 Sch.6 para.11, SI 2014/3255
Art.7
Reg.3E, amended: SI 2014/884 Reg.4
Reg.14, amended: SI 2014/1623 Reg.2
Reg.15, amended: SI 2014/884 Reg.4, SI
2014/3255 Art.7
Reg.25, amended: SI 2014/1913 Reg.15, SI
2014/3117 Reg.19
Reg.46, amended: SI 2014/2309 Reg.2
Reg.48, amended: SI 2014/884 Reg.4
Reg.52, amended: SI 2014/3255 Art.7
Reg.69, applied: SI 2014/1230 Reg.32,
Reg.33
Reg.69A, applied: SI 2014/1230 Reg.32,
Reg.33
Reg.69B, applied: SI 2014/1230 Reg.32,
Reg.33
Reg.70, applied: SI 2014/1230 Reg.32
Reg.79, amended: SI 2014/147 Art.8
Reg.85A, amended: SI 2014/902 Reg.3, SI
2014/2735 Reg.3
Reg.98, amended: SI 2014/591 Reg.4, SI
2014/3255 Art.7
Reg.105, amended: SI 2014/591 Reg.4, SI
2014/1913 Reg.11, SI 2014/3117 Reg.15
Reg.105, applied: SI 2014/1913 Reg.11, SI
2014/3117 Reg.15
Reg.105, revoked (in part): SI 2014/1913
Reg.11, SI 2014/3117 Reg.15
Reg.113, amended: SI 2014/1913 Reg.12, SI
2014/3117 Reg.16
Reg.113, applied: SI 2014/1913 Reg.12, SI
2014/3117 Reg.16
Reg.113, revoked (in part): SI 2014/1913
Reg.12, SI 2014/3117 Reg.16
Reg.141, amended: SI 2014/2309 Reg.3
Reg.145, applied: SI 2014/516 Sch.12
Reg.146C, amended: SI 2014/2309 Reg.3
Reg.146G, applied: SI 2014/516 Sch.12
Reg.169, amended: SI 2014/879 Art.74
Reg.172, amended: SI 2014/516 Art.20
Sch.1 Part I para.1, referred to: SI 2014/147
Art.9
Sch.1 Part I para.2, substituted: SI 2014/516
Sch.9

Sch.1 Part II para.4, amended: SI 2014/516
Art.19
Sch.1 Part III para.14, amended: SI
2014/2888 Reg.3
Sch.1 Part III para.15, amended: SI
2014/2888 Reg.3
Sch.1 Part III para.16, amended: SI
2014/2888 Reg.3
Sch.1 Part IV, substituted: SI 2014/516
Sch.10
Sch.1 Part IVA para.20H, amended: SI
2014/2888 Reg.3
Sch.1 Part IVA para.20I, amended: SI
2014/2888 Reg.3
Sch.1 Part IVB para.20M, substituted: SI
2014/516 Sch.11
Sch.2 para.5, applied: SI 2014/516 Sch.12
Sch.2 para.6, applied: SI 2014/516 Sch.12,
SI 2014/1230 Reg.29
Sch.2 para.7, applied: SI 2014/516 Sch.12,
SI 2014/1230 Reg.29
Sch.2 para.9, applied: SI 2014/516 Sch.12
Sch.2 para.10, applied: SI 2014/516 Sch.12
Sch.2 para.11, amended: SI 2014/591 Reg.4
Sch.2 para.11, applied: SI 2014/516 Sch.12
Sch.2 para.13, applied: SI 2014/1230 Reg.29
Sch.2 para.14, applied: SI 2014/1230 Reg.29
Sch.2 para.17, amended: SI 2014/516 Art.19,
SI 2014/2888 Reg.3
Sch.5 para.4, applied: SI 2014/516 Sch.12
Sch.5 para.14, applied: SI 2014/516 Sch.12
Sch.5A para.3, applied: SI 2014/516 Sch.12
Sch.7, applied: SI 2014/1913 Reg.13, SI
2014/3117 Reg.17
Sch.7 para.2A, amended: SI 2014/591 Reg.4
Sch.7 paraA.4, added: SI 2014/1913 Reg.13
Sch.7 paraA.4, revoked (in part): SI
2014/1913 Reg.13
Sch.7 para.4, amended: SI 2014/3255 Art.7
Sch.7 paraA.5, added: SI 2014/3117 Reg.17
Sch.7 paraA.5, revoked (in part): SI
2014/3117 Reg.17
Sch.7 para.5, amended: SI 2014/3255 Art.7
Sch.7 para.26, amended: SI 2014/852 Art.6
Sch.7 para.56, amended: SI 2014/513 Sch.1
para.5
Sch.7 para.75, added: SI 2014/2103 Art.4
Sch.8, applied: SI 2014/1913 Reg.14, SI
2014/3117 Reg.18
Sch.8 paraA.4, added: SI 2014/1913 Reg.14

Sch.8 paraA.4, revoked (in part): SI
2014/1913 Reg.14

Sch.8 paraA.5, added: SI 2014/3117 Reg.18

Sch.8 paraA.5, revoked (in part): SI
2014/3117 Reg.18

Sch.8 para.60, amended: SI 2014/513 Sch.1
para.5

Sch.8 para.64, added: SI 2014/2103 Art.4

**251. National Health Service (Clinical
Negligence Scheme) Regulations 1996**

Reg.1, amended: SI 2014/933 Reg.2

Reg.3, amended: SI 2014/3090 Sch.1 para.1

Reg.3, revoked (in part): SI 2014/933 Reg.3

Reg.4, amended: SI 2014/933 Reg.4

263. Charter Trustees Regulations 1996

Reg.15, revoked (in part): SI 2014/580 Art.3

275. Gas (Northern Ireland) Order 1996

Art.7, applied: SI 2014/1458 Art.5

Art.15B, amended: SI 2014/892 Sch.1
para.218

Art.15B, applied: SI 2014/559

Art.15B, referred to: SI 2014/892 Sch.2
para.2

Art.17A, amended: SI 2014/892 Sch.1
para.219

Art.17A, referred to: SI 2014/892 Sch.2
para.2

Art.18, amended: SI 2014/892 Sch.1
para.220

Art.23, amended: SI 2014/892 Sch.1
para.221

Art.27, amended: SI 2014/892 Sch.1
para.221

**282. Merchant Shipping (Prevention of
Pollution) (Law of the Sea Convention) Order
1996**

Art.2, enabled: SI 2014/3076, SI 2014/3306

**301. A282 Trunk Road (Dartford East Tunnel)
(Weight Restriction) Order 1996**

revoked: SI 2014/2518 Art.5

varied: SI 2014/2333 Art.5, SI 2014/3458
Art.7

**341. Health and Safety (Safety Signs and
Signals) Regulations 1996**

Reg.7, substituted: SI 2014/469 Sch.3
para.64

**449. Gas Act 1986 (Exemptions) (No.1) Order
1996**

revoked: SI 2014/528 Sch.1

**465. New Town (East Kilbride) (Transfer of
Property, Rights and Liabilities) Order 1996**

Art.2, see *Bavaird v Sir Robert McAlpine
Ltd* 2014 S.C. 322 (IH (Ex Div)), Lady
Paton

Art.3, see *Bavaird v Sir Robert McAlpine
Ltd* 2014 S.C. 322 (IH (Ex Div)), Lady
Paton

**471. Gas Act 1986 (Exemptions) (No.2) Order
1996**

revoked: SI 2014/528 Sch.1

**513. Act of Adjournal (Criminal Procedure
Rules) 1996**

see *Speirs (Allan) v HM Advocate* 2014
S.C.L. 58 (HCJ), The Lord Justice Clerk
(Carloway)

Sch.2 Appendix, amended: SSI 2014/162

Sch.1, SSI 2014/349 Sch.1 Part 1, Sch.1 Part
2

Sch.2 Part VII, added: SSI 2014/242 r.3

Sch.2 Part VII, added: SSI 2014/162 r.2

Sch.2 para.59.4, see *HM Advocate v Sinclair
(Angus Robertson)* [2014] HCJAC 131, 2014
S.L.T. 1092 (HCJ), The Lord Justice Clerk
(Carloway)

**588. Civil Courts (Amendment) (No.2) Order
1996**

revoked: SI 2014/820 Sch.1

**615. Education (Areas to which Pupils and
Students Belong) Regulations 1996**

Reg.2, amended: SI 2014/2103 Art.5

Reg.4, amended: SI 2014/2103 Art.5

Reg.5, amended: SI 2014/2103 Art.5

Reg.7, amended: SI 2014/2103 Art.5

**711. Local Government Pension Scheme
(Environment Agency) Regulations 1996**

Reg.2, applied: SI 2014/525 Reg.25

800. Pensions Increase (Review) Order 1996

referred to: SI 2014/668 Sch.1

Art.6, substituted: SI 2014/107 Sch.1

para.56, SI 2014/3229 Sch.6 para.35

**802. A21 Trunk Road (Tonbridge Bypass to
Pembury Bypass Dualling) Order 1996**

revoked: SI 2014/1330 Art.2

**808. A21 Trunk Road (Tonbridge Bypass to
Pembury Bypass Dualling) (Detrunking) Order
1996**

revoked: SI 2014/1337 Art.2

825. Pipelines Safety Regulations 1996

Reg.13A, applied: SI 2014/3109 Sch.1

890. Marking of Plastic Explosives for Detection Regulations 1996
    revoked: SI 2014/1638 Sch.14 Part 2
    Reg.6, substituted: SI 2014/469 Sch.3
    para.65

972. Special Waste Regulations 1996
    applied: SSI 2014/4 Reg.4
    Reg.18, applied: SSI 2014/319 Sch.1 para.5,
    Sch.2 para.8, Sch.3 para.5, Sch.4 para.5

1080. Buying Agency Trading Fund (Amendment) Order 1996
    Art.2, varied: SI 2014/2708 Art.5

1141. Juries (Northern Ireland) Order 1996
    Art.2, amended: SI 2014/1116 Art.11
    Art.4, amended: SI 2014/1116 Art.11
    Art.6, amended: SI 2014/1116 Art.11
    Art.26A, amended: SI 2014/1116 Art.11
    Art.26B, amended: SI 2014/1116 Art.11
    Art.26C, amended: SI 2014/1116 Art.11

1172. Occupational Pension Schemes (Contracting-out) Regulations 1996
    Reg.1, applied: SSI 2014/164 Reg.95
    Reg.1, revoked (in part): SI 2014/107 Sch.1
    para.17, SI 2014/3229 Sch.6 para.12
    Reg.26, amended: SI 2014/107 Sch.1
    para.17, SI 2014/3229 Sch.6 para.12
    Reg.55, amended: SI 2014/560 Sch.3 para.5,
    SI 2014/3229 Sch.3 para.3
    Reg.55, disapplied: SI 2014/3229 Sch.2
    para.6
    Reg.57, amended: SI 2014/107 Sch.1
    para.17, SI 2014/3229 Sch.6 para.12
    Reg.58, amended: SI 2014/107 Sch.1
    para.17, SI 2014/3229 Sch.6 para.12
    Reg.59, amended: SI 2014/107 Sch.1
    para.17, SI 2014/3229 Sch.6 para.12
    Reg.60, applied: SI 2014/1964 Reg.164, SI
    2014/2848 Reg.83, Reg.166
    Reg.69B, amended: SI 2014/107 Sch.1
    para.17, SI 2014/560 Sch.3 para.5, SI
    2014/3229 Sch.3 para.3, Sch.6 para.12
    Reg.69B, disapplied: SI 2014/3229 Sch.2
    para.6

1243. National Park Authorities (England) Order 1996
    Sch.1 Part 1, substituted: SI 2014/571 Sch.1
    Sch.1 Part 2, amended: SI 2014/571 Art.2

1299. Proceeds of Crime (Northern Ireland) Order 1996
    Art.8, see *R. v Mackle (Plunkett Jude)*
    [2014] UKSC 5, [2014] A.C. 678 (SC), Lord
    Neuberger JSC
    Art.8, applied: SI 2014/3141 Reg.24
    Art.31, applied: SI 2014/3141 Reg.23

1354. Gas Act 1986 (Exemptions) (No.3) Order 1996
    revoked: SI 2014/528 Sch.1

1462. Contracting-out (Transfer and Transfer Payment) Regulations 1996
    Sch.2 para.1, amended: SI 2014/107 Sch.1
    para.18, SI 2014/3229 Sch.6 para.13
    Sch.2 para.6, amended: SI 2014/107 Sch.1
    para.18, SI 2014/3229 Sch.6 para.13

1499. Food Labelling Regulations 1996
    revoked (in part): SI 2014/1855 Sch.6 Part 2,
    SI 2014/2303 Sch.6 Part 2, SSI 2014/312
    Sch.4 Part 2
    Reg.1, revoked (in part): SI 2014/1855 Sch.6
    Part 1, SI 2014/2303 Sch.6 Part 1, SSI
    2014/312 Sch.4 Part 1
    Reg.2, amended: SI 2014/1855 Sch.6 Part 1,
    Sch.7 para.11, SI 2014/2303 Sch.6 Part 1,
    Sch.7 para.11
    Reg.2, revoked (in part): SI 2014/2303 Sch.6
    Part 1
    Reg.3, amended: SI 2014/1855 Sch.7
    para.12, SI 2014/2303 Sch.7 para.12
    Reg.3, revoked (in part): SI 2014/1855 Sch.6
    Part 1, SI 2014/2303 Sch.6 Part 1
    Reg.4, amended: SI 2014/1855 Sch.7 para.2,
    SI 2014/2303 Sch.7 para.2
    Reg.4, revoked (in part): SI 2014/1855 Sch.6
    Part 1, SI 2014/2303 Sch.6 Part 1
    Reg.5, revoked (in part): SI 2014/1855 Sch.6
    Part 1, SI 2014/2303 Sch.6 Part 1
    Reg.6, revoked (in part): SI 2014/1855 Sch.6
    Part 1, SI 2014/2303 Sch.6 Part 1
    Reg.7, revoked (in part): SI 2014/1855 Sch.6
    Part 1, SI 2014/2303 Sch.6 Part 1
    Reg.8, revoked (in part): SI 2014/1855 Sch.6
    Part 1, SI 2014/2303 Sch.6 Part 1
    Reg.9, revoked (in part): SI 2014/1855 Sch.6
    Part 1, SI 2014/2303 Sch.6 Part 1
    Reg.10, revoked (in part): SI 2014/1855
    Sch.6 Part 1, SI 2014/2303 Sch.6 Part 1
    Reg.11, revoked (in part): SI 2014/1855
    Sch.6 Part 1, SI 2014/2303 Sch.6 Part 1

Reg.12, revoked (in part): SI 2014/1855
Sch.6 Part 1, SI 2014/2303 Sch.6 Part 1
Reg.13, revoked (in part): SI 2014/1855
Sch.6 Part 1, SI 2014/2303 Sch.6 Part 1
Reg.14, revoked (in part): SI 2014/1855
Sch.6 Part 1, SI 2014/2303 Sch.6 Part 1
Reg.15, revoked (in part): SI 2014/1855
Sch.6 Part 1, SI 2014/2303 Sch.6 Part 1
Reg.16, revoked (in part): SI 2014/1855
Sch.6 Part 1, SI 2014/2303 Sch.6 Part 1
Reg.17, revoked (in part): SI 2014/1855
Sch.6 Part 1, SI 2014/2303 Sch.6 Part 1
Reg.17A, revoked (in part): SI 2014/1855
Sch.6 Part 1, SI 2014/2303 Sch.6 Part 1
Reg.18, revoked (in part): SI 2014/1855
Sch.6 Part 1, SI 2014/2303 Sch.6 Part 1
Reg.19, revoked (in part): SI 2014/1855
Sch.6 Part 1, SI 2014/2303 Sch.6 Part 1
Reg.20, revoked (in part): SI 2014/1855
Sch.6 Part 1, SI 2014/2303 Sch.6 Part 1
Reg.21, revoked (in part): SI 2014/1855
Sch.6 Part 1, SI 2014/2303 Sch.6 Part 1
Reg.22, revoked (in part): SI 2014/1855
Sch.6 Part 1, SI 2014/2303 Sch.6 Part 1
Reg.23, revoked (in part): SI 2014/1855
Sch.6 Part 1, SI 2014/2303 Sch.6 Part 1
Reg.24, revoked (in part): SI 2014/1855
Sch.6 Part 1, SI 2014/2303 Sch.6 Part 1
Reg.25, revoked (in part): SI 2014/1855
Sch.6 Part 1, SI 2014/2303 Sch.6 Part 1
Reg.26, revoked (in part): SI 2014/1855
Sch.6 Part 1, SI 2014/2303 Sch.6 Part 1
Reg.27, revoked (in part): SI 2014/1855
Sch.6 Part 1, SI 2014/2303 Sch.6 Part 1
Reg.28, revoked (in part): SI 2014/1855
Sch.6 Part 1, SI 2014/2303 Sch.6 Part 1
Reg.29, revoked (in part): SI 2014/1855
Sch.6 Part 1, SI 2014/2303 Sch.6 Part 1
Reg.30, revoked (in part): SI 2014/1855
Sch.6 Part 1, SI 2014/2303 Sch.6 Part 1
Reg.31, revoked (in part): SI 2014/1855
Sch.6 Part 1, SI 2014/2303 Sch.6 Part 1
Reg.32, revoked (in part): SI 2014/1855
Sch.6 Part 1, SI 2014/2303 Sch.6 Part 1
Reg.33, revoked (in part): SI 2014/1855
Sch.6 Part 1, SI 2014/2303 Sch.6 Part 1
Reg.34, revoked (in part): SI 2014/1855
Sch.6 Part 1, SI 2014/2303 Sch.6 Part 1
Reg.34A, revoked (in part): SI 2014/1855
Sch.6 Part 1, SI 2014/2303 Sch.6 Part 1

Reg.34B, revoked (in part): SI 2014/1855
Sch.6 Part 1, SI 2014/2303 Sch.6 Part 1
Reg.34C, revoked (in part): SI 2014/1855
Sch.6 Part 1, SI 2014/2303 Sch.6 Part 1
Reg.35, revoked (in part): SI 2014/1855
Sch.6 Part 1, SI 2014/2303 Sch.6 Part 1
Reg.36, revoked (in part): SI 2014/1855
Sch.6 Part 1, SI 2014/2303 Sch.6 Part 1
Reg.37, revoked (in part): SI 2014/1855
Sch.6 Part 1, SI 2014/2303 Sch.6 Part 1
Reg.38, revoked (in part): SI 2014/1855
Sch.6 Part 1, SI 2014/2303 Sch.6 Part 1
Reg.39, revoked (in part): SI 2014/1855
Sch.6 Part 1, SI 2014/2303 Sch.6 Part 1
Reg.40, revoked (in part): SI 2014/1855
Sch.6 Part 1, SI 2014/2303 Sch.6 Part 1
Reg.41, amended: SI 2014/1855 Sch.7
para.3, SI 2014/2303 Sch.7 para.3
Reg.41, revoked (in part): SI 2014/1855
Sch.6 Part 1, SI 2014/2303 Sch.6 Part 1
Reg.44, revoked (in part): SI 2014/1855
Sch.6 Part 1, SI 2014/2303 Sch.6 Part 1, SSI
2014/312 Sch.4 Part 1
Reg.46, revoked (in part): SI 2014/1855
Sch.6 Part 1, SI 2014/2303 Sch.6 Part 1
Reg.49, revoked (in part): SI 2014/1855
Sch.6 Part 1, SI 2014/2303 Sch.6 Part 1
Reg.50, revoked (in part): SI 2014/1855
Sch.6 Part 1, SI 2014/2303 Sch.6 Part 1
Sch.AA1, revoked (in part): SI 2014/1855
Sch.6 Part 1, SI 2014/2303 Sch.6 Part 1, SSI
2014/312 Sch.4 Part 1
Sch.8 Part I, amended: SI 2014/1855 Sch.6
Part 1, Sch.7 para.13, SI 2014/2303 Sch.6
Part 1, SSI 2014/312 Sch.4 Part 1, Sch.5
para.2
Sch.8 Part I, substituted: SI 2014/2303 Sch.7
para.13
Sch.9, revoked (in part): SI 2014/1855 Sch.6
Part 1, SI 2014/2303 Sch.6 Part 1, SSI
2014/312 Sch.4 Part 1
1502. Food (Lot Marking) Regulations 1996
Reg.2, amended: SI 2014/1855 Sch.7 para.5,
SI 2014/2303 Sch.7 para.5, SSI 2014/312
Sch.5 para.3
Reg.2, substituted: SI 2014/1855 Sch.7
para.15, SI 2014/2303 Sch.7 para.15
Reg.4, amended: SI 2014/1855 Sch.7
para.16, SI 2014/2303 Sch.7 para.16, SSI
2014/312 Sch.5 para.3

1513. Health and Safety (Consultation with Employees) Regulations 1996
applied: SI 2014/3352 Sch.2 para.30
Sch.2 para.3, amended: SI 2014/431 Sch.1 para.17
Sch.2 para.3A, added: SI 2014/431 Sch.1 para.18

1527. Landfill Tax Regulations 1996
Reg.31, amended: SI 2014/707 Reg.3

1564. Protection of Water Against Agricultural Nitrate Pollution (Scotland) Regulations 1996
Reg.2, amended: SSI 2014/373 Reg.4, Reg.5

1629. United Nations Arms Embargoes (Former Yugoslavia) (Amendment) Order 1996
revoked: SI 2014/2711 Sch.1

1655. Occupational Pension Schemes (Disclosure of Information) Regulations 1996
Reg.6, referred to: SI 2014/1711 Reg.78
Reg.7, referred to: SI 2014/1711 Reg.78
Reg.11, disapplied: SI 2014/1711 Reg.78
Sch.2 para.4, referred to: SI 2014/1711 Reg.78
Sch.2 para.16, referred to: SI 2014/1711 Reg.78
Sch.2 para.17, referred to: SI 2014/1711 Reg.78

1656. Work in Compressed Air Regulations 1996
Reg.8, applied: SI 2014/2936 Sch.1 para.4
Reg.12, applied: SI 2014/2936 Sch.1 para.4

1667. Charities (The Royal School for the Blind) Order 1996
Part 3 para.4, amended: SI 2014/1815 Sch.1 para.6

1685. Police (Promotion) Regulations 1996
Reg.2, amended: SI 2014/2373 Reg.3
Reg.3, amended: SI 2014/2373 Reg.4
Sch.1 para.5, amended: SI 2014/2373 Reg.5

1715. Occupational Pension Schemes (Scheme Administration) Regulations 1996
Part IV, applied: SI 2014/1711 Reg.68
Reg.3, applied: SI 2014/1711 Reg.40
Reg.4, amended: SI 2014/540 Reg.2
Reg.7, amended: SI 2014/107 Sch.1 para.19
Reg.16A, substituted: SI 2014/3138 Reg.7

1738. Deregulation (Industrial and Provident Societies) Order 1996
Art.3, revoked: 2014 c.14 Sch.7
Art.7, revoked: 2014 c.14 Sch.7
Art.12, revoked: 2014 c.14 Sch.7

1847. Occupational Pension Schemes (Transfer Values) Regulations 1996
Reg.1, amended: SI 2014/1711 Reg.32
Reg.6, referred to: SI 2014/1711 Reg.31
Reg.7, amended: SI 2014/1711 Reg.32
Reg.7A, amended: SI 2014/1711 Reg.32
Reg.7B, amended: SI 2014/1711 Reg.32
Reg.7C, amended: SI 2014/1711 Reg.32
Reg.7D, amended: SI 2014/1711 Reg.32
Reg.19, applied: SI 2014/1711 Reg.30

1880. Local Authorities (Contracting Out of Tax Billing, Collection and Enforcement Functions) Order 1996
referred to: SI 2014/856 Art.3
Art.1, amended: SI 2014/600 Sch.1 para.6
Art.2, amended: SI 2014/856 Art.2
Art.25, amended: SI 2014/600 Sch.1 para.6
Art.25, substituted: SI 2014/600 Sch.1 para.6
Art.42, amended: SI 2014/600 Sch.1 para.6
Art.42, substituted: SI 2014/600 Sch.1 para.6
Art.58, amended: SI 2014/600 Sch.1 para.6
Art.58, substituted: SI 2014/600 Sch.1 para.6
Art.70, amended: SI 2014/600 Sch.1 para.6

1919. Employment Rights (Northern Ireland) Order 1996
see *Crawford v Department for Employment and Learning* [2014] NICA 26, [2014] I.R.L.R. 626 (CA (NI)), Girvan LJ
Art.40, see *Anakaa v Firstsource Solutions Ltd* [2014] NICA 57, [2014] I.R.L.R. 941 (CA (NI)), Girvan LJ
Art.59, varied: 2014 c.6 s.126
Art.68A, amended: SI 2014/308 Sch.1 para.3
Art.120, varied: 2014 c.6 s.126
Art.121, varied: 2014 c.6 s.126
Art.132A, amended: SI 2014/308 Sch.1 para.3
Art.135, amended: SI 2014/308 Sch.1 para.3
Art.233, see *Crawford v Department for Employment and Learning* [2014] NICA 26, [2014] I.R.L.R. 626 (CA (NI)), Girvan LJ

1921. Industrial Tribunals (Northern Ireland) Order 1996
Art.20, amended: SI 2014/308 Sch.1 para.4, SI 2014/1614 Reg.9

1995. Chessington Computer Centre Trading Fund (Revocation) Order 1996
varied: SI 2014/2708 Art.5

2089. Carriage of Dangerous Goods by Rail Regulations 1996
revoked: SI 2014/1637 Sch.4 Part 1

2095. Carriage of Dangerous Goods by Road Regulations 1996
revoked: SI 2014/1637 Sch.4 Part 1

2154. Merchant Shipping (Prevention of Oil Pollution) Regulations 1996
referred to: SSI 2014/324 Sch.1 para.8
Reg.1, amended: SI 2014/3306 Sch.2 para.2

2447. Advice and Assistance (Scotland) Regulations 1996
see *Donaldson v Scottish Legal Aid Board* [2014] CSIH 31, 2014 S.C. 689 (IH (Ex Div)), Lady Paton
Reg.8B, see *Donaldson v Scottish Legal Aid Board* [2014] CSIH 31, 2014 S.C. 689 (IH (Ex Div)), Lady Paton
Reg.16, amended: SSI 2014/90 Sch.1 Part 3
Sch.2 para.5, amended: SSI 2014/90 Sch.1 Part 3
Sch.3 Part I para.1A, added: SSI 2014/257 Reg.2

2483. HMSO Trading Fund (Revocation) Order 1996
varied: SI 2014/2708 Art.5

2489. Local Authorities Traffic Orders (Procedure) (England and Wales) Regulations 1996
Reg.9, see *AA and Sons Ltd v Slough BC* [2014] EWHC 1127 (Admin), [2014] R.T.R. 29 (QBD (Admin)), Green J

2579. Civil Courts (Amendment No 3) Order 1996
revoked: SI 2014/820 Sch.1

2745. Social Security Benefit (Computation of Earnings) Regulations 1996
Reg.2, amended: SI 2014/107 Sch.1 para.20, SI 2014/3229 Sch.6 para.14
Reg.2, referred to: SI 2014/516 Art.6
Reg.7, referred to: SI 2014/516 Art.6

2795. Gas Act 1986 (Exemptions) (No.4) Order 1996
revoked: SI 2014/528 Sch.1

2803. Employment Tribunals (Interest on Awards in Discrimination Cases) Regulations 1996
see *BAE Systems (Operations) Ltd v Konczak* [2014] I.R.L.R. 676 (EAT), Judge Hand Q.C.
Reg.3, see *BAE Systems (Operations) Ltd v Konczak* [2014] I.R.L.R. 676 (EAT), Judge Hand Q.C.

2881. Maritime Security (Jersey) Order 1996
revoked: SI 2014/265 Art.3

2890. Housing Renewal Grants Regulations 1996
Reg.2, amended: SI 2014/107 Sch.1 para.21
Reg.19, amended: SI 2014/1829 Reg.3
Reg.31, amended: SI 2014/1913 Reg.11, SI 2014/3117 Reg.15
Reg.31, applied: SI 2014/1913 Reg.11, SI 2014/3117 Reg.15
Reg.31, revoked (in part): SI 2014/1913 Reg.11, SI 2014/3117 Reg.15
Reg.38, amended: SI 2014/1913 Reg.12, SI 2014/3117 Reg.16
Reg.38, applied: SI 2014/1913 Reg.12, SI 2014/3117 Reg.16
Reg.38, revoked (in part): SI 2014/1913 Reg.12, SI 2014/3117 Reg.16
Sch.3, applied: SI 2014/1913 Reg.13, SI 2014/3117 Reg.17
Sch.3 paraA.4, added: SI 2014/1913 Reg.13
Sch.3 paraA.4, revoked (in part): SI 2014/1913 Reg.13
Sch.3 paraA.5, added: SI 2014/3117 Reg.17
Sch.3 paraA.5, revoked (in part): SI 2014/3117 Reg.17
Sch.3 para.22, amended: SI 2014/852 Art.7
Sch.3 para.59, amended: SI 2014/513 Sch.1 para.6
Sch.4, applied: SI 2014/1913 Reg.14, SI 2014/3117 Reg.18
Sch.4 paraA.4, added: SI 2014/1913 Reg.14
Sch.4 paraA.4, revoked (in part): SI 2014/1913 Reg.14
Sch.4 paraA.5, added: SI 2014/3117 Reg.18
Sch.4 paraA.5, revoked (in part): SI 2014/3117 Reg.18

2907. Child Support Departure Direction and Consequential Amendments Regulations 1996
see *Hakki v Secretary of State for Work and Pensions* [2014] EWCA Civ 530, [2014] B.T.C. 22 (CA (Civ Div)), Longmore LJ
Reg.12, amended: SI 2014/1386 Reg.4

3010. Merchant Shipping (Dangerous or Noxious Liquid Substances in Bulk) Regulations 1996
Reg.2, amended: SI 2014/3306 Sch.2 para.3

3047. Surface Waters (Abstraction for Drinking Water) (Classification) (Scotland) Regulations 1996
revoked: SSI 2014/364 Reg.50

3126. Occupational Pension Schemes (Winding Up) Regulations 1996
> Reg.12, applied: SI 2014/1711 Reg.10
> Reg.13, varied: SI 2014/1711 Reg.12

3147. Employment Protection (Continuity of Employment) Regulations 1996
> Reg.2, amended: SI 2014/386 Sch.1 para.1

3195. Social Security (Child Maintenance Bonus) Regulations 1996
> Reg.1, amended: SI 2014/107 Sch.1 para.22, SI 2014/3229 Sch.6 para.15

3204. Homelessness (Suitability of Accommodation) Order 1996
> see *Birmingham City Council v Balog* [2013] EWCA Civ 1582, [2014] H.L.R. 14 (CA (Civ Div)), Sullivan LJ

1997

8. Channel Tunnel Rail Link (Qualifying Authorities) Order 1997
> revoked: SI 2014/1332 Art.2

194. Assured Tenancies and Agricultural Occupancies (Forms) Regulations 1997
> Reg.3, amended: SI 2014/1900 Sch.2 para.2
> Sch.1, added: SI 2014/1900 Sch.2 para.3
> Sch.1, amended: SI 2014/374 Reg.2, SI 2014/1900 Sch.2 para.3
> Sch.1, substituted: SI 2014/1900 Sch.2 para.3

272. United Nations Arms Embargoes (Dependent Territories) (Amendment) Order 1997
> revoked: SI 2014/2711 Sch.1

273. United Nations Arms Embargoes (Rwanda) (Amendment) Order 1997
> revoked: SI 2014/2711 Sch.1

291. Act of Sederunt (Child Care and Maintenance Rules) 1997
> Part 3 r.3.49, amended: SSI 2014/201 r.5
> Part 5, added: SSI 2014/201 r.4
> Part 5 r.5.1, amended: SSI 2014/201 r.4
> Part 5 r.5.2, amended: SSI 2014/201 r.4
> Part 5 r.5.4, amended: SSI 2014/201 r.4
> r.3.48, see *C v Authority Reporter* 2014 Fam. L.R. 72 (Sh Ct (Glasgow)), Sheriff Principal C A L Scott, QC
> Sch.1, amended: SSI 2014/201 r.5, Sch.1

311. Teachers (Compensation for Redundancy and Premature Retirement) Regulations 1997
> Part III, applied: SI 2014/512 Reg.101
> Reg.3, applied: SI 2014/512 Reg.101
> Reg.16, amended: SI 2014/107 Sch.1 para.23
> Reg.16, revoked (in part): SI 2014/107 Sch.1 para.23

319. Local Authorities (Capital Finance) Regulations 1997
> Reg.16, referred to: SI 2014/3352 Reg.8

346. Merchant Shipping (Disqualification of Holder of Seaman's Certificates) Regulations 1997
> applied: SI 2014/1613 Reg.38

347. Merchant Shipping (Section 63 Inquiries) Rules 1997
> applied: SI 2014/1613 Reg.38

361. Civil Courts (Amendment) Order 1997
> revoked: SI 2014/820 Sch.1

420. Town and Country Planning (Determination of Appeals by Appointed Persons) (Prescribed Classes) Regulations 1997
> Reg.3, amended: SI 2014/552 Reg.6

562. Merchant Shipping (Light Dues) Regulations 1997
> Sch.2 Part II para.3, amended: SI 2014/527 Reg.2

627. Housing Act 1996 (Consequential Amendments) (No.2) Order 1997
> Sch.1 para.1, revoked: 2014 c.14 Sch.7

634. Pensions Increase (Review) Order 1997
> referred to: SI 2014/668 Sch.1
> Art.6, substituted: SI 2014/107 Sch.1
> para.56, SI 2014/3229 Sch.6 para.35

728. Council Tax (Exempt Dwellings) (Scotland) Order 1997
> Sch.1 para.2, see *City of Edinburgh Council v Lothian Valuation Appeal Committee* [2014] CSIH 32, [2014] R.A. 410 (IH (Ex Div)), Lady Paton
> Sch.1 para.4, see *City of Edinburgh Council v Lothian Valuation Appeal Committee* [2014] CSIH 32, [2014] R.A. 410 (IH (Ex Div)), Lady Paton
> Sch.1 para.7, see *City of Edinburgh Council v Lothian Valuation Appeal Committee* [2014] CSIH 32, [2014] R.A. 410 (IH (Ex Div)), Lady Paton

784. Occupational Pension Schemes (Discharge of Liability) Regulations 1997
    Reg.1, revoked (in part): SI 2014/107 Sch.1 para.24, SI 2014/3229 Sch.6 para.16
    Reg.4, amended: SI 2014/540 Reg.3
    Reg.11, amended: SI 2014/107 Sch.1 para.24, SI 2014/3229 Sch.6 para.16

818. National Health Service (Optical Charges and Payments) Regulations 1997
    Reg.1, amended: SI 2014/2015 Reg.2
    Reg.8, amended: SI 2014/460 Reg.4
    Reg.12, applied: SI 2014/462 Reg.3
    Reg.17, applied: SI 2014/462 Reg.3
    Sch.1, amended: SI 2014/462 Reg.2
    Sch.2 para.1, amended: SI 2014/462 Reg.2
    Sch.2 para.2, amended: SI 2014/462 Reg.2
    Sch.3, substituted: SI 2014/462 Sch.1

821. Channel Tunnel Rail Link (Planning Appeals) Regulations 1997
    revoked: SI 2014/1333 Reg.2

831. Lifts Regulations 1997
    Reg.2, amended: SI 2014/469 Sch.3 para.67
    Sch.15 para.1, amended: SI 2014/469 Sch.3 para.68
    Sch.15 para.8, amended: SI 2014/469 Sch.3 para.68

869. Race Relations (Northern Ireland) Order 1997
    applied: SI 2014/1183, SI 2014/2874
    referred to: 2014 c.22 s.33

1033. Criminal Procedure and Investigations Act 1996 (Code of Practice) (No.2) Order 1997
    applied: SI 2014/1610 r.22_9

1085. Civil Courts (Amendment) (No.2) Order 1997
    revoked: SI 2014/820 Sch.1

1156. Stamp Duty and Stamp Duty Reserve Tax (Open-ended Investment Companies) Regulations 1997
    applied: SI 2014/1932 Reg.1
    Reg.4A, revoked (in part): SI 2014/1932 Reg.3

1160. Hedgerows Regulations 1997
    applied: SI 2014/3263 Sch.2 para.5
    Reg.5, applied: SI 2014/2950 Art.33, SI 2014/3223 Sch.1 para.13, SI 2014/3331 Art.27
    Reg.5, disapplied: SI 2014/3263 Sch.2 para.2
    Reg.6, applied: SI 2014/3328 Art.3

    Reg.6, varied: SI 2014/1599 Art.6, SI 2014/1873 Art.8, SI 2014/2950 Art.7
    Reg.7, applied: SI 2014/3331 Art.27

1183. Social Security (Recovery of Benefits) (Northern Ireland) Order 1997
    Art.2, amended: 2014 c.1 Sch.1 para.10
    Art.3, amended: 2014 c.1 Sch.1 para.11
    Art.3A, amended: 2014 c.1 Sch.1 para.18
    Art.8, applied: SI 2014/916 Reg.26
    Art.10A, added: 2014 c.1 Sch.1 para.12
    Art.11, amended: 2014 c.1 Sch.1 para.16
    Art.12, amended: 2014 c.1 Sch.1 para.13
    Art.13, amended: 2014 c.1 Sch.1 para.14, Sch.1 para.16
    Art.15, amended: 2014 c.1 Sch.1 para.15, Sch.1 para.16
    Art.16, amended: 2014 c.1 Sch.1 para.16
    Art.21, amended: 2014 c.1 Sch.1 para.16
    Art.22, amended: 2014 c.1 Sch.1 para.16
    Art.23, amended: 2014 c.1 Sch.1 para.16
    Art.25, amended: 2014 c.1 Sch.1 para.20

1347. Trunk Roads (Restricted Roads) (Kirkcudbrightshire) (Variation) Order 1997
    revoked: SSI 2014/247 Art.4

1431. Distress for Customs and Excise Duties and Other Indirect Taxes Regulations 1997
    revoked (in part): SI 2014/600 Sch.1 Part 2

1466. Registration of Overseas Births and Deaths (Amendment) Regulations 1997
    revoked: SI 2014/511 Reg.17

1508. Merchant Shipping (Crew Accommodation) Regulations 1997
    referred to: SI 2014/1613 Reg.30
    Reg.3, amended: SI 2014/1614 Reg.10

1531. Railways (Heathrow Express Temporary Network) (Exemptions) Order 1997
    revoked: SI 2014/3244 Sch.2

1612. Local Government Pension Scheme Regulations 1997
    disapplied: SI 2014/525 Reg.26
    revoked: SI 2014/525 Sch.1
    Reg.13, referred to: SI 2014/525 Reg.8
    Reg.28, applied: SI 2014/525 Reg.12
    Reg.35, applied: SI 2014/525 Sch.2 para.4, Sch.2 para.5
    Reg.42, applied: SI 2014/525 Reg.17
    Reg.42B, added: SI 2014/560 Sch.3 para.17
    Reg.42B, amended: SI 2014/3061 Sch.1 para.11
    Reg.42C, added: SI 2014/560 Sch.3 para.17

Reg.42D, added: SI 2014/3061 Sch.1
para.11

Reg.55, applied: SI 2014/525 Reg.11,
Reg.15, Sch.2 para.7

Reg.60, applied: SI 2014/525 Reg.15

Reg.66, applied: SI 2014/525 Reg.15

Reg.83, applied: SI 2014/525 Reg.15

Reg.108A, applied: SI 2014/525 Reg.21

Reg.122A, applied: SI 2014/525 Reg.21

Reg.123, applied: SI 2014/525 Sch.2 para.4

Sch.8, referred to: SI 2014/525 Reg.26

1892. Family Law Act 1996 (Commencement No 2) Order 1997

Art.3, revoked (in part): 2014 c.6 s.18

Art.4, revoked: 2014 c.6 s.18

1980. Local Authority Accounts (Scotland) Amendment Regulations 1997

revoked: SSI 2014/200 Reg.4

1984. Rent Officers (Housing Benefit Functions) Order 1997

Art.4B, amended: SI 2014/3126 Art.2

Sch.3B para.2, amended: SI 2014/3126 Art.2

Sch.3B para.6, amended: SI 2014/3126 Sch.1

1995. Rent Officers (Housing Benefit Functions) (Scotland) Order 1997

Art.4B, amended: SI 2014/3126 Art.3

Sch.3B para.2, amended: SI 2014/3126 Art.3

Sch.3B para.6, amended: SI 2014/3126 Sch.2

2073. Animal By-Products (Identification) (Amendment) Regulations 1997

revoked: SI 2014/517 Reg.28

2182. Foods Intended for Use in Energy Restricted Diets for Weight Reduction Regulations 1997

Reg.3, amended: SI 2014/1855 Sch.7
para.18, SI 2014/2303 Sch.7 para.18, SSI
2014/312 Sch.5 para.4

2196. Gaming Duty Regulations 1997

Reg.5, amended: SI 2014/1930 Reg.4

2310. Civil Courts (Amendment No 3) Order 1997

revoked: SI 2014/820 Sch.1

2329. Procurement of Air Navigation Equipment (Technical Specifications) Regulations 1997

revoked: SI 2014/3225 Reg.3

2348. Registration of Births, Still-births, Deaths and Marriages (Prescription of Forms) (Scotland) Regulations 1997

Sch.11, amended: SSI 2014/141 Sch.1

Sch.17, amended: SSI 2014/306 Sch.8

2349. Marriage (Prescription of Forms) (Scotland) Regulations 1997

Sch.1, amended: SSI 2014/306 Sch.4

Sch.2, amended: SSI 2014/306 Sch.5

Sch.3, amended: SSI 2014/306 Sch.6

Sch.4, amended: SSI 2014/306 Sch.7

2400. Zebra, Pelican and Puffin Pedestrian Crossings Regulations and General Directions 1997

Reg.24, see *Brooks v Blackpool BC* [2013]
EWHC 3735 (Admin), (2014) 178 J.P. 79
(QBD (Admin)), Haddon-Cave J

2427. Gas Act 1986 (Exemption) Order 1997

revoked: SI 2014/528 Sch.1

2439. Vehicle Excise Duty (Immobilisation, Removal and Disposal of Vehicles) Regulations 1997

Reg.2, amended: SI 2014/2358 Sch.2 para.2

Reg.6, amended: SI 2014/2358 Sch.2 para.3

Reg.12, amended: SI 2014/2358 Sch.2
para.4

Reg.15, amended: SI 2014/2358 Sch.2
para.5

2567. Merchant Shipping (Oil Pollution Preparedness, Response and Cooperation Convention) Order 1997

Art.2, enabled: SI 2014/3306

2762. Civil Courts (Amendment No 4) Order 1997

revoked: SI 2014/820 Sch.1

2776. Diving at Work Regulations 1997

Reg.2, amended: SI 2014/469 Sch.3 para.69

Reg.6, applied: SI 2014/2936 Sch.1 para.4

Reg.7, amended: SI 2014/469 Sch.3 para.69

Sch.1, amended: SI 2014/469 Sch.3 para.69

2813. Social Security (Penalty Notice) Regulations 1997

Reg.2, amended: SI 2014/591 Reg.5

2946. London Docklands Development Corporation (Planning Functions) Order 1997

revoked: SI 2014/683 Sch.1

2962. Merchant Shipping and Fishing Vessels (Health and Safety at Work) Regulations 1997

Part VII, added: SI 2014/1616 Reg.2

Reg.2, amended: SI 2014/1616 Reg.2

Reg.3, amended: SI 2014/1616 Reg.2

Reg.7, amended: SI 2014/1616 Reg.2

Reg.11A, added: SI 2014/1616 Reg.2

Reg.13A, added: SI 2014/1616 Reg.2

Reg.15, amended: SI 2014/1616 Reg.2

Reg.16, amended: SI 2014/1616 Reg.2
Reg.17, amended: SI 2014/1616 Reg.2
Reg.19, amended: SI 2014/1616 Reg.2
Reg.21, amended: SI 2014/1616 Reg.2
Reg.24, amended: SI 2014/1616 Reg.2
Reg.27, amended: SI 2014/1616 Reg.2
Reg.27A, added: SI 2014/1616 Reg.2
Reg.28, amended: SI 2014/1616 Reg.2
Reg.28A, added: SI 2014/1616 Reg.2
Reg.29, amended: SI 2014/1616 Reg.2
Sch.1, added: SI 2014/1616 Reg.2
3022. Merchant Shipping (ISM Code) (Ro-Ro Passenger Ferries) Regulations 1997
revoked: SI 2014/1512 Reg.1
3032. Copyright and Rights in Databases Regulations 1997
Sch.2 para.15, amended: SI 2014/549 Sch.1 para.27

1998

84. Urban Development Corporations in England (Planning Functions) Order 1998
revoked: SI 2014/683 Sch.1
105. Council Tax (Prescribed Classes of Dwellings) (Wales) Regulations 1998
Sch.1 para.3, amended: SI 2014/107 Sch.2 para.1
141. Bread and Flour Regulations 1998
Reg.2, amended: SI 2014/1855 Sch.7 para.20, SI 2014/2303 Sch.7 para.20, SSI 2014/312 Sch.5 para.5
Reg.5, revoked (in part): SI 2014/1855 Sch.6 Part 1, SI 2014/2303 Sch.6 Part 1, SSI 2014/312 Sch.4 Part 1, Sch.5 para.5
Reg.11, revoked (in part): SI 2014/1855 Sch.6 Part 1, SI 2014/2303 Sch.6 Part 1, SSI 2014/312 Sch.4 Part 1
364. Local Government Pension Scheme (Transitional Provisions) (Scotland) Regulations 1998
applied: SSI 2014/233 Reg.3, Reg.17, Reg.22, Reg.24
varied: SSI 2014/233 Reg.24
Reg.22, disapplied: SSI 2014/233 Reg.24
366. Local Government Pension Scheme (Scotland) Regulations 1998
applied: SSI 2014/233 Reg.3, Reg.17, Reg.22, Reg.24
revoked: SSI 2014/233 Sch.1

varied: SSI 2014/233 Reg.24
Reg.12, referred to: SSI 2014/233 Reg.8
Reg.22, applied: SSI 2014/233 Reg.1
Reg.27, applied: SSI 2014/233 Reg.12
Reg.34, applied: SSI 2014/233 Sch.2 para.4, Sch.2 para.5
Reg.41, referred to: SSI 2014/233 Reg.17
Reg.54, applied: SSI 2014/233 Reg.11, Reg.15, Sch.2 para.7
Reg.59, applied: SSI 2014/233 Reg.15
Reg.65, applied: SSI 2014/233 Reg.15
Reg.82, applied: SSI 2014/233 Reg.15
Reg.108, applied: SSI 2014/233 Reg.21
Reg.123, applied: SSI 2014/233 Sch.2 para.4
Reg.124, applied: SSI 2014/233 Reg.21
Reg.128, disapplied: SSI 2014/233 Reg.24
494. Health and Safety (Enforcing Authority) Regulations 1998
Reg.1A, added: SI 2014/469 Sch.3 para.71
Reg.2, amended: SI 2014/469 Sch.3 para.72, SI 2014/3248 Sch.5 para.8
Reg.2, applied: SI 2014/2418 Sch.1
Reg.2A, added: SI 2014/469 Sch.3 para.73
Reg.2A, applied: SI 2014/2418 Sch.1
Reg.3, amended: SI 2014/469 Sch.3 para.74
Reg.3, disapplied: SI 2014/1663 Reg.30
Reg.4, amended: SI 2014/469 Sch.3 para.75
Reg.4, revoked (in part): SI 2014/1638 Sch.13 para.17, Sch.14 Part 2
Reg.4A, added: SI 2014/469 Sch.3 para.76
Reg.5, amended: SI 2014/469 Sch.3 para.77
Reg.6, amended: SI 2014/469 Sch.3 para.78
Reg.6, substituted: SI 2014/469 Sch.3 para.78
Reg.6A, added: SI 2014/469 Sch.3 para.79
Sch.2 para.14, added: SI 2014/1639 Sch.2 para.1
503. Pensions Increase (Review) Order 1998
referred to: SI 2014/668 Sch.1
Art.6, substituted: SI 2014/107 Sch.1
para.56, SI 2014/3229 Sch.6 para.35
504. Building Societies (Accounts and Related Provisions) Regulations 1998
Sch.9 para.3, revoked (in part): SI 2014/48 Reg.2
Sch.9 para.4, amended: SI 2014/48 Reg.2
562. Income-related Benefits (Subsidy to Authorities) Order 1998
Art.4, amended: SI 2014/1667 Art.2
Sch.1, substituted: SI 2014/1667 Sch.1

Sch.4A Part III, substituted: SI 2014/1667 Sch.2

Sch.4A Part V, substituted: SI 2014/1667 Sch.3

642. National Health Service (Optical Charges and Payments) (Scotland) Regulations 1998

Reg.17, applied: SSI 2014/61 Reg.3

Reg.19, amended: SSI 2014/61 Reg.2

Sch.1, amended: SSI 2014/61 Reg.2

Sch.2, substituted: SSI 2014/61 Sch.1

Sch.3 para.1, amended: SSI 2014/61 Reg.2

Sch.3 para.2, amended: SSI 2014/61 Reg.2

649. Scheme for Construction Contracts (England and Wales) Regulations 1998

see *Brighton University v Dovehouse Interiors Ltd* [2014] EWHC 940 (TCC), [2014] B.L.R. 432 (QBD (TCC)), Carr J

Sch.1, see *Aspect Contracts (Asbestos) Ltd v Higgins Construction Plc* [2013] EWCA Civ 1541, [2014] 1 W.L.R. 1220 (CA (Civ Div)), Longmore LJ

Sch.1 para.23, see *Aspect Contracts (Asbestos) Ltd v Higgins Construction Plc* [2013] EWCA Civ 1541, [2014] 1 W.L.R. 1220 (CA (Civ Div)), Longmore LJ

687. Scheme for Construction Contracts (Scotland) Regulations 1998

see *T Clarke (Scotland) Ltd v Mmaxx Underfloor Heating Ltd* [2014] CSOH 62, [2014] B.L.R. 341 (OH), Lord Woolman

879. Agriculture Act 1986 (Commencement No 6) Order 1998

revoked: SI 2014/1924 Sch.1

1056. Merchant Shipping (Oil Pollution Preparedness, Response and Co-operation Convention) Regulations 1998

Reg.5, amended: SI 2014/3306 Sch.2 para.4

1065. Federal Republic of Yugoslavia (United Nations Sanctions) Order 1998

revoked: SI 2014/2711 Sch.1

1275. Right to Purchase (Prescribed Persons) (Scotland) Amendment Order 1998

revoked: 2014 asp 14 s.1

1351. Enforcement of Road Traffic Debts (Certificated Bailiffs) (Amendment) Regulations 1998

revoked: SI 2014/600 Sch.1 Part 2

1398. Food Labelling (Amendment) Regulations 1998

Reg.1, revoked (in part): SI 2014/1855 Sch.6 Part 1, SI 2014/2303 Sch.6 Part 1, SSI 2014/312 Sch.4 Part 1

Reg.2, revoked (in part): SI 2014/1855 Sch.6 Part 2, SI 2014/2303 Sch.6 Part 2

Reg.3, revoked (in part): SI 2014/1855 Sch.6 Part 1, SI 2014/2303 Sch.6 Part 1, SSI 2014/312 Sch.4 Part 1

Reg.11, revoked (in part): SI 2014/1855 Sch.6 Part 2, SI 2014/2303 Sch.6 Part 2, SSI 2014/312 Sch.4 Part 2

Reg.12, revoked (in part): SI 2014/1855 Sch.6 Part 1, SI 2014/2303 Sch.6 Part 1, SSI 2014/312 Sch.4 Part 1

Sch.1, revoked (in part): SI 2014/1855 Sch.6 Part 1, SI 2014/2303 Sch.6 Part 1, SSI 2014/312 Sch.4 Part 1

1451. National Health Service Superannuation Scheme (Scotland) (Additional Voluntary Contributions) Regulations 1998

Reg.2, amended: SSI 2014/154 Reg.35

Reg.3, amended: SSI 2014/154 Reg.36

Reg.4, amended: SSI 2014/154 Reg.37

Reg.6, amended: SSI 2014/154 Reg.38

Reg.10, amended: SSI 2014/154 Reg.39

Reg.11, amended: SSI 2014/154 Reg.40

Reg.14, amended: SSI 2014/154 Reg.41

Reg.15, amended: SSI 2014/154 Reg.42

Reg.18, amended: SSI 2014/293 Sch.1 para.4

Reg.19, amended: SSI 2014/154 Reg.43

Reg.20, amended: SSI 2014/154 Reg.44

1471. A35 Trunk Road (Wilmington) (30 and 40 Miles Per Hour Speed Limits) Order 1998

Sch.2, varied: SI 2014/2148 Art.2

Sch.3, varied: SI 2014/2148 Art.2

1500. Merchant Shipping (Control of Pollution) (SOLAS) Order 1998

enabled: SI 2014/1512

1501. United Nations Arms Embargoes (Amendment) (Sierra Leone) Order 1998

revoked: SI 2014/2711 Sch.1

1502. United Nations Arms Embargoes (Dependent Territories) (Amendment) (Sierra Leone) Order 1998

revoked: SI 2014/2711 Sch.1

1504. Criminal Justice (Children) (Northern Ireland) Order 1998

Art.12, applied: SI 2014/3141 Reg.110

1506. Social Security (Northern Ireland) Order 1998
Part II, applied: 2014 c.28 s.59
Art.9, applied: SI 2014/881 Reg.2
Art.10, applied: 2014 c.28 s.37
Art.13, amended: SI 2014/886 Art.4

1561. Merchant Shipping (International Safety Management (ISM) Code) Regulations 1998
applied: SI 2014/1512 Reg.18
revoked: SI 2014/1512 Reg.1
Reg.19, applied: SI 2014/1512 Reg.18

1594. National Health Service (Scotland) (Injury Benefits) Regulations 1998
Reg.2, amended: SSI 2014/154 Reg.31
Reg.4, amended: SSI 2014/154 Reg.32
Reg.8, amended: SSI 2014/154 Reg.33
Reg.20, amended: SSI 2014/293 Sch.1 para.5

1678. Children (Performances) (Miscellaneous Amendments) Regulations 1998
revoked (in part): SI 2014/3309 Sch.1, SSI 2014/372 Reg.32

1713. Faculty Jurisdiction (Appeals) Rules 1998
Part II r.4, applied: SI 2014/2072 Sch.1 Part TABLEa
Part IV r.17, applied: SI 2014/2072 Sch.1 Part TABLEa
Part V r.19, applied: SI 2014/2072 Sch.1 Part TABLEa

1728. Social Security (Categorisation of Earners) Amendment Regulations 1998
revoked: SI 2014/635 Sch.1

1760. Education (Student Support) (Northern Ireland) Order 1998
Art.3, applied: SI 2014/2929 Reg.4

1779. Gas Act 1986 (Exemption) Order 1998
revoked: SI 2014/528 Sch.1

1833. Working Time Regulations 1998
applied: SI 2014/480 Reg.9
see *Benkharbouche v Embassy of Sudan* [2014] 1 C.M.L.R. 40 (EAT), Langstaff J;
see *R. (on the application of United Road Transport Union) v Secretary of State for Transport* [2013] EWCA Civ 962, [2014] R.T.R. 9 (CA (Civ Div)), Jackson LJ
Reg.2, see *Truslove v Scottish Ambulance Service* [2014] I.C.R. 1232 (EAT (SC)), Langstaff J
Reg.13, see *Sood Enterprises Ltd v Healy* [2014] 2 C.M.L.R. 15 (EAT (SC)), Lady Stacey

Reg.13A, see *Sood Enterprises Ltd v Healy* [2014] 2 C.M.L.R. 15 (EAT (SC)), Lady Stacey
Reg.16, amended: SI 2014/3322 Reg.3
Reg.18, amended: SI 2014/308 Sch.1 para.5
Reg.24, see *Truslove v Scottish Ambulance Service* [2014] I.C.R. 1232 (EAT (SC)), Langstaff J
Reg.28, amended: SI 2014/469 Sch.3 para.81, SI 2014/480 Reg.9
Reg.30, amended: SI 2014/386 Sch.1 para.3
Reg.30B, added: SI 2014/386 Sch.1 para.4
Reg.35, amended: SI 2014/386 Sch.1 para.5, SI 2014/431 Sch.1 para.19
Sch.3 para.1, applied: SI 2014/480 Reg.9
Sch.3 para.2, amended: SI 2014/107 Sch.1 para.25, SI 2014/3229 Sch.6 para.17
Sch.3 para.8, amended: SI 2014/469 Sch.3 para.82

1870. Individual Savings Account Regulations 1998
Reg.2, amended: 2014 c.26 Sch.8 para.85, Sch.8 para.144, SI 2014/654 Reg.3, SI 2014/1450 Reg.3
Reg.2C, amended: SI 2014/654 Reg.4
Reg.2D, amended: SI 2014/1450 Reg.4
Reg.4, amended: SI 2014/1450 Reg.5
Reg.4A, amended: SI 2014/1450 Reg.8
Reg.4C, revoked: SI 2014/1450 Reg.9
Reg.4D, revoked: SI 2014/1450 Reg.10
Reg.4ZA, amended: SI 2014/654 Reg.5, SI 2014/1450 Reg.6
Reg.4ZA, revoked (in part): SI 2014/1450 Reg.6
Reg.4ZB, amended: SI 2014/654 Reg.6, SI 2014/1450 Reg.7
Reg.4ZE, amended: SI 2014/654 Reg.7
Reg.5C, amended: SI 2014/1450 Reg.11
Reg.5DB, amended: SI 2014/1450 Reg.12
Reg.5E, amended: SI 2014/1450 Reg.13
Reg.7, amended: 2014 c.26 Sch.8 para.86, Sch.8 para.145, SI 2014/654 Reg.8, SI 2014/1450 Reg.14
Reg.7, revoked (in part): SI 2014/1450 Reg.14
Reg.8, amended: SI 2014/654 Reg.9, SI 2014/1450 Reg.15
Reg.8, revoked (in part): SI 2014/654 Reg.9, SI 2014/1450 Reg.15
Reg.9, amended: SI 2014/1450 Reg.16
Reg.10, amended: SI 2014/1450 Reg.17

Reg.12, amended: SI 2014/654 Reg.10, SI 2014/1450 Reg.18

Reg.12, revoked (in part): SI 2014/1450 Reg.18

Reg.14, amended: SI 2014/654 Reg.11

Reg.21, amended: SI 2014/1450 Reg.19

Reg.21, revoked (in part): SI 2014/1450 Reg.19

Reg.22, amended: SI 2014/1450 Reg.20

Reg.23, revoked: SI 2014/1450 Reg.21

Reg.24, amended: SI 2014/1450 Reg.22

Reg.24, revoked (in part): SI 2014/1450 Reg.22

Reg.25, amended: SI 2014/1450 Reg.23

Reg.26, amended: SI 2014/1450 Reg.24

Reg.31, amended: SI 2014/654 Reg.12, SI 2014/1450 Reg.25

Reg.34, amended: 2014 c.26 Sch.8 para.87

1880. Civil Courts (Amendment) Order 1998

revoked: SI 2014/820 Sch.1

1908. Dartford-Thurrock Crossing Regulations 1998

Reg.1, amended: SI 2014/2949 Reg.3

Reg.2, amended: SI 2014/2949 Reg.4

Reg.4, amended: SI 2014/2949 Reg.5

Reg.5, amended: SI 2014/2949 Reg.6

Reg.6, amended: SI 2014/2949 Reg.7

Reg.11, revoked: SI 2014/2949 Reg.8

Sch.1, substituted: SI 2014/2949 Reg.9

1941. Firearms Rules 1998

r.3, revoked (in part): SI 2014/1239 r.3

r.4, amended: SI 2014/1239 r.4

r.4, revoked (in part): SI 2014/1239 r.4

r.5, amended: SI 2014/1239 r.5

r.5, revoked (in part): SI 2014/1239 r.5

r.6, revoked (in part): SI 2014/1239 r.6

r.6, substituted: SI 2014/1239 r.6

r.7, amended: SI 2014/1239 r.7

Sch.1 Part I, amended: SI 2014/1239 Sch.1

Sch.1 Part II, amended: SI 2014/1239 Sch.2

Sch.1 Part IV, amended: SI 2014/1239 Sch.3

2306. Provision and Use of Work Equipment Regulations 1998

Reg.4, see *Hay v Advanced Stairlifts (Scotland) Ltd* [2014] CSOH 118, 2014 Rep. L.R. 102 (OH), Lady Stacey; see *Hide v Steeplechase Co (Cheltenham) Ltd* [2013] EWCA Civ 545, [2014] 1 All E.R. 405 (CA (Civ Div)), Longmore LJ

Reg.5, applied: SI 2014/3248 Reg.15

Reg.6, amended: SI 2014/3248 Sch.5 para.11

Reg.6, applied: SI 2014/3248 Reg.15

2307. Lifting Operations and Lifting Equipment Regulations 1998

Reg.9, amended: SI 2014/3248 Sch.5 para.9

2409. Prohibition of Keeping or Release of Live Fish (Specified Species) Order 1998

revoked (in part): SI 2014/143 Art.4

2410. Olive Oil (Marketing Standards) (Amendment) Regulations 1998

revoked: SI 2014/195 Reg.20

2451. Gas Safety (Installation and Use) Regulations 1998

Reg.16, applied: SI 2014/3109 Sch.1

2514. Merchant Shipping (Passenger Ship Construction Ships of Classes I, II and II(A)) Regulations 1998

Reg.2, disapplied: SI 2014/1512 Reg.5

2535. Religious Character of Schools (Designation Procedure) Regulations 1998

referred to: SI 2014/3261

Reg.3, applied: SI 2014/1132 Reg.62

2572. Family Law Act 1996 (Commencement) (No.3) Order 1998

Art.4, revoked: 2014 c.6 s.18

2771. Merchant Shipping (Vessels in Commercial Use for Sport or Pleasure) Regulations 1998

Reg.2, amended: SI 2014/1614 Reg.11

Sch.1, amended: SI 2014/1614 Reg.11

Sch.2, amended: SI 2014/1614 Reg.11

2793. European Communities (Designation) (No.3) Order 1998

Sch.1, amended: SI 2014/1362 Sch.1

2864. Fees for Inquiries (Standard Daily Amount) Regulations 1998

revoked (in part): SI 2014/692 Sch.1

2910. Civil Courts (Amendment) (No.2) Order 1998

revoked: SI 2014/820 Sch.1

3132. Civil Procedure Rules 1998

applied: SI 2014/2604 r.9

see *Adlington v ELS International Lawyers LLP (In Administration)* [2014] 1 Costs L.R. 105 (QBD (Birmingham)), Judge Oliver-Jones QC; see *Bank of Ireland v Philip Pank Partnership* [2014] EWHC 284 (TCC), [2014] 2 Costs L.R. 301 (QBD (TCC)), Stuart-Smith J; see *Bentine v Bentine* [2013] EWHC 3098 (Ch), [2014] 1 All E.R. 983

(Ch D), Proudman J; see *Elsevier Ltd v Munro* [2014] EWHC 2728 (QB), [2014] 5 Costs L.O. 797 (QBD), Warby J; see *G (An Adult) (Costs), Re* [2014] EWCOP 5, [2014] C.O.P.L.R. 432 (CP), Sir James Munby PFD; see *Harrison v Laidlaw* [2014] EWHC 35 (Ch), [2014] C.P. Rep. 20 (Ch D), Master Bowles; see *Hayes v Hayes* [2014] EWHC 2694 (Ch), [2014] Bus. L.R. 1238 (Ch D), Nugee J; see *Luckwell v Limata* [2014] EWHC 536 (Fam), [2014] 2 F.L.R. 1252 (Fam Div), Holman J; see *R. (on the application of Bar Standards Board) v Disciplinary Tribunal of the Council of the Inns of Court* [2014] EWHC 1570 (Admin), [2014] 4 All E.R. 759 (QBD (Admin)), Moses LJ; see *Salekipour v Parmar* [2013] EWCA Civ 1376, [2014] 1 Costs L.O. 81 (CA (Civ Div)), Arden LJ; see *Sharbatly v Shagroon* [2013] EWHC 3756 (Fam), [2014] 2 F.L.R. 209 (Fam Div), Parker J

Part 2 r.2.1, amended: SI 2014/407 r.4
Part 2 r.2.3, amended: SI 2014/407 r.4, r.5
Part 2 r.2.4, amended: SI 2014/407 r.4, r.5
Part 3 r.3.4, amended: SI 2014/407 r.6
Part 3 r.3.5, amended: SI 2014/407 r.6
Part 3 r.3.5A, substituted: SI 2014/407 r.6
Part 3 r.3.6A, added: SI 2014/407 r.6
Part 3 r.3.8, amended: SI 2014/1233 r.3
Part 3 r.3.12, amended: SI 2014/867 r.4
Part 3 r.3.15, amended: SI 2014/867 r.5
Part 5 r.5.2, revoked (in part): SI 2014/867 r.6
Part 6 r.6.31, amended: SI 2014/2948 r.4
Part 6 r.6.33, amended: SI 2014/2948 r.4
Part 8 r.8.1, amended: SI 2014/407 r.7
Part 12 r.12.4, amended: SI 2014/407 r.4
Part 12 r.12.5A, substituted: SI 2014/407 r.8
Part 12 r.12.6, amended: SI 2014/407 r.4
Part 13 r.13.1, amended: SI 2014/407 r.9
Part 13 r.13.4, amended: SI 2014/407 r.9
Part 14 r.14.1, amended: SI 2014/407 r.10
Part 14 r.14.2, amended: SI 2014/407 r.10
Part 14 r.14.4, amended: SI 2014/407 r.10
Part 14 r.14.5, amended: SI 2014/407 r.10
Part 14 r.14.6, amended: SI 2014/407 r.10
Part 14 r.14.7, amended: SI 2014/407 r.10
Part 14 r.14.7A, substituted: SI 2014/407 r.10
Part 14 r.14.9, amended: SI 2014/407 r.10
Part 14 r.14.10, amended: SI 2014/407 r.10

Part 14 r.14.11, amended: SI 2014/407 r.10
Part 14 r.14.12, amended: SI 2014/407 r.10
Part 14 r.14.13, amended: SI 2014/407 r.10
Part 14 r.14.14, amended: SI 2014/407 r.4
Part 16 r.16.3, amended: SI 2014/407 r.11
Part 21 r.21.1, amended: SI 2014/407 r.12
Part 21 r.21.12, amended: SI 2014/3299 r.5
Part 23 r.23.2, amended: SI 2014/407 r.13
Part 25 r.25.1, amended: SI 2014/407 r.4
Part 25 r.25.2, amended: SI 2014/407 r.4
Part 25 r.25.4, amended: SI 2014/407 r.4
Part 25 r.25.5, amended: SI 2014/407 r.4
Part 26 r.26.1, amended: SI 2014/407 r.14
Part 26 r.26.2, amended: SI 2014/407 r.14
Part 26 r.26.2A, amended: SI 2014/407 r.14, SI 2014/867 r.7
Part 26 r.26.2A, substituted: SI 2014/407 r.14
Part 26 r.26.3, amended: SI 2014/407 r.14
Part 26 r.26.4A, added: SI 2014/407 r.14
Part 26 r.26.5, amended: SI 2014/407 r.14
Part 30 r.30.1, amended: SI 2014/407 r.4, r.15
Part 30 r.30.2, amended: SI 2014/407 r.15
Part 30 r.30.2, revoked (in part): SI 2014/407 r.15
Part 30 r.30.3, amended: SI 2014/407 r.4, r.15, SI 2014/3299 r.6
Part 30 r.30.4, amended: SI 2014/407 r.15
Part 30 r.30.5, amended: SI 2014/2044 r.4
Part 30 r.30.6, amended: SI 2014/407 r.15
Part 30 r.30.7, amended: SI 2014/407 r.15
Part 30 r.30.8, amended: SI 2014/407 r.4
Part 31, varied: SI 2014/1610 r.61_9
Part 34 r.34.13, amended: SI 2014/407 r.4
Part 35 r.35.4, amended: SI 2014/2044 r.5
Part 36, substituted: SI 2014/3299 Sch.1
Part 36 r.36.10A, amended: SI 2014/2044 r.6
Part 36 r.36.14, amended: SI 2014/2044 r.6
Part 36 r.36.14A, amended: SI 2014/2044 r.6
Part 37 r.37.3, amended: SI 2014/3299 r.8
Part 40 r.40.8A, added: SI 2014/407 r.16
Part 40 r.40.9A, added: SI 2014/407 r.16
Part 40 r.40.13A, added: SI 2014/407 r.16
Part 40 r.40.14A, added: SI 2014/407 r.16
Part 42 r.42.1, amended: SI 2014/407 r.17
Part 44 r.44.1, amended: SI 2014/407 r.4, r.18
Part 44 r.44.9, amended: SI 2014/3299 r.9
Part 45 r.45.8, amended: SI 2014/867 r.8

Part 45 r.45.19, amended: SI 2014/2044 r.7,
SI 2014/3299 r.10
Part 45 r.45.20, amended: SI 2014/3299 r.10
Part 45 r.45.24, amended: SI 2014/3299 r.10
Part 45 r.45.26, amended: SI 2014/3299 r.10
Part 45 r.45.29F, amended: SI 2014/2044
r.7, SI 2014/3299 r.10
Part 45 r.45.29I, amended: SI 2014/2044 r.7,
SI 2014/3299 r.10
Part 45 r.45.30, amended: SI 2014/407 r.19
Part 45 r.45.33, amended: SI 2014/407 r.4
Part 45 r.45.34, amended: SI 2014/407 r.4
Part 45 r.45.35, amended: SI 2014/407 r.4
Part 46 r.46.8, amended: SI 2014/407 r.4
Part 47 r.47.3, amended: SI 2014/407 r.4
Part 47 r.47.4, amended: SI 2014/407 r.20
Part 47 r.47.15, amended: SI 2014/407 r.4
Part 47 r.47.20, amended: SI 2014/3299 r.11
Part 47 r.47.22, amended: SI 2014/407 r.4
Part 50 r.50, amended: SI 2014/407 r.4
Part 52, applied: SI 2014/1610 r.64_3,
r.76_13
Part 52 r.52.1, amended: SI 2014/407 r.4
Part 52 r.52.3, amended: SI 2014/407 r.4,
r.21, SI 2014/879 Art.76, SI 2014/2044 r.8
Part 52 r.52.5A, added: SI 2014/2044 r.8
Part 52 r.52.9, amended: SI 2014/2044 r.8
Part 52 r.52.12, amended: SI 2014/3299 r.12
Part 52 r.52.13, amended: SI 2014/407 r.4,
SI 2014/879 Art.76
Part 52 r.52.14, amended: SI 2014/407 r.4
Part 52 r.52.15, amended: SI 2014/2044 r.8
Part 52 r.52.15A, added: SI 2014/2044 r.8
Part 52 r.52.17, amended: SI 2014/407 r.4
Part 52 r.52.21, added: SI 2014/407 r.21
Part 54, added: SI 2014/610 r.3
Part 54 r.54.21, amended: SI 2014/2044 r.9
Part 54 r.54.22, amended: SI 2014/1233 r.4
Part 55 r.55.3, amended: SI 2014/407 r.22
Part 55 r.55.5, amended: SI 2014/407 r.22
Part 55 r.55.11, amended: SI 2014/407 r.22
Part 55 r.55.16, amended: SI 2014/407 r.22
Part 55 r.55.26, amended: SI 2014/867 r.9
Part 55 r.55.27, amended: SI 2014/867 r.10
Part 56 r.56.2, amended: SI 2014/407 r.23
Part 57, amended: SI 2014/2044 r.10
Part 57, added: SI 2014/2044 Sch.1
Part 57 r.57.1, amended: SI 2014/407 r.24,
SI 2014/2044 r.10
Part 57 r.57.2, amended: SI 2014/407 r.4,
r.24

Part 57 r.57.9, amended: SI 2014/407 r.24
Part 57 r.57.16, amended: SI 2014/2044 r.10
Part 60 r.60.4, amended: SI 2014/407 r.25
Part 61 r.61.2, amended: SI 2014/407 r.26
Part 63 r.63.13, amended: SI 2014/407 r.27
Part 63 r.63.14, amended: SI 2014/407 r.27
Part 63 r.63.19, amended: SI 2014/407 r.4,
r.27
Part 65, amended: SI 2014/2044 r.11
Part 65 r.65.3, amended: SI 2014/407 r.28
Part 65 r.65.6, amended: SI 2014/407 r.4
Part 65 r.65.10, revoked (in part): SI
2014/407 r.28
Part 65 r.65.12, amended: SI 2014/407 r.28
Part 65 r.65.14, amended: SI 2014/407 r.28
Part 65 r.65.21, amended: SI 2014/407 r.4
Part 65 r.65.28, amended: SI 2014/407 r.28
Part 65 r.65.31, amended: SI 2014/407 r.4
Part 65 r.65.42, amended: SI 2014/2044 r.11
Part 65 r.65.43, amended: SI 2014/407 r.28,
SI 2014/2044 r.11
Part 65 r.65.44, amended: SI 2014/2044 r.11
Part 65 r.65.45, amended: SI 2014/2044 r.11
Part 65 r.65.46, amended: SI 2014/2044 r.11
Part 65 r.65.47, amended: SI 2014/407 r.4,
SI 2014/2044 r.11
Part 65 r.65.48, amended: SI 2014/2044 r.11
Part 65 r.65.49, amended: SI 2014/2044 r.11
Part 66 r.66.6, amended: SI 2014/867 r.11
Part 66 r.66.6, revoked (in part): SI 2014/867
r.11
Part 67 r.67.3, amended: SI 2014/407 r.4,
r.29
Part 68 r.68.2, amended: SI 2014/407 r.4
Part 70 r.70.1, amended: SI 2014/407 r.30
Part 70 r.70.2A, added: SI 2014/407 r.30
Part 70 r.70.3, amended: SI 2014/407 r.4,
r.30
Part 70 r.70.5, amended: SI 2014/407 r.4,
r.30
Part 71 r.71.2, amended: SI 2014/407 r.31
Part 71 r.71.8, amended: SI 2014/407 r.31
Part 72 r.72.3, amended: SI 2014/407 r.32
Part 72 r.72.7, amended: SI 2014/407 r.4,
r.32
Part 73 r.73.3, amended: SI 2014/407 r.4,
r.33
Part 73 r.73.10, amended: SI 2014/407 r.33
Part 73 r.73.17, amended: SI 2014/407 r.4
Part 74, amended: SI 2014/407 r.34
Part 74, added: SI 2014/3299 r.13

Part 74 r.74.1, amended: SI 2014/407 r.4, SI 2014/2948 r.5, SI 2014/3299 r.13

Part 74 r.74.2, amended: SI 2014/407 r.34

Part 74 r.74.3, amended: SI 2014/2948 r.5

Part 74 r.74.3, revoked (in part): SI 2014/2948 r.5

Part 74 r.74.3A, added: SI 2014/2948 r.5

Part 74 r.74.4, amended: SI 2014/2948 r.5

Part 74 r.74.4A, added: SI 2014/2948 r.5

Part 74 r.74.5, amended: SI 2014/2948 r.5

Part 74 r.74.6, amended: SI 2014/2948 r.5

Part 74 r.74.7A, added: SI 2014/2948 r.5

Part 74 r.74.8, amended: SI 2014/2948 r.5

Part 74 r.74.9, substituted: SI 2014/2948 r.5

Part 74 r.74.10, amended: SI 2014/2948 r.5

Part 74 r.74.11, amended: SI 2014/2948 r.5

Part 74 r.74.11A, added: SI 2014/2948 r.5

Part 74 r.74.12, amended: SI 2014/407 r.4, SI 2014/2948 r.5

Part 74 r.74.17, amended: SI 2014/407 r.4

Part 74 r.74.18, amended: SI 2014/407 r.4

Part 74 r.74.19, amended: SI 2014/2948 r.5

Part 74 r.74.19, revoked (in part): SI 2014/2948 r.5

Part 75 r.75.1, amended: SI 2014/407 r.35

Part 75 r.75.2, amended: SI 2014/407 r.35

Part 75 r.75.3, amended: SI 2014/407 r.35

Part 75 r.75.5A, amended: SI 2014/407 r.4

Part 75 r.75.6, amended: SI 2014/407 r.35

Part 75 r.75.6, revoked (in part): SI 2014/407 r.35

Part 75 r.75.7, amended: SI 2014/407 r.35

Part 75 r.75.7, revoked (in part): SI 2014/407 r.35

Part 75 r.75.8, amended: SI 2014/407 r.35

Part 75 r.75.9, amended: SI 2014/407 r.35

Part 75 r.75.10, amended: SI 2014/407 r.35

Part 81 r.81.1, amended: SI 2014/407 r.4

Part 81 r.81.9, amended: SI 2014/3299 r.14

Part 81 r.81.12, amended: SI 2014/407 r.4

Part 81 r.81.13, amended: SI 2014/867 r.12

Part 81 r.81.15, amended: SI 2014/2044 r.12

Part 81 r.81.18, amended: SI 2014/407 r.4, SI 2014/867 r.13

Part 81 r.81.31, amended: SI 2014/407 r.4

Part 81 r.81.33, amended: SI 2014/407 r.4

Part 81 r.81.34, amended: SI 2014/407 r.4

Part 81 r.81.35, amended: SI 2014/867 r.14

Part 81 r.81.37, amended: SI 2014/867 r.15

Part 82 r.82.31, amended: SI 2014/407 r.4

Part 83, added: SI 2014/407 Sch.1

Part 83, amended: SI 2014/867 r.16

Part 83 r.83.2, amended: SI 2014/867 r.17

Part 83 r.83.2A, added: SI 2014/867 r.18

Part 83 r.83.6, substituted: SI 2014/2044 r.13

Part 83 r.83.9, amended: SI 2014/2044 r.13

Part 84, added: SI 2014/482 Sch.1

Part 87, added: SI 2014/3299 Sch.2

Pt 13., see *Newland Shipping and Forwarding Ltd v Toba Trading FZC* [2014] EWHC 210 (Comm), [2014] 2 Costs L.R. 279 (QBD (Comm)), Hamblen J

Pt 18., see *Harrison v Laidlaw* [2014] EWHC 35 (Ch), [2014] C.P. Rep. 20 (Ch D), Master Bowles; see *Secretary of State for Health v Servier Laboratories Ltd* [2013] EWCA Civ 1234, [2014] 1 W.L.R. 4383 (CA (Civ Div)), Laws LJ; see *XYZ v Various Companies* [2013] EWHC 3643 (QB), [2014] 2 Costs L.O. 197 (QBD), Thirlwall J

Pt 20., see *Harrison v Technical Sign Co Ltd* [2013] EWCA Civ 1569, [2014] P.N.L.R. 15 (CA (Civ Div)), Moore-Bick LJ; see *Isis Investments Ltd v Oscatello Investments Ltd* [2013] EWCA Civ 1493, [2014] Bus. L.R. 341 (CA (Civ Div)), Longmore LJ; see *Wagenaar v Weekend Travel Ltd (t/a Ski Weekend)* [2014] EWCA Civ 1105, [2014] C.P. Rep. 46 (CA (Civ Div)), Laws LJ

Pt 21., see *Dunhill v Burgin* [2014] UKSC 18, [2014] 1 W.L.R. 933 (SC), Lady Hale DPSC

Pt 23., see *Yates v Revenue and Customs Commissioners* [2014] EWHC 2311 (QB), [2014] P.I.Q.R. P24 (QBD), Master McCloud

Pt 24., see *Akerman-Livingstone v Aster Communities Ltd (formerly Flourish Homes Ltd)* [2014] EWCA Civ 1081, [2014] 1 W.L.R. 3980 (CA (Civ Div)), Arden LJ; see *Ansari v Knowles* [2013] EWCA Civ 1448, [2014] C.P. Rep. 9 (CA (Civ Div)), Moore-Bick LJ; see *Simpson (t/a Harrow Solicitors and Advocates) v Godson* [2013] EWCA Civ 1339, [2014] 1 Costs L.O. 77 (CA (Civ Div)), Moore-Bick LJ

Pt 29., see *Kershaw v Roberts* [2014] EWHC 1037 (Ch), [2014] 3 Costs L.R. 536 (Ch D), Hickinbottom J

Pt 31., see *Secretary of State for Health v Servier Laboratories Ltd* [2013] EWCA Civ

1234, [2014] 1 W.L.R. 4383 (CA (Civ Div)),
Laws LJ; see *Solicitor General v Dodd*
[2014] EWHC 240 (QB), [2014] F.S.R. 27
(QBD), Andrews J; see *Tchenguiz v
Director of the Serious Fraud Office* [2013]
EWHC 2128 (QB), [2014] 1 W.L.R. 1476
(QBD), Eder J; see *Tchenguiz-Imerman v
Imerman* [2012] EWHC 4047 (Fam), [2014]
1 F.L.R. 232 (Fam Div), Moylan J
Pt 32., see *Central Trading & Exports Ltd v
Fioralba Shipping Co* [2014] EWHC 2397
(Comm), [2014] 2 Lloyd's Rep. 449 (QBD
(Comm)), Males J
Pt 35., see *Beauty Star Ltd v Janmohamed*
[2014] EWCA Civ 451, [2014] C.P. Rep. 34
(CA (Civ Div)), Laws LJ; see *Mengiste v
Endowment Fund for the Rehabilitation of
Tigray* [2013] EWCA Civ 1003, [2014] C.P.
Rep. 5 (CA (Civ Div)), Arden LJ; see
Rogers v Hoyle [2014] EWCA Civ 257,
[2014] 3 W.L.R. 148 (CA (Civ Div)), Arden
LJ; see *Wall v Mutuelle de Poitiers
Assurances* [2014] EWCA Civ 138, [2014] 1
W.L.R. 4263 (CA (Civ Div)), Longmore LJ
Pt 36., see *Courtwell Properties Ltd v
Greencore PF (UK) Ltd* [2014] EWHC 184
(TCC), [2014] 2 Costs L.O. 289 (QBD
(TCC)), Akenhead J; see *Jopling v
Leavesley* [2013] EWCA Civ 1605, [2014]
W.T.L.R. 807 (CA (Civ Div)), Elias LJ
Pt 40., see *Beauty Star Ltd v Janmohamed*
[2014] EWCA Civ 451, [2014] C.P. Rep. 34
(CA (Civ Div)), Laws LJ
Pt 44., see *Lakatamia Shipping Co Ltd v Su*
[2014] EWHC 796 (Comm), [2014] 3 Costs
L.R. 532 (QBD (Comm)), Hamblen J; see
Rubin v Rubin [2014] EWHC 611 (Fam),
[2014] 1 W.L.R. 3289 (Fam Div), Mostyn J;
see *Sharbatly v Shagroon* [2013] EWHC
3756 (Fam), [2014] 2 F.L.R. 209 (Fam Div),
Parker J
Pt 47., see *French v Hartman* [2014] EWHC
1682 (QB), [2014] 6 Costs L.O. 829 (QBD),
Green J
Pt 54., see *Hamnett v Essex CC* [2014]
EWHC 246 (Admin), [2014] 1 W.L.R. 2562
(QBD (Admin)), Singh J; see *R. (on the
application of Ellaway) v Cardiff CC* [2013]
EWHC 2907 (Admin), [2014] Env. L.R. 12
(QBD (Admin)), Judge Curran QC

Pt 6., see *American Leisure Group Ltd v
Garrard* [2014] EWHC 2101 (Ch), [2014] 1
W.L.R. 4102 (Ch D), David Richards J
Pt 72., see *Taurus Petroleum Ltd v State Oil
Marketing Co of the Ministry of Oil, Iraq*
[2013] EWHC 3494 (Comm), [2014] 1 All
E.R. (Comm) 942 (QBD (Comm)), Field J
Pt 79., see *Bank Mellat v HM Treasury*
[2014] A.C. 700 (SC), Lord Neuberger PSC
Pt 8., see *Hamnett v Essex CC* [2014]
EWHC 246 (Admin), [2014] 1 W.L.R. 2562
(QBD (Admin)), Singh J; see *Various
Claimants v News Group Newspapers Ltd*
[2013] EWHC 2119 (Ch), [2014] Ch. 400
(Ch D), Mann J
r.1.1, see *Hallam Estates Ltd v Baker* [2014]
EWCA Civ 661, [2014] C.P. Rep. 38 (CA
(Civ Div)), Jackson LJ; see *Lord McAlpine
of West Green v Bercow* [2013] EWHC 981
(QB), [2014] E.M.L.R. 3 (QBD), Tugendhat
J; see *Yeo v Times Newspapers Ltd* [2014]
EWHC 2853 (QB), [2014] 5 Costs L.O. 823
(QBD), Warby J
r.1.3, see *Denton v TH White Ltd* [2014]
EWCA Civ 906, [2014] 1 W.L.R. 3926 (CA
(Civ Div)), Lord Dyson MR; see *Hallam
Estates Ltd v Baker* [2014] EWCA Civ 661,
[2014] C.P. Rep. 38 (CA (Civ Div)), Jackson
LJ; see *Lord McAlpine of West Green v
Bercow* [2013] EWHC 981 (QB), [2014]
E.M.L.R. 3 (QBD), Tugendhat J; see
*Owners and/or Bailees of the Panamax Star
v Owners of the Auk* [2013] EWHC 4076
(Admlty), [2014] 1 Lloyd's Rep. 606 (QBD
(Admlty)), Hamblen J
r.1.4, see *Mann v Mann* [2014] EWHC 537
(Fam), [2014] 1 W.L.R. 2807 (Fam Div),
Mostyn J
r.2.6, see *Hills Contractors and Construction
Ltd v Struth* [2013] EWHC 1693 (TCC),
[2014] 1 W.L.R. 1 (QBD (TCC)), Ramsey J
r.3.1, see *Bank of Ireland v Gill* [2013]
EWHC 2996 (Ch), [2014] B.P.I.R. 156 (Ch
D), Asplin J; see *Chartwell Estate Agents
Ltd v Fergies Properties SA* [2014] EWCA
Civ 506, [2014] C.P. Rep. 36 (CA (Civ
Div)), Laws LJ; see *Hallam Estates Ltd v
Baker* [2014] EWCA Civ 661, [2014] C.P.
Rep. 38 (CA (Civ Div)), Jackson LJ; see
*Hills Contractors and Construction Ltd v
Struth* [2013] EWHC 1693 (TCC), [2014] 1

W.L.R. 1 (QBD (TCC)), Ramsey J; see *McTear v Englehard* [2014] EWHC 722 (Ch), [2014] 3 Costs L.R. 493 (Ch D), Richard Spearman QC; see *Mitchell v News Group Newspapers Ltd* [2013] EWCA Civ 1537, [2014] 1 W.L.R. 795 (CA (Civ Div)), Lord Dyson MR; see *Newland Shipping and Forwarding Ltd v Toba Trading FZC* [2014] EWHC 1986 (Comm), [2014] 4 Costs L.R. 688 (QBD (Comm)), Males J; see *Newland Shipping and Forwarding Ltd v Toba Trading FZC* [2014] EWHC 210 (Comm), [2014] 2 Costs L.R. 279 (QBD (Comm)), Hamblen J; see *SET Select Energy GmbH v F&M Bunkering Ltd* [2014] EWHC 192 (Comm), [2014] 1 Lloyd's Rep. 652 (QBD (Comm)), Blair J; see *Thevarajah v Riordan* [2014] EWCA Civ 14, [2014] C.P. Rep. 19 (CA (Civ Div)), Richards LJ; see *Utilise TDS Ltd v Cranstoun Davies* [2014] EWHC 834 (Ch), [2014] 3 Costs L.O. 417 (Ch D (Manchester)), Judge Hodge Q.C.; see *Various Claimants v News Group Newspapers Ltd* [2013] EWHC 2119 (Ch), [2014] Ch. 400 (Ch D), Mann J; see *XYZ v Various Companies* [2013] EWHC 3643 (QB), [2014] 2 Costs L.O. 197 (QBD), Thirlwall J

r.3.4, see *Barclay Pharmaceuticals Ltd v Waypharm LP* [2013] EWHC 503 (Comm), [2014] 2 All E.R. (Comm) 82 (QBD (Comm)), Gloster J; see *Binns v Firstplus Financial Group Plc* [2013] EWHC 2436 (QB), [2014] Bus. L.R. 110 (QBD), Judge Jeremy Richardson QC; see *Fairford Group Ltd Plc (In Liquidation) v Revenue and Customs Commissioners* [2014] UKUT 329 (TCC), [2014] B.V.C. 529 (UT (Tax)), Simon J; see *Grant v Hayes* [2014] EWHC 2646 (Ch), [2014] B.P.I.R. 1455 (Ch D), Nugee J; see *Karpov v Browder* [2013] EWHC 3071 (QB), [2014] E.M.L.R. 8 (QBD), Simon J; see *McTear v Englehard* [2014] EWHC 722 (Ch), [2014] 3 Costs L.R. 493 (Ch D), Richard Spearman QC

r.3.5, see *Prince Abdulaziz v Apex Global Management Ltd* [2014] UKSC 64, [2014] 1 W.L.R. 4495 (SC), Lord Neuberger PSC

r.3.8, see *Adlington v ELS International Lawyers LLP (In Administration)* [2014] 1 Costs L.R. 105 (QBD (Birmingham)), Judge

Oliver-Jones QC; see *Chartwell Estate Agents Ltd v Fergies Properties SA* [2014] EWCA Civ 506, [2014] C.P. Rep. 36 (CA (Civ Div)), Laws LJ; see *Chartwell Estate Agents Ltd v Fergies Properties SA* [2014] EWHC 438 (QB), [2014] 2 Costs L.R. 353 (QBD), Globe J; see *Denton v TH White Ltd* [2014] EWCA Civ 906, [2014] 1 W.L.R. 3926 (CA (Civ Div)), Lord Dyson MR; see *Hallam Estates Ltd v Baker* [2014] EWCA Civ 661, [2014] C.P. Rep. 38 (CA (Civ Div)), Jackson LJ; see *MA Lloyd & Sons Ltd (t/a KPM Marine) v PPC International Ltd (t/a Professional Powercraft)* [2014] EWHC 41 (QB), [2014] 2 Costs L.R. 256 (QBD), Turner J

r.3.9, see *1,3 and 5 Argall Avenue, Re* [2014] EWHC 2981 (Ch), [2014] 5 Costs L.R. 915 (Ch D), Barling J; see *Adlington v ELS International Lawyers LLP (In Administration)* [2014] 1 Costs L.R. 105 (QBD (Birmingham)), Judge Oliver-Jones QC; see *Associated Electrical Industries Ltd v Alstom UK* [2014] EWHC 430 (Comm), [2014] 3 Costs L.R. 415 (QBD (Comm)), Andrew Smith J; see *Bank of Ireland v Philip Pank Partnership* [2014] EWHC 284 (TCC), [2014] 2 Costs L.R. 301 (QBD (TCC)), Stuart-Smith J; see *British Gas Trading Ltd v Oak Cash and Carry Ltd* [2014] EWHC 4058 (QB), [2014] 6 Costs L.R. 1122 (QBD), McGowan J; see *Caliendo v Mishcon de Reya* [2014] EWHC 3414 (Ch), [2014] 6 Costs L.O. 935 (Ch D), Hildyard J; see *Chartwell Estate Agents Ltd v Fergies Properties SA* [2014] EWCA Civ 506, [2014] C.P. Rep. 36 (CA (Civ Div)), Laws LJ; see *Chartwell Estate Agents Ltd v Fergies Properties SA* [2014] EWHC 438 (QB), [2014] 2 Costs L.R. 353 (QBD), Globe J; see *Denton v TH White Ltd* [2014] EWCA Civ 906, [2014] 1 W.L.R. 3926 (CA (Civ Div)), Lord Dyson MR; see *Durrant v Chief Constable of Avon and Somerset* [2013] EWCA Civ 1624, [2014] 1 W.L.R. 4313 (CA (Civ Div)), Richards LJ; see *Forstater v Python (Monty) Pictures Ltd* [2013] EWHC 3759 (Ch), [2014] 1 Costs L.R. 36 (Ch D), Norris J; see *Hills Contractors and Construction Ltd v Struth* [2013] EWHC 1693 (TCC), [2014] 1 W.L.R.

1 (QBD (TCC)), Ramsey J; see *Karbhari v Ahmed* [2013] EWHC 4042 (QB), [2014] 1 Costs L.R. 151 (QBD (Preston)), Turner J; see *Lakatamia Shipping Co Ltd v Su* [2014] EWHC 275 (Comm), [2014] 2 Costs L.R. 307 (QBD (Comm)), Hamblen J; see *Leeds City Council v Revenue and Customs Commissioners* [2014] UKUT 350 (TCC), [2014] B.V.C. 531 (UT (Tax)), Judge Colin Bishopp; see *MA Lloyd & Sons Ltd (t/a KPM Marine) v PPC International Ltd (t/a Professional Powercraft)* [2014] EWHC 41 (QB), [2014] 2 Costs L.R. 256 (QBD), Turner J; see *McTear v Englehard* [2014] EWHC 722 (Ch), [2014] 3 Costs L.R. 493 (Ch D), Richard Spearman QC; see *Mid-East Sales Ltd v United Engineering and Trading Co (PVT) Ltd* [2014] EWHC 1457 (Comm), [2014] 2 All E.R. (Comm) 623 (QBD (Comm)), Burton J; see *Mitchell v News Group Newspapers Ltd* [2013] EWCA Civ 1537, [2014] 1 W.L.R. 795 (CA (Civ Div)), Lord Dyson MR; see *Newland Shipping and Forwarding Ltd v Toba Trading FZC* [2014] EWHC 210 (Comm), [2014] 2 Costs L.R. 279 (QBD (Comm)), Hamblen J; see *Porter Capital Corp v Masters* [2014] 3 Costs L.R. 528 (Ch D), Nicholas Strauss QC; see *Revenue and Customs Commissioners v McCarthy and Stone (Developments) Ltd* [2014] UKUT 196 (TCC), [2014] S.T.C. 973 (UT (Tax)), Judge Greg Sinfield; see *SC DG Petrol Srl v Vitol Broking Ltd* [2013] EWHC 3920 (Comm), [2014] 2 Costs L.R. 205 (QBD (Comm)), Robin Knowles QC; see *Summit Navigation Ltd v Generali Romania Asigurare Reasigurare SA* [2014] EWHC 398 (Comm), [2014] 1 W.L.R. 3472 (QBD (Comm)), Leggatt J; see *Thevarajah v Riordan* [2014] EWCA Civ 14, [2014] C.P. Rep. 19 (CA (Civ Div)), Richards LJ; see *Ultimate Products Ltd v Woolley* [2014] EWHC 2706 (Ch), [2014] 5 Costs L.O. 787 (Ch D), Christopher Pymont, Q.C.; see *Utilise TDS Ltd v Cranstoun Davies* [2014] EWHC 834 (Ch), [2014] 3 Costs L.O. 417 (Ch D (Manchester)), Judge Hodge Q.C.; see *Wyche v Careforce Group Plc* [2013] EWHC 3282 (Comm), [2014] 1 Costs L.R. 1 (QBD (Comm)), Walker J

r.3.13, see *Bank of Ireland v Philip Pank Partnership* [2014] EWHC 284 (TCC), [2014] 2 Costs L.R. 301 (QBD (TCC)), Stuart-Smith J; see *Rattan v UBS AG* [2014] EWHC 665 (Comm), [2014] 3 Costs L.R. 488 (QBD (Comm)), Males J; see *Utilise TDS Ltd v Cranstoun Davies* [2014] EWHC 834 (Ch), [2014] 3 Costs L.O. 417 (Ch D (Manchester)), Judge Hodge Q.C.
r.3.14, see *Bank of Ireland v Philip Pank Partnership* [2014] EWHC 284 (TCC), [2014] 2 Costs L.R. 301 (QBD (TCC)), Stuart-Smith J; see *Mitchell v News Group Newspapers Ltd* [2013] EWCA Civ 1537, [2014] 1 W.L.R. 795 (CA (Civ Div)), Lord Dyson MR; see *Rattan v UBS AG* [2014] EWHC 665 (Comm), [2014] 3 Costs L.R. 488 (QBD (Comm)), Males J; see *Utilise TDS Ltd v Cranstoun Davies* [2014] EWHC 834 (Ch), [2014] 3 Costs L.O. 417 (Ch D (Manchester)), Judge Hodge Q.C.; see *Wain v Gloucestershire CC* [2014] EWHC 1274 (TCC), [2014] 4 Costs L.O. 585 (QBD (TCC)), Judge David Grant
r.6.3, see *Hills Contractors and Construction Ltd v Struth* [2013] EWHC 1693 (TCC), [2014] 1 W.L.R. 1 (QBD (TCC)), Ramsey J
r.6.9, see *Murrills v Berlanda* [2014] EWCA Civ 6, [2014] C.P. Rep. 21 (CA (Civ Div)), Kitchin LJ
r.6.15, see *American Leisure Group Ltd v Garrard* [2014] EWHC 2101 (Ch), [2014] 1 W.L.R. 4102 (Ch D), David Richards J; see *Bullitt Mobile Ltd v Sonim Technologies* [2013] EWHC 3367 (IPEC), [2014] F.S.R. 23 (IPEC), Birss J; see *Deutsche Bank AG v Sebastian Holdings Inc* [2014] EWHC 112 (Comm), [2014] 1 All E.R. (Comm) 733 (QBD (Comm)), Cooke J; see *Societe pour la Recherche, la Production, le Transport, la Transformation et la Commercialisation des Hydrocarbures SpA (Sonatrach) v Statoil Natural Gas LLC (Statoil)* [2014] EWHC 875 (Comm), [2014] 2 All E.R. (Comm) 857 (QBD (Comm)), Flaux J
r.6.32, see *Bullitt Mobile Ltd v Sonim Technologies* [2013] EWHC 3367 (IPEC), [2014] F.S.R. 23 (IPEC), Birss J
r.6.33, see *Bullitt Mobile Ltd v Sonim Technologies* [2013] EWHC 3367 (IPEC), [2014] F.S.R. 23 (IPEC), Birss J; see *Fern*

Computer Consultancy Ltd v Intergraph Cadworx & Analysis Solutions Inc [2014] EWHC 2908 (Ch), [2014] Bus. L.R. 1397 (Ch D), Mann J; see *Young v Anglo American South Africa Ltd* [2014] EWCA Civ 1130, [2014] Bus. L.R. 1434 (CA (Civ Div)), Lord Dyson MR
r.6.40, see *Embassy of Brazil v de Castro Cerqueira* [2014] 1 W.L.R. 3718 (EAT), Lewis J
r.6.41, see *Murrills v Berlanda* [2014] EWCA Civ 6, [2014] C.P. Rep. 21 (CA (Civ Div)), Kitchin LJ
r.7.2, see *Hills Contractors and Construction Ltd v Struth* [2013] EWHC 1693 (TCC), [2014] 1 W.L.R. 1 (QBD (TCC)), Ramsey J
r.7.4, see *Hills Contractors and Construction Ltd v Struth* [2013] EWHC 1693 (TCC), [2014] 1 W.L.R. 1 (QBD (TCC)), Ramsey J
r.7.5, see *American Leisure Group Ltd v Garrard* [2014] EWHC 2101 (Ch), [2014] 1 W.L.R. 4102 (Ch D), David Richards J; see *Euro-Asian Oil SA v Abilo (UK) Ltd* [2013] EWHC 485 (Comm), [2014] 1 All E.R. (Comm) 162 (QBD (Comm)), Burton J
r.7.6, see *American Leisure Group Ltd v Garrard* [2014] EWHC 2101 (Ch), [2014] 1 W.L.R. 4102 (Ch D), David Richards J; see *Euro-Asian Oil SA v Abilo (UK) Ltd* [2013] EWHC 485 (Comm), [2014] 1 All E.R. (Comm) 162 (QBD (Comm)), Burton J; see *Lincolnshire CC v Mouchel Business Services Ltd* [2014] EWHC 352 (TCC), [2014] B.L.R. 347 (QBD (TCC)), Stuart-Smith J
r.13.3, see *Mid-East Sales Ltd v United Engineering and Trading Co (PVT) Ltd* [2014] EWHC 1457 (Comm), [2014] 2 All E.R. (Comm) 623 (QBD (Comm)), Burton J; see *Newland Shipping and Forwarding Ltd v Toba Trading FZC* [2014] EWHC 1986 (Comm), [2014] 4 Costs L.R. 688 (QBD (Comm)), Males J; see *Power v Godfrey* [2013] EWHC 4359 (Ch), [2014] B.P.I.R. 484 (Ch D), Morgan J; see *Samara v MBI Partners UK Ltd* [2014] EWHC 563 (QB), [2014] 3 Costs L.R. 457 (QBD), Silber J
r.16.2, see *Travis Perkins Trading Co Ltd v Caerphilly CBC* [2014] EWHC 1498 (TCC), [2014] B.L.R. 465 (QBD (TCC)), Akenhead J

r.16.5, see *Symes v St George's Healthcare NHS Trust* [2014] EWHC 2505 (QB), [2014] Med. L.R. 449 (QBD), Simon Picken Q.C.
r.17.1, see *San Vicente v Secretary of State for Communities and Local Government* [2013] EWCA Civ 817, [2014] 1 W.L.R. 966 (CA (Civ Div)), Lloyd LJ
r.17.4, see *Bellinger v Mercer Ltd* [2014] EWCA Civ 996, [2014] 1 W.L.R. 3597 (CA (Civ Div)), Lord Dyson MR; see *Chandra v Brooke North (A Firm)* [2013] EWCA Civ 1559, [2014] T.C.L.R. 1 (CA (Civ Div)), Laws LJ; see *Co-operative Group Ltd v Birse Developments Ltd* [2014] EWCA Civ 707, [2014] B.L.R. 477 (CA (Civ Div)), Tomlinson LJ; see *San Vicente v Secretary of State for Communities and Local Government* [2013] EWCA Civ 817, [2014] 1 W.L.R. 966 (CA (Civ Div)), Lloyd LJ
r.18.1, see *XYZ v Various Companies* [2013] EWHC 3643 (QB), [2014] 2 Costs L.O. 197 (QBD), Thirlwall J
r.19.4A, see *R. (on the application of Boots Management Services Ltd) v Central Arbitration Committee* [2014] EWHC 65 (Admin), [2014] I.R.L.R. 278 (QBD (Admin)), Keith J
r.19.5, see *Insight Group Ltd v Kingston Smith (A Firm)* [2012] EWHC 3644 (QB), [2014] 1 W.L.R. 1448 (QBD), Leggatt J; see *Nemeti v Sabre Insurance Co Ltd* [2013] EWCA Civ 1555, [2014] C.P. Rep. 16 (CA (Civ Div)), Sir Terence Etherton C
r.19.7, see *Archer v Travis Perkins Plc* [2014] EWHC 1362 (Ch), [2014] Pens. L.R. 311 (Ch D), Rose J
r.21.1, see *Zarbafi v Zarbafi* [2014] EWCA Civ 1267, [2014] 1 W.L.R. 4122 (CA (Civ Div)), Rimer LJ
r.21.2, see *Dunhill v Burgin* [2014] UKSC 18, [2014] 1 W.L.R. 933 (SC), Lady Hale DPSC
r.21.4, see *Dunhill v Burgin* [2014] UKSC 18, [2014] 1 W.L.R. 933 (SC), Lady Hale DPSC
r.21.7, see *Zarbafi v Zarbafi* [2014] EWCA Civ 1267, [2014] 1 W.L.R. 4122 (CA (Civ Div)), Rimer LJ
r.21.10, see *Dunhill v Burgin* [2014] UKSC 18, [2014] 1 W.L.R. 933 (SC), Lady Hale DPSC

r.23.3, see *Groarke v Fontaine* [2014] EWHC 1676 (QB), [2014] 4 Costs L.R. 670 (QBD), Sir David Eady

r.23.5, see *Hallam Estates Ltd v Baker* [2014] EWCA Civ 661, [2014] C.P. Rep. 38 (CA (Civ Div)), Jackson LJ

r.23.11, see *MA Lloyd & Sons Ltd (t/a KPM Marine) v PPC International Ltd (t/a Professional Powercraft)* [2014] EWHC 41 (QB), [2014] 2 Costs L.R. 256 (QBD), Turner J; see *Webb Resolutions Ltd v E-Surv Ltd* [2014] EWHC 49 (QB), [2014] 1 Costs L.R. 182 (QBD), Turner J

r.25.1, see *McLennan Architects Ltd v Jones* [2014] EWHC 2604 (TCC), [2014] T.C.L.R. 6 (QBD (TCC)), Akenhead J

r.25.7, see *Comic Enterprise Ltd v Twentieth Century Fox Film Corp* [2014] EWHC 2286 (Ch), [2014] E.T.M.R. 51 (Ch D), Roger Wyand QC

r.25.12, see *Diag Human SE v Czech Republic* [2013] EWHC 3190 (Comm), [2014] 1 All E.R. (Comm) 605 (QBD (Comm)), Burton J; see *Northampton Regional Livestock Centre Co v Cowling* [2013] EWHC 1720 (QB), [2014] 1 Costs L.O. 15 (QBD), Stewart J

r.25.13, see *GSM Export (UK) Ltd (In Administration) v Revenue and Customs Commissioners* [2014] UKUT 457 (TCC), [2014] B.V.C. 539 (UT (Tax)), Judge Roger Berner; see *Harrison v Laidlaw* [2014] EWHC 35 (Ch), [2014] C.P. Rep. 20 (Ch D), Master Bowles; see *Kirkpatrick v Snoozebox Ltd* [2014] B.C.C. 477 (QBD), Master Leslie; see *Konkola Copper Mines Plc v U&M Mining Zambia Ltd* [2014] EWHC 2146 (Comm), [2014] 2 Lloyd's Rep. 507 (QBD (Comm)), Eder J; see *Northampton Regional Livestock Centre Co v Cowling* [2013] EWHC 1720 (QB), [2014] 1 Costs L.O. 15 (QBD), Stewart J; see *Seakom Ltd v Knowledgepool Group Ltd* [2014] EWCA Civ 1164, [2014] 5 Costs L.R. 820 (CA (Civ Div)), Gloster LJ

r.26.4, see *Mann v Mann* [2014] EWHC 537 (Fam), [2014] 1 W.L.R. 2807 (Fam Div), Mostyn J

r.27.14, see *Akhtar v Boland (Costs)* [2014] EWCA Civ 943, [2014] C.P. Rep. 41 (CA (Civ Div)), Gloster LJ

r.31.10, see *Tchenguiz-Imerman v Imerman* [2012] EWHC 4047 (Fam), [2014] 1 F.L.R. 232 (Fam Div), Moylan J

r.31.16, see *Smith v Secretary of State for Energy and Climate Change* [2013] EWCA Civ 1585, [2014] 1 W.L.R. 2283 (CA (Civ Div)), Longmore LJ

r.31.17, see *Hussain v King Edward VII Hospital* [2013] EWCA Civ 1863, (2014) 136 B.M.L.R. 54 (CA (Civ Div)), Longmore LJ; see *Tchenguiz v Director of the Serious Fraud Office* [2014] EWHC 1315 (Comm), [2014] Lloyd's Rep. F.C. 539 (QBD (Comm)), Eder J; see *Yates v Revenue and Customs Commissioners* [2014] EWHC 2311 (QB), [2014] P.I.Q.R. P24 (QBD), Master McCloud

r.31.20, see *Tchenguiz v Director of the Serious Fraud Office* [2014] EWCA Civ 1129, [2014] C.P. Rep. 45 (CA (Civ Div)), Longmore LJ

r.31.22, see *Alphasteel Ltd (In Liquidation) v Shirkhani* [2013] EWCA Civ 1272, [2014] C.P. Rep. 1 (CA (Civ Div)), Tomlinson LJ; see *DB Schenker Rail (UK) Ltd v Schunk GmbH* [2014] CAT 2, [2014] Comp. A.R. 205 (CAT), Marcus Smith QC; see *IG Index Ltd v Cloete* [2014] EWCA Civ 1128, [2014] C.P. Rep. 44 (CA (Civ Div)), Arden LJ; see *Tchenguiz v Director of the Serious Fraud Office* [2014] EWHC 1315 (Comm), [2014] Lloyd's Rep. F.C. 539 (QBD (Comm)), Eder J

r.32.2, see *MacLennan v Morgan Sindall (Infrastructure) Plc* [2013] EWHC 4044 (QB), [2014] 1 W.L.R. 2462 (QBD), Green J

r.32.5, see *Hayes v Hayes* [2014] EWHC 2694 (Ch), [2014] Bus. L.R. 1238 (Ch D), Nugee J

r.32.10, see *Chartwell Estate Agents Ltd v Fergies Properties SA* [2014] EWCA Civ 506, [2014] C.P. Rep. 36 (CA (Civ Div)), Laws LJ; see *Chartwell Estate Agents Ltd v Fergies Properties SA* [2014] EWHC 438 (QB), [2014] 2 Costs L.R. 353 (QBD), Globe J; see *Karbhari v Ahmed* [2013] EWHC 4042 (QB), [2014] 1 Costs L.R. 151 (QBD (Preston)), Turner J; see *MA Lloyd & Sons Ltd (t/a KPM Marine) v PPC International Ltd (t/a Professional Powercraft)* [2014] EWHC 41 (QB), [2014]

2 Costs L.R. 256 (QBD), Turner J; see *McTear v Englehard* [2014] EWHC 722 (Ch), [2014] 3 Costs L.R. 493 (Ch D), Richard Spearman QC

r.35.4, see *BMG (Mansfield) Ltd v Galliford Try Construction Ltd* [2013] EWHC 3183 (TCC), [2014] C.P. Rep. 3 (QBD (TCC)), Edwards-Stuart J; see *McTear v Englehard* [2014] EWHC 722 (Ch), [2014] 3 Costs L.R. 493 (Ch D), Richard Spearman QC

r.35.15, see *Cary v Commissioner of Police of the Metropolis* [2014] EWCA Civ 987, [2014] C.P. Rep. 42 (CA (Civ Div)), Arden LJ

r.36.10, see *Haynes v Department for Business, Innovation and Skills* [2014] EWHC 643 (QB), [2014] 3 Costs L.R. 475 (QBD), Jay J; see *Jopling v Leavesley* [2013] EWCA Civ 1605, [2014] W.T.L.R. 807 (CA (Civ Div)), Elias LJ; see *PGF II SA v OMFS Co 1 Ltd* [2013] EWCA Civ 1288, [2014] 1 W.L.R. 1386 (CA (Civ Div)), Maurice Kay LJ

r.36.11, see *Evans v Royal Wolverhampton Hospitals NHS Foundation Trust* [2014] EWHC 3185 (QB), [2014] 6 Costs L.O. 899 (QBD), Leggatt J

r.36.14, see *Elsevier Ltd v Munro* [2014] EWHC 2728 (QB), [2014] 5 Costs L.O. 797 (QBD), Warby J; see *Feltham v Freer Bouskell (Costs)* [2013] EWHC 3086 (Ch), [2014] 1 Costs L.O. 29 (Ch D), Charles Hollander Q.C.; see *Greenwich Millennium Village Ltd v Essex Services Group Plc (formerly Essex Electrical Group Ltd)* [2014] EWHC 1099 (TCC), [2014] T.C.L.R. 4 (QBD (TCC)), Coulson J; see *Quiet Moments Ltd, Re* [2014] EWCA Civ 1536, [2014] 6 Costs L.R. 1106 (CA (Civ Div)), Sir Terence Etherton; see *Rehill v Rider Holdings Ltd* [2014] EWCA Civ 42, [2014] 3 Costs L.R. 405 (CA (Civ Div)), Lewison LJ; see *Thinc Group Ltd v Kingdom* [2013] EWCA Civ 1306, [2014] C.P. Rep. 8 (CA (Civ Div)), Arden LJ

r.38.6, see *Forstater v Python (Monty) Pictures Ltd* [2013] EWHC 3759 (Ch), [2014] 1 Costs L.R. 36 (Ch D), Norris J; see *R. (on the application of Smoke Club Ltd) v Network Rail Infrastructure Ltd* [2013]

EWHC 3830 (Admin), [2014] 2 Costs L.O. 123 (QBD (Admin)), Ouseley J

r.40.12, see *A (A Child) (Judgment Corrections), Re* [2014] EWCA Civ 871, [2014] 1 W.L.R. 4453 (CA (Civ Div)), Patten LJ

r.43.2, see *Yeo v Times Newspapers Ltd* [2014] EWHC 2853 (QB), [2014] 5 Costs L.O. 823 (QBD), Warby J

r.44.2, see *FH Brundle v Perry* [2014] EWHC 979 (IPEC), [2014] 4 Costs L.O. 576 (IPEC), Judge Hacon; see *Forstater v Python (Monty) Pictures Ltd* [2013] EWHC 3759 (Ch), [2014] 1 Costs L.R. 36 (Ch D), Norris J; see *Jones v Secretary of State for Energy and Climate Change* [2014] EWCA Civ 363, [2014] 3 All E.R. 956 (CA (Civ Div)), Patten LJ; see *M v M (Costs)* [2013] EWHC 3372 (Fam), [2014] 1 F.L.R. 499 (Fam Div), Eleanor King J; see *Northrop Grumman Mission Systems Europe Ltd v BAE Systems (Al Diriyah C4I) Ltd* [2014] EWHC 3148 (TCC), [2014] T.C.L.R. 8 (QBD (TCC)), Ramsey J; see *Quiet Moments Ltd, Re* [2014] EWCA Civ 1536, [2014] 6 Costs L.R. 1106 (CA (Civ Div)), Sir Terence Etherton

r.44.3, see *Cussens v Realreed Ltd* [2013] EWHC 1229 (QB), [2014] 1 W.L.R. 275 (QBD), Andrew Smith J; see *Rehill v Rider Holdings Ltd* [2014] EWCA Civ 42, [2014] 3 Costs L.R. 405 (CA (Civ Div)), Lewison LJ; see *Speciality Produce Ltd v Secretary of State for the Environment, Food and Rural Affairs* [2014] EWCA Civ 225, [2014] C.P. Rep. 29 (CA (Civ Div)), Longmore LJ; see *Walker Construction (UK) Ltd v Quayside Homes Ltd* [2014] EWCA Civ 93, [2014] 1 C.L.C. 121 (CA (Civ Div)), Laws LJ

r.44.3B, see *1,3 and 5 Argall Avenue, Re* [2014] EWHC 2981 (Ch), [2014] 5 Costs L.R. 915 (Ch D), Barling J; see *Forstater v Python (Monty) Pictures Ltd* [2013] EWHC 3759 (Ch), [2014] 1 Costs L.R. 36 (Ch D), Norris J; see *Ultimate Products Ltd v Woolley* [2014] EWHC 2706 (Ch), [2014] 5 Costs L.O. 787 (Ch D), Christopher Pymont, Q.C.

r.44.4, see *Finglands Coachways Ltd v O'Hare* [2014] EWHC 1513 (QB), [2014] 4 Costs L.O. 668 (QBD), Cranston J

r.44.12A, see *Tasleem v Beverley* [2013] EWCA Civ 1805, [2014] 1 W.L.R. 3567 (CA (Civ Div)), Sir Terence Etherton C

r.44.13, see *Wagenaar v Weekend Travel Ltd (t/a Ski Weekend)* [2014] EWCA Civ 1105, [2014] C.P. Rep. 46 (CA (Civ Div)), Laws LJ

r.44.14, see *Rehill v Rider Holdings Ltd* [2014] EWCA Civ 42, [2014] 3 Costs L.R. 405 (CA (Civ Div)), Lewison LJ; see *Wagenaar v Weekend Travel Ltd (t/a Ski Weekend)* [2014] EWCA Civ 1105, [2014] C.P. Rep. 46 (CA (Civ Div)), Laws LJ

r.44.15, see *Caliendo v Mishcon de Reya* [2014] EWHC 3414 (Ch), [2014] 6 Costs L.O. 935 (Ch D), Hildyard J; see *Ultimate Products Ltd v Woolley* [2014] EWHC 2706 (Ch), [2014] 5 Costs L.O. 787 (Ch D), Christopher Pymont, Q.C.; see *Yeo v Times Newspapers Ltd* [2014] EWHC 2853 (QB), [2014] 5 Costs L.O. 823 (QBD), Warby J

r.44.16, see *Wagenaar v Weekend Travel Ltd (t/a Ski Weekend)* [2014] EWCA Civ 1105, [2014] C.P. Rep. 46 (CA (Civ Div)), Laws LJ

r.44.17, see *Wagenaar v Weekend Travel Ltd (t/a Ski Weekend)* [2014] EWCA Civ 1105, [2014] C.P. Rep. 46 (CA (Civ Div)), Laws LJ

r.45.30, see *FH Brundle v Perry* [2014] EWHC 979 (IPEC), [2014] 4 Costs L.O. 576 (IPEC), Judge Hacon

r.45.32, see *FH Brundle v Perry* [2014] EWHC 979 (IPEC), [2014] 4 Costs L.O. 576 (IPEC), Judge Hacon

r.45.41, see *Venn v Secretary of State for Communities and Local Government* [2013] EWHC 3546 (Admin), [2014] J.P.L. 447 (QBD (Admin)), Lang J

r.46.2, see *X Local Authority v Trimega Laboratories Ltd* [2014] 2 F.L.R. 232 (Fam Div), Judge Williams

r.47.6, see *1,3 and 5 Argall Avenue, Re* [2014] EWHC 2981 (Ch), [2014] 5 Costs L.R. 915 (Ch D), Barling J

r.47.9, see *Hallam Estates Ltd v Baker* [2014] EWCA Civ 661, [2014] C.P. Rep. 38 (CA (Civ Div)), Jackson LJ

r.47.11, see *Tasleem v Beverley* [2013] EWCA Civ 1805, [2014] 1 W.L.R. 3567 (CA (Civ Div)), Sir Terence Etherton C

r.48.1, see *Wagenaar v Weekend Travel Ltd (t/a Ski Weekend)* [2014] EWCA Civ 1105, [2014] C.P. Rep. 46 (CA (Civ Div)), Laws LJ

r.48.2, see *Wagenaar v Weekend Travel Ltd (t/a Ski Weekend)* [2014] EWCA Civ 1105, [2014] C.P. Rep. 46 (CA (Civ Div)), Laws LJ

r.48.6, see *R. (on the application of Bar Standards Board) v Disciplinary Tribunal of the Council of the Inns of Court* [2014] EWHC 1570 (Admin), [2014] 4 All E.R. 759 (QBD (Admin)), Moses LJ

r.52.3, see *R. (on the application of Grace) v Secretary of State for the Home Department* [2014] EWCA Civ 1091, [2014] 1 W.L.R. 3432 (CA (Civ Div)), Lord Dyson MR; see *Webb Resolutions Ltd v E-Surv Ltd* [2014] EWHC 49 (QB), [2014] 1 Costs L.R. 182 (QBD), Turner J

r.52.9, see *Universal Enterprises (EU) Ltd v Revenue and Customs Commissioners* [2014] S.T.C. 1515 (UT (Tax)), Judge Colin Bishopp

r.52.9A, see *Akhtar v Boland (Costs)* [2014] EWCA Civ 943, [2014] C.P. Rep. 41 (CA (Civ Div)), Gloster LJ; see *JE (Jamaica) v Secretary of State for the Home Department* [2014] EWCA Civ 192, [2014] C.P. Rep. 24 (CA (Civ Div)), Laws LJ; see *JJ Food Service Ltd v Zulhayir* [2013] EWCA Civ 1304, [2014] C.P. Rep. 15 (CA (Civ Div)), Rimer LJ

r.52.10, see *A (A Child) (Judgment Corrections), Re* [2014] EWCA Civ 871, [2014] 1 W.L.R. 4453 (CA (Civ Div)), Patten LJ

r.52.11, see *A (A Child) (Intractable Contact Dispute: Human Rights Violations), Re* [2013] EWCA Civ 1104, [2014] 1 F.L.R. 1185 (CA (Civ Div)), Aikens LJ; see *Symes v St George's Healthcare NHS Trust* [2014] EWHC 2505 (QB), [2014] Med. L.R. 449 (QBD), Simon Picken Q.C.

r.54.1, see *R. (on the application of Boots Management Services Ltd) v Central Arbitration Committee* [2014] EWHC 2930

(Admin), [2014] I.R.L.R. 887 (QBD
(Admin)), Sir Brian Keith
r.54.12, see *R. (on the application of Grace)
v Secretary of State for the Home
Department* [2014] EWCA Civ 1091, [2014]
1 W.L.R. 3432 (CA (Civ Div)), Lord Dyson
MR
r.54.14, see *R. (on the application of Boots
Management Services Ltd) v Central
Arbitration Committee* [2014] EWHC 2930
(Admin), [2014] I.R.L.R. 887 (QBD
(Admin)), Sir Brian Keith
r.55.8, see *Akerman-Livingstone v Aster
Communities Ltd (formerly Flourish Homes
Ltd)* [2014] EWCA Civ 1081, [2014] 1
W.L.R. 3980 (CA (Civ Div)), Arden LJ
r.58.5, see *Associated Electrical Industries
Ltd v Alstom UK* [2014] EWHC 430
(Comm), [2014] 3 Costs L.R. 415 (QBD
(Comm)), Andrew Smith J
r.58.14, see *Summit Navigation Ltd v
Generali Romania Asigurare Reasigurare
SA* [2014] EWHC 398 (Comm), [2014] 1
W.L.R. 3472 (QBD (Comm)), Leggatt J
r.61.11, see *Cosmotrade SA v Kairos
Shipping Ltd* [2014] EWCA Civ 217, [2014]
1 W.L.R. 3883 (CA (Civ Div)), Rimer LJ
r.62.18, see *Honeywell International Middle
East Ltd v Meydan Group LLC* [2014]
EWHC 1344 (TCC), [2014] 2 Lloyd's Rep.
133 (QBD (TCC)), Ramsey J
r.63.14, see *Bullitt Mobile Ltd v Sonim
Technologies* [2013] EWHC 3367 (IPEC),
[2014] F.S.R. 23 (IPEC), Birss J
r.64.2, see *Holden-Hindley v Holden-
Hindley* [2013] EWHC 3053 (Ch), [2014]
W.T.L.R. 275 (Ch D), Roth J
r.72.2, see *Merchant International Co Ltd v
Natsionalna Aktsionerna Kompaniia
Naftogaz Ukrainy* [2014] EWHC 391
(Comm), [2014] 1 C.L.C. 271 (QBD
(Comm)), Blair J; see *Taurus Petroleum Ltd
v State Oil Marketing Co of the Ministry of
Oil, Iraq* [2013] EWHC 3494 (Comm),
[2014] 1 All E.R. (Comm) 942 (QBD
(Comm)), Field J
Sch.1, applied: SI 2014/1610 r.19_8, r.19_9
Sch.1 Part 17, revoked: SI 2014/407 r.37
Sch.1 Part 45, revoked: SI 2014/407 r.37
Sch.1 Part 46, revoked: SI 2014/407 r.37
Sch.1 Part 47, revoked: SI 2014/407 r.37

Sch.1 Part 54, revoked: SI 2014/3299 r.16
Sch.1 Part 113, revoked: SI 2014/407 r.37
Sch.1 Part 116, applied: SI 2014/1610
r.40_7, r.40_8
Sch.2 Part 1 para.6, amended: SI 2014/867
r.3, r.19
Sch.2 Part 16, revoked: SI 2014/867 r.20
Sch.2 Part 22, revoked: SI 2014/407 r.38
Sch.2 Part 24, revoked: SI 2014/407 r.38
Sch.2 Part 25, revoked: SI 2014/407 r.38
Sch.2 Part 26, revoked: SI 2014/407 r.38
Sch.2 Part 27 para.1, amended: SI 2014/407
r.39
Sch.2 Part 27 para.2, amended: SI 2014/407
r.39
Sch.2 Part 27 para.2, revoked (in part): SI
2014/407 r.39
Sch.2 Part 27 para.3, amended: SI 2014/407
r.39
Sch.2 Part 27 para.4, amended: SI 2014/407
r.39
Sch.2 Part 27 para.4, revoked (in part): SI
2014/879 Art.77
Sch.2 Part 27 para.5, amended: SI 2014/407
r.39
Sch.2 Part 27 para.6, amended: SI 2014/407
r.39
Sch.2 Part 27 para.7, amended: SI 2014/407
r.4, r.39
Sch.2 Part 27 para.7A, amended: SI
2014/407 r.39
Sch.2 Part 27 para.7B, amended: SI
2014/407 r.4
Sch.2 Part 27 para.8, revoked: SI 2014/407
r.39
Sch.2 Part 27 para.10, amended: SI
2014/407 r.4, r.39
Sch.2 Part 27 para.11, amended: SI
2014/407 r.4
Sch.2 Part 27 para.13, amended: SI
2014/407 r.39
Sch.2 Part 27 para.14, amended: SI
2014/407 r.4, r.39
Sch.2 Part 27 para.15, amended: SI
2014/407 r.39
Sch.2 Part 27 para.16, amended: SI
2014/407 r.4, r.39
Sch.2 Part 27 para.17, revoked: SI 2014/407
r.39
Sch.2 Part 27 para.19, amended: SI
2014/407 r.4, r.39

Sch.2 Part 27 para.20, amended: SI
2014/407 r.39
Sch.2 Part 27 para.22, amended: SI
2014/407 r.39
Sch.2 Part 28 paraA.1, added: SI 2014/407
r.40
Sch.2 Part 28 para.1, amended: SI 2014/867
r.21
Sch.2 Part 28 para.1A, added: SI 2014/407
r.40
Sch.2 Part 28 para.2, amended: SI 2014/867
r.21
Sch.2 Part 28 para.4, amended: SI 2014/867
r.21
Sch.2 Part 28 para.5, amended: SI 2014/867
r.21
Sch.2 Part 28 para.7, amended: SI 2014/867
r.3, r.21
Sch.2 Part 28 para.8, amended: SI 2014/867
r.21
Sch.2 Part 28 para.9, amended: SI 2014/867
r.3
Sch.2 Part 28 para.10, amended: SI
2014/867 r.21
Sch.2 Part 28 para.11, revoked (in part): SI
2014/867 r.21
Sch.2 Part 28 para.12, revoked: SI 2014/867
r.21
Sch.2 Part 28 para.13, amended: SI
2014/867 r.21
Sch.2 Part 28 para.13, revoked (in part): SI
2014/867 r.21
Sch.2 Part 28 para.14, amended: SI
2014/867 r.21
Sch.2 Part 33, revoked: SI 2014/407 r.38
Sch.2 Part 39 para.1, amended: SI 2014/867
r.22
Sch.2 Part 39 para.2, amended: SI 2014/867
r.22
Sch.2 Part 39 para.5, amended: SI 2014/867
r.3, r.22
Sch.2 Part 39 para.6, amended: SI 2014/867
r.22
Sch.2 Part 39 para.7, amended: SI 2014/867
r.22
Sch.2 Part 39 para.9, amended: SI 2014/867
r.22
Sch.2 Part 39 para.10, amended: SI
2014/867 r.22
Sch.2 Part 39 para.11, amended: SI
2014/867 r.22

Sch.2 Part 39 para.13A, amended: SI
2014/867 r.3, r.22
Sch.2 Part 39 para.19, amended: SI
2014/867 r.22
Sch.2 Part 44 para.4, amended: SI 2014/867
r.3, r.23
Sch.2 Part 49 para.19, amended: SI
2014/867 r.3, r.24

**3175. Corporation Tax (Instalment Payments)
Regulations 1998**
applied: 2014 c.26 s.119
Reg.2, amended: SI 2014/2409 Reg.2
Reg.3, amended: SI 2014/2409 Reg.2
Reg.6, applied: 2014 c.26 s.119
Reg.7, applied: 2014 c.26 s.119
Reg.8, applied: 2014 c.26 s.119
Reg.9, applied: 2014 c.26 s.119
Reg.10, applied: 2014 c.26 s.119
Reg.11, applied: 2014 c.26 s.119
Reg.13, applied: 2014 c.26 s.119

1999

**3. Social Security (Categorisation of Earners)
Amendment Regulations 1999**
revoked: SI 2014/635 Sch.1

**71. Allocation of Housing and Homelessness
(Review Procedures) Regulations 1999**
Reg.8, see *Mohamoud v Birmingham City
Council* [2014] EWCA Civ 227, [2014]
H.L.R. 22 (CA (Civ Div)), Moore-Bick LJ;
see *NJ v Wandsworth LBC* [2013] EWCA
Civ 1373, [2014] P.T.S.R. 497 (CA (Civ
Div)), Lewison LJ

**107. Channel Tunnel Rail Link (Assessment of
Environmental Effects) Regulations 1999**
revoked: SI 2014/1333 Reg.2

216. Civil Courts (Amendment) Order 1999
revoked: SI 2014/820 Sch.1

**280. Federal Republic of Yugoslavia (United
Nations Sanctions) (Amendment) Order 1999**
revoked: SI 2014/2711 Sch.1

**293. Town and Country Planning
(Environmental Impact Assessment) (England
and Wales) Regulations 1999**
Reg.2, see *R. (on the application of Corbett)
v Cornwall Council* [2013] EWHC 3958
(Admin), [2014] P.T.S.R. 727 (QBD
(Admin)), Lewis J; see *R. (on the
application of Ellaway) v Cardiff CC* [2013]

EWHC 2907 (Admin), [2014] Env. L.R. 12 (QBD (Admin)), Judge Curran QC

Reg.19, see *R. (on the application of Corbett) v Cornwall Council* [2013] EWHC 3958 (Admin), [2014] P.T.S.R. 727 (QBD (Admin)), Lewis J

Sch.2, see *R. (on the application of Evans) v Basingstoke and Deane BC* [2013] EWCA Civ 1635, [2014] 1 W.L.R. 2034 (CA (Civ Div)), Aikens LJ

Sch.3 para.1, see *R. (on the application of Thakeham Village Action Ltd) v Horsham DC* [2014] EWHC 67 (Admin), [2014] Env. L.R. 21 (QBD (Admin)), Lindblom J

Sch.4, see *R. (on the application of Corbett) v Cornwall Council* [2013] EWHC 3958 (Admin), [2014] P.T.S.R. 727 (QBD (Admin)), Lewis J

327. Town and Country Planning (Costs of Inquiries etc.) (Standard Daily Amount) Regulations 1999

revoked (in part): SI 2014/692 Sch.1

400. Welfare of Animals (Slaughter or Killing) (Amendment) Regulations 1999

revoked (in part): SI 2014/951 Reg.46, SI 2014/1240 Reg.47

491. Criminal Legal Aid (Fixed Payments) (Scotland) Regulations 1999

Reg.2, amended: SSI 2014/366 Reg.4

Reg.4, amended: SSI 2014/366 Reg.5, Reg.6, Reg.7

Reg.4A, amended: SSI 2014/366 Reg.8

Sch.1A, amended: SSI 2014/366 Reg.10

Sch.1 Part 1, amended: SSI 2014/366 Reg.9

Sch.1B Part 1, amended: SSI 2014/366 Reg.11

522. Pensions Increase (Review) Order 1999

referred to: SI 2014/668 Sch.1

Art.6, substituted: SI 2014/107 Sch.1 para.56, SI 2014/3229 Sch.6 para.35

584. National Minimum Wage Regulations 1999

Reg.3, see *Esparon (t/a Middle West Residential Care Home) v Slavikovska* [2014] I.C.R. 1037 (EAT), Judge Serota QC; see *Whittlestone v BJP Home Support Ltd* [2014] I.C.R. 275 (EAT), Langstaff J

Reg.11, amended: SI 2014/2485 Reg.3

Reg.12, amended: SI 2014/546 Reg.2, SI 2014/2103 Art.6

Reg.13, amended: SI 2014/2485 Reg.3, SI 2014/2832 Reg.3

Reg.15, see *Esparon (t/a Middle West Residential Care Home) v Slavikovska* [2014] I.C.R. 1037 (EAT), Judge Serota QC; see *Whittlestone v BJP Home Support Ltd* [2014] I.C.R. 275 (EAT), Langstaff J

Reg.36, amended: SI 2014/2485 Reg.3

611. Housing (Right to Buy) (Cost Floor) (Scotland) Order 1999

revoked: 2014 asp 14 s.1

654. European Communities (Designation) Order 1999

Sch.1, amended: SI 2014/2705 Art.7

662. Water (Northern Ireland) Order 1999

Art.29A, amended: SI 2014/892 Sch.1 para.222

671. Social Security Contributions (Transfer of Functions, etc.) (Northern Ireland) Order 1999

Art.7, amended: 2014 c.7 s.6

Art.7, varied: 2014 c.6 s.126

Art.10, varied: 2014 c.6 s.126

Art.13, varied: 2014 c.6 s.126

672. National Assembly for Wales (Transfer of Functions) Order 1999

Art.2, applied: SI 2014/1515

Sch.1, amended: 2014 c.21 Sch.7 para.127, Sch.10 para.19

Sch.1, applied: SI 2014/1515

681. Magistrates Courts (Hearsay Evidence in Civil Proceedings) Rules 1999

r.3, applied: SI 2014/1610 r.50_6

728. Prison Rules 1999

Part I r.2, amended: SI 2014/2169 r.2

Part II r.7, amended: SI 2014/2169 r.2

Part II r.9, amended: SI 2014/2169 r.2

Part II r.55A, amended: SI 2014/2169 r.2

Part II r.59, amended: SI 2014/2169 r.2

r.7, see *R. v Mahmood (Asad)* [2013] EWCA Crim 2356, [2014] 1 Cr. App. R. 31 (CA (Crim Div)), Fulford LJ

r.34, see *R. v Mahmood (Asad)* [2013] EWCA Crim 2356, [2014] 1 Cr. App. R. 31 (CA (Crim Div)), Fulford LJ

r.35A, see *R. v Mahmood (Asad)* [2013] EWCA Crim 2356, [2014] 1 Cr. App. R. 31 (CA (Crim Div)), Fulford LJ

743. Control of Major Accident Hazards Regulations 1999

Reg.2, amended: SI 2014/469 Sch.3 para.84

Reg.3, disapplied: SI 2014/1637 Reg.3

Reg.7, amended: SI 2014/469 Sch.3 para.85

Reg.15, amended: SI 2014/469 Sch.3
para.86
Reg.16, amended: SI 2014/469 Sch.3
para.87
Reg.19, amended: SI 2014/469 Sch.3
para.88
Reg.20, amended: SI 2014/469 Sch.3
para.89
Reg.22, amended: SI 2014/469 Sch.3
para.90
Sch.1, amended: SI 2014/162 Reg.2

747. Food Labelling (Amendment) Regulations 1999

Reg.1, revoked (in part): SI 2014/1855 Sch.6
Part 1, SI 2014/2303 Sch.6 Part 1, SSI
2014/312 Sch.4 Part 1
Reg.2, revoked (in part): SI 2014/1855 Sch.6
Part 2, SI 2014/2303 Sch.6 Part 2
Reg.3, revoked (in part): SI 2014/1855 Sch.6
Part 1, SI 2014/2303 Sch.6 Part 1, SSI
2014/312 Sch.4 Part 1
Reg.11, revoked (in part): SI 2014/1855
Sch.6 Part 2, SI 2014/2303 Sch.6 Part 2
Reg.12, revoked (in part): SI 2014/1855
Sch.6 Part 1, SI 2014/2303 Sch.6 Part 1, SSI
2014/312 Sch.4 Part 1

873. National Health Service (Liabilities to Third Parties Scheme) Regulations 1999

Reg.1, amended: SI 2014/931 Reg.2
Reg.3, amended: SI 2014/3090 Sch.1 para.1
Reg.4, amended: SI 2014/931 Reg.3
Reg.7, amended: SI 2014/931 Reg.4
Reg.8, amended: SI 2014/931 Reg.5
Reg.9, amended: SI 2014/931 Reg.6
Reg.9, revoked (in part): SI 2014/931 Reg.6

874. National Health Service (Property Expenses Scheme) Regulations 1999

Reg.1, amended: SI 2014/932 Reg.2
Reg.3, amended: SI 2014/3090 Sch.1 para.1
Reg.4, amended: SI 2014/932 Reg.3
Reg.7, amended: SI 2014/932 Reg.4
Reg.8, amended: SI 2014/932 Reg.5
Reg.8, revoked (in part): SI 2014/932 Reg.5

892. Barnet and Chase Farm Hospitals National Health Service Trust (Establishment) Order 1999

applied: SI 2014/1597 Art.2

904. Prosecution of Offences Act 1985 (Specified Proceedings) Order 1999

Sch.1 Part 1 para.16A, added: SI 2014/1229
Art.2

913. North West London Hospitals National Health Service Trust (Establishment) Order 1999

revoked: SI 2014/2524 Art.8

929. Act of Sederunt (Summary Applications, Statutory Applications and Appeals etc Rules) 1999

Part 3, added: SSI 2014/302 r.7
Part 3, added: SSI 2014/371 r.4
r.2.31, see *Chief Constable of the Police
Service of Scotland v R* [2014] CSIH 8, 2014
S.C. 448 (IH (2 Div)), The Lord Justice
Clerk (Carloway)
Sch.1, amended: SSI 2014/302 r.7, SSI
2014/371 Sch.3

930. Wireless Telegraphy (Exemption) Regulations 1999

see *Recall Support Services Ltd v Secretary
of State for Culture Media and Sport* [2013]
EWHC 3091 (Ch), [2014] 2 C.M.L.R. 2 (Ch
D), Rose J

980. Distraint by Authorised Officers (Fees, Costs and Charges) Regulations 1999

revoked (in part): SI 2014/600 Sch.1 Part 2

991. Social Security and Child Support (Decisions and Appeals) Regulations 1999

Reg.1, amended: SI 2014/107 Sch.1 para.26,
SI 2014/1097 Reg.12, SI 2014/3229 Sch.6
para.18
Reg.3, amended: SI 2014/1097 Reg.12
Reg.6, amended: SI 2014/1097 Reg.12
Reg.7, amended: SI 2014/1097 Reg.12

1011. Civil Courts (Amendment) (No.2) Order 1999

revoked: SI 2014/820 Sch.1

1022. Insolvency (Amendment) (No.2) Rules 1999

Sch.1 para.11, see *Lehman Brothers
International (Europe) (In Administration),
Re* [2014] EWHC 1687 (Ch), [2014] Bus.
L.R. 1186 (Ch D (Companies Ct)), David
Richards J

1027. Social Security Contributions (Decisions and Appeals) Regulations 1999

Reg.3, varied: 2014 c.6 s.126
Reg.4, varied: 2014 c.6 s.126
Reg.11, varied: 2014 c.6 s.126
Reg.12, varied: 2014 c.6 s.126

1053. Non-Road Mobile Machinery (Emission of Gaseous and Particulate Pollutants) Regulations 1999
Reg.2, amended: SI 2014/1309 Reg.3
Sch.9 Part 2 para.8, amended: SI 2014/1309 Reg.4

1085. Fees in the Registers of Scotland Amendment Order 1999
revoked: SSI 2014/188 Sch.2

1136. Miscellaneous Food Additives (Amendment) Regulations 1999
Reg.14, amended: SI 2014/1855 Sch.6 Part 1, SI 2014/2303 Sch.6 Part 1, SSI 2014/312 Sch.4 Part 1
Reg.14, revoked (in part): SI 2014/1855 Sch.6 Part 1, SI 2014/2303 Sch.6 Part 1, SSI 2014/312 Sch.4 Part 1

1319. Scotland Act 1998 (Cross-Border Public Authorities) (Specification) Order 1999
Sch.1, amended: 2014 c.12 Sch.11 para.102, SI 2014/1924 Sch.1

1347. Act of Sederunt (Proceedings for Determination of Devolution Issues Rules) 1999
Art.2, amended: 2014 c.29 s.4

1380. North and West Salmon Fishery District Designation Order 1999
Art.2, applied: SSI 2014/327 Sch.1
Art.4, applied: SSI 2014/327 Sch.1
Sch.1, applied: SSI 2014/327 Sch.1
Sch.3, applied: SSI 2014/327 Sch.1

1381. Conon Salmon Fishery District Designation Order 1999
Art.2, applied: SSI 2014/327 Sch.1
Art.4, applied: SSI 2014/327 Sch.1
Sch.1, applied: SSI 2014/327 Sch.1

1382. Lochaber Salmon Fishery District Designation Order 1999
Art.2, applied: SSI 2014/327 Sch.1
Sch.1, applied: SSI 2014/327 Sch.1

1441. Education (Inspection of Nursery Education) (Wales) Regulations 1999
Reg.4, amended: SI 2014/1212 Reg.2

1483. Food Labelling (Amendment) (No.2) Regulations 1999
revoked (in part): SI 2014/1855 Sch.6 Part 1, SI 2014/2303 Sch.6 Part 1, SSI 2014/312 Sch.4 Part 1

1513. Olive Oil (Designations of Origin) Regulations 1999
revoked: SI 2014/195 Reg.20

1549. Public Interest Disclosure (Prescribed Persons) Order 1999
applied: SI 2014/2418 Art.2
revoked: SI 2014/2418 Art.2
Sch.1, amended: SI 2014/469 Sch.3 para.190, SI 2014/549 Sch.1 para.25, SI 2014/596 Art.2, SI 2014/1815 Sch.1 para.7

1603. Contaminants in Food (Amendment) Regulations 1999
revoked (in part): SI 2014/1855 Sch.6 Part 1, SI 2014/2303 Sch.6 Part 1, SSI 2014/312 Sch.4 Part 1

1619. General Teaching Council for Wales (Constitution) Regulations 1999
revoked: SI 2014/2365 Sch.1

1621. Registration of Marriages (Welsh Language) Regulations 1999
Sch.1, amended: SI 2014/107 Sch.1 para.27

1672. Public Gas Transporter Pipe-line Works (Environmental Impact Assessment) Regulations 1999
Reg.1, amended: SI 2014/557 Reg.2

1736. Visiting Forces and International Headquarters (Application of Law) Order 1999
Sch.6, amended: SI 2014/1638 Sch.13 para.18

1747. Scotland Act 1998 (Cross-Border Public Authorities) (Adaptation of Functions etc.) Order 1999
Sch.1, amended: 2014 c.12 Sch.11 para.102, SI 2014/1924 Sch.1
Sch.11, revoked: SI 2014/1924 Sch.1
Sch.21, revoked: 2014 c.12 Sch.11 para.102

1750. Scotland Act 1998 (Transfer of Functions to the Scottish Ministers etc.) Order 1999
Sch.1, amended: 2014 c.12 s.109
Sch.5 para.3, revoked: 2014 c.12 s.109
Sch.5 para.18, revoked (in part): 2014 c.12 s.109

1820. Scotland Act 1998 (Consequential Modifications) (No.2) Order 1999
Sch.2 Part I para.124, revoked: 2014 c.12 Sch.11 para.102

2001. Pressure Equipment Regulations 1999
Reg.2, amended: SI 2014/469 Sch.3 para.92
Sch.8 para.1, amended: SI 2014/469 Sch.3 para.93

2024. Quarries Regulations 1999
Reg.2, amended: SI 2014/1638 Sch.13 para.19

Reg.3, amended: SI 2014/3248 Sch.5
para.12
Sch.5 Part II, amended: SI 2014/1637 Sch.4
Part 1

**2083. Unfair Terms in Consumer Contracts
Regulations 1999**

see *West v Ian Finlay and Associates* [2014]
EWCA Civ 316, [2014] B.L.R. 324 (CA
(Civ Div)), Moore-Bick LJ
Reg.3, amended: SI 2014/549 Sch.1 para.26
Reg.5, see *West v Ian Finlay and Associates*
[2014] EWCA Civ 316, [2014] B.L.R. 324
(CA (Civ Div)), Moore-Bick LJ
Reg.8, see *West v Ian Finlay and Associates*
[2014] EWCA Civ 316, [2014] B.L.R. 324
(CA (Civ Div)), Moore-Bick LJ
Reg.10, amended: SI 2014/549 Sch.1
para.26
Reg.12, amended: SI 2014/549 Sch.1
para.26
Reg.13, amended: SI 2014/549 Sch.1
para.26
Reg.14, amended: SI 2014/549 Sch.1
para.26
Reg.15, amended: SI 2014/549 Sch.1
para.26

**2228. Environmental Impact Assessment
(Forestry) (England and Wales) Regulations
1999**

Reg.4, disapplied: SI 2014/3263 Sch.2
para.2
Reg.20, applied: SI 2014/3223 Sch.1 para.11
Reg.22, disapplied: SI 2014/3263 Sch.2
para.2

2360. Distress for Rent (Amendment) Rules 1999

revoked: SI 2014/600 Sch.1 Part 2

**2463. Mines (Control of Ground Movement)
Regulations 1999**

revoked (in part): SI 2014/3248 Sch.4 Part 1
Reg.5, applied: SI 2014/3248 Reg.71

**2564. Distress for Rent (Amendment) (No.2)
Rules 1999**

revoked: SI 2014/600 Sch.1 Part 2

2639. Gas Act 1986 (Exemptions) Order 1999

revoked: SI 2014/528 Sch.1

**2720. Neath to Abergavenny Trunk Road (A465)
(Abergavenny to Hirwaun Dualling and Slip
Roads) and East of Abercynon to East of
Dowlais Road (A4060), Cardiff to Glan Conwy
Trunk Road (A470) (Connecting Roads) Order
1999**

Art.6, amended: SI 2014/2716 Art.2
Sch.2 para.4, substituted: SI 2014/2716 Art.3
Sch.2 para.22, added: SI 2014/2716 Art.4
Sch.3, amended: SI 2014/2716 Art.5
Sch.4, amended: SI 2014/2716 Art.6

**2864. Motor Vehicles (Driving Licences)
Regulations 1999**

Reg.3, amended: SI 2014/3190 Reg.3
Reg.7, amended: SI 2014/613 Reg.3
Reg.7, revoked (in part): SI 2014/3190
Reg.4
Reg.9, amended: SI 2014/613 Reg.4
Reg.21A, added: SI 2014/3190 Reg.5
Reg.22, amended: SI 2014/480 Reg.6
Reg.23A, amended: SI 2014/1816 Reg.2
Reg.24, amended: SI 2014/3190 Reg.6
Reg.27, amended: SI 2014/1816 Reg.2
Reg.28, amended: SI 2014/1816 Reg.2
Reg.28A, amended: SI 2014/1816 Reg.2
Reg.30, substituted: SI 2014/1816 Reg.2
Reg.31, amended: SI 2014/480 Reg.6
Reg.32, amended: SI 2014/480 Reg.6
Reg.33, amended: SI 2014/480 Reg.6
Reg.34, amended: SI 2014/480 Reg.6
Reg.35, amended: SI 2014/480 Reg.6
Reg.36, amended: SI 2014/480 Reg.6
Reg.37, amended: SI 2014/613 Reg.5
Reg.38, amended: SI 2014/3190 Reg.7
Reg.45, amended: SI 2014/613 Reg.6, SI
2014/3190 Reg.8
Reg.72, amended: SI 2014/613 Reg.7
Sch.2 Part 1, amended: SI 2014/613 Reg.8
Sch.3 Part 1, amended: SI 2014/2580 Reg.2
Sch.7 Part 3 paraE, amended: SI 2014/613
Reg.9
Sch.7 Part 4 paraE, amended: SI 2014/613
Reg.9
Sch.8 Part 3, amended: SI 2014/613 Reg.10
Sch.8 Part 3 paraH, added: SI 2014/613
Reg.10
Sch.8 Part 4, amended: SI 2014/613 Reg.10
Sch.8 Part 4 paraH, added: SI 2014/613
Reg.10
Sch.9, amended: SI 2014/613 Sch.1, SI
2014/3190 Reg.9, Sch.1

2892. Nuclear Reactors (Environmental Impact Assessment for Decommissioning) Regulations 1999

Reg.2, amended: SI 2014/469 Sch.3 para.96
Reg.4, amended: SI 2014/469 Sch.3 para.95
Reg.5, amended: SI 2014/469 Sch.3 para.95
Reg.6, amended: SI 2014/469 Sch.3 para.95
Reg.7, amended: SI 2014/469 Sch.3 para.95
Reg.8, amended: SI 2014/469 Sch.3 para.95
Reg.9, amended: SI 2014/469 Sch.3 para.95
Reg.10, amended: SI 2014/469 Sch.3 para.95
Reg.11, amended: SI 2014/469 Sch.3 para.95
Reg.12, amended: SI 2014/469 Sch.3 para.95
Reg.13, amended: SI 2014/469 Sch.3 para.95
Reg.15, amended: SI 2014/469 Sch.3 para.95
Reg.16, amended: SI 2014/469 Sch.3 para.97

2932. Rail Vehicle Accessibility (Serco Metrolink T68A Vehicles) Exemption Order 1999

revoked: SI 2014/3244 Sch.2

2979. Financial Markets and Insolvency (Settlement Finality) Regulations 1999

Reg.2, amended: SI 2014/3348 Sch.3 para.7
Reg.25, amended: SI 2014/2947 Sch.4 para.5

3026. Gas Act 1986 (Exemptions) (No.4) (Amendment) Order 1999

revoked: SI 2014/528 Sch.1

3089. Gas Act 1986 (Exemptions) (No.2) Order 1999

revoked: SI 2014/528 Sch.1

3107. Motor Fuel (Composition and Content) Regulations 1999

Reg.5A, amended: SI 2014/3076 Reg.3

3147. Welfare Reform and Pensions (Northern Ireland) Order 1999

Art.26, applied: SI 2014/3138 Reg.4
Art.26, referred to: 2014 c.26 Sch.6 para.1

3185. General Teaching Council for Wales (Constitution) (Amendment) Regulations 1999

revoked: SI 2014/2365 Sch.1

3186. Distress for Rent (Amendment) (No.3) Rules 1999

revoked: SI 2014/600 Sch.1 Part 2

3187. Civil Courts (Amendment) (No.3) Order 1999

revoked: SI 2014/820 Sch.1

3232. Ionising Radiations Regulations 1999

Reg.2, amended: SI 2014/469 Sch.3 para.99
Reg.4, amended: SI 2014/3248 Sch.5 para.10
Reg.5, amended: SI 2014/469 Sch.3 para.101
Reg.6, amended: SI 2014/469 Sch.3 para.102
Reg.21, amended: SI 2014/469 Sch.3 para.100
Reg.22, amended: SI 2014/469 Sch.3 para.103
Reg.25, amended: SI 2014/469 Sch.3 para.104
Reg.32, amended: SI 2014/469 Sch.3 para.100
Reg.36, amended: SI 2014/469 Sch.3 para.100
Reg.37, amended: SI 2014/469 Sch.3 para.100
Reg.39, amended: SI 2014/469 Sch.3 para.100
Reg.40, amended: SI 2014/469 Sch.3 para.100
Reg.41, amended: SI 2014/469 Sch.3 para.100
Sch.3, amended: SI 2014/469 Sch.3 para.100
Sch.4 Part II para.13, amended: SI 2014/469 Sch.3 para.100
Sch.4 Part II para.14, amended: SI 2014/469 Sch.3 para.100
Sch.4 Part II para.18, amended: SI 2014/469 Sch.3 para.100
Sch.4 Part II para.19, amended: SI 2014/469 Sch.3 para.100
Sch.4 Part II para.20, amended: SI 2014/469 Sch.3 para.100
Sch.4 Part II para.22, amended: SI 2014/469 Sch.3 para.100
Sch.8 Part I, amended: SI 2014/469 Sch.3 para.100

3242. Management of Health and Safety at Work Regulations 1999

see *Kennedy v Cordia (Services) LLP* [2014] CSIH 76, 2014 S.L.T. 984 (IH (Ex Div)), Lady Smith
Reg.3, applied: SI 2014/1638 Sch.11 para.3, SI 2014/3248 Reg.9, Reg.54, Reg.57

Reg.3, see *Kennedy v Cordia (Services) LLP*
[2014] CSIH 76, 2014 S.L.T. 984 (IH (Ex
Div)), Lady Smith

**3263. Distraint by Collectors (Fees, Costs and
Charges) (Stamp Duty Penalties) Regulations
1999**

revoked (in part): SI 2014/600 Sch.1 Part 2

**3312. Maternity and Parental Leave etc
Regulations 1999**

Reg.13, revoked (in part): SI 2014/3221
Reg.3
Reg.15, substituted: SI 2014/3221 Reg.4
Reg.18, amended: SI 2014/3221 Reg.5
Sch.2 para.2, amended: SI 2014/3221 Reg.6
Sch.2 para.2, revoked (in part): SI
2014/3221 Reg.6

**3323. Transnational Information and
Consultation of Employees Regulations 1999**

Reg.27, amended: SI 2014/386 Sch.1 para.7
Reg.27A, added: SI 2014/386 Sch.1 para.8
Reg.41, amended: SI 2014/386 Sch.1 para.9,
SI 2014/431 Sch.1 para.20

2000

**10. Children (Performances) Amendment
Regulations 2000**

revoked: SI 2014/3309 Sch.1

128. Pressure Systems Safety Regulations 2000

Reg.2, amended: SI 2014/3248 Sch.5
para.13

**212. National Health Service Trusts (Trust
Funds Appointment of Trustees) Order 2000**

Art.1, amended: SI 2014/1905 Art.2
Art.3, amended: SI 2014/1905 Art.2
Art.4, revoked: SI 2014/1905 Art.2
Sch.1, amended: SI 2014/1905 Art.2

**290. Consumer Credit (Credit Reference
Agency) Regulations 2000**

Sch.2, amended: SI 2014/366 Art.7

**309. Competition Act 1998 (Determination of
Turnover for Penalties) Order 2000**

Art.3, amended: SI 2014/549 Sch.1 para.2

**413. Data Protection (Subject Access
Modification) (Health) Order 2000**

Art.4, amended: SI 2014/2747 Art.2, Art.3

**414. Data Protection (Subject Access
Modification) (Education) Order 2000**

Art.4, amended: SI 2014/2747 Art.4

**415. Data Protection (Subject Access
Modification) (Social Work) Order 2000**

Sch.1 para.2, amended: SI 2014/2747 Art.5

**419. Data Protection (Miscellaneous Subject
Access Exemptions) Order 2000**

Sch.1 Part III, amended: SI 2014/2747 Art.6

**432. Greater London Authority
(Disqualification) Order 2000**

Sch.1 Part I para.7A, added: SI 2014/469
Sch.3 para.191
Sch.1 Part II para.20A, added: SI 2014/469
Sch.3 para.191

**619. National Health Service Pension Scheme
(Additional Voluntary Contributions)
Regulations 2000**

Reg.2, amended: SI 2014/78 Reg.18
Reg.2A, added: SI 2014/78 Reg.19
Reg.15, amended: SI 2014/78 Reg.20

**620. National Health Service (Charges for Drugs
and Appliances) Regulations 2000**

Reg.3, amended: SI 2014/545 Reg.2
Reg.4, amended: SI 2014/545 Reg.2
Reg.4A, amended: SI 2014/545 Reg.2
Reg.5, amended: SI 2014/545 Reg.2
Reg.6, amended: SI 2014/545 Reg.2
Reg.6A, amended: SI 2014/545 Reg.2
Reg.6B, amended: SI 2014/545 Reg.2
Sch.1, amended: SI 2014/545 Reg.2
Sch.1, referred to: SI 2014/545 Reg.3

**656. Food Standards Act 1999 (Transitional and
Consequential Provisions and Savings) (England
and Wales) Regulations 2000**

Reg.10, revoked (in part): SI 2014/951
Reg.46, SI 2014/1240 Reg.47
Sch.8 Part III, revoked (in part): SI 2014/951
Reg.46, SI 2014/1240 Reg.47

672. Pensions Increase (Review) Order 2000

referred to: SI 2014/668 Sch.1
Art.6, substituted: SI 2014/107 Sch.1
para.56, SI 2014/3229 Sch.6 para.35

**688. Social Security (Maternity Allowance)
(Earnings) Regulations 2000**

Reg.2, amended: SI 2014/3255 Art.8

**727. Social Security Contributions
(Intermediaries) Regulations 2000**

Reg.7, amended: SI 2014/3159 Reg.6

**728. Social Security Contributions
(Intermediaries) (Northern Ireland) Regulations
2000**

Reg.7, amended: SI 2014/3159 Reg.7

729. Social Fund Winter Fuel Payment Regulations 2000
> Reg.1, amended: SI 2014/107 Sch.1 para.28, SI 2014/3229 Sch.6 para.19
> Reg.2, amended: SI 2014/3270 Reg.2
> Sch.1, added: SI 2014/3270 Reg.2

824. Community Legal Service (Cost Protection) Regulations 2000
> see *Murphy v Rayner* [2013] EWHC 3878 (Ch), [2014] 1 W.L.R. 677 (Ch D), Nicholas Strauss QC
> Reg.5, amended: SI 2014/879 Art.78
> Reg.5, see *Murphy v Rayner* [2013] EWHC 3878 (Ch), [2014] 1 W.L.R. 677 (Ch D), Nicholas Strauss QC

1038. General Osteopathic Council (Application for Registration and Fees) Rules Order of Council 2000
> Sch.1, amended: SI 2014/598 Sch.1

1054. Pension Sharing (Pension Credit Benefit) Regulations 2000
> Reg.7, applied: SI 2014/1964 Reg.92, Reg.96, SI 2014/2336 Reg.49

1059. Ionising Radiation (Medical Exposure) Regulations 2000
> Reg.2, amended: 2014 c.23 Sch.8 para.1
> Reg.2, revoked (in part): 2014 c.23 Sch.8 para.1

1106. United Nations (Sanctions) (Amendment) Order 2000
> revoked: SI 2014/2711 Sch.1

1111. Airports Act 1986 (Jersey) Order 2000
> applied: SI 2014/2713

1481. Distress for Rent (Amendment) Rules 2000
> revoked: SI 2014/600 Sch.1 Part 2

1482. Civil Courts (Amendment) Order 2000
> revoked: SI 2014/820 Sch.1

1551. Part-time Workers (Prevention of Less Favourable Treatment) Regulations 2000
> see *Ministry of Justice v O'Brien* [2014] I.C.R. 773 (EAT), Sir David Keene
> Reg.8, amended: SI 2014/386 Sch.1 para.11
> Reg.8A, added: SI 2014/386 Sch.1 para.12

1556. Eritrea and Ethiopia (United Nations Sanctions) Order 2000
> revoked: SI 2014/2711 Sch.1

1625. Town and Country Planning Appeals (Determination by Inspectors) (Inquiries Procedure) (England) Rules 2000
> r.7, see *Hopkins Development Ltd v Secretary of State for Communities and Local Government* [2014] EWCA Civ 470, [2014] P.T.S.R. 1145 (CA (Civ Div)), Jackson LJ
> r.16, see *Hopkins Development Ltd v Secretary of State for Communities and Local Government* [2014] EWCA Civ 470, [2014] P.T.S.R. 1145 (CA (Civ Div)), Jackson LJ

1626. Town and Country Planning (Hearings Procedure) (England) Rules 2000
> see *San Vicente v Secretary of State for Communities and Local Government* [2013] EWCA Civ 817, [2014] 1 W.L.R. 966 (CA (Civ Div)), Lloyd LJ; see *San Vicente v Secretary of State for Communities and Local Government* [2013] EWHC 2713 (Admin), [2014] J.P.L. 217 (QBD (Admin)), Collins J

1631. A477 Trunk Road (Llanddowror, Carmarthenshire) (Restricted Roads 40 mph Speed Limit) Order 2000
> varied: SI 2014/1058 Art.6

1786. Disabled Persons (Badges for Motor Vehicles) (Wales) Regulations 2000
> Part III, amended: SI 2014/3082 Reg.2
> Reg.2, amended: SI 2014/3082 Reg.2
> Reg.4, amended: SI 2014/3082 Reg.2
> Reg.8, amended: SI 2014/3082 Reg.2
> Reg.9, amended: SI 2014/3082 Reg.2
> Reg.11, revoked: SI 2014/3082 Reg.2
> Sch.1, revoked: SI 2014/3082 Reg.2

1820. Eritrea and Ethiopia (United Nations Sanctions) (Amendment) Order 2000
> revoked: SI 2014/2711 Sch.1

1866. Medical Food (Wales) Regulations 2000
> Reg.3, amended: SI 2014/1102 Reg.2

1926. Social Security (Work-focused Interviews for Lone Parents) and Miscellaneous Amendments Regulations 2000
> Reg.2C, amended: SI 2014/1097 Reg.13
> Reg.2ZA, amended: SI 2014/1097 Reg.13
> Reg.2ZA, revoked (in part): SI 2014/1097 Reg.13
> Reg.4, amended: SI 2014/1097 Reg.13
> Reg.4, revoked (in part): SI 2014/1097 Reg.13
> Reg.6, amended: SI 2014/1097 Reg.13
> Reg.7, amended: SI 2014/1097 Reg.13
> Reg.7, applied: SI 2014/1097 Reg.8
> Reg.8, amended: SI 2014/1097 Reg.13
> Reg.8, applied: SI 2014/1097 Reg.8

2047. Faculty Jurisdiction Rules 2000
referred to: SI 2014/2072 Sch.1 Part TABLE
2048. Faculty Jurisdiction (Care of Places of Worship) Rules 2000
applied: SI 2014/2072 Sch.1 Part TABLE
2088. Supply of New Cars Order 2000
amended: SI 2014/549 Sch.1 para.3
Art.1, amended: SI 2014/549 Sch.1 para.3
Art.4, amended: SI 2014/549 Sch.1 para.3
Art.14, amended: SI 2014/549 Sch.1 para.3
2110. Foreign Package Holidays (Tour Operators and Travel Agents) Order 2000
Art.7, amended: SI 2014/549 Sch.1 para.4
2121. Education (National Curriculum) (Temporary Exceptions for Individual Pupils) (England) Regulations 2000
Reg.1, amended: SI 2014/2103 Art.7
Reg.3, amended: SI 2014/2103 Art.7
Reg.4, amended: SI 2014/2103 Art.7
Reg.10, amended: SI 2014/2103 Art.7
2129. Tonnage Tax (Training Requirement) Regulations 2000
applied: SI 2014/2394 Reg.2
Reg.15, amended: SI 2014/2394 Reg.3
Reg.21, amended: SI 2014/2394 Reg.3
2254. Food Irradiation Provisions (England) Regulations 2000
revoked: SI 2014/1855 Sch.6 Part 1
2334. Consumer Protection (Distance Selling) Regulations 2000
Reg.3, amended: SI 2014/549 Sch.1 para.28
Reg.26, amended: SI 2014/549 Sch.1 para.28
Reg.26A, amended: SI 2014/549 Sch.1 para.28
Reg.27, amended: SI 2014/549 Sch.1 para.28
Reg.28, amended: SI 2014/549 Sch.1 para.28
Reg.29, amended: SI 2014/549 Sch.1 para.28
2384. Children (Performances) (Amendment) (No.2) Regulations 2000
revoked: SI 2014/3309 Sch.1
2664. Trunk Road (Llandybie, Dyfed) (Speed Limits) Order 1978 (Variation) Order 2000
revoked: SI 2014/2893 Art.4
2724. Immigration (Designation of Travel Bans) Order 2000
Sch.1, substituted: SI 2014/1849 Sch.1

2737. Distress for Rent (Amendment No 2) Rules 2000
revoked: SI 2014/600 Sch.1 Part 2
2738. Civil Courts (Amendment No 2) Order 2000
revoked: SI 2014/820 Sch.1
2792. Fixed Penalty Order 2000
Sch.1, amended: SI 2014/259 Art.2
2831. Genetically Modified Organisms (Contained Use) Regulations 2000
applied: SI 2014/1663 Reg.33
revoked: SI 2014/1663 Reg.35
Reg.8, applied: SI 2014/1663 Reg.33
Reg.9, applied: SI 2014/1663 Reg.33
Reg.11, applied: SI 2014/1663 Reg.33
Reg.14, applied: SI 2014/1663 Reg.33
Reg.15, applied: SI 2014/1663 Reg.33
Reg.18, applied: SI 2014/1663 Reg.33
2853. Local Authorities (Functions and Responsibilities) (England) Regulations 2000
Sch.4, see *R. (on the application of Buck) v Doncaster MBC* [2013] EWCA Civ 1190, [2014] P.T.S.R. 111 (CA (Civ Div)), Master of the Rolls
3027. School Government (Terms of Reference)(Wales) Regulations 2000
referred to: SI 2014/2677 Reg.3
Reg.7, applied: SI 2014/1132 Reg.62
3042. Energy Crops Regulations 2000
revoked: SI 2014/3263 Sch.5
3043. Rural Enterprise Regulations 2000
revoked: SI 2014/3263 Sch.5
3044. England Rural Development Programme (Enforcement) Regulations 2000
applied: SI 2014/3263 Reg.35
revoked: SI 2014/3263 Sch.5
Reg.2, applied: SI 2014/3263 Reg.35
3045. Vocational Training Grants (Agriculture and Forestry) Regulations 2000
revoked: SI 2014/3263 Sch.5
3046. Agricultural Processing and Marketing Grants Regulations 2000
revoked: SI 2014/3263 Sch.5
3089. Town and Country Planning (Costs of Inquiries etc.) (Standard Daily Amount) (England) Regulations 2000
revoked: SI 2014/692 Sch.1
3164. Reporting of Suspicious Marriages and Registration of Marriages (Miscellaneous Amendments) Regulations 2000
Reg.1, amended: SI 2014/1660 Reg.2

Reg.2, amended: SI 2014/1660 Reg.2

3206. Gas Act 1986 (Exemptions) (No.4) (Amendment) Order 2000

revoked: SI 2014/528 Sch.1

3278. Magistrates Courts Warrants (Specification of Provisions) Order 2000

Art.2, revoked (in part): SI 2014/879 Art.79

3323. Coffee Extracts and Chicory Extracts (England) Regulations 2000

Reg.2, amended: SI 2014/1855 Sch.7 para.22

Reg.5, amended: SI 2014/1855 Sch.7 para.23

Reg.6, revoked: SI 2014/1855 Sch.6 Part 1

Reg.11, revoked (in part): SI 2014/1855 Sch.6 Part 1

3352. Welfare of Animals (Slaughter or Killing) (Amendment) (England) Regulations 2000

revoked: SI 2014/1240 Reg.47

3371. Young Offender Institution Rules 2000

Part I r.2, amended: SI 2014/2169 r.3

Part II r.4, amended: SI 2014/2169 r.3

Part II r.5, amended: SI 2014/2169 r.3

Part II r.60A, amended: SI 2014/2169 r.3

Part II r.65, amended: SI 2014/2169 r.3

2001

155. Child Support (Maintenance Calculations and Special Cases) Regulations 2001

Reg.1, amended: SI 2014/107 Sch.1 para.29, SI 2014/3229 Sch.6 para.20

Reg.4, amended: SI 2014/884 Reg.3

Reg.5, applied: SI 2014/614 Reg.4

Reg.13, amended: SI 2014/1386 Reg.5

Sch.Part II para.4, amended: SI 2014/3255 Art.9

218. Strategic Rail Authority (Licence Exemption) Order 2001

revoked: SI 2014/3244 Sch.2

238. Detention Centre Rules 2001

r.34, see *R. (on the application of DK) v Secretary of State for the Home Department* [2014] EWHC 3257 (Admin), [2014] Med. L.R. 510 (QBD (Admin)), Haddon-Cave J

319. Competition Act 1998 (Public Transport Ticketing Schemes Block Exemption) Order 2001

Art.3, amended: SI 2014/549 Sch.1 para.5

Art.17, amended: SI 2014/549 Sch.1 para.5

Art.18, amended: SI 2014/549 Sch.1 para.5

Art.19, amended: SI 2014/549 Sch.1 para.5

Art.20, amended: SI 2014/549 Sch.1 para.5

Art.21, amended: SI 2014/549 Sch.1 para.5

341. Representation of the People (England and Wales) Regulations 2001

Reg.15, amended: SI 2014/3161 Reg.3

Reg.16, substituted: SI 2014/3161 Reg.4

Reg.25, amended: SI 2014/3161 Reg.5

Reg.32, amended: SI 2014/3161 Reg.6

Reg.35, amended: SI 2014/1234 Reg.2

Reg.35A, added: SI 2014/1234 Reg.3

Reg.45G, applied: SI 2014/1805 Reg.2, SI 2014/1806 Reg.2

Reg.45H, revoked: SI 2014/1805 Reg.3

Reg.102, applied: SI 2014/2764 Reg.2

431. England Rural Development Programme (Enforcement) (Amendment) Regulations 2001

applied: SI 2014/3263 Reg.35

revoked: SI 2014/3263 Sch.5

497. Representation of the People (Scotland) Regulations 2001

Reg.15, amended: SI 2014/3124 Reg.3

Reg.16, substituted: SI 2014/3124 Reg.4

Reg.25, amended: SI 2014/3124 Reg.5

Reg.32, amended: SI 2014/3124 Reg.6

Reg.35A, added: SI 2014/3124 Reg.7

Reg.45F, applied: SI 2014/1805 Reg.2, SI 2014/1806 Reg.2

Reg.45G, revoked: SI 2014/1805 Reg.3

Reg.101, applied: SI 2014/2764 Reg.2

544. Financial Services and Markets Act 2000 (Regulated Activities) Order 2001

Part II, applied: SI 2014/1850 Art.12

Art.3, amended: SI 2014/366 Art.2, SI 2014/1850 Art.3

Art.4, amended: SI 2014/1292 Art.6

Art.4, referred to: SI 2014/1292 Art.7

Art.9AC, added: SI 2014/366 Art.2

Art.14, referred to: SI 2014/2080 Art.2, Art.4, Art.8

Art.15, applied: SI 2014/2080 Art.4

Art.19, applied: SI 2014/2080 Art.4

Art.20, amended: SI 2014/366 Art.2

Art.21, referred to: SI 2014/2080 Art.2

Art.24, amended: SI 2014/366 Art.2

Art.36, amended: SI 2014/366 Art.2

Art.36A, amended: SI 2014/1448 Art.2

Art.36G, amended: SI 2014/366 Art.2

Art.36G, substituted: SI 2014/366 Art.2

Art.36H, amended: SI 2014/366 Art.2

Art.36IA, added: SI 2014/366 Art.2

Art.39, amended: SI 2014/366 Art.2

Art.39C, amended: SI 2014/366 Art.2

Art.39F, referred to: SI 2014/334 Art.2

Art.39H, amended: SI 2014/366 Art.2

Art.39I, amended: SI 2014/1850 Art.4

Art.39I, revoked (in part): SI 2014/1850 Art.4

Art.39J, amended: SI 2014/366 Art.2

Art.39L, amended: SI 2014/366 Art.2

Art.39L, substituted: SI 2014/366 Art.2

Art.44, amended: SI 2014/366 Art.2

Art.50, amended: SI 2014/366 Art.2

Art.51A, amended: SI 2014/366 Art.2

Art.51A, substituted: SI 2014/366 Art.2

Art.51ZA, referred to: SI 2014/1292 Art.7

Art.51ZC, referred to: SI 2014/1292 Art.7

Art.52A, amended: SI 2014/366 Art.2

Art.52A, substituted: SI 2014/366 Art.2

Art.55, amended: SI 2014/366 Art.2

Art.60B, amended: SI 2014/1850 Art.5

Art.60B, referred to: SI 2014/334 Art.2

Art.60C, amended: SI 2014/366 Art.2, SI 2014/1850 Art.6

Art.60D, amended: SI 2014/366 Art.2

Art.60E, amended: SI 2014/366 Art.2, SI 2014/1740 Art.2

Art.60F, amended: SI 2014/366 Art.2, SI 2014/1850 Art.7

Art.60G, amended: SI 2014/366 Art.2

Art.60JA, added: SI 2014/366 Art.2

Art.60K, amended: SI 2014/366 Art.2

Art.60K, substituted: SI 2014/366 Art.2

Art.60L, amended: SI 2014/366 Art.2, SI 2014/1850 Art.8

Art.60LA, added: SI 2014/366 Art.2

Art.60LA, amended: SI 2014/1850 Art.9

Art.60LB, added: SI 2014/1850 Art.10

Art.60N, amended: SI 2014/366 Art.2

Art.60R, amended: SI 2014/366 Art.2

Art.60R, substituted: SI 2014/366 Art.2

Art.63A, amended: SI 2014/366 Art.2

Art.63E, amended: SI 2014/366 Art.2

Art.63I, amended: SI 2014/366 Art.2

Art.63M, amended: SI 2014/366 Art.2

Art.65, amended: SI 2014/366 Art.2

Art.72G, added: SI 2014/366 Art.2

Art.76, amended: SI 2014/1815 Sch.1 para.8

Art.77, applied: SI 2014/3350 Art.4

Art.89D, substituted: SI 2014/366 Art.2

Art.89E, amended: SI 2014/366 Art.2

s.art II Art.60S, added: SI 2014/366 Art.2

Sch.4A, added: SI 2014/1850 Art.11

664. Pensions Increase (Review) Order 2001

referred to: SI 2014/668 Sch.1

Art.6, substituted: SI 2014/107 Sch.1

para.56, SI 2014/3229 Sch.6 para.35

776. Magistrates Courts (Blood Tests) (Amendment) Rules 2001

revoked: SI 2014/879 Sch.1

838. Climate Change Levy (General) Regulations 2001

Part II, amended: 2014 c.26 Sch.20 para.8

Part III, amended: 2014 c.26 Sch.20 para.8

Reg.2, amended: 2014 c.26 Sch.20 para.8

Reg.8, amended: 2014 c.26 Sch.20 para.8

Reg.11, amended: 2014 c.26 Sch.20 para.8

Reg.11, revoked (in part): 2014 c.26 Sch.20 para.8

Reg.12, amended: 2014 c.26 Sch.20 para.8

Reg.33, amended: 2014 c.26 Sch.20 para.8

Reg.34, amended: 2014 c.26 Sch.20 para.8

Reg.35, amended: 2014 c.26 Sch.20 para.8

Reg.35, revoked (in part): 2014 c.26 Sch.20 para.8

Sch.1, amended: 2014 c.26 Sch.20 para.8

Sch.1 para.2, amended: 2014 c.26 Sch.20 para.8

Sch.1 para.3, amended: 2014 c.26 Sch.20 para.8

Sch.1 para.5, amended: 2014 c.26 Sch.20 para.8

Sch.1 para.6, amended: 2014 c.26 Sch.20 para.8

Sch.1 para.6, revoked (in part): 2014 c.26 Sch.20 para.8

853. Transport Act 2000 (Civil Aviation Authority Pension Scheme) Order 2001

disapplied: SI 2014/3229 Sch.2 para.6

961. European Communities (Designation) Order 2001

Sch., amended: SI 2014/1362 Sch.1

1002. Housing Benefit and Council Tax Benefit (Decisions and Appeals) Regulations 2001

Reg.1, amended: SI 2014/107 Sch.1 para.30, SI 2014/3229 Sch.6 para.21

Reg.7, amended: SI 2014/213 Reg.2

Reg.8, amended: SI 2014/213 Reg.2

1004. Social Security (Contributions) Regulations 2001

applied: SI 2014/2929 Reg.4, SI 2014/3051 Reg.33

Reg.9, varied: 2014 c.6 s.126
Reg.10, amended: SI 2014/569 Reg.3
Reg.11, amended: SI 2014/569 Reg.4
Reg.14, applied: SI 2014/3051 Reg.39
Reg.15, applied: SI 2014/3051 Reg.39
Reg.25, applied: SI 2014/3051 Reg.32
Reg.27, applied: SI 2014/3051 Reg.32
Reg.40A, added: SI 2014/3159 Reg.5
Reg.44, applied: SI 2014/3050 Reg.36, SI 2014/3051 Reg.29
Reg.56A, added: SI 2014/2746 Reg.4
Reg.67A, substituted: SI 2014/608 Reg.3
Reg.94B, added: SI 2014/3196 Reg.2
Reg.114, amended: SI 2014/572 Reg.2
Reg.114A, added: SI 2014/572 Reg.2
Reg.125, amended: SI 2014/634 Reg.2
Reg.145, applied: SI 2014/3051 Reg.33
Reg.146, applied: SI 2014/3134 Reg.6
Sch.3, applied: SI 2014/3051 Reg.32
Sch.3 Part V para.5, amended: SI 2014/3228 Reg.3
Sch.3 Part VIII para.3A, added: SI 2014/608 Reg.4
Sch.3 Part VIII para.14A, added: SI 2014/3228 Reg.4
Sch.3 Part X para.25, added: SI 2014/3159 Reg.5
Sch.4A, varied: 2014 c.6 s.126
Sch.4 Part I para.1, amended: SI 2014/608 Reg.6, SI 2014/2397 Reg.3
Sch.4 Part II para.7, varied: 2014 c.6 s.126
Sch.4 Part II para.9, varied: 2014 c.6 s.126
Sch.4 Part III para.10, amended: SI 2014/1016 Reg.2
Sch.4 Part III para.11, amended: SI 2014/1016 Reg.2, SI 2014/2397 Reg.3
Sch.4 Part III para.11, varied: 2014 c.6 s.126
Sch.4 Part III para.11ZA, amended: SI 2014/1016 Reg.2
Sch.4 Part III para.17, revoked (in part): SI 2014/992 Art.10
Sch.4 Part III para.17A, amended: SI 2014/992 Art.10
Sch.4 Part III para.18, amended: SI 2014/992 Art.10
Sch.4 Part III para.18, revoked (in part): SI 2014/992 Art.10
Sch.4 Part III para.20, amended: SI 2014/992 Art.10
Sch.4 Part III para.21A, amended: SI 2014/608 Reg.7

Sch.4 Part III para.21D, amended: SI 2014/608 Reg.8
Sch.4 Part III para.21E, amended: SI 2014/608 Reg.9
Sch.4 Part III para.21EA, amended: SI 2014/2397 Reg.3
Sch.4 Part III para.21G, added: SI 2014/2397 Reg.3
Sch.4 Part III para.22, revoked (in part): SI 2014/2397 Reg.3
Sch.4 Part III para.22, varied: 2014 c.6 s.126
Sch.4 Part III para.25, revoked: SI 2014/2397 Reg.3
Sch.4 Part III para.26, amended: 2014 c.7 s.7
Sch.4 Part IV para.31, amended: SI 2014/608 Reg.10
Sch.4A para.13, revoked: SI 2014/2397 Reg.3
Sch.4A para.15, varied: 2014 c.6 s.126
Sch.4B para.3, varied: 2014 c.6 s.126
Sch.4B para.6, revoked: SI 2014/2397 Reg.3
Sch.7 Part II, amended: SI 2014/2397 Reg.3

1062. Financial Services and Markets Act 2000 (Collective Investment Schemes) Order 2001
Sch.para.21, amended: SI 2014/1815 Sch.1 para.9

1077. Community Legal Service (Funding) (Counsel in Family Proceedings) Order 2001
Art.2, amended: SI 2014/2864 Art.2
Art.2C, amended: SI 2014/2864 Art.2
Art.4, amended: SI 2014/2864 Art.2
Art.5, amended: SI 2014/2864 Art.2
Art.8, amended: SI 2014/2864 Art.2
Art.15, amended: SI 2014/2864 Art.2

1085. Social Security (Inherited SERPS) Regulations 2001
Reg.1, amended: SI 2014/3213 Art.5

1177. Financial Services and Markets Act 2000 (Carrying on Regulated Activities by Way of Business) Order 2001
Art.6, amended: SI 2014/3340 Art.2

1184. European Parliamentary Elections (Franchise of Relevant Citizens of the Union) Regulations 2001
Reg.4, amended: SI 2014/1803 Reg.3
Reg.4, revoked (in part): 2014 c.13 s.14
Reg.5, amended: SI 2014/1803 Reg.4
Reg.6, amended: SI 2014/1803 Reg.5
Reg.6, revoked (in part): 2014 c.13 s.14
Reg.8, amended: SI 2014/1803 Reg.6
Reg.10, amended: SI 2014/1803 Reg.7

Sch., amended: SI 2014/1803 Reg.8

1201. Financial Services and Markets Act 2000 (Exemption) Order 2001

Sch.Part II para.19, revoked: SI 2014/366 Art.8

Sch.Part III para.39, revoked: SI 2014/366 Art.8

Sch.Part IV para.44, amended: SI 2014/506 Art.2

Sch.Part IV para.47, revoked: SI 2014/366 Art.8

Sch.Part IV para.52, amended: SI 2014/366 Art.8

Sch.Part IV para.52, revoked (in part): SI 2014/366 Art.8

Sch.Part IV para.55, added: SI 2014/506 Art.2

1217. Financial Services and Markets Act 2000 (Appointed Representatives) Regulations 2001

Reg.2, amended: SI 2014/206 Reg.2

Reg.3, amended: SI 2014/206 Reg.2, SI 2014/366 Art.9

Reg.5, added: SI 2014/206 Reg.2

1228. Open-Ended Investment Companies Regulations 2001

Reg.13, amended: SI 2014/107 Sch.1 para.31, SI 2014/3229 Sch.6 para.22

1232. Food Irradiation Provisions (Wales) Regulations 2001

revoked: SI 2014/2303 Sch.6 Part 1

1294. Northern Ireland Act 1998 (Designation of Public Authorities) Order 2001

Sch.1, amended: SI 2014/1924 Sch.1

1296. Justices and Justices Clerks (Costs) Regulations 2001

Reg.2, amended: SI 2014/879 Art.80

1323. Additional Pension and Social Security Pensions (Home Responsibilities) (Amendment) Regulations 2001

Reg.5A, amended: SI 2014/591 Reg.6

Reg.5C, added: SI 2014/591 Reg.6

1330. Barnet, Enfield and Haringey Mental Health National Health Service Trust (Establishment) Order 2001

Art.4, amended: SI 2014/1903 Art.2

1420. Financial Services and Markets Act 2000 (Service of Notices) Regulations 2001

Reg.1, amended: SI 2014/549 Sch.1 para.29

1440. Coffee Extracts and Chicory Extracts (Wales) Regulations 2001

Reg.2, amended: SI 2014/2303 Sch.7 para.22

Reg.5, amended: SI 2014/2303 Sch.7 para.23

Reg.6, revoked: SI 2014/2303 Sch.6 Part 1

Reg.11, revoked (in part): SI 2014/2303 Sch.6 Part 1

1633. A55 Trunk Road (Holyhead, Anglesey) (50 mph Speed Limit &amp Prohibition of Pedestrians) Order 2001

Art.3, varied: SI 2014/2649 Art.7

1712. Tobacco Products Regulations 2001

see *R. v Mackle (Plunkett Jude)* [2014] UKSC 5, [2014] A.C. 678 (SC), Lord Neuberger JSC

Reg.13, see *R. v Tatham (Philip)* [2014] EWCA Crim 226, [2014] Lloyd's Rep. F.C. 354 (CA (Crim Div)), Sir Brian Leveson PQBD

1744. General Social Care Council (Appointments and Procedure) Regulations 2001

Reg.10, amended: SI 2014/1815 Sch.1 para.10

1768. Railways (Closure Provisions) (Exemptions) (St Pancras) Order 2001

revoked: SI 2014/3244 Sch.2

2188. Financial Services and Markets Act 2000 (Disclosure of Confidential Information) Regulations 2001

applied: SI 2014/3085 Reg.13

Reg.2, amended: SI 2014/3348 Sch.3 para.8

Reg.8, amended: SI 2014/3348 Sch.3 para.8

Reg.9, amended: SI 2014/3348 Sch.3 para.8

Reg.10A, added: SI 2014/3348 Sch.3 para.8

Reg.11, amended: SI 2014/3348 Sch.3 para.8

Sch.1 Part 1, amended: SI 2014/549 Sch.1 para.30, SI 2014/883 Reg.2, SI 2014/2879 Reg.7, SI 2014/3348 Sch.3 para.8

Sch.1 Part 2, amended: SI 2014/3348 Sch.3 para.8

Sch.1 Part 3, amended: SI 2014/3348 Sch.3 para.8

Sch.2, amended: SI 2014/549 Sch.1 para.30, SI 2014/883 Reg.2

Sch.3, amended: SI 2014/549 Sch.1 para.30

Sch.3, revoked (in part): SI 2014/549 Sch.1 para.30

**2283. Standards Committees (Wales)
Regulations 2001**
  Reg.2, amended: SI 2014/3061 Sch.1 para.8
**2340. Discretionary Housing Payments (Grants)
Order 2001**
  Art.3, amended: SI 2014/1667 Art.2
  Art.7, amended: SI 2014/1667 Art.2
  Art.7, revoked (in part): SSI 2014/298 Art.2
**2501. Inspection of Education and Training
(Wales) Regulations 2001**
  Reg.2, amended: SI 2014/1212 Reg.3
  Reg.4, amended: SI 2014/1212 Reg.3
**2541. Capital Allowances (Energy-saving Plant
and Machinery) Order 2001**
  Art.2, amended: SI 2014/1868 Art.3
  Art.3, amended: SI 2014/1868 Art.4
**2564. Life Sentences (Northern Ireland) Order
2001**
  Art.3, see *Corey's Application for Judicial
  Review, Re* [2014] A.C. 516 (SC), Lord
  Mance JSC
  Art.6, see *Corey's Application for Judicial
  Review, Re* [2014] A.C. 516 (SC), Lord
  Mance JSC
  Art.9, see *Corey's Application for Judicial
  Review, Re* [2014] A.C. 516 (SC), Lord
  Mance JSC
**2599. Northern Ireland Assembly (Elections)
Order 2001**
  Art.6, amended: 2014 c.13 s.5
  Art.6B, amended: 2014 c.13 s.5
  Sch.1, amended: 2014 c.13 s.5, SI
  2014/1116 Art.12, SI 2014/1804 Art.2
  Sch.2, amended: SI 2014/1804 Art.3
**2617. Financial Services and Markets Act 2000
(Mutual Societies) Order 2001**
  Art.7, amended: SI 2014/1815 Sch.1 para.11
  Sch.3 Part III para.214, revoked: 2014 c.14
  Sch.7
**2743. Education (Grants) (Music, Ballet and
Choir Schools) (England) Regulations 2001**
  Reg.4, amended: SI 2014/852 Art.8
**2748. Transport (Scotland) Act 2001 (Conditions
attached to PSV Operator's Licence and
Competition Test for Exercise of Bus Functions)
Order 2001**
  Art.2, amended: SI 2014/549 Sch.1 para.31
  Art.4, amended: SI 2014/549 Sch.1 para.31
  Art.5, amended: SI 2014/549 Sch.1 para.31
  Art.6, amended: SI 2014/549 Sch.1 para.31
  Art.7, amended: SI 2014/549 Sch.1 para.31

  Art.10, amended: SI 2014/549 Sch.1 para.31
  Art.14, amended: SI 2014/549 Sch.1 para.31
**2857. Education (Grants etc.) (Dance and
Drama) (England) Regulations 2001**
  revoked: SI 2014/80 Sch.1
**2879. Value Added Tax (Refund of Tax to
Museums and Galleries) Order 2001**
  Sch.1, amended: SI 2014/2858 Sch.1
**2975. Radiation (Emergency Preparedness and
Public Information) Regulations 2001**
  Reg.18A, amended: SI 2014/469 Sch.3
  para.105
  Reg.18B, added: SI 2014/469 Sch.3 para.105
**2993. Competition Act 1998 (Section 11
Exemption) Regulations 2001**
  Reg.2, amended: SI 2014/549 Sch.1 para.6
  Reg.3, amended: SI 2014/549 Sch.1 para.6
**3020. Common Agricultural Policy (Paying
Agencies Competent Authority and Co-
ordinating Body) Regulations 2001**
  revoked: SI 2014/3260 Reg.5
**3022. Excise Duty Points (Duty Suspended
Movements of Excise Goods) Regulations 2001**
  Reg.7, see *Butlers Ship Stores Ltd v Revenue
  and Customs Commissioners* [2014] S.T.C.
  732 (UT (Tax)), Lord Glennie
**3084. Financial Services and Markets Act 2000
(Gibraltar) Order 2001**
  Art.1, amended: SI 2014/1292 Art.3
  Art.2, amended: SI 2014/1292 Art.3
  Art.3, amended: SI 2014/1292 Art.3
  Art.4, amended: SI 2014/1292 Art.3
**3119. A5 Trunk Road (Nesscliffe) (24 Hour
Clearway) Order 2001**
  revoked: SI 2014/2469 Art.6
**3139. Organic Farming (England Rural
Development Programme) (Amendment)
Regulations 2001**
  revoked: SI 2014/3263 Sch.5
**3198. Common Agricultural Policy (Protection
of Community Arrangements) (Amendment)
Regulations 2001**
  revoked: SI 2014/3263 Sch.5
**3209. Merchant Shipping (Domestic Passenger
Ships) (Safety Management Code) Regulations
2001**
  Reg.3, amended: SI 2014/1512 Reg.17
**3270. Electricity (Class Exemptions from the
Requirement for a Licence) Order 2001**
  Art.3, applied: SI 2014/1458 Art.5
  Sch.4, applied: SI 2014/1458 Art.5

3384. Local Authorities (Standing Orders) (England) Regulations 2001
applied: SI 2014/165 Reg.4
Reg.2, amended: SI 2014/165 Reg.3
Reg.3, amended: SI 2014/165 Reg.3
Reg.3, revoked (in part): SI 2014/165 Reg.3
Reg.4, amended: SI 2014/165 Reg.2, Reg.3
Reg.4, substituted: SI 2014/165 Reg.2
Sch.1 Part I para.1, amended: SI 2014/165 Reg.3
Sch.1 Part I para.3, amended: SI 2014/165 Reg.3
Sch.1 Part II para.1, amended: SI 2014/165 Reg.3
Sch.1 Part III, revoked: SI 2014/165 Reg.3
Sch.1 Part IV, amended: SI 2014/165 Reg.3
Sch.2 Part I, amended: SI 2014/165 Reg.3
Sch.2 Part I para.1, amended: SI 2014/165 Reg.3
Sch.2 Part I para.8, amended: SI 2014/165 Reg.3
Sch.2 Part I para.15, added: SI 2014/165 Reg.2
Sch.2 Part II para.1, amended: SI 2014/165 Reg.3
Sch.2 Part II para.6, amended: SI 2014/165 Reg.3
Sch.2 Part II para.11, added: SI 2014/165 Reg.2
Sch.2 Part III, added: SI 2014/165 Reg.2

3438. Litigants in Person (Costs and Expenses) (Magistrates Courts) Order 2001
Art.3, amended: SI 2014/879 Art.81

3442. Colours in Food (Amendment) (England) Regulations 2001
revoked: SI 2014/1855 Sch.6 Part 1

3495. European Communities (Designation) (No.3) Order 2001
Art.2, revoked (in part): SI 2014/1890 Art.6
Sch.1, amended: SI 2014/1362 Sch.1, SI 2014/1890 Art.6

3510. Seeds (National Lists of Varieties) Regulations 2001
Sch.1 Part I para.2, amended: SI 2014/487 Reg.3

3649. Financial Services and Markets Act 2000 (Consequential Amendments and Repeals) Order 2001
Art.183, revoked: 2014 c.14 Sch.7

3830. Welfare of Animals (Slaughter or Killing) (Amendment) (England) Regulations 2001
revoked: SI 2014/1240 Reg.47

3900. England Rural Development Programme (Project Variations) Regulations 2001
revoked: SI 2014/3263 Sch.5

3909. Colours in Food (Amendment)(Wales) Regulations 2001
revoked: SI 2014/2303 Sch.6 Part 1

3928. Civil Jurisdiction and Judgments (Authentic Instruments and Court Settlements) Order 2001
Art.1, amended: SI 2014/2947 Sch.3 para.2
Art.2, amended: SI 2014/2947 Sch.3 para.3
Art.3, amended: SI 2014/2947 Sch.3 para.4

3929. Civil Jurisdiction and Judgments Order 2001
Art.2, amended: SI 2014/2947 Sch.2 para.2
Sch.1 para.1, amended: SI 2014/879 Art.83, SI 2014/2947 Sch.2 para.3
Sch.1 para.1, revoked (in part): SI 2014/2947 Sch.2 para.3
Sch.1 para.2, amended: SI 2014/2947 Sch.2 para.3
Sch.1 para.2A, added: SI 2014/2947 Sch.2 para.3
Sch.1 para.3, amended: SI 2014/879 Art.84
Sch.1 para.3, revoked (in part): SI 2014/879 Art.84, SI 2014/2947 Sch.2 para.3
Sch.1 para.4, amended: SI 2014/2947 Sch.2 para.3
Sch.1 para.5, amended: SI 2014/879 Art.85, SI 2014/2947 Sch.2 para.3
Sch.1 para.5, revoked (in part): SI 2014/2947 Sch.2 para.3
Sch.1 para.6, revoked: SI 2014/2947 Sch.2 para.3
Sch.1 para.7, amended: SI 2014/2947 Sch.2 para.3
Sch.1 para.8, amended: SI 2014/2947 Sch.2 para.3
Sch.1 para.9, amended: SI 2014/2947 Sch.2 para.3
Sch.1 para.10, amended: SI 2014/2947 Sch.2 para.3
Sch.1 para.11, amended: SI 2014/2947 Sch.2 para.3

3952. Rail Vehicle Accessibility (Croydon Tramlink Class CR4000 Vehicles) Exemption Order 2001
Art.4, amended: SI 2014/3244 Art.3

Art.4, revoked (in part): SI 2014/3244 Art.3
Art.7, revoked: SI 2014/3244 Art.3
Art.9, revoked: SI 2014/3244 Art.3

3965. Care Homes Regulations 2001
Reg.18, see *Esparon (t/a Middle West*
Residential Care Home) v Slavikovska
[2014] I.C.R. 1037 (EAT), Judge Serota QC

3967. Children's Homes Regulations 2001
see *Liverpool City Council v SG* [2014]
EWCOP 10, [2014] C.O.P.L.R. 585 (CP),
Holman J
Reg.2, amended: SI 2014/2103 Art.8
Reg.11, see *Liverpool City Council v SG*
[2014] EWCOP 10, [2014] C.O.P.L.R. 585
(CP), Holman J
Reg.12B, amended: SI 2014/2103 Art.8
Reg.17, see *Liverpool City Council v SG*
[2014] EWCOP 10, [2014] C.O.P.L.R. 585
(CP), Holman J
Reg.17A, see *Liverpool City Council v SG*
[2014] EWCOP 10, [2014] C.O.P.L.R. 585
(CP), Holman J
Reg.17B, see *Liverpool City Council v SG*
[2014] EWCOP 10, [2014] C.O.P.L.R. 585
(CP), Holman J
Sch.3, amended: SI 2014/2103 Art.8

3997. Misuse of Drugs (Designation) Order 2001
Sch.1 Part I para.1, amended: SI 2014/1274
Art.2, SI 2014/1376 Art.2, SI 2014/3276
Art.2

3998. Misuse of Drugs Regulations 2001
Reg.6A, amended: SI 2014/2081 Reg.3
Sch.1 para.1, amended: SI 2014/1275 Reg.3,
SI 2014/1377 Reg.3, SI 2014/3277 Reg.3,
Reg.4
Sch.2 para.1, amended: SI 2014/1275 Reg.4,
SI 2014/3277 Reg.5
Sch.3 para.1, amended: SI 2014/1275 Reg.5
Sch.4 Part I para.1, amended: SI 2014/1275
Reg.6, SI 2014/3277 Reg.6

4022. Social Security (Loss of Benefit)
Regulations 2001
Reg.3ZA, applied: SI 2014/1230 Reg.36
Reg.3ZB, applied: SI 2014/1230 Reg.38
Reg.3ZB, disapplied: SI 2014/1230 Reg.35
Reg.3ZB, varied: SI 2014/1230 Reg.37
Reg.17, applied: SI 2014/1230 Reg.36

4025. Civil Courts (Amendment) Order 2001
revoked: SI 2014/820 Sch.1

4026. Distress for Rent (Amendment) Rules 2001
revoked: SI 2014/600 Sch.1 Part 2

4027. Aggregates Levy (Registration and
Miscellaneous Provisions) Regulations 2001
Reg.3, amended: SI 2014/836 Reg.3
Reg.3, revoked (in part): SI 2014/836 Reg.3

2002

63. Genetically Modified Organisms (Contained
Use) (Amendment) Regulations 2002
revoked: SI 2014/1663 Reg.35

111. Al-Qa'ida and Taliban (United Nations
Measures) Order 2002
revoked: SI 2014/2711 Sch.1

233. Police Act 1997 (Criminal Records)
Regulations 2002
Reg.2, amended: SI 2014/2122 Reg.2
Reg.3A, added: SI 2014/239 Reg.2
Reg.4B, added: SI 2014/239 Reg.2
Reg.5A, amended: SI 2014/955 Reg.2
Reg.5B, amended: SI 2014/955 Reg.2, SI
2014/2103 Art.9
Reg.5B, substituted: SI 2014/955 Reg.2
Reg.5C, amended: SI 2014/955 Reg.2, SI
2014/2122 Reg.2
Reg.5C, revoked (in part): SI 2014/955
Reg.2
Reg.5C, substituted: SI 2014/955 Reg.2
Reg.9, amended: SI 2014/239 Reg.2

253. Nursing and Midwifery Order (2001) 2002
applied: SI 2014/3215 Reg.2, Reg.3
Art.7, applied: SI 2014/3139, SI 2014/3139
Sch.1
Art.7, enabled: SI 2014/3139
Art.9, amended: SI 2014/1887 Sch.1 para.24
Art.10, amended: SI 2014/1887 Sch.1
para.25
Art.12A, added: SI 2014/1887 Sch.1 para.26
Art.12A, amended: SI 2014/3272 Art.3
Art.25, amended: SI 2014/3272 Art.4
Art.26, amended: SI 2014/3272 Art.5
Art.26A, added: SI 2014/3272 Art.6
Art.29, see *Adegbulugbe v Nursing and*
Midwifery Council [2013] EWHC 3301
(Admin), (2014) 135 B.M.L.R. 171 (QBD
(Admin)), Andrews J
Art.30, amended: SI 2014/3272 Art.7
Art.31, amended: SI 2014/3272 Art.8
Art.31, revoked (in part): SI 2014/3272 Art.8
Art.33, amended: SI 2014/1887 Sch.1
para.27

Art.33, applied: SI 2014/3139 Sch.1
Art.33, enabled: SI 2014/3139
Art.37, amended: SI 2014/1887 Sch.1
para.28, SI 2014/3272 Art.9
Art.37, revoked (in part): SI 2014/3272 Art.9
Art.38, see *D v Nursing and Midwifery
Council* [2014] CSIH 90, 2014 S.L.T. 1069
(IH (Ex Div)), Lady Paton
Art.47, applied: SI 2014/3139, SI 2014/3139
Sch.1
Art.47, enabled: SI 2014/3139
Art.48, applied: SI 2014/3139
Sch.4, amended: SI 2014/1887 Sch.1 para.29

**254. Health and Social Work Professions Order
2002**
Art.7, applied: SI 2014/532, SI 2014/532
Sch.1
Art.7, enabled: SI 2014/532
Art.7, referred to: SI 2014/532
Art.9, amended: SI 2014/1887 Sch.1 para.12
Art.10, amended: SI 2014/1887 Sch.1
para.13
Art.11A, added: SI 2014/1887 Sch.1 para.14
Art.33, amended: SI 2014/1887 Sch.1
para.15
Art.37, amended: SI 2014/1887 Sch.1
para.16
Art.38, amended: SI 2014/1887 Sch.1
para.17
Art.41, applied: SI 2014/532, SI 2014/532
Sch.1
Art.41, enabled: SI 2014/532
Art.41, referred to: SI 2014/532, SI
2014/532 Sch.1
Art.42, applied: SI 2014/532
Sch.3 para.1, amended: SI 2014/1887 Sch.1
para.18

318. Electronic Signatures Regulations 2002
Reg.2, applied: SSI 2014/83 Reg.3

324. Care Homes (Wales) Regulations 2002
Reg.2, amended: SI 2014/107 Sch.2 para.2

**452. Town and Country Planning (Costs of
Inquiries etc.) (Standard Daily Amount)
(England) Regulations 2002**
revoked: SI 2014/692 Sch.1

**501. Excise Goods (Accompanying Documents)
Regulations 2002**
Reg.5, see *Butlers Ship Stores Ltd v Revenue
and Customs Commissioners* [2014] S.T.C.
732 (UT (Tax)), Lord Glennie

**505. Electoral Commission (Limit on Public
Awareness Expenditure) Order 2002**
revoked: SI 2014/510 Art.3

**646. Common Agricultural Policy Support
Schemes (Appeals) Regulations 2002**
revoked: SI 2014/3263 Sch.5

699. Pensions Increase (Review) Order 2002
referred to: SI 2014/668 Sch.1
Art.6, substituted: SI 2014/107 Sch.1
para.56, SI 2014/3229 Sch.6 para.35

**794. Ministry of Agriculture, Fisheries and Food
(Dissolution) Order 2002**
Art.3, revoked (in part): SI 2014/1924 Sch.1

**919. Registration of Social Care and
Independent Health Care (Wales) Regulations
2002**
Reg.2, amended: SI 2014/107 Sch.2 para.3

**1311. National Health Service (Compensation for
Premature Retirement) Regulations 2002**
Reg.2, amended: SI 2014/78 Reg.22
Reg.2A, added: SI 2014/78 Reg.23

1355. Offshore Chemicals Regulations 2002
applied: SI 2014/1599 Sch.10 para.9, Sch.11
para.8, SI 2014/1873 Sch.13 para.9, Sch.14
para.5, SI 2014/2594 Sch.2 para.8, Sch.3
para.8, SI 2014/2950 Sch.9 para.8, SI
2014/3331 Sch.8 para.11
referred to: SSI 2014/324 Sch.1 para.9

**1438. Health Service (Control of Patient
Information) Regulations 2002**
referred to: 2014 c.23 s.110
Reg.1, amended: 2014 c.23 Sch.8 para.3
Reg.5, amended: 2014 c.23 s.117
Reg.5, applied: 2014 c.23 Sch.7 para.8
Reg.5, substituted: 2014 c.23 s.117
Reg.6, amended: 2014 c.23 s.117

**1472. Animal By-Products (Identification)
(Amendment) (Wales) Regulations 2002**
revoked: SI 2014/517 Reg.28

**1703. Social Security (Jobcentre Plus Interviews)
Regulations 2002**
Reg.4A, amended: SI 2014/1097 Reg.14
Reg.4A, revoked (in part): SI 2014/1097
Reg.14
Reg.5, amended: SI 2014/1097 Reg.14
Reg.5, revoked (in part): SI 2014/1097
Reg.14
Reg.6, amended: SI 2014/1097 Reg.14
Reg.8, amended: SI 2014/1097 Reg.14
Reg.11, amended: SI 2014/1097 Reg.14
Reg.12, amended: SI 2014/1097 Reg.14

Reg.12, applied: SI 2014/1097 Reg.8
Reg.12A, added: SI 2014/1097 Reg.14
1792. State Pension Credit Regulations 2002
applied: SI 2014/2672 Sch.1 para.40
Reg.1, amended: SI 2014/107 Sch.1 para.32, SI 2014/591 Reg.7, SI 2014/3229 Sch.6 para.23, SI 2014/3255 Art.10
Reg.2, amended: SI 2014/902 Reg.4
Reg.6, amended: SI 2014/516 Art.21
Reg.6, applied: SI 2014/516 Sch.13
Reg.7, amended: SI 2014/516 Art.21
Reg.7, applied: SI 2014/516 Sch.13
Reg.15, amended: SI 2014/3255 Art.10
Reg.15, revoked (in part): SI 2014/3255 Art.10
Reg.15, varied: 2014 c.6 s.126
Reg.17A, amended: SI 2014/591 Reg.7, SI 2014/3255 Art.10
Reg.17A, revoked (in part): SI 2014/3255 Art.10
Reg.17A, varied: 2014 c.6 s.126
Reg.18, amended: SI 2014/591 Reg.7
Reg.24, amended: SI 2014/591 Reg.7
Sch.1 Part I para.1, amended: SI 2014/2888 Reg.3
Sch.1 Part I para.2, amended: SI 2014/2888 Reg.3
Sch.2 para.1, amended: SI 2014/2888 Reg.3
Sch.2 para.2, amended: SI 2014/3255 Art.10
Sch.2 para.6, applied: SI 2014/516 Sch.13
Sch.2 para.7, applied: SI 2014/516 Sch.13
Sch.2 para.8, applied: SI 2014/516 Sch.13
Sch.2 para.9, amended: SI 2014/591 Reg.7
Sch.2 para.9, applied: SI 2014/516 Sch.13
Sch.2 para.14, amended: SI 2014/516 Art.21, SI 2014/2888 Reg.3
Sch.3 para.1, amended: SI 2014/516 Art.21
Sch.3 para.2, applied: SI 2014/516 Sch.13
Sch.5 Part I para.23C, amended: SI 2014/513 Sch.1 para.7
Sch.6 para.4, amended: SI 2014/2888 Reg.3
1837. Penalties for Disorderly Behaviour (Amount of Penalty) Order 2002
Sch.1 Part II, amended: SI 2014/1383 Art.2
1915. Child Support Appeals (Jurisdiction of Courts) Order 2002
Art.3, applied: SI 2014/840 r.5
1970. Exchange Gains and Losses (Bringing into Account Gains or Losses) Regulations 2002
Reg.13, amended: SI 2014/3325 Reg.2

2005. Working Tax Credit (Entitlement and Maximum Rate) Regulations 2002
Reg.5, amended: SI 2014/3255 Art.11
Reg.5, revoked (in part): SI 2014/3255 Art.11
Reg.5, varied: 2014 c.6 s.126
Reg.9, revoked (in part): SI 2014/658 Reg.2
Reg.14, amended: SI 2014/2924 Reg.4
Sch.1 Part 1 para.9, substituted: SI 2014/2924 Reg.4
Sch.2, amended: SI 2014/384 Art.4, SI 2014/845 Reg.3
2006. Tax Credits (Definition and Calculation of Income) Regulations 2002
Part 2, varied: SI 2014/1230 Sch.1 para.15
Reg.2, varied: SI 2014/1230 Sch.1 para.12
Reg.3, amended: SI 2014/658 Reg.4
Reg.3, revoked (in part): SI 2014/658 Reg.4
Reg.3, varied: SI 2014/1230 Sch.1 para.13
Reg.4, amended: SI 2014/658 Reg.4, SI 2014/2924 Reg.5, SI 2014/3255 Art.12
Reg.4, varied: 2014 c.6 s.126, SI 2014/1230 Sch.1 para.14
Reg.6, varied: SI 2014/1230 Sch.1 para.16
Reg.7, amended: SI 2014/658 Reg.4, SI 2014/3255 Art.12
Reg.7, varied: SI 2014/1230 Sch.1 para.17
Reg.8, varied: SI 2014/1230 Sch.1 para.18
Reg.10, varied: SI 2014/1230 Sch.1 para.19
Reg.11, varied: SI 2014/1230 Sch.1 para.20
Reg.12, varied: SI 2014/1230 Sch.1 para.21
Reg.13, varied: SI 2014/1230 Sch.1 para.22
Reg.18, varied: SI 2014/1230 Sch.1 para.23
Reg.19, amended: SI 2014/513 Sch.1 para.8
2007. Child Tax Credit Regulations 2002
Reg.2, amended: SI 2014/1231 Reg.3
Reg.2, referred to: SI 2014/3219 Sch.1 para.2
Reg.3, applied: SI 2014/3219 Sch.1 para.3
Reg.5, amended: SI 2014/1231 Reg.3, SI 2014/2924 Reg.3
Reg.7, amended: SI 2014/384 Art.3, SI 2014/845 Reg.2
Reg.8, amended: SI 2014/2924 Reg.3
2008. Tax Credits (Income Thresholds and Determination of Rates) Regulations 2002
Reg.2, varied: SI 2014/1230 Sch.1 para.25
Reg.3, amended: SI 2014/845 Reg.4
Reg.7, varied: SI 2014/1230 Sch.1 para.26
Reg.8, amended: SI 2014/845 Reg.4
Reg.8, varied: SI 2014/1230 Sch.1 para.27

2013. Electronic Commerce (EC Directive) Regulations 2002

Reg.2, see *Paramount Home Entertainment International Ltd v British Sky Broadcasting Ltd* [2013] EWHC 3479 (Ch), [2014] E.C.D.R. 7 (Ch D), Arnold J

2014. Tax Credits (Claims and Notifications) Regulations 2002

applied: SI 2014/1230 Reg.6, Reg.16

Reg.4, varied: SI 2014/1230 Sch.1 para.29

Reg.11, varied: SI 2014/1230 Sch.1 para.30

Reg.12, varied: SI 2014/1230 Sch.1 para.31

Reg.13, varied: SI 2014/1230 Sch.1 para.32

Reg.15, varied: SI 2014/1230 Sch.1 para.33

Reg.18, applied: SI 2014/1230 Reg.16

Reg.33, varied: SI 2014/1230 Sch.1 para.34

2034. Fixed-term Employees (Prevention of Less Favourable Treatment) Regulations 2002

Reg.7, amended: SI 2014/386 Sch.1 para.14

Reg.7A, added: SI 2014/386 Sch.1 para.15

2064. Education (Grants etc.) (Dance and Drama) (England) (Amendment) Regulations 2002

revoked: SI 2014/80 Sch.1

2071. Education (Special Educational Needs) (City Colleges) (England) Regulations 2002

Reg.1, amended: SI 2014/2103 Art.10

Reg.2, amended: SI 2014/2103 Art.10

Reg.4, substituted: SI 2014/2103 Art.10

2125. Merchant Shipping (Hours of Work) Regulations 2002

Reg.2, amended: SI 2014/308 Reg.2

Reg.2, revoked (in part): SI 2014/308 Reg.2

Reg.3, substituted: SI 2014/308 Reg.2

Reg.3A, added: SI 2014/308 Reg.2

Reg.3A, amended: SI 2014/386 Sch.1 para.17, SI 2014/431 Sch.1 para.22

Reg.4, substituted: SI 2014/308 Reg.2

Reg.7, amended: SI 2014/308 Reg.2

Reg.9, amended: SI 2014/308 Reg.2

Reg.10, revoked: SI 2014/1614 Reg.12

Reg.11, amended: SI 2014/308 Reg.2

Reg.12, substituted: SI 2014/308 Reg.2

Reg.12A, added: SI 2014/308 Reg.2

Reg.13, amended: SI 2014/308 Reg.2

Reg.14, substituted: SI 2014/308 Reg.2

Reg.14A, added: SI 2014/308 Reg.2

Reg.14A, amended: SI 2014/1614 Reg.12

Reg.15, amended: SI 2014/308 Reg.2

Reg.16, amended: SI 2014/308 Reg.2

Reg.17, revoked: SI 2014/308 Reg.2

Reg.17A, added: SI 2014/308 Reg.2

Reg.18, amended: SI 2014/308 Reg.2

Reg.19, amended: SI 2014/308 Reg.2

Reg.20, amended: SI 2014/308 Reg.2

Reg.20, revoked (in part): SI 2014/1614

Reg.12

Reg.22, added: SI 2014/308 Reg.2

Reg.22, amended: SI 2014/431 Sch.1 para.23

Reg.22A, added: SI 2014/431 Sch.1 para.24

Reg.23, amended: SI 2014/386 Sch.1 para.18, SI 2014/431 Sch.1 para.25

2173. Tax Credits (Payments by the Commissioners) Regulations 2002

Reg.7, varied: SI 2014/1230 Sch.1 para.36

2375. National Health Service (Functions of Strategic Health Authorities and Primary Care Trusts and Administration Arrangements) (England) Regulations 2002

see *R. (on the application of A) v Secretary of State for Health* [2014] EWHC 1364 (Admin), [2014] Med. L.R. 246 (QBD (Admin)), King J; see *R. (on the application of Ealing LBC) v NHS England* [2013] EWHC 3255 (Admin), (2014) 135 B.M.L.R. 128 (QBD (Admin)), Mitting J

2533. Atomic Energy (Americium) Order 2002

revoked: SI 2014/469 Sch.3 para.210

2586. Lymington Harbour Revision (Constitution) Order 2002

applied: SI 2014/1076 Art.3, Art.7, Art.16

Art.14, amended: SI 2014/1076 Art.23

Art.15, revoked: SI 2014/1076 Art.23

2633. Transfer of Functions (Civil Defence) Order 2002

Art.2, varied: SI 2014/2708 Art.5

2664. A483 Trunk Road (Southern Approach to Tycroes, Ammanford, Carmarthenshire) (40 50 mph Speed Limit) Order 2002

revoked: SI 2014/1455 Art.4

2676. Control of Lead at Work Regulations 2002

Reg.2, amended: SI 2014/469 Sch.3 para.106

Reg.9, amended: SI 2014/469 Sch.3 para.106

Reg.10, amended: SI 2014/469 Sch.3 para.106

Reg.15, amended: SI 2014/469 Sch.3 para.106

2677. Control of Substances Hazardous to Health Regulations 2002
  applied: SI 2014/3248 Reg.44
  Reg.2, amended: SI 2014/469 Sch.3 para.107
  Reg.5, revoked (in part): SI 2014/3248 Sch.4 Part 2
  Reg.10, amended: SI 2014/469 Sch.3 para.107
  Reg.11, amended: SI 2014/469 Sch.3 para.107
  Reg.18, amended: SI 2014/469 Sch.3 para.107

2684. Town and Country Planning (Enforcement) (Hearings Procedure) (England) Rules 2002
  r.2, amended: SI 2014/553 Art.2
  r.3, amended: SI 2014/553 Art.2
  r.9, amended: SI 2014/553 Art.2

2685. Town and Country Planning (Enforcement) (Determination by Inspectors) (Inquiries Procedure) (England) Rules 2002
  r.2, amended: SI 2014/553 Art.3
  r.3, amended: SI 2014/553 Art.3
  r.11, amended: SI 2014/553 Art.3

2686. Town and Country Planning (Enforcement) (Inquiries Procedure) (England) Rules 2002
  r.2, amended: SI 2014/553 Art.4
  r.3, amended: SI 2014/553 Art.4
  r.13, amended: SI 2014/553 Art.4

2742. Road Vehicles (Registration and Licensing) Regulations 2002
  Reg.6, revoked: SI 2014/2358 Sch.1 para.2
  Reg.7, revoked: SI 2014/2358 Sch.1 para.3
  Reg.8, revoked: SI 2014/2358 Sch.1 para.4
  Reg.9, substituted: SI 2014/2358 Sch.1 para.5
  Reg.16, amended: SI 2014/2358 Sch.1 para.6
  Reg.16, revoked (in part): SI 2014/2358 Sch.1 para.6
  Reg.19, substituted: SI 2014/2358 Sch.1 para.7
  Reg.20, revoked (in part): SI 2014/2358 Sch.1 para.8
  Reg.23, amended: SI 2014/2676 Reg.3
  Reg.23, revoked (in part): SI 2014/2676 Reg.3
  Reg.24, amended: SI 2014/2676 Reg.4

Reg.24, revoked (in part): SI 2014/2676 Reg.4
Reg.26, revoked (in part): SI 2014/2358 Sch.1 para.9
Reg.31, revoked: SI 2014/2358 Sch.1 para.10
Reg.33, amended: SI 2014/2358 Sch.1 para.11
Reg.33, revoked (in part): SI 2014/2358 Sch.1 para.11
Reg.40, amended: SI 2014/2358 Sch.1 para.12
Reg.41, amended: SI 2014/2358 Sch.1 para.13
Reg.41, revoked (in part): SI 2014/2358 Sch.1 para.13
Reg.42, revoked (in part): SI 2014/2358 Sch.1 para.14
Reg.42, substituted: SI 2014/2358 Sch.1 para.14
Sch.2 para.4, applied: 2014 c.26 Sch.18 para.15, Sch.18 para.17, Sch.18 para.18
Sch.2 para.4A, applied: 2014 c.26 Sch.18 para.17, Sch.18 para.18
Sch.2 para.4B, applied: 2014 c.26 Sch.18 para.17, Sch.18 para.18
Sch.2 para.4C, applied: 2014 c.26 Sch.18 para.17, Sch.18 para.18
Sch.2 para.4D, applied: 2014 c.26 Sch.18 para.17, Sch.18 para.18
Sch.2 para.5, applied: 2014 c.26 Sch.18 para.15
Sch.2 para.12, amended: SI 2014/480 Reg.7
Sch.2 para.13, amended: SI 2014/2116 Reg.3
Sch.4 Part I para.1, amended: SI 2014/2358 Sch.1 para.15
Sch.4 Part II para.3, revoked: SI 2014/2358 Sch.1 para.15
Sch.4 Part III para.7, revoked: SI 2014/2358 Sch.1 para.15
Sch.6 Part I para.1, substituted: SI 2014/2358 Sch.1 para.16
Sch.6 Part I para.3, amended: SI 2014/2358 Sch.1 para.16
Sch.6 Part I para.5, amended: SI 2014/2358 Sch.1 para.16
Sch.6 Part I para.6, amended: SI 2014/2358 Sch.1 para.16

**2761. Olive Oil (Marketing Standards)
(Amendment) Regulations 2002**
revoked: SI 2014/195 Reg.20
**2776. Dangerous Substances and Explosive
Atmospheres Regulations 2002**
applied: SI 2014/1637 Reg.18
Reg.3, revoked (in part): SI 2014/3248 Sch.4
Part 2
Reg.7, applied: SI 2014/3248 Reg.21,
Reg.22, Reg.23, Reg.29, Reg.31
Reg.17, applied: SI 2014/1637 Reg.24
Reg.17, revoked (in part): SI 2014/1637
Sch.4 Part 1
Sch.6 Part 1 para.2, revoked: SI 2014/1637
Sch.4 Part 1
Sch.7 Part 1, amended: SI 2014/1637 Sch.4
Part 1
**2788. Paternity and Adoption Leave Regulations
2002**
applied: SI 2014/3096 Reg.3, Reg.4
Reg.2, amended: SI 2014/2112 Reg.3, SI
2014/3206 Reg.4
Reg.2, varied: SI 2014/3096 Reg.6
Reg.3, varied: SI 2014/3096 Reg.7
Reg.4, amended: SI 2014/2112 Reg.4
Reg.4, varied: SI 2014/3096 Reg.8
Reg.8, amended: SI 2014/2112 Reg.5, SI
2014/3206 Reg.5
Reg.8, varied: SI 2014/3096 Reg.9
Reg.9, varied: SI 2014/3096 Reg.10
Reg.10, varied: SI 2014/3096 Reg.11
Reg.11, varied: SI 2014/3096 Reg.12
Reg.13, amended: SI 2014/2112 Reg.6
Reg.15, amended: SI 2014/2112 Reg.7, SI
2014/3206 Reg.6
Reg.15, revoked (in part): SI 2014/2112
Reg.7
Reg.15, varied: SI 2014/3096 Reg.13
Reg.16, varied: SI 2014/3096 Reg.14
Reg.17, varied: SI 2014/3096 Reg.14
Reg.18, varied: SI 2014/3096 Reg.15
Reg.20, varied: SI 2014/3096 Reg.16
Reg.22, amended: SI 2014/2112 Reg.8, SI
2014/3206 Reg.7
Reg.22, varied: SI 2014/3096 Reg.17
Reg.26, amended: SI 2014/2112 Reg.9
Reg.28, amended: SI 2014/2112 Reg.10,
Reg.11
Reg.29, amended: SI 2014/2112 Reg.12,
Reg.13

**2812. Freedom of Information Act 2000
(Commencement No 2) Order 2002**
Sch.1 Part I, amended: SI 2014/1924 Sch.1
**2818. Statutory Paternity Pay and Statutory
Adoption Pay (Weekly Rates) Regulations 2002**
Reg.2, amended: SI 2014/147 Art.5
Reg.3, amended: SI 2014/147 Art.5
**2820. Statutory Paternity Pay and Statutory
Adoption Pay (Administration) Regulations 2002**
Reg.11, amended: SI 2014/2934 Reg.25,
Reg.26
**2821. Statutory Paternity Pay and Statutory
Adoption Pay (Persons Abroad and Mariners)
Regulations 2002**
Reg.1, amended: SI 2014/3134 Reg.13,
Reg.14, SI 2014/3255 Art.13
Reg.1, varied: 2014 c.6 s.126
Reg.2, amended: SI 2014/3255 Art.13
Reg.5, amended: SI 2014/3255 Art.13
Reg.5, varied: 2014 c.6 s.126
**2822. Statutory Paternity Pay and Statutory
Adoption Pay (General) Regulations 2002**
referred to: SI 2014/2862 Reg.2
Reg.2, amended: SI 2014/2934 Reg.4
Reg.2, varied: SI 2014/2934 Reg.7
Reg.3, varied: SI 2014/2934 Reg.8
Reg.5A, added: SI 2014/2862 Reg.4
Reg.6, amended: SI 2014/2862 Reg.5
Reg.9, amended: SI 2014/2862 Reg.6
Reg.11, varied: SI 2014/2934 Reg.9
Reg.11A, added: SI 2014/2862 Reg.7
Reg.11A, varied: SI 2014/2934 Reg.10
Reg.12, amended: SI 2014/2862 Reg.8
Reg.12, varied: SI 2014/2934 Reg.11
Reg.13, varied: SI 2014/2934 Reg.12
Reg.14, varied: SI 2014/2934 Reg.13
Reg.15, amended: SI 2014/2862 Reg.9
Reg.15, varied: SI 2014/2934 Reg.14
Reg.16, varied: SI 2014/2934 Reg.15
Reg.20, varied: SI 2014/2934 Reg.16
Reg.21, varied: SI 2014/2934 Reg.17
Reg.22, amended: SI 2014/2934 Reg.5
Reg.22, varied: SI 2014/2934 Reg.18
Reg.23, varied: SI 2014/2934 Reg.19
Reg.24, varied: SI 2014/2934 Reg.20
Reg.25, varied: SI 2014/2934 Reg.21
Reg.29, varied: SI 2014/2934 Reg.22
Reg.30, varied: SI 2014/2934 Reg.23
Reg.34, amended: SI 2014/386 Sch.1
para.19
Reg.40, varied: SI 2014/2934 Reg.24

2836. Employment (Northern Ireland) Order 2002

Art.8, varied: 2014 c.6 s.126
Art.9, varied: 2014 c.6 s.126
Art.11, varied: 2014 c.6 s.126
Art.12, varied: 2014 c.6 s.126
Art.13, varied: 2014 c.6 s.126

2843. Northern Ireland Act 1998 (Modification of Enactments) Order 2002

Art.7, revoked: SI 2014/1924 Sch.1

2848. Double Taxation Relief (Taxes on Income) (The United States of America) Order 2002

see *Macklin v Revenue and Customs Commissioners* [2014] S.F.T.D. 290 (FTT (Tax)), Judge John Walters Q.C.

2978. School Companies Regulations 2002

Reg.28, substituted: SI 2014/2923 Reg.2

3026. Forest Reproductive Material (Great Britain) Regulations 2002

Reg.2, amended: SI 2014/1833 Reg.3
Reg.14, amended: SI 2014/1833 Reg.4
Reg.17, amended: SI 2014/1833 Reg.5
Reg.18, substituted: SI 2014/1833 Reg.6
Reg.19, amended: SI 2014/1833 Reg.7
Reg.25, substituted: SI 2014/1833 Reg.8
Reg.32, amended: SI 2014/1833 Reg.9
Sch.13, substituted: SI 2014/1833 Reg.10

3045. Sale and Supply of Goods to Consumers Regulations 2002

Reg.2, amended: SI 2014/549 Sch.1 para.7

3047. Statutory Payment Schemes (Electronic Communications) Regulations 2002

Reg.1, varied: 2014 c.6 s.126

3061. European Communities (Rights against Insurers) Regulations 2002

Reg.3, see *McLaughlin v Morrison* 2014 S.L.T. 111 (OH), Lord Jones; see *Nemeti v Sabre Insurance Co Ltd* [2013] EWCA Civ 1555, [2014] C.P. Rep. 16 (CA (Civ Div)), Sir Terence Etherton C

3113. Traffic Signs Regulations and General Directions 2002

applied: SI 2014/3105 Sch.1, SI 2014/3110 Sch.1, SI 2014/3112 Sch.1, SSI 2014/10 Art.2, Art.3, Art.4, SSI 2014/11 Art.2, SSI 2014/16 Art.3, Art.6, SSI 2014/17 Art.3, Art.4, Art.5, SSI 2014/18 Art.3, Art.4, Art.5, SSI 2014/19 Art.3, Art.4, Art.5, SSI 2014/20 Art.3, Art.4, Art.5, SSI 2014/45 Art.3, Art.4, Art.5, SSI 2014/46 Art.3, Art.4, Art.5, SSI 2014/47 Art.3, Art.4, Art.5, SSI 2014/48

Art.3, Art.4, Art.5, SSI 2014/75 Art.3, Art.4, Art.5, SSI 2014/76 Art.3, Art.4, Art.5, SSI 2014/77 Art.3, Art.4, Art.5, SSI 2014/78 Art.3, Art.4, Art.5, SSI 2014/82 Art.2, SSI 2014/104 Art.3, Art.4, Art.5, SSI 2014/105 Art.3, Art.4, Art.5, SSI 2014/106 Art.3, Art.4, Art.5, SSI 2014/107 Art.3, Art.4, Art.5, SSI 2014/120 Art.2, SSI 2014/124 Art.2, Art.3, Art.4, SSI 2014/128 Art.2, SSI 2014/133 Art.3, Art.4, Art.5, SSI 2014/134 Art.3, Art.5, SSI 2014/135 Art.3, Art.4, Art.5, SSI 2014/136 Art.3, Art.4, Art.5, SSI 2014/138 Art.2, SSI 2014/156 Art.2, Art.3, Art.4, SSI 2014/175 Art.2, SSI 2014/177 Art.2, Art.3, Art.4, SSI 2014/178 Art.3, Art.4, Art.5, SSI 2014/179 Art.3, Art.4, Art.5, SSI 2014/180 Art.3, Art.4, Art.5, SSI 2014/181 Art.3, Art.4, Art.5, SSI 2014/182 Art.2, SSI 2014/195 Art.3, SSI 2014/199 Art.2, SSI 2014/203 Art.2, SSI 2014/205 Art.2, SSI 2014/206 Art.3, Art.4, Art.5, SSI 2014/207 Art.3, Art.4, Art.5, SSI 2014/208 Art.3, Art.4, Art.5, SSI 2014/209 Art.3, Art.4, Art.5, SSI 2014/211 Art.2, Art.3, SSI 2014/216 Art.2, SSI 2014/223 Art.2, SSI 2014/228 Art.3, Art.4, Art.5, Art.6, SSI 2014/234 Art.3, Art.4, Art.5, SSI 2014/235 Art.3, Art.4, Art.5, SSI 2014/236 Art.3, Art.4, Art.5, SSI 2014/237 Art.3, Art.4, Art.5, SSI 2014/241 Art.2, SSI 2014/244 Art.3, SSI 2014/245 Art.3, Art.4, Art.5, SSI 2014/248 Art.2, SSI 2014/259 Art.2, SSI 2014/266 Art.2, SSI 2014/280 Art.2, SSI 2014/286 Art.2, Art.3, Art.4, SSI 2014/288 Art.2, SSI 2014/329 Art.3, Art.4, Art.5, SSI 2014/330 Art.3, Art.4, Art.5, SSI 2014/331 Art.3, Art.4, Art.5, SSI 2014/332 Art.3, Art.4, Art.5, SSI 2014/340 Art.2, SSI 2014/380 Art.2, SSI 2014/381 Art.3, Art.4, Art.5, SSI 2014/382 Art.3, Art.4, Art.5, SSI 2014/383 Art.4, Art.5, SSI 2014/384 Art.4, Art.5, SSI 2014/385 Art.2

Part I, applied: SSI 2014/240 Art.3, Art.4, Art.5

Reg.002, applied: SSI 2014/253 Art.4, Art.5, SSI 2014/254 Art.4, Art.5, SSI 2014/255 Art.4, Art.5, SSI 2014/256 Art.4, Art.5, SSI 2014/270 Art.4, Art.5, SSI 2014/271 Art.4, Art.5, SSI 2014/273 Art.4, Art.5, SSI 2014/275 Art.4, Art.5, SSI 2014/276 Art.3, SSI 2014/299 Art.2

Reg.023, applied: SSI 2014/253 Art.3, Art.5, SSI 2014/254 Art.3, SSI 2014/255 Art.3, Art.5, SSI 2014/256 Art.3, Art.5, SSI 2014/270 Art.3, Art.5, SSI 2014/271 Art.3, Art.5, SSI 2014/273 Art.3, Art.5, SSI 2014/275 Art.3, Art.5, SSI 2014/276 Art.2, Art.3

Reg.024, applied: SSI 2014/253 Art.3, SSI 2014/254 Art.3, SSI 2014/255 Art.3, SSI 2014/256 Art.3

3119. Tax Credits (Notice of Appeal) Regulations 2002

revoked (in part): SI 2014/886 Art.3

Reg.2, amended: SI 2014/886 Art.3

3133. Proceeds of Crime Act 2002 (Enforcement in different parts of the United Kingdom) Order 2002

Art.6, applied: SI 2014/1610 r.57_4, r.57_5, r.57_6

3150. Company Directors Disqualification (Northern Ireland) Order 2002

applied: SI 2014/1132 Sch.7 para.7, SI 2014/2709 Sch.2 para.7

Art.2, amended: SI 2014/892 Sch.1 para.224

Art.10, applied: SI 2014/882 Reg.5

Art.12, amended: SI 2014/892 Sch.1 para.225

Art.13A, amended: SI 2014/892 Sch.1 para.226

Art.13B, amended: SI 2014/892 Sch.1 para.227

Art.13C, amended: SI 2014/892 Sch.1 para.228

Art.13D, amended: SI 2014/892 Sch.1 para.229

Art.20, amended: SI 2014/892 Sch.1 para.230

Art.21, amended: SI 2014/892 Sch.1 para.231

Art.22, amended: SI 2014/892 Sch.1 para.232

3178. Education (Pupil Exclusions and Appeals) (Maintained Schools) (England) Regulations 2002

Reg.6, see *SA v Camden LBC Independent Appeal Panel* [2013] EWHC 3152 (Admin), [2014] E.L.R. 29 (QBD (Admin)), Nicola Davies J

3207. Flexible Working (Procedural Requirements) Regulations 2002

revoked: 2014 c.6 s.132

Reg.15, amended: SI 2014/431 Sch.1 para.27

Reg.15, applied: SI 2014/382 Art.4

Reg.15A, added: SI 2014/431 Sch.1 para.28

3236. Flexible Working (Eligibility, Complaints and Remedies) Regulations 2002

revoked: SI 2014/1398 Reg.2

Reg.2, amended: SI 2014/852 Art.9

Reg.3, amended: SI 2014/852 Art.9

2003

12. A1 Trunk Road (New Road, Sandy, Bedfordshire) (Prohibition of "U Turns) Order 2003

revoked: SI 2014/741 Art.4

25. Prohibition of Keeping or Release of Live Fish (Specified Species) (Amendment) (England) Order 2003

revoked: SI 2014/143 Art.4

37. Motor Vehicles (Compulsory Insurance) (Information Centre and Compensation Body) Regulations 2003

Reg.13, see *Bloy v Motor Insurers' Bureau* [2013] EWCA Civ 1543, [2014] Lloyd's Rep. I.R. 75 (CA (Civ Div)), Sir Terence Etherton C

74. Wireless Telegraphy (Exemption) Regulations 2003

see *Recall Support Services Ltd v Secretary of State for Culture Media and Sport* [2013] EWHC 3091 (Ch), [2014] 2 C.M.L.R. 2 (Ch D), Rose J

82. Proceeds of Crime Act 2002 (Appeals under Part 2) Order 2003

applied: SI 2014/1610 r.71_5, r.71_8

referred to: SI 2014/1610 r.71_1

Art.6, applied: SI 2014/1610 r.72_1, r.71_2

Art.7, applied: SI 2014/1610 r.71_2, r.71_3

Art.8, referred to: SI 2014/1610 r.71_6, r.71_7

Art.12, applied: SI 2014/1610 r.71_10

Art.15, referred to: SI 2014/1610 r.71_10

239. Allocation of Housing (Wales) Regulations 2003

Reg.4, revoked: SI 2014/2603 Reg.7

282. Income and Corporation Taxes (Electronic Communications) Regulations 2003

Reg.1, amended: SI 2014/489 Reg.3

Reg.2, amended: SI 2014/489 Reg.4

Reg.3, amended: SI 2014/489 Reg.5, Reg.6
Reg.5, amended: SI 2014/489 Reg.7

333. Proceeds of Crime Act 2002
(Commencement No 5, Transitional Provisions,
Savings and Amendment) Order 2003
see *R. v Onuigbo (aka Okoronkwo)*
(Unoamaka) [2014] EWCA Crim 65, [2014]
Lloyd's Rep. F.C. 302 (CA (Crim Div)),
Pitchford LJ
Art.3, applied: SI 2014/3141 Reg.20
Art.4, applied: SI 2014/3141 Reg.24
Art.5, applied: SI 2014/3141 Reg.19
Art.6, applied: SI 2014/3141 Reg.23
Art.10, applied: SI 2014/3141 Reg.19,
Reg.20, Reg.23, Reg.24

389. General Teaching Council for Wales
(Constitution) (Amendment) Regulations 2003
revoked: SI 2014/2365 Sch.1

403. Nuclear Industries Security Regulations
2003
applied: SI 2014/469 Sch.1 para.4, Sch.4
para.24
Reg.2, amended: SI 2014/469 Sch.3 para.2,
Sch.3 para.3, Sch.3 para.210
Reg.2, applied: SI 2014/469 Sch.1 para.1
Reg.2, disapplied: SI 2014/469 Sch.1 para.1
Reg.3, applied: SI 2014/469 Sch.1 para.1
Reg.3, disapplied: SI 2014/469 Sch.1 para.1
Reg.4, amended: SI 2014/469 Sch.3 para.2,
Sch.3 para.4, SI 2014/526 Reg.3
Reg.4, revoked (in part): SI 2014/469 Sch.3
para.4, Sch.3 para.210
Reg.5, amended: SI 2014/469 Sch.3 para.2
Reg.6, amended: SI 2014/469 Sch.3 para.2
Reg.7, amended: SI 2014/469 Sch.3 para.2
Reg.8, amended: SI 2014/469 Sch.3 para.2,
Sch.3 para.5
Reg.8, revoked (in part): SI 2014/469 Sch.3
para.5, Sch.3 para.210
Reg.9, amended: SI 2014/469 Sch.3 para.2
Reg.10, amended: SI 2014/469 Sch.3 para.2
Reg.11, amended: SI 2014/469 Sch.3 para.2,
Sch.3 para.6
Reg.12, revoked: SI 2014/469 Sch.3 para.7,
Sch.3 para.210
Reg.13, amended: SI 2014/469 Sch.3 para.2
Reg.14, amended: SI 2014/469 Sch.3 para.2
Reg.15, amended: SI 2014/469 Sch.3 para.2
Reg.16, amended: SI 2014/469 Sch.3 para.2
Reg.17, amended: SI 2014/469 Sch.3 para.2
Reg.18, amended: SI 2014/469 Sch.3 para.2

Reg.19, amended: SI 2014/469 Sch.3 para.2
Reg.20, amended: SI 2014/469 Sch.3 para.2
Reg.21, amended: SI 2014/469 Sch.3 para.2,
Sch.3 para.8
Reg.22, amended: SI 2014/469 Sch.3 para.2,
Sch.3 para.9
Reg.23, revoked: SI 2014/469 Sch.3 para.10,
Sch.3 para.210
Reg.25, amended: SI 2014/469 Sch.3
para.11
Reg.25, applied: SI 2014/469 Sch.1 para.4
Reg.25A, added: SI 2014/469 Sch.3 para.12
Reg.27, substituted: SI 2014/469 Sch.3
para.14
Reg.28, amended: SI 2014/469 Sch.3
para.15
Reg.29, added: SI 2014/469 Sch.3 para.16

413. Marriage (Northern Ireland) Order 2003
applied: SI 2014/1110 Art.14

418. Audit and Accountability (Northern
Ireland) Order 2003
Art.4D, amended: 2014 c.2 Sch.12 para.58

419. Energy (Northern Ireland) Order 2003
Art.2, amended: SI 2014/892 Sch.1 para.234
Art.7, amended: SI 2014/892 Sch.1 para.235
Art.8A, amended: SI 2014/892 Sch.1
para.236
Art.8A, revoked (in part): SI 2014/892 Sch.1
para.236
Art.13, amended: SI 2014/892 Sch.1
para.237
Art.15, amended: SI 2014/892 Sch.1
para.238
Art.18, amended: SI 2014/892 Sch.1
para.239
Art.23, amended: SI 2014/892 Sch.1
para.240
Art.63, amended: SI 2014/631 Sch.2 para.9,
SI 2014/892 Sch.1 para.241
Art.63, revoked (in part): SI 2014/892 Sch.1
para.241
Sch.2 para.5, amended: SI 2014/892 Sch.1
para.243
Sch.2 para.5, referred to: SI 2014/892 Sch.2
para.2

431. Health and Personal Social Services
(Quality, Improvement and Regulation)
(Northern Ireland) Order 2003
Part III, applied: 2014 c.23 s.51, s.73

435. Access to Justice (Northern Ireland) Order 2003
Sch.2 para.2, amended: SI 2014/3298 Reg.5
464. Town and Country Planning (Costs of Inquiries etc.) (Standard Daily Amount) (England) Regulations 2003
revoked: SI 2014/692 Sch.1
474. Food Labelling (Amendment) (England) Regulations 2003
revoked: SI 2014/1855 Sch.6 Part 1
480. A487 Trunk Road (Southern Approach to Llanfarian, Aberystwyth, Ceredigion) (40 mph Speed Limit) Order 2003
varied: SI 2014/1501 Art.7
499. Social Security Contributions and Benefits Act 1992 (Application of Parts 12ZA, 12ZB and 12ZC to Adoptions from Overseas) Regulations 2003
amended: SI 2014/2857 Reg.3
Reg.1, amended: SI 2014/2857 Reg.4
Reg.2, amended: SI 2014/3255 Art.14
Reg.2, varied: 2014 c.6 s.126
Reg.4, added: SI 2014/2857 Reg.5
Sch.1, amended: SI 2014/3255 Art.14
Sch.3, added: SI 2014/2857 Sch.1
507. School Organisation Proposals by the Learning and Skills Council for England Regulations 2003
Reg.2, amended: SI 2014/2103 Art.11
Reg.9, amended: SI 2014/2103 Art.11
Reg.10, amended: SI 2014/2103 Art.11
Reg.16, amended: SI 2014/2103 Art.11
Reg.18, amended: SI 2014/2103 Art.11
Reg.22, amended: SI 2014/2103 Art.11
Reg.23, amended: SI 2014/2103 Art.11
Sch.3 Part 3 para.13, amended: SI 2014/2103 Art.11
527. Police Regulations 2003
applied: SI 2014/3362 Reg.9
Reg.3, amended: SI 2014/2372 Reg.3
Reg.7, see *Panayiotou v Kernaghan* [2014] I.R.L.R. 500 (EAT), Lewis J
Reg.10, amended: SI 2014/2372 Reg.4
Reg.12, amended: SI 2014/2372 Reg.5
Reg.13, amended: SI 2014/2372 Reg.6
548. British Nationality (General) Regulations 2003
Reg.14, amended: 2014 c.22 Sch.9 para.71
Sch.2A para.1, amended: SI 2014/1465
Reg.3

609. A483 Trunk Road (Gresford Interchange, Wrexham) (Derestriction) Order 2003
varied: SI 2014/810 Art.7
628. National Assistance (Sums for Personal Requirements) (England) Regulations 2003
Reg.2, amended: SI 2014/582 Reg.2
653. Tax Credits (Immigration) Regulations 2003
Reg.3, amended: SI 2014/658 Reg.3
654. Tax Credits (Residence) Regulations 2003
Reg.3, amended: SI 2014/1511 Reg.6
Reg.3, varied: SI 2014/1230 Sch.1 para.38
658. Immigration (Notices) Regulations 2003
Reg.2, amended: SI 2014/2768 Reg.2
Reg.3, revoked: SI 2014/2768 Reg.2
Reg.4, amended: SI 2014/2768 Reg.2
Reg.4, revoked (in part): SI 2014/2768 Reg.2
Reg.5, amended: SI 2014/2768 Reg.2
Reg.5, revoked (in part): SI 2014/2768 Reg.2
Reg.7, amended: SI 2014/2768 Reg.2
Reg.7, revoked (in part): SI 2014/2768 Reg.2
681. Pensions Increase (Review) Order 2003
referred to: SI 2014/668 Sch.1
Art.6, substituted: SI 2014/107 Sch.1
para.56, SI 2014/3229 Sch.6 para.35
733. Social Security (Categorisation of Earners) Amendment (Northern Ireland) Regulations 2003
revoked: SI 2014/635 Sch.1
736. Social Security (Categorisation of Earners) Amendment Regulations 2003
revoked: SI 2014/635 Sch.1
832. Food Labelling (Amendment) (Wales) Regulations 2003
revoked: SI 2014/2303 Sch.6 Part 1
838. Entry Level Agri-Environment Scheme (Pilot) (England) Regulations 2003
revoked: SI 2014/3263 Sch.5
907. Local Authorities (Charges for Specified Welfare Services) (England) Regulations 2003
applied: SI 2014/2672 Sch.1 para.37, Sch.2 para.29
916. Child Benefit and Guardian's Allowance (Decisions and Appeals) Regulations 2003
Reg.2, amended: SI 2014/886 Art.5
Reg.28, amended: SI 2014/886 Art.5
Reg.29A, amended: SI 2014/886 Art.5
Reg.30, amended: SI 2014/886 Art.5

Reg.31, amended: SI 2014/886 Art.5
Reg.31, revoked (in part): SI 2014/886 Art.5
Reg.32, amended: SI 2014/886 Art.5
Reg.32, revoked (in part): SI 2014/886 Art.5

921. Paternity and Adoption Leave (Adoption from Overseas) Regulations 2003
Reg.4, amended: SI 2014/3092 Reg.23
Reg.7, amended: SI 2014/3092 Reg.24
Reg.9, amended: SI 2014/3092 Reg.25

962. Tax Credits Act 2002 (Commencement No 4, Transitional Provisions and Savings) Order 2003
Art.2, revoked (in part): SI 2014/1848 Art.2

1038. Education (National Curriculum) (Key Stage 2 Assessment Arrangements) (England) Order 2003
Art.9, amended: SI 2014/2103 Art.12

1039. Education (National Curriculum) (Key Stage 3 Assessment Arrangements) (England) Order 2003
Art.6, amended: SI 2014/2103 Art.13

1076. Medicines and Healthcare Products Regulatory Agency Trading Fund Order 2003
referred to: SI 2014/432
Sch.1, applied: SI 2014/432

1082. Ammonium Nitrate Materials (High Nitrogen Content) Safety Regulations 2003
Reg.11, amended: SI 2014/469 Sch.3 para.108

1173. Adoption (Bringing Children into the United Kingdom) Regulations 2003
see *A County Council v M* [2013] EWHC 1501 (Fam), [2014] 1 F.L.R. 881 (Fam Div), Peter Jackson J

1185. Immigration (Passenger Transit Visa) Order 2003
revoked: SI 2014/2702 Sch.2
Sch.1, amended: SI 2014/1513 Art.2

1247. Criminal Justice (Northern Ireland) Order 2003
applied: SI 2014/3141 Reg.98
Art.6, applied: SI 2014/3141 Reg.98

1326. Government Resources and Accounts Act 2000 (Audit of Public Bodies) Order 2003
Art.13, revoked: SI 2014/1924 Sch.1
Sch.1, amended: SI 2014/1924 Sch.1

1368. Enterprise Act 2002 (Super-complaints to Regulators) Order 2003
Art.2, amended: SI 2014/549 Sch.1 para.8

1369. Enterprise Act 2002 (Merger Prenotification) Regulations 2003
Reg.4, revoked: SI 2014/549 Sch.1 para.9
Reg.5, amended: SI 2014/549 Sch.1 para.9
Reg.7, amended: SI 2014/549 Sch.1 para.9
Reg.8, amended: SI 2014/549 Sch.1 para.9
Reg.8, revoked (in part): SI 2014/549 Sch.1 para.9
Reg.8, varied: SI 2014/549 Sch.2 para.2
Reg.9, revoked: SI 2014/549 Sch.1 para.9
Reg.14, amended: SI 2014/549 Sch.1 para.9

1370. Enterprise Act 2002 (Merger Fees and Determination of Turnover) Order 2003
applied: SI 2014/534 Art.12
Art.2, amended: SI 2014/534 Art.3
Art.3, amended: SI 2014/534 Art.4
Art.3, applied: SI 2014/534 Art.12
Art.3, revoked (in part): SI 2014/534 Art.4
Art.4, amended: SI 2014/534 Art.5
Art.5, amended: SI 2014/534 Art.6
Art.6, amended: SI 2014/534 Art.7
Art.7, substituted: SI 2014/534 Art.8
Art.8, amended: SI 2014/534 Art.9
Art.9, applied: SI 2014/534 Art.12
Art.9, substituted: SI 2014/534 Art.10
Art.10, applied: SI 2014/534 Art.12
Art.10, revoked: SI 2014/534 Art.11

1371. Competition Commission (Penalties) Order 2003
revoked: SI 2014/559 Art.5

1372. Competition Appeal Tribunal Rules 2003
r.8, see *Somerfield Stores Ltd v Office of Fair Trading* [2014] EWCA Civ 400, [2014] U.K.C.L.R. 1215 (CA (Civ Div)), Laws LJ
r.26, see *Groupe Eurotunnel SA v Competition Commission* [2014] Comp. A.R. 77 (CAT), Marcus Smith QC

1373. OFT Registers of Undertakings and Orders (Available Hours) Order 2003
revoked: SI 2014/558 Art.3

1387. Food Supplements (England) Regulations 2003
Reg.2, amended: SI 2014/1855 Sch.7 para.25
Reg.6, amended: SI 2014/1855 Sch.7 para.26
Reg.7, amended: SI 2014/1855 Sch.7 para.27

1399. Enterprise Act 2002 (Part 8 Designated Enforcers Criteria for Designation, Designation of Public Bodies as Designated Enforcers and Transitional Provisions) Order 2003
    Art.3, amended: SI 2014/549 Sch.1 para.10

1417. Land Registration Rules 2003
    Part 4 r.31, varied: SI 2014/2708 Art.5
    Sch.1, amended: SI 2014/834 Sch.3 para.4, SI 2014/2371 Art.2
    Sch.5, amended: SI 2014/834 Sch.3 para.5

1563. Specified Sugar Products (England) Regulations 2003
    Reg.2, amended: SI 2014/1855 Sch.7 para.29
    Reg.5, amended: SI 2014/1855 Sch.7 para.30
    Reg.6, revoked: SI 2014/1855 Sch.6 Part 1
    Reg.10, revoked (in part): SI 2014/1855 Sch.6 Part 1

1572. Health Professions Council (Registration and Fees) Rules Order of Council 2003
    Sch.1, added: SI 2014/1887 Sch.1 para.20, Sch.1 para.21, Sch.1 para.22
    Sch.1, amended: SI 2014/532 Sch.1

1592. Enterprise Act 2002 (Protection of Legitimate Interests) Order 2003
    applied: SI 2014/891 Art.23
    varied: SI 2014/891 Art.20
    Art.1, amended: SI 2014/891 Art.3
    Art.3, amended: SI 2014/891 Art.4
    Art.4, amended: SI 2014/891 Art.5
    Art.5, amended: SI 2014/891 Art.6
    Art.5, applied: SI 2014/891 Art.20, Art.21
    Art.5A, added: SI 2014/891 Art.7
    Art.6, amended: SI 2014/891 Art.8
    Art.7, amended: SI 2014/891 Art.9
    Art.8, amended: SI 2014/891 Art.10
    Art.9, amended: SI 2014/891 Art.11
    Art.11, amended: SI 2014/891 Art.12
    Art.12, amended: SI 2014/891 Art.13
    Art.13, amended: SI 2014/891 Art.14
    Art.14, amended: SI 2014/891 Art.15
    Art.14, revoked (in part): SI 2014/891 Art.15
    Sch.1, amended: SI 2014/891 Art.16
    Sch.1, revoked (in part): SI 2014/891 Art.16
    Sch.2, amended: SI 2014/891 Art.17
    Sch.2 para.1, applied: SI 2014/891 Art.23
    Sch.2 para.1, revoked: SI 2014/891 Art.17
    Sch.2 para.2, amended: SI 2014/891 Art.17
    Sch.2 para.2, applied: SI 2014/891 Art.23
    Sch.2 para.3, amended: SI 2014/891 Art.17

    Sch.2 para.4, amended: SI 2014/891 Art.17
    Sch.2 para.5, amended: SI 2014/891 Art.17
    Sch.2 para.7, amended: SI 2014/891 Art.17
    Sch.2 para.8, amended: SI 2014/891 Art.17
    Sch.2 para.10, amended: SI 2014/891 Art.17
    Sch.2 para.11, amended: SI 2014/891 Art.17
    Sch.3 para.1, amended: SI 2014/891 Art.18
    Sch.3 para.1, applied: SI 2014/559
    Sch.3 para.1, revoked (in part): SI 2014/891 Art.18
    Sch.3 para.2, amended: SI 2014/891 Art.18
    Sch.4 para.3, amended: SI 2014/891 Art.19
    Sch.4 para.7, amended: SI 2014/891 Art.19
    Sch.4 para.15, revoked (in part): SI 2014/891 Art.19
    Sch.4 para.18, added: SI 2014/891 Art.19

1595. Enterprise Act 2002 (Anticipated Mergers) Order 2003
    Art.4, amended: SI 2014/549 Sch.1 para.11

1659. Cocoa and Chocolate Products (England) Regulations 2003
    Reg.2, amended: SI 2014/1855 Sch.7 para.32
    Reg.5, amended: SI 2014/1855 Sch.7 para.33
    Reg.6, amended: SI 2014/1855 Sch.7 para.34
    Reg.7, revoked (in part): SI 2014/1855 Sch.6 Part 1
    Reg.11, revoked (in part): SI 2014/1855 Sch.6 Part 1

1660. Employment Equality (Religion or Belief) Regulations 2003
    Reg.3, see *Mba v Merton LBC* [2013] EWCA Civ 1562, [2014] 1 W.L.R. 1501 (CA (Civ Div)), Maurice Kay LJ

1661. Employment Equality (Sexual Orientation) Regulations 2003
    see *Innospec Ltd v Walker* [2014] I.C.R. 645 (EAT), Langstaff J

1662. Education (School Teachers Qualifications) (England) Regulations 2003
    Sch.2 Part 1 para.13B, substituted: SI 2014/2697 Reg.3

1709. Education (School Teachers Prescribed Qualifications, etc) Order 2003
    Art.5, amended: SI 2014/1063 Art.2
    Art.5, revoked (in part): SI 2014/1063 Art.2

1719. Food Supplements (Wales) Regulations 2003

Reg.2, amended: SI 2014/2303 Sch.7
para.25
Reg.6, amended: SI 2014/2303 Sch.7
para.26
Reg.7, amended: SI 2014/2303 Sch.7
para.27
1729. Disease Control (England) Order 2003
applied: SI 2014/2337 Art.10
1847. Coast Protection (Notices) (Wales)
Regulations 2003
Reg.5, amended: 2014 c.29 s.4
1849. Animal By-Products (Identification)
(Amendment) (Wales) Regulations 2003
revoked: SI 2014/517 Reg.28
1857. Enforcement of Road Traffic Debts
(Certificated Bailiffs) (Amendment) Regulations
2003
revoked: SI 2014/600 Sch.1 Part 2
1858. Distress for Rent (Amendment) Rules 2003
revoked: SI 2014/600 Sch.1 Part 2
1888. European Communities (Designation)
(No.3) Order 2003
Sch.1, amended: SI 2014/1362 Sch.1
1902. Wireless Telegraphy (Limitation of
Number of Licences) Order 2003
revoked: SI 2014/774 Art.2
1964. Education (Modification of Enactments
Relating to Employment) (England) Order 2003
see *Birmingham City Council v Emery*
[2014] E.L.R. 203 (EAT), Mitting J; see
Davies v Haringey LBC [2014] EWHC 3393
(QB), [2014] B.L.G.R. 743 (QBD),
Supperstone J
1987. Service Charges (Consultation
Requirements) (England) Regulations 2003
see *BDW Trading Ltd v South Anglia*
Housing Ltd [2013] EWHC 2169 (Ch),
[2014] 1 W.L.R. 920 (Ch D), Nicholas
Strauss QC; see *Voyvoda v Grosvenor West*
End Properties [2014] L. & T.R. 10 (UT
(Lands)), Jeremy Sullivan QC
Reg.3, see *BDW Trading Ltd v South Anglia*
Housing Ltd [2013] EWHC 2169 (Ch),
[2014] 1 W.L.R. 920 (Ch D), Nicholas
Strauss QC
1994. Education (Mandatory Awards)
Regulations 2003
Sch.3 Part 3 para.7, amended: SI 2014/107
Sch.1 para.33
2075. Meat Products (England) Regulations 2003
revoked: SI 2014/3001 Reg.8

Reg.6, referred to: SI 2014/1603 Sch.3
para.2
Sch.2, referred to: SI 2014/1603 Sch.3 para.2
2076. Capital Allowances (Environmentally
Beneficial Plant and Machinery) Order 2003
Art.2, amended: SI 2014/1869 Art.3
2097. Insolvency Act 1986 (Prescribed Part)
Order 2003
applied: SI 2014/229 Sch.5 para.1
2141. Distress for Rent (Amendment No 2) Rules
2003
revoked: SI 2014/600 Sch.1 Part 2
2162. A11 Trunk Road (Chalk Hill to Barton
Mills, Suffolk) (50 Miles per Hour Speed Limit)
2003
revoked: SI 2014/2198 Art.3
2243. Honey (England) Regulations 2003
Reg.2, amended: SI 2014/1855 Sch.7
para.36
Reg.4, amended: SI 2014/1855 Sch.7
para.37
Reg.6, revoked: SI 2014/1855 Sch.6 Part 1
Reg.10, revoked (in part): SI 2014/1855
Sch.6 Part 1
2306. Channel Tunnel Rail Link (Nomination)
(Amendment) Order 2003
revoked: SI 2014/1332 Art.2
2314. Religious Character of Schools
(Designation Procedure) (Independent Schools)
(England) Regulations 2003
referred to: SI 2014/1024, SI 2014/2320, SI
2014/2342, SI 2014/3361
2329. Classical Swine Fever (England) Order
2003
revoked: SI 2014/1894 Sch.5
2382. National Health Service (Travel Expenses
and Remission of Charges) Regulations 2003
Reg.5, amended: SI 2014/545 Reg.4, SI
2014/2667 Reg.2
Reg.5, applied: SI 2014/2667 Reg.5
2426. Privacy and Electronic Communications
(EC Directive) Regulations 2003
applied: SI 2014/1825 Art.3
2456. Classical Swine Fever (Wales) Order 2003
revoked: SI 2014/1894 Sch.5
2498. Copyright and Related Rights Regulations
2003
Reg.11, revoked: SI 2014/1372 Sch.1
para.14
Reg.16, revoked: SI 2014/1372 Sch.1
para.14

Reg.23, revoked: SI 2014/1384 Sch.1 para.8
Sch.1 Part 2 para.22, revoked: SI 2014/1384
Sch.1 para.8

2499. Copyright (Visually Impaired Persons) Act 2002 (Commencement) Order 2003
revoked: SI 2014/1384 Sch.1 para.8

2577. Olive Oil (Marketing Standards) Regulations 2003
revoked: SI 2014/195 Reg.20
Reg.10, applied: SI 2014/195 Reg.18

2613. Council Tax and Non-Domestic Rating (Demand Notices) (England) Regulations 2003
Sch.2 Part 1 para.7, substituted: SI 2014/404 Reg.3
Sch.2 Part 3 para.3, substituted: SI 2014/404 Reg.4

2628. Immigration (Passenger Transit Visa) (Amendment No 2) Order 2003
revoked: SI 2014/2702 Sch.2

2647. Food (Provisions relating to Labelling) (England) Regulations 2003
revoked: SI 2014/1855 Sch.6 Part 1

2682. Income Tax (Pay As You Earn) Regulations 2003
applied: SI 2014/2396 Reg.1, SI 2014/2929 Reg.4
Reg.2, amended: SI 2014/992 Art.9, SI 2014/2689 Reg.3
Reg.2, revoked (in part): SI 2014/472 Reg.3
Reg.14C, added: SI 2014/2689 Reg.4
Reg.23, amended: SI 2014/2689 Reg.5
Reg.28, amended: SI 2014/2689 Reg.5
Reg.66, amended: SI 2014/2689 Reg.6
Reg.67B, amended: SI 2014/472 Reg.4
Reg.67D, amended: SI 2014/472 Reg.5
Reg.67E, amended: SI 2014/472 Reg.6
Reg.67G, amended: SI 2014/1017 Reg.2
Reg.67H, amended: SI 2014/1017 Reg.2
Reg.67I, added: SI 2014/2396 Reg.2
Reg.69, amended: SI 2014/1017 Reg.2
Reg.69A, added: SI 2014/472 Reg.7
Reg.70, varied: 2014 c.6 s.126
Reg.72, amended: SI 2014/992 Art.9
Reg.72, revoked (in part): SI 2014/992 Art.9
Reg.72E, amended: SI 2014/472 Reg.8
Reg.72F, amended: SI 2014/472 Reg.9
Reg.81, amended: SI 2014/992 Art.9
Reg.81, revoked (in part): SI 2014/992 Art.9
Reg.82, revoked: SI 2014/992 Art.9
Reg.84, amended: SI 2014/992 Art.9
Reg.84A, added: SI 2014/474 Reg.2

Reg.97ZA, added: 2014 c.26 s.17
Reg.141, amended: SI 2014/472 Reg.10
Reg.142, substituted: SI 2014/472 Reg.11
Reg.143, amended: SI 2014/472 Reg.12, Reg.13
Reg.144, amended: SI 2014/472 Reg.14, SI 2014/2689 Reg.5
Reg.145, revoked: SI 2014/472 Reg.15
Reg.146, revoked: SI 2014/472 Reg.16
Reg.147A, added: SI 2014/472 Reg.17
Reg.161, amended: SI 2014/2689 Reg.7
Reg.206, amended: SI 2014/472 Reg.18
Reg.207, revoked (in part): SI 2014/472 Reg.19
Reg.218, amended: SI 2014/992 Art.9
Reg.219, amended: SI 2014/992 Art.9
Sch.A1 para.21, amended: SI 2014/472 Reg.20

2754. Animal By-Products (Identification) (Amendment) (Wales) (No.2) Regulations 2003
revoked: SI 2014/517 Reg.28

2834. Channel Tunnel Rail Link (Nomination) (Amendment) (No.2) Order 2003
revoked: SI 2014/1332 Art.2

2837. Stamp Duty Land Tax (Administration) Regulations 2003
Reg.29, revoked: SI 2014/600 Sch.1 para.7, Sch.1 Part 2
Sch.3, revoked: SI 2014/600 Sch.1 para.7, Sch.1 Part 2

2896. Thurrock Development Corporation (Area and Constitution) Order 2003
revoked: SI 2014/1181 Art.2

2913. African Swine Fever (England) Order 2003
revoked: SI 2014/1894 Sch.5

2994. Department for Transport (Driver Licensing and Vehicle Registration Fees) Order 2003
applied: SI 2014/2580

3037. Cocoa and Chocolate Products (Wales) Regulations 2003
Reg.2, amended: SI 2014/2303 Sch.7 para.29
Reg.5, amended: SI 2014/2303 Sch.7 para.30
Reg.6, amended: SI 2014/2303 Sch.7 para.31
Reg.7, revoked (in part): SI 2014/2303 Sch.6 Part 1

Reg.11, revoked (in part): SI 2014/2303
Sch.6 Part 1
3044. Honey (Wales) Regulations 2003
Reg.2, amended: SI 2014/2303 Sch.7
para.33
Reg.4, amended: SI 2014/2303 Sch.7
para.34
Reg.6, revoked: SI 2014/2303 Sch.6 Part 1
Reg.10, revoked (in part): SI 2014/2303
Sch.6 Part 1
**3047. Specified Sugar Products (Wales)
Regulations 2003**
Reg.2, amended: SI 2014/2303 Sch.7
para.36
Reg.5, amended: SI 2014/2303 Sch.7
para.37
Reg.6, revoked: SI 2014/2303 Sch.6 Part 1
Reg.10, revoked (in part): SI 2014/2303
Sch.6 Part 1
**3049. Merchant Shipping (Working Time Inland
Waterways) Regulations 2003**
Reg.4, amended: SI 2014/386 Sch.1 para.21,
SI 2014/431 Sch.1 para.29
Reg.18, amended: SI 2014/386 Sch.1
para.22
Reg.18A, added: SI 2014/386 Sch.1 para.23
Reg.19, amended: SI 2014/386 Sch.1
para.24, SI 2014/431 Sch.1 para.29
3102. Export (Penalty) Regulations 2003
Reg.9F, amended: SI 2014/1264 Art.9
**3103. Extradition Act 2003 (Commencement and
Savings) Order 2003**
Art.2, applied: SI 2014/1610 r.2_1
Art.3, applied: SI 2014/1610 r.2_1
**3146. Local Authorities (Capital Finance and
Accounting) (England) Regulations 2003**
Reg.30J, added: SI 2014/1375 Reg.3
**3207. Processed Cereal-based Foods and Baby
Foods for Infants and Young Children
(England) Regulations 2003**
applied: SI 2014/3001 Reg.3
Reg.8, amended: SI 2014/1855 Sch.7
para.39
**3226. Financial Collateral Arrangements (No.2)
Regulations 2003**
Reg.3, amended: SI 2014/3348 Sch.3 para.9
Reg.12, amended: SI 2014/3348 Sch.3
para.9
Reg.18A, added: SI 2014/3348 Sch.3 para.9

**3239. Local Authorities (Capital Finance and
Accounting) (Wales) Regulations 2003**
Reg.18, amended: SI 2014/481 Reg.3
Reg.24A, substituted: SI 2014/481 Reg.4
**3272. Welfare of Animals (Slaughter or Killing)
(Amendment) (England) Regulations 2003**
revoked: SI 2014/1240 Reg.47
3273. African Swine Fever (Wales) Order 2003
revoked: SI 2014/1894 Sch.5
**3284. Designation of Schools Having a Religious
Character (Independent Schools) (England)
(No.2) Order 2003**
Sch.1, amended: SI 2014/2342 Sch.2
**3319. Conduct of Employment Agencies and
Employment Businesses Regulations 2003**
Reg.27A, added: SI 2014/3351 Reg.2
**3335. Extradition Act 2003 (Part 3 Designation)
Order 2003**
Art.2, revoked (in part): SI 2014/834 Sch.3
para.6
**3372. A483 Trunk Road (Newbridge By Pass,
Wrexham County Borough) (Derestriction)
Order 2003**
varied: SI 2014/810 Art.8

2004

**22. A477 Trunk Road (Red Roses,
Carmarthenshire) (40 MPH Speed Limit) Order
2004**
varied: SI 2014/1058 Art.6
102. Price Marking Order 2004
Art.1, amended: SI 2014/1855 Sch.7 para.41
**249. Food (Provisions relating to Labelling)
(Wales) Regulations 2004**
revoked: SI 2014/2303 Sch.6 Part 1
**291. National Health Service (General Medical
Services Contracts) Regulations 2004**
Reg.2, amended: SI 2014/465 Reg.3
Reg.26B, substituted: SI 2014/465 Reg.4
Reg.26C, substituted: SI 2014/465 Reg.4
Sch.6 Part 1 para.6A, added: SI 2014/465
Reg.5
Sch.6 Part 1 para.11, substituted: SI
2014/465 Reg.6
Sch.6 Part 1 para.12, amended: SI 2014/465
Reg.7
Sch.6 Part 3 para.39A, amended: SI
2014/2721 Reg.2

Sch.6 Part 5 para.74, added: SI 2014/465
Reg.8
Sch.6 Part 5 para.76ZA, added: SI
2014/2721 Reg.3
Sch.6 Part 9 para.122, amended: SI
2014/1887 Sch.2 para.1
Sch.6 Part 9 para.123, amended: SI
2014/1887 Sch.2 para.1

293. European Parliamentary Elections Regulations 2004

Reg.11, amended: SI 2014/923 Reg.2
Reg.15, enabled: SI 2014/325
Reg.52, applied: SI 2014/704 Art.6
Reg.120, enabled: SI 2014/1129
Reg.122A, amended: SI 2014/923 Reg.3
Sch.1 Part 3 para.23, amended: SI 2014/923
Reg.2
Sch.2 Part 2 para.17, amended: SI 2014/923
Reg.2
Sch.2 Part 2 para.26, amended: SI 2014/923
Reg.4
Sch.2 Part 2 para.31A, amended: SI
2014/923 Reg.4
Sch.2 Part 4 para.41, amended: SI 2014/923
Reg.2
Sch.2 Part 4 para.42, applied: SI 2014/704
Art.6
Sch.2 Part 4 para.54A, amended: SI
2014/923 Reg.4
Sch.2 Part 4 para.67, amended: SI 2014/923
Reg.4
Sch.2 Part 4 para.70, applied: SI 2014/704
Art.6
Sch.3 Part 1 para.8, amended: SI 2014/923
Reg.5
Sch.3 Part 1 para.8, applied: SI 2014/704
Art.6
Sch.3 Part 1 para.14, amended: SI 2014/923
Reg.5
Sch.3 Part 1 para.24, amended: SI 2014/923
Reg.5
Sch.3 Part 1 para.28, applied: SI 2014/704
Art.6
Sch.3 Part 1 para.29, applied: SI 2014/704
Art.5
Sch.3 Part 2 para.13, amended: SI 2014/923
Reg.5
Sch.3 Part 2 para.23, amended: SI 2014/923
Reg.5
Sch.6 Part 3 para.10, amended: SI
2014/1803 Reg.53

294. Representation of the People (Combination of Polls) (England and Wales) Regulations 2004

Appendix 1., added: SI 2014/920 Sch.1
Reg.2, amended: SI 2014/920 Reg.2
Reg.4, amended: SI 2014/920 Reg.2
Reg.5, amended: SI 2014/920 Reg.2
Reg.8, amended: SI 2014/920 Reg.2
Sch.2 para.3, amended: SI 2014/920 Reg.2
Sch.2 para.9, substituted: SI 2014/920 Reg.3
Sch.2 para.22, amended: SI 2014/920 Reg.2
Sch.2 para.28, substituted: SI 2014/920
Reg.4
Sch.2 para.29, substituted: SI 2014/920
Reg.5

314. Processed Cereal-based Foods and Baby Foods for Infants and Young Children (Wales) Regulations 2004

applied: SI 2014/3087 Reg.3
Reg.8, amended: SI 2014/2303 Sch.7
para.39

352. Petroleum Licensing (Exploration and Production) (Seaward and Landward Areas) Regulations 2004

Reg.3, disapplied: SI 2014/1686 Reg.2
Sch.6, disapplied: SI 2014/1686 Reg.2

353. Insurers (Reorganisation and Winding Up) Regulations 2004

Reg.2, amended: SI 2014/1815 Sch.1
para.12
Reg.2, varied: SI 2014/229 Sch.5 para.1A
Reg.17, amended: SI 2014/1815 Sch.1
para.12

400. High Court Enforcement Officers Regulations 2004

Reg.13, amended: SI 2014/600 Sch.1 para.8
Reg.13, revoked (in part): SI 2014/600 Sch.1
para.8
Reg.15, revoked: SI 2014/600 Sch.1 para.8,
Sch.1 Part 2
Sch.3, applied: SI 2014/600 Art.4
Sch.3, referred to: SI 2014/600 Art.4
Sch.3, revoked: SI 2014/600 Sch.1 para.8,
Sch.1 Part 2
Sch.4, revoked: SI 2014/600 Sch.1 para.8,
Sch.1 Part 2

478. National Health Service (General Medical Services Contracts) (Wales) Regulations 2004

Reg.2, amended: SI 2014/2291 Reg.3
Sch.6 Part 3 para.49, amended: SI
2014/2291 Reg.3
Sch.6 Part 4, amended: SI 2014/2291 Reg.3

Sch.6 Part 4 para.64, amended: SI
2014/2291 Reg.3
Sch.6 Part 9 para.120, amended: SI
2014/1887 Sch.2 para.5
Sch.6 Part 9 para.121, amended: SI
2014/1887 Sch.2 para.5

**572. Street Works (Inspection Fees) (England)
(Amendment) Regulations 2004**
applied: SI 2014/466 Sch.1, SI 2014/3109
Sch.1, SI 2014/3310 Sch.1

**577. Designation of Schools Having a Religious
Character (Independent Schools) (England)
(No.3) Order 2004**
Sch.1, amended: SI 2014/3361 Sch.2

**590. Common Agricultural Policy Non-IACS
Support Schemes (Appeals) (England)
Regulations 2004**
revoked: SI 2014/3263 Sch.5

593. Insolvency Proceedings (Fees) Order 2004
Art.6, amended: SI 2014/583 Art.2
Sch.2 para.2, amended: SI 2014/583 Art.3

**627. National Health Service (Personal Medical
Services Agreements) Regulations 2004**
Reg.2, amended: SI 2014/465 Reg.9
Reg.10, see *Pitalia v NHS Commissioning
Board* [2014] EWCA Civ 474, (2014) 138
B.M.L.R. 89 (CA (Civ Div)), Aikens LJ
Reg.18B, substituted: SI 2014/465 Reg.10
Sch.5 Part 1 para.9, substituted: SI 2014/465
Reg.11
Sch.5 Part 1 para.10, amended: SI 2014/465
Reg.12
Sch.5 Part 2 para.13A, added: SI 2014/465
Reg.13
Sch.5 Part 3 para.38A, amended: SI
2014/2721 Reg.4
Sch.5 Part 5 para.70A, added: SI 2014/465
Reg.14
Sch.5 Part 5 para.72ZA, added: SI
2014/2721 Reg.5
Sch.5 Part 9 para.113, amended: SI
2014/1887 Sch.2 para.2
Sch.5 Part 9 para.114, amended: SI
2014/1887 Sch.2 para.2

**629. National Health Service (General Medical
Services Contracts) (Prescription of Drugs etc.)
Regulations 2004**
Sch.2, amended: SI 2014/1625 Reg.2

**643. Police (Complaints and Misconduct)
Regulations 2004**
see *R. (on the application of the Chief
Constable of West Yorkshire) v Independent
Police Complaints Commission* [2013]
EWHC 2698 (Admin), [2014] P.T.S.R. 242
(QBD (Admin)), Judge Jeremy Richardson
QC

**683. Leasehold Valuation Tribunals (Fees)
(Wales) Regulations 2004**
Reg.8, amended: SI 2014/107 Sch.2 para.4,
SI 2014/287 Reg.2
Reg.8, revoked (in part): SI 2014/287 Reg.2

**684. Service Charges (Consultation
Requirements) (Wales) Regulations 2004**
Reg.2, amended: SI 2014/107 Sch.2 para.5

686. Kimberley Process (Fees) Regulations 2004
revoked: SI 2014/1684 Reg.5

**753. ACAS Arbitration Scheme (Great Britain)
Order 2004**
Sch.1 Part VII para.26, amended: SI
2014/386 Sch.1 para.25

**756. Civil Aviation (Working Time) Regulations
2004**
Reg.18, amended: SI 2014/431 Sch.1
para.31
Reg.19, added: SI 2014/431 Sch.1 para.32

758. Pensions Increase (Review) Order 2004
referred to: SI 2014/668 Sch.1
Art.6, substituted: SI 2014/107 Sch.1
para.56, SI 2014/3229 Sch.6 para.35

**770. Social Security (Contributions,
Categorisation of Earners and Intermediaries)
(Amendment) Regulations 2004**
Reg.34, revoked (in part): SI 2014/635 Sch.1

**865. General Medical Services and Personal
Medical Services Transitional and
Consequential Provisions Order 2004**
Art.1, see *Pitalia v NHS Commissioning
Board* [2014] EWCA Civ 474, (2014) 138
B.M.L.R. 89 (CA (Civ Div)), Aikens LJ
Art.58, see *Pitalia v NHS Commissioning
Board* [2014] EWCA Civ 474, (2014) 138
B.M.L.R. 89 (CA (Civ Div)), Aikens LJ
Art.68, see *Pitalia v NHS Commissioning
Board* [2014] EWCA Civ 474, (2014) 138
B.M.L.R. 89 (CA (Civ Div)), Aikens LJ

**940. Trunk Road (Llandybie, Dyfed) (Speed
Limits) Order 1978 (Variation) Order 2004**
revoked: SI 2014/2893 Art.5

1022. National Health Service (General Medical Services Contracts) (Prescription of Drugs Etc.) (Wales) Regulations 2004

    Sch.2, amended: SI 2014/109 Reg.2

1031. Medicines for Human Use (Clinical Trials) Regulations 2004

    applied: 2014 c.23 s.112

    referred to: 2014 c.23 s.110, SI 2014/1638 Sch.2 para.7

    Reg.5, amended: 2014 c.23 s.116

1034. Crime (International Co-operation) Act 2003 (Designation of Prosecuting Authorities) Order 2004

    Art.2, amended: SI 2014/834 Sch.3 para.7

1045. Credit Institutions (Reorganisation and Winding up) Regulations 2004

    Part 6, added: SI 2014/3348 Sch.3 para.10

    Reg.2, amended: SI 2014/3348 Sch.3 para.10

    Reg.3, amended: SI 2014/3348 Sch.3 para.10

    Reg.10, amended: SI 2014/3348 Sch.3 para.10

    Reg.18, amended: SI 2014/3348 Sch.3 para.10

    Reg.19, amended: SI 2014/3348 Sch.3 para.10

    Reg.21, amended: SI 2014/3348 Sch.3 para.10

    Reg.29, amended: SI 2014/3348 Sch.3 para.10

    Reg.34, substituted: SI 2014/3348 Sch.3 para.10

    Reg.35, substituted: SI 2014/3348 Sch.3 para.10

    Reg.36, amended: SI 2014/3348 Sch.3 para.10

    Reg.38, amended: SI 2014/3348 Sch.3 para.10

1077. Competition Act 1998 (Concurrency) Regulations 2004

    applied: SI 2014/536 Reg.12

    revoked: SI 2014/536 Reg.12

1078. Competition Act 1998 (Appealable Decisions and Revocation of Notification of Excluded Agreements) Regulations 2004

    Reg.2, amended: SI 2014/549 Sch.1 para.12

1219. Accession (Immigration and Worker Registration) Regulations 2004

    see *Revenue and Customs Commissioners v Spiridonova* [2014] NICA 63 (CA (NI)), Morgan LCJ

1255. Nuclear Safeguards (Notification) Regulations 2004

    applied: SI 2014/469 Sch.1 para.2

    amended: SI 2014/469 Sch.3 para.18

    Reg.2, amended: SI 2014/469 Sch.3 para.19

    Reg.4, amended: SI 2014/469 Sch.3 para.18

    Reg.5, amended: SI 2014/469 Sch.3 para.18, Sch.3 para.20

    Reg.6, amended: SI 2014/469 Sch.3 para.18, Sch.3 para.21

1261. Competition Act 1998 and Other Enactments (Amendment) Regulations 2004

    Reg.3, amended: SI 2014/549 Sch.1 para.13

    Reg.3, revoked (in part): SI 2014/549 Sch.1 para.13

    Reg.8, amended: SI 2014/549 Sch.1 para.13

1267. European Parliamentary Elections (Northern Ireland) Regulations 2004

    Reg.2, amended: SI 2014/1803 Reg.10

    Reg.7, amended: SI 2014/1803 Reg.11

    Reg.8, amended: SI 2014/1803 Reg.12

    Reg.9, amended: SI 2014/1803 Reg.13

    Reg.11, amended: SI 2014/1803 Reg.14

    Reg.16, applied: SI 2014/794 Art.2

    Reg.16, enabled: SI 2014/794

    Reg.18, amended: SI 2014/1803 Reg.15

    Reg.58, amended: SI 2014/1803 Reg.16

    Reg.80, amended: SI 2014/1803 Reg.17

    Sch.1 Part II para.17, applied: SI 2014/794 Art.2

    Sch.1 Part III para.29, amended: SI 2014/1803 Reg.19

    Sch.1 Part III para.30, amended: SI 2014/1803 Reg.20

    Sch.1 Part III para.33, amended: SI 2014/1803 Reg.21

    Sch.1 Part III para.42, amended: SI 2014/1803 Reg.22

    Sch.1 Part III para.43A, added: SI 2014/1803 Reg.23

    Sch.1 Part III para.50, amended: SI 2014/1803 Reg.24

    Sch.1 Part V para.66, amended: SI 2014/1803 Reg.25

    Sch.1 Part V para.67, amended: SI 2014/1803 Reg.26

Sch.1 Part VIII, amended: SI 2014/1803
Reg.27, Sch.1
Sch.2 Part I para.2, amended: SI 2014/1803
Reg.29
Sch.2 Part I para.2A, amended: SI
2014/1803 Reg.30
Sch.2 Part I para.2B, substituted: SI
2014/1803 Reg.31
Sch.2 Part I para.3, substituted: SI
2014/1803 Reg.32
Sch.2 Part I para.7, amended: SI 2014/1803
Reg.33
Sch.2 Part I para.13, amended: SI 2014/1803
Reg.34
Sch.2 Part I para.14, amended: SI 2014/1803
Reg.35
Sch.2 Part II para.15, amended: SI
2014/1803 Reg.36
Sch.2 Part II para.17, substituted: SI
2014/1803 Reg.37
Sch.2 Part II para.18, amended: SI
2014/1803 Reg.38
Sch.2 Part II para.20, amended: SI
2014/1803 Reg.39
Sch.2 Part II para.21, amended: SI
2014/1803 Reg.40
Sch.2 Part II para.26, amended: SI
2014/1803 Reg.41
Sch.2 Part II para.26A, added: SI 2014/1803
Reg.42
Sch.2 Part II para.29, substituted: SI
2014/1803 Reg.43
Sch.2 Part II para.36, amended: SI
2014/1803 Reg.44
Sch.2 Part III, added: SI 2014/1803 Reg.45
Sch.2 Part III, amended: SI 2014/1803
Reg.45
Sch.4 Part III para.10, substituted: SI
2014/1803 Reg.47
Sch.4 Part III para.11, amended: SI
2014/1803 Reg.48
Sch.6 para.6, amended: SI 2014/1803
Reg.50
Sch.6 para.12A, added: SI 2014/1803
Reg.51
Sch.6 para.22, added: SI 2014/1803 Reg.52
Sch.6 para.22, amended: SI 2014/1803
Reg.52

**1280. Mersey Docks and Harbour Company
(Liverpool Landing Stage Extension) Harbour
Revision Order 2004**
Art.16, varied: SI 2014/2708 Art.5
**1300. Measuring Instruments (EEC
Requirements) (Fees) Regulations 2004**
Sch.1, amended: SI 2014/568 Reg.3
**1304. Immigration (Passenger Transit Visa)
(Amendment) Order 2004**
revoked: SI 2014/2702 Sch.2
1396. Meat Products (Wales) Regulations 2004
revoked: SI 2014/3087 Reg.8
**1404. Plant Health (Export Certification)
(England) Order 2004**
Art.2, amended: SI 2014/609 Art.2
Sch.3, substituted: SI 2014/609 Art.2
Sch.4, substituted: SI 2014/609 Art.2
1450. Child Trust Funds Regulations 2004
Reg.2, amended: SI 2014/649 Reg.3, SI
2014/1815 Sch.1 para.13
Reg.9, amended: SI 2014/649 Reg.4, SI
2014/1453 Reg.3
Reg.12, amended: SI 2014/649 Reg.5, SI
2014/1453 Reg.4
Reg.18A, amended: SI 2014/649 Reg.6
**1512. Food Labelling (Amendment) (England)
Regulations 2004**
revoked: SI 2014/1855 Sch.6 Part 1
**1517. Enterprise Act 2002 (Bodies Designated to
make Super-complaints) Order 2004**
Sch.1, amended: SI 2014/631 Sch.1 para.22
**1642. London Thames Gateway Development
Corporation (Area and Constitution) Order
2004**
revoked: SI 2014/1181 Art.2
**1654. Nursing and Midwifery Council (Fees)
Rules Order of Council 2004**
Sch.1, amended: SI 2014/3139 Sch.1
**1713. Fishing Vessels (Working Time Sea-
fishermen) Regulations 2004**
Reg.4, amended: SI 2014/386 Sch.1 para.27,
SI 2014/431 Sch.1 para.33
Reg.19, amended: SI 2014/386 Sch.1
para.28
Reg.19A, added: SI 2014/386 Sch.1 para.29
Reg.20, amended: SI 2014/386 Sch.1
para.30, SI 2014/431 Sch.1 para.33
**1756. Adult Placement Schemes (Wales)
Regulations 2004**
Reg.2, amended: SI 2014/107 Sch.2 para.6

1761. Nursing and Midwifery Council (Fitness to Practise) Rules Order of Council 2004
> see *White v Nursing and Midwifery Council* [2014] EWHC 520 (Admin), [2014] Med. L.R. 205 (QBD (Admin)), Mitting J

1767. Nursing and Midwifery Council (Education, Registration and Registration Appeals) Rules Order of Council 2004
> Sch.1, added: SI 2014/1887 Sch.1 para.31, Sch.1 para.32
> Sch.1, amended: SI 2014/1887 Sch.1 para.31, Sch.1 para.33

1769. Justification of Practices Involving Ionising Radiation Regulations 2004
> Reg.18, amended: SI 2014/469 Sch.3 para.109
> Reg.22, amended: SI 2014/469 Sch.3 para.109

1809. Street Works (Inspection Fees) (Amendment) (Wales) Regulations 2004
> applied: SI 2014/3311 Sch.1

1818. Uranium Enrichment Technology (Prohibition on Disclosure) Regulations 2004
> Reg.1, amended: SI 2014/469 Sch.3 para.23
> Reg.3, amended: SI 2014/469 Sch.3 para.24
> Reg.4, amended: SI 2014/469 Sch.3 para.25
> Reg.5, amended: SI 2014/469 Sch.3 para.26
> Reg.6, amended: SI 2014/469 Sch.3 para.27

1861. Employment Tribunals (Constitution and Rules of Procedure) Regulations 2004
> see *Crossland v OCS Group Ltd* [2014] EWCA Civ 678, [2014] 5 Costs L.R. 791 (CA (Civ Div)), Rimer LJ
> Sch.1 para.4, see *Pallet Route Solutions Ltd v Morris* [2014] I.C.R. 394 (EAT), Langstaff J
> Sch.1 para.6, see *Pallet Route Solutions Ltd v Morris* [2014] I.C.R. 394 (EAT), Langstaff J
> Sch.1 para.8, see *Pallet Route Solutions Ltd v Morris* [2014] I.C.R. 394 (EAT), Langstaff J
> Sch.1 para.9, see *Pallet Route Solutions Ltd v Morris* [2014] I.C.R. 394 (EAT), Langstaff J
> Sch.1 para.18, see *Scott v Russell* [2013] EWCA Civ 1432, [2014] 1 Costs L.O. 95 (CA (Civ Div)), Laws LJ
> Sch.1 para.33, see *Pallet Route Solutions Ltd v Morris* [2014] I.C.R. 394 (EAT), Langstaff J
> Sch.1 para.34, see *MWH UK Ltd v Wise (Inspector of Health and Safety)* [2014] EWHC 427 (Admin), [2014] A.C.D. 96 (QBD (Admin)), Popplewell J; see *Pallet Route Solutions Ltd v Morris* [2014] I.C.R. 394 (EAT), Langstaff J
> Sch.1 para.38, see *Ladak v DRC Locums Ltd* [2014] I.R.L.R. 851 (EAT), Judge David Richardson

1980. Sudan (Restrictive Measures) (Overseas Territories) (Amendment) Order 2004
> revoked: SI 2014/2707 Art.1

2033. Health Professions (Operating Department Practitioners and Miscellaneous Amendments) Order 2004
> Art.6, revoked: SI 2014/879 Sch.1

2035. Courts Act 2003 (Consequential Amendments) Order 2004
> applied: SI 2014/1610 r.2_1

2065. Biofuels and Other Fuel Substitutes (Payment of Excise Duties etc.) Regulations 2004
> Reg.7, amended: SI 2014/471 Reg.3
> Sch.1 para.1, amended: SI 2014/471 Reg.4
> Sch.1 para.2, amended: SI 2014/471 Reg.4

2066. Courts Act 2003 (Commencement No 6 and Savings) Order 2004
> applied: SI 2014/1610 r.2_1

2068. Competition Appeal Tribunal (Amendment and Communications Act Appeals) Rules 2004
> r.1, amended: SI 2014/549 Sch.1 para.14
> r.3, amended: SI 2014/549 Sch.1 para.14
> r.5, amended: SI 2014/549 Sch.1 para.14

2095. Financial Services (Distance Marketing) Regulations 2004
> amended: SI 2014/208 Art.3
> Reg.2, amended: SI 2014/208 Art.3
> Reg.17, amended: SI 2014/208 Art.3
> Reg.18, amended: SI 2014/208 Art.3
> Reg.19, amended: SI 2014/208 Art.3
> Reg.20, amended: SI 2014/208 Art.3
> Reg.21, amended: SI 2014/208 Art.3
> Reg.22, amended: SI 2014/208 Art.3

2110. Merchant Shipping (Vessel Traffic Monitoring and Reporting Requirements) Regulations 2004
> Reg.12, amended: SI 2014/3306 Sch.2 para.5

2187. Children and Family Court Advisory and Support Service (Reviewed Case Referral) Regulations 2004
Reg.2, amended: SI 2014/879 Art.86

2205. Town and Country Planning (Transitional Arrangements) (England) Regulations 2004
revoked: SI 2014/692 Sch.1

2245. Potatoes Originating in Egypt (Wales) Regulations 2004
Reg.2, amended: SI 2014/1463 Reg.2
Reg.3, amended: SI 2014/1463 Reg.2

2326. European Public Limited-Liability Company Regulations 2004
Reg.5, substituted: SI 2014/2382 Reg.12
Reg.6, substituted: SI 2014/2382 Reg.13
Reg.7, substituted: SI 2014/2382 Reg.14
Reg.8, substituted: SI 2014/2382 Reg.15
Reg.9, substituted: SI 2014/2382 Reg.16
Reg.10, substituted: SI 2014/2382 Reg.17
Reg.10A, added: SI 2014/2382 Reg.18
Reg.11, substituted: SI 2014/2382 Reg.19
Reg.11A, added: SI 2014/2382 Reg.20
Reg.13A, amended: SI 2014/2382 Reg.21
Reg.15, amended: SI 2014/2382 Reg.22
Reg.68, substituted: SI 2014/2382 Reg.23
Reg.70, amended: SI 2014/2382 Reg.24
Reg.72, amended: SI 2014/2382 Reg.25
Reg.77, amended: SI 2014/2382 Reg.26
Reg.80C, amended: SI 2014/2382 Reg.27
Reg.82, amended: SI 2014/2382 Reg.28
Reg.85, substituted: SI 2014/2382 Reg.29
Reg.85A, added: SI 2014/2382 Reg.30
Reg.86, amended: SI 2014/2382 Reg.31
Reg.87, amended: SI 2014/2382 Reg.32
Reg.88, amended: SI 2014/2382 Reg.33
Sch.1, revoked: SI 2014/2382 Reg.34
Sch.4 para.2, substituted: SI 2014/2382 Reg.35

2333. ACAS (Flexible Working) Arbitration Scheme (Great Britain) Order 2004
Sch.1 Part VII para.26, amended: SI 2014/386 Sch.1 para.31

2355. Town and Country Planning (London Borough of Camden) Special Development (Amendment) Order 2004
revoked: SI 2014/683 Sch.1

2424. Road Traffic (Permitted Parking Area and Special Parking Area) (County of Cambridgeshire) (City of Cambridge) Order 2004
revoked: SI 2014/3205 Art.2

2443. Business Improvement Districts (England) Regulations 2004
Reg.6, amended: SI 2014/3199 Reg.2
Sch.4 para.1, amended: SI 2014/600 Sch.1 para.9
Sch.4 para.9, amended: SI 2014/600 Sch.1 para.9
Sch.4 para.10, amended: SI 2014/600 Sch.1 para.9
Sch.4 para.13, amended: SI 2014/600 Sch.1 para.9
Sch.4 para.14, amended: SI 2014/600 Sch.1 para.9
Sch.5 Part 002 para.8, amended: SI 2014/3199 Reg.2

2543. Inheritance Tax (Delivery of Accounts) (Excepted Estates) Regulations 2004
Reg.4, amended: SI 2014/488 Reg.2

2558. Food Labelling (Amendment) (Wales) Regulations 2004
revoked: SI 2014/2303 Sch.6 Part 1

2608. General Medical Council (Fitness to Practise) Rules Order of Council 2004
see *R. (on the application of Hibbert) v General Medical Council* [2013] EWHC 3596 (Admin), [2014] Med. L.R. 84 (QBD (Admin)), Simler J
Sch.1, added: SI 2014/1270 Sch.1
Sch.1, amended: SI 2014/1270 Sch.1
Sch.1, substituted: SI 2014/1270 Sch.1

2609. General Medical Council (Voluntary Erasure and Restoration following Voluntary Erasure) Regulations Order of Council 2004
Sch.1, added: SI 2014/1272 Sch.1
Sch.1, amended: SI 2014/1272 Sch.1

2612. General Medical Council (Restoration following Administrative Erasure) Regulations Order of Council 2004
Sch.1, added: SI 2014/1276 Sch.1
Sch.1, amended: SI 2014/1276 Sch.1

2661. Olive Oil (Marketing Standards) (Amendment) Regulations 2004
revoked: SI 2014/195 Reg.20

2751. Competition Act 1998 (Office of Fair Trading's Rules) Order 2004
revoked: SI 2014/458 Art.3

2783. Education (National Curriculum) (Key Stage 1 Assessment Arrangements) (England) Order 2004
Art.7, amended: SI 2014/2103 Art.14

2824. Food Labelling (Amendment) (England) (No.2) Regulations 2004
revoked: SI 2014/1855 Sch.6 Part 1

2876. A55 Trunk Road (Penmaenmawr &mdash Conwy Morfa, Conwy) (Derestriction) Order 2004
disapplied: SI 2014/3377 Art.12
varied: SI 2014/827 Art.12, SI 2014/915 Art.9

3022. Food Labelling (Amendment) (No.2) (Wales) Regulations 2004
revoked: SI 2014/2303 Sch.6 Part 1

3120. Non-Contentious Probate Fees Order 2004
Sch.1, amended: SI 2014/876 Art.2
Sch.1A para.1, amended: SI 2014/513 Sch.1 para.9, SI 2014/590 Art.6

3202. Water Mergers (Modification of Enactments) Regulations 2004
Reg.3, amended: SI 2014/549 Sch.1 para.22
Reg.4, amended: SI 2014/549 Sch.1 para.22
Reg.6, amended: SI 2014/549 Sch.1 para.22
Reg.7, revoked: SI 2014/549 Sch.1 para.22
Reg.8, amended: SI 2014/549 Sch.1 para.22
Reg.8, revoked (in part): SI 2014/549 Sch.1 para.22
Reg.10A, added: SI 2014/549 Sch.1 para.22
Reg.11, amended: SI 2014/549 Sch.1 para.22
Reg.12, amended: SI 2014/549 Sch.1 para.22
Reg.13, amended: SI 2014/549 Sch.1 para.22
Reg.13A, added: SI 2014/549 Sch.1 para.22
Reg.15, amended: SI 2014/549 Sch.1 para.22
Reg.16, revoked: SI 2014/549 Sch.1 para.22
Reg.17, amended: SI 2014/549 Sch.1 para.22
Reg.17, revoked (in part): SI 2014/549 Sch.1 para.22
Reg.25, revoked: SI 2014/549 Sch.1 para.22
Reg.26, amended: SI 2014/549 Sch.1 para.22
Reg.28, amended: SI 2014/549 Sch.1 para.22
Reg.29, amended: SI 2014/549 Sch.1 para.22
Reg.30, amended: SI 2014/549 Sch.1 para.22
Reg.30A, added: SI 2014/549 Sch.1 para.22

Reg.32, amended: SI 2014/549 Sch.1 para.22

3206. Water Mergers (Determination of Turnover) Regulations 2004
Reg.3, amended: SI 2014/549 Sch.1 para.23
Sch.1 para.6, amended: SI 2014/549 Sch.1 para.23
Sch.1 para.9, amended: SI 2014/549 Sch.1 para.23

3233. Enterprise Act 2002 (Commencement No 7 and Transitional Provisions and Savings) Order 2004
Art.5, amended: SI 2014/549 Sch.1 para.15

3256. Loan Relationships and Derivative Contracts (Disregard and Bringing into Account of Profits and Losses) Regulations 2004
Reg.2, amended: SI 2014/3188 Reg.8
Reg.3, amended: SI 2014/3188 Reg.8
Reg.3, revoked (in part): SI 2014/3188 Reg.3
Reg.4, amended: SI 2014/3188 Reg.8
Reg.4A, amended: SI 2014/3188 Reg.4, Reg.8
Reg.4A, revoked (in part): SI 2014/3188 Reg.4
Reg.4C, amended: SI 2014/3188 Reg.5
Reg.5, amended: SI 2014/3188 Reg.8
Reg.6, applied: SI 2014/3188 Reg.9
Reg.6, substituted: SI 2014/3188 Reg.6
Reg.6A, applied: SI 2014/3188 Reg.9
Reg.7, amended: SI 2014/3188 Reg.8
Reg.8, amended: SI 2014/3188 Reg.8
Reg.9, amended: SI 2014/3188 Reg.8
Reg.9, revoked (in part): SI 2014/3188 Reg.8
Reg.9A, added: SI 2014/3188 Reg.7
Reg.9A, amended: SI 2014/3188 Reg.7, Reg.8
Reg.10, amended: SI 2014/3188 Reg.8
Reg.11, amended: SI 2014/3188 Reg.8
Reg.12, amended: SI 2014/3188 Reg.8
Reg.12A, added: SI 2014/3325 Reg.3
Reg.12A, applied: SI 2014/3325 Reg.1

3271. Loan Relationships and Derivative Contracts (Change Of Accounting Practice) Regulations 2004
Reg.2, amended: SI 2014/3187 Reg.4
Reg.3, amended: SI 2014/3325 Reg.4
Reg.3B, amended: SI 2014/3187 Reg.4
Reg.3C, amended: SI 2014/3187 Reg.3, Reg.4

Reg.4, amended: SI 2014/3187 Reg.4
Reg.5, amended: SI 2014/3187 Reg.4

3280. Common Agricultural Policy Single Payment and Support Schemes (Cross Compliance) (Wales) Regulations 2004
revoked: SI 2014/3223 Sch.3
varied: SI 2014/3223 Reg.15
Sch.1 para.27, substituted: SI 2014/371 Reg.3
Sch.1 para.28, added: SI 2014/371 Reg.4

3328. European Communities (Designation) (No.7) Order 2004
Sch.1, amended: SI 2014/1362 Sch.1

3337. Air Navigation (Overseas Territories) (Environmental Standards) Order 2004
revoked: SI 2014/2926 Art.2

3344. Food with Added Phytosterols or Phytostanols (Labelling) (England) Regulations 2004
revoked: SI 2014/1855 Sch.6 Part 1

3363. Freedom of Information (Removal and Relaxation of Statutory Prohibitions on Disclosure of Information) Order 2004
Art.8, revoked: 2014 c.2 Sch.1 Part 2

3367. Plant Health (Phytophthora kernovii Management Zone) (England) Order 2004
revoked: SI 2014/2875 Art.2

3370. West Northamptonshire Development Corporation (Area and Constitution) Order 2004
revoked: SI 2014/1181 Art.2
Art.2, revoked: SI 2014/1181 Art.2

3391. Environmental Information Regulations 2004
applied: SI 2014/2012 Reg.12
see *Fish Legal v Information Commissioner (C-279/12)* [2014] Q.B. 521 (ECJ (Grand Chamber)), Judge Skouris (President); see *R. (on the application of Evans) v Attorney General* [2014] EWCA Civ 254, [2014] Q.B. 855 (CA (Civ Div)), Lord Dyson MR
Reg.5, see *R. (on the application of Evans) v Attorney General* [2014] EWCA Civ 254, [2014] Q.B. 855 (CA (Civ Div)), Lord Dyson MR
Reg.12, applied: SI 2014/1663 Reg.28
Reg.13, applied: SI 2014/1663 Reg.28

3426. Information and Consultation of Employees Regulations 2004
Reg.29, amended: SI 2014/386 Sch.1 para.33

Reg.29A, added: SI 2014/386 Sch.1 para.34
Reg.40, amended: SI 2014/386 Sch.1 para.35

2005

37. Supply of Extended Warranties on Domestic Electrical Goods Order 2005
Art.9, amended: SI 2014/549 Sch.1 para.16
Art.10, amended: SI 2014/549 Sch.1 para.16

41. Licensing Act 2003 (Personal licences) Regulations 2005
Reg.6, amended: SI 2014/3284 Reg.2
Reg.7, amended: SI 2014/3284 Reg.2
Sch.2, amended: SI 2014/3284 Sch.1

42. Licensing Act 2003 (Premises licences and club premises certificates) Regulations 2005
see *R. (on the application of D&D Bar Services Ltd) v Romford Magistrates' Court* [2014] EWHC 344 (Admin), [2014] L.L.R. 761 (QBD (Admin)), Judge Blackett
Reg.38, see *R. (on the application of D&D Bar Services Ltd) v Romford Magistrates' Court* [2014] EWHC 344 (Admin), [2014] L.L.R. 761 (QBD (Admin)), Judge Blackett
Reg.39, see *R. (on the application of D&D Bar Services Ltd) v Romford Magistrates' Court* [2014] EWHC 344 (Admin), [2014] L.L.R. 761 (QBD (Admin)), Judge Blackett

44. Licensing Act 2003 (Hearings) Regulations 2005
Reg.34, amended: SI 2014/2341 Reg.2

79. Licensing Act 2003 (Fees) Regulations 2005
Reg.8, substituted: SI 2014/1371 Reg.8

215. Local Authorities (Contracting Out of BID Levy Billing, Collection and Enforcement Functions) Order 2005
Art.1, amended: SI 2014/600 Sch.1 para.6
Art.9, amended: SI 2014/600 Sch.1 para.6
Art.9, substituted: SI 2014/600 Sch.1 para.6
Art.17, amended: SI 2014/600 Sch.1 para.6

230. Asylum and Immigration Tribunal (Procedure) Rules 2005
applied: SI 2014/2604 r.46
revoked: SI 2014/2604 r.45
r.14, see *N v Advocate General for Scotland* [2014] UKSC 30, [2014] 1 W.L.R. 2064 (SC), Lord Neuberger PSC
r.17, see *SM (Withdrawal of Appealed Decision: Effect: Pakistan)* [2014] UKUT 64

(IAC), [2014] Imm. A.R. 662 (UT (IAC)),
Judge Peter Lane
r.45, see *AAN (Veil: Afghanistan)* [2014]
UKUT 102 (IAC), [2014] Imm. A.R. 756
(UT (IAC)), McCloskey J; see *N v Advocate
General for Scotland* [2014] UKSC 30,
[2014] 1 W.L.R. 2064 (SC), Lord Neuberger
PSC

255. Pensions (Northern Ireland) Order 2005
Art.34, see *Pensions Regulator v Desmond*
[2014] Pens. L.R. 9 (CA (NI)), Morgan LCJ
Art.91, see *Pensions Regulator v Desmond*
[2014] Pens. L.R. 9 (CA (NI)), Morgan LCJ
Art.97, see *Pensions Regulator v Desmond*
[2014] Pens. L.R. 9 (CA (NI)), Morgan LCJ

**269. Representation of the People (Variation of
Limits of Candidates Election Expenses) Order
2005**
revoked: SI 2014/1870 Art.7

**368. Accounts and Audit (Wales) Regulations
2005**
revoked: SI 2014/3362 Reg.30

384. Criminal Procedure Rules 2005
applied: SI 2014/1610 r.2_1

389. Adoption Agencies Regulations 2005
Reg.2, amended: SI 2014/1492 Reg.8, SI
2014/1556 Reg.3
Reg.12, amended: SI 2014/1556 Reg.4
Reg.12A, added: SI 2014/1556 Reg.5
Reg.12B, applied: SI 2014/2934 Reg.3, SI
2014/3050 Reg.3, SI 2014/3051 Reg.2, SI
2014/3052 Reg.3, SI 2014/3134 Reg.2
Reg.14, amended: SI 2014/852 Art.10, SI
2014/1556 Reg.6
Reg.18, amended: SI 2014/1556 Reg.7
Reg.19A, applied: SI 2014/1492 Reg.5
Reg.19A, substituted: SI 2014/1492 Reg.9
Reg.30B, applied: SI 2014/3050 Reg.3
Reg.30G, applied: SI 2014/1492 Reg.5
Reg.30G, substituted: SI 2014/1492 Reg.10
Reg.32, amended: SI 2014/1556 Reg.8
Reg.33, applied: SI 2014/2934 Reg.3, SI
2014/3050 Reg.3, SI 2014/3051 Reg.2, SI
2014/3134 Reg.2
Reg.35, amended: SI 2014/2103 Art.15
Sch.1A, added: SI 2014/1492 Reg.11
Sch.1A, applied: SI 2014/1492 Reg.3
Sch.1A, referred to: SI 2014/1492 Reg.4
Sch.1 Part 1 para.12, amended: SI
2014/2103 Art.15
Sch.4B, added: SI 2014/1492 Reg.12

Sch.4B, applied: SI 2014/1492 Reg.3

**392. Adoptions with a Foreign Element
Regulations 2005**
applied: SI 2014/1795 Reg.9
Part 3, applied: SI 2014/1795 Reg.9
Reg.10, applied: SI 2014/1795 Reg.9
Reg.22, amended: SI 2014/2103 Art.16

**395. Rail Vehicle Accessibility (Croydon
Tramlink Class CR4000 Vehicles) Exemption
(Amendment) Order 2005**
revoked: SI 2014/3244 Sch.2

**437. Armed Forces Early Departure Payments
Scheme Order 2005**
Art.4, amended: SI 2014/2958 Art.4
Art.12, amended: SI 2014/2958 Art.5

438. Armed Forces Pension Scheme Order 2005
applied: SI 2014/2336 Reg.71
Sch.1, added: SI 2014/2958 Art.3, SI
2014/3061 Sch.1 para.15, Sch.2 para.1, SI
2014/3255 Art.15
Sch.1, amended: SI 2014/560 Sch.3 para.7,
SI 2014/2958 Art.3, SI 2014/3061 Sch.2
para.1, SI 2014/3255 Art.15
Sch.1, applied: SI 2014/560 Sch.2 para.4, SI
2014/3229 Sch.2 para.5
Sch.1, substituted: SI 2014/107 Sch.1
para.34

**449. Pension Protection Fund (Hybrid Schemes)
(Modification) Regulations 2005**
Reg.2, applied: SI 2014/1711 Reg.53

**454. Social Security (Graduated Retirement
Benefit) Regulations 2005**
Sch.1, amended: SI 2014/516 Art.8

**492. Immigration (Passenger Transit Visa)
(Amendment) Order 2005**
revoked: SI 2014/2702 Sch.2

545. Justices Clerks Rules 2005
r.2, amended: SI 2014/879 Art.88
r.3, amended: SI 2014/879 Art.89
r.3A, revoked: SI 2014/879 Art.90
Sch.2, revoked: SI 2014/879 Art.90

**553. Justices of the Peace (Size and
Chairmanship of Bench) Rules 2005**
applied: SI 2014/1610 r.37_1, SI 2014/2867
Sch.1 para.1
r.3, amended: SI 2014/879 Art.91

554. Local Justice Areas Order 2005
Sch.1, amended: SI 2014/322 Art.4, SI
2014/1899 Art.4, SI 2014/2867 Art.4

560. Asylum and Immigration Tribunal (Fast Track Procedure) Rules 2005
>   applied: SI 2014/2604 r.46
>   revoked: SI 2014/2604 r.45

588. Court Security Officers (Designation) Regulations 2005
>   applied: SI 2014/786 Art.4

590. Pension Protection Fund (Entry Rules) Regulations 2005
>   Reg.1, amended: SI 2014/1711 Reg.58
>   Reg.2, see *FSS Pension Trustees Ltd, Re*
>   [2014] EWHC 1397 (Ch), [2014] Pens. L.R.
>   303 (Ch D), Newey J
>   Reg.2, amended: SI 2014/1711 Reg.58
>   Reg.2, referred to: SI 2014/1711 Reg.43
>   Reg.5, amended: SI 2014/1815 Sch.1
>   para.14
>   Reg.5A, added: SI 2014/1664 Reg.2
>   Reg.6, amended: SI 2014/1664 Reg.2
>   Reg.6, varied: SI 2014/229 Sch.5 para.2
>   Reg.9, varied: SI 2014/229 Sch.5 para.2
>   Reg.21, amended: SI 2014/1711 Reg.58

598. Local Government (Best Value) Performance Indicators and Performance Standards (England) Order 2005
>   Sch.2, amended: SI 2014/2103 Art.17

617. Courts Act 2003 (Consequential Provisions) (No.2) Order 2005
>   Sch.1 para.30, revoked: SI 2014/879 Sch.1

639. Road Transport (Working Time) Regulations 2005
>   see *R. (on the application of United Road Transport Union) v Secretary of State for Transport* [2013] EWCA Civ 962, [2014] R.T.R. 9 (CA (Civ Div)), Jackson LJ

649. Transfer of Employment (Pension Protection) Regulations 2005
>   Reg.1, amended: SI 2014/540 Reg.4
>   Reg.2, amended: SI 2014/540 Reg.4
>   Reg.3, substituted: SI 2014/540 Reg.4

669. Pension Protection Fund (Review and Reconsideration of Reviewable Matters) Regulations 2005
>   Reg.2, see *West of England Ship Owners Insurance Services Ltd Retirement Benefits Scheme, Re* [2014] EWHC 20 (Ch), [2014] Pens. L.R. 167 (Ch D (Companies Ct)), Andrew Spink, Q.C.
>   Sch.1, amended: SI 2014/1711 Reg.61

670. Pension Protection Fund (Compensation) Regulations 2005
>   Reg.1, amended: SI 2014/107 Sch.1 para.35,
>   SI 2014/3229 Sch.6 para.24
>   Reg.3, varied: SI 2014/1711 Reg.59
>   Reg.13A, added: SI 2014/1711 Reg.60
>   Reg.15B, amended: SI 2014/1711 Reg.60
>   Reg.15ZA, added: SI 2014/1711 Reg.60
>   Reg.25, amended: SI 2014/1711 Reg.60
>   Reg.25, revoked (in part): SI 2014/1711
>   Reg.60

672. Pension Protection Fund (Valuation) Regulations 2005
>   Reg.5, applied: SI 2014/1711 Reg.45

677. Education (Grants etc.) (Dance and Drama) (England) (Amendment) Regulations 2005
>   revoked: SI 2014/80 Sch.1

678. Occupational Pension Schemes (Employer Debt) Regulations 2005
>   Reg.5, applied: SI 2014/1711 Reg.23
>   Reg.8, applied: SI 2014/1711 Reg.19
>   Reg.9, applied: SI 2014/1711 Reg.62
>   Reg.10, amended: SI 2014/540 Reg.5
>   Reg.14, applied: SI 2014/1711 Reg.19

684. Companies Act 1985 (Power to Enter and Remain on Premises Procedural) Regulations 2005
>   applied: SI 2014/574 Reg.2

691. Adoption Support Services Regulations 2005
>   Part 1A, added: SI 2014/1563 Reg.4
>   Reg.2, amended: SI 2014/1563 Reg.3

735. Work at Height Regulations 2005
>   see *Yates v National Trust* [2014] EWHC 222 (QB), [2014] P.I.Q.R. P16 (QBD), Nicol J

758. Non-Domestic Rating (Alteration of Lists and Appeals) (Wales) Regulations 2005
>   Reg.14, see *Roberts (Valuation Officer) v West Coast Marine (Pwllheli) Ltd* [2014] R.A. 1 (UT (Lands)), Martin Rodger Q.C.

858. Pensions Increase (Review) Order 2005
>   referred to: SI 2014/668 Sch.1
>   Art.6, substituted: SI 2014/107 Sch.1
>   para.56, SI 2014/3229 Sch.6 para.35

890. Adoption Information and Intermediary Services (Pre-Commencement Adoptions) Regulations 2005
>   Reg.2, amended: SI 2014/2696 Reg.3
>   Reg.2A, added: SI 2014/2696 Reg.4

Reg.4, amended: SI 2014/2696 Reg.5

Reg.5, amended: SI 2014/2696 Reg.6

Reg.5, revoked (in part): SI 2014/2696
Reg.6

Reg.5A, added: SI 2014/2696 Reg.7

Reg.8, amended: SI 2014/2696 Reg.8

Reg.8, revoked (in part): SI 2014/2696
Reg.8

Reg.9, substituted: SI 2014/2696 Reg.9

Reg.10, amended: SI 2014/2696 Reg.10

Reg.11, amended: SI 2014/2696 Reg.11

Reg.12, amended: SI 2014/2696 Reg.12

Reg.16, amended: SI 2014/2696 Reg.13

**894. Hazardous Waste (England and Wales)
Regulations 2005**

Reg.8, amended: 2014 c.29 s.4

Reg.9, amended: 2014 c.29 s.4

**899. Food Labelling (Amendment) (England)
Regulations 2005**

revoked: SI 2014/1855 Sch.6 Part 1

**902. Crime and Disorder Act 1998 (Service of
Prosecution Evidence) Regulations 2005**

applied: SI 2014/1610 r.3_26, r.9_15, r.14_1

**963. Criminal Justice (Sentencing) (Programme
and Electronic Monitoring Requirements) Order
2005**

revoked: SI 2014/669 Sch.1

Art.3, amended: SI 2014/163 Art.3

Sch.1, amended: SI 2014/163 Art.4

Sch.2, amended: SI 2014/163 Art.5

**985. Criminal Procedure and Investigations Act
1996 (Code of Practice) Order 2005**

applied: SI 2014/1610 r.22_9

**1074. Regulatory Reform (National Health
Service Charitable and Non-Charitable Trust
Accounts and Audit) Order 2005**

Art.4, revoked: 2014 c.2 Sch.1 Part 2

**1082. Manufacture and Storage of Explosives
Regulations 2005**

applied: SI 2014/1638 Reg.47

revoked: SI 2014/1638 Sch.14 Part 2

Reg.2, amended: SI 2014/469 Sch.3
para.111

Reg.3, amended: SI 2014/469 Sch.3
para.112

Reg.5, amended: SI 2014/469 Sch.3
para.113

Reg.5, applied: SI 2014/1638 Reg.47

Reg.11, amended: SI 2014/469 Sch.3
para.114

Reg.11, applied: SI 2014/1638 Reg.47

Reg.11A, added: SI 2014/469 Sch.3
para.115

Reg.13, amended: SI 2014/469 Sch.3
para.116

Reg.13, applied: SI 2014/1638 Reg.16,
Reg.47

Reg.13A, added: SI 2014/469 Sch.3
para.117

Reg.14, amended: SI 2014/469 Sch.3
para.118

Reg.14, applied: SI 2014/1638 Reg.47

Reg.16, amended: SI 2014/469 Sch.3
para.119

Reg.23, amended: SI 2014/469 Sch.3
para.120

Reg.26, applied: SI 2014/1638 Reg.47

Reg.27, applied: SI 2014/1638 Reg.16,
Reg.47

Sch.1 para.1, amended: SI 2014/469 Sch.3
para.121

Sch.1 para.4, added: SI 2014/469 Sch.3
para.121

Sch.4 para.8, amended: SI 2014/469 Sch.3
para.122

**1093. Control of Vibration at Work Regulations
2005**

Reg.2, amended: SI 2014/469 Sch.3
para.123

1109. Special Guardianship Regulations 2005

Sch.1 para.1, amended: SI 2014/2103 Art.18

**1127. Extradition Act 2003 (Part 3 Designation)
(Amendment) Order 2005**

Art.2, revoked (in part): SI 2014/834 Sch.3
para.8

**1130. Crime (International Co-operation) Act
2003 (Designation of Prosecuting Authorities)
(Amendment) Order 2005**

Art.2, revoked (in part): SI 2014/834 Sch.3
para.9

**1133. Revenue and Customs (Inspections)
Regulations 2005**

Reg.2, amended: SI 2014/834 Sch.3 para.10

**1140. Passenger and Goods Vehicles (Recording
Equipment) (Tachograph Card Fees)
Regulations 2005**

Sch.1, amended: SI 2014/2557 Reg.2

Sch.2, amended: SI 2014/2557 Reg.2

**1224. Food with Added Phytosterols or
Phytostanols (Labelling) (Wales) Regulations
2005**

revoked: SI 2014/2303 Sch.6 Part 1

Reg.2, amended: SI 2014/440 Reg.2

1258. Sudan (United Nations Measures) (Overseas Territories) Order 2005

revoked: SI 2014/2707 Art.1

1309. Food Labelling (Amendment) (Wales) Regulations 2005

revoked: SI 2014/2303 Sch.6 Part 1

1312. Business Improvement Districts (Wales) Regulations 2005

Sch.4 para.1, amended: SI 2014/600 Sch.1 para.10

Sch.4 para.10, amended: SI 2014/600 Sch.1 para.10

Sch.4 para.13, amended: SI 2014/600 Sch.1 para.10

Sch.4 para.14, amended: SI 2014/600 Sch.1 para.10

1313. Adoption Agencies (Wales) Regulations 2005

applied: SI 2014/1795 Reg.9

Part 3, applied: SI 2014/1795 Reg.9

Part 5, applied: SI 2014/1795 Reg.9

Part 6, applied: SI 2014/1795 Reg.9

Part 7, applied: SI 2014/1795 Reg.9

Reg.2, amended: SI 2014/567 Reg.2

Reg.3, substituted: SI 2014/567 Reg.2

Reg.14, amended: SI 2014/852 Art.11

Reg.19, amended: SI 2014/852 Art.11

Reg.28, applied: SI 2014/2934 Reg.3, SI 2014/3050 Reg.3, SI 2014/3051 Reg.2, SI 2014/3134 Reg.2

1437. Education (Pupil Information) (England) Regulations 2005

Reg.2, amended: SI 2014/2103 Art.19

Reg.3, amended: SI 2014/2103 Art.19

Sch.2 para.2, amended: SI 2014/2103 Art.19

1478. General Optical Council (Registration Rules) Order of Council 2005

Sch.1, substituted: SI 2014/1887 Sch.1 para.8

1512. Adoption Support Services (Local Authorities) (Wales) Regulations 2005

Reg.3, applied: SI 2014/1795 Reg.9

Reg.7, applied: SI 2014/1795 Reg.9

1513. Special Guardianship (Wales) Regulations 2005

Sch.1 para.3, amended: SI 2014/3061 Sch.1 para.9

Sch.1 para.4, amended: SI 2014/3061 Sch.1 para.9

1529. Financial Services and Markets Act 2000 (Financial Promotion) Order 2005

Art.15, amended: SI 2014/366 Art.10

Art.16, amended: SI 2014/366 Art.10

Art.28B, amended: SI 2014/366 Art.10

Art.29, amended: SI 2014/366 Art.10

Art.34, amended: SI 2014/506 Art.3

Art.35, amended: SI 2014/1815 Sch.1 para.15

Art.35, substituted: SI 2014/1815 Sch.1 para.15

Art.55A, amended: SI 2014/366 Art.10

Art.55B, added: SI 2014/506 Art.3

Art.61, amended: SI 2014/366 Art.10

Art.72F, added: SI 2014/208 Art.4

Sch.1 Part I para.4B, amended: SI 2014/366 Art.10

Sch.1 Part I para.4C, amended: SI 2014/366 Art.10

Sch.1 Part I para.10BA, amended: SI 2014/366 Art.10

Sch.1 Part I para.10BB, amended: SI 2014/366 Art.10

Sch.1 Part I para.11, amended: SI 2014/366 Art.10

Sch.1 Part II para.14, amended: SI 2014/1815 Sch.1 para.15

Sch.1 Part II para.28, amended: SI 2014/366 Art.10

1541. Regulatory Reform (Fire Safety) Order 2005

applied: SI 2014/3283 Sch.1 para.12

see *R. v Wilson (Michael)* [2013] EWCA Crim 1780, [2014] Q.B. 704 (CA (Crim Div)), Gross LJ

Art.4, amended: SI 2014/469 Sch.3 para.124

Art.32, see *R. v Wilson (Michael)* [2013] EWCA Crim 1780, [2014] Q.B. 704 (CA (Crim Div)), Gross LJ

1643. Control of Noise at Work Regulations 2005

Reg.2, amended: SI 2014/469 Sch.3 para.125

1646. Electricity and Gas Appeals (Designation and Exclusion) Order 2005

revoked: SI 2014/1293 Sch.1

Art.4, amended: SI 2014/549 Sch.1 para.32

1654. Nuclear Industries Security (Fees) Regulations 2005

Reg.2, amended: SI 2014/469 Sch.3 para.149, Sch.3 para.210

Reg.3, amended: SI 2014/469 Sch.3
para.150
Reg.4, amended: SI 2014/469 Sch.3
para.151
Sch.1, amended: SI 2014/469 Sch.3 para.152

1715. Climate Change Levy (Fuel Use and Recycling Processes) Regulations 2005

Sch.1 Part A para.1, amended: 2014 c.26
Sch.20 para.9
Sch.1 Part A para.2, amended: 2014 c.26
Sch.20 para.9
Sch.1 Part B para.18, revoked: 2014 c.26
Sch.20 para.9
Sch.1 Part B para.26, revoked: 2014 c.26
Sch.20 para.9
Sch.1 Part B para.26A, added: SI 2014/844
Reg.3
Sch.1 Part B para.27, revoked: 2014 c.26
Sch.20 para.9
Sch.1 Part B para.32, revoked: 2014 c.26
Sch.20 para.9
Sch.1 Part B para.34, revoked: 2014 c.26
Sch.20 para.9
Sch.1 Part B para.36, revoked: 2014 c.26
Sch.20 para.9

1788. Community Interest Company Regulations 2005

Part 2A, amended: SI 2014/1815 Sch.1
para.16
Reg.2, amended: SI 2014/1815 Sch.1
para.16, SI 2014/2483 Reg.3
Reg.6A, amended: SI 2014/1815 Sch.1
para.16
Reg.17, amended: SI 2014/2483 Reg.4
Reg.18, revoked: SI 2014/2483 Reg.5
Reg.20, revoked: SI 2014/2483 Reg.6
Reg.22, amended: SI 2014/2483 Reg.7
Reg.22, revoked (in part): SI 2014/2483
Reg.7
Reg.27, substituted: SI 2014/2483 Reg.8
Sch.1 para.1, amended: SI 2014/1815 Sch.1
para.16
Sch.2 para.1, amended: SI 2014/1815 Sch.1
para.16
Sch.3 para.1, amended: SI 2014/1815 Sch.1
para.16

1902. Motor Cars (Driving Instruction) Regulations 2005

applied: SI 2014/480 Reg.8, SI 2014/2216
Reg.3
Reg.2, amended: SI 2014/2216 Reg.2

Reg.12, amended: SI 2014/2216 Reg.2
Reg.12, revoked (in part): SI 2014/2216
Reg.2
Reg.17, amended: SI 2014/1816 Reg.7
Reg.18, amended: SI 2014/480 Reg.8
Sch.4, substituted: SI 2014/480 Sch.2 para.1
Sch.5, substituted: SI 2014/480 Sch.2 para.1
Sch.6, substituted: SI 2014/480 Sch.2 para.1

1983. Age-Related Payments Regulations 2005

Part 2, applied: SI 2014/2672 Sch.2 para.32

1986. Financial Assistance Scheme Regulations 2005

applied: SI 2014/1711 Reg.70
varied: SI 2014/1711 Reg.72
Reg.2, amended: SI 2014/107 Sch.1 para.36,
SI 2014/3229 Sch.6 para.25
Reg.2, applied: SI 2014/1711 Reg.72
Reg.9, amended: SI 2014/837 Reg.2
Reg.9, applied: SI 2014/1711 Reg.70
Reg.13, amended: SI 2014/1815 Sch.1
para.17
Reg.22, applied: SI 2014/1711 Reg.72
Reg.27, applied: SI 2014/1711 Reg.72
Reg.29, applied: SI 2014/1711 Reg.72
Reg.31, applied: SI 2014/1711 Reg.72

1996. Registration of Civil Partnerships (Fees) Order 2005

revoked: SI 2014/1789 Art.3

1999. M275 and M27 Motorway (Speed Limit) Regulations 2005

revoked: SI 2014/790 Reg.2

2042. Civil Contingencies Act 2004 (Contingency Planning) Regulations 2005

Reg.54A, added: SI 2014/469 Sch.3
para.192

2045. Income Tax (Construction Industry Scheme) Regulations 2005

Reg.7A, added: SI 2014/472 Reg.21
Reg.8, varied: 2014 c.6 s.126
Reg.14, revoked: SI 2014/992 Art.11
Reg.15, revoked: SI 2014/992 Art.11
Reg.56, revoked (in part): SI 2014/992
Art.11
Reg.56, varied: 2014 c.6 s.126
Reg.58, amended: SI 2014/992 Art.11

2054. Remand in Custody (Effect of Concurrent and Consecutive Sentences of Imprisonment) Rules 2005

see *R. v Leacock (Mark)* [2013] EWCA
Crim 1994, [2014] 2 Cr. App. R. (S.) 12 (CA
(Crim Div)), Lord Thomas LCJ

2055. Offshore Petroleum Activities (Oil Pollution Prevention and Control) Regulations 2005
    referred to: SSI 2014/324 Sch.1 para.11

2114. Civil Partnership Act 2004 (Amendments to Subordinate Legislation) Order 2005
    Sch.1 para.9, revoked (in part): SI 2014/80 Sch.1

2291. Cardiff to Glan Conwy Trunk Road (A470) (Blaenau Ffestiniog to Cancoed Improvement) Order 2005
    Art.3, amended: 2014 c.29 s.4

2339. Community Design Regulations 2005
    Reg.1A, amended: SI 2014/2400 Reg.3

2415. NHS Business Services Authority (Awdurdod Gwasanaethau Busnes y GIG) Regulations 2005
    Reg.10, amended: SI 2014/1815 Sch.1 para.18

2466. Genetically Modified Organisms (Contained Use) (Amendment) Regulations 2005
    revoked: SI 2014/1663 Reg.35

2517. Plant Health (Forestry) Order 2005
    Art.2, amended: SI 2014/2420 Art.3
    Art.5, amended: SI 2014/2420 Art.4
    Art.6, amended: SI 2014/2420 Art.5
    Art.8, amended: SI 2014/2420 Art.6
    Art.12, amended: SI 2014/2420 Art.7
    Art.18, amended: SI 2014/2420 Art.8
    Art.19, amended: SI 2014/2420 Art.9
    Art.20, amended: SI 2014/2420 Art.10
    Art.21, amended: SI 2014/2420 Art.11
    Art.31, amended: SI 2014/2420 Art.12
    Art.32, amended: SI 2014/2420 Art.13
    Art.40, amended: SI 2014/2420 Art.14
    Art.41, amended: SI 2014/2420 Art.15
    Art.42, amended: SI 2014/2420 Art.16
    Sch.1, amended: SI 2014/2420 Art.17
    Sch.1A, added: SI 2014/2420 Art.18
    Sch.2 Part A, amended: SI 2014/2420 Art.19
    Sch.2 Part B, amended: SI 2014/2420 Art.19
    Sch.4 Part A, amended: SI 2014/2420 Art.20
    Sch.4 Part B, amended: SI 2014/2420 Art.20
    Sch.4 Part C, amended: SI 2014/2420 Art.20
    Sch.5 Part A para.2, amended: SI 2014/2420 Art.21
    Sch.5 Part A para.2A, revoked (in part): SI 2014/2420 Art.21
    Sch.5 Part A para.3, amended: SI 2014/2420 Art.21

Sch.5 Part A para.4, amended: SI 2014/2420 Art.21
Sch.5 Part B para.1A, added: SI 2014/2420 Art.21
Sch.6 Part A para.5, revoked (in part): SI 2014/2420 Art.22
Sch.6 Part B para.2, substituted: SI 2014/2420 Art.22
Sch.6 Part B para.3, amended: SI 2014/2420 Art.22
Sch.7 Part A para.5, revoked (in part): SI 2014/2420 Art.23
Sch.7 Part B para.2, substituted: SI 2014/2420 Art.23
Sch.7 Part B para.4, amended: SI 2014/2420 Art.23

2530. Plant Health (England) Order 2005
    Part 7A, revoked: SI 2014/979 Art.4
    Art.2, amended: SI 2014/2385 Art.3
    Art.2, referred to: SI 2014/601 Reg.8
    Art.5, amended: SI 2014/2385 Art.4
    Art.8, amended: SI 2014/2385 Art.5
    Art.12, amended: SI 2014/2385 Art.6
    Art.12, applied: SI 2014/601 Reg.2
    Art.19, amended: SI 2014/979 Art.3, SI 2014/2385 Art.7
    Art.20, amended: SI 2014/2385 Art.8
    Art.21, amended: SI 2014/2385 Art.9
    Art.22, amended: SI 2014/2385 Art.10
    Art.24, amended: SI 2014/2385 Art.11
    Art.29, amended: SI 2014/2385 Art.12
    Art.40, referred to: SI 2014/601 Reg.4
    Art.42, amended: SI 2014/2385 Art.13
    Sch.1 Part A, amended: SI 2014/2385 Art.14
    Sch.1 Part B, amended: SI 2014/979 Art.4, SI 2014/2385 Art.14
    Sch.1 Part C, added: SI 2014/2385 Art.14
    Sch.2 Part A, amended: SI 2014/2385 Art.15
    Sch.2 Part B, amended: SI 2014/2385 Art.15
    Sch.4 Part A, amended: SI 2014/2385 Art.16
    Sch.4 Part B, amended: SI 2014/2385 Art.16
    Sch.4 Part C, amended: SI 2014/2385 Art.16
    Sch.5 Part A para.1, amended: SI 2014/2385 Art.17
    Sch.5 Part A para.2, amended: SI 2014/2385 Art.17
    Sch.5 Part A para.2A, substituted: SI 2014/2385 Art.17
    Sch.5 Part A para.3, substituted: SI 2014/2385 Art.17

Sch.5 Part B para.5, amended: SI 2014/2385 Art.17

Sch.6 Part A para.4, substituted: SI 2014/2385 Art.18

Sch.6 Part A para.7, amended: SI 2014/2385 Art.18

Sch.6 Part A para.8, amended: SI 2014/2385 Art.18

Sch.6 Part B paraA.1, added: SI 2014/2385 Art.18

Sch.7 Part A para.4, substituted: SI 2014/2385 Art.19

Sch.7 Part A para.7, amended: SI 2014/2385 Art.19

Sch.7 Part A para.8, amended: SI 2014/2385 Art.19

Sch.7 Part B para.2, substituted: SI 2014/2385 Art.19

Sch.7 Part B para.3, amended: SI 2014/2385 Art.19

Sch.7 Part B para.8, amended: SI 2014/2385 Art.19

2531. NHS Blood and Transplant (Gwaed a Thrawsblaniadau'r GIG) Regulations 2005

Reg.10, amended: SI 2014/1815 Sch.1 para.19

2751. Supply of Relevant Veterinary Medicinal Products Order 2005

Art.2, amended: SI 2014/549 Sch.1 para.17

Art.7, amended: SI 2014/549 Sch.1 para.17

Art.8, amended: SI 2014/549 Sch.1 para.17

2761. Civil Partnership (Registration Abroad and Certificates) Order 2005

Art.5, amended: SI 2014/1107 Art.3

Art.6, amended: SI 2014/1107 Art.4

Art.10, amended: SI 2014/1107 Art.5

Art.10, revoked (in part): SI 2014/1107 Art.5

Art.14, amended: SI 2014/3181 Sch.2 para.2

Art.17, amended: SI 2014/1107 Art.6

Art.17, applied: SI 2014/1789 Sch.1

2798. Criminal Justice Act 2003 (Mandatory Life Sentences Appeals in Transitional Cases) Order 2005

applied: SI 2014/1610 r.65_1, r.68_11, r.65_5, r.68_12

Art.12, applied: SI 2014/1610 r.74_1, r.74_2

Art.15, applied: SI 2014/1610 r.74_2

2903. Greenhouse Gas Emissions Trading Scheme (Amendment) and National Emissions Inventory Regulations 2005

Part 3, substituted: SI 2014/3075 Reg.2

Part 5, revoked: SI 2014/3075 Reg.2

Reg.2, revoked (in part): SI 2014/3075 Reg.2

Reg.5, applied: SI 2014/3075 Reg.3

Reg.13A, added: SI 2014/3075 Reg.2

Reg.14, amended: SI 2014/3075 Reg.2

Reg.17, amended: SI 2014/3075 Reg.2

Sch.1, revoked: SI 2014/3075 Reg.2

2914. Government of Maintained Schools (Wales) Regulations 2005

applied: SI 2014/2709 Reg.21

Part 7, varied: SI 2014/2709 Sch.3 para.1

Reg.34, referred to: SI 2014/1132 Reg.81

Reg.39, varied: SI 2014/2709 Sch.3 para.2, Sch.3 para.3

Reg.41, varied: SI 2014/2709 Sch.3 para.4

Reg.42, varied: SI 2014/2709 Sch.3 para.5

Reg.43, varied: SI 2014/2709 Sch.3 para.6

Reg.44, varied: SI 2014/2709 Sch.3 para.7

Reg.44A, varied: SI 2014/2709 Sch.3 para.8

Reg.45, varied: SI 2014/2709 Sch.3 para.9

Reg.46, varied: SI 2014/2709 Sch.3 para.10

Reg.49, varied: SI 2014/2709 Sch.3 para.11

Reg.50, varied: SI 2014/2709 Sch.3 para.12

Reg.51, varied: SI 2014/2709 Sch.3 para.13

Reg.52, varied: SI 2014/2709 Sch.3 para.14

Reg.55, amended: SI 2014/1609 Reg.3

Reg.55, varied: SI 2014/2709 Sch.3 para.15

Reg.57, varied: SI 2014/2709 Sch.3 para.15

Reg.58, varied: SI 2014/2709 Sch.3 para.16

Reg.59, varied: SI 2014/2709 Sch.3 para.17

Reg.63, varied: SI 2014/2709 Sch.3 para.18

2915. Governor Allowances (Wales) Regulations 2005

applied: SI 2014/1132 Sch.10 para.1

2918. Licensing Act 2003 (Permitted Temporary Activities) (Notices) Regulations 2005

Reg.3, amended: SI 2014/1371 Reg.7

Sch.1, amended: SI 2014/2417 Sch.1

2923. Civil Courts (Amendment) Order 2005

revoked: SI 2014/820 Sch.1

3061. Social Fund Maternity and Funeral Expenses (General) Regulations 2005

Reg.3, amended: SI 2014/107 Sch.1 para.37, SI 2014/852 Art.12, SI 2014/3229 Sch.6 para.26

Reg.3A, amended: SI 2014/852 Art.12

3167. Registration of Civil Partnerships (Fees) (No.2) Order 2005

revoked: SI 2014/1789 Art.3

3172. Water Services etc (Scotland) Act 2005 (Consequential Provisions and Modifications) Order 2005
    Art.5, amended: SI 2014/892 Sch.1 para.245
    Art.5, applied: SI 2014/559
    Art.5, referred to: SI 2014/892 Sch.2 para.2
    Art.10, amended: SI 2014/892 Sch.1 para.246
    Art.10, referred to: SI 2014/892 Sch.2 para.2

3174. Reporting of Suspicious Civil Partnerships Regulations 2005
    Reg.2, amended: SI 2014/1660 Reg.3

3176. Civil Partnership (Registration Provisions) Regulations 2005
    Reg.9, amended: SI 2014/3061 Sch.1 para.10
    Reg.13, applied: SI 2014/3181 Reg.21
    Reg.14, applied: SI 2014/3181 Reg.21
    Reg.15, amended: SI 2014/3181 Sch.2 para.1
    Reg.17, applied: SI 2014/3181 Reg.21
    Sch.2, added: SI 2014/107 Sch.1 para.38
    Sch.2, amended: SI 2014/107 Sch.1 para.38

3180. Criminal Justice (International Co-operation) Act 1990 (Enforcement of Overseas Forfeiture Orders) Order 2005
    Art.3, amended: SI 2014/834 Sch.3 para.12
    Art.15, amended: SI 2014/834 Sch.3 para.13

3181. Proceeds of Crime Act 2002 (External Requests and Orders) Order 2005
    applied: SI 2014/1610 r.57_14
    Part 2, applied: SI 2014/1893 Art.19
    Part 4, applied: SI 2014/1893 Art.19
    Art.6, amended: SI 2014/834 Sch.3 para.15
    Art.18, amended: SI 2014/834 Sch.3 para.16
    Art.20, amended: SI 2014/3141 Reg.4
    Art.34, amended: SI 2014/834 Sch.3 para.17
    Art.66, amended: SI 2014/3141 Reg.4
    Art.106, amended: SI 2014/3141 Reg.4
    Art.141R, amended: SI 2014/834 Sch.3 para.18
    Art.213, amended: SI 2014/834 Sch.3 para.19
    Pt 5., see *United States v Abacha* [2014] EWHC 993 (Comm), [2014] Lloyd's Rep. F.C. 392 (QBD (Comm)), Field J

3200. School Councils (Wales) Regulations 2005
    Reg.2, varied: SI 2014/1132 Sch.9 para.1, Sch.9 para.2, Sch.9 para.3
    Reg.3, varied: SI 2014/1132 Sch.9 para.4, Sch.9 para.5, Sch.9 para.6, Sch.9 para.7

    Reg.4, varied: SI 2014/1132 Sch.9 para.8, Sch.9 para.9
    Reg.7, varied: SI 2014/1132 Sch.9 para.10

3262. Healthy Start Scheme and Welfare Food (Amendment) Regulations 2005
    applied: SI 2014/3099 Reg.2

3320. Hydrocarbon Oil Duties (Reliefs for Electricity Generation) Regulations 2005
    Reg.2, amended: SI 2014/713 Reg.3
    Sch.2, substituted: SI 2014/713 Reg.4

3361. National Health Service (General Dental Services Contracts) Regulations 2005
    see *NHS Commissioning Board (NHS England) v Bargain Dentist.Com* [2014] EWHC 1994 (QB), [2014] Med. L.R. 301 (QBD), Elisabeth Laing J
    Reg.2, amended: SI 2014/443 Reg.3
    Sch.2 Part 1 para.1, amended: SI 2014/443 Reg.3
    Sch.3 Part 10 para.81, amended: SI 2014/1887 Sch.2 para.8
    Sch.3 Part 10 para.82, amended: SI 2014/1887 Sch.2 para.8
    Sch.3 para.55, see *NHS Commissioning Board (NHS England) v Bargain Dentist.Com* [2014] EWHC 1994 (QB), [2014] Med. L.R. 301 (QBD), Elisabeth Laing J
    Sch.3 para.56, see *NHS Commissioning Board (NHS England) v Bargain Dentist.Com* [2014] EWHC 1994 (QB), [2014] Med. L.R. 301 (QBD), Elisabeth Laing J
    Sch.4 para.16, revoked: SI 2014/443 Reg.3

3365. Representations Procedure (Children) (Wales) Regulations 2005
    revoked: SI 2014/1795 Reg.26

3366. Social Services Complaints Procedure (Wales) Regulations 2005
    revoked: SI 2014/1794 Reg.23

3367. Common Agricultural Policy Single Payment and Support Schemes (Cross Compliance) (Wales) (Amendment) Regulations 2005
    revoked: SI 2014/3223 Sch.3

3373. National Health Service (Personal Dental Services Agreements) Regulations 2005
    Reg.2, amended: SI 2014/443 Reg.4
    Sch.2 Part 1 para.1, amended: SI 2014/443 Reg.4

Sch.3 Part 10 para.79, amended: SI
2014/1887 Sch.2 para.9
Sch.3 Part 10 para.80, amended: SI
2014/1887 Sch.2 para.9
Sch.4 para.2, amended: SI 2014/443 Reg.4
Sch.4 para.15, revoked: SI 2014/443 Reg.4

3377. Occupational Pension Schemes (Scheme Funding) Regulations 2005

Reg.2, applied: SI 2014/1711 Reg.62
Reg.2, varied: SI 2014/1711 Reg.66
Reg.8, varied: SI 2014/1711 Reg.66
Reg.9, varied: SI 2014/1711 Reg.66
Sch.2 para.1, applied: SI 2014/1711 Reg.62
Sch.2 para.4, applied: SI 2014/1711 Reg.62
Sch.2 para.7, applied: SI 2014/1711 Reg.62

3381. Occupational Pension Schemes (Cross-border Activities) Regulations 2005

Reg.2, applied: SI 2014/1711 Reg.77
Reg.4, applied: SI 2014/1711 Reg.77
Reg.5, applied: SI 2014/1711 Reg.77
Reg.6, applied: SI 2014/1711 Reg.77
Reg.9, applied: SI 2014/1711 Reg.77
Reg.10, applied: SI 2014/1711 Reg.77

3436. Education (Grants etc.) (Dance and Drama) (England) (Amendment) (No.2) Regulations 2005

revoked: SI 2014/80 Sch.1

3454. Registered Pension Schemes (Accounting and Assessment) Regulations 2005

Reg.4, amended: SI 2014/1928 Reg.3
Reg.5, amended: SI 2014/1928 Reg.4
Reg.8, amended: SI 2014/1928 Reg.5,
Reg.6, Reg.7

3477. National Health Service (Dental Charges) Regulations 2005

Reg.2, amended: SI 2014/443 Reg.5
Reg.4, amended: SI 2014/545 Reg.5
Reg.13A, amended: SI 2014/545 Reg.5

2006

5. Public Contracts Regulations 2006

see *Draper v Lincolnshire CC* [2014]
EWHC 2388 (Admin), [2014] B.L.G.R. 673
(QBD (Admin)), Collins J; see *Travis
Perkins Trading Co Ltd v Caerphilly CBC*
[2014] EWHC 1498 (TCC), [2014] B.L.R.
465 (QBD (TCC)), Akenhead J
Reg.47D, see *Travis Perkins Trading Co Ltd
v Caerphilly CBC* [2014] EWHC 1498

(TCC), [2014] B.L.R. 465 (QBD (TCC)),
Akenhead J
Sch.1, amended: SI 2014/834 Sch.3 para.20

6. Utilities Contracts Regulations 2006

Reg.3, see *NATS (Services) Ltd v Gatwick
Airport Ltd* [2014] EWHC 3133 (TCC),
[2014] B.L.R. 697 (QBD (TCC)), Ramsey J
Reg.45G, see *NATS (Services) Ltd v Gatwick
Airport Ltd* [2014] EWHC 3133 (TCC),
[2014] B.L.R. 697 (QBD (TCC)), Ramsey J

18. Performances (Moral Rights, etc.) Regulations 2006

Sch.1 para.9, amended: SI 2014/1384 Sch.1
para.8

31. Food Hygiene (Wales) Regulations 2006

Reg.17, amended: SI 2014/3080 Reg.2
Reg.32A, revoked: SI 2014/1858 Reg.2
Sch.1, amended: SI 2014/1858 Reg.2
Sch.3 para.2, amended: SI 2014/1858 Reg.2
Sch.4 para.8, amended: SI 2014/2303 Sch.7
para.41
Sch.6A, revoked: SI 2014/1858 Reg.2
Sch.6 para.1A, added: SI 2014/3080 Reg.2
Sch.6 para.7A, added: SI 2014/3080 Reg.2
Sch.6 para.8, amended: SI 2014/3080 Reg.2
Sch.7 para.12, revoked: SI 2014/2303 Sch.6
Part 1

33. Occupational Pension Schemes (Early Leavers Cash Transfer Sums and Contribution Refunds) Regulations 2006

Reg.1, amended: SI 2014/1711 Reg.35
Reg.2, amended: SI 2014/1711 Reg.35
Reg.2A, amended: SI 2014/1711 Reg.35
Reg.2B, amended: SI 2014/1711 Reg.35
Reg.2C, amended: SI 2014/1711 Reg.35
Reg.4, amended: SI 2014/1711 Reg.35

136. Pension Benefits (Insurance Company Liable as Scheme Administrator) Regulations 2006

Reg.2, amended: 2014 c.30 Sch.1 para.30

179. Foot-and-Mouth Disease (Wales) Order 2006

applied: SI 2014/1894 Reg.4
Art.3, amended: SI 2014/517 Sch.2 para.1
Art.26, amended: SI 2014/517 Sch.2 para.1
Art.27, amended: SI 2014/517 Sch.2 para.1
Sch.4 Part 2 para.20, amended: SI 2014/517
Sch.2 para.1
Sch.4 Part 3 para.33, amended: SI 2014/517
Sch.2 para.1

Sch.5 Part 1 para.2, amended: SI 2014/517
Sch.2 para.1
Sch.5 Part 1 para.3, amended: SI 2014/517
Sch.2 para.1
Sch.5 Part 1 para.5, amended: SI 2014/517
Sch.2 para.1
Sch.5 Part 1 para.6, amended: SI 2014/517
Sch.2 para.1
Sch.5 Part 1 para.7, amended: SI 2014/517
Sch.2 para.1
Sch.5 Part 1 para.8, amended: SI 2014/517
Sch.2 para.1

180. Foot-and-Mouth Disease (Control of Vaccination) (Wales) Regulations 2006
Sch.1 Part 3 para.18, amended: SI 2014/517
Sch.2 para.2

182. Foot-and-Mouth Disease (England) Order 2006
applied: SI 2014/1894 Reg.4

207. Pensions Schemes (Application of UK Provisions to Relevant Non-UK Schemes) Regulations 2006
Part 4, added: 2014 c.30 Sch.1 para.96
Reg.5, amended: 2014 c.30 Sch.1 para.96
Reg.6, revoked (in part): 2014 c.30 Sch.1 para.33
Reg.7, revoked (in part): 2014 c.30 Sch.1 para.33
Reg.14, amended: 2014 c.30 Sch.1 para.33
Reg.14, revoked (in part): 2014 c.30 Sch.1 para.33
Reg.15, amended: 2014 c.30 Sch.1 para.96

208. Pension Schemes (Information Requirements Qualifying Overseas Pension Schemes, Qualifying Recognised Overseas Pensions Schemes and Corresponding Relief) Regulations 2006
Reg.3, amended: 2014 c.30 Sch.1 para.97

213. Housing Benefit Regulations 2006
applied: SI 2014/1230 Reg.6, Reg.10, SI 2014/3094 Art.6
see *R. (on the application of MA) v Secretary of State for Work and Pensions* [2014] EWCA Civ 13, [2014] P.T.S.R. 584 (CA (Civ Div)), Lord Dyson MR
Part 3 regA.13, amended: SI 2014/212 Reg.3
Reg.B13, see *R. (on the application of MA) v Secretary of State for Work and Pensions* [2014] EWCA Civ 13, [2014] P.T.S.R. 584 (CA (Civ Div)), Lord Dyson MR

Reg.2, amended: SI 2014/107 Sch.1 para.40, SI 2014/213 Reg.3, SI 2014/591 Reg.8, SI 2014/3229 Sch.6 para.27, SI 2014/3255 Art.17
Reg.6, amended: SI 2014/3255 Art.17
Reg.7, see *Obrey v Secretary of State for Work and Pensions* [2013] EWCA Civ 1584, [2014] H.L.R. 12 (CA (Civ Div)), Laws LJ
Reg.9, see *R. (on the application of Whapples) v Birmingham CrossCity Clinical Commissioning Group* [2014] EWHC 2647 (Admin), [2014] P.T.S.R. 1413 (QBD (Admin)), Sales J
Reg.10, amended: SI 2014/539 Reg.2, SI 2014/902 Reg.5
Reg.10, applied: SI 2014/2603 Reg.5
Reg.28, amended: SI 2014/213 Reg.3, SI 2014/2888 Reg.3, SI 2014/3255 Art.17
Reg.28, varied: 2014 c.6 s.126
Reg.34, amended: SI 2014/213 Reg.3
Reg.35, amended: SI 2014/591 Reg.8, SI 2014/3255 Art.17
Reg.35, applied: SI 2014/2672 Reg.14
Reg.36, amended: SI 2014/3255 Art.17
Reg.38, amended: SI 2014/213 Reg.3
Reg.39, amended: SI 2014/213 Reg.3
Reg.42, amended: SI 2014/591 Reg.8, SI 2014/1913 Reg.11, SI 2014/3117 Reg.15
Reg.42, applied: SI 2014/1913 Reg.11, SI 2014/3117 Reg.15
Reg.42, revoked (in part): SI 2014/1913 Reg.11, SI 2014/3117 Reg.15
Reg.49, amended: SI 2014/1913 Reg.12, SI 2014/3117 Reg.16
Reg.49, applied: SI 2014/1913 Reg.12, SI 2014/3117 Reg.16
Reg.49, revoked (in part): SI 2014/1913 Reg.12, SI 2014/3117 Reg.16
Reg.74, amended: SI 2014/516 Art.17, SI 2014/2888 Reg.3
Reg.75C, amended: SI 2014/771 Reg.3
Reg.75E, amended: SI 2014/3255 Art.17
Reg.75H, added: SI 2014/771 Reg.3
Reg.83, applied: SI 2014/1230 Reg.6, SI 2014/3094 Art.6
Reg.87, amended: SI 2014/213 Reg.3
Sch.1 Part 1 para.2, amended: SI 2014/516 Art.17
Sch.1 Part 2 para.6, amended: SI 2014/516 Art.17

Sch.3 Part 1 para.1, referred to: SI 2014/147 Art.7

Sch.3 Part 1 para.2, substituted: SI 2014/516 Sch.5

Sch.3 Part 2 para.3, amended: SI 2014/516 Art.17

Sch.3 Part 3 para.13, amended: SI 2014/213 Reg.3, SI 2014/2888 Reg.3

Sch.3 Part 3 para.14, amended: SI 2014/213 Reg.3, SI 2014/2888 Reg.3

Sch.3 Part 3 para.15, amended: SI 2014/213 Reg.3

Sch.3 Part 3 para.16, amended: SI 2014/213 Reg.3, SI 2014/2888 Reg.3

Sch.3 Part 4, amended: SI 2014/516 Sch.6

Sch.3 Part 6 para.25, amended: SI 2014/516 Art.17

Sch.3 Part 6 para.26, amended: SI 2014/516 Art.17

Sch.5, applied: SI 2014/1913 Reg.13, SI 2014/3117 Reg.17

Sch.5 para.2A, amended: SI 2014/591 Reg.8

Sch.5 paraA.4, added: SI 2014/1913 Reg.13

Sch.5 paraA.4, revoked (in part): SI 2014/1913 Reg.13

Sch.5 paraA.5, added: SI 2014/3117 Reg.17

Sch.5 paraA.5, revoked (in part): SI 2014/3117 Reg.17

Sch.5 para.25, amended: SI 2014/852 Art.13

Sch.5 para.57, amended: SI 2014/513 Sch.1 para.10

Sch.5 para.66, added: SI 2014/2103 Art.20

Sch.6, applied: SI 2014/1913 Reg.14, SI 2014/3117 Reg.18

Sch.6 paraA.4, added: SI 2014/1913 Reg.14

Sch.6 paraA.4, revoked (in part): SI 2014/1913 Reg.14

Sch.6 paraA.5, added: SI 2014/3117 Reg.18

Sch.6 paraA.5, revoked (in part): SI 2014/3117 Reg.18

Sch.6 para.58, amended: SI 2014/513 Sch.1 para.10

Sch.6 para.61, added: SI 2014/2103 Art.20

214. Housing Benefit (Persons who have attained the qualifying age for state pension credit) Regulations 2006

applied: SI 2014/1230 Reg.6, Reg.10, SI 2014/3094 Art.6

Reg.2, amended: SI 2014/107 Sch.1 para.41, SI 2014/591 Reg.9, SI 2014/3229 Sch.6 para.28, SI 2014/3255 Art.18

Reg.6, amended: SI 2014/3255 Art.18

Reg.10, amended: SI 2014/902 Reg.6

Reg.10, applied: SI 2014/2603 Reg.5

Reg.29, amended: SI 2014/3255 Art.18

Reg.29, revoked (in part): SI 2014/3255 Art.18

Reg.29, varied: 2014 c.6 s.126

Reg.31, amended: SI 2014/213 Reg.4, SI 2014/2888 Reg.3, SI 2014/3255 Art.18

Reg.31, varied: 2014 c.6 s.126

Reg.34, amended: SI 2014/213 Reg.4

Reg.35, amended: SI 2014/591 Reg.9, SI 2014/3255 Art.18

Reg.35, applied: SI 2014/2672 Reg.14

Reg.35, revoked (in part): SI 2014/3255 Art.18

Reg.35, varied: 2014 c.6 s.126

Reg.36, amended: SI 2014/3255 Art.18

Reg.39, amended: SI 2014/213 Reg.4

Reg.40, amended: SI 2014/213 Reg.4

Reg.41, amended: SI 2014/591 Reg.9

Reg.42, amended: SI 2014/591 Reg.9

Reg.55, amended: SI 2014/516 Art.18

Reg.64, applied: SI 2014/1230 Reg.6, SI 2014/3094 Art.6

Reg.68, amended: SI 2014/213 Reg.4

Sch.1 Part 1 para.2, amended: SI 2014/516 Art.18

Sch.1 Part 2 para.6, amended: SI 2014/516 Art.18

Sch.3 Part 1 para.1, substituted: SI 2014/516 Sch.7

Sch.3 Part 2 para.3, amended: SI 2014/516 Art.18

Sch.3 Part 3 para.6, amended: SI 2014/213 Reg.4, SI 2014/2888 Reg.3

Sch.3 Part 3 para.7, amended: SI 2014/213 Reg.4

Sch.3 Part 3 para.8, amended: SI 2014/213 Reg.4

Sch.3 Part 4, substituted: SI 2014/516 Sch.8

Sch.4 para.5, amended: SI 2014/2888 Reg.3

Sch.6 Part 1 para.26D, amended: SI 2014/513 Sch.1 para.11

Sch.6 Part 1 para.26F, added: SI 2014/2103 Art.21

215. Council Tax Benefit Regulations 2006

Reg.18, varied: 2014 c.6 s.126

216. Council Tax Benefit (Persons who have attained the qualifying age for state pension credit) Regulations 2006
  Reg.19, varied: 2014 c.6 s.126
  Reg.21, varied: 2014 c.6 s.126
  Reg.25, varied: 2014 c.6 s.126
217. Housing Benefit and Council Tax Benefit (Consequential Provisions) Regulations 2006
  Sch.3 para.4, amended: SI 2014/212 Reg.2
  Sch.3 para.6, referred to: SI 2014/2603 Reg.5
223. Child Benefit (General) Regulations 2006
  Reg.1, amended: SI 2014/1231 Reg.2
  Reg.3, amended: SI 2014/1231 Reg.2, SI 2014/2924 Reg.2
  Reg.23, amended: SI 2014/1511 Reg.3
  Reg.27, see *Revenue and Customs Commissioners v Spiridonova* [2014] NICA 63 (CA (NI)), Morgan LCJ
  Reg.27, amended: SI 2014/1511 Reg.4
246. Transfer of Undertakings (Protection of Employment) Regulations 2006
  applied: 2014 c.2 Sch.1 para.1, 2014 c.20 s.6, SSI 2014/164 Reg.93
  disapplied: 2014 c.2 Sch.1 para.1
  referred to: 2014 c.23 s.118
  see *Ellis v Cabinet Office* [2014] EWHC 2049 (Ch), [2014] Pens. L.R. 681 (Ch D), Rose J; see *Heron v Sefton MBC* [2014] Eq. L.R. 130 (EAT), Mitting J; see *Horizon Security Services Ltd v Ndeze* [2014] I.R.L.R. 854 (EAT), Judge Eady QC; see *Kavanagh v Crystal Palace FC 2000 Ltd* [2013] EWCA Civ 1410, [2014] 1 All E.R. 1033 (CA (Civ Div)), Maurice Kay LJ; see *Manchester College v Hazel* [2014] EWCA Civ 72, [2014] I.C.R. 989 (CA (Civ Div)), Moore-Bick LJ; see *Robert Sage Ltd (t/a Prestige Nursing Care Ltd) v O'Connell* [2014] I.R.L.R. 428 (EAT), Slade J
  Reg.2, applied: SSI 2014/164 Reg.93
  Reg.3, amended: SI 2014/16 Reg.5
  Reg.3, disapplied: SSI 2014/164 Reg.93
  Reg.3, see *Robert Sage Ltd (t/a Prestige Nursing Care Ltd) v O'Connell* [2014] I.R.L.R. 428 (EAT), Slade J
  Reg.4, amended: SI 2014/16 Reg.6
  Reg.4, referred to: SI 2014/1139 Reg.5
  Reg.4, see *Robert Sage Ltd (t/a Prestige Nursing Care Ltd) v O'Connell* [2014] I.R.L.R. 428 (EAT), Slade J

  Reg.4A, added: SI 2014/16 Reg.7
  Reg.5, referred to: SI 2014/1139 Reg.5
  Reg.7, amended: SI 2014/16 Reg.8
  Reg.7, see *Kavanagh v Crystal Palace FC 2000 Ltd* [2013] EWCA Civ 1410, [2014] 1 All E.R. 1033 (CA (Civ Div)), Maurice Kay LJ; see *Manchester College v Hazel* [2014] EWCA Civ 72, [2014] I.C.R. 989 (CA (Civ Div)), Moore-Bick LJ; see *RR Donnelley Global Document Solutions Group Ltd v Besagni* [2014] I.C.R. 1008 (EAT), Slade J
  Reg.9, amended: SI 2014/16 Reg.9
  Reg.10, applied: SI 2014/1139 Reg.5
  Reg.11, amended: SI 2014/16 Reg.10
  Reg.12, amended: SI 2014/386 Sch.1 para.37, SI 2014/853 Art.2
  Reg.13, amended: SI 2014/16 Reg.11
  Reg.13, referred to: SI 2014/3352 Sch.2 para.30
  Reg.13, see *Allen v Morrisons Facilities Services Ltd* [2014] I.C.R. 792 (EAT), Slade J
  Reg.13A, added: SI 2014/16 Reg.11
  Reg.14, see *Allen v Morrisons Facilities Services Ltd* [2014] I.C.R. 792 (EAT), Slade J
  Reg.15, amended: SI 2014/16 Reg.11, SI 2014/853 Art.2
  Reg.15, see *Allen v Morrisons Facilities Services Ltd* [2014] I.C.R. 792 (EAT), Slade J
  Reg.16, amended: SI 2014/386 Sch.1 para.38
  Reg.16A, added: SI 2014/853 Art.2
  Sch.1 para.10, amended: SI 2014/386 Sch.1 para.39
264. Community Benefit Societies (Restriction on Use of Assets) Regulations 2006
  Sch.2 para.3, revoked: SI 2014/574 Reg.7
265. Friendly and Industrial and Provident Societies Act 1968 (Audit Exemption) (Amendment) Order 2006
  revoked: 2014 c.14 Sch.7
349. Occupational and Personal Pension Schemes (Consultation by Employers and Miscellaneous Amendment) Regulations 2006
  Sch.1 para.4, amended: SI 2014/386 Sch.1 para.41
  Sch.1 para.4A, added: SI 2014/386 Sch.1 para.42

Sch.1 para.12, amended: SI 2014/386 Sch.1
para.43
**354. Enterprise Act 2002 (Enforcement
Undertakings) Order 2006**
Art.4, amended: SI 2014/549 Sch.1 para.18
**355. Enterprise Act 2002 (Enforcement
Undertakings and Orders) Order 2006**
Art.4, amended: SI 2014/549 Sch.1 para.19
Art.4, revoked (in part): SI 2014/549 Sch.1
para.19
**371. Licensing of Houses in Multiple
Occupation (Prescribed Descriptions) (England)
Order 2006**
see *Bristol City Council v Digs (Bristol) Ltd*
[2014] EWHC 869 (Admin), [2014] H.L.R.
30 (QBD (Admin)), Burnett J
Art.3, see *Bristol City Council v Digs
(Bristol) Ltd* [2014] EWHC 869 (Admin),
[2014] H.L.R. 30 (QBD (Admin)), Burnett J
**489. National Health Service (Personal Dental
Services Agreements) (Wales) Regulations 2006**
Sch.2 Part 1 para.1, amended: SI 2014/872
Reg.3
Sch.3 Part 10 para.79, amended: SI
2014/1887 Sch.2 para.11
Sch.3 Part 10 para.80, amended: SI
2014/1887 Sch.2 para.11
**490. National Health Service (General Dental
Services Contracts) (Wales) Regulations 2006**
Sch.2 Part 1 para.1, amended: SI 2014/872
Reg.2
Sch.3 Part 10 para.81, amended: SI
2014/1887 Sch.2 para.10
Sch.3 Part 10 para.82, amended: SI
2014/1887 Sch.2 para.10
**491. National Health Service (Dental Charges)
(Wales) Regulations 2006**
Reg.4, amended: SI 2014/461 Reg.2
**493. Immigration (Passenger Transit Visa)
(Amendment) Order 2006**
revoked: SI 2014/2702 Sch.2
**499. Registered Pension Schemes (Transfer of
Sums and Assets) Regulations 2006**
Reg.4, amended: SI 2014/1449 Reg.2
Reg.12, amended: 2014 c.30 Sch.1 para.34,
Sch.2 para.16
501. Fines Collection Regulations 2006
applied: SI 2014/1610 r.52_1
Reg.30, amended: SI 2014/879 Art.92
Reg.30, revoked (in part): SI 2014/879
Art.92

**557. Health and Safety (Enforcing Authority for
Railways and Other Guided Transport Systems)
Regulations 2006**
Reg.2, amended: SI 2014/469 Sch.3
para.126, SI 2014/3248 Sch.5 para.14
Reg.3, amended: SI 2014/469 Sch.3
para.126
Reg.4, amended: SI 2014/469 Sch.3
para.126
Reg.5A, added: SI 2014/469 Sch.3 para.126
Sch.1 para.13, revoked: SI 2014/469 Sch.3
para.210
**558. Occupational Pension Schemes (Fraud
Compensation Levy) Regulations 2006**
Reg.7, applied: SI 2014/1711 Reg.50
**567. Registered Pension Schemes (Provision of
Information) Regulations 2006**
Reg.2, amended: SI 2014/1843 Reg.3
Reg.3, amended: 2014 c.30 Sch.1 para.35,
Sch.1 para.90, SI 2014/1843 Reg.4
Reg.5B, revoked: 2014 c.30 Sch.1 para.35
Reg.11, amended: SI 2014/1843 Reg.5
Reg.11, substituted: SI 2014/1843 Reg.5
Reg.14A, amended: 2014 c.30 Sch.1 para.88
Reg.14A, applied: SI 2014/2848 Reg.180
Reg.14B, amended: 2014 c.30 Sch.1 para.89
Reg.14ZA, added: 2014 c.30 Sch.1 para.87
Reg.16, amended: 2014 c.30 Sch.1 para.35
Reg.17, amended: 2014 c.30 Sch.1 para.35
Reg.19, added: 2014 c.26 Sch.5 para.11
**569. Registered Pension Schemes (Splitting of
Schemes) Regulations 2006**
Reg.3, applied: SI 2014/2848 Reg.177
Sch.3, applied: SI 2014/2848 Reg.177
**572. Taxation of Pension Schemes (Transitional
Provisions) Order 2006**
Art.18, amended: 2014 c.26 Sch.5 para.12
Art.23C, amended: 2014 c.26 s.42, 2014
c.30 Sch.1 para.72
Art.25C, amended: 2014 c.30 Sch.1 para.69
**580. Pension Protection Fund (General and
Miscellaneous Amendments) Regulations 2006**
applied: SI 2014/1711 Reg.48, Reg.49
Reg.1, amended: SI 2014/107 Sch.1 para.42,
SI 2014/3229 Sch.6 para.29
Reg.19A, applied: SI 2014/1711 Reg.48,
Reg.49
601. Air Navigation (General) Regulations 2006
Reg.11, substituted: SI 2014/3302 Sch.1
para.6

602. Elections (Policy Development Grants Scheme) Order 2006
    Sch.1, substituted: SI 2014/556 Sch.1 para.1, Sch.1 para.2

606. Naval, Military and Air Forces Etc (Disablement and Death) Service Pensions Order 2006
    applied: SI 2014/916 Sch.2
    referred to: SI 2014/505
    Sch.1 Part II, amended: SI 2014/505 Sch.1
    Sch.1 Part III, amended: SI 2014/505 Sch.2
    Sch.1 Part IV, amended: SI 2014/505 Sch.3
    Sch.2 Part II, amended: SI 2014/505 Sch.4
    Sch.2 Part III, amended: SI 2014/505 Sch.5
    Sch.6 Part II, amended: SI 2014/107 Sch.1 para.43, SI 2014/3229 Sch.6 para.30

659. Weights and Measures (Packaged Goods) Regulations 2006
    Reg.2, amended: SI 2014/2975 Reg.36
    Reg.3, amended: SI 2014/2975 Reg.37
    Sch.6, revoked: SI 2014/2975 Reg.38

741. Pensions Increase (Review) Order 2006
    referred to: SI 2014/668 Sch.1
    Art.6, substituted: SI 2014/107 Sch.1 para.56, SI 2014/3229 Sch.6 para.35

758. Gender Recognition (Application Fees) Order 2006
    Sch.1 para.1, amended: SI 2014/513 Sch.1 para.12, SI 2014/590 Art.6

759. Occupational Pension Schemes (Modification of Schemes) Regulations 2006
    Reg.3, amended: SI 2014/107 Sch.1 para.44, SI 2014/560 Sch.3 para.6, SI 2014/3229 Sch.3 para.4, Sch.6 para.31
    Reg.3, disapplied: SI 2014/3229 Sch.2 para.6
    Reg.7, amended: SI 2014/560 Sch.3 para.6, SI 2014/3229 Sch.3 para.4
    Reg.7, disapplied: SI 2014/3229 Sch.2 para.6
    Reg.7ZA, added: SI 2014/107 Sch.1 para.44, SI 2014/3229 Sch.6 para.31

802. Occupational Pension Schemes (Payments to Employer) Regulations 2006
    Reg.2, amended: SI 2014/1711 Reg.39
    Reg.4, referred to: SI 2014/1711 Reg.38
    Reg.18, referred to: SI 2014/1711 Reg.36

873. Staffing of Maintained Schools (Wales) Regulations 2006
    Reg.3, amended: SI 2014/1609 Reg.2

Reg.3, varied: SI 2014/1132 Sch.8 para.1, Sch.8 paraA.1
Reg.4, varied: SI 2014/1132 Sch.8 para.2
Reg.6, varied: SI 2014/1132 Sch.8 para.3
Reg.7, revoked (in part): SI 2014/1609 Reg.2
Reg.7, varied: SI 2014/1132 Sch.8 para.4, Sch.8 para.5, Sch.8 para.6, Sch.8 para.7
Reg.7A, added: SI 2014/1609 Reg.2
Reg.7A, varied: SI 2014/1132 Sch.8 para.4, Sch.8 para.7
Reg.9, varied: SI 2014/1132 Sch.8 para.8
Reg.9A, varied: SI 2014/1132 Sch.8 para.9
Reg.9B, varied: SI 2014/1132 Sch.8 para.9
Reg.10, amended: SI 2014/1609 Reg.2
Reg.10, applied: SI 2014/1132 Reg.63
Reg.10, varied: SI 2014/1132 Sch.8 para.10
Reg.12, varied: SI 2014/1132 Sch.8 para.11
Reg.15A, varied: SI 2014/1132 Sch.8 para.11, Sch.8 para.12
Reg.16, varied: SI 2014/1132 Sch.8 para.13
Reg.17, applied: SI 2014/1132 Reg.67
Reg.17, varied: SI 2014/1132 Sch.8 para.11, Sch.8 para.14
Reg.18, varied: SI 2014/1132 Sch.8 para.12, Sch.8 para.15, Sch.8 para.16
Reg.18A, varied: SI 2014/1132 Sch.8 para.17
Reg.19, varied: SI 2014/1132 Sch.8 para.18, Sch.8 para.19, Sch.8 para.20
Reg.20, varied: SI 2014/1132 Sch.8 para.8
Reg.20A, varied: SI 2014/1132 Sch.8 para.9
Reg.23, varied: SI 2014/1132 Sch.8 para.21, Sch.8 para.22
Reg.24, amended: SI 2014/1609 Reg.2
Reg.24, applied: SI 2014/1132 Reg.63
Reg.24, varied: SI 2014/1132 Sch.8 para.23
Reg.24A, varied: SI 2014/1132 Sch.8 para.4, Sch.8 para.12, Sch.8 para.24
Reg.26, varied: SI 2014/1132 Sch.8 para.11
Reg.26A, varied: SI 2014/1132 Sch.8 para.17
Reg.27, varied: SI 2014/1132 Sch.8 para.4
Reg.28, varied: SI 2014/1132 Sch.8 para.25
Reg.29, applied: SI 2014/1132 Reg.67
Reg.29, varied: SI 2014/1132 Sch.8 para.4
Reg.32, varied: SI 2014/1132 Sch.8 para.4, Sch.8 para.26, Sch.8 para.27
Reg.33, varied: SI 2014/1132 Sch.8 para.28
Reg.34, applied: SI 2014/1132 Reg.63
Reg.34, varied: SI 2014/1132 Sch.8 para.28

Reg.35, varied: SI 2014/1132 Sch.8 para.29

932. Police (Injury Benefit) Regulations 2006

Reg.7, amended: SI 2014/79 Reg.11

Reg.13, amended: SI 2014/79 Reg.12

Reg.20, amended: SI 2014/79 Reg.13

Sch.5 para.2, amended: SI 2014/79 Reg.14

964. Authorised Investment Funds (Tax) Regulations 2006

applied: SI 2014/685 Reg.2

Reg.14A, revoked: SI 2014/1932 Reg.4

Reg.14E, amended: SI 2014/685 Reg.7

Reg.14F, revoked: SI 2014/685 Reg.7

Reg.69F, amended: SI 2014/518 Reg.3

Reg.69F, revoked (in part): SI 2014/518 Reg.3

Sch.1 Part 1, amended: SI 2014/518 Reg.3

Sch.1 Part 2, amended: SI 2014/685 Reg.7

965. Child Benefit (Rates) Regulations 2006

Reg.2, amended: SI 2014/384 Art.2

987. Serious Organised Crime and Police Act 2005 (Application and Modification of Certain Enactments to Designated Staff of SOCA) Order 2006

revoked: SI 2014/1704 Art.9

1003. Immigration (European Economic Area) Regulations 2006

applied: SI 2014/1976 Reg.4, SI 2014/2761 Reg.4

see *R. (on the application of Nouazli) v Secretary of State for the Home Department* [2013] EWCA Civ 1608, [2014] 1 W.L.R. 3313 (CA (Civ Div)), Moore-Bick LJ; see *RM (Zimbabwe) v Secretary of State for the Home Department* [2013] EWCA Civ 775, [2014] 1 W.L.R. 2259 (CA (Civ Div)), Longmore LJ; see *Sannie v Secretary of State for the Home Department* [2013] EWCA Civ 1638, [2014] Imm. A.R. 703 (CA (Civ Div)), Sir Terence Etherton C

Part 3, applied: SI 2014/581 Sch.3 para.2

Reg.2, amended: SI 2014/1976 Sch.1 para.1

Reg.2, applied: SI 2014/2604 r.23

Reg.3, see *Babajanov (Continuity of Residence: Immigration (EEA) Regulations 2006), Re* [2014] Imm. A.R. 196 (UT (IAC)), Judge Allen

Reg.6, amended: SI 2014/1451 Reg.3, SI 2014/2761 Reg.3

Reg.6, applied: SI 2014/1451 Reg.4, SI 2014/2603 Reg.4, Reg.6, SI 2014/2761 Reg.4

Reg.11, amended: SI 2014/1976 Sch.1 para.2

Reg.13, applied: SI 2014/2603 Reg.4, Reg.6

Reg.15, applied: SI 2014/2603 Reg.4, Reg.6

Reg.15, see *Babajanov (Continuity of Residence: Immigration (EEA) Regulations 2006), Re* [2014] Imm. A.R. 196 (UT (IAC)), Judge Allen

Reg.15A, applied: SI 2014/2603 Reg.4, Reg.6

Reg.15A, see *Hines v Lambeth LBC* [2014] EWCA Civ 660, [2014] 1 W.L.R. 4112 (CA (Civ Div)), Sullivan LJ; see *Mensah v Salford City Council* [2014] EWHC 3537 (Admin), (2014) 17 C.C.L. Rep. 492 (QBD (Admin)), Lewis J

Reg.15B, amended: SI 2014/1976 Sch.1 para.3

Reg.17, see *Sannie v Secretary of State for the Home Department* [2013] EWCA Civ 1638, [2014] Imm. A.R. 703 (CA (Civ Div)), Sir Terence Etherton C

Reg.19, amended: SI 2014/1976 Sch.1 para.4

Reg.19, see *ZZ (France) v Secretary of State for the Home Department* [2014] EWCA Civ 7, [2014] Q.B. 820 (CA (Civ Div)), Lord Dyson MR

Reg.21, see *R. (on the application of Nouazli) v Secretary of State for the Home Department* [2013] EWCA Civ 1608, [2014] 1 W.L.R. 3313 (CA (Civ Div)), Moore-Bick LJ; see *Sannie v Secretary of State for the Home Department* [2013] EWCA Civ 1638, [2014] Imm. A.R. 703 (CA (Civ Div)), Sir Terence Etherton C

Reg.22, amended: 2014 c.22 Sch.1 para.2, SI 2014/1976 Sch.1 para.5

Reg.24, see *R. (on the application of Nouazli) v Secretary of State for the Home Department* [2013] EWCA Civ 1608, [2014] 1 W.L.R. 3313 (CA (Civ Div)), Moore-Bick LJ

Reg.24AA, added: SI 2014/1976 Sch.1 para.6

Reg.29, amended: SI 2014/1976 Sch.1 para.7

Reg.29AA, added: SI 2014/1976 Sch.1 para.8

Sch.1, enabled: SI 2014/2604

Sch.2 para.3, amended: SI 2014/1976 Sch.1 para.9

Sch.2 para.4, applied: SI 2014/2604 r.16

1030. Cross-Border Insolvency Regulations 2006

see *Pan Ocean Co Ltd, Re* [2014] EWHC 2124 (Ch), [2014] Bus. L.R. 1041 (Ch D (Companies Ct)), Morgan J

Reg.2, see *Pan Ocean Co Ltd, Re* [2014] EWHC 2124 (Ch), [2014] Bus. L.R. 1041 (Ch D (Companies Ct)), Morgan J

1031. Employment Equality (Age) Regulations 2006

Reg.3, see *Lockwood v Department of Work and Pensions* [2013] EWCA Civ 1195, [2014] 1 All E.R. 250 (CA (Civ Div)), Rimer LJ

Sch.6 para.11, applied: SI 2014/382 Art.4

Sch.6 para.12, applied: SI 2014/382 Art.4

1116. Criminal Justice Act 1988 (Reviews of Sentencing) Order 2006

applied: SI 2014/1610 r.70_1

Sch.1 para.2, amended: SI 2014/1651 Art.2

Sch.1 para.4, amended: SI 2014/1651 Art.2

1161. Seed Potatoes (England) Regulations 2006

applied: SI 2014/601 Reg.3

Reg.8, applied: SI 2014/601 Reg.3

Reg.9, applied: SI 2014/601 Reg.3

1200. Welfare of Animals (Slaughter or Killing) (Amendment) (England) Regulations 2006

revoked: SI 2014/1240 Reg.47

1248. Merchant Shipping (Prevention of Air Pollution from Ships) Order 2006

Art.2, enabled: SI 2014/3076, SI 2014/3306

Art.3, enabled: SI 2014/3076, SI 2014/3306

1260. Human Tissue Act 2004 (Ethical Approval, Exceptions from Licensing and Supply of Information about Transplants) Regulations 2006

Reg.1, amended: 2014 c.23 Sch.8 para.8

Reg.3, amended: SI 2014/1459 Reg.11

1275. Local Authorities (Standing Orders) (Wales) Regulations 2006

Reg.2, amended: SI 2014/1514 Reg.3

Reg.5, amended: SI 2014/1514 Reg.4

Reg.5, revoked (in part): SI 2014/1514 Reg.4

Reg.6, revoked: SI 2014/1514 Reg.5

Reg.7, substituted: SI 2014/1514 Reg.6

Reg.8, amended: SI 2014/1514 Reg.7

Reg.9, amended: SI 2014/1514 Reg.8

Reg.9, applied: SI 2014/1514 Reg.12

Reg.9, revoked (in part): SI 2014/1514 Reg.8

Sch.1 Part 1, amended: SI 2014/1514 Reg.9

Sch.1 Part 1, substituted: SI 2014/1514 Reg.9

Sch.1 Part 2 para.3, revoked (in part): SI 2014/1514 Reg.9

Sch.3 Part 1, added: SI 2014/1514 Reg.10

Sch.3 Part 1, substituted: SI 2014/1514 Reg.10

Sch.3 Part 2, added: SI 2014/1514 Reg.10

Sch.3 Part 2, substituted: SI 2014/1514 Reg.10

Sch.3 Part 3, revoked: SI 2014/1514 Reg.10

Sch.4, added: SI 2014/1514 Reg.11

Sch.4, amended: SI 2014/1514 Reg.11

Sch.4, referred to: SI 2014/1514 Reg.12

Sch.4, substituted: SI 2014/1514 Reg.11

1294. Allocation of Housing and Homelessness (Eligibility) (England) Regulations 2006

Reg.2, amended: SI 2014/435 Reg.2

Reg.2, revoked (in part): SI 2014/435 Reg.2

Reg.3, amended: SI 2014/435 Reg.2

Reg.4, amended: SI 2014/435 Reg.2

Reg.4, revoked (in part): SI 2014/435 Reg.2

Reg.5, amended: SI 2014/435 Reg.2

Reg.6, amended: SI 2014/435 Reg.2

Reg.6, revoked (in part): SI 2014/435 Reg.2

1466. Transport and Works (Applications and Objections Procedure) (England and Wales) Rules 2006

applied: SI 2014/310, SI 2014/1604, SI 2014/2027, SI 2014/3102

Sch.5, amended: SI 2014/469 Sch.3 para.193

1542. Civil Courts (Amendment) Order 2006

revoked: SI 2014/820 Sch.1

1643. Plant Health (Wales) Order 2006

Part 7A, revoked: SI 2014/1186 Art.4

Art.2, amended: SI 2014/521 Art.3, SI 2014/2368 Art.3

Art.6, amended: SI 2014/521 Art.4

Art.8, amended: SI 2014/521 Art.5, SI 2014/2368 Art.4

Art.12, amended: SI 2014/521 Art.6, SI 2014/2368 Art.5

Art.12, applied: SI 2014/1792 Reg.2

Art.19, amended: SI 2014/521 Art.7, SI 2014/1186 Art.3

Art.21, amended: SI 2014/521 Art.8, SI 2014/2368 Art.6

Art.22, amended: SI 2014/521 Art.9, SI 2014/2368 Art.7

Art.24, amended: SI 2014/521 Art.10

Art.32, applied: SI 2014/3223 Sch.1 para.7

Art.40, referred to: SI 2014/1792 Reg.4

Art.44A, added: SI 2014/1463 Reg.3

Art.45, amended: SI 2014/1463 Reg.3

Art.46, substituted: SI 2014/1463 Reg.3

Sch.1 Part A, amended: SI 2014/521 Art.11, SI 2014/2368 Art.8

Sch.1 Part B, amended: SI 2014/1186 Art.4, SI 2014/2368 Art.8

Sch.2 Part A, amended: SI 2014/2368 Art.9

Sch.2 Part B, amended: SI 2014/521 Art.12, SI 2014/2368 Art.9

Sch.3, amended: SI 2014/521 Art.13

Sch.4 Part A, amended: SI 2014/521 Art.14, SI 2014/2368 Art.10

Sch.4 Part B, amended: SI 2014/521 Art.14, SI 2014/2368 Art.10

Sch.4 Part C, amended: SI 2014/2368 Art.10

Sch.5 Part A para.1, amended: SI 2014/2368 Art.11

Sch.5 Part A para.2, amended: SI 2014/2368 Art.11

Sch.5 Part A para.2A, added: SI 2014/521 Art.15

Sch.5 Part A para.2A, substituted: SI 2014/2368 Art.11

Sch.5 Part A para.3, substituted: SI 2014/2368 Art.11

Sch.5 Part A para.8, added: SI 2014/521 Art.15

Sch.5 Part B para.5, amended: SI 2014/2368 Art.11

Sch.6 Part A para.3B, added: SI 2014/521 Art.16

Sch.6 Part A para.4, substituted: SI 2014/2368 Art.12

Sch.6 Part A para.7, amended: SI 2014/2368 Art.12

Sch.6 Part A para.8, amended: SI 2014/2368 Art.12

Sch.6 Part A para.8, substituted: SI 2014/521 Art.16

Sch.6 Part A para.10, added: SI 2014/521 Art.16

Sch.6 Part B paraA.1, added: SI 2014/2368 Art.12

Sch.7 Part A para.3B, added: SI 2014/521 Art.17

Sch.7 Part A para.4, substituted: SI 2014/2368 Art.13

Sch.7 Part A para.7, amended: SI 2014/2368 Art.13

Sch.7 Part A para.8, amended: SI 2014/2368 Art.13

Sch.7 Part A para.8, substituted: SI 2014/521 Art.17

Sch.7 Part A para.10, added: SI 2014/521 Art.17

Sch.7 Part B para.2, substituted: SI 2014/2368 Art.13

Sch.7 Part B para.3, amended: SI 2014/2368 Art.13

Sch.7 Part B para.8, amended: SI 2014/2368 Art.13

Sch.8 Part A para.1, substituted: SI 2014/1463 Reg.4

Sch.8 Part A para.5, amended: SI 2014/1463 Reg.4

Sch.8 Part B para.1, substituted: SI 2014/1463 Reg.4

Sch.8 Part B para.5, amended: SI 2014/1463 Reg.4

1701. Plant Health (Export Certification) (Wales) Order 2006

Art.2, amended: SI 2014/1759 Art.2

Sch.3, substituted: SI 2014/1759 Art.2

Sch.4, substituted: SI 2014/1759 Art.2

1714. Education (School Inspection) (Wales) Regulations 2006

Reg.6, amended: SI 2014/1212 Reg.4

Reg.8, amended: SI 2014/1212 Reg.4

Reg.10, amended: SI 2014/1212 Reg.4

Reg.14, substituted: SI 2014/1212 Reg.4

Reg.16, amended: SI 2014/1212 Reg.4

1751. Education (Pupil Registration) (England) Regulations 2006

applied: SI 2014/3283 Sch.1 para.15

1811. Firefighters Compensation Scheme (England) Order 2006

Sch.1, added: SI 2014/447 Sch.1 para.1, Sch.1 para.2, Sch.1 para.7, Sch.1 para.9, Sch.1 para.10, Sch.1 para.11

Sch.1, amended: SI 2014/447 Sch.1 para.1, Sch.1 para.2, Sch.1 para.3, Sch.1 para.4, Sch.1 para.5, Sch.1 para.6, Sch.1 para.7, Sch.1 para.8, Sch.1 para.9, Sch.1 para.10, Sch.1 para.11

Sch.1, revoked: SI 2014/447 Sch.1 para.7, Sch.1 para.8

Sch.1, substituted: SI 2014/447 Sch.1 para.1, Sch.1 para.7

1924. Double Taxation Relief (Taxes on Income) (Japan) Order 2006

Sch.1, referred to: SI 2014/1881 Art.2

1947. Work and Families (Northern Ireland) Order 2006

Art.11, varied: 2014 c.6 s.126

1975. Registered Designs Rules 2006

Part 1 r.2A, added: SI 2014/2405 r.3

2002. Electricity Act 1989 (Exemption from the Requirement for an Interconnector Licence) Order 2006

Art.2, amended: SI 2014/2587 Art.2

Art.3, amended: SI 2014/2587 Art.2

Art.3, revoked (in part): SI 2014/2587 Art.2

2059. European Cooperative Society (Involvement of Employees) Regulations 2006

Reg.30, amended: SI 2014/386 Sch.1 para.45

Reg.30A, added: SI 2014/386 Sch.1 para.46

Reg.41, amended: SI 2014/386 Sch.1 para.47, SI 2014/431 Sch.1 para.34

Sch.3 para.18, amended: SI 2014/431 Sch.1 para.34

2135. Serious Organised Crime and Police Act 2005 (Appeals under Section 74) Order 2006

applied: SI 2014/1610 r.65_1, r.68_11, r.65_5, r.68_12

Art.15, applied: SI 2014/1610 r.74_1, r.74_2

Art.18, applied: SI 2014/1610 r.74_2

Art.19, applied: SI 2014/1610 r.74_3

Art.20, applied: SI 2014/1610 r.74_2

2167. Dover Harbour Revision Order 2006

Art.5, referred to: SI 2014/2720 Art.8, Art.10

Art.7, applied: SI 2014/2720 Art.7

Art.19, applied: SI 2014/2720 Art.9

2170. Immigration (Continuation of Leave) (Notices) Regulations 2006

Reg.2, see *Ahmadi (S.47 Decision: Validity: Sapkota: Afghanistan), Re* [2013] EWCA Civ 512, [2014] 1 W.L.R. 401 (CA (Civ Div)), Sullivan LJ

2298. England Rural Development Programme (Closure of Project-Based Schemes) Regulations 2006

revoked: SI 2014/3263 Sch.5

2321. African Development Fund (Multilateral Debt Relief Initiative) Order 2006

Art.3, amended: SI 2014/2457 Art.2

2323. International Development Association (Multilateral Debt Relief Initiative) Order 2006

Art.3, amended: SI 2014/3056 Art.2

2522. Environmental Impact Assessment (Agriculture) (England) (No.2) Regulations 2006

Reg.4, disapplied: SI 2014/3263 Sch.2 para.2

Reg.9, disapplied: SI 2014/3263 Sch.2 para.2

Reg.26, disapplied: SI 2014/3263 Sch.2 para.2

Reg.28, disapplied: SI 2014/3263 Sch.2 para.2

2524. Coventry and Warwickshire Partnership National Health Service Trust (Establishment) Order 2006

Art.1, amended: SI 2014/360 Art.2

Art.3, amended: SI 2014/360 Art.3

Art.4, amended: SI 2014/360 Art.4

Art.5, substituted: SI 2014/360 Art.5

2645. Allocation of Housing (Wales) (Amendment) Regulations 2006

revoked: SI 2014/2603 Reg.7

2646. Homelessness (Wales) Regulations 2006

revoked: SI 2014/2603 Reg.7

2697. Plant Health (Fees) (Forestry) Regulations 2006

Sch.3, substituted: SI 2014/589 Reg.3

Sch.3A, substituted: SI 2014/589 Reg.4

Sch.4, substituted: SI 2014/589 Reg.5

2786. Wireless Telegraphy (Limitation of Number of Licences) (Amendment) Order 2006

revoked: SI 2014/774 Art.2

2788. Asylum and Immigration Tribunal (Procedure) (Amendment) Rules 2006

revoked: SI 2014/2604 r.45

2789. Asylum and Immigration Tribunal (Fast Track Procedure) (Amendment) Rules 2006

revoked: SI 2014/2604 r.45

2810. Mental Capacity Act 2005 (Appropriate Body) (England) Regulations 2006

Reg.2, amended: 2014 c.23 Sch.8 para.9

2815. Nuclear Industries Security (Amendment) Regulations 2006

Reg.8, revoked: SI 2014/469 Sch.3 para.210

2824. Selective Licensing of Houses (Specified Exemptions) (Wales) Order 2006

Art.2, amended: SI 2014/107 Sch.2 para.7

2831. Common Agricultural Policy Single Payment and Support Schemes (Cross Compliance) (Wales) (Amendment) Regulations 2006

revoked: SI 2014/3223 Sch.3

2881. A1 and A14 Trunk Roads (Brampton Hut Interchange, Cambridgeshire) (40 Miles Per Hour Speed Limit) Order 2006

Sch.1, varied: SI 2014/1046 Art.3

2913. Scotland Act 1998 (River Tweed) Order 2006

Art.2, disapplied: 2014 c.21 s.61

2917. Royal Marines Terms of Service Regulations 2006

Reg.2, amended: SI 2014/3068 Reg.6

Reg.3, amended: SI 2014/3068 Reg.7

Reg.8, substituted: SI 2014/3068 Reg.8

2918. Royal Navy Terms of Service (Ratings) Regulations 2006

Reg.2, amended: SI 2014/3068 Reg.3

Reg.3, amended: SI 2014/3068 Reg.4

Reg.8, substituted: SI 2014/3068 Reg.5

2920. Civil Courts (Amendment No.2) Order 2006

revoked: SI 2014/820 Sch.1

2929. Seed Potatoes (Wales) Regulations 2006

applied: SI 2014/1792 Reg.3

Reg.8, applied: SI 2014/1792 Reg.3

Reg.9, applied: SI 2014/1792 Reg.3

2950. Merchant Shipping (Prevention of Pollution by Sewage and Garbage) Order 2006

Art.3, enabled: SI 2014/3306

Art.4, enabled: SI 2014/3306

Art.5, enabled: SI 2014/3306

2993. Regional Transport Planning (Wales) Order 2006

revoked: SI 2014/2178 Art.4

3095. Enterprise Act 2002 (Enforcement Undertakings) (No.2) Order 2006

Art.4, amended: SI 2014/549 Sch.1 para.20

3103. Inspection of the Careers and Related Services (Wales) Regulations 2006

Reg.4, amended: SI 2014/1212 Reg.5

Reg.7, amended: SI 2014/1212 Reg.5

3278. Representation of the People (Combination of Polls) (England and Wales) (Amendment) Regulations 2006

Reg.4, revoked (in part): SI 2014/920 Reg.7

3296. Taxation of Securitisation Companies Regulations 2006

Reg.8, applied: SI 2014/1831 Art.3

3304. Local Elections (Principal Areas) (England and Wales) Rules 2006

r.2, amended: SI 2014/494 r.2

Sch.2, added: SI 2014/494 r.3

Sch.2, amended: SI 2014/494 r.3, Sch.1

Sch.2, referred to: SI 2014/918 Art.1

Sch.2, substituted: SI 2014/494 r.3

Sch.3, added: SI 2014/494 r.4

Sch.3, amended: SI 2014/494 r.4, Sch.2

Sch.3, referred to: SI 2014/918 Art.1

Sch.3, substituted: SI 2014/494 r.4

3305. Local Elections (Parishes and Communities) (England and Wales) Rules 2006

r.2, amended: SI 2014/492 r.2

Sch.2, added: SI 2014/492 r.3

Sch.2, amended: SI 2014/492 r.3, Sch.1

Sch.2, referred to: SI 2014/919 Art.1

Sch.2, substituted: SI 2014/492 r.3

Sch.3, added: SI 2014/492 r.4

Sch.3, amended: SI 2014/492 r.4, Sch.2

Sch.3, referred to: SI 2014/919 Art.1

Sch.3, substituted: SI 2014/492 r.4

3309. Avian Influenza (H5N1 in Poultry) (Wales) Order 2006

Art.2, amended: SI 2014/517 Sch.2 para.3

Art.3, amended: SI 2014/517 Sch.2 para.3

Art.14, amended: SI 2014/517 Sch.2 para.3

3310. Avian Influenza (H5N1 in Wild Birds) (Wales) Order 2006

Art.2, amended: SI 2014/517 Sch.2 para.4

Art.13, amended: SI 2014/517 Sch.2 para.4

Sch.1 Part 4 para.13, amended: SI 2014/517 Sch.2 para.4

Sch.1 Part 5 para.14, amended: SI 2014/517 Sch.2 para.4

Sch.1 Part 5 para.15, amended: SI 2014/517 Sch.2 para.4

3322. Compensation (Claims Management Services) Regulations 2006

Part 11, added: SI 2014/3239 Reg.2

Part 11, applied: SI 2014/3239 Reg.3

Reg.3, amended: SI 2014/3239 Reg.2

Reg.5, revoked (in part): SI 2014/3239 Reg.2

Reg.14, amended: SI 2014/3239 Reg.2

Reg.14, applied: SI 2014/3239 Reg.3

Reg.14A, added: SI 2014/3239 Reg.2

Reg.36, applied: SI 2014/3239 Reg.3

3336. Water and Sewerage Services (Northern Ireland) Order 2006

Art.5, amended: SI 2014/892 Sch.1 para.248

Art.6, amended: SI 2014/892 Sch.1 para.249
Art.23, amended: SI 2014/892 Sch.1
para.250
Art.23, applied: SI 2014/559
Art.23, referred to: SI 2014/892 Sch.2 para.2
Art.27, amended: SI 2014/892 Sch.1
para.251
Art.27, referred to: SI 2014/892 Sch.2 para.2
Art.28, amended: SI 2014/892 Sch.1
para.252
Art.29, amended: SI 2014/892 Sch.1
para.253
Art.56, amended: SI 2014/892 Sch.1
para.253
Art.60, amended: SI 2014/892 Sch.1
para.254
Art.253, amended: SI 2014/892 Sch.1
para.255
Art.259, amended: SI 2014/892 Sch.1
para.256
Art.265, amended: SI 2014/631 Sch.2
para.10, SI 2014/892 Sch.1 para.257
Art.265, revoked (in part): SI 2014/892
Sch.1 para.257

**3342. Agricultural Subsidies and Grants
Schemes (Appeals) (Wales) Regulations 2006**
Reg.3, applied: SI 2014/1835 Reg.3
Sch.1 para.18, added: SI 2014/2894 Reg.2

**3343. Rural Development Programmes (Wales)
Regulations 2006**
revoked: SI 2014/3223 Sch.3
varied: SI 2014/3223 Reg.15
Reg.1, applied: SI 2014/3223 Reg.15
Reg.2, referred to: SI 2014/3223 Reg.15

**3367. Olive Oil (Marketing Standards)
(Amendment) Regulations 2006**
revoked: SI 2014/195 Reg.20

**3375. Clifton Suspension Bridge Tolls (Revision)
Order 2006**
revoked: SI 2014/926 Art.3

3415. Police Pensions Regulations 2006
Reg.7, amended: SI 2014/381 Reg.3

**3432. Firefighters Pension Scheme (England)
Order 2006**
Sch.1, added: SI 2014/445 Sch.1 para.1,
Sch.1 para.2, Sch.1 para.3, Sch.1 para.4,
Sch.1 para.5, Sch.1 para.6, Sch.1 para.9,
Sch.1 para.10, Sch.1 para.11, Sch.1 para.12,
Sch.1 para.13, Sch.1 para.14, Sch.1 para.15,
Sch.1 para.16, Sch.1 para.17, SI 2014/560
Sch.3 para.17

Sch.1, amended: SI 2014/445 Sch.1 para.1,
Sch.1 para.2, Sch.1 para.3, Sch.1 para.4,
Sch.1 para.5, Sch.1 para.6, Sch.1 para.7,
Sch.1 para.8, Sch.1 para.9, Sch.1 para.10,
Sch.1 para.11, Sch.1 para.12, Sch.1 para.14
Sch.1, substituted: SI 2014/445 Sch.1 para.3,
Sch.1 para.12

2007

**75. Rural Development (Enforcement)
(England) Regulations 2007**
applied: SI 2014/3263 Reg.9, Reg.35
revoked: SI 2014/3263 Sch.5
Reg.1, applied: SI 2014/3263 Reg.35
Reg.2, applied: SI 2014/3263 Reg.35

**79. Sulphur Content of Liquid Fuels (England
and Wales) Regulations 2007**
Reg.2, substituted: SI 2014/1975 Reg.3
Reg.4, substituted: SI 2014/1975 Reg.4
Reg.5, substituted: SI 2014/1975 Reg.5
Reg.6, substituted: SI 2014/1975 Reg.6
Reg.9, added: SI 2014/1975 Reg.7
Sch.1, amended: SI 2014/1975 Reg.8
Sch.1 para.1, amended: SI 2014/1975 Reg.8
Sch.1 para.2, amended: SI 2014/1975 Reg.8
Sch.2, revoked: SI 2014/1975 Reg.9

107. Assisted Areas Order 2007
revoked: SI 2014/1508 Art.4

**115. Personal Injuries (NHS Charges)
(Amounts) Regulations 2007**
Reg.2, amended: SI 2014/204 Reg.2

**121. National Health Service (Free Prescriptions
and Charges for Drugs and Appliances) (Wales)
Regulations 2007**
Reg.2, amended: SI 2014/2291 Reg.4

**191. Quick-frozen Foodstuffs (England)
Regulations 2007**
Reg.2, amended: SI 2014/1855 Sch.7
para.43
Reg.5, amended: SI 2014/1855 Sch.7
para.44

**236. National Assembly for Wales
(Representation of the People) Order 2007**
Art.34, amended: 2014 c.29 s.3
Sch.5 Part 2 para.9, amended: 2014 c.29 s.3

**292. Guarantees of Origin of Electricity
Produced from High-efficiency Cogeneration
Regulations 2007**
Reg.2, amended: SI 2014/1403 Reg.5

Reg.3, amended: SI 2014/1403 Reg.5
Reg.5, amended: SI 2014/1403 Reg.5
Reg.10, amended: SI 2014/1403 Reg.5
Sch.1 para.7, amended: SI 2014/1403 Reg.5
Sch.2, revoked: SI 2014/1403 Reg.5

307. Review of Children's Cases (Wales) Regulations 2007
Sch.1 para.5, amended: SI 2014/852 Art.14

310. Placement of Children (Wales) Regulations 2007
Reg.6, amended: SI 2014/852 Art.15
Reg.9, amended: SI 2014/852 Art.15

320. Construction (Design and Management) Regulations 2007
Reg.4, see *MWH UK Ltd v Wise (Inspector of Health and Safety)* [2014] EWHC 427 (Admin), [2014] A.C.D. 96 (QBD (Admin)), Popplewell J
Reg.19, amended: SI 2014/469 Sch.3 para.127
Reg.20, see *MWH UK Ltd v Wise (Inspector of Health and Safety)* [2014] EWHC 427 (Admin), [2014] A.C.D. 96 (QBD (Admin)), Popplewell J
Reg.21, amended: SI 2014/469 Sch.3 para.127
Sch.1, amended: SI 2014/469 Sch.3 para.127

339. Traffic Management (Guidance on Intervention Criteria) (England) Order 2007
applied: SI 2014/3310 Sch.1, SI 2014/3311 Sch.1
referred to: SI 2014/466 Sch.1

388. Accounts and Audit (Wales) (Amendment) Regulations 2007
revoked: SI 2014/3362 Reg.30

389. Quick-frozen Foodstuffs (Wales) Regulations 2007
Reg.2, amended: SI 2014/2303 Sch.7 para.43
Reg.5, amended: SI 2014/2303 Sch.7 para.44

398. Commissioner for Older People in Wales Regulations 2007
Reg.4, amended: 2014 c.29 s.4
Reg.11, amended: 2014 c.29 s.4

399. Local Authorities (Executive Arrangements) (Functions and Responsibilities) (Wales) Regulations 2007
Sch.1, amended: SI 2014/3362 Reg.29

402. Welfare of Animals (Slaughter or Killing) (Amendment) (England) Regulations 2007
revoked: SI 2014/1240 Reg.47

448. Diseases of Animals (Approved Disinfectants) (England) Order 2007
applied: SI 2014/1894 Reg.15

457. Commons (Registration of Town or Village Greens) (Interim Arrangements) (England) Regulations 2007
applied: SI 2014/3038 Reg.14, Reg.54
revoked (in part): SI 2014/3038 Reg.54
see *Church Commissioners for England v Hampshire CC* [2013] EWHC 1933 (Admin), [2014] A.C.D. 21 (QBD (Admin)), Collins J; see *Church Commissioners for England v Hampshire CC* [2014] EWCA Civ 634, [2014] 1 W.L.R. 4555 (CA (Civ Div)), Arden LJ
Reg.5, see *Church Commissioners for England v Hampshire CC* [2014] EWCA Civ 634, [2014] 1 W.L.R. 4555 (CA (Civ Div)), Arden LJ

461. Competition Commission (Water Industry) Penalties Order 2007
revoked: SI 2014/559 Art.5

463. Childcare Act 2006 (Childcare Assessments) Regulations 2007
Reg.1, amended: SI 2014/2103 Art.22

464. Education and Inspections Act 2006 (Prescribed Education and Training etc) Regulations 2007
Reg.4, revoked: SI 2014/80 Sch.1

478. NHS Direct National Health Service Trust (Establishment) Order 2007
revoked: SI 2014/588 Art.2

529. Cattle Identification Regulations 2007
Sch.2, applied: SI 2014/112 Sch.1 para.1

572. Rent Repayment Orders (Supplementary Provisions) (England) Regulations 2007
substituted: SI 2014/2888 Reg.9
Reg.1, amended: SI 2014/2888 Reg.9
Reg.2, amended: SI 2014/2888 Reg.9

583. Commons (Severance of Rights) (Wales) Order 2007
revoked: SI 2014/219 Art.5
Art.2, applied: SI 2014/219 Art.6

605. Vehicle Drivers (Certificates of Professional Competence) Regulations 2007
Reg.2, amended: SI 2014/2264 Reg.3
Reg.5, amended: SI 2014/1816 Reg.4

Reg.5A, amended: SI 2014/1816 Reg.5, SI
2014/2264 Reg.4
Reg.5B, amended: SI 2014/1816 Reg.6
Reg.6, amended: SI 2014/2264 Reg.5
Reg.6A, amended: SI 2014/2264 Reg.6
Reg.6A, substituted: SI 2014/2264 Reg.6
Reg.6B, added: SI 2014/2264 Reg.7

**650. Royal Air Force Terms of Service
Regulations 2007**
Reg.3, amended: SI 2014/3068 Reg.12
Reg.4, amended: SI 2014/3068 Reg.13
Reg.4, revoked (in part): SI 2014/3068
Reg.13
Reg.5, revoked: SI 2014/3068 Reg.14
Reg.6, amended: SI 2014/3068 Reg.15
Reg.6, revoked (in part): SI 2014/3068
Reg.15
Reg.7, revoked: SI 2014/3068 Reg.16
Reg.10, amended: SI 2014/3068 Reg.17
Reg.11, revoked: SI 2014/3068 Reg.18
Reg.12, amended: SI 2014/3068 Reg.19
Reg.12, revoked (in part): SI 2014/3068
Reg.19
Reg.13, substituted: SI 2014/3068 Reg.20
Reg.14, substituted: SI 2014/3068 Reg.21
Reg.15, amended: SI 2014/3068 Reg.22
Reg.16, revoked: SI 2014/3068 Reg.23

**694. Her Majesty's Chief Inspector of
Education, Children's Services and Skills (Fees
and Frequency of Inspections) (Children's
Homes etc.) Regulations 2007**
Reg.14, amended: SI 2014/670 Reg.3
Reg.15, amended: SI 2014/670 Reg.4
Reg.16, amended: SI 2014/670 Reg.5
Reg.17, amended: SI 2014/670 Reg.6
Reg.18, amended: SI 2014/670 Reg.7

**707. Criminal Justice Act 2003 (Surcharge)
Order 2007**
see *R. v de Brito (Paulo Aguiar)* [2013]
EWCA Crim 1134, [2014] 1 Cr. App. R. (S.)
38 (CA (Crim Div)), Keith J
Art.3, see *R. v de Brito (Paulo Aguiar)*
[2013] EWCA Crim 1134, [2014] 1 Cr. App.
R. (S.) 38 (CA (Crim Div)), Keith J

**722. Childcare (Supply and Disclosure of
Information) (England) Regulations 2007**
Reg.2, substituted: SI 2014/1921 Reg.25
Reg.4, amended: SI 2014/1921 Reg.26
Reg.5, amended: SI 2014/1921 Reg.27
Reg.6, amended: SI 2014/1921 Reg.28
Reg.6, substituted: SI 2014/1921 Reg.28

Reg.7, amended: SI 2014/1921 Reg.29
Reg.7, substituted: SI 2014/1921 Reg.29
Reg.8, amended: SI 2014/1921 Reg.30
Reg.9, amended: SI 2014/1921 Reg.31
Sch.4, added: SI 2014/1921 Reg.32

740. Tuberculosis (England) Order 2007
applied: SI 2014/2383 Art.25
revoked: SI 2014/2383 Art.24
Art.3, amended: SI 2014/714 Art.2
Art.3A, added: SI 2014/714 Art.2
Art.8, amended: SI 2014/714 Art.2
Art.9, amended: SI 2014/714 Art.2
Art.10, amended: SI 2014/714 Art.2
Art.19, amended: SI 2014/714 Art.2
Sch.1 para.2, revoked: SI 2014/714 Art.2

**783. Town and Country Planning (Control of
Advertisements) (England) Regulations 2007**
Reg.6, see *Stadium Capital Holdings No.2
Ltd v Secretary of State for Communities and
Local Government* [2013] EWHC 3548
(Admin), [2014] J.P.L. 533 (QBD (Admin)),
Collins J
Reg.8, see *Stadium Capital Holdings No.2
Ltd v Secretary of State for Communities and
Local Government* [2013] EWHC 3548
(Admin), [2014] J.P.L. 533 (QBD (Admin)),
Collins J

786. Civil Courts (Amendment) Order 2007
revoked: SI 2014/820 Sch.1

**792. Employee Share Schemes (Electronic
Communication of Returns and Information)
Regulations 2007**
revoked: 2014 c.26 Sch.8 para.88

801. Pensions Increase (Review) Order 2007
referred to: SI 2014/668 Sch.1
Art.6, substituted: SI 2014/107 Sch.1
para.56, SI 2014/3229 Sch.6 para.35

**812. General Teaching Council for Wales
(Constitution) (Amendment) Regulations 2007**
revoked: SI 2014/2365 Sch.1

**833. Mental Capacity Act 2005 (Appropriate
Body) (Wales) Regulations 2007**
Reg.2, amended: 2014 c.23 Sch.8 para.10

**834. Pension Protection Fund (Contributions
Equivalent Premium) Regulations 2007**
revoked: 2014 c.19 Sch.13 para.37

**835. Asylum and Immigration Tribunal
(Procedure) (Amendment) Rules 2007**
revoked: SI 2014/2604 r.45

842. Cattle Identification (Wales) Regulations 2007
Sch.3 Part 1 para.3, amended: SI 2014/517
Sch.2 para.5

871. Producer Responsibility Obligations (Packaging Waste) Regulations 2007
Reg.40, applied: SSI 2014/319 Sch.1 para.9, Sch.2 para.14, Sch.3 para.9
Sch.2 para.6, amended: SI 2014/2890 Reg.2
Sch.2 para.6A, amended: SI 2014/2890 Reg.2

913. Electricity (Single Wholesale Market) (Northern Ireland) Order 2007
Art.10, amended: SI 2014/892 Sch.1 para.258

916. Road Traffic (Northern Ireland) Order 2007
Sch.5 para.6, amended: 2014 c.22 Sch.9 para.65

930. Serious Organised Crime and Police Act 2005 (Designated Sites under Section 128) Order 2007
Art.2, amended: SI 2014/411 Art.2
Art.2, revoked (in part): SI 2014/411 Art.2
Sch.3, revoked: SI 2014/411 Art.2
Sch.5, substituted: SI 2014/2263 Art.2

934. Regulation of Investigatory Powers (Authorisations Extending to Scotland) Order 2007
Sch.1, amended: SI 2014/467 Art.3

945. Business Premises Renovation Allowances Regulations 2007
Reg.2, amended: SI 2014/1687 Reg.3
Reg.3, amended: SI 2014/1687 Reg.4
Reg.4, amended: SI 2014/1687 Reg.5
Reg.5, amended: SI 2014/1687 Reg.6

957. School Governance (Constitution) (England) Regulations 2007
Sch.6 para.9, amended: SI 2014/1257 Reg.5

970. Common Agricultural Policy Single Payment and Support Schemes (Cross-compliance) (Wales) (Amendment) Regulations 2007
revoked: SI 2014/3223 Sch.3

972. Designation of Schools Having a Religious Character (Wales) Order 2007
revoked: SI 2014/3261 Art.2

1013. Local Elections (Communities) (Welsh Forms) Order 2007
Art.3, amended: SI 2014/919 Art.2
Art.4, amended: SI 2014/919 Art.2

Art.9, amended: SI 2014/919 Art.2
Sch.2, amended: SI 2014/919 Sch.1
Sch.3, amended: SI 2014/919 Sch.2
Sch.4, amended: SI 2014/919 Sch.3
Sch.5, amended: SI 2014/919 Sch.4

1015. Local Elections (Principal Areas) (Welsh Forms) Order 2007
Art.3, amended: SI 2014/918 Art.2
Art.4, amended: SI 2014/918 Art.2
Art.9, amended: SI 2014/918 Art.2
Sch.2, amended: SI 2014/918 Sch.1
Sch.3, amended: SI 2014/918 Sch.2
Sch.4, amended: SI 2014/918 Sch.3
Sch.5, amended: SI 2014/918 Sch.4

1024. Local Authorities (Mayoral Elections) (England and Wales) Regulations 2007
Reg.2, amended: SI 2014/370 Reg.3
Reg.3, amended: SI 2014/370 Reg.2
Reg.3, revoked (in part): SI 2014/370 Reg.2
Reg.4, substituted: SI 2014/370 Reg.2
Reg.5, amended: SI 2014/370 Reg.4
Sch.1, added: SI 2014/370 Reg.5
Sch.1, amended: SI 2014/370 Reg.2, Reg.5, Sch.1
Sch.1, substituted: SI 2014/370 Reg.5
Sch.2, amended: SI 2014/370 Reg.6
Sch.2A, revoked: SI 2014/370 Reg.2
Sch.3, added: SI 2014/370 Reg.7
Sch.3, amended: SI 2014/370 Reg.2, Reg.7, Sch.2
Sch.3, substituted: SI 2014/370 Reg.7
Sch.3A, revoked: SI 2014/370 Reg.2
Sch.4 para.1, amended: SI 2014/370 Reg.8

1040. Notification of Marketing of Food for Particular Nutritional Uses (Wales) Regulations 2007
Reg.2, amended: SI 2014/1102 Reg.3
Reg.3, amended: SI 2014/1102 Reg.3

1065. Education (Information About Children in Alternative Provision) (England) Regulations 2007
Reg.2, amended: SI 2014/2103 Art.23

1069. Education (Pupil Referral Units) (Application of Enactments) (Wales) Regulations 2007
Sch.1 Part 2 para.14, amended: SI 2014/1609 Reg.5
Sch.1 Part 2 para.16, added: SI 2014/2677 Reg.10

1072. Firefighters Pension Scheme (Wales) Order 2007
  Sch.1, added: SI 2014/560 Sch.3 para.17
  Sch.1, amended: SI 2014/523 Art.3

1073. Firefighters Compensation Scheme (Wales) Order 2007
  Sch.1, added: SI 2014/3256 Sch.1 para.1,
  Sch.1 para.2, Sch.1 para.7, Sch.1 para.9,
  Sch.1 para.10, Sch.1 para.11
  Sch.1, amended: SI 2014/3256 Sch.1 para.1,
  Sch.1 para.2, Sch.1 para.3, Sch.1 para.4,
  Sch.1 para.5, Sch.1 para.6, Sch.1 para.7,
  Sch.1 para.8, Sch.1 para.9, Sch.1 para.10,
  Sch.1 para.11
  Sch.1, applied: SI 2014/3256 Art.3
  Sch.1, revoked: SI 2014/3256 Sch.1 para.7,
  Sch.1 para.8
  Sch.1, substituted: SI 2014/3256 Sch.1
  para.1, Sch.1 para.7

1104. National Health Service (Travelling Expenses and Remission of Charges) (Wales) Regulations 2007
  Reg.5, amended: SI 2014/460 Reg.5
  Sch.1, amended: SI 2014/1099 Reg.3

1166. Local Government Pension Scheme (Benefits, Membership and Contributions) Regulations 2007
  applied: SI 2014/525 Reg.14, Reg.22
  revoked: SI 2014/525 Sch.1
  Reg.4, referred to: SI 2014/525 Reg.14
  Reg.8, applied: SI 2014/525 Reg.4, Reg.8,
  Reg.10, Reg.17
  Reg.12, applied: SI 2014/525 Reg.3, Sch.2
  para.4
  Reg.12A, applied: SI 2014/525 Reg.3
  Reg.12B, applied: SI 2014/525 Sch.2 para.4
  Reg.13, applied: SI 2014/525 Reg.11
  Reg.14, applied: SI 2014/525 Reg.11,
  Reg.15
  Reg.18, applied: SI 2014/525 Sch.2 para.4,
  Sch.2 para.5
  Reg.20, applied: SI 2014/525 Reg.4, Reg.12,
  Reg.17
  Reg.30, applied: SI 2014/525 Sch.2 para.1
  Reg.30A, applied: SI 2014/525 Sch.2 para.1
  Reg.32, applied: SI 2014/525 Reg.17
  Reg.35, applied: SI 2014/525 Reg.17
  Reg.38, applied: SI 2014/525 Reg.24
  Reg.39, amended: SI 2014/44 Reg.3

1167. Consumer Credit (Information Requirements and Duration of Licences and Charges) Regulations 2007
  see *JP Morgan Chase Bank NA v Northern Rock (Asset Management) Plc* [2014]
  EWHC 291 (Ch), [2014] 1 W.L.R. 2197 (Ch D), Simon Monty Q.C.
  Reg.1A, added: SI 2014/2369 Reg.2
  Reg.2, amended: SI 2014/2369 Reg.2
  Reg.4, amended: SI 2014/2369 Reg.2
  Reg.10A, added: SI 2014/2369 Reg.2
  Reg.26, amended: SI 2014/366 Art.11
  Reg.41A, added: SI 2014/2369 Reg.2
  Sch.1 Part 1 para.3A, added: SI 2014/2369
  Reg.2
  Sch.1 Part 2A, substituted: SI 2014/2369
  Reg.2
  Sch.1 Part 2A para.4A, amended: SI
  2014/2369 Reg.2
  Sch.3 Part 5, amended: SI 2014/366 Art.11
  Sch.5 Part 1 para.6, amended: SI 2014/366
  Art.11

1174. Criminal Defence Service (Funding) Order 2007
  see *Lord Chancellor v Ahmed* [2013] EWHC
  3642 (QB), [2014] 1 Costs L.R. 21 (QBD),
  Andrews J; see *Maclaverty Cooper Atkins v Lord Chancellor* [2014] EWHC 1387 (QB),
  [2014] 4 Costs L.R. 629 (QBD), Akenhead
  J; see *R. v Connors (Costs)* [2014] 5 Costs
  L.R. 942 (Sen Cts Costs Office), Costs Judge
  C Campbell; see *R. v Jalibaghodelehzi*
  [2014] 4 Costs L.R. 781 (Sen Cts Costs
  Office), Costs Judge Gordon-Saker; see *R. v Napper (Costs)* [2014] 5 Costs L.R. 947
  (Sen Cts Costs Office), Costs Judge J
  Simons
  Art.11, see *R. v Banfield (Shirley)* [2014]
  EWCA Crim 1824, [2014] 5 Costs L.R. 896
  (CA (Crim Div)), Lord Thomas LCJ
  Art.26, see *R. v Connors (Costs)* [2014] 5
  Costs L.R. 942 (Sen Cts Costs Office), Costs
  Judge C Campbell; see *R. v Nettleton (Costs)* [2014] 2 Costs L.R. 387 (Sen Cts
  Costs Office), Costs Judge Campbell
  Art.30, see *Maclaverty Cooper Atkins v Lord Chancellor* [2014] EWHC 1387 (QB),
  [2014] 4 Costs L.R. 629 (QBD), Akenhead J
  Sch.1 Pt 1 para.3, see *Lord Chancellor v Ahmed* [2013] EWHC 3642 (QB), [2014] 1
  Costs L.R. 21 (QBD), Andrews J

Sch.1 Pt 4 para.14, see *R. v French (Costs)*
[2014] 4 Costs L.R. 786 (Sen Cts Costs
Office), Costs Judge C Campbell
Sch.1 Pt 5, see *R. v Connors (Costs)* [2014]
5 Costs L.R. 942 (Sen Cts Costs Office),
Costs Judge C Campbell
Sch.2, see *Maclaverty Cooper Atkins v Lord
Chancellor* [2014] EWHC 1387 (QB),
[2014] 4 Costs L.R. 629 (QBD), Akenhead
J; see *R. v Garness (Costs)* [2014] 1 Costs
L.R. 201 (Sen Cts Costs Office), Costs Judge
Gordon-Saker; see *R. v Napper (Costs)*
[2014] 5 Costs L.R. 947 (Sen Cts Costs
Office), Costs Judge J Simons
Sch.2 Pt 1 para.1, see *Maclaverty Cooper
Atkins v Lord Chancellor* [2014] EWHC
1387 (QB), [2014] 4 Costs L.R. 629 (QBD),
Akenhead J; see *R. v Osoteko (Costs)*
[2014] 1 Costs L.R. 190 (Sen Cts Costs
Office), Costs Judge Simons
Sch.2 Pt 1 para.3, see *R. v Garness (Costs)*
[2014] 1 Costs L.R. 201 (Sen Cts Costs
Office), Costs Judge Gordon-Saker
Sch.2 Pt 2 para.8, see *Maclaverty Cooper
Atkins v Lord Chancellor* [2014] EWHC
1387 (QB), [2014] 4 Costs L.R. 629 (QBD),
Akenhead J
Sch.2 Pt 2B para.10, see *Tuckers Solicitors v
Lord Chancellor* [2013] EWHC 3817 (QB),
[2014] 1 Costs L.R. 29 (QBD), Andrews J
Sch.2 Pt 3 para.15, see *Maclaverty Cooper
Atkins v Lord Chancellor* [2014] EWHC
1387 (QB), [2014] 4 Costs L.R. 629 (QBD),
Akenhead J; see *R. v Osoteko (Costs)*
[2014] 1 Costs L.R. 190 (Sen Cts Costs
Office), Costs Judge Simons
**1182. Government of Wales Act 2006 (Local
Government (Contracts) Act 1997)
(Modifications) Order 2007**
Art.2, amended: 2014 c.29 s.4
**1263. Equality Act (Sexual Orientation)
Regulations 2007**
see *Cary v Commissioner of Police of the
Metropolis* [2014] EWCA Civ 987, [2014]
C.P. Rep. 42 (CA (Civ Div)), Arden LJ
**1269. National Assembly for Wales (Transfer of
Property, Rights and Liabilities) Order 2007**
Art.3, amended: 2014 c.29 s.4
Art.7, amended: 2014 c.29 s.4
Art.8, amended: 2014 c.29 s.4
Art.9, amended: 2014 c.29 s.4

**1270. Government of Wales Act 2006
(Transitional Provisions) Order 2007**
Art.2, amended: 2014 c.29 s.4
**1333. A40 Trunk Road (Monmouth,
Monmouthshire) (50 MPH Speed Limit) Order
2007**
varied: SI 2014/1500 Art.6, SI 2014/2466
Art.8
**1357. Local Authority Adoption Service (Wales)
Regulations 2007**
Sch.1 para.10, amended: SI 2014/1794
Reg.24, SI 2014/1795 Reg.27
**1388. Government of Wales Act 2006
(Consequential Modifications and Transitional
Provisions) Order 2007**
Sch.1 para.4, amended: 2014 c.29 s.4
Sch.1 para.18, amended: 2014 c.29 s.4
Sch.1 para.19, amended: 2014 c.29 s.4
Sch.1 para.20, amended: 2014 c.29 s.4
Sch.1 para.49, amended: 2014 c.29 s.4
Sch.1 para.50, amended: 2014 c.29 s.4
Sch.1 para.59, amended: 2014 c.29 s.4
Sch.1 para.61, amended: 2014 c.29 s.4
Sch.1 para.63, amended: 2014 c.29 s.4
Sch.1 para.66, amended: 2014 c.29 s.4
Sch.1 para.70, amended: 2014 c.29 s.4
Sch.1 para.71, amended: 2014 c.29 s.4
Sch.1 para.72, amended: 2014 c.29 s.4
Sch.1 para.75, amended: 2014 c.29 s.4
Sch.1 para.76, amended: 2014 c.29 s.4
Sch.1 para.78, amended: 2014 c.29 s.4
Sch.1 para.79, amended: 2014 c.29 s.4
Sch.1 para.80, amended: 2014 c.29 s.4
Sch.1 para.81, amended: 2014 c.29 s.4
Sch.1 para.82, amended: 2014 c.29 s.4
Sch.1 para.83, amended: 2014 c.29 s.4
Sch.1 para.84, amended: 2014 c.29 s.4
Sch.1 para.86, amended: 2014 c.29 s.4
Sch.1 para.87, amended: 2014 c.29 s.4
Sch.1 para.97, amended: 2014 c.29 s.4
Sch.1 para.102, amended: 2014 c.29 s.4
Sch.1 para.103, amended: 2014 c.29 s.4
Sch.1 para.104, amended: 2014 c.29 s.4
Sch.1 para.107, amended: 2014 c.29 s.4
Sch.1 para.113, amended: 2014 c.29 s.4
Sch.1 para.116, amended: 2014 c.29 s.4
Sch.1 para.117, amended: 2014 c.29 s.4
Sch.1 para.118, amended: 2014 c.29 s.4
Sch.1 para.119, amended: 2014 c.29 s.4
Sch.1 para.125, amended: 2014 c.29 s.4
Sch.1 para.126, amended: 2014 c.29 s.4

Sch.1 para.127, amended: 2014 c.29 s.4
Sch.1 para.128, amended: 2014 c.29 s.4
Sch.1 para.129, amended: 2014 c.29 s.4
Sch.1 para.130, amended: 2014 c.29 s.4
Sch.1 para.131, amended: 2014 c.29 s.4
Sch.1 para.132, amended: 2014 c.29 s.4
Sch.1 para.133, amended: 2014 c.29 s.4
Sch.1 para.134, amended: 2014 c.29 s.4
Sch.1 para.137, amended: 2014 c.29 s.4
Sch.1 para.140, amended: 2014 c.29 s.4
Sch.1 para.145, amended: 2014 c.29 s.4
Sch.1 para.146, amended: 2014 c.29 s.4
Sch.1 para.147, amended: 2014 c.29 s.4
Sch.1 para.149, amended: 2014 c.29 s.4
Sch.1 para.150, amended: 2014 c.29 s.4
Sch.1 para.151, amended: 2014 c.29 s.4
Sch.1 para.152, amended: 2014 c.29 s.4
Sch.1 para.154, amended: 2014 c.29 s.4
Sch.1 para.155, amended: 2014 c.29 s.4

1440. Mersey Docks and Harbour Company (Seaforth River Terminal) Harbour Revision Order 2007
Art.20, varied: SI 2014/2708 Art.5

1509. Control of Cash (Penalties) Regulations 2007
Reg.4F, amended: SI 2014/1264 Art.10

1518. Marine Works (Environmental Impact Assessment) Regulations 2007
applied: SSI 2014/224 Art.10

1523. Human Tissue (Quality and Safety for Human Application) Regulations 2007
Reg.4, amended: SI 2014/2883 Reg.2

1609. Justices of the Peace (Training and Development Committee) Rules 2007
applied: SI 2014/2867 Sch.1 para.1
referred to: SI 2014/879 Art.102
r.2, amended: SI 2014/879 Art.94
r.18, amended: SI 2014/879 Art.95
r.31, amended: SI 2014/879 Art.96
r.31, applied: SI 2014/840 r.11, r.12
r.35, amended: SI 2014/879 Art.97
r.35, referred to: SI 2014/879 Art.103
r.37, amended: SI 2014/879 Art.98
r.38, amended: SI 2014/879 Art.99
r.39, amended: SI 2014/879 Art.100
r.40, amended: SI 2014/879 Art.101
r.41, amended: SI 2014/879 Art.100

1610. Family Proceedings Courts (Constitution of Committees and Right to Preside) Rules 2007
applied: SI 2014/842 r.6, SI 2014/879 Art.102

revoked: SI 2014/879 Sch.1
r.10, applied: SI 2014/879 Art.103

1611. Youth Courts (Constitution of Committees and Right to Preside) Rules 2007
applied: SI 2014/1610 r.37_1, SI 2014/2867 Sch.1 para.1

1627. Animals and Animal Products (Import and Export) (Wales) (Laboratories, Circuses and Avian Quarantine) Regulations 2007
Reg.10, amended: 2014 c.29 s.4
Reg.14, amended: 2014 c.29 s.4
Sch.1, amended: 2014 c.29 s.4

1631. Addition of Vitamins, Minerals and Other Substances (England) Regulations 2007
Reg.4, amended: SI 2014/1855 Sch.7 para.7, Sch.7 para.46

1711. Transfrontier Shipment of Waste Regulations 2007
applied: SI 2014/861 Reg.23
Reg.2, revoked: SI 2014/861 Reg.3
Reg.4, amended: SI 2014/861 Reg.4
Reg.4A, added: SI 2014/861 Reg.5
Reg.6, substituted: SI 2014/861 Reg.6
Reg.7, substituted: SI 2014/861 Reg.7
Reg.10, amended: SI 2014/861 Reg.8
Reg.14, amended: SI 2014/861 Reg.9
Reg.46, revoked (in part): SI 2014/861 Reg.10
Reg.49A, added: SI 2014/861 Reg.11
Reg.50, substituted: SI 2014/861 Reg.12
Reg.59, amended: SI 2014/861 Reg.13
Reg.59A, amended: SI 2014/861 Reg.14
Reg.59B, added: SI 2014/861 Reg.15
Sch.A1, added: SI 2014/861 Sch.1
Sch.1, amended: SI 2014/861 Reg.17
Sch.1 para.1, revoked: SI 2014/861 Reg.17
Sch.2, revoked: SI 2014/861 Reg.18
Sch.3 para.2, amended: SI 2014/861 Reg.19
Sch.4 para.1, revoked: SI 2014/861 Reg.20
Sch.5 Part 1 para.1, substituted: SI 2014/861 Reg.21
Sch.5 Part 1 para.5, amended: SI 2014/861 Reg.21
Sch.5 Part 1 para.6, amended: SI 2014/861 Reg.21
Sch.5 Part 2, substituted: SI 2014/861 Reg.21
Sch.5 Part 2A, added: SI 2014/861 Reg.21

1744. Court of Protection Rules 2007
see *A Local Authority v K* [2013] EWHC 242 (COP), [2014] 1 F.C.R. 209 (CP), Cobb

J; see *X (Deprivation of Liberty), Re* [2014]
EWCOP 25, [2014] C.O.P.L.R. 674 (CP),
Sir James Munby PFD; see *X (Deprivation
of Liberty), Re* [2014] EWCOP 37, (2014)
17 C.C.L. Rep. 464 (CP), Sir James Munby
PFD
r.73, see *G (An Adult), Re* [2014] EWCOP
1361, [2014] C.O.P.L.R. 416 (CP), Sir
James Munby PFD; see *X (Deprivation of
Liberty), Re* [2014] EWCOP 37, (2014) 17
C.C.L. Rep. 464 (CP), Sir James Munby
PFD
r.75, see *G (An Adult), Re* [2014] EWCOP
1361, [2014] C.O.P.L.R. 416 (CP), Sir
James Munby PFD
r.87, see *O (Court of Protection:
Jurisdiction), Re* [2013] EWHC 3932
(COP), [2014] Fam. 197 (CP), Sir James
Munby PFD
r.92, see *A Local Authority v K* [2013]
EWHC 242 (COP), [2014] 1 F.C.R. 209
(CP), Cobb J
r.140, see *UF, Re* [2013] EWHC 4289
(COP), [2014] C.O.P.L.R. 93 (CP), Charles J
r.141, see *X (Deprivation of Liberty), Re*
[2014] EWCOP 37, (2014) 17 C.C.L. Rep.
464 (CP), Sir James Munby PFD
r.156, see *E, Re* [2014] EWCOP 27, [2014]
Med. L.R. 417 (CP), Senior Judge Denzil
Lush; see *JS v KB* [2014] EWHC 483
(COP), [2014] C.O.P.L.R. 275 (CP), Cobb J
r.157, see *E, Re* [2014] EWCOP 27, [2014]
Med. L.R. 417 (CP), Senior Judge Denzil
Lush; see *G (An Adult) (Costs), Re* [2014]
EWCOP 5, [2014] C.O.P.L.R. 432 (CP), Sir
James Munby PFD
r.159, see *E, Re* [2014] EWCOP 27, [2014]
Med. L.R. 417 (CP), Senior Judge Denzil
Lush; see *G (An Adult) (Costs), Re* [2014]
EWCOP 5, [2014] C.O.P.L.R. 432 (CP), Sir
James Munby PFD; see *JS v KB* [2014]
EWHC 483 (COP), [2014] C.O.P.L.R. 275
(CP), Cobb J
r.172, see *A (A Patient) (Court of
Protection: Appeal), Re* [2013] EWCA Civ
1661, [2014] 1 W.L.R. 3773 (CA (Civ Div)),
Moses LJ
r.181, see *A (A Patient) (Court of
Protection: Appeal), Re* [2013] EWCA Civ
1661, [2014] 1 W.L.R. 3773 (CA (Civ Div)),
Moses LJ

1745. Court of Protection Fees Order 2007
Sch.2 para.1, amended: SI 2014/513 Sch.1
para.13, SI 2014/590 Art.3
Sch.2 para.17, amended: SI 2014/590 Art.3
**1772. Early Years Foundation Stage (Learning
and Development Requirements) Order 2007**
Art.2, amended: SI 2014/913 Art.3
Art.5, amended: SI 2014/913 Art.4
Art.6, amended: SI 2014/913 Art.5
Art.6A, added: SI 2014/913 Art.6
Art.7, substituted: SI 2014/913 Art.7
**1797. Childcare Providers (Information, Advice
and Training) Regulations 2007**
revoked: SI 2014/2319 Reg.5
Reg.4, amended: SI 2014/2103 Art.24
**1870. Education (Provision of Full-Time
Education for Excluded Pupils) (England)
Regulations 2007**
Reg.3, amended: SI 2014/3216 Reg.2
Reg.4, amended: SI 2014/3216 Reg.2
Reg.5, amended: SI 2014/2103 Art.25
**1894. Coal Mines (Control of Inhalable Dust)
Regulations 2007**
revoked (in part): SI 2014/3248 Sch.4 Part 1
Reg.4, applied: SI 2014/3248 Reg.71
**1895. Civil Aviation (Access to Air Travel for
Disabled Persons and Persons with Reduced
Mobility) Regulations 2007**
revoked: SI 2014/2833 Reg.2
see *Hook v British Airways Plc* [2014]
UKSC 15, [2014] A.C. 1347 (SC), Lord
Neuberger PSC
Reg.9, see *Hook v British Airways Plc*
[2014] UKSC 15, [2014] A.C. 1347 (SC),
Lord Neuberger PSC
**1933. Mobile Roaming (European Communities)
Regulations 2007**
Reg.4, amended: SI 2014/2715 Reg.2
Reg.5A, added: SI 2014/2715 Reg.3
**1951. Street Works (Registers, Notices,
Directions and Designations) (England)
Regulations 2007**
applied: SI 2014/941 Sch.1, SI 2014/3105
Sch.1, SI 2014/3310 Sch.1, SI 2014/3311
Sch.1
referred to: SI 2014/466 Sch.1, SI 2014/3110
Sch.1, SI 2014/3310 Sch.1, SI 2014/3311
Sch.1
varied: SI 2014/3105 Sch.1, SI 2014/3106
Sch.1, SI 2014/3107 Sch.1, SI 2014/3108

Sch.1, SI 2014/3109 Sch.1, SI 2014/3110
Sch.1, SI 2014/3112 Sch.1
Reg.16, applied: SI 2014/466 Sch.1, SI
2014/3107 Sch.1, SI 2014/3310 Sch.1, SI
2014/3311 Sch.1

1984. Addition of Vitamins, Minerals and Other Substances (Wales) Regulations 2007
Reg.4, amended: SI 2014/2303 Sch.7 para.7,
Sch.7 para.46

2003. Heather and Grass etc Burning (England) Regulations 2007
Reg.2, applied: SI 2014/3263 Sch.2 para.3
Reg.5, applied: SI 2014/3263 Sch.2 para.3
Reg.5, disapplied: SI 2014/3263 Sch.2
para.2
Reg.6, applied: SI 2014/3263 Sch.2 para.3
Reg.6, disapplied: SI 2014/3263 Sch.2
para.2

2005. Reciprocal Enforcement of Maintenance Orders (United States of America) Order 2007
Art.6, referred to: SI 2014/879 Art.59
Sch.1 para.3, revoked: SI 2014/879 Art.106
Sch.1 para.6, revoked (in part): SI 2014/879
Art.107
Sch.1 para.15, amended: SI 2014/879
Art.108
Sch.1 para.16, amended: SI 2014/879
Art.109
Sch.2, added: SI 2014/879 Art.116
Sch.2, amended: SI 2014/879 Art.112,
Art.113, Art.114, Art.115, Art.116, Art.117
Sch.2, revoked: SI 2014/879 Art.111,
Art.112, Art.114

2006. Recovery of Maintenance (United States of America) Order 2007
Art.3, amended: SI 2014/879 Art.118

2044. Welsh Forms of Oaths and Affirmations (Government of Wales Act 2006) Order 2007
amended: 2014 c.29 s.4

2080. Nutrition and Health Claims (England) Regulations 2007
Reg.5, amended: SI 2014/1855 Sch.7 para.9,
Sch.7 para.48
Reg.8, revoked: SI 2014/1855 Sch.6 Part 1

2142. National Assembly for Wales (Diversion of Functions) (No.2) Order 2007
Art.2, amended: 2014 c.29 s.4
Art.4, amended: 2014 c.29 s.4

2157. Money Laundering Regulations 2007
applied: SI 2014/631 Art.5
Reg.4, amended: SI 2014/506 Art.4

Reg.23, amended: SI 2014/631 Sch.3 para.2
Reg.23, applied: SI 2014/631 Art.5
Reg.23, revoked (in part): SI 2014/631 Sch.3
para.2
Reg.32, amended: SI 2014/631 Sch.3 para.2
Reg.32, revoked (in part): SI 2014/631 Sch.3
para.2
Reg.34, applied: SI 2014/631 Sch.3 para.5,
Sch.3 para.6
Reg.42, applied: SI 2014/631 Sch.3 para.5,
Sch.3 para.6
Reg.43, applied: SI 2014/631 Sch.3 para.6,
Sch.3 para.7
Reg.43, varied: SI 2014/631 Sch.3 para.6
Reg.43A, varied: SI 2014/631 Sch.3 para.6
Reg.43B, varied: SI 2014/631 Sch.3 para.6
Reg.43D, varied: SI 2014/631 Sch.3 para.6
Reg.43E, varied: SI 2014/631 Sch.3 para.6
Reg.43F, amended: SI 2014/1264 Art.11
Reg.44, applied: SI 2014/631 Sch.3 para.7
Reg.46, amended: SI 2014/834 Sch.3
para.21

2158. Categories of Gaming Machine Regulations 2007
Reg.3, amended: SI 2014/45 Reg.2
Reg.4, amended: SI 2014/45 Reg.2
Reg.5, amended: SI 2014/45 Reg.2

2192. Remote Gaming Duty Regulations 2007
Reg.3, applied: SI 2014/2257 Reg.5
Reg.4, applied: SI 2014/2257 Reg.5

2193. Enterprise Act 2002 (Disclosure of Information for Civil Proceedings etc.) Order 2007
Art.2, amended: SI 2014/549 Sch.1 para.21

2194. Companies Act 2006 (Commencement No 3, Consequential Amendments, Transitional Provisions and Savings) Order 2007
Sch.4 Part 3 para.29, revoked: 2014 c.14
Sch.7

2314. Assembly Learning Grant (Further Education) Regulations 2007
Reg.2, amended: 2014 c.29 s.4
Reg.3, amended: 2014 c.29 s.4

2324. Education (School Performance Information) (England) Regulations 2007
Reg.2, amended: SI 2014/2103 Art.26
Sch.6 para.11, amended: SI 2014/2103
Art.26
Sch.6 para.12, amended: SI 2014/2103
Art.26
Sch.7 para.6, amended: SI 2014/2103 Art.26

Sch.7 para.7, amended: SI 2014/2103 Art.26
Sch.7 para.8, amended: SI 2014/2103 Art.26
Sch.7 para.9, amended: SI 2014/2103 Art.26
2329. Gambling Act 2005 (Advertising of Foreign Gambling) Regulations 2007
revoked: 2014 c.17 s.3
2359. Education (Nutritional Standards and Requirements for School Food) (England) Regulations 2007
revoked: SI 2014/1603 Reg.11
Reg.2, amended: SI 2014/1855 Sch.7 para.50, SI 2014/3001 Sch.3 para.2
Sch.1, amended: SI 2014/3001 Sch.3 para.3
Sch.2 para.4, amended: SI 2014/3001 Sch.3 para.4
Sch.3 Part 1 para.3, amended: SI 2014/3001 Sch.3 para.5
Sch.5, amended: SI 2014/3001 Sch.3 para.6
2441. Community Legal Service (Funding) Order 2007
Art.3, amended: SI 2014/1818 Art.2
Sch.1 Part 001, amended: SI 2014/1818 Art.2
Sch.1 Part 003, amended: SI 2014/1818 Art.2
Sch.2 Part 001, amended: SI 2014/1818 Art.2
Sch.2 Part 002, amended: SI 2014/1818 Art.2
Sch.3 para.16, revoked: SI 2014/1818 Art.2
Sch.4 Part 1 para.1, amended: SI 2014/1818 Art.2
Sch.4 Part 2, amended: SI 2014/1818 Art.2
Sch.4 Part 2 para.59, amended: SI 2014/1818 Art.2
Sch.4 Part 2 para.60, amended: SI 2014/1818 Art.2
Sch.4 Part 2 para.60A, added: SI 2014/1818 Art.2
Sch.4 Part 2 para.61, amended: SI 2014/1818 Art.2
2461. Welfare of Animals (Slaughter or Killing) (Amendment) (Wales) Regulations 2007
revoked: SI 2014/951 Reg.46
2585. Commons (Deregistration and Exchange Orders) (Interim Arrangements) (England) Regulations 2007
applied: SI 2014/3038 Reg.14
revoked (in part): SI 2014/3038 Reg.54

2598. Manufacture and Storage of Explosives and the Health and Safety (Enforcing Authority) (Amendment and Supplementary Provisions) Regulations 2007
revoked: SI 2014/1638 Sch.14 Part 2
2611. Nutrition and Health Claims (Wales) Regulations 2007
Reg.3, amended: SI 2014/1102 Reg.4
Reg.5, amended: SI 2014/2303 Sch.7 para.9, Sch.7 para.48
Reg.8, revoked: SI 2014/2303 Sch.6 Part 1
2621. Family Proceedings Courts (Constitution of Committees and Right to Preside) (Amendment) Rules 2007
revoked: SI 2014/879 Sch.1
2785. Natural Mineral Water, Spring Water and Bottled Drinking Water (England) Regulations 2007
Reg.2, amended: SI 2014/1855 Sch.7 para.52
Reg.22, revoked (in part): SI 2014/1855 Sch.6 Part 1
2803. Diseases of Animals (Approved Disinfectants) (Wales) Order 2007
applied: SI 2014/1894 Reg.15
2920. Channel Tunnel Rail Link (Nomination) (Amendment) Order 2007
revoked: SI 2014/1332 Art.2
2933. Environmental Impact Assessment (Agriculture) (Wales) Regulations 2007
Reg.11, amended: 2014 c.29 s.4
Reg.12, amended: 2014 c.29 s.4
2974. Companies (Cross-Border Mergers) Regulations 2007
see *Sigma Tau Pharmaceutical Ltd, Re* [2013] EWHC 3279 (Ch), [2014] B.C.C. 70 (Ch D), Rose J
Reg.2, see *Olympus UK Ltd, Re* [2014] EWHC 1350 (Ch), [2014] Bus. L.R. 816 (Ch D (Companies Ct)), Hildyard J; see *Sigma Tau Pharmaceutical Ltd, Re* [2013] EWHC 3279 (Ch), [2014] B.C.C. 70 (Ch D), Rose J
Reg.3A, varied: SI 2014/3348 Art.218
Reg.11, see *Olympus UK Ltd, Re* [2014] EWHC 1350 (Ch), [2014] Bus. L.R. 816 (Ch D (Companies Ct)), Hildyard J
Reg.13, see *Olympus UK Ltd, Re* [2014] EWHC 1350 (Ch), [2014] Bus. L.R. 816 (Ch D (Companies Ct)), Hildyard J

Reg.16, see *Sigma Tau Pharmaceutical Ltd, Re* [2013] EWHC 3279 (Ch), [2014] B.C.C. 70 (Ch D), Rose J

Reg.45, amended: SI 2014/386 Sch.1 para.49

Reg.45A, added: SI 2014/386 Sch.1 para.50

Reg.62, amended: SI 2014/386 Sch.1 para.51

Sch.2 para.18, amended: SI 2014/386 Sch.1 para.52

3131. A428 Trunk Road (Caxton Common to Hardwick, Cambridgeshire) (De-Restriction) Order 2007

Sch.1, varied: SI 2014/1027 Art.3

3153. Rating Lists (Valuation Date) (Wales) Order 2007

revoked: SI 2014/2917 Art.3

3165. Natural Mineral Water, Spring Water and Bottled Drinking Water (Wales) Regulations 2007

Reg.2, amended: SI 2014/2303 Sch.7 para.50

Reg.22, revoked (in part): SI 2014/2303 Sch.6 Part 1

3170. Asylum and Immigration Tribunal (Procedure) (Amendment No 2) Rules 2007

revoked: SI 2014/2604 r.45

3175. Police and Criminal Evidence Act 1984 (Application to Revenue and Customs) Order 2007

Art.14, revoked: SI 2014/788 Art.3

Sch.1, amended: SI 2014/788 Art.4

3290. Immigration (Restrictions on Employment) Order 2007

Art.4, substituted: SI 2014/1183 Art.3

Art.5, amended: SI 2014/1183 Art.4

Art.6, amended: SI 2014/1183 Art.5

Art.6, revoked (in part): SI 2014/1183 Art.5

Art.7, amended: SI 2014/1183 Art.6

Sch.1 Part LIST_A para.1, amended: SI 2014/1183 Art.8

Sch.1 Part LIST_A para.2, amended: SI 2014/1183 Art.8

Sch.1 Part LIST_A para.3, amended: SI 2014/1183 Art.7, Art.8

Sch.1 Part LIST_A para.4, amended: SI 2014/1183 Art.7

Sch.1 Part LIST_A para.5, amended: SI 2014/1183 Art.8

Sch.1 Part LIST_A para.6, amended: SI 2014/1183 Art.8

Sch.1 Part LIST_A para.7, amended: SI 2014/1183 Art.7, Art.8

Sch.1 Part LIST_A para.13, amended: SI 2014/1183 Art.7

Sch.1 Part LIST_A para.13, revoked: SI 2014/1183 Art.8

Sch.1 Part LIST_B, substituted: SI 2014/1183 Art.9

Sch.1 Part LIST_B para.2, amended: SI 2014/1183 Art.7

Sch.1 Part LIST_B para.3, amended: SI 2014/1183 Art.7

Sch.1 Part LIST_B para.4, amended: SI 2014/1183 Art.7

Sch.1 Part LIST_B para.6, amended: SI 2014/1183 Art.7

Sch.1 Part LIST_B para.7, amended: SI 2014/1183 Art.7

Sch.1 Part LIST_B para.8, amended: SI 2014/1183 Art.7

3291. Patents Rules 2007

Part 2 r.19, amended: SI 2014/2401 r.3

Part 2 r.19, substituted: SI 2014/578 r.2

Part 3 r.36, amended: SI 2014/2401 r.4, r.5

Part 3 r.39, amended: SI 2014/2401 r.6

Part 3 r.41A, added: SI 2014/2401 r.7

Part 4 r.44, amended: SI 2014/2401 r.9

Part 8 r.93, amended: SI 2014/2401 r.10

Sch.4 Part 1, amended: SI 2014/2401 r.8

3298. Transfer of Funds (Information on the Payer) Regulations 2007

Reg.12F, amended: SI 2014/1264 Art.12

Reg.15, amended: SI 2014/834 Sch.3 para.22

3372. Traffic Management Permit Scheme (England) Regulations 2007

applied: SI 2014/466 Sch.1, SI 2014/941 Sch.1, SI 2014/3105 Sch.1, SI 2014/3106 Sch.1, SI 2014/3107 Sch.1, SI 2014/3110 Sch.1, SI 2014/3112 Sch.1, SI 2014/3310 Sch.1, SI 2014/3311 Sch.1

referred to: SI 2014/941 Sch.1, SI 2014/3105 Sch.1, SI 2014/3106 Sch.1, SI 2014/3110 Sch.1, SI 2014/3112 Sch.1

Part 3, applied: SI 2014/3108 Sch.1, SI 2014/3112 Sch.1

Part 5, applied: SI 2014/3105 Sch.1, SI 2014/3110 Sch.1, SI 2014/3112 Sch.1

Part 7, applied: SI 2014/941 Sch.1, SI 2014/3106 Sch.1

Part 8, applied: SI 2014/466 Art.4, SI
2014/941 Art.4, SI 2014/2460 Art.4, SI
2014/2462 Art.4, SI 2014/3105 Art.4, SI
2014/3106 Art.4, SI 2014/3107 Art.4, SI
2014/3108 Art.4, SI 2014/3109 Art.4, SI
2014/3110 Art.4, SI 2014/3112 Art.4, SI
2014/3310 Art.4, Sch.1, SI 2014/3311 Art.4
Reg.3, applied: SI 2014/941 Sch.1, SI
2014/3310 Sch.1
Reg.3, referred to: SI 2014/3310 Sch.1
Reg.5, applied: SI 2014/941 Sch.1
Reg.7, applied: SI 2014/466 Sch.1, SI
2014/3310 Sch.1, SI 2014/3311 Sch.1
Reg.9, applied: SI 2014/941 Sch.1, SI
2014/3109 Sch.1
Reg.10, applied: SI 2014/941 Sch.1, SI
2014/3105 Sch.1, SI 2014/3107 Sch.1, SI
2014/3110 Sch.1, SI 2014/3112 Sch.1, SI
2014/3310 Sch.1
Reg.10, referred to: SI 2014/941 Sch.1, SI
2014/3105 Sch.1, SI 2014/3110 Sch.1, SI
2014/3112 Sch.1
Reg.11, applied: SI 2014/941 Sch.1, SI
2014/3310 Sch.1
Reg.12, applied: SI 2014/941 Sch.1
Reg.13, applied: SI 2014/3105 Sch.1, SI
2014/3110 Sch.1, SI 2014/3112 Sch.1, SI
2014/3310 Sch.1
Reg.15, applied: SI 2014/941 Sch.1, SI
2014/3105 Sch.1, SI 2014/3107 Sch.1, SI
2014/3110 Sch.1, SI 2014/3310 Sch.1
Reg.16, applied: SI 2014/3310 Sch.1
Reg.17, applied: SI 2014/941 Sch.1
Reg.18, applied: SI 2014/941 Sch.1, SI
2014/3105 Sch.1, SI 2014/3110 Sch.1, SI
2014/3112 Sch.1, SI 2014/3310 Sch.1
Reg.18, referred to: SI 2014/941 Sch.1
Reg.19, applied: SI 2014/941 Sch.1, SI
2014/3105 Sch.1, SI 2014/3110 Sch.1, SI
2014/3112 Sch.1
Reg.21, applied: SI 2014/3106 Sch.1, SI
2014/3107 Sch.1
Reg.23, referred to: SI 2014/941 Sch.1
Reg.29, referred to: SI 2014/941 Sch.1
Reg.30, applied: SI 2014/941 Sch.1, SI
2014/3107 Sch.1, SI 2014/3310 Sch.1
Reg.30, referred to: SI 2014/3310 Sch.1
Reg.31, applied: SI 2014/3310 Sch.1
Reg.31, referred to: SI 2014/466 Sch.1, SI
2014/3310 Sch.1

Reg.33, applied: SI 2014/3106 Sch.1, SI
2014/3107 Sch.1, SI 2014/3108 Sch.1, SI
2014/3109 Sch.1
Reg.40, applied: SI 2014/941 Sch.1, SI
2014/3310 Sch.1
Sch.1, applied: SI 2014/3107 Sch.1
Sch.1, referred to: SI 2014/941 Sch.1

3382. Army Terms of Service Regulations 2007
Reg.5, amended: SI 2014/3068 Reg.9
Reg.6, substituted: SI 2014/3068 Reg.10
Reg.8, amended: SI 2014/3068 Reg.11

**3479. Energy Act 2004 (Designation of Publicly
Owned Companies) Order 2007**
revoked: SI 2014/1391 Art.2

**3490. Childcare Act 2006 (Provision of
Information to Parents) (England) Regulations
2007**
Reg.1, amended: SI 2014/1921 Reg.3
Sch.1 para.1, amended: SI 2014/1921 Reg.4

**3538. Environmental Permitting (England and
Wales) Regulations 2007**
Reg.38, see *R. v Morgan (Christopher Lynn)*
[2013] EWCA Crim 1307, [2014] 1 W.L.R.
3450 (CA (Crim Div)), Aikens LJ; see
*Walker and Son (Hauliers) Ltd v
Environment Agency* [2014] EWCA Crim
100, [2014] 4 All E.R. 825 (CA (Crim Div)),
Lord Thomas LCJ

**3544. Legislative and Regulatory Reform
(Regulatory Functions) Order 2007**
Sch.1 Part 1, amended: SI 2014/469 Sch.3
para.194, SI 2014/549 Sch.1 para.33, SI
2014/860 Art.2
Sch.1 Part 2, amended: SI 2014/469 Sch.3
para.194, SI 2014/517 Sch.2 para.6, SI
2014/860 Art.2

**3573. Infant Formula and Follow-on Formula
(Wales) Regulations 2007**
Reg.2, amended: SI 2014/123 Reg.2, SI
2014/1102 Reg.5
Reg.8, amended: SI 2014/123 Reg.2
Reg.9, substituted: SI 2014/123 Reg.2
Reg.13, amended: SI 2014/1102 Reg.5
Reg.15, amended: SI 2014/123 Reg.2
Reg.16, amended: SI 2014/123 Reg.2

2008

132. Immigration (Employment of Adults Subject to Immigration Control) (Maximum Penalty) Order 2008
Art.2, amended: SI 2014/1262 Art.2
216. Rating Lists (Valuation Date) (England) Order 2008
revoked: SI 2014/2841 Art.3
238. Local Government Pension Scheme (Transitional Provisions) Regulations 2008
revoked: SI 2014/525 Sch.1
Reg.3, applied: SI 2014/525 Sch.2 para.6
Reg.4, applied: SI 2014/525 Sch.2 para.6
Reg.15, applied: SI 2014/525 Reg.24
239. Local Government Pension Scheme (Administration) Regulations 2008
applied: SI 2014/525 Reg.14, Reg.22
revoked: SI 2014/525 Sch.1
Reg.4, applied: SI 2014/525 Reg.5
Reg.7, applied: SI 2014/525 Reg.5
Reg.8B, applied: SI 2014/525 Reg.5, Reg.6
Reg.9, amended: SI 2014/44 Reg.5
Reg.12, applied: SI 2014/525 Reg.5
Reg.13, amended: SI 2014/44 Reg.6
Reg.14, applied: SI 2014/525 Reg.5
Reg.16, applied: SI 2014/525 Sch.2 para.6
Reg.17, applied: SI 2014/525 Reg.10
Reg.23, applied: SI 2014/525 Reg.11, Reg.15
Reg.36, applied: SI 2014/1012 Art.11
Reg.38, substituted: SI 2014/44 Reg.7
Reg.40, applied: SI 2014/525 Reg.24
Reg.40A, applied: SI 2014/525 Sch.2 para.4
Reg.46, applied: SI 2014/525 Reg.10
Reg.70, applied: SI 2014/525 Reg.3
Reg.84, applied: SI 2014/525 Sch.2 para.4
Reg.87, applied: SI 2014/525 Reg.10
Sch.4 Part 1 para.2B, applied: SI 2014/525 Reg.19
346. Regulated Covered Bonds Regulations 2008
applied: SI 2014/1195 Art.2
Reg.42, applied: SI 2014/1195 Art.2
386. Non-Domestic Rating (Unoccupied Property) (England) Regulations 2008
Reg.4, see *Pall Mall Investments (London) Ltd v Gloucester City Council* [2014] EWHC 2247 (Admin), [2014] P.T.S.R. 1184 (DC), Pitchford LJ

465. Products of Animal Origin (Disease Control) (England) Regulations 2008
applied: SI 2014/1894 Reg.30
Reg.3, amended: SI 2014/1894 Reg.43
Sch.1 para.1, amended: SI 2014/1894 Reg.43
Sch.1 para.3, revoked: SI 2014/1894 Reg.43
Sch.1 para.5, revoked: SI 2014/1894 Reg.43
517. Meat Products (England) (Amendment) Regulations 2008
revoked: SI 2014/3001 Reg.8
565. Insurance Accounts Directive (Miscellaneous Insurance Undertakings) Regulations 2008
Reg.2, amended: SI 2014/1815 Sch.1 para.20
Reg.4, amended: SI 2014/1815 Sch.1 para.20
Reg.6, amended: SI 2014/1815 Sch.1 para.20
Reg.7, amended: SI 2014/1815 Sch.1 para.20
Reg.14, amended: SI 2014/1815 Sch.1 para.20
Reg.14, substituted: SI 2014/1815 Sch.1 para.20
Sch.1 para.1, amended: SI 2014/1815 Sch.1 para.20
Sch.1 para.3, amended: SI 2014/1815 Sch.1 para.20
Sch.2 para.1, amended: SI 2014/1815 Sch.1 para.20
Sch.2 para.3, amended: SI 2014/1815 Sch.1 para.20
574. Serious Organised Crime and Police Act 2005 and Serious Crime Act 2007 (Consequential and Supplementary Amendments to Secondary Legislation) Order 2008
Sch.1 para.6, revoked (in part): SI 2014/834
Sch.3 para.23
649. Occupational Pension Schemes (Internal Dispute Resolution Procedures Consequential and Miscellaneous Amendments) Regulations 2008
applied: SI 2014/2848 Reg.148, Reg.163
653. National Health Service Pension Scheme Regulations 2008
Part 2, added: SI 2014/570 Reg.35
Reg.1, amended: SI 2014/78 Reg.10

Reg.1, amended: SI 2014/78 Reg.11, SI 2014/570 Reg.20, SI 2014/1607 Reg.9

Reg.1, amended: SI 2014/570 Reg.22

Reg.1, amended: SI 2014/570 Reg.24

Reg.1, amended: SI 2014/570 Reg.31

Reg.1, amended: SI 2014/78 Reg.14, SI 2014/570 Reg.36

Reg.1, amended: SI 2014/570 Reg.40

Reg.1, amended: SI 2014/570 Reg.46

Reg.1A, added: SI 2014/78 Reg.12

Reg.1A, added: SI 2014/78 Reg.15

Reg.2, amended: SI 2014/570 Reg.23

Reg.2, amended: SI 2014/570 Reg.25, SI 2014/1607 Reg.10

Reg.2, amended: SI 2014/570 Reg.42, SI 2014/1607 Reg.14

Reg.3, amended: SI 2014/570 Reg.19

Reg.3, amended: SI 2014/1607 Reg.13

Reg.4, amended: SI 2014/570 Reg.26, SI 2014/1607 Reg.11

Reg.4, amended: SI 2014/570 Reg.43

Reg.5, amended: SI 2014/570 Reg.41

Reg.5, amended: SI 2014/570 Reg.44, SI 2014/1607 Reg.15

Reg.6, amended: SI 2014/570 Reg.27

Reg.6, amended: SI 2014/570 Reg.29

Reg.6, amended: SI 2014/570 Reg.45

Reg.7, amended: SI 2014/570 Reg.28

Reg.7, amended: SI 2014/570 Reg.37

Reg.9, amended: SI 2014/570 Reg.32

Reg.9, amended: SI 2014/570 Reg.38

Reg.9A, added: SI 2014/570 Reg.33

Reg.9A, amended: SI 2014/1607 Reg.12

Reg.9A, added: SI 2014/570 Reg.47

Reg.9A, amended: SI 2014/1607 Reg.16

Reg.10, amended: SI 2014/78 Reg.13

Reg.10, amended: SI 2014/78 Reg.16

Reg.11, amended: SI 2014/570 Reg.30

Reg.12A, added: SI 2014/570 Reg.21

Reg.13, amended: SI 2014/570 Reg.39

Reg.14, amended: SI 2014/570 Reg.34

Reg.14, amended: SI 2014/570 Reg.48, SI 2014/1607 Reg.17

711. Pensions Increase (Review) Order 2008

referred to: SI 2014/668 Sch.1

Art.6, substituted: SI 2014/107 Sch.1 para.56, SI 2014/3229 Sch.6 para.35

713. Meat Products (Wales) (Amendment) Regulations 2008

revoked: SI 2014/3087 Reg.8

788. Local Authorities (Model Code of Conduct) (Wales) Order 2008

see *Heesom v Public Services Ombudsman for Wales* [2014] EWHC 1504 (Admin), [2014] 4 All E.R. 269 (QBD (Admin)), Hickinbottom J

Sch.1, amended: SI 2014/1815 Sch.1 para.21

794. Employment and Support Allowance Regulations 2008

applied: SI 2014/1230 Reg.31

Reg.1, revoked (in part): SI 2014/3255 Art.20

Reg.2, amended: SI 2014/107 Sch.1 para.45, SI 2014/884 Reg.5, SI 2014/3229 Sch.6 para.32, SI 2014/3255 Art.20

Reg.5, applied: SI 2014/1230 Reg.20

Reg.20, amended: SI 2014/884 Reg.5

Reg.30, applied: SI 2014/1230 Reg.21

Reg.34, see *Secretary of State for Work and Pensions v Brade* [2014] CSIH 39, 2014 S.C. 742 (IH (Ex Div)), Lady Smith

Reg.35, see *Secretary of State for Work and Pensions v Brade* [2014] CSIH 39, 2014 S.C. 742 (IH (Ex Div)), Lady Smith

Reg.43, amended: SI 2014/3255 Art.20

Reg.63, applied: SI 2014/1230 Reg.30, Reg.31

Reg.70, amended: SI 2014/902 Reg.7

Reg.82, revoked: SI 2014/3255 Art.20

Reg.82A, added: SI 2014/3255 Art.20

Reg.95, amended: SI 2014/591 Reg.10, SI 2014/3255 Art.20

Reg.144, amended: SI 2014/2309 Reg.2

Reg.144, disapplied: SI 2014/2309 Reg.4

Sch.3, see *Secretary of State for Work and Pensions v Brade* [2014] CSIH 39, 2014 S.C. 742 (IH (Ex Div)), Lady Smith

Sch.4 Part 1, referred to: SI 2014/147 Art.11

Sch.4 Part 2 para.6, amended: SI 2014/2888 Reg.3

Sch.4 Part 3 para.11, substituted: SI 2014/516 Sch.14

Sch.4 Part 4 para.12, amended: SI 2014/147 Art.11

Sch.4 Part 4 para.13, amended: SI 2014/516 Art.22

Sch.6 para.2, amended: SI 2014/3255 Art.20

Sch.6 para.7, applied: SI 2014/516 Sch.15

Sch.6 para.8, applied: SI 2014/516 Sch.15, SI 2014/1230 Reg.29

Sch.6 para.9, applied: SI 2014/516 Sch.15,
SI 2014/1230 Reg.29
Sch.6 para.11, applied: SI 2014/516 Sch.15
Sch.6 para.12, applied: SI 2014/516 Sch.15
Sch.6 para.13, amended: SI 2014/591
Reg.10
Sch.6 para.13, applied: SI 2014/516 Sch.15
Sch.6 para.15, applied: SI 2014/1230 Reg.29
Sch.6 para.16, applied: SI 2014/1230 Reg.29
Sch.6 para.19, amended: SI 2014/516 Art.22,
SI 2014/2888 Reg.3
Sch.8 para.4, amended: SI 2014/3255 Art.20
Sch.8 para.5, amended: SI 2014/3255 Art.20
Sch.8 para.26, amended: SI 2014/852 Art.16
Sch.8 para.53, amended: SI 2014/513 Sch.1
para.14
Sch.8 para.67, added: SI 2014/2103 Art.27
Sch.9 para.56, amended: SI 2014/513 Sch.1
para.14
Sch.9 para.59, added: SI 2014/2103 Art.27

**817. Government Resources and Accounts Act
2000 (Audit of Public Bodies) Order 2008**
Art.4, revoked: 2014 c.2 Sch.1 Part 2

**912. Offender Management Act 2007
(Consequential Amendments) Order 2008**
Sch.1 Part 2 para.26, revoked (in part): 2014
c.2 Sch.1 Part 2
Sch.1 Part 2 para.27, revoked (in part): 2014
c.2 Sch.1 Part 2

944. Specified Animal Pathogens Order 2008
applied: SI 2014/1894 Reg.4

**946. Proceeds of Crime Act 2002 (Investigations
in England, Wales and Northern Ireland Code of
Practice) Order 2008**
applied: SI 2014/1893 Art.35

**948. Companies Act 2006 (Consequential
Amendments etc) Order 2008**
Sch.1 Part 1 para.1, revoked (in part): 2014
c.14 Sch.7, SI 2014/1924 Sch.1
Sch.1 Part 1 para.4, revoked: 2014 c.14
Sch.7
Sch.1 Part 1 para.23, revoked: 2014 c.2
Sch.1 Part 2

**974. Childcare (Early Years Register)
Regulations 2008**
Reg.2, amended: SI 2014/912 Reg.3
Reg.4, amended: SI 2014/912 Reg.4
Sch.1 Part 1 para.1A, added: SI 2014/912
Reg.5
Sch.1 Part 1 para.3, amended: SI 2014/912
Reg.5

Sch.1 Part 1 para.3A, amended: SI 2014/912
Reg.5
Sch.1 Part 1 para.9, amended: SI 2014/912
Reg.5
Sch.1 Part 1 para.11, amended: SI 2014/912
Reg.5
Sch.2 Part 1 para.1A, added: SI 2014/912
Reg.6
Sch.2 Part 1 para.2, amended: SI 2014/912
Reg.6
Sch.2 Part 1 para.8, substituted: SI 2014/912
Reg.6
Sch.2 Part 1 para.11, amended: SI 2014/912
Reg.6
Sch.2 Part 1 para.12, amended: SI 2014/912
Reg.6
Sch.2 Part 1 para.14, amended: SI 2014/912
Reg.6

**975. Childcare (General Childcare Register)
Regulations 2008**
Part 2, substituted: SI 2014/912 Reg.8
Part 4, substituted: SI 2014/912 Reg.15
Reg.2, amended: SI 2014/912 Reg.9
Reg.5, amended: SI 2014/912 Reg.10
Reg.7, amended: SI 2014/912 Reg.11
Reg.8, amended: SI 2014/912 Reg.12
Reg.8A, added: SI 2014/912 Reg.13
Reg.9, amended: SI 2014/912 Reg.14
Reg.12, amended: SI 2014/912 Reg.16
Reg.13, amended: SI 2014/912 Reg.17
Reg.14, amended: SI 2014/912 Reg.18
Reg.14A, added: SI 2014/912 Reg.19
Sch.1, amended: SI 2014/912 Reg.20
Sch.1 Part 1 para.1A, added: SI 2014/912
Reg.20
Sch.1 Part 1 para.3, amended: SI 2014/912
Reg.20
Sch.1 Part 1 para.4A, added: SI 2014/912
Reg.20
Sch.1 Part 1 para.6, amended: SI 2014/912
Reg.20
Sch.1 Part 1 para.8, amended: SI 2014/912
Reg.20
Sch.2, amended: SI 2014/912 Reg.21
Sch.2 Part 1 para.1A, added: SI 2014/912
Reg.21
Sch.2 Part 1 para.2, amended: SI 2014/912
Reg.21
Sch.2 Part 1 para.5, substituted: SI 2014/912
Reg.21

Sch.2 Part 1 para.8, amended: SI 2014/912
Reg.21
Sch.2 Part 1 para.9, amended: SI 2014/912
Reg.21
Sch.2 Part 1 para.11, amended: SI 2014/912
Reg.21
Sch.3 para.1A, added: SI 2014/912 Reg.22
Sch.3 para.2, amended: SI 2014/912 Reg.22
Sch.3 para.2, revoked (in part): SI 2014/912
Reg.22
Sch.3 para.3, amended: SI 2014/912 Reg.22
Sch.3 para.6, substituted: SI 2014/912
Reg.22
Sch.3 para.6A, added: SI 2014/912 Reg.22
Sch.3 para.8, amended: SI 2014/912 Reg.22
Sch.3 para.8, revoked (in part): SI 2014/912
Reg.22
Sch.3 para.11, substituted: SI 2014/912
Reg.22
Sch.3 para.12, amended: SI 2014/912
Reg.22
Sch.3 para.13, substituted: SI 2014/912
Reg.22
Sch.3 para.13A, added: SI 2014/912 Reg.22
Sch.3 para.16, revoked: SI 2014/912 Reg.22
Sch.3 para.17, amended: SI 2014/912
Reg.22, SI 2014/2103 Art.28
Sch.3 para.18, amended: SI 2014/912
Reg.22
Sch.3 para.24, amended: SI 2014/912
Reg.22
Sch.3 para.25, amended: SI 2014/912
Reg.22
Sch.3 para.26, amended: SI 2014/912
Reg.22
Sch.3 para.28, amended: SI 2014/912
Reg.22
Sch.3 para.29, amended: SI 2014/912
Reg.22
Sch.6, amended: SI 2014/912 Reg.23
Sch.6 para.4, substituted: SI 2014/912
Reg.23
Sch.6 para.5, amended: SI 2014/912 Reg.23
Sch.6 para.10, revoked (in part): SI
2014/912 Reg.23
Sch.6 para.14, amended: SI 2014/912
Reg.23
Sch.6 para.17, revoked: SI 2014/912 Reg.23
Sch.6 para.18, amended: SI 2014/912
Reg.23, SI 2014/2103 Art.28

Sch.6 para.19, amended: SI 2014/912
Reg.23
Sch.6 para.26, amended: SI 2014/912
Reg.23
Sch.6 para.27, amended: SI 2014/912
Reg.23
Sch.6 para.29, amended: SI 2014/912
Reg.23
Sch.6 para.31, amended: SI 2014/912
Reg.23
Sch.6 para.32, amended: SI 2014/912
Reg.23
Sch.6 para.33, amended: SI 2014/912
Reg.23

976. Childcare (Early Years and General Childcare Registers) (Common Provisions) Regulations 2008
Reg.5, amended: SI 2014/1921 Reg.6
Reg.6, amended: SI 2014/1921 Reg.7
Reg.7A, added: SI 2014/1921 Reg.8
Reg.8, amended: SI 2014/1921 Reg.9

979. Childcare (Exemptions from Registration) Order 2008
Art.2, amended: SI 2014/913 Art.9
Art.3, amended: SI 2014/913 Art.10

1052. Magistrates Courts Fees Order 2008
Sch.1, substituted: SI 2014/875 Sch.1
Sch.2 para.1, amended: SI 2014/513 Sch.1
para.15, SI 2014/590 Art.6

1053. Civil Proceedings Fees Order 2008
applied: SI 2014/1610 r.17_31
see *Page v Hewetts Solicitors* [2013] EWHC
2845 (Ch), [2014] W.T.L.R. 479 (Ch D),
Hildyard J
Art.1, amended: SI 2014/874 Art.2
Art.2, amended: SI 2014/874 Art.2
Art.3, amended: SI 2014/874 Art.2
Sch.1, amended: SI 2014/590 Art.4, SI
2014/1834 Art.3, SI 2014/2059 Art.2
Sch.1, substituted: SI 2014/874 Sch.1
Sch.2, applied: SI 2014/1610 r.17_31
Sch.2 para.1, amended: SI 2014/513 Sch.1
para.16, SI 2014/590 Art.4, SI 2014/1834
Art.4

1054. Family Proceedings Fees Order 2008
Art.2, amended: SI 2014/877 Art.2
Sch.1, amended: SI 2014/590 Art.5
Sch.1, substituted: SI 2014/877 Sch.1
Sch.2 para.1, amended: SI 2014/513 Sch.1
para.17, SI 2014/590 Art.5

1081. Heather and Grass etc Burning (Wales) Regulations 2008
    Reg.2, amended: 2014 c.29 s.4
    Reg.7, applied: SI 2014/3223 Sch.1 para.9
    Reg.10, amended: 2014 c.29 s.4

1083. Local Government Pension Scheme (Amendment) Regulations 2008
    revoked: SI 2014/525 Sch.1

1088. Asylum and Immigration Tribunal (Procedure) (Amendment) Rules 2008
    revoked: SI 2014/2604 r.45

1089. Asylum and Immigration Tribunal (Fast Track Procedure) (Amendment) Rules 2008
    revoked: SI 2014/2604 r.45

1160. Teesport Harbour Revision Order 2008
    Art.20, varied: SI 2014/2708 Art.5

1184. Mental Health (Hospital, Guardianship and Treatment) (England) Regulations 2008
    Reg.3, see *K v Kingswood Centre Hospital Managers* [2014] EWCA Civ 1332, [2014] Med. L.R. 497 (CA (Civ Div)), Moore-Bick LJ

1185. General Ophthalmic Services Contracts Regulations 2008
    Reg.16, amended: SI 2014/418 Reg.3
    Sch.1 Part 8 para.51, amended: SI 2014/1887 Sch.2 para.12

1186. Primary Ophthalmic Services Regulations 2008
    Reg.3, amended: SI 2014/418 Reg.2, SI 2014/545 Reg.6, SI 2014/2667 Reg.3
    Reg.3, applied: SI 2014/2667 Reg.6

1188. Food Labelling (Declaration of Allergens) (England) Regulations 2008
    revoked: SI 2014/1855 Sch.6 Part 1

1216. Criminal Justice (Northern Ireland) Order 2008
    Art.40, applied: SI 2014/3141 Reg.107
    Art.40, varied: SI 2014/3141 Reg.97
    Art.44, applied: SI 2014/3141 Reg.107
    Art.79, applied: SI 2014/3141 Reg.110

1263. Offender Management Act 2007 (Approved Premises) Regulations 2008
    revoked: SI 2014/1198 Reg.2

1268. Food Labelling (Declaration of Allergens) (Wales) Regulations 2008
    revoked: SI 2014/2303 Sch.6 Part 1

1270. Specified Animal Pathogens (Wales) Order 2008
    applied: SI 2014/1894 Reg.4

1275. Products of Animal Origin (Disease Control) (Wales) Regulations 2008
    applied: SI 2014/1894 Reg.30
    Reg.3, amended: SI 2014/1894 Reg.43
    Sch.1 para.1, amended: SI 2014/1894 Reg.43
    Sch.1 para.3, revoked: SI 2014/1894 Reg.43
    Sch.1 para.5, revoked: SI 2014/1894 Reg.43

1276. Business Protection from Misleading Marketing Regulations 2008
    Reg.2, amended: SI 2014/549 Sch.1 para.34
    Reg.3, see *Oldham MBC v Worldwide Marketing Solutions Ltd* [2014] EWHC 1910 (QB), [2014] P.T.S.R. 1072 (QBD), Phillips J
    Reg.4, see *Oldham MBC v Worldwide Marketing Solutions Ltd* [2014] EWHC 1910 (QB), [2014] P.T.S.R. 1072 (QBD), Phillips J
    Reg.5, see *Oldham MBC v Worldwide Marketing Solutions Ltd* [2014] EWHC 1910 (QB), [2014] P.T.S.R. 1072 (QBD), Phillips J
    Reg.13, amended: SI 2014/549 Sch.1 para.34
    Reg.14, amended: SI 2014/549 Sch.1 para.34
    Reg.15, amended: SI 2014/549 Sch.1 para.34
    Reg.17, amended: SI 2014/549 Sch.1 para.34
    Reg.18, see *Oldham MBC v Worldwide Marketing Solutions Ltd* [2014] EWHC 1910 (QB), [2014] P.T.S.R. 1072 (QBD), Phillips J
    Reg.19, amended: SI 2014/549 Sch.1 para.34
    Reg.20, amended: SI 2014/549 Sch.1 para.34

1277. Consumer Protection from Unfair Trading Regulations 2008
    see *R. v King (Scott)* [2014] EWCA Crim 621, [2014] 2 Cr. App. R. (S.) 54 (CA (Crim Div)), Fulford LJ; see *R. v X Ltd* [2013] EWCA Crim 818, [2014] 1 W.L.R. 591 (CA (Crim Div)), Leveson LJ
    Part 4A, added: SI 2014/870 Reg.3
    Reg.2, amended: SI 2014/549 Sch.1 para.35, SI 2014/870 Reg.2

Reg.3, see *R. v X Ltd* [2013] EWCA Crim 818, [2014] 1 W.L.R. 591 (CA (Crim Div)), Leveson LJ

Reg.5, see *R. v X Ltd* [2013] EWCA Crim 818, [2014] 1 W.L.R. 591 (CA (Crim Div)), Leveson LJ

Reg.8, see *R. v X Ltd* [2013] EWCA Crim 818, [2014] 1 W.L.R. 591 (CA (Crim Div)), Leveson LJ

Reg.9, see *R. v X Ltd* [2013] EWCA Crim 818, [2014] 1 W.L.R. 591 (CA (Crim Div)), Leveson LJ

Reg.12, see *R. v King (Scott)* [2014] EWCA Crim 621, [2014] 2 Cr. App. R. (S.) 54 (CA (Crim Div)), Fulford LJ; see *R. v X Ltd* [2013] EWCA Crim 818, [2014] 1 W.L.R. 591 (CA (Crim Div)), Leveson LJ

Reg.13, see *R. v King (Scott)* [2014] EWCA Crim 621, [2014] 2 Cr. App. R. (S.) 54 (CA (Crim Div)), Fulford LJ

Reg.19, amended: SI 2014/549 Sch.1 para.35, SI 2014/870 Reg.4

Reg.27A, substituted: SI 2014/870 Reg.4

Reg.29, amended: SI 2014/870 Reg.4

Sch.1 para.12, see *R. v X Ltd* [2013] EWCA Crim 818, [2014] 1 W.L.R. 591 (CA (Crim Div)), Leveson LJ

Sch.1 para.22, see *R. v King (Scott)* [2014] EWCA Crim 621, [2014] 2 Cr. App. R. (S.) 54 (CA (Crim Div)), Fulford LJ

1317. Drinking Milk (England) Regulations 2008

Reg.9, revoked: SI 2014/1855 Sch.6 Part 1

1319. Electoral Administration Act 2006 (Regulation of Loans etc Northern Ireland) Order 2008

Art.5, substituted: 2014 c.13 s.2

Sch.1, amended: 2014 c.13 s.2

1331. Architects (Recognition of European Qualifications etc and Saving and Transitional Provision) Regulations 2008

Reg.26, revoked: SI 2014/4 Art.3

1338. Abortion (Amendment) (Wales) Regulations 2008

Reg.2, amended: 2014 c.29 s.4

Reg.3, amended: 2014 c.29 s.4

Reg.4, amended: 2014 c.29 s.4

1503. A282 Trunk Road (Dartford-Thurrock Crossing and Approach Roads) (Speed Limits) Order 2008

revoked: SI 2014/2519 Art.4

1512. Commissioner for Older People in Wales (Amendment) Regulations 2008

Reg.2, amended: 2014 c.29 s.4

Reg.3, amended: 2014 c.29 s.4

1596. Social Security (Recovery of Benefits) (Lump Sum Payments) Regulations 2008

Reg.1, amended: SI 2014/1456 Sch.1 para.2

Reg.4, amended: SI 2014/1456 Sch.1 para.3

Reg.4, substituted: SI 2014/1456 Sch.1 para.3

Reg.4A, added: SI 2014/1456 Sch.1 para.4

Reg.6, amended: SI 2014/1456 Sch.1 para.5

Reg.7, amended: SI 2014/1456 Sch.1 para.6

Reg.9, amended: SI 2014/1456 Sch.1 para.7

Reg.10, amended: SI 2014/1456 Sch.1 para.8

Reg.10, applied: SI 2014/916 Reg.26

Reg.12, amended: SI 2014/1456 Sch.1 para.9

Reg.12A, added: SI 2014/1456 Sch.1 para.10

Reg.13, amended: SI 2014/1456 Sch.1 para.11

Reg.14, amended: SI 2014/1456 Sch.1 para.12

Reg.16, amended: SI 2014/1456 Sch.1 para.13

Reg.17, amended: SI 2014/1456 Sch.1 para.14

Reg.19, amended: SI 2014/1456 Sch.1 para.15

Sch.1 para.1, amended: SI 2014/1456 Sch.1 para.16

Sch.1 para.4, amended: SI 2014/1456 Sch.1 para.16

Sch.1 para.6, amended: SI 2014/1456 Sch.1 para.16

Sch.1 para.7, amended: SI 2014/1456 Sch.1 para.16

Sch.1 para.11, amended: SI 2014/1456 Sch.1 para.16

Sch.1 para.12, amended: SI 2014/1456 Sch.1 para.16

Sch.1 para.13, amended: SI 2014/1456 Sch.1 para.16

Sch.1 para.15, amended: SI 2014/1456 Sch.1 para.16

Sch.1 para.18, amended: SI 2014/1456 Sch.1 para.16

1597. Supply of Machinery (Safety) Regulations 2008
 Reg.2, amended: SI 2014/469 Sch.3
 para.129
 Reg.21, amended: SI 2014/469 Sch.3
 para.129
 Reg.27, revoked (in part): SI 2014/3248
 Sch.4 Part 2
 Sch.5, amended: SI 2014/469 Sch.3 para.130
 Sch.5 para.1, amended: SI 2014/469 Sch.3
 para.130
 Sch.5 para.3A, added: SI 2014/469 Sch.3
 para.130
 Sch.5 para.7, amended: SI 2014/469 Sch.3
 para.130
 Sch.5 para.8, amended: SI 2014/469 Sch.3
 para.130

1598. Home Loss Payments (Prescribed Amounts) (England) Regulations 2008
 revoked: SI 2014/1966 Reg.3

1647. European Parliament (House of Lords Disqualification) Regulations 2008
 Reg.4, disapplied: 2014 c.24 s.6

1660. Cross-border Railway Services (Working Time) Regulations 2008
 Reg.17, amended: SI 2014/386 Sch.1
 para.54
 Reg.17A, added: SI 2014/386 Sch.1 para.55
 Reg.18, amended: SI 2014/386 Sch.1
 para.56

1732. Education (National Curriculum) (Foundation Stage) (Wales) Order 2008
 revoked: SI 2014/1996 Art.2

1741. Representation of the People (Northern Ireland) Regulations 2008
 referred to: SI 2014/1808 Reg.1
 Reg.3, amended: SI 2014/1808 Reg.2
 Reg.9, substituted: SI 2014/1808 Reg.3
 Reg.20, amended: 2014 c.13 s.15
 Reg.20, revoked (in part): 2014 c.13 s.15
 Reg.22, amended: 2014 c.13 s.15
 Reg.25, revoked (in part): 2014 c.13 s.14
 Reg.26A, added: SI 2014/1808 Reg.4
 Reg.27, amended: SI 2014/1808 Reg.5
 Reg.29, substituted: SI 2014/1808 Reg.6
 Reg.30, amended: SI 2014/1808 Reg.7
 Reg.36, amended: SI 2014/1808 Reg.8
 Reg.37, amended: SI 2014/1808 Reg.9
 Reg.38A, added: SI 2014/1808 Reg.10
 Reg.39, amended: SI 2014/1808 Reg.11
 Reg.41, amended: 2014 c.13 s.20

 Reg.41, applied: 2014 c.13 s.20
 Reg.43, amended: 2014 c.13 s.20
 Reg.43, applied: 2014 c.13 s.20
 Reg.50A, added: SI 2014/1808 Reg.12
 Reg.51, amended: SI 2014/1808 Reg.13
 Reg.53, amended: SI 2014/1808 Reg.14
 Reg.53A, added: SI 2014/1808 Reg.15
 Reg.53D, applied: SI 2014/1805 Reg.2, SI 2014/1806 Reg.2
 Reg.55, amended: SI 2014/1808 Reg.16
 Reg.55A, amended: SI 2014/1808 Reg.17
 Reg.55B, substituted: SI 2014/1808 Reg.18
 Reg.56, substituted: SI 2014/1808 Reg.19
 Reg.60, amended: SI 2014/1808 Reg.20
 Reg.66, amended: SI 2014/1808 Reg.21
 Reg.67, amended: SI 2014/1808 Reg.13
 Reg.72, amended: SI 2014/1808 Reg.22
 Reg.73, amended: SI 2014/1808 Reg.23
 Reg.75, amended: SI 2014/1808 Reg.24
 Reg.76, amended: SI 2014/1808 Reg.25
 Reg.81, amended: SI 2014/1808 Reg.26
 Reg.81A, added: SI 2014/1808 Reg.27
 Reg.84, substituted: SI 2014/1808 Reg.28
 Reg.91, amended: SI 2014/1808 Reg.29
 Reg.93, amended: SI 2014/1808 Reg.30
 Reg.109, amended: SI 2014/1808 Reg.13
 Reg.114, amended: SI 2014/1808 Reg.31
 Sch.3, added: SI 2014/1808 Reg.32
 Sch.3, amended: SI 2014/1808 Reg.32, Sch.2

1792. European Communities (Designation) (No.2) Order 2008
 Art.3, revoked: SI 2014/1362 Sch.1

1804. Childcare (Fees) Regulations 2008
 Reg.3, amended: SI 2014/1921 Reg.11
 Reg.4, amended: SI 2014/1921 Reg.12
 Reg.5, amended: SI 2014/1921 Reg.13
 Reg.6, amended: SI 2014/1921 Reg.14

1816. Cancellation of Contracts made in a Consumer's Home or Place of Work etc Regulations 2008
 see *Gibbs Gillespie (A Partnership) v Sturch* [2014] EWCA Civ 392, [2014] E.C.C. 31 (CA (Civ Div)), Kitchin LJ
 Reg.5, see *Robertson v Swift* [2014] UKSC 50, [2014] 1 W.L.R. 3438 (SC), Lady Hale JSC; see *Salat v Barutis* [2013] EWCA Civ 1499, [2014] E.C.C. 2 (CA (Civ Div)), Moore-Bick LJ

Reg.6, see *Gibbs Gillespie (A Partnership) v Sturch* [2014] EWCA Civ 392, [2014] E.C.C. 31 (CA (Civ Div)), Kitchin LJ
Reg.7, see *Robertson v Swift* [2014] UKSC 50, [2014] 1 W.L.R. 3438 (SC), Lady Hale JSC; see *Salat v Barutis* [2013] EWCA Civ 1499, [2014] E.C.C. 2 (CA (Civ Div)), Moore-Bick LJ
Reg.8, see *Robertson v Swift* [2014] UKSC 50, [2014] 1 W.L.R. 3438 (SC), Lady Hale JSC
Reg.17, see *Salat v Barutis* [2013] EWCA Civ 1499, [2014] E.C.C. 2 (CA (Civ Div)), Moore-Bick LJ

1863. Serious Crime Act 2007 (Appeals under Section 24) Order 2008
applied: SI 2014/1610 r.65_1, r.65_5, r.68_11
Part 3, applied: SI 2014/1610 r.76_1, r.76_4
Art.14, applied: SI 2014/1610 r.76_1, r.76_4
Art.15, applied: SI 2014/1610 r.76_6
Art.16, applied: SI 2014/1610 r.76_8
Art.17, applied: SI 2014/1610 r.76_9
Art.18, applied: SI 2014/1610 r.76_10
Art.31, applied: SI 2014/1610 r.76_1

1890. Welsh Language Schemes (Public Bodies) Order 2008
Sch.1, amended: SI 2014/549 Sch.1 para.55, SI 2014/3184 Sch.1 para.18

1898. Gas and Electricity (Consumer Complaints Handling Standards) Regulations 2008
Reg.2, amended: SI 2014/631 Sch.1 para.23
Reg.8, amended: SI 2014/631 Sch.1 para.23
Reg.9, amended: SI 2014/631 Sch.1 para.23

1907. Whole of Government Accounts (Designation of Bodies) (No.2) Order 2008
Sch.1, amended: 2014 c.29 s.4

1911. Limited Liability Partnerships (Accounts and Audit) (Application of Companies Act 2006) Regulations 2008
Reg.24, added: SI 2014/1815 Sch.1 para.22
Reg.24, amended: SI 2014/1815 Sch.1 para.22

1961. Commons Registration (England) Regulations 2008
revoked: SI 2014/3038 Reg.54

1963. Mesothelioma Lump Sum Payments (Conditions and Amounts) Regulations 2008
Sch.1, amended: SI 2014/868 Reg.2

1978. Proceeds of Crime Act 2002 (Investigative Powers of Prosecutors in England, Wales and Northern Ireland Code of Practice) Order 2008
applied: SI 2014/1893 Art.35

2034. Crossrail (Qualifying Authorities) Order 2008
Art.3, added: SI 2014/1367 Art.3

2036. Crossrail (Nomination) Order 2008
Art.5, added: SI 2014/1367 Art.2

2038. London Waste and Recycling Board Order 2008
Art.21, revoked (in part): 2014 c.2 Sch.1 Part 2

2175. Crossrail (Fees for Requests for Planning Approval) Regulations 2008
Reg.8, added: SI 2014/1382 Reg.2

2268. Gas and Electricity Regulated Providers (Redress Scheme) Order 2008
Art.2, amended: SI 2014/2378 Art.2

2298. Fire and Rescue Services (National Framework) (Wales) Order 2008
Art.2, amended: 2014 c.29 s.4

2349. Nitrate Pollution Prevention Regulations 2008
Reg.18, applied: SI 2014/3263 Sch.2 para.4
Reg.20, disapplied: SI 2014/3263 Sch.2 para.2

2425. Local Government Pension Scheme (Miscellaneous) Regulations 2008
revoked: SI 2014/525 Sch.1

2427. Wireless Telegraphy (Mobile Communication Services on Aircraft) (Exemption) Regulations 2008
revoked: SI 2014/953 Reg.2

2512. Felixstowe Branch Line and Ipswich Yard Improvement Order 2008
applied: SI 2014/1821 Art.6, Sch.1
Art.2, applied: SI 2014/1821 Art.15
Art.45, applied: SI 2014/1821 Art.15
Art.50, applied: SI 2014/1821 Art.15
Art.51, applied: SI 2014/1821 Art.8, Art.9
Sch.6, applied: SI 2014/1821 Art.6, Art.15
Sch.9, applied: SI 2014/1821 Art.15
Sch.9 para.2, applied: SI 2014/1821 Art.13

2551. Child Support Information Regulations 2008
Reg.6, amended: SI 2014/879 Art.121

2562. Air Navigation (Jersey) Order 2008
applied: SI 2014/2713 Art.2
revoked: SI 2014/2713 Art.2

2685. Tribunal Procedure (First-tier Tribunal) (Social Entitlement Chamber) Rules 2008
    applied: SI 2014/916 Reg.25
    Part 2 r.19, substituted: SI 2014/2128 r.35
    Part 3 r.22, amended: SI 2014/514 r.22
    r.27, see *M v Advocate General for Scotland*
    2014 S.L.T. 475 (OH), Lord Boyd of
    Duncansby

2698. Tribunal Procedure (Upper Tribunal) Rules 2008
    Part 1 r.1, amended: SI 2014/514 r.4, SI
    2014/2128 r.4
    Part 2 r.5, amended: SI 2014/514 r.5, SI
    2014/2128 r.5
    Part 2 r.5, revoked (in part): SI 2014/2128
    r.5
    Part 2 r.10, amended: SI 2014/514 r.6
    Part 2 r.12, revoked (in part): SI 2014/2128
    r.6
    Part 2 r.19, substituted: SI 2014/2128 r.7
    Part 3 r.21, amended: SI 2014/514 r.7, SI
    2014/2128 r.8
    Part 3 r.21, revoked (in part): SI 2014/2128
    r.8
    Part 3 r.22, amended: SI 2014/514 r.8, SI
    2014/1505 r.3, SI 2014/2128 r.9
    Part 3 r.22A, added: SI 2014/2128 r.10
    Part 3 r.24, amended: SI 2014/2128 r.11
    Part 3 r.26B, amended: SI 2014/514 r.9, r.10
    Part 4 r.30, amended: SI 2014/514 r.11
    Part 5 r.36A, amended: SI 2014/2128 r.12
    Part 5 r.37, amended: SI 2014/2128 r.13
    Part 6 r.40, amended: SI 2014/2128 r.14
    Part 6 r.40A, amended: SI 2014/1505 r.4
    Part 6 r.40A, revoked: SI 2014/2128 r.15
    r.2, see *Leeds City Council v Revenue and*
    Customs Commissioners [2014] UKUT 350
    (TCC), [2014] B.V.C. 531 (UT (Tax)),
    Judge Colin Bishopp; see *SM (Withdrawal*
    of Appealed Decision: Effect: Pakistan)
    [2014] UKUT 64 (IAC), [2014] Imm. A.R.
    662 (UT (IAC)), Judge Peter Lane
    r.5, see *AAN (Veil: Afghanistan)* [2014]
    UKUT 102 (IAC), [2014] Imm. A.R. 756
    (UT (IAC)), McCloskey J; see *Revenue and*
    Customs Commissioners v McCarthy and
    Stone (Developments) Ltd [2014] UKUT 196
    (TCC), [2014] S.T.C. 973 (UT (Tax)), Judge
    Greg Sinfield; see *Universal Enterprises*
    (EU) Ltd v Revenue and Customs

Commissioners [2014] S.T.C. 1515 (UT
(Tax)), Judge Colin Bishopp
    r.8, see *Universal Enterprises (EU) Ltd v*
    Revenue and Customs Commissioners
    [2014] S.T.C. 1515 (UT (Tax)), Judge Colin
    Bishopp
    r.10, see *Leeds City Council v Revenue and*
    Customs Commissioners [2014] UKUT 350
    (TCC), [2014] B.V.C. 531 (UT (Tax)),
    Judge Colin Bishopp; see *Softhouse*
    Consulting Ltd v Revenue and Customs
    Commissioners [2014] UKUT 197 (TCC),
    [2014] B.V.C. 511 (UT (Tax)), Judge Colin
    Bishopp
    r.17, see *SM (Withdrawal of Appealed*
    Decision: Effect: Pakistan) [2014] UKUT 64
    (IAC), [2014] Imm. A.R. 662 (UT (IAC)),
    Judge Peter Lane
    r.17A, see *SM (Withdrawal of Appealed*
    Decision: Effect: Pakistan) [2014] UKUT 64
    (IAC), [2014] Imm. A.R. 662 (UT (IAC)),
    Judge Peter Lane
    r.22, see *Softhouse Consulting Ltd v Revenue*
    and Customs Commissioners [2014] UKUT
    197 (TCC), [2014] B.V.C. 511 (UT (Tax)),
    Judge Colin Bishopp
    r.23, see *Revenue and Customs*
    Commissioners v McCarthy and Stone
    (Developments) Ltd [2014] UKUT 196
    (TCC), [2014] S.T.C. 973 (UT (Tax)), Judge
    Greg Sinfield
    r.24, see *Earlsferry Thistle Golf Club v*
    Revenue and Customs Commissioners
    [2014] UKUT 250 (TCC), [2014] S.T.C.
    2498 (UT (Tax)), Lord Tyre
    Sch.1 para.4, amended: SI 2014/2128 r.16
    Sch.3, amended: SI 2014/514 r.12
    Sch.3 para.1, amended: SI 2014/514 r.13
    Sch.3 para.3, amended: SI 2014/514 r.13
    Sch.3 para.7, amended: SI 2014/514 r.13
    Sch.3 para.9, amended: SI 2014/514 r.13

2699. Tribunal Procedure (First-tier Tribunal) (Health, Education and Social Care Chamber) Rules 2008
    Part 1 r.1, amended: SI 2014/2128 r.20
    Part 2 r.11, amended: SI 2014/2128 r.21
    Part 2 r.17, amended: SI 2014/2128 r.22
    Part 3 r.19, amended: SI 2014/2128 r.23
    Part 3 r.20, amended: SI 2014/2128 r.24
    Part 3 r.21, amended: SI 2014/2128 r.25
    Part 3 r.24, amended: SI 2014/2128 r.26

Part 3 r.26, amended: SI 2014/2128 r.27
Part 4 r.32, amended: SI 2014/514 r.17
Part 4 r.34, substituted: SI 2014/514 r.18
Part 4 r.37, amended: SI 2014/514 r.19
Part 4 r.39, amended: SI 2014/514 r.20
Sch.1, amended: SI 2014/2128 r.28

2701. Cardiff to Glan Conwy Trunk Road (A470) (Penloyn to Tan Lan Improvement) Order 2008
Art.3, amended: 2014 c.29 s.4
Art.4, amended: 2014 c.29 s.4

2713. Bail (Electronic Monitoring of Requirements) (Responsible Officer) Order 2008
revoked: SI 2014/669 Sch.1
Art.2, amended: SI 2014/163 Art.7
Sch.1, amended: SI 2014/163 Art.8

2768. Criminal Justice (Sentencing) (Curfew Condition) Order 2008
revoked: SI 2014/669 Sch.1
Art.2, amended: SI 2014/163 Art.10
Sch.1, amended: SI 2014/163 Art.11

2770. Non-Domestic Rating (Small Business Relief) (Wales) Order 2008
Art.7, amended: SI 2014/372 Art.2
Art.11, amended: SI 2014/372 Art.2
Art.11A, amended: SI 2014/372 Art.2

2829. Gambling Act 2005 (Advertising of Foreign Gambling) (Amendment) (No.2) Regulations 2008
revoked: 2014 c.17 s.3

2836. Allocation and Transfer of Proceedings Order 2008
revoked: SI 2014/879 Sch.1

2852. REACH Enforcement Regulations 2008
Reg.2, amended: SI 2014/469 Sch.3 para.132, SI 2014/2882 Reg.2
Reg.3, amended: SI 2014/469 Sch.3 para.133
Reg.3A, added: SI 2014/469 Sch.3 para.134
Reg.6, amended: SI 2014/469 Sch.3 para.135
Reg.8B, added: SI 2014/2882 Reg.2
Reg.11, amended: SI 2014/2882 Reg.2
Reg.17, amended: SI 2014/469 Sch.3 para.136
Reg.21, amended: SI 2014/469 Sch.3 para.137
Sch.1, amended: SI 2014/469 Sch.3 para.138
Sch.2 para.2, amended: SI 2014/469 Sch.3 para.139

Sch.3 Part 1 para.1, amended: SI 2014/3248
Sch.5 para.15
Sch.3 Part 3 para.1, amended: SI 2014/1638
Sch.13 para.21
Sch.5B, added: SI 2014/2882 Reg.2
Sch.6 Part 2, amended: SI 2014/469 Sch.3 para.140
Sch.6 Part 2 para.9, amended: SI 2014/469 Sch.3 para.140
Sch.6 Part 2 para.9B, added: SI 2014/469 Sch.3 para.140
Sch.7 Part 3, amended: SI 2014/469 Sch.3 para.141
Sch.7 Part 3 para.3, amended: SI 2014/469 Sch.3 para.141
Sch.8 Part 2, amended: SI 2014/469 Sch.3 para.142
Sch.8 Part 2 para.2, amended: SI 2014/469 Sch.3 para.142

2860. Companies Act 2006 (Commencement No 8, Transitional Provisions and Savings) Order 2008
applied: SI 2014/3348 Art.220
Sch.2, amended: 2014 c.29 s.4
Sch.2 para.43A, varied: SI 2014/3348 Art.220
Sch.2 para.114A, amended: 2014 c.29 s.4

2869. Political Donations and Regulated Transactions (Anonymous Electors) Regulations 2008
revoked: SI 2014/1806 Reg.3

2908. Crossrail (Planning Appeals) (Written Representations Procedure) (England) Regulations 2008
Reg.13, added: SI 2014/1382 Reg.3

2924. Merchant Shipping (Prevention of Air Pollution from Ships) Regulations 2008
Reg.2, amended: SI 2014/3076 Reg.2, SI 2014/3306 Sch.2 para.6
Reg.25, amended: SI 2014/3076 Reg.2
Reg.32, amended: SI 2014/3076 Reg.2
Reg.38, added: SI 2014/3076 Reg.2
Sch.2A para.1, amended: SI 2014/3076 Reg.2
Sch.2A para.2, amended: SI 2014/3076 Reg.2
Sch.2A para.3, amended: SI 2014/3076 Reg.2
Sch.2A para.4, amended: SI 2014/3076 Reg.2

Sch.2A para.5, amended: SI 2014/3076
Reg.2
Sch.2A para.7, amended: SI 2014/3076
Reg.2
Sch.2A para.7, revoked (in part): SI
2014/3076 Reg.2
Sch.2A para.10, amended: SI 2014/3076
Reg.2
2975. Rail Vehicle Accessibility Exemption Orders (Parliamentary Procedures) Regulations 2008
Reg.2, applied: SI 2014/3244
Reg.5, applied: SI 2014/2660
2989. Local Government Pension Scheme (Amendment) (No.2) Regulations 2008
revoked: SI 2014/525 Sch.1
2995. Judicial Appointments Order 2008
Sch.2, amended: SI 2014/2898 Art.3
2998. Pre-release Access to Official Statistics Order 2008
Sch.1 Part 1 para.3, amended: 2014 c.29 s.4
Sch.1 Part 2 para.15, amended: 2014 c.29 s.4
3004. Local Loans (Increase of Limit) Order 2008
revoked: 2014 c.26 s.300
3048. Immigration (Biometric Registration) Regulations 2008
Reg.3, applied: SI 2014/581 Sch.3 para.2
3087. Transfrontier Shipment of Radioactive Waste and Spent Fuel Regulations 2008
Sch.1 Part 1 para.2, amended: SI 2014/469 Sch.3 para.143
Sch.1 Part 2 para.6, amended: SI 2014/469 Sch.3 para.143
3093. School Information (England) Regulations 2008
Reg.2, amended: SI 2014/2103 Art.29
Sch.4 para.10, substituted: SI 2014/2103 Art.29
3100. Smoke Control Areas (Authorised Fuels) (Wales) Regulations 2008
revoked: SI 2014/684 Reg.3
3117. European Communities (Designation) (No.4) Order 2008
revoked: SI 2014/1362 Art.4
3128. United Nations Arms Embargoes (Rwanda) (Amendment) Order 2008
revoked: SI 2014/2711 Sch.1

3138. London To Fishguard Trunk Road (A40) (Penblewin To Slebech Park Improvement) Order 2008
Art.5, amended: 2014 c.29 s.4
3151. Tax Credits Act 2002 (Transitional Provisions) Order 2008
Art.3, revoked (in part): SI 2014/1848 Art.4
3154. Transmissible Spongiform Encephalopathies (Wales) Regulations 2008
Reg.2, amended: SI 2014/517 Sch.2 para.7
Reg.4, amended: SI 2014/517 Sch.2 para.7
3206. Spirit Drinks Regulations 2008
Sch.2 Part 2, amended: SI 2014/1855 Sch.7 para.54
3231. Export Control Order 2008
Sch.1, amended: SI 2014/702 Art.2
Sch.1 Part 2, substituted: SI 2014/702 Art.2
Sch.2, substituted: SI 2014/1069 Sch.1
Sch.3, amended: SI 2014/1069 Art.2
Sch.3, substituted: SI 2014/1069 Art.2
Sch.4 Part 2, amended: SI 2014/2357 Art.13
Sch.4 Part 4, amended: SI 2014/2357 Art.13
3245. Local Government Pension Scheme (Administration) (Amendment) Regulations 2008
revoked: SI 2014/525 Sch.1
3257. Merchant Shipping (Prevention of Pollution by Sewage and Garbage from Ships) Regulations 2008
referred to: SSI 2014/324 Sch.1 para.12
Reg.2, amended: SI 2014/3306 Sch.2 para.7

2009

138. Hill Farm Allowance Regulations 2009
revoked: SI 2014/112 Reg.9
198. Immigration (Passenger Transit Visa) (Amendment) Order 2009
revoked: SI 2014/2702 Sch.2
209. Payment Services Regulations 2009
applied: SI 2014/1195 Art.2, SI 2014/1825 Art.3, SI 2014/2418 Sch.1
Part 9, amended: SI 2014/549 Sch.1 para.36
Reg.2, amended: SI 2014/549 Sch.1 para.36
Reg.52, amended: SI 2014/366 Art.12
Reg.52, applied: SI 2014/366 Art.13
Reg.92A, added: SI 2014/366 Art.12
Reg.93, applied: SI 2014/1195 Art.2
Reg.98, amended: SI 2014/549 Sch.1 para.36

Reg.99, amended: SI 2014/549 Sch.1
para.36
Reg.100, amended: SI 2014/549 Sch.1
para.36
Reg.102, amended: SI 2014/549 Sch.1
para.36
Reg.103, amended: SI 2014/549 Sch.1
para.36
Reg.104, amended: SI 2014/549 Sch.1
para.36
Reg.105, amended: SI 2014/549 Sch.1
para.36
Reg.106, amended: SI 2014/549 Sch.1
para.36
Reg.107, amended: SI 2014/549 Sch.1
para.36
Reg.108, amended: SI 2014/549 Sch.1
para.36
Reg.109, amended: SI 2014/549 Sch.1
para.36
Reg.114, amended: SI 2014/549 Sch.1
para.36
Reg.117, amended: SI 2014/549 Sch.1
para.36
Reg.119, amended: SI 2014/549 Sch.1
para.36
Sch.4A, added: SI 2014/366 Art.12
Sch.5 Part 1 para.3, amended: SI 2014/366
Art.12
Sch.5 Part 1 para.7, amended: SI 2014/366
Art.12

**214. Companies (Disclosure of Address)
Regulations 2009**
Sch.1, amended: SI 2014/469 Sch.3
para.195, SI 2014/549 Sch.1 para.37, SI
2014/631 Sch.2 para.11

**216. Ozone-Depleting Substances
(Qualifications) Regulations 2009**
Reg.5, applied: SSI 2014/319 Sch.2 para.18
Reg.6, applied: SSI 2014/319 Sch.2 para.18
Reg.9, applied: SSI 2014/319 Sch.2 para.18

**273. Tribunal Procedure (First-tier Tribunal)
(Tax Chamber) Rules 2009**
r.2, see *Revenue and Customs
Commissioners v Ingenious Games LLP*
[2014] UKUT 62 (TCC), [2014] S.T.C. 1416
(UT (Tax)), Sales J
r.5, see *Eclipse Film Partners No.35 LLP v
Revenue and Customs Commissioners*
[2014] EWCA Civ 184, [2014] C.P. Rep. 26
(CA (Civ Div)), Moses LJ

r.8, see *Fairford Group Ltd Plc (In
Liquidation) v Revenue and Customs
Commissioners* [2014] UKUT 329 (TCC),
[2014] B.V.C. 529 (UT (Tax)), Simon J
r.9, see *MCashback Software 6 LLP v
Revenue and Customs Commissioners*
[2014] S.F.T.D. 510 (FTT (Tax)), Judge
Jonathan Cannan
r.10, see *Eclipse Film Partners No.35 LLP v
Revenue and Customs Commissioners*
[2014] EWCA Civ 184, [2014] C.P. Rep. 26
(CA (Civ Div)), Moses LJ; see *Reddrock
Ltd v Revenue and Customs Commissioners*
[2014] UKUT 61 (TCC), [2014] S.T.C. 1643
(UT (Tax)), David Richards J; see *Tarafdar
(t/a Shah Indian Cuisine) v Revenue and
Customs Commissioners* [2014] UKUT 362
(TCC), [2014] B.V.C. 533 (UT (Tax)),
Judge Roger Berner
r.18, see *288 Group Ltd v Revenue and
Customs Commissioners* [2014] S.F.T.D.
592 (FTT (Tax)), Judge Barbara Mosedale;
see *General Healthcare Group Ltd v
Revenue and Customs Commissioners*
[2014] UKFTT 353 (TC), [2014] S.F.T.D.
1026 (FTT (Tax)), Judge Roger Berner
r.38, see *Rosenbaum's Executor v Revenue
and Customs Commissioners* [2014]
W.T.L.R. 351 (FTT (Tax)), Judge Guy
Brannan

275. Appeals (Excluded Decisions) Order 2009
Art.3, see *Singh v Secretary of State for the
Home Department* [2014] EWCA Civ 438,
[2014] 1 W.L.R. 3585 (CA (Civ Div)),
Arden LJ

**309. Local Authority Social Services and
National Health Service Complaints (England)
Regulations 2009**
applied: SI 2014/3090 Art.6, SI 2014/3218
Art.5
see *R. (on the application of Bhatti) v Bury
MBC* [2013] EWHC 3093 (Admin), (2014)
17 C.C.L. Rep. 64 (QBD (Admin)), Judge
Pelling QC

**319. Banking Act 2009 (Third Party
Compensation Arrangements for Partial
Property Transfers) Regulations 2009**
Reg.1, amended: SI 2014/1830 Reg.2, SI
2014/3329 Art.126
Reg.2, amended: SI 2014/3329 Art.126
Reg.4, substituted: SI 2014/3329 Art.126

Reg.5, amended: SI 2014/3329 Art.126
Reg.6, amended: SI 2014/3329 Art.126
Reg.8, amended: SI 2014/3329 Art.126
Reg.9, amended: SI 2014/3329 Art.126
322. Banking Act 2009 (Restriction of Partial Property Transfers) Order 2009
Art.1, amended: SI 2014/1831 Art.4, SI 2014/3329 Art.125
Art.2, amended: SI 2014/1828 Art.13, SI 2014/3329 Art.125
Art.8, amended: SI 2014/3329 Art.125
Art.9, revoked: SI 2014/3329 Art.125
Art.9A, added: SI 2014/1831 Art.4
Art.10, amended: SI 2014/3329 Art.125
Art.12, amended: SI 2014/3329 Art.125
393. Allocation of Housing and Homelessness (Eligibility) (Wales) Regulations 2009
revoked: SI 2014/2603 Reg.7
404. Finance Act 2008, Schedule 36 (Appointed Day and Savings) Order 2009
see *R. (on the application of Derrin Brother Properties Ltd) v Revenue and Customs Commissioners* [2014] EWHC 1152 (Admin), [2014] S.T.C. 2238 (QBD (Admin)), Simler J
Art.3, see *R. (on the application of Derrin Brother Properties Ltd) v Revenue and Customs Commissioners* [2014] EWHC 1152 (Admin), [2014] S.T.C. 2238 (QBD (Admin)), Simler J
447. Local Government Pension Scheme (Administration) (Amendment) Regulations 2009
revoked: SI 2014/525 Sch.1
463. Aquatic Animal Health (England and Wales) Regulations 2009
Reg.6, applied: SI 2014/3303 Reg.3
470. Education (Student Loans) (Repayment) Regulations 2009
Part 3, applied: SI 2014/651 Reg.1
Reg.23, amended: SI 2014/651 Reg.3
Reg.29, amended: SI 2014/651 Reg.4
Reg.29, revoked (in part): SI 2014/651 Reg.4
Reg.58, amended: SI 2014/651 Reg.5
Reg.59B, amended: SI 2014/651 Reg.6
Reg.59E, amended: SI 2014/651 Reg.7
Reg.59F, amended: SI 2014/651 Reg.8
Reg.59G, amended: SI 2014/651 Reg.9
Reg.63, amended: SI 2014/651 Reg.10
Reg.68, amended: SI 2014/651 Reg.11

Reg.76, amended: SI 2014/651 Reg.12
491. Road Safety (Financial Penalty Deposit) Order 2009
Sch.1 Part 1, amended: SI 2014/267 Art.2
492. Road Safety (Financial Penalty Deposit) (Appropriate Amount) Order 2009
Art.1, amended: SI 2014/2766 Art.2
Sch.1 Part 1, amended: SI 2014/802 Art.2, SI 2014/2766 Art.3
Sch.2, amended: SI 2014/2766 Art.4
510. Designation of Schools Having a Religious Character (Independent Schools) (England) Order 2009
Sch.1, amended: SI 2014/2342 Sch.2
648. Electricity and Gas Appeals (Designation and Exclusion) Order 2009
revoked: SI 2014/1293 Sch.1
665. Co-ordination of Regulatory Enforcement (Enforcement Action) Order 2009
Art.2, amended: SI 2014/573 Art.2, SI 2014/3070 Art.2
Art.2, revoked (in part): SI 2014/573 Art.2, SI 2014/3070 Art.2
Art.3, amended: SI 2014/573 Art.2
692. Pensions Increase (Review) Order 2009
referred to: SI 2014/668 Sch.1
Art.6, substituted: SI 2014/107 Sch.1
para.56, SI 2014/3229 Sch.6 para.35
693. Health and Safety (Miscellaneous Amendments and Revocations) Regulations 2009
Reg.2, amended: SI 2014/1638 Sch.13 para.22
Reg.2, revoked (in part): SI 2014/1638 Sch.13 para.22, Sch.14 Part 2
Sch.1 para.1, revoked: SI 2014/1638 Sch.14 Part 2
Sch.1 para.4, revoked: SI 2014/1638 Sch.14 Part 2
711. Department for Transport (Fees) Order 2009
Sch.1 Part 2 para.7, referred to: SI 2014/2118
Sch.1 Part 3 para.21, referred to: SI 2014/2114
Sch.1 Part 3 para.24, referred to: SI 2014/2114
Sch.1 Part 3 para.28, referred to: SI 2014/2115
Sch.1 Part 3 para.32, referred to: SI 2014/2115

Sch.1 Part 3 para.36, referred to: SI
2014/2115
Sch.1 Part 4 para.42, referred to: SI
2014/2116
Sch.1 Part 5 para.44, referred to: SI
2014/2119
Sch.2, referred to: SI 2014/2114, SI
2014/2115, SI 2014/2116, SI 2014/2118, SI
2014/2119

**716. Chemicals (Hazard Information and
Packaging for Supply) Regulations 2009**
Reg.7, amended: SI 2014/1637 Sch.4 para.8

**774. Financial Services and Markets Act 2000
(Controllers) (Exemption) Order 2009**
Art.6A, amended: SI 2014/366 Art.14

**779. Local Health Boards (Constitution,
Membership and Procedures) (Wales)
Regulations 2009**
Reg.3, referred to: SI 2014/566 Reg.5
Reg.17, amended: SI 2014/1815 Sch.1
para.23

**781. European Parliamentary Elections (Welsh
Forms) Order 2009**
revoked: SI 2014/704 Art.3

785. Renewables Obligation Order 2009
applied: SI 2014/893 Art.24, SI 2014/2043
Reg.16
Part 5, amended: SI 2014/893 Art.6
Art.2, amended: SI 2014/893 Art.2
Art.3, amended: SI 2014/893 Art.3
Art.17AB, substituted: SI 2014/893 Art.4
Art.21A, added: SI 2014/893 Art.5
Art.23A, added: SI 2014/893 Art.6
Art.24, amended: SI 2014/893 Art.7
Art.24, revoked (in part): SI 2014/893 Art.7
Art.25, substituted: SI 2014/893 Art.8
Art.26, amended: SI 2014/893 Art.9
Art.30B, amended: SI 2014/893 Art.10
Art.41, amended: SI 2014/893 Art.11
Art.53, amended: SI 2014/893 Art.12
Art.54, amended: SI 2014/893 Art.13
Art.54A, amended: SI 2014/893 Art.14
Art.54B, added: SI 2014/893 Art.15
Art.57, amended: SI 2014/893 Art.16
Art.58, substituted: SI 2014/893 Art.17
Art.58A, amended: SI 2014/893 Art.19
Art.58B, added: SI 2014/893 Art.20
Art.58ZA, amended: SI 2014/893 Art.18
Art.60, amended: SI 2014/893 Art.21
Sch.A2 para.3, amended: SI 2014/893 Art.22
Sch.3A para.2, amended: SI 2014/893 Art.23

**805. Building Societies (Insolvency and Special
Administration) Order 2009**
Sch.1 Part 3 para.32ZA, added: SI
2014/3344 Art.5

**847. Zimbabwe (Financial Sanctions)
Regulations 2009**
Reg.3, substituted: SI 2014/383 Reg.3
Reg.3A, added: SI 2014/383 Reg.4
Reg.4, revoked: SI 2014/383 Reg.6
Reg.15, amended: SI 2014/383 Reg.5

**858. Family Proceedings Courts (Miscellaneous
Amendments) Rules 2009**
r.6, amended: 2014 c.29 s.4

**859. Data Retention (EC Directive) Regulations
2009**
applied: 2014 c.27 s.1, SI 2014/2042 Reg.14
revoked: SI 2014/2042 Reg.14
Sch.1, applied: 2014 c.27 s.2, SI 2014/2042
Reg.3

**871. Access to Justice Act 1999 (Destination of
Appeals) (Family Proceedings) Order 2009**
Art.2, revoked: SI 2014/879 Art.122
Art.4, revoked (in part): SI 2014/879 Art.122
Art.10, revoked: SI 2014/879 Art.122

873. Distress for Rent (Amendment) Rules 2009
revoked: SI 2014/600 Sch.1 Part 2

**890. Waste Batteries and Accumulators
Regulations 2009**
Reg.11, applied: SSI 2014/319 Sch.2 para.16
Reg.13, applied: SSI 2014/319 Sch.2 para.16
Reg.16, applied: SSI 2014/319 Sch.2 para.16
Reg.27, applied: SSI 2014/319 Sch.2 para.16
Reg.29, applied: SSI 2014/319 Sch.2 para.16
Reg.89, applied: SSI 2014/319 Sch.2 para.16

**975. Proceeds of Crime Act 2002 (References to
Financial Investigators) Order 2009**
Sch.1, amended: SI 2014/467 Art.5, SI
2014/549 Sch.1 para.38

**1025. Local Government Pension Scheme
(Amendment) Regulations 2009**
revoked: SI 2014/525 Sch.1

**1069. European Parliamentary Elections
(Returning Officers Charges) (Great Britain and
Gibraltar) Order 2009**
revoked: SI 2014/325 Art.3

**1077. European Parliamentary Elections (Local
Returning Officers Charges) (England, Wales
and Gibraltar) Order 2009**
revoked: SI 2014/325 Art.3

1085. Company and Business Names (Miscellaneous Provisions) Regulations 2009
> Sch.2 para.3, amended: SI 2014/1815 Sch.1 para.24

1107. Armed Forces (Protection of Children of Service Families) Regulations 2009
> Reg.5, amended: SI 2014/852 Art.17

1114. Upper Tribunal (Lands Chamber) Fees Order 2009
> Sch.2 para.1, amended: SI 2014/513 Sch.1 para.18, SI 2014/590 Art.6

1120. European Parliamentary Elections (Local Returning Officers Charges) (Scotland) Order 2009
> revoked: SI 2014/325 Art.3

1143. European Parliamentary Elections (Returning Officer's Charges) (Northern Ireland) Order 2009
> revoked: SI 2014/794 Art.3

1171. Registered Pension Schemes (Authorised Payments) Regulations 2009
> Reg.3A, added: 2014 c.26 Sch.5 para.6
> Reg.6, amended: 2014 c.26 s.42
> Reg.6, applied: SSI 2014/164 Reg.33
> Reg.8, amended: 2014 c.26 s.42
> Reg.10, amended: 2014 c.26 s.42
> Reg.10, substituted: 2014 c.30 Sch.1 para.73
> Reg.11, amended: 2014 c.26 s.42
> Reg.11, applied: SSI 2014/164 Reg.33, SSI 2014/217 Reg.168, SSI 2014/292 Reg.168
> Reg.11, referred to: SI 2014/512 Reg.174
> Reg.11A, amended: 2014 c.26 s.42
> Reg.12, amended: 2014 c.26 s.42
> Reg.12, applied: SSI 2014/164 Reg.33, SSI 2014/217 Reg.168, SSI 2014/292 Reg.168
> Reg.12, referred to: SI 2014/512 Reg.174

1182. Health Care and Associated Professions (Miscellaneous Amendments and Practitioner Psychologists) Order 2009
> Art.7, applied: SI 2014/936 Art.2, SI 2014/1981 Art.2
> Art.7, enabled: SI 2014/936, SI 2014/1981

1229. Immigration (Passenger Transit Visa) (Amendment) (No.3) Order 2009
> revoked: SI 2014/2702 Sch.2

1233. Immigration (Passenger Transit Visa) (Amendment) (No.4) Order 2009
> revoked: SI 2014/2702 Sch.2

1299. Swine Vesicular Disease Regulations 2009
> revoked: SI 2014/1894 Sch.5

1302. Infrastructure Planning (National Policy Statement Consultation) Regulations 2009
> revoked: SI 2014/692 Sch.1
> Reg.3, amended: SI 2014/631 Sch.1 para.24

1348. Carriage of Dangerous Goods and Use of Transportable Pressure Equipment Regulations 2009
> applied: SI 2014/469 Sch.1 para.3, Sch.4 para.24, SI 2014/1637 Reg.21, SI 2014/1639 Reg.4
> disapplied: SI 2014/1638 Reg.2, Reg.3
> Reg.2, amended: SI 2014/469 Sch.3 para.28
> Reg.7, amended: SI 2014/1638 Sch.13 para.23
> Reg.12, amended: SI 2014/469 Sch.3 para.28
> Reg.14, amended: SI 2014/1639 Sch.2 para.2
> Reg.25, amended: SI 2014/469 Sch.3 para.28
> Reg.25, applied: SI 2014/1638 Reg.35
> Reg.27, disapplied: SI 2014/469 Sch.1 para.3
> Reg.29, disapplied: SI 2014/469 Sch.1 para.3
> Reg.32, substituted: SI 2014/469 Sch.3 para.28
> Reg.32A, added: SI 2014/469 Sch.3 para.28
> Sch.3 para.1, disapplied: SI 2014/469 Sch.1 para.3
> Sch.3 para.3, disapplied: SI 2014/469 Sch.1 para.3

1352. General Teaching Council for Wales (Constitution) (Amendment) Regulations 2009
> revoked: SI 2014/2365 Sch.1

1372. Swine Vesicular Disease (Wales) Regulations 2009
> revoked: SI 2014/1894 Sch.5

1385. Public Health Wales National Health Service Trust (Membership and Procedure) Regulations 2009
> Reg.1, amended: SI 2014/1815 Sch.1 para.25

1505. Fishguard to Bangor Trunk Road (A487) (Porthmadog, Minffordd and Tremadog Bypass and De-trunking) Order 2009
> Art.3, amended: 2014 c.29 s.4
> Art.4, amended: 2014 c.29 s.4
> Art.5, amended: 2014 c.29 s.4

1547. Childcare (Disqualification) Regulations 2009
Reg.4, amended: SI 2014/1921 Reg.16
Reg.5, amended: SI 2014/1921 Reg.17
Reg.6, amended: SI 2014/1921 Reg.18
Reg.7, amended: SI 2014/1921 Reg.19
Reg.8, amended: SI 2014/1921 Reg.20
Reg.9, amended: SI 2014/1921 Reg.21
Reg.10, amended: SI 2014/1921 Reg.22
Reg.12, amended: SI 2014/1921 Reg.23

1551. Marketing of Fresh Horticultural Produce (Wales) Regulations 2009
Reg.9, amended: 2014 c.29 s.4
Reg.10, amended: 2014 c.29 s.4
Reg.11, amended: 2014 c.29 s.4
Reg.13, amended: 2014 c.29 s.4

1554. Childcare (Provision of Information About Young Children) (England) Regulations 2009
Reg.2, amended: SI 2014/2103 Art.30, SI 2014/3197 Reg.3
Reg.4, amended: SI 2014/3197 Reg.4
Reg.4A, added: SI 2014/3197 Reg.5
Reg.5, substituted: SI 2014/3197 Reg.6
Sch.1 Part 2 para.12, amended: SI 2014/3197 Reg.7

1557. Meat (Official Controls Charges) (Wales) Regulations 2009
Reg.2, amended: SI 2014/951 Sch.6 para.1

1563. Education (Individual Pupil Information) (Prescribed Persons) (England) Regulations 2009
Reg.2, amended: SI 2014/2103 Art.31

1574. Meat (Official Controls Charges) (England) Regulations 2009
Reg.2, amended: SI 2014/1240 Sch.6 para.4

1580. Swine Vesicular Disease (Wales) (Amendment) Regulations 2009
revoked: SI 2014/1894 Sch.5

1586. Education (Outturn Statements) (England) Regulations 2009
Reg.2, amended: SI 2014/2103 Art.32

1603. Supreme Court Rules 2009
see *Bank Mellat v HM Treasury* [2014] A.C. 700 (SC), Lord Neuberger PSC
Part 1 r.3, amended: 2014 c.29 s.4
r.27, see *Bank Mellat v HM Treasury* [2014] A.C. 700 (SC), Lord Neuberger PSC
r.29, see *Bank Mellat v HM Treasury* [2014] A.C. 700 (SC), Lord Neuberger PSC

1606. Education and Skills Act 2008 (Commencement No 4, Commencement No 3 (Amendment), Transitory and Saving Provisions) Order 2009
Art.5, revoked: SI 2014/3364 Sch.1

1771. Common Agricultural Policy Single Payment and Support Schemes (Horticulture) Regulations 2009
revoked: SI 2014/3259 Reg.15

1801. Overseas Companies Regulations 2009
Sch.1, amended: SI 2014/469 Sch.3
para.196, SI 2014/549 Sch.1 para.39, SI 2014/631 Sch.2 para.12

1803. Registrar of Companies and Applications for Striking Off Regulations 2009
Reg.8, amended: SI 2014/2382 Reg.36

1804. Limited Liability Partnerships (Application of Companies Act 2006) Regulations 2009
Reg.8, applied: SI 2014/3140 Reg.2
Reg.8, enabled: SI 2014/3140
Reg.17, applied: SI 2014/3140 Reg.2
Reg.46, varied: SI 2014/3348 Art.218
Reg.50, added: SI 2014/1602 Art.3
Reg.50, amended: SI 2014/1602 Art.3
Reg.50, substituted: SI 2014/1602 Art.3
Reg.63, amended: SI 2014/3209 Reg.20
Reg.81, enabled: SI 2014/3140

1887. Community Care, Services for Carers and Children's Services (Direct Payments) (England) Regulations 2009
applied: SI 2014/1652 Reg.8
Reg.7, applied: SI 2014/829 Sch.1 para.22
Reg.8, applied: SI 2014/829 Sch.1 para.23
Reg.9, applied: SI 2014/829 Sch.1 para.24
Reg.10, applied: SI 2014/829 Sch.1 para.25
Reg.11, applied: SI 2014/829 Sch.1 para.26
Reg.12, applied: SI 2014/829 Sch.1 para.27
Reg.17, applied: SI 2014/829 Sch.1 para.28
Reg.18, applied: SI 2014/829 Sch.1 para.29

1914. Heavy Goods Vehicles (Charging for the Use of Certain Infrastructure on the Trans-European Road Network) Regulations 2009
Reg.2, amended: SI 2014/2437 Reg.2
Reg.3, amended: SI 2014/2437 Reg.2
Reg.4, amended: SI 2014/2437 Reg.2
Reg.4, substituted: SI 2014/2437 Reg.2
Reg.4A, added: SI 2014/2437 Reg.2
Reg.5, substituted: SI 2014/2437 Reg.2
Reg.6, revoked: SI 2014/2437 Reg.2
Reg.8, amended: SI 2014/2437 Reg.2

Reg.9, amended: SI 2014/2437 Reg.2
Reg.10, substituted: SI 2014/2437 Reg.2
Reg.12, amended: SI 2014/2437 Reg.2
Reg.12A, added: SI 2014/2437 Reg.2
Reg.13, amended: SI 2014/2437 Reg.2
Reg.13, revoked (in part): SI 2014/2437
Reg.2
Reg.14, amended: SI 2014/2437 Reg.2
Reg.15, amended: SI 2014/2437 Reg.2
Reg.16, substituted: SI 2014/2437 Reg.2
Reg.17, amended: SI 2014/2437 Reg.2
Reg.17, revoked (in part): SI 2014/2437
Reg.2
Reg.18, amended: SI 2014/2437 Reg.2
Reg.18, revoked (in part): SI 2014/2437
Reg.2
Reg.19, revoked: SI 2014/2437 Reg.2
Reg.20, substituted: SI 2014/2437 Reg.2
Reg.20A, added: SI 2014/2437 Reg.2
Reg.21, amended: SI 2014/2437 Reg.2
1917. Overseas Companies (Execution of Documents and Registration of Charges) Regulations 2009
Reg.4, see *Habas Sinai Ve Tibbi Gazlar Istihsal Endustrisi v VSC Steel Co Ltd* [2013] EWHC 4071 (Comm), [2014] 1 Lloyd's Rep. 479 (QBD (Comm)), Hamblen J
1931. Solicitors (Non-Contentious Business) Remuneration Order 2009
applied: SI 2014/2072 Sch.1 para.3
1941. Companies Act 2006 (Consequential Amendments, Transitional Provisions and Savings) Order 2009
Sch.1 para.14, revoked: 2014 c.14 Sch.7
Sch.1 para.16, revoked: 2014 c.14 Sch.7
Sch.1 para.173, revoked: 2014 c.2 Sch.1 Part 2
1973. Whole of Government Accounts (Designation of Bodies) Order 2009
Sch.1, amended: 2014 c.29 s.4
1976. Tribunal Procedure (First-tier Tribunal) (General Regulatory Chamber) Rules 2009
applied: SI 2014/631 Sch.3 para.6
see *Browning v Information Commissioner* [2014] EWCA Civ 1050, [2014] 1 W.L.R. 3848 (CA (Civ Div)), Maurice Kay LJ
Part 3 r.22, amended: SI 2014/2128 r.18
r.5, see *Browning v Information Commissioner* [2014] EWCA Civ 1050,

[2014] 1 W.L.R. 3848 (CA (Civ Div)), Maurice Kay LJ
r.35, see *Browning v Information Commissioner* [2014] EWCA Civ 1050, [2014] 1 W.L.R. 3848 (CA (Civ Div)), Maurice Kay LJ
2018. Commons Registration (England) (Amendment) Regulations 2009
revoked: SI 2014/3038 Reg.54
2023. Family Law Act 1996 (Forced Marriage)(Relevant Third Party) Order 2009
see *Bedfordshire Constabulary v RU* [2013] EWHC 2350 (Fam), [2014] Fam. 69 (Fam Div), Holman J
2048. Port Security Regulations 2009
applied: SI 2014/8 Art.3, Art.4, Sch.2 para.3, SI 2014/82 Art.3, Sch.2 para.3, SI 2014/577 Art.3, Art.4, Sch.2 para.3, SI 2014/604 Art.3, Art.4, Sch.2 para.3, SI 2014/1811 Art.2, Art.3, Art.4, Sch.2 para.3, SI 2014/2007 Art.3, Sch.2 para.3
Reg.2, applied: SI 2014/8 Art.2, SI 2014/577 Art.2, SI 2014/604 Art.2, SI 2014/2007 Art.2
2056. Armed Forces (Powers of Stop and Search, Search, Seizure and Retention) Order 2009
Art.2, amended: SI 2014/934 Art.2
2108. Ecclesiastical Offices (Terms of Service) Regulations 2009
applied: SI 2014/895 Sch.2 para.4
Reg.9, amended: SI 2014/431 Sch.1 para.36
Reg.9A, added: SI 2014/431 Sch.1 para.37
Reg.30, amended: SI 2014/2083 Reg.2
Reg.32, applied: SI 2014/895 Sch.2 para.4
2131. Supreme Court Fees Order 2009
Sch.2 para.1, amended: SI 2014/513 Sch.1 para.19, SI 2014/590 Art.6
2158. Assembly Learning Grant (Further Education) Regulations 2009
Reg.2, amended: 2014 c.29 s.4
Reg.3, amended: 2014 c.29 s.4
2163. Eggs and Chicks (England) Regulations 2009
Reg.3, amended: SI 2014/1855 Sch.7 para.56
Sch.2 Part 2, amended: SI 2014/1855 Sch.7 para.57
2263. Infrastructure Planning (Environmental Impact Assessment) Regulations 2009
applied: SI 2014/3331 Art.32
referred to: SI 2014/3328 Art.3
Reg.3, applied: SI 2014/3328

2264. Infrastructure Planning (Applications Prescribed Forms and Procedure) Regulations 2009
applied: SI 2014/909, SI 2014/1052, SI 2014/1599, SI 2014/1796, SI 2014/1873, SI 2014/2269, SI 2014/2384, SI 2014/2434, SI 2014/2637, SI 2014/2846, SI 2014/2935, SI 2014/3331
Reg.5, amended: SI 2014/2381 Reg.2
Sch.1, amended: SI 2014/469 Sch.3 para.197

2268. Non-Domestic Rating (Alteration of Lists and Appeals) (England) Regulations 2009
Reg.4, see *GPS (Great Britain) Ltd v Bird (Valuation Officer)* [2014] R.A. 145 (UT (Lands)), NJ Rose, FRICS; see *Pearce's Appeal, Re* [2014] UKUT 291 (LC), [2014] R.A. 341 (UT (Lands)), Martin Rodger Q.C.
Reg.6, see *Mayday Optical Co Ltd v Kendrick (Valuation Officer)* [2014] R.A. 45 (UT (Lands)), Judge Huskinson
Reg.8, see *Mayday Optical Co Ltd v Kendrick (Valuation Officer)* [2014] R.A. 45 (UT (Lands)), Judge Huskinson
Reg.14, see *BMC Properties and Management Ltd v Jackson (Valuation Officer)* [2014] UKUT 93 (LC), [2014] R.A. 309 (UT (Lands)), Martin Rodger Q.C.

2269. Valuation Tribunal for England (Council Tax and Rating Appeals) (Procedure) Regulations 2009
Reg.38, see *Metis Apartments Ltd v Grace (Valuation Officer)* [2014] R.A. 222 (VT), Graham Zellick Q.C. (President); see *SC v East Riding of Yorkshire Council* [2014] R.A. 279 (VT), Graham Zellick Q.C. (President)

2270. Council Tax (Alteration of Lists and Appeals) (England) Regulations 2009
Reg.3, see *Kelderman v Valuation Office Agency* [2014] EWHC 1592 (Admin), [2014] R.V.R. 323 (QBD (Admin)), Nicol J
Reg.11, see *Kelderman v Valuation Office Agency* [2014] EWHC 1592 (Admin), [2014] R.V.R. 323 (QBD (Admin)), Nicol J

2401. European Public Limited-Liability Company (Employee Involvement) (Great Britain) Regulations 2009
Reg.28, amended: SI 2014/386 Sch.1 para.58
Reg.28A, added: SI 2014/386 Sch.1 para.59

Reg.39, amended: SI 2014/386 Sch.1 para.60, SI 2014/431 Sch.1 para.38

2455. Civil Courts (Amendment) Order 2009
revoked: SI 2014/820 Sch.1

2460. National Savings Bank (Investment Deposits) (Limits) (Amendment) Order 2009
revoked: SI 2014/484 Art.3

2476. Companies Act 2006 and Limited Liability Partnerships (Transitional Provisions and Savings) (Amendment) Regulations 2009
Reg.2, amended: 2014 c.29 s.4

2538. Food Labelling (Nutrition Information) (England) Regulations 2009
revoked: SI 2014/1855 Sch.6 Part 1

2578. Local Authorities (Case and Interim Case Tribunals and Standards Committees) (Amendment) (Wales) Regulations 2009
Reg.4, amended: 2014 c.29 s.4

2615. Company, Limited Liability Partnership and Business Names (Sensitive Words and Expressions) Regulations 2009
revoked: SI 2014/3140 Reg.7
Sch.2 Part 1, amended: 2014 c.29 s.4
Sch.2 Part 2, amended: 2014 c.29 s.4

2680. School Staffing (England) Regulations 2009
see *Davies v Haringey LBC* [2014] EWHC 3393 (QB), [2014] B.L.G.R. 743 (QBD), Supperstone J
Reg.3, amended: SI 2014/798 Reg.2
Reg.12, see *Birmingham City Council v Emery* [2014] E.L.R. 203 (EAT), Mitting J
Reg.16, see *Birmingham City Council v Emery* [2014] E.L.R. 203 (EAT), Mitting J
Reg.19, see *Davies v Haringey LBC* [2014] EWHC 3393 (QB), [2014] B.L.G.R. 743 (QBD), Supperstone J
Reg.20, see *Birmingham City Council v Emery* [2014] E.L.R. 203 (EAT), Mitting J

2705. Food Labelling (Nutrition Information) (Wales) Regulations 2009
revoked: SI 2014/2303 Sch.6 Part 1

2767. RTM Companies (Model Articles) (England) Regulations 2009
Reg.2, see *Fairhold Mercury Ltd v HQ (Block 1) Action Management Co Ltd* [2014] L. & T.R. 5 (UT (Lands)), Martin Rodger Q.C.
Sch.1, see *Fairhold Mercury Ltd v HQ (Block 1) Action Management Co Ltd* [2014]

L. & T.R. 5 (UT (Lands)), Martin Rodger
Q.C.
**2796. Merchant Shipping (Anti-Fouling Systems)
Regulations 2009**
    Reg.2, amended: SI 2014/3306 Sch.2 para.8
**2816. Public Transport Users Committee for
Wales (Establishment) Order 2009**
    revoked: SI 2014/595 Art.3
    Art.3, applied: SI 2014/595 Art.3
**2818. Pre-release Access to Official Statistics
(Wales) Order 2009**
    Sch.1 para.1, amended: 2014 c.29 s.4
2824. Aerosol Dispensers Regulations 2009
    Reg.3, amended: SI 2014/1130 Reg.3
**2950. Youth Rehabilitation Order (Electronic
Monitoring Requirement) Order 2009**
    revoked: SI 2014/669 Sch.1
    Art.2, amended: SI 2014/163 Art.13
    Sch.1, amended: SI 2014/163 Art.14
**2958. Government of Wales Act 2006
(Consequential Modifications, Transitional
Provisions and Saving) Order 2009**
    Art.3, amended: 2014 c.29 s.4
    Art.4, amended: 2014 c.29 s.4
    Art.6, amended: 2014 c.29 s.4
    Art.9, amended: 2014 c.29 s.4
    Art.11, amended: 2014 c.29 s.4
**2970. Rail Passengers Rights and Obligations
(Exemptions) Regulations 2009**
    revoked: SI 2014/2793 Reg.6
**2971. Mutual Societies (Transfers of Business)
(Tax) Regulations 2009**
    Reg.2, amended: SI 2014/1815 Sch.1 para.26
    Reg.3, amended: SI 2014/1815 Sch.1 para.26
    Reg.19, amended: SI 2014/1815 Sch.1 para.26
    Reg.22, amended: SI 2014/1815 Sch.1 para.26
    Reg.30, amended: SI 2014/1815 Sch.1 para.26
    Reg.32, amended: SI 2014/1815 Sch.1 para.26
**2982. Company, Limited Liability Partnership
and Business Names (Public Authorities)
Regulations 2009**
    Sch.1, amended: SI 2014/469 Sch.3 para.198
**2995. Limited Liability Partnerships
(Amendment) (No.2) Regulations 2009**
    Reg.2, amended: 2014 c.29 s.4

2999. Provision of Services Regulations 2009
    Reg.15, amended: SI 2014/1937 Reg.2
    Reg.38, amended: SI 2014/1937 Reg.2
3001. Offshore Funds (Tax) Regulations 2009
    applied: SI 2014/685 Reg.2
    Reg.17, amended: SI 2014/1931 Reg.2
    Reg.48, amended: SI 2014/1931 Reg.2
    Reg.80, amended: SI 2014/685 Reg.8
    Reg.81, revoked: SI 2014/685 Reg.8
    Sch.3 Part 2, amended: SI 2014/685 Reg.8
**3013. Double Taxation Relief and International
Tax Enforcement (Virgin Islands) Order 2009**
    Sch.1, referred to: SI 2014/1359 Art.2
3015. Air Navigation Order 2009
    applied: SI 2014/774 Sch.6 Part 2, SI
    2014/1599 Sch.1 para.8, SI 2014/1873 Sch.1
    para.7, SI 2014/2594 Sch.1 para.7, SI
    2014/2950 Sch.9 para.17, Sch.10 para.16, SI
    2014/3331 Sch.1 para.3
    Art.6, applied: SI 2014/2936 Sch.1 para.9
    Art.11, amended: SI 2014/3302 Art.5
    Art.11A, added: SI 2014/3302 Art.6
    Art.12, amended: SI 2014/3302 Art.7
    Art.13, amended: SI 2014/3302 Art.8
    Art.14, amended: SI 2014/3302 Art.9
    Art.15, amended: SI 2014/3302 Art.10
    Art.15, revoked (in part): SI 2014/3302 Art.10
    Art.25, amended: SI 2014/3302 Art.11
    Art.35, amended: SI 2014/3302 Art.12
    Art.36E, amended: SI 2014/3302 Art.13
    Art.36G, amended: SI 2014/3302 Art.14
    Art.36I, amended: SI 2014/3302 Art.15
    Art.36J, amended: SI 2014/3302 Art.16
    Art.37, amended: SI 2014/3302 Art.17
    Art.37, revoked (in part): SI 2014/3302 Art.17
    Art.39, amended: SI 2014/3302 Art.18
    Art.39, revoked (in part): SI 2014/3302 Art.18
    Art.40, substituted: SI 2014/3302 Art.19
    Art.41, amended: SI 2014/3302 Art.20
    Art.43, amended: SI 2014/3302 Art.21
    Art.49, amended: SI 2014/3302 Art.22
    Art.86, amended: SI 2014/3302 Art.23
    Art.87, substituted: SI 2014/3302 Art.24
    Art.88, amended: SI 2014/3302 Art.25
    Art.93, amended: SI 2014/3302 Art.26
    Art.97, substituted: SI 2014/3302 Art.27
    Art.103, amended: SI 2014/3302 Art.28
    Art.104, amended: SI 2014/3302 Art.29

Art.112, amended: SI 2014/3302 Art.30
Art.117, amended: SI 2014/3302 Art.31
Art.118, amended: SI 2014/3302 Art.32
Art.118, substituted: SI 2014/3302 Art.32
Art.119, amended: SI 2014/3302 Art.33
Art.121, amended: SI 2014/3302 Art.34
Art.122, amended: SI 2014/3302 Art.35
Art.123, substituted: SI 2014/3302 Art.36
Art.124, amended: SI 2014/3302 Art.37
Art.125, substituted: SI 2014/3302 Art.38
Art.131, amended: SI 2014/3302 Art.39
Art.140, amended: SI 2014/3302 Art.40
Art.144, amended: SI 2014/3302 Art.41
Art.149, substituted: SI 2014/3302 Art.42
Art.150, amended: SI 2014/3302 Art.43
Art.156, amended: SI 2014/3302 Art.44
Art.158, amended: SI 2014/3302 Art.45
Art.160, amended: SI 2014/3302 Art.75
Art.161, enabled: SI 2014/13, SI 2014/14, SI
2014/28, SI 2014/36, SI 2014/88, SI
2014/89, SI 2014/90, SI 2014/139, SI
2014/140, SI 2014/141, SI 2014/142, SI
2014/214, SI 2014/215, SI 2014/216, SI
2014/272, SI 2014/273, SI 2014/274, SI
2014/275, SI 2014/318, SI 2014/437, SI
2014/438, SI 2014/439, SI 2014/700, SI
2014/746, SI 2014/783, SI 2014/809, SI
2014/848, SI 2014/849, SI 2014/850, SI
2014/943, SI 2014/944, SI 2014/945, SI
2014/1002, SI 2014/1003, SI 2014/1005, SI
2014/1006, SI 2014/1007, SI 2014/1008, SI
2014/1070, SI 2014/1140, SI 2014/1141, SI
2014/1142, SI 2014/1143, SI 2014/1144, SI
2014/1191, SI 2014/1192, SI 2014/1193, SI
2014/1194, SI 2014/1196, SI 2014/1235, SI
2014/1278, SI 2014/1281, SI 2014/1304, SI
2014/1495, SI 2014/1528, SI 2014/1555, SI
2014/1558, SI 2014/1577, SI 2014/1578, SI
2014/1579, SI 2014/1580, SI 2014/1657, SI
2014/1802, SI 2014/1817, SI 2014/1840, SI
2014/1938, SI 2014/1939, SI 2014/1973, SI
2014/2206, SI 2014/2389, SI 2014/2391, SI
2014/2392, SI 2014/2393, SI 2014/2450, SI
2014/2486, SI 2014/2520, SI 2014/2669
Art.205, amended: SI 2014/3302 Art.60
Art.207, amended: SI 2014/3302 Art.61
Art.208A, amended: SI 2014/3302 Art.62
Art.211, amended: SI 2014/3302 Art.63
Art.211A, added: SI 2014/3302 Art.64
Art.212, amended: SI 2014/3302 Art.65
Art.214, amended: SI 2014/3302 Art.66

Art.214A, amended: SI 2014/3302 Art.67
Art.215, amended: SI 2014/3302 Art.68
Art.218, amended: SI 2014/3302 Art.69
Art.223, substituted: SI 2014/508 Art.3
Art.224, revoked (in part): SI 2014/508 Art.4
Art.225, substituted: SI 2014/508 Art.5
Art.226, amended: SI 2014/3302 Art.46,
Art.70
Art.228, amended: SI 2014/508 Art.6
Art.230, substituted: SI 2014/508 Art.7
Art.232, amended: SI 2014/3302 Art.47
Art.232A, added: SI 2014/3302 Art.48
Art.233, revoked: SI 2014/3302 Art.49
Art.239, amended: SI 2014/3302 Art.50
Art.241, amended: SI 2014/3302 Art.51
Art.246, amended: SI 2014/2920 Art.4
Art.246A, added: SI 2014/1888 Art.2
Art.250, amended: SI 2014/3302 Art.52
Art.255, amended: SI 2014/2920 Art.5, SI
2014/3302 Art.53, Art.71, Art.76
Art.257, amended: SI 2014/3302 Art.54
Art.260, amended: SI 2014/3302 Art.55
Art.261, amended: SI 2014/3302 Art.56
Sch.4 para.5, amended: SI 2014/3302 Art.77
Sch.7 Part A, amended: SI 2014/3302 Art.57
Sch.13 Part A, added: SI 2014/3302 Art.58,
Art.72
Sch.13 Part A, amended: SI 2014/3302
Art.78
Sch.13 Part A, substituted: SI 2014/3302
Art.58
Sch.13 Part B, added: SI 2014/3302 Art.58,
Art.72, Art.78
Sch.13 Part B, amended: SI 2014/3302
Art.58, Art.72
Sch.13 Part B, substituted: SI 2014/3302
Art.58
Sch.13 Part C, added: SI 2014/3302 Art.58,
Art.72, Art.78
Sch.13 Part C, amended: SI 2014/508 Art.3,
SI 2014/3302 Art.58
Sch.13 Part C, substituted: SI 2014/3302
Art.58
3112. Care Quality Commission (Registration) Regulations 2009
Reg.12, applied: SI 2014/2936 Sch.5
Reg.14, applied: SI 2014/2936 Sch.5
Reg.25, applied: SI 2014/2936 Sch.5
3150. Local Government Pension Scheme (Miscellaneous) Regulations 2009
revoked: SI 2014/525 Sch.1

3151. Child Support (Management of Payments and Arrears) Regulations 2009
  Reg.2, amended: SI 2014/1386 Reg.6
  Reg.3, amended: SI 2014/1386 Reg.6
  Reg.3A, added: SI 2014/1386 Reg.6
  Reg.11, amended: SI 2014/1386 Reg.6
  Reg.11, varied: SI 2014/1621 Reg.2
3157. INSPIRE Regulations 2009
  Reg.11, amended: 2014 c.29 s.4
3192. LONDON TO FISHGUARD TRUNK ROAD (A40) (IMPROVEMENT AT THE KELL, TREFFGARNE) ORDER 2009
  Art.3, amended: 2014 c.29 s.4
3214. European Communities (Designation) (No.5) Order 2009
  Art.5, revoked: SI 2014/1362 Sch.1
3219. Sheep and Goats (Records, Identification and Movement) (England) Order 2009
  referred to: SI 2014/331
  Art.2, amended: SI 2014/331 Art.3
  Art.7, amended: SI 2014/331 Art.4
  Art.9, amended: SI 2014/331 Art.5
  Art.10, amended: SI 2014/331 Art.6
  Art.21, amended: SI 2014/331 Art.7
  Art.21, applied: SI 2014/112 Sch.1 para.4
  Art.22, substituted: SI 2014/331 Art.8
  Art.23, substituted: SI 2014/331 Art.9
  Art.24, applied: SI 2014/112 Sch.1 para.4
  Art.26, revoked (in part): SI 2014/331 Art.10
  Art.28, amended: SI 2014/331 Art.11
  Art.43, added: SI 2014/331 Art.12
3225. Smoke Control Areas (Authorised Fuels) (Wales) (Amendment) Regulations 2009
  revoked: SI 2014/684 Reg.3
3235. Food Enzymes Regulations 2009
  Reg.7, revoked: SI 2014/1855 Sch.6 Part 1
3238. Food Additives (England) Regulations 2009
  Reg.18, revoked (in part): SI 2014/3001
  Reg.8
3255. Official Feed and Food Controls (England) Regulations 2009
  Reg.2, amended: SI 2014/2748 Reg.2
  Sch.1, amended: SI 2014/2748 Reg.2
3256. Education (Local Curriculum for Pupils in Key Stage 4) (Wales) Regulations 2009
  Reg.4, substituted: SI 2014/42 Reg.2
  Reg.5, revoked: SI 2014/42 Reg.2
  Reg.11, amended: SI 2014/42 Reg.2

3263. Common Agricultural Policy Single Payment and Support Schemes (Integrated Administration and Control System) Regulations 2009
  applied: SI 2014/3263 Reg.3, Reg.35
  revoked: SI 2014/3263 Sch.5
  Reg.2, applied: SI 2014/3223 Reg.15, SI 2014/3263 Reg.35
3270. Rural Development Programmes (Wales) (Amendment) Regulations 2009
  revoked: SI 2014/3223 Sch.3
3319. Allocation and Transfer of Proceedings (Amendment) Order 2009
  revoked: SI 2014/879 Sch.1
3320. Civil Courts (Amendment No 2) Order 2009
  revoked: SI 2014/820 Sch.1
3344. Eels (England and Wales) Regulations 2009
  Part 4, applied: 2014 c.21 Sch.8 para.30
  Reg.26, referred to: 2014 c.21 Sch.8 para.20
3359. Assembly Learning Grants (European University Institute) (Wales) Regulations 2009
  revoked: SI 2014/3037 Reg.4
3365. Agriculture (Cross compliance) (No.2) Regulations 2009
  applied: SI 2014/3263 Reg.35
  revoked: SI 2014/3263 Sch.5
3375. Cardiff to Glan Conwy Trunk Road (A470) (Cwm-bach to Newbridge-on-Wye) Order 2009
  Art.3, amended: 2014 c.29 s.4
  Art.4, amended: 2014 c.29 s.4
3376. Official Feed and Food Controls (Wales) Regulations 2009
  Reg.2, amended: SI 2014/2714 Reg.2
  Sch.1, amended: SI 2014/2714 Reg.2
3377. Food Enzymes (Wales) Regulations 2009
  Reg.7, revoked: SI 2014/2303 Sch.6 Part 1
3420. A40/A48 Trunk Roads(Pensarn Roundabout, Carmarthen) (40 mph Speed Limit) Order 2009
  varied: SI 2014/3416 Art.7

2010

5. Employers Duties (Registration and Compliance) Regulations 2010
  Reg.3, amended: SI 2014/1815 Sch.1 para.27

38. Common Agricultural Policy Single Payment and Support Schemes (Cross Compliance) (Wales) (Amendment) Regulations 2010
revoked: SI 2014/3223 Sch.3
39. Common Agricultural Policy Single Payment and Support Schemes (Appeals) Regulations 2010
applied: SI 2014/3263 Reg.35
revoked: SI 2014/3263 Sch.5
Reg.2, applied: SI 2014/3263 Reg.35
42. First-tier Tribunal (Gambling) Fees Order 2010
Sch.2 para.1, amended: SI 2014/513 Sch.1
para.20, SI 2014/590 Art.6
44. Tribunal Procedure (Amendment No 2) Rules 2010
r.23, revoked: SI 2014/2604 r.45
76. National Health Service (Functions of the First-tier Tribunal relating to Primary Medical, Dental and Ophthalmic Services) Regulations 2010
Reg.5, amended: SI 2014/443 Reg.2
93. Agency Workers Regulations 2010
see *Moran v Ideal Cleaning Services Ltd* [2014] 2 C.M.L.R. 37 (EAT), Singh J
Reg.3, see *Moran v Ideal Cleaning Services Ltd* [2014] 2 C.M.L.R. 37 (EAT), Singh J
Reg.7, see *Moran v Ideal Cleaning Services Ltd* [2014] 2 C.M.L.R. 37 (EAT), Singh J
Reg.18, amended: SI 2014/386 Sch.1 para.62
Reg.18A, added: SI 2014/386 Sch.1 para.63
102. Infrastructure Planning (Interested Parties) Regulations 2010
Sch.1, amended: SI 2014/469 Sch.3 para.199
103. Infrastructure Planning (Examination Procedure) Rules 2010
applied: SI 2014/909, SI 2014/1052, SI 2014/1599, SI 2014/1796, SI 2014/1873, SI 2014/2269, SI 2014/2434, SI 2014/2637, SI 2014/2846, SI 2014/2935, SI 2014/3331
104. Infrastructure Planning (Compulsory Acquisition) Regulations 2010
Sch.2, amended: SI 2014/469 Sch.3 para.200
150. Ordinary Statutory Paternity Pay (Adoption), Additional Statutory Paternity Pay (Adoption) and Statutory Adoption Pay (Adoptions from Overseas) (Persons Abroad and Mariners) Regulations 2010
Reg.4, varied: 2014 c.6 s.126

151. Statutory Paternity Pay and Statutory Adoption Pay (Persons Abroad and Mariners) Regulations 2002 (Amendment) Regulations 2010
Reg.3, varied: 2014 c.6 s.126
Reg.5, varied: 2014 c.6 s.126
153. Social Security Contributions and Benefits Act 1992 (Application of Parts 12ZA and 12ZB to Adoptions from Overseas) Regulations 2003 (Amendment) Regulations 2010
Reg.2, varied: 2014 c.6 s.126
155. Employee Study and Training (Procedural Requirements) Regulations 2010
Reg.17, amended: SI 2014/431 Sch.1 para.40
Reg.17A, added: SI 2014/431 Sch.1 para.41
167. Hill Farm Allowance Regulations 2010
applied: SI 2014/112 Reg.4, Reg.5
196. Pension Protection Fund and Occupational Pension Schemes (Miscellaneous Amendments) Regulations 2010
Reg.2, referred to: 2014 c.19 s.45
Reg.8, referred to: 2014 c.19 s.45
231. Pharmacy Order 2010
Art.32, disapplied: SI 2014/1887 Sch.3 para.20
Art.32, substituted: SI 2014/1887 Sch.1 para.35
Art.37, amended: SI 2014/1887 Sch.1 para.36
Art.39, amended: SI 2014/1887 Sch.1 para.37
288. Community Health Councils (Constitution, Membership and Procedures) (Wales) Regulations 2010
Reg.27, see *R. (on the application of Flatley) v Hywel Dda University Local Health Board* [2014] EWHC 2258 (Admin), (2014) 140 B.M.L.R. 1 (QBD (Admin)), Hickinbottom J
428. Welsh Ministers (Transfer of Fire and Rescue Service Equipment) Order 2010
Art.1, amended: 2014 c.29 s.4
432. Rail Vehicle Accessibility (Non-Interoperable Rail System) Regulations 2010
referred to: SI 2014/2660 Art.4
Sch.1 Part 1 para.9, referred to: SI 2014/2660 Art.3
Sch.1 Part 1 para.10, referred to: SI 2014/2660 Art.3
Sch.1 Part 1 para.12, referred to: SI 2014/2660 Art.3

Sch.1 Part 1 para.14, referred to: SI
2014/2660 Art.3
Sch.1 Part 1 para.18, referred to: SI
2014/2660 Art.3

**440. Registration of Civil Partnerships (Fees)
(Amendment) Order 2010**
revoked: SI 2014/1789 Art.3

**441. Registration of Births, Deaths and
Marriages (Fees) Order 2010**
Sch.1, substituted: SI 2014/1790 Art.2

**480. Regulation of Investigatory Powers
(Communications Data) Order 2010**
applied: SI 2014/1610 r.6_27
Sch.2 Part 2, amended: SI 2014/549 Sch.1
para.40

**490. Conservation of Habitats and Species
Regulations 2010**
applied: SI 2014/1873 Art.39, SI 2014/2935
Art.22
referred to: SI 2014/2933 Art.16
see *Elliott v Secretary of State for
Communities and Local Government* [2013]
EWCA Civ 703, [2014] Env. L.R. 1 (CA
(Civ Div)), Laws LJ; see *R. (on the
application of Gate) v Secretary of State for
Transport* [2013] EWHC 2937 (Admin),
[2014] J.P.L. 383 (QBD (Admin)), Turner J;
see *Royal Society for the Protection of Birds
v Secretary of State for Communities and
Local Government* [2014] EWHC 1523
(Admin), [2014] Env. L.R. 30 (QBD
(Admin)), Ouseley J; see *Royal Society for
the Protection of Birds v Secretary of State
for Environment Food & Rural Affairs*
[2014] EWHC 1645 (Admin), [2014] Env.
L.R. 29 (QBD (Admin)), Mitting J
Reg.8, referred to: SI 2014/3303 Reg.5
Reg.53, applied: SI 2014/2935 Sch.11
para.31
Reg.53, see *Elliott v Secretary of State for
Communities and Local Government* [2013]
EWCA Civ 703, [2014] Env. L.R. 1 (CA
(Civ Div)), Laws LJ
Reg.61, applied: SI 2014/2933 Art.16
Reg.61, see *Royal Society for the Protection
of Birds v Secretary of State for
Communities and Local Government* [2014]
EWHC 1523 (Admin), [2014] Env. L.R. 30
(QBD (Admin)), Ouseley J
Reg.62, see *Forest of Dean Friends of the
Earth v Forest of Dean DC* [2013] EWHC

1567 (Admin), [2014] Env. L.R. 3 (QBD
(Admin)), Edwards-Stuart J
Reg.73, disapplied: SI 2014/2933 Art.16
Reg.102, see *Forest of Dean Friends of the
Earth v Forest of Dean DC* [2013] EWHC
1567 (Admin), [2014] Env. L.R. 3 (QBD
(Admin)), Edwards-Stuart J

**493. Employment Relations Act 1999
(Blacklists) Regulations 2010**
Reg.7, amended: SI 2014/386 Sch.1 para.65
Reg.10, amended: SI 2014/386 Sch.1
para.65
Reg.18, added: SI 2014/386 Sch.1 para.66

**521. Regulation of Investigatory Powers
(Directed Surveillance and Covert Human
Intelligence Sources) Order 2010**
applied: SI 2014/1610 r.6_27
Art.3, amended: SI 2014/467 Art.2
Sch.1 Part 1, amended: 2014 c.29 s.4, SI
2014/467 Sch.1, SI 2014/549 Sch.1 para.41

**528. Local Government Pension Scheme
(Amendment) Regulations 2010**
revoked: SI 2014/525 Sch.1

**540. Common Agricultural Policy Single
Payment and Support Schemes Regulations 2010**
applied: SI 2014/3259 Reg.15
revoked: SI 2014/3259 Reg.15

**630. Marine and Coastal Access Act 2009
(Commencement No 1, Consequential,
Transitional and Savings Provisions) (England
and Wales) Order 2010**
Art.5, amended: 2014 c.29 s.4
Art.9, amended: 2014 c.29 s.4

**637. Assembly Learning Grant (Further
Education) (Amendment) Regulations 2010**
Reg.3, amended: 2014 c.29 s.4
Reg.5, amended: 2014 c.29 s.4

**638. Federation of Maintained Schools and
Miscellaneous Amendments (Wales) Regulations
2010**
Part 1, revoked: SI 2014/1132 Reg.2
Part 4, applied: SI 2014/1132 Reg.2
Sch.1, revoked: SI 2014/1132 Reg.2

**644. Tax Credits Act 2002 (Transitional
Provisions) Order 2010**
Art.3, revoked (in part): SI 2014/1848 Art.3

**672. Authorisation of Frequency Use for the
Provision of Mobile Satellite Services (European
Union) Regulations 2010**
applied: SI 2014/774 Sch.4 para.2

675. Environmental Permitting (England and Wales) Regulations 2010

applied: SI 2014/1599 Sch.9 para.4, SI 2014/2434 Art.14, Sch.8 para.4, SI 2014/2935 Sch.9 para.102, SI 2014/2950 Art.15, SI 2014/3328 Art.14

varied: 2014 c.20 Sch.1 para.6

see *Sweeney v Westminster Magistrates' Court* [2014] EWHC 2068 (Admin), (2014) 178 J.P. 336 (DC), Pitchford LJ

Reg.2, amended: SI 2014/517 Sch.2 para.9, SI 2014/2852 Reg.3

Reg.5, amended: SI 2014/2852 Reg.4

Reg.10, amended: SI 2014/255 Reg.3

Reg.12, applied: SI 2014/909 Art.18, SI 2014/1052 Art.17, SI 2014/1796 Art.17, SI 2014/1873 Art.20, SI 2014/2027 Art.13, SI 2014/2269 Art.15, SI 2014/2434 Art.14, SI 2014/2441 Art.18, SI 2014/2637 Art.16, SI 2014/2935 Art.20, SI 2014/2950 Art.15, SI 2014/3102 Art.16, SI 2014/3223 Sch.1 para.3, SI 2014/3331 Art.12

Reg.12, disapplied: SI 2014/1599 Art.13, SI 2014/3263 Sch.2 para.2

Reg.12, see *R. v Southern Water Services Ltd* [2014] EWCA Crim 120, [2014] 2 Cr. App. R. (S.) 29 (CA (Crim Div)), Lord Thomas LCJ

Reg.20, amended: SI 2014/255 Reg.4

Reg.21, amended: SI 2014/255 Reg.5

Reg.24, amended: SI 2014/255 Reg.6

Reg.28, amended: SI 2014/255 Reg.7

Reg.28, revoked (in part): SI 2014/255 Reg.7

Reg.32, amended: SI 2014/255 Reg.8

Reg.35, amended: SI 2014/255 Reg.9

Reg.35, applied: SI 2014/3223 Sch.1 para.3

Reg.35, disapplied: SI 2014/3263 Sch.2 para.2

Reg.38, applied: SI 2014/2384 Art.19

Reg.38, see *R. v Southern Water Services Ltd* [2014] EWCA Crim 120, [2014] 2 Cr. App. R. (S.) 29 (CA (Crim Div)), Lord Thomas LCJ

Reg.46, revoked (in part): SI 2014/255 Reg.10

Reg.60, amended: SI 2014/2852 Reg.5

Reg.61, amended: SI 2014/2852 Reg.6

Reg.61, substituted: SI 2014/2852 Reg.6

Reg.64, amended: SI 2014/2852 Reg.7

Reg.64, substituted: SI 2014/2852 Reg.7

Reg.74, amended: SI 2014/2852 Reg.8

Sch.1 Part 1 para.3, amended: SI 2014/255 Reg.11

Sch.1 Part 1 para.4, amended: SI 2014/255 Reg.11

Sch.1 Part 2, revoked (in part): SI 2014/255 Reg.11

Sch.1 Part 2, amended: SI 2014/255 Reg.11

Sch.1 Part 2 para.1, amended: SI 2014/255 Reg.11

Sch.1 Part 2 para.1, revoked (in part): SI 2014/517 Sch.2 para.9

Sch.1 Part 2 para.2, revoked: SI 2014/255 Reg.11

Sch.2 para.1, amended: SI 2014/2852 Reg.9

Sch.2 para.1, substituted: SI 2014/2852 Reg.9

Sch.2 para.2, amended: SI 2014/2852 Reg.9

Sch.2 para.2, substituted: SI 2014/2852 Reg.9

Sch.2 para.4, substituted: SI 2014/2852 Reg.9

Sch.2 para.4A, added: SI 2014/2852 Reg.9

Sch.2 para.5, amended: SI 2014/255 Reg.12

Sch.2 para.5, substituted: SI 2014/2852 Reg.9

Sch.2 para.5A, added: SI 2014/2852 Reg.9

Sch.2 para.9, amended: SI 2014/2852 Reg.9

Sch.3 Part 1 para.11, amended: 2014 c.29 s.4

Sch.3 Part 2 para.2, substituted: SI 2014/2852 Reg.10

Sch.3 Part 2 para.2A, added: SI 2014/2852 Reg.10

Sch.3 Part 3 para.3, substituted: SI 2014/2852 Reg.11

Sch.3 Part 3 para.3A, added: SI 2014/2852 Reg.11

Sch.3 Part 3 para.4, added: SI 2014/255 Reg.13

Sch.4 para.4, varied: SI 2014/2708 Art.5

Sch.5 Part 1 para.5, amended: SI 2014/255 Reg.14

Sch.5 Part 1 para.9, amended: SI 2014/255 Reg.14

Sch.5 Part 1 para.16, amended: SI 2014/255 Reg.14

Sch.9A, added: SI 2014/255 Sch.1

Sch.9 para.3, revoked: SI 2014/255 Reg.15

Sch.14 para.1, amended: SI 2014/255 Reg.17

Sch.19 para.3, added: SI 2014/255 Reg.18

Sch.20 para.13, amended: SI 2014/255
Reg.19
Sch.20 para.13, revoked (in part): SI
2014/255 Reg.19
Sch.22, applied: SI 2014/3223 Sch.1 para.3
Sch.22, disapplied: SI 2014/3263 Sch.2
para.2
Sch.24 para.1, amended: SI 2014/255
Reg.20, SI 2014/2852 Reg.12

**683. Accounts and Audit (Wales) (Amendment)
Regulations 2010**
revoked: SI 2014/3362 Reg.30

**698. Electricity (Standards of Performance)
Regulations 2010**
Reg.3, amended: SI 2014/631 Sch.1 para.25
Reg.24, amended: SI 2014/631 Sch.1
para.25
Reg.25, amended: SI 2014/631 Sch.1
para.25
Sch.2 para.1, amended: SI 2014/631 Sch.1
para.25

**713. Valuation Tribunal for Wales Regulations
2010**
Reg.27, amended: SI 2014/554 Reg.2
Reg.29, amended: SI 2014/554 Reg.2

**737. Merchant Shipping (Maritime Labour
Convention) (Medical Certification) Regulations
2010**
Reg.2, amended: SI 2014/1614 Reg.13
Reg.3, revoked: SI 2014/1614 Reg.13
Reg.5, amended: SI 2014/1614 Reg.13
Reg.8, amended: SI 2014/1614 Reg.13
Reg.10, amended: SI 2014/1614 Reg.13
Reg.12, amended: SI 2014/1614 Reg.13
Reg.13, amended: SI 2014/1614 Reg.13
Reg.14, amended: SI 2014/1614 Reg.13
Reg.16, amended: SI 2014/1614 Reg.13

**768. CRC Energy Efficiency Scheme Order
2010**
Art.14, amended: 2014 c.29 s.4
Art.73, amended: 2014 c.29 s.4
Sch.3 Part 2 para.7, amended: 2014 c.29 s.4
Sch.3 Part 3 para.12, amended: 2014 c.29 s.4
Sch.5 Part 1 para.4, amended: 2014 c.29 s.4
Sch.6 Part 1, amended: 2014 c.29 s.4
Sch.6 Part 1 para.1, amended: 2014 c.29 s.4
Sch.10 para.3, amended: 2014 c.29 s.4
Sch.10 para.4, amended: 2014 c.29 s.4

**772. Occupational and Personal Pension
Schemes (Automatic Enrolment) Regulations
2010**
Reg.12, applied: SI 2014/512 Reg.15
Reg.32I, amended: SI 2014/715 Reg.2
Reg.36, amended: SI 2014/715 Reg.2

**781. Health and Social Care Act 2008
(Regulated Activities) Regulations 2010**
revoked: SI 2014/2936 Reg.25
Reg.21, varied: SI 2014/2936 Reg.26
Reg.22, see *Esparon (t/a Middle West
Residential Care Home) v Slavikovska*
[2014] I.C.R. 1037 (EAT), Judge Serota QC
Reg.27, applied: SI 2014/2936 Reg.26
Sch.1 para.7, referred to: SI 2014/1788 Sch.1

**782. UK Border Agency (Complaints and
Misconduct) Regulations 2010**
Reg.46, amended: SI 2014/834 Sch.3
para.25
Reg.61, amended: SI 2014/834 Sch.3
para.26
Reg.62, amended: SI 2014/834 Sch.3
para.27
Reg.63, amended: SI 2014/834 Sch.3
para.28
Reg.70, amended: SI 2014/834 Sch.3
para.29

**790. Retention of Knives in Court Regulations
2010**
applied: SI 2014/786 Art.4

**828. Banking Act 2009 (Inter-Bank Payment
Systems) (Disclosure and Publication of
Specified Information) Regulations 2010**
Sch.1, amended: SI 2014/549 Sch.1 para.42

**832. Armed Forces (Redundancy, Resettlement
and Gratuity Earnings Schemes) (No.2) Order
2010**
Art.2, amended: SI 2014/3255 Art.21
Art.6, amended: SI 2014/3255 Art.21
Art.21, amended: SI 2014/3255 Art.21
Art.23, amended: SI 2014/107 Sch.1 para.46

**844. Housing and Regeneration Act 2008
(Registration of Local Authorities) Order 2010**
Sch.1 para.9, revoked: 2014 c.2 Sch.12
para.123
Sch.1 para.52, revoked: 2014 c.2 Sch.12
para.123
Sch.2 para.24, revoked: 2014 c.2 Sch.1 Part
2

860. Licensing Act 2003 (Mandatory Licensing Conditions) Order 2010
    Art.3, amended: SI 2014/2440 Art.2
    Sch.1, substituted: SI 2014/2440 Sch.1
    Sch.1 para.1, disapplied: SI 2014/2440 Art.3

866. Housing and Regeneration Act 2008 (Consequential Provisions) Order 2010
    Sch.2 para.1, revoked: 2014 c.14 Sch.7
    Sch.2 para.119, revoked: 2014 c.14 Sch.7

900. Animal Gatherings (Wales) Order 2010
    Art.8, amended: SI 2014/517 Sch.2 para.8

948. Community Infrastructure Levy Regulations 2010
    Part 10, applied: SI 2014/385 Reg.14
    Reg.2, amended: SI 2014/385 Reg.3
    Reg.2, revoked (in part): SI 2014/385 Reg.3
    Reg.6, applied: SI 2014/2384 Sch.19 para.7
    Reg.8, amended: SI 2014/385 Reg.4
    Reg.8, revoked (in part): SI 2014/385 Reg.4
    Reg.9, amended: SI 2014/385 Reg.4
    Reg.11, amended: SI 2014/385 Reg.5
    Reg.13, amended: SI 2014/385 Reg.5
    Reg.14, see *R. (on the application of Fox Strategic Land and Property Ltd) v Chorley BC* [2014] EWHC 1179 (Admin), [2014] J.P.L. 1152 (QBD (Admin)), Lindblom J
    Reg.14, amended: SI 2014/385 Reg.5
    Reg.16, applied: SI 2014/385 Reg.14
    Reg.40, substituted: SI 2014/385 Reg.6
    Reg.42A, added: SI 2014/385 Reg.7
    Reg.46, amended: SI 2014/385 Reg.7
    Reg.47, amended: SI 2014/385 Reg.7
    Reg.49, substituted: SI 2014/385 Reg.7
    Reg.49A, added: SI 2014/385 Reg.7
    Reg.50, substituted: SI 2014/385 Reg.7
    Reg.51, amended: SI 2014/385 Reg.7
    Reg.52, amended: SI 2014/385 Reg.7
    Reg.53, amended: SI 2014/385 Reg.7
    Reg.54A, added: SI 2014/385 Reg.7
    Reg.55, revoked (in part): SI 2014/385 Reg.7
    Reg.56, amended: SI 2014/385 Reg.7
    Reg.57, amended: SI 2014/385 Reg.7
    Reg.57, revoked (in part): SI 2014/385 Reg.7
    Reg.58A, amended: SI 2014/385 Reg.8
    Reg.59B, amended: SI 2014/385 Reg.8
    Reg.61, amended: SI 2014/385 Reg.8
    Reg.62, amended: SI 2014/385 Reg.8
    Reg.64, amended: SI 2014/385 Reg.9

    Reg.64, revoked (in part): SI 2014/385 Reg.9
    Reg.64A, amended: SI 2014/385 Reg.9
    Reg.65, amended: SI 2014/385 Reg.9
    Reg.65, applied: SI 2014/385 Reg.14
    Reg.66, amended: SI 2014/385 Reg.9
    Reg.67, amended: SI 2014/385 Reg.9
    Reg.73A, added: SI 2014/385 Reg.9
    Reg.74, amended: SI 2014/385 Reg.9
    Reg.74A, amended: SI 2014/385 Reg.9
    Reg.74B, added: SI 2014/385 Reg.9
    Reg.75, amended: SI 2014/385 Reg.9
    Reg.84, amended: SI 2014/385 Reg.10
    Reg.112, amended: SI 2014/385 Reg.11
    Reg.113, amended: SI 2014/385 Reg.11
    Reg.114, amended: SI 2014/385 Reg.11
    Reg.116A, added: SI 2014/385 Reg.11
    Reg.120, amended: SI 2014/385 Reg.11
    Reg.122, see *R. (on the application of Hampton Bishop PC) v Herefordshire Council* [2013] EWHC 3947 (Admin), [2014] B.L.G.R. 209 (QBD (Admin)), Hickinbottom J; see *R. (on the application of Thakeham Village Action Ltd) v Horsham DC* [2014] EWHC 67 (Admin), [2014] Env. L.R. 21 (QBD (Admin)), Lindblom J
    Reg.123, amended: SI 2014/385 Reg.12
    Reg.124, varied: SI 2014/2708 Art.5
    Reg.128A, amended: SI 2014/385 Reg.13

959. Care Planning, Placement and Case Review (England) Regulations 2010
    Reg.2, amended: SI 2014/852 Art.18, SI 2014/2103 Art.33
    Reg.5, substituted: SI 2014/1917 Reg.3
    Reg.8ZA, added: SI 2014/1556 Reg.10
    Reg.22A, added: SI 2014/1556 Reg.11
    Reg.22A, applied: SI 2014/2934 Reg.3, SI 2014/3050 Reg.3, SI 2014/3051 Reg.2, SI 2014/3052 Reg.3, SI 2014/3134 Reg.2
    Reg.42, amended: SI 2014/1917 Reg.4
    Sch.1 para.2, amended: SI 2014/1556 Reg.12
    Sch.1 para.2, referred to: SI 2014/3352 Reg.16
    Sch.2A para.9, amended: SI 2014/1556 Reg.12
    Sch.7 para.14, added: SI 2014/1917 Reg.5

976. Northern Ireland Act 1998 (Devolution of Policing and Justice Functions) Order 2010
    Sch.3 para.5, revoked: 2014 c.12 Sch.11 para.102

985. Human Fertilisation and Embryology (Parental Orders) Regulations 2010

see *J v G (Parental Orders)* [2013] EWHC 1432 (Fam), [2014] 1 F.L.R. 297 (Fam Div), Theis J

Reg.6, revoked: SI 2014/879 Art.124

Sch.4, amended: SI 2014/879 Art.125

988. Crossrail (Devolution of Functions) Order 2010

referred to: SI 2014/310 Sch.6 para.2

990. Teachers Pensions Regulations 2010

disapplied: SI 2014/512 Sch.3 para.31

Part 4, substituted: SI 2014/2651 Reg.10

Part 5, applied: SI 2014/512 Sch.3 para.32

Reg.2A, added: SI 2014/560 Sch.3 para.17

Reg.2A, amended: SI 2014/3061 Sch.1 para.11

Reg.2B, added: SI 2014/560 Sch.3 para.17

Reg.2C, added: SI 2014/3061 Sch.1 para.11

Reg.7, amended: SI 2014/424 Reg.3, SI 2014/3255 Art.22

Reg.9, amended: SI 2014/424 Reg.4

Reg.13, amended: SI 2014/2651 Reg.3, Reg.4

Reg.13, applied: SI 2014/512 Sch.1 para.2

Reg.14, applied: SI 2014/512 Sch.1 para.3

Reg.14A, added: SI 2014/424 Reg.5

Reg.14A, amended: SI 2014/2651 Reg.5

Reg.14F, amended: SI 2014/2651 Reg.6

Reg.15, amended: SI 2014/3255 Art.22

Reg.16, amended: SI 2014/2651 Reg.7

Reg.16, applied: SI 2014/512 Sch.3 para.51

Reg.17, amended: SI 2014/2651 Reg.8

Reg.19, applied: SI 2014/512 Sch.3 para.54

Reg.22, amended: SI 2014/3255 Art.22

Reg.22, applied: SI 2014/512 Sch.3 para.50

Reg.26, applied: SI 2014/512 Sch.3 para.32

Reg.30, amended: SI 2014/2651 Reg.9

Reg.39, applied: SI 2014/512 Sch.3 para.32

Reg.40, amended: SI 2014/3255 Art.22

Reg.43, amended: SI 2014/3255 Art.22

Reg.44, amended: SI 2014/2651 Reg.11

Reg.51, amended: SI 2014/2651 Reg.12

Reg.55, amended: SI 2014/2651 Reg.13

Reg.59, amended: SI 2014/2651 Reg.14

Reg.60, applied: SI 2014/512 Sch.3 para.44

Reg.64, substituted: SI 2014/2651 Reg.15

Reg.65, applied: SI 2014/512 Sch.3 para.39

Reg.71, amended: SI 2014/2651 Reg.16

Reg.79, applied: SI 2014/512 Sch.3 para.40

Reg.83, applied: SI 2014/512 Sch.3 para.44

Reg.94, amended: SI 2014/2651 Reg.17

Reg.95, amended: SI 2014/3255 Art.22

Reg.95, applied: SI 2014/512 Sch.3 para.41

Reg.98, amended: SI 2014/3255 Art.22

Reg.117, amended: SI 2014/2651 Reg.18

Reg.119, amended: SI 2014/2651 Reg.19

Reg.123, substituted: SI 2014/2651 Reg.20

Reg.131, amended: SI 2014/3255 Art.22

Sch.1, amended: SI 2014/424 Reg.6, SI 2014/2651 Reg.3, Reg.21, SI 2014/3255 Art.22

Sch.2 Part 1 para.2, amended: SI 2014/2651 Reg.22

Sch.2 Part 1 para.3, amended: SI 2014/2651 Reg.3

Sch.2 Part 1 para.14A, added: SI 2014/424 Reg.7

Sch.2 Part 3 para.25, amended: SI 2014/2651 Reg.3

Sch.2 Part 3 para.26, added: SI 2014/2651 Reg.22

Sch.3 para.2, amended: SI 2014/424 Reg.8, SI 2014/2651 Reg.23

Sch.3 para.4, amended: SI 2014/2651 Reg.23

Sch.4 para.2, applied: SI 2014/512 Sch.3 para.31

Sch.4 para.4, amended: SI 2014/2651 Reg.24

Sch.4 para.11, amended: SI 2014/2651 Reg.24

Sch.6 Part 2 para.11, substituted: SI 2014/2651 Reg.25

Sch.6 Part 2 para.13, amended: SI 2014/2651 Reg.25

Sch.6 Part 3 para.14, amended: SI 2014/2651 Reg.25

Sch.6 Part 3 para.15, amended: SI 2014/2651 Reg.25

Sch.7 para.3, amended: SI 2014/2651 Reg.26

Sch.9, applied: SI 2014/512 Sch.3 para.41

Sch.9 Part 2 para.6, amended: SI 2014/2651 Reg.27

Sch.9 Part 3 para.7, amended: SI 2014/2651 Reg.27

Sch.9 Part 3 para.7, revoked (in part): SI 2014/2651 Reg.27

Sch.10 Part 1 para.2, amended: SI 2014/2651 Reg.28

Sch.13 Part 3 para.8, substituted: SI
2014/2651 Reg.29
Sch.13 Part 5 para.26, amended: SI
2014/2651 Reg.29

**995. Human Fertilisation and Embryology
(Disclosure of Information for Research
Purposes) Regulations 2010**
Reg.2, amended: 2014 c.23 Sch.8 para.11

**1013. Consumer Credit (Disclosure of
Information) Regulations 2010**
Reg.1, applied: SI 2014/208 Art.6
Reg.1, referred to: SI 2014/366 Art.15
Sch.1, applied: SI 2014/366 Art.15
Sch.1 para.5, amended: SI 2014/208 Art.5
Sch.3, applied: SI 2014/366 Art.15
Sch.3 para.5, amended: SI 2014/208 Art.5

**1014. Consumer Credit (Agreements)
Regulations 2010**
Reg.4, see *Bassano v Toft* [2014] EWHC
377 (QB), [2014] E.C.C. 14 (QBD),
Popplewell J
Reg.5, see *Bassano v Toft* [2014] EWHC
377 (QB), [2014] E.C.C. 14 (QBD),
Popplewell J
Sch.1, amended: SI 2014/366 Art.16
Sch.1, applied: SI 2014/366 Art.17

**1051. Whole of Government Accounts
(Designation of Bodies) Order 2010**
Sch.1, amended: 2014 c.29 s.4

**1056. Additional Statutory Paternity Pay
(General) Regulations 2010**
Reg.2, varied: 2014 c.6 s.126
Reg.23, varied: 2014 c.6 s.126
Reg.26, amended: SI 2014/386 Sch.1
para.67
Reg.31, varied: 2014 c.6 s.126

**1060. Additional Statutory Paternity Pay
(Weekly Rates) Regulations 2010**
Reg.2, amended: SI 2014/147 Art.5

**1080. Apprenticeships, Skills, Children and
Learning Act 2009 (Consequential Amendments)
(England and Wales) Order 2010**
Sch.1 Part 2 para.98, revoked: 2014 c.2
Sch.1 Part 2

**1140. Control of Artificial Optical Radiation at
Work Regulations 2010**
Reg.1, amended: SI 2014/469 Sch.3
para.144

**1156. Education (Educational Provision for
Improving Behaviour) Regulations 2010**
Reg.3, amended: SI 2014/2103 Art.34

Reg.5, amended: SI 2014/2103 Art.34
Reg.6, amended: SI 2014/2103 Art.34

**1228. Merchant Shipping (Ship-to-Ship
Transfers) Regulations 2010**
Reg.5A, amended: SI 2014/3306 Sch.2
para.9

1379. Tuberculosis (Wales) Order 2010
Art.2, amended: SI 2014/632 Art.2
Art.2A, added: SI 2014/632 Art.2
Art.12, amended: SI 2014/632 Art.2
Art.13, amended: SI 2014/632 Art.2
Art.14, amended: SI 2014/632 Art.2
Art.21, amended: SI 2014/632 Art.2

**1461. Civil Enforcement of Parking
Contraventions (City and County of Cardiff)
Designation Order 2010**
Sch.1, substituted: SI 2014/2722 Sch.1

1492. Drinking Milk (Wales) Regulations 2010
Reg.9, revoked: SI 2014/2303 Sch.6 Part 1

**1617. General Pharmaceutical Council
(Registration Rules) Order of Council 2010**
Sch.1, added: SI 2014/1887 Sch.1 para.39,
Sch.1 para.40, Sch.1 para.41

1671. Eggs and Chicks (Wales) Regulations 2010
Reg.3, amended: SI 2014/2303 Sch.7
para.52
Sch.2 Part 2, amended: SI 2014/2303 Sch.7
para.53

**1703. Child Minding and Day Care
(Disqualification) (Wales) Regulations 2010**
Reg.2, amended: 2014 c.29 s.4

**1704. Cancellation of Student Loans for Living
Costs Liability (Wales) Regulations 2010**
applied: SI 2014/1314 Reg.5

**1762. A465 Trunk Road (Glanbaiden Junction,
Gilwern,Monmouthshire) (50 mph Speed Limit)
Order 2010**
varied: SI 2014/3420 Art.7

**1780. Poultry Compartments (Wales) Order
2010**
Art.4, amended: 2014 c.29 s.4

**1797. Assembly Learning Grants (European
University Institute) (Wales) (Amendment)
Regulations 2010**
revoked: SI 2014/3037 Reg.4

**1813. Revenue and Customs (Complaints and
Misconduct) Regulations 2010**
Reg.40, amended: SI 2014/834 Sch.3
para.31
Reg.52, amended: SI 2014/834 Sch.3
para.32

Reg.67, amended: SI 2014/834 Sch.3
para.33
Reg.68, amended: SI 2014/834 Sch.3
para.34
Reg.74, amended: SI 2014/834 Sch.3
para.35

1892. Common Agricultural Policy Single Payment and Support Schemes (Wales) Regulations 2010
revoked: SI 2014/3223 Sch.3

1904. Taxes (Definition of Charity) (Relevant Territories) Regulations 2010
Sch.1, amended: SI 2014/1807 Reg.2

1907. Employment and Support Allowance (Transitional Provisions, Housing Benefit and Council Tax Benefit) (Existing Awards) (No.2) Regulations 2010
applied: SI 2014/1230 Reg.23, Reg.24,
Reg.26
Reg.4, applied: SI 2014/1230 Reg.23,
Reg.24
Reg.7, applied: SI 2014/1230 Reg.23

1930. Occupational Pension Schemes (Levies) (Amendment) Regulations 2010
Reg.2, referred to: 2014 c.19 s.45

1997. Education (Independent School Standards) (England) Regulations 2010
Reg.2, amended: SI 2014/2103 Art.35
Sch.1 Part 1 para.2, amended: SI 2014/2103
Art.35
Sch.1 Part 2 para.5, substituted: SI
2014/2374 Reg.2
Sch.1 Part 6 para.24, amended: SI
2014/2103 Art.35

2078. Rural Development (Enforcement) (England) (Amendment) Regulations 2010
applied: SI 2014/3263 Reg.35
revoked: SI 2014/3263 Sch.5

2088. Electricity (Connection Standards of Performance) Regulations 2010
Reg.2, amended: SI 2014/631 Sch.1 para.26
Reg.18, amended: SI 2014/631 Sch.1
para.26
Sch.2 para.1, amended: SI 2014/631 Sch.1
para.26

2090. Local Government Pension Scheme (Miscellaneous) Regulations 2010
revoked: SI 2014/525 Sch.1

2132. Equality Act 2010 (Sex Equality Rule) (Exceptions) Regulations 2010
Reg.4, amended: SI 2014/1711 Reg.75

Reg.4, varied: SI 2014/1711 Reg.74

2133. Equality Act (Age Exceptions for Pension Schemes) Order 2010
see *Palmer v Royal Bank of Scotland Plc*
[2014] I.C.R. 1288 (EAT), Langstaff J

2172. Environmental Permitting (England and Wales) (Amendment) (No.2) Regulations 2010
applied: SI 2014/3331 Sch.12 para.61

2184. Town and Country Planning (Development Management Procedure) (England) Order 2010
Art.16, see *R. (on the application of HS2 Action Alliance Ltd) v Secretary of State for Transport* [2014] EWHC 2759 (Admin),
[2014] P.T.S.R. 1334 (QBD (Admin)),
Lindblom J
Art.25, see *R. (on the application of HS2 Action Alliance Ltd) v Secretary of State for Transport* [2014] EWHC 2759 (Admin),
[2014] P.T.S.R. 1334 (QBD (Admin)),
Lindblom J
Art.29, see *R. (on the application of HS2 Action Alliance Ltd) v Secretary of State for Transport* [2014] EWHC 2759 (Admin),
[2014] P.T.S.R. 1334 (QBD (Admin)),
Lindblom J
Art.30, amended: SI 2014/564 Art.8
Sch.5, amended: SI 2014/469 Sch.3 para.201
Sch.5 para.1, amended: SI 2014/469 Sch.3
para.201
Sch.6, amended: SI 2014/1532 Art.2

2214. Building Regulations 2010
Part 5, amended: SI 2014/579 Reg.2
Reg.2, amended: SI 2014/110 Reg.3, SI
2014/579 Reg.2
Reg.12, amended: SI 2014/579 Reg.2
Reg.20, amended: SI 2014/579 Reg.2
Reg.20, revoked (in part): SI 2014/579
Reg.2
Reg.20A, added: SI 2014/579 Reg.2
Reg.21, amended: SI 2014/110 Reg.4
Reg.25C, added: SI 2014/110 Reg.5
Reg.26A, added: SI 2014/110 Reg.6
Reg.27A, added: SI 2014/110 Reg.7
Reg.28, substituted: SI 2014/110 Reg.8
Reg.43, amended: SI 2014/579 Reg.2
Reg.47, amended: SI 2014/110 Reg.9, SI
2014/579 Reg.2
Sch.2 Part CLASS para.1, substituted: SI
2014/1638 Sch.13 para.24

Sch.3, amended: SI 2014/579 Sch.1 Part 1,
SI 2014/2362 Reg.2
Sch.3A, added: SI 2014/579 Sch.1 Part 2
Sch.3A, amended: SI 2014/2362 Reg.2
Sch.4 para.1, amended: SI 2014/579 Reg.2

2215. Building (Approved Inspectors etc.)
Regulations 2010
Reg.5A, added: SI 2014/58 Reg.3
Reg.7, substituted: SI 2014/58 Reg.4
Reg.8, amended: SI 2014/110 Reg.12, SI 2014/579 Reg.3
Reg.8, revoked (in part): SI 2014/579 Reg.3
Reg.20, amended: SI 2014/110 Reg.13, SI 2014/579 Reg.3
Reg.30, revoked (in part): SI 2014/58 Reg.5
Sch.1, added: SI 2014/58 Reg.6
Sch.1, revoked: SI 2014/58 Reg.6
Sch.1, substituted: SI 2014/58 Reg.6
Sch.2 para.5, revoked (in part): SI 2014/58 Reg.7
Sch.2 para.6, substituted: SI 2014/58 Reg.7
Sch.3 para.6, substituted: SI 2014/58 Reg.8
Sch.4 para.5, substituted: SI 2014/58 Reg.9

2450. Social Security (Contributions)
(Amendment No 5) Regulations 2010
Reg.3, varied: 2014 c.6 s.126
Reg.4, varied: 2014 c.6 s.126

2451. Social Security Contributions (Decisions
and Appeals) (Amendment) Regulations 2010
Reg.2, varied: 2014 c.6 s.126

2493. Statutory Payment Schemes (Electronic
Communications) (Amendment) Regulations
2010
Reg.3, varied: 2014 c.6 s.126

2494. Tax Credits (Miscellaneous Amendments)
(No.2) Regulations 2010
Reg.3, varied: 2014 c.6 s.126
Reg.5, varied: 2014 c.6 s.126

2495. Income Tax (Construction Industry
Scheme) (Amendment No 2) Regulations 2010
Reg.3, varied: 2014 c.6 s.126
Reg.4, varied: 2014 c.6 s.126

2496. Income Tax (Pay As You Earn)
(Amendment No 2) Regulations 2010
Reg.3, varied: 2014 c.6 s.126

2512. Wireless Telegraphy (Exemption and
Amendment) Regulations 2010
Reg.5, amended: SI 2014/1484 Reg.2
Reg.9, added: SI 2014/1484 Reg.2

2571. Care Leavers (England) Regulations 2010
Reg.3, amended: SI 2014/852 Art.19

Reg.5, amended: SI 2014/1917 Reg.7
Sch.1 para.11, added: SI 2014/1917 Reg.8

2574. Child Minding and Day Care (Wales)
Regulations 2010
Sch.2 Part 2 para.21, amended: SI 2014/107
Sch.2 para.8

2600. Tribunal Procedure (Upper Tribunal)
(Lands Chamber) Rules 2010
Part 3 r.21, amended: SI 2014/514 r.15
r.2, see *Dickinson v Network Rail*
Infrastructure Ltd [2014] UKUT 372 (LC)
(UT (Lands)), Sir Keith Lindblom P
r.10, see *Dickinson v Network Rail*
Infrastructure Ltd [2014] UKUT 372 (LC)
(UT (Lands)), Sir Keith Lindblom P

2617. Ecodesign for Energy-Related Products
Regulations 2010
Sch.1 para.4, amended: SI 2014/1290 Reg.2

2653. Tribunal Procedure (Amendment No 3)
Rules 2010
r.4, revoked: SI 2014/2604 r.45

2655. First-tier Tribunal and Upper Tribunal
(Chambers) Order 2010
Art.5A, amended: SI 2014/1901 Art.2
Art.13, amended: SI 2014/1901 Art.2

2677. International Tax Enforcement (Anguilla)
Order 2010
Sch.1 Part 1, referred to: SI 2014/1357 Art.2

2679. International Tax Enforcement (Turks
and Caicos Islands) Order 2010
Sch.1 Part 1, referred to: SI 2014/1360 Art.2

2680. International Tax Enforcement (Gibraltar)
Order 2010
Sch.1 Part 1, referred to: SI 2014/1356 Art.2

2691. Scottish Parliament (Constituencies and
Regions) Order 2010
revoked: SI 2014/501 Art.4

2724. A487 Trunk Road (Blaenannerch,
Ceredigion) (40 mph Speed Limit) Order 2010
varied: SI 2014/454 Art.7

2817. Flavourings in Food (England)
Regulations 2010
Reg.7, revoked: SI 2014/1855 Sch.6 Part 1

2818. Rate of Bereavement Benefits Regulations
2010
Reg.2, amended: SI 2014/516 Art.13
Reg.3, amended: SI 2014/516 Art.13

2840. Genetically Modified Organisms
(Contained Use) (Amendment) Regulations 2010
revoked: SI 2014/1663 Reg.35

2854. Veterinary Surgeons and Veterinary Practitioners (Registration) Regulations Order of Council 2010
revoked: SI 2014/3493 Art.3, Sch.1

2860. Political Parties, Elections and Referendums (Civil Sanctions) Order 2010
Art.4, amended: SI 2014/335 Art.2
Art.5, amended: SI 2014/335 Art.3
Sch.2 Part 1, amended: SI 2014/2448 Art.2

2880. Single Use Carrier Bags Charge (Wales) Regulations 2010
Sch.1 para.1, amended: SI 2014/2291 Reg.5

2906. Education and Skills Act 2008 (Commencement No 7 and Transitory Provisions) Order 2010
Art.3, revoked: SI 2014/3364 Sch.1

2911. Legal Services Act 2007 (Levy) (No.2) Rules 2010
r.2, amended: SI 2014/1185 r.3
r.3, amended: SI 2014/1185 r.4
r.4, amended: SI 2014/1185 r.5
r.5, amended: SI 2014/1185 r.6
r.6, amended: SI 2014/1185 r.7
r.6, revoked (in part): SI 2014/1185 r.7
r.8, amended: SI 2014/1185 r.8

2919. Education (Independent Educational Provision in England) (Provision of Information) Regulations 2010
Sch.1 Part 3 para.5, amended: SI 2014/2103 Art.36

2922. Flavourings in Food (Wales) Regulations 2010
Reg.7, revoked: SI 2014/2303 Sch.6 Part 1

2941. Agriculture (Cross compliance) (No.2) Regulations 2009 (Amendment) Regulations 2010
revoked: SI 2014/3263 Sch.5

2955. Family Procedure Rules 2010
applied: SI 2014/667 r.45, SI 2014/3296 r.15
disapplied: SI 2014/667 r.45, SI 2014/3296 r.15
referred to: SI 2014/543 Reg.4
see *C (A Child) (Prohibited Steps Order: Procedural Irregularity), Re* [2013] EWCA Civ 1412, [2014] 1 W.L.R. 2182 (CA (Civ Div)), Sullivan LJ
Part 1 r.1.4, amended: SI 2014/843 r.3
Part 2 r.2.3, amended: SI 2014/667 r.3, SI 2014/843 r.4, SI 2014/3296 r.3
Part 2 r.2.3, disapplied: SI 2014/3296 r.15

Part 2 r.2.3, revoked (in part): SI 2014/667 r.3, SI 2014/3296 r.3
Part 2 r.2.5, amended: SI 2014/667 r.4
Part 2 r.2.6, amended: SI 2014/667 r.5
Part 2 r.2.6, revoked (in part): SI 2014/667 r.5
Part 2 r.2.7, substituted: SI 2014/667 r.6
Part 3, substituted: SI 2014/843 r.5
Part 3 r.3.2, referred to: SI 2014/603 Sch.1
Part 3 r.3.4, amended: SI 2014/3296 r.4
Part 4 r.4.1, referred to: SI 2014/603 Sch.1
Part 4 r.4.3, referred to: SI 2014/603 Sch.1
Part 4 r.4.7, referred to: SI 2014/603 Sch.1
Part 6 r.6.24, referred to: SI 2014/603 Sch.1
Part 6 r.6.26, referred to: SI 2014/603 Sch.1
Part 6 r.6.32, referred to: SI 2014/603 Sch.1
Part 6 r.6.36, referred to: SI 2014/603 Sch.1
Part 7 r.7.8, amended: SI 2014/843 r.6, SI 2014/3296 r.5
Part 7 r.7.8, revoked (in part): SI 2014/843 r.6
Part 7 r.7.11, amended: SI 2014/524 r.3
Part 7 r.7.12, amended: SI 2014/843 r.7
Part 7 r.7.12, revoked (in part): SI 2014/843 r.7
Part 7 r.7.13, substituted: SI 2014/3296 r.6
Part 7 r.7.14, referred to: SI 2014/603 Sch.1
Part 7 r.7.19, amended: SI 2014/843 r.8
Part 7 r.7.20, amended: SI 2014/843 r.9
Part 7 r.7.20, referred to: SI 2014/603 Sch.1
Part 7 r.7.22, amended: SI 2014/843 r.10
Part 7 r.7.22, revoked (in part): SI 2014/843 r.10
Part 7 r.7.25, revoked: SI 2014/843 r.11
Part 7 r.7.26, amended: SI 2014/524 r.4
Part 7 r.7.30, referred to: SI 2014/603 Sch.1
Part 7 r.7.32, referred to: SI 2014/603 Sch.1
Part 7 r.7.32, revoked (in part): SI 2014/843 r.12
Part 8 r.8.20, referred to: SI 2014/603 Sch.1
Part 8 r.8.25, amended: SI 2014/3296 r.7
Part 8 r.8.26, amended: SI 2014/3296 r.8
Part 9, substituted: SI 2014/667 r.11
Part 9 r.9.2, revoked: SI 2014/667 r.7
Part 9 r.9.10, amended: SI 2014/843 r.13
Part 9 r.9.10, revoked (in part): SI 2014/843 r.13
Part 9 r.9.14, amended: SI 2014/667 r.8
Part 9 r.9.15, amended: SI 2014/843 r.14
Part 9 r.9.18, amended: SI 2014/667 r.9
Part 9 r.9.18, referred to: SI 2014/603 Sch.1

Part 9 r.9.20, referred to: SI 2014/603 Sch.1
Part 9 r.9.21A, added: SI 2014/667 r.10
Part 9 r.9.23, revoked: SI 2014/667 r.12
Part 9 r.9.26, referred to: SI 2014/603 Sch.1
Part 9 r.9.26C, added: SI 2014/667 r.13
Part 10 r.10.3, referred to: SI 2014/603 Sch.1
Part 10 r.10.6, amended: SI 2014/667 r.14
Part 10 r.10.6, referred to: SI 2014/603 Sch.1
Part 10 r.10.7, referred to: SI 2014/603 Sch.1
Part 10 r.10.11, amended: SI 2014/3296 r.9
Part 10 r.10.12, substituted: SI 2014/667 r.15
Part 11 r.11.15, substituted: SI 2014/667 r.16
Part 12 r.12.2, amended: SI 2014/843 r.15
Part 12 r.12.2, revoked (in part): SI 2014/843 r.15
Part 12 r.12.3, amended: SI 2014/843 r.16
Part 12 r.12.3, referred to: SI 2014/603 Sch.1
Part 12 r.12.4, referred to: SI 2014/603 Sch.1
Part 12 r.12.5, amended: SI 2014/843 r.17
Part 12 r.12.5, referred to: SI 2014/603 Sch.1
Part 12 r.12.5, revoked (in part): SI 2014/843 r.17
Part 12 r.12.6, amended: SI 2014/843 r.18
Part 12 r.12.6, referred to: SI 2014/603 Sch.1
Part 12 r.12.8, amended: SI 2014/843 r.20
Part 12 r.12.8, substituted: SI 2014/843 r.19
Part 12 r.12.12, referred to: SI 2014/603 Sch.1
Part 12 r.12.13, referred to: SI 2014/603 Sch.1
Part 12 r.12.14, amended: SI 2014/843 r.21
Part 12 r.12.14, referred to: SI 2014/603 Sch.1
Part 12 r.12.15, amended: SI 2014/843 r.22
Part 12 r.12.15, referred to: SI 2014/603 Sch.1
Part 12 r.12.19, referred to: SI 2014/603 Sch.1
Part 12 r.12.21, referred to: SI 2014/603 Sch.1
Part 12 r.12.22, referred to: SI 2014/603 Sch.1
Part 12 r.12.22, substituted: SI 2014/843 r.23
Part 12 r.12.23, referred to: SI 2014/603 Sch.1
Part 12 r.12.23, substituted: SI 2014/843 r.24
Part 12 r.12.25, substituted: SI 2014/843 r.25
Part 12 r.12.26, substituted: SI 2014/843 r.26
Part 12 r.12.26A, added: SI 2014/843 r.27
Part 12 r.12.29, referred to: SI 2014/603 Sch.1

Part 12 r.12.31, referred to: SI 2014/603 Sch.1
Part 12 r.12.33, amended: SI 2014/843 r.28
Part 12 r.12.42A, added: SI 2014/3296 r.10
Part 12 r.12.73, referred to: SI 2014/603 Sch.1
Part 12 r.12.75, amended: SI 2014/843 r.29
Part 13 r.13.1, amended: SI 2014/843 r.30
Part 13 r.13.3, referred to: SI 2014/603 Sch.1
Part 13 r.13.5, referred to: SI 2014/603 Sch.1
Part 13 r.13.8, referred to: SI 2014/603 Sch.1
Part 13 r.13.9, referred to: SI 2014/603 Sch.1
Part 13 r.13.14, referred to: SI 2014/603 Sch.1
Part 13 r.13.16, referred to: SI 2014/603 Sch.1
Part 13 r.13.21, referred to: SI 2014/603 Sch.1
Part 13 r.13.22, referred to: SI 2014/603 Sch.1
Part 14 r.14.1, amended: SI 2014/843 r.31
Part 14 r.14.2, referred to: SI 2014/603 Sch.1
Part 14 r.14.2, substituted: SI 2014/843 r.32
Part 14 r.14.3, amended: SI 2014/843 r.33, r.34
Part 14 r.14.3, referred to: SI 2014/603 Sch.1
Part 14 r.14.5, referred to: SI 2014/603 Sch.1
Part 14 r.14.6, referred to: SI 2014/603 Sch.1
Part 14 r.14.7, referred to: SI 2014/603 Sch.1
Part 14 r.14.8, amended: SI 2014/843 r.35
Part 14 r.14.8, referred to: SI 2014/603 Sch.1
Part 14 r.14.9, referred to: SI 2014/603 Sch.1
Part 14 r.14.10, referred to: SI 2014/603 Sch.1
Part 14 r.14.13, amended: SI 2014/843 r.36
Part 14 r.14.14, referred to: SI 2014/603 Sch.1
Part 14 r.14.16, referred to: SI 2014/603 Sch.1
Part 14 r.14.18, amended: SI 2014/843 r.37
Part 14 r.14.18, referred to: SI 2014/603 Sch.1
Part 14 r.14.20, referred to: SI 2014/603 Sch.1
Part 14 r.14.25, amended: SI 2014/843 r.38
Part 14 r.14.26, amended: SI 2014/843 r.39
Part 14 r.14.26, referred to: SI 2014/603 Sch.1
Part 14 r.14.27, referred to: SI 2014/603 Sch.1
Part 15 r.15.6, referred to: SI 2014/603 Sch.1

Part 15 r.15.8, referred to: SI 2014/603 Sch.1

Part 15 r.15.9, referred to: SI 2014/603 Sch.1

Part 16 r.16.3, referred to: SI 2014/603 Sch.1

Part 16 r.16.4, referred to: SI 2014/603 Sch.1

Part 16 r.16.11, referred to: SI 2014/603 Sch.1

Part 16 r.16.21, referred to: SI 2014/603 Sch.1

Part 16 r.16.24, referred to: SI 2014/603 Sch.1

Part 16 r.16.30, referred to: SI 2014/603 Sch.1

Part 16 r.16.33, referred to: SI 2014/603 Sch.1

Part 16 r.16.34, referred to: SI 2014/603 Sch.1

Part 16 r.16.38, amended: SI 2014/843 r.40, r.41

Part 16 r.16.39, amended: SI 2014/843 r.42

Part 17 r.17.2, amended: SI 2014/843 r.43

Part 17 r.17.2, revoked (in part): SI 2014/843 r.43

Part 17 r.17.3, referred to: SI 2014/603 Sch.1

Part 17 r.17.4, referred to: SI 2014/603 Sch.1

Part 18 r.18.3, referred to: SI 2014/603 Sch.1

Part 18 r.18.4, referred to: SI 2014/603 Sch.1

Part 18 r.18.5, referred to: SI 2014/603 Sch.1

Part 18 r.18.8, referred to: SI 2014/603 Sch.1

Part 18 r.18.9, referred to: SI 2014/603 Sch.1

Part 19 r.19.1, referred to: SI 2014/603 Sch.1

Part 19 r.19.4, referred to: SI 2014/603 Sch.1

Part 19 r.19.6, referred to: SI 2014/603 Sch.1

Part 19 r.19.8, referred to: SI 2014/603 Sch.1

Part 19 r.19.9, referred to: SI 2014/603 Sch.1

Part 21 r.21.2, referred to: SI 2014/603 Sch.1

Part 22 r.22.1, referred to: SI 2014/603 Sch.1

Part 22 r.22.3, referred to: SI 2014/603 Sch.1

Part 22 r.22.5, referred to: SI 2014/603 Sch.1

Part 22 r.22.7, referred to: SI 2014/603 Sch.1

Part 22 r.22.9, referred to: SI 2014/603 Sch.1

Part 23 r.23.4, referred to: SI 2014/603 Sch.1

Part 23 r.23.6, referred to: SI 2014/603 Sch.1

Part 23 r.23.9, amended: SI 2014/667 r.17

Part 23 r.23.9, referred to: SI 2014/603 Sch.1

Part 24 r.24.3, referred to: SI 2014/603 Sch.1

Part 24 r.24.4, referred to: SI 2014/603 Sch.1

Part 24 r.24.7, referred to: SI 2014/603 Sch.1

Part 24 r.24.11, referred to: SI 2014/603 Sch.1

Part 24 r.24.13, referred to: SI 2014/603 Sch.1

Part 25 r.25.1, revoked: SI 2014/843 r.44

Part 25 r.25.2, amended: SI 2014/843 r.45

Part 25 r.25.4, referred to: SI 2014/603 Sch.1

Part 25 r.25.4, substituted: SI 2014/843 r.46

Part 25 r.25.5, amended: SI 2014/843 r.47

Part 25 r.25.6, substituted: SI 2014/843 r.48

Part 25 r.25.7, amended: SI 2014/843 r.49

Part 25 r.25.8, amended: SI 2014/843 r.50

Part 25 r.25.8, referred to: SI 2014/603 Sch.1

Part 25 r.25.10, referred to: SI 2014/603 Sch.1

Part 25 r.25.11, referred to: SI 2014/603 Sch.1

Part 25 r.25.16, referred to: SI 2014/603 Sch.1

Part 25 r.25.19, amended: SI 2014/843 r.51

Part 25 r.25.19, revoked (in part): SI 2014/843 r.51

Part 25 r.25.20, amended: SI 2014/667 r.18

Part 26 r.26.3, referred to: SI 2014/603 Sch.1

Part 27 r.27.2, amended: SI 2014/667 r.19

Part 27 r.27.2, revoked (in part): SI 2014/667 r.19

Part 27 r.27.3, referred to: SI 2014/603 Sch.1

Part 27 r.27.7, referred to: SI 2014/603 Sch.1

Part 29 r.29.1, referred to: SI 2014/603 Sch.1

Part 29 r.29.4, referred to: SI 2014/603 Sch.1

Part 29 r.29.11, referred to: SI 2014/603 Sch.1

Part 29 r.29.14, referred to: SI 2014/603 Sch.1

Part 29 r.29.19, added: SI 2014/667 r.20

Part 29 r.29.19, applied: SI 2014/840 r.13

Part 29 r.29.19, referred to: SI 2014/603 Sch.1

Part 30, applied: SI 2014/667 r.45

Part 30 r.30.1, amended: SI 2014/667 r.21

Part 30 r.30.3, amended: SI 2014/667 r.22, SI 2014/3296 r.11

Part 30 r.30.3, revoked (in part): SI 2014/667 r.22

Part 30 r.30.4, amended: SI 2014/667 r.23

Part 30 r.30.4, revoked (in part): SI 2014/667 r.23

Part 30 r.30.5, amended: SI 2014/667 r.24

Part 30 r.30.13, amended: SI 2014/667 r.25

Part 30 r.30.14, amended: SI 2014/667 r.26

Part 31, amended: SI 2014/524 r.5

Part 31 r.31.1, amended: SI 2014/524 r.6

Part 31 r.31.2, amended: SI 2014/524 r.7

Part 31 r.31.3, amended: SI 2014/524 r.8

Part 31 r.31.8, amended: SI 2014/524 r.9
Part 31 r.31.12, amended: SI 2014/524 r.10
Part 31 r.31.14, amended: SI 2014/524 r.11
Part 32 r.32.10A, amended: SI 2014/667 r.27
Part 33, amended: SI 2014/667 r.38
Part 33 r.33.1, amended: SI 2014/667 r.28
Part 33 r.33.2, amended: SI 2014/667 r.29
Part 33 r.33.4, amended: SI 2014/667 r.30
Part 33 r.33.5, substituted: SI 2014/667 r.31
Part 33 r.33.10, amended: SI 2014/667 r.32
Part 33 r.33.11, amended: SI 2014/667 r.33
Part 33 r.33.14, amended: SI 2014/667 r.34
Part 33 r.33.17, amended: SI 2014/667 r.35
Part 33 r.33.18, revoked: SI 2014/667 r.36
Part 33 r.33.19, substituted: SI 2014/667 r.37
Part 33 r.33.20, amended: SI 2014/667 r.39
Part 33 r.33.21, revoked: SI 2014/667 r.40
Part 33 r.33.23, substituted: SI 2014/667 r.41
Part 33 r.33.24, amended: SI 2014/667 r.42
Part 33 r.33.25, amended: SI 2014/667 r.43
Part 37, added: SI 2014/667 Sch.1
Part 37 r.37.1, amended: SI 2014/3296 r.12
Part 37 r.37.9, amended: SI 2014/843 r.52,
SI 2014/3296 r.13
Part 37 r.37.9, referred to: SI 2014/603 Sch.1
Part 38, added: SI 2014/3296 r.14
Pt 28., see *M v M (Costs)* [2013] EWHC
3372 (Fam), [2014] 1 F.L.R. 499 (Fam Div),
Eleanor King J; see *X Local Authority v
Trimega Laboratories Ltd* [2014] 2 F.L.R.
232 (Fam Div), Judge Williams
Pt 33., see *Constantinides v Constantinides*
[2013] EWHC 3688 (Fam), [2014] 1 W.L.R.
1934 (Fam Div), Holman J
Pt 9., see *Mann v Mann* [2014] EWHC 537
(Fam), [2014] 1 W.L.R. 2807 (Fam Div),
Mostyn J
r.1.1, see *A (Abduction: Child's Objections
to Return), Re* [2014] EWCA Civ 554,
[2014] 1 W.L.R. 4326 (CA (Civ Div)),
Moore-Bick LJ; see *H-L (A Child) (Care
Proceedings: Expert Evidence), Re* [2013]
EWCA Civ 655, [2014] 1 W.L.R. 1160 (CA
(Civ Div)), Sir James Munby PFD; see *S (A
Child) (Split Hearing: Fact Finding), Re*
[2014] EWCA Civ 25, [2014] 1 F.L.R. 1421
(CA (Civ Div)), Tomlinson LJ
r.2.3, see *Tchenguiz-Imerman v Imerman
(Application for Joinder)* [2012] EWHC
4277 (Fam), [2014] 1 F.L.R. 865 (Fam Div),
Moylan J

r.3.3, see *Mann v Mann* [2014] EWHC 537
(Fam), [2014] 1 W.L.R. 2807 (Fam Div),
Mostyn J
r.4.1, see *F (A Child) (Return Order: Power
to Revoke), Re* [2014] EWHC 1780 (Fam),
[2014] 1 W.L.R. 4375 (Fam Div), Mostyn J
r.9.11, see *Tchenguiz-Imerman v Imerman
(Application for Joinder)* [2012] EWHC
4277 (Fam), [2014] 1 F.L.R. 865 (Fam Div),
Moylan J
r.9.26B, see *Tchenguiz-Imerman v Imerman
(Application for Joinder)* [2012] EWHC
4277 (Fam), [2014] 1 F.L.R. 865 (Fam Div),
Moylan J
r.12.37, see *X (Deprivation of Liberty), Re*
[2014] EWCOP 37, (2014) 17 C.C.L. Rep.
464 (CP), Sir James Munby PFD
r.14.3, see *G (A Child) (Non-relative Carer:
Joinder to Adoption Proceedings), Re* [2014]
EWCA Civ 432, [2014] 3 W.L.R. 1719 (CA
(Civ Div)), Sullivan LJ
r.18.11, see *Practice Guidance (Fam Ct:
Duration of Ex Parte (Without Notice)
Orders)* [2014] 3 F.C.R. 402 (Fam Ct), Sir
James Munby PFD
r.25.1, see *F (A Child) (Abduction:
Art.13(b): Psychiatric Assessment), Re*
[2014] EWCA Civ 275, [2014] 2 F.L.R.
1115 (CA (Civ Div)), Sullivan LJ; see *H-L
(A Child) (Care Proceedings: Expert
Evidence), Re* [2013] EWCA Civ 655,
[2014] 1 W.L.R. 1160 (CA (Civ Div)), Sir
James Munby PFD; see *S (Parenting
Assessment), Re* [2014] 2 F.L.R. 575 (CC
(Bournemouth)), Sir James Munby PFD
r.25.11, see *JG (A Child) v Legal Services
Commission* [2014] EWCA Civ 656, [2014]
5 Costs L.O. 708 (CA (Civ Div)), Richards
LJ
r.25.12, see *JG (A Child) v Legal Services
Commission* [2014] EWCA Civ 656, [2014]
5 Costs L.O. 708 (CA (Civ Div)), Richards
LJ
r.27.11, see *Al-Hilli (Reporting Restrictions),
Re* [2013] EWHC 2190 (Fam), [2014] 1
F.L.R. 403 (Fam Div), Baker J
r.28.2, see *M v M (Costs)* [2013] EWHC
3372 (Fam), [2014] 1 F.L.R. 499 (Fam Div),
Eleanor King J

r.28.3, see *M v M (Costs)* [2013] EWHC
3372 (Fam), [2014] 1 F.L.R. 499 (Fam Div),
Eleanor King J
r.29.15, see *P v P (Divorce: Financial
Remedy Order)* [2014] EWHC 1101 (Fam),
[2014] 1 W.L.R. 4607 (Fam Div), Eleanor
King J

2956. Somalia (Asset-Freezing) Regulations 2010
Sch.1 para.5, amended: 2014 c.29 s.4

**2969. National Assembly for Wales
(Disqualification) Order 2010**
Sch.1 Part 1, amended: SI 2014/549 Sch.1
para.56

**2975. Double Taxation Relief and International
Tax Enforcement (Federal Republic of
Germany) Order 2010**
Sch.1, referred to: SI 2014/1874 Art.2
Sch.1 Part 1, substituted: SI 2014/1874
Sch.1

**2979. Double Taxation Relief and International
Tax Enforcement (Belgium) Order 2010**
Sch.1, substituted: SI 2014/1875 Sch.1

**3023. Financial Services and Markets Act 2000
(Administration Orders Relating to Insurers)
Order 2010**
Art.2, varied: SI 2014/229 Sch.5 para.3
Art.3, varied: SI 2014/229 Sch.5 para.3

**3048. Submarine Pipelines (Designated Owners)
Order 2010**
revoked: SI 2014/422 Art.2

2011

**94. M4 Motorway (West of Junction 23A
(Magor) to East of Junction 29 (Castleton))
(Variable Speed Limits) Regulations 2011**
varied: SI 2014/158 Art.5

99. Electronic Money Regulations 2011
applied: SI 2014/1195 Art.2, SI 2014/2418
Sch.1
Reg.59A, added: SI 2014/366 Art.18
Reg.60, applied: SI 2014/1195 Art.2
Sch.2A, added: SI 2014/366 Art.18
Sch.3 Part 1 para.2, revoked (in part): SI
2014/366 Art.18
Sch.3 Part 1 para.3, amended: SI 2014/366
Art.18
Sch.3 Part 1 para.8, amended: SI 2014/366
Art.18

**122. Legal Services Act 2007 (Disclosure of
Restricted Information) Order 2011**
Sch.1, amended: SI 2014/549 Sch.1 para.43

**209. Criminal Procedure and Investigations Act
1996 (Defence Disclosure Time Limits)
Regulations 2011**
applied: SI 2014/1610 r.22_9, r.3_26
referred to: SI 2014/1610 r.2_3

232. Gas (Exemptions) Order 2011
Art.5, applied: SI 2014/1458 Art.5

**234. CRC Energy Efficiency Scheme
(Amendment) Order 2011**
Art.19, amended: 2014 c.29 s.4

**236. Films Co-Production Agreements
(Amendment) Order 2011**
revoked: SI 2014/1561 Art.3

**245. Investment Bank Special Administration
Regulations 2011**
see *MF Global UK Ltd (In Special
Administration), Re* [2013] EWHC 2556
(Ch), [2014] 1 W.L.R. 1558 (Ch D), David
Richards J; see *MF Global UK Ltd (In
Special Administration), Re* [2014] EWHC
2222 (Ch), [2014] Bus. L.R. 1156 (Ch D
(Companies Ct)), Richards J

**300. Police Act 1996 (Equipment) Regulations
2011**
Reg.2, amended: SI 2014/395 Reg.2
Reg.4, added: SI 2014/395 Reg.2

**402. Food Labelling (Declaration of Allergens)
(England) Regulations 2011**
revoked: SI 2014/1855 Sch.6 Part 1

**445. Immigration and Nationality (Fees) Order
2011**
applied: SI 2014/581, SI 2014/581 Reg.10,
SI 2014/922, SI 2014/2398
referred to: SI 2014/2771 Art.13
revoked: 2014 c.22 Sch.9 para.74
Art.2, amended: SI 2014/205 Art.2, SI
2014/2038 Art.2
Art.3, amended: SI 2014/205 Art.2, SI
2014/2038 Art.2
Art.3, applied: SI 2014/581 Reg.3, Reg.4,
Reg.5, Reg.6, SI 2014/922 Reg.3, Reg.4,
Reg.5, Reg.6
Art.4, amended: SI 2014/205 Art.2
Art.4, applied: SI 2014/581 Reg.6, Reg.8, SI
2014/922 Reg.5, Reg.8, Reg.9
Art.5, amended: SI 2014/205 Art.2, SI
2014/2038 Art.2

Art.5, applied: SI 2014/581 Reg.4, Reg.5,
Reg.6, Reg.8, SI 2014/922 Reg.5
Art.6, applied: SI 2014/581 Reg.7, SI
2014/922 Reg.7
Art.7, applied: SI 2014/922 Reg.9

463. Seed Marketing Regulations 2011
Sch.1, amended: SI 2014/487 Reg.4

465. Food Labelling (Declaration of Allergens) (Wales) Regulations 2011
revoked: SI 2014/2303 Sch.6 Part 1

517. Armed Forces and Reserve Forces (Compensation Scheme) Order 2011
applied: SI 2014/916 Sch.2, SI 2014/1230 Reg.24
Art.12, substituted: SI 2014/412 Art.2
Art.15, referred to: SI 2014/2672 Sch.1 para.18
Art.24A, amended: SI 2014/412 Art.2
Art.24D, amended: SI 2014/412 Art.2
Art.29, referred to: SI 2014/2672 Sch.1 para.19
Art.31, referred to: SI 2014/2672 Sch.1 para.19
Sch.3 Part 1, amended: SI 2014/412 Art.4, Art.5, Art.6, Art.7, Art.8, Art.9, Sch.1

548. Libya (Financial Sanctions) Order 2011
Sch.1 para.5, amended: 2014 c.29 s.4

561. Local Government Pension Scheme (Benefits, Membership and Contributions) (Amendment) Regulations 2011
revoked: SI 2014/525 Sch.1

564. Marine Licensing (Application Fees) Regulations 2011
revoked: SI 2014/615 Reg.8

582. Arrangements for Placement of Children by Voluntary Organisations and Others (England) Regulations 2011
Reg.7, amended: SI 2014/852 Art.20
Sch.4 para.2, amended: SI 2014/2103 Art.37

593. Mutual Societies (Electronic Communications) Order 2011
Art.22, revoked: 2014 c.14 Sch.7
Art.24, revoked: 2014 c.14 Sch.7

605. Libya (Asset-Freezing) Regulations 2011
Sch.1 para.5, amended: 2014 c.29 s.4

668. Stamp Duty and Stamp Duty Reserve Tax (European Multilateral Clearing Facility N.V.) Regulations 2011
revoked: SI 2014/9 Reg.5

692. Tuberculosis (Wales) Order 2011
Art.2, amended: SI 2014/632 Art.3

Art.2A, added: SI 2014/632 Art.3
Art.9, amended: SI 2014/632 Art.3
Art.10, amended: SI 2014/632 Art.3
Art.16, amended: SI 2014/632 Art.3

695. Regional Flood and Coastal Committees (England and Wales) Regulations 2011
Reg.11, amended: 2014 c.29 s.4

702. Finance Act 2009, Schedules 55 and 56 (Income Tax Self Assessment and Pension Schemes) (Appointed Days and Consequential and Savings Provisions) Order 2011
Art.22, revoked: SI 2014/3269 Art.5

712. Qualifying Care Relief (Specified Social Care Schemes) Order 2011
Art.5, amended: SI 2014/852 Art.21

734. Independent Health Care (Wales) Regulations 2011
Reg.25, amended: 2014 c.23 Sch.8 para.12

750. Terrorist Asset-Freezing etc Act 2010 (Overseas Territories) Order 2011
Sch.2 para.10, amended: 2014 c.29 s.4

761. London Insolvency District (Central London County Court) Order 2011
revoked: SI 2014/818 Art.2

827. Pensions Increase (Review) Order 2011
referred to: SI 2014/668 Sch.1
Art.6, substituted: SI 2014/107 Sch.1 para.56, SI 2014/3229 Sch.6 para.35

885. Student Fees (Amounts) (Wales) Regulations 2011
Reg.3, amended: SI 2014/2071 Reg.3
Reg.4, substituted: SI 2014/2071 Reg.4
Reg.5, added: SI 2014/2071 Reg.5

887. Egypt (Asset-Freezing) Regulations 2011
Sch.1 para.5, amended: 2014 c.29 s.4

888. Tunisia (Asset-Freezing) Regulations 2011
Sch.1 para.5, amended: 2014 c.29 s.4

908. Greater Manchester Combined Authority Order 2011
Art.3, applied: SI 2014/1112 Art.2

935. Road Traffic Exemptions (Special Forces) (Variation and Amendment) Regulations 2011
Reg.3, applied: SI 2014/12 Art.6, SI 2014/29 Art.8, SI 2014/30 Art.6, SI 2014/33 Art.5, SI 2014/37 Art.6, SI 2014/38 Art.6, SI 2014/50 Art.8, SI 2014/53 Art.7, SI 2014/56 Art.6, SI 2014/57 Art.6, SI 2014/60 Art.6, SI 2014/61 Art.7, SI 2014/62 Art.7, SI 2014/67 Art.9, SI 2014/70 Art.4, SI 2014/71 Art.5, SI 2014/75 Art.8, SI 2014/83 Art.6, SI 2014/85 Art.6, SI 2014/87 Art.9, SI 2014/99 Art.6, SI

2014/102 Art.6, SI 2014/103 Art.6, SI
2014/104 Art.6, SI 2014/134 Art.6, SI
2014/138 Art.6, SI 2014/151 Art.4, SI
2014/155 Art.6, SI 2014/156 Art.7, SI
2014/157 Art.8, SI 2014/169 Art.8, SI
2014/170 Art.6, SI 2014/172 Art.6, SI
2014/174 Art.6, SI 2014/189 Art.6, SI
2014/190 Art.4, SI 2014/222 Art.6, SI
2014/223 Art.5, SI 2014/224 Art.6, SI
2014/225 Art.5, SI 2014/226 Art.6, SI
2014/228 Art.6, SI 2014/232 Art.6, SI
2014/233 Art.6, SI 2014/244 Art.5, SI
2014/246 Art.7, SI 2014/248 Art.6, SI
2014/252 Art.5, SI 2014/281 Art.6, SI
2014/283 Art.6, SI 2014/284 Art.7, SI
2014/289 Art.6, SI 2014/293 Art.5, SI
2014/294 Art.7, SI 2014/295 Art.8, SI
2014/297 Art.5, SI 2014/298 Art.6, SI
2014/300 Art.6, SI 2014/302 Art.6, SI
2014/304 Art.6, SI 2014/309 Art.6, SI
2014/311 Art.6, SI 2014/342 Art.6, SI
2014/343 Art.6, SI 2014/346 Art.6, SI
2014/352 Art.6, SI 2014/365 Art.6, SI
2014/391 Art.6, SI 2014/392 Art.6, SI
2014/393 Art.6, SI 2014/394 Art.6, SI
2014/396 Art.18, SI 2014/397 Art.12, SI
2014/398 Art.6, SI 2014/401 Art.9, SI
2014/405 Art.6, SI 2014/419 Art.7, SI
2014/425 Art.6, SI 2014/428 Art.6, SI
2014/429 Art.8, SI 2014/653 Art.8, SI
2014/655 Art.6, SI 2014/657 Art.6, SI
2014/665 Art.6, SI 2014/671 Art.7, SI
2014/672 Art.6, SI 2014/673 Art.5, SI
2014/674 Art.11, SI 2014/679 Art.7, SI
2014/680 Art.7, SI 2014/681 Art.7, SI
2014/689 Art.6, SI 2014/701 Art.6, SI
2014/718 Art.5, SI 2014/719 Art.6, SI
2014/734 Art.9, SI 2014/740 Art.6, SI
2014/747 Art.9, SI 2014/758 Art.6, SI
2014/759 Art.7, SI 2014/763 Art.6, SI
2014/764 Art.7, SI 2014/767 Art.5, SI
2014/770 Art.6, SI 2014/773 Art.7, SI
2014/775 Art.6, SI 2014/778 Art.6, SI
2014/799 Art.6, SI 2014/803 Art.7, SI
2014/858 Art.6, SI 2014/937 Art.11, SI
2014/947 Art.7, SI 2014/948 Art.7, SI
2014/957 Art.5, SI 2014/960 Art.7, SI
2014/961 Art.8, SI 2014/967 Art.6, SI
2014/968 Art.6, SI 2014/977 Art.7, SI
2014/978 Art.14, SI 2014/980 Art.6, SI
2014/983 Art.7, SI 2014/984 Art.9, SI

2014/985 Art.6, SI 2014/989 Art.6, SI
2014/993 Art.12, SI 2014/999 Art.7, SI
2014/1010 Art.6, SI 2014/1018 Art.10, SI
2014/1026 Art.5, SI 2014/1041 Art.6, SI
2014/1048 Art.5, SI 2014/1072 Art.7, SI
2014/1079 Art.6, SI 2014/1080 Art.6, SI
2014/1081 Art.7, SI 2014/1104 Art.6, SI
2014/1109 Art.6, SI 2014/1113 Art.7, SI
2014/1122 Art.6, SI 2014/1125 Art.6, SI
2014/1145 Art.7, SI 2014/1147 Art.7, SI
2014/1150 Art.9, SI 2014/1159 Art.11, SI
2014/1160 Art.5, SI 2014/1163 Art.6, SI
2014/1166 Art.9, SI 2014/1168 Art.6, SI
2014/1170 Art.6, SI 2014/1172 Art.6, SI
2014/1174 Art.8, SI 2014/1175 Art.8, SI
2014/1214 Art.6, SI 2014/1216 Art.9, SI
2014/1218 Art.7, SI 2014/1223 Art.7, SI
2014/1224 Art.10, SI 2014/1225 Art.5, SI
2014/1228 Art.12, SI 2014/1279 Art.6, SI
2014/1284 Art.7, SI 2014/1297 Art.9, SI
2014/1298 Art.7, SI 2014/1299 Art.8, SI
2014/1301 Art.7, SI 2014/1302 Art.8, SI
2014/1305 Art.8, SI 2014/1306 Art.4, SI
2014/1307 Art.7, SI 2014/1312 Art.6, SI
2014/1320 Art.7, SI 2014/1322 Art.7, SI
2014/1336 Art.4, SI 2014/1342 Art.8, SI
2014/1343 Art.10, SI 2014/1346 Art.8, SI
2014/1348 Art.7, SI 2014/1392 Art.6, SI
2014/1469 Art.6, SI 2014/1476 Art.9, SI
2014/1486 Art.6, SI 2014/1488 Art.5, SI
2014/1489 Art.10, SI 2014/1490 Art.6, SI
2014/1496 Art.7, SI 2014/1547 Art.6, SI
2014/1569 Art.6, SI 2014/1570 Art.4, SI
2014/1582 Art.6, SI 2014/1634 Art.7, SI
2014/1642 Art.8, SI 2014/1647 Art.8, SI
2014/1654 Art.8, SI 2014/1655 Art.5, SI
2014/1656 Art.4, SI 2014/1658 Art.7, SI
2014/1672 Art.9, SI 2014/1679 Art.7, SI
2014/1680 Art.9, SI 2014/1681 Art.8, SI
2014/1690 Art.11, SI 2014/1692 Art.5, SI
2014/1695 Art.8, SI 2014/1696 Art.7, SI
2014/1700 Art.7, SI 2014/1701 Art.5, SI
2014/1733 Art.6, SI 2014/1735 Art.8, SI
2014/1736 Art.6, SI 2014/1744 Art.7, SI
2014/1745 Art.7, SI 2014/1749 Art.6, SI
2014/1757 Art.6, SI 2014/1783 Art.5, SI
2014/1784 Art.5, SI 2014/1841 Art.7, SI
2014/1856 Art.10, SI 2014/1861 Art.7, SI
2014/1863 Art.6, SI 2014/1927 Art.4, SI
2014/1935 Art.5, SI 2014/1949 Art.6, SI
2014/1950 Art.7, SI 2014/1951 Art.5, SI

2014/1952 Art.6, SI 2014/1956 Art.7, SI
2014/1968 Art.10, SI 2014/1970 Art.6, SI
2014/1974 Art.6, SI 2014/1978 Art.7, SI
2014/1979 Art.7, SI 2014/1982 Art.6, SI
2014/1984 Art.7, SI 2014/1988 Art.4, SI
2014/2001 Art.7, SI 2014/2002 Art.6, SI
2014/2003 Art.8, SI 2014/2004 Art.6, SI
2014/2008 Art.7, SI 2014/2032 Art.7, SI
2014/2033 Art.5, SI 2014/2037 Art.5, SI
2014/2041 Art.6, SI 2014/2048 Art.7, SI
2014/2052 Art.9, SI 2014/2053 Art.6, SI
2014/2066 Art.6, SI 2014/2088 Art.13, SI
2014/2089 Art.8, SI 2014/2090 Art.8, SI
2014/2091 Art.7, SI 2014/2092 Art.5, SI
2014/2094 Art.6, SI 2014/2098 Art.6, SI
2014/2102 Art.4, SI 2014/2105 Art.6, SI
2014/2138 Art.8, SI 2014/2153 Art.6, SI
2014/2156 Art.4, SI 2014/2159 Art.12, SI
2014/2163 Art.6, SI 2014/2168 Art.6, SI
2014/2170 Art.6, SI 2014/2171 Art.6, SI
2014/2173 Art.7, SI 2014/2183 Art.6, SI
2014/2188 Art.6, SI 2014/2189 Art.7, SI
2014/2192 Art.6, SI 2014/2193 Art.10, SI
2014/2195 Art.6, SI 2014/2214 Art.6, SI
2014/2217 Art.7, SI 2014/2219 Art.6, SI
2014/2221 Art.11, SI 2014/2253 Art.5, SI
2014/2256 Art.9, SI 2014/2266 Art.7, SI
2014/2274 Art.12, SI 2014/2276 Art.10, SI
2014/2282 Art.12, SI 2014/2285 Art.9, SI
2014/2286 Art.6, SI 2014/2292 Art.8, SI
2014/2293 Art.9, SI 2014/2298 Art.6, SI
2014/2302 Art.6, SI 2014/2312 Art.8, SI
2014/2314 Art.8, SI 2014/2318 Art.5, SI
2014/2324 Art.6, SI 2014/2331 Art.8, SI
2014/2334 Art.4, SI 2014/2343 Art.27, SI
2014/2345 Art.6, SI 2014/2346 Art.23, SI
2014/2351 Art.5, SI 2014/2352 Art.6, SI
2014/2353 Art.4, SI 2014/2360 Art.6, SI
2014/2390 Art.5, SI 2014/2408 Art.5, SI
2014/2412 Art.7, SI 2014/2414 Art.14, SI
2014/2421 Art.5, SI 2014/2425 Art.5, SI
2014/2426 Art.6, SI 2014/2427 Art.6, SI
2014/2428 Art.9, SI 2014/2432 Art.9, SI
2014/2433 Art.4, SI 2014/2453 Art.6, SI
2014/2471 Art.8, SI 2014/2476 Art.7, SI
2014/2479 Art.9, SI 2014/2480 Art.7, SI
2014/2487 Art.5, SI 2014/2499 Art.7, SI
2014/2500 Art.7, SI 2014/2506 Art.8, SI
2014/2510 Art.6, SI 2014/2512 Art.13, SI
2014/2517 Art.6, SI 2014/2521 Art.9, SI
2014/2525 Art.6, SI 2014/2536 Art.10, SI

2014/2537 Art.6, SI 2014/2538 Art.10, SI
2014/2541 Art.6, SI 2014/2545 Art.4, SI
2014/2546 Art.12, SI 2014/2547 Art.9, SI
2014/2549 Art.6, SI 2014/2551 Art.10, SI
2014/2563 Art.5, SI 2014/2564 Art.5, SI
2014/2569 Art.5, SI 2014/2571 Art.7, SI
2014/2581 Art.8, SI 2014/2585 Art.11, SI
2014/2593 Art.7, SI 2014/2596 Art.7, SI
2014/2599 Art.8, SI 2014/2600 Art.8, SI
2014/2601 Art.7, SI 2014/2608 Art.6, SI
2014/2626 Art.9, SI 2014/2630 Art.7, SI
2014/2633 Art.7, SI 2014/2637 Art.11, SI
2014/2638 Art.5, SI 2014/2639 Art.4, SI
2014/2644 Art.6, SI 2014/2645 Art.6, SI
2014/2654 Art.5, SI 2014/2663 Art.11, SI
2014/2675 Art.7, SI 2014/2681 Art.6, SI
2014/2683 Art.6, SI 2014/2684 Art.6, SI
2014/2685 Art.6, SI 2014/2695 Art.7, SI
2014/2699 Art.6, SI 2014/2700 Art.7, SI
2014/2723 Art.6, SI 2014/2743 Art.9, SI
2014/2752 Art.12, SI 2014/2758 Art.8, SI
2014/2779 Art.10, SI 2014/2782 Art.11, SI
2014/2784 Art.9, SI 2014/2785 Art.6, SI
2014/2787 Art.6, SI 2014/2792 Art.6, SI
2014/2797 Art.7, SI 2014/2801 Art.6, SI
2014/2802 Art.6, SI 2014/2804 Art.6, SI
2014/2814 Art.8, SI 2014/2815, SI
2014/2815 Art.5, SI 2014/2819 Art.5, SI
2014/2820 Art.7, SI 2014/2826 Art.8, SI
2014/2834 Art.7, SI 2014/2835, SI
2014/2835 Art.10, SI 2014/2870 Art.9, SI
2014/2876 Art.9, SI 2014/2877 Art.5, SI
2014/2878 Art.5, SI 2014/2901 Art.5, SI
2014/2951 Art.7, SI 2014/2952 Art.12, SI
2014/2955 Art.6, SI 2014/2959 Art.6, SI
2014/2967 Art.7, SI 2014/2969 Art.6, SI
2014/2972 Art.6, SI 2014/2988 Art.6, SI
2014/2990 Art.6, SI 2014/2992 Art.8, SI
2014/2999 Art.6, SI 2014/3000 Art.6, SI
2014/3003 Art.7, SI 2014/3005 Art.6, SI
2014/3006 Art.4, SI 2014/3013 Art.6, SI
2014/3016 Art.7, SI 2014/3023 Art.6, SI
2014/3024 Art.6, SI 2014/3028 Art.7, SI
2014/3030 Art.6, SI 2014/3031 Art.7, SI
2014/3032 Art.6, SI 2014/3034 Art.7, SI
2014/3035 Art.6, SI 2014/3039 Art.4, SI
2014/3040 Art.6, SI 2014/3041 Art.3, SI
2014/3042 Art.5, SI 2014/3044 Art.7, SI
2014/3045 Art.12, SI 2014/3047 Art.6, SI
2014/3048 Art.6, SI 2014/3049 Art.6, SI
2014/3064 Art.8, SI 2014/3121 Art.6, SI

2014/3123 Art.8, SI 2014/3131 Art.6, SI
2014/3132 Art.11, SI 2014/3136 Art.6, SI
2014/3151 Art.6, SI 2014/3153 Art.10, SI
2014/3154 Art.6, SI 2014/3173 Art.12, SI
2014/3174 Art.5, SI 2014/3175 Art.8, SI
2014/3176 Art.6, SI 2014/3353 Art.13, SI
2014/3370 Art.6, SI 2014/3371 Art.7, SI
2014/3375 Art.7, SI 2014/3386 Art.4, SI
2014/3394 Art.4, SI 2014/3403 Art.7, SI
2014/3410 Art.9, SI 2014/3419 Art.7, SI
2014/3421 Art.5, SI 2014/3423 Art.5, SI
2014/3425 Art.5, SI 2014/3429 Art.7, SI
2014/3434 Art.7, SI 2014/3438 Art.7, SI
2014/3446 Art.8, SI 2014/3450 Art.6, SI
2014/3454 Art.7, SI 2014/3455 Art.6, SI
2014/3458 Art.6, SI 2014/3464 Art.6, SI
2014/3471 Art.6, SI 2014/3473 Art.6, SI
2014/3475 Art.7, SI 2014/3476 Art.6, SI
2014/3478 Art.5, SI 2014/3481 Art.7, SI
2014/3483 Art.10, SI 2014/3494 Art.6, SI
2014/3497 Art.7, SI 2014/3498 Art.6, SI
2014/3504 Art.6, SI 2014/3505 Art.6, SSI
2014/10 Art.6, SSI 2014/17 Art.7, SSI
2014/18 Art.7, SSI 2014/19 Art.7, SSI
2014/20 Art.7, SSI 2014/45 Art.7, SSI
2014/46 Art.7, SSI 2014/47 Art.7, SSI
2014/48 Art.7, SSI 2014/75 Art.7, SSI
2014/76 Art.7, SSI 2014/77 Art.7, SSI
2014/78 Art.7, SSI 2014/96 Art.3, SSI
2014/97 Art.4, SSI 2014/104 Art.7, SSI
2014/105, SSI 2014/106 Art.7, SSI
2014/107, SSI 2014/124 Art.6, SSI 2014/125
Art.3, SSI 2014/126 Art.3, SSI 2014/133
Art.7, SSI 2014/134 Art.7, SSI 2014/135
Art.6, SSI 2014/177 Art.7, SSI 2014/178
Art.7, SSI 2014/179 Art.7, SSI 2014/180
Art.7, SSI 2014/181 Art.7, SSI 2014/195
Art.4, SSI 2014/198 Art.4, SSI 2014/204
Art.4, SSI 2014/205 Art.3, SSI 2014/206
Art.7, SSI 2014/207 Art.7, SSI 2014/208
Art.7, SSI 2014/209 Art.7, SSI 2014/211
Art.5, SSI 2014/216 Art.3, SSI 2014/222
Art.4, SSI 2014/228 Art.8, SSI 2014/234
Art.7, SSI 2014/235 Art.7, SSI 2014/236
Art.7, SSI 2014/237 Art.7, SSI 2014/240
Art.7, SSI 2014/245 Art.7, SSI 2014/253
Art.7, SSI 2014/254 Art.7, SSI 2014/255
Art.7, SSI 2014/256 Art.7, SSI 2014/270
Art.7, SSI 2014/271 Art.7, SSI 2014/273
Art.7, SSI 2014/275 Art.7, SSI 2014/276

Art.5, SSI 2014/286 Art.7, SSI 2014/329
Art.7, SSI 2014/330 Art.7, SSI 2014/331
Art.7, SSI 2014/332 Art.7, SSI 2014/381
Art.7, SSI 2014/382 Art.7, SSI 2014/383
Art.7, SSI 2014/384 Art.7, SSI 2014/385
Art.3

936. Marine Licensing (Notices Appeals) Regulations 2011
  Reg.1, applied: SI 2014/2555 Art.10
  Reg.5, applied: SI 2014/2555 Art.10
962. Social Care Charges (Means Assessment and Determination of Charges) (Wales) Regulations 2011
  Reg.5, amended: SI 2014/666 Reg.5
  Reg.14, amended: SI 2014/666 Reg.5
963. Social Care Charges (Direct Payments) (Means Assessment and Determination of Reimbursement or Contribution) (Wales) Regulations 2011
  Reg.5, amended: SI 2014/666 Reg.6
  Reg.16, amended: SI 2014/666 Reg.6
964. Social Care Charges (Review of Charging Decisions) (Wales) Regulations 2011
  Reg.9, amended: SI 2014/1794 Reg.24
988. Waste (England and Wales) Regulations 2011
  see *Skrytek v Secretary of State for Communities and Local Government* [2013] EWCA Civ 1231, [2014] Env. L.R. 15 (CA (Civ Div)), Maurice Kay LJ
  Part 10A, added: SI 2014/656 Reg.7
  Reg.24, amended: SI 2014/656 Reg.3
  Reg.29, amended: SI 2014/656 Reg.4
  Reg.32, amended: SI 2014/656 Reg.5
  Reg.35, amended: SI 2014/656 Reg.6
1006. Mobile Homes (Written Statement) (England) Regulations 2011
  Sch.1, amended: SI 2014/5 Reg.18, SI 2014/549 Sch.1 para.44
1016. Care Homes (Wales) (Miscellaneous Amendments) Regulations 2011
  Reg.3, amended: 2014 c.29 s.4
1033. Warm Home Discount Regulations 2011
  Reg.14, amended: SI 2014/695 Reg.2
1044. Access to Justice Act 1999 (Destination of Appeals) (Family Proceedings) Order 2011
  Art.1, amended: SI 2014/602 Art.3
  Art.1, varied: SI 2014/956 Art.11
  Art.2, amended: SI 2014/602 Art.3
  Art.2, revoked (in part): SI 2014/602 Art.3
  Art.2, varied: SI 2014/956 Art.11

Art.3, revoked: SI 2014/602 Art.3
Art.3, varied: SI 2014/956 Art.11

1064. Equality Act 2010 (Statutory Duties) (Wales) Regulations 2011
Reg.19, amended: 2014 c.29 s.4

1086. Ivory Coast (Asset-Freezing) Regulations 2011
Sch.1 para.5, amended: 2014 c.29 s.4

1128. Wireless Telegraphy (Licence Charges) Regulations 2011
Sch.2, amended: SI 2014/1295 Reg.3

1129. Iran (Asset-Freezing) Regulations 2011
Sch.1 para.5, amended: 2014 c.29 s.4

1197. Trade in Animals and Related Products Regulations 2011
Reg.3, substituted: SI 2014/3158 Sch.1 para.13
Reg.11, applied: SI 2014/1894 Reg.4

1268. Whole of Government Accounts (Designation of Bodies) Order 2011
Sch.1, amended: 2014 c.29 s.4

1325. A46 Trunk Road (M69 Junction, North of Coventry) (50 Miles Per Hour Speed Limit) Order 2011
revoked: SI 2014/136 Art.7

1329. Magistrates Courts (Enforcement or Variation of Orders Made in Family Proceedings and Miscellaneous Provisions) Rules 2011
revoked: SI 2014/879 Sch.1

1349. Employment and Support Allowance (Work-Related Activity) Regulations 2011
Reg.3, amended: SI 2014/1097 Reg.15

1366. Immigration Services Commissioner (Application Fee) Order 2011
Art.3, amended: SI 2014/2847 Art.2
Art.5, amended: SI 2014/2847 Art.2
Art.6A, added: SI 2014/2847 Art.2

1433. Rural Development Programme (Transfer and Appeals) (England) Regulations 2011
applied: SI 2014/3263 Reg.35
revoked: SI 2014/3263 Sch.5
Reg.3, applied: SI 2014/3263 Reg.35

1460. Allocation and Transfer of Proceedings (Amendment) Order 2011
revoked: SI 2014/879 Sch.1

1465. Civil Courts (Amendment) Order 2011
revoked: SI 2014/820 Sch.1

1484. Civil Jurisdiction and Judgments (Maintenance) Regulations 2011
Sch.1 Part 1 para.1, amended: SI 2014/879 Art.127

Sch.1 Part 2 para.4, amended: SI 2014/879 Art.128
Sch.1 Part 3 para.6, amended: SI 2014/879 Art.129
Sch.1 Part 3 para.7, amended: SI 2014/879 Art.130
Sch.1 Part 4 para.8, amended: SI 2014/879 Art.131
Sch.1 Part 5 para.11, amended: SI 2014/879 Art.132
Sch.1 Part 5 para.11, revoked (in part): SI 2014/879 Art.132
Sch.7 para.28, referred to: SI 2014/879 Art.45

1495. Family Proceedings Courts (Constitution of Committees and Right to Preside) (Amendment) Rules 2011
revoked: SI 2014/879 Sch.1

1524. Energy Information Regulations 2011
Sch.1 para.1, amended: SI 2014/1290 Reg.3

1542. Distress for Rent (Amendment) Rules 2011
revoked: SI 2014/600 Sch.1 Part 2

1553. Immigration (Passenger Transit Visa)(Amendment) Order 2011
revoked: SI 2014/2702 Sch.2

1556. National Health Service (Charges to Overseas Visitors) Regulations 2011
see *Ahmad v Secretary of State for the Home Department* [2014] EWCA Civ 988, [2014] 3 C.M.L.R. 45 (CA (Civ Div)), Arden LJ
Reg.23, amended: SI 2014/1534 Reg.2

1568. Contracting Out (Local Authorities Social Services Functions) (England) Order 2011
revoked: SI 2014/829 Art.5

1593. Welsh Language Commissioner (Appointment) Regulations 2011
Reg.2, amended: 2014 c.29 s.4

1609. Civil Courts (Amendment No 2) Order 2011
revoked: SI 2014/820 Sch.1

1627. Education (Non-Maintained Special Schools) (England) Regulations 2011
Sch.1 Part 2 para.29, amended: SI 2014/2103 Art.38
Sch.1 Part 2 para.34, amended: SI 2014/2103 Art.38

1654. Cancellation of Student Loans for Living Costs Liability (Wales) Regulations 2011
applied: SI 2014/1314 Reg.5

1656. Olympic Route Network Designation (Amendment) Order 2011
  revoked: SI 2014/3184 Sch.1 para.19

1689. Ministerial and other Salaries Act 1975 (Amendment) Order 2011
  Sch.1, varied: SI 2014/2708 Art.5

1734. Court Funds Rules 2011
  Part 1 r.2, amended: SI 2014/879 Art.133

1751. Registered Pension Schemes (Miscellaneous Amendments) Regulations 2011
  Reg.8, revoked (in part): 2014 c.26 s.42

1792. Registered Pension Schemes (Prescribed Requirements of Flexible Drawdown Declaration) Regulations 2011
  revoked: 2014 c.30 Sch.1 para.32

1797. Registered Pension Schemes (Provision of Information) (Amendment) (No.2) Regulations 2011
  Reg.4, revoked (in part): 2014 c.30 Sch.1 para.35
  Reg.5, revoked: 2014 c.30 Sch.1 para.35

1824. Town and Country Planning (Environmental Impact Assessment) Regulations 2011
  see *R. (on the application of Marton-cum-Grafton Parish Council) v North Yorkshire CC* [2013] EWHC 2406 (Admin), [2014] Env. L.R. 10 (QBD (Admin)), Judge Gosnell; see *Wakil (t/a Orya Textiles) v Hammersmith and Fulham LBC* [2013] EWHC 2833 (Admin), [2014] Env. L.R. 14 (QBD (Admin)), Lindblom J
  Reg.2, see *R. (on the application of Save Britain's Heritage) v Secretary of State for Communities and Local Government* [2013] EWHC 2268 (Admin), [2014] Env. L.R. 9 (QBD (Admin)), Stadlen J; see *Wakil (t/a Orya Textiles) v Hammersmith and Fulham LBC* [2013] EWHC 2833 (Admin), [2014] Env. L.R. 14 (QBD (Admin)), Lindblom J
  Reg.3, see *Highland Council v Scottish Ministers* [2014] CSIH 74 (IH (1 Div)), The Lord President (Gill)
  Reg.4, see *R. (on the application of Embleton Parish Council) v Northumberland CC* [2013] EWHC 3631 (Admin), [2014] Env. L.R. 16 (QBD (Admin)), Judge Behrens

1885. Carriage of Dangerous Goods and Use of Transportable Pressure Equipment (Amendment) Regulations 2011
  Reg.13, revoked: SI 2014/469 Sch.3 para.210
  Reg.17, revoked (in part): SI 2014/1638 Sch.13 para.25, Sch.14 Part 2
  Sch.1 para.3, revoked: SI 2014/1638 Sch.13 para.25, Sch.14 Part 2

1893. Afghanistan (Asset-Freezing) Regulations 2011
  Sch.1 para.5, amended: 2014 c.29 s.4

1939. School Governors Annual Reports (Wales) Regulations 2011
  Reg.5, amended: SI 2014/2677 Reg.11
  Sch.2 para.19, added: SI 2014/2677 Reg.11

1943. Head Teacher's Report to Parents and Adult Pupils (Wales) Regulations 2011
  Reg.2, amended: SI 2014/1998 Reg.2
  Reg.3, amended: SI 2014/1998 Reg.2
  Reg.4, revoked (in part): SI 2014/1998 Reg.2
  Reg.4A, added: SI 2014/1998 Reg.2
  Sch.1 Part 1 para.1, substituted: SI 2014/1998 Reg.2
  Sch.1 Part 4A, revoked: SI 2014/1998 Reg.2
  Sch.1 Part 5, added: SI 2014/1998 Reg.2

1986. Education (Student Support) Regulations 2011
  see *R. (on the application of Kebede) v Secretary of State for Business, Innovation and Skills* [2013] EWHC 2396 (Admin), [2014] P.T.S.R. 92 (QBD (Admin)), Burnett J; see *R. (on the application of Tigere) v Secretary of State for Business, Innovation and Skills* [2014] EWCA Civ 1216, [2014] H.R.L.R. 26 (CA (Civ Div)), Laws LJ
  Part 5, applied: SI 2014/1530 Reg.47, Sch.2 para.11
  Reg.2, amended: SI 2014/2765 Reg.3
  Reg.5, amended: SI 2014/2765 Reg.4
  Reg.12, amended: SI 2014/2765 Reg.5
  Reg.13, amended: SI 2014/2765 Reg.6
  Reg.19, amended: SI 2014/2765 Reg.7
  Reg.23, amended: SI 2014/2765 Sch.1
  Reg.38, amended: SI 2014/2765 Reg.8
  Reg.40, substituted: SI 2014/2765 Reg.9
  Reg.41, amended: SI 2014/2765 Reg.10
  Reg.41, revoked (in part): SI 2014/2765 Reg.10
  Reg.42, amended: SI 2014/1766 Reg.10

Reg.44, amended: SI 2014/2765 Sch.1
Reg.45, amended: SI 2014/2103 Art.39, SI
2014/2765 Reg.11, Sch.1
Reg.46, amended: SI 2014/2765 Sch.1
Reg.69, amended: SI 2014/2765 Reg.12
Reg.72, amended: SI 2014/2765 Sch.1
Reg.73, amended: SI 2014/2765 Sch.1
Reg.74, amended: SI 2014/2765 Sch.1
Reg.75, amended: SI 2014/2765 Sch.1
Reg.76, amended: SI 2014/2765 Sch.1
Reg.77, amended: SI 2014/2765 Sch.1
Reg.78, amended: SI 2014/2765 Sch.1
Reg.79, amended: SI 2014/2765 Sch.1
Reg.80, amended: SI 2014/2765 Sch.1
Reg.81, amended: SI 2014/2765 Sch.1
Reg.87, amended: SI 2014/2765 Sch.1
Reg.105, amended: SI 2014/2765 Sch.1
Reg.124, amended: SI 2014/2765 Reg.13
Reg.127, amended: SI 2014/2765 Reg.14
Reg.139, amended: SI 2014/2765 Reg.15
Reg.141, amended: SI 2014/2765 Reg.16
Reg.144, amended: SI 2014/2765 Reg.17
Reg.147, amended: SI 2014/2765 Reg.18
Reg.159, amended: SI 2014/2765 Reg.19
Reg.159, revoked (in part): SI 2014/2765
Reg.19
Reg.161, amended: SI 2014/2765 Reg.20
Reg.165A, added: SI 2014/2765 Reg.21
Reg.166, amended: SI 2014/2765 Reg.22
Sch.4 para.1, amended: SI 2014/1766
Reg.11
Sch.4 para.4, amended: SI 2014/1766
Reg.11
Sch.4 para.5, amended: SI 2014/1766
Reg.11
Sch.4 para.5, revoked (in part): SI
2014/1766 Reg.11
Sch.4 para.9, amended: SI 2014/2765 Sch.1
2059. Patents Act 1977 (Amendment)
Regulations 2011
revoked: SI 2014/1385 Reg.3
2064. Allocation and Transfer of Proceedings
(Amendment No 2) Order 2011
revoked: SI 2014/879 Sch.1
2097. Civil Courts (Amendment No 3) Order
2011
revoked: SI 2014/820 Sch.1
2208. Buying Agency Trading Fund
(Amendment) Order 2011
revoked: SI 2014/561 Art.3

2260. Equality Act 2010 (Specific Duties)
Regulations 2011
Sch.1, amended: SI 2014/469 Sch.3
para.204, SI 2014/3090 Sch.1 para.1, SI
2014/3184 Sch.1 para.20
2261. Air Traffic Controller Licensing (National
Supervisory Authority) Regulations 2011
revoked: SI 2014/2920 Art.2
2292. Alien and Locally Absent Species in
Aquaculture (England and Wales) Regulations
2011
Reg.7, applied: SI 2014/143 Art.1
Reg.29, revoked (in part): SI 2014/143 Art.4
2323. Health Research Authority (Establishment
and Constitution) Order 2011
revoked: 2014 c.23 s.109
2341. Health Research Authority Regulations
2011
revoked: 2014 c.23 s.109
Reg.7, applied: SI 2014/3090 Art.4
2344. Upper Tribunal (Immigration and Asylum
Chamber) (Judicial Review) (England and
Wales) Fees Order 2011
Sch.1, amended: SI 2014/878 Art.2
Sch.2 para.1, amended: SI 2014/513 Sch.1
para.21, SI 2014/590 Art.6
2377. Animal By-Products (Enforcement) (No.2)
(Wales) Regulations 2011
revoked: SI 2014/517 Reg.28
2379. Trade in Animals and Related Products
(Wales) Regulations 2011
Reg.3, substituted: SI 2014/3158 Sch.1
para.15
Reg.11, applied: SI 2014/1894 Reg.4
2687. Legislative Reform (Industrial and
Provident Societies and Credit Unions) Order
2011
Art.3, revoked: 2014 c.14 Sch.7
Art.8, revoked (in part): 2014 c.14 Sch.7
Art.9, revoked: 2014 c.14 Sch.7
2704. Electricity and Gas (Internal Markets)
Regulations 2011
Reg.51, amended: SI 2014/3332 Reg.8, SI
2014/3333 Reg.5
Sch.3, revoked: SI 2014/3332 Reg.4
Sch.4, revoked: SI 2014/3332 Reg.7
2711. Health and Social Care Act 2008
(Regulated Activities) (Amendment) Regulations
2011
revoked: SI 2014/2936 Reg.25

2742. Al-Qaida (Asset-Freezing) Regulations 2011
Sch.1 para.5, amended: 2014 c.29 s.4

2749. Postal Services (Appeals to the Competition Commission) (Investigations and Extension of Time Limits) Order 2011
applied: SI 2014/549 Sch.2 para.6, Sch.2 para.7
Art.2, amended: SI 2014/549 Sch.1 para.45
Art.3, amended: SI 2014/549 Sch.1 para.45
Art.3, applied: SI 2014/559
Art.4, amended: SI 2014/549 Sch.1 para.45
Art.5, amended: SI 2014/549 Sch.1 para.45

2752. West Northamptonshire Development Corporation (Area and Constitution) (Amendment) Order 2011
revoked: SI 2014/1181 Art.2

2840. Tribunal Procedure (Amendment) (No.2) Rules 2011
revoked: SI 2014/2604 r.45

2841. First-tier Tribunal (Immigration and Asylum Chamber) Fees Order 2011
applied: SI 2014/2604 r.9

2860. Renewable Heat Incentive Scheme Regulations 2011
applied: SI 2014/928 Reg.12, Reg.39, SI 2014/2043 Reg.16
Reg.2, amended: SI 2014/1413 Reg.3
Reg.4, amended: SI 2014/1413 Reg.4
Reg.5, amended: SI 2014/1413 Reg.5
Reg.6, amended: SI 2014/1413 Reg.6
Reg.7, amended: SI 2014/1413 Reg.7
Reg.8, substituted: SI 2014/1413 Reg.8
Reg.8A, added: SI 2014/1413 Reg.9
Reg.9, substituted: SI 2014/1413 Reg.10
Reg.9A, added: SI 2014/1413 Reg.11
Reg.11, revoked (in part): SI 2014/1413 Reg.12
Reg.12, amended: SI 2014/1413 Reg.13
Reg.13, substituted: SI 2014/1413 Reg.14
Reg.15, amended: SI 2014/1413 Reg.15
Reg.17B, added: SI 2014/1413 Reg.16
Reg.22, amended: SI 2014/1413 Reg.17
Reg.23, amended: SI 2014/928 Reg.72
Reg.23, substituted: SI 2014/1413 Reg.18
Reg.25, amended: SI 2014/1413 Reg.19
Reg.25, revoked (in part): SI 2014/1413 Reg.19
Reg.26, amended: SI 2014/1413 Reg.20
Reg.26A, added: SI 2014/1413 Reg.21
Reg.27, amended: SI 2014/1413 Reg.22

Reg.28, amended: SI 2014/1413 Reg.23
Reg.28, revoked (in part): SI 2014/1413 Reg.23
Reg.29, amended: SI 2014/1413 Reg.24
Reg.30, amended: SI 2014/1413 Reg.25
Reg.31, amended: SI 2014/1413 Reg.26
Reg.33, amended: SI 2014/1413 Reg.27
Reg.34, amended: SI 2014/1413 Reg.28
Reg.37, substituted: SI 2014/1413 Reg.29
Reg.37A, amended: SI 2014/1413 Reg.30
Reg.37B, amended: SI 2014/1413 Reg.31
Reg.37C, amended: SI 2014/1413 Reg.32
Reg.37D, amended: SI 2014/1413 Reg.33
Reg.37E, amended: SI 2014/1413 Reg.34
Reg.37F, added: SI 2014/1413 Reg.35
Reg.39, amended: SI 2014/1413 Reg.36
Reg.39A, amended: SI 2014/1413 Reg.37
Reg.39B, added: SI 2014/1413 Reg.38
Reg.40, amended: SI 2014/1413 Reg.39
Reg.41, amended: SI 2014/1413 Reg.40
Reg.42, amended: SI 2014/1413 Reg.41
Reg.43, substituted: SI 2014/1413 Reg.42
Reg.43A, added: SI 2014/1413 Reg.43
Reg.50, amended: SI 2014/1413 Reg.44
Sch.1 para.1, amended: SI 2014/1413 Reg.45
Sch.3, amended: SI 2014/1413 Reg.46
Sch.3A, added: SI 2014/1413 Reg.47
Sch.4, substituted: SI 2014/1413 Reg.48
Sch.5, substituted: SI 2014/1413 Reg.49

2866. Legal Services Act 2007 (Designation as a Licensing Authority) (No.2) Order 2011
Sch.2, amended: SI 2014/879 Sch.1

2883. Non-Commercial Movement of Pet Animals Order 2011
Part 2A, added: SI 2014/3158 Art.8
Art.2, amended: SI 2014/3158 Art.3
Art.2, revoked (in part): SI 2014/3158 Art.3
Art.3, amended: SI 2014/3158 Art.4
Art.4, amended: SI 2014/3158 Art.5
Art.5, amended: SI 2014/3158 Art.6
Art.6, amended: SI 2014/3158 Art.7
Art.11, amended: SI 2014/3158 Art.9
Art.13, amended: SI 2014/3158 Art.10
Art.16, amended: SI 2014/3158 Art.11
Art.19, substituted: SI 2014/3158 Art.12
Art.22, amended: SI 2014/3158 Art.13

2909. Smoke Control Areas (Authorised Fuels) (Wales) (Amendment) Regulations 2011
revoked: SI 2014/684 Reg.3

2910. Tax Credits Act 2002 (Further Commencement and Transitional Provisions) Order 2011

    revoked: SI 2014/1848 Art.4

2914. Local Authorities (Referendums)(Petitions)(England) Regulations 2011

    Part 2, applied: SI 2014/2172 Reg.3

2925. Export Control (Sudan and South Sudan Sanctions) and (Miscellaneous Amendments) Regulations 2011

    Reg.1, revoked: SI 2014/3258 Reg.2

    Reg.9, revoked: SI 2014/3258 Reg.2

2936. Wine Regulations 2011

    Reg.19, revoked (in part): SI 2014/1855

    Sch.6 Part 1, Sch.6 Part 2, SSI 2014/312

    Sch.4 Part 2

2940. School Teacher Appraisal (Wales) Regulations 2011

    applied: SI 2014/2709 Reg.22

    Reg.3, amended: SI 2014/2677 Reg.12

    Reg.12, amended: SI 2014/2677 Reg.12

    Reg.26, amended: SI 2014/2677 Reg.12

    Reg.39, amended: SI 2014/2677 Reg.12

2941. Common Agricultural Policy Single Payment and Support Schemes (Cross Compliance) (Wales) (Amendment) Regulations 2011

    revoked: SI 2014/3223 Sch.3

2947. Parole Board Rules 2011

    Part 2 r.5, amended: SI 2014/240 r.3

    Part 2 r.5, revoked (in part): SI 2014/240 r.3

2999. Investment Trust (Approved Company) (Tax) Regulations 2011

    applied: SI 2014/685 Reg.2

    Reg.32, amended: SI 2014/685 Reg.9

    Reg.33, revoked: SI 2014/685 Reg.9

3066. Railways (Interoperability) Regulations 2011

    Reg.2, amended: SI 2014/3217 Reg.2

2012

8. School Admissions (Admission Arrangements and Co-ordination of Admission Arrangements) (England) Regulations 2012

    Reg.1, amended: SI 2014/2886 Reg.3

    Reg.2, amended: SI 2014/2886 Reg.4

    Reg.3, revoked (in part): SI 2014/2886 Reg.5

    Reg.5, amended: SI 2014/2886 Reg.6

    Reg.6, amended: SI 2014/2886 Reg.7

    Reg.13, amended: SI 2014/2886 Reg.8

    Reg.14, amended: SI 2014/2886 Reg.9

    Reg.15, amended: SI 2014/2886 Reg.10

    Reg.17, substituted: SI 2014/2886 Reg.11

    Reg.18, amended: SI 2014/2886 Reg.12

    Reg.19, amended: SI 2014/2886 Reg.13

    Reg.23, substituted: SI 2014/2886 Reg.14

    Reg.27, amended: SI 2014/2886 Reg.15

    Reg.28, substituted: SI 2014/2886 Reg.16

    Reg.29, substituted: SI 2014/2886 Reg.17

    Sch.4, amended: SI 2014/2886 Reg.18

10. School Admissions (Infant Class Sizes) (England) Regulations 2012

    applied: SI 2014/3352 Sch.2 para.11

    Reg.2, amended: SI 2014/2103 Art.40

    Sch.1 para.1, amended: SI 2014/852 Art.22

    Sch.1 para.2, substituted: SI 2014/2103 Art.40

    Sch.1 para.4, amended: SI 2014/852 Art.22

66. Agriculture (Miscellaneous Amendments) Regulations 2012

    revoked: SI 2014/3263 Sch.5

    Reg.3, applied: SI 2014/3263 Reg.35

116. Immigration (Passenger Transit Visa) (Amendment) Order 2012

    revoked: SI 2014/2702 Sch.2

129. Syria (European Union Financial Sanctions) Regulations 2012

    Sch.1 para.5, amended: 2014 c.29 s.4

148. Non-Domestic Rating (Small Business Rate Relief) (England) Order 2012

    Art.3, amended: SI 2014/43 Art.2

    Art.4, amended: SI 2014/43 Art.2

    Art.4, substituted: SI 2014/43 Art.2

169. General Teaching Council for Wales (Constitution) (Amendment) Regulations 2012

    revoked: SI 2014/2365 Sch.1

178. Forest Law Enforcement, Governance and Trade Regulations 2012

    Reg.5A, added: SI 2014/2339 Reg.2

206. Special Educational Needs (Direct Payments) (Pilot Scheme) Order 2012

    Art.4, substituted: SI 2014/166 Art.2

    Sch.1 Part 2 para.3, amended: SI 2014/166 Art.2

245. Seed Marketing (Wales) Regulations 2012

    Sch.1, amended: SI 2014/519 Reg.2

320. Education (Wales) Measure 2009 (Commencement No.3 and Transitional Provisions) Order 2012
Art.4, revoked: SI 2014/3267 Reg.2
321. Education (Wales) Measure 2009 (Pilot) Regulations 2012
revoked: SI 2014/3267 Reg.2
323. Local Authorities (Conduct of Referendums)(England) Regulations 2012
Reg.4, applied: SI 2014/924 Reg.1
Reg.6, amended: SI 2014/924 Reg.3
Sch.3 Part 4 para.12, amended: SI 2014/924 Reg.4
Sch.3 Part 4 para.19, amended: SI 2014/924 Reg.5
Sch.3 Part 5 para.21, amended: SI 2014/924 Reg.6
Sch.3 Part 5 para.26, amended: SI 2014/924 Reg.7
Sch.3 Part 6 para.36, amended: SI 2014/924 Reg.8
Sch.3 Part 8, amended: SI 2014/924 Sch.1
Sch.4 para.1, amended: SI 2014/924 Reg.10, Reg.11, Sch.2
Sch.5 Part 4 para.12, amended: SI 2014/924 Reg.12
Sch.5 Part 4 para.17, amended: SI 2014/924 Reg.13
Sch.5 Part 4 para.20, substituted: SI 2014/924 Reg.14
Sch.5 Part 4 para.21, substituted: SI 2014/924 Reg.15
Sch.5 Part 5 para.23, amended: SI 2014/924 Reg.16
Sch.5 Part 5 para.28, amended: SI 2014/924 Reg.17
Sch.5 Part 6 para.38, amended: SI 2014/924 Reg.18
Sch.5 Part 8, amended: SI 2014/924 Sch.1, Sch.3
336. Local Authorities (Elected Mayors)(Elections, Terms of Office and Casual Vacancies)(England) Regulations 2012
Reg.2, amended: SI 2014/2172 Reg.2
Reg.3, amended: SI 2014/2172 Reg.2
Reg.3, disapplied: SI 2014/2172 Reg.3
361. Sudan and South Sudan (Restrictive Measures) (Overseas Territories) Order 2012
revoked: SI 2014/2707 Art.1

444. Local Authorities (Conduct of Referendums) (Council Tax Increases) (England) Regulations 2012
Reg.4, applied: SI 2014/925 Reg.1
Reg.4, revoked (in part): SI 2014/231 Reg.2
Reg.5, applied: SI 2014/925 Reg.1
Reg.5, revoked (in part): SI 2014/231 Reg.2
Reg.6, applied: SI 2014/925 Reg.1
Reg.6, revoked (in part): SI 2014/231 Reg.2
Reg.12, amended: SI 2014/925 Reg.3
Sch.3, added: SI 2014/925 Reg.5, Reg.6, Reg.7
Sch.3, amended: SI 2014/925 Sch.1
Sch.3, substituted: SI 2014/925 Reg.4
Sch.4 para.1, amended: SI 2014/925 Reg.9, Reg.10, Sch.2
Sch.5, added: SI 2014/925 Reg.14, Reg.15, Reg.16
Sch.5, amended: SI 2014/925 Sch.1, Sch.3
Sch.5, substituted: SI 2014/925 Reg.11, Reg.12, Reg.13
501. Welfare of Animals (Slaughter or Killing) (Amendment) (England) Regulations 2012
revoked: SI 2014/1240 Reg.47
516. Judicial Pensions (Contributions) Regulations 2012
Reg.3, amended: SI 2014/483 Reg.3
531. Residential Property Tribunal Procedures and Fees (Wales) Regulations 2012
Reg.2, amended: SI 2014/2553 Sch.1 para.1
Reg.4, amended: SI 2014/2553 Sch.1 para.2
Reg.5, amended: SI 2014/2553 Sch.1 para.3
Reg.7, amended: SI 2014/2553 Sch.1 para.4
Reg.11, revoked: SI 2014/2553 Sch.1 para.5
Reg.12, amended: SI 2014/2553 Sch.1 para.6
Reg.14, amended: SI 2014/2553 Sch.1 para.7
Reg.21, amended: SI 2014/2553 Sch.1 para.8
Reg.22, amended: SI 2014/2553 Sch.1 para.9
Reg.35, amended: SI 2014/2553 Sch.1 para.10
Reg.40, amended: SI 2014/2553 Sch.1 para.11
Reg.45, amended: SI 2014/2553 Sch.1 para.12
Reg.46, amended: SI 2014/2553 Sch.1 para.13

Reg.47, amended: SI 2014/2553 Sch.1
para.14
Reg.47, revoked (in part): SI 2014/2553
Sch.1 para.14
Reg.49, amended: SI 2014/107 Sch.2 para.9,
SI 2014/286 Reg.2
Reg.49, revoked (in part): SI 2014/286
Reg.2
Sch.1 Part 001 para.13, amended: SI
2014/286 Reg.2
Sch.1 Part 001 para.19, amended: SI
2014/286 Reg.2
Sch.1 Part 003, amended: SI 2014/2553
Sch.1 para.15
Sch.1 Part 003 para.50, amended: SI
2014/2553 Sch.1 para.15
Sch.1 Part 003 para.51, amended: SI
2014/2553 Sch.1 para.15
Sch.1 Part 003 para.52, amended: SI
2014/2553 Sch.1 para.15
Sch.1 Part 003 para.53, amended: SI
2014/2553 Sch.1 para.15
Sch.1 Part 003 para.54, amended: SI
2014/2553 Sch.1 para.15
Sch.1 Part 003 para.55, amended: SI
2014/2553 Sch.1 para.15
Sch.1 Part 003 para.56, amended: SI
2014/2553 Sch.1 para.15
Sch.1 Part 003 para.56, revoked (in part): SI
2014/2553 Sch.1 para.15
Sch.1 Part 003 para.57, amended: SI
2014/2553 Sch.1 para.15
Sch.1 Part 003 para.58, amended: SI
2014/2553 Sch.1 para.15
Sch.1 Part 003 para.59, amended: SI
2014/2553 Sch.1 para.15
Sch.1 Part 003 para.60, amended: SI
2014/2553 Sch.1 para.15
Sch.1 Part 003 para.61, revoked: SI
2014/2553 Sch.1 para.15
Sch.1 Part 003 para.62, added: SI 2014/2553
Sch.1 para.15
560. Teachers Disciplinary (England)
Regulations 2012
Reg.6, amended: SI 2014/1685 Reg.2
Reg.12A, added: SI 2014/1685 Reg.2
Reg.13, amended: SI 2014/1685 Reg.2
605. Town and Country Planning (Tree
Preservation)(England) Regulations 2012
Reg.14, applied: SI 2014/1052 Art.37

632. Control of Asbestos Regulations 2012
Reg.2, amended: SI 2014/469 Sch.3
para.145
Reg.19, amended: SI 2014/469 Sch.3
para.145
Reg.22, amended: SI 2014/469 Sch.3
para.145
Reg.33, amended: SI 2014/469 Sch.3
para.145
642. Allocation and Transfer of Proceedings
(Amendment) Order 2012
revoked: SI 2014/879 Sch.1
643. Civil Courts (Amendment) Order 2012
revoked: SI 2014/820 Sch.1
686. Isle of Anglesey Local Authorities (Change
to the Years of Ordinary Elections) Order 2012
revoked: SI 2014/3033 Art.4
687. Postal Services Act 2011 (Transfer of
Accrued Pension Rights) Order 2012
applied: SI 2014/500 Art.2
Art.15, added: SI 2014/500 Art.6
Sch.1, disapplied: SI 2014/3229 Sch.2 para.6
Sch.1 Part I para.1, amended: SI 2014/500
Art.6
Sch.1 Part I para.2A, added: SI 2014/560
Sch.3 para.17, SI 2014/3061 Sch.2 para.9
Sch.1 Part I para.2A, amended: SI
2014/3061 Sch.1 para.11
Sch.1 Part I para.2B, added: SI 2014/560
Sch.3 para.17
Sch.1 Part I para.2C, added: SI 2014/3061
Sch.1 para.11
Sch.1 Part I para.3, amended: SI 2014/500
Art.6
Sch.1 Part I para.5, amended: SI 2014/500
Art.6
Sch.1 Part I para.6, amended: SI 2014/500
Art.6
Sch.1 Part I para.7, amended: SI 2014/500
Art.6
Sch.1 Part I para.8, amended: SI 2014/500
Art.6
Sch.1 Part I para.9, amended: SI 2014/500
Art.6
Sch.1 Part I para.10, amended: SI 2014/500
Art.6
Sch.1 Part I para.11, amended: SI 2014/500
Art.6
Sch.1 Part I para.12, amended: SI 2014/500
Art.6

Sch.1 Part I para.14, amended: SI 2014/500 Art.6
Sch.1 Part I para.15, amended: SI 2014/500 Art.6
Sch.1 Part I para.16, amended: SI 2014/500 Art.6
Sch.1 Part I para.17, amended: SI 2014/500 Art.6
Sch.1 Part I para.18, amended: SI 2014/500 Art.6
Sch.1 Part II para.3, amended: SI 2014/500 Art.6
Sch.1 Part II para.4, amended: SI 2014/500 Art.6
Sch.1 Part II para.5, amended: SI 2014/500 Art.6
Sch.1 Part II para.6, amended: SI 2014/500 Art.6
Sch.1 Part II para.7, amended: SI 2014/500 Art.6
Sch.1 Part II para.8, amended: SI 2014/500 Art.6
Sch.1 Part II para.11, amended: SI 2014/500 Art.6
Sch.1 Part II para.13, amended: SI 2014/500 Art.6
Sch.1 Part II para.15, amended: SI 2014/500 Art.6
Sch.1 Part III para.2, amended: SI 2014/500 Art.6
Sch.1 Part III para.4, amended: SI 2014/500 Art.6
Sch.1 Part IV para.2, amended: SI 2014/500 Art.6
Sch.1 Part IV para.3, amended: SI 2014/500 Art.6
Sch.1 Part IV para.4, amended: SI 2014/500 Art.6
Sch.1 Part IV para.5, amended: SI 2014/500 Art.6
Sch.1 Part IV para.9, amended: SI 2014/500 Art.6
Sch.1 Part IV para.13, amended: SI 2014/500 Art.6
Sch.1 Part IV para.14, amended: SI 2014/500 Art.6
Sch.1 Part IV para.15, amended: SI 2014/500 Art.6
Sch.1 Part IV para.16, amended: SI 2014/500 Art.6

Sch.1 Part IV para.17, amended: SI 2014/500 Art.6
Sch.1 Part IV para.18, amended: SI 2014/500 Art.6
Sch.1 Part IV para.20, amended: SI 2014/500 Art.6
Sch.1 Part V para.2, amended: SI 2014/500 Art.6
Sch.1 Part V para.3, amended: SI 2014/500 Art.6
Sch.1 Part V para.4, amended: SI 2014/500 Art.6
Sch.1 Part V para.5, amended: SI 2014/500 Art.6
Sch.1 Part V para.7, amended: SI 2014/500 Art.6
Sch.1 Part V para.8, amended: SI 2014/500 Art.6
Sch.1 Part V para.9, amended: SI 2014/500 Art.6
Sch.1 Part V para.10, amended: SI 2014/500 Art.6
Sch.1 Part V para.12, amended: SI 2014/500 Art.6
Sch.1 Part V para.13, amended: SI 2014/500 Art.6
Sch.1 Part V para.17, amended: SI 2014/500 Art.6
Sch.1 Part V para.18, amended: SI 2014/500 Art.6
Sch.1 Part VII para.1, amended: SI 2014/500 Art.6
Sch.1 Part IX para.3, amended: SI 2014/500 Art.6
Sch.1 Part IX para.4, amended: SI 2014/500 Art.6
Sch.1 Part IX para.5, amended: SI 2014/500 Art.6
Sch.1 Part IX para.6, amended: SI 2014/500 Art.6
Sch.1 Part IX para.8, amended: SI 2014/500 Art.6
Sch.1 Part IX para.9, amended: SI 2014/500 Art.6
Sch.1 Part IX para.10, amended: SI 2014/500 Art.6
Sch.2 para.2, amended: SI 2014/500 Art.6
Sch.2 para.3, amended: SI 2014/500 Art.6
Sch.2 para.4, amended: SI 2014/500 Art.6
Sch.2 para.6, amended: SI 2014/500 Art.6
Sch.2 para.7, amended: SI 2014/500 Art.6

Sch.2 para.10, amended: SI 2014/500 Art.6
Sch.2 para.11, amended: SI 2014/500 Art.6
Sch.2 para.12, amended: SI 2014/500 Art.6
Sch.2 para.13, amended: SI 2014/500 Art.6
Sch.2 para.15, amended: SI 2014/500 Art.6
Sch.2 para.16, amended: SI 2014/500 Art.6
Sch.2 para.17, amended: SI 2014/500 Art.6
Sch.2 para.19, amended: SI 2014/500 Art.6
Sch.2 para.20, amended: SI 2014/500 Art.6
Sch.3 para.10, amended: SI 2014/500 Art.6
Sch.4 Part II para.12, amended: SI 2014/500
Art.6

700. Housing (Scotland) Act 2010
(Consequential Provisions and Modifications)
Order 2012
Sch.1 Part 1 para.6, revoked: 2014 c.14
Sch.7

734. Housing (Right to Buy) (Limit on Discount)
(England) Order 2012
referred to: SI 2014/1378 Art.3
revoked: SI 2014/1378 Art.4
Art.3, revoked: SI 2014/1378 Art.4

752. Welsh Language Board (Transfer of Staff,
Property, Rights and Liabilities) Order 2012
Art.2, amended: 2014 c.29 s.4
Art.3, amended: 2014 c.29 s.4

757. Social Security (Miscellaneous
Amendments) Regulations 2012
Reg.3, varied: 2014 c.6 s.126
Reg.5, varied: 2014 c.6 s.126
Reg.7, varied: 2014 c.6 s.126
Reg.8, varied: 2014 c.6 s.126
Reg.9, varied: 2014 c.6 s.126
Reg.10, varied: 2014 c.6 s.126

761. Registration of Civil Partnerships (Fees)
(Amendment) Order 2012
revoked: SI 2014/1789 Art.3

762. Education (Specified Work) (England)
Regulations 2012
Reg.3, amended: SI 2014/3255 Art.25

771. Immigration (Passenger Transit
Visa)(Amendment)(No.2) Order 2012
revoked: SI 2014/2702 Sch.2

782. Pensions Increase (Review) Order 2012
referred to: SI 2014/668 Sch.1
Art.6, substituted: SI 2014/107 Sch.1
para.56, SI 2014/3229 Sch.6 para.35

795. National Savings Bank (Investment
Deposits) (Limits) (Amendment) Order 2012
revoked: SI 2014/484 Art.3

798. Consular Fees Order 2012
Art.3, amended: SI 2014/1110 Art.20, SI
2014/3265 Art.20
Sch.1 Part 1, amended: SI 2014/1110 Art.21,
SI 2014/3265 Art.21
Sch.1 Part 2, amended: SI 2014/509 Art.2

801. Town and Country Planning (Development
Management Procedure) (Wales) Order 2012
Art.27, applied: SI 2014/2693 Reg.5
Art.27, referred to: SI 2014/593 Reg.5
Art.28A, added: SI 2014/1772 Art.2
Art.29, amended: SI 2014/1772 Art.2
Art.29, applied: SI 2014/2693 Reg.5
Sch.4, amended: SI 2014/469 Sch.3 para.207

821. Social Security (Contributions)
(Amendment No 3) Regulations 2012
Sch.1, varied: 2014 c.6 s.126

901. National Health Service Trust Development
Authority (Establishment and Constitution)
Order 2012
applied: 2014 c.2 Sch.13 para.9, Sch.13
para.12, Sch.13 para.13

921. Care Quality Commission (Registration)
and (Additional Functions) and Health and
Social Care Act 2008 (Regulated Activities)
(Amendment) Regulations 2012
Reg.11, revoked: SI 2014/2936 Reg.25

922. National Health Service Trust Development
Authority Regulations 2012
Reg.13, amended: SI 2014/1815 Sch.1
para.28

925. Iran (European Union Financial Sanctions)
Regulations 2012
Reg.9A, amended: SI 2014/105 Reg.3
Reg.10, amended: SI 2014/105 Reg.4
Sch.1 para.5, amended: 2014 c.29 s.4

938. Early Years Foundation Stage (Welfare
Requirements) Regulations 2012
Reg.2, amended: SI 2014/912 Reg.25
Reg.4, amended: SI 2014/912 Reg.26
Reg.5, substituted: SI 2014/912 Reg.27
Reg.5A, added: SI 2014/912 Reg.28
Reg.6, substituted: SI 2014/912 Reg.29
Reg.8, amended: SI 2014/912 Reg.30
Reg.10, amended: SI 2014/912 Reg.31

956. Young People's Learning Agency Abolition
(Consequential Amendments to Subordinate
Legislation) (England) Order 2012
Art.8, revoked: SI 2014/80 Sch.1

961. Localism Act 2011 (Consequential Amendments) Order 2012
> Sch.1 para.1, revoked: 2014 c.14 Sch.7

1033. School Discipline (Pupil Exclusions and Reviews) (England) Regulations 2012
> Reg.6, see *R. (on the application of CR) v Independent Review Panel of Lambeth LBC* [2014] EWHC 2461 (Admin), [2014] E.L.R. 359 (QBD (Admin)), Collins J

1034. School Governance (Constitution) (England) Regulations 2012
> Reg.2, revoked: SI 2014/1257 Reg.2
> Reg.4, substituted: SI 2014/1257 Reg.2
> Reg.6, amended: SI 2014/1257 Reg.2
> Reg.8, amended: SI 2014/1257 Reg.2
> Reg.9, amended: SI 2014/1257 Reg.2
> Reg.15, substituted: SI 2014/1257 Reg.2
> Sch.1 para.12, added: SI 2014/1257 Reg.2
> Sch.3 para.4, substituted: SI 2014/1257 Reg.2
> Sch.4 para.13, amended: SI 2014/1257 Reg.6

1035. School Governance (Federations) (England) Regulations 2012
> Reg.2, substituted: SI 2014/1257 Reg.3
> Reg.3, substituted: SI 2014/1257 Reg.3
> Reg.4, revoked (in part): SI 2014/1257 Reg.3
> Reg.14, amended: SI 2014/1257 Reg.3
> Reg.16, amended: SI 2014/1257 Reg.3
> Reg.17, amended: SI 2014/1257 Reg.3
> Reg.21, amended: SI 2014/1257 Reg.3
> Reg.22A, added: SI 2014/1257 Reg.3
> Sch.1 para.2, amended: SI 2014/1257 Reg.3
> Sch.2 para.11, added: SI 2014/1257 Reg.3
> Sch.4 para.2, revoked: SI 2014/1257 Reg.3
> Sch.4 para.7, added: SI 2014/1257 Reg.3

1108. Health Research Authority (Amendment) Regulations 2012
> revoked: SI 2014/3090 Sch.1 para.2

1109. Health Research Authority (Establishment and Constitution) Amendment Order 2012
> revoked: SI 2014/3090 Sch.1 para.2

1128. Postal Services Act 2011 (Disclosure of Information) Order 2012
> Art.3, amended: SI 2014/469 Sch.3 para.205, SI 2014/549 Sch.1 para.46, SI 2014/631 Sch.1 para.27
> Art.4, amended: SI 2014/469 Sch.3 para.205, SI 2014/549 Sch.1 para.46

1204. Police (Complaints and Misconduct) Regulations 2012
> Reg.29A, added: SI 2014/2406 Reg.2
> Reg.36, amended: SI 2014/2406 Reg.2

1273. Health Education England (Establishment and Constitution) Order 2012
> revoked: 2014 c.23 s.96

1290. Health Education England Regulations 2012
> revoked: 2014 c.23 s.96
> Reg.13, amended: SI 2014/1815 Sch.1 para.29

1301. Guinea-Bissau (Asset-Freezing) Regulations 2012
> Sch.1 para.5, amended: 2014 c.29 s.4

1363. Tribunal Procedure (Amendment No 2) Rules 2012
> r.9, revoked (in part): SI 2014/2128 r.39

1375. Fishing Boats (Satellite-Tracking Devices and Electronic Reporting) (England) Scheme 2012
> Art.13, amended: SI 2014/3363 Art.2

1391. Tuberculosis (England) (Amendment) Order 2012
> revoked: SI 2014/2383 Art.24

1404. Road Vehicles (Construction and Use) (Amendment) Regulations 2012
> revoked: SI 2014/1862 Reg.3

1464. Relevant Authorities (Disclosable Pecuniary Interests) Regulations 2012
> Reg.1, amended: SI 2014/1815 Sch.1 para.30

1489. Iraq (Asset-Freezing) Regulations 2012
> Sch.1 para.5, amended: 2014 c.29 s.4

1501. Quality and Safety of Organs Intended for Transplantation Regulations 2012
> Reg.3, amended: SI 2014/1459 Reg.3
> Reg.6, amended: SI 2014/1459 Reg.4
> Reg.12, amended: SI 2014/1459 Reg.5
> Reg.13, amended: SI 2014/1459 Reg.6
> Reg.16, amended: SI 2014/1459 Reg.7
> Reg.18, amended: SI 2014/1459 Reg.8
> Reg.27, amended: SI 2014/1459 Reg.9
> Reg.27, revoked (in part): SI 2014/1459 Reg.9
> Sch.2 para.3, added: SI 2014/1459 Reg.10

1507. Sudan (Asset-Freezing) Regulations 2012
> revoked: SI 2014/1826 Reg.18

1508. Republic of Guinea (Asset-Freezing) Regulations 2012
> Sch.1 para.5, amended: 2014 c.29 s.4

1511. Democratic Republic of the Congo (Asset-Freezing) Regulations 2012
Sch.1 para.5, amended: 2014 c.29 s.4

1513. Health and Social Care Act 2008 (Regulated Activities) (Amendment) Regulations 2012
revoked: SI 2014/2936 Reg.25

1515. Eritrea (Asset-Freezing) Regulations 2012
Sch.1 para.5, amended: 2014 c.29 s.4

1516. Liberia (Asset-Freezing) Regulations 2012
Sch.1 para.5, amended: 2014 c.29 s.4

1517. Lebanon and Syria (Asset-Freezing) Regulations 2012
Sch.1 para.5, amended: 2014 c.29 s.4

1518. Cancellation of Student Loans for Living Costs Liability (Wales) Regulations 2012
applied: SI 2014/1314 Reg.5

1532. Immigration Appeals (Family Visitor) Regulations 2012
revoked (in part): 2014 c.22 Sch.9 para.37

1652. Health and Safety (Fees) Regulations 2012
Reg.1, amended: SI 2014/469 Sch.3 para.154, SI 2014/1638 Sch.13 para.27, SI 2014/3248 Sch.4 Part 2
Reg.2, revoked (in part): SI 2014/3248 Sch.4 Part 2
Reg.8, amended: SI 2014/469 Sch.3 para.155
Reg.9, amended: SI 2014/469 Sch.3 para.156, SI 2014/1637 Sch.4 para.9, SI 2014/1638 Sch.13 para.28, SI 2014/1639 Sch.2 para.3
Reg.9, revoked (in part): SI 2014/1639 Sch.3 Part 2
Reg.10, substituted: SI 2014/1637 Sch.4 para.9
Reg.11, amended: SI 2014/469 Sch.3 para.157
Reg.12, substituted: SI 2014/469 Sch.3 para.158
Reg.13, amended: SI 2014/1663 Reg.34
Reg.16, amended: SI 2014/469 Sch.3 para.159
Reg.17, amended: SI 2014/469 Sch.3 para.160
Reg.24, amended: SI 2014/469 Sch.3 para.161, SI 2014/1663 Reg.34
Reg.24, revoked (in part): SI 2014/469 Sch.3 para.161
Sch.1, revoked (in part): SI 2014/3248 Sch.4 Part 2

Sch.7, amended: SI 2014/469 Sch.3 para.162
Sch.8, substituted: SI 2014/1638 Sch.13 para.29
Sch.8 Part 1, substituted: SI 2014/1638 Sch.13 para.29
Sch.8 Part 2, substituted: SI 2014/1638 Sch.13 para.29
Sch.8 Part 3, revoked: SI 2014/1639 Sch.3 Part 2
Sch.8 Part 3A, added: SI 2014/1639 Sch.2 para.3
Sch.8 Part 4, substituted: SI 2014/1637 Sch.4 para.9
Sch.8 Part 5, revoked: SI 2014/1639 Sch.3 Part 2
Sch.8 Part 8, substituted: SI 2014/1638 Sch.13 para.29
Sch.10, amended: SI 2014/1663 Reg.34
Sch.13, amended: SI 2014/469 Sch.3 para.163

1663. Immigration (Designation of Travel Bans) (Amendment) Order 2012
revoked: SI 2014/1849 Sch.2

1696. Criminal Justice Act 2003 (Surcharge) Order 2012
see *R. v Bailey (Wayne)* [2013] EWCA Crim 1551, [2014] 1 Cr. App. R. (S.) 59 (CA (Crim Div)), Leveson LJ; see *R. v de Brito (Paulo Aguiar)* [2013] EWCA Crim 1134, [2014] 1 Cr. App. R. (S.) 38 (CA (Crim Div)), Keith J
Art.7, see *R. v de Brito (Paulo Aguiar)* [2013] EWCA Crim 1134, [2014] 1 Cr. App. R. (S.) 38 (CA (Crim Div)), Keith J
Sch.1, amended: SI 2014/2120 Art.2

1726. Criminal Procedure Rules 2012
see *DLA Piper UK LLP v BDO LLP* [2013] EWHC 3970 (Admin), [2014] 1 W.L.R. 4425 (QBD (Admin)), Moses LJ
Part 17, applied: SI 2014/1610 r.2_1
Part 17, varied: SI 2014/1610 r.2_1
r.76.2, see *R. (on the application of Gray) v Aylesbury Crown Court* [2013] EWHC 500 (Admin), [2014] 1 W.L.R. 818 (QBD (Admin)), Toulson, L.J.

1734. Charities (Exception from Registration) (Amendment) Regulations 2012
revoked: SI 2014/242 Reg.3

1741. Statutory Auditors (Amendment of Companies Act 2006 and Delegation of Functions etc) Order 2012

    Art.9, amended: SI 2014/2009 Art.10

1755. Syria (Restrictive Measures) (Overseas Territories) Order 2012

    Art.2, amended: SI 2014/269 Art.3

    Art.8, amended: SI 2014/269 Art.4

    Art.8A, amended: SI 2014/269 Art.5

    Art.15A, added: SI 2014/269 Art.6

    Art.19, revoked: SI 2014/269 Art.7

    Art.33, amended: SI 2014/269 Art.8

    Art.43, amended: SI 2014/269 Art.9

    Art.43, revoked (in part): SI 2014/269 Art.9

    Sch.2 para.1, amended: SI 2014/269 Art.10

    Sch.2 para.2, amended: SI 2014/269 Art.10

    Sch.2 para.3, amended: SI 2014/269 Art.10

    Sch.2 para.4, revoked: SI 2014/269 Art.10

    Sch.4 para.1, amended: SI 2014/269 Art.11

    Sch.4 para.2, amended: SI 2014/269 Art.11

    Sch.4 para.3, amended: SI 2014/269 Art.11

    Sch.4 para.4, revoked: SI 2014/269 Art.11

    Sch.5, substituted: SI 2014/269 Art.12

1770. International Recovery of Maintenance (Hague Convention 2007) (Rules of Court) Regulations 2012

    Reg.2, revoked: SI 2014/879 Art.134

1796. Armed Forces (Enhanced Learning Credit Scheme and Further and Higher Education Commitment Scheme) Order 2012

    Art.2, amended: SI 2014/3255 Art.26

1803. Whole of Government Accounts (Designation of Bodies) Order 2012

    Sch.1, amended: 2014 c.29 s.4

1809. Treaty of Lisbon (Changes in Terminology or Numbering) Order 2012

    Sch.1 Part 2, amended: SI 2014/1855 Sch.6

    Part 1, SI 2014/3001 Reg.8

    Sch.1 Part 4, amended: SI 2014/3087 Reg.8

1812. Oxfordshire (Electoral Changes) Order 2012

    Art.2, amended: SI 2014/23 Art.5, SI 2014/24 Art.5

    Art.5, revoked: SI 2014/24 Art.5

    Art.12, revoked: SI 2014/23 Art.5

1818. Further Education Loans Regulations 2012

    Reg.2, amended: SI 2014/1766 Reg.3

    Reg.3, amended: SI 2014/1766 Reg.4

    Reg.4, revoked (in part): SI 2014/290 Reg.3

    Reg.4, substituted: SI 2014/1766 Reg.5

    Reg.5, amended: SI 2014/1766 Reg.6

    Reg.5, revoked (in part): SI 2014/290 Reg.4

    Reg.9, amended: SI 2014/1766 Reg.7

    Reg.15, amended: SI 2014/1766 Reg.8

1821. Housing (Right to Manage) (England) Regulations 2012

    Reg.17, amended: SI 2014/1815 Sch.1 para.31

1848. Customs Disclosure of Information and Miscellaneous Amendments Regulations 2012

    Reg.4, amended: SI 2014/834 Sch.3 para.36

1876. Sexual Offences Act 2003 (Notification Requirements) (England and Wales) Regulations 2012

    Reg.12, see *R. (on the application of Prothero) v Secretary of State for the Home Department* [2013] EWHC 2830 (Admin), [2014] 1 W.L.R. 1195 (DC), Sir John Thomas PQBD

1897. Gaming Duty (Amendment) Regulations 2012

    revoked: SI 2014/1930 Reg.3

1903. Natural Resources Body for Wales (Establishment) Order 2012

    Art.11, applied: SI 2014/861 Reg.23

1916. Human Medicines Regulations 2012

    referred to: SI 2014/1638 Sch.2 para.7

    Reg.2, referred to: SI 2014/1638 Sch.2 para.6, Sch.2 para.7

    Reg.48, amended: SI 2014/1878 Reg.3

    Reg.49, amended: SI 2014/1878 Reg.4, Reg.5

    Reg.50, amended: SI 2014/1878 Reg.4, Reg.6

    Reg.57A, added: SI 2014/1878 Reg.7

    Reg.59, amended: SI 2014/1878 Reg.4, Reg.8

    Reg.62, amended: SI 2014/1878 Reg.4

    Reg.65A, added: SI 2014/1878 Reg.9

    Reg.66A, added: SI 2014/1878 Reg.10

    Reg.68, amended: SI 2014/1878 Reg.4, Reg.11

    Reg.69, amended: SI 2014/1878 Reg.4, Reg.12

    Reg.71, amended: SI 2014/1878 Reg.4, Reg.13

    Reg.75, amended: SI 2014/1878 Reg.4, Reg.14

    Reg.76, amended: SI 2014/1878 Reg.4

    Reg.77, amended: SI 2014/1878 Reg.4

    Reg.80A, added: SI 2014/1878 Reg.15

Reg.95A, added: SI 2014/1878 Reg.16

Reg.96, amended: SI 2014/1878 Reg.4

Reg.97, substituted: SI 2014/1878 Reg.17

Reg.98, amended: SI 2014/1878 Reg.4

Reg.101, amended: SI 2014/1878 Reg.4

Reg.165, amended: SI 2014/490 Reg.3

Reg.172, amended: SI 2014/1878 Reg.18

Reg.177, amended: SI 2014/1878 Reg.19

Reg.191A, added: SI 2014/1878 Reg.20

Reg.195, amended: SI 2014/1878 Reg.21

Reg.213, amended: SI 2014/490 Reg.4, SI 2014/1878 Reg.22

Reg.213, revoked (in part): SI 2014/490 Reg.4

Reg.214, amended: SI 2014/490 Reg.5

Reg.217, amended: SI 2014/490 Reg.5

Reg.217A, added: SI 2014/490 Reg.6

Reg.218, amended: SI 2014/490 Reg.7, SI 2014/1878 Reg.23

Reg.219, amended: SI 2014/490 Reg.5, Reg.8

Reg.224, amended: SI 2014/490 Reg.5

Reg.225, amended: SI 2014/490 Reg.5

Reg.240, amended: SI 2014/490 Reg.5

Reg.242, amended: SI 2014/490 Reg.5

Reg.253, amended: SI 2014/490 Reg.5

Reg.294, amended: SI 2014/1878 Reg.24

Reg.346, amended: SI 2014/490 Reg.9, SI 2014/1878 Reg.25

Sch.1 Part 1 para.1, amended: SI 2014/490 Reg.10

Sch.8A, added: SI 2014/1878 Reg.26

Sch.17 Part 1, amended: SI 2014/1878 Reg.27

Sch.17 Part 2, amended: SI 2014/1878 Reg.27

Sch.17 Part 3, amended: SI 2014/490 Reg.11

Sch.17 Part 5, amended: SI 2014/1878 Reg.27

Sch.27 Part 1 para.13, amended: SI 2014/1878 Reg.28

Sch.27 Part 1 para.14, substituted: SI 2014/1878 Reg.28

Sch.30 para.7, amended: SI 2014/1878 Reg.29

1917. Police and Crime Commissioner Elections Order 2012

applied: SI 2014/1963 Art.5

Art.2, varied: SI 2014/1963 Art.7

Art.4, amended: SI 2014/921 Art.4

Art.4, revoked (in part): SI 2014/921 Art.4

Art.8, amended: SI 2014/921 Art.5

Art.52, amended: SI 2014/1963 Art.3

Art.52, varied: SI 2014/1963 Art.8, Art.9

Sch.1 para.1, amended: SI 2014/921 Art.6

Sch.1 para.2, amended: SI 2014/921 Art.7

Sch.2 Part 1 para.1, amended: SI 2014/921 Art.8

Sch.2 Part 1 para.5, amended: SI 2014/921 Art.9

Sch.2 Part 1 para.6, amended: SI 2014/921 Art.10

Sch.2 Part 2 para.14, amended: SI 2014/921 Art.11

Sch.2 Part 2 para.15A, added: SI 2014/921 Art.12

Sch.2 Part 2 para.16, amended: SI 2014/921 Art.13

Sch.2 Part 2 para.20, amended: SI 2014/921 Art.14

Sch.2 Part 2 para.26, amended: SI 2014/921 Art.15

Sch.2 Part 3 para.28, amended: SI 2014/921 Art.16

Sch.2 Part 3 para.30, amended: SI 2014/921 Art.17

Sch.2 Part 3 para.30, revoked (in part): SI 2014/921 Art.17

Sch.2 Part 3 para.35, substituted: SI 2014/921 Art.18

Sch.2 Part 3 para.42A, added: SI 2014/921 Art.19

Sch.2 Part 3 para.45, revoked (in part): SI 2014/921 Art.20

Sch.2 Part 3 para.48, amended: SI 2014/921 Art.21

Sch.2 Part 3 para.48, revoked (in part): SI 2014/921 Art.21

Sch.2 Part 3 para.50, revoked: SI 2014/921 Art.22

Sch.2 Part 3 para.51, amended: SI 2014/921 Art.23

Sch.2 Part 3 para.52, revoked: SI 2014/921 Art.24

Sch.2 Part 3 para.54, amended: SI 2014/921 Art.25

Sch.2 Part 3 para.55, amended: SI 2014/921 Art.26

Sch.2 Part 3 para.57, amended: SI 2014/921 Art.27

Sch.2 Part 3 para.57, revoked (in part): SI 2014/921 Art.27

Sch.2 Part 3 para.59, amended: SI 2014/921
Art.28
Sch.2 Part 3 para.59A, added: SI 2014/921
Art.29
Sch.2 Part 4 para.60, amended: SI 2014/921
Art.30, Sch.1
Sch.3 Part 1 para.1, amended: SI 2014/921
Art.31
Sch.3 Part 1 para.2, revoked: SI 2014/921
Art.32
Sch.3 Part 3 para.30, amended: SI 2014/921
Art.33
Sch.3 Part 3 para.32, substituted: SI
2014/921 Art.34
Sch.3 Part 3 para.34, amended: SI 2014/921
Art.35
Sch.3 Part 3 para.39, amended: SI 2014/921
Art.36
Sch.3 Part 3 para.49, amended: SI 2014/921
Art.37
Sch.3 Part 8 para.70, amended: SI 2014/921
Art.38, Sch.2
Sch.4 Part 2 para.12, revoked (in part): SI
2014/921 Art.39
Sch.4 Part 3 para.25, added: SI 2014/921
Art.40
Sch.4 Part 3 para.25, amended: SI 2014/921
Art.40
Sch.4 Part 3 para.25, revoked: SI 2014/921
Art.40
Sch.4 Part 3 para.27, added: SI 2014/921
Art.41
Sch.4 Part 3 para.31, amended: SI 2014/921
Art.42
Sch.4 Part 3 para.31, substituted: SI
2014/921 Art.42
Sch.4 Part 3 para.33, amended: SI 2014/921
Art.43
Sch.4 Part 3 para.33, revoked (in part): SI
2014/921 Art.43
Sch.4 Part 3 para.39, added: SI 2014/921
Art.44
Sch.4 Part 3 para.39, amended: SI 2014/921
Art.44
Sch.4 Part 3 para.42, amended: SI 2014/921
Art.45
Sch.4 Part 4 para.45, amended: SI 2014/921
Art.46
Sch.8 Part 1, varied: SI 2014/1963 Art.10
Sch.8 Part 1 para.1, amended: SI 2014/1963
Art.4

Sch.8 Part 1 para.1, varied: SI 2014/1963
Art.10
Sch.8 Part 1 para.2, amended: SI 2014/1963
Art.4
Sch.8 Part 1 para.5, amended: SI 2014/1963
Art.4
Sch.8 Part 1 para.6, varied: SI 2014/1963
Art.10
Sch.8 Part 1 para.8, varied: SI 2014/1963
Art.10
Sch.8 Part 1 para.10, varied: SI 2014/1963
Art.10
Sch.8 Part 1 para.11, varied: SI 2014/1963
Art.10
Sch.8 Part 1 para.13, amended: SI
2014/1963 Art.4
Sch.8 Part 1 para.13, varied: SI 2014/1963
Art.10
Sch.8 Part 1 para.14, varied: SI 2014/1963
Art.10
Sch.10 para.1, amended: SI 2014/921 Art.47
Sch.10 para.3, amended: SI 2014/921 Art.48
**1943. School Premises (England) Regulations
2012**
Reg.9, applied: SI 2014/1603 Reg.6
**1954. Civil Courts (Amendment) (No.2) Order
2012**
revoked: SI 2014/820 Sch.1
**1955. Allocation and Transfer of Proceedings
(Amendment) (No.2) Order 2012**
revoked: SI 2014/879 Sch.1
**1976. Climate Change Agreements
(Administration) Regulations 2012**
Reg.5, amended: SI 2014/2872 Reg.2
**1989. Local Government Pension Scheme
(Miscellaneous) Regulations 2012**
revoked: SI 2014/525 Sch.1
**2031. Neighbourhood Planning (Referendums)
Regulations 2012**
Reg.6, amended: SI 2014/333 Reg.3
Sch.3, added: SI 2014/333 Reg.4, Reg.5,
Reg.6, Reg.7
Sch.3, amended: SI 2014/333 Sch.1
Sch.4 Part 1, amended: SI 2014/333 Reg.9,
Reg.10, Sch.2
Sch.4 Part 2 para.2, amended: SI 2014/333
Reg.11
Sch.4 Part 2 para.7, amended: SI 2014/333
Reg.11
Sch.4 Part 3 para.16, amended: SI 2014/333
Reg.11

Sch.4 Part 3 para.19, amended: SI 2014/333 Reg.11

Sch.4 Part 3 para.22, amended: SI 2014/333 Reg.11

Sch.5, added: SI 2014/333 Reg.13, Reg.14, Reg.15, Reg.16

Sch.5, amended: SI 2014/333 Sch.1, Sch.3

Sch.5, substituted: SI 2014/333 Reg.12

Sch.6 Part 5 para.23, amended: SI 2014/333 Reg.18

Sch.6 Part 11, amended: SI 2014/333 Sch.4

Sch.7, added: SI 2014/333 Reg.20, Reg.28, Reg.29, Reg.30, Reg.31

Sch.7, amended: SI 2014/333 Reg.20, Reg.24, Reg.26, Reg.27, Sch.5

Sch.7, revoked: SI 2014/333 Reg.21, Reg.22, Reg.23, Reg.25, Reg.27

Sch.7, substituted: SI 2014/333 Reg.22, Reg.24, Reg.31

Sch.8, amended: SI 2014/333 Reg.33

2034. A38 Trunk Road (Hilliard's Cross to Branston Interchange, Staffordshire) (30 Miles Per Hour Speed Limit and Derestriction) Order 2012

revoked: SI 2014/1034 Art.6

2058. Immigration (Designation of Travel Bans) (Amendment No 2) Order 2012

revoked: SI 2014/1849 Sch.2

2059. Local Authorities (Mayoral Elections) (England and Wales) (Amendment) Regulations 2012

revoked: SI 2014/370 Reg.2

2079. Green Deal Framework (Disclosure, Acknowledgment, Redress etc.) Regulations 2012

Reg.52, amended: SI 2014/549 Sch.1 para.47

2089. Local Authorities (Executive Arrangements) (Meetings and Access to Information) (England) Regulations 2012

Reg.4, amended: SI 2014/2095 Reg.5

Reg.20, revoked (in part): SI 2014/2095 Reg.5

2105. Green Deal (Qualifying Energy Improvements) Order 2012

Sch.1, amended: SI 2014/2020 Art.2

2234. Protection of Freedoms Act 2012 (Commencement No 3) Order 2012

Art.13, amended: SI 2014/831 Art.2

2261. Schools Forums (England) Regulations 2012

Reg.1, amended: SI 2014/2103 Art.41, SI 2014/3352 Reg.3

Reg.4, amended: SI 2014/3352 Reg.3

Reg.6, substituted: SI 2014/3352 Reg.3

Reg.10, amended: SI 2014/3352 Reg.3

2272. Street Works (Charges for Unreasonably Prolonged Occupation of the Highway) (England) (Amendment) Regulations 2012

applied: SI 2014/3109 Sch.1

2276. Immigration and Nationality (Cost Recovery Fees) (Amendment) Regulations 2012

revoked: 2014 c.22 Sch.9 para.74

2319. Town and Country Planning (Compensation) (Wales) (No.2) Regulations 2012

revoked: SI 2014/593 Reg.7

2421. Assets of Community Value (England) Regulations 2012

Reg.5, amended: SI 2014/1815 Sch.1 para.32

2522. Disclosure and Barring Service (Core Functions) Order 2012

Art.2, amended: SI 2014/238 Art.2

2631. Police (Performance) Regulations 2012

Reg.4, amended: SI 2014/2403 Reg.2

Reg.12, amended: SI 2014/2403 Reg.2

Reg.13, amended: SI 2014/2403 Reg.2

Reg.30, amended: SI 2014/2403 Reg.2

Reg.31, amended: SI 2014/2403 Reg.2

Reg.38, amended: SI 2014/2403 Reg.2

Reg.39, amended: SI 2014/2403 Reg.2

Reg.40, amended: SI 2014/2403 Reg.2

2632. Police (Conduct) Regulations 2012

Reg.10A, added: SI 2014/3347 Reg.2

2655. Collaboration Between Education Bodies (Wales) Regulations 2012

Reg.3, amended: SI 2014/1132 Reg.92

Reg.4, amended: SI 2014/1132 Reg.92

Reg.7, amended: SI 2014/1132 Reg.92

2675. Mobile Homes (Written Statement) (Wales) Regulations 2012

revoked: SI 2014/1762 Reg.4

Sch.1, amended: SI 2014/549 Sch.1 para.57

2677. Child Support Maintenance Calculation Regulations 2012

Reg.11, amended: SI 2014/1386 Reg.7

Reg.12, amended: SI 2014/1386 Reg.7

Reg.14, amended: SI 2014/1386 Reg.7

Reg.44, amended: SI 2014/884 Reg.3

2685. General Medical Council (Licence to Practise and Revalidation) Regulations Order of Council 2012

Sch.1, added: SI 2014/1273 Sch.1
Sch.1, amended: SI 2014/1273 Sch.1
Sch.1, substituted: SI 2014/1273 Sch.1

2782. Feed-in Tariffs Order 2012

applied: SI 2014/2043 Reg.16
Art.17A, added: SI 2014/1601 Art.2
Sch.2 para.1, amended: SI 2014/2865 Art.2
Sch.2 para.2, amended: SI 2014/2865 Art.2
Sch.2 para.2A, added: SI 2014/2865 Art.2
Sch.2 para.5, amended: SI 2014/2865 Art.2

2814. International Recovery of Maintenance (Hague Convention 2007 etc.) Regulations 2012

Sch.1 para.1, revoked (in part): SI 2014/879 Art.137
Sch.1 para.2, amended: SI 2014/879 Art.138
Sch.1 para.3, amended: SI 2014/879 Art.139
Sch.1 para.3, revoked (in part): SI 2014/879 Art.139
Sch.1 para.7, amended: SI 2014/879 Art.140
Sch.1 para.7, revoked (in part): SI 2014/879 Art.140
Sch.2 para.2, amended: SI 2014/879 Art.142
Sch.2 para.2, revoked (in part): SI 2014/879 Art.142
Sch.2 para.3, amended: SI 2014/879 Art.143
Sch.2 para.10, amended: SI 2014/879 Art.144
Sch.4 para.3, amended: SI 2014/879 Art.145

2840. Customs (Inspections by Her Majesty's Inspectors of Constabulary and the Scottish Inspectors) Regulations 2012

Reg.6, amended: SI 2014/907 Reg.4
Reg.6, revoked (in part): SI 2014/907 Reg.4
Sch.1 Part 1, amended: SI 2014/907 Reg.5

2885. Council Tax Reduction Schemes (Prescribed Requirements) (England) Regulations 2012

Reg.2, amended: SI 2014/3255 Art.27, SI 2014/3312 Reg.2
Reg.4, substituted: SI 2014/107 Sch.1 para.54
Reg.6, amended: SI 2014/3312 Reg.2
Reg.10, amended: SI 2014/3255 Art.27
Reg.12, amended: SI 2014/3312 Reg.2
Sch.1 Part 3 para.8, amended: SI 2014/3312 Reg.2
Sch.1 Part 6 para.16, amended: SI 2014/3255 Art.27

Sch.1 Part 6 para.16, revoked (in part): SI 2014/3255 Art.27
Sch.1 Part 6 para.16, varied: 2014 c.6 s.126
Sch.1 Part 6 para.18, amended: SI 2014/3255 Art.27, SI 2014/3312 Reg.2
Sch.1 Part 6 para.18, revoked (in part): SI 2014/3255 Art.27
Sch.1 Part 6 para.18, varied: 2014 c.6 s.126
Sch.1 Part 6 para.19, amended: SI 2014/3255 Art.27
Sch.1 Part 6 para.22, amended: SI 2014/3312 Reg.2
Sch.1 Part 6 para.23, amended: SI 2014/3312 Reg.2
Sch.1 Part 6 para.25, amended: SI 2014/3255 Art.27, SI 2014/3312 Reg.2
Sch.1 Part 6 para.25, varied: 2014 c.6 s.126
Sch.1 Part 6 para.28, amended: SI 2014/3312 Reg.2
Sch.1 Part 6 para.29, amended: SI 2014/3312 Reg.2
Sch.1 Part 6 para.30, amended: SI 2014/3312 Reg.2
Sch.2 Part 1 para.1, amended: SI 2014/448 Reg.2, SI 2014/3312 Reg.2
Sch.2 Part 1 para.2, amended: SI 2014/3312 Reg.2
Sch.2 Part 2 para.3, amended: SI 2014/448 Reg.2
Sch.2 Part 4, amended: SI 2014/3312 Reg.2
Sch.3 para.1, amended: SI 2014/3312 Reg.2
Sch.4 para.5, amended: SI 2014/3312 Reg.2
Sch.4 para.6, amended: SI 2014/3312 Reg.2
Sch.5 para.19, amended: SI 2014/3312 Reg.2
Sch.6 Part 1 para.21, amended: SI 2014/3312 Reg.2
Sch.6 Part 1 para.22, amended: SI 2014/3312 Reg.2
Sch.6 Part 1 para.29, revoked (in part): SI 2014/513 Sch.1 para.22
Sch.6 Part 1 para.29ZA, added: SI 2014/513 Sch.1 para.22

2886. Council Tax Reduction Schemes (Default Scheme) (England) Regulations 2012

Sch.1, varied: 2014 c.6 s.126

2920. Town and Country Planning (Fees for Applications, Deemed Applications, Requests and Site Visits) (England) Regulations 2012

applied: SI 2014/2026 Reg.3
Reg.14, amended: SI 2014/2026 Reg.2

Reg.14, applied: SI 2014/2026 Reg.3
Reg.16, applied: SI 2014/3328 Art.3
Sch.1 Part 1 para.11, amended: SI 2014/357 Reg.2
Sch.1 Part 2, amended: SI 2014/357 Reg.2

2965. Council Tax (Exempt Dwellings) (England) (Amendment) Order 2012
Art.2, see *A2Dominion Housing Group Ltd v Hammersmith and Fulham LBC* [2014] R.V.R. 268 (VT), Graham Zellick Q.C. (President)

2991. School and Early Years Finance (England) Regulations 2012
revoked: SI 2014/3352 Reg.2

2994. Benefit Cap (Housing Benefit) Regulations 2012
see *R. (on the application of JS) v Secretary of State for Work and Pensions* [2013] EWHC 3350 (QB), [2014] P.T.S.R. 23 (QBD (Admin)), Elias LJ; see *R. (on the application of JS) v Secretary of State for Work and Pensions* [2014] EWCA Civ 156, [2014] P.T.S.R. 619 (CA (Civ Div)), Lord Dyson MR

2996. National Health Service Commissioning Board and Clinical Commissioning Groups (Responsibilities and Standing Rules) Regulations 2012
Reg.1, amended: SI 2014/1611 Reg.2
Reg.10, amended: SI 2014/452 Reg.2
Reg.16, amended: SI 2014/3215 Reg.5
Reg.20, amended: SI 2014/1611 Reg.3
Reg.21, applied: SI 2014/2821 Reg.3, Reg.5
Reg.22, applied: SI 2014/2821 Reg.3, Reg.5
Reg.24, applied: SI 2014/2821 Reg.3, Reg.5
Reg.28, amended: SI 2014/1611 Reg.3
Reg.29, amended: SI 2014/1611 Reg.3
Reg.30, amended: SI 2014/1611 Reg.3
Reg.32A, amended: SI 2014/1611 Reg.4
Reg.32B, amended: SI 2014/1611 Reg.4
Reg.41, amended: SI 2014/1611 Reg.5
Sch.1 para.4, amended: SI 2014/2103 Art.42
Sch.1 para.8, amended: SI 2014/2103 Art.42
Sch.3 Part 1, revoked: SI 2014/452 Reg.2
Sch.3 Part 2, amended: SI 2014/91 Reg.2
Sch.4 para.22A, added: SI 2014/452 Reg.3
Sch.4 para.57A, added: SI 2014/452 Reg.3
Sch.5 para.6, amended: SI 2014/1611 Reg.6

2999. Climate Change Agreements (Eligible Facilities) Regulations 2012
Reg.2, amended: SI 2014/1318 Reg.2

Sch.1 para.37, added: SI 2014/1318 Reg.2

3007. Employment Rights (Increase of Limits) Order 2012
revoked: SI 2014/382 Art.2

3010. Immigration (Designation of Travel Bans) (Amendment No 3) Order 2012
revoked: SI 2014/1849 Sch.2

3018. Electricity and Gas (Energy Companies Obligation) Order 2012
applied: SI 2014/3219 Art.27
Art.2, amended: SI 2014/1131 Art.3, SI 2014/2897 Art.3, SI 2014/3231 Art.3
Art.3, amended: SI 2014/3231 Art.4
Art.8A, added: SI 2014/3231 Art.5
Art.12, amended: SI 2014/1131 Art.4, SI 2014/3231 Art.6
Art.12, revoked (in part): SI 2014/1131 Art.4
Art.13, amended: SI 2014/1131 Art.5, SI 2014/3231 Art.7
Art.13, applied: SI 2014/3219 Art.27
Art.13, revoked (in part): SI 2014/1131 Art.5
Art.14, amended: SI 2014/3231 Art.8
Art.14, revoked (in part): SI 2014/3231 Art.8
Art.15, applied: SI 2014/3219 Art.27
Art.16, amended: SI 2014/1131 Art.6, SI 2014/2897 Art.4, SI 2014/3231 Art.9
Art.16, applied: SI 2014/3219 Art.28
Art.16, revoked (in part): SI 2014/1131 Art.6, SI 2014/3231 Art.9
Art.17, amended: SI 2014/2897 Art.5
Art.17, applied: SI 2014/3219 Art.29
Art.18, amended: SI 2014/2897 Art.6
Art.19, applied: SI 2014/3219 Art.28
Art.19A, added: SI 2014/3231 Art.10
Art.19B, applied: SI 2014/3219 Art.11
Art.19D, applied: SI 2014/3219 Art.11
Art.20, amended: SI 2014/3231 Art.11
Art.21, amended: SI 2014/3231 Art.12
Art.21A, added: SI 2014/1131 Art.7
Art.21A, amended: SI 2014/3231 Art.14
Art.21ZA, added: SI 2014/3231 Art.13
Art.22, amended: SI 2014/1131 Art.8, SI 2014/3231 Art.15
Art.24, amended: SI 2014/3231 Art.16
Sch.1 para.1, amended: SI 2014/1131 Art.9
Sch.1 para.2, amended: SI 2014/1131 Art.9
Sch.1 para.3, added: SI 2014/1131 Art.9

3022. Agricultural Holdings (Units of Production) (Wales) Order 2012
revoked: SI 2014/41 Art.3

3027. Common Agricultural Policy Single Payment and Support Schemes (Amendment) Regulations 2012

revoked: SI 2014/3259 Reg.15

3032. Restriction of the Use of Certain Hazardous Substances in Electrical and Electronic Equipment Regulations 2012

Reg.23, amended: SI 2014/1771 Reg.4

Reg.23, revoked (in part): SI 2014/1771 Reg.4

3038. Greenhouse Gas Emissions Trading Scheme Regulations 2012

Reg.3, amended: SI 2014/3125 Reg.2

Reg.17, amended: SI 2014/3125 Reg.3

Reg.20, amended: SI 2014/3125 Reg.4

Reg.32, amended: SI 2014/3125 Reg.5

Reg.32A, added: SI 2014/3125 Reg.6

Reg.33, amended: SI 2014/3125 Reg.7

Reg.33A, added: SI 2014/3125 Reg.8

Reg.34, amended: SI 2014/3125 Reg.9

Reg.35, amended: SI 2014/3125 Reg.10

Reg.37, amended: SI 2014/3125 Reg.11

Reg.42, revoked: SI 2014/3125 Reg.12

Reg.42A, added: SI 2014/3125 Reg.13

Reg.54, amended: SI 2014/3125 Reg.14

Reg.60, amended: SI 2014/3125 Reg.15

Reg.61, amended: SI 2014/3125 Reg.16

Reg.63, amended: SI 2014/3125 Reg.17

Reg.64, amended: SI 2014/3125 Reg.18

Reg.87, amended: SI 2014/3125 Reg.19

Reg.87AA, added: SI 2014/3125 Reg.19

Sch.1 para.3, varied: SI 2014/2708 Art.5

Sch.7 para.1A, added: SI 2014/3125 Reg.20

Sch.8 para.5, amended: SI 2014/3125 Reg.21

Sch.8 para.8, amended: SI 2014/3125 Reg.21

Sch.8 para.9, added: SI 2014/3125 Reg.21

Sch.10 para.1, amended: SI 2014/3125 Reg.22

3040. Housing Benefit (Amendment) Regulations 2012

see *R. (on the application of MA) v Secretary of State for Work and Pensions* [2014] EWCA Civ 13, [2014] P.T.S.R. 584 (CA (Civ Div)), Lord Dyson MR

3042. Child Maintenance and Other Payments Act 2008 (Commencement No 10 and Transitional Provisions) Order 2012

Art.3, amended: SI 2014/1635 Art.6

Art.3, disapplied: SI 2014/1635 Art.6

Art.5, disapplied: SI 2014/1635 Art.6

3093. Common Agricultural Policy Single Payment and Support Schemes (Wales) (Amendment) Regulations 2012

revoked: SI 2014/3223 Sch.3

3098. Civil Legal Aid (Procedure) Regulations 2012

Reg.2, amended: SI 2014/1824 Reg.2

Reg.20, amended: SI 2014/1824 Reg.2

Reg.23, amended: SI 2014/1824 Reg.2

Reg.31, amended: SI 2014/1824 Reg.2

Reg.33, amended: SI 2014/814 Reg.2

Reg.33, revoked (in part): SI 2014/814 Reg.2

Reg.34, amended: SI 2014/814 Reg.3

Reg.37, applied: SI 2014/131 Reg.6, SI 2014/607 Reg.6

Reg.42, amended: SI 2014/814 Reg.4

Reg.67, amended: SI 2014/1824 Reg.2

3110. Consumer Rights (Payment Surcharges) Regulations 2012

Reg.3, amended: SI 2014/549 Sch.1 para.48

Reg.4, referred to: SI 2014/2908 Sch.1

Reg.7, amended: SI 2014/549 Sch.1 para.48

Reg.7, referred to: SI 2014/2908 Sch.1

Reg.9, amended: SI 2014/549 Sch.1 para.48

3118. Energy Performance of Buildings (England and Wales) Regulations 2012

Reg.4, amended: SI 2014/880 Reg.3

Reg.9, amended: SI 2014/880 Reg.4

Reg.11, amended: SI 2014/880 Reg.5

Reg.14, amended: SI 2014/880 Reg.6

Reg.28, amended: SI 2014/880 Reg.7

Reg.32, amended: SI 2014/880 Reg.8

Reg.34, amended: SI 2014/880 Reg.9

Reg.35, amended: SI 2014/880 Reg.10

Reg.36, amended: SI 2014/880 Reg.11

Reg.38, amended: SI 2014/880 Reg.12

3122. Payments in Euro (Credit Transfers and Direct Debits) Regulations 2012

Reg.15, applied: SI 2014/1195 Art.2

3144. Council Tax Reduction Schemes and Prescribed Requirements (Wales) Regulations 2012

applied: SI 2014/825 Reg.3, SI 2014/856 Art.3

Sch.1 Part 4 para.10, varied: 2014 c.6 s.126

Sch.1 Part 4 para.19, varied: 2014 c.6 s.126

Sch.6 Part 4 para.21, varied: 2014 c.6 s.126

3174. Designation of Schools Having a Religious Character (Independent Schools) (England) (No.3) Order 2012
    Sch.1, amended: SI 2014/1024 Sch.2, SI 2014/3361 Sch.2

2013

    7. Scotland Act 2012 (Transitional and Consequential Provisions) Order 2013
        Art.2, see *Rondos (Michal) v HM Advocate* [2014] HCJAC 119 (HCJ), Lady Paton
    9. Criminal Legal Aid (General) Regulations 2013
        Reg.9, see *Chelmsford County Court v Ramet* [2014] EWHC 56 (Fam), [2014] 2 F.L.R. 1081 (Fam Div), Sir James Munby PFD; see *King's Lynn and West Norfolk Council v Bunning* [2013] EWHC 3390 (QB), [2014] 2 All E.R. 1095 (QBD), Blake J

    104. Civil Legal Aid (Merits Criteria) Regulations 2013
        see *Bhatia Best Ltd v Lord Chancellor* [2014] EWHC 746 (QB), [2014] 1 W.L.R. 3487 (QBD), Silber J
        Reg.2, amended: SI 2014/131 Reg.2
        Reg.43, revoked (in part): SI 2014/131 Reg.2
        Reg.56, revoked (in part): SI 2014/131 Reg.2
        Reg.58, amended: SI 2014/131 Reg.2
        Reg.58, revoked (in part): SI 2014/131 Reg.2
        Reg.60, amended: SI 2014/131 Reg.2
        Reg.61, amended: SI 2014/131 Reg.2
        Reg.61, revoked (in part): SI 2014/131 Reg.2
        Reg.64, revoked (in part): SI 2014/131 Reg.2
        Reg.66, amended: SI 2014/131 Reg.2
        Reg.67, amended: SI 2014/131 Reg.2
        Reg.68, amended: SI 2014/131 Reg.2
        Reg.69, amended: SI 2014/131 Reg.2
        Reg.75, revoked (in part): SI 2014/131 Reg.2
    105. Pension Protection Fund and Occupational Pension Schemes (Levy Ceiling and Compensation Cap) Order 2013
        revoked: SI 2014/10 Art.5

164. Belarus (Asset-Freezing) Regulations 2013
    Sch.1 para.5, amended: 2014 c.29 s.4
165. Financial Services and Markets Act 2000 (Prescribed Financial Institutions) Order 2013
    Art.1, amended: SI 2014/3348 Sch.3 para.11
    Art.2, amended: SI 2014/3348 Sch.3 para.11
217. Accounts and Audit (Wales) (Amendment) Regulations 2013
    revoked: SI 2014/3362 Reg.30
240. Health and Safety at Work etc Act 1974 (Application outside Great Britain) Order 2013
    applied: SI 2014/1638 Reg.3, SI 2014/1639 Reg.1, SI 2014/3248 Reg.1
249. Immigration and Nationality (Fees) (Amendment) Order 2013
    revoked: 2014 c.22 Sch.9 para.74
276. Jobseeker's Allowance (Schemes for Assisting Persons to Obtain Employment) Regulations 2013
    Reg.3, amended: SI 2014/2103 Art.43
    Reg.3, applied: SI 2014/1913 Reg.4
    Reg.5, applied: SI 2014/1913 Reg.6
349. National Health Service (Pharmaceutical and Local Pharmaceutical Services) Regulations 2013
    Reg.13, amended: SI 2014/417 Reg.3
    Reg.15, amended: SI 2014/417 Reg.4
    Reg.17, amended: SI 2014/417 Reg.5
    Reg.18, amended: SI 2014/417 Reg.6
    Reg.20, amended: SI 2014/417 Reg.7
    Reg.24, amended: SI 2014/417 Reg.8
    Reg.26, amended: SI 2014/417 Reg.9
    Reg.31, amended: SI 2014/417 Reg.10
    Reg.32, amended: SI 2014/417 Reg.11
    Reg.33, amended: SI 2014/417 Reg.12
    Reg.34, amended: SI 2014/417 Reg.13
    Reg.34, revoked (in part): SI 2014/417 Reg.13
    Reg.40, amended: SI 2014/417 Reg.14
    Reg.64, amended: SI 2014/417 Reg.15
    Reg.64, disapplied: SI 2014/417 Reg.16
    Reg.64, referred to: SI 2014/417 Reg.16
    Sch.2 Part 1 para.7, amended: SI 2014/417 Reg.17
    Sch.2 Part 2 para.13, amended: SI 2014/417 Reg.17
    Sch.2 Part 5 para.31, amended: SI 2014/417 Reg.17
    Sch.2 Part 5 para.32, amended: SI 2014/417 Reg.17

Sch.4 Part 2 para.12, amended: SI 2014/417
Reg.18
Sch.5 para.11, amended: SI 2014/417
Reg.19
Sch.9 para.11, amended: SI 2014/417
Reg.20
376. Universal Credit Regulations 2013
applied: SI 2014/1230 Reg.19, Reg.21,
Reg.28, Reg.30, Reg.32
Part 4, applied: SI 2014/1230 Reg.19,
Reg.20, Reg.21, Reg.22, Reg.23, Reg.24,
Reg.26, Reg.27
Part 5, applied: SI 2014/1230 Reg.22,
Reg.27, SI 2014/3219 Sch.1 para.1
Part 8, applied: SI 2014/1230 Reg.30,
Reg.32
Reg.2, amended: SI 2014/597 Reg.2, SI
2014/884 Reg.6, SI 2014/2888 Reg.3, SI
2014/3255 Art.28
Reg.2, varied: 2014 c.6 s.126
Reg.4, applied: SI 2014/3219 Sch.1 para.1
Reg.5, applied: SI 2014/1230 Reg.28
Reg.15, amended: SI 2014/2887 Reg.3
Reg.19, applied: SI 2014/1230 Reg.24
Reg.21, amended: SI 2014/2887 Reg.3
Reg.21, revoked (in part): SI 2014/2887
Reg.3
Reg.22A, added: SI 2014/2887 Reg.3
Reg.24, amended: SI 2014/2888 Reg.3
Reg.24, applied: SI 2014/3037 Reg.25
Reg.27, applied: SI 2014/1230 Reg.19,
Reg.21, Reg.22, Reg.23, Reg.24, Reg.26,
Reg.27, SI 2014/3037 Reg.25
Reg.27, disapplied: SI 2014/1230 Reg.19,
Reg.21, Reg.23, Reg.24, Reg.26
Reg.28, applied: SI 2014/1230 Reg.20,
Reg.21
Reg.28, disapplied: SI 2014/1230 Reg.19,
Reg.20, Reg.21, Reg.22, Reg.23, Reg.24,
Reg.26, Reg.27
Reg.31, applied: SI 2014/2319 Reg.3
Reg.32, amended: SI 2014/3255 Art.28
Reg.32, varied: 2014 c.6 s.126
Reg.33, amended: SI 2014/2887 Reg.2
Reg.34, amended: SI 2014/2887 Reg.2
Reg.34A, added: SI 2014/2887 Reg.2
Reg.36, amended: SI 2014/516 Sch.16
Reg.36, applied: SI 2014/1230 Reg.36
Reg.36, referred to: SI 2014/147 Art.13
Reg.37, amended: SI 2014/597 Reg.2
Reg.38, disapplied: SI 2014/1230 Reg.23

Reg.39, amended: SI 2014/597 Reg.2
Reg.40, amended: SI 2014/597 Reg.2
Reg.55, amended: SI 2014/2888 Reg.4, SI
2014/3255 Art.28
Reg.55, revoked (in part): SI 2014/3255
Art.28
Reg.55, varied: 2014 c.6 s.126
Reg.57, amended: SI 2014/2888 Reg.4
Reg.61, substituted: SI 2014/2888 Reg.4
Reg.62, substituted: SI 2014/2888 Reg.4
Reg.66, applied: SI 2014/1230 Reg.10,
Reg.25
Reg.73, amended: SI 2014/2887 Reg.4
Reg.73, disapplied: SI 2014/1230 Reg.10
Reg.77, amended: SI 2014/2888 Reg.4
Reg.79, applied: SI 2014/1230 Reg.9
Reg.79, referred to: SI 2014/1230 Reg.9
Reg.90, amended: SI 2014/2888 Reg.4
Reg.91, amended: SI 2014/1097 Reg.16
Reg.91A, added: SI 2014/1097 Reg.16
Reg.92, amended: SI 2014/902 Reg.8
Reg.98, amended: SI 2014/597 Reg.2, SI
2014/2888 Reg.8
Reg.99, amended: SI 2014/597 Reg.2, SI
2014/2888 Reg.8
Reg.101, amended: SI 2014/597 Reg.2
Reg.101, applied: SI 2014/1230 Reg.32
Reg.101, varied: SI 2014/1230 Reg.30
Reg.102, amended: SI 2014/597 Reg.2
Reg.102, applied: SI 2014/1230 Reg.33
Reg.103, amended: SI 2014/597 Reg.2
Reg.104, amended: SI 2014/597 Reg.2
Reg.104, applied: SI 2014/1230 Reg.31
Reg.107, applied: SI 2014/1230 Reg.34
Reg.111, applied: SI 2014/1230 Reg.32
Reg.111, varied: SI 2014/1230 Reg.32
Reg.116, amended: SI 2014/597 Reg.2
Sch.1 para.1, amended: SI 2014/771 Reg.2
Sch.1 para.3, amended: SI 2014/771 Reg.2
Sch.1 para.3, revoked (in part): SI 2014/771
Reg.2
Sch.1 para.3A, added: SI 2014/771 Reg.2
Sch.4 Part 1 para.2, amended: SI 2014/771
Reg.2
Sch.4 Part 3 para.7, amended: SI 2014/597
Reg.2
Sch.4 Part 3 para.14, amended: SI 2014/516
Art.24
Sch.4 Part 3 para.15, amended: SI
2014/2888 Reg.3

Sch.4 Part 4 para.24, applied: SI 2014/516
Sch.17
Sch.4 Part 5 para.33, applied: SI 2014/516
Sch.17
Sch.4 Part 5 para.35, applied: SI 2014/516
Sch.17
Sch.4 Part 5 para.36, applied: SI 2014/516
Sch.17
Sch.5, applied: SI 2014/1230 Reg.29
Sch.5 Part 1 para.2, amended: SI 2014/597
Reg.2
Sch.5 Part 3 para.5, applied: SI 2014/1230
Reg.29
Sch.5 Part 3 para.5, disapplied: SI
2014/1230 Reg.29
Sch.5 Part 4 para.10, applied: SI 2014/516
Sch.17
Sch.5 Part 4 para.10, revoked (in part): SI
2014/597 Reg.2
Sch.5 Part 4 para.11, amended: SI 2014/597
Reg.2
Sch.5 Part 4 para.11, applied: SI 2014/516
Sch.17
Sch.5 Part 4 para.12, amended: SI 2014/597
Reg.2
Sch.5 Part 4 para.12, applied: SI 2014/516
Sch.17
Sch.5 Part 4 para.13, amended: SI 2014/597
Reg.2

377. Social Security (Personal Independence Payment) Regulations 2013
Reg.24, amended: SI 2014/516 Art.10

378. Jobseeker's Allowance Regulations 2013
Reg.2, amended: SI 2014/3255 Art.29
Reg.15, amended: SI 2014/597 Reg.3
Reg.18, amended: SI 2014/597 Reg.3
Reg.19, amended: SI 2014/597 Reg.3
Reg.20, amended: SI 2014/597 Reg.3
Reg.21, amended: SI 2014/597 Reg.3
Reg.36, amended: SI 2014/2309 Reg.2
Reg.39, amended: SI 2014/884 Reg.6
Reg.43, amended: SI 2014/3255 Art.29
Reg.49, amended: SI 2014/147 Art.10
Reg.58, amended: SI 2014/597 Reg.3, SI
2014/3255 Art.29

379. Employment and Support Allowance Regulations 2013
Reg.2, amended: SI 2014/107 Sch.1 para.55,
SI 2014/3229 Sch.6 para.34
Reg.16, amended: SI 2014/884 Reg.6
Reg.48, amended: SI 2014/1097 Reg.17

Reg.49, amended: SI 2014/597 Reg.4
Reg.51, amended: SI 2014/597 Reg.4
Reg.52, amended: SI 2014/597 Reg.4
Reg.62, amended: SI 2014/147 Art.12, SI
2014/516 Art.23
Reg.75, revoked: SI 2014/3255 Art.30
Reg.75A, added: SI 2014/3255 Art.30
Reg.80, amended: SI 2014/597 Reg.4, SI
2014/3255 Art.30
Reg.85, amended: SI 2014/2309 Reg.2

380. Universal Credit, Personal Independence Payment, Jobseeker's Allowance and Employment and Support Allowance (Claims and Payments) Regulations 2013
applied: SI 2014/209 Art.2, SI 2014/1230
Reg.6, SI 2014/1583 Art.2, SI 2014/2321
Art.2, SI 2014/3067 Art.2
Reg.6, referred to: SI 2014/1452 Art.3, SI
2014/1923 Art.3, SI 2014/3094 Art.7
Reg.6, revoked: SI 2014/2887 Reg.3
Reg.9, amended: SI 2014/2887 Reg.3
Reg.9, applied: SI 2014/1230 Reg.6, Reg.7,
Reg.8, Reg.17, SI 2014/1452 Art.3, SI
2014/1923 Art.3, SI 2014/3094 Art.7
Reg.9, referred to: SI 2014/1452 Art.3, SI
2014/1923 Art.3
Reg.26, amended: SI 2014/2887 Reg.3
Reg.26, applied: SI 2014/1230 Reg.9
Reg.26, revoked (in part): SI 2014/2887
Reg.3
Reg.26, varied: SI 2014/1230 Reg.15
Reg.46, amended: SI 2014/2888 Reg.5
Reg.57, applied: SI 2014/1230 Reg.16
Reg.57, referred to: SI 2014/1230 Reg.16
Sch.5 para.9, amended: SI 2014/485 Reg.3
Sch.6, applied: SI 2014/1230 Reg.18
Sch.6 para.3, applied: SI 2014/1230 Reg.18
Sch.6 para.4, amended: SI 2014/2888 Reg.6
Sch.6 para.5, amended: SI 2014/2888 Reg.6
Sch.6 para.7, amended: SI 2014/2888 Reg.6
Sch.6 para.11, amended: SI 2014/597 Reg.5
Sch.6 para.11, revoked (in part): SI
2014/597 Reg.5
Sch.6 para.12, amended: SI 2014/597 Reg.5
Sch.6 para.12, revoked (in part): SI
2014/597 Reg.5
Sch.7 para.1, amended: SI 2014/612 Reg.15
Sch.7 para.2, amended: SI 2014/612 Reg.15
Sch.7 para.3, amended: SI 2014/612 Reg.15
Sch.7 para.4, amended: SI 2014/612 Reg.15
Sch.7 para.5, amended: SI 2014/612 Reg.15

381. Universal Credit, Personal Independence Payment, Jobseeker's Allowance and Employment and Support Allowance (Decisions and Appeals) Regulations 2013
Reg.26, amended: SI 2014/597 Reg.6
382. Rent Officers (Universal Credit Functions) Order 2013
Art.2, amended: SI 2014/3126 Art.4
Art.4, amended: SI 2014/3126 Art.4
Sch.1 para.4, amended: SI 2014/3126 Art.4
Sch.1 para.6, amended: SI 2014/3126 Sch.3
383. Social Security (Payments on Account of Benefit) Regulations 2013
Reg.5, amended: SI 2014/2888 Reg.5
Reg.9, substituted: SI 2014/2888 Reg.5
Reg.18, substituted: SI 2014/2888 Reg.5
384. Social Security (Overpayments and Recovery) Regulations 2013
applied: SI 2014/3280 Art.5
Reg.2, referred to: SI 2014/3280 Art.5
Reg.2, revoked (in part): SI 2014/3280 Art.6
Reg.3, referred to: SI 2014/3280 Art.5
386. Universal Credit (Transitional Provisions) Regulations 2013
revoked: SI 2014/1230 Reg.3
Reg.5, referred to: SI 2014/209 Art.2
415. Civil Courts (Amendment) Order 2013
revoked: SI 2014/820 Sch.1
418. Payment to Treasury of Penalties (Enforcement Costs) Order 2013
Art.2, amended: SI 2014/2879 Reg.8
419. Financial Services and Markets Act 2000 (Qualifying EU Provisions) Order 2013
Art.1, amended: SI 2014/3348 Sch.3 para.12
Art.2, amended: SI 2014/2879 Reg.9, SI 2014/3348 Sch.3 para.12
Art.3, amended: SI 2014/2879 Reg.9, SI 2014/3348 Sch.3 para.12
Art.4, amended: SI 2014/2879 Reg.9
Art.5, amended: SI 2014/2879 Reg.9, SI 2014/3348 Sch.3 para.12
Art.6, amended: SI 2014/2879 Reg.9, SI 2014/3348 Sch.3 para.12
421. Allocation and Transfer of Proceedings (Amendment) Order 2013
revoked: SI 2014/879 Sch.1
422. Civil Legal Aid (Remuneration) Regulations 2013
Reg.2, amended: SI 2014/7 Reg.2, SI 2014/586 Reg.2, SI 2014/1389 Reg.2, SI 2014/1824 Reg.3

Reg.5, amended: SI 2014/607 Reg.2
Reg.5A, added: SI 2014/607 Reg.2
Reg.5A, amended: SI 2014/1824 Reg.3
Reg.6, amended: SI 2014/607 Reg.2
Reg.7, amended: SI 2014/607 Reg.2
Reg.8, amended: SI 2014/1389 Reg.2
Reg.12, amended: SI 2014/607 Reg.2
Sch.1 para.1, amended: SI 2014/586 Sch.1 para.1
Sch.1 Part 1 para.2A, added: SI 2014/7 Reg.2
Sch.1 Part 1 para.3, amended: SI 2014/7 Reg.2, SI 2014/586 Sch.1 para.1
Sch.1 Part 3, amended: SI 2014/586 Sch.1 para.2
Sch.3 Part 1, amended: SI 2014/586 Reg.2, SI 2014/1389 Reg.2
Sch.3 para.2, added: SI 2014/1389 Reg.2
Sch.3 Part 2, amended: SI 2014/586 Reg.2
435. Criminal Legal Aid (Remuneration) Regulations 2013
Reg.9, see *R. v Banfield (Shirley)* [2014] EWCA Crim 1824, [2014] 5 Costs L.R. 896 (CA (Crim Div)), Lord Thomas LCJ
Reg.17A, added: SI 2014/2422 Sch.1
Reg.21, amended: SI 2014/2422 Reg.2
Reg.22, amended: SI 2014/2422 Reg.2
Sch.1 Part 3 para.6, substituted: SI 2014/2422 Reg.2
Sch.1 Part 4 para.9, substituted: SI 2014/2422 Reg.2
Sch.2 Part 2 para.4, substituted: SI 2014/2422 Reg.2
Sch.2 Part 2 para.6, amended: SI 2014/415 Sch.1 para.2
Sch.2 Part 2 para.7, amended: SI 2014/415 Sch.1 para.3, Sch.1 para.4
Sch.2 Part 2 para.8, amended: SI 2014/415 Sch.1 para.5
Sch.2 Part 2 para.9, amended: SI 2014/415 Sch.1 para.6
Sch.2 Part 3 para.10, substituted: SI 2014/2422 Reg.2
Sch.2 Part 3 para.11, amended: SI 2014/415 Sch.1 para.7
Sch.2 Part 5 para.19, amended: SI 2014/415 Sch.1 para.8
Sch.2 Part 6 para.27, amended: SI 2014/415 Sch.1 para.9
Sch.3 para.7, amended: SI 2014/415 Sch.2 para.2

Sch.4 para.2, amended: SI 2014/415 Sch.3 para.2, Sch.3 para.3

Sch.4 para.3, amended: SI 2014/415 Sch.3 para.4, Sch.3 para.5, Sch.3 para.6, Sch.3 para.7

Sch.4 para.4, amended: SI 2014/415 Sch.3 para.8, Sch.3 para.9

Sch.4 para.5, amended: SI 2014/415 Sch.3 para.10, Sch.3 para.11

Sch.4 para.6, amended: SI 2014/415 Sch.3 para.12

Sch.4 para.7, amended: SI 2014/415 Sch.3 para.13, Sch.3 para.14

Sch.4 para.8, amended: SI 2014/415 Sch.3 para.15

Sch.4 para.9, amended: SI 2014/415 Sch.3 para.16

Sch.4 para.10, amended: SI 2014/415 Sch.3 para.17

Sch.4 para.11, amended: SI 2014/415 Sch.3 para.18, Sch.3 para.19, Sch.3 para.20

Sch.4 para.12, amended: SI 2014/415 Sch.3 para.21

449. Identification and Traceability of Explosives Regulations 2013

revoked: SI 2014/1638 Sch.14 Part 2

Reg.8, amended: SI 2014/469 Sch.3 para.146

452. Non-Domestic Rating (Rates Retention) Regulations 2013

Sch.4 para.1, amended: SI 2014/96 Reg.2

Sch.4 para.1A, added: SI 2014/96 Reg.2

461. National Health Service (Optical Charges and Payments) Regulations 2013

Reg.8, amended: SI 2014/545 Reg.7, SI 2014/2667 Reg.4

Reg.8, applied: SI 2014/2667 Reg.7

Reg.12, applied: SI 2014/418 Reg.5

Reg.18, applied: SI 2014/418 Reg.5

Reg.20, amended: SI 2014/418 Reg.4

Reg.20, applied: SI 2014/418 Reg.5

Sch.1, amended: SI 2014/418 Reg.4

Sch.1, applied: SI 2014/418 Reg.5

Sch.2 para.1, amended: SI 2014/418 Reg.4

Sch.2 para.2, amended: SI 2014/418 Reg.4

Sch.3, amended: SI 2014/418 Reg.4

466. Food (Miscellaneous Amendment and Revocation) (England) Regulations 2013

revoked: SI 2014/1855 Sch.6 Part 1

477. Tribunal Procedure (Amendment) Rules 2013

r.27, amended: SI 2014/2128 r.37

480. Civil Legal Aid (Financial Resources and Payment for Services) Regulations 2013

Reg.5, see *UF, Re* [2013] EWHC 4289 (COP), [2014] C.O.P.L.R. 93 (CP), Charles J

Reg.5, amended: SI 2014/812 Reg.2, SI 2014/2701 Reg.2

Reg.27, amended: SI 2014/2701 Reg.2

486. Operation of Air Services in the Community (Pricing etc.) Regulations 2013

Reg.3, amended: SI 2014/549 Sch.1 para.49

Reg.4, amended: SI 2014/549 Sch.1 para.49

Reg.5, amended: SI 2014/549 Sch.1 para.49

492. Inter-authority Recoupment (England) Regulations 2013

Reg.4, amended: SI 2014/2103 Art.44

Reg.5, amended: SI 2014/2103 Art.44

494. Plant Health (Fees) (England) Regulations 2013

revoked: SI 2014/601 Reg.9

496. Financial Services Act 2012 (Mutual Societies) Order 2013

Sch.2, revoked: 2014 c.14 Sch.7

503. Civil Legal Aid (Statutory Charge) Regulations 2013

Reg.2, amended: SI 2014/1824 Reg.4

504. Financial Services and Markets Act 2000 (Over the Counter Derivatives, Central Counterparties and Trade Repositories) Regulations 2013

Reg.52, amended: SI 2014/905 Reg.2

507. Recovery of Costs (Remand to Youth Detention Accommodation) Regulations 2013

Reg.3, amended: SI 2014/562 Reg.2, SI 2014/981 Reg.2, SI 2014/2931 Reg.2

531. Gloucestershire Care Services National Health Service Trust (Establishment) Order 2013

Art.1, amended: SI 2014/358 Art.2

Art.4, amended: SI 2014/358 Art.3

Art.5, substituted: SI 2014/358 Art.4

Art.6, revoked: SI 2014/358 Art.5

Art.7, revoked: SI 2014/358 Art.5

537. Transfer of Functions (Chequers and Dorneywood Estates) Order 2013

Art.2, varied: SI 2014/2708 Art.5

Art.3, varied: SI 2014/2708 Art.5

Art.4, varied: SI 2014/2708 Art.5

Art.5, varied: SI 2014/2708 Art.5

Art.6, varied: SI 2014/2708 Art.5

544. National Health Service (Dental Charges) (Wales) (Amendment) Regulations 2013
revoked: SI 2014/461 Reg.3

545. Food (Miscellaneous Amendment and Revocation) (Wales) Regulations 2013
revoked: SI 2014/2303 Sch.6 Part 1

561. Smoke Control Areas (Exempted Fireplaces) (Wales) Order 2013
revoked: SI 2014/694 Art.3

562. Smoke Control Areas (Authorised Fuels) (Wales) (Amendment) Regulations 2013
revoked: SI 2014/684 Reg.3

574. Social Security Benefits Up-rating Order 2013
revoked: SI 2014/516 Art.25

588. Council Tax Reduction Schemes (Detection of Fraud and Enforcement) (Wales) Regulations 2013
Reg.2, amended: SI 2014/825 Reg.2

594. Health and Social Care Act 2012 (Consequential Amendments) Order 2013
Art.4, revoked: 2014 c.2 Sch.1 Part 2

599. Social Security Benefits Up-rating Regulations 2013
revoked: SI 2014/618 Reg.6

600. Companies Act 2006 (Amendment of Part 25) Regulations 2013
Reg.6, referred to: SI 2014/3344 Art.3

602. Police and Fire Reform (Scotland) Act 2012 (Consequential Provisions and Modifications) Order 2013
Art.14, amended: 2014 c.12 Sch.11 para.101
Sch.1 para.5, revoked (in part): 2014 c.12 Sch.11 para.102

604. Pensions Increase (Review) Order 2013
referred to: SI 2014/668 Sch.1
Art.6, substituted: SI 2014/107 Sch.1
para.56, SI 2014/3229 Sch.6 para.35

614. Criminal Legal Aid (Determinations by a Court and Choice of Representative) Regulations 2013
Reg.4, see *King's Lynn and West Norfolk Council v Bunning* [2013] EWHC 3390 (QB), [2014] 2 All E.R. 1095 (QBD), Blake J
Reg.7, see *King's Lynn and West Norfolk Council v Bunning* [2013] EWHC 3390 (QB), [2014] 2 All E.R. 1095 (QBD), Blake J

617. Immigration and Nationality (Cost Recovery Fees) Regulations 2013
revoked: SI 2014/581 Reg.11

628. Legal Aid (Information about Financial Resources) Regulations 2013
Sch.1 para.5A, added: SI 2014/901 Reg.2

631. National Assistance (Sums for Personal Requirements) and National Assistance (Assessment of Resources) (Amendment) (Wales) Regulations 2013
Reg.2, revoked: SI 2014/666 Reg.3

667. Automatic Enrolment (Earnings Trigger and Qualifying Earnings Band) Order 2013
Art.3, revoked: SI 2014/623 Art.4

675. Lancashire County Council (Torrisholme to the M6 Link (A683 Completion of Heysham to M6 Link Road)) Order 2013
see *R. (on the application of Gate) v Secretary of State for Transport* [2013] EWHC 2937 (Admin), [2014] J.P.L. 383 (QBD (Admin)), Turner J

677. Housing (Right to Buy) (Limit on Discount) (England) Order 2013
referred to: SI 2014/1378 Art.3
revoked: SI 2014/1378 Art.4

678. Immigration (Designation of Travel Bans) (Amendment) Order 2013
revoked: SI 2014/1849 Sch.2

693. A55 Trunk Road (Glan Conwy Conwy Morfa, Conwy County Borough) (Temporary 70 mph Speed Limit) Order 2013
varied: SI 2014/915 Art.7, SI 2014/2467 Art.5

737. Non-Domestic Rating (Levy and Safety Net) Regulations 2013
Reg.5, amended: SI 2014/822 Reg.3
Sch.1 para.1, amended: SI 2014/822 Reg.4, Reg.5, Reg.6, Reg.7
Sch.1 para.2, amended: SI 2014/822 Reg.8, Reg.9
Sch.1 para.2, substituted: SI 2014/822 Reg.9
Sch.2, amended: SI 2014/822 Reg.10

749. Immigration and Nationality (Fees) Regulations 2013
revoked: SI 2014/922 Reg.12

755. Natural Resources Body for Wales (Functions) Order 2013
Sch.4 para.377, revoked: SI 2014/255 Reg.21

760. Electoral Registration (Disclosure of Electoral Registers) Regulations 2013
    Reg.2, amended: SI 2014/450 Reg.2

763. Trade Union and Labour Relations (Consolidation) Act 1992 (Amendment) Order 2013
    see *University College Union v University of Stirling* [2014] CSIH 5, 2014 S.C. 414 (IH (Ex Div)), Lord Brodie

765. Education (European Institutions) and Student Support (Wales) Regulations 2013
    revoked: SI 2014/1895 Reg.2

777. Legal Deposit Libraries (Non-Print Works) Regulations 2013
    Reg.26, applied: SI 2014/1384 Sch.1 para.9

795. Zimbabwe (Financial Sanctions) (Suspension) Regulations 2013
    revoked: SI 2014/383 Reg.7

898. National Health Service (Pharmaceutical Services) (Wales) Regulations 2013
    Reg.2, amended: SI 2014/2291 Reg.6

920. Diocese of York (Educational Endowments) (Ellerton Priory Church of England School) Order 2013
    Art.1, amended: SI 2014/942 Art.2
    Art.2, amended: SI 2014/942 Art.2
    Art.7, added: SI 2014/942 Art.2

971. Offshore Combustion Installations (Pollution Prevention and Control) Regulations 2013
    referred to: SSI 2014/324 Sch.1 para.18

977. A494 Trunk Road (River Dee Bridge, Queensferry, Flintshire) (Temporary 50 mph Speed Limit) Order 2013
    varied: SI 2014/915 Art.18

981. Mobile Homes (Selling and Gifting) (England) Regulations 2013
    Reg.2, amended: SI 2014/5 Reg.19
    Reg.7, amended: SI 2014/5 Reg.19, SI 2014/442 Reg.7
    Reg.11, revoked: SI 2014/5 Reg.19

983. Welfare Reform Act 2012 (Commencement No 9 and Transitional and Transitory Provisions and Commencement No 8 and Savings and Transitional Provisions (Amendment)) Order 2013
    applied: SI 2014/2887 Reg.5
    referred to: SI 2014/209 Art.3, SI 2014/1583 Art.3

Art.2, amended: SI 2014/1452 Art.4, SI 2014/1661 Art.4, SI 2014/1923 Art.4, SI 2014/3067 Art.6, SI 2014/3094 Art.7
Art.2, varied: SI 2014/1583 Art.2
Art.3, amended: SI 2014/1452 Art.5, SI 2014/1923 Art.4, SI 2014/3094 Art.7
Art.3, applied: SI 2014/209 Art.3, SI 2014/1583 Art.3, SI 2014/2321 Art.3, SI 2014/3094 Art.3
Art.3, revoked (in part): SI 2014/1452 Art.5
Art.3A, added: SI 2014/1452 Art.5
Art.3A, amended: SI 2014/1661 Art.4
Art.3A, applied: SI 2014/209 Art.3, SI 2014/1583 Art.3, SI 2014/2321 Art.3, SI 2014/3094 Art.3
Art.3A, substituted: SI 2014/1923 Art.4
Art.3A, varied: SI 2014/209 Art.3
Art.4, amended: SI 2014/1923 Art.4, SI 2014/3094 Art.7
Art.4, applied: SI 2014/209 Art.4, Art.5, SI 2014/1583 Art.4, SI 2014/2321 Art.4, Art.5, SI 2014/3094 Art.4
Art.4, referred to: SI 2014/209 Art.5, SI 2014/1583 Art.4, Art.5, SI 2014/2321 Art.4, SI 2014/3094 Art.4, Art.5
Art.4, substituted: SI 2014/1452 Art.6
Art.5, amended: SI 2014/1923 Art.4, SI 2014/3067 Art.6
Art.5, applied: SI 2014/209 Art.4, SI 2014/1583 Art.4, Art.5, SI 2014/1923 Art.5, SI 2014/2321 Art.4, SI 2014/3094 Art.4
Art.5, revoked (in part): SI 2014/3094 Art.7
Art.5, substituted: SI 2014/1452 Art.7
Art.5, varied: SI 2014/3094 Art.4
Art.5A, added: SI 2014/1452 Art.8
Art.5A, amended: SI 2014/2321 Art.7
Art.6, amended: SI 2014/1452 Art.9
Art.6, applied: SI 2014/209 Art.5
Art.6, revoked (in part): SI 2014/1452 Art.9
Art.6, varied: SI 2014/1452 Art.17
Art.9, amended: SI 2014/1452 Art.10
Art.9, applied: SI 2014/209 Art.5, SI 2014/2321 Art.5, SI 2014/3094 Art.5
Art.9, referred to: SI 2014/1452 Art.17
Art.10, amended: SI 2014/3067 Art.7
Art.10, applied: SI 2014/3067 Art.7
Art.11, amended: SI 2014/1452 Art.11, SI 2014/3067 Art.7
Art.11, referred to: SI 2014/1452 Art.11, Art.17
Art.12, amended: SI 2014/3067 Art.7

Art.13, amended: SI 2014/1452 Art.12, SI 2014/3067 Art.7

Art.13, referred to: SI 2014/1452 Art.12, Art.17

Art.15, amended: SI 2014/1452 Art.13

Art.15, referred to: SI 2014/1452 Art.17

Art.18, amended: SI 2014/1452 Art.13

Art.18, referred to: SI 2014/1452 Art.17

Art.22, amended: SI 2014/1452 Art.14

Art.22, referred to: SI 2014/1452 Art.17

Art.24, added: SI 2014/1452 Art.15

Sch.2, referred to: SI 2014/209 Art.3, SI 2014/1583 Art.3, SI 2014/3094 Art.6

Sch.4 para.21, amended: SI 2014/147 Art.12

Sch.5, added: SI 2014/1452 Art.16

Sch.5, applied: SI 2014/1923 Art.5

Sch.5, varied: SI 2014/209 Art.4

Sch.5 para.1, amended: SI 2014/1661 Art.4

Sch.5 para.1, revoked (in part): SI 2014/1923 Art.4

Sch.5 para.3, amended: SI 2014/1661 Art.4

Sch.5 para.3, revoked (in part): SI 2014/1661 Art.4

Sch.5 para.4, amended: SI 2014/1661 Art.4

Sch.5 para.4, substituted: SI 2014/1923 Art.4

Sch.5 para.6, amended: SI 2014/1661 Art.4

Sch.5 para.6, varied: SI 2014/1583 Art.2

Sch.5 para.7, amended: SI 2014/1661 Art.4

Sch.5 para.8, amended: SI 2014/1661 Art.4, SI 2014/1923 Art.4

1023. A27 Trunk Road (Portfield Roundabout Bognor Road Roundabout) (Temporary Restriction and Prohibition of Traffic) Order 2013

revoked: SI 2014/300 Art.7

1102. Town and Country Planning (Compensation) (England) Regulations 2013

Reg.2, amended: SI 2014/565 Reg.2

1119. CRC Energy Efficiency Scheme Order 2013

Art.3, amended: SI 2014/502 Art.2

Art.12, amended: SI 2014/502 Art.3

Art.14, amended: 2014 c.29 s.4

Art.24, amended: SI 2014/502 Art.4

Art.25, amended: SI 2014/502 Art.4

Art.26, amended: SI 2014/502 Art.3

Art.74, amended: SI 2014/502 Art.5

Art.82, applied: SSI 2014/319 Sch.2 para.24

Sch.1 Part 1 para.1, amended: SI 2014/502 Art.6

Sch.1 Part 2 para.4, amended: SI 2014/502 Art.6

Sch.1 Part 5 para.14, amended: SI 2014/502 Art.6

Sch.1 Part 5 para.15, amended: SI 2014/502 Art.6

Sch.1 Part 5 para.16, amended: SI 2014/502 Art.6

Sch.1 Part 5 para.29A, added: SI 2014/502 Art.6

Sch.1 Part 7 para.32, amended: SI 2014/502 Art.6

Sch.1 Part 7 para.34, substituted: SI 2014/502 Art.6

Sch.2 Part 1 para.2, amended: SI 2014/502 Art.7

Sch.2 Part 2 para.7, amended: 2014 c.29 s.4

Sch.2 Part 3 para.12, amended: 2014 c.29 s.4

Sch.4 para.4, amended: 2014 c.29 s.4

Sch.5 Part 1, amended: 2014 c.29 s.4

Sch.5 Part 1 para.1, amended: 2014 c.29 s.4

1122. M54 Motorway (Junction 1 to Junction 3) (Temporary Restriction and Prohibition of Traffic) Order 2013

Art.2, amended: SI 2014/2243 Art.5

1141. School Admissions (Infant Class Sizes) (Wales) Regulations 2013

Sch.1 para.1, amended: SI 2014/852 Art.23

Sch.1 para.4, amended: SI 2014/852 Art.23

1163. Official Statistics Order 2013

Sch.1, amended: SI 2014/549 Sch.1 para.50

1169. Tribunal Procedure (First-tier Tribunal) (Property Chamber) Rules 2013

Part 1 r.1, amended: SI 2014/2128 r.30

Part 5 r.45, revoked: SI 2014/2128 r.31

Part 5 r.47, amended: SI 2014/2128 r.32

1179. First-tier Tribunal (Property Chamber) Fees Order 2013

Sch.1, amended: SI 2014/182 Art.2, SI 2014/1900 Sch.2 para.5, Sch.2 para.6

Sch.2 para.1, amended: SI 2014/513 Sch.1 para.23, SI 2014/590 Art.6

1188. Tribunal Procedure (Amendment No 3) Rules 2013

see *Dickinson v Network Rail Infrastructure Ltd* [2014] UKUT 372 (LC) (UT (Lands)), Sir Keith Lindblom P

1237. Employment Tribunals (Constitution and Rules of Procedure) Regulations 2013

see *Pallet Route Solutions Ltd v Morris* [2014] I.C.R. 394 (EAT), Langstaff J

Reg.6, amended: SI 2014/271 Reg.2
Reg.8, amended: SI 2014/271 Reg.3
Reg.14, revoked (in part): SI 2014/611
Reg.2
Sch.1 para.1, amended: SI 2014/271 Reg.5,
Reg.6, SI 2014/468 Reg.2
Sch.1 para.10, amended: SI 2014/271 Reg.7
Sch.1 para.12, amended: SI 2014/271 Reg.8
Sch.1 para.33, amended: SI 2014/271 Reg.9
Sch.1 para.74, see *Ladak v DRC Locums Ltd*
[2014] I.R.L.R. 851 (EAT), Judge David
Richardson
Sch.1 para.88, amended: 2014 c.29 s.4
Sch.1 para.98, amended: 2014 c.29 s.4
Sch.1 para.105A, added: SI 2014/468 Reg.2
Sch.2 para.5, revoked (in part): SI 2014/271
Reg.10

1387. Construction Products Regulations 2013
Sch.5 para.4, revoked (in part): SSI
2014/364 Reg.50

**1389. Electricity and Gas (Market Integrity and
Transparency) (Enforcement etc.) Regulations
2013**
Reg.44, enabled: SI 2014/514

**1396. Cancellation of Student Loans for Living
Costs Liability (Wales) Regulations 2013**
applied: SI 2014/1314 Reg.5

**1455. Enterprise and Regulatory Reform Act
2013 (Commencement No 1, Transitional
Provisions and Savings) Order 2013**
Art.4, revoked (in part): SI 2014/2481 Art.3

**1460. Accession of Croatia (Immigration and
Worker Authorisation) Regulations 2013**
Reg.1, amended: SI 2014/530 Reg.2
Reg.2, amended: SI 2014/530 Reg.2
Reg.5, applied: SI 2014/2603 Reg.4, Reg.6
Reg.5, substituted: SI 2014/530 Reg.2
Reg.7, amended: SI 2014/530 Reg.2

**1471. Reporting of Injuries, Diseases and
Dangerous Occurrences Regulations 2013**
Reg.2, amended: SI 2014/1638 Sch.13
para.31, SI 2014/3248 Sch.5 para.16
Reg.3, amended: SI 2014/3248 Sch.5
para.16
Reg.13, amended: SI 2014/3248 Sch.5
para.16
Sch.2 Part 1 para.5, amended: SI 2014/1638
Sch.13 para.31
Sch.2 Part 3 para.29, amended: SI
2014/3248 Sch.5 para.16

Sch.2 Part 3 para.40, amended: SI
2014/3248 Sch.5 para.16
Sch.2 Part 3 para.43, amended: SI
2014/3248 Sch.5 para.16

**1482. Justice and Security Act 2013
(Commencement, Transitional and Saving
Provisions) Order 2013**
Art.4, see *R. (on the application of Ignaoua)
v Secretary of State for the Home
Department* [2013] EWCA Civ 1498, [2014]
1 W.L.R. 651 (CA (Civ Div)), Lord Dyson
MR

**1487. National Curriculum (Exceptions for First,
Second, Third and Fourth Key Stages)
(England) Regulations 2013**
Reg.2, amended: SI 2014/1866 Reg.3, SI
2014/3286 Reg.2

**1493. A27 Trunk Road (Arundel Road,
Crockerhill) (Temporary Prohibition of Traffic)
Order 2013**
revoked: SI 2014/1785 Art.5

**1506. Biocidal Products and Chemicals
(Appointment of Authorities and Enforcement)
Regulations 2013**
Reg.9, amended: SI 2014/469 Sch.3
para.147

**1511. Welfare Reform Act 2012
(Commencement No 11 and Transitional and
Transitory Provisions and Commencement No 9
and Transitional and Transitory Provisions
(Amendment)) Order 2013**
applied: SI 2014/2887 Reg.5
referred to: SI 2014/1923 Art.5, SI
2014/3067 Art.7
Art.2, amended: SI 2014/1452 Art.18, SI
2014/1661 Art.5, SI 2014/1923 Art.6, SI
2014/3067 Art.4, Art.6
Art.2, referred to: SI 2014/1661 Art.4
Art.3, amended: SI 2014/1452 Art.18, SI
2014/1661 Art.5, SI 2014/1923 Art.6
Art.3, referred to: SI 2014/1661 Art.4
Art.3, revoked (in part): SI 2014/1452 Art.18
Art.4, amended: SI 2014/1661 Art.5, SI
2014/1923 Art.6, SI 2014/3067 Art.6
Art.4, substituted: SI 2014/1452 Art.18
Art.5, amended: SI 2014/1452 Art.18, SI
2014/1923 Art.6
Art.5, varied: SI 2014/1452 Art.17

1554. Criminal Procedure Rules 2013
applied: SI 2014/1610 r.2_1
revoked: SI 2014/1610

see *DPP v Gowing* [2013] EWHC 4614
(Admin), (2014) 178 J.P. 181 (DC), Beatson
LJ; see *Practice Direction (Criminal
Proceedings: Various Changes)* [2013]
EWCA Crim 2328, [2014] 1 W.L.R. 35 (CA
(Crim Div)), Lord Thomas LCJ; see *R. v
Baybasin (Mehmet Sirin)* [2013] EWCA
Crim 2357, [2014] 1 W.L.R. 2112 (CA
(Crim Div)), Lord Thomas LCJ; see *R. v
Swinbourne (Frank Paul)* [2013] EWCA
Crim 2329, (2014) 178 J.P. 34 (CA (Crim
Div)), Fulford LJ
r.1.1, see *DPP v Jarman* [2013] EWHC
4391 (Admin), (2014) 178 J.P. 89 (QBD
(Admin)), Beatson LJ
r.3.3, see *DPP v Gowing* [2013] EWHC
4614 (Admin), (2014) 178 J.P. 181 (DC),
Beatson LJ
r.14.2, see *R. v Stocker (Keith Anthony)*
[2013] EWCA Crim 1993, [2014] 1 Cr. App.
R. 18 (CA (Crim Div)), Hallett LJ
r.16.2, see *R. v Jolleys (Robert) Ex p. Press
Association* [2013] EWCA Crim 1135,
[2014] 1 Cr. App. R. 15 (CA (Crim Div)),
Leveson LJ
r.76.8, see *DPP v Radziwilowicz* [2014]
EWHC 2283 (Admin), (2014) 178 J.P. 432
(DC), Sir Brian Leveson PQBD

**1617. National Health Service (Direct Payments)
Regulations 2013**
applied: SI 2014/1652 Reg.8

**1624. School Governance (Roles, Procedures and
Allowances) (England) Regulations 2013**
Reg.13, amended: SI 2014/1257 Reg.4
Reg.14, amended: SI 2014/1257 Reg.4
Reg.16, substituted: SI 2014/1257 Reg.4
Reg.25, amended: SI 2014/1257 Reg.4
Sch.1 para.1, amended: SI 2014/1257 Reg.4
Sch.1 para.2, amended: SI 2014/1257 Reg.4
Sch.1 para.3, amended: SI 2014/1257 Reg.4

**1674. Judicial Discipline (Prescribed
Procedures) Regulations 2013**
revoked: SI 2014/1919 Reg.25

1675. Bathing Water Regulations 2013
Reg.6, applied: SI 2014/1067
Sch.2 Part 1, amended: SI 2014/2363 Reg.2
Sch.2 Part 2, amended: SI 2014/1067 Reg.2

**1700. Plant Health (Fees) (Wales) Regulations
2013**
revoked: SI 2014/1792 Reg.9

**1745. Immigration (Designation of Travel Bans)
(Amendment No 2) Order 2013**
revoked: SI 2014/1849 Sch.2

1768. Fish Labelling Regulations 2013
Reg.2, amended: SI 2014/3104 Reg.2
Reg.3, amended: SI 2014/3104 Reg.2
Reg.4, revoked: SI 2014/3104 Reg.2
Reg.6, amended: SI 2014/3104 Reg.2
Reg.6, revoked (in part): SI 2014/3104
Reg.2
Reg.7, amended: SI 2014/3104 Reg.2
Reg.8, amended: SI 2014/3104 Reg.2
Reg.9, amended: SI 2014/3104 Reg.2
Sch.1 Part 1 para.1, amended: SI 2014/3104
Reg.2
Sch.1 Part 2 para.2, amended: SI 2014/3104
Reg.2

**1773. Alternative Investment Fund Managers
Regulations 2013**
Reg.2, amended: SI 2014/1292 Art.4
Reg.10, applied: SI 2014/2418 Sch.1
Reg.22, amended: SI 2014/1292 Art.4
Reg.71, amended: SI 2014/1292 Art.4
Reg.72, amended: SI 2014/1292 Art.4
Reg.74, amended: SI 2014/1292 Art.4
Reg.75, amended: SI 2014/1292 Art.4
Reg.78, amended: SI 2014/1292 Art.4

**1783. Road User Charging Schemes (Penalty
Charges, Adjudication and Enforcement)
(England) Regulations 2013**
Reg.6, amended: SI 2014/81 Reg.3
Reg.9, amended: SI 2014/81 Reg.4

**1785. Merchant Shipping (Maritime Labour
Convention) (Survey and Certification)
Regulations 2013**
Reg.2, amended: SI 2014/1614 Reg.14
Reg.4, amended: SI 2014/1614 Reg.14
Reg.11, amended: SI 2014/1614 Reg.14
Reg.15, amended: SI 2014/1614 Reg.14
Reg.17, amended: SI 2014/1614 Reg.14

**1796. Whole of Government Accounts
(Designation of Bodies) Order 2013**
Sch.1, amended: 2014 c.29 s.4

**1797. Alternative Investment Fund Managers
(Amendment) Regulations 2013**
Sch.1 para.1, amended: SI 2014/1292 Art.5
Sch.1 para.1, revoked (in part): SI
2014/1292 Art.5

1813. Protection of Freedoms Act 2012 (Destruction, Retention and Use of Biometric Data) (Transitional, Transitory and Saving Provisions) Order 2013

Art.5, varied: SI 2014/1704 Art.5

1860. Child Maintenance and Other Payments Act 2008 (Commencement No 11 and Transitional Provisions) Order 2013

Art.3, amended: SI 2014/1635 Art.7

Art.3, disapplied: SI 2014/1635 Art.7

Art.5, disapplied: SI 2014/1635 Art.7

1877. Democratic People's Republic of Korea (European Union Financial Sanctions) Regulations 2013

Sch.1 para.5, amended: 2014 c.29 s.4

1881. Financial Services and Markets Act 2000 (Regulated Activities) (Amendment) (No.2) Order 2013

Art.12, amended: SI 2014/506 Art.5

Art.20, amended: SI 2014/506 Art.5

Art.20, disapplied: SI 2014/366 Art.13

Art.30, substituted: SI 2014/376 Art.3

Art.37, amended: SI 2014/376 Art.4

Art.38, amended: SI 2014/376 Art.5

Art.39, amended: SI 2014/376 Art.6

Art.39, revoked (in part): SI 2014/376 Art.6

Art.40, amended: SI 2014/376 Art.7

Art.40, revoked (in part): SI 2014/376 Art.7

Art.44, amended: SI 2014/376 Art.8

Art.45, amended: SI 2014/376 Art.9

Art.48, amended: SI 2014/208 Art.7

Art.48A, added: SI 2014/208 Art.7

Art.56, amended: SI 2014/366 Art.19, SI 2014/376 Art.10, SI 2014/1446 Art.2

Art.56, revoked (in part): SI 2014/1446 Art.2

Art.58, amended: SI 2014/208 Art.7, SI 2014/366 Art.19, SI 2014/2632 Art.2

Art.59, amended: SI 2014/208 Art.7, SI 2014/835 Art.2

Art.59, revoked (in part): SI 2014/835 Art.2

Art.59A, added: SI 2014/208 Art.7

Sch.1 Part 2 para.32, varied: SI 2014/631 Sch.3 para.3

Sch.1 Part 2 para.40, revoked (in part): SI 2014/366 Art.19

1893. Employment Tribunals and the Employment Appeal Tribunal Fees Order 2013

Art.12, amended: SI 2014/590 Art.2

Sch.2, amended: SI 2014/468 Reg.3, SI 2014/590 Sch.1

Sch.3 para.1, amended: SI 2014/513 Sch.1 para.24, SI 2014/590 Art.2

1896. Reservoirs Act 1975 (Exemptions, Appeals and Inspections) (England) Regulations 2013

Reg.3, amended: SI 2014/3248 Sch.5 para.17

1918. Legal Officers (Annual Fees) Order 2013

revoked: SI 2014/895 Art.4

Sch.1 Part TABLE, amended: SI 2014/896 Sch.1

1922. Ecclesiastical Judges, Legal Officers and Others (Fees) Order 2013

revoked: SI 2014/2072 Art.3

1932. School Teachers Pay and Conditions Order 2013

revoked: SI 2014/2045 Art.3

1962. International Tax Compliance (United States of America) Regulations 2013

revoked: SI 2014/1506 Reg.29

1984. Healthy Eating in Schools (Nutritional Standards and Requirements) (Wales) Regulations 2013

Reg.2, amended: SI 2014/2303 Sch.7 para.55, SI 2014/3087 Sch.3 para.2

Sch.3 para.8, amended: SI 2014/3087 Sch.3 para.3

1999. M20 Motorway (Junctions 4 7) (Temporary Restriction and Prohibition of Traffic) Order 2013

revoked: SI 2014/405 Art.7

2012. Export Control (Syria Sanctions) Order 2013

Art.3, amended: SI 2014/1896 Art.2

Art.12A, added: SI 2014/1896 Art.2

Art.17, amended: SI 2014/1896 Art.2

2033. Veterinary Medicines Regulations 2013

Reg.2, referred to: SI 2014/1638 Sch.2 para.6

Sch.5 para.20, amended: SI 2014/599 Reg.3

Sch.5 para.29, amended: SI 2014/599 Reg.3

Sch.5 para.31, amended: SI 2014/599 Reg.3

Sch.7 Part 2 para.17, amended: SI 2014/599 Reg.4

Sch.7 Part 6 para.50, amended: SI 2014/599 Reg.4

Sch.7 Part 6 para.51, substituted: SI 2014/599 Reg.4

2094. Education (Information About Individual Pupils) (England) Regulations 2013

Reg.2, amended: SI 2014/852 Art.24, SI 2014/2103 Art.45

Sch.1 Part 1 para.13, amended: SI 2014/852
Art.24

**2111. Smoke Control Areas (Authorised Fuels)
(England) (No.2) Regulations 2013**
revoked: SI 2014/491 Reg.3

**2112. Smoke Control Areas (Exempted
Fireplaces) (England) (No.2) Order 2013**
revoked: SI 2014/504 Art.3

**2124. Government of Maintained Schools
(Training Requirements for Governors) (Wales)
Regulations 2013**
Reg.2, amended: SI 2014/1132 Reg.93, SI
2014/2225 Reg.2
Reg.4, amended: SI 2014/1132 Reg.93
Reg.4, applied: SI 2014/1132 Sch.7 para.12
Reg.5, amended: SI 2014/1132 Reg.93, SI
2014/2225 Reg.2
Reg.7, revoked: SI 2014/1132 Reg.93

**2127. Government of Maintained Schools (Clerk
to a Governing Body) (Wales) Regulations 2013**
Reg.2, amended: SI 2014/1132 Reg.94
Reg.3, amended: SI 2014/1132 Reg.94
Reg.4, amended: SI 2014/1132 Reg.94

2139. Fish Labelling (Wales) Regulations 2013
referred to: SI 2014/3079 Reg.3
Reg.2, amended: SI 2014/3079 Reg.2
Reg.4, amended: SI 2014/3079 Reg.2
Reg.4, revoked (in part): SI 2014/3079
Reg.2
Reg.5, applied: SI 2014/3079 Reg.3
Reg.6, applied: SI 2014/3079 Reg.3
Reg.7, applied: SI 2014/3079 Reg.3
Sch.1 Part 1 para.1, applied: SI 2014/3079
Reg.3
Sch.1 Part 2 para.2, applied: SI 2014/3079
Reg.3

**2140. Town and Country Planning (Section 62A
Applications) (Procedure and Consequential
Amendments) Order 2013**
Part 6, added: SI 2014/1532 Art.6
Part 7, added: SI 2014/1532 Art.7
Art.2, amended: SI 2014/1532 Art.4
Art.14, amended: SI 2014/1532 Art.5
Sch.3, added: SI 2014/1532 Art.8
Sch.4, added: SI 2014/1532 Art.9

**2189. A2070 Trunk Road (Bad Munstereifel
Road) (Temporary Restriction and Prohibition
of Traffic)(No.2) Order 2013**
revoked: SI 2014/2102 Art.5

**2210. Food Additives, Flavourings, Enzymes and
Extraction Solvents (England) Regulations 2013**
Reg.20, revoked: SI 2014/1855 Sch.6 Part 1

**2216. Gangmasters Licensing (Exclusions)
Regulations 2013**
Sch.1 Part 2 para.12, amended: SI
2014/2124 Reg.2
Sch.1 Part 2 para.12, substituted: SI
2014/1240 Sch.6 para.5

**2232. Education (National
Curriculum)(Attainment Targets and
Programmes of Study)(England) Order 2013**
Art.2, amended: SI 2014/1867 Art.3, SI
2014/1941 Art.3, SI 2014/3285 Art.3
Art.3, amended: SI 2014/1867 Art.4, SI
2014/1941 Art.4, SI 2014/3285 Art.4
Art.5, amended: SI 2014/1867 Art.5, SI
2014/1941 Art.5
Art.6, amended: SI 2014/1867 Art.6, SI
2014/1941 Art.6, SI 2014/3285 Art.5

**2259. Registered Pension Schemes and Overseas
Pension Schemes (Miscellaneous Amendments)
Regulations 2013**
Reg.3, amended: 2014 c.30 Sch.1 para.97

**2302. Courts and Tribunals Fee Remissions
Order 2013**
see *R. (on the application of Unison) v Lord
Chancellor* [2014] EWHC 218 (Admin),
[2014] I.C.R. 498 (DC), Moses LJ

**2356. Local Government Pension Scheme
Regulations 2013**
applied: SI 2014/525 Reg.3, Reg.4, Reg.12,
Reg.14, Reg.17, Reg.19, Reg.24, SI
2014/1012 Art.11, SI 2014/1146 Reg.11
Reg.2, applied: SI 2014/525 Reg.3, SI
2014/1146 Reg.11
Reg.3, applied: SI 2014/525 Reg.5, Reg.7
Reg.3, disapplied: SI 2014/525 Reg.5
Reg.3A, added: SI 2014/1146 Reg.3
Reg.3A, applied: SI 2014/1146 Reg.11
Reg.3A, referred to: SI 2014/1146 Reg.11
Reg.4, amended: SI 2014/1146 Reg.4
Reg.6, disapplied: SI 2014/525 Reg.7
Reg.9, applied: SI 2014/525 Reg.4, Sch.2
para.4
Reg.11, referred to: SI 2014/525 Reg.8
Reg.15, amended: SI 2014/3255 Art.31
Reg.16, amended: SI 2014/3255 Art.31
Reg.16, applied: SI 2014/525 Reg.4, Reg.8,
Reg.11, Sch.2 para.4

Reg.17, applied: SI 2014/525 Reg.4, Reg.11, Reg.15

Reg.17, disapplied: SI 2014/525 Reg.15

Reg.18, applied: SI 2014/525 Reg.7, Reg.14

Reg.20, applied: SI 2014/525 Reg.8

Reg.20, disapplied: SI 2014/525 Reg.8

Reg.21, applied: SI 2014/525 Reg.8

Reg.22, applied: SI 2014/525 Sch.2 para.6

Reg.30, applied: SI 2014/525 Reg.4, Reg.11, Sch.2 para.1, Sch.2 para.5

Reg.31, applied: SI 2014/525 Reg.4, Reg.11

Reg.32, referred to: SI 2014/525 Sch.2 para.4

Reg.33, applied: SI 2014/525 Reg.13

Reg.33, varied: SI 2014/525 Reg.15

Reg.35, applied: SI 2014/525 Reg.11

Reg.37, disapplied: SI 2014/525 Reg.12

Reg.38, applied: SI 2014/525 Reg.11

Reg.39, applied: SI 2014/525 Reg.4, Reg.12

Reg.40, applied: SI 2014/525 Reg.17

Reg.41, applied: SI 2014/525 Reg.17

Reg.60, applied: SI 2014/525 Sch.2 para.2

Reg.64, amended: SI 2014/1146 Reg.5

Reg.64, varied: SI 2014/863 Art.14, SI 2014/865 Art.17, SI 2014/1012 Art.17

Reg.70, applied: SI 2014/525 Reg.22

Reg.72, applied: SI 2014/525 Reg.23

Reg.103, amended: SI 2014/1146 Reg.6

Reg.104, added: SI 2014/1146 Reg.7

Reg.104, applied: SI 2014/1146 Reg.11

Sch.1, amended: SI 2014/44 Reg.9, SI 2014/3255 Art.31

Sch.1, referred to: SI 2014/525 Reg.3

Sch.1, revoked (in part): SI 2014/3255 Art.31

Sch.1, varied: SI 2014/525 Reg.17

Sch.2 Part 1 para.24, added: SI 2014/1012 Art.18

Sch.2 Part 1 para.25, added: SI 2014/863 Art.15

Sch.2 Part 2 para.14, added: SI 2014/1146 Reg.8

Sch.2 Part 3 para.8, amended: SI 2014/1146 Reg.9

Sch.2 Part 4, amended: SI 2014/44 Reg.10, SI 2014/525 Reg.26

Sch.3 Part 1 para.1, amended: SI 2014/863 Art.15

Sch.3 Part 2 para.4, amended: SI 2014/1012 Art.18, SI 2014/1146 Reg.10

2388. Extradition Act 2003 (Designation of Prosecutors) (England and Wales and Northern Ireland) Order 2013

Sch.1, amended: SI 2014/834 Sch.3 para.37

2429. Electricity and Gas Appeals (Designation and Exclusion) Order 2013

revoked: SI 2014/1293 Sch.1

2568. M1 and M6 Motorways and the A14 Trunk Road (Catthorpe) (Temporary Restriction and Prohibition of Traffic) Order 2013

revoked: SI 2014/1164 Art.18

2591. Food Additives, Flavourings, Enzymes and Extraction Solvents (Wales) Regulations 2013

Reg.20, revoked: SI 2014/2303 Sch.6 Part 1

2605. Proceeds of Crime Act 2002 (External Investigations) Order 2013

Art.2, amended: SI 2014/834 Sch.3 para.38

2607. Agricultural Holdings (Units of Production) (England) Order 2013

revoked: SI 2014/2712 Art.3

2629. A404 Trunk Road (Burchett's Green Junction Handy Cross Interchange) (Temporary Prohibition of Traffic) Order 2013

revoked: SI 2014/2675 Art.8

2655. Designation of Rural Primary Schools (England) Order 2013

revoked: SI 2014/2650 Art.3

2657. Welfare Reform Act 2012 (Commencement No 13 and Transitional and Transitory Provisions) Order 2013

applied: SI 2014/2887 Reg.5

referred to: SI 2014/1923 Art.5, SI 2014/3067 Art.7

Art.2, amended: SI 2014/1452 Art.19, SI 2014/1661 Art.6, SI 2014/1923 Art.7, SI 2014/3067 Art.6

Art.2, referred to: SI 2014/1661 Art.4

Art.2, revoked (in part): SI 2014/1923 Art.7

Art.3, amended: SI 2014/1452 Art.19, SI 2014/1661 Art.6, SI 2014/1923 Art.7

Art.3, referred to: SI 2014/1661 Art.4

Art.3, revoked (in part): SI 2014/1452 Art.19

Art.4, amended: SI 2014/1661 Art.6, SI 2014/1923 Art.7, SI 2014/3067 Art.6

Art.4, substituted: SI 2014/1452 Art.19

Art.6, amended: SI 2014/1452 Art.19, SI 2014/1661 Art.6

2734. Occupational and Personal Pension Schemes (Disclosure of Information) Regulations 2013

Reg.2, amended: SI 2014/1711 Reg.79
Reg.5, disapplied: SI 2014/1711 Reg.78
Reg.15, applied: SI 2014/1711 Reg.67
Reg.16A, added: SI 2014/1711 Reg.79
Reg.19, amended: SI 2014/1711 Reg.79
Reg.19, applied: SSI 2014/164 Reg.17
Reg.25, amended: SI 2014/1711 Reg.79
Sch.2 Part 1 para.16A, added: SI 2014/1711 Reg.79
Sch.2 Part 2 para.28A, added: SI 2014/1711 Reg.79
Sch.3 Part 3, referred to: SI 2014/1711 Reg.78
Sch.4, referred to: SI 2014/1711 Reg.78
Sch.5, referred to: SI 2014/1711 Reg.78
Sch.6, amended: SI 2014/1711 Reg.79
Sch.6 Part 2 para.6, amended: SI 2014/1711 Reg.79
Sch.6 Part 2 para.6A, added: SI 2014/1711 Reg.79
Sch.6 Part 3 para.16A, added: SI 2014/1711 Reg.79
Sch.8 Part 5 para.16, referred to: SI 2014/1711 Reg.78

2750. Fruit Juices and Fruit Nectars (Wales) Regulations 2013

Sch.15 para.1, revoked: SI 2014/2303 Sch.6 Part 1

2775. Fruit Juices and Fruit Nectars (England) Regulations 2013

Sch.15 para.1, revoked: SI 2014/1855 Sch.6 Part 1

2780. M1 and M6 Motorways and the A14 Trunk Road (Catthorpe) (Temporary Restriction and Prohibition of Traffic) Order 2013 Variation Order 2013

revoked: SI 2014/1164 Art.18

2819. Unauthorised Unit Trusts (Tax) Regulations 2013

applied: SI 2014/685 Reg.2, Reg.3
Reg.3, amended: SI 2014/585 Reg.3
Reg.24, amended: SI 2014/685 Reg.10
Reg.27, amended: SI 2014/585 Reg.4
Reg.29A, added: SI 2014/585 Reg.5

2828. Housing Benefit and Universal Credit (Size Criteria) (Miscellaneous Amendments) Regulations 2013

see *R. (on the application of MA) v Secretary of State for Work and Pensions* [2014] EWCA Civ 13, [2014] P.T.S.R. 584 (CA (Civ Div)), Lord Dyson MR

2846. Welfare Reform Act 2012 (Commencement No 14 and Transitional and Transitory Provisions) Order 2013

applied: SI 2014/2887 Reg.5
referred to: SI 2014/1923 Art.5, SI 2014/3067 Art.7
Art.2, amended: SI 2014/1452 Art.20, SI 2014/1661 Art.7, SI 2014/1923 Art.8, SI 2014/3067 Art.6
Art.2, referred to: SI 2014/1661 Art.4
Art.2, revoked (in part): SI 2014/1923 Art.8
Art.3, amended: SI 2014/1452 Art.20, SI 2014/1661 Art.7, SI 2014/1923 Art.8
Art.3, referred to: SI 2014/1661 Art.4
Art.3, revoked (in part): SI 2014/1452 Art.20
Art.4, amended: SI 2014/1661 Art.7, SI 2014/1923 Art.8, SI 2014/3067 Art.6
Art.4, substituted: SI 2014/1452 Art.20
Art.5, amended: SI 2014/1452 Art.20, SI 2014/1661 Art.7
Art.5, varied: SI 2014/1452 Art.17

2870. Air Navigation (Overseas Territories) Order 2013

Art.3, amended: SI 2014/2925 Art.3, Art.12
Art.5, amended: SI 2014/2925 Art.4
Art.8, amended: SI 2014/2925 Art.5
Art.15, disapplied: SI 2014/2925 Art.3
Art.16, amended: SI 2014/2925 Art.3
Art.18, amended: SI 2014/3281 Art.3
Art.20A, added: SI 2014/3281 Art.4
Art.35, amended: SI 2014/2925 Art.12
Art.36, amended: SI 2014/2925 Art.12
Art.74, amended: SI 2014/2925 Art.6
Art.94, amended: SI 2014/2925 Art.7
Art.138, amended: SI 2014/2925 Art.8
Art.154A, added: SI 2014/2925 Art.9
Art.155, amended: SI 2014/2925 Art.10
Art.156, amended: SI 2014/2925 Art.10
Art.188, amended: SI 2014/2925 Art.11

2875. Foreign Marriage (Amendment) Order 2013

revoked (in part): SI 2014/1110 Art.17

2952. Animal By-Products (Enforcement) (England) Regulations 2013
    applied: SI 2014/1894 Reg.30, Sch.3 para.3, Sch.3 para.13

2979. Enterprise and Regulatory Reform Act 2013 (Commencement No 4 and Saving Provision) Order 2013
    Art.3, amended: SI 2014/824 Art.2
    Art.3, revoked: SI 2014/824 Art.2
    Art.3A, added: SI 2014/824 Art.2
    Art.3A, substituted: SI 2014/2481 Art.4

2996. Food Safety and Hygiene (England) Regulations 2013
    Reg.2, amended: SI 2014/2748 Reg.3
    Reg.19, amended: SI 2014/2885 Reg.2
    Reg.35, revoked: SI 2014/2748 Reg.3
    Reg.41, amended: SI 2014/2885 Reg.2
    Sch.1, amended: SI 2014/2748 Reg.3
    Sch.2, substituted: SI 2014/2748 Reg.3
    Sch.3 para.2, revoked: SI 2014/2748 Reg.3
    Sch.3 para.14, amended: SI 2014/2748 Reg.3
    Sch.3 para.14, revoked (in part): SI 2014/2748 Reg.3
    Sch.4 para.8, amended: SI 2014/1855 Sch.7 para.59
    Sch.6 para.1A, added: SI 2014/2885 Reg.2
    Sch.6 para.7A, added: SI 2014/2885 Reg.2
    Sch.6 para.8, amended: SI 2014/2885 Reg.2
    Sch.8, revoked: SI 2014/2748 Reg.3

3026. Smoke Control Areas (Exempted Fireplaces) (England) (No.2) (Amendment) Order 2013
    revoked: SI 2014/504 Art.3

3029. Council Tax Reduction Schemes and Prescribed Requirements (Wales) Regulations 2013
    Reg.2, amended: SI 2014/66 Reg.3
    Reg.8, amended: SI 2014/66 Reg.4
    Reg.28, amended: SI 2014/66 Reg.5
    Reg.28, revoked (in part): SI 2014/66 Reg.5
    Sch.1 Part 2 para.3, amended: SI 2014/66 Reg.6
    Sch.1 Part 4 para.10, varied: 2014 c.6 s.126
    Sch.1 Part 4 para.19, amended: SI 2014/66 Reg.6
    Sch.1 Part 4 para.19, varied: 2014 c.6 s.126
    Sch.1 Part 4 para.24, amended: SI 2014/66 Reg.6
    Sch.2 Part 1 para.1, amended: SI 2014/66 Reg.7

Sch.2 Part 1 para.2, amended: SI 2014/66 Reg.7
Sch.2 Part 4, amended: SI 2014/66 Reg.7
Sch.5 Part 1 para.21, amended: SI 2014/66 Reg.8
Sch.5 Part 1 para.22, amended: SI 2014/66 Reg.8
Sch.5 Part 1 para.28, revoked (in part): SI 2014/513 Sch.1 para.25
Sch.5 Part 1 para.28A, added: SI 2014/513 Sch.1 para.25
Sch.5 Part 2 para.33, added: SI 2014/66 Reg.8
Sch.6 Part 2 para.5, amended: SI 2014/66 Reg.9
Sch.6 Part 4 para.25, amended: SI 2014/66 Reg.9
Sch.7 Part 1 para.1, amended: SI 2014/66 Reg.10
Sch.7 Part 1 para.3, amended: SI 2014/66 Reg.10
Sch.7 Part 3 para.10, amended: SI 2014/66 Reg.10
Sch.7 Part 4, amended: SI 2014/66 Reg.10
Sch.7 Part 6 para.23, amended: SI 2014/66 Reg.10
Sch.7 Part 6 para.24, amended: SI 2014/66 Reg.10
Sch.9 para.30, amended: SI 2014/852 Art.25
Sch.9 para.59, amended: SI 2014/513 Sch.1 para.25
Sch.10 para.2A, added: SI 2014/66 Reg.11
Sch.10 para.12, amended: SI 2014/66 Reg.11
Sch.10 para.60, amended: SI 2014/513 Sch.1 para.25
Sch.10 para.63, added: SI 2014/66 Reg.11
Sch.11 Part 2 para.9, amended: SI 2014/66 Reg.12
Sch.11 Part 2 para.10, amended: SI 2014/66 Reg.12

3035. Council Tax Reduction Schemes (Default Scheme) (Wales) Regulations 2013
    Sch.1, added: SI 2014/66 Reg.15, Reg.16, Reg.23, Reg.31, Reg.32, SI 2014/513 Sch.1 para.26
    Sch.1, amended: SI 2014/66 Reg.14, Reg.15, Reg.17, Reg.18, Reg.19, Reg.20, Reg.21, Reg.22, Reg.23, Reg.24, Reg.25, Reg.27, Reg.28, Reg.29, Reg.30, Reg.31, SI 2014/513 Sch.1 para.26, SI 2014/852 Art.26

Sch.1, revoked: SI 2014/66 Reg.16, SI
2014/513 Sch.1 para.26
Sch.1, substituted: SI 2014/66 Reg.16,
Reg.26, Reg.31, Reg.32
Sch.1, varied: 2014 c.6 s.126

**3050. Plant Health (Fees) (England)
(Amendment) Regulations 2013**
revoked: SI 2014/601 Reg.9

**3103. CRC Energy Efficiency Scheme
(Allocation of Allowances for Payment)
Regulations 2013**
Reg.7, amended: SI 2014/495 Reg.2, SI
2014/3262 Reg.2
Reg.7, revoked (in part): SI 2014/3262
Reg.2
Reg.9, amended: SI 2014/3262 Reg.2

**3104. School and Early Years Finance (England)
Regulations 2013**
Reg.10, applied: SI 2014/3352 Reg.9
Reg.11, applied: SI 2014/3352 Reg.8
Reg.16, applied: SI 2014/3352 Reg.19
Sch.2 Part 1, applied: SI 2014/3352 Sch.2
para.5
Sch.2 Part 2 para.8, applied: SI 2014/3352
Reg.8
Sch.2 Part 2 para.11, applied: SI 2014/3352
Reg.8
Sch.2 Part 5, referred to: SI 2014/3352 Reg.8

**3109. School Organisation (Establishment and
Discontinuance of Schools) Regulations 2013**
Reg.2, amended: SI 2014/2103 Art.46

**3110. School Organisation (Prescribed
Alterations to Maintained Schools) (England)
Regulations 2013**
Reg.2, amended: SI 2014/2103 Art.47

**3113. Waste Electrical and Electronic
Equipment Regulations 2013**
Reg.11, amended: SI 2014/1771 Sch.2 Part 1
Reg.13, amended: SI 2014/1771 Sch.1
para.1
Reg.14, amended: SI 2014/1771 Sch.2 Part 1
Reg.16, amended: SI 2014/1771 Reg.2,
Sch.2 Part 1
Reg.17, amended: SI 2014/1771 Sch.2 Part 1
Reg.18, amended: SI 2014/1771 Sch.2 Part 1
Reg.19, amended: SI 2014/1771 Sch.1
para.2
Reg.20, amended: SI 2014/1771 Sch.1
para.3
Reg.21, amended: SI 2014/1771 Sch.1
para.4

Reg.22, amended: SI 2014/1771 Sch.1
para.5
Reg.23, amended: SI 2014/1771 Sch.1
para.6
Reg.24, amended: SI 2014/1771 Sch.1
para.7
Reg.25, amended: SI 2014/1771 Sch.2 Part 1
Reg.26, amended: SI 2014/1771 Sch.2 Part 1
Reg.27, amended: SI 2014/1771 Sch.1
para.8
Reg.28, amended: SI 2014/1771 Sch.2 Part 1
Reg.30, amended: SI 2014/1771 Sch.1
para.9
Reg.31, amended: SI 2014/1771 Sch.1
para.10
Reg.32, amended: SI 2014/1771 Sch.2 Part 1
Reg.33, amended: SI 2014/1771 Reg.2
Reg.34, amended: SI 2014/1771 Sch.2 Part 1
Reg.35, amended: SI 2014/1771 Sch.1
para.11
Reg.36, amended: SI 2014/1771 Sch.1
para.12
Reg.37, amended: SI 2014/1771 Reg.2,
Sch.1 para.13
Reg.38, amended: SI 2014/1771 Reg.2,
Sch.1 para.14
Reg.39, amended: SI 2014/1771 Sch.1
para.15
Reg.40, amended: SI 2014/1771 Sch.1
para.16
Reg.41, amended: SI 2014/1771 Sch.1
para.17
Reg.42, amended: SI 2014/1771 Sch.1
para.18
Reg.44, amended: SI 2014/1771 Sch.1
para.19
Reg.45, amended: SI 2014/1771 Sch.1
para.20
Reg.47, amended: SI 2014/1771 Sch.2 Part 1
Reg.48, amended: SI 2014/1771 Sch.1
para.21
Reg.51, substituted: SI 2014/1771 Reg.2
Reg.53, amended: SI 2014/1771 Reg.2,
Sch.1 para.22
Reg.54, amended: SI 2014/1771 Sch.1
para.23
Reg.55, amended: SI 2014/1771 Reg.2,
Sch.2 Part 1
Reg.56, amended: SI 2014/1771 Sch.1
para.24

Reg.57, amended: SI 2014/1771 Reg.2,
Sch.2 Part 1
Reg.58, amended: SI 2014/1771 Sch.2 Part 1
Reg.60, amended: SI 2014/1771 Sch.1
para.25
Reg.61, amended: SI 2014/1771 Reg.2,
Sch.2 Part 1
Reg.62, amended: SI 2014/1771 Reg.2,
Sch.2 Part 1
Reg.63, amended: SI 2014/1771 Sch.1
para.26
Reg.64, amended: SI 2014/1771 Sch.2 Part 1
Reg.66, amended: SI 2014/1771 Sch.1
para.27
Reg.67, amended: SI 2014/1771 Sch.1
para.28
Reg.69, amended: SI 2014/1771 Reg.2,
Sch.2 Part 1
Reg.70, amended: SI 2014/1771 Sch.2 Part 1
Reg.71, amended: SI 2014/1771 Sch.2 Part 1
Reg.72, amended: SI 2014/1771 Sch.1
para.29
Reg.74, amended: SI 2014/1771 Sch.2 Part 1
Reg.75, amended: SI 2014/1771 Reg.2
Reg.76, amended: SI 2014/1771 Reg.2,
Sch.2 Part 1
Reg.77, amended: SI 2014/1771 Sch.2 Part 1
Reg.78, amended: SI 2014/1771 Reg.2,
Sch.2 Part 1
Reg.79, amended: SI 2014/1771 Sch.2 Part 1
Reg.80, amended: SI 2014/1771 Sch.1
para.30, Sch.2 Part 1
Reg.81, amended: SI 2014/1771 Reg.2,
Sch.2 Part 1
Reg.88, amended: SI 2014/1771 Reg.2,
Sch.2 Part 1
Reg.89, amended: SI 2014/1771 Sch.2 Part 1
Reg.90, applied: SSI 2014/319 Sch.2 para.25
Reg.91, substituted: SI 2014/1771 Reg.2
Sch.10 Part 3 para.19, amended: SI
2014/1771 Sch.2 Part 2
Sch.11 Part 1 para.5, revoked: SI 2014/1771
Reg.2
Sch.11 Part 2 para.9, amended: SI
2014/1771 Sch.1 para.31
Sch.11 Part 2 para.10, amended: SI
2014/1771 Sch.1 para.31
Sch.11 Part 2 para.11, amended: SI
2014/1771 Sch.1 para.31
Sch.11 Part 2 para.12, amended: SI
2014/1771 Sch.1 para.31

Sch.11 Part 2 para.13, amended: SI
2014/1771 Sch.1 para.31
Sch.11 Part 2 para.14, amended: SI
2014/1771 Sch.1 para.31
Sch.11 Part 2 para.15, amended: SI
2014/1771 Sch.1 para.31
Sch.11 Part 2 para.16, amended: SI
2014/1771 Sch.1 para.31
Sch.11 Part 2 para.17, amended: SI
2014/1771 Sch.1 para.31
Sch.11 Part 2 para.18, amended: SI
2014/1771 Sch.1 para.31
Sch.11 Part 2 para.19, amended: SI
2014/1771 Sch.1 para.31
Sch.11 Part 2 para.20, amended: SI
2014/1771 Sch.1 para.31
Sch.11 Part 2 para.22, amended: SI
2014/1771 Sch.1 para.31
Sch.11 Part 2 para.23, amended: SI
2014/1771 Sch.1 para.31
Sch.11 Part 2 para.24, amended: SI
2014/1771 Sch.1 para.31
Sch.11 Part 2 para.25, amended: SI
2014/1771 Sch.1 para.31
Sch.11 Part 3 para.28, amended: SI
2014/1771 Sch.2 Part 2
Sch.11 Part 3 para.29, amended: SI
2014/1771 Sch.2 Part 2
Sch.11 Part 3 para.30, amended: SI
2014/1771 Sch.2 Part 2
Sch.11 Part 3 para.31, amended: SI
2014/1771 Sch.2 Part 2
Sch.11 Part 3 para.32, amended: SI
2014/1771 Sch.2 Part 2
Sch.11 Part 3 para.33, amended: SI
2014/1771 Sch.2 Part 2
Sch.11 Part 3 para.34, amended: SI
2014/1771 Sch.2 Part 2
Sch.11 Part 3 para.35, amended: SI
2014/1771 Sch.2 Part 2
Sch.11 Part 3 para.36, amended: SI
2014/1771 Sch.2 Part 2
Sch.11 Part 3 para.38, amended: SI
2014/1771 Sch.2 Part 2
Sch.14 para.1, amended: SI 2014/1771 Sch.1
para.32
Sch.14 para.2, amended: SI 2014/1771 Sch.1
para.32
Sch.14 para.3, amended: SI 2014/1771 Sch.1
para.32

Sch.14 para.4, amended: SI 2014/1771 Sch.1 para.32

3115. Capital Requirements Regulations 2013
Reg.7, revoked (in part): SI 2014/3348 Sch.3 para.13

3134. Consumer Contracts (Information, Cancellation and Additional Charges) Regulations 2013
referred to: SI 2014/2908 Sch.1
Reg.35, amended: SI 2014/870 Reg.9
Sch.1, amended: SI 2014/870 Reg.9
Sch.2, amended: SI 2014/870 Reg.9
Sch.4 para.4, amended: SI 2014/870 Reg.9
Sch.4 para.9, amended: SI 2014/870 Reg.9

3156. Local Elections (Northern Ireland) Order 2013
Sch.1 para.7, amended: SI 2014/1116 Art.10
Sch.1 para.13A, added: SI 2014/1116 Art.10
Sch.1 para.23, amended: SI 2014/1116 Art.10

3168. Enterprise Act 2002 (Part 8 EU Infringements) Order 2013
revoked: SI 2014/2908 Art.2

3177. Education (Student Support) (Wales) Regulations 2013
Reg.2, amended: SI 2014/1712 Reg.3
Reg.5, amended: SI 2014/1712 Reg.4
Reg.6, amended: SI 2014/1712 Reg.5
Reg.69, applied: SI 2014/1464 Art.2
Reg.74, applied: SI 2014/1464 Art.2
Reg.93, amended: SI 2014/1712 Reg.6
Reg.97, amended: SI 2014/1712 Reg.7
Reg.99, amended: SI 2014/1712 Reg.8
Reg.100, amended: SI 2014/1712 Reg.9
Reg.101, amended: SI 2014/1712 Reg.10
Sch.3, applied: SI 2014/1464 Art.2

3186. HGV Road User Levy (HMRC Information Gateway) Regulations 2013
Reg.2, revoked (in part): 2014 c.26 s.93

3193. Local Authority (Duty to Secure Early Years Provision Free of Charge) Regulations 2013
revoked: SI 2014/2147 Reg.9
Reg.1, amended: SI 2014/1705 Reg.2

3197. Electoral Registration and Administration Act 2013 (Transitional Provisions) Order 2013
applied: SI 2014/2764 Reg.2
Art.1, amended: SI 2014/449 Art.3
Art.4A, added: SI 2014/449 Art.4
Art.6, amended: SI 2014/449 Art.5
Art.7, applied: SI 2014/3178 Art.4

3198. Representation of the People (England and Wales) (Description of Electoral Registers and Amendment) Regulations 2013
Reg.22, added: SI 2014/1234 Reg.4

3206. Representation of the People (Scotland) (Description of Electoral Registers and Amendment) Regulations 2013
Reg.1, amended: SI 2014/1250 Reg.3
Reg.22, added: SI 2014/1250 Reg.4

3220. Energy Efficiency (Eligible Buildings) Regulations 2013
Reg.2, amended: SI 2014/1403 Reg.11

3231. Agriculture (Cross compliance) (No.2) (Amendment) Regulations 2013
revoked: SI 2014/3263 Sch.5

3235. Single Common Market Organisation (Consequential Amendments) Regulations 2013
Reg.6, revoked (in part): SI 2014/1855 Sch.6 Part 1, Sch.6 Part 2, SSI 2014/312 Sch.4 Part 1, Sch.4 Part 2

3238. A55 Trunk Road (Conwy Tunnel, Conwy) (Temporary Traffic Prohibitions and Restrictions) (No 2) Order 2013
revoked: SI 2014/2892 Art.10

3246. Severn Bridges Tolls Order 2013
revoked: SI 2014/3313 Art.3

3271. M4 Motorway (Brynglas Tunnels, Newport) (Temporary Traffic Restriction &amp Prohibitions) (No.2) Order 2013
revoked: SI 2014/2308 Art.4

3287. M5 Motorway (Junctions 11A-12) (Temporary Restriction and Prohibition of Traffic) (Number 2) Order 2013
Art.2, varied: SI 2014/420 Art.2
Art.3, varied: SI 2014/420 Art.2

2014

1. Taking Control of Goods (Fees) Regulations 2014
applied: SI 2014/600 Art.4, SI 2014/3204 Sch.4 para.10, Sch.4 para.13, Sch.4 para.14
Reg.5, applied: SI 2014/600 Art.4, SI 2014/3204 Sch.4 para.13
Reg.6, applied: SI 2014/600 Art.4

5. Mobile Homes (Site Rules) (England) Regulations 2014
Reg.10, amended: SI 2014/3073 Reg.2

13. Air Navigation (Restriction of Flying) (Salthouse, Norfolk) Regulations 2014
revoked: SI 2014/36 Reg.2
Reg.2, amended: SI 2014/28 Reg.2
Sch.1, amended: SI 2014/14 Reg.2, SI 2014/28 Reg.2
Sch.1, applied: SI 2014/14
Sch.1, referred to: SI 2014/28

14. Air Navigation (Restriction of Flying) (Salthouse, Norfolk) (Amendment) Regulations 2014
revoked: SI 2014/36 Reg.2

16. Collective Redundancies and Transfer of Undertakings (Protection of Employment) (Amendment) Regulations 2014
see *RR Donnelley Global Document Solutions Group Ltd v Besagni* [2014] I.C.R. 1008 (EAT), Slade J

17. Lymington Harbour (Works) Revision Order 2014
applied: SI 2014/1076 Art.3, Art.7, Art.16

28. Air Navigation (Restriction of Flying) (Salthouse, Norfolk) (Amendment No 2) Regulations 2014
revoked: SI 2014/36 Reg.2

47. Machine Games Duty (Types of Machine) Order 2014
revoked: 2014 c.26 s.124

99. A2 Trunk Road (Brenley Corner Interchange Thanington Interchange) (Temporary Restriction and Prohibition of Traffic) Order 2014
revoked: SI 2014/2541 Art.7

106. Marriage of Same Sex Couples (Registration of Buildings and Appointment of Authorised Persons) Regulations 2014
Reg.4, amended: SI 2014/1791 Reg.2
Reg.9, amended: SI 2014/1791 Reg.2

112. Uplands Transitional Payment Regulations 2014
Reg.2, referred to: SI 2014/2712 Sch.1
Reg.3, applied: SI 2014/2712 Sch.1
Reg.5, applied: SI 2014/2712 Sch.1

143. Prohibition of Keeping or Release of Live Fish (Specified Species) (England) Order 2014
Art.1, amended: SI 2014/3342 Art.2
Art.1A, added: SI 2014/3342 Art.2
Art.2, amended: SI 2014/3342 Art.2
Sch.1 Part 1, substituted: SI 2014/3342 Sch.1

144. Football Spectators (2014 World Cup Control Period) Order 2014
Art.3, amended: SI 2014/220 Art.2

147. Welfare Benefits Up-rating Order 2014
Art.8, referred to: SI 2014/516 Art.6

163. Criminal Justice (Electronic Monitoring) (Responsible Person) Order 2014
revoked: SI 2014/669 Sch.1

169. M4 Motorway (Junctions 10 11) (Temporary Restriction and Prohibition of Traffic) Order 2014
revoked: SI 2014/1654 Art.10

205. Immigration and Nationality (Fees) (Amendment) Order 2014
revoked: 2014 c.22 Sch.9 para.74

209. Welfare Reform Act 2012 (Commencement No 16 and Transitional and Transitory Provisions) Order 2014
applied: SI 2014/2887 Reg.5
referred to: SI 2014/1923 Art.5, SI 2014/3067 Art.7
Art.2, amended: SI 2014/1452 Art.21, SI 2014/1661 Art.8, SI 2014/1923 Art.9, SI 2014/3067 Art.6
Art.2, referred to: SI 2014/1661 Art.4
Art.2, revoked (in part): SI 2014/1923 Art.9
Art.3, amended: SI 2014/1452 Art.21, SI 2014/1661 Art.8, SI 2014/1923 Art.9
Art.3, referred to: SI 2014/1661 Art.4
Art.3, revoked (in part): SI 2014/1452 Art.21
Art.4, amended: SI 2014/1661 Art.8, SI 2014/1923 Art.9, SI 2014/3067 Art.6
Art.4, substituted: SI 2014/1452 Art.21
Art.5, amended: SI 2014/1452 Art.21, SI 2014/1661 Art.8
Art.5, varied: SI 2014/1452 Art.17

225. A1(M) Motorway (Junction 17 Fletton Parkway, City of Peterborough) Northbound (Temporary Restriction and Prohibition of Traffic) Order 2014
Art.2, varied: SI 2014/2272 Art.2

229. Co-operative and Community Benefit Societies and Credit Unions (Arrangements, Reconstructions and Administration) Order 2014
amended: SI 2014/1815 Sch.1 para.33
Art.1, amended: SI 2014/1815 Sch.1 para.33, SI 2014/1822 Art.3
Art.13, substituted: SI 2014/1822 Art.4
Sch.1 Part 1 para.1, amended: SI 2014/1822 Art.5

Sch.1 Part 2 para.3, amended: SI 2014/1822 Art.5

Sch.1 Part 2 para.5, amended: SI 2014/1822 Art.5

Sch.1 Part 2 para.6, amended: SI 2014/1822 Art.5

Sch.1 Part 2 para.7, amended: SI 2014/1822 Art.5

Sch.1 Part 3 para.12, amended: SI 2014/1822 Art.5

Sch.1 Part 3 para.14, amended: SI 2014/1822 Art.5

Sch.1 Part 3 para.18, amended: SI 2014/1822 Art.5

Sch.1 Part 3 para.26, amended: SI 2014/1822 Art.5

Sch.1 Part 3 para.33, amended: SI 2014/1822 Art.5

Sch.1 Part 3 para.34, amended: SI 2014/1822 Art.5

Sch.1 Part 4 para.38, amended: SI 2014/1822 Art.5

Sch.1 Part 4 para.40, amended: SI 2014/1822 Art.5

Sch.2 para.1, amended: SI 2014/1822 Art.6

Sch.2 para.3, amended: SI 2014/1822 Art.6

Sch.2 para.5, amended: SI 2014/1822 Art.6

Sch.2 para.6, amended: SI 2014/1822 Art.6

Sch.4 Part 1 para.2, amended: SI 2014/1822 Art.7

Sch.4 Part 2 para.9, amended: SI 2014/1822 Art.7

Sch.4 Part 2 para.19, amended: SI 2014/1822 Art.7

Sch.4 Part 3 para.41, amended: SI 2014/1822 Art.7

Sch.4 Part 3 para.51, amended: SI 2014/1822 Art.7

Sch.5 para.1A, added: SI 2014/1822 Art.8

Sch.5 para.3, amended: SI 2014/1822 Art.8

253. Enterprise and Regulatory Reform Act 2013 (Commencement No 5, Transitional Provisions and Savings) Order 2014

applied: SI 2014/271 Reg.11

254. Employment Tribunals (Early Conciliation Exemptions and Rules of Procedure) Regulations 2014

Sch.1 para.4, substituted: SI 2014/847 Reg.2

265. Maritime Security (Jersey) Order 2014

Art.2, varied: SI 2014/322 Art.4

271. Employment Tribunals (Constitution and Rules of Procedure) (Amendment) Regulations 2014

Reg.2, amended: SI 2014/787 Reg.3

Reg.3, amended: SI 2014/787 Reg.4

300. A27 Trunk Road (Portfield Roundabout Bognor Road Roundabout) (Temporary Restriction and Prohibition of Traffic) Order 2014

revoked: SI 2014/2037 Art.6

366. Financial Services and Markets Act 2000 (Regulated Activities) (Amendment) Order 2014

Art.1, amended: SI 2014/506 Art.6

Art.3, revoked (in part): SI 2014/506 Art.6

Art.19, amended: SI 2014/506 Art.6

371. Common Agricultural Policy Single Payment and Support Schemes (Cross Compliance) (Wales) (Amendment) Regulations 2014

revoked: SI 2014/3223 Sch.3

398. A47 Trunk Road (Trowse Interchange to Brundall, Norfolk) (Temporary Restriction and Prohibition of Traffic and Pedestrians) Order 2014

revoked: SI 2014/2699 Art.7

407. Civil Procedure (Amendment) Rules 2014

r.4, amended: SI 2014/1233 r.5

416. Enterprise and Regulatory Reform Act 2013 (Commencement No 6, Transitional Provisions and Savings) Order 2014

Sch.1 para.4, applied: SI 2014/549 Sch.2 para.1

Sch.1 para.6, applied: SI 2014/549 Sch.2 para.1

421. Certification of Enforcement Agents Regulations 2014

Reg.8, applied: SI 2014/482 r.5

Reg.12, applied: SI 2014/482 r.5

458. Competition Act 1998 (Competition and Markets Authority's Rules) Order 2014

Sch.1 para.5, applied: SI 2014/536 Reg.9

Sch.1 para.10, applied: SI 2014/536 Reg.9

Sch.1 para.15, applied: SI 2014/536 Reg.9

469. Energy Act 2013 (Office for Nuclear Regulation) (Consequential Amendments, Transitional Provisions and Savings) Order 2014

Sch.2 para.1, revoked: SI 2014/1638 Sch.14 Part 2

Sch.3 Part 3 para.46, revoked: SI 2014/1638 Sch.14 Part 2

Sch.3 Part 3 para.53, revoked: SI 2014/1638
Sch.14 Part 2
Sch.3 Part 3 para.110, revoked: SI
2014/1638 Sch.14 Part 2
Sch.3 Part 3 para.146, revoked: SI
2014/1638 Sch.14 Part 2
**491. Smoke Control Areas (Authorised Fuels)
(England) Regulations 2014**
revoked: SI 2014/2366 Reg.3
**497. Ukraine (Sanctions) (Overseas Territories)
Order 2014**
revoked: SI 2014/1100 Art.1
**504. Smoke Control Areas (Exempted
Fireplaces) (England) Order 2014**
revoked: SI 2014/2404 Art.3
**507. Ukraine (European Union Financial
Sanctions) Regulations 2014**
Sch.1 para.5, amended: 2014 c.29 s.4
512. Teachers Pension Scheme Regulations 2014
Reg.2, amended: SI 2014/2652 Reg.3
Reg.3, amended: SI 2014/2652 Reg.4, SI
2014/3255 Art.32
Reg.3, revoked (in part): SI 2014/3255
Art.32
Reg.7, amended: SI 2014/2652 Reg.5
Reg.9, amended: SI 2014/2652 Reg.6
Reg.19, amended: SI 2014/2652 Reg.7
Reg.23, amended: SI 2014/3255 Art.32
Reg.31, amended: SI 2014/2652 Reg.8
Reg.33, amended: SI 2014/3255 Art.32
Reg.34, amended: SI 2014/3255 Art.32
Reg.39, amended: SI 2014/3255 Art.32
Reg.41, amended: SI 2014/2652 Reg.9
Reg.117, amended: SI 2014/2652 Reg.10
Reg.143, amended: SI 2014/3255 Art.32
Reg.147, amended: SI 2014/2652 Reg.11
Reg.147, revoked (in part): SI 2014/2652
Reg.11
Reg.150, amended: SI 2014/2652 Reg.12, SI
2014/3255 Art.32
Reg.154, amended: SI 2014/2652 Reg.13
Reg.174, amended: SI 2014/2652 Reg.14
Reg.182, amended: SI 2014/2652 Reg.15
Reg.184, amended: SI 2014/3255 Art.32
Reg.185, substituted: SI 2014/2652 Reg.16
Reg.189, amended: SI 2014/3255 Art.32
Reg.192, substituted: SI 2014/2652 Reg.17
Reg.196, amended: SI 2014/2652 Reg.18
Reg.200, amended: SI 2014/2652 Reg.19
Reg.201, amended: SI 2014/2652 Reg.20

Reg.201, revoked (in part): SI 2014/2652
Reg.20
Reg.203, amended: SI 2014/2652 Reg.21
Reg.205, amended: SI 2014/2652 Reg.22
Reg.209, amended: SI 2014/2652 Reg.23
Reg.209, revoked (in part): SI 2014/2652
Reg.23
Reg.211, amended: SI 2014/2652 Reg.24
Reg.219, amended: SI 2014/2652 Reg.25, SI
2014/3255 Art.32
Reg.220, amended: SI 2014/2652 Reg.26
Reg.223, amended: SI 2014/2652 Reg.27
Reg.225, added: SI 2014/2652 Reg.28
Sch.1 Part 1 para.1, amended: SI 2014/2652
Reg.29
Sch.1 Part 1 para.5, amended: SI 2014/2652
Reg.29
Sch.1 Part 2 para.10, amended: SI
2014/2652 Reg.29
Sch.1 Part 3 para.25, amended: SI
2014/2652 Reg.29
Sch.1 Part 4 para.35, added: SI 2014/2652
Reg.29
Sch.2 Part 1 para.3, amended: SI 2014/2652
Reg.30
Sch.2 Part 4 para.29, amended: SI
2014/2652 Reg.31
Sch.3 Part 1 para.1, amended: SI 2014/2652
Reg.32
Sch.3 Part 2 para.11, amended: SI
2014/2652 Reg.33
Sch.3 Part 3 para.14, amended: SI
2014/2652 Reg.34
Sch.3 Part 3 para.15, amended: SI
2014/2652 Reg.34
Sch.3 Part 3 para.16, amended: SI
2014/2652 Reg.34
Sch.3 Part 4 para.21, amended: SI
2014/2652 Reg.35
Sch.3 Part 4 para.21, revoked (in part): SI
2014/2652 Reg.35
Sch.3 Part 4 para.22, amended: SI
2014/2652 Reg.36
Sch.3 Part 7 para.31, amended: SI
2014/2652 Reg.37
Sch.3 Part 7 para.32, amended: SI
2014/2652 Reg.38
Sch.3 Part 7 para.39, amended: SI
2014/2652 Reg.39
Sch.3 Part 7 para.39A, added: SI 2014/2652
Reg.40

Sch.3 Part 7 para.40, amended: SI 2014/2652 Reg.41

Sch.3 Part 7 para.41, amended: SI 2014/2652 Reg.42

Sch.3 Part 7 para.41, revoked (in part): SI 2014/2652 Reg.42

Sch.3 Part 7 para.41A, added: SI 2014/2652 Reg.43

Sch.3 Part 7 para.43, amended: SI 2014/2652 Reg.44

Sch.3 Part 7 para.43, revoked (in part): SI 2014/2652 Reg.44

Sch.3 Part 7 para.43A, added: SI 2014/2652 Reg.45

Sch.3 Part 7 para.44, amended: SI 2014/2652 Reg.46

Sch.3 Part 7 para.45, amended: SI 2014/2652 Reg.47

Sch.3 Part 8 para.50, amended: SI 2014/2652 Reg.48

Sch.3 Part 8 para.51, amended: SI 2014/2652 Reg.49

Sch.3 Part 8 para.52, added: SI 2014/2652 Reg.49

Sch.3 Part 8 para.54, amended: SI 2014/2652 Reg.50

Sch.3 Part 8 para.55, added: SI 2014/2652 Reg.51

Sch.4, added: SI 2014/2652 Reg.52

517. Animal By-Products (Enforcement) (Wales) Regulations 2014

applied: SI 2014/1894 Reg.30, Sch.3 para.3

525. Local Government Pension Scheme (Transitional Provisions, Savings and Amendment) Regulations 2014

Reg.19, disapplied: SI 2014/1146 Reg.11

531. Government Resources and Accounts Act 2000 (Estimates and Accounts) Order 2014

Sch.1, added: SI 2014/3314 Sch.1

Sch.1, amended: SI 2014/3314 Art.2, Sch.1, Sch.2, Sch.3

560. Marriage (Same Sex Couples) Act 2013 (Consequential and Contrary Provisions and Scotland) Order 2014

Art.5, revoked: SI 2014/3168 Art.4

574. Co-operative and Community Benefit Societies and Credit Unions (Investigations) Regulations 2014

Reg.2, amended: 2014 c.29 s.4

581. Immigration and Nationality (Cost Recovery Fees) Regulations 2014

referred to: SI 2014/2771 Art.13

revoked: 2014 c.22 Sch.9 para.74

Reg.2, amended: SI 2014/2398 Reg.2

Reg.5, amended: SI 2014/2398 Reg.2

Reg.6, amended: SI 2014/2398 Reg.2

Reg.8, substituted: SI 2014/2398 Reg.2

Sch.3 para.2, amended: SI 2014/2398 Reg.2

Sch.3 para.3, added: SI 2014/2398 Reg.2

Sch.4 para.2, amended: SI 2014/2398 Reg.2

Sch.6, substituted: SI 2014/2398 Reg.2

587. Central African Republic (European Union Financial Sanctions) Regulations 2014

Sch.1 para.5, amended: 2014 c.29 s.4

593. Town and Country Planning (Compensation) (Wales) Regulations 2014

revoked: SI 2014/2693 Reg.7

601. Plant Health (Fees) (England) Regulations 2014

Reg.2, amended: SI 2014/3243 Reg.3

Sch.2, substituted: SI 2014/3243 Reg.4

603. Justices Clerks and Assistants Rules 2014

Sch.1, amended: SI 2014/841 Sch.1

614. Child Support (Ending Liability in Existing Cases and Transition to New Calculation Rules) Regulations 2014

Reg.1, amended: SI 2014/1386 Reg.8

Reg.6, amended: SI 2014/1386 Reg.8

615. Marine Licensing (Application Fees) Regulations 2014

referred to: SI 2014/2555 Sch.1

Reg.6, amended: SI 2014/950 Reg.2

693. Ukraine (European Union Financial Sanctions) (No.2) Regulations 2014

Sch.1 para.5, amended: 2014 c.29 s.4

700. Air Navigation (Restriction of Flying) (Farnborough Air Show) Regulations 2014

Reg.3, amended: SI 2014/1973 Reg.2

714. Tuberculosis (England) (Amendment) Order 2014

revoked: SI 2014/2383 Art.24

827. A55 Trunk Road (Pen-y-clip Tunnel, Conwy County Borough) (Temporary Traffic Prohibitions &amp Restriction) Order 2014

revoked: SI 2014/3377 Art.16

828. Guardian's Allowance Up-rating Order 2014

applied: SI 2014/881 Reg.2, Reg.3

838. Guardian's Allowance Up-rating (Northern Ireland) Order 2014
applied: SI 2014/881 Reg.2, Reg.3

840. Family Court (Composition and Distribution of Business) Rules 2014
referred to: SI 2014/956 Art.10
Part 2 r.5, applied: SI 2014/956 Art.10
Part 5 r.12A, added: SI 2014/3297 r.3
Part 5 r.16, amended: SI 2014/3297 r.4
Part 5 r.19, applied: SI 2014/956 Art.10
Part 5 r.20, referred to: SI 2014/603 Sch.1
Sch.1, amended: SI 2014/3297 r.5
Sch.1, substituted: SI 2014/3297 r.5
Sch.2, amended: SI 2014/3297 r.6

842. Family Court (Constitution of Committees Family Panels) Rules 2014
applied: SI 2014/956 Art.8, SI 2014/2867 Sch.1 para.1

863. Barnsley, Doncaster, Rotherham and Sheffield Combined Authority Order 2014
Art.3, applied: SI 2014/1112 Art.2

864. West Yorkshire Combined Authority Order 2014
Art.3, applied: SI 2014/1112 Art.2

865. Halton, Knowsley, Liverpool, St Helens, Sefton and Wirral Combined Authority Order 2014
Art.3, applied: SI 2014/1112 Art.2

867. Civil Procedure (Amendment No 4) Rules 2014
r.25, amended: SI 2014/1233 r.6

879. Crime and Courts Act 2013 (Family Court Consequential Provision) (No.2) Order 2014
applied: SI 2014/956 Art.8

886. Tax Credits, Child Benefit and Guardian's Allowance Reviews and Appeals Order 2014
Art.1, enabled: SI 2014/2881

889. Children and Families Act 2014 (Commencement No 2) Order 2014
Art.4A, added: SI 2014/1134 Art.2
Art.5, revoked (in part): SI 2014/1134 Art.2

916. Diffuse Mesothelioma Payment Scheme Regulations 2014
Sch.4, amended: SI 2014/917 Reg.2

922. Immigration and Nationality (Fees) Regulations 2014
referred to: SI 2014/2771 Art.13
revoked: 2014 c.22 Sch.9 para.74

952. Energy Efficiency (Building Renovation and Reporting) Regulations 2014
Reg.4, amended: SI 2014/1403 Reg.12

985. A14 Trunk Road (Junction 31 Girton to Junction 37 Exning) and the A428 Trunk Road/M11 Motorway (Girton Interchange) (Cambridgeshire) (Temporary Restriction and Prohibition of Traffic) Order 2014
revoked: SI 2014/2008 Art.8

1012. Durham, Gateshead, Newcastle Upon Tyne, North Tyneside, Northumberland, South Tyneside and Sunderland Combined Authority Order 2014
Art.3, applied: SI 2014/1112 Art.2

1064. A465 Trunk Road (Hirwaun, Rhondda Cynon Taf) (Prohibition of Right Hand Turns) Order 2014
varied: SI 2014/2853 Art.4

1095. M42 Motorway and A45 Trunk Road (M42 Junction 6, Solihull) (Temporary Restriction and Prohibition of Traffic) Order 2014
revoked: SI 2014/3382 Art.7

1110. Consular Marriages and Marriages under Foreign Law Order 2014
revoked: SI 2014/3265 Art.18

1132. Federation of Maintained Schools (Wales) Regulations 2014
Sch.8 paraA.1, added: SI 2014/1609 Reg.4
Sch.8 para.4, amended: SI 2014/1609 Reg.4
Sch.8 para.5, revoked: SI 2014/1609 Reg.4
Sch.8 para.7, substituted: SI 2014/1609 Reg.4

1143. Air Navigation (Restriction of Flying) (Giro d'Italia Stage 2) Regulations 2014
referred to: SI 2014/1192
Reg.3, amended: SI 2014/1192 Reg.2

1144. Air Navigation (Restriction of Flying) (Giro d'Italia Stage 1) Regulations 2014
referred to: SI 2014/1191
Reg.3, amended: SI 2014/1191 Reg.2

1200. A494 and A550 Trunk Roads (Queensferry Interchange to Deeside Park Interchange, Flintshire) (Temporary Traffic Prohibitions and 40 MPH Speed Limit) Order 2014
Art.1, amended: SI 2014/1201 Art.2

1230. Universal Credit (Transitional Provisions) Regulations 2014
Reg.2, amended: SI 2014/1626 Reg.3
Reg.5, amended: SI 2014/1626 Reg.3
Reg.6, amended: SI 2014/1626 Reg.3
Reg.6, varied: SI 2014/3094 Art.6
Reg.7, amended: SI 2014/1626 Reg.3, SI 2014/2887 Reg.3

Reg.8, amended: SI 2014/1626 Reg.3
Reg.11, varied: SI 2014/3094 Art.6
Reg.12A, added: SI 2014/1626 Reg.4
Reg.14, amended: SI 2014/1626 Reg.3
Reg.22, amended: SI 2014/1626 Reg.5
Reg.23, amended: SI 2014/1626 Reg.5
Reg.23, revoked (in part): SI 2014/1626
Reg.5
Reg.25, amended: SI 2014/1626 Reg.5
Reg.26, amended: SI 2014/1626 Reg.5
Reg.36, amended: SI 2014/1626 Reg.6
Reg.37, added: SI 2014/1626 Reg.6
Sch.1, added: SI 2014/1626 Reg.4

1240. Welfare of Animals at the Time of Killing Regulations 2014
revoked: SI 2014/1258 Reg.2

1257. School Governance (Constitution and Federations) (England) (Amendment) Regulations 2014
Reg.1, amended: SI 2014/1959 Reg.2

1261. Financial Services and Markets Act 2000 (Transparency) Regulations 2014
revoked: SI 2014/3293 Reg.6

1273. General Medical Council (Licence to Practise and Revalidation) (Amendment) Regulations Order of Council 2014
Art.2, added: SI 2014/1270 Sch.1
Art.2, amended: SI 2014/1270 Sch.1
Art.2, substituted: SI 2014/1270 Sch.1

1292. Alternative Investment Fund Managers Order 2014
Part 2, amended: SI 2014/1313 Art.2
Art.1, amended: SI 2014/1313 Art.2
Art.7, amended: SI 2014/1313 Art.2

1378. Housing (Right to Buy) (Limit on Discount) (England) Order 2014
Art.4, substituted: SI 2014/1865 Art.2

1386. Child Support (Consequential and Miscellaneous Amendments) Regulations 2014
Reg.1, amended: SI 2014/1621 Reg.3
Reg.2, amended: SI 2014/1621 Reg.3
Reg.6, amended: SI 2014/1621 Reg.3
Reg.6, revoked (in part): SI 2014/1621
Reg.3

1410. A500 Trunk Road and M6 Motorway (Barthomley, Cheshire) (Temporary Restriction and Prohibition of Traffic) (Slip Road) Order 2014
revoked: SI 2014/3130 Art.10

1457. Public Lending Right Scheme 1982 (Commencement of Variations) Order 2014
Art.1, revoked (in part): SI 2014/1945 Art.2

1513. Immigration (Passenger Transit Visa) (Amendment) Order 2014
revoked: SI 2014/2702 Sch.2

1528. Air Navigation (Restriction of Flying) (Jet Formation Display Teams) (No.4) Regulations 2014
Sch.1, amended: SI 2014/2389 Reg.3

1530. Special Educational Needs and Disability Regulations 2014
applied: SI 2014/2270 Art.5, Art.6, Art.20, Art.27
varied: SI 2014/2270 Art.23
Part 3, varied: SI 2014/2270 Art.21
Reg.5, varied: SI 2014/2270 Art.5, Art.6
Reg.10, applied: SI 2014/2270 Art.27
Reg.10, disapplied: SI 2014/2270 Art.7
Reg.10, varied: SI 2014/2270 Art.22
Reg.13, disapplied: SI 2014/2270 Art.7
Reg.20, amended: SI 2014/2096 Reg.3
Reg.27, varied: SI 2014/2270 Art.24

1546. A14 Trunk Road (Junction 26 St Ives to Junction 29 Bar Hill, Cambridgeshire) (Temporary Prohibition of Traffic) Order 2014
revoked: SI 2014/2008 Art.8

1558. Air Navigation (Restriction of Flying) (Ascot) Regulations 2014
Reg.3, amended: SI 2014/1939 Reg.3

1583. Welfare Reform Act 2012 (Commencement No 17 and Transitional and Transitory Provisions) Order 2014
applied: SI 2014/2887 Reg.5
referred to: SI 2014/1923 Art.5, SI 2014/3067 Art.7
Art.2, amended: SI 2014/1661 Art.9, SI 2014/1923 Art.10, SI 2014/3067 Art.5, Art.6
Art.2, referred to: SI 2014/1661 Art.4
Art.3, amended: SI 2014/1923 Art.10
Art.3, referred to: SI 2014/1661 Art.4
Art.4, amended: SI 2014/1923 Art.10, SI 2014/3067 Art.6

1603. Requirements for School Food Regulations 2014
Reg.2, amended: SI 2014/3001 Sch.3 para.8
Sch.3 para.2, amended: SI 2014/3001 Sch.3 para.9

1610. Criminal Procedure Rules 2014
r.14.2, see *R. v Powell (Carl Michael)*
[2014] EWCA Crim 642, [2014] 1 W.L.R.
2757 (CA (Crim Div)), Jackson LJ
1638. Explosives Regulations 2014
Reg.2, amended: SI 2014/3248 Sch.5
para.18
Reg.3, amended: SI 2014/3248 Sch.5
para.18
Reg.3, revoked (in part): SI 2014/3248 Sch.4
Part 2
Reg.7, applied: SI 2014/3248 Reg.30
Reg.13, applied: SI 2014/3248 Reg.73
Reg.16, amended: SI 2014/3248 Sch.5
para.18
Reg.23, applied: SI 2014/3248 Reg.73
Reg.31, amended: SI 2014/3248 Sch.5
para.18
Reg.47, amended: SI 2014/3248 Sch.5
para.18
Sch.1 para.1, amended: SI 2014/3248 Sch.5
para.18
Sch.5 para.8, amended: SI 2014/3248 Sch.5
para.18
Sch.11 Part 1 para.1, amended: SI
2014/3248 Sch.5 para.18
**1641. Gambling (Licensing and Advertising) Act
2014 (Transitional Provisions) Order 2014**
Art.2, amended: SI 2014/1675 Art.2
Art.3, amended: SI 2014/2646 Art.3, SI
2014/2665 Art.2
Art.5, amended: SI 2014/2646 Art.3
Art.6, amended: SI 2014/2646 Art.3
Art.7, amended: SI 2014/2646 Art.3
**1652. Special Educational Needs (Personal
Budgets) Regulations 2014**
Reg.2, amended: SI 2014/2096 Reg.2
Reg.4A, added: SI 2014/2096 Reg.2
Reg.14, amended: SI 2014/2096 Reg.2
**1657. Air Navigation (Restriction of Flying)
(Auchterarder) Regulations 2014**
Reg.3, amended: SI 2014/1938 Reg.3
**1667. Income-related Benefits (Subsidy to
Authorities) and Discretionary Housing
Payments (Grants) Amendment Order 2014**
Art.2, revoked (in part): SSI 2014/298 Art.2
**1705. Local Authority (Duty to Secure Early
Years Provision Free of Charge) (Amendment)
Regulations 2014**
revoked: SI 2014/2147 Reg.9

**1752. M4 Motorway (Junctions 8/9 10)
(Temporary Prohibition of Traffic) Order 2014**
revoked: SI 2014/2412 Art.9
**1777. Legal Aid, Sentencing and Punishment of
Offenders Act 2012 (Alcohol Abstinence and
Monitoring Requirements) Piloting Order 2014**
applied: SI 2014/1787 Art.2
**1795. Representations Procedure (Wales)
Regulations 2014**
referred to: SI 2014/1794 Reg.11
**1802. Air Navigation (Restriction of Flying)
(Watnall) Regulations 2014**
revoked: SI 2014/1817 Reg.2
**1820. Immigration Act 2014 (Commencement No
1, Transitory and Saving Provisions) Order 2014**
Art.4, revoked: SI 2014/2771 Art.14
**1826. Sudan (European Union Financial
Sanctions) Regulations 2014**
Sch.1 para.5, amended: 2014 c.29 s.4
**1827. South Sudan (European Union Financial
Sanctions) Regulations 2014**
Sch.1 para.5, amended: 2014 c.29 s.4
**1831. Banking Act 2009 (Banking Group
Companies) Order 2014**
Art.2, amended: SI 2014/3329 Art.127
**1835. Common Agricultural Policy Basic
Payment Scheme (Provisional Payment Region
Classification) (Wales) Regulations 2014**
Reg.2, amended: SI 2014/2367 Reg.2
Reg.3, amended: SI 2014/2367 Reg.2
Reg.3, revoked (in part): SI 2014/2367
Reg.2
Sch.1, substituted: SI 2014/2367 Sch.1
**1840. Air Navigation (Restriction of Flying)
(Newport) Regulations 2014**
Reg.3, amended: SI 2014/2206 Reg.3
**1867. Education (National
Curriculum)(Attainment Targets and
Programmes of Study)(England)(Amendment)
Order 2014**
revoked: SI 2014/1941 Art.7
**1974. A14 Trunk Road (Junction 16
Catworth/Molesworth to Junction 24
Godmanchester, Cambridgeshire) (Temporary
Restriction and Prohibition of Traffic) Order
2014**
Art.4, varied: SI 2014/2488 Art.2
**2011. Contracts for Difference (Allocation)
Regulations 2014**
applied: SI 2014/2012 Reg.5

2012. Contracts for Difference (Standard Terms) Regulations 2014
 Reg.12, applied: SI 2014/2511 Reg.16
2013. Electricity Market Reform (General) Regulations 2014
 Reg.11, applied: SI 2014/2011 Reg.26
 Reg.12, applied: SI 2014/2011 Reg.26
2035. A3 Trunk Road (Ripley By-Pass) (Temporary Prohibition of Traffic) Order 2014
 Art.2, amended: SI 2014/2419 Art.2
2042. Data Retention Regulations 2014
 revoked: 2014 c.27 s.8
2043. Electricity Capacity Regulations 2014
 applied: SI 2014/3354 Reg.6, Reg.32
 Part 10, applied: SI 2014/3354 Reg.11, Reg.19
 Part 10, applied: SI 2014/3354 Reg.11, Reg.30, Reg.32
 Reg.2, amended: SI 2014/3354 Sch.2 para.2
 Reg.3, amended: SI 2014/3354 Sch.2 para.3
 Reg.4, amended: SI 2014/3354 Sch.2 para.4
 Reg.40, applied: SI 2014/3354 Reg.7
 Reg.41, amended: SI 2014/3354 Sch.2 para.5
 Reg.41, applied: SI 2014/3354 Reg.8
 Reg.42, applied: SI 2014/3354 Reg.8
 Reg.44, amended: SI 2014/3354 Sch.2 para.6
 Reg.45, amended: SI 2014/3354 Sch.2 para.7
 Reg.47, amended: SI 2014/3354 Sch.2 para.8
 Reg.53, varied: SI 2014/3354 Reg.26
 Reg.55, applied: SI 2014/3354 Reg.28
 Reg.55, disapplied: SI 2014/3354 Reg.26
 Reg.56, disapplied: SI 2014/3354 Reg.26
 Reg.58, varied: SI 2014/3354 Reg.26
 Reg.67, amended: SI 2014/3354 Sch.2 para.9
 Reg.77, amended: SI 2014/3354 Sch.2 para.10
 Reg.80, amended: SI 2014/3354 Sch.2 para.10
 Reg.81, amended: SI 2014/3354 Sch.2 para.11
 Sch.1 para.2, amended: SI 2014/3354 Sch.2 para.12
 Sch.1 para.6, amended: SI 2014/3354 Sch.2 para.13
 Sch.1 para.7, applied: SI 2014/3354 Reg.21
 Sch.2, applied: SI 2014/3354 Reg.2

 Sch.2 para.1, amended: SI 2014/3354 Sch.2 para.14
2054. Ukraine (European Union Financial Sanctions) (No.3) Regulations 2014
 Reg.3, amended: SI 2014/2445 Reg.3, Reg.4
 Reg.3A, added: SI 2014/2445 Reg.5
 Reg.3A, amended: SI 2014/3230 Reg.2
 Reg.3B, amended: SI 2014/3230 Reg.2
 Reg.3C, added: SI 2014/3230 Reg.3
 Reg.4, amended: SI 2014/2445 Reg.6
 Sch.1 para.5, amended: 2014 c.29 s.4
2147. Local Authority (Duty to Secure Early Years Provision Free of Charge) Regulations 2014
 Reg.3, applied: SI 2014/3352 Reg.16
2234. Whole of Government Accounts (Designation of Bodies) Order 2014
 Sch.1, amended: 2014 c.29 s.4
2257. General Betting, Pool Betting and Remote Gaming Duties (Registration, Records and Agents) Regulations 2014
 Reg.3, amended: SI 2014/2912 Reg.6
 Reg.4, amended: SI 2014/2912 Reg.6
2321. Welfare Reform Act 2012 (Commencement No 19 and Transitional and Transitory Provisions and Commencement No 9 and Transitional and Transitory Provisions (Amendment)) Order 2014
 applied: SI 2014/2887 Reg.5
 referred to: SI 2014/3067 Art.7
 Art.2, amended: SI 2014/3067 Art.6
 Art.4, amended: SI 2014/3067 Art.6
2328. Armed Forces Early Departure Payments Scheme Regulations 2014
 Reg.19, applied: SI 2014/2336 Reg.58
2336. Armed Forces Pension Regulations 2014
 applied: SI 2014/2328 Reg.9, Reg.10, Reg.13, Reg.14, Reg.15
 Reg.3, amended: SI 2014/3255 Art.33
 Reg.4, applied: SI 2014/2328 Reg.3
 Reg.24, amended: SI 2014/3255 Art.33
 Reg.24, applied: SI 2014/2328 Reg.5
 Reg.43, applied: SI 2014/2328 Reg.16, Reg.19
 Reg.51, applied: SI 2014/2328 Reg.8, Reg.16, Reg.19
 Reg.52, applied: SI 2014/2328 Reg.8, Reg.16, Reg.19
 Reg.60, applied: SI 2014/2328 Reg.19

2338. Tuberculosis (Deer and Camelid) Slaughter and Compensation (England) Order 2014
    Art.4, applied: SI 2014/2337 Art.18

2342. Designation of Schools Having a Religious Character (Independent Schools) (England) (No.2) Order 2014
    Sch.1, amended: SI 2014/3361 Art.5, Sch.2

2357. Export Control (Russia, Crimea and Sevastopol Sanctions) Order 2014
    Art.2, amended: SI 2014/2932 Art.3
    Art.3, amended: SI 2014/2932 Art.3
    Art.5A, added: SI 2014/2932 Art.3
    Art.9, amended: SI 2014/2932 Art.3
    Art.11, amended: SI 2014/2932 Art.3

2379. Education and Skills Act 2008 (Commencement No 10 and Transitory Provisions) Order 2014
    Art.3, revoked: SI 2014/3364 Sch.1

2391. Air Navigation (Restriction of Flying) (RAF Fairford, Gloucestershire) Regulations 2014
    Reg.3, amended: SI 2014/2450 Reg.3, Reg.4

2398. Immigration and Nationality (Cost Recovery Fees) (Amendment) Regulations 2014
    revoked: 2014 c.22 Sch.9 para.74

2418. Public Interest Disclosure (Prescribed Persons) Order 2014
    Sch.1, amended: SI 2014/3294 Art.6

2444. Gambling (Licensing and Advertising) Act 2014 (Commencement No.1) Order 2014
    Art.2, amended: SI 2014/2646 Art.2

2590. Anti-social Behaviour, Crime and Policing Act 2014 (Commencement No 7, Saving and Transitional Provisions) Order 2014
    Art.3, amended: SI 2014/2754 Art.3
    Art.4, amended: SI 2014/2754 Art.4
    Art.5A, added: SI 2014/2754 Art.5

2594. Burbo Bank Extension Offshore Wind Farm Order 2014
    applied: SI 2014/3301
    Art.6, amended: SI 2014/3301 Sch.1
    Sch.1 Part 3 para.2, revoked: SI 2014/3301 Sch.1
    Sch.1 Part 3 para.3, amended: SI 2014/3301 Sch.1

2608. A421 Trunk Road (Bedford Southern Bypass, Bedfordshire) (Temporary Restriction and Prohibition of Traffic) Order 2014
    revoked: SI 2014/2792 Art.7

2671. Care and Support (Deferred Payment) Regulations 2014
    applied: SI 2014/2670 Reg.5

2672. Care and Support (Charging and Assessment of Resources) Regulations 2014
    Reg.7, applied: SI 2014/2673 Reg.3
    Sch.2 para.2, applied: SI 2014/2670 Reg.5

2710. Russia, Crimea and Sevastopol (Sanctions) (Overseas Territories) Order 2014
    Art.8A, added: SI 2014/2919 Art.3
    Art.13, amended: SI 2014/2919 Art.4, Art.5
    Art.14, amended: SI 2014/2919 Art.4
    Art.20, amended: SI 2014/2919 Art.4
    Sch.2 para.1, amended: SI 2014/2919 Art.4

2771. Immigration Act 2014 (Commencement No 3, Transitional and Saving Provisions) Order 2014
    Art.9, applied: SI 2014/2928 Art.2

2792. A421 Trunk Road (Bedford Southern Bypass, Bedfordshire) (Temporary Restriction and Prohibition of Traffic) (No.2) Order 2014
    revoked: SI 2014/2999 Art.7

2824. Care and Support (Independent Advocacy Support) Regulations 2014
    revoked: SI 2014/2889 Reg.8

2848. Firefighters Pension Scheme (England) Regulations 2014
    Reg.3, amended: SI 2014/3255 Art.34
    Reg.3, revoked (in part): SI 2014/3255 Art.34
    Reg.18, amended: SI 2014/3255 Art.34
    Reg.113, amended: SI 2014/3255 Art.34

2887. Universal Credit (Digital Service) Amendment Regulations 2014
    referred to: SI 2014/3094 Art.7

2948. Civil Procedure (Amendment No 7) Rules 2014
    r.5, amended: SI 2014/3299 r.17

3001. Products Containing Meat etc (England) Regulations 2014
    Reg.5, applied: SI 2014/1603 Sch.3 para.2
    Reg.5, referred to: SI 2014/1603 Sch.3 para.2
    Sch.1, referred to: SI 2014/1603 Sch.3 para.2

3050. Shared Parental Leave Regulations 2014
    applied: SI 2014/3096 Reg.5
    Part 3, varied: SI 2014/3092 Reg.7
    Reg.2, varied: SI 2014/3092 Reg.7, Reg.9, SI 2014/3096 Reg.20
    Reg.3, varied: SI 2014/3092 Reg.7, Reg.10, SI 2014/3096 Reg.21

Reg.5, applied: SI 2014/3053 Reg.4, SI
2014/3054 Reg.6
Reg.20, varied: SI 2014/3092 Reg.11, SI
2014/3096 Reg.22
Reg.21, varied: SI 2014/3092 Reg.12, SI
2014/3096 Reg.23
Reg.23, varied: SI 2014/3092 Reg.13, SI
2014/3096 Reg.24
Reg.24, varied: SI 2014/3092 Reg.14, SI
2014/3096 Reg.25
Reg.25, varied: SI 2014/3092 Reg.15, SI
2014/3096 Reg.26
Reg.26, varied: SI 2014/3092 Reg.16, SI
2014/3096 Reg.27
Reg.28, varied: SI 2014/3092 Reg.17, SI
2014/3096 Reg.28
Reg.32, varied: SI 2014/3096 Reg.29
Reg.34, varied: SI 2014/3092 Reg.18, SI
2014/3096 Reg.30
Reg.35, varied: SI 2014/3092 Reg.19, SI
2014/3096 Reg.31
Reg.36, varied: SI 2014/3092 Reg.20, SI
2014/3096 Reg.32
Sch.1 Part 2, varied: SI 2014/3092 Reg.7
Sch.1 Part 2 para.10, varied: SI 2014/3092
Reg.21, SI 2014/3096 Reg.33

**3051. Statutory Shared Parental Pay (General)
Regulations 2014**
Part 3, applied: SI 2014/3093 Reg.3
Reg.2, applied: SI 2014/3093 Reg.3
Reg.2, varied: SI 2014/3093 Reg.5, Reg.6,
SI 2014/3097 Reg.4
Reg.3, applied: SI 2014/3093 Reg.3
Reg.3, varied: SI 2014/3097 Reg.5
Reg.4, applied: SI 2014/3054 Reg.4
Reg.5, applied: SI 2014/3053 Reg.3, SI
2014/3054 Reg.5
Reg.17, varied: SI 2014/3093 Reg.7, SI
2014/3097 Reg.6
Reg.18, varied: SI 2014/3093 Reg.8, SI
2014/3097 Reg.7
Reg.19, applied: SI 2014/3097 Reg.10
Reg.19, varied: SI 2014/3093 Reg.9, SI
2014/3097 Reg.8, Reg.10
Reg.20, varied: SI 2014/3093 Reg.10, SI
2014/3097 Reg.9, Reg.10
Reg.21, applied: SI 2014/3097 Reg.10
Reg.21, varied: SI 2014/3097 Reg.10
Reg.23, varied: SI 2014/3093 Reg.11, SI
2014/3097 Reg.11

Reg.24, varied: SI 2014/3093 Reg.12, SI
2014/3097 Reg.12
Reg.29, varied: SI 2014/3093 Reg.13, SI
2014/3097 Reg.13
Reg.31, varied: SI 2014/3093 Reg.14, SI
2014/3097 Reg.14
Reg.32, varied: SI 2014/3093 Reg.15, SI
2014/3097 Reg.15
Reg.33, applied: SI 2014/3134 Reg.4, Reg.5
Sch.1 Part 2, applied: SI 2014/3093 Reg.3
Sch.1 Part 2 para.12, varied: SI 2014/3093
Reg.16, SI 2014/3097 Reg.16

**3052. Maternity and Adoption Leave
(Curtailment of Statutory Rights to Leave)
Regulations 2014**
applied: SI 2014/3092 Reg.3
referred to: SI 2014/3092 Reg.3
varied: SI 2014/3092 Reg.3
Reg.2, varied: SI 2014/3092 Reg.5, SI
2014/3096 Reg.18
Reg.3, varied: SI 2014/3092 Reg.6, SI
2014/3096 Reg.19

**3140. Company, Limited Liability Partnership
and Business Names (Sensitive Words and
Expressions) Regulations 2014**
Sch.2 Part 1, amended: 2014 c.29 s.4
Sch.2 Part 2, amended: 2014 c.29 s.4

**3141. Criminal Justice and Data Protection
(Protocol No 36) Regulations 2014**
Part 6, applied: SSI 2014/337 Sch.1 para.9
Reg.3, amended: SI 2014/3191 Reg.2
Reg.5, amended: SI 2014/3191 Reg.2
Reg.8, amended: SI 2014/3191 Reg.2
Reg.18, amended: SI 2014/3191 Reg.2
Reg.40, amended: SI 2014/3191 Reg.2
Reg.60, amended: SI 2014/3191 Reg.2
Reg.67, amended: SI 2014/3191 Reg.2
Reg.71, amended: SI 2014/3191 Reg.2
Reg.85, applied: SI 2014/3300 Reg.19
Reg.88, applied: SSI 2014/337 Sch.2 para.14
Reg.91, amended: SI 2014/3191 Reg.2
Reg.107, applied: SSI 2014/337 Sch.2
para.14
Reg.110, amended: SI 2014/3191 Reg.2
Sch.1 para.1, amended: SI 2014/3191 Reg.2
Sch.1 para.4, amended: SI 2014/3191 Reg.2
Sch.2 para.1, amended: SI 2014/3191 Reg.2
Sch.2 para.4, amended: SI 2014/3191 Reg.2
Sch.4 Part 1, amended: SI 2014/3191 Reg.2

3269. Finance Act 2009, Schedules 55 and 56 and Sections 101 and 102 (Stamp Duty Reserve Tax) (Appointed Days, Consequential and Transitional Provision) Order 2014
    amended: SI 2014/3346 Art.2
    Art.1, amended: SI 2014/3346 Art.2
    Art.3, amended: SI 2014/3346 Art.2
3330. Banking Act 2009 (Mandatory Compensation Arrangements Following Bail-in) Regulations 2014
    Reg.12, amended: SI 2014/3344 Art.6
3349. Yemen (European Union Financial Sanctions) Regulations 2014
    Sch.1 para.5, amended: 2014 c.29 s.4